Funding Public Schools in the United States, Indian Country, and US Territories (Second Edition)

A Volume in:
Conducting Research in Education Finance:
Methods, Measurement, and Policy Perspectives

Series Editors:
David C. Thompson
R. Craig Wood
National Education Finance Academy

Conducting Research in Education Finance: Methods, Measurement, and Policy Perspectives

Series Editors:
David C. Thompson
Kansas State University

R. Craig Wood
University of Florida

National Education Finance Academy

Books in This Series:

Charter School Funding Considerations (2022)
Christine Rienstra Kiracofe, Marilyn A. Hirth, & Tom Hutton

Higher Education Finance Research:
Policy, Politics, and Practice (2014)
Mary P. McKeown-Moak & Christopher M. Mullin

Funding Public Schools in the United States, Indian Country, and US Territories (Second Edition)

Philip Westbrook
Eric A. Houck
R. Craig Wood
David C. Thompson

INFORMATION AGE PUBLISHING, INC.
Charlotte, NC • www.infoagepub.com

Library of Congress Cataloging-In-Publication Data

The CIP data for this book can be found on the Library of Congress website (loc.gov).

Paperback: 979-8-88730-268-3
Hardcover: 979-8-88730-269-0
E-Book: 979-8-88730-270-6

Printed in the United States of America

CONTENTS

Preface: Splitting the Atom of Sovereignty: Financing America's Public Schools...xi
William E. Thro

Introduction: Creating a Scholarly Ecosystem for School Finance Studies xv
Eric A. Houck, Philip Westbrook,
R. Craig Wood, and David C. Thompson

PART I
SCHOOL FINANCE MECHANISMS
OF THE FIFTY STATES

1. **Alabama** 3
Amy Dagley and Philip Westbrook

2. **Alaska** 19
Amy Dagley and Amy Lujan

3. **Arizona** 33
Daniel W. Eadens and Gayle A. Blanchard

4. **Arkansas** 49
Steve Bounds

5. **California** 71
   Ann Blankenship-Knox, Paul Jessup, and Bob Blattner

6. **Colorado** 91
   E. Glenn McClain, Jr. and Spencer C. Weiler

7. **Connecticut** 107
   Michael Morton and George Sinclair

8. **Delaware** 125
   Christopher Brooks

9. **Florida** 141
   R. Craig Wood

10. **Georgia** 169
    David G. Martínez, Lauren G. Epps, and Patrick D. Bennett

11. **Hawai'i** 187
    Brenda Mendiola

12. **Idaho** 199
    David C. Thompson

13. **Illinois** 213
    Michael A. Jacoby, Benjamin Boer, and Melissa Figueira

14. **Indiana** 231
    Marilyn A. Hirth and Daniel Hile

15. **Iowa** 249
    Ain A. Grooms

16. **Kansas** 263
    Kellen J. Adams, S. Craig Neuenswander,
    and David C. Thompson

17. **Kentucky** 283
    William E. Thro

18. **Louisiana** 297
   *Janet M. Pope, Dannie P. Garrett, III, Markey W. Pierré, and
   Wendy Baudoin*

19. **Maine** 315
   Sharda Jackson Smith

20. **Maryland** 329
   Chelsea E. Haines

21. **Massachusetts** 345
   David Danning

22. **Michigan** 365
   Brett Geier and Scott Sawyer

23. **Minnesota** 381
   Nicola A. Alexander

24. **Mississippi** 401
   Spencer D. Stone

25. **Missouri** 409
   R. Craig Wood and Kai Cui

26. **Montana** 421
   Lou L. Sabina and Devon Viola

27. **Nebraska** 429
   *Joel Applegate, Bryce Wilson, Kellen J. Adams,
   and David C. Thompson*

28. **Nevada** 441
   Jacob D. Skousen and R. Karlene McCormick-Lee

29. **New Hampshire** 455
   Osnat Zaken

30. **New Jersey** 469
   R. Craig Wood and Kai Cui

31. **New Mexico**...485
    Marianna Olivares and Cristóbal Rodríguez

32. **New York**...497
    Brian O. Brent and Karen J. DeAngelis

33. **North Carolina** 517
    Eric A. Houck, Walter Hart, and Jim R. Watson

34. **North Dakota** 529
    Eric A. Houck

35. **Ohio** 541
    Barbara M. De Luca and Steven A. Hinshaw

36. **Oklahoma**...555
    Jeffrey Maiden and Shawn Hime

37. **Oregon**..567
    Andy Saultz and Alyssa Nestler

38. **Pennsylvania** 577
    Andrew L. Armagost and Timothy J. Shrom

39. **Rhode Island**...603
    Jacob D. Skousen

40. **South Carolina**..623
    Mazen Aziz and Henry Tran

41. **South Dakota** 637
    Wade Pogany and Tyler Pickner

42. **Tennessee**...651
    Lisa G. Driscoll

43. **Texas** 663
    Catherine E. Knepp and Mary P. McKeown-Moak

44. **Utah** 683
     W. Bryan Bowles and Robert W. Smith

45. **Vermont**.. 703
     Tammy Kolbe and D. Akol Aguek

46. **Virginia** 721
     William Owings and Leslie S. Kaplan

47. **Washington** 737
     David S. Knight, Pooya Almasi, and JoLynne Berge

48. **West Virginia**... 757
     Keith A. Butcher

49. **Wisconsin** 771
     Lisa Lambert Snodgrass

50. **Wyoming** 793
     Neil Theobald

PART II

SCHOOL FINANCE IN INDIAN COUNTRY, US TERRITORIES, AND THE DISTRICT OF COLUMBIA

51. **District of Columbia**.. 805
     Michael C. Petko

52. **Indian Country**.. 837
     Alex RedCorn, Meredith L. McCoy, and Hollie J. Mackey

53. **U.S. Territories**.. 867
     Lou L. Sabina and Anna Peters

PREFACE

SPLITTING THE ATOM OF SOVEREIGNTY

Financing America's Public Schools

William E. Thro

The Framers split the atom of sovereignty. It was the genius of their idea that our citizens would have two political capacities, one state and one federal, each protected from incursion by the other. The resulting Constitution created a legal system unprecedented in form and design, establishing two orders of government, each with its own direct relationship, its own privity, its own set of mutual rights and obligations to the people who sustain it and are governed by it. It is appropriate to recall these origins, which instruct us as to the nature of the two different governments created and confirmed by the Constitution.

—*Justice Anthony Kennedy[1]*

In America, the People—not the Queen or the Parliament or the Party or the Faith—are sovereign.[2] This notion of the People being sovereign has profound implications.[3] First, because the People, not the legislature or the government, are sovereign, fundamental principles can "be lifted out of the lawmaking and other governmental processes and institutions of government and set above them."[4] The

Funding Public Schools in the United States, Indian Country,
and US Territories (Second Edition), pages xi–xiv.
Copyright © 2023 by Information Age Publishing
www.infoagepub.com

xi

Constitution becomes "a fixed fundamental law superior to ordinary legislation."[5] Second, because the People are sovereign, the People may allocate portions of "their sovereign power to their different representatives and agents at both the state and national levels."[6] This division of sovereignty between the States and the National Government "is a defining feature of our Nation's constitutional blueprint."[7] The division of power between *dual sovereigns*, the States and the National Government, is reflected throughout the Constitution's text,[8] as well as its structure.[9]

> Just as the separation and independence of the coordinate branches of the Federal Government serve to prevent the accumulation of excessive power in any one branch, a healthy balance of power between the States and the Federal Government will reduce the risk of tyranny and abuse from either front."[10] Phrased differently, although the People, in the exercise of their sovereignty, granted vast power to the National Government, the National Government remains one of enumerated, hence limited, powers.[11] Indeed, "that those limits may not be mistaken, or forgotten, the constitution is written.[12]

Because "the federal balance is too essential a part of our constitutional structure and plays too vital a role in securing freedom,"[13] the Supreme Court has intervened to support the sovereign prerogatives of both the States and the National Government. In order to preserve the sovereignty of the National Government, the Court has prevented the States from imposing term limits on members of Congress,[14] and instructing members of Congress as to how to vote on certain issues.[15] Similarly, the Courts has invalidated state laws infringing on the right to travel,[16] that undermine the Nation's foreign policy,[17] and exempting a State from generally applicable regulations of interstate commerce.[18]

Conversely, "the preservation of the States, and the maintenance of their governments, are as much within the design and care of the Constitution as the preservation of the Union and the maintenance of the National Government. The Constitution, in all its provisions, looks to an indestructible Union, composed of indestructible States."[19] Recognizing that "the States retain substantial sovereign powers under our constitutional scheme, powers with which Congress does not readily interfere,"[20] and that "the erosion of state sovereignty is likely to occur a step at a time,"[21] the National Government may not compel the States to pass particular legislation,[22] to require state officials to enforce federal law,[23] to dictate the location of the State Capitol,[24] or to regulate purely local matters.[25]

This division of sovereignty manifests itself in the sphere of public education. Although education is not a fundamental right under the United States Constitution,[26] every State Constitution has a provision mandating, at a minimum, that the State provide a system of free public schools.[27] Because the States' have different histories, economies, political cultures, and values, the responses of the States reflect the diversity of the Republic. There is no single approach. Every State—and every sovereign Tribe—is unique.

In this book, my colleagues in the National Education Finance Academy describe how each State and each sovereign Tribe have approached the problem of education finance. The result is a book that provides a brief overview or introduction to education throughout the Nation.

—William E. Thro
President
National Education Finance Academy, 2022–23

ENDNOTES

[1] U.S. Term Limits, Inc. v. Thornton, 514 U.S. 779, 838–39 (1995).

[2] Gordon S. Wood, Power and Liberty: Constitutionalism in the American Revolution 18–26, 92–95 (2021).

[3] Id. at 95.

[4] Id. at 46.

[5] Id. at 49.

[6] Id. at 95.

[7] Federal Maritime Commission v. South Carolina State Ports Authority, 535 U.S. 743, 751 (2002).

[8] Printz, v. United States, 521 U.S. 898, 919 (1997).

[9] Alde v. Maine, 527 U.S. 706, 714–15 (1999).

[10] Gregory v. Ashcroft, 501 U.S. 452, 458 (1991).

[11] McCulloch v. Maryland, 17 U.S. (4 Wheat.) 316, 405 (1819).

[12] Marbury v. Madison, 5 U.S. (1 Cranch) 137, 176 (1803).

[13] United States v. Lopez, 514 U.S. 549, 578 (1995) (Kennedy, J., joined by O'Connor, J., concurring).

[14] U.S. Term Limits, 514 U.S. at 800-01.

[15] Cook v. Gralike, 531 U.S. 510, 519–22 (2001).

[16] Saenz v. Roe, 526 U.S. 489 (1999).

[17] Crosby v. National Foreign Trade Council, 530 U.S. 363, 372-74 (2000).

[18] Reno v. Condon, 528 U.S. 141, 150 (2000).

[19] Texas v. White, 74 U.S. (7 Wall.) 700, 725 (1868).

[20] Gregory, 501 U.S. at 461.

[21] South Carolina v. Baker, 485 U.S. 505, 533 (1988) (O'Connor, J., dissenting).

[22] New York v. United States, 505 U.S. 144, 162 (1992).

[23] Printz, 521 U.S. at 935.

[24] Coyle v. Smith, 221 U.S. 559, 579 (1911).

[25] United States v. Morrison, 529 U.S. 598, 617–19 (2000); Lopez, 514 U.S. at 561 n.3.

[26] San Antonio Indep. Sch. Dist. v. Rodriguez, 411 U.S. 1, 33 (1973). Of course, the Court recognized "education is perhaps the most important function of state and local governments" because "it is doubtful that any child may reasonably be expected to succeed in life if he is denied the opportunity of an education." Brown v. Board of Educ., 347 U.S. 483, 493 (1954). Indeed, the Court has stressed "the importance of education in maintaining our basic institutions ..." Plyler v. Doe, 457 U.S. 202, 221 (1982). Wisconsin v. Yoder, 406 U.S. 205, 213 (1972) ("Providing public schools ranks at the very apex of the function of a State"); Abington Sch. Dist. v. Schempp, 374 U.S. 203, 230 (1963) (Brennan, J., concurring) ("Americans regard the public schools as a most vital civic institution for the preservation of a democratic system of government").

[27] See Ala. Const. art 14; § 256; Alaska Const. art. VII, § 1; Ariz. Const. art. XI; § 1; Ark. Const. art. XIV, sec 1; Cal. Const. art. IX, § 5; Colo. Const. art. IX; § 2; Conn. Const. art. VIII; § 1; Del. Const. art. X, § 1; Fla. Const. art. IX; § 1; Ga. Const. art. VIII, § VII, ¶ 1; Haw. Const. art. X, § 1; Idaho Const. art. IX, § 1; Ill. Const. art. X, § 1; Ind. Const. art. VIII, sec. 1; Iowa Const. art. IX, § 3; Kan. Const. art. VI, § 1; Ky. Const. § 183; La. Const. art. VIII, § 1; Me. Const. art. 8, § 1; Md.

Const. art. VIII, § 1; Mass. Const. pt. 2, ch. 5; Mich. Const. art. VIII, § 2; Minn. Const. art. XIII, § 1; Miss. Const. art. VIII, § 201; Mo. Const. art. 9. § 1(a); Mont. Const. art. X, § 1; Neb. Const. art. VII, § 1; Nev. Const. art. XI, § 2; N.H. Const. pt. 2, art. 83; N.J. Const. art. VIII, § 4; N.M. Const. art. XII, § 1; N.Y. Const. art. XI, § 1; N.C. Const. art. IX, § 2; N.D. Const. art. VII, § 1; Ohio Const. art. VI, § 3; Okla. Const. art. XIII, § 1; Or. Const. art. VIII, § 3; Pa. Const. art. III, § 14, R.I. Const. art. XII, § 1; S.C. Const. art. XI, § 3; S.D. Const. art. VIII, § 1; Tenn. Const. art. XI, § 12; Tex. Const. art. VII, § 1; Utah Const. art. X, § 1; Vt. Const. ch. 2, § 68; Va. Const. art. VIII, § 1; Wash. Const. art. IX, § 1; W.Va. Const. art. XII, § 1; Wis. Const. art. X, § 3; Wyo. Const. art. VII, § 1.

INTRODUCTION

CREATING A SCHOLARLY ECOSYSTEM FOR SCHOOL FINANCE STUDIES

Eric A. Houck
University of North Carolina at Chapel Hill

Philip Westbrook
University of Alabama

R. Craig Wood
University of Florida

David C. Thompson
Kansas State University

We welcome you to the second edition of this book. We are excited to update the First Edition of this work, which catalogues the basic funding infrastructure of each of the 50 US states, the District of Columbia, the US Territories, and Native nations who share geography with the United States.

The First Edition of this book filled a much-needed hole in the academic ecosystem of education finance and affiliated studies. While overviews of state systems were maintained online and in journal articles, these overviews were not codified into a unified reference work with wide distribution and organizational

Funding Public Schools in the United States, Indian Country,
and US Territories (Second Edition), pages xv–xviii.
Copyright © 2023 by Information Age Publishing
www.infoagepub.com

support.[1] The First Edition was supported with the backing of the National Education Finance Academy (NEFA): both from the energy of its members in writing and editing the book chapters, and the wisdom and energy of leadership in providing this book as a membership benefit.

Since publication of the First Edition, a number of developments within the field of education finance have served to necessitate a Second Edition. First, legislative changes have impacted funding mechanisms in multiple states. School finance litigation decisions have impacted funding mechanisms in Washington, Pennsylvania, and North Carolina, to name a few examples.[2]

Second, levels of funding have changed as state-level bureaucrats and policymakers begin to understand recent academic findings that increases in school funding as well as the delivery of school funding impact student short- and long-term outcomes both in academic performance and other quality of life measures.[3]

Third, the COVID-19 pandemic altered both the levels of funding from federal courses as well as state supplemental funds, but in some cases also altered the structured by which school funding was distributed. For example, states began rethinking predicating funding on attendance figures and shifting to enrollment based headcounts.[4]

The second edition of this book captures changes to school funding mechanisms impacting US public school students resulting from these (and other) exogenous factors.

The first edition of this book also made a contribution to the scholarly discussion of school finance and funding through the inclusion of a chapter addressing school funding structures across Indian Country. In addition to providing basic fiscal information, this chapter called for scholars to rethink and expand their conceptions of what is included in a national census of school funding mechanisms. This second edition expands this position by including a chapter on education funding in US Territories.

The chapter on Indian Country is also updated in the Second Edition. After hearing questions from non-Native scholars about the use of the term *Indian Country* to describe the provision of educational resources to Native nations, communities, and other affiliated Indian organizations, the chapter authors speak to the use of the term as appropriately broad so as to acknowledge that funding for Native American populations is derived from varying combinations of tribal nation, state, federal, and local sources, and that the complex interactions of these funding models and mechanisms creates unique challenges for educators of Native students.[5] In order to accomplish this, the chapter authors also wrote to provide historical, legal and cultural context for the existence of these current structures. [6] As with the first edition, we are extremely thankful for this chapter and proud to have a small role in bringing this scholarship to the attention of the school finance community.[7]

The second edition of this work also integrates more neatly into NEFA's initiatives to educate scholars and policymakers about the need for accurate and timely reporting on state-level school funding mechanisms. If, as Cubberly noted in 1906, "the problem of sufficient revenue lies aback of every other problem," then academic work in the economics of education, educational administration, educational law and many other subfields requires a passing acquaintance to the school funding mechanisms in use across the nation.[8] Over the last few years, NEFA has hosted "State of the State" updates at its annual conference, resuscitated after a brief hiatus by the work of Cathy Sielke of the University of Georgia, among others.[9] In partnership with the *Journal of Education Finance and* the *Journal of Education Human Resources*, these State of the States reports are now published annually by the journal, with a companion website at the NEFA homepage.[10]

While authors attempted to include the most accurate financial information available at the time of authorship, readers are encouraged to confirm state information from the state departments of education or government finance agencies as budgets frequently change. The complexity of education finance systems also makes summarizing finance numbers difficult as there are often variances and exceptions to formulas.

By placing both this book and the State of the States under the auspices of NEFA, leaders in the field have sought to create a system to support each other through what we think of as a scholarly ecosystem: a series of publications whereby education finance scholars can use to both support their work of inquiry into education finance related issues, as well as a consistent outlet for policy scholarship on education funding mechanisms across the nation. It is our hope that this volume, supplemented by State of the States updates, will serve as a first source for both education finance scholas, and education policy researchers more broadly as they seek to contextualize their inquiries into state-level educational policy-making and implementation.

As an editorial team, we would like to thank NEFA for its work in support of this volume as well as each of the chapter authors for their dedication to understanding the role of school funding mechanisms in allocating resources within states. We would like to acknowledge the *Journal of Education Finance* and *Journal of Education Human Resources* for their support of the State of the States reports, and the editorial team at Information Age Publishing for their thoughtful review and support of the final product.

ENDNOTES

[1] Verstegen, D. A., & Jordan, T. S. (2009). A fifty-state survey of school finance policies and programs: An overview. Journal of Education Finance, 213–230; Verstegen, D. A. (2011). Public education finance systems in the United States and funding policies for populations with special educational needs. Education Policy Analysis Archives/Archivos Analíticos de Políticas Educativas, 19, 1–30. See also the Education Commission of the States funding info page at https://www.ecs.org/research-reports/key-issues/funding/.

[2] McCleary, et ux., et al. v. State of Washington, 84362-7; William Penn SD et al. v. Pa. Dept. of Education et al. (Pa. Commonwealth Court, 2018); Leandro v. State of North Carolina 488 S.E.2d 249 (1997).

[3] Jackson, C. K., Johnson, R. C., & Persico, C. (2016). The Effects of School Spending on Educational and Economic Outcomes: Evidence from School Finance Reforms. The Quarterly Journal of Economics, 131(1), 157–218.

[4] Gordon, N., & Reber, S. (2020). Federal aid to school districts during the COVID-19 recession. National Tax Journal, 73(3), 781–804; Gordon, N., & Reber, S. (2022). Were Federal COVID Relief Funds for Schools Enough?. Tax Policy and the Economy, 36(1), 123–157; Tran, H., Buckman, D., Bynoe, T. & Vesely, R. (2022). School finance during the COVID-19 pandemic: How are states responding in FY21? Journal of Education Finance, 47(5).

[5] In addition the term "Indian Country" is a US governmental designation as well as a preferred term of use for many indigenous scholars.

[6] See, for additional context: McCoy, M. L., & Villeneuve, M. (2020). Reconceiving schooling: Centering Indigenous experimentation in Indian education history. History of Education Quarterly, 60(4), 487–519 and RedCorn, A. (2020). Liberating sovereign potential: A working education capacity building model for Native Nations. Journal of School Leadership, 30(6), 493–518.

[7] For additional context, please see https://www.ncai.org/tribalnations/introduction/Indian_Country_101_Updated_February_2019.pdf.

[8] Cubberly, E. (1906). School Funds and Their Apportionment. New York: Teachers College. Columbia University.

[9] See, for example: Sielke, C., Dayton, J., Holmes, C. T., Jefferson, A., & Fowler, W. (2001). Public school finance programs of the United States and Canada: 1998–1999. American Education Finance Association and National Center for Education Statistics, Education Finance Division. Retrieved August, 12, 2002.

[10] See here: https://www.nationaledfinance.com/journal_of_ed_finance_475.php.

PART I

SCHOOL FINANCE MECHANISMS
OF THE FIFTY STATES

CHAPTER 1

ALABAMA

Amy Dagley
University of Alabama at Birmingham

Philip Westbrook
University of Alabama

GENERAL BACKGROUND

Alabama has had seven constitutions since the state was first established in 1819. The first, the Constitution of 1819, known as the Frontier Constitution, established public schools in Alabama.[1] Based on the principles of the Land Ordinance Act of 1785 and the Northwest Ordinance Act of 1787, the sixteenth section of each township was set aside for public schools and one township, or 36 sections, was reserved for the use of a seminary of learning. Each sixteenth section of land belonged to the individual township, and one of the earliest acts of the new state was to allow each township to lease the sixteenth section of land to provide for public schools. The original act was modified numerous times, but the most critical were: extending leases and extending time of payment, allowing townships to sell the land, and requiring proceeds from the lands to be invested in the state bank and the interest to be solely used to support schools.[2] By 1840, the legislature required the state bank to pay $200,000 annually to schools, which exceeded the fair interest rate and was typical for the times—Alabama was relying on the state bank

Funding Public Schools in the United States, Indian Country,
and US Territories (Second Edition), pages 3–17.
Copyright © 2023 by Information Age Publishing
www.infoagepub.com

to cover all expenses of government.[3] By 1843 the state bank went bankrupt,[4] and the entire income of the public school fund was cut off by the bank's failure.[5] Since the State guaranteed the bank stock, the principal of the public school fund, which was represented by certificates, became a permanent charge on the State.[6] However, it was difficult for the state comptroller to collect outstanding notes due to lease extensions and land that had been exploited.[7] The Public Education Act of 1854 created the first statewide system of public schools by establishing the 'Education Fund,' and transferring the management of the school fund from the state comptroller to the new position of state superintendent.[8]

The Constitution of 1861, known as the Secession Constitution, repeated basic philosophies of the 1819 Constitution regarding public education. Education languished in the devastation of the Civil War.[9]

The Constitution of 1865, known as the Reorganization Constitution, preserved the sixteenth section land endowment for public schools. However, with the state struggling to provide basic services little attention could be provided to public education.[10]

The Constitution of 1868, known as the Reconstruction Constitution, encouraged and strengthened public education by calling for a free education for children "…between the ages of five and twenty-one years," including both white and black children, created a state board of education, preserved the sixteenth section lands for public schools, empowered local school boards to levy taxes for schools, and appropriated one-fifth of state revenue for public education.[11]

The Constitution of 1875, known as the Conservative Constitution, abolished the state board of education, consolidated power in the hands of an elected state superintendent, required separate schools for white and "children of citizens of African descent," reduced expenditures, and limited taxes.[12]

The Constitution of 1901, known as the Disenfranchising Constitution, returned white rule to the state, disenfranchised black citizens, and consolidated power in the state legislature by greatly limiting the local control of counties and municipalities. Until November 2022 this constitution was considered to be the longest in the United States and possibly the longest in the world, having been amended nearly 1,000 times. The Constitution of 1901 maintained Alabama in a post-Civil War and emerging industrial economy mindset. The constitution contained outdated language on segregated schools stating that "…separate schools shall be provided for white and colored children, and no child of either race shall be permitted to attend a school of the other race"[13] as well as language from a 1956 amendment to Section 260,[14] passed after *Brown v. Board of Education of Topeka*[15] to allow, not require, the state legislature to provide for education where and under what conditions as the legislature determines, and allow children to attend schools for their own race.

In November of 2022 Alabama citizens voted to approve a "new" constitution that reorganized the 1901 Constitution so similar subjects were located together, arranged local amendments by county, removed duplicative and repealed provisions, consolidated provisions regarding economic development, and removed racist language.[16] The Constitution of 2022 does not change the property tax structure or any other aspects of the Constitution of 1901.

DESCRIPTIVE STATISTICS

For FY 2022, Alabama has 67 county school districts, 71 city school districts, and since some charter schools are considered local education agencies there are eight charter schools included in the system count for a total of 146 public school systems in the state. District size ranged from 424 students in Linden City to 49,923 students in Mobile County. More than half of the school districts in Alabama have a total enrollment of less than 3,000 students, and three districts have enrollments greater than 30,000.[17]

The school systems are serving 717,988 students in K–12 for FY 2022. This represents a 1.3% statewide decrease in student numbers since the 2019–2020 school year, or pre-pandemic. Some school systems were impacted more than this number would reveal. One hundred and two districts reported decreased enrollment and more than 36% of those had more than a 5% decrease in enrollment compared to two years before. Of those districts reporting more than a 5% decrease in enrollment, 70.3% of them were seen in systems with predominantly Black student populations. Conecuh County saw the biggest decrease in enrollment at 24.7% since 2019–2020, with Selma City experiencing the second largest decrease at 17.1%. Alternatively, eight systems increased their student numbers by 5% or more, with the largest increase by percentage recorded with Chickasaw City Schools at 85.7% and the second largest increase in Limestone County at 36.6%. These substantial increases in enrollment will be discussed later in the section on virtual schools.

CURRENT POLITICAL CLIMATE

The Alabama legislature is composed of 105 members of the House of Representatives and 35 members in the Senate. The Republican Party controls both chambers of the legislature and the office of the governor.[18] A regular session of the legislature is limited to 30 days within 105 calendar days, and the governor can call special sessions to address specific subjects. Alabama's fiscal year runs October 1 through September 30 which makes budgeting more complex since it matches neither the academic year nor the employee contract year. Alabama is one of only four states that do not use a July 1—June 30 fiscal year.[19]

SOURCES OF REVENUE

Approximately 91% of total appropriated revenues in the state of Alabama are earmarked.[20] Alabama operates primarily from six major operating funds, two of which handle most state business: the General Fund and the Education Trust Fund. Only two other states, Michigan and Utah, have separate funds for education. Alabama's General Fund is supported by over 40 tax sources, the largest being insurance company premium tax, use tax, sumptuary taxes, and ad valorem tax. The General Fund provides for nearly all state functions other than education. The Education Trust Fund (ETF) is the largest operating fund in the state. Revenues credited to the ETF are used to provide for K–12 public schools, higher education, and other education-related agencies.

THE EDUCATION TRUST FUND

The Education Trust Fund was created in 1927 'for educational purposes only' and 'for the support, maintenance, and development of public education and capital improvements relating to educational facilities.' It levied revenue sources for education and set them apart as a special fund for education.[21] The ETF receives funds from nine tax sources, the largest being state income tax, followed by state sales tax, state utility tax, and a state use tax.[22] In addition to supporting education, appropriations from the ETF also support the Mental Health Fund and the Public Welfare Trust Fund. Monies on deposit in the ETF are annually appropriated by the state legislature. Table 1.1 provides a description of ETF receipts for the Fiscal Years 2018–2022.

The Education Trust Fund Rolling Reserve Act[23] establishes the maximum amount that may be legislatively appropriated in any fiscal year. This maximum amount, known as a 'Fiscal Year Appropriation Cap,' is calculated by taking the

TABLE 1.1. Education Trust Fund Receipts, 2018–2022

	ACTUAL			ESTIMATED	
	FY 2018	FY 2019	FY 2020	FY 2021	FY 2022
Income Tax	4,208,436,407	4,548,470,728	4,657,167,331	4,624,505,962	4,777,404,584
Sales Tax	1,908,442,757	2,013,911,327	2,084,997,958	2,119,186,793	2,203,243,739
Utility Tax	395,433,474	401,311,660	388,005,781	395,000,000	400,000,000
Use Tax	177,141,487	184,991,767	229,956,798	238,731,179	246,920,534
Insurance Premium Tax	30,993,296	30,993,296	30,993,295	0*	0*
Beer Tax	21,871,510	22,594,709	22,313,700	22,179,818	22,046,739
Mobile Telecommunications Tax	10,402,546	11,924,392	9,804,424	8,627,894	7,592,547
All Other	843,902	1,078,324	16,332,453	1,045,141	997,506
Grand Total	**6,753,565,379**	**7,215,276,203**	**7,439,571,740**	**7,409,276,787**	**7,658,205,649**

Insurance premium tax deposited in General Fund per Act 2019–392.

Source: Alabama Department of Finance, Executive Budget Office, Fiscal Year 2022. https://budget.alabama.gov/executive_budget_document/

sum of the total amount of revenue deposited into the ETF for the highest 14 years out of the last 15 years. The cap may be adjusted if the legislature passes legislation adding revenue to the ETF, but by no more than 95% of anticipated new revenue as described by the fiscal note attached to the legislative act.

The act further requires that revenues in excess of the appropriation cap be placed in an account known as the ETF Rainy Day Fund Account. The ETF Rainy Day Fund has two different subaccounts: (1) The ETF Budget Stabilization Fund, and (2) the ETF Advancement and Technology Fund. The Budget Stabilization Fund is first funded at a rate of 1% of the previous year's ETF appropriations until the fund reaches 7.5% of the previous year's appropriation to be used in times in which there is a shortfall in the revenue needed to meet budget allocations. The ETF Advancement and Technology Fund is the excess over the required funds for the Budget Stabilization Fund and is to be appropriated in an independent supplemental appropriation bill once the balance of this fund is at $10 million. These funds are to be used for (1) repairs or deferred maintenance of facilities, (2) classroom instruction support, (3) insurance for facilities, (4) transportation, or (5) technology.[24]

Prior to the pandemic, Alabama proposed more than $390 million in additional funds to the education budget, but the uncertainty of the pandemic impacted the final budget. The state cut $300 million from the proposed FY 2021 education budget, including a 3% teacher pay raise, and $20 million in new funding for early childhood development.[25] The final FY 2021 education budget still saw an increase of $91 million over the previous year with total appropriations of $7.2 billion.[26] The allocation provided a 2% raise for teachers, and 6–12 grade math and science teachers will be paid more on a new salary schedule.[27] The FY 2022 appropriations for public K–12 schools is $7.7 billion.[28] This is an increase of 6.3 percent over the FY 2021 budget.

DISTRIBUTION FORMULAS

Alabama's current funding distribution model for public K–12 schools is known as the Foundation Program. This Foundation Program was created in 1995 by the state legislature to replace the old 1935 Foundation Program that was commonly referred to as the 'State Minimum Program,' which was considered both inadequate and inequitable.[29]

The Foundation Program is an equalization grant in that funds are disbursed based on the needs and ability of local school systems to generate funding for schools. The Foundation Program is a partnership funded by local monies through property tax and by the state through the Education Trust Fund. Each local school system is required to contribute the equivalent of ten mills ad valorem tax based on local millage rate yield. This amount of local money is considered the state-required match in the state-local partnership for funding schools. This equalization grant requires each system to participate at a basic level of support according to the fiscal capacity of each community, and the formula determines funding primarily based on student enrollment.

Foundation Program funds are distributed to school systems based on two main sources of data: (1) the Average Daily Membership (ADM) of a school system, and (2) the Local Education Agency Personnel Report System (LEAPS Report). System ADM is the average daily enrollment for a system during the first twenty scholastic days after Labor Day of the preceding school year. ADM is collected by the State Department of Education through the system's student database. ADM is calculated for each school in the system using the formula:

Pupil Days for the 20 School Days after Labor Day/ 20 = ADM

Each school system is required to file a report on personnel called the Local Education Agency Personnel System Report (LEAPS Report) which lists all personnel, their highest degree, years of experience, salary, and work assignments. This report ensures that Foundation Program funded personnel are (1) properly certified to teach in the fields assigned, and (2) personnel are assigned to complete work as funded by the legislature. The LEAPS Report is submitted annually to the Alabama State Department of Education by each school system. School systems report all personnel, including staff funded by local or federal funds. All Foundation Program units must be employed in the school in which they are earned, or Foundation funds must be returned to the state. Districts may add personnel using local funds as determined by the local board of education. The cost of the Foundation Program is computed using salaries and fringe benefits, classroom instructional support, other current expenses, and student growth.[30]

SALARIES AND FRINGE BENEFITS

The Foundation Program funds salaries and fringe benefits for teacher units and other personnel. Funds are distributed to support teacher units using a formula with divisors for each grade level. These divisors are provided in Table 1.2. The divisors include an adjustment for weighting special education and career technical education in order to determine the number of teacher units a school "earns." The formula for determining teacher units is calculated by:

ADM (for each grade) / Divisor = Derived Units

It should be noted that the divisors in Table 1.2 are unrelated to teacher-student ratios in schools. Once the number of state calculated units is determined, the units are converted to dollars based on the state's Minimum Salary Schedule for Teachers, which is based on the highest degree earned and years of experience. The matrix is determined annually in the ETF appropriations. For FY 2022, the Foundation Program funding includes a 2% pay raise for all employees.[31]

TABLE 1.2 Grade Divisors for FY 2022

Grade	Divisor
Grades K–3	14.25
Grades 4–6	20.43
Grades 7–8	19.70
Grades 9–12	17.95

In addition to funding teacher units earned by school systems, the Foundation Program may be used to employ career and technical education certified teachers. A weighted formula provides career tech administrators and counselors for school systems having career tech schools. Other career tech funds are provided by the federal government or local school system funds. In 2021, 82.17% of high school students were enrolled in at least one CTE class.[32]

Additional funds are provided through extension increases to support administrators, counselors, librarians, and career and technical education administrators. The Foundation Program also provides funds for fringe benefits, which are computed based on salaries for program units at rates determined by the legislature or as required by state or federal law. Detailed information about employee benefits is addressed below in the section "Employee Benefits."

CLASSROOM INSTRUCTIONAL SUPPORT

The Foundation Program provides funding for classroom instructional support costs for student materials, technology, library enhancement, professional development, and textbooks. All of the costs are calculated per unit, except textbooks which are based on ADM. For FY 2022, student materials are funded at $700 per unit ($32,792,872), technology at $500 per unit ($23,423,480), library enhancement at $157.72 per unit ($7,388,691), professional development at $100 per unit (4,684,696), and textbooks at $75 per ADM (53,988,537).[33] These funds may only be spent for the designated allocation. Student material funds are given directly to each teacher for use in the classroom and purchases must be consistent with school technology and professional development plans. Expenditure of funds for library enhancement and technology must be based on school plans, developed by a committee, and require a majority vote.

OTHER CURRENT EXPENSES

The Foundation Program provides funds for a category called 'Other Current Expenses' which is a catch-all for non-transportation support employees (all employees related to transportation are funded in a separate allocation). This includes secretarial and bookkeeping staff, custodial staff, teacher aides, and other noncertified employees who are not specifically allocated in a separate line item in the Foundation Program. This line item is calculated by unit based on a fixed amount determined by the legislature. For FY 2022 this is $20,702 per unit for a total of $969,814,790. This money has more flexibility than the other allocations and is usually expended on operating costs or salaries for support positions.

STUDENT GROWTH

In 2021, Alabama's legislature amended how the cost of the Foundation Program is determined by adding student growth as an allowable cost.[34] The allowance for student growth is determined by multiplying the combined allowances of salaries, fringe benefits, classroom instructional support, and other current expenses on a per student basis by the net year over year growth of ADM for non-virtual students for the preceding two years. Growth that is attributable to full-time virtual students shall be funded at a rate determined by the Alabama Department of Education based on the average cost to districts in educating virtual students. Full-time virtual school students who reside out of district are considered full-time virtual students for computing the Foundation Program allowance.[35]

TRANSPORTATION

Alabama has a funding formula for transportation of public school pupils that provides funding for (1) a fleet of buses; (2) fuel; (3) bus driver and other employee salaries; (4) employee benefits including healthcare and pension; and (5) maintenance. Transportation is funded by a cost reimbursement formula for students who live more than two miles from the local school; however, most school systems provide optional transportation to children living closer than two miles at the expense of the local system.

The Alabama Fleet Renewal program provides school systems with funding for each bus that is ten years old or less. For FY 2022 this amount is $7,581 per bus.[36] Districts may use the funds to purchase or lease new school buses. School systems are reimbursed for fuel based on the actual number of miles driven as calculated in the system's Route Report. Consideration is given for the type of route driven (general transportation, special education transport, choice transport, midday transport to special schools and career centers, etc.) and the number of students transported. The cost of employees including bus drivers, supervisors, support workers, bus aides for special needs students, and maintenance, is calculated in the plan.

For FY 2022 the total amount of state funding for Fleet Renewal is $7,581 per bus for a total of $48,495,657, while the total amount for Transportation Operations is $331,941,251.[37] In 2021 there were 9,934 school buses covering 486,890 daily route miles transporting 354,094 students at an annual cost of $1,151.14 per child.[38]

TECHNOLOGY

Alabama requires a technology coordinator for each school district, this is provided with a special line item of $12,551,084 for FY 2022. In addition, FY 2022 provides $500 per teacher unit for the purchase of technology.[39]

SCHOOL NURSES

Alabama provides school nurses with an appropriation allocated for each system to receive one school nurse at a base salary determined by the legislature plus additional funding based on the ADM of the school system. For FY 2022 the total allocation is $40,672,957.[40]

SPECIAL EDUCATION

The Alabama Foundation Program funds teacher units earned by school systems which may be used to employ special education teachers. The Foundation Program does not provide weighted per-pupil funding for special needs children; however, the ETF includes special allocation for (1) preschool special education and (2) a catastrophic fund for the support of individual special education students to which the system may apply for additional funding for unbudgeted expenses related to severe needs of a special education child.

Preschool Special Education. Alabama funds preschool for special education services for children with disabilities in an amount determined annually by the state legislature per Act No. 1991-474. School systems report the number of children ages 3–5 with special needs who attend preschool, and the allocation is divided per school system by ADM. The preschool special education program is a specific line item in the ETF allocation.

Special Education Catastrophic Fund Allocation. Alabama provides a catastrophic fund allocation that serves as a pool of money to which school systems can apply based on extreme expenses related to individual special education students who were not considered in the regular school budget. This fund is limited, and systems must justify an exceptional case supporting additional state funding. The funds are distributed by the SDE until the pool of money is exhausted. The catastrophic fund allocation is a specific line item in the ETF allocation and was $5 million for FY 2021.[41]

CAPITAL OUTLAY AND DEBT SERVICE

Alabama provides support for capital outlay and debt service through an allocation in the Education Trust Fund (ETF). For FY 2022 the Capital Purchase is $210,000,000 and the Debt Service is $532,864. Each school system is required to contribute 0.450926 mills to receive the Capital Purchase allocation from the state in FY 2022, and the total allocation is $29,552,370.[42] Capital Outlay funds are distributed based on a complex formula that considers the system's yield of three mills ad valorem tax divided by the system's ADM to determine the millage yield per pupil. Systems are ranked, and funds are distributed by an equalization grant that considers the differences in capacity of each system.

EMPLOYEE BENEFITS

The state administers the Teacher Retirement System of Alabama (TRS), a defined benefit plan, established in 1941for all full-time employees in state-supported education institutions.[43] The legislature ensures the system is fully funded by setting actuarially determined employer contribution rates in the Education Trust Fund budget. There are currently two tiers of membership: Members who were employed prior to January 1, 2013, known as Tier 1 members, and members employed on or after January 1, 2013, known as Tier 2 members. These plans provide both disability and service retirement to members and qualified survivor beneficiaries. The Tier 1 member contribution rate is 7.5% of total salary, and the employer contribution for FY 2022 is 12.43%.[44] Tier 1 members may retire with 25 years of service at any age, or after ten years of service at age 60. The Tier 2 member contribution rate is 6.2% of total salary,[45] and the employer rate is 11.32%. Tier 2 members cannot collect retirement until age 62 and after a minimum of ten years of service credit. There is no option for Tier 2 members to retire before age 62, even with 30 years of service.

Education employees may elect to participate in the Public Education Employees' Health Insurance Plan (PEEHIP) which was established in 1983.[46] The state funds the employer contribution at $800 per month per employee. The FY 2021 employer contribution budget amount is $952.4 million.[47] The TRS and PEEHIP Boards of Control set monthly premiums, which are an additional source of funding for the insurance program. The PEEHIP Board is composed of 15 members who are elected or hold office ex officio. Board members serve as the trustees of the funds and are responsible for administration of the retirement system.[48] Education employees participate in Social Security and Medicare; the employer contribution rate is 6.20% and 1.45% respectively. The employer contribution to unemployment compensation for 2019 is 0.1250%.[49] The state funds five sick leave days and two personal days per year for each employee, although many local districts elect to provide more. The state provides compensation for substitutes for certified employees at a rate of $95.00 per day.

CHARTER SCHOOLS

In 2015, Alabama passed the Alabama School Choice and Student Opportunity Act to establish a process for the formation of charter schools in the state. There are two options for charters: start-up charters or conversion charters. Start-up charter school functions as a local education agency (LEA), while a conversion charter remains as part of the LEA in which it existed as a public school prior to converting to charter status.[50] Start-up charter schools may be authorized by the Alabama Public Charter School Commission, an independent state agency composed of political appointees, or by the local board of education where the charter wishes to open. Local boards of education must be approved by the state department of education as a charter school authorizer before approving a charter application. As of FY 2022, there are only six school districts who are charter authorizers,[51] eight start-up charter schools, and one conversion charter school operating in the state.[52] One charter school had its charter revoked in 2021. Charter schools are required to have an independent certified public accountant complete an audit of the school's finances annually, according to the same requirements for all public schools in the state. As a result of the audit, the audit report and management letter must be sent to the charter authorizer to provide oversight.

The first charter school opened in Mobile in 2017, and a unique public charter school opened in August 2018 in affiliation with The University of West Alabama, a public university located in rural Sumter County. Critics noted the irony in the timing of the announcement, in that the largest private school in the county (Sumter Academy) which was established in 1970 as one of many Christian academies created following federal desegregation orders in the years after *Brown v Board of Education*, announced it would be closing its doors.[53] The most recent charter school to open in the state raised some eyebrows as well. In the fall of 2021, the Magic City Acceptance Academy, an LGBTQ affirming 6–12 grade school, opened its doors after its application was denied three times previously. The charter application was first denied by Birmingham City Schools, then the appeal made to the Commission was denied. A second application was submitted directly to the Commission the following year and was denied again after four of the eight commissioners at the meeting abstained from the vote, three voted to approve, and one voted against the application.[54] There was considerable press around these denials, particularly when the Commission approved a charter application rated 50 points lower by an independent assessment than the Magic City Acceptance Academy application.[55] Eventually the Commission approved the charter in a 7-2 vote. It is worth noting, while the school partners with the Magic City Acceptance Center and is an LGBTQ affirming school, its admission processes and instructional practices are advertised to be inclusive of all students.

NONPUBLIC SCHOOL FUNDING

Alabama residents may donate money to nonprofit organizations known as Scholarship Granting Organizations (SGOs) in lieu of paying state taxes, as established by the Alabama Accountability Act, for K–12 students to attend public or private schools.[56] Eligibility is based on family income being 185% or less of the federal poverty level. The scholarship can currently support up to 4000 students with the current cap of $30 million.[57] Proportionally, 90% of the money is going to religious schools. There are 158 private schools eligible to participate in the SGOs, the majority mention religion in their name or curriculum.

VIRTUAL EDUCATION

By the 2016–2017 school year, each school board was required to adopt a policy to provide a virtual education option for grades 9 to 12 as "an online pathway for earning a high school diploma."[58] Full-time students in a virtual program are counted as part of the local schools ADM, participate in state testing, may participate in extracurricular activities, and are subject to the same requirements imposed by the state athletic association where the local board permits inter-system transfers for athletics.[59] The law places no requirement on local systems to use the state provided program or to contract with a vendor, therefore, each system has created its own virtual experience. While every system provides a virtual option for high school courses by law, only 14 systems have developed 15 stand-alone virtual schools in the state that are reporting attendance separately from other schools in the system in the 2021–2022 ADM count,[60] compared to only seven virtual schools reporting ADM separately in the 2019–2020 count. Of the 14 systems reporting, seven virtual schools accept students across the state of Alabama. Three of those seven districts reported significant increases in district enrollment in the 2021–2022 ADM counts which appear to be attributed to the virtual schools. The three largest virtual schools in the state are also housed in the same three districts reporting significant district enrollment increases: Limestone County, Eufaula City, and Chickasaw City.

The largest virtual school in the state is in Limestone County, which accounted for 43% of the district's enrollment in 2021–2022, compared to 21.5% two years before. As mentioned previously in this chapter, Limestone County saw the second largest percentage increase in enrollment in the state over the previous two years. Eufaula City Schools has the second largest virtual school in the state, with over 4,000 students enrolled. This represents over 64% of the students enrolled in the district. The third largest virtual school in the state is in Chickasaw City Schools. As mentioned earlier in the chapter, Chickasaw City had the largest percentage increase in system enrollment in the state (over 85%), and this appears to be attributed to its virtual school. However, much like other districts in the state, Chickasaw City did not report virtual school enrollment separate from the school it was housed in until the 2021–2022 ADM count. Yet, district enrollment more than doubled in 2020–2021 in Chickasaw City, and the increase from the 2019–2020 school year to the 2021–2022 school year appears to be accounted for by the virtual school enrollment reported in the 2021–2022 ADM count, making the virtual school in Chickasaw City serving over 62% of the district's total enrollment numbers.

It is important to note that not all school systems operating virtual schools saw increases in student enrollment. In fact, the two districts with the largest decreases in enrollment, as noted earlier in this chapter, were Conecuh County and Selma City which both operate virtual schools. However, Conecuh County's virtual school is available to students residing across the state of Alabama. Conecuh County saw a district enrollment decrease of nearly 25% over the last two years, while its virtual school enrollment decreased by over 40%. In the 2021–2022

ADM count, the virtual school in Conecuh County serves nearly 27% of the students enrolled in the district.

These shifts in enrollment for systems providing virtual education across the state influenced the legislature to add student growth considerations for Foundation Program funding in 2021. However, the Alabama Department of Education determines the rate of funding for net growth of full-time virtual students, based on the average cost to districts in educating virtual students.

FEDERAL COVID-19 FUNDING

Alabama received a combined $3.14 billion in COVID-19 relief funds from three rounds of federal emergency funding for public elementary and secondary schools.[61] Funds were distribution by the state to school districts according to the districts' individual plans.[62] Additionally, the governor provided $8.9 million to scholarship granting organizations from federal COVID-19 relief funds for students to attend private K–12 schools.[63]

ENDNOTES

[1]   Alabama Legislature, Constitution of 1819, http://www.legislature.state.al.us/aliswww/history/constitutions/1819/1819.html.

[2]   Stephen Weeks, "History of Public School Education in Alabama," United States Bureau of Education, Bulletin 1915, no. 12, whole no. 637 (1915), https://files.eric.ed.gov/fulltext/ED541810.pdf.

[3]   Ibid., Weeks, 1915, p. 28.

[4]   Ira Harvey, "School Finance for the Alabama Superintendent," Alabama Superintendents Academy, Alabama State Department of Education, 2015, http://uasa.ua.edu/uploads/3/0/1/2/30128295/finance_reference_2015_122115.pdf.

[5]   Ibid., Weeks, 1915, p. 28.

[6]   Ibid., Weeks, 1915, p. 34.

[7]   Ibid., Weeks, 1915, p. 35.

[8]   Ibid., Harvey, 2015, and Weeks, 1915.

[9]   Alabama Legislature, Constitution of 1861, http://www.legislature.state.al.us/aliswww/history/constitutions/1861/1861.html.

[10] Alabama Legislature, Constitution of 1865, http://www.legislature.state.al.us/aliswww/history/constitutions/1865/1865.html.

[11] Alabama Legislature, Constitution of 1868, http://www.legislature.state.al.us/aliswww/history/constitutions/1868/1868all.html.

[12] Alabama Legislature, Constitution of 1875, http://www.legislature.state.al.us/aliswww/history/constitutions/1875/1875.html.

[13] Alabama Legislature, Constitution of 1901, http://alisondb.legislature.state.al.us/alison/codeofalabama/constitution/1901/toc.htm.

[14] Amendment 111, proposed by Act 1956-82.

[15] Brown v. Board of Education of Topeka, 347 U.S. 483 (1954).

[16] Alabama Office of the Governor, "State of Alabama Proclamation by the Governor," (November 28, 2022), https://governor.alabama.gov/assets/2022/11/2022-11-28-Post-Election-Proclamation-Recompilation-of-Constitution.pdf

[17] Alabama Department of Education, "ADM by System and School, School Year 2021–2022," 2021, https://www.alabamaachieves.org/reports-data/financial-reports/.

[18] National Conference of State Legislatures (NCSL), "Legislatures At-A-Glance," (July 14, 2021), https://www.ncsl.org/research/about-state-legislatures/legislatures-at-a-glance.aspx.

[19] National Conference of State Legislatures (NCSL), "FY 2022 State Budget Status," (November 19, 2021), https://www.ncsl.org/research/fiscal-policy/fy-2022-state-budget-status.aspx.

[20] Alabama Department of Finance, Executive Budget Office, "General Budget Information," (2021), https://budget.alabama.gov/general-budget-info/.

[21] Ibid., Harvey, 2015.

[22] Alabama Department of Finance, Executive Budget Office, "State of Alabama Executive Budget Report FY 2022," 2021, https://budget.alabama.gov/executive_budget_document/.

[23] The Education Trust Fund Rolling Reserve Act, Act 2011-3 as amended by Act 2015-538, see Code of Alabama of 1975 §29-9.

[24] Alabama Legislative Services Agency, Fiscal Division. "Budget Fact Book FY 2021," 2021, http://lsa.state.al.us/PDF/Fiscal/BudgetFactBook/2021_Budget_Fact_Book.pdf.

[25] Caroline Beck, "Ivey Signs State Budgets into Law," WBRC, Alabama Daily News, May 18, 2020, https://www.wbrc.com/2020/05/18/ivey-signs-state-budgets-into-law/.

[26] Alabama Legislative Services Agency, Fiscal Division, "Budget Fact Book, FY 2021," https://alison.legislature.state.al.us/LSA-fiscal-archived-publications, and Alabama Legislature, "Education Trust Fund Appropriations Comparison Sheet for FY 2021—HB 187 (Act 2020-169)," https://alison.legislature.state.al.us/LSA-fiscal-archived-spreadsheets.

[27] Alabama Legislature, An Act to Establish the Teacher Excellence and Accountability for Mathematics and Science (TEAMS) Salary Schedule Program, 2021 Ala. Acts 2021-340, S. 327.

[28] Alabama Legislature, "Education Trust Fund Appropriations Comparison Sheet for FY 2022—SB 189 (Act 2021-342)," and "State General Fund Appropriations Comparison Sheet for FY 2022—HB 309 (Act 2021-479)," https://alison.legislature.state.al.us/LSA-fiscal-archived-spreadsheets.

[29] Ibid., Harvey, 2015, and Code of Alabama of 1975, § 16-13-230.

[30] Code of Alabama of 1975, §16-13-231, as amended by Act 2021-166 (SB 9).

[31] Alabama Department of Education, Financial Reports, Foundation Reports, "FY 2022 State Allocation," 2021, https://www.alabamaachieves.org/reports-data/financial-reports/.

[32] Alabama Department of Education, "Quick Facts 2021," 2021, https://www.alabamaachieves.org/communication/quick-facts/.

[33] Ibid., Alabama State Department of Education, "FY 2022 State Allocation," 2021.

[34] Code of Alabama of 1975, §16-13-231, as amended by Act 2021-166 (SB 9). Alabama Administrative Code 290-2-1-.01(1)(e).

[35] ALSDE Memo FY21-3050.

[36] Ibid., Alabama Department of Education, "FY 2022 State Allocation," 2021, https://www.alabamaachieves.org/reports-data/financial-reports/.

[37] Ibid., Alabama Department of Education, "FY 2022 State Allocation," 2021.

[38] Ibid., Alabama State Department of Education, "Quick Facts 2021," 2021.

[39] Ibid., Alabama Department of Education, "FY 2022 State Allocation," 2021.

[40] Ibid., Alabama Department of Education, "FY 2022 State Allocation," 2021.

[41] Ibid., Alabama Legislative Services Agency, "Budget Fact Book FY 2021," 2021.

[42] Ibid., Alabama Department of Education, "FY 2022 State Allocation," 2021.

[43] The Retirement Systems of Alabama, "Teachers' Retirement System," 2021, https://www.rsa-al.gov/index.php/trs/.

[44] Ibid., Alabama Department of Education, "FY 2022 State Allocation," 2021.

[45] Alabama Legislature, An Act to Amend the Teacher's Retirement System. H. 93 of 202 regular session, submitted to governor.

[46] The Retirement Systems of Alabama, "Public Education Employees' Health Insurance Plan," 2021, https://www.rsa-al.gov/peehip/.

[47] Ibid., Alabama Legislative Services Agency, "Budget Fact Book FY 2021," 2021.

[48] Retirement Systems of Alabama, "PEEHIP Board of Control," 2021, https://www.rsa-al.gov/peehip/board-of-control/.

49 Ibid., Alabama Department of Education, "FY 2022 State Allocation," 2021.

50 Code of Alabama of 1975, §16-6F-9(a)(5) and (6).

51 Alabama Department of Education, "Charter School," 2021, https://www.alabamaachieves.org/charter-schools/.

52 Ibid., Alabama Department of Education, "ADM by System and School, School Year 2021–2022," 2021.

53 Trisha Powell Crain, "Alabama Commission Approves Two New Public Charter Schools," AL.COM, June 27, 2017, http://www.al.com/news/index.ssf/2017/06/alabama_commission_approves_tw.html.

54 Trisha Powell Crain, "Alabama's LGBTQ Charter School Denied Again by State Commission," AL.COM, Sep. 10, 2020, https://www.al.com/news/2020/09/alabamas-lgbtq-charter-school-denied-again-by-state-commission.html.

55 Kyle Whitmire, "Opinion: Proposed LGBTQ Charter School Scored High Marks, Alabama Rejected It Anyway," AL.COM, Sep. 21, 2020, https://www.al.com/news/2020/09/proposed-lgbtq-charter-school-scored-high-marks-alabama-rejected-it-anyway.html.

56 Alabama Accountability Act, 2015, Ch. 434, SB 71, https://www.revenue.alabama.gov/wp-content/uploads/2022/05/Act2015-434.pdf.

57 Trisha Powell Crain, "Alabama School Choice Scholarship Funds Students to Attend Religious Private Schools," Alabama Education Lab, August 1, 2022, https://www.al.com/education-lab/2022/08/alabama-school-choice-scholarships-funds-students-to-attend-religious-private-schools.html.

58 Code of Alabama of 1975, §16-46A-1(a)(1).

59 Code of Alabama of 1975, §16-46A-2.

60 Note: Baldwin County has two virtual schools, Baldwin County Elementary Virtual School serving K–8, and Baldwin County Virtual Schools serving 9–12 grades.

61 61. https://aplusala.org/blog/2022/05/12/how-to-use-the-a-covid-school-spending-tracker

62 National Conference of State Legislatures, "Elementary and Secondary School Emergency Relief Fund Tracker," December 20, 2021, https://www.ncsl.org/ncsl-in-dc/standing-committees/education/cares-act-elementary-and-secondary-school-emergency-relief-fund-tracker.aspx.

63 Trisha Powell Crain, "Alabama School Choice Scholarship Funds Students to Attend Religious Private Schools," Alabama Education Lab, August 1, 2022, https://www.al.com/education-lab/2022/08/alabama-school-choice-scholarships-funds-students-to-attend-religious-private-schools.html.

CHAPTER 2

ALASKA

Amy Dagley
University of Alabama at Birmingham

Amy Lujan
Alaska Association of School Business Officials

BACKGROUND

In 1959, Alaska became the 49th state of the United States. At the time of statehood, there were municipal and territorial schools serving the urban population, while rural schools were either operated by the territory or the federal Bureau of Indian Affairs (BIA). Article VII, Section I of the Alaska Constitution states, "The legislature shall by general law establish and maintain a system of public schools open to all children of the State, and may provide for other public education institutions." This signaled the state's intent to unify the dual systems into one statewide school system.[1] The cost of taking over BIA schools with state-funded schools was prohibitive, and the state did not achieve the goal until three decades later.

In 1962, the Alaska State Legislature established Alaska's first foundation program.[2] Under this plan, the state departed from the past practice of reimbursing school districts for expenses and instead funded districts based on 'basic need.' A

Funding Public Schools in the United States, Indian Country,
and US Territories (Second Edition), pages 19–32.
Copyright © 2023 by Information Age Publishing
www.infoagepub.com
All rights of reproduction in any form reserved.

local contribution was also required; area cost differentials were factored in; and there was a deduction for federal impact aid funds[3] received by districts. These characteristics carry through to the current state K-12 foundation formula funding program.

During the 1970s and 1980s, foundation programs based on instructional units were implemented. In rural areas, Regional Education Attendance Areas (REAAs) were formed in 1975, which provided for locally elected school boards. The REAAs also received funding through the foundation program, so public schools across the state were finally funded by one program. The passage of Senate Bill 36 in 1998 moved the state to a school aid formula based on the number of students per school. The use of funding communities and instructional units in the prior formula was abandoned. To ease the transition, approximately $21 million in new funding was injected into the formula, and a supplemental funding floor was implemented which would erode over time.[4]

The 1998 formula was adjusted in subsequent years in various ways. The most significant adjustments were following the recommendations of the Joint Legislative Education Funding Task Force (JLEFT), which issued its reports in 2007.[5] Again, the legislature was able to inject new funding into the formula to ease the transition. The resulting formula currently in use is reviewed in the section, Distribution Formulas.

As the state progressed towards its goal of replacing its dual education system with a single state-wide system, the state faced challenges as to whether or not it was delivering equitable education opportunities for all Alaska students. Focusing on these disparities, the state was sued by representatives of rural schools on several occasions, the most notable being *Hootch v. Alaska State-Operated School System*, a.k.a. "the Molly Hootch case," that challenged the states' practice of not providing secondary schools in many rural villages.[6] The lack of local access to rural secondary schools resulted in students attending boarding school far from home. Although the Molly Hootch case failed in the Alaska Supreme Court, it was later settled out-of-court by consent decree and obligated the state to provide primary and secondary schools in many rural villages.[7] While the state began to open secondary schools across the state, disparities in funding capital projects between urban and rural schools plagued the state. In 1999, a superior court agreed with the plaintiffs in *Kasayulie v. State* that the state's methods for funding capital projects were discriminatory against rural schools and therefore unconstitutional.[8] In order to understand why Alaska struggled with funding public education, one must understand how Alaska's geographic size and population distribution have created unique challenges for the state.

The ten largest school districts in the nation, by square miles, are located in the geographically largest state in the country: Alaska. Alaska is larger than the next three largest states combined: Texas, California, and Montana. While Alaska makes up nearly 20% of the United States, it is one of the least populated states. Population estimates in 2020 were nearly 729,000, with over 54% of the population located in the Anchorage and Matanuska-Susitna economic region.[9] Alaska's K-12 funding formula must fund 53 school districts and one state-run boarding school, Mt. Edgecumbe High School.[10] These school districts range from single-site districts to districts with sprawling geography. For example, an area slightly larger than the state of Minnesota is served by a single school district, the North Slope Borough School District. Due to the geography of the state, it is not surprising that logistics and transportation are an extreme challenge in Alaska, with many communities in the state accessible only by air and perhaps seasonally by water. Pupil transportation by small, chartered planes to sporting events and other school activities is common, and several school districts own airplanes.

For FY 2021, district size in the state ranged from just 11 students in the Pelican City School District to 41,902 in the Anchorage School District. More than half of all districts (30) had a total enrollment of fewer than 500 students, and just five districts had enrollments greater than 5,000.[11] Three years ago, there were only four districts with enrollment over 5,000. Galena City School District more than doubled its enrollment numbers in 2021 to more than 9,000, due to its statewide correspondence school. This will be explored more in depth later in the chapter.

CURRENT POLITICAL CLIMATE

The Alaska Legislature has 20 members in the Senate and 40 members in the House of Representatives. The Senate currently has 13 Republicans and 7 Democrats, and three-fourths of the Senate are male. There are 21 Republicans, 16 Democrats, 2 non-affiliated, and 1 independent in the House, and more than 67% are male. The current Governor is a Republican, as is the majority in the Senate; however, since 2016 Alaska has had a bipartisan governing coalition in the House. The judiciary is selected using the Judicial Merit Selection System, a process created by the Alaska Constitution, whereby the Alaska Judicial Council submits two or more qualified applicants to the Governor who then has 45 days to appoint one to the position. After serving a specified period of time, the judge must stand for approval in a general election on a non-partisan ballot.

Alaska teachers are unionized in nearly all school districts and are most commonly represented by the National Education Association (NEA). There are also unions for education support professionals in many Alaskan districts, which are often local associations or may be affiliated with a national association. NEA-Alaska includes 12,000 members in 51 school districts and supports district-by-district contract negotiations. They also advocate in the state legislature and provide various services. One of the most significant of these is the NEA-sponsored Public Education Health Trust, which began in 1996.

In addition to NEA, various advocacy groups have a strong voice at the state level. These include the Alaska Council of School Administrators (ACSA), which is made up of superintendent, principal and school business official member associations, and the Alaska Association of School Boards (AASB). The Alaska Municipal League (AML) is also involved on issues that overlap with municipal funding concerns. All of these associations have strong membership statewide. From the grassroots level, Great Alaska Schools has advocated on numerous issues.

SOURCES OF REVENUE

The state relies on four major sources of revenue: investment revenue, federal revenue, petroleum revenue, and non-petroleum revenue. Investment revenue comes primarily from the Alaska Permanent Fund and the Constitutional Budget Reserve Fund. Non-petroleum revenue comes from taxes, licenses and permits, fines, etc. Alaska has no state-wide sales tax or personal income tax to generate revenue. The state relies heavily on revenues generated by the oil and gas industry which has caused a crisis in funding state services for the last several years, due to both declining prices and declining output. The state funding crisis has made the relatively high percentage of the state budget devoted to K-12 education a target for funding reductions.

Although it is the largest state in the union, only a small portion of land in Alaska is subject to a property tax. Cities and boroughs have taxing authority; therefore, 24 municipalities (cities and boroughs) levy a property tax, and 107 municipalities levy a general sales tax.[12] Since municipalities have taxing authority, they are required to contribute education funding to their dependent school districts of the equivalent value of a 2.65 mill tax levy on the full and true value of the taxable real and personal property in the district, not to exceed 45% of the district's basic need for the preceding fiscal year.[13] Taxable value is established by the state assessor and may differ from the valuations determined at the local level. However, Regional Education Attendance Areas (REAAs) do not provide this local contribution and are not able to tax locally. This has created some controversy over local contribution. Some say that REAAs do not contribute; however, districts also contribute up to 90% of eligible federal Impact Aid funding, which is a sizable contribution for many REAAs. The federal Title VII Impact Aid program provides funds to school districts for children of parents living and/or working on federal property in-lieu of local tax revenues.[14] The $91.5 million in Impact Aid that figured in the funding formula for FY 2021 is not an insignificant amount, particularly in relation to the size of these districts. In FY 2021, all but twelve Alaskan districts had an Impact Aid deduction in the funding formula. Contribution of Impact Aid funds as well as a local contribution based on mill rates by municipalities with taxing authority and dependent school districts provides an equalization mechanism in the funding formula within the parameters of federal law.

On the other side of the debate, city and borough school districts are restricted in the amount they can contribute to their local districts above the required minimum contribution. The calculation of a maximum contribution is directly related to the ability of the state to deduct eligible Impact Aid within the state formula. The federal government mandates this 'disparity testing.' This results in frustration for residents of city and borough districts when they fund their local districts 'to the cap' and are unable to increase funding unless state funding is also increased. However, if the maximum contribution caps were removed, the state would no longer be able to deduct eligible Impact Aid in the funding calculations.

In June 2021, the U.S. Department of Education notified the Alaska Department of Education and Early Development (DEED) that the state did not meet the requirements in section 7009(b) of the Elementary and Secondary Education Act of 1965, and Alaska was not eligible to consider a portion of Impact Aid payments as local resources in determining state funding. This was determined after the state failed the 'disparity test' calculated on FY 2020 data by having a funding differential of more than 25% between districts. The dispute centers around whether pupil transportation funding should be included in the disparity test calculation; it has not been included in the past. DEED has requested a hearing to appeal the decision. If the U.S. Department of Education no longer allows Alaska to continue deducting Impact Aid as part of the state formula, it will upset the foundation formula and significant revisions may be considered.

DISTRIBUTION FORMULAS

The current funding formula[15] is student-based and covers K-12, plus pre-kindergarten special education. The process begins with Average Daily Membership (ADM), determined by an annual 20-day student count period ending on the fourth Friday in October. The Department of Education and Early Development (DEED) tightly controls the count procedure and subsequent verification of data. The ADM is then adjusted through six calculations to reach the Adjusted Average Daily Membership (AADM):[16]

- Step 1—Adjust: ADM for School Size;
- Step 2—Apply: District Cost Factor;
- Step 3—Apply: Special Needs Factor;
- Step 4—Apply: Vocational & Technical Funding;
- Step 5—Add: Intensive Services Count;
- Step 6—Add: Correspondence Student Counts

Step 1—School Size Adjustment

This step is the most complex adjustment. The purpose is to adjust for cost differences based on school size so that the smaller schools receive additional operational funds and larger schools are adjusted downward, assuming economies of scale.

First, correspondence students are subtracted from a school's ADM. Next, there are guidelines for determining how school districts with enrollments less than 425 will be accounted for within the calculation. There are also special provisions for alternative and charter schools. Finally, ADM is adjusted as shown in Table 2.1.

TABLE 2.1. ADM Adjustment for School Size.

School Size	Formula
10-19.99	39.60
20-29.99	$39.60 + (1.62 \times (ADM—20))$
30-74.99	$55.80 + (1.49 \times (ADM—30))$
75-149.99	$122.85 + (1.27 \times (ADM—75))$
150-249.99	$218.10 + (1.08 \times (ADM—150))$
250-399.99	$326.10 + (0.97 \times (ADM—250))$
400-749.99	$471.60 + (0.92 \times (ADM—400))$
Over 750	$793.60 + (0.84 \times (ADM—750))$

Next, a hold-harmless provision may apply if total district ADM adjusted for school size has decreased 5% or more compared to the prior year. If so, the drop in ADM is phased in over three years.

Step 2—District Cost Factors

Cost factors are specific to each school district, and range from 1.000 to 2.116, with the Anchorage School District currently set as the base at 1.000. At this step of the formula, the district's school size adjusted ADM is multiplied by the district's cost factor. The multipliers were set by statute based on a 2005 study by the Institute for Social and Economic Research (ISER).[17] In a 2015 report reviewing the school funding program, it was suggested there may be a need to review and revise the District Cost Factors set for each district, which may become outdated over time.[18] It is important to note that in the past when new cost factors were implemented, winners and losers were appeased by the injection of additional funds into the formula, which is a difficult challenge when state budgets are tight.

Step 3—Special Needs Funding

Vocational, special education (except intensive special education), gifted/talented education, and bilingual/bicultural education are block-funded. At this step of the formula, the previously adjusted ADM is now multiplied by the Special Needs factor of 1.2. The block funding approach is a departure from the method in prior formulas of calculating special needs entitlement based on individual student counts in these programs. Currently, only prekindergarten special needs students must be specifically identified for inclusion in the regular count, along with identification of intensive needs students (see Step 5 below).

Step 4—Vocational and Technical Funding

Funding at this step is also referred to as Career & Technical Education (CTE) funding. These funds are intended to assist districts in providing CTE instruction to students in grades 7 through 12. At this step of the formula, the previously adjusted ADM is now multiplied by the CTE factor of 1.015. Again, this a departure from prior formulas which relied on individual student counts for this type of funding.

At this step the consolidation of schools provision is also calculated when one or more schools are consolidated within a community. The reduction is phased in over four years, with the first two years being offset by 100%, the third year by 66%, and the fourth year by 33%.

Step 5—Intensive Services Funding

In the case of Intensive Services Funding, the basis for calculation is an actual count of students receiving intensive services who are enrolled on the last day of the 20-day student count period and who have an Individual Education Plan (IEP) in place. State regulations strictly define the qualification of students for the Intensive Services, high-needs classification. At this step of the formula, the district's intensive student count is multiplied by 13. This calculation is added to the previously adjusted ADM.

Step 6—Correspondence Programs

Funding for correspondence programs is calculated by multiplying the correspondence ADM by 90%. Note that correspondence student counts were excluded from the preceding calculations beginning in Step 1. At this step of the formula, the correspondence calculation is now added to the previously adjusted ADM to get the final Adjusted Average Daily Membership (AADM).

Basic Need

The next step is to multiply the AADM by the Base Student Allocation (BSA) to determine Basic Need. For FY 2022, the BSA is $5,930.

The BSA is the figure that is most commonly debated each year in the state legislature. It has been flat funded at $5,930 since FY 2017. However, due to the calculations in Steps 1-6, the effect of a change to the BSA will vary widely among districts, even those with a similar number of students enrolled. For the FY 2022 projection, the total Basic Need for the Alaska K-12 Foundation Formula program is $1.5 billion.[19]

Other Formula Funding Elements

The required contribution is subtracted from Basic Need for city and borough school districts. For the FY 2022 projection, the total required local contribution statewide is $274 million. Boroughs and municipalities may also choose to fund their local districts an additional amount above the required local contribution, up to the level of 23% of basic need, or a 2-mill equivalent of the full and true value of the taxable and real property within the district, whichever is greater. However, once a district reaches the level of the greater of these two calculations, they are funding 'to the cap,' an issue discussed earlier in the 'Sources of Revenue' section.

As referenced previously, the federal Title VII Impact Aid program provides funds to school districts for children of parents living and/or working on federal property in-lieu of local tax revenues. After deductions, 90% of the eligible funds are subtracted from Basic Need. For FY 2021, the total eligible federal Impact Aid received in the state was $127 million, of which $91.5 million was subtracted from Basic Need.[20] For the FY 2022 projection, the total eligible federal Impact Aid received in the state may be $103.6 million, of which $74.9 million may be subtracted from Basic Need.[21] This depends on the outcome of the appeal DEED has filed with the U.S. Department of Education. In the final step, a Quality School Grant in the amount of AADM x $16 is added.

To summarize the final calculations in the Alaska K-12 Foundation Funding Formula:

Basic Need—Required Local Contribution—Deductible Impact Aid + Quality Schools Grant = Total State Entitlement

For the FY 2022 projection, the Total State Entitlement across all 53 school districts plus Mt. Edgecumbe, the state-operated boarding school, is $1.2 billion.[22] Of this total, the largest district in the state (Anchorage School District) is projected to receive $323 million (26.6%) based on an unadjusted projected student count of nearly 44,406.74 (34.9%). The five largest districts in the state combined (Anchorage, Matanuska-Susitna Borough, Fairbanks, Kenai Peninsula Borough, and Juneau) are projected to receive $703.1 million (57.9%) based on an unadjusted projected student count of just over 87,000 (68.6%). These statistics reflect a large number of small schools in the remaining 48 districts, plus Mt. Edgecumbe. In total, state funding for FY 2021 supported 494 schools, 71 of which had enrollments of less than 25 students as of October 1, 2020.[23]

Additional detail on these calculations, including projected funding by the school district, can be found in the *Public School Funding Program Overview* which is updated annually by the Alaska Department of Education and Early Development.[24]

Other K-12 State Funding

In addition to the K-12 Foundation Funding Formula, the state provides funding to school districts through other funding mechanisms. Most notably, this funding includes pupil transportation, capital projects, and retirement system funding. Capital projects and retirement system funding are discussed in separate sections below.

For pupil transportation, districts receive funding on a per-pupil basis, with the per-pupil amount based on a calculation of actual district transportation expenses. For FY 2021, the total amount of pupil transportation funding to 48 districts was $65.3 million, and FY 2022 is projected to be $71.4 million.[25]

Funding Issues

Several times in recent years, legislators have wanted to increase K-12 funding but have not wanted to make the increase 'permanent' by increasing the Base Student Allocation in the funding formula. This has resulted in special funding allocations outside the formula. In some cases, this made good sense, such as when energy costs spiked and the impact was thought to be temporary. However, education advocates are unified in calling for increases to the Base Student Allocation to support the bulk of K-12 expenditures, since the funding formula is seen as the fair way to allocate funding across the K-12 system as a whole.

Another issue that may affect the ability to deliver effective instruction is the lack of any funding adjustment for at-risk or low-income students. This was noted as atypical, compared to other states with student-centered funding formulas, in a report commissioned by the legislature.[26] The report also documented significant variation among Alaskan districts with regard to percentages of low-income students.[27] High rates of suicide and adverse childhood experiences in Alaska clearly indicate the challenges to educators from at-risk student populations.[28]

Instructional advocates have also pointed out that Alaska is falling behind in its funding for prekindergarten, which research has shown is highly beneficial for future educational achievement.[29] To date, the state has funded prekindergarten only through very limited grant programs and for prekindergarten special needs services. Some local districts have chosen to fund prekindergarten programs with their own resources.

CAPITAL OUTLAY AND DEBT SERVICE

There are three mechanisms for state funding of capital projects: (1) School Construction and Major Maintenance Grants; (2) State Aid for School Construction in REAAs, and the Small Municipal School District Grant Program; and (3) the Debt Reimbursement Program. For the period FY 2011—FY 2021, the state-funded over $1 billion in school construction and $423 million in major maintenance. However, the state funding crisis due to low oil prices has resulted in significant reductions in funding over the past several years, with just $27.4 million in combined construction and maintenance funding in FY 2020, no state funding in FY 2021 for construction and only $34,277 for maintenance. The reductions are even more apparent when comparing two recent multi-year periods: FY 2011 to FY 2014 compared to the last seven years, FY 2015 to FY 2021. During the first four years, the state spent a total of $1.1 billion, while over the last seven years the state spent $320 million on construction and major maintenance.[30] Furthermore, the legislature placed a complete moratorium on approving projects for the Debt Reimbursement Program from 2015 to 2025. Reimbursement rates have also been reduced in recent years, and debt reimbursement was vetoed by the current governor. These changes leave local taxpayers with the bill for a larger share of existing bond debt than expected. It may also make taxpayers less likely to fund future bond proposals. Due to the declining condition of school facilities over time, these program reductions are a major concern for school district administrators.

EMPLOYEE BENEFITS

The state administers two retirement funding systems that serve school district employees, the Teacher Retirement System (TRS) and the Public Employees Retirement System (PERS). Benefits in both systems have been reduced significantly for new employees over the past three decades, with different tiers implemented. Most significantly, as of July 2006, all new employees are enrolled in a defined contribution system, as opposed to the previous defined benefit plans. Due in part to miscalculations by actuarial consultants, the state is faced with a multi-billion-dollar pension shortfall. When addressing this shortfall, it was decided that school districts and municipalities would not be required to pay escalating amounts toward this shortfall; rather, district rates for the pension plans would be fixed and the state would make 'on-behalf' payments toward the pension plans. In FY 2020 pension payments made on behalf of school districts totaled about $157.2 million.[31] Note that these pension payments are in addition to the contributions by school districts and individuals toward the pension system, which are calculated as a percentage of payroll expense.

CHARTER SCHOOL FUNDING

In 1995, Alaska passed the Charter School Act, which has been amended three times since it was passed. Charter schools are public schools in Alaska. They operate as a school in the local district in which they are located, yet they can also serve as a distance learning or correspondence school for homeschool students or even as a boarding charter school, though there are currently no boarding charter schools in the state.[32] When a charter school is established it may apply for a one time grant for educational services, but no additional state funding is given directly to a charter school. Once established within Alaskan districts, specific contracts with the charter schools are negotiated at the local district level. Therefore, the districts receive funds for students in charter schools according to the state funding formula but the allocated funding and operating mechanisms for each charter are variable, within certain parameters set in statute. For example, the school district can keep an amount determined by DEED for indirect costs, which is limited to a maximum of 4% of direct expenditures. There are no specific reporting requirements of charter school financial data to the state. As of October 1, 2020, there were 8,354 students in 31 charter schools across the state; however some of these students are being served through the charter school as homeschool or correspondence students.[33] Of the 31 charter schools in the state, 15 are located in the Anchorage and Matanuska-Susitna Valley, i.e., geographically close to each other and to high population centers.

VIRTUAL EDUCATION

Due to its far-flung distances, Alaskans have long been involved with virtual education, whether by delivery of paper-based lessons to students in remote locations or early experiments with video conferencing, though the latter has been hindered by lack of bandwidth in many locations. The DEED administered a correspondence program through FY 2007, when these efforts were taken up entirely by individual districts. Over time, district-based correspondence programs grew to serve students statewide and outside the state.

Alaskan students involved in correspondence programs may also attend brick and mortar-based programs for some coursework and extra-curricular activities. In this case, the data checking mechanisms incorporated into the state foundation funding program prevent double-counting of enrollment and provide that enrollment funding be split. Therefore, correspondence programs can be used flexibly to provide a mix of educational opportunities.

With the COVID-19 pandemic, use of virtual education increased in Alaska and around the nation. Many students transferred to correspondence programs, to avoid the uncertain schedule of brick and mortar-based programs. As mentioned earlier in this chapter, Galena City Schools more than doubled district enrollment for FY 2021 with 9,399 students enrolled in the district and a whopping 9,249 of them enrolled in the correspondence school, Interior Distance Education of Alaska (IDEA).[34] According to statewide enrollment data for the 2021 student count, 2,183 students left public school in Alaska compared to the previous year, and 7,819 students moved to different districts. This is based on 35 districts reporting enrollment decreases while 17 districts reported gains.[35] In examining those differences, it appears that 7,559 of those 7,819 students could be accounted for in six districts, which all had significant increases in correspondence school enrollment: Galena City (75.1% or 4,031 students), Yukon-Koyukuk (117.2% or 2,346 students), Nenana City (32.3% or 471 students), Craig City (54.9% or 311 students), Denali Borough (21.6% or 216 students), and Chugach (35.7% or 184). These six districts represent 96.7% of the gain for all 17 districts reporting increases. In addition, 22 school districts reported a 5% or more enrollment drop, triggering the state's hold harmless clause. Only time will tell if these shifts in enrollment were temporary or if they signal a new trend in education in the state.

FEDERAL COVID-19 FUNDING

Alaska's DEED received approximately $505.2 million total from federal COVID-19 relief funding.[36] More than $174.6 millions (34%) of those funds is to be distributed to Anchorage Schools, and four districts will receive the smallest shares at $100,000 each (Aleutians East Borough, Pelican, Skagway, and Yakutat). Alaska districts have indicated they plan to use the various COVID-19 relief funding packages to address specific needs related to the pandemic. Some districts are using the funds to pay for technology (e.g., devices and internet access for disadvantaged students), fulltime virtual teacher positions, blended learning course development, and sanitation. However, it is too early to determine exactly how all the funds will be spent across the state. In order to allow districts to comply with federal spending deadlines, the limitation on general fund balance carryover was suspended temporarily.

CONCLUDING COMMENTS

The State of Alaska's K-12 Foundation Funding program features a comprehensive formula that addresses the large variations in school size, district size and location of schools, including some of the most remote locations in the United States. The 2015 study commissioned by the Legislature resulted in some recommendations, but none of the recommendations were critical to the integrity of the funding formula.[37] However, the state's diversity is the biggest threat to the long-term viability of the carefully balanced formula. As population migrates to urban centers, can the state continue to afford schools with small enrollments in far-flung villages? Is this in the best interest of students? The current dispute between the State of Alaska and US DOE over the Impact Aid disparity test also relates to the state's diversity. The dispute centers around the entirely separate funding mechanism for pupil transportation, which the state argues is necessary because of stark differences among school districts.

Viewed from a local level, the greatest difficulties posed by the current funding system relate to timing. The state legislature typically does not finalize the base student allocation funding amount for the next school year until the end of the legislative session, which ends in April but is sometimes extended into the late spring or summer. Consequently, districts must often proceed with hiring and planning for the next fiscal year without knowing the final state funding level. The other significant planning variable is the student count, which is not known until October when the 20-day count is taken. After all the reconciliations from the fall student count are completed, a district's funding for the fiscal year ending in June may not be finalized until as late as March of that same year.

School district administrators have advocated for an earlier commitment to the base student allocation and for changes in the timing of the student count that is figured into the funding formula. In most years however, legislators fall back on using education funding as an end-of-session bargaining chip, since it is one of the largest components of the state budget.

While it is reasonable to expect that there will be significant changes to Alaska's K-12 funding formula in the future, the authors are hopeful that school funding experts will be consulted, along with Alaska school business officials, so that the outcome will be a funding mechanism that addresses the needs of this unique state.

ENDNOTES

[1] Gordon Harrison, "Alaska's Constitution: A Citizen's Guide, 5th edition." Alaska Legislative Affairs Agency. (2021). http://akleg.gov/docs/pdf/citizens_guide.pdf

[2] J. Livey. and G. Keiser, "Public School Financing in Alaska." House Research Agency—Alaska State Legislature. (1987). http://archives2.legis.state.ak.us/PublicImageServer.cgi?lra/SAC_86-87/87-400001M.pdf

[3] Title VIII of the Elementary and Secondary Education Act of 1965 authorizes the federal government to compensate school districts for any impact on either the district's revenue or expenditures resulting from federal presence in the district. In Alaska, this includes Native lands, military bases, low rent housing and other federal facilities.

[4] Alaska Department of Education and Early Development, "Alaska's Public School Funding Formula: A Report to the Alaska State Legislature." (2001). https://education.alaska.gov/publications/FundingFormulaSB36Report.docx

[5] Joint Legislative Education Funding Task Force, "Report to the Governor and Legislature." (2007). https://library.alaska.gov/asp/edocs/2007/09/ocn173495965.pdf

[6] Hootch v. Alaska State-Operated School System, 536 P.2d 793 (Alaska 1975).

[7] Tobeluk v. Lind, 589 P.2d 873 (Alaska 1979).

[8] Kasayulie v. State, Case no. 3AN-97-3782 Civil (Alaska Superior Court 1999), consent decree signed in September 2011.

[9] Alaska Department of Labor and Workforce Development. "Research and Analysis: Population Estimates." (2020). https://live.laborstats.alaska.gov/pop/index.cfm.

[10] . Amy Dagley, "Alaska," Journal of Education Finance, volume 46, issue 3 (2021): 244-245.

[11] Alaska Department of Education and Early Development, "District Enrollment by Grade as of October 1, 2020." (2021). https://education.alaska.gov/Stats/enrollment/1-%20Enrollment%20by%20District%20by%20Grade%202020-21.xlsx or https://education.alaska.gov/data-center

[12] Department of Commerce, Community, and Economic Development. "Alaska Tax Facts, Office of the State Assessor." https://www.commerce.alaska.gov/web/dcra/officeofthestateassessor/alaskataxfacts.aspx

[13] Alaska Statute 14.17.410(b)(2).

[14] Formerly Title VIII of the Elementary and Secondary Education Act (ESEA) of 1965, currently Title VII under ESEA, as amended by Every Student Succeeds Act of 2015.

[15] Alaska Statute 14.17.410

[16] Alaska Department of Education and Early Development. "Public School Funding Program Overview," 2021. https://education.alaska.gov/SchoolFinance/docs/ADA%20Funding%20Program%20Overview%202022_eff1-2021.pdf; Legislative Finance Division. Citizen's Guide to K-12 Funding in Alaska: Informational Paper 21-2. 2020. https://www.legfin.akleg.gov/InformationalPapers/19-2CitizensGuideToK12.pdf

[17] Bradford Tuck, Matthew Berman, and Alexandra Hill of Institute of Social and Economic Research. "Alaska School District Cost Study Update," 2005. https://pubs.iseralaska.org/media/7705ea52-6fde-4d7f-b180-14da7f94f7a6/final_School_Cost_Update.pdf

[18] Justin Silverstein, Amanda Brown, and Mark Fermanich of Augenblick, Palaich and Associates, "Review of Alaska's School Funding Program," 2015. http://apaconsulting.net/wp-content/uploads/2015/07/AlaskaFunding2015.pdf

[19] Alaska Department of Education and Early Development. "FY2022 Foundation Formula PROJECTION," prepared by School Finance November 20, 2020. https://education.alaska.gov/schoolfinance/foundationfunding

[20] Alaska Department of Education and Early Development. "FY2021 Foundation Formula - FINAL," prepared August 31, 2021. https://education.alaska.gov/schoolfinance/foundationfunding

[21] Alaska Department of Education and Early Development. "FY2022 Foundation Formula PROJECTION," prepared by School Finance November 20, 2021. https://education.alaska.gov/schoolfinance/foundationfunding

22 Alaska Department of Education and Early Development. "FY2022 Foundation Formula PRO-JECTION," prepared by School Finance November 20, 2020. https://education.alaska.gov/school-finance/foundationfunding

23 Alaska Department of Education and Early Development. "School Enrollment by Grade as of October 1, 2020," 2021. http://education.alaska.gov/data-center

24 Alaska Department of Education and Early Development. "Public School Funding Program Overview," 2021. https://education.alaska.gov/SchoolFinance/docs/ADA%20Funding%20Program%20Overview%202022_eff1-2021.pdf

25 Alaska Department of Education and Early Development, "Pupil Transportation Grant by District FY2013 to FY2022," April 20, 2021. https://education.alaska.gov/SchoolFinance/docs/GrantBy_District_FY05-FY22_Projected.xlsx.

26 Silverstein, et. al (2015), p. 38.

27 Ibid, p. 42.

28 Alaska Department of Health and Social Services, "Adverse Childhood Experiences—Overcoming ACEs in Alaska," 2014. http://dhss.alaska.gov/commissioner/Documents/MentalHealth/StrengtheningSystem-CompPlan_Goal1_2020-24.pdf

29 Brookings Institution Pre-Kindergarten Task Force, "The Current State of Scientific Knowledge on Pre-Kindergarten Effects," 2017. https://www.brookings.edu/wp-content/uploads/2017/04/duke_prekstudy_final_4-4-17_hires.pdf

30 Alaska Department of Education and Early Development. "School Capital Project Funding Under SB237: A Report to the Legislature," 2021. https://education.alaska.gov/facilities/pdf/Final_SB237_Report2021.pdf

31 Alaska Department of Education and Early Development. "Audited FY2020 Revenues," 2021. http://education.alaska.gov/SchoolFinance/OperatingFund/20AuditedRevenues.xlsx, or https://education.alaska.gov/schoolfinance/budgetsactual

32 Alaska Statutes 14.03.255

33 Alaska Department of Education and Early Development. "School Enrollment by Grade as of October 1, 2020." http://education.alaska.gov/Stats/enrollment/2-%20Enrollment%20by%20School%20by%20Grade%202020-21.xlsx

34 Alaska Department of Education and Early Development. "School Enrollment by Grade as of October 1, 2020." http://education.alaska.gov/Stats/enrollment/2-%20Enrollment%20by%20School%20by%20Grade%202020-21.xlsx

35 Alaska Department of Education and Early Development. "School Enrollment by Grade as of October 1, 2019." http://education.alaska.gov/stats/enrollment/2-Enrollment-by-School-by-Grade-2019-20.xlsx

36 Alaska Department of Education and Early Development, "COVID-19 Federal Relief Funding for Alaska School Districts," Updated September 1, 2021. https://education.alaska.gov/arp-state-plan/9.1.2021%20COVID%20Relief%20Funds%20-%20School%20District%20Allocations.pdf

37 .Justin Silverstein, Amanda Brown, and Mark Fermanich of Augenblick, Palaich and Associates, "Review of Alaska's School Funding Program," 2015. http://apaconsulting.net/wp-content/uploads/2015/07/AlaskaFunding2015.pdf

CHAPTER 3

ARIZONA

Daniel W. Eadens

University of Central Florida

Gayle A. Blanchard

Northern Arizona University

GENERAL BACKGROUND

According to Article 11 Section 1 of the Arizona State Constitution "requires the legislature to establish a 'general and uniform' public school system" and Section 10 of that same Article requires,

> The revenue for the maintenance of the respective state educational institutions shall be derived from the investment of the proceeds of the sale, and from the rental of such lands as have been set aside by the enabling act approved June 20, 1910, or other legislative enactment of the United States, for the use and benefit of the respective state educational institutions. In addition to such income the legislature shall make such appropriations, to be met by taxation, as shall insure the proper maintenance of all state educational institutions, and shall make such special appropriations as shall provide for their development and improvement. (Arizona State Legislature, n.d.).[1]

Funding Public Schools in the United States, Indian Country,
and US Territories (Second Edition), pages 33–47.
Copyright © 2023 by Information Age Publishing
www.infoagepub.com
All rights of reproduction in any form reserved.

The language is mostly clear, however, the words in the last sentence are subject to interpretation. Arizona has had an equalization formula since the 1970s. According to Chuck Essigs, Director of Governmental Relations for the Arizona Association of School Board Officials (2018), prior to 1980 (Laws 1980, 2nd S.S., Ch. 9), there was unlimited overrides with no time limits, no limit on transportation spending, the county paid employer's retirement and social security for certified employees, 7% annual increases in regular education and special education per pupil formula, separate budgets for regular and special education transportation, and districts were allowed a $.30/.60 levy. However, in 1980 and beyond, revenue control limits (RCLs) were set, equalization of budget limits occurred for 1981/82 through 1985/86 81-82 minus 20% of variation removed each year, and transportation was not included. Regarding the transportation formula(TSL) there was no equalization and no serious movement to revise it since then and students could travel to any district and count towards state funding. However, in 1994 open enrollment became mandated with required policies.[2]

The Arizona State Senate Issue Brief (2018) wrote that due to the plethora of court cases in other states, "Arizona began reforming its school finance system to address the potential unconstitutionality of its system and reestablish a 'general and uniform' public school system" and that the statutory formula from 1980, modified in 1985 to eliminate district funding disparities and increase state funding, is the current system, which is designed to "*equalize* per-pupil spending among school districts, taking into account student enrollment and property values" (p. 1). Furthermore, spending is capped, and each district approximately gets that same amount of funding for each students.[3]

Descriptive Statistics

According to the 2020-2021 Arizona Report Card, there are more than 1,111,000 students that attend publicly funded K-12 schools. "Approximately 874,000 of those students attend one of more than 2,000 district public schools, with the remaining 237,000 attending one of more than 700 charter schools in the state."

Of the 60,176 K-12 Arizona teachers currently in classrooms, 49,941 work in district K-12 schools and 10,235 work in charter schools. Currently there are an additional 37,271 certified teachers in the state that are either serving in positions outside of a classroom or not working within the education system.[4]

CURRENT POLITICAL CLIMATE

The current political climate in Arizona might best be described as strained. " In 2020 Arizona voted for a Democratic presidential candidate for the first time in almost 25 years, has two Democratic senators for the first time in almost 70 years, but also voted for one of the most deeply conservative Republican state legislatures in decades."[5]

No state in the country has cut school funding more than Arizona. Between 2008 and 2014, state lawmakers cut funding per student by 36.6 percent, according to a national analysis by the non-partisan Center on Budget and Policy Priorities.[6]

The political leaders in the state of Arizona have continued their mantra of no new taxes, no new consistent funding sources for schools, greater school choice options and proposed legislation for the expansion of vouchers. These actions along with ongoing litigation for school capital funding and no support for teacher raises, resulted in a 2018 Red for Ed teacher walkout, supported by the Arizona Education Association (AEA), the state's professional organization. Membership for this group is voluntary and the AEA does not engage in collective bargaining, as Arizona is a right to work state.

Ongoing K-12 challenges include continued litigation for school capital funding, proposition 208 (a 2020 voter approved tax on high income earners) and the threat of a mid-year funding reduction due to an aggregate spending limit based on constitutional language from the 1980s. Additionally, "Arizona's 54th Legislature, 2nd Regular Session, adjourned Sine Die at 12:21 AM May 26, 2020, without sufficiently addressing the impending challenges related to COVID-19.» [7] This lack of legislative action further fuels the divide between educational organizations and the state leaders.

SOURCES OF REVENUE

Arizona has a primarily student-based formula. A base amount is assigned for a student with no unique circumstances or special needs. Increased funding (weights) are provided to increase funding for specific categories of students. The current base funding amount per student for FY 2021 was $4,305.73. Arizona does not provide increased funding for students in poverty.[8]

Arizona sets a ceiling for local property tax rates, as well as a level above which voter approval is required. School districts require voter approval to raise more than the rate sufficient to reach their formula amount and, even with voter approval, are to 15% above their formula amount for operating costs.

DISTRIBUTION FORMULAS

General Fund

While some wealthy school districts in Arizona with high property values could generate their own funding, "most school districts require revenues in the form of Basic State Aid in order to receive full funding under the statutory formula" (The Arizona State Senate Issue Brief, 2016, p. 1).[9] The current district funding formula is:

Equalization Base - Qualifying Tax Rate = Equalization Assistance

Equalization Assistance - State Equalization Tax Rate = Basic State Aid

The following is a description of each of the element in the formula, based on information from the (The Arizona State Senate Issue Brief, 2018, pp. 2-5).

The first part of the formula is the Equalization Base. Essentially this is the limits of each district's spending and is derived by adding the Base Support Level (BSL), Transportation Support Level (TSL), and District Additional Assistance (DAA).

Equalization Base = BSL + TSL+ DAA

BSL includes capital and weights. The BSL adds weights for Special Education (SPED), high School Students, English Language Learners (EL), K-3 students, and small and isolated school districts. In FY 2010, SPED weights were calculated by multiplying the number of diagnoses times the BSL. For example, students with multiple disabilities sever sensory impairment were weighted 7.947, Orthopedic Impairment 6.773, Visual Impairment 4.806, Hearing Impairment, 4.771, Moderate Intellectual Disability, 4.421, Developmental delay, Mild Intellectual Disability, Speech and Language Impairment, and Other Health Impaired were all weighted at 0.003.

District unweighted (actual student count), per particular range of grades, student count times a specified legislated amount yields the DAA. The formula looks at student counts in three size categories: less than 100, between 100 and 600, and more than 600 and three different grade level bands.

DAA = Unweighted Student Count x Per Pupil Amount

The legislative set amount, adjusted annually for inflation, multiplied by daily mileage of bus routes, tokens, and passes, is the Transportation Support Level (TSL), not to be confused with the Transportation Revenue Control Limit, option to asses additional to the property tax for costs greater than the TSL.

TSL = $ Amount x Route Miles (eligible students) + Tokens/Passes

The BSL is a school district's total from their Weighted Student Count (WSC) multiplied by the Base Level Amount (BLA) multiplied by the Teacher Experience Index (TEI). District size and location (rural, urban, suburban), certain grade levels (Group A) and student characteristics (Group B) determine the WSC. The per student amount set by the legislature and adjusted for inflation are the Base Level Amount (BLA).

BSL = WSC x BLA x 1.0125 x TEI

FY 2021 Base Level Amount = $4,305.73

$4,359.55 with 1/25% teacher compensation

Qualifying Tax Rate (QTR), adjusted annually, is the primary property tax rate set by the legislature to determine how much funding districts receive from the state and is multiplied by the Net Assessed Value (NAV) to determine amount of state aid. In smaller rural communities, typically where there are fewer businesses and lower property taxes collected, is where basic state aid from the state's general fund makes up the difference that local property taxes do not generate enough, due to the equalization base funding being greater than the QTR times the NAV. There reverse is true in wealthier communities and cities where QTR times NAV is less than the equalization base and the property tax rates are set. Additionally, property owners are assessed a State Equalization Tax Rate (SETR). Yields from the primary property tax and minimum qualifying tax rate, which are levied and collected by each county, goes directly into Arizona's State General Fund. Districts are eligible for equalization assistance if the revenue from the QTR does not exceeds the district's equalization base.

QTR > Equalization Base = No Equalization Assistance

Equalization Base > QTR = Equalization Assistance

Equalization Assistance > SETR = Basic State Aid

SCHOOL FACILITIES AND CAPITAL OUTLAY

Arizona Supreme court declared the 1994 Arizona Capital Funding System unconstitutional based on *Roosevelt v. Bishop*. Essentially, funding disparities between districts was unequalized. According to the Arizona State Senate Issue Brief (2018, Aug. 3),[10]

In 1994, Arizona's system of school capital finance was declared unconstitutional by a court decision in Roosevelt v. Bishop because it failed to conform to the state Constitution's "general and uniform" clause. The Arizona Supreme Court opined that the system relied too heavily on secondary property tax revenue, which is driven by property value, and created an unequalized system with funding disparities between school districts. The state twice attempted to address the Court's ruling, first in 1996 through an amended system based on the original financing system, and again in 1997 with the creation of a new system, the Assistance to Build Classrooms program. In *Hull v. Albrecht*, the Court rejected both proposals and imposed on the state a deadline of June 30, 1998, to develop a constitutional system of school capital finance or risk closure of K-12 public schools. On July 9, 1998, during a special session, legislation was passed reforming the way traditional K-12 public schools (not including charter schools) finance capital investment and construction in Arizona. This legislation was called Students Fair and Immediate Resources for

Students. Today, commonly known as Students FIRST. Since 1998, the Students FIRST program has served as Arizona's school capital finance system, funded in part by Proposition 301 revenues dedicated from the state transaction privilege tax, state trust land revenues and annual legislative appropriations to the School Facilities Board (SFB). p. 1

There are three programs in Students FIRST, administered by the SFB, and they deal with emergency deficiency corrections, building renewals, and new school construction. While the emergency deficiency fund dried, the building renewal program was funded via formula from FY 1999-2008, but was replaced by an amount in FY 2009. The brief listed new school construction originally under the FY 2014 formula (No. of Pupils x Square Foot Per Pupil, x Cost per Square Foot) but later changed,

From FY 2009 through FY 2013, the Legislature placed a moratorium on all new school construction but exempted lease-to purchase authority and land acquisition. The moratorium was lifted in FY 2014. Finally, in FY 2011 SFB issued Qualified School Construction Bonds, as authorized by the federal American Reinvestment and Recovery Act of 2009, to finance $91 million worth of lease-to-own transactions that funded the construction of five new schools and additional space for three schools. (p. 4)

FOOD SERVICE

According to Olson (2009), "districts are permitted to operate school meal programs on a nonprofit basis to children in attendance at the school. All revenues collected in the operation of a school district's school meal program must be deposited in the district's school meal program fund" (p. 55).

TEACHER RETIREMENT

The Arizona State Retirement System (ASRS) contribution rate is 12.41% for retirement, long term disability, and health insurance. As of June 30, 2020, ASRS active education membership represented 52% from public schools, 2% charter schools, 8% universities and 4% community colleges totaling 66% in ASRS Public Education. As of FY 2020, there was $42.2 billion in its investments. (Arizona State Retirement System (ASRS) 2021).[11]

SPECIAL EDUCATION

Funding for special education was finally mandated in 1993, but not effective until SY 1976/77. Essigs (2018) said that 90% of the excess cost was placed in the 1974 state funding formula and that the formula changed after that a year later. He furthered that in SY 1980/81 Group A component was added and 85% of special education students were funded based on the total students in the district. [12]

COMPENSATORY EDUCATION

There is a fund for compensatory instruction that was established in 2006 and designed to "to improving the English proficiency of English language learners. The programs may include individual or small group instruction, extended day classes, summer school, or intercession school" (Olson, 2009, p. 52)[13]

EARLY CHILDHOOD AND GIFTED EDUCATION

"Like federal grants, the state also funds special projects in addition to the formula based funding of the foundation system. The state projects, however, are significantly less expensive than the ESEA Title I and IDEA Part B grants" (Olson, 2009, p. 52).[14] A few of these special projects were grants for vocational education, early childhood education, adult education, dropout prevention, gifted, and family literacy.

BILINGUAL EDUCATION

The state General Fund special line-item funds the structured English immersion program which was initiated in 2006. Revenues are distributed based on each school's request "to provide instruction to English language learners" (Olson, 2009, p. 52).[15]

OTHER CATEGORICAL PROGRAMS

Assistance to School Districts for Children of State Employees, Certificates of Educational Convenience, and Special Education Fund are three Other State Aid programs that The Arizona State Senate Issue Brief listed (2018, p. 6).[16] The latter fund covers special education student's costs at schools of deaf and blind, state hospitals, disabled programs, and residential facilities that are private when placed by the state.

CHARTER SCHOOLS

Essigs (2018) provided the following information on Charter School funding.[17] The proposed voucher law became the charter school law in 1994. He said initially the original formula was exactly the same for charter schools as it was for public schools. Charters have surged in Arizona. In 1998 charters captured 4.3% of average daily membership in Arizona and districts had 95.7%. Charter enrollment rose to 18,000 students from Data from Oct. 1, 2020 showing an 18,000 student increase from the previous year, according to the Arizona State Board for Charter Schools—March 2021 newsletter. It was projected that in 20/21 charters would have 20.1% and districts 79.9%. In 2017 charter school shares of state revenue was $1.3 billion with 170K students and districts had $3.4 billion of the state revenue and have 928K students. In SY 1996/97 a transportation formula was set at $174 per student, now it is $261 and is permanently part of additional assistance for charters that was added in 1997/98.

The funding and ADE Annual Report for FY 2020 was released and offered this relevant information comparing public and charter schools[18]:

- According to the Arizona Joint Legislative Budget Committee (JLBC), for FY 2020 the average daily membership (ADM) for charter schools totaled 202,633 while District Public Schools ADM totaled 918,624.
- For FY 2020, Arizona charter schools captured 22% of the Average Daily Membership (ADM) while district public schools maintained 78% ADM. •Charter School ADM was 202,633 and District Public Schools ADM was 918,624.
- When comparing the equalization formula funding for FY 2020, charter school revenue was just over $1.5 billion as compared to district public schools at almost $6 billion. Per pupil amounts are as follows: charter schools $7,690, district public schools $6,387. •When considering all reported funding: maintenance and operation (M & 0), capital and other funding from state, federal and local sources, charter revenue climbed to nearly $2 billion and district public schools reached just over $10 billion. Per pupil amounts are as follows: charter schools $9,845, district public schools $11,153. (JLBC Staff Overview of K-12 per pupil funding for school districts and charter schools, 2021)

The following is a description of each of the elements in the formula based on information from the (The Arizona State Senate Issue Brief, 2018, p. 4). Since charter schools do not have taxing authority and have no other revenue from local taxpayer sources, they are eligible for state aid from the state General Fund and there is no equalization assistance. The formula only has two parts.

$$\text{Charter School Funding} = BSL + CAA$$

While the BSL is the same as above, minus TEI, Charter Additional Assistance (CAA) is statutorily assigned and is similar to DAA.

$$CAA = \text{unweighted count x per pupil amount}$$

PRIVATE SCHOOLS, TAX CREDITS, DEDUCTIONS, EXEMPTIONS

Laux and Jensen (2018) reported the following information about state aid to private schools and tax credits, deductions, and exemptions. They said private school tuition income tax credit was started in 1998 for individuals. Then, in 2006 corporate tax credits were added. As of 2011, public school funds can be diverted to provide Empowerment Scholarship Accounts (ESAs) and Student Tuition Organizations (STOs) for private school tuition, that is when the empowerment scholar savings accounts began and was expanded in future years. Both ESAs and STOs provide an option for families to opt out or public school. Arizona, in 1998, created the first tax credits for citizens that donate to an STO, which is a scholarship award for private schools. Currently there are over 90 STOs and it continues to expand, Donations are allowed by corporations. While families are limited on the annual amount they can donate, corporations can donate up to their entire tax liability. The state fiscal impact is that the state revenues are reduced as individual and corporate income tax earn credits. The corporate credit cap was increased to $10 million a year plus 20% annual increase in 2006. There is no maximum amount a corporation may contribute, but the state does assign an overall donation cap every year. Corporate Tax Credits are allowed on a first come, first serve basis until the cap is reached. The cap for fiscal year 2021-2022 is $135 million.[19]

Ellen, Lozano, and O'Brien (2018) gave this information about ESAs. In FY 2018, there were approximately 5,000 using the ESA program, about $75 million (Arizona Department of Education, 2021). As of March 31, 2021 there are 9,831 active ESA students. A.R.S. 15-2402(B)(4) outlines what is and is not permitted to be used with ESA funds, mainly they are used for private school tuition, textbooks, curricular material, and tutoring and ESA contracts must be renewed annually, Arizona Department of Education disperses the funds quarterly to applicant's parents on a prepaid debit card. Amounts could range annually from $3k to $30K and is about 90% of what the state would normally pay the district.

ESA expansion cap is limited to .5% (about 5,000 students) for all Arizona students until 2020 and the additional costs to Arizona state general fund annually for ESA expansion is substantial, $2.1 million in 2018. ESAs in Arizona are funded at 90% of the state's per pupil funding (100% for low income students). Currently, there are 10 categories of eligibility for ESA. As it stands now, any ESA funds that were unused, up to $2,000 annually, may be converted into a Coverdell Education Savings Account for college. Student may not use an ESA while they receive an STO scholarship or tax credit scholarship simultaneously. This year there is a new IRS Charitable contribution regulation that restricts claims to only the amounts above the State tax credits.[20]

LOCAL SCHOOL REVENUE

Neighborhood elections are opportunities for local citizens to supplement their school funding with overrides, bonds, and line item property taxes such as adjacent ways, desegregation, transportation, prevention. Bonds and overrides, pending voter approval, can increase district funding, although this is not allowed for Charters. Overrides are typically for seven years, but at the end of the fifth year they begin decreasing. Maintenance and operations (M & O) overrides, commonly used for staff and salaries, can be approved in Arizona up to 15% of the M & O budget. Capitol overrides can be approved up to 5%. Bond funding amounts and usage are restricted specifically for individual projects such as busses, new buildings and renovations and must be audited annually. The use of bonds, for capital

TABLE 3.1. Education General Fund Annual Expenditure: FY2014-2022

	FY 2014	FY 2015	FY 2016	FY 2017	FY 2018	FY 2019	FY 2020	FY 2021	FY 2022
EDUCATION									
Arts, Arizona Commission on the	0	0	0	0	0	0	0	0	0
Charter Schools, State Board for	786,900	896,400	1,024,300	997,300	1,069,800	1,077,900	2,200,000	2,152,100	2,103,000
Community Colleges, Arizona (36)	69,508,700	71,906,400	54,373,200	54,312,700	55,086,500	57,236,600	95,681,800	66,645,400	108,904,700
Deaf and the Blind, School for the	21,418,500	21,921,300	21,378,100	21,616,900	21,800,700	21,457,000	23,255,200	23,865,500	23,255,700
Education, State Board of (58)	0	0	1,139,100	921,700	953,500	906,200	1,038,000	1,334,300	2,340,000
Education, Department of (7) (58)	3,661,757,100	3,831,124,100	3,939,909,800	4,079,045,400	4,201,507,900	4,675,275,400	5,192,791,800	5,599,591,900	5,910,547,300
Historical Society, Arizona (64)	3,155,000	3,156,000	3,157,000	2,723,100	3,179,800	3,195,000	3,107,600	3,195,600	2,906,000
Historical Society, Prescott	826,000	809,000	825,800	824,500	840,200	827,600	832,600	867,700	900,600
Medical Student Loans Board	0	0	0	0	0	0	0	0	0
Postsecondary Education, Commission for (23)	1,396,800	1,396,800	1,396,800	1,396,800	1,848,900	1,646,800	1,680,000	1,680,900	1,680,900
School Capital Facilities, State Board for	0	0	0	0	0	0	0	0	0
School Facilities Board (30)	191,646,800	178,355,700	230,378,000	227,889,600	302,240,700	261,617,500	353,509,100	273,994,700	290,809,500
Universities/Board of Regents									
Board of Regents (23)	21,902,600	24,928,400	21,928,400	21,928,400	6,909,300	6,898,100	22,395,100	22,480,000	29,916,000
Arizona State University - Tempe/DPC (68)	270,228,200	290,102,200	315,844,800	305,397,600	320,256,600	328,775,800	334,270,600	324,717,400	385,261,900
Arizona State University - East Campus (68)	22,704,200	25,853,400	28,095,600	0	0	0	0	0	0
Arizona State University - West Campus (68)	33,328,100	33,328,100	39,024,400	0	0	0	0	0	0
Arizona State University - Other	0	0	0	0	0	0	0	0	0
Northern Arizona University	109,245,000	118,281,200	131,452,600	105,227,000	108,612,700	112,095,700	117,250,900	109,804,600	135,452,400
University of Arizona - Main Campus (5) (64)	208,501,000	209,341,200	241,652,500	197,059,600	199,600,900	208,836,400	215,808,900	207,722,200	250,739,100
University of Arizona - Health Sciences Center (18)	69,585,300	69,585,300	85,170,200	68,859,800	69,437,700	68,897,700	76,897,900	76,897,700	76,897,700
University of Arizona - Other	0	0	0	0	0	0	0	0	0
University Medical Center/Post Secondary Education Board	0	0	0	0	0	0	0	0	0
Subtotal Universities/Regents	735,494,400	771,419,800	863,168,500	698,472,400	704,817,200	725,503,700	766,623,400	741,621,900	878,267,100
TOTAL EDUCATION	4,685,990,200	4,880,985,500	5,116,750,600	5,088,200,400	5,293,345,200	5,748,743,700	6,442,230,600	6,714,950,000	7,221,714,800

Source: Education General Fund Annual Expenditure. (2021, August 27). FY 2014-2022. State Department of (38)(57). 631,817. The Joint Legislative Budget Committee. https://www.azleg.gov/jlbc/gfhistoricalspending.pdf

expenditures, are restricted to the information on the ballot and the voter information guide and must be nearly all used within the three years. Additionally, some
districts can obtain Indian Gaming funds and Proposition 301 (which increased
the state's sale tax by 0.6 cents) and was approved by Arizona voters and requires
Arizona to provide extra educational funds.

EARMARKED STATE REVENUES

The information in this section is according to (The Arizona State Senate Issue
Brief, 2018, p. 5).[21] When designated Arizona state trust lands are sold, the funds
are placed in the Permanent State School Fund (investment earnings, lease proceeds, and interest on land purchases) to offset the state General Fund costs for
Basic Sate Aid. Proposition 123, initiated in 2010 and ruled on in 2014, required
the state to increase the base level based on inflation. The 2015 settlement, voter
approved in 2016, increase land trust distribution from 2.5 to 6.9 percent through
FY 2025. Additionally, an automatic homeowner's rebate helps Additional State
Aid to districts.

FEDERAL COVID-19 FUNDING

Of the $190.5 billion allocated by the federal government to the Elementary and
Secondary Schools Emergency Relief fund (ESSER), Arizona received over
$4 billion from the three separate federal relief packages. For Arizona these
three packages, comprised of Coronavirus Aid, Relief and Economic Security
(CARES) Act, the Coronavirus Response and Relief Supplemental Appropriations Act, 2021 (CRRSA), and The American Rescue Plan Act. Combined they
reflect the following allocations:

ESSER I: $277,422,944

ESSER II: $1,149,715,947

ESSER III: $ 2,582,098,697

The funds are highly flexible and are designed to address local relief, prevention and preparation, and recovery efforts relative to responding to COVID-19.
The majority of the dollars went directly to districts and schools, while the Arizona Department of Education designated the required set asides to statewide
strategic projects in order to support the needs of schools and increase learning
opportunities.[22]

LEA Allocations

The Arizona Department of Education used set aside funds of $112.4 million to
ensure a base level of relief. Every public school and non-profit charter school in

Arizona was guaranteed to receive relief funding of a minimum of $150,000, with $175,000 guaranteed for rural school districts and charter schools, and $200,000 guaranteed for the most remote school districts and charter schools.

In addition to the ESSER I and II funds, school districts could apply for state set aside funds from the ESSER III funds. The Arizona Department of Education identified the following three focus areas for this competitive application process: 1) enrichment and reinforcements for learning, 2) mental, behavior and physical health support for students and educators, and 3) student and family re-engagement.

The Arizona Department of Education partnered with outside agencies such as Achieve60AZ, College Success Arizona, Expect More Arizona and the Arizona School Administrators Association to identify and develop resources to support LEAs, and to meet local stakeholder engagement requirements under ESSER III.

An evidenced-based clearing house of resources was developed and shared with LEAs This clearing house provides evidence-based interventions to address academic and social-emotional learning loss. Additionally, the Arizona Department of Education initiated ongoing webinars and trainings that provided the knowledge and steps for districts in order to address submissions, requirements and expenditures.

Statewide Projects

Statewide projects and initiatives were funded through the required set aside of ESSER funds. Projects and allocations are based on seven identified areas.[23]

1. Baseline levels of relief for all public schools
   - $112.4 million to ensure a baseline level of relief funding for all schools and career and technical education districts.
2. Increase proficiency for all students and close achievement gaps.
   - $9.6 million – Partnership with ASU Prep Digital: Math Momentum
   - $1 million – Funding for Arizona's Office of Indian Education
   - $500,000 – Special Education Cost Study
   - $500,000– Holistic Youth Transformation Program: New Pathways for Youth
   - $300,000 – Time is Now Youth Mentorship: Big Brothers, Big Sisters $100,000 – Opportunities for Youth
3. Educator recruitment and retention
   - $5 million -Northern Arizona University and the Arizona K12 Center: Arizona Teacher Residency Program
   - $1 million - Northern Arizona University Dine Institute Teacher Fellows
   - $1 million - Arizona State University Preparing Educators for Arizona's Indigenous Communities (PEAIC)

- $1 million –University of Arizona Indigenous Teacher Education Program (ITEP)
- $500,000 – Partnership with University of Arizona's Center for Recruitment and Retention of Math Educators for Professional Development

4. Safe and healthy schools
  - $21.3 Million – Addition of 140 School Counselor & Social Worker Positions through the School Safety Grant Program
  - $3 million –PAX Good Behavior Game Training
  - $470,000 –Trauma Sensitive Training and Support for Schools

5. Serving Arizona school communities and families through the pandemic
  - $5 million – Special Education Compensatory Services Fund
  - $2.3 Million – Support for Community-Based Organizations, YMCA, and Boys & Girls Club
  - $1 million –Parent Educator Academy

6. Bridging the digital divide and providing access to digital resources
  - $6.5 Million – Partnership with Discovery Education
  - $3 Million –Office of Digital Teaching and Learning (ODTL)
  - $2.5 million –ASU Prep Digital: Arizona Virtual Teacher Institute
  - $1.5 Million – Partnership Expanding Rural Broadband
  - $853,000 – Laptop and Hotspot Partnership with City of Phoenix
  - $15,000 – Kajeet Hotspots for Students & Families

7. Post secondary access and attainment
  - Nearly $2 million dollars to address college and career counseling, FAFSA completion rates and training.

Governor's Emergency Education Relief Fund (GEER)

The Arizona Department of Education reports the state of Arizona received over $69 million dollars under the Governor's Emergency Education Relief Fund. The purpose of these funds is to provide additional support to K-12 and Higher Education institutions that have been most significantly impacted by COVID-19. These funds cannot be used by states to replace state aid.[24]

GEER Fund Projects

- $40 million to expand broadband in rural communities to bridge the digital divide
- $20 million to bring in extra support for high-need schools through Acceleration Academies
- $6 million for the Arizona Teachers Academy to assist with the teacher shortage
- $1 million in microgrants to support innovative programs to continue educating Arizona students

- $1 million for vehicles for the Arizona School for the Deaf and the Blind
- $700,000 for leadership development through Beat the Odds Leadership Academy
- $500,000 for tutoring from Teach for America to provide tutoring to kids most in need in schools most impacted across the state

SUMMARY

Arizona's school funding model is based on an equalization formula. While the base support level of funding for each student is initially the same, more funds are added to district's with certain students such as English language learners and those with special needs, which receive additional weighted funding based on varying exceptionalities. Additionally, new and growing school districts are authorized additional funding for facilities, voters have opportunity to increase property tax for schools, and can supplement property taxes to create additional support for local schools. Finally, districts that fail to raise enough tax base funding are given state aid. Nationally, Arizona continues to trail all other states in per-pupil funding. "The SARS-CoV-2 (COVID-19) pandemic further hurt state revenue, and the impending shortfall will likely impact educational review." [25]

ENDNOTES

[1] Article 11, Section 1 of the Arizona Constitution requires the legislature to establish a "general and uniform" public school system. Arizona State Senate Issue Brief. (2018, Aug. 3). Arizona's school finance system. Retrieved from https://www.azleg.gov/Briefs/Senate/ARIZONA%27S%20SCHOOL%20FINANCE%20SYSTEM%202018.pdf

[2] Chuck Essigs, (2018, September 5). *How things got this way: A brief history of recent Arizona school finance*. Power point presented at The Arizona School Board Association's 42nd Annual Law Conference in Phoenix Arizona. Unpublished.

[3] Arizona State Senate Issue Brief. (2018, Aug. 3). Arizona's school finance system. Retrieved from https://www.azleg.gov/Briefs/Senate/ARIZONA%27S%20SCHOOL%20FINANCE%20SYSTEM%202018.pdf

[4] Arizona Department of Education, *AZ School Report Cards*. Retrieved from https://azreportcards.azed.gov/state-report

[5] The London School of Economics and Political Science, *LSE US Centre's daily blog on American Politics and Policy*. Retrieved from : https://blogs.lse.ac.uk/usappblog/2021/01/21/what-happened-arizona-turned-blue-in-the-2020-presidential-election-but-the-republicans-still-control-the-state/

[6] Center on Budget and Policy Priority. (Nov. 2016). *School Funding in Arizona Still Well Below 2008 Level* Retrieved from https://www.cbpp.org/sites/default/files/atoms/files/11-1-16sfp-fact-sheets-az.pdf

[7] Martínez, David, G. "Arizona." *Journal of Education Finance* 46, no. 3 (2021): 246-248. muse.jhu.edu/article/786652.

[8] Arizona State Senate Fact Sheet for H.B. 2902/S.B. 1675 Retrieved from https://www.azleg.gov/legtext/54leg/2R/summary/S.1685-2902RULES_ASENACTED.DOCX.htm

[9] Arizona State Senate Issue Brief. (2018, Aug 3). Arizona's school finance system. Retrieved from https://www.azleg.gov/Briefs/Senate/ARIZONA%27S%20SCHOOL%20FINANCE%20SYSTEM%202018.pdf

[10] Arizona State Senate Issue Brief. (2018, August 3). Students First. Retrieved from https://www.azleg.gov/Briefs/Senate/STUDENTS%20FIRST%202018.pdf

[11] Arizona State Retirement System. (2021). *Popular Annual Financial Report FY 2020.* Retrieved from *https://www.azasrs.gov/sites/default/files/Popular%20Annual%20Financial%20Report%20 FY%202020.pdf*

[12] Essigs, Chuck. (2018, September 5). *How things got this way: A brief history of recent Arizona school finance.* Power point presented at The Arizona School Board Association's 42nd Annual Law Conference in Phoenix Arizona. Unpublished.

[13] [14, 15] Olson, J. (2009, December). Arizona school finance. Arizona Tax Research Association. Retrieved from https://www.tanqueverdeschools.org/Downloads/ATRA-Arizona_School_Finance. pdf

[16] Arizona State Senate Issue Brief. (2018, August 3). Students First. Retrieved from https://www. azleg.gov/Briefs/Senate/STUDENTS%20FIRST%202018.pdf

[17] Essigs, Chuck. (2018, September 5). *How things got this way: A brief history of recent Arizona school finance.* Power point presented at The Arizona School Board Association's 42nd Annual Law Conference in Phoenix Arizona. Unpublished.

[18] Arizona Department of Education (2021), *Superintendent's Annual Reports.* Retrieved from https://www.azed.gov/finance/reports

[19] Laux, S. & Jensen, L. (2018, September 5). *Student tuition organizations: What are they, who do they benefit, and what is the true cost?* Power point presented at The Arizona School Board Association's 42nd Annual Law Conference in Phoenix Arizona. Unpublished.

[20] Ellen, J., Lozano, M., & O'Brien, C. (2018, September 5). *Empowerment scholarship accounts.* Power point presented at The Arizona School Board Association's 42nd Annual Law Conference in Phoenix Arizona. Unpublished.

[21] Arizona State Senate Issue Brief. (2018, August 3). Students First. Retrieved from https://www. azleg.gov/Briefs/Senate/STUDENTS%20FIRST%202018.pdf

[22] National Conference of State Legislatures (NCSL). *Elementary and Secondary School Emergency Relief Fund Tracker (Jan. 2022).* Retrieved from https://www.ncsl.org/ncsl-in-dc/standing-committees/education/cares-act-elementary-and-secondary-school-emergency-relief-fund-tracker.aspx

[23] Arizona Department of Education. *ADE ESSER Set Asides (n.d.).* Retrieved from https://www. azed.gov/esser-setaside

[24] Arizona Department of Education, *GEER Fund* (n.d.) Retrieved from: https://www.azed.gov/ cares/geer

[25] Martínez, Davíd, G. "Arizona." *Journal of Education Finance* 46, no. 3 (2021): 246-248. muse. jhu.edu/article/786652

CHAPTER 4

ARKANSAS

Steve Bounds

Arkansas Tech University

GENERAL OVERVIEW

Arkansas became the 25th state to be admitted to the union, being admitted in June 1836. Its constitution was revised five times with the current version being adopted in 1874. Article 14, Section 1 of the constitution which addresses education in the state begins, "Intelligence and virtue being the safeguards of liberty and the bulwark of a free and good government, the State shall ever maintain a general, suitable and efficient system of free public schools and shall adopt all suitable means to secure to the people the advantages and opportunities of education."

Arkansas is predominantly a rural state with 234 school districts and 27 charter schools. Total enrollment for 2020-2021 was 473,861 students with 24,085 of them being enrolled in charter schools. District enrollment ranged from 286 students to 21,796 students. The median enrollment was 923 students. Two-thirds of the districts had enrollments less than 1500 students and half had enrollments less than 1000. Enrollment has been steady, only slightly increasing 0.2% over the past ten years. Table 4.1 displays enrollment numbers covering a ten-year period. Student composition by ethnicity was 60% White, 20% Black, 14% Hispanic, and 6% other ethnicities. Arkansas employed 34,027 teachers of which 84% were

Funding Public Schools in the United States, Indian Country,
and US Territories (Second Edition), pages 49–69.
Copyright © 2023 by Information Age Publishing
www.infoagepub.com

TABLE 4.1. Total Public School Enrollment by Academic Year

Academic Year	Enrollment
2012-13	471,867
2013-14	474,995
2014-15	476,083
2015-16	476,049
2016-17	477,268
2017-18	479,258
2018-19	478,318
2019-20	479,432
2020-21	473,861
2021-22	484,662

White, 14% were Black, 1% were Hispanic, and 1% were other ethnicities. Table 4.2 displays a current classification of Arkansas public P-12 school districts organized by district size and poverty.

Political Climate

The state's governance system consists of the executive branch, legislature, and judicial system. The voters elect a governor, a lieutenant governor and several cabinet-level positions: secretary of state, attorney general, treasurer, auditor, and land commissioner. The governor appoints qualified individuals to lead various state boards, committees, and departments. The lieutenant governor is elected separately from the governor and can be from a different political party, though this rarely happens.

TABLE 4.2. Classification of Arkansas Public K-12 Districts

	# of Districts	District Avg ADM	Total ADM	District Avg. FRPL %
District Size				
Small (750 or Fewer)	92	529	48,470	80.5%
Medium (751-5,000)	127	1,786	225,580	69.5%
Large (5,001+)	15	11,409	170,564	59.5%
Poverty				
Low Poverty (<70%)	102	2,368	240,801	52.3%
Medium Poverty (70%-<90%)	54	1,992	107,035	74.6%
High Poverty (90%+)	78	1,250	96,778	99.6%

Source: Arkansas Department of Education, State Aid Notice; Child Nutrition Unit, Audited Free and Reduced-Price Lunch; Office of Innovation for Education (2022).

The General Assembly of Arkansas is the state legislature. The legislature is a bicameral body composed of the upper house Arkansas Senate with 35 members, and the lower Arkansas House of Representatives with 100 members. The legislature and governorship were predominantly controlled by the Democratic Party until recently. In the 2012 election cycle control of the Senate shifted from Democratic control to Republican for the first time in the history of the state. Republicans also took control of the House and the governor's office in that election and have maintained control since. Currently, the state has a Republican governor, 78 Republican House members, and 27 Republican Senate members. Republican lawmakers hold the clear majority with only 22 Democrat House members, 7 Democrat Senate members, and 1 Independent Senate member.

The state operates on a biennial budget cycle. The Arkansas legislature convenes its regular session on the second Monday in January of every odd numbered year. The fiscal session, where most school finance issues are addressed, is convened on the second Monday in February of every even numbered year. The sequence of key events in the budget process is as follows: Budget instructions are sent to state agencies in May of the year preceding the start of the new biennium. State agencies submit their budget requests to the governor in July. Agency hearings are held between August and October. The governor submits his or her proposed budget to the state legislature in November.

The state legislature adopts a budget between January and April. The budget must be passed by a three-fourths majority. The governor is required by statute to submit a balanced budget; however, the legislature is not legally required to pass a balanced budget.

School Finance Litigation

No significant school finance litigation has occurred in the state since 1992. In 1983, the Arkansas Supreme Court ruled in *Dupree v. Alma School District*[1] that the state's funding formula was unconstitutional. While this specific ruling did not address the level of financial support that was legally mandated, it made clear that the state of Arkansas' duty is to distribute educational funds in an equitable manner. The *Dupree* ruling as well as the federal government's *A Nation at Risk*[2] report gave definite momentum to then Governor Bill Clinton's education agenda during his second presidential term. The Education Standards Committee, which was headed by then state first lady Hillary Rodham Clinton, concentrated on achieving better teacher quality, a more rigorous curriculum, a longer school year, and smaller class sizes in the state of Arkansas. Governor Clinton connected school consolidation to these new standards and was able to raise the state sales tax by 1% to fund his public P-12 education reforms.

In 1992, the Lakeview School District filed suit alleging that the state's formula for distributing education funds to public schools remained inequitable. The trial court found that the school finance distribution formula violated the state's constitutional provisions but stayed its order to give the Arkansas General Assembly additional time to enact a constitutional school funding system. After several unsuccessful attempts to resolve the issue, a compliance trial was held in 2000. Other public school districts throughout the state joined the suit, alleging that Arkansas' school funding system was both inequitable and inadequate. The court agreed but left the choice of legal remedy to the legislative and executive branches.

In 2001, ongoing education reform was impacted by the school funding lawsuit *Lake View School District*[3] and the federal education reform initiative of *The No Child Left Behind Act*.[4] The state legislature enacted comprehensive legislation to modify the state's school funding formula, increasing teacher pay, improving school facilities, and imposing an extensive standardized testing program. These reforms significantly improved the condition of public education in the state and the *Lakeview* case was finally decided in the Arkansas Supreme Court in 2004.[5]

The focus of state policymakers on reforming public education and enhancing funding continued during the years 2007 – 2015. For example, during the Eighty-sixth General Assembly, the state approved the largest single capital expenditure for public P-12 education in Arkansas history by committing $456 million to improve school facilities. The Arkansas Constitution provides that the state "shall ever maintain a general, suitable and efficient system of free public schools and shall adopt all suitable means to secure to the people the advantages and opportunities of education."[6] Thus, the two primary Arkansas Supreme Court decisions interpreting the state's constitutional school funding provisions are the *Dupree* and *Lake View* decisions. In order to comply, the Arkansas General Assembly created the Joint Committee on Educational Adequacy during the 2003 regular legislative session and charged it with conducting an adequacy study.[7] The Adequacy Study statute requires the House and Senate Education Committees to evaluate the entire spectrum of public education every two years to determine whether students receive equal opportunity for an adequate education. Based on the recommendations and additional information, the Subcommittee refined the funding levels established in the state's foundation funding matrix, and in 2006, the Arkansas General Assembly increased Arkansas's foundation funding rate.[8]

SOURCES OF REVENUE

Arkansas public P-12 schools receive many different types of funding. In Fiscal Year 2021, Arkansas school districts and open-enrollment charter schools received approximately $5.7 billion in total revenue[9] of which $2.3 billion was provided through the state's foundation formula. Currently, foundation funding is the primary method of public education funding in Arkansas.[10] Foundation funding is based on a district's average daily membership (ADM). Each year, the state distributes foundation funding to each of its 234 school districts on a per-pupil basis. The school fiscal year begins July 1 and ends June 30 of the year following. The notation FY 2021, or FY21, indicates the fiscal year that ends in June 2021.

Local Funding

In Arkansas, local taxes are collected through eight local revenue sources including *property taxes-current* (received July-December); *property relief sales tax*; *property tax by 6/30* (Received January-June); *property relief tax 6/30*; *property tax-delinquent*; *excess commission*; *land redemption in state sales*; *penalties/interest on tax*.

The property tax rate is imposed upon the district's property owners and is based on the assessed value of their property. Property is classified as real or personal. Real property is real estate, including land and homes. Personal property may include other property not considered real. Real property may be further divided into agricultural, commercial, or utility for taxation purposes. *Real, personal* and *utility* taxes comprise three main categories. Real, personal and utility assessments are added together to create the Total Assessment for a school district, reflected in the following formula:

$$Real + Personal + Utility = Total\ Assessment$$

Based on Article 14 of the Arkansas Constitution, a public school district is required to charge a minimum of 25 mills, known as the Uniform Rate of Tax (URT), dedicated to maintenance and operation.[11] The local school district has the option to increase its millage rate by having voters within the district vote on additional mills. To estimate the amount of taxes a district could receive, the amount of Total Assessment is multiplied by the millage rate.

Property tax usually constitutes the bulk of local income. Assessed value (AV) is based on a percentage (20%) of fair market value (FMV) of the property. The tax rate is expressed as mills per $1000 of assessed value and a mill is one-tenth of a cent. Other lesser sources of local revenue include earnings on investments, food service sales, land redemption sales, in lieu of taxes, tuition payments, athletic gate receipts, and rental of facilities, to name a few.

Arkansas statutes require reassessment of property values every three to five years. As a result, a district's assessed valuation typically increases. As an example, Arkansas school districts' assessed valuation increased 5.75 billion dollars between FY13 and FY18, an increase of 13.3%.

DISTRIBUTION FORMULAS

State Foundation Funding

Arkansas school foundation funding is unrestricted, meaning that Arkansas does not specify what school districts may or may not purchase with state appropriated monies. The policy is intended to provide flexibility for the specific financial needs of each school district, allowing some districts the fiscal discretion to spend more on teacher salaries, for example, while other districts may have higher transportation funding needs. Foundation funding is comprised of two main sources: the uniform rate of tax (URT) and the state foundation funding aid. The URT is a constitutionally mandated minimum millage rate, or property tax rate that school districts must levy at the local level. This rate is set at 25 mills and the revenue generated is used specifically for school operations.

State foundation funding aid is provided to make up the difference between the amount of money raised through the URT and the foundation funding rate set by the Arkansas legislature. The two smaller components of foundation funding are the 98% URT Actual Collection Adjustment and other types of funding collectively considered miscellaneous funds. The 98% URT adjustment funding is state money used to supplement districts, whereas actual URT collections are less than 98% of what was anticipated based on assessments. This funding ensures that districts receive at least 98% of their total URT funding when the county is unable to collect the full amount from its citizens. Miscellaneous funds are monies school districts receive from "federal forest reserves, federal grazing rights, federal mineral rights, federal impact aid, federal flood control, wildlife refuge funds, and severance taxes," that are "in lieu of taxes and local sales and use taxes dedicated to education."[12] Among districts statewide in FY21, the URT made up approximately 35% of the state's total foundation funding, while state foundation funding aid covered about 64%. However, these percentages varied greatly among individual school districts. For the state's charter schools, which currently have no tax base from which to collect funds, the entire foundation funding amount is covered by state foundation funding aid.[13] Table 4.3 reflects foundation funding levels per pupil from FY16 and projected to FY23.

The primary revenue types for funding Arkansas public K-12 schools include five main sources:

- *Foundation Funding* primarily consists of property tax revenues (uniform rate of tax, or URT) and the state aid portion of foundation funding (the components of foundation funding are described later in this chapter);

TABLE 4.3. Foundation Funding Per Pupil

Fiscal Year	Per Student
2016	$6,584
2017	$6,646
2018	$6,713
2019	$6,781
2020	$6,899
2021	$7,018
2022	$7,182
2023	$7,349

Source: State of Arkansas, Bureau of Legislative Research (2022).

- *Other Unrestricted Funds* including state funding such as enrollment growth, declining enrollment, and isolated school funding and local revenue sources in excess of URT. School districts have broad authority to spend these funds for their educational needs without limitation;
- *State Restricted Funds* including state categorical funds, as well as funding for magnet school programs, early childhood education, adult education, career education, special education, academic facilities and other grants for specific programs;
- *Federal Revenues* including Title I funding, the Individuals with Disabilities Education Act (IDEA), Part B funding, school lunch and breakfast grant funds and other federal grant funding;
- *Other Funding Sources* including the sale of bonds for construction activities, loans, insurance compensation for loss of assets, other gains from disposals of assets and other miscellaneous funding.

Arkansas' K-12 education foundation funding formula, often referred to as "the matrix," is used to determine the per-pupil level of foundation funding disbursed to each school district in the state. Each year, Arkansas legislators involved in the state's adequacy study determine the dollar amount necessary to fund each line item of the foundation funding formula (matrix) based on the money needed to adequately fund school districts' educational needs. The state's matrix formula is not intended to reimburse schools for actual expenditures but rather provide a methodology for determining an adequate funding level allowing schools to meet state accreditation standards as well as to adequately educate the state's students. The matrix calculates per-pupil funding based on the cost of personnel and other resources needed to operate a prototypical school of 500 students. Unlike the foundation funding rate, the matrix is not established in state statute: instead, it is used as a tool to set the state's foundation funding rate.

The matrix is divided into two basic sections: (1) the number of people needed for funding a prototypical school of 500 students; and (2) costs associated with all needed resources for a school district. Table 4.4 displays the four components that comprise foundation funding in Arkansas. From 2011 to 2020, state founda-

TABLE 4.4. Arkansas Formula Foundation Funding Components, 2020

Foundation Funding Components	District Total	% of Total	Charter Total	% of Total
URT	$1,246,334,339	38.9%	$0	0%
State Foundation Funding Aid	$1,927,329,045	60.1%	$141,706,492	100%
98% Adjustment	$20,619,275	0.6%	$0	0%
Miscellaneous	$13,537,614	0.4%	$0	0%
Total	$3,207,811,273		$141,706,492	

Source: State of Arkansas, Bureau of Legislative Research (2021).

TABLE 4.5. Matrix Formula: Personnel Needed for Sample Prototypical School of 500 Students

	Matrix Item	2019 FTEs per 500 students
Classroom Teachers	Kindergarten	2.00
	Grades 1-3	5.00
	Grades 4-12	13.80
	Non-Core	4.14
	Subtotal	24.94
Pupil Support Staff	Special Education	2.90
	Instructional Facilitators	2.50
	Library Media Specialist	0.85
	Counselors & Nurses	2.50
	Subtotal	8.75
Administration	Principal	1.00
	Secretary	1.00
	Total	35.69

Source: State of Arkansas, Bureau of Legislative Research (2020).

TABLE 4.6. Funding Needed for School-Level Salaries, School-Level Resources, and District-Level Resources

School-Level Salaries	Salary & Benefits	Per-Student Funding Amt.
Classroom Teachers	$65,811	$3,282.65
Pupil Support Staff	$65,811	$1,151.75
Principal	$99,012	$198.10
Secretary	$40,855	$81.70
School-Level Resources		
Technology		$250.00
Instructional Materials		$183.10
Extra Duty Funds		$66.20
Supervisory Aides		$50.00
Substitutes		$71.80
District-Level Resources		
Operations & Maintenance		$685.00
Transportation		$321.20
Central Office		$438.80

Source: State of Arkansas, Bureau of Legislative Research (2020).

TABLE 4.7. State Funding for the Arkansas Department of Education

| Fiscal Year | Dept. of Education Public School Fund Account | General Education Fund-Dept. Education Fund Account | Educational Excellence Trust Fund | | Educational Facilities Partnership Fund | Educational Ad-equacy Fund | Total All Selected Funds |
			Dept. of Education Public School Fund Account	Dept. of Education Fund Account	Account and Dept. of Public School Academic Facilities & Transp. Fund Account		
2005	$1,587,868,208	$11,841,192	$165,146,201	$809,075	$20,439,774	$442,872,886	$2,228,977,336
2006	$1,664,928,944	$13,536,267	$178,219,239	$873,122	$54,214,982	$426,505,888	$2,338,278,442
2007	$1,722,737,993	$13,433,942	$191,219,957	$936,815	$90,976,326	$448,450,030	$2,467,755,062
2008	$1,830,265,989	$15,799,231	$200,422,877	$981,901	$502,643,494	$438,730,903	$2,988,844,395
2009	$1,843,274,503	$14,769,806	$193,587,342	$948,413	$51,585,902	$433,090,041	$2,537,256,006
2010	$1,790,947,911	$17,529,999	$190,786,665	$934,692	$36,916,527	$411,286,403	$2,448,402,197
2011	$1,829,267,307	$15,167,661	$180,391,694	$883,765	$57,704,295	$451,110,054	$2,534,524,776
2012	$1,882,316,142	$15,701,088	$188,051,836	$921,294	$58,528,882	$438,147,425	$2,583,666,667
2013	$1,936,432,524	$15,471,687	$193,026,506	$945,665	$62,465,585	$444,832,631	$2,653,174,598
2014	$1,980,965,210	$16,578,345	$195,093,479	$955,792	$84,858,082	$456,647,180	$2,735,098,088
2015	$2,072,170,259	$16,587,878	$199,766,427	$978,685	$51,071,087	$460,221,761	$2,800,796,097
2016	$2,113,356,522	$16,162,434	$202,031,412	$989,781	$98,785,465	$477,029,412	$2,908,355,026
2017	$2,136,234,690	$16,162,434	$210,504,218	$1,031,291	$59,633,327	$488,716,784	$2,912,282,744
2018	$2,110,560,691	$16,162,434	$215,134,282	$1,053,974	$150,579,640	$504,750,501	$2,998,241,522
2019	$2,156,934,175	$15,677,561	$222,454,322	$1,089,836	$61,355,437	$467,249,996	$2,924,761,327
2020	$2,169,729,298	$16,298,264	$226,827,803	$1,111,263	$62,387,201	$595,416,316	$3,071,770,145

Source: State of Arkansas, Bureau of Legislative Research (2020).

tion aid consistently made up 64-65% of foundation funding, while URT made up 34-35%. State foundation aid in 2021 was at about 60% of foundation funding. Table 4.5 illustrates the first section of the state's matrix formula, the number of people needed for the prototypical school of 500 students. Table 4.6 illustrates the second component of the state's matrix formula, which specifies the cost of the staff described in the first section of the matrix, as well as the cost of all other needed resources. The matrix is divided into three cost categories, including (1) school-level salaries of teachers and other pupil support staff, (2) school-level resources, including instructional materials and technology-related expenses, and (3) district-level resources, including funding for operations and maintenance and transportation expenses.

Table 4.7 details the level of state funding made available to the Arkansas Department of Education (ADE) from FY05 through FY20, specifically for P-12 education. For FY23, the legislature allocated $3,233,266,080 to ADE.

CATEGORICAL FUNDING

Special Education Funding

Special needs, or categorical, funding is pursuant to state statute.[14] During FY17 school year, Arkansas public school districts spent $436.8 million on special education services, or approximately $7,481 per pupil with a classified disability. The state's open-enrollment charter schools spent $5.8 million on special education services, or approximately $4,523 per pupil with a disability. Those figures should not be mistaken to reflect the total cost of educating students with disabilities because they do not include all expenditures districts incurred behalf of all students, such as the cost of principal salaries or utilities. These figures represent only the expenditures specific to special education services or students. Arkansas primarily uses monies obtained through the local millage and foundation funding matrix for special education funding purposes. Local and state aid monies are deposited to the general fund and coded to special education expenditures as needed.

In addition to local and foundation funds being used to support special education, monies from other categorical funds are also used, including the following specific school fund categories: Isolated, Student Growth, and/or Declining Enrollment funds, state National School Lunch, English Language Learner, and Professional Development funds, Special Education Services funds which are designed to help districts and charters pay for special education supervisors and extended-year services for students with disabilities, Residential Treatment funds for special education provided to students in residential treatment centers, youth shelters, juvenile detention centers, and other minor state special education funding sources such as the Arkansas School Recognition Program and Professional Quality Enhancement Teacher & Administrator Induction Program (PATHWISE) program.

In Arkansas, some students are classified as high-cost special education pupils. Nationally, approximately 5% of special education students are classified as high-

TABLE 4.8.   Special Education Spending: By Source of Funds FY18

Source	Public K-12 Schools	Public Charter Schools
Foundation and local funds	$270,476,393	$3,091,394
Isolated, Student Growth, Declining Enrollment	$870,360	$13,462
Categorical funds	$3,031,885	$38,810
Special Education Services	$2,656,613	$15,420
Residential Treatment	$5,675,123	$0
Catastrophic Loss	$11,506,253	$34,201
Other State Special Ed Funding	$23,577	$0
Early childhood special education	$3,264,783	$11,519
Desegregation	$2,065,749	$0

cost. Once a school district spends more than $15,000 on specialized resources for a student, the district may apply for catastrophic loss funding. The state of Arkansas pays 80% of special education costs beyond $15,000 up to $50,000 and 50% of costs over $50,000 up to $100,000.[15] Table 4.8 lists the special education expenditures from various state funding sources for FY18 for public K-12 districts in Arkansas.

Alternative Learning Environment (ALE), English Language Learners (ELL), National School Lunch State Categorical (NSL) and Professional Development (PD) are considered state categorical funds. The expenditure of funds from each of these categories is restricted. Allowable expenditures for each category are specified in law and/or rules. A school district may transfer funds received from any categorical fund source to another categorical fund source. Per-pupil state categorical funding is provided in addition to per-pupil foundation funding. There is a limit to the amount of categorical funds a district can carry over in a fiscal year. Districts carrying over balances larger than allowed may be required to surrender those unspent excess funds. Districts must expend a minimum of 85% of the current NSL of the current year NSL funding. The total aggregate balance of categorical funds at year-end may not exceed 20%.

In addition to these funds, Arkansas public schools can apply for Medicaid and Arkansas Medicaid Administrative Claiming (ARMAC) reimbursement. Medicaid is a federally funded program allowing districts to be reimbursed for medical services provided as part of an Individualized Education Plan (IEP). ARMAC is a federally funded program that helps school districts cover the cost of administrative activities related to Medicaid or other health services. Other special education funds are restricted accounts to be used only for special education purposes.

Two major sources of federal special education funds provided to the state to be distributed to school districts include the Special Education School Age – Section 611 Allocations and the Special Education Federal Preschool – Section 619 Allocations accounts. During the 2017-18 school year, approximately

TABLE 4.9. Special Education Funds Distributed
to Arkansas K-12 Public Schools

School Year	Funds Distributed
2013-14	33,715,146
2014-15	33,441,371
2015-16	34,050,823
2016-17	33,652,335
2017-18	38,249,554
2018-19	39,211,930
2019-20	40,181,382
2020-21	60,134,638

$117,332,895 and $5,372,923 of Section 611 and Section 619 funds, respectively, were available to the state of Arkansas. Local allocations to LEAs are based on a formula that determines the amount per special education pupil for each individual district. Key elements of the formula include a base amount from the previous year, a population component based on the number of eligible students, and a poverty component based on free/reduced lunch status. Table 4.9 lists funds distributed to Arkansas public schools.

Alternative Learning Environment

An Alternative Learning Environment (ALE) program must comply with state law and relevant Arkansas Department of Education (ADE) rules.[16] It is important to point out that for ALE funding eligibility, a student must be enrolled in an eligible ALE program for a minimum of 20 consecutive days per school year. In FY22, ALE funding for each school year was $4,794 multiplied by the district's eligible ALE students' full-time equivalence (FTE) in the previous year[17] as defined in 4.06 of the ADE Rules Governing the Distribution of Student Special Needs Funding and the Determination of Allowable Expenditures of Those Funds – May 2016. The FTE is calculated by dividing the number of days each student was enrolled in the ALE by the total number of days in the school year (typically 178) and multiplying the result by the number of enrolled course minutes divided by the number of minutes in a day. Examples are as follows:

$$\text{Student "B" FTE} = (89/178) \times (216/360) = .30$$
$$\text{Student "C" FTE} (178/178) \times (360/360) = 1.0$$

To calculate ALE funding, multiply the total full-time equivalent (FTE) (1.3) by the per-student ALE funding amount ($4,794). 1.3 X $4,794 = $6,232.

ENGLISH LANGUAGE LEARNERS

English Language Learners (ELL) are students identified as not proficient in the English language based on approved English proficiency assessment instruments which measure proficiency in and comprehension of English in reading, writing, speaking, and listening.[18] The ELL funding amount is the amount authorized by law multiplied by the district's identified ELL pupil population in the current school year. In FY22, ELL funding for each school year was $359 multiplied by the number of identified ELL students, with the pupil count verified on October 1.

Enhanced Student Achievement Funding

Enhanced Student Achievement Funding is distributed to districts based on the number of identified national school lunch students. For a school district in which ninety percent (90%) or more of the previous school year's enrolled students are national school lunch students, the amount of per-student Enhanced Student Achievement Funding for the FY22 school year was set at $1,594 and for the FY23 school year was $1,613. For districts in which at least 70% but less than 90% are national school lunch students, the amount of per-student Enhanced Student Achievement Funding for the FY22 school year was $1,063 and for the FY23 school year was $1,076. For districts in which less than 70% of the students are national school lunch students, the amount of per-student Enhanced Student Achievement Funding for the FY22 school year was $532 and for the FY23 school year was $538. The per-student Enhanced Student Achievement Funding for an open-enrollment public charter school is based upon the current school year enrollment instead of the previous year. If a district's percentage should change so that it either gains or losses Enhanced Student Achievement Funds per identified student, the gain or loss is distributed over a three-year period.

Student Growth Funding

To help ease the potential financial burden resulting from rapid increases in student populations, a school district with enrollment growth in quarterly average daily membership (ADM) compared to its prior-year three quarter average daily membership may be eligible for student growth funding.[19] Student growth funding is calculated as the ADM increase in each quarter compared to the prior 3-quarter year ADM.

For example, using the data in Table 4.10 to calculate Sample School District's student growth funding for FY22 where FF represents the foundation funding amount per ADM allocated to the district, we use the formula:

[(FY21 4th Quarter ADM – FY20 3-Quarter ADM) *times* FF] +
[(FY22 1st Quarter ADM – FY21 3-Quarter ADM) *times* FF] +
[(FY22 2nd Quarter ADM – FY21 3-Quarter ADM) *times* FF] +
[(FY22 3rd Quarter ADM – FY21 3-Quarter ADM) *times* FF]

TABLE 4.10.   Data Illustrating Student Growth

FY20 3-Quarter ADM	528.16	FY21 quarter 4 ADM	541.11	Growth in Quarter 4	12.95
FY21 3-quarter ADM	540.19	FY22 quarter 1 ADM	552.33	Growth in Quarter 1	12.14
FY21 3-quarter ADM	540.19	FY22 quarter 2 ADM	549.08	Growth in Quarter 2	8.89
FY21 3-quarter ADM	540.19	FY22 quarter 3 ADM	539.02	Growth in Quarter 3	No growth
Total ADM Growth					33.98

Source: Arkansas School Finance Manual 2021-2022 (2021).

Student Growth Funding
= Total ADM Growth x Foundation Funding
= 33.98 x $1,795.50 = $61,011

Arkansas school districts may expend student growth funding on any eligible school purpose while maintaining the student growth revenue code. No district can receive both declining enrollment funding and student growth funding, and no district can receive both declining enrollment and special needs isolated funding. Therefore, a district will receive the larger amount of either declining enrollment funding or the sum of Student Growth Funding and Special Needs Isolated Funding.

Declining Enrollment Funding

Declining enrollment funding is defined as the amount of state financial aid provided to an eligible school district from funds made available for the decline in the average daily membership of the school district in the preceding school year compared to the school year before the preceding school year.[20] Declining enrollment funding is equal to the three-quarter ADM of the prior year, subtracted from the average of the three-quarter ADMs of the prior fiscal year and the fiscal year prior to the prior fiscal year, multiplied by the current per-student foundation funding amount. For example, to calculate declining student enrollment funding for FY22, the formula would be calculated:

((870.28 + 851.34)/2) - 851.34 = 9.47
9.47 x FY22 per student foundation funding
9.47 x $7,182 = $68,014 declining enrollment funding

Isolated Funding

Isolated Funding is addressed in Arkansas law and specifically states that (a) Undistributed funds under this section and §§ 6-20-601 and 6-20- 603 shall be distributed on an equal basis per school district to each school district that is eligible to receive funds under subsections; or (b) Funds distributed under subdivision shall be used by the school district only for transportation costs of the isolated school areas in the school district.[21] To be considered an isolated district, the district must meet four of the five criteria: (1) Distance of 12 miles or more by hard-surfaced highway from the high school of the district to the nearest adjacent high school in an adjoining district; (2) Density ratio of transported students is less than 3 students per square mile; (3) Total area of the district is 95 square miles or greater; (4) Less than 50% of bus routes are on hard-surfaced roads; (5) There are geographic barriers such as lakes, rivers, and mountain ranges that would impede travel.

General Transportation

Similar to special education funding, Arkansas mainly uses monies obtained through the local millage and foundation funding matrix for transportation-related expenses. Local and state aid monies are deposited to the General Fund and coded to transportation expenditures, as needed. In the foundation funding matrix, transportation is funded at $321.20 per pupil for FY22 and FY23. This money, although considered transportation aid in the funding matrix, is not restricted money and can be spent for other purposes.

The state provides Enhanced Transportation Funding to school districts facing higher than normal costs to provide transportation for students to and from school. For FY23, the state allocated $7,200,000 for enhanced transportation funding. Enhanced transportation funding is not restricted money and can be spent for other purposes. The method utilized to determine and allocate the enhanced funding is based on a relatively secret statistical analysis of transportation behavior of all school districts in Arkansas and incorporates ADM, daily route miles, and the number of actual bus riders. Superintendents must wait for the state to determine how much each school district receives since they have no way to predict an amount. For example, District 1 and District 2 are neighboring rural districts consisting of 235 and 298 square miles, respectively, and an ADM of 1,363 and 601, respectively. District 1 received $5,112 while District 2 received $50,512 in enhanced transportation funding. Table 4.11 illustrates transportation expenses for Arkansas public school districts from FY13 to FY22.

Professional Development

During FY22 and subsequent years, the professional development funding per-student is an amount up to $40.80 multiplied by the school district's prior-year three-quarter average daily membership (ADM). A portion of the $40.80 is used to fund statewide professional development programs each year. The funding amount per-pupil provided directly to a school district is calculated after removing the portion corresponding to statewide programs. For FY22, the amount of per-student professional development funding excluding statewide programs was $36.00. This amount is provided on the preliminary state aid notice each year.

TABLE 4.11. Transportation Expenses

Fiscal Years	Enhanced Transportation Funds	Transportation Expenses
2013	N/A	$199,822,772
2014	N/A	$203,025,960
2015	N/A	$197,320,327
2016	N/A	$198,542,601
2017	$3,088,374	$199,531,255
2018	$3,000,000	$209,585,665
2019	$3,000,000	$211,288,868
2020	$5,000,000	$201,107,043
2021	$5,000,000	$202,697,555
2022	$5,937,098	

To calculate professional development funding, the state multiplies prior-year three-quarter ADM by the per-pupil professional development funding amount. For example, for a school district with FY21 three-quarter ADM of 629.17 and a per-student professional development funding rate for FY22 of $36.00, the professional development funding amount would be calculated as follows:

$$629.17 \text{ X } \$36.00 = \$22,650$$

CAPITAL OUTLAY AND DEBT SERVICE

Bonded debt assistance is restricted funding to be used exclusively for the payment of bonded debt. The calculation of bonded debt assistance is based on a school district's principal and interest payment schedule in effect and on file with the Department of Education (ADE).[22] ACA § 6-20-2503 attributes 90% of each school district's outstanding bonded debt to the financing of academic facilities. However, the law provides for a school district to submit documentation if more than 90% of its outstanding bonded debt was issued in support of academic facilities.

This established percentage of 90% or more is applied to each district's fiscal year principal and interest bonded debt payment from the January 1, 2005 debt schedule. The resulting 'adjusted 1/1/05 scheduled debt payment' is divided by the total assessed value of the district multiplied by 1,000 to calculate the required debt service mills. This product is multiplied by the state wealth index[23] and is different from the facilities wealth index[24] multiplied by the prior year three-quarter average daily membership (ADM) and multiplied by a funding factor of $18.03.

EMPLOYEE BENEFITS

Healthcare

Arkansas teachers and staff may participate in the state's voluntary cost-sharing health insurance program. Participating districts are required to pay a specific portion of the health insurance premium while the state and employee also contribute to the premium payment. In FY22, the state offered three levels of healthcare plans: Premium, Classic, and Basic. The total monthly premium for the Basic plan was $328.71. The district was required to pay a minimum of $168.52 and the state paid $98.93 leaving the employee to pay $61.26. Districts have the option of paying more, thereby lowering the cost to the employee. A recent change in state law has raised the minimum district contribution to $300 per month.

Retirement

Teachers in Arkansas enter into the state's Teacher Retirement System (TRS) upon being hired at an Arkansas public school. The Arkansas Teacher Retirement System is a defined benefit plan. Teachers are eligible to retire based on their age and years of service: a) 28 or more years of service at any age; b) 25 to 27 years of service at any age (reduced benefits); or, c) Five to 24 years of service at age 60. Teachers contribute 6% of their salaries to the state retirement fund, which gains interest over time. Their employers contribute 15% of their salaries, but that percentage does not gain interest.

CHARTER SCHOOLS

In Arkansas there are two basic types of public charter schools. An *open-enrollment charter school* is a public charter school run by a governmental entity, an institution of higher learning or a tax-exempt non-sectarian organization. Open enrollment schools can draw students from across district boundaries. A *district conversion charter school* is a public school converted to a public charter school. Conversion schools can only draw students from within the school district's boundaries. In FY22 there were 35 conversion charter schools and 13 open-enrollment charter schools operating in Arkansas. Public charter schools receive funding in the same manner as public schools except that they do not have assessed valuation property and do not receive property taxes.[13] In FY20, public charter schools in Arkansas received nearly $142 million in foundation funding, nearly 7% of the total sent to all schools.

NONPUBLIC SCHOOL FUNDING

Arkansas does not provide any direct funding to nonpublic schools. In certain situations, Federal funds may indirectly be utilized by nonpublic schools. These funds typically require public schools to invite nonpublic schools to participate in specific activities such as professional development.

TABLE 4.12. Arkansas' Foundation Matrix Funding Formula Trends Fiscal Years 2005 through projected 2019

Updated March 30, 2017	FY05	FY06	FY07	FY08	FY09	FY10	FY11	FY12	FY13	FY14	FY15	FY16	FY17	FY18	FY19
Matrix Calculations															
School Size	500.0	599.0	500.0	500.0	500.0	500.0	500.0	500.0	500.0	500.0	500.0	500.0	500.0	500.0	500.0
K = 8% of students	40.0	49.0	40.0	40.0	40.0	40.0	40.0	40.0	40.0	40.0	40.0	40.0	40.0	40.0	40.0
Grades 1-3 = 23% of students	115.0	115.0	115.0	115.0	115.0	115.0	115.0	115.0	115.0	115.0	115.0	115.0	115.0	115.0	115.0
Grades 4-12 = 69% of students	345.0	345.0	345.0	345.0	345.0	345.0	345.0	345.0	345.0	345.0	345.0	345.0	345.0	345.0	345.0
Staffing Ratios															
K PT ratio = 20:1	2.0	2.0	2.0	2.0	2.0	2.0	2.0	2.0	2.0	2.0	2.0	2.0	2.0	2.0	2.0
Grades 1-3 PT ratio = 23:1	5.0	5.0	5.0	5.0	5.0	2.0	5.0	5.0	5.0	5.0	5.0	5.0	5.0	5.0	5.0
Grades 4-12 PT ratio = 25:1	13.8	13.8	13.8	13.8	13.8	13.8	13.8	13.8	13.8	13.8	13.8	13.8	13.8	13.8	13.8
PAM = 20% of classroom	4.2	4.2	4.2	4.1	4.14	4.14	4.1	4.1	4.1	4.14	4.14	4.1	4.14	4.1	4.14
Total Classroom Teachers	25.0	25.0	25.0	24.94	24.94	24.94	24.94	24.94	24.94	24.94	24.94	24.94	24.94	24.94	24.94
Special Ed Teachers	2.9	2.9	2.9	2.9	2.9	2.9	2.9	2.9	2.9	2.9	2.9	2.9	2.9	2.9	2.9
Instructional Facilitators	2.5	2.5	2.5	2.5	2.5	2.5	2.5	2.5	2.5	2.5	2.5	2.5	2.5	2.5	2.5
Librarian/Media Specialist	0.7	0.7	0.7	0.825	0.825	0.825	0.825	0.825	0.825	0.825	0.0825	0.85	0.85	0.85	0.85
Guidance Counselor & Nurse	2.5	2.5	2.5	2.5	2.5	2.5	2.5	2.5	2.5	2.5	2.5	2.5	2.5	2.5	2.5
Total Pupil Support Personnel	8.6	8.6	8.6	8.725	8.725	8.725	8.725	8.725	8.725	8.725	8.725	8.75	8.75	8.75	8.75
SUBTOTAL	33.6	33.6	33.665	33.665	33.665	35.665	33.665	33.665	33.665	33.665	33.665	33.69	33.69	33.69	33.69
Principal	1.0	1.0	1.0	1.0	1.0	1.0	1.0	1.0	1.0	1	1.0	1.0	1	1	1
Secretary	0.0	0.0	0.0	1.0	1.0	1.0	1.0	1.0	1.0	1	1.0	1.0	1	1	1
Total School-Level Personnel	34.6	35.6	34.6	33.665	35.665	35.665	35.665	35.665	35.665	35.665	35.665	35.69	35.69	35.69	35.69
School-Level Salaries															
Teacher Salary + Benefits	$48,750	$50,581	$52,321	$54,888	$55,954	$57,073	$58,214	$59,378	$60,566	$61,839	$63,130	$63,663	$64,196	$64,998	$65,811
Per Student Matrix Expenditure	$3,271	$3,399	$3,516	$3,696	$3,767	$3,843	$3,920	$3,998	$4,078	$4,164	$4,290	$4,290	$4,326	$4,377	$4,434
Principal Salary + Benefits	$72,000	$73,500	$76,335	$86,168	$87,860	$89,617	$91,409	$92,127	$95,102	$96,686	$99,012	$99,012	$99,012	$99,012	$99,012
Per Student Matrix Expenditure	$144	$147	$153	$172	$176	$179	$183	$187	$190	$194	$198	$198	$198	$198	$198
School-level secretary	$-	$-	$-	$34,751	$35,415	$36,123	$36,845	$37,582	$38,334	$39,213	$40,031	$40,031	$40,031	$40,451	$40,855
Per Student Matrix Expenditure	$-	$-	$-	$70	$71	$72	$74	$75	$77	$79	$801	$80	$80	$81	$82
School-Level Salaries Per Student	$3,415	$3,551	$3,669	$3,937	$4,014	$4,094	$4,176	$4,260	$4,345	$4,436	$4,529	$4,568	$4,604	$4,659	$4,715

School-Level Resources

Technology	$ 250	$ 216	$ 185	$ 220	$ 201	$ 205	$ 209	$ 213	$ 218	$ 222	$ 226	$ 238	$ 250	$ 250	$ 250
Instructional Materials	$ 250	$ 259	$ 268	$ 160	$ 163	$ 17	$ 170	$ 173	$ 177	$ 180	$ 183	$ 183	$ 183	$ 183	$ 183
Extra Duty Funds	$ 90	$ 94	$ 97	$ 50	$ 51	$ 52	$ 53	$ 54	$ 55	$ 56	$ 57	$ 61	$ 65	$ 66	$ 66
Supervisory Aides	$ 35	$ 36	$ 37	$ 49	$ 50	$ 21	$ 26	$ 54	$ 55	$ 56	$ 57	$ 50	$ 50	$ 50	$ 50
Substitutes	$ 63	$ 57	$ 59	$ 59	$ 59	$ 60	$ 61	$ 63	$ 64	$ 65	$ 66	$ 68	$ 69	$ 70	$ 72
Teacher Continuing Ed Pay (5 Days)	$ 101	$ 93	$ 96												
School-Level Resources Per Student	$ 789	$ 755	$ 742	$ 538	$ 525	$ 535	$ 546	$ 557	$ 568	$ 579	$ 589	$ 600	$ 617	$ 619	$ 621

Carry-Forward

Operations & Maintenance				$ 581	$ 581	$ 593	$ 605	$ 617	$ 629	$ 640	$ 652	$ 665	$ 665	$ 675	$ 685
Central Office				$ 376	$ 384	$ 391	$ 399	$ 407	$ 415	$ 423	$ 430	$ 430	$ 439	$ 439	$ 439
Transportation				$ 286	$ 286	$ 292	$ 298	$ 304	$ 310	$ 316	$ 321	$ 321	$ 321	$ 321	$ 321
Carry-Forward Per Student	$ 1,152	$ 1,180	$ 1,206	$ 1,243	$ 1,251	$ 1,276	$ 1,301	$ 1,327	$ 1,354	$ 1,378	$ 1,403	$ 1,416	$ 1,425	$ 1,435	$ 1,445
Foundation Per Pupil Expenditures	$ 5,356	$ 5,486	$ 5,620	$ 5,719	$ 5,789	$ 5,905	$ 6,023	$ 6,144	$ 6,267	$ 6,393	$ 6,521	$ 6,584	$ 6,646	$ 6,713	$ 6,781
Adjustments (Cushion/Retirement)	$ 44	$ 42	$ 42	$ -	$ -	$ -	$ -	$ -	$ -	$ -	$ -	$ -	$ -	$ -	$ -
Matrix Foundation Per Student	$ 5,400	$ 5,528	$ 5,662	$ 5,719	$ 5,789	$ 5,905	$ 6,023	$ 6,144	$ 6,267	$ 6,393	$ 6,521	$ 6,584	$ 6,646	$ 6,713	$ 6,781
Increase per ADM		$ 128	$ 134	$ 57	$ 70	$ 116	$ 118	$ 121	$ 123	$ 126	$ 128	$ 63	$ 62	$ 67	$ 68
%		2	2	1	1	2	2	2	2	2	2	1	1	1	1
Enhanced Funding Per Student				$ 51	$ 87	$ 35	$ -	$ -	$ -	$ -	$ -	$ -	$ -	$ -	$ -
Total Foundation Funding	$ 5,400	$ 5,528	$ 5,662	$ 5,770	$ 5,876	$ 5,940	$ 6,023	$ 6,144	$ 6,267	$ 6,393	$ 6,521	$ 6,584	$ 6,646	$ 6,713	$ 6,781

VIRTUAL EDUCATION

Arkansas Virtual Academy, an open-enrollment charter school, is the oldest provider of online education in Arkansas. It has an enrollment of nearly 4,000 students though enrollment swelled during the COVID-19 pandemic. Being a charter school, it receives funding like other public charter schools.

FEDERAL COVID-19 FUNDS

Arkansas districts received $115,882,774 in Elementary and Secondary School Emergency Relief (ESSER) I funds, $502,215,668 in ESSER II monies, and $1,128,707,964 in American Rescue Plan (ARP) funds during the COVID pandemic. In addition, the state received $30,664,782 for the Governor's Emergency Education Relief (GEER) fund. Most districts used the funds for personal protective equipment (PPE), cleaning and sanitizing materials, and similar supplies necessary to maintain school operations during the pandemic. Equipment and supplies to support remote learning were also a significant use of the funds. For the most part, Arkansas schools remained open during the pandemic and in-school attendance was relatively high.

SUMMARY

Table 4.12 summarizes Arkansas' foundation matrix funding formula trends for FY05 through FY19 and shows expenditures including school-level salaries as well as district and school-level resources. Finally, and overall, Arkansas P-12 school districts and open enrollment charter schools received about $5.7 billion in total revenue during FY17. Foundation funding clearly made up the largest percentage of that revenue (56%) followed by federal revenue (11%) and state restricted funds (10%). One measure of the adequacy of Arkansas' education funding system is its total per-pupil spending, whereby nationally Arkansas ranks 34th and its per-pupil expenditure is more than $1,600 below national average.[25]

NOTES

1   651 S.W.2d 90 (1983).
2   United States. National Commission on Excellence in Education. *A Nation at Risk : The Imperative for Educational Reform : A Report to the Nation and the Secretary of Education,* United States Department of Education. Washington, D.C. :The Commission : [Supt. of Docs., U.S. G.P.O. distributor], 1983.
3   351 Ark. 31 SW3d 472 (2002).
4   P.L. 107-110 (2001).
5   *Lake View School District No. 25 v. Huckabee,* 189 S.W.3d 1 (Ark. 2004).
6   Ark. Const. art. 14, § 1.
7   Allen Odden, Lawrence Picus, and Mark Fermanich (2003). *An Evidence-based Approach to School Finance Adequacy in Arkansas. Report* prepared for the Arkansas Joint Committee on Education Adequacy. Retrieved from http://www.arkleg.state.ar.us/education/K12/AdequacyReportYears/2003%20Final%20Arkansas%20Report%2009_01_2 003.pdf

8 Adequacy Study Oversight Subcommittee, A Report on Legislative Hearings For the 2006 Interim Study on Educational Adequacy, Final Report and Recommendations, January 22, 2007.

9 State of Arkansas, Bureau of Legislative Research (2020).

10 A.C.A. § 6-20-2301 et seq.

11 Ark. Cont. Art 14.

12 Ark. § 6-20-2303(12)(A).

13 Bounds, Steve. "Arkansas." Journal of Education Finance 46, no. 3 (2021): 249+. Gale OneFile: Nursing and Allied Health (accessed July 22, 2022). https://link.gale.com/apps/doc/A659749010/PPNU?u=akstateu1&sid=summon&xid=cbd60944.

14 A.C.A. §6-20-2301 et seq. *See*: "Rules Governing the Distribution of Student Special Needs Funding and the Determination of Allowable Expenditures of Those Funds" (May 2016).

15 Michael Griffith, *State Funding Programs for High-Cost Special Education Students* (May 2008). Retrieved from: https://www.ecs.org/clearinghouse/78/10/7810.pdf

16 A.C.A §6-48-101 et seq.

17 Rule 4.06 of the ADE "Rules Governing the Distribution of Student Special Needs Funding and the Determination of Allowable Expenditures of Those Funds" (May 2016).

18 Ibid, Rule 3.11 of the ADE (2016).

19 Arkansas Department of Education (ADE) Act 741, "Rules Governing the Calculation Methods for Declining Enrollment and Student Growth Funding for Public School Districts" (2017). Retrieved from: http://adecm.arkansas.gov/ViewApprovedMemo.aspx?Id=3304

20 Arkansas Department of Education (ADE), "Rules Governing the Calculation Methods for Declining Enrollment and Student Growth Funding for Public School Districts" (2020). Retrieved from: http://www.arkansased.org/public/userfiles/Legal/LegalCurrent%20Rules/ade_296_declining_2020_current.pdf

21 A.C.A. §6-20-601 *et seq.*

22 A.C.A. § 6-20-2503.

23 A.C.A. § 6-20-2503(a)(6).

24 A.C.A. § 6-20-2502.

25 National Center for Education Statistics, *Revenues and Expenditures for Public Elementary and Secondary Education: School Year 2014-15* (Fiscal Year 2015). Retrieved from: https://nces.ed.gov/pubs2018/2018301.pdf

CHAPTER 5

CALIFORNIA

Ann Blankenship-Knox
University of Redlands

Paul Jessup
University of Redlands

Bob Blattner
Principal, Blattner & Associates

GENERAL BACKGROUND

California's role in school funding has been infamous since the 1970s. The 1971 *Serrano v. Priest*[1] state supreme court decision placed California on the map in terms of school funding debates and constitutional supports. The *Serrano* decision shifted the focus of school finance reform from federal courts to state-level constitutional provisions, effectively proving that strict interpretation of state education articles could substitute for elusive federal protections. Indeed, the *Serrano* ruling launched a national reform wave that persists today, so that states' school aid plans are typically first subjected to judicial scrutiny on the basis of strength of education article language, albeit still with varying outcomes. Under these conditions, California led the way in defining the tensions and disputes surrounding state responsibility for funding public schools, so much so that today's legal ar-

Funding Public Schools in the United States, Indian Country, and US Territories (Second Edition), pages 71–89.
Copyright © 2023 by Information Age Publishing
www.infoagepub.com

guments still echo the challenge that a child's education may not depend on the accident of residence.[2]

Despite the dire and cataclysmic projections during the late winter and early spring of 2020 which forecasted tens of billions of dollars in lost tax revenue due to the pandemic, California's economy and resulting tax revenues remained strong. That fiscal strength led to a record $124.3 billion in funding for all K-12 education programs - $80.4 billion from the Proposition 98 funds and $43.9 billion from other federal, state, and local sources. California's public school funding remains the largest single portion of the state's budget, capturing roughly 40% of the state's general fund revenues.[3]

In grand overview, the annual state budget is put in place by the state legislature and the governor. The budget cycle begins when the governor submits to the legislature an itemized proposed budget on or before January 10th.[4] The Senate Budget and Fiscal Review Committee and the Assembly Budget Committee conduct hearings on Governor's proposed budget bill in late February.[5] The governor proposes budget revisions in May based on updated information about state revenues. After considering the governor's initial and revised budget proposals, the two houses of the state legislature, currently overwhelmingly Democratic in composition, work together with the governor to finalize a version of the budget bill that can pass in each house by a simple majority vote.[6] The legislature must pass a budget bill on or before June 15th and send it to the governor for signature. [7] The governor can reduce or eliminate individual spending items before approving the final budget.[8]

Overall, the state budget directs how education funds are appropriated. At the local level, budgets are approved by local school boards after public hearings.[9] But the impact of *Serrano,* combined with the emaciated yields of local property taxes (now capped at 1%) after passage of Proposition 13 in 1978[10], have given local school boards very little control over their revenues.[11] Proposition 13, officially titled the People's Initiative to Limit Property Taxation, was a ballot measure to amend the state Constitution to roll back and reduce property tax rates. The initiative was championed by anti-tax crusaders Howard Jarvis and Paul Gann and overwhelmingly passed by the California electorate in June of 1978. Overnight, property taxes across the state were slashed by nearly 60% resulting in a shift in the burden of funding the state's roughly 1,000 public school districts from the local tax revenue (property taxes) and taxing authorities (school boards) to the state's general fund and legislature. Along with that shift in funding responsibility came a shift in school policy authorities, resulting in a significant loss of local programmatic control.

California's funding system is extraordinarily centralized at the state level, and at the heart of it beats Proposition 98[12], a Constitutional Amendment narrowly passed by voters more than 30 years ago to protect funding levels for K-14 public schools.[13]

Proposition 98

Proposition 98 calculates a minimum funding guarantee for K-14 schools[14] based on various "tests" that weigh the impact of fiscal and demographic inputs (state tax revenues, per capita personal income, local property taxes, public school enrollment, and more).[15] The three tests that determine K-14 funding are as follows[16]:

Test 1: K-14 education must receive a minimum percentage of General Fund revenues (currently about 38%);

Test 2: K-14 education must receive at least the same amount of state aide and local property tax dollars as received in the prior year (adjusted for changes in K-12 attendance and the percent change in per capita personal income); or

Test 3: K-14 education must receive at least the same amount of state aide and local property tax dollars as received in the prior year (adjusted for changes in K-12 attendance and the percent change in per capita General Fund revenue plus .5%.[17]

To fund Proposition 98, property taxes generated locally for schools are combined with revenue from the state's General Fund, with the statewide mix currently at about 70/30 State GF to LPT. Some districts (at this time about 100) actually generate more in Local Property Taxes than they receive in State funding, and these "Basic Aid" districts get to keep that excess amount, often reaching $5,000 or more per student above the state's funding level.[18]

Test 1	Test 2	Test 3
Share of General Fund Revenue	Change in Per Capita Personal Income (PCPI)	Change in General Fund Revenue

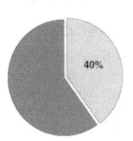

	PCPI	General Fund
40%	ADA	ADA
	Prior-Year Funding	Prior-Year Funding

| Guarantee based on share of state General Fund revenue going to K-14 education in 1986-87. | Guarantee based on prior-year funding level adjusted for year-over-year changes in K-12 attendance and California PCPI. | Guarantee based on prior-year funding level adjusted for year-over-year changes in K-12 attendance and state General Fund revenue. |

ADA = average daily attendance.

Source: https://lao.ca.gov/Publications/Report/4466

FIGURE 5.1.   Three Proposition 98 "Tests"

As a fiscal safety net, Proposition 98 has its shortcomings. Just two years after its passage, another Constitutional Amendment (Proposition 111) severely weakened its provisions by adding a 3rd "test" basically allowing automatic suspension of the minimum guarantee if state tax growth cannott support it.[19] Now, however, because of Test 3, because it is based on year-to-year changes rather than longer-term trends, and because state tax collections are increasingly volatile, the minimum guarantee is subject to enormous swings—usually negative. There is a constitutional promise—the "Maintenance Factor"—to get funding back on track eventually.[20] But that can take years and the billions lost in the meantime are never recovered.[21] Proposition 98 almost always determines the funding ceiling these days, not the floor as it was intended to be. Its stated goal of pushing California into a top-10 state in terms of high funding and low class size is almost forgotten. But maligned as it often is, and while it only defines the size of the funding pot, not how that pot is spent, Proposition 98 still looms over budgeting for public schools in California.

BASIC SUPPORT PROGRAM[22]

In 2013-14, California implemented a new public education finance system called Local Control Funding Formula (LCFF), replacing a system that had been in place for approximately 40 years.[23] Prior to 2013, schools were funded through a mixture of general purpose grants and more than 50 categorical grants.[24] LCFF greatly simplified the school finance system while attempting to improve equity, transparency, and performance in public schools.[25] For school districts and charter schools, LCFF provides local educational agencies (LEAs) with uniform base grants and with supplemental and concentration grants based on their student demographic profile.[26]

Base Grants for School Districts and Charter Schools Under LCFF

Base grants are distributed to school districts and charter schools to cover recurring general operational costs, such as teacher and administrator salaries, books, supplies, etc.[27] Base grants are calculated based on the average daily attendance[28] based on the grade span of the pupil.[29] Base grant amounts for each grade span were initially set for the 2013-14 school year as follows: grades K-3 ($6,845); grades 4-6 ($6,947); grades 7-8 ($7,154); and, grades 9-12 ($8,289). The base grant is determined each year by adding cost of living adjustments (COLA) to the prior year's base grant (before grade span adjustments).[30] For grades K-3 and 9-12, the base grants are further augmented by applying grade span adjustments of 10.4% and 2.6% respectively.[31] Table 5.1 shows how the 2021-22 base grants (and adjusted base grants) were calculated based on the 2017-18 base grants, the COLA, and the grade span adjustments.

TABLE 5.1. Base Grant Funding, Education Code (EC) Section 42238.02(d)

Grade Span	2020-21 Base Grant per ADA	2021-22 COLA (1.7%)	Grade Span Adjustments (K-3: 10.4% 9-12: 2.6%)	2021-22 Base Grant/ Adjusted Base Grant per ADA
K-3	$8,503	$144	$899	$9,546
4-6	$7,818	$133	N/A	$7,951
7-8	$8,050	$137	N/A	$8,187
9-12	$9,572	$163	$253	$9,988

Source: California Department of Education. Funding Rates and Information, Fiscal Year 2021-22: Principal Apportionment funding rates and other fiscal information for fiscal year 2021-22.

Supplemental and Concentration Grants for School Districts and Charter Schools Under LCFF

In addition to base grants that are calculated based on average daily attendance of all students, school districts and charter schools may also receive additional program funds for distribution to districts to support district populations of students who are in the foster care system or who are classified as homeless, students who are classified as English learners, and students who are classified as low-income based on their qualification for free or reduced-price meals.[32] These students, referred to as "unduplicated pupils," are counted only once, even if they may be classified in more than one of the covered categories.[33] The number of unduplicated pupils, collectively referred to as the "unduplicated count," entitle a school district to supplemental grants, and potentially and concentration grants if the count reaches a certain threshold.[34]

School districts receive supplemental grants for all of their unduplicated pupils. The supplemental grant is calculated by multiplying 20% of the adjusted base grant multiplied by the unduplicated count (as a percent of the total school district population). For example, if a high school district had a population 1200 students (based on ADA) for the 2018-19 school year had an unduplicated count amounting to 17% of that population, the supplemental grant would be calculated as follows:

If a school district has a significant unduplicated count (in excess of 55% of the student population) meaning it has a high concentration of students who may

TABLE 5.2. Example Calculation of Supplemental Grant

Grade level	Adjusted Base Grant (see Table 5.1)	20% of Adjusted Base Grant	Unduplicated Count (17% of district population)	Supplemental Grant
9-12	$9,988	$1,998	204	$407,592

TABLE 5.3. Example Calculation of Concentration Grant

Grade level	Adjusted Base Grant (see Table 1.1 above)	65% of Adjusted Base Grant	Unduplicated Count in Excess of 55% (12% of district population)	Supplemental Grant
9-12	$9,988	$6,492	144	$934,848

needed additional supports to be successful in the public school system, it will also receive concentration funding.[35] Concentration funding is calculated by multiplying 65% of the adjusted base grant by the unduplicated count (as a percent of the total school district population) that exceeds 55%.[36] For example, if the same high school district mentioned in the example above had an unduplicated count amounting to 67% of its population (rather than 17%), the concentration grant would be calculated as follows:

To get a clear picture of how the base grant and the supplemental and concentration grants work together, see Table 5.3 that provides a calculation of total education grant funding for the high school district mentioned above, with 67% of its students classified as unduplicated pupils.

Local Control Accountability Plan (LCAP)

The LCAP is a three-year plan that describes how the school district will support positive student outcomes for state and local priorities, particularly for unduplicated pupils.[37] Using a template provided by the State,[38] each school district provides a full accounting of how their LCFF funds are spent and how each expenditure supports the State's eight educational priorities:

TABLE 5.4. Example Calculation of Total Local Control Funding Formula Grant (Based on 67% Unduplicated Count)

Funding Source	Adjusted Base Grant (see Table 1.1 above)	Portion of Adjusted Base Grant	Total Number of Students	Number of Unduplicated Pupils	Supplemental Grant
Adjusted Base Grant	$9,988	N/A	1200	N/A	$11,985,600
Supplemental Grant	N/A	$1,998	N/A	204	$407,592
Concentration Grant	N/A	$4,994	N/A	144	$934,848
Total					$13,328,040

1. Appropriate basic educational supports, in the form of appropriately cre-
    dentialed teachers, standards-aligned instructional materials, and school
    facilities that are maintained in good repair;[39]
2. Implementation of academic content and performance standards;[40]
3. Parental involvement and family engagement;[41]
4. Academic achievement for all students;[42]
5. Student engagement;[43]
6. Positive school climate;[44]
7. Access to and enrollment in a broad course of study;[45] and,
8. Other student outcomes.[46]

Priorities one, two, and seven address the basic conditions of learning, priorities
four and eight address student outcomes, and priorities three, five, and six address
community engagement.

Each LCAP is intended to tell the story of where a school district has been,
where it is, and where it is trying to go. It includes a narrative statement, school
district progress and goals, identification of performance gaps, plans of action,
identification of services, and planned expenditures.[47] At the beginning of the
three-year LCAP process, the school district, in consultation with members of
the community,[48] establishes a set of goals on which they want to focus for that
period. Each goal is aligned to state and local priorities and the district identifies
annual measurable outcomes on which to evaluate progress.[49] The plan is modified and updated in the two years between LCAP drafting years.[50] Every year, the
LCAP or a modification/revision of the LCAP must be approved by the governing
district board of education on or before July 1st of each year.[51] Within five days of
adoption, the LCAP and the budget are then sent to the county superintendent of
schools for final approval.[52] While the LCAP was initially intended to provide a
clar and concise summary of district budget priorities for non-experts, over time,
these documents have grown ever longer and more complicated.

California School Dashboard and Statewide System of Support

State funding for education is tied to the California School Dashboard,[53] an
accountability system aimed at continuous improvement for the purpose of providing information about how well local education agencies and schools are meeting the needs of the state's diverse student population.[54] The California School
Dashboard provides educators, parents, and community members open access to
aggregated education data on schools and districts.[55] Building on the Dashboard,
the budget provides funding to support school districts identified with consistently
low-performing student subgroups and connects them to a network of resources
available through the companion Statewide System of Support.[56]

Revenue Sources

While LCFF represents a dramatic departure from previous education spending plans, the funding mechanism is not new. Once the LCFF amount is calculated, an LEA is first funded using local property taxes. If the local property tax revenues are insufficient to reach the LCFF level, as they are from more than 90% of the State's LEAs, then the state provides additional funds up to the LCFF funding level.[57] If the property taxes raised in a particular community exceed the LCFF funding level, the LEA does not receive any LCFF funds from the state but is permitted to keep the extra property tax revenues generated.[58]

Gap Appropriations

LCFF itself did not create a new source of revenue; it only regulates how state revenues are distributed and managed.[59] And it directs the distribution of additional money for students classified as high-need; in 2018-19, 62.48% of California's students qualified as high-need according to LCFF.[60] When LCFF passed, Governor Brown estimated that it would cost approximately $60 billion to fully fund the system, about $21 billion more than was previously allocated for education.[61] This dramatic increase in funding required a transition period, during which time LEAs received their pre-LCFF funding plus an portion of the difference towards their full-funding target.[62] The gap funding transition period was predicted to take seven years. However, as a result of strong growth in tax receipts, Governor Brown was able to ensure that LCFF was fully funded before he left office in 2018.[63]

Falling Enrollment

A four-year run of significant declines in public school enrollment through 2020-21 is predicted to continue until the 2030s, a trend that will have profound implications for education funding at the local, state, and federal levels.[64] Total statewide enrollment will drop during that time from just over 6 Million to under 5.5 Million, with more than half of that decline (278,000) occurring in Los Angeles County alone. (Compare to 15 years ago, when statewide enrollment was over 6.3 Million.) While 20 of the state's 58 counties will see some growth, that will be nominal – the largest growth is to occur in San Joaquin County, with a total increase of only 6,100 students. This decline – if it occurs, remember these are only projections – will have significant impacts and will probably lead to some policy changes of greater or lesser impact. For local education agencies currently funded by the state on a per-ADA basis, it means a reduction in funding – *on the natural*. But changes may be forthcoming to somehow mitigate the issue, particularly for large urban districts.

Categorical Funding

A decades-long move to eliminate state-directed, restricted "categorical" program funding was abruptly reversed in the course of a few months during the Spring of 2021, as billions in new revenue for schools was identified. While many advocated for these dollars to be spent on buying down school district obligations (such as employee benefits), or for being sent as unrestricted funding to schools, Governor Newsom and the State Legislature instead invested in dozens of new, restricted categorical programs addressing a wide range of activities they identified as high priorities.[65]

Federal Stimulus Funding

The Coronavirus Aid, Relief, and Economic Security (CARES) Act provided states with $30.75 billion in emergency funding and streamlined waivers giving State educational agencies increased flexibility to respond to COVID-19.[66] The funds were distributed through the Elementary and Secondary School Emergency Relief Fund (California's allocation was $1,647,306,127) and the Governor's Emergency Education Relief Fund (California's allocation was $355,227,235).[67] The funding was distributed to Local Education Agencies to address costs associated with their response to the COVID-19 pandemic[68].

BUDGET ACT OF 2021-22

As the largest program funded by the state's General Fund, public school funding is a significant focus in every budget.[69] On June 28, 2021, Governor Gavin Newsom signed the Budget Act for the 2021-22 school (and fiscal) year.[70] The budget package included $124.3 billion for TK-14 education,[71] with per-pupil spending of $23,089 in 2021-22.[72] The 2021-22 Budget Act also included the following allocations:

- Proposition 98: In January 2021, Govenor Newsom made conservative projections for the K-14 Proposition 98 minimum funding guarantee.[73] However, as a result of significant increases in state revenues, the Budget Act of 2021 included much higher Proposition 98 funding levels.[74] Consequently, the final K-12 per pupil spending level ended up being significantly higher than the 2020-21 per pupil spending level, and the spending levels proposed in January 2021.

- Early Childhood Education and Child Care

  The 2021-22 budget includes significant resources towards adopting universal TK "as part of a mixed delivery system for early education."[75] The budget included $200 million to expand the California state preschool programs and an additional $100 million to support preschool teacher training and professional development.[76] The hope is that universal pre-school will be phased in over a five-year period and LEAs will start receiving funding to establish universal preschool programs as early as 2022-23.[77]

- Community Schools

    The 2021-22 budget expanded the California Community Schools Partnership Program (CCSPP), providing it with $4.8 billion in Proposition 98 funding (to be distributed through 2027-28). It aligns CCSPP with Heathy Start best practices and includes $141.8 million for LEAs to create regional technical assistance centers.[78]

- Expanded Learning Opportunities

    The 2021-22 budget provides resources for the creation of an Expanded Learning Opportunities program for funding after school and summer school enrichment programs in communities with high concentrations of unduplicated count students.[79] Like the After School Education and Safety (ASES) program, the Expanded Learning Opportunities program will include eduational elements, such as turtoring and homework assistance and supplemental instruction in STEAM[80] content, CTE[81], and physical fitness.[82]

- Educator Preparation, Retention, and Professional Development

    The 2021-22 budget package includes resources for a number of programs aimed at preparing, recuiting, and retaining high-quality teachers, administrators, and classified state in public K-12 schools across California. Some programs included in this package include grants to enhance educator effectiveness, grants for teachers who commit to teaching in high-priority schools, resources for teacher residency programs, grants for classified employees to earn a teaching crediential, professional development for school leaders, and professional development for teachers in specific focus areas.[83]

- Universal School Meals Program

    The 2021-22 budget funds a new program, the Universal School Meals Program (USMP). The USMP will help schools cover the cost of providing breakfast and lunch for all students, regardless of family income.[84] USMP also provides one-time resources for schools to upgrade kitchen facilities and equipment and train food service employees on healthy food preparation. The universal provision of school meals makes it more difficult for LEAs to collect income data for the purposes of supplemental and concentration grant funding.

- Special Education

    The 2021-22 budget includes investments in special education services. Beyond the $396.9 million allocated to base rate special education funding, the budget includes allocations for early intervention services for preschool-aged students, learning recovery support for students with special needs, dispute resolution services for special education services complaints, and additional district-based special projects.[85]

SUMMARY

California's school finance system is complex and accounts for nearly half of the state's annual general fund spending. The funding reforms of 2014 sought to improve resources for the state's most vulnerable students and provide LEAs with more control of and accountability for their education resources. Longitudinal data for recent past years shows increasing education revenue from multiple sources. Figure 5.2 graphically demonstrates how LCFF has steadily increased education funding between 2015 and 2020. Figure 5.3 parses those same data to a per-pupil view.

Still, funding for California's approximately 6 million students is the subject of considerable criticism. Despite decades of nearly continuous school finance litigation and significant increases in funding levels, critics argue that schools are at least standing still if not regressing in terms of pupil performance.[86] A 2018 survey[87] of school superintendents across the state found general support for the LCFF, but with considerable dissatisfaction relating to numerous elements of state support. More specifically, many administrators strongly favored the tenets of the LCFF, but were concerned about the administrative burden, inadequate base funding, and lack of flexibility regarding use of supplemental and concentration funds.[88] Superintendents expressed concern regarding stakeholder engagement and the timeliness of the Dashboard. Unsurprisingly, school district context played a huge role in relative satisfaction with the LCFF, with favorability increasing as school district size increased – conversely, the smaller the district, the greater the dissatisfaction with perceptions involving administrative burden and losses perceived from elimination of categorical programs. Overall, a large majority (78%) regarded the LCFF as underfunded related to its goals and expectations, despite acknowledgment (69%) that LCFF's increased funding had been essential to successes so far.[89]

Outsider criticism of California school finance reform has been strong as well. While all sides generally regard the state as having made progress through increased focus and spending, critics argue that LCFF funding does not necessarily help unduplicated pupils as intended.[90] Critics also argue that there is still a lack of transparency, accountability, understandability, and disparities when microanalyzing equal access to high-quality resources under LCFF.[91]

At the core, all sides appear to agree in recognizing the complexity and size of the California school funding system[92] – a system containing over 6 million chil-

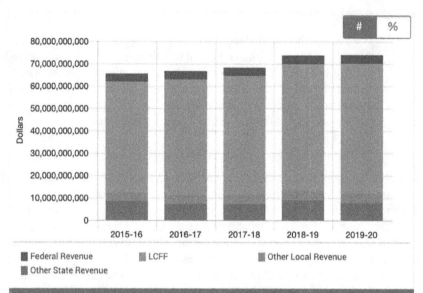

General Fund Revenues by Category	2015-16	2016-17	2017-18	2018-19	2019-20
Federal Revenue	3,687,318,716	3,713,861,887	3,783,136,273	4,026,224,148	3,927,723,277
LCFF	49,380,261,403	51,969,710,049	53,080,128,136	56,387,896,655	57,834,069,666
Other Local Revenue	3,758,004,134	3,740,358,903	4,083,147,736	4,283,797,467	4,220,209,318
Other State Revenue	8,716,419,235	7,243,016,284	7,279,640,363	9,028,256,604	7,977,081,605
Total	65,542,003,488	66,666,947,123	68,226,052,508	73,726,174,874	73,959,083,866

Chart Notes   Source

Note: California implemented the Local Control Funding Formula (LCFF) in 2013-14. Prior to 2013-14, the "LCFF" section of this graph refers to what were known as "Revenue Limit" sources under the previous school finance system. This graph displays the main sources of revenue by type for California school districts over the past five years. The General Fund is the chief operating fund for school districts, and most of the district's financial transactions flow through this fund.

Source: https://www.ed-data.org/state/CA

FIGURE 5.2 California School Revenue Sources, Amounts and Trends, Fiscal Years 2016-2020

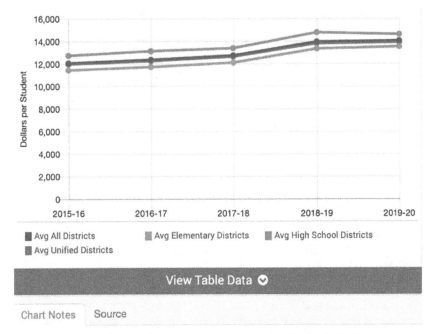

This chart shows per-student General Fund revenues for all California districts by type over the past five years. The General Fund is the chief operating fund for school districts and most financial transactions flow through this fund. For more information about the financial reports on Ed-Data, see our help article.

Source: https://www.ed-data.org/state/CA

FIGURE 5.3.   California Per-Student Revenue Trends Fiscal Years 2016-2020

dren, with 60% coming from low income backgrounds, 19% classified as English Language learners, and 12% with special needs.[93] Above all, large achievement gaps exist which the LCFF intends to redress. Certainly, the flood of one-time or limited-time funds associated with the unexpected revenue surpluss will provide schools with some short term opportunity. What happens next is yet to be seen.

ENDNOTES

1   5 Cal.3d 584 (1971) (Serrano I); subsequent litigation followed in Serrano v. Priest, 18 Cal.3d 728 (1976) (Serrano II); and Serrano v. Priest, 20 Cal.3d 25 (1977) (Serrano III). For a more complete synopsis of subsequent California finance litigation through 2018, see California, SchoolFunding. Info: A Project of the Center for Educational Equity at Teachers College, http://schoolfunding.info/ litigation-map/california/#1484003321788-7f4cb732-5834 (last visited Oct. 22, 2021).

2   Id., Serrano I, 5 Cal.3d at 589, stating "...makes the quality of education for school age children in California, including Plaintiff Children, a function of the wealth of the children's parents and neighbors, as measured by the tax base of the school district in which said children reside."

[3] In California, community colleges are funded with K-12 schools rather than with public 4-year institutions (University of California and California State University Systems). In the 2021-22 budget, $5 billion was allocated for community colleges, with $3.5 billion for community college apportionments and categorical programs and an additional $1.5 billion in deferals of systems funding. Joint Analysis: Enacted 2021-22 Budget, Cal. Community Colleges (July 13, 2021), https://www.cccco.edu/-/media/CCCCO-Website/College-Finance-and-Facilities/Budget-News/July-2021/Joint-Analysis-Enacted-Budget_2021-22.pdf?la=en&hash=1A85666B435AE-C55D9B7BCC62D31135247196AFB

[4] Cal. Const., art. IV, § 12(a). If the governor's budget includes proposed expenditures that exceed anticipated revenues, the Governor must recommend sources of additional revenue.

[5] Committee hearings generally begin soon after they receive the "Analysis of the Budget Bill" from the Legislative Analyst. The Legislative Analyst is appointed by the Joint Legislative Budget Committee and is charged with providing a nonpartisan analysis and recommendations for changes to the Governor's proposed budget. California's Budget Process, State of Cal. Dep't of Fin., http://www.dof.ca.gov/budget/Budget_Process/index.html (last visited Oct. 22, 2021).

[6] Id.

[7] Cal. Const., art. IV, § 12(b)(3).

[8] Education Budget, Cal. Dep't of Educ., https://www.cde.ca.gov/fg/fr/eb/ (last visited Oct. 22, 2021).

[9] Cal. Educ. Code § 42127 (a)(1) (West 2019).

[10] Cal. Const., art. XIIIA .On June 6, 1978, voters passed Proposition 13, reducing property tax rates on homes, businesses, and farms. Proposition 13 limits increases in assessed property value and caps property tax and ad valorem property tax rates to 1% of the full cash value at the time of acquisition. What is Proposition 13? California Tax Data, https://www.californiataxdata.com/pdf/Prop13.pdf (last visited Jan. 31, 2019); A Historical Review of Proposition 98, Legislative Analyst's Office (Jan. 18, 2017), https://lao.ca.gov/Publications/Report/3526#Formulas.

[11] Local parcel taxes are an exception, being levied on an equal amount per property parcel upon approval of 2/3s of the voters, with the revenue essentially unrestricted. From the first attempt in 1983 through 2020, there have been almost 2,000 parcel tax elections (many being re-authorizations as they are usually levied only for a short term), with about 57% passing, generally – though not exclusively – in more affluent communities, often in the San Francisco Bay Area. Parcel Tax Elections in California, Ballotpedia, https://ballotpedia.org/Parcel_tax_elections_in_California (last visited Oct. 19, 2021).

[12] Cal. Educ. Code § 41206 (West 2021).

[13] Cal. Const., art. XIIIB; Cal. Const., art. XVI.

[14] K-12 schools receive about 89% of the Proposition 98 funds, with the remaining going to community colleges.

[15] Proposition 98 Primer, Legislative Analyst's Office (Feb. 2005), https://lao.ca.gov/2005/prop_98_primer/prop_98_primer_020805.htm.

[16] Id. The test used depends on how the economy and General Fund revenues grow annually.

[17] Proposition 98 Sets a Minimum Funding Guarantee for Education (Policy Brief), EdSource (Mar. 2009), https://edsource.org/wp-content/publications/PolicyBriefR3.pdf.

[18] The 2021-22 contains about $30 Billion in discretionary spending for Proposition 98 (K-14 schools), of which only about $4 billion is ongoing – the rest being one-time in nature. The 2021-22 Budget: Overview of the Spending Plan, The Legislative Analyst's Office (Aug. 2021), https://lao.ca.gov/reports/2021/4448/2021-Spending-Plan-082421.pdf

[19] The original version allowed political suspension, but only by a two-thirds vote of the legislature and a governor's signature.

[20] Cal. Const., art. XVI; Cal. Educ. Code § 41207.2 (West 2021).

[21] During the Great Recession, for instance, the Maintenance Factor exceeded $10 Billion per year.

22 See generally, Education Budget, Cal. Dep't of Educ. (Aug. 17, 2021), https://www.cde.ca.gov/fg/fr/eb/; also, Local Control Funding Formula Overview, Cal. Dep't of Educ (Sept. 10, 2021) https://www.cde.ca.gov/fg/aa/lc/.

23 Local Control Funding Formula Overview, Cal. Dep't of Educ. (Sept. 10, 2021) https://www.cde.ca.gov/fg/aa/lc/.

24 Id.

25 Local Control Funding Formula: LCFF Dictates How State Funds Flow to Schools, Ed100 (Aug. 2017), https://ed100.org/lessons/lcff.

26 Cal. Educ. Code § 42238.02 (West 2021).

27 Local Control Funding Formula Overview, Cal. Dep't of Educ. (Sept. 10, 2021) https://www.cde.ca.gov/fg/aa/lc/; Cal. Educ. Code § 42238.03 (West 2021) (setting forth how base entitlement rates are calculated).

28 Local Control Funding Formula Overview, Cal. Dep't of Educ. (Sept. 10, 2021) https://www.cde.ca.gov/fg/aa/lc/.

29 Cal. Educ. Code § 42238.02(d) (West 2021).

30 Cost-of-living adjustments (COLA) rates are set each year as part of the budget negotiation process. The Governor presents an estimated COLA in the budget he or she submits in January. LCFF and COLA, Cal. Dep't of Educ. (July 22, 2021), https://www.cde.ca.gov/fg/aa/pa/lcffcola.asp. Under California law, the COLA is linked to the national price index developed by the Bureau of Economic Analysis for the U.S. Department of Commerce. "Due to the significant increase in revenues projected for 2020-21 and 2021-22, there is a corresponding increase in LCFF funding levels. The budget package reflects an LCFF increase of $3.2 billion, 5.07 percent over 2019-20 levels. This reflects a 2.31 percent cost-of-living (COLA adjustment for 2020-21, a 1.70 percent COLA adjustment for 2021-22, and a $520 million (1 percent) increase in LCFF base funding. Budget Act for 2021-22: Information, Cal. Dep't of Educ. (Oct. 5, 2021), https://www.cde.ca.gov/fg/fr/eb/yr21ltr0811.asp.

31 Cal. Educ. Code § 42238.02(d)(2)-(3) (West 2021). The adjustment of 10.4% for K-3 grades is to help reduce class size and the 2.6% adjustment for high school grades is to help off-set the cost of career-technical education.

32 Cal. Educ. Code § 42238.02 (West 2021).

33 Id.

34 Id. at (e).

35 The LCFF Concentration Grant was first proposed in 2007 in a white paper by Alan Bersin, Michael Kirst, and Goodwin Liu, calling for it to be applied for districts with more than 50% of their students eligible for Free/Reduced Price Meals. Alan Bersin, Michael W. Kirst, & Goodwin Liu, Getting Beyond the Facts: Reforming California School Finance [Issue Brief], Univ. of Cal., Berkley Law School (Apr. 2008), https://www.law.berkeley.edu/files/GBTFissuebriefFINAL.pdf. While it cited "some evidence" of substantial impact of poverty at that level, other studies have refuted this premise. And the standard for compensatory funding addressing concentrated poverty is generally a 40% Census rate. A PPIC report from 2013 concurred with the 40% standard, and their analysis found that in California "a 40 percent threshold in the Census poverty rate would be similar to using a 90 percent threshold in the free and reduced price lunch program." Heather Rose & Margaret Weston, California School District Revenue and Student Poverty: Moving Toward a Weighted Pupil Funding Formula, Public Policy Inst. of California (Feb. 2013), https://www.ppic.org/wp-content/uploads/content/pubs/report/R_213HRR.pdf. Additionally, this study noted "concern" about applying a Concentration Grant formula at the district, as opposed to a site, level, because "in California, poverty is not always equally distributed across schools within a district." Id. So there is no defensible rationale to export the Concentration Grant's 55% eligibility threshold and its districtwide-funding standard to other programs. Note that the statewide "unduplicated count" percentage, 62%, is actually higher than the Concentration Grant threshold. California Public Schools, Educ. Data Partnership, https://www.ed-data.org/state/CA (last visited Oct. 28, 2021).

ᴰue to a last-minute political deal , the Concentration Grant funding per ADA was set at a rate two-and-a-half times as great as the Supplemental Grant's, even though they serve identical students. This wasn't always the case. For 18 months, for all three iterations of the LCFF from its initial proposal (under a different name) in January 2012 through the 2013 May Revision, the funding per-ADA for the Supplemental and Concentration Grants were identical. First there was a 37% augmentation to the Base Grant for each, then it was cut to 20% for each a year later, then bumped up to 35% five months after that – again, each time, both grants were treated the same. But in the final deal, cut just weeks before it was signed into law on July 1, 2013, the Supplemental Grant add-on was slashed by almost half, to 20%, and the Concentration Grant augmentation was pushed up to 50%, with the threshold for Concentration Grant eligibility increased to 55%. This last-minute reduction in the Supplemental Grant augmentation disadvantaged the Unduplicated Count pupils in districts receiving little or no Concentration Grant funding. Currently, more than three quarters of a million Unduplicated Count students attend LEAs ineligible for any Concentration Grants; a quarter million more are in Concentration Grant-eligible districts with an Unduplicated Count percentage of less than 60%.

[36] Id. at (f). Prior to 2021-22, the concentration grant multiplier was 50% of the base grant. The concentration grant multiplier was increased to 65% as part of the 2021-22 budget. Budget Act for 2021-22: Information, Cal. Dep't of Educ. (Oct. 5, 2021), https://www.cde.ca.gov/fg/fr/eb/yr21ltr0811.asp.

[37] Cal. Educ. Code § 52060 et seq. (West 2021); Local Control Accountability Plan (LCAP), Cal. Dep't of Educ. (Aug. 20, 2021), https://www.cde.ca.gov/re/lc/.

[38] Cal. Educ. Code § 52060(a) (West 2021).

[39] Id. at (d)(1).

[40] Id. Specifically, this goal relates to the implementation of Common Core State Standards for all students, including English learners. See LCFF and LCAP State Priority Areas, San Juan Unified Sch. Dist., https://www.sanjuan.edu/Page/23613 (last visited Oct. 22, 2021).

[41] Id. at (d)(3).

[42] Id. at (d)(4). Measures of this include standardized test scores, Academic Performance Index (API) scores, percent of student population who are college and career ready, ELs who become English proficient, and Advance Placement (AP) test passage rates. LCFF and LCAP State Priority Areas, San Juan Unified Sch. Dist., https://www.sanjuan.edu/Page/23613 (last visited Oct. 22, 2021).

[43] Id. at (d)(5). Measures of this include student attendance rates, chronic absenteeism rates, and dropout rates. LCFF and LCAP State Priority Areas, San Juan Unified Sch. Dist., https://www.sanjuan.edu/Page/23613 (last visited Oct. 22, 2021).

[44] Id. at (d)(6). Measures of this include student suspension and expulsion rates and other local measures of climate, such as student feedback and climate survey results.

[45] Id. at (d)(7). The broad course of study includes all subject areas described in Cal. Educ. Code § 51210, 51220(a)-(i) (West 2021).

[46] Id. at (d)(8). Specifically, this refers to pupil outcomes in the broad course of study described in the previous footnote.

[47] Local Control Accountability Plan (LCAP), Cal. Dep't of Educ. (Aug. 20, 2021), https://www.cde.ca.gov/re/lc/.

[48] The superintendent, with the support and help of their staff, drafts the LCAP. Cal. Educ. Code § 52062(a)(1) (West 2021). The superintendent presents the LCAP to the parent advisory committee (established pursuant to Cal. Educ. Code § 52063) and the English learner parent advisory committee (also established pursuant to Cal. Educ. Code § 52063) for review and comment. The superintendent is also required to give members of the community an opportunity to give feedback on the LCAP (Cal. Educ. Code § 52062(a)(3)) before submitting the LCAP to the governing board of the school district for adoption. (Cal. Educ. Code § 52062(a)). In an effort to ensure that additional funding is used to benefit the unduplicated pupils, school districts often seek out more extensive community feedback on the programing funded by supplemental and concentration grants. They

may solicit participation of a large group of parents, teachers, classified employees, and community members to serve on LCAP advisory committees.

[49] Id. The district measures outcomes using both state and local matrices.

[50] Cal. Educ. Code § 52062 (West 2021).

[51] Cal. Educ. Code § 52061 (West 2021). The school board must hold at least one public hearing to allow the public to review the LCAP and make recommendations or comments before it is adopted. Cal. Educ. Code § 52062(b)(1) (West 2021). The school board adopts the LCAP in a public meeting (after and not on the same day as the public comment meeting) during which they also adopt the school district budget. Cal. Educ. Code § 52062(b)(2) (West 2021).

[52] Cal. Educ. Code § 52070 (West 2021). A school district's budget cannot be approved and funded until the county superintendent of schools reviews the school district LCAP and confirms that it complies with the LCAP requirements.

[53] California School Dashboard and System of Support, Cal. Dep't of Educ. (Sept. 22, 2021), https://www.cde.ca.gov/ta/ac/cm/.

[54] Budget Act for 2021-22: Information, Cal. Dep't of Educ. (Oct. 5, 2021), https://www.cde.ca.gov/fg/fr/eb/yr21ltr0811.asp.

[55] California School Dashboard, https://www.caschooldashboard.org (last visited Oct. 25, 2021). The Dashboard provides information on student achievement scores, student discipline, absenteeism rates, graduation rates, and college and career readiness. The Dashboard also allows these statistics to be further broken down by race and for English learners, special education, foster/homeless students, and low-income students.

[56] California's System of Support, Cal. Dep't of Educ. (Oct. 22, 2021), https://www.cde.ca.gov/sp/sw/tl/csss.asp.

[57] Local Control Funding Formula: LCFF Dictates How State Funds Flow to School Districts, Ed100, https://ed100.org/lessons/lcff (last visited Oct. 25, 2021).

[58] Id.

[59] Id.

[60] Id.; California Public Schools, Educ. Data Partnership, https://www.ed-data.org/state/CA (last visited Oct. 28, 2021).

[61] Id. Proposition 30 (The Schools and Local Public Safety Protection Act of 2012) was approved by voters the same year LCFF passed. It temporarily increased personal income tax and sales and use tax rates to provide additional revenue for public elementary and secondary schools and community colleges. It expired in 2016, at which time Proposition 55 (The California Children's Education and Heath Care Protection Act of 2016) was approved to extend the increases to personal income tax rates on earnings over $250,000 to provide continued revenue for elementary and secondary schools and community colleges through fiscal year 2030-31. A.B.1808, 2017-18 Reg. Sess. (Cal. 2018).

[62] Id.

[63] Budget Act for 2021-22: Information, Cal. Dep't of Educ. (Oct. 5, 2021), https://www.cde.ca.gov/fg/fr/eb/yr21ltr0811.asp.

[64] California Public K-12 Graded Enrollment and High School Graduate Projections by County–2021 Series, State of Ca. Dept. of Finance (June 2021), https://www.dof.ca.gov/Forecasting/Demographics/Projections/Public_K-12_Graded_Enrollment/. There has been an extended ADA hold-harmless provision during the COVID pandemic. The continued natural decline in enrollment means that eliminating these hold-harmless extensions will cause even more fiscal distress than might usually be the case, so there may be some legislative revisions to address the issue. For instance, this could result in a switch from attendance-based to enrollment-based funding – something urban districts have been pushing for years in California. Under Proposition 98's, total statewide funding for schools is independent of enrollment – meaning that statewide declining enrollment actually increases funding per student. And there is also the Prop 98 bump that is part of the transition to universal TK. Absent an economic downturn, there should be resources to address declining enrollment if the political will is there, as it probably will be given the political

clout of many large declining enrollment districts. Federal funding is largely per-student based, so California will naturally see some reductions in federal dollars.

[65] Newsom's May Revision Proposes 'Historic' $93.7B for Education, EdCal (May 24, 2021), https://edcal.acsa.org/newsoms-may-revision-proposes-historic-93.7b-for-education

[66] Federal Stimulus Funding, Cal. Dep't of Educ. (Dec. 31, 2021) , https://www.cde.ca.gov/fg/cr/

[67] Id.

[68] Id.

[69] Education Budget, Cal. Dep't of Educ. (Aug. 17, 2021), https://www.cde.ca.gov/fg/fr/eb/index.asp; Budget Act for 2021-22: Information, Cal. Dep't of Educ. (Oct 5, 2021), https://www.cde.ca.gov/fg/fr/eb/yr21ltr0811.asp

[70] Budget Act for 2021-22: Information, Cal. Dep't of Educ. (Oct. 5, 2021), https://www.cde.ca.gov/fg/fr/eb/yr21ltr0811.asp. See also, Mazen Aziz & Oscar Jimenez-Castellanos, California, 46(3) J. of Educ. Fin. 251 (2021).

[71] Inclusive of all public funding sources (federal, state, and local).

[72] Id. Per pupil spending indicated here is an average rate, across grade spans. The comparable 2020-21 per pupil spending rate was $16,881; this is a significant increase in per pupil spending.

[73] Id. The Governor's January budget projected Prop 98 funding at $79.5 billion (2019-20), $82.8 billion (2020-21), and $88.1 billion (2021-22).

[74] Id. Instead of the funding levels listed above, the Prop 98 funding levels were estimated to be $79.3 billion (2019-20), $93.4 billion. (2020-21), and $93.7 billion (2021-22). The increased revenues also resulted in significant deposits into the Public School System Stabalization Account ($1.9 billion for 2020-21 and $2.6 billion for 2021-22, totaling $4.5 billion).

[75] Id.

[76] Id.

[77] Id. The goal is to have universal preschool fully implemented by 2025-26. Should these universal preschool goals be met, Prop 98 minimum funding may be "rebenched" to provide ongoing financial support for preschool programs.

[78] Id.

[79] Id.

[80] Science, technology, engineering, art, and math.

[81] Career and technical education.

[82] Id. The Expanded Learning Opportunites programs will offer at least nine hours of in-person before or after school instruction on school days and on at least 30 non-schooldays during intersession periods.

[83] Id. Professional development funds are specifically designated for learning acceleration in mathematics, literacy, and language development, social and emotional learning, early mathematics, and mental health and wellness.

[84] Id. Unver the USMP, schools will be required to apply for federal meal provisions to maximize federal meal reimbursement. The state will cover any remaining or unreimbursed costs up to the federal free per-meal rate.

[85] Id. Special project funds are designated for Riverside County Office of Education and the El Dorado County Office of Education, in support of the Supporting Inclusive Practices Project.

[86] John Affeldt, California Needs a New Master Plan to Close the Education Equity Gap, EdSource (Oct. 31, 2018), https://edsource.org/2018/california-needs-another-master-plan-to-close-the-education-equity-gap/604068.

[87] Julie A. Marsh & Julia E. Koppich, Superintendents Speak: Implementing the Local Control Funding Formula (LCFF), PACE (June 27, 2018), https://www.documentcloud.org/documents/4561241-LCFF-Supt-Survey-2018.html.

[88] Id.

[89] Id.

90 Nadra Kareem Nittle, Why School Funding Will Always Be Imperfect, The Atlantic (Aug. 24, 2016), https://www.theatlantic.com/education/archive/2016/08/will-there-ever-be-a-perfect-way-to-fund-schools/497069/

91 See, e.g., Matt Barnum, How New Evidence Bolsters the Case for California's Education Policy Rebellion, Chalkbeat (Feb. 8, 2018), https://www.chalkbeat.org/posts/us/2018/02/08/how-new-evidence-bolsters-the-case-for-californias-education-policy-rebellion/; see also, Susan Ferriss, Will New Funding Formula Move Schools Toward Education Equity? KQED (Feb. 8, 2017), https://www.kqed.org/news/11305666/will-new-funding-formula-move-schools-towards-education-equity.

92 The 2018-19 Budget: K-12 Education in Context, Legislative Analyst's Office (Jan. 26, 2018), https://lao.ca.gov/Publications/Report/3736

93 CalFacts 2018, Legislative Analyst's Office, https://lao.ca.gov/reports/2018/3905/calfacts-2018.pdf (last visited Jan. 31, 2019).

CHAPTER 6

COLORADO

E. Glenn McClain, Jr.
Weld RE-7 School District

Spencer C. Weiler
Brigham Young University

GENERAL BACKGROUND

Colorado was granted statehood and enacted its first constitution in 1876.[1] However, public schools started to dot the territory as early as 1861 and the funding for these early schools was exclusively based off of local revenues.[2] By the turn of the twentieth century, public schools increased the services provided to students to include a high school curriculum and, with these increases in the overall quality of the educational experience for school-aged children, state aid was included to augment local efforts to fund schools.[3] Eventually, state sales and income tax revenues were used to supplement the overall funding for public education.[4] By the time Colorado entered the twenty-first century, state aid accounted for roughly 60% of the total funding for public education, despite efforts to equally distribute the tax burden for public education between state and local tax revenues. Two anti-tax constitutional amendments contribute to the overall overreliance on state aid to fund public education.[5]

Funding Public Schools in the United States, Indian Country,
and US Territories (Second Edition), pages 91–106.
Copyright © 2023 by Information Age Publishing
www.infoagepub.com

The primary focus of this chapter is on providing readers with a thorough understanding of Colorado's funding formula for public education. The discussion will touch on an array of topics, including the general fund, special education, transportation, the marijuana tax and school facilities, virtual/online schools, special levies, and the state retirement system. The discussion will then move to summarize the major school finance lawsuits that originated in the state of Colorado.

BASIC SUPPORT PROGRAM

The current funding formula for Colorado was enacted in 1994.[6] Recently, advocates for public education have contended that the current state funding formula is antiquated and needs to be revised to reflect the current fiscal realities of providing all students "a thorough and uniform"[7] educational experience in the 21st century.[8] During the 2018 legislative session, there was a bill that, if passed, would have completely altered funding for public education, but the bill failed to garner sufficient public support in the form of tax increases. The educational community in Colorado continues to seek ways to infuse new revenue into the state's public education system. Since 2018 there have been three statewide ballot issues that have not passed, but some minor headway has been made through passage of sin-taxes that have bolstered funding for rural school districts and early childhood education.

GENERAL FUND

The state funding formula, entitled the Public School Finance Act of Colorado, determines the per pupil funding for the 178 school districts and the state charter schools that are chartered by the Charter School Institute.[9] The amount of money school districts and charter schools receive for public education is referred to as the total program. A school district's or charter school's total program is determined by a student count formula and the student count in Colorado is conducted on or around October 1 each year.[10] The formula for the total program is expressed in the following equation:

(Funded Pupil Count X Total Per-pupil Funding) + At-risk Funding + Online Funding + Budget Stabilization Factor = TOTAL PROGRAM[11]

The total per-pupil funding is, in effect, the base funding level for each full-time equivalency (FTE) student.[12] For the 2020-2021 school year, the base funding was $7,083.61.[13] The state funding formula includes weights that add to the base per pupil funding. These weights include:

1. Cost of Living: This weight provides additional revenue to school districts located in regions of the state with above average cost of living indices. The state cost of living factor is based on the mean scores from

the Denver and Boulder communities.[14] The cost of living factor ranges from 1.012 to 1.650 in Colorado.[15]

2.   Personnel Costs: Certain school districts have made choices regarding staffing levels and, as a result, the percent of the school district's total program allocated to personnel costs exceeds the state average of 80%. The state funding formula provides additional funding to school districts where the personnel costs amount to more than 80% of the school district's total program.[16] The personnel cost factor ranges from 1.010 to 2.243.[17]

3.   Size: In rural Colorado there are small school districts that serve less than 100 students. These school districts are required to fully staff a building even though there may be less than 10 students in any classroom. The state's funding formula allocates additional resources to smaller school districts to ensure they can properly serve the students living in these geographically isolated areas of the state.[18] The size factor ranges from 1.0297 to 2.3958.[19]

As a result of these weights, the base per-pupil funding varies from school district to school district, based on cost of living, personnel, and size.

The state funding formula also provides additional resources to school districts with higher percentages of students that qualify for free and reduced meals. The statewide average of students qualifying for free and reduced meals is roughly 40% and school districts that exceed that percentage receive additional at-risk funding.[20] The state refers to this additional funding as the concentration factor, which will be discussed in greater detail below.

Finally, the budget stabilization factor (BS) serves to reduce the overall impact of the weights to the state funding formula. In essence, the budget stabilization factor reduces the state aid for public education to ensure that the state funding commitment does not exceed the state revenues. The formula for budget stabilization is:

(Total program after BS/Total program before BS)—1 = BS Factor reduction

The minimum total program funding, on a per-pupil basis, for the 2021–2022 school year was $7,225.28.[21] It should be noted that the BS Factor does not negatively impact school districts that do not rely on state aid to meet the total program.

External Forces on the General Fund

Colorado voters approved two state constitutional amendments that work together to drive down the local contribution to public education and negatively impact the general fund for public education. As a result, state aid is forced to backfill lost local revenue funds instead of supplementing these funds to ensure all students have access to an adequate educational opportunity. The result of these two constitutional amendments is that the desired balance between state and local contributions[22] to public education has proven unattainable. These two amendments, namely the Gallagher Amendment and the Taxpayer Bill of Rights, are discussed in this section.

The Gallagher Amendment was adopted in 1982 to stabilize property tax rates by establishing a static relationship between the overall revenues generated from residential and nonresidential properties.[23] The purpose of the Gallagher Amendment, to stabilize residential property rates, was a commendable goal, but the actual implementation resulted in unintended consequences. Specifically, after Gallagher was passed, the overall number and value of each residential property increased at a faster rate than nonresidential properties. As a result, the taxable portion for residential properties fell from 21% in 1982 to 7.96% today while taxation rates on nonresidential properties have remained constant over this same period, a rate of 29%.[24] In November 2020, a statewide referred measure passed that repealed Gallagher and the static property assessment ratios; however, the effects of almost forty years of reduced property taxing capacity are still felt in K-12 funding.

From 1982 until 1992, when Colorado voters approved the Colorado's Taxpayer Bill of Rights (TABOR),[25] all Colorado school districts levied 40.8 mills on property owners. As the taxable portion of residential properties fell (currently at 7.15% for residential and 29% for non-residential properties), the local contribution to public education decreased and was supplanted by state aid. However, TABOR put an end to this practice since one of the key components of the amendment was that all proposed tax increases must be approved by voters. County commissioners and school district officials could no longer increase mill levies without first obtaining permission from voters. As a result, starting in 1992 the local contribution to the total program for public education in Colorado has slowly decreased and state revenues are required to supplant lost local revenues. Research suggests that TABOR and Gallagher, together, are depriving public education of over $2 billion annually.[26]

Local Contribution

The local contribution to Colorado's funding formula is derived from two primary sources: property taxes and specific ownership taxes.[27] Property tax rates are determined based on two key factors: 1) the net assessed value of all of the properties within a given school district, and 2) the local share, as mandated by the state, to the school district's total program. The net assessed value of each school district in the state varies greatly, as would be expected, and these variances may result in inequities in Colorado's funding formula. To stabilize declining property tax rates throughout the state, in 2007 legislation was enacted that capped the maximum mill levy rate at 27 mills and froze all mill levy rates below 27. As a result, the range of mill levy rates in Colorado school districts is 1.68 to 27 mills. For the 2021-2022 school year, local property tax revenues for public education accounted for $2.94 billion dollars, or 31% of the $7.989 billion budget for public education in the state.

The specific ownership tax refers to vehicle registration tax.[28] These taxes are collected at the county level and then dispersed to the local school districts. The specific ownership tax only generated $195 million for the 2021-2022 school year, or $220.78 per student.[29]

The local contribution to a school district's total program ranges from 0%[30] to 100%. The reason for this variation in local contribution stems from the progressive nature of the state's funding formula. In essence, the state recognizes there are school districts in Colorado that are property poor, or school districts with inadequate net assessed values. In response, the state provides property poor school districts with a greater percentage of state aid.

Compensatory Education

In addition to the factors detailed in the section on the general fund, Colorado's funding formula recognizes that certain students require additional resources to ensure they are fully capable of being successful in school. Specifically, Colorado provides school districts with additional recourses for each student that is classified as:

1. A student with a disability—Colorado allocates $167 million to meet the unique educational needs of students with disabilities. These funds are distributed to local school districts, based on the needs of students they serve. Typically, school districts receive $1,250 for each student that qualifies for special education services the previous year.[31] Starting in the 2018-19 school year, the state provided school districts with an additional $1,876 for "students with more intensive special-education needs."[32]

2. Gifted and talented student services—The state funding formula provides school districts with $12.1 million to school districts to help with the identification process of potential gifted and talented students and curriculum enrichment.[33]

3. English language learners—English language learners make up roughly 14% of the entire student population in Colorado. The state allocates $48 million annually to support the educational attainment of English learning students, or $52.65 per student.[34]

4. Students at risk of dropping out of school—Relying on free and reduced numbers as an approximate for at-risk students, the state provides school districts with $494 million. School districts receive an additional 12% of the base per pupil funding for each student classified as at-risk.[35] When school districts have a percentage of students qualifying for free and reduced lunch that exceeds the state average, they become eligible for the concentration factor, which provides additional at-risk funding.

Special Education

As detailed in Colorado's Exceptional Children's Education Act (ECEA), state educators strive to provide appropriate educational opportunities to all students and the goal is to provide these opportunities in the least restrictive environment.[36] School districts are required to provide services to all students with disabilities that qualify for special education services from the age of three to 21.

Services for students with disabilities are provided by school districts, specialized day programs, residential programs, and private programs. The appropriate services for an individual student is dictated by the student's academic or emotional needs and the ability of the local school district to meet those needs.

On or around December 1 of each year, school districts report to the state the number of students receiving special education services and the percent of services each student receives. These data are then used by state officials to generate a special education budget for each school district for the following school year. Once school district officials receive the special education budget from the state, a budget is developed for each school within the school district. This school specific budget for special education services will include personnel expenditures, including both teachers and paraprofessionals, and funding for specific or specialized programs.

General Transportation

On average, roughly 42% of students rely on transportation services to get to and from school each day. School districts throughout the state own over 6,000 buses that travel over 58 million miles annually. To help offset the costs associated with transporting students to and from school, the state established the Public School Transportation Fund.[37] These funds are not intended to cover the cost of purchasing a new bus,[38] but do provide school districts with a transportation reimbursement, in the form of a $0.37 refund per mile traveled. The $0.37 reimbursement amounts to 40% of the total travel expense. School district efforts to fund the remaining 60% of the transportation expense include drawing the funds from the total program, charging families a transportation fee,[39] or building into a mill levy override a line for transportation.

Transportation is not required by state law,[40] but the general practice is to provide transportation for students that are forced to cross dangerous intersections or who live outside of a reasonable walking distance from school. It should be noted that charter schools are not required to provide transportation to students. However, if charter school officials decide to provide transportation to students, then all the rules and regulations placed on traditional public schools apply to charter schools.[41]

School Facilities/Marijuana Tax

Most school districts, when needing to remodel an existing building or to build a new facility, approach voters to approve a bond initiative. However, there are several school districts in Colorado where the tax base is insufficient to generate the necessary resources required for the construction of a new facility. As a result, the state established the Building Excellent Schools Today (B.E.S.T.) Grant program.[42] The B.E.S.T. Grant was created when a lawsuit was filed against the state contending the state funding formula was unconstitutional as a result of the inequities related to replacing or remodeling school facilities.[43] As a part of the settlement in this case, the state agreed to put $190 million aside as a matching fund for school districts in need of assistance related to facility expenses. The B.E.S.T. Grant also receives resources from the state's land trust funds, the state's lottery, marijuana taxes, and earned interest each year.

School districts with facility projects apply to the state for B.E.S.T. funds. The B.E.S.T. board uses a set of criteria to approve facility projects. Matching funds are granted based on a formula using local wealth, as measured by the school district's net assessed value. The B.E.S.T. board prioritizes facility projects where a school district's net assessed value is limited. Since its inception in 2000, the B.E.S.T. Grant has received over $2.8 billion in requests and has been able to fund $1.2 billion in capital construction projects.

Starting in 2014, the state of Colorado began to collect taxes on sales of marijuana products for recreational use. In 2017, marijuana tax revenues amounted to $247 million, with $100 million going into public education.[44] The first $40 million in tax revenues from the sales of marijuana goes to the B.E.S.T. grant program to aid with addressing the facility needs across the state. The remaining tax revenues from marijuana sales are allocated into the Public School Permanent Fund and the State Public School Fund.[45]

Career and Technical Education

Funding for Career and Technical Education (CTE) is provided to school districts on a per-pupil basis and the funds are used to provide instruction, materials, equipment, and related services.[46] Specifically, the state provides school districts with up to 80% of the first $1,250 spent on CTE needs on a per pupil basis and 50% of any costs that exceed the initial $1,250.

Virtual Education

During the 2017-2018 school year, there were 21,246 Colorado students enrolled in an online educational program.[47] The two most common options are online charter schools, which typically span multiple school districts, and online options offered to students through the local school district. The funding for online programs differs, based on the services being provided.[48] For the cross-school district charter schools, the state's funding formula provides a reduced per pupil

TABLE 6.1. Federal COVID Stimulus Funding, Colorado

CARES Act ESSER I	CRF	CRRSA ACT ESSER II	ARP Act ESSER III
$120,993,782	$510,000,000	$519,324,311	$1,166,328,632

expenditure, which is, on average, 10% less than the minimum per pupil funding for the state.[49] Students enrolled in online schools that are sponsored by a local school district generate the same per pupil funding for the school district as traditional brick and mortar students.

Federal COVID Stimulus Funding

In response to the COVID-19 pandemic, the United States Congress passed three stimulus bills that included funding for education: the Coronavirus Aid, Relief, and Economic Security (CARES) Act (March 2020); the Coronavirus Response and Relief Supplemental Appropriations (CRRSA) Act (December 2020); and the American Rescue Plan (ARP) Act (March 2021). Each stimulus bill provided funding for the Elementary and Secondary School Emergency Relief (ESSER) fund and the Governor's Emergency Education Relief (GEER) fund.[50]

The CARES Act established the $150 billion Coronavirus Relief Fund (CRF) to support states with COVID-19 related expenses incurred between March 1 and December 30, 2020. Colorado Governor Jared Polis directed $510 million from the state's CRF to the Colorado Department of Education to be awarded to school districts, the Charter School Institute, the Colorado School for the Deaf and the Blind and facility schools on a per pupil basis. Additionally, each Boards of Cooperative Educational Services (BOCES) in the state received $25,000.

Colorado funding from these special once-in-a-generation funds are summarized in Table 6.1.

In general, 90% of each of the above funds were distributed through the Title I formula and 10% was held in a state reserve fund and distributed through a grant program administered by the Colorado Department of Education's Commissioner of Education. Allowable uses include but are not limited or required:

- Child nutrition including universal free lunch/meals,
- COVID-19 prevention strategies to safely reopen schools and maximize in-person learning,
- Address the impact of lost instructional time by supporting the implementation of evidence-based interventions that respond to students' social, emotional, and academic needs,
- Address the disproportionate impact of COVID-19 on historically marginalized students, students from low-income backgrounds, students with disabilities, English learners, students who are migratory, students expe-

riencing homelessness, students in correctional facilities, and students in foster care,

- Serve the mental health needs of students,
- Provide integrated student supports,
- Provide students with evidence-based summer learning and enrichment programs,
- Connect K-12 students to high-quality home internet,
- Stabilize and diversify the educator workforce and rebuild the educator pipeline,
- School facility repairs and improvements, and
- Additional equipment that could improve access for students including school transportation vehicles.[51]

School officials are currently focused on providing equitable and adequate educational opportunities that address the impact of COVID-19 on students, educators, and staff, focusing on evidence-based strategies for: 1) Meeting students' social, emotional, mental and physical health, and academic needs, including through meeting basic student needs; reengaging students; and providing access to a safe and inclusive learning environment; 2) Addressing the impact of COVID-19 on students' opportunity to learn, including closing the digital divide; implementing strategies for accelerating learning; effectively using data; and addressing resource inequities; and 3) Supporting educator and staff well-being and stability, including stabilizing a diverse and qualified educator workforce.

Special Levies

Colorado school districts are authorized to approach voters to approve a mill levy override (MLO), but the maximum amount a school district can seek in a mill levy override is 25% of the school district's total program.[52] To date, 114 of the 178 school districts have voter approved mill levy overrides. Due to the wide variance in local wealth, Colorado has some districts where it is virtually impossible to enhance revenue through the MLO process. The legislature, through a Legislative Interim Committee, is examining methodologies that the State of Colorado could implement to equalize MLO revenue through matching funds. The equalization of MLO revenue is predicated upon a stable and sustainable revenue source.

School districts may also seek voter approval to secure Special Building and Technology Funds in the form of 10 additional mills for up to three years' time.[53] These funds are specifically designated for the purchase of land, construction expenses, purchasing facilities, maintaining existing facilities, security expenses, and expenses related to technology.

Capital Outlay

School districts have several options to cover capital projects. One option, which is no longer required in state law, is to set a portion of the total program, on a per pupil basis, aside to cover capital projects. For large-scale capital projects, school districts have the following options:

1. Bonded indebtedness[54]—School districts seeking to issue bonds hold an election in which local voters approve or reject a ballot initiative that would raise funds necessary for extensive capital needs. Bonds include a principal loan amount and interest payments. The state does impose a cap on the total amount of bond indebtedness for school districts and the cap is 20%[55] (25% for school districts with rapidly increasing student populations) of the net assessed value for the school district.[56]

2. Loan Program for Capital Improvements[57]—Reserved for school districts that are deemed as growth school districts, the loan program allows eligible school districts to apply for loans from the state treasurer, pending approval from local voters. These funds are then used to address immediate capital improvement needs in the school district, such as the purchase of portable classrooms.

3. Supplemental Capital Construction, Technology and Maintenance Fund[58]—School district officials can choose to approach voters seeking permission to obtain additional mills for technology (upgrade and replacement) and maintenance needs. These monies represent an ongoing cash fund for the school district to address technology and facility needs.

Food Services

The state allows school districts to provide students with an array of food services, including: after-school snack program, emergency feeding, fresh fruit and vegetable program, National School Lunch Program, School Breakfast Program, seamless summer option, and summer food service program.[59] The state reimburses school districts based on the number of students served in each of the programs. The reimbursement rate varies from program to program. Historically, school districts received $0.37 per student that participates in the National School Lunch Program each day, $0.30 per student that participates in the School Breakfast Program, $0.20 per student eligible for the Special Milk Program, and $0.08 per student in the after-school snack program. Once the COVID-19 pandemic hit, meals were made available to all students for free and this practice remains in place during the 2021-2022 school year.

State Funding for Non-Public Schools

The Colorado Constitution specifically states, "Neither the general assembly, nor any county, city, town, township, school district or other public corporation, shall ever make any appropriation, or pay from any public fund or moneys whatsoever, anything in aid of any church or sectarian society, or for any sectarian purpose."[60] In short, state law specifically prohibits the allocation of public funds to any non-public school.

Other State Aid

As was discussed above, the state funding formula recognizes the need to provide school districts with additional support for students that are at-risk, gifted and talented, non-English speaking students, and students with disabilities. The state provides financial support to school districts to provide these students with the educational support they require.[61]

Capital Improvement

Prior to fully appreciating the effects of the Great Recession in Colorado, state law required school districts to take a portion of the total program, on a per pupil basis, and set these funds aside for capital improvement projects. However, in 2009 this requirement was eliminated and school districts could continue the practice or could roll the funds that would have been designated for capital improvement projects into the total program for instructional needs. The long-term impact of this decision remains to be seen, but potentially alarming trends are already surfacing throughout the state. Some school districts are opting to roll traditional capital improvement projects, such as re-roofing or re-carpeting a school building, into bond initiatives. As a result, voters are being asked to pay interest on top of the cost of these capital improvement expenditures. In addition, a trend of school districts seeking bonds in excess of $500 million is becoming more commonplace in Colorado and it is expected that this trend of large bond amounts will continue into the future.

Retirement

Colorado's retirement system, dubbed the Public Employee Retirement Association (PERA),[62] is a pre-funded retirement program, or a retirement program where employees and employers contribute a percentage each employee's monthly income into the plan. Currently the employee contributes 10.5% and the employer contributes 20.9%.[63] The monthly funds are used to make payouts to retired individuals that are drawing from PERA and are invested to generate interest for PERA. The process is overseen by PERA's Board of Trustees.[64]

There are over 630,000 people, or one in every ten people in Colorado, that are either contributing to or drawing a retirement from PERA. When a PERA eligible employee retires, this person's actual monthly payment is based on a few factors, including: the highest average salary of the employee, which is currently based on the average of the three highest annual salaries, and the total number of years the employee contributed to PERA.

In 2010, after the Great Recession hit Colorado, PERA's overall value fell by $11 billion, or 26%. In response, the state increased the minimum required contributions for employees and employers. In addition, the overall benefits that employees would receive were reduced. However, despite assurances that these measures would fix PERA, in 2021 PERA has over $31 billion in unfunded liabilities. The unfunded liability is a source of concern throughout the state since it is feared that another economic downturn could bankrupt PERA.

To ensure PERA remained fiscally viable, the state's General Assembly explored several remedies that would ensure PERA remains solvent. The solutions for fixing PERA included: reducing the annual cost of living adjustment from 2% to 1.5%,[65] increasing the employee contribution from 8% to 11%, increasing the employer contribution from 20% to 22%, and increasing the eligible retirement window from 30 years in the system to age 65. It is anticipated that with these changes PERA will become fiscally solvent in 30 years.

REVENUE

The revenues for public education in Colorado are derived from three sources: local taxes, state taxes, and federal title funds. The local revenues to public education are generated through property and specific ownership taxes, or vehicle registration. The local revenue sources generate $2.94 billion, or 31% of the total funding for public education in Colorado.[66]

State revenues are generated from an array of taxes: Sales, Insurance Premium, Income, Corporate, and Cigarette. Sales and Income Taxes generate over 91% of the state revenues.[67] State revenues accounts for $4.8 billion, or 61% of the total funding for public education in Colorado.

The federal contribution for public education in Colorado is primarily generated from federal income tax and federal dollars are aimed at providing historically disadvantaged students with the necessary support to be successful in school. The federal funds are rolled into different federal programs, such as the Every Student Succeeds Act. Title funds, which are embedded in the Every Student Succeeds Act, are specifically designed to support students at risk of dropping out of school, English learners, and rural school districts. Federal dollars amount to $620.8 million, or 6.03% of the total funding for public education in Colorado.

SCHOOL FINANCE LITIGATION IN COLORADO

Colorado has experienced several lawsuits filed over the years contending that the state's funding formula fails to properly fund public education. Some of the cases were adjudicated while others were settled. There are two landmark decisions that help to illustrate the overall landscape in Colorado related to the state's role in funding public education in a "thorough and uniform"[68] fashion. Each case is briefly discussed below.

In 1977, a group of plaintiffs filed a lawsuit, entitled *Lujan v. Colorado State Board of Education*,[69] against the state Board of Education contending that the state's funding formula at the time perpetuated disparities in school district funding that, ultimately, deprived certain students an equal access to education. The trial court ruled in favor of the plaintiffs, but the state supreme court reversed that ruling. In its ruling, the state supreme court held that the state's education clause of "thorough and uniform" did not guarantee students "absolute equality in educational services or expenditures." The ruling also upheld local control as a constitutional justification for funding disparities between school districts.

As was stated previously in this chapter, in 1994 the state enacted a new funding formula for public education. In 2005, the School Finance Act of 1994 was challenged in the *Lobato v. State*[70] lawsuit. In *Lobato*, the plaintiffs' claim centered on evidence that the state funding formula failed to provide all students with a "thorough and uniform" educational experience. Specifically, the plaintiffs' arguments centered on the educational needs of students with disabilities, English language learners, and the need for preschool and full-day kindergarten, along with transportation services, for all students. The claim was initially dismissed by the District Court and that decision was appealed. The appellate ruling sided with the plaintiffs, claiming that the state's funding formula was irrational and unconstitutional.

The appellate ruling was subsequently appealed to the state Supreme Court. The state Supreme Court first set out to define the educational clause standard of "thorough and uniform." The state Supreme Court defined thorough and uniform as "a free public school system that is of a quality marked by completeness, is comprehensive, and is consistent across the state" and then applied the claims in *Lobato* to this definition. The state Supreme Court ruled that the current funding formula is constitutional since the array of statutes governing public education are applied uniformly to all 178 school districts.

In a third lawsuit, which was initiated in 2007, the Colorado Supreme Court wrestled with the constitutional interplay between TABOR, the state School Finance Act, and the balance between state and local revenues. The Colorado Supreme Court determined that the Colorado Department of Education (CDE) erroneously and unconstitutionally reduced local school mill levies during the 1990s and early 2000s. In effect, the CDE's actions resulted in wide ranges in mill levies between school districts across the state, which eliminated any semblance of a uniform mill levy. Districts that passed ballot issues allowing for the retention of revenues should have maintained their mill levies rates and local taxing capacity, but this did not happen. Recently the state general assembly worked to address this inequity. State lawmakers enacted a statute that provides a mechanism for addressing this inequity between school districts in terms of mill levy rates.

SUMMARY

Public education is the second greatest item on the state's general fund, as illustrated in Table 6.2. The state of Colorado spends 34% of its general fund on P-20

TABLE 6.2. State Operating Budget, General Fund, FY 2019-2020

Program	General Fund Appropriation	Percent of Total General Fund
Human Services/Health Care	$13,033,600,000	40.1%
Higher Education	$4,875,500,000	15.0%
Correctional/Judicial	$1,828,600,000	5.6%
Education (K-12)	$6,185,900,000	19.0%
Transportation	$2,112,000,000	6.5%
General Government	$672,900,000	2.1%
Other	$3,807,000,000	11.7%
TOTAL	$35,515,800,000	100.0%

Mesa County Board of County Commissioners v. State, unpublished decision, available at: https://caselaw.findlaw.com/co-supreme-court/1413147.html

educational services. However, the current trajectory for the state's general fund does not appear to be sustainable under TABOR. The state cannot continue to allocate 34% of the general fund to P-20 educational needs (which is already down from 47% in 2018) and, at the same time, address the transportation, health care, and correctional needs throughout the state.

ENDNOTES

[1] Carl Abbott, Colorado: A History of the Centennial State 114-116 (Colorado Associated University Press, 1976).

[2] Wilbur Fisk Stone (editor), History of Colorado: Illustrated 586 (The S. J. Clarke Publishing Company, 1918).

[3] LeRoy R. Hafen and Ann Hafen, The Colorado Story: A History of Your State and Mine 436 (The Old West Publishing Company, 1953).

[4] Id.

[5] Spencer C. Weiler and Gabriel R. Serna, Colorado, Journal of Education Finance 40, no. 3 (2015): 307.

[6] C.R.S. 22-54-101.

[7] Colo. Const. (1876), Article IX, §2.

[8] Some state politicians had intimated that students attending public education need to receive a "world class" education to be prepared to function in the 21st century economy.

[9] C.R.S. 22-54-101.

[10] C.R.S. 22-54-104.3. State law requires school districts to conduct the student count on a set day each year and that day occurs within an eleven-day period around October 1.

[11] Colorado Department of Education (CDE), Understanding Colorado School Finance and Categorical Program Funding (July 2017).

[12] C.R.S. 22-54-104.3.

[13] CDE, supra note 11, at 3. See also Financing of Public Schools for Fiscal Year 2021-22 (2021). Available at: https://leg.colorado.gov/publications/financing-public-schools-fy-2021-22. The current base funding figure represents a $679 increase from 2017-2018, when this chapter was first published. See also Tommy E. Jackson and Tamela C. Thomas, Colorado, 46 J. Ed. Fin. 254 (2021), 254.

[14] C.R.S. 22-54.5-208.

[15] CDE, supra note 11, at 3.

[16] C.R.S. 22-54.5- 205.

[17] CDE, supra note 11, at 3.

[18] C.R.S. 22-54-122.

[19] CDE, supra note 11, at 4.

[20] C.R.S. 22-54-136.

[21] CDE, supra note 11, at 5.

[22] The desired balance between state and local aid used to support public education is 50/50.

[23] Colo. Const. Art. X, §3.

[24] Colorado Department of Treasury (n.d.), Constitutional Provisions, available at: http://www.colorado.gov/cs/Satellite/Treasury/TR/1196935260080

[25] Colo. Const. Art. X, §20.

[26] Gabriel R. Serna and Spencer C. Weiler, Tempered Optimism in Colorado: 2015 State-of-the-States. Journal of Education Finance, 387-390, at 389.

[27] C.R.S. 22-54-106.

[28] C.R.S. 22-54-106.

[29] School Finance Unit (n.d.). Available at: https://www.cde.state.co.us/cdefinance#:~:text=In%20budget%20year%202018%2D19,property%20taxes%20(%242.36%20billion).

[30] The total program for all traditional public school districts includes a local contribution, which varies from school district to school district. However, there are a few non-traditional school districts in the state, including state sponsored charter schools and school of the deaf and blind, that do not receive any funds generated from local property and specific ownership taxes. That is why we are reporting a range of 0% to 100%.

[31] C.R.S. 22-20-101.

[32] EdBuild, Funding for Students with Disabilities (n.d.), at 1. Available at: https://cosfp.org/wp-content/uploads/edbuild_-co_-_sped_-_final.pdf

[33] C.R.S. 22-20-104.5.

[34] C.R.S. 22-24-101. The per student number is based on the entire state student population. There are roughly 135,818 students in Colorado who qualify for ELL services. When the ELL student population is divided into the $48 million, the per pupil figure changes to $353.41.

[35] C.R.S. 22-20 through C.R.S. 22-29.

[36] C.R.S. 22-20-102.

[37] C.R.S. 22-51-101.

[38] School districts have several options when it comes to purchasing new transportation vehicles that includes general fund, transportation mill levy, capital project funds, grants, bonds, and mill levy overrides.

[39] Voters must approve a proposed transportation fee before it is enacted by a school board.

[40] C.R.S. 4204-R-200.03.

[41] C.R.S. 22-30.5-103.

[42] C.R.S. 22-43.7-101.

[43] Giardino v. Colorado Board of Education, No. 98-CV-0246 (Denver Dist. Ct. 1998).

[44] Colorado Department of Revenue, Marijuana Tax Data, available at: https://www.colorado.gov/pacific/revenue/colorado-marijuana-tax-data; see also Houck, E. A. & Midkiff, B. C. (2018). Advocacy Coalitions and Colorado's Legalization of Recreational Marijuana: A Discourse Analysis. Journal of Education Finance. 44(2), 115-139.

[45] During the 2021 legislative session, the state General Assembly temporarily reallocated a portion of the marijuana tax revenues from the B.E.S.T. grant program to the total program for general education purposes. In addition, in November 2021, Colorado voters will be asked to consider a marijuana tax increase that would be used for a new program, similar to B.E.S.T., that would fund instructional needs.

[46] C.R.S. 23-8-101.

[47] Colorado Department of Education, Online Summary Report (2019), at 5. Available at: https://www.cde.state.co.us/sites/default/files/docs/onlinelearning/Final_Summary%20Report%20for%20Online%20Schools%20and%20Programs.pdf. Due to COVID-19, the online enrollment figures in Colorado are in a constant state of flux.

[48] C.R.S. 22-30.7-107.

[49] C.R.S. 22-54-104 (4.5).

[50] The ESSER funds direct 90% of the total state allocation to local education agencies based on Title I formula, with the remaining 10% earmarked for state reserve funds. The GEER funds are largely discretionary programs for governors to use as emergency support for early childhood through higher education.

[51] Colorado Department of Education, Federal COVID Education Funding (n.d.), available at: http://www.cde.state.co.us/caresact

[52] C.R.S. 22-54-108. The state caps the mill levy override for school districts that are designated as small attendance centers at 30%. School districts with enrollments less than 300 students qualify as small attendance centers.

[53] C.R.S. 22-45-103(1)(d).

[54] C.R.S. 22-42-102.

[55] The state allows school districts to use the greater of 20% of net assessed value or 6% of actual value as the cap.

[56] C.R.S. 22-42-104.

[57] C.R.S. 22-2-125.

[58] C.R.S. 22-54-108.7.

[59] C.R.S. 22-54-123.

[60] Colo. Const. Article IX, § 7.

[61] C.R.S. 22-24-101.

[62] C.R.S. 24-51-101.

[63] C.R.S. 24-51-401. In July 1, 2022, the employee contribution will increase to 10.5%.

[64] C.R.S. 24-51-202.

[65] The cost of living adjustment is on a trigger that is designed to respond to current economic trends.

[66] In 2019, the local contribution was 34.1% of the total funding for public education and generated $2.41 billion.

[67] Joint Budget Committee, Appropriations Report Fiscal Year 2017-18, at 10.

[68] Colo. Const. (1876), Article IX, §2.

[69] Lujan v. Colorado State Board of Education, 649 P.2d 1005 (1982).

[70] Lobato v. State, 304 P.3d 1132 (2013).

CHAPTER 7

CONNECTICUT

Michael Morton
School and State Finance Project

George Sinclair
School and State Finance Project

GENERAL BACKGROUND[1]

Despite a long history of supporting public education and the inclusion of a School Fund in its 1818 constitution to financially support public or "common" schools,[2] the Connecticut Constitution did not formally recognize the responsibility of state government to provide public education for the state's students until 1965 when a new state constitution was approved by a referendum and adopted. The 1965 constitution, which remains the state's constitution, amended Article Eighth to include the following provision:

> There shall always be free public elementary and secondary schools in the state. The general assembly shall implement this principle by appropriate legislation.[3]

While Article Eighth of the Connecticut Constitution formally recognizes the right of the state's students to attend a free public school, it does not include any mention regarding the required quality of a public school, the level at which a

Funding Public Schools in the United States, Indian Country, and US Territories (Second Edition), pages 107–124.
Copyright © 2023 by Information Age Publishing
www.infoagepub.com
107

school must be funded, or the mechanism(s) by which a school should be funded. The answers to these questions were left for the state legislature, and often the judicial branch, to address.

Significant Court Cases

Beginning in the 1700s and its time as a British colony, Connecticut provided some funding to its communities to support the schooling of their children. The funding was often marginal and based on the number of students educated by a community. By the 1970s, Connecticut's sole support to local public schools was a flat grant based on the district's Average Daily Membership.[4] This grant peaked in 1975 at $250 per student. The vast majority of district funding instead came from local property tax revenue. In 1977, as the result of a legal challenge to the state's heavy reliance on the property tax for school funding, the Connecticut Supreme Court ruled in *Horton v. Meskill* that the state's education financing mechanism violated the education rights clause and the equal protection clause of the state constitution because it allowed "property wealthy" towns to spend more on education with less effort, impeding children's constitutional rights to an equal education.[5]

The Court also ruled the State had a constitutional obligation to make up for the disparities in town wealth, however, the Court did not address the overall level or sufficiency of state education aid nor did it propose specific remedies to address the disparities. Rather, the Court ruled it is up to the legislature to devise a constitutional system for funding the state's public schools.[6]

Connecticut's General Assembly adopted the state's first major education equalization funding formula, the Guaranteed Tax Base (GTB) grant, in 1979,[7] which was challenged by the *Horton* plaintiffs in 1985. While the GTB grant survived the legal challenge,[8] it was ultimately replaced in 1988 by the Education Cost Sharing (ECS) grant.[9]

After years of changes and revisions,[10] the ECS formula and Connecticut's education finance system was once again the subject of a legal challenge in the case of *Connecticut Coalition for Justice in Education Funding (CCJEF) v. Rell.* The case wound its way through Connecticut's judicial branch for over a decade before a Hartford Superior Court judge ruled partially in favor of CCJEF in 2016 and found Connecticut's K-12 education system in violation of students' constitutional right to an adequate education. The judge ordered the legislature to develop a plan within 180 days to address the parts of Connecticut's education system that he found unconstitutional.[11]

On appeal, the Connecticut Supreme Court ruled 4-3 in favor of the State of Connecticut and rejected each of the legal claims made by CCJEF.[12] In reversing the superior court's decision, the Court found Connecticut provided a minimally adequate education sufficient to satisfy the state's constitution and held that:

Although Connecticut has 'an imperfect public educational system,' [i]t is not the function of the courts...to create educational policy or to attempt by judicial fiat to eliminate all of the societal deficiencies that continue to frustrate the state's educational efforts ... [T]he function of the courts is to determine whether the narrow and specific criteria for a minimally adequate educational system under [Connecticut's] state constitution have been satisfied.[13]

Prior to the Connecticut Supreme Court's 2018 ruling in *CCJEF v. Rell*, the General Assembly overhauled the ECS formula in an attempt to make the system more equitable and to phase in greater funding for the state's lower-wealth, higher-need districts.[14]

Another court case of significance to school finance in Connecticut is *Sheff v. O'Neill*. In 1989, a group of city and suburban parents filed suit on behalf of their 18 children against then-Governor William O'Neill. The plaintiffs argued that public schools in Hartford were segregated, underfunded, and denied students in the Hartford area their constitutional right to an adequate and equal education due to the disparities in the distribution of funding and resources between communities of color in Hartford and the adjacent, majority white suburbs.[15]

In 1996, the Connecticut Supreme Court found Hartford's public schools to be racially segregated and in violation of the state constitution's anti-segregation provision. The Court found the racial segregation deprived the plaintiff's children of their right to substantially equal educational opportunity.[16] In response to the Court's ruling in *Sheff v. O'Neill*, the Connecticut General Assembly passed legislation that, among other things, created a two-way, voluntary integration program featuring a new regional magnet school system and an expanded interdistrict transfer program.[17] As detailed throughout this chapter, the creation of the magnet school system, and the stipulated agreements that have occurred in the *Sheff v. O'Neill* case since the Connecticut Supreme Court's 1996 ruling, play a significant role in the structure and function of Connecticut's school finance system.

Enrollment & Demographics

Connecticut has 149 local public school districts, 17 regional public school districts, 21 public charter schools, five Regional Educational Service Centers (RESCs) that operate interdistrict magnet schools, and one technical and education career system that operates 17 technical high schools and other programs.

For the 2020-21 school year, Connecticut's public school enrollment was 513,079. Over the past decade, the state's student enrollment consistently declined – dropping by approximately eight percent (45,299 students).[18] Simultaneously, the number of economically disadvantaged students (as measured by eligibility for free or reduced-price lunch) served by Connecticut's public school districts increased 11.5 percent to 219,172 (42.7 percent of total enrollment). The state's English Learner population also increased significantly during the same time period – growing by approximately 40 percent to 42,474 students (8.3 percent of total enrollment). Additionally, the number of students requiring special education services increased from 2011-12 to 2020-21 by 23 percent to 83,623 (16.3 percent of total enrollment).[19] Connecticut districts that educate the greatest percentages of economically disadvantaged students, English Learners, and students with disabilities also educate the largest numbers of these higher-need students.[20] These districts also tend to have larger percentages of BIPOC[21] students.

Approximately 50 percent of Connecticut students self-identify as BIPOC and 50 percent self-identify as white.[22] Below is a list of Connecticut's total student enrollment by race/ethnicity for the 2020-21 school year.

- American Indian or Alaska Native: 0.25%
- Asian: 5.22%
- Black or African American: 12.72%
- Hispanic/Latino of any Race: 27.78%
- Native Hawaiian or Other Pacific Islander: 0.10%
- Two or More Races: 4.03%
- White: 49.90%

Serving Connecticut's students are nearly 97,000 certified and non-certified teachers, administrators, paraprofessionals, and support staff. For the 2020-21 school year, the vast majority of Connecticut's educators identified as white (89.9 percent) with 4.3 percent identifying as Hispanic or Latino and 4.1 percent identifying as Black or African American.[23]

Spending

Total K-12 education spending in Connecticut from all sources was more than $12 billion for the most recent year of record.[24] Spending per student for the 2019-20 school year varied greatly across Connecticut's school districts, with a low of $13,132 and a high of $46,735. The state average for district per-student spending was $17,838.[25]

CURRENT POLITICAL CLIMATE

The Connecticut General Assembly is bicameral legislative body comprised of a 151-member House of Representatives and a 36-member State Senate. As of November 2021, the Democratic Party controls the House by a margin of 43 members, and the Senate by a margin of 12 members. The state's executive branch is headed by Governor Ned Lamont, also a Democrat, who appoints commissioners of state agencies (including the State Department of Education) with approval from the General Assembly. In addition to the Governor, the state has four elected constitutional officers: Secretary of the State, Treasurer, Comptroller, and Attorney General. All are elected to four-year terms, and currently, all offices are held by Democrats.

Connecticut's legislative process operates on a biennial schedule. In odd-numbered years, the legislature must enact a balanced state budget for the next two fiscal years. In even-numbered years, the General Assembly convenes for a shorter legislative session that is intended to be limited to budget adjustments for the current biennium. Connecticut's fiscal years run from July 1 to June 30.

Union Representation & Engagement

There is a broad collection of various education advocacy and interest groups in Connecticut, including the state's two prominent teachers' unions: the Connecticut Education Association (CEA) and the state affiliate of the American Federation of Teachers (AFT).[26] Both unions have historically been key Democratic allies.

Other Advocacy & Interest Groups

Other active interest groups include: the Connecticut Association of Public School Superintendents; the Connecticut Association of Boards of Education; the Connecticut Charter School Association; the RESC Alliance; the Connecticut Conference of Municipalities; and the Connecticut Council of Small Towns.

Current School Finance Legislation

The 1996 Connecticut Supreme Court ruling in *Sheff v. O'Neill*[27] resulted in legislation intended to encourage voluntary steps toward racial integration, partially through the establishment of magnet and regional charter schools.[28] In January 2020, the parties in the case agreed to a new stipulated agreement that runs through June 2022 and provides a pathway for potentially ending the litigation and judicial oversight of the case. Among its many components, the stipulated agreement: creates 1,052 new magnet school seats, including nearly 600 reserved for Hartford resident students; provides $1.1 million for the development of new magnet school themes; provides $800,000 over two years for academic and social support to Hartford students participating in the Open Choice program; provides $300,000 to incentivize suburban districts to increase the number of Open Choice seats they make available for Hartford students by 20 percent; and requires the State Department of Education to develop a long-term school choice plan for *Sheff* programs.[29]

SOURCES OF REVENUE

Local and regional public school districts in Connecticut primarily receive funding from two main sources: local property tax revenue and state aid.[30] The local contribution is distributed by the town to the school district, as Connecticut's school districts are fiscally dependent on their local municipalities and have no taxing authority.[31] Additionally, towns must rely on local property tax revenue to support education and other services because state law prohibits them from levying other taxes. State aid is primarily distributed through the state's ECS formula, which distributes education equalization aid to municipalities for their local and/ or regional public school districts based on a variety of student and community need-based factors. However, it is important to note that only local and regional public schools receive state aid through ECS, while other funding formulas are used for choice programs such as charter and magnet schools.

In 2019, 58.5 percent of Connecticut's total education funding came from local property taxes, and 37.2 percent came from state aid. Federal funding makes up a small percentage (4.3 percent) of total revenue for local and regional school districts. School districts may also receive additional funding through tuition and other sources.[32]

The percentages of state and local funding vary greatly from district to district depending on a number of factors including how many higher-need students a district is educating, and the ability of the district's town to raise local property tax revenue. As a result, higher-need, lower-income districts generally have to rely more on state education aid for funding. For example, in Hartford, where nearly 80 percent of the student population is eligible for free or reduced-price lunch (FRPL), the state provides over 70 percent of the city's education funding. Contrarily, 20 percent of the student population in Greenwich is eligible for FRPL and less than one percent of the district's education funding comes from the state. Often, wealthier districts also spend more per student. In 2019-20, Greenwich spent $22,645 per student, compared to Hartford's $17,496.[33]

DISTRIBUTION FORMULAS

Regular Education Program

The State of Connecticut distributes state education funding to public schools through a variety of formulas and grants. Currently, Connecticut's legislature uses more than 10 different funding formulas to determine how much money public schools should receive. These formulas range in complexity and differ based on the type of public school being funded.

The primary source of state education funding in Connecticut is the ECS grant,[34] which provides approximately $2 billion in funding annually to local and regional public school districts. Charter schools, magnet schools, and other types of types of school choice programs do not receive funding from the ECS grant.

Based on the current biennial state budget passed by the Connecticut General Assembly, the ECS grant will provide approximately $2.14 billion in FY 2022, and $2.18 billion in FY 2023, to the state's municipalities for the operation of their local and/or regional public school districts.[35] As the agency overseeing K-12 public education, the CSDE receives and distributes the ECS grant directly to Connecticut's municipalities, which then pass the grant through to their respective district(s). All towns are guaranteed some funding from the ECS grant, even when the calculated result of the grant's formula is that a town would not be entitled to receive ECS grant funding. This guarantee is the result of the ECS formula's Minimum Aid Ratio, which is 10 percent for Alliance Districts (the state's 33 lowest-performing districts) and one percent for all other districts.[36]

The ECS grant is calculated using the ECS formula, which is made up of several different components, including: the foundation, student need-based weights, the Base Aid Ratio, and the phase-in schedule. While not based on a specific calculation or estimation, the formula's foundation amount is intended to represent the estimated cost of educating a general education student who does not have any additional learning needs. The foundation amount is currently $11,525 per student.[37] Additionally, the foundation "incorporates" the State's share of general special education funding, resulting in approximately 22 percent of the ECS foundation amount being attributable to special education.[38]

The ECS formula contains three "need-student" weights, which increase per-student state education aid for students with additional learning needs.[39] Below is a description of each of the weights in the ECS formula.

- Low-Income Student Weight
    - Increases foundation amount by 30 percent for students who live in economically disadvantaged households as measured by eligibility for free or reduced-price lunch (FRPL).
- Concentrated Poverty Weight
    - Increases foundation amount an additional 15 percent (for a total of 45 percent) for economically disadvantaged students residing in districts where 60 percent or more of the enrollment is considered economically disadvantaged.
    - Weight applies only to a district's low-income students above the 60-percent level.
- English Learner Weight
    - Increases foundation amount by 25 percent for students who are identified as needing additional English-language skills.

The Base Aid Ratio is the variable in the ECS formula that determines each community's ability to financially support its public schools. The Base Aid Ratio acts as an equity metric to distribute state education funding through the ECS formula, with the towns with the least ability to fund their public schools receiving the most state aid. The Base Aid Ratio uses two elements to calculate a town's ability to fund its public schools: a property wealth factor and an income wealth factor. The property wealth factor counts for 70% in determining a town's Base Aid Ratio and is determined using a town's Equalized Net Grand List per Capita (ENGLPC), compared to the state median town ENGLPC. The income wealth factor counts for 30% and is determined using a town's Median Household Income (MHI), compared to the state median MHI.[40] The ECS formula also adds additional funding for communities that have one of the highest Public Investment

Communities (PIC) index scores. Under the formula, if a town has one of the 19 highest PIC index scores, the town receives a bonus of three to six percentage points to its Base Aid Ratio — resulting in increased state education aid to the town.[41]

Finally, the ECS formula contains a Regional District Bonus, which provides additional funding to towns that send students to a regional school district or one of Connecticut's three endowed academies. The Regional District Bonus is scaled based on the number of student grades educated by the regional school district or endowed academy. Towns receive $100 for each student and each grade sent to a regional school district or endowed academy.[42]

The ECS formula is currently being phased in over time with the phase-in schedule differing between towns receiving — according to the formula — an increase in ECS funding over their fiscal year 2017 grants and those receiving a decrease. The phase-in began in FY 2019 and, for towns receiving increases, will be complete in FY 2028.[43]

As part of the Connecticut state budget for FYs 2022 and 2023, towns that are overfunded according to the ECS formula and would normally experience decreases in their ECS funding are "held harmless" for two years. This means instead of having their funding reduced, these towns will receive the same funding for FYs 2022 and 2023 as they did in FY 2021. The formula's phase-out schedule will resume in FY 2024 and proceed until full funding is reached in FY 2030.[44]

There is also a hold harmless provision for Alliance Districts, the 33 lowest-performing school districts in Connecticut. Alliance Districts that would otherwise receive a decrease in state education aid, according to the ECS formula, are permanently held harmless at their fiscal year 2017 ECS grant amounts.[45]

School Choice Funding Formulas

While the ECS formula is used to fund local and regional public school districts, Connecticut uses 10 additional formulas to distribute state education funding to public schools of choice. Specifically, the State uses five different formulas for magnet schools, two different formulas for charter schools, and individual formulas for the Connecticut Technical Education and Career System, agriscience programs, and the Open Choice program.[46]

Special Education

Outside the approximately 22 percent of the ECS grant's foundation amount that is attributed to special education, state funding for special education is limited. In total, Connecticut's municipalities annually assume 65 percent, or $1.3 billion, of the state's total special education expenses.[47] However, the State does provide funding for special education through the Excess Cost grant, which is meant to assist districts in paying for special education expenses for students with extraordinary needs.

Local and regional school districts are eligible for partial reimbursement from the State for students who require services that cumulatively exceed the school district's "basic contribution," or the portion of a student's education that the school district is responsible for. The basic contribution is all costs up to 4.5 times the district's previous year's average expenditure per student. The Excess Cost grant also reimburses school districts for students placed through state agency placements.[48] In these cases, the basic contribution is 100 percent of the school district's previous year's net current expenditure per student.[49]

Students whose services qualify for Excess Cost grant reimbursement make up less than one percent of the total number of Connecticut public school students.[50] However, the State of Connecticut currently appropriates approximately $140 million dollars for the Excess Cost grant,[51] which is less than is necessary to fully fund all costs over the 4.5 times threshold. As a result, the CSDE divides the total Excess Cost appropriation by the total amount requested by districts to determine the amount by which grants will be prorated.

Transportation

Connecticut requires local boards of education to provide "reasonable and desirable" transportation to students between the ages of 5 and 21, who have not yet graduated high school.[52,53] However, Connecticut does not have any statutory definition of reasonable and desirable transportation. Local and regional school districts are also required to provide all resident students who attend private, nonprofit schools located in the district with the same transportation services afforded to students attending public schools. This only applies when the majority of students attending the private school are residents of the host district.[54]

Until 2016, the State reimbursed school districts on a sliding scale of 0 – 60 percent based on local wealth tied to legislative appropriations.[55] However, with the exception of funding for interdistrict magnet school transportation, no funds have been appropriated for school transportation in recent years.

CAPITAL OUTLAY AND DEBT SERVICE

School construction in Connecticut is primarily funded by the State through the sale of general obligation (GO) bonds. School construction projects paid for through bonding are approved by the General Assembly during the biennial budget process. Once authorized by the legislature, the State Bond Commission votes to allocate the funds. The State Bond Commission is chaired by the Governor, who sets the agenda for the Commission's meetings.[56] In FY 2019, the State allocated $259 million in bonding to education and libraries, which represented 8.6 percent of all bonds issued.[57]

In order to receive state assistance for school construction, towns must first vote to allow the local board of education to apply for school building project grants through the Department of Administrative Services (DAS). The legislature has the authority to determine which projects are ultimately approved.[58] If approved, the state reimburses construction costs for local and regional districts on a scale between 10 and 70 percent for new construction, and 20 and 80 percent for renovations.[59] How much a district is reimbursed is based on town wealth, measured by a town's Adjusted Equalized Net Grand List per Capita. Certain school types are eligible for more reimbursement, such as "diversity schools," which are intended to be a solution to racial segregation and are eligible for 80 percent reimbursement for new construction.[60]

Most of Connecticut's school districts are fiscally dependent on their local municipalities, which levy taxes to support the district's operations. Although they cannot levy taxes, Connecticut's 17 regional school districts are considered fiscally independent as they are authorized to issue bonds with voter approval and set their own budgets independently from municipal governments.[61]

Generally, charter schools are responsible for procuring and funding their own facilities, and many charter schools lease their facilities. Charter school construction funds are not granted specifically in Connecticut's statutes. Instead, funds are authorized by the legislature on an ad hoc basis. When funds are made available by the General Assembly, governing bodies of state charter schools can apply for grants from the CSDE for either new school buildings, general improvements to school buildings, or repayment of debt incurred for school building projects.[62] Funding for charter school construction projects comes from the State Bond Commission's authority to issue bonds.[63]

Interdistrict magnet school building projects, developed for the purpose of increasing student diversity, are eligible to have up to 80 percent of the costs of construction reimbursed by the State.[64] Prior to 2012, magnet schools built for the purpose of assisting the State in meeting its requirements under the *Sheff v. O'Neill* stipulated agreements were eligible to be reimbursed for up to 100 percent of the costs associated with the school's construction.[65] The rate for these programs was reduced from 100 percent to 80 percent by Conn. Acts 12-120.

EMPLOYEE BENEFITS

Connecticut's Teachers' Retirement System (TRS) is a defined benefit plan that disburses a fixed pension benefit to participating teachers upon retirement.[66] As of the end of FY 2020, TRS had 50,951 active members and 38,540 retirees and beneficiaries. The average age of an active member was 45 years with 14 years of service and an annual salary of $83,368. The average annual pension was $58,406 for normal retirement and $51,750 for early retirement.[67]

Connecticut's TRS has been in operation since 1939 and is currently funded by the State of Connecticut and contributions from teachers. Active teachers currently contribute seven percent of their salary to TRS,[68] with the State of Connecticut responsible for making the entire employer contribution in the form of its actuarially determined employer contribution (ADEC). The State's contribution comes in the form of an annual appropriation from Connecticut's General Fund.[69] If the calculated contribution is not high enough to prevent growth in TRS' unfunded actuarial liabilities, the State is also responsible for these additional liabilities.[70]

Connecticut does not require any local contributions to TRS although most TRS members are employees, or former employees, of local and regional boards of education. Although most TRS members are municipal employees, the pension system is managed at the state level and local contributions are not required. This means that although salaries are set through collective bargaining agreements at the local level, retirement benefit rates are negotiated at the state level.

TRS members, and their local district employers, also do not contribute to Social Security. In Connecticut, the decision to opt-out of Social Security for TRS members was made in the 1950s when the members of TRS voted against participating in the program.[71] In 1959, the Connecticut General Assembly passed a law prohibiting current and future TRS members from holding a referendum to reverse this decision, which still applies to current Connecticut teachers.[72] While TRS members do not contribute to Social Security, they do pay 1.45 percent of their earnings to support Medicare costs and contribute 1.25 percent of their salary to the TRS retiree health insurance fund.[73]

As of the end of FY 2020, the TRS had $18.1 billion in unfunded actuarial liabilities and a funded ratio of 51.3 percent,[74] making it the fifth lowest funded state teachers' pension system in the country.[75] The system's unfunded liabilities are primarily the result of mistakes of the past, including decades of no state contributions, the state not making its full ADEC when it did make contributions, and overly optimistic assumed rates of return.[76]

During its 2019 regular legislative session, the Connecticut General Assembly made a number of changes to the TRS to financially stabilize the system and address the large ADEC payments the State was expected to make in the coming years.[77] The changes made include:

- Re-amortizing the system's unfunded liabilities over a 30-year period;
- Creating a Teachers' Retirement Fund Bonds Special Capital Reserve Fund backed by a General Fund surplus and lottery receipts;
- Reducing the TRS assumed rate of return from eight percent to 6.9 percent;
- Limiting credited interest on mandatory contributions to four percent annually; and
- Altering the mechanism for re-amortizing the unfunded liability of potential benefit increases.

Assuming a 6.9 percent return, the changes are projected to reduce the State's aggregate ADEC from FY 2020 to FY 2032 by $6.6 billion, but will ultimately require a net increase of $15.6 billion in ADEC payments over the period of FY 2020 to FY 2049.[78]

CHARTER SCHOOL FUNDING

There are two types of charter schools in Connecticut: local charter schools and state charter schools. A local charter school is a public school, or part of a public school, that has been converted into a charter school, and is approved by the local and state boards of education.[79] State charter schools are established as charter schools, approved by the State Board of Education, and operated independently of the local or regional school district.[80] During the 2020-21 school year, there was only one local charter school in Connecticut and 21 state charter schools, serving approximately 11,000 students, or roughly two percent of total public school enrollment.[81]

Connecticut funds state charter schools through a per-student grant paid directly to the school. In FYs 2017 and 2018, state charter schools received $11,000 per student.[82] In FY 2019, those grants were increased to $11,250 per student, and in FYs 2022-23 state charter schools will receive $11,525 per student, which is equivalent to the ECS formula's foundation amount for local and regional public schools. Additionally, for the 2022-23 biennium, state charter schools will receive weighted funding consistent with the student-need weights that are part of the ECS formula. This weighted funding will be phased-in, which will result in state charter school students receiving 14.76 percent of their full weighted funding amount at the end of the biennium.[83] Additionally, newly approved state charter schools may receive a state grant of up to $75,000 if they help the State meet its obligations under the 1996 *Sheff v. O'Neill* ruling.[84]

State charter schools are responsible for providing special education services to enrolled students. A student's local school district must hold a planning and placement meeting with representatives from the charter school, and the student's resident town is required to pay the charter school the reasonable cost of educating the student.[85] However, the charter school is legally responsible for ensuring the student receives the special education services as mandated by the student's individualized education program, regardless of whether the services are provided by the charter school or local school district, and regardless of whether or not the charter school is actually being reimbursed by the municipality.

Local charter schools may receive state funding of up to $3,000 per student. However, this funding is paid to the host municipality rather than the school itself.[86] The school district where a student lives is responsible for annual payments to the charter school in the amount specified in its charter. This amount includes reasonable special education costs.[87] For students who live in the district where the local charter school is located, the school district where the local charter school is located is responsible for providing funding equal to the per-pupil expenditure from two fiscal years prior, multiplied by the number of resident students attending the charter school in the current fiscal year.[88] The State may award initial start-up grants of up to $500,000 to a town with a newly established local charter school.[89]

NONPUBLIC SCHOOL FUNDING

Connecticut does not generally provide funding to nonpublic schools. However, there are three endowed academies in the state that receive state funding. Endowed academies are privately governed and managed, but, in general, must follow the same laws and regulations as traditional public schools[90] and are subject to school accountability reporting from the CSDE.[91]

Endowed academies are eligible to receive state reimbursement for school construction projects if the school's host municipality qualifies under the standard school construction bonding process.[92] Endowed academies primarily receive their funding through tuition, which may either be paid privately on behalf of the students or paid for by the sending town.[93]

VIRTUAL EDUCATION

Prior to the COVID-19 pandemic and its impacts on public education, K-12 virtual education was used scarcely, if at all, by Connecticut school districts. Like districts across the country, Connecticut districts moved to fully remote learning during the spring semester of the 2019-20 school year to help prevent the spread of COVID-19, and many districts continued offering remote learning throughout the 2020-21 school year.

In response to the pandemic and the widespread use of remote learning, the Connecticut General Assembly passed several measures during its 2021 regular legislative session concerning remote learning and virtual education offerings for students. One of these new measures authorizes boards of education, beginning with the 2022-23 school year, to provide remote learning to students in grades 9-12 if the boards (1) comply with standards developed by the CSDE and (2) adopt a student attendance policy that meets certain requirements.[94]

By July 1, 2023, the CSDE is also required to develop a plan for a K-12 statewide remote learning school that, among other requirements, must take into account the recommendations of a new 17-member Remote Learning Commission, which was established to analyze and provide recommendations about remote learning, and produce a report about remote learning's impact on students' educational attainment, physical and emotional development, and access to special services.[95]

FEDERAL COVID-19 FUNDING

As part of the three stimulus and relief packages passed by Congress in response to the COVID-19 pandemic, the State of Connecticut has been awarded more than $1.7 billion in federal funds for K-12 education. The vast majority of these federal funds have come from the Elementary and Secondary School Emergency Relief (ESSER) Fund. Table 7.1 outlines the ESSER funding awarded to Connecticut under each stimulus and relief package, and how much has been allocated to the state's local educational agencies or set aside by the CSDE.

TABLE 7.1. Connecticut's ESSER Fund Allocations by Stimulus/Relief Package

Relief/Stimulus Package	Total CT ESSER Allocations	CT ESSER LEA Allocations	CT State Set Aside Allocations
CARES Act (ESSER I)	$111.1 million	$99.9 million	$11.1 million
CRRSA Act (ESSER II)	$494.4 million	$443.2 million	$49.2 million
ARP Act (ESSER III)	$1.1 billion	$995.3 million	$110.5 million
Total	$1.7 billion	$1.5 billion	$170.8 million

ESSER funding provided to Connecticut's districts under the CARES Act ranged from $10.3 million for Hartford Public Schools to $2,524 for Norfolk Public Schools.[96] In April 2020, the CSDE established statewide priority uses for ESSER funds in order to meet the critical needs of students brought on by the coronavirus pandemic. The statewide priority areas were:

- Equitable Access to Technology;
- Equitable Access to High Quality Online Curriculum Including Necessary Supports;
- Remediation/Compensatory Education; and
- Social/Emotional Well-Being.[97]

ESSER funding provided to Connecticut's districts under the CRRSA Act ranged from $45.7 million for Hartford Public Schools to $11,191 for Norfolk Public Schools. In January 2021, the CSDE established state-level priority areas for uses of ESSER II funds provided under the CRRSA Act. The priority areas are listed below, along with how much ESSER II funding Connecticut districts, in total, plan to spend on the priority area.

- Academic Supports, Learning Loss, Learning Acceleration and Recovery ($230 million;
- Family and Community Connections ($22.9 million);
- School Safety and Social-Emotional Well-Being of the "Whole Student" and of School Staff ($74 million); and
- Remote Learning, Staff Development, and the Digital Divide ($54.5 million).[98]

ENDNOTES

[1] We would like to acknowledge the work of Dr. Leslie DeNardis in crafting the chapter for the first edition of this work.

[2] Conn. Const. art. Eighth, § 4.

[3] Conn. Const. art. Eighth, § 1.

[4] DeNardis, L. (2020). Connecticut. Journal of Education Finance, 45(3), 273.

[5] Horton v. Meskill, 172 Conn. 615 (1977).

[6] Ibid.

7   Conn. Acts 79-128

8   Horton v. Meskill, 195 Conn. 24 (1985).

9   Conn. Acts 88-358

10 School and State Finance Project. (2021). History of School Finance in Connecticut. New Haven, CT: Author. Retrieved from https://ctschoolfinance.org/resource-assets/History-of-School-Finance-in-Connecticut.pdf.

11 Memorandum of Decision, Connecticut Coalition for Justice in Education Funding, Inc. v. Rell, Superior Court, judicial district of Hartford, Docket No. XO7 HHD-CV-14-5037565-S (September 7, 2016). Retrieved from http://civilinquiry.jud.ct.gov/DocumentInquiry/DocumentInquiry.aspx?DocumentNo=11026151.

12 Connecticut Coalition for Justice in Education Funding, Inc. v. Rell, 327 Conn. 650 (2018).

13 Ibid.

14 Conn. Acts 17-2 (June Special Session)

15 Complaint, Sheff v. O'Neill, Superior Court, judicial district of Hartford/New Britain at Hartford (April 26, 1989).

16 Sheff v. O'Neill, 238 Conn. 1, 678 A.2d 1267 (1996).

17 Conn. Acts 97-290.

18 Please note that while Connecticut's public school enrollment has consistently declined in recent years, enrollment numbers for the 2020-21 school year may be impacted by the COVID-19 pandemic and the effects it had on classroom learning and public education.

19 EdSight. (n.d.). Public School Enrollment. Available from https://edsight.ct.gov/.

20 School and State Finance Project. (2021). Mismatch Between Funding & Student Needs in Connecticut. Hamden, CT: Author. Retrieved from https://ctschoolfinance.org/resource-assets/Mismatch-Between-Funding-and-Student-Needs.pdf.

21 BIPOC is an acronym that stands for "Black, Indigenous, People of Color." It is used to refer to individuals who self-identify as American Indian or Alaska Native; Asian; Black or African American; Hispanic/Latino of any race; Native Hawaiian or other Pacific Islander; or two or more races.

22 EdSight. (n.d.). Public School Enrollment. Available from https://edsight.ct.gov/.

23 EdSight. (n.d.). Educator Race/Ethnicity. Available from https://edsight.ct.gov/.

24 U.S. Census Bureau. (2021). Table 1: Summary of Public Elementary-Secondary School System Finances by State: Fiscal Year 2019. 2019 Annual Survey of School System Finances. Washington, DC: Author. Available from https://www2.census.gov/programs-surveys/school-finances/tables/2019/secondary-education-finance/ elsec19_sumtables.xls.

25 Connecticut State Department of Education. (n.d.). Per Pupil Expenditures by Function (District), 2019-2020. Available from https://edsight.ct.gov/.

26 Connecticut State Department of Education. (n.d.). Educational Organizations in CT. Retrieved from https://portal.ct.gov/SDE/Educational-Organizations-in-CT.

27 Sheff v. O'Neill, 238 Conn. 1, 678 A.2d 1267 (1996).

28 Conn. Acts 97-290

29 State of Connecticut, Office of the Governor. (2020, January 10). Attorney General Tong, Governor Lamont Announce Breakthrough Sheff v. O'Neill Settlement [Press release]. Retrieved from https://portal.ct.gov/Office-of-the-Governor/ News/Press-Releases/2020/01-2020/Attorney-General-Tong-Governor-Lamont-Announce-Breakthrough-Sheff-v-ONeillSettlement.

30 U.S. Census Bureau. (2021). Table 1: Summary of Public Elementary-Secondary School System Finances by State: Fiscal Year 2019. 2019 Annual Survey of School System Finances. Washington, DC: Author. Available from https://www2.census.gov/programs-surveys/school-finances/tables/2019/secondary-education-finance/ elsec19_sumtables.xls.

31 Connecticut School Finance Project. (2019). FAQs: Fiscally Independent School Districts. New Haven, CT: Author. Retrieved from http://ctschoolfinance.org/resource-assets/Fiscally-Independent-School-Districts-FAQ.pdf.

32 U.S. Census Bureau. (2021). Table 1: Summary of Public Elementary-Secondary School System Finances by State: Fiscal Year 2019. 2019 Annual Survey of School System Finances. Wash-

ington, DC: Author. Available from https://www2.census.gov/programs-surveys/school-finances/tables/2019/secondary-education-finance/ elsec19_sumtables.xls.

[33] School and State Finance Project. (2021). Mismatch Between Funding & Student Needs in Connecticut. Hamden, CT: Author. Retrieved from https://ctschoolfinance.org/resource-assets/Mismatch-Between-Funding-and-Student-Needs.pdf.

[34] Jackson Smith, S. (2021). Connecticut. Journal of Education Finance, 46(3), 257-259.

[35] Conn. Acts 21-2 (June Special Session)

[36] Conn. Gen. Statutes ch. 172, § 10-262f(2).

[37] Conn. Gen. Statutes ch. 172, § 10-262f(9).

[38] Connecticut General Assembly, Office of Fiscal Analysis and the Office of Legislative Research. (2014). CT Special Education Funding [PowerPoint slides]. Hartford, CT: Author. Retrieved from http://www2.housedems.ct.gov/MORE/SPED/pubs/OFA-OLR_Presentation_2013-01-23.pdf.

[39] Conn. Gen. Statutes ch. 172, § 10-262f(25).

[40] Conn. Gen. Statutes ch. 172, § 10-262f(44).

[41] Conn. Gen. Statutes ch. 172, § 10-262f(46).

[42] Conn. Gen. Statutes ch. 172, § 10-262f(19).

[43] Conn. Gen. Statutes ch. 172, § 10-262h.

[44] Conn. Acts 21-2 (June Special Session)

[45] Conn. Gen. Statutes ch. 172, § 10-262h.

[46] School and State Finance Project. (n.d.). How Connecticut Funds Education. Retrieved from https://ctschoolfinance.org/issues/how-ct-funds-education.

[47] Connecticut State Department of Education. (2018). LEA Special Education Expenditures. Hartford, CT: Author. Available from https://ctschoolfinance.org/resources/lea-special-education-expenditures-2003-17-ct-state-department-of-education.

[48] Conn. Gen. Statutes ch. 165, §§ 10-76g(a)-76g(b).

[49] Conn. Gen. Statutes ch. 165, § 10-76d(e).

[50] EdSight. (n.d.). Public School Enrollment. Available from https://edsight.ct.gov/.

[51] Conn. Acts 21-2 (June Special Session)

[52] Conn. Gen. Statutes ch. 168, § 10-186.

[53] Conn. Gen. Statutes ch. 170, § 10-220.

[54] Conn. Gen. Statutes ch. 172, § 10-281.

[55] Conn. Gen. Statutes ch. 172, § 10-266m.

[56] Pinho, R. (2015). Connecticut's Bonding Process (2015-R-0058). Hartford, CT: Connecticut General Assembly, Office of Legislative Research. Retrieved from https://www.cga.ct.gov/2015/rpt/pdf/2015-R-0068.pdf.

[57] Lembo, K. (2019). Budgetary/Statutory Basis (GAAP Based Budgeting) Annual Report, For the Fiscal Year Ended June 30, 2019. Hartford, CT: State of Connecticut, Office of the State Comptroller. Retrieved from https://www.osc.ct.gov/reports/annual/2019/Annual2019.pdf.

[58] Conn. Gen. Statutes ch. 173, § 10-283.

[59] Conn. Gen. Statutes ch. 173, § 10-285a(a).

[60] Conn. Gen. Statutes ch. 173, § 10-286h.

[61] Connecticut School Finance Project. (2019). FAQs: Fiscally Independent School Districts. New Haven, CT: Author. Retrieved from http://ctschoolfinance.org/resource-assets/Fiscally-Independent-School-Districts-FAQ.pdf.

[62] Conn. Gen. Statutes ch. 164, § 10-66hh(a).

[63] Conn. Gen. Statutes ch. 164, § 10-66jj.

[64] Conn. Gen. Statutes ch. 172, §10-286h.

[65] Conn. Gen. Statutes ch. 172, §10-264h.

[66] Campbell, J., Gellman, C., & Moran, J. (2010). State Employees and Teachers' Retirement Systems (2010-R-0268). Hartford, CT: Connecticut General Assembly, Office of Legislative Research. Retrieved from https://www.cga.ct.gov/2010/rpt/2010-R-0268.htm.

67 Connecticut General Assembly, Office of Fiscal Analysis. (2020). OFA Fact Sheet: Teachers' Retirement System (TRS). Hartford, CT: Author. Retrieved from http://ctstatefinance.org/assets/uploads/files/OFA-Fact-Sheet-TRS-November-2020.pdf.

68 Ibid.

69 Lembo, K. (2017). Annual Report of the State Comptroller, FY 2017. Hartford, CT: State of Connecticut, Office of the State Comptroller. Retrieved from http://www.osc.ct.gov/reports/annual/2017/Budgetary2017.pdf.

70 State of Connecticut Teachers' Retirement System Viability Commission. (2018). Report of the Commission. Hartford, CT: Author. Retrieved from http://www.ct.gov/trb/lib/trb/formsandpubs/CT_TRS_Viability_Commission_Report_03192019.pdf.

71 Moran, J.D. (2017). Teachers and Social Security (2017-R-0212). Hartford, CT: Connecticut General Assembly, Office of Legislative Research. Retrieved from https://www.cga.ct.gov/2017/rpt/pdf/2017-R0212.pdf.

72 Ibid.

73 Connecticut General Assembly, Office of Fiscal Analysis. (2020). OFA Fact Sheet: Teachers' Retirement System (TRS). Hartford, CT: Author. Retrieved from http://ctstatefinance.org/assets/uploads/files/OFA-Fact-Sheet-TRS-November-2020.pdf.

74 Ibid.

75 Public Plans Data. (n.d.). Plan Data: Connecticut Teachers. Retrieved from https://publicplansdata.org/quick-facts/by-pension-plan/plan/?ppd_id=17.

76 Aubry, J., & Munnell, A.H. (2015). *Final Report on Connecticut's State Employees Retirement System and Teachers' Retirement System.* Chestnut Hill, MA: Center for Retirement Research at Boston College. Retrieved from http://crr.bc.edu/wp-content/uploads/2015/11/Final-Report-on-CT-SERS-and-TRS_November-2015.pdf.

77 Conn. Acts 19-117

78 State of Connecticut, Office of Policy and Management. (2019). Actuarial Projections for Governor Ned Lamont's Proposed Changes to Teachers' Retirement System. Hartford, CT: Author. Retrieved from http://ctstatefinance.org/assets/uploads/files/Actuarial-Projections-for-Governor-Lamont-Proposed-TRSChanges.xlsx.

79 Conn. Gen. Statutes ch. 164, § 10-66aa (2).

80 Conn. Gen. Statutes ch. 164, § 10-66aa (3).

81 EdSight. (n.d.). Public School Enrollment. Available from https://edsight.ct.gov/.

82 Connecticut State Department of Education. (2020). Biennial Report on the Operation of Charter Schools in Connecticut. Hartford, CT: Author. Retrieved from https://portal.ct.gov/-/media/SDE/CharterSchools/Biennial_Report_Operation_of_CharterSchools.pdf?la=en.

83 Conn. Acts 21-2 (June Special Session).

84 Conn. Gen. Statutes ch. 164, § 10-66ee(l).

85 Conn. Gen. Statutes ch. 164, § 10-66ee(d)(3).

86 Conn. Gen. Statutes ch. 164, § 10-66ee(c).

87 Conn. Gen. Statutes ch. 164, § 10-66ee(b)(1).

88 Conn. Gen. Statutes ch. 164, § 10-66ee(b)(2).

89 Conn. Gen. Statutes ch. 164, § 10-66nn(a).

90 Moran, J. (2016). Woodstock Academy and Other Private Academies that Serve as Public Schools (2016- R-0121). Hartford, CT: Connecticut General Assembly, Office of Legislative Research. Retrieved from https://www.cga.ct.gov/2016/rpt/pdf/2016-R-0121.pdf.

91 Connecticut State Department of Education. (2018). District Profile and Performance Report for School Year 2017-18: Norwich Free Academy District. Hartford, CT: Author. Retrieved from http://edsight.ct.gov/ Output/District/HighSchool/9010022_201718.pdf.

92 Moran, J. (2016). Woodstock Academy and Other Private Academies that Serve as Public Schools (2016- R-0121). Hartford, CT: Connecticut General Assembly, Office of Legislative Research. Retrieved from https://www.cga.ct.gov/2016/rpt/pdf/2016-R-0121.pdf.

93 Conn. Gen. Statutes ch. 164, § 10-34.

[94] Conn. Acts 21-46

[95] Conn. Acts 21-2 (June Special Session)

[96] School and State Finance Project. (2021). COVID-19 Relief Funding for Education. Retrieved from https://ctschoolfinance.org/issues/esser-funding.

[97] State of Connecticut, State Board of Education. (2020). State Level Priorities: Sustaining Local School District Capacity & Providing Equity and Access to a High Quality Education for All Children. Hartford, CT: Author. Retrieved from https://portal.ct.gov/-/media/SDE/Digest/2019-20/CSDE-K-12-Funding-Priorities.pdf.

[98] School and State Finance Project. (2021). COVID-19 Relief Funding for Education. Retrieved from https://ctschoolfinance.org/issues/esser-funding.

CHAPTER 8

DELAWARE

Christopher Brooks
University of North Carolina at Chapel Hill

GENERAL BACKGROUND AND DEMOGRAPHICS

Delaware is a small but wealthy state, and its state educational system generally reflects this fact.[1] Article X of the current state constitution, adopted in 1897, addresses the state's role in public education, requiring that "the General Assembly shall provide for the establishment and maintenance of a general and efficient system of free public schools" and that "the General Assembly shall make provision for the annual payment... equitably apportioned among the school districts of the State.[2]" This mandate is described as relatively lenient, establishing some basic standards that the educational system must meet while lacking specific language about what such a system is meant to achieve.[3]

Delaware has a total 215 public schools, approximately 10 percent of which are charter schools, organized into 19 school districts across its 3 counties. 16 of these districts are traditional K-12 districts and the other 3 are special county-wide districts that manage vocational-technical education. While there has been some interest in reducing the number of districts in the relatively small state,[4] a state commissioned task force concluded that a theoretical reduction to one traditional K-12 district per county offered little potential savings and was thus inadvisable.[5]

Funding Public Schools in the United States, Indian Country,
and US Territories (Second Edition), pages 125–140.
Copyright © 2023 by Information Age Publishing
www.infoagepub.com

There were approximately 138,000 students in the state of Delaware in the 2021-22 school year. Table 8.1 describes the demographics of these students. Delaware has experienced a steady increase in overall enrollment, from 130.6 thousand pupils in 2011 to 138.4 thousand in 2021.[6] This growth was driven by large increases in the number of Hispanic and multiracial students in the state, with other racial/ethnic groups being relatively stable or slightly declining over the past six years.[7]

Delaware has an overall graduation rate of 89 percent, slightly above the national average of 86 percent.[8] While Delaware does have meaningful gaps in graduation rates between White students and Black and Hispanic students, they are among the smallest in the U.S., at 5 and 3 percentage points respectively.[9]

Delaware uses the common-core-aligned Smarter Balanced testing standards that are also employed by 10 other states in grades 3-8,[10] and pre-COVID proficiency rates in math and English were 53 percent in English and 44 percent in math.[11] In 2021, proficiency was down to 41 percent in English and 26 percent in math, although these rates are likely resulting from low participation rates and the ongoing impacts of the COVID pandemic.[12] The state was roughly average in 4th and 8th grade math and reading scores in the 2019 administration of the National Assessment of Educational Progress.[13]

The state of Delaware employed nearly 10,000 teachers (full time equivalencies) in the 2021 school year. Delaware's teacher workforce, relative to the student population, is disproportionately White and female. Approximately 80 percent of teachers are White, 11 percent are Black, and only 4 percent are Hispanic, with all other racial/ethnic categories comprising the remaining 5 percent.[14] A 2017 report

TABLE 8.1.   Student Demographics in Delaware, 2021

Race/Ethnicity	
American Indian or Alaska Native	0.41%
Asian American	4.27%
Black or African American	30.05%
Hispanic or Latino	18.25%
Multi-Racial	4.62%
Native Hawaiian or Other Pacific Islander	0.14%
White or Caucasian	42.25%
Residence	
Foster Care	0.21%
Homeless	1.19%
Military Family	1.36%
Other Characteristics	
English Learners	9.58%
Low Income	26.73%
Students with Disabilities	16.76%

Source: Delaware DoE (2021b) https://reportcard.doe.k12.de.us/
detail.html#aboutpage?scope=state&district=0&school=0

by the state's Teacher and Leader Effectiveness Branch found that these representational gaps between teachers of color and students of color existed in every district in the state and that the racial/ethnic diversity of teachers was temporally stagnant, despite an increasingly diverse student body.[15] This may be partly attributable to disparities in retention rates, with Black and Hispanic early career teachers being retained at lower rates than their White peers.[16]

POLITICAL CLIMATE

The Delaware state government is comprised of an executive branch headed by the state governor, currently John Carney (D), a judiciary branch headed by the Delaware Supreme Court, and a bicameral legislative branch, comprised of a 41 member House of Representatives and a 21 seat Senate. Since 1993, both the governorship and state senate have been controlled by the Democratic Party, and since 2009 Democrats have also controlled the House of Representatives.

Delaware's fiscal year begins on the first of July and the annual budgeting timeline is prescribed by the Delaware State Code. The general operating budget process starts with state organizations submitting proposals to the state Office of Management and Budget (OMB) by November 15th. Then the OMB compiles and reviews these proposals and sends a proposed budget to the Governor by December 15th. The OMB and Governor then review, approve, and develop a budget proposal and budget appropriations which are then submitted to the General Assembly by February 1st.[17] The FY2022 operating budget was $4.7 billion, and approximate 5 percent increase over FY 2021.[18]

The state of Delaware has a separate capital expenditures budget, which includes school capital expenditures and improvements. This funding is formally titled the annual Bond and Capital Improvements Act but is colloquially referred to as the Bond Bill. The Bond Bill is by tradition passed in the same deadline sequence as the general budget, although there are no strict requirements for passage dates. For FY 2022, this bond amounted to $1.35 billion, an increase of over $400 million dollars over FY 2021, and included $181 million towards school construction and renovation.[19]

The final type of budget in Delaware is the Grant-in-Aid budget, which is used to appropriate supplemental funding for non-profit organizations that serve citizens of Delaware. The most recent Grant-in-Aid bill was $63.2 million, the largest in state history.[20] The funds appropriated generally do not concern education in a narrow sense, but do include monies for family and youth services, adult education, and various education advocacy groups.

These annual budgets are also supplemented by one-time spending, and due to recent budget surpluses, the FY 2022 supplemental bill was large, amounting to $221 million. These funds included one-time bonuses ($54.6 M) and pension ($15.3M) investments for state employees, funds for school-based health centers ($10k), and the development of Pre-K standards ($45k).[21]

As with any state, non-government actors play a prominent role in Delaware's education policy. Delaware is not a right-to-work state, and efforts by some counties and localities to institute such policies were quashed by the state legislature in 2018.[22] Staff and teachers are represented by the Delaware State Educators Association (DSEA). The organization is part of the National Educators Association and has local unions within each school district. State regulations regarding teacher unions are listed in Delaware Code Chapter 14 Section 40.[23] The state has mandatory bargaining between the Delaware State Educators Association. The state does however prohibit public school employees from striking. In a comparative report published by the Fordham Institute 2012, Delaware was categorized as having strong unions, ranking 19th overall.[24]

Many other organizations are also involved in the politics of education in Delaware. The Rodel Foundation of Delaware, itself an educational interest group, compiled a more exhaustive list of primary stakeholders than there is space in this chapter to discuss.[25] This resource offers a good starting point for further investigation into educational stakeholders in the state. Organizations include professional or sector organizations, like the Delaware Association of School Administrators, business organizations, like the Delaware Business Roundtable Education Committee, non-profit institutes and foundations, like The Caesar Rodney Institute or Longwood Foundation, and government commissions and boards, like the Delaware Professional Standards Board or the Delaware State Parent Advisory Council.

The Delaware Public Integrity Commission is a codified government organization which tracks lobbying of the state government that crosses minimum direct expenditure thresholds. While overall lobbying was down significantly in 2020 due to COVID-19 and totaled approximately $28k, 3 of the 6 most frequently disclosed lobbying employers were directly or adjacently associated with education (The Delaware Charter School Network, Delaware State Chamber of Commerce, Delaware Business Roundtable Education Committee), cumulatively representing 10 percent of all total disclosures.[26]

State Litigation

Until recently Delaware was among the few states that had never experienced school finance litigation. However, in 2018 the American Civil Liberties Union (ACLU) sued the state of Delaware on behalf of Delawareans for Educational Opportunity and the Delaware NAACP on grounds of educational inadequacy. In *Delawareans for Educational Opportunity v. Carney,*[27] the suit alleged failure by the legislature to fund education fairly and adequately across schools in the state, violating the state's constitutional guarantee that all children receive a general and efficient education (a less prominent portion of the suit pertained to the reassessment of property tax value, which is discussed later in the chapter.) More particularly, plaintiffs alleged that the state had failed to provide for students from low-income families, students with disabilities, and English language learners (EL) with the resources needed for an adequate education. Unlike most states,

Delaware provided no explicitly weighted funding in formula for schools that serve higher proportions of low-income students and English language learners.

In October 2018, a chancery court denied the state's motion to dismiss the suit. The court noted that Delaware schools enrolling the most disadvantaged students tend to have larger class sizes, fewer specialists and counselors, and insufficient dual language resources and that Delaware's schools might be perceived as segregated by race and class.[28] The court concluded that the constitutional requirement for a "general and efficient system of free public schools" required that the system "educate students and produces educated citizens," something that would need to be demonstrated as occurring by the state in trial.[29]

The court also went to the issue of equity, remarking that decisions in 31 other states' courts had taken interest in qualitative dimensions of equity and adequacy and that 13 other states with similar constitutional provisions had considered equity and adequacy suits. The Delaware court related the case to *Brown v. Board of Education*,[30] drawing parallels between segregation and inadequate and ineffective schooling.[31]

After the initial filing, Delaware implemented two new funding mechanisms. The first is the Student Success Block, which began in 2018-19 and totaled approximately $5 million in annual funding. The Student Success Block provides additional funding to schools based on the number of students with disabilities in grades K-3 and additionally funds one reading specialist in each high-need elementary school.[32] The larger and newer initiative is "Opportunity Funding," a program that was allocated $25 million in the 2019-20 school year for sending supplemental discretionary funding to districts based on the number of English Learner students ($500 per pupil) and low-income students ($300 per student) in a district, with additional funding earmarked specifically for mental health services in schools.[33] These funds occurred outside of the normal funding system through special legislation and represented the first attempts by the state to offer explicitly weighted funding to low-income and English Learning Students.

These new avenues of distributing funds directly addressed the specific funding issues cited by the plaintiffs in their original complaint, and the litigation was settled prior to final ruling.[34] The binding settlement included specific agreements for the continuation and expansion of Opportunity Funding until it more than doubles, reaching $60 million by School year 2024-25.[35] At this point, total Opportunity Funding becomes attached to pupil counts, with the required total funding amount being calculated in fiscal year x by the following:

$$Opp.\,Funding = \left(\frac{\$55\ million}{\#\ low\ inc.\ pupils + \#\ EL\ pupils\ in\ FY\ 2025}\right) * \#\ low\ inc.\ pupils + \#\ EL\ pupils\ in\ FYx$$

Other requirements of the settlement include that Opportunity Funds not supplant existing funding programs, that at least $5 million go to schools with 60% Low Income students and/or 20% English Learner students for mental health or reading supports, and that each district must report on how Opportunity Funds are used at the school level. Legislation to implement these Opportunity Funding levels were passed in June 2021.[36]

There were six other large matters addressed in the settlement. (1) K-3 special education students must receive differentiated resource allocation rates like those provided for special education students in grades 4-12. (2) the establishment of an Ombudspersons program for each county to investigate and resolve parental or student complaints regarding discipline, access to school programs, and other forms of different or unfair treatment. (3) increased funding for the state pre-k Early Childhood Assistance Program in FY 2024 and 2025. (4) $4 million in FY 2023, 2024 and 2025 for the recruitment and retention of teachers in high-needs schools. (5) an independent and non-obligating assessment of the Delaware public school finance system to be completed by 2024. And (6) a new equity statement attached to request of Issuance of a Certificate of Necessity for capital construction and renovation that records the demographic information of students who will attend or benefit from proposed capital expenditures. The required funding for FY 2022 was implemented in the subsequent budget bill in compliance with the settlement.[37]

SOURCES OF REVENUE

Like most states, Delaware utilizes federal, state, and local monies for public schools. The most recent annual financial report comes from the 2018-19 school year, in which local funds comprised 59.5 percent of educational revenue, with 32.7 percent generated locally and 7.9 percent coming from the federal government.[38] This share has been relatively unchanged over the past decade,[39] although overall educational spending has increased substantially.[40] In the 2022 budget, the state Department of Education received $1.71 billion of the total $4.7 billion state budget.[41]

Local funds come from property taxes, whose rates are determined by local school districts according to Delaware code.[42] The amount of local tax depends on both tax rates and the assessed value of the property within the school district, which is determined by the county.

The state incentivizes certain local property tax rates through a component of the state funding formula known as Division III. Districts receive money based on their local tax revenue contributions towards education, relative to the revenues across the state. The baseline expected contribution is known as the 'authorized amount', but this value is adjusted depending on local factors like poverty rates and wealth, to ensure districts with less assessed value still receive funds in recognition of tax effort. If a district meets its expected contribution, it receives a full portion of the Division III funds allocated for it. This effort-based incentive helps maintain the 70-30 state-local ratio for school funding.

Local property value assessment was the subject of the less prominent 'county track' of *Delawareans for Educational Opportunity v Carney*. Property values had not been reassessed in decades and failed to account for the economic growth and change of the state.[43] In this portion of the suit, the court found that Delaware's reliance on decades old property tax valuations were unconstitutional and as of April 2021, all three counties have agreed to begin the process of reassessing property value for the tax levying process. [44] Plaintiffs argued that the outdated property value assessment meant those living in what are presently lower value properties were expected to pay excess taxes due to valuations that occurred as far back as the 1970s. As the opinion noted:

> One third of the funding for Delaware's public schools comes from local taxes. When school districts levy local taxes, they are required to use the assessment rolls prepared by Delaware's three counties. If there are problems with the counties' assessment rolls, then those problems affect the school districts' ability to levy local taxes.[45]

In updating the property assessment, the tax burden of local revenue generation is expected to better reflect the present property value and thus more equitable distribute the local cost of education.

DISTRIBUTION FORMULAS

Delaware designates funds through a three-part Division system.[46] This Division system is a resource-allocation model in which funding for specific positions, like teachers, nurses, or principals, are prescriptively allocated based on the number of students in the district, with some weight given to those students with special education needs. Therefore, state money is generally directed for specific purposes, with local jurisdictions only have significant spending autonomy on Division III funding, locally raised money, and some outside of the formula programs.

Division I funds are designated for employees of school districts according to the state salary schedule.[47] Funding units for a teacher are assigned based on the number of students in specific grades and who have specific needs as displayed in Table 8.2. Because fewer students in special education are needed to qualify for a unit of funding, this effectively represents a weighted funding formula that provides greater resources to districts that serve greater numbers of students in special education. In accordance with the *Delawareans v. Carney* settlement, special education students in grades K-3 will receive equal weighting as special education students in grades 4-12 by the 2023-24 school year.

TABLE 8.2. Number of Pupils Needed for a District to Qualify for a Teacher Funding 'Unit'

Preschool	12.8
K-3	16.2
K-3 Special Education	12.2
4-12 Regular Education	20
4-12 Basic Special Education (Basic)	8.4
Pre-K-12 Intensive Special Education (Intensive)	6
Pre-K-12 Complex Special Education (Complex)	2.6

Source: Delaware Title 14 Chapter 17 2021

The state's allocation is typically designed to provide approximately 70 percent of all teacher salaries.[48] Other positions (principals, nurses, and driver education specialists) are also determined by the number of pupils or units, with requirements varying by position (see Table 8.3). Ninety-eight percent of Division I funding for staff must be used in the school that 'earned' it, although this requirement can be waived through the local school board. Division I funding was $1.134 billion in FY 2022, approximately 89.3 percent of the money spent on the three divisions.[49]

Division II funds are designated for school and energy costs excluding student transportation and debt service.[50] This includes purchasing textbooks, furniture, and classroom equipment. Districts receive one unit of Division II funding for

TABLE 8.3. Number of Pupils Needed for a District to Qualify for a Funding 'Unit'

Superintendent	1 per district, with salary calculated by number of Div. 1 units in district
Assistant Superintendent	1 for each 300 Div. 1 units; maximum of 2
Directors	1 for the first 200 Div. 1 units; 1 for each 100 Div. 1 Units beyond the first 200; maximum of 6
Supervisors	1 for each 150 Div. 1 units.
Supervisors of transportation	1 for districts with more than 7,000 transported pupils
Supervisors of school lunch	1 for every district with less than 500 Div. 1 units; 1 for every 500 Div. 1 units beyond 500 Div. 1 units
Principal	1 for first 15 or more Div. 1 units in a building
Assistant Principal 1	1 for first 30 or more Div. 1 units; 0.65 for 25 to less than 30 Div. 1 units
Assistant Principal 2	1 for first 55 or more Div. 1 units; 0.65 for 50 to less than 55 Div. 1 units
Assistant Principal 3	1 for first each 20 Div. 1 units beyond the first 55 Div. 1 units
Administrative, Financial, or Other Secretaries	1 for 10 Div. 1 units for first 100 Units; 1 for 12 Div. 1 units beyond 100 units
Nurses	1 for each 40 Div. 1 units in district; at least 1 per building
Specialist—Visiting Teacher*	1 for each 250 Div. 1 units
Specialist—Driver Education Teacher*	1 for every 125 10th grade pupils in district
Physical Therapists, Occupational Therapists, Speech Language Pathologists, School Psychologists or Other Related Services Specialists	1 12-month for every 3 Complex Special Education; 1 11-month for every group of 5.5 children counted as intensive; 1 10-month at a rate of 1 for every group of 57 children counted in the K-3, grades 4-12 (regular education) and the basic units*

* Specialists are earned at the school level and are to be used to hire specialists relative to the needs of the student populations in said school.
Source: Delaware Title 14 Chapter 13 2021

TABLE 8.4. Non-Division/Outside-the-Formula School Funding in Fiscal Year 2022

Fund	FY22 $ Amount	Description
Selected Other Items		
General Contingency	$17.53M	Money held for unforeseen expenses or emergencies
Opportunity Fund	$33.5M	Provides additional funding for English learner and low-income students on a per-pupil basis
Related Services s for Students with Disabilities	$4.17M	1 unit for every 57 Division 1 units of regular education students; 1 unit for every 5.5 pre-K-12 intensive special education; 1 unit for each 3 units of pre-K-12 complex special education. Used to support statewide deaf-blind programs and can be flexibly used to support services or materials for students with disabilities.
Mental Health Services	$4M	1 unit for every 700 students in grades K-5. Can be used for mental health therapists, counselors, social workers, and psychologist. Funding ratio reduces annually until FY 2024 wherein districts receive 1 unit for every 250 students in grades K-5
Educational Sustainment Fund	$28.15M	Allocated based on enrollment and can be used for any local purpose
Skills, Knowledge and Responsibility Pay Supplement	$6.74M	Funding for the supplements associated with mentor stipends and National Board Certifications.
Student Discipline Program	$5.34M	Statewide for severe discipline.
World Language Expansion	$1.65M	For districts implementing world language expansion in elementary schools
School/County Ombudsman	$1M	Provides three Ombudspersons, one to serve in each county, per the finance case settlement.
Block Grants		
Student Success Block Grant	$3.97M	Provides additional funding to schools based on the number of students with disabilities in grades K-3 and additionally funds one reading specialist in each high-need elementary school
Academic Excellence Block Grant	$48.54M	1 unit for every 250 students. Can be used for a broad range of educational services
Technology Block Grant	$3.77M	Allocated based on Division I units. Used for technology maintenance and support
Transportation	$131.84M	Formula distributes money to go towards the transportation of students

Information adapted from the Delaware Fiscal Year 2022 Appropriations Act (HB 250) and Delaware Title 14

every one unit of Division I funding. Each Division II unit was worth $611.77 for All Other Costs and $2,299.64 for Energy in fiscal year 2022.[51] In fiscal year 2022, Division II funding was $34.26 million, approximately 2.7 percent of total division funding.[52] 90 percent of non-energy funding must be distributed to the school that 'earns' those units, although this requirement can be waived by local districts with permission by the state. Vocational programs which require a lot of energy can receive additional Division II funding.

Division III, known as educational advancement funding, can be used at the district's discretion for education purposes. In fiscal year 2020, Division III funding was $101.632 million, or approximately 8.0 percent of total division funding.[53] As described previously, districts receive money based on the 'effort' of local tax revenue contributions towards education, adjusted for a districts 'ability' to raise the expected local contribution to education. If a district meets its expected contribution, it receives a full portion of the Division III funds allocated for it. This has an equalizing effect on locally generated discretionary educational revenue, since low property value districts can set similar tax rates as their high value peers and still receive comparable funding that reduces the gap between high and low wealth districts. Without Division III funding, high property wealth districts would be able to raise significantly more money than low wealth districts at similar tax burden rates, creating inequality in funding due to the assessed value of the property within a district.

Delaware's annual budget also contains a number of significant non-division, or non-formula school funding mechanisms, like "Education Block Grants," "Public School Transportation" and an array of "Other Items" that cover a breadth of purposes. "Other Items" can vary by year, but typically include efforts to support disadvantaged students and fund student and instructional resources. It also now includes the Opportunity Fund for low income and EL students that is the centerpiece of the *Delawareans v. Carney* settlement. Education Block Grants similarly cover a breadth of funding interests, including educational technology, teacher professional development, and flexible funds to meet local school needs. A selection of non-Division funding items, including funding amounts and descriptions of purpose can be seen in Table 8.4. The over $320 million allocated in these funds is a substantial addition to the $1.27 billion Divisions I-III spending.

OTHER EDUCATIONAL EXPENDITURES

Capital Outlay and Debt Services

The process of state spending on capital projects is covered above, but capital projects are not entirely funded by the state. Delaware funds at least 60, and up to 80, percent of major capital construction projects, depending on the local district's ability to pay.[54] Minor Capital improvements follow a similar pattern, but with a fixed 60-40 state-district split.[55] Capital projects require local referendum, and total outstanding bonds cannot exceed a certain threshold of the overall assessed property value of a district at a given time.[56] The state's debt service for local schools is included in Other Elective Spending in the annual budget and in FY2022 is $73.04M.[57] These monies are categorized as Appropriated Special Funds, rather than General Funds, because they are devoted to the specific restrictions of agreed upon capital financing with local school districts.[58]

Employee Benefits

Delaware school employees are entitled to 1 day of sick leave per month of employment annually (10-month employees get 10 days of sick leave, 11-month get 11, 12 get 12).[59] State employees also get 12 weeks of paid parental leave after 1 year of employment.[60] Employees are required to participate in the State Employee's Pension fund. Employees are eligible for full retirement with either (1) 5 years of service and attaining age 62, (2) fifteen years of service and attaining age 60, or (3) 30 years of service regardless of age.[61] Pension payouts are based on the years of service and the average of the three highest years of salary.[62] The FY 2022 budget saw an increase in pensions benefits of 1-3 percent and a one-time $500 bonus due to budget surpluses.[63] Health insurance is offered to school employees through the state and are grouped with Department of Education, Technical Community College, Delaware State University employees.[64] Other benefits, like, dental, vision, prescription, life, and long-term disability are offered either through an employee's school, the state, or both.[65]

Charter School Funding

Delaware passed legislation allowing for charter schools in 1995.[66] There are 23 charter schools in Delaware in the 2021-22 school year, a majority of which are primary K-5/6/7 schools.[67] Charter schools are funded similarly to traditional public schools, with a mix of state and local spending, and receive resources based on the same three Division system as traditional schools. However, the state does not provide money for charter school facilities.[68]

Nonpublic School Funding

The state of Delaware does not provide any public funding, vouchers, or Education Savings accounts to private schools.[69] Private and homeschools mist register with the Delaware Department of Education, but the Department does not accredit or monitor the curriculum of these schools.[70]

Virtual Education

The state of Delaware has not enacted any legislation in recent years regarding Virtual Education as a long-term alternative to traditional in-person schooling,[71] and there is no statewide system or explicit support for such an alternative.[72] However, individual districts can offer such alternatives. For example, the Christina

School District offers the Christina School District Virtual Academy which is an entirely online alternative to traditional K-12 schooling.[73] The Virtual Academy is built on the distance learning model developed for the COVID pandemic, but the option remained open in the 2021-22 school year despite the state's general transition back to in-person learning, with some indication that it will be a permanent option going forward.[74]

Federal Covid Funding

Delaware received hundreds of millions of dollars in COVID relief from the federal government through the Elementary and Secondary School Emergency Relief (ESSER) Fund I ($43.49M), II ($182,89M), and III ($410.73M). ESSER I money must be used by the end of 2022, ESSER II by the end of 2023, and ESSER II by the end of 2024.

Ninety percent of ESSER funds must be distributed to local school districts, with the remaining 10 percent being used to address COVID at the state level. For ESSER I, the state used its $4.3M to invest in remote instruction technology and direct funds to low-income students for meals, technology, and summer learning materials.[75] For ESSER II, the state used its $18.3M for learning resources to address learning loss, including tutoring, online learning resources, programs for English language learning students, and socioemotional services.[76]

ESSER III was part of the Biden administrations American Rescue Plan, and funds were fully released after spending plans were approved by the federal Department of Education. Delaware's plan was accepted in 2021 and it outlined using the state's $41M funds to (1) reopen for in-person instruction in the 2021-22 school year following all CDC guidelines, (2) develop a voluntary vaccination program for all teachers and staff, (3) address learning loss through the implementation of evidence-based interventions, (4) invest in afterschool and summer learning programs, and (5) meet socioemotional health needs for students.[77] LEA's received guidance from the state to use the remaining money for similar purposes and are required to use at least 20 percent to address learning loss, but otherwise have significant discretion on how funds are used. District- and charter-level had to also be submitted and approved by the Delaware Department of Education and are available through the department's website.[78] As an example of the range of uses, Brandywine school district received $24 million in ESSER III funding and are implementing instructional technology and coaches, surveillance camera upgrades, resources like clothes, school supplies and food and housing assistance, tutoring support for English Learning students, contracts for mental health services, and in-person and remote summer programming, among many other things.[79]

ENDNOTES

1 I would like to thank David C. Thompson and R. Craig Wood for their work on the first edition of this chapter; the first edition's chapter: Staff Writer. "Delaware." In Funding Public Schools in the United States and Indian Country, edited by David C. Thompson, R. Craig Wood, S. Craig Neuenswander, and Randy D. Watson, 1st ed., 101–12. Charlotte, NC: Information Age Publishing, Inc, 2019.

2 "The Delaware Constitution," art. X § 1-2 (1897), https://delcode.delaware.gov/constitution/constitution-11.html#TopOfPage.

3 National Conference of State Legislatures, "The State Role in Education Finance" (Washington D.C., Referencing a system for evaluating and cataloguing of state education articles by William Thro), http://www.ncsl.org/research/education/state-role-in-education-finance.aspx.

4 Larry Nagengast, "Delaware's New Dept. of Education under Susan Bunting," Delaware First Media, March 10, 2017, https://www.delawarepublic.org/education/2017-03-10/delawares-new-dept-of-education-under-susan-bunting.

5 Jessica Bies, "Task Force: Consolidating Delaware School Districts Not Recommended, Will Not Save Money," The News Journal, accessed October 26, 2021, https://www.delawareonline.com/story/news/education/2018/05/15/task-force-consolidating-delawares-school-districts-doesnt-make-sense/612054002/.

6 Rodel Foundation, "Delaware Public School Students (2020-21)," Rodel, 2021, https://rodelde.org/ataglance/.

7 Delaware DoE, "Student Enrollment," Delaware Open Data Portal, 2021, https://data.delaware.gov/Education/Student-Enrollment/6i7v-xnmf.

8 NCES, "Public High School Graduation Rates," National Center for Education Statistics, 2021, https://nces.ed.gov/programs/coe/indicator/coi.

9 Ibid.

10 Catherine Gewertz, "Which States Are Using PARCC or Smarter Balanced?," Education Week, February 16, 2017, https://www.edweek.org/teaching-learning/which-states-are-using-parcc-or-smarter-balanced.

11 "2019 State Assessment Results Released," Delaware Department of Education, accessed November 18, 2021, https://www.doe.k12.de.us/site/http%3A%2F%2Fwww.doe.k12.de.us%2Fsite%2F-Default.aspx%3FPageType%3D3%26DomainID%3D4%26PageID%3D1%26ViewID%3D6446e e88-d30c-497e-9316-3f8874b3e108%26FlexDataID%3D23950.

12 "2021 State Assessment Results Released," State of Delaware News, August 10, 2021, https://news.delaware.gov/2021/08/10/2021-state-assessment-results-released/.

13 NAEP, "NAEP State Profiles," The Nation's Report Card, 2019, https://www.nationsreportcard.gov/profiles/stateprofile.

14 Delaware DoE, "Educator Characteristics," Delaware Open Data Portal, 2021, https://data.delaware.gov/Education/Educator-Characteristics/t9ya-d7ak.

15 Teacher and Leader Effectiveness Branch, "'The Set': Racial Diversity in DE's Teacher and School Leader Workforce" (Delaware Dept. of Education, 2017), https://www.doe.k12.de.us/cms/lib/DE01922744/Centricity/domain/37/the%20set%20monthly%20data%20briefs/The%20June%202017%20Set%20-%20Racial%20Diversity.pdf.

16 Ibid.

17 DE OMB, "Budget and Accounting Policy Chapter 1 - Introduction" (Wilmington, Delaware: State of Delaware Office of Management and Budget, October 2021), https://budget.delaware.gov/accounting-manual/documents/chapter01.pdf?ver=1029.

18 "Fiscal Year 2022 Appropriations Act," Pub. L. No. 250, § 54, 83 Laws of Delaware (2021), https://legis.delaware.gov/BillDetail?LegislationId=78941.

19 "Fiscal Year 2022 Bond and Capital Improvements Act," Pub. L. No. 200, § 56, 83 Laws of Delaware (2021), https://legis.delaware.gov/BillDetail?LegislationId=79011.

20 "An Act Making Appropriations for Certain Grants-in-Aid for the Fiscal Year Ending June 30, 2022," Pub. L. No. 265, § 57, 83 Laws of Delaware (2021), https://legis.delaware.gov/BillDetail?LegislationId=79013.

21 "An Act Making a One-Time Supplemental Appropriation for the Fiscal Year Ending June 30, 2022 to the Office of Budget and Management," Pub. L. No. 251, § 55, 83 Laws of Delaware (2021), https://legis.delaware.gov/BillDetail?LegislationId=78942.

22 Scott Goss, "Delaware Legislature Passes Bill to Kill Right-to-Work in Sussex County," The News Journal, June 2018, https://www.delawareonline.com/story/news/politics/2018/06/22/delaware-legislature-trumps-right-work-sussex-county/724727002/.

23 "Public School Employment Relations Act," 14, 40 Delaware Code § (2019), https://delcode.delaware.gov/title14/c040/index.html.

24 Amber Winkler, Janie Scull, and Dara Zeehandelaar, "How Strong Are U.S. Teacher Unions? A State by State Comparison" (Thomas B. Fordham Institute, 2012), https://files.eric.ed.gov/fulltext/ED537563.pdf.

25 "Key Stakeholders in Delaware Education Policy" (Wilmington, Delaware: Rodel Foundation of Delaware, 2016), http://www.rodelfoundationde.org/wp-content/uploads/2016/04/29.-Key-stakeholders-brief.pdf.

26 "Lobbying Activity GA Session 151," Delaware Public Integrity Reporting System, 2021, https://pirs.delaware.gov/#/lobbyingactivity/list.

27 Memorandum Opinion., 2018-0029–VCL Civil Action (Court of Chancery of the State of Delaware 2018).

28 DELAWAREANS FOR EDUCT'L OPP. v. Carney, 199 A. 3d 109 (Del: Court of Chancery 2018). p. 14-44.

29 ibid. p. 8-9

30 Brown v. Board of Education, 347 US 483 (Supreme Court 1954).

31 DELAWAREANS FOR EDUCT'L OPP. v. Carney, 199 A. 3d. p. 109.

32 Sy Doan et al., "Evaluation of Delaware's Opportunity Funding and Student Success Block Grant Programs: Early Implementation" (Santa Monica, CA: RAND Corporation, 2021), https://doi.org/10.7249/RRA230-1. p. ix.

33 "Opportunity Funding 101," Rodel (blog), October 28, 2019, 101, http://rodelde.org/opportunity-funding-101/.as national research shows us. But how money is spent matters just as how much—as long as the how is driven by local context and needs. Now that the school year is underway and next year's budget cycle is about to begin, let's check in on the status of the state's Opportunity Funding investment and put this progress into the broader context of school funding efforts to provide resources for low-income and English leaner students. What is Opportunity Funding? This year Governor John Carney proposed, and the legislature passed, a three-year, $60 million Opportunity Funding investment of targeted resources toward Delaware's most disadvantaged students. This funding is an evolution of the administration's previous Opportunity Grants initiative. It marked Delaware's first foray into some kind of per-pupil "weighted funding" mechanism to help schools better support students that data show need extra help, like low-income and English learner students. Through Opportunity Funding, every district will receive a per-pupil appropriation of $300 for every low-income student and $500 for every English learner student that they can spend as they choose (according to plans approved by the Department of Education

34 Settlement Stipulation and [Proposed] Order, C.A. No. 2018-0029-VCL State Track (2020).

35 ibid. p. 3-4.

36 "An Act to Amend the Delaware Code Relating to Educational Opportunity Funding," Pub. L. No. 56, § 53, 83 Laws of Delaware (2021), https://legis.delaware.gov/BillDetail?LegislationId=48348.

37 Fiscal Year 2022 Appropriations Act.

38 "Fiscal District Financial Report Regular School" (Wilmington, Delaware: Delaware Dept. of Education, 2020), https://www.doe.k12.de.us/site/handlers/filedownload.ashx?moduleinstanceid=11358&dataid=24493&FileName=Fiscal%20district%20financial%20report%20REGULAR%20SCHOOL_V3.pdf.

39 "Delaware School Finance 101" (Wilmington, Delaware: Delaware Dept. of Education, 2015).

40 "Current Expenditures for Public Elementary and Secondary Education, by State or Jurisdiction: Selected Years, 1969-70 through 2017-18," National Center for Education Statistics (National Center for Education Statistics, 2020), https://nces.ed.gov/programs/digest/d20/tables/dt20_236.25.asp.

41 Fiscal Year 2022 Appropriations Act.

42 "Local School Taxes," 14, 19 Delaware Code § 1902 (2019), https://delcode.delaware.gov/title14/c040/index.html.

43 Jackson, Tommy E. "Delaware." Journal of Education Finance 46, no. 3 (2021): 260–62.

44 In re Delaware Public Schools Litigation (County Track), 239 A. 3d 451 (Del: Court of Chancery 2020).

45 Ibid. p. 2

46 "State Appropriations," 14, 17 Delaware Code § 1702 (2019), https://delcode.delaware.gov/title14/c017/index.html.

47 Ibid.

48 "Delaware School Finance 101."

49 Fiscal Year 2022 Appropriations Act. p. 55

50 State Appropriations. § 1702.

51 Ibid.

52 Fiscal Year 2022 Appropriations Act. p. 55

53 State Appropriations. § 1702.

54 "Delaware School Finance 101." p. 11.

55 Ibid.

56 "Local School Bonds," 14, 21 Delaware Code § (2019), https://delcode.delaware.gov/title14/c021/index.html.

57 Fiscal Year 2022 Appropriations Act. p. 14.

58 "Budget and Accounting Policy Chapter 3 - Delaware's Accounting Framework" (Wilmington, Delaware: State of Delaware Office of Management and Budget, October 2021), https://budget.delaware.gov/accounting-manual/documents/chapter01.pdf?ver=1029.

59 "Salaries and Working Conditions of School Employees," 14, 13 Delaware Code § 1318 (2019), https://delcode.delaware.gov/title14/c013/index.html.

60 "Health and Wellbeing," Delaware Employment Link, accessed November 20, 2021, https://delawarestatejobs.com/benefits/health.shtml.

61 "State Employees' FAQ's," State of Delaware Office of Pensions, 2017, https://open.omb.delaware.gov/FAQs-SEPP.shtml.

62 "State Employee Pension Calculator," State of Delaware Office of Pensions, 2017, https://open.omb.delaware.gov/pensionPlans/StateEmp/Calculator/calculator_sep.shtml.

63 Mark Eichmann, "Delaware Operating Budget Approved, but Lots of Legislation Left for State Lawmakers," WHYY, 2021, https://whyy.org/articles/delaware-operating-budget-approved-but-lots-of-legislation-left-for-state-lawmakers/.

64 "DOE, K12, DTCC & DSU Employees," Delaware Department of Human Resources, 2019, 12, https://dhr.delaware.gov/benefits/education/index.shtml.

65 "Resource Document for Education Employees" (Wilmington, Delaware: Delaware Department of Human Resources, 2021), https://dhr.delaware.gov/benefits/education/documents/resource-document.pdf?ver=0615.

66 "The Delaware Charter Schools Network," Delaware Charter Schools Network, accessed November 20, 2021, http://www.decharternetwork.org/About-Us.

67 "List of Active Charter Schools," Delaware Department of Education, 2021, https://www.doe.k12.de.us/Page/http%3A%2F%2Fwww.doe.k12.de.us%2Fsite%2Fdefault.aspx%3FPageID%3D1910.

68 "What Is a Charter School?," Delaware Charter School Network, 2021, http://www.decharternetwork.org/About-Us/What-is-a-Charter-School.

[69] "50-State Comparison: Private School Choice," Education Commission of the States, March 24, 2021, https://www.ecs.org/50-state-comparison-private-school-choice/.

[70] "Homeschool and Private School Considerations," Delaware Department of Education, 2020, https://www.doe.k12.de.us/Page/http%3A%2F%2Fwww.doe.k12.de.us%2Fsite%2Fdefault.aspx-%3FPageID%3D4079.

[71] Ben Erwin, "Virtual School Policies," Policy Snapshot (Education Commission of the States, 2019), https://www.ecs.org/wp-content/uploads/Virtual-School-Policies.pdf.

[72] "Snapshot 2019: A Review of K-12 Online, Blended, and Digital Learning" (Durango, Colorado: Digital Learning Collaborative, 2019), https://static1.squarespace.com/static/59381b9a17bffc68b-f625df4/t/5df14d464ba53f72845791b2/1576095049441/DLC-KP-Snapshot2019.pdf.

[73] "Virtual Academy," Christina School District, 2021, https://www.christinak12.org/http%3A%2F%2Fwww.christinak12.org%2Fsite%2Fdefault.aspx%3FPageID%3D4836.

[74] Matt Hooke, "Christina Plans to Offer Virtual Option Even after the Pandemic," Newark Post, 2021, https://www.newarkpostonline.com/news/christina-plans-to-offer-virtual-option-even-after-the-pandemic/article_1b6ae3c7-904c-52d7-8451-43d6c370aa00.html.

[75] "Elementary and Secondary School Emergency Relief Fund Tracker," National Conference of State Legislatures, 2021, https://www.ncsl.org/ncsl-in-dc/standing-committees/education/cares-act-elementary-and-secondary-school-emergency-relief-fund-tracker.aspx.

[76] "GEER/ESSER II Plan Summary" (2021: Delaware Dept. of Education, 2021), https://www.doe.k12.de.us/cms/lib/DE01922744/Centricity/Domain/511/ESSER-GEER%20II%20FINAL%20Spending%20Plan%20Summary%20031521.pdf.

[77] "Delaware ARP ESSER State Plan Highlights" (Office of Elementary and Secondary Education, 2021), https://oese.ed.gov/files/2021/07/Delaware-ARP-ESSER-State-Plan-Highlights-v2-072121.pdf.

[78] "ESSER Funding / Emergency ESSER Funding," Delaware Department of Education, 2021, https://www.doe.k12.de.us/Page/http%3A%2F%2Fwww.doe.k12.de.us%2Fsite%2Fdefault.aspx-%3FPageID%3D4458.

[79] "Brandywine School District Initial ESSER II & ESSER III Plan" (New Castle County, Delaware: Brandywine School District, June 2021), https://www.brandywineschools.org/cms/lib/DE50000195/Centricity/Domain/4/BSD%20Initial%20ESSER%20II%20and%20III%20Plan%20Overview_6.21.21.pdf.

CHAPTER 9

FLORIDA

R. Craig Wood
University of Florida

GENERAL BACKGROUND

The Florida constitution states, "The education of children is a fundamental value of the people of the State of Florida. It is, therefore, a paramount duty of the state to make adequate provision for the education of all children residing within its borders. Adequate provision shall be made by law for a uniform, efficient, safe, secure and high quality system of free public schools that allows students to obtain a high quality education."[1]

In 1973, the Florida legislature enacted the Florida Education Finance Program (FEFP) and established state policy regarding equalized funding to guarantee to each student in the public education system the availability of programs and services appropriate to his or her educational needs that are substantially equal to those available to any similar student, notwithstanding geographic difference and varying local economic factors.[2] To equalize educational opportunities, the FEFP formula recognized: (1) varying local property tax bases; (2) varying education program costs; (3) varying costs of living; and (4) varying costs of equivalent educational programs due to sparsity and dispersion of student populations.

Funding Public Schools in the United States, Indian Country,
and US Territories (Second Edition), pages 141–168.
Copyright © 2023 by Information Age Publishing
www.infoagepub.com

The current FEFP is the primary mechanism for funding the operating costs of Florida school districts. FEFP funds are primarily generated by multiplying the number of full-time equivalent (FTE) students in each of the funded education programs by cost factors to obtain a weighted FTE. Weighted FTE is then multiplied by a base student allocation and by a district cost differential to determine the base funding from state and local FEFP funds. Program cost factors represent relative cost differences among the FEFP programs.

BASIC SUPPORT PROGRAM

Source of Funds for School Districts

In 2018-19, school districts receive approximately 40% of financial support from state sources, 49% from local sources, and 11% from federal sources.

State Support

The major portion of state support is distributed through the FEFP. Taxes from multiple sources are deposited in the state's General Revenue Fund. The predominant tax source is the 6% sales tax on goods and services.

The Florida Legislature established the Education Enhancement Trust Fund (EETF), which includes the net proceeds of the Florida Lottery and the tax proceeds on slot machines in Broward and Miami-Dade counties. Lottery proceeds were used to fund the $40,616,014 appropriation that provides the cash and debt service requirements for the Classrooms First and 1997 School Capital Outlay Bond Program, $128,652,817 for debt service for the Class Size Reduction and Educational Facilities Lottery Revenue Bond Program and $91,116,464 for school district workforce education.[3]

The Florida Constitution establishes a limit of 18 students in prekindergarten through grade 3 classrooms, 22 students in grades 4-8 classrooms and 25 students in grades 9-12 classrooms. The Class Size Reduction categorical was established to fund this requirement exclusively from state funds.[4]

The Florida constitution authorizes certain revenues to be used by school districts for capital outlay purposes. The state constitution guarantees a stated annual amount for each district from proceeds of licensing motor vehicles, referred to as Capital Outlay and Debt Service (CO&DS) funds. The constitution provides that school districts may share in the proceeds from gross receipts taxes referred to as Public Education Capital Outlay (PECO) funds as provided by legislative appropriation.[5]

Local Support

Local revenue for school support is derived almost entirely from property taxes levied by Florida's 67 counties, each of which constitutes a school district. Each district must levy a required local effort millage against its assessed valuation. The state legislature sets the required local effort. Each district's share of the state-required local effort is determined by a statutory procedure that is initiated by certification of the property tax valuation of each district. Millage rates are also adjusted because required local effort may not exceed 90% of a district's total FEFP entitlement.

Based on the 2020 tax roll provided by the Florida Department of Revenue, the commissioner certified the required millage of each district on July 17, 2020. The state average millage was set at 3.720, and certifications for the 67 school districts varied from 3.846 (Jackson) to 1.555 mills (Monroe) due to the assessment ratio adjustment and the 90 percent limitation. The 90 percent limitation reduced the required local effort of six districts. The districts and the adjusted millage rates were Collier (2.768), Franklin (3.177), Monroe (1.555), Sarasota (3.711), Sumter (3.090) and Walton (2.434).

The department is required to calculate the Prior Period Funding Adjustment Millage (PPFAM), which is levied by a school district if, in a prior year, the full amount of required local effort funds were not collected due to changes in property values, or if a prior year's final taxable value has not been certified for the current year's tax levy. The commissioner calculates the amount of the unrealized required local effort funds from the prior period and the millage required to generate that amount. This levy is in addition to the required local effort millage certified by the commissioner but does not affect the calculation of the current year's required local effort. The funds generated by this levy are not included in the district's FEFP allocation.[6]

School boards may set discretionary tax levies of the following types:

1. Current operation—The Florida Legislature set the maximum discretionary current operating millage for 2020-21 at 0.748 mills.[7] If the revenue from 1.5 mills is insufficient to meet the payments due under a lease-purchase agreement entered into before June 30, 2009, by a district school board or to meet other critical district fixed capital outlay needs, the board may levy an additional 0.25 mills for fixed capital outlay in lieu of levying an equivalent amount of the discretionary mills for operations.[8]

2. Capital outlay and maintenance—School boards may levy up to 1.5 mills if the funds appropriated through the Charter School Capital Outlay Allocation were less than the average charter school capital outlay funds per unweighted FTE student for the 2018-19 fiscal year, multiplied by the estimated number of charter school students for the applicable fiscal year and adjusted by changes in the Consumer Price Index, charter schools will also receive a portion of the revenue from the 1.5 discretionary millage levied by the school district. In 2020-21, school districts are not required to share revenue from the 1.5 discretionary millage levy because the legislature appropriated $169,600,000 for the Charter School Capital Outlay Allocation, which meets the funding requirement

for charter schools does not prohibit a school district from sharing any 1.5 discretionary millage revenue with charter schools, the amount appropriated does not require a school district to do so.[9]

School boards may expend funds raised by the 1.5-mill capital outlay levy for the following:

- The educational plant—Costs of construction, renovation, remodeling, maintenance, and repair of the educational plant. This also includes the maintenance, renovation, and repair of leased facilities to correct deficiencies.
- Expenditures that are directly related to the delivery of student instruction—Purchase, lease or lease-purchase of equipment, educational plants and construction materials directly related to the delivery of student instruction.
- Conversion of space—Rental or lease of existing buildings or space within existing buildings, originally constructed or used for purposes other than education, for conversion to use as educational facilities.
- A new school's library media center collection—Opening day collection for the library media center of a new school.
- School buses—Purchase, lease-purchase or lease of school buses or the payment to a private entity to offset the cost of school buses.
- Servicing of payments related to lease-purchase agreements—Servicing of payments related to lease-purchase agreements issued for any purpose under authority of prior enactments of this law. Costs associated with the lease-purchase of equipment, educational plants and school buses may include the issuance of certificates of participation and the servicing of payments related to such certificates. Only three-fourths of the proceeds from this millage can be obligated to lease-purchase agreements unless the lease-purchase agreements were entered into before June 30, 2009.
- Equipment, computers, enterprise resource software—Purchase or lease of new and replacement equipment: enterprise resource software applications that are classified as capital assets in accordance with definitions of the Governmental Accounting Standards Board, have a useful life of at least five years and are used to support district-wide administration or state-mandated reporting requirements; computer hardware, including electronic hardware and other hardware devices necessary for gaining access to or enhancing the use of electronic content and resources.[10]

School boards are authorized to expend up to $150 per unweighted FTE student from revenue generated by the 1.5 mill capital outlay millage levy for:

1. The purchase, lease-purchase, or lease of driver's education vehicles; motor vehicles used for the maintenance or operation of plants and

equipment; security vehicles; or vehicles used in storing or distributing materials and equipment.[11]

2. Payment of the cost of premiums, as defined or property and casualty insurance necessary to insure school district educational and ancillary plants. As used in this paragraph, casualty insurance has the same meaning. This means that casualty insurance may only be for burglary and theft, glass, boiler and machinery, leakage and fire extinguishing equipment and elevators. Operating revenues that are made available through the payment of property and casualty insurance premiums from revenues generated under this subsection may be expended only for nonrecurring operational expenditures of the school district.[12]

Violation of these expenditure provisions will result in an equal dollar reduction of FEFP funds in the year following an audit citation.

If revenue from the 1.5 mill levy were insufficient to make payments due under a lease-purchase agreement entered prior to June 30, 2009, or to meet other critical district capital outlay needs, a district school board may levy up to 0.25 mills for fixed capital outlay in lieu of levying an equivalent amount of the 0.748 discretionary operating millage for operations.[13]

In addition to levies established by the school board, qualified electors may vote an additional millage levy for operations and/or capital outlay purposes for a period not to exceed two years.[14]

Statutes provide for an additional levy, not to exceed four years, for traditional and charter school operational purposes to be authorized by the electorate through a local referendum or in conjunction with a general election. This voted levy and the levies established by the school board must not exceed 10 mills in total. This levy is distinguished from the constitutional authority for voted millage noted in the previous paragraph because it is for operations only, may be approved for up to four years instead of two years, and is included in the 10-mill limit established by the state constitution. Funds generated by this levy must be shared with charter schools based on each charter school's proportionate share of a district's total unweighted FTE.[15]

School districts are authorized to sell bonds for capital outlay projects to be repaid from local property taxes.[16]

Budgeted revenues from local taxes are determined by applying millage levies to 96% of the school taxable value of property. School board adoption of millage levies is governed by the advertising and public meeting requirements.[17]

This surtax, obtained via referendum, may take effect on the first day of any month but may not take effect until at least 60 days after the date of approval by the electors. The resolution providing for imposition of the surtax shall set forth a plan for use of the proceeds for fixed capital expenditures or fixed capital costs associated with the construction, reconstruction or improvement of school facilities and campuses that have a useful life expectancy of five or more years. The

TABLE 9.1.   Florida Schedule of Millages

Type of Millage	Statutory Authority	Established By	Uses
Required Local Effort	FRS §1011.62(4)	Commissioner	Operating
Prior Period Funding Adjustment	FRS §1011.62(4)(e)	Commissioner	Operating
Current Operating Discretionary-Max .748 Mills	FRS §1011.71(1)	School Board	Operating
Local Capital Improve- ment-Max 1.5 Mills	FRS §1011.71 (2)	School Board	Capital Improvements
Capital Improvement Discretionary-Max .25 Mills	FRS §1011.71(3)	School Board	Lease=purchase pay- ments/ meet fixed capital outlay in lieu of operating discre- tionary millage
Operating or Capital (Not to Exceed 2 yrs)	FRS §1011.73(1)	Voter Referendum	Not specified
Additional Millage (Not to Exceed 4 yrs)	FRS §1011.73(2)	Voter Referendum	Operating
Debt Service	Fl. Const. Art. VII, sec 12, FRS §200.001(3) (e)	Voter Referendum	Not Specified

plan shall address any land acquisition, land improvement, design, and related engineering costs. Additionally, the plan shall include the costs of retrofitting and providing for technology implementation, including hardware and software, for the various sites within the school district.[18]

Surtax revenues may be used for the purpose of servicing bond indebtedness to finance authorized projects and any interest that accrues thereto may be held in trust to finance such projects. Neither the proceeds of the surtax nor any interest accrued thereto shall be used for operational expenditures. The Florida Depart- ment of Revenue distributes the surtax revenue to the school board imposing the tax.

The governing authority in each county is authorized to levy a discretionary sales surtax of 0.5 percent or 1 percent if approval were obtained by referen- dum. If the governing bodies of the municipalities representing a majority of the county's population adopt uniform resolutions establishing the rate of the surtax and calling for a referendum on the surtax, the levy of the surtax shall be placed on the ballot and shall take effect if approved by a majority of the electors of the county voting in the referendum on the surtax. The surtax may not be levied for more than 15 years. The proceeds of the surtax authorized by this subsection and any accrued interest shall be expended by the school district to finance, plan, and construct infrastructure.[19]

Developmental research schools (lab schools) at state universities are classified for funding as special school districts, as is the Florida Virtual School. Because these special districts have no taxing authority, the state provides the same dollar amount per student for the 0.748 discretionary operating millage revenues as is generated for district students by the tax base of the district where the school is located. For 2020-21, the contribution for the discretionary operating millage is $25,552,581 (2020-21 FEFP Second Calculation). There is no required local effort for special school districts; therefore, special districts are funded entirely with state funds.

Federal Support—The Florida State Board of Education may approve plans for cooperating with the federal government in carrying out any phase of the education program and must provide for the proper administration of funds apportioned to the state from federal appropriations. The commissioner recommends policies for administering funds appropriated from federal sources to the state for any education purpose and provides for the execution of plans and policies.

School districts receive funds from the federal government directly and through the state as an administering agency. School districts may receive federal funds from various agencies such as the Department of Labor, Veterans Administration, Department of Interior, Department of Education, Department of Defense and Department of Agriculture.

Federal funding also supports the Every Student Succeeds Act program, which establishes accountability measures for public schools to ensure that students in all schools are reaching proficiency in reading and mathematics (replaced the No Child Left Behind program effective for the 2017-18 school year); Individuals with Disabilities Education Act programs, which support education services for students with physical and mental challenges; Workforce Investment Act and Carl D. Perkins Career and Technical Education Act programs, which improve the quality of career and technical education in Florida.

Federal funds are typically used to supplement state and local funds authorized by the Florida Legislature to support various education programs.

On March 27, 2020, the Coronavirus Aid, Relief, and Economic Security (CARES) Act was signed into law to provide significant financial support to mediate the impact that COVID-19 has had on schools. The act includes $770.2 million in Elementary and Secondary School Emergency Relief (ESSER) funds that may be spent at considerable discretion by Florida school districts, but are particularly intended to support remote learning, especially for disadvantaged and at-risk students and their teachers. Each school district has the discretion to determine how much of this funding to draw down in a given fiscal year, based on its needs. In addition, the Governor's Emergency Education Relief (GEER) program, supported by CARES, provides $64 million for summer recovery to reduce academic achievement gaps exacerbated by COVID-19 and $30 million to cover schools' increased costs for cleaning and sanitation due to COVID-19.

Requirements for FEFP Participation

Each district participating in the state appropriations for the FEFP must provide evidence of its effort to maintain an adequate school program throughout the district and must meet at least the requirements cited below:

1. Maintain adequate and accurate records, including a system of internal accounts for individual schools, and file with the department, in correct and proper form, on or before the date due, each annual or periodic report that is required by the Florida Administrative Code.
2. Operate all schools for a term of 180 actual teaching days or the equivalent on an hourly basis. Upon written application, the Florida State Board of Education may prescribe procedures for altering this requirement.
3. Provide written contracts for all instructional personnel.
4. Expend funds for salaries in accordance with a salary schedule or schedules adopted by the school board, in accordance with Florida Statutes and the F.A.C.
5. Observe all requirements of the Florida State Board of Education relating to the preparation, adoption, and execution of budgets for the district school system.
6. Levy the required local effort millage rate on the taxable value for school purposes of the district.
7. Maintain an ongoing, systematic evaluation of the education program needs of the district and develop a comprehensive annual and long-range plan for meeting those ne

DISTRIBUTING STATE DOLLARS

Determining Gross State and Local FEFP for Florida School Districts

FTE STUDENTS

X

PROGRAM COST FACTORS

=

WEIGHTED FTE STUDENTS

X

BASE STUDENT ALLOCATION

X

DISTRICT COST DIFFERENTIAL

=

BASE FUNDING

+

DEPT. OF JUVENILE JUSTICE SUPPLEMENT

+

DECLINING ENROLLMENT SUPPLEMENT

+

SPARSITY SUPPLEMENT

+

STATE FUNDED DISCRETIONARY CONTRIBUTION

+

0.748 MILLS DISCRETIONARY COMPRESSION

+

SAFE SCHOOLS

+

READING PROGRAMS

+

SUPPLEMENTAL ACADEMIC INSTRUCTION

+

ESE GUARANTEED ALLOCATION

+

INSTRUCTIONAL MATERIALS

+

TEACHERS CLASSEROOM SUPPLY ASSSISTANCE

+

STUDENT TRANSPORTATION

+

VIRTUAL EDUCATION CONTRIBUTION

+

DIGITAL CLASSROOMS ALLOCATION

+

FEDERALLY CONNECTED STUDENT SUPPLEMENT

+

MENTAL HEALTH ASSISTANCE ALLOCTION

+

TOTAL FUNDS COMPRESSION & HOLD HARMLESS ALLOCATION

+

TEACHER SALARY INCREASE ALLOCATION

+

TURNAROUND SUPPLEMENTAL SERICES ALLOCATION

=

GROSS STATE & LOCAL FEFP DOLLARS

-

REQUIRED LOCAL EFFORT

=

GROSS STATE FEFP

+

ADJUSTMENTS

=

NET FEFP ALLOCATION

+

CATEGORICAL AID PROGRAMS

=

TOTAL STATE FUNDING

FTE Students

An FTE student for FEFP funding purposes is one student in membership in one or more FEFP programs for a school year or its equivalent. The time equivalent for a school year is listed below by grade group.

Standard School

1. Student in grades 4 through 12—900 hours of instruction
2. Student in kindergarten through grade 3 or in an authorized prekindergarten ESE program—720 hours of instruction

State Funding

Funding for FTE membership in programs scheduled beyond the regular 180-day term is limited, as described later in this section.

For purposes of calculating the FTE student membership, a student is considered in membership until he or she withdraws or until the eleventh consecutive school day of his or her absence. A student is eligible for FTE student membership reporting if both of the following conditions are satisfied:

1. The student is in program membership at least one day during the survey period in an approved course of study as defined in the Course Code Directory, excluding non-instructional activities as defined in the Florida Administrative Code: and
2. The student is in attendance at least one day during the survey period or one of the six scheduled meetings preceding the survey period when students were in attendance in school.

   Note: For year-round schools, if the student's track were out of school during survey week, the last week the track was in session becomes survey week.

The FTE generated by a student for the purposes of FEFP funding is limited to 1.0 FTE during the 180-day school year.

Dual enrollment is the enrollment of an eligible secondary student or home education student in a postsecondary course earning credit toward completion of high school and a career certificate, or toward an associate or baccalaureate degree [20] (Dual enrollment courses may be taught at Florida public secondary or postsecondary schools, or eligible Florida private secondary or postsecondary schools. Credit must be earned at both institutions. The course must offer credit leading to a high school diploma and a career certificate or an associate or baccalaureate degree. Career education dual enrollment is available for secondary students seeking a degree or certificate from a complete job preparatory program but is not intended to sustain student enrollment in isolated career courses. Early admission is a form of dual enrollment through which eligible secondary students enroll in an eligible postsecondary institution on a full-time basis in courses that are creditable toward the high school diploma and the associate or baccalaureate degree. Participation in the early admission program is limited to students who have completed a minimum of six semesters of full-time secondary enrollment, including studies undertaken in the ninth grade. Dual enrollment students earn the Grades 9-12 Basic Cost Factor at the home school while dually enrolled elsewhere. Each of these forms of dual enrollment is included in the calculation of FTE students.

School districts are required to pay public postsecondary institutions the standard tuition rate per credit hour when dual enrollment course instruction takes place on a postsecondary institution's campus and the course is taken during the fall or spring term. When dual enrollment course instruction is provided at a high school site by postsecondary institution faculty, school districts must reimburse postsecondary institutions the proportion of salary and benefits used to provide the instruction.[21]

School districts are not responsible for any costs to postsecondary institutions for dual enrollment courses that are offered by postsecondary institutions but provided on high school sites by school district faculty.

Students in kindergarten through grade 12 who are enrolled for more than six semesters in practical arts courses or exploratory courses, designed to expose them to a broad range of occupations to guide their academic and occupational plans, as defined shall not be counted as FTE students for such instruction. Students in grades 6-8 who are enrolled in career education courses shall be counted as Basic Grades 6-8. Only students in grades 9-12 who are enrolled in career education courses are reported in Program 300, Career Education. [22]

During the year, at least four FTE student membership surveys must be conducted under the administrative direction of, and on the schedule provided by, the commissioner. In addition to the four surveys, Survey 5 collects end-of-year student academic data. specifies that the number of FTE student membership surveys shall not exceed nine in a fiscal year. The commissioner has established four FTE student enrollment surveys for the 2020-21 school year and these surveys are scheduled for July 6-10, 2020; October 5-9, 2020; February 8-12, 2021; and June 14-18, 2021. [23]

The commissioner has the authority to establish for any school district or school an alternate period for an FTE student membership survey within eight weeks subsequent to the regular statewide survey period. Evidence must be submitted by the school district indicating that an abnormal fluctuation in student membership may occur at the time of the statewide survey period to warrant an alternate survey period. The commissioner must limit consideration of "abnormal fluctuation" to changes of more than 25 percent in any school or 5 percent in any district between the FTE student membership at the time of the regular statewide survey and the alternate survey period. The "abnormal fluctuation" must be caused by factors such as major student boycotts; civil disturbances; in- or out-migration in agricultural, industrial, or federal installations or contractors; or providential causes beyond the control of the district school board. district school boards are required to request alternate FTE surveys for DJJ programs experiencing fluctuations in student enrollment. Any request for an alternate survey period must be made prior to the original survey period. [24]

Classification for special program FTE requires: (1) proper qualification of students, (2) proper qualification of teachers and (3) appropriate subject matter in accordance with the F.A.C.

FTE Recalibration and the Common Student Identifier

All FTE student enrollment is capped at 1.0 FTE per student for the year except FTE reported by DJJ students beyond the 180-day school year. School districts report all FTE student enrollment, and the department combines all FTE student enrollment reported for the student by all school districts, including FLVS. The department then recalibrates all reported FTE student enrollment for each student to 1.0 FTE if the total reported FTE exceeds 1.0.

When a student is served by multiple school districts or moves from one district to another, that student should retain the same student identifier in every school district.

The process for calculating FTE within a single survey has the following provisions:

1. If a student identifier were reported by more than one school district, then all reported FTE is gathered, recalibrated, and funded.
2. If a student identifier were reported by only one school district, and there is no student record with similar demographics, then the FTE is recalibrated and funded only to the reporting school district.
3. If a student identifier were reported by only one school district, and there is a student record with similar or matching demographics reported by another school district, and at least one of the school districts reported less than 0.2 FTE, then all reported FTE is gathered, recalibrated, and funded.
4. If a student identifier were reported by only one school district and there were a student record with similar or matching demographics reported by another school district, none of the school districts reported less than 0.2 FTE, and the student identifiers do not have entry codes during survey week, then the FTE will be recalibrated and funded separately
5. If a student identifier were reported by only one school district and there were a student record with similar or matching demographics reported by another school district, none of the school districts reported less than 0.2 FTE, and at least one of the student identifiers has an entry code

during survey week, then all reported FTE is gathered, recalibrated, and funded.

The process for calculating FTE across multiple surveys has the following provisions: If a student identifier were reported in both surveys 2 and 3, then the FTE for the student identifier were processed in a manner similar to that for a single survey. For a student identifier that is not reported in both surveys 2 and 3, the FTE for that student identifier is gathered, recalibrated to 0.5 FTE and funded.

Program Cost Factors and Weighted FTE

Program cost factors assure that each program receives an equitable share of funds in relation to its relative cost per student. Through the annual program cost report, districts report the expenditures for each FEFP program. The cost per FTE student of each FEFP program is used to produce an index of relative costs, with the cost per FTE of Basic, Grades 4-8, established as the 1.000 base. To minimize the fluctuation in program cost factors, the Florida Legislature typically uses a three-year average in computing cost factors.

Multiplying the FTE students for a program by its cost factor produces "weighted FTE." This calculation weights the FTE to reflect the relative costs of the programs, as represented by the program cost factors. Program cost factors established for use in 2020-21 are as follows:

SE students in Levels 4 and 5 are reported with the appropriate cost factor (weight) for their respective levels. ESE students who are not classified in Level 4 or 5 are reported in the applicable Basic Program "with ESE services." Additional funding for these students is provided by the ESE Guaranteed Allocation component of the FEFP formula.

To provide for the planned use of FEFP funds, the Florida Legislature has established the following combination of programs during the 180-day regular school year and summer school:

1. Basic Education Programs
2. Exceptional Student Education for Support Levels 4 and 5 English for Speakers of Other Languages

Grades 9-12 Career Education Programs

Prekindergarten through grade 12 courses offered beyond the regular 180-day school year, including intersessions, except DJJ programs, Juveniles Incompetent to Proceed programs, and FLVS courses, do not generate FEFP funding; however, the FTE for intersession and summer school courses is reported so that the department may include this data in its statistical reports.

For the purpose of course completion and credit recovery pursuant to ss. 1002.45 and 1003.498, F.S., virtual instruction programs and virtual charter schools may operate beyond the regular 180-day school year.[25]

Weighted FTE Cap

Program Group 2 has an enrollment ceiling (cap) that is established based on each district's estimates of FTE in each FEFP program. District estimates are reviewed and approved by a state enrollment estimating conference. The appropriated FTE in each program is multiplied by the program's cost factor. The resulting weighted FTE, aggregated by program group, establishes the group cap. After actual FTE is reported, Group 2 FTE in excess of the cap receive a program cost factor of 1.0. A statewide cap of 400,208.72 weighted FTE was set for Group 2 for the 2020-21 fiscal year.

Additional Weighted FTE

All FTE provided in this section is in addition to the recalibrated FTE calculation.

Small District ESE Supplement

Supplemental funding is provided for districts that have fewer than 10,000 FTE and fewer than three FTE students in ESE Support Levels 4 and 5. This supplement is limited to the statewide value of 43.35 weighted FTE. The commissioner shall set the value of the supplemental FTE based on documented evidence of the difference in the cost of the service and the FEFP funding. The supplemental value for a district shall not exceed three FTE for each of these support levels (ESE Support Levels 4 and 5).

Small, Isolated High School Supplement

High schools with at least 28 students and no more than 100 students in grades 9-12 and that are no closer than 28 miles to the nearest high school may qualify for an isolated school supplement. A district elementary school may also qualify if:

- The school serves a primary configuration of kindergarten through grade 5 but may also include prekindergarten or grades 6 through 8.
- The school is located at least 35 miles by the shortest route from another elementary school within the school has been serving students primarily in basic studies.
- The school has a student population in which at least 75 percent of the students are eligible for free or reduced-price school lunch; and
- The school has a membership of at least 28, but not more than 100.

Districts with qualifying schools must levy the maximum discretionary operating millage in order to receive the supplement.[26]

Bonus FTE Programs

An additional value of 0.16 FTE shall be reported by school districts for each student in Advanced Placement (AP) classes who earns a score of three or higher on each College Board AP Subject examination, provided he or she has been taught in an AP class in the prior year. A value of 0.3 FTE shall be reported for each student who receives a College Bo.[27] A value of 0.16 additional FTE is to be calculated for each student enrolled in an International Baccalaureate (IB) course who receives a score of four or higher on the subject examination. An Advanced International Certificate of Education (AICE) student earns an additional 0.16 if he or she receives a score of "E" on a full-credit subject exam or an additional 0.08 FTE if he or she is enrolled in a half-credit class and earns a score of "E" or higher on the subject exam. A value of 0.3 FTE should be calculated for each student who receives an IB or AICE diploma.

From the funding generated by the bonus FTE of these programs,[28] districts are required to distribute bonuses to certain classroom teachers as follows:

1. International Baccalaureate—A bonus of $50 is earned by an IB teacher for each student in each IB course who receives a score of four or higher on the IB examination. An additional bonus of $500 is earned by the IB teacher in a school designated with a performance grade category of "D" or "F" who has at least one student scoring four or higher on the IB subject examination. Bonuses awarded under this paragraph shall be in addition to any regular wages or other bonuses the teacher received or is scheduled to receive.

2. Advanced International Certificate of Education—A teacher earns a $50 bonus for each student in the full-credit AICE course who receives a score of "E" or higher on the subject exam and a $25 bonus for each student in each half-credit AICE course who receives a score of "E" or higher on the subject examination. Additional bonuses of $500 and $250 for full-credit and half-credit courses, respectively, shall be awarded to AICE teachers in a school designated with a performance grade category of "D" or "F" who have at least one student passing the subject examination in that class. Bonuses awarded under this paragraph shall be in addition to any regular wages or other bonuses the teacher received or is scheduled to receive.

3. Advanced Placement—A $50 bonus is earned by an AP teacher for each student in each AP course who receives a score of three or higher on the College Board AP Examination. An additional bonus of $500 is earned by the AP teacher in a school designated with a performance grade category of "D" or "F" who has at least one student scoring three or higher

on the College Board AP subject examination. Bonuses awarded under this paragraph shall be in addition to any regular wages or other bonuses the teacher received or is scheduled to receive.

4.   Career and Professional Education Act (CAPE)

Pursuant to additional FTE shall be calculated as follows:[29]

- A value of 0.025 FTE shall be calculated for CAPE Digital Tool certificates earned by students in elementary and middle school grades. [30]
- A value of 0.1 or 0.2 FTE shall be calculated for each student who completes a career-themed course as defined in or courses with embedded CAPE industry certifications and who is issued an industry certification identified annually on the CAPE Industry Certification Funding List approved in accordance with rule 6A-6.0573, F.A.C. A value of 0.2 FTE student membership shall be calculated for each student who is issued a CAPE Industry Certification that has a statewide articulation agreement for college credit approved by the State Board of Education. For CAPE industry certifications that do not articulate for college credit, the department shall assign an FTE value of 0.1 for each certification.
- A value of 0.3 FTE student membership shall be calculated for student completion of the courses and the embedded certifications identified on the CAPE Industry Certification Funding List and approved by the commissioner.[31]
- A value of 0.5 FTE student membership shall be calculated for CAPE Acceleration Industry Certifications that articulate for 15 to 29 college credit hours.
- A value of 1.0 FTE student membership shall be calculated for CAPE Acceleration Industry Certifications that articulate for 30 or more college credit hours. These include CAPE Acceleration Industry Certifications approved by the commissioner.[32] Middle grades students who earn additional FTE membership for a CAPE Digital Tool certificate may not use the previously funded examination to satisfy the requirements for earning an industry certification. Additional FTE membership for an elementary or middle grades student shall not exceed 0.1 FTE for certificates or certifications earned within the same fiscal year. The Florida State Board of Education shall include the assigned values on the CAPE Industry Certification Funding List, in accordance with the F.A.C. Such value shall be added to the total FTE student membership for grades 6 through 12 in the subsequent year.[33] CAPE industry certifications earned through dual enrollment must be reported and funded Nevertheless, if a student earns a certification through a dual enrollment course, and the certification is not a fundable certification on the postsecondary certification funding list, or the dual enrollment certification is earned as a result of an agreement between a school district and a nonpublic postsecondary institution, the bonus value

shall be funded in the same manner as other nondual enrollment course industry certifications. In such cases, the school district may provide for an agreement between the postsecondary institution may enter into an agreement for equitable distribution of the bonus funds.[34]

Statute also allows provides for the following teacher bonuses:[35]

- $25 for each student taught by a teacher who provided instruction in a course that led to the student's attainment of an industry certification on the CAPE Industry Certification Funding List with a weight of 0.1 FTE.
- $50 for each student taught by a teacher who provided instruction in a course that led to the student's attainment of an industry certification on the CAPE Industry Certification Funding List with a weight of 0.2 FTE.
- $75 for each student taught by a teacher who provided instruction in a course that led to the student's attainment of an industry certification on the CAPE Industry Certification Funding List with a weight of 0.3 FTE.
- $100 for each student taught by a teacher who provided instruction in a course that led to the student's attainment of an industry certification on the CAPE Industry Certification Funding List with a weight of 0.5 or 1.0 FTE.

Bonuses awarded pursuant to this paragraph shall be provided to teachers who are employed by the school district in the year in which the additional FTE student membership calculation is included in the calculation. Any bonus awarded to a teacher under this paragraph is in addition to any regular wages or other bonuses the teacher received or is scheduled to receive.

Early High School Graduation

Statutes authorize the addition of 0.25 FTE to each district's total FTE for each student who earns 24 credits and graduates one semester in advance of the student's cohort and an additional 0.50 FTE for each student who earns 24 credits and graduates one year or more in advance of the student's cohort.[36]

Dual Enrollment

Students who are enrolled in an early college program earn 0.16 FTE, and those students who are not enrolled in an early college program earn 0.08 FTE upon completion of a general education course through the dual enrollment program with a grade of "A" or better. In addition, students with a 3.0 grade point average or better who receive an associate degree through the dual enrollment program following completion of courses taken in 2020-21 earn 0.3 FTE. School districts must allocate at least half of the funds received from dual enrollment bonus FTE funding to the schools that generated the funds.[37]

Base Student Allocation

The BSA from state and local funds is determined annually by the Florida Legislature and is a component in the calculation of Base Funding. For the 2020-21 fiscal year, the BSA is $4,319.49.

District Cost Differential

Statutes require the commissioner to annually compute DCDs by adding each district's Florida Price Level Index for the most recent three years and dividing the sum by three.[38] The result is multiplied by 0.800 and divided by 100, and 0.200 is added to the product to obtain the DCD. This serves to limit the factor's adjustment to 80 percent of the index (i.e., the approximate percentage of district salary costs to total operating costs). The three-year averaging reduces the immediate impact on districts of fluctuations in the index.

Base Funding

Base Funding is derived from the product of the weighted FTE students, multiplied by the BSA and the DCD.

Florida Department of Juvenile Justice Supplement

The total kindergarten through grade 12 weighted FTE student membership in juvenile justice education programs in each school district shall be multiplied by the amount of the state average class-size reduction factor multiplied by the district's cost differential. An amount equal to the sum of this calculation shall be allocated in the FEFP to each school district to supplement other sources of funding for students in juvenile justice education programs.

Declining Enrollment Supplement

The declining enrollment supplement is determined by comparing the unweighted FTE for the current year to the unweighted FTE of the prior year. In those districts where there is a decline in unweighted FTE, 25 percent of the decline is multiplied by the prior-year base funding per unweighted FTE. This amount is the declining enrollment supplement for the district. Chapter 2020-114, Laws of Florida, suspended this supplement for the 2020-21 fiscal year.

Sparsity Supplement

The FEFP recognizes the relatively higher operating cost of smaller districts due to sparse student populations through a statutory formula in which the variable factor is a sparsity index. This index is computed by dividing the FTE of the district by the number of permanent senior high school centers. For districts with FTE student memberships between 20,000 and 24,000, the number of high school centers is reduced to four. The number of high school centers is reduced to three for districts with fewer than 20,000 FTE students. By General Appropriations Act proviso, participation is limited to districts of 24,000 or fewer FTE students. There are four adjustments to the initial sparsity computation, including a wealth adjustment. This supplement is limited to $55,500,000 statewide for the 2020-21 fiscal year.

State-Funded Discretionary Contribution

Developmental research schools (lab schools) and FLVS are established as separate school districts for purposes of FEFP funding. Statutes authorize the calculation and allocation of funds for the lab schools in lieu of discretionary local tax revenue that is generated for district students by the tax base of the district where the school is located. The FLVS discretionary contribution is calculated by multiplying the maximum allowable non-voted discretionary millage for operations by the value of 96 percent of the current year's taxable value for school purposes for the state; dividing this product by the total FTE student membership of the state; and multiplying this quotient by the FTE student membership of the school. Funds for the discretionary contribution are appropriated from state funds in the General Appropriations Act.[39]

0.748 Mills Discretionary Compression

If any school district levies the full 0.748 mill levy, and it generates an amount of funds per unweighted FTE student that is less than the state average amount per unweighted FTE student, the school district shall receive a discretionary millage compression supplement that, when added to the funds generated by the district's 0.748 mill levy, shall be equal to the state average.[40]

Safe Schools

The General Appropriations Act provides $180,000,000 for Safe Schools activities in the 2020-21 fiscal year. These funds guarantee each district a minimum of $250,000. Of the remaining amount, one-third shall be allocated to school districts based on the latest official Florida Crime Index provided by the Florida Department of Law Enforcement, and two-thirds shall be allocated based on each district's share of the state's total unweighted student enrollment. Safe Schools funds are to be used by school districts to help them with establishing a school resource officer program. Each district must report to the department by October 15 that all of its public schools have completed a security risk assessment. If a district school board, through its adopted policies, procedures, or actions, denies a charter school access to any safe school officer options the school district must assign a school resource office or school safety officer to the charter school. Under such circumstances, the charter school's share of the costs of the school resource officer or school safety officer may not exceed the safe school allocation funds provided to the charter school and shall be retained by the school district.[41]

Reading Program

Funds in the amount of $130,000,000 are provided for a K-12 comprehensive, district-wide system of research- based reading instruction for the 2020-21 fiscal year. The amount of $115,000 shall be allocated to each district, and the remaining balance shall be allocated based on each district's proportion of the total K-12 base funding. Districts with one or more of the schools on the list of 300 lowest-performing elementary schools based on the state reading assessment must use each of those schools' portion of the allocation to provide an additional hour of intensive reading instruction for each day of the entire school year for the students in each school. The additional hour may be provided within the school day. This additional hour of instruction must be provided by teachers or reading specialists who are effective in teaching reading. Students enrolled in these schools who have level 4 or 5 reading assessment scores may choose to participate in the additional hour of instruction on an optional basis. ESE centers shall not be included in the 300 schools. The Florida State Board of Education shall withhold funds from a school district that fails to comply with this requirement.[42]

Supplemental Academic Instruction

The Supplemental Academic Instruction (SAI) component of the FEFP formula provides funding of $723,869,528 (as of the second calculation of the FEFP) for the 2020-21 fiscal year. School districts with schools earning a "D" or "F" grade must use such schools' portion of SAI funds to implement intervention and support strategies for school improvement and for salary incentives. Each school district with one or more of the 300 lowest performing elementary schools based on a three-year average of the state reading assessment data must use that school's portion of the allocation to provide an additional hour of intensive reading instruction each day for the students in the school. This additional hour of instruction must be provided by teachers or reading specialists who are effective in teaching reading, or by a kindergarten through grade 5 mentoring reading program that is supervised by a teacher who is effective at teaching reading. Students enrolled in these schools who have level 4 or 5 reading assessment scores may choose to participate in the additional hour of instruction on an optional basis. ESE centers shall not be included in the 300 schools.

The funds for the SAI allocation shall consist of a base amount with a workload adjustment based on changes in FTE.

Exceptional Student Education (ESE) Guaranteed Allocation

ESE services for students whose level of service is less than Support Levels 4 and 5 are funded through the ESE Guaranteed Allocation. The students generate FTE funding using the appropriate Basic Program weight for their grade level. This allocation provides for the additional services needed for exceptional students. District allocations from the appropriation of $1,092,394,272 are recalculated during the year based on actual student membership from FTE surveys. School districts that have provided education services in 2019-20 for exceptional education students who are residents of other districts shall not discontinue providing such services without the prior approval of the department.

Instructional Materials

For 2020-21, $236,574,333 is provided to purchase instructional materials, including $12,492,403 for library media materials, $3,414,590 for science lab materials and supplies, $10,590,529 for dual enrollment instructional materials and $3,193,706 for digital instructional materials for students with disabilities.

Florida Teachers Classroom Supply Assistance Program

This appropriation provides an allocation to each school district based on the prorated total of each school district's share of the total kindergarten through grade 12 unweighted FTE student enrollment. Funds are to be used only by classroom teachers for the purchase of classroom instructional materials and supplies for use in teaching students. An appropriation of $54,143,375 is allocated for the Florida Teachers Classroom Supply Assistance Program in 2020-21.[43]

Student Transportation

To provide transportation services in school districts in support of student learning, $449,966,033 is appropriated for Student Transportation in 2020-21. The formula contains the following provisions in the state allocation for student transportation: (1) students with special transportation needs earn a higher rate of funding than base students; (2) base funding for each district is established by the district's proportionate share of the total statewide students eligible for transportation; and (3) indices are applied that modify the base funding amount to reward more efficient bus utilization, compensate for rural population density and adjust funding based on the cost of living.[44]

Virtual Education Contribution

The virtual education contribution shall be allocated pursuant to the statutory guidelines. The contribution shall be based on $5,230 per FTE student.[45]

Digital Classrooms Allocation

Funds in the amount of $8,000,000 are provided to school districts to support school district and school efforts to integrate technology in classroom teaching and learning to ensure students have access to high-quality electronic and digital instructional materials and resources and empower classroom teachers to help students succeed. The amount of $100,000 shall be allocated to each district, and the remaining balance shall be allocated based on each school district's share of the total kindergarten through grade 12 unweighted FTE student enrollment. Twenty percent of the funds provided may be used for professional development, including in-state conference attendance or online coursework, to enhance the use of technology for digital instructional strategies. Other eligible uses include acquiring and maintaining items on the eligible services list authorized by the federal E-rate program and acquiring computer and device hardware and associated software.[46]

Federally Connected Student Supplement

A district's total Federally Connect Student Supplement allocation is the sum of the student allocation and an exempt property allocation. As of the 2020-21 Second Calculation, a statewide total of $13,861,617 has been provided for the Federally Connected Student Supplement. The Federally Connected Student Supplement was created to provide supplemental funding for school districts to support the education of students connected with federally owned military installations, National Aeronautics and Space Administration property and Indian lands. To be eligible for this supplement, the district must be eligible for federal Impact Aid Program funds under s. 8003 of Title VIII of the Elementary and Secondary Education Act of 1965. The student allocation is calculated based on the number of students reported for federal Impact Aid Program funds who meet specific criteria. The total number of qualifying federally connected students is multiplied by a percentage of the base student allocation as determined annually in the FEFP Conference Report. The total number of students with disabilities is multiplied by an additional percentage of the base student allocation. The exempt property allocation is equal to the tax-exempt value of federal impact aid lands multiplied by the capital outlay millage authorized and levied.[47]

Mental Health Assistance Allocation

Funds in the amount of $100,000,000 are provided to help establish or expand school-based mental health care. Each school district will receive a minimum of $100,000, and the remaining balance will be distributed proportionally to districts based on their total unweighted student enrollment.

Before receiving funds, school districts are required to annually develop and submit a plan outlining the local program and planned expenditures to their school boards for approval. Charter schools are eligible to receive a proportionate share of the district's allocation by submitting a plan to their governing body for approval and providing the approved plan to their district. The department will distribute the district's allocated funds upon the district's submission of an approved plan, including approved plans of all charter schools. The allocated funds may not supplant funds that are provided for mental health assistance from other operating funds and may not be used to increase salaries or provide bonuses.[48]

Funding Compression and Hold Harmless Allocation

The amount of $68,000,000 was appropriated for the Funding Compression and Hold Harmless Allocation in 2020-21 to provide additional funding for school districts whose funds per unweighted FTE student in the prior fiscal year were less than the statewide average or whose district cost differential in the current year is less than the prior year. Funds shall be allocated based on the requirements of s. 1011.62(17), F.S.

For the 2020-21 allocation, 25 percent of the difference between the district's prior-year funds per FTE student and the state average shall be used to determine the allocation. A district's allocation shall not be greater than $100 per FTE student.

Districts that do not receive a funding compression allocation are held harmless for any decrease to the district cost differential. The hold harmless allocation is calculated by applying a factor of 11.03 to the district's weighted FTE and the BSA.

Turnaround School Supplemental Services Allocation

The amount of $45,473,810 is appropriated to provide eligible schools with funds to improve the overall academic and community welfare of students and their families, pursuant to Eligible schools include district-managed turnaround schools earning two consecutive grades of "D" or a grade of "F," district-managed turnaround schools that earn a grade of "C" or higher and are no longer in turnaround status, and schools that earn three consecutive grades below a "C." Eligible activities may include tutorial and after-school programs, student counseling, nutrition education, parental counseling and an extended school day and school year. Service models should encourage students to complete high school and attend college or career training, set high academic expectations, and inspire character development. Eligible schools will receive up to $500 per FTE student. Upon receipt of school grades, the department provides school districts with a list of preliminary allocations for qualifying schools, which are recalculated in subsequent FEFP calculations.[49]

Teacher Salary Increase Allocation

The sum of $500,000,000 in recurring funds is provided for the Teacher Salary Increase Allocation.[50] Eighty percent of these funds are provided for school districts to increase the salaries of all full- time district and charter school classroom teachers (including certified pre-kindergarten teachers funded through the FEFP, but not including substitute teachers) to at least $47,500 or the maximum amount achievable based on the district's allocation. Twenty percent of this allocation, along with any unused funds from the 80 percent, is to provide salary increases to full-time classroom teachers who did not receive an increase or received an increase of less than 2 percent, or other full-time instructional personnel excluding substitute teachers.

School districts must submit board-approved salary distribution plans to the department by October 2020 indicating how they plan to distribute Teacher Salary Increase Allocation funds. In addition, they must submit a preliminary report to the department detailing planned expenditures of the Teacher Salary Increase Allocation by December 1, 2020, and a final report by August 1, 2021. The department will use district data in its February 1, 2021, report to the Governor, President of the Senate and Speaker of the House on the planned statewide expenditure of Teacher Salary Increase Allocation funds.

Required Local Effort

The district required local effort is subtracted from the state and local FEFP dollars. The amount of required local effort that each district must provide to participate in the FEFP is calculated as described in the following paragraphs.

Adjusted required local effort from ad valorem taxes for 2020-21 was set in the Second Calculation at $8,016,904,590. Using the certified 2020 tax roll from the Florida Department of Revenue, the commissioner computed and certified the required local effort millage rate for each district. For the current fiscal year FEFP calculation, each district's contribution for required local effort is the product of the certified mills multiplied by 96 percent of the taxable value for school purposes of the district.

The amount produced by applying the average computed required local effort millage rate of 3.720 to the certified tax roll is adjusted by an equalization factor for each district.[51] The purpose of this adjustment is to offset variations among districts in the level of assessment of property. The Florida Department of Revenue provides the commissioner with its most recent determination of the assessment level of the prior year's assessment roll for each district and for the state. A millage rate is computed based on the positive or negative variation of each district from the state average assessment level. The millage rate resulting from application of this equalization factor is added to the state average required local effort millage. The sum of these two rates becomes each district's certified required local effort millage. Developmental research schools and FLVS have no taxing authority. Therefore, state funds are used to provide the required local effort, as well as equivalent discretionary local revenue, for these schools.

Adjustments

The department is authorized to make adjustments in the allocation of funds to a district for adjudication of litigation, arithmetical errors, assessment roll change, FTE student membership errors or allocation errors revealed in an audit report. An under-allocation in a prior year caused by a school district's error may not be the basis for a positive allocation adjustment for the current year.

If state revenue collections were not sufficient to fund the amount appropriated for the FEFP, a special session may be held to reduce the appropriation and allocations. If the program calculates an amount that exceeds the appropriation, a proration of available funds will be deducted from districts' calculated funding in proportion to each district's relative share of state and local FEFP dollars. This procedure preserves equity in the distribution of available dollars.

If appropriated funds for the FEFP were inadvertently omitted in the FEFP Conference Report, these funds will be added in a later calculation as an additional allocation. The allocation of these funds will be determined by the Florida Education Finance Program Appropriation Allocation Conference.[52]

Categorical Program Funds

Categorical program funds are added to the FEFP allocation that is distributed to districts. Categorical programs include the Class Size Reduction Program and the District Discretionary Lottery and Florida School Recognition Program.

Class Size Reduction

As a result of the voter-approved amendment to Article IX, s. 1, of the Florida Constitution, regarding class size reduction, additional operating and capital outlay funds were appropriated to assist districts in their efforts to not exceed the class size maximums. Beginning with the 2010-11 school year, Florida classrooms could have no more than 18 students in prekindergarten through grade 3, 22 students in grades 4-8 and 25 students in grades 9-12. If a district school board determines that it is impractical, educationally unsound or disruptive to student learning, students who enroll after the October student membership survey may be temporarily assigned to a class that exceeds the maximums cited. Up to three students may be assigned to a teacher in the kindergarten through grade 3 group. Up to five students may be assigned to a teacher in the grades 4-8 and 9-12 groups.

For 2020-21, the class size reduction appropriation is $3,145,795,385 for operations. These funds are used by districts primarily to hire teachers to meet class size requirements. The class size reduction allocation factors for the 2020-21 fiscal year for the operating categorical program are as follows: $1,301.57 (grades PreK-3), $887.80 (grades 4-8) and $889.95 (grades 9-12) per weighted FTE student.

District Discretionary Lottery and Florida School Recognition Program Funds

No funding was appropriated to this program for 2020-21. When funded, the Florida School Recognition Program provides monetary awards to schools that earn an "A" grade, improve at least one performance grade from the previous year or sustain the previous year's improvement of more than one letter grade. District Discretionary Lottery and Florida School Recognition Program funds remaining after funding the Florida School Recognition Program are allocated to school districts based on each district's proportionate share of the FEFP base funding entitlement (WFTE x BSA x DCD).

FEFP CALCULATION SCHEDULE

The FEFP is calculated five times throughout the year to arrive at each year's final appropriation. These calculations are as follows:

1. First Calculation—This calculation is completed by the Florida Legislature. District allocations for July 10 are based on this calculation.
2. Second Calculation—This calculation is made upon receipt of the certified tax roll from the Florida Department of Revenue as provided[53] for in District allocations for July 26 through January are based on this calculation.
3. Third Calculation—This calculation is made upon receipt of districts' October survey FTE counts. District allocations for January through April are based on this calculation. (District current-year July and October and prior-year June FTE amounts are summed with a February estimate derived from annualization factors provided by each school district.)
4. Fourth Calculation—This calculation is made upon receipt of districts' February FTE counts and estimated June FTE. District allocations for April through June are based on this calculation.
5. Final Calculation—This calculation is made upon receipt of districts' June FTE counts. Prior-year adjustments in the following fiscal year are completed based on a comparison of this Final Calculation to the Fourth Calculation.

With each calculation, districts are sent a detailed report of the input data and results.

SUMMARY

The state of Florida is project to have nearly 22 million residents by year end 2021. Only the states of California and Texas have larger populations. As such, Florida is the third most populated state. The state has 67 school districts organized along county lines. Additionally, Florida has the largest virtual school in the nation as well as growing programs for parents choosing private schools. The primary mechanism for funding public schools is the Florida Education Finance Program, first created tin the early 1970s. Although heavily amended in the ensuring years the formula's basic conceptual framework has remained the same and has withstood numerous constitutional challenges. With the current Governor, Commissioner of Education, and current Legislature the growth of charter, vouchers, tax credits and various options are expected to grow over time.

TABLE 9.2.   Determining Gross State and Local FEFP for Florida School Districts

Programs	Current Cost Factors
K-Grades 1,2,3	1.124
Grades 4,5,6,7,8	1.0000
Grades 9,10,11,12	1.012
K, Grades 1,2,3 with ESE Services	1.124
Grades 4,5,6,7,8 with ESE Services	1.000
Grades 9,10,11,12 with ESE Services	1.012
ESE Support Level 4	3.644
ESE Support Level 5	5.462
English for Speakers of Other Languages	1.184
Programs for Grades 9-12 Career Education	1.012

ENDNOTES

[1]   Florida Constitution, Art. IX, sec. 1.
[2]   This chapter is largely adapted from various Florida Department of Education documents most notably, in large part, 2020-21 Funding for Florida School Districts, Florida Dept. of Educ., available at http://www.fldoe.org/fefp.
[3]   FRS §1004.02(25). The District Lottery and School Recognition Program was not funded for 2020-21
[4]   FL Const. Art. IX, sec. 1.
[5]   FL Const. Art. XII sec. 9(d) and sec. 9(a)(2).
[6]   FRS §1011.62(4)(e).
[7]   FRS §1011.71(1).
[8]   FRS §1011.71(3).
[9]   See, FRS §§1011.71(2), 1013.62(1), 1013.62(1), 1013.62(1).
[10] FRS §§1011.71(2)(a)-(k).
[11] FRS §1011.71(5).
[12] FRS §§627.403, 624.605(1)(d), (f), (g), (h) and (m).
[13] FRS §§1011.71(3), 011.71(1).
[14] Florida Const., Art. VII, sec. 9 and FRS §1011.73(1).
[15] FRS §§1011.71(9), 1011.73(2), 1011.71(9).
[16] Florida Const., Art. VII, sec. 12, and FRS §§200.001(3)(e), 1010.40-1010.55, F.S.
[17] FRS, §§200, (Determination of Millage).
[18] FRS §212.055(6).
[19] FRS §212.055(2).
[20] FRS §1007.271.
[21] FRS §1007.271(21
[22] FRS §1003.01(4)(a).
[23] Rule 6A-1.0451(4), F.A.C., FRS §1011.62(1)(a).
[24] See F.A.C. 6A-1.0451, F.A.C.
[25] FRS, §§1002.45, 1003.498, and 1011.61(1)(c)2.

[26] FRS §1011.62(1)(h).

[27] FRS §1003.4282.

[28] FRS §§1011.62(1)(l), (m), (n) and (o).

[29] FRS §1011.62(1)(o).

[30] FRS §1003.493(1)(b).

[31] FRS §§1003.4203(5)(a) and 1008.44.

[32] FRS §§1003.4203(5)(b) and 1008.44.

[33] FRS §1011.80.

[34] FRS §1011.62(1)(o).

[35] FRS §1011.62(1)(o).

[36] FRS §§1011.62(1)(p), 1003.4281, 1003.4281.

[37] FRS §§1007.273, 1011.62(i).

[38] FRS §1011.62(2).

[39] FRS §§1002.32(9), 1011.71(1).

[40] FRS §1011.62(5).

[41] FRS §§1008.22(3), 011.62(9),1008.32.

[42] FRS §§1008.22(3), 1011.62(9), and 1008.32.

[43] FRS §012.71.

[44] FRS §011.68.

[45] FRS §011.62(11).

[46] FRS §1001.20(4)(a)1.b.

[47] FRS §§1011.62(13) and 1011.71(2).

[48] FRS §1011.62(16).

[49] FRS §011.62(21).

[50] FRS §1011.62(18).

[51] FRS §1011.62(4)(b).

[52] FRS §1011.65.

[53] FRS §1011.62(4).

CHAPTER 10

GEORGIA

Davíd G. Martínez
University of South Carolina

Lauren G. Epps
University of South Carolina

Patrick D. Bennett
University of South Carolina

GENERAL BACKGROUND

Among the United States of Americas (US) educational landscape, Georgia stands out for its historical significance. Georgia was unique as the last of the British Colonies, establishing fiscal support in the House of Commons for public infrastructure of the state including schools.[1] This influenced how the colonists of Georgia authored the initial constitution of 1777 to include Article LIV which stated, "schools shall be erected in each county, and supported at the general expense of the State, as the legislature shall hereafter point out."[2] By 1785 Georgia has established a *Senatus Academicus* that oversaw not only the bourgeoning University system, but was also charged with recommending what types of schools would operate throughout the state, and what curriculum would be taught.[3] In 1817 the Georgia legislature passed a funding resolution, colloquially known as

Funding Public Schools in the United States, Indian Country,
and US Territories (Second Edition), pages 169–185.
Copyright © 2023 by Information Age Publishing
www.infoagepub.com

the *Poor School Fund,* to offset the cost of tuition in support of schools designed to teach enslaved peoples Christianity.[4] In 1821 an *Academic Fund* was established by the state of Georgia and by 1837, the *Poor School Fund* was merged with the *Academic Fund* into the *Common School Fund.*[5] A significant provision formally establishing free public schools in Georgia passed in 1858 at the behest of Governor Joseph Emerson Brown.[6] Governor Browns' amendments to the states' educational provisions established a consistent funding source directed discretely at White children, not generally poor children as previous law had established.[7] This historical artifact informs the landscape of free public education in Georgia, for whom it was available, and how the states political leaders mediated the availability of schools. By 1830 Georgia policy makers passed legislation prohibiting the teaching of enslaved peoples to read or write model after South Carolina's statutes.[8] Amongst the colonies anti-literacy laws prohibiting the education of enslaved peoples was commonplace, and by some historical accounts Georgia laid the framework for the 1830s statutes by the late 1700s and Savannah officially passed prohibition by 1817.[9] While officially Georgia worked to prohibit the education of its Black Community, within the community itself abolitionists such as Mathilda Taylor, Mary Woodhouse, and Jane Deaveaux, worked to upend the educational oppression, setting up schools in secret for enslaved peoples.[10]

The Civil War disrupted further efforts to reify free public education in the state, however, the Georgia policymakers in the remnants of the war and in accordance with previous policy set up a system of public schools across Georgia.[11] The state statute provided instruction for any free White persons between the ages of 6 and 21. The Georgia state constitution of 1868 codified language to support all children between the ages of 6 and 18 as entitled to benefit from the compulsory school fund set up by the state.[12] In 1880 Ware High School, the first high school for Black students opened in Augusta. By 1890 only about 1% of Black children attended schools, and *Plessy v. Ferguson* (1896) set the structure for continued educational persecution of Black children in Georgia.[13] Racial segregation of education between Black and White students continued well into the early 1900s and in 1924 the first high school for Black students opened in Atlanta. The Georgia Equalization Act passed in 1926 and equalized state level school funds across the state.

In 1937 Georgia passed House Bill 123 that established a seven-month school year, and House Bill 141 that provided funding for textbooks to compulsory public schools. House Bill 125 (1937) also helped to establish the state board of education.[14] In 1937 Georgia also passed legislation that provided public state funds to school for Black children. The 1945 changes to Georgia's constitution changed how the school system of Georgia was administered, providing oversight to the state itself.[15] In 1949 the state of Georgia passed the passed the Minimum Program for Education Act that set up the structure of its current minimum foundation program but continued its segregationist policies. One of the major complications in the history of Georgia public schools is segregation which continued in

Georgia until the *Brown vs. Board of Education of Topeka* (1954) which forced schools nationally to desegregate.[16] Segregation continued through 1971 when the landmark decision of *Swann v. Charlotte-Mecklenburg Board of Education* (1971) forced all schools in Georgia to finally desegregate.

The current mechanism to fund schools was established in 1985 when the Georgia General Assembly passed the Quality Basic Education act (QBE). The QBE's purpose is to provide more equitable funding to all of Georgia's students and is largely responsible for funding schools today. Later in this chapter we will outline the school funding mechanism in detail. The next section, however, defines some important constitutional language.

Notable Constitutional Language

The legal framework for Georgia's education system is codified in the constitution, and Georgia's code of laws. The constitution of Georgia states in Art. VIII, § I, paragraph I:

> Paragraph I. Public education; free public education prior to college or postsecondary level; support by taxation. The provision of an adequate public education for the citizens shall be a primary obligation of the State of Georgia. Public education for the citizens prior to the college or postsecondary level shall be free and shall be provided for by taxation. The expense of other public education shall be provided for in such manner and in such amount as may be provided by law.[17]

The Georgia state constitution also provides a framework for the establishment and maintenance of their public school system and governance including Art. VIII, § V, paragraph I and II:

> Paragraph I. School systems continued; consolidation of school systems authorized; new independent school systems prohibited. Authority is granted to county and area boards of education to establish and maintain public schools within their limits,[18]

and

> Paragraph II. Boards of education. Each school system shall be under the management and control of a board of education, the members of which shall be elected as provided by law.[19]

Concurrently, Georgia Code of Laws Title 20 Article 6 outlines the educational provisions of the state including admission to a free program of instruction that ensures all of Georgia's students have access to a quality education and ample opportunities to develop the necessary competencies for lifelong learning and to maintain good physical and mental health so that Georgians may actively participate in the governing process and their community; see Code 1981, § 20-2-131.1 and § 20-2-133.a.[20]

Legally Georgia has an obligation to provide a free basic public education, however, challenges can arise due to the amorphous language which absolves Georgia of its responsibility so long as any county or area board is operating "within their limits." Georgia's education is also held to a subjective standard of "quality," in its constitutional language, defaulting to the Georgia Department of Education and the Georgia State Board of Education for guidance on learning standards; Code 1981, § 20-2-140. The Georgia Department of Education outlines the learning standards framework, and areas of concentration for its standards of excellence including:

1. Computer Science,
2. Career, Technical, and Agricultural Education Career Clusters/Pathways,
3. English Language Arts,
4. Fine Arts,
5. Health,
6. Mathematics,
7. Physical Education,
8. Science,
9. Social Studies,
10. World Languages.[21]

Descriptive Statistics

Georgia currently educates approximately 1,686,318 students through the Georgia Department of Education: 742,320 in elementary school, 413,448 in middle school, and 530,550 in high school (Georgia Department of Education, 2022).[22] The majority of students in Georgia are Black, White and LatinX. Approximately 37.4% of all students in Georgia are White, 36.5% are Black, and 17.1% of students are LatinX (i.e. reported as Hispanic by Georgia)[23]. In 2021-2022 56.2% of students in Georgia were eligible for free or reduced lunch, 12.1% approximately 204,000 were eligible for special education services, and 8.9% of Georgia's students are English learners.[24] Table 10.1 shows the enrollment trends in Georgia from the 2011-2012 school year to the 2020-2021 school year. As Table 10.1 shows, the total enrollment in Georgia has remained consistent and had minor changes year to year from approximately 1,685,000 to a peak of approximately 1,770,000 in 2019-2020. The Asian student population has seen the largest net change from 57,165 in 2011-2012 to 77,060 in 2020-2021.

In 2021-2022 Georgia had 2,306 schools, across 219 total school districts; 21 city systems, 159 county systems, 29 state and commission charter schools, and 3 state schools. For the 2021-2022 school year there were 119,492 teachers, 3.6% (i.e. 4,247) of which have 30+ years of teaching experience, 21% who have at least 21 (i.e. 25,121) years of experience, and 32.7 (i.e. 39,015) of which have at least 11 years of experience.[25] Table 10.2 includes salient staff level staffing information. From Table 10.2 we see that the pupil teacher ratio has remained consistent

TABLE 10.1. State Level Descriptive Information Enrollment 2011-2012 to 2020-2021

Race/Ethnicity	2021	2020	2019	2018	2017	2016	2015	2014	2013	2012
Asian or Asian/Pacific Islander Students	77060	76516	74722	72392	69456	66453	63491	61100	59067	57165
Black	631012	643308	646675	648917	649332	648758	644467	637740	628849	623601
Indigenous	3335	3385	3396	3440	3461	3453	3592	3733	3576	3732
LatinX	295523	295154	283847	275991	267498	256082	244113	228901	217122	205317
Nat. Hawaiian or Other Pacific Isl. Students	1741	1771	1776	1839	1877	1967	2010	2005	1869	1803
White	649197	679024	689552	701424	710792	721134	730041	736619	740789	743258
Two or More Races	72147	70499	67234	64639	61930	59390	56723	53811	52060	50140
Total Enrollment	1730015	1769657	1767202	1768642	1764346	1757237	1744437	1723909	1703332	1685016

Note: U.S. Department of Education, National Center for Education Statistics, Common Core of Data (CCD), State Nonfiscal Public Elementary/Secondary Education Survey.

United States Department of Education, National Center for Education Statistics, Common Core of Data (CCD), "State Nonfiscal Public Elementary/Secondary Education Survey," Access November 22, 2022 https://nces.ed.gov/ccd/elsi/tableGenerator.aspx.

TABLE 10.2. State Level Descriptive Information Teachers/Admin 2011-2012 to 2020-2021

	2021	2020	2019	2018	2017	2016	2015	2014	2013	2012
Pupil-Teacher Ratio	14.65	15.02	15.08	15.24	15.37	15.55	15.65	15.75	15.57	15.16
Total District Admin.	3025.5	3059.4	2934.7	2710.6	2532.6	2411.1	2435.2	2419.7	2359.9	2257.3
Total FTE (Teachers)	118059.1	117836.9	117159.3	116021.7	114762.5	113031	111469.8	109441	109364.9	111133.3

Note: U.S. Department of Education, National Center for Education Statistics, Common Core of Data (CCD), State Nonfiscal Public Elementary/Secondary Education Survey.

United States Department of Education, National Center for Education Statistics, Common Core of Data (CCD), "State Nonfiscal Public Elementary/Secondary Education Survey," Access November 22, 2022 https://nces.ed.gov/ccd/elsi/tableGenerator.aspx.

over time and in 2020-2021 was 14.65. The total number of administrators in the state has increased from 2257 in 2011-2012 to 3025 in 2020-2021 representing an approximately 34% increase in administrators. By comparison, while the teacher FTE has increased from 111,133 to 118,059 in the same time, this represents a 6.23% increase. The average beginning teacher salary in the state is $44,048 and the average overall teacher salary is $60,543. The 2021-2022 Georgia state salary schedule reports that new teachers with no years of experience have an annual income of $35,217, while a teacher with a Ph.D. and 21 or more years of experience have a salary of approximately $77,000.[26]

CURRENT POLITICAL CLIMATE

The Georgia state General Assembly consists of two chambers the House of Representatives (House) and the Senate. There are currently 180 house members representing Georgia's districts; 77 members affiliated with the Democratic party and 103 members affiliated with the Republican party.[27] Until his passing on November 16th, 2022 David Ralston served as 73rd Speaker of Georgia's House of Representatives. Jan Jones replaced David Ralston as the 74th Speaker Pro Tempore.[28] The Georgia State Senate consists of 56 members; 22 members affiliated with the Democratic party and 34 members affiliated with the Republican party.[29] Currently, Geoff Duncan serves as the Lieutenant Governor, while Senator Butch Miller serves as the Senate President Pro Tempore. At the Federal level, Georgia is represented by 14 members; 6 members affiliated with the Democratic party and 8 members affiliated with the Republican party.[30] Georgia also has two Senate representatives, the Reverend Raphael Warnock and Jon Ossof.[31]

The legislative calendar of Georgia is dictated by the constitution section 4 of article III which states the General Assembly must convene by the second Monday of January. The session is capped at a maximum of 40 days. Each year two appropriations bills are set forth by Georgia's General Assembly and signed by the Governor. The first bills reconciles the previous years budget, while the second bill proposes the subsequent years budget.[32] In September at the start of the budgeting process all state agencies are required to submit budgets to the Office of Planning and Budget (OPB). The Governor's Office then proposes an omnibus revenue estimate. OPB then reviews all budget requests and the Governor's Office outlines the details of the omnibus budget plan in the Governor's Budget Report.[33] The budget is then outlined in a House and Senate omnibus bill and once passed the Governor has 40 days to review, amend, and both bills into law. The entire process begins on July 1st and ends on June 30th of the next year.

School Finance Litigation

Georgia has had some school finance litigation due to the school finance disparity that exists across the state. In 1981 McDaniel v. Thomas was set before the Georgia State Supreme Court who decided that although there were school finance disparities across districts maintained the state school finance system did not violate the equal protection clause of the United States constitution or the Georgia constitutions educational clauses. Furthermore, the court found that despite the school finance disparity that did exist, education was not a fundamental right, and that Georgia had autonomy over how their system of schools, and thus the system of school finance, functioned.[34] The Georgia State Supreme Court once again heard school finance case in 2014, *Gaddy v. Georgia Department of Revenue*. This case stemmed from challenges to Georgia's tax-credit voucher program which plaintiffs asserted violated the states' constitutional provisions and allowed individuals and businesses to receive a Georgia income tax credit for donations made to approved scholarships maintained by private or public organizations. Ultimately the Georgia Supreme Court dismissed the case.[35]

In 2022, Georgia joined a class with 21 other states and brought litigation against the United States Department of Agriculture (USDA) asserting that its new policies applying the definition of discrimination too broad. In 2022 the USDA changed its policy on discrimination stating that discrimination based on sex found in Title IX of the Education Amendments of 1972, and in the Food and Nutrition Act of 2008, and Supplemental Nutrition Assistance Program (SNAP), includes discrimination based on sexual orientation and gender identity.[36] States found to break this policy would be excluded from the USDA federal school lunch program, and funding associated with the program. The 22 states seeking relief from the policy which include Indiana, Alabama, Alaska, Arizona, Arkansas, Georgia, Kansas, Kentucky, Louisiana, Mississippi, Missouri, Montana, Nebraska, Ohio, Oklahoma, South Carolina, South Dakota, Tennessee, Texas, Utah, Virginia, and West Virginia.

Most recently, August of 2022, seven charter schools from DeKalb County Georgia filed a motion against the DeKalb County School Districts claiming the district:

1. is not funding the charter schools at or above the minimum funding levels,
2. is not providing the charter school an equal share of the state austerity funds restored in the state budget,
3. is withholding funds at the charter schools' academic year midterm,
4. is not providing the charter school's their share of federal funds for special needs students and teacher development, and
5. is improperly withholding 3% of the charter school's funding through various fees without providing the stipulated services.[37]

The Plaintiffs seek damages of approximately $21 million, the difference of $54 million and $33 million. This amount is the proportion of funding lost after austerity funding cuts were restored from the Spring 2021 Georgia Department of Education midterm allocation sheets.

SOURCES OF REVENUE

Georgia funds its public schools through State, Federal, and Local sources. In FY 2022 Georgia's Governor allocated $27,252,569,596 in total state revenue. The FY 2022 budget includes nearly $290,280,797 in cuts from the FY 2020 budget of $27,542,850,393.[38] Of this total budget, the Governor allocated $10,212,899,126 to the Department of Education in FY 2022, a decrease of $431,928,498 from the $10,644,827,624 in FY 2020. It should be noted the Governor increased the allocation to the Department of Education in FY 2022 from FY 2021; FY 2021 allocation $9,632,727,015. The largest proportion of state funding is directly related to income and sales tax levies.[39]

The constitution of Georgia states in Art. VIII, § VI, paragraph I:

> The board of education of each school system shall annually certify to its fiscal authority or authorities a school tax not greater than 20 mills per dollar for the support and maintenance of education. Said fiscal authority or authorities shall annually levy said tax upon the assessed value of all taxable property within the territory served by said school system, provided that the levy made by an area board of education, which levy shall not be greater than 20 mills per dollar, shall be in such amount and within such limits as may be prescribed by local law applicable thereto.[40]

Furthermore, paragraph IV states:

> The board of education of each school district in a county in which no independent school district is located may by resolution and the board of education of each county school district and the board of education of each independent school district located within such county may by concurrent resolutions impose, levy, and collect a sales and use tax for educational purposes of such school districts conditioned upon approval by a majority of the qualified voters residing within the limits of the local taxing jurisdiction voting in a referendum thereon. This tax shall be at the rate of 1 percent and shall be imposed for a period of time not to exceed five years, but in all other respects, except as otherwise provided in this Paragraph, shall correspond to and be levied in the same manner as the tax provided for by Article 3 of Chapter 8 of Title 48 of the Official Code of Georgia Annotated, relating to the special county 1 percent sales and use tax, as now or hereafter amended. Proceedings for the reimposition of such tax shall be in the same manner as proceedings for the initial imposition of the tax, but the newly authorized tax shall not be imposed until the expiration of the tax then in effect.[41]

This language then imposes a 20 mill local property tax limit for education which can not be increased without voter approval. Local school boards also have the option to increase sales tax by 1% for 5 years through voter approval for earmarked projects. In terms of local tax revenue levies, all property is required to be assessed at 40% of the fair market value unless otherwise specified by law. (*see* GA Code § 48-5-7.2). Fair market value is defined as "the amount a knowledge-

TABLE 10.3. Revenue Information

State Name	2020	2019	2018	2017	2016	2015	2014	2013	2012
Tot. Fed. Rev. PP	$1,101	$1,118	$1,067	$1,091	$1,063	$1,083	$1,078	$1,094	$1,140
Tot. Loc. Rev. PP	$6,015	$5,783	$5,397	$5,146	$4,983	$4,814	$4,705	$4,702	$4,846
Tot. Stat. Rev. PP	$6,348	$5,865	$5,683	$5,350	$5,118	$4,864	$4,593	$4,474	$4,471
Tot. Rev. PP	$13,464	$12,766	$12,147	$11,587	$11,164	$10,761	$10,377	$10,270	$10,457
Tot. Fed. Rev.	$1,947,637,547	$1,975,862,393	$1,887,694,221	$1,925,205,326	$1,867,231,698	$1,888,388,350	$1,858,226,568	$1,864,121,079	$1,920,091,556
Tot. Loc. Rev.	$10,644,994,979	$10,219,619,555	$9,544,980,211	$9,078,707,246	$8,756,084,878	$8,398,327,339	$8,111,683,409	$8,008,602,668	$8,166,228,905
Tot. Stat. Rev.	$11,234,259,226	$10,365,335,031	$10,051,396,015	$9,439,804,455	$8,993,751,655	$8,485,439,552	$7,918,497,451	$7,620,091,826	$7,533,980,009
Tot. Rev.	$23,826,891,752	$22,560,816,979	$21,484,070,447	$20,443,717,027	$19,617,068,231	$18,772,155,241	$17,888,407,428	$17,492,815,573	$17,620,300,470

Note: U.S. Department of Education, National Center for Education Statistics, Common Core of Data (CCD), State Nonfiscal Public Elementary/Secondary Education Survey.
United States Department of Education, National Center for Education Statistics, Common Core of Data (CCD), "State Nonfiscal Public Elementary/Secondary Education Survey," Access November 22, 2022 https://nces.ed.gov/ccd/elsi/tableGenerator.aspx.

able buyer would pay for the property and a willing seller would accept for the property at an arm's length, bona fide sale," (*see* GA Code 48-5-2).

Trends Over Time

Georgia's revenue allocations in all three major categories, Local, State, and Federal have increased year to year. The local share of revenue per-pupil has increased from $4,846 in 2012 to $6,015 in 2020. Concurrently the state share of per-pupil revenue has increased from $4,471 in 2012 to $6,348 in 2020. Invariably the change has supported the decrease in federal funding during this time. From Table 10.3 we see the federal share of revenue was $1,140 in 2012 and decreased to $1,101 in 2020. Georgia's districts have seen an increase in total revenue from all sources as well, from $10,457 in 2012 to $13,464 in 2020. Table 10.3 also presents information related to the aggregate increases in overall revenue in the three major categories. While aggregate revenue is important, per-pupil revenue provides the most salient information for comparisons. One note, Georgia as a whole has increased its total revenue availability for education from $17,620,300,470 in 2012 to $23,826,891,752. This is a $6,206,591,282 approximately 35% in aggregate revenue increases.

DISTRIBUTION FORMULA

One of the fundamental challenges associated with educating Georgia's students are the resources necessary for every child to meet the learning standards set by Georgia state policy. The major mechanism to fund student in Georgia is the Quality Basic Education (QBE) school formula. The QBE was passed in 1985 through Georgia's The Quality Basic Education (QBE) act.[42] The Quality Basic Education Act (QBE), provides the framework for funding schools as it relates to GA Code § 20-2-161. The purpose of the QBE is to provide all students an equitable public education including access to the necessary resources that ensures all students have an opportunity to participate in a quality program of instruction (GA CODE § 20-2-131). The current QBE formula includes Direct Instructional Cost that includes salaries, benefits, and materials such as textbooks, travel, and equipment. The QBE also includes Indirect Instructional Costs that include revenue for district and school administration, maintenance and operation, funding for 20 additional days of instruction, any media associated with schools and operations costs. The FY 2022 total QBE allocation is $5,751.10.[43] Historically the QBE is rarely fully funded, and in FY 2022 the Georgia State General Assembly has cut $383,024,889 from the QBE.[44]

There is also equalization association with the QBE distribution. At the local level the QBE requires communities to fund a portion of the education of students through property tax revenue. The local requirement is five mills levied on each community's property tax base. The state calculates levies using an equalization adjustment on the actual property tax value, and all sales, to account for differences in valuation between communities.[45] Recently, Georgia decreased the equalization program by $164 million and capped how much school districts can raise through property taxes.[46] Georgia also funds students through weighted category adjustments. Table 10.4 provides an overview of the current weights as reported by the Georgia Department of Education.

Table 10.5 provides long term expenditure trends for Georgia. While Table 10.3 provided an over view of how much funding is available per-pupil and to the states schools overall, Table 10.5 provide an overview of how much is spent per student. We see from Table 10.5 total per-pupil expenditures have increased from 2012 to 2020, $10,365.00 to $13,146.00. Table 10.5 also shows that the direct share of per-pupil expenditures on instruction have increased as well from $5,734.00 in 2012 to $7,116.00 in 2020. Table 10.5 also shows the aggregate state level expenditures for salaries and benefits. From Table 10.5 we see there are aggregate expenditure increases from 2012 to 2020.

Transportation

The state of Georgia is required by state law to provide transportation for students through their local school districts (GA CODE § 20-2-188). State aid is provided according to a schedule of standard transportation costs and a schedule of variable transportation costs. The FY 2022 budget includes $188 million for

TABLE 10.4.   Student Weights by Category

Program	Weight
Kindergarten	1.6719
Grades 1-3	1.2945
Grades 4-5	1.0389
Grades 6-8	1.1378
Grades 9-12	1.0000
Kindergarten Early Intervention Program (EIP)	2.0670
Grades 1-3 EIP	1.8174
Grades 4-5 EIP	1.8119
Gifted Education	1.6790
Remedial Education	1.3573
CTAE (Voc. Lab)	1.1832
SPED Funding Level I	2.411
SPED Funding Level II	2.8390
SPED Funding Level III	3.6173
SPED Funding Level IV	5.8684
SPED Funding Level V	2.4733

Note: All category weights provided by the Georgia Department of Education file:///Users/davidgmartinez/Desktop/Georgia%20 Chapter/FY2022%20FTE%20Categories%20and%20Weights.pdf

TABLE 10.5. Expenditures 2012-2020

Expenditures	2020	2019	2018	2017	2016	2015	2014	2013	2012
Inst. Exp. PP	$7,116.00	$6,767.00	$6,558.00	$6,269.00	$6,084.00	$5,855.00	$5,659.00	$5,656.00	$5,734.00
Tot. Exp. PP	$13,146.00	$12,571.00	$12,061.00	$11,531.00	$11,015.00	$10,692.00	$10,334.00	$10,235.00	$10,365.00
Debt Serv. Exp.	$883,548,914	$749,461,113	$864,680,656	$858,920,299	$804,556,893	$831,515,274	$917,209,518	$1,043,684,867	$1,142,192,560
Tot. Cap. Out-lay Exp.	$2,305,631,677	$2,149,475,416	$2,006,622,738	$1,959,953,379	$1,842,276,457	$1,880,047,724	$1,650,630,128	$1,633,451,105	$1,566,185,288
Tot. Inst. Exp. (Benefits)	$3,606,884,061	$3,353,485,596	$3,124,257,136	$2,824,023,682	$2,674,847,588	$2,494,344,333	$2,375,341,210	$2,294,936,983	$2,231,870,911
Tot. Inst. Exp. (Salary)	$8,029,858,061	$7,593,628,961	$7,475,744,008	$7,297,730,655	$6,932,397,673	$6,689,670,637	$6,483,312,636	$6,489,862,795	$6,626,114,113

Note: U.S. Department of Education, National Center for Education Statistics, Common Core of Data (CCD), State Nonfiscal Public Elementary/Secondary Education Survey.

United States Department of Education, National Center for Education Statistics, Common Core of Data (CCD), "State Nonfiscal Public Elementary/Secondary Education Survey," Access November 22, 2022 https://nces.ed.gov/ccd/elsi/tableGenerator.aspx.

the Department of Education to updated 1,747 school buses with safer models. The Georgia budget for busses has declined from 54% of the cost of education in 1991 to 16% in 2020.[47] Georgia was also recently awarded a $51.1 million Federal Grant to purchase electric school buses. This funding is allocated through the United States Environmental Protection Agency.

Retirement

Georgia has a robust teacher retirement system. The Teachers' Retirement System (TRS) is the retirement fund for public school teachers, state university employees, and others in educational environments.[48] The TRS was established in 1943 by the state legislature to provide retirement security for educator. The TRS is funded through both individual and employer contributions, 6% and 19.81% respectively.

CAPITAL OUTLAY AND DEBT SERVICE

Georgia funds capital outlay through several mechanisms. The first is a capital outlay program which all local educational agencies (LEA) can use, the second is a low wealth capital outlay funding system, and the third is an advanced capital outlay funding program. The capital outlay allocation is determined through student FTE, a five-year projection of student FTE, and the needs of the LEA.[49] Furthermore, an LEAs share of capital outlay funding is computed by multiplying the annual authorization level by the ratio of the local need to the total state need as determined by the Local Facilities Plans (LFP). The local LEA board is then responsible to apply for funding with the following criteria as quoted from 160-5-4-.03 Applications for State Capital Outlay Funding:

1. The proposed facilities improvements coordinated with the instructional program as outlined in the LFP.
2. Cost estimates adjusted to current construction costs as necessary.
3. The instructional and support space needs for each facility priority.
4. The estimated construction start date.[50]

All LEAs nationally also account for their debt service. In general debt service revenue is restricted, committed, or assigned for the payment of general long-term debt. Table 10.5 provides the long-term trend of capital outlay expenditures and debt service. From Table 10.5 we see that debt has decreased from 2012, $1,142,192,560, to 2020, $883,548,914. Local reduction of debt allows for school districts to operate with greater amounts of revenue that is not previously earmarked. Table 10.5 also shows that capital outlay funding has increased from 2012 to 2020, $1,566,185,288 to $2,305,631,677 respectively.

CHARTER SCHOOL FUNDING

Georgia currently has a burgeoning charter network that has now reached approximately 43 schools which serve 38,000 students. Georgia's first authorized charter school was instituted in 1993 and Georgia's charter school law was amended in 1998, expanding school choice across the state.[51] Georgia's Charter Schools Act (1998), O.C.G.A. § 20-2-2060, established Georgia's Charter school program. Subsequently the Charter School Commission who authorizes all state charter schools in accordance with Article 31A of O.C.G.A. Title 20 was established in 2012 through House Bill 797 via constitutional mandate.

Charter school revenue is allocated through the QBE formula, outlined above, and is supplemented through State Charter School Supplement (SCSS) funding. House Bill 787 (2018) established the SCSS to offset any revenue disparities between Georgia's charters schools and traditional public schools (TPS). Since Georgia charter schools are ineligible to receive funding from local tax levies, the Georgia State Legislature passed House Bill 787 (2018). House Bill 910 (2021), the Georgia State Congressional House reconciliation bill, included $93 million in QBE adjustments to fund the states estimated 11,926 student increase in charter school enrollment.[52] This reflected an approximately 69% increase from FY 2021. House Bill 910 also includes $233,602 in grants to fund charter school expansion and $14.6 million to offset the cost of two new charter schools. This bill also included $3.2 million in funding for the Special Needs Scholarship. In 2007 Georgia established a school voucher program, the Special Needs Scholarship, through O.C.G.A. §§ 20-2:2110-2118. This program enables parents of a student with disabilities to receive a voucher which offsets the cost of attending a private school.[53]

The charter school movement in Georgia has continued to expand and in October of 2022 received $38,295,000 through the U.S. Department of Education Charter Schools Program (CSP) State Entity grant competition.[54] has awarded a grant of $38,295,000 through the FY22 Charter Schools Program (CSP) State Entity grant competition to the State Charter Schools Foundation of Georgia (SCSF) to support the creation, replication, and expansion of high-quality charter schools throughout Georgia. The Georgia Governor Brian Kemp also allocated $4.1 million to the Georgia Strategic Charter School Growth Initiative earmarked for charter school expansion including grants to support high quality Georgia charter schools.[55] Finally, the Georgia State Legislature passed House Bill 1215 (2022) which strengthened the policy that supports charter schools. House Bill 1215 discretely requires TPS to provide more exact budget calculations to fund charter schools as equitably as possible through the charter funding mechanisms, the bill allows for transfers from TPS to charters after the start of the school year, it strengthens the language of charter schools to include most school choice models, and it removes performance audits from virtual state charters. In total, these policy language changes, and increases in funding, help to continue the expansion of charter schools in Georgia.[56]

FEDERAL COVID-19 FUNDING

The COVID-19 pandemic forced many states to contend with a myriad of complications. Part of the pandemic was the reality that schools provide a great deal of services to a large part of the Georgia community almost daily, and that these services are difficult to maintain given the realities of budgeting and the available funding. The United States Federal Government to support all states passed legislation to mediate the complications associated with the pandemic. Georgia received $457,169,852 in ESSER I funds through the Coronavirus Aid, Relief & Economic Security (CARES) Act, $1,892,092,618 in ESSER II funds through the Coronavirus Response & Relief Supplemental Appropriations (CRRSA) Act, and $4,252,431,691 in ESSER III funds through the American Rescue Plan (ARP) Act.[57] In total approximately $6 billion was approved to support Georgia's schools.[58] Recently, the Georgia Partnership for Excellence in Education (GPEE) published a report outlining how districts were spending their funds.[59] The report outlines the top areas of concern for LEAs including, IT & Infrastructure including software, staffing challenges including incentive to recruit and retain staff, summer learning programs. The average per-pupil allocation of ESSER funding is $3,450. Nationally there is growing concern about the school level staffing challenges most districts now face. ESSER funds were used to address these challenges, and to maintain the operation of schools.[60]

ENDNOTES

[1] Kilpatrick, William H. "The Beginnings of the Public School System in Georgia." The Georgia Historical Quarterly 5, no. 3 (1921): 3-19.

[2] Yale Law school, "Constitution of Georgia; February 5, 1777," The Avalon Project, Yale University, accessed November 22, 2022, https://avalon.law.yale.edu/18th_century/ga02.asp.

[3] Kilpatrick, William H. "The Beginnings of the Public School System in Georgia." The Georgia Historical Quarterly 5, no. 3 (1921): 3-19.

[4] Walker, Eugene. "The History of Georgia Public Schools." Accessed November 22, 2022, https://www.columbusstate.edu/archives/_docs/gah/1991/01-17.pdf.

[5] Kilpatrick, William H. "The Beginnings of the Public School System in Georgia." The Georgia Historical Quarterly 5, no. 3 (1921): 3-19.

[6] United States Department of the Interior National Park Service, "Public Elementary and Secondary Schools in Georgia, 1868-1971," accessed November 22, 2022 https://www.dca.ga.gov/sites/default/files/historicschools.pdf.

[7] Id.

[8] Christopher, Brown M., and Lisa Delpit. The politics of curricular change: Race, hegemony, and power in education. Vol. 131. Peter Lang, 2005.

[9] Id.

[10] Johnson, Whittington B. "Free African-American women in Savannah, 1800-1860: Affluence and autonomy amid adversity." The Georgia Historical Quarterly 76, no. 2 (1992): 260-283; Georgia Historical Society, "Educator of Slave Children," Access November 22, 2022, https://georgiahistory.com/education-outreach/online-exhibits/featured-historical-figures/mother-mathilda-beasley/educator-of-slave-children/.

[11] Kilpatrick, William H. "The Beginnings of the Public School System in Georgia." The Georgia Historical Quarterly 5, no. 3 (1921): 3-19.

[12] Georgia Constitution. Title XII, Article V, Section 1300. "The Beneficiaries of the Educational Fund." Access November 22, 2022, https://digitalcommons.law.uga.edu/ga_code/10/.

[13] United States Department of the Interior National Park Service, "Public Elementary and Secondary Schools in Georgia, 1868-1971," accessed November 22, 2022 https://www.dca.ga.gov/sites/default/files/historicschools.pdf.

[14] Id.

[15] Id.

[16] Valien, P. (1955). The Desegregation Decision—One Year Afterward—A Critical Summary. The Journal of Negro Education, 24(3), 388-396; Brown v. Board of Education of Topeka, 347 U.S. 483 (1954)

[17] Georgia Constitution. Article VIII, Section I, paragraph I. "Public Education." Access November 22, 2022, https://law.justia.com/constitution/georgia/conart8.html.

[18] Georgia Constitution. Article VIII, Section V, paragraph I. "Local School Systems." Access November 22, 2022, https://law.justia.com/constitution/georgia/conart8.html.

[19] Georgia Constitution. Article VIII, Section V, paragraph II. "Local School Systems." Access November 22, 2022, https://law.justia.com/constitution/georgia/conart8.html.

[20] State of Georgia, "Title 20. Education," accessed November 28, 2022, http://ga.elaws.us/law/20.

[21] Georgia Department of Education, "Learning Standards Framework Index," accessed November 22, 2022, https://case.georgiastandards.org.

[22] Georgia Department of Education, "Quick Facts About Georgia Public Education 2021-22," accessed November 22, 2022, https://www.gadoe.org/External-Affairs-and-Policy/communications/Documents/Quick%20Facts%202021-2022.pdf.

[23] Id.

[24] Id.

[25] Georgia Department of Education, "Quick Facts About Georgia Public Education 2021-22," accessed November 22, 2022, https://www.gadoe.org/External-Affairs-and-Policy/communications/Documents/Quick%20Facts%202021-2022.pdf.

[26] Georgia Department of Education, "Teacher Salaries," access November 22, 2022 https://www.gadoe.org/Finance-and-Business-Operations/Budget-Services/Pages/default.aspx.

[27] Georgia House of Representatives, "Representatives," access November 22, 2022 https://www.legis.ga.gov/members/house.

[28] Georgia House of Representatives, "Office of the Speaker, " access November 22, 2022 https://www.legis.ga.gov/house/speaker.

[29] Balletopia, "Georgia State Senate," access November 22, 2022 https://ballotpedia.org/Georgia_State_Senate.

[30] United States House of Representatives, "List of Representatives," access November 22, 2022 https://www.house.gov/representatives#state-georgia.

[31] United States Senate, "States in the Senate|Georgia," access November 22, 2022 https://www.senate.gov/states/GA/intro.htm.

[32] Governor's Office of Planning and Budget, "The Budget Process," access November 22, 2022 https://opb.georgia.gov/budget-information/budget-process.

[33] Governor's Office of Planning and Budget, "Governor's Budget Reports," access November 22, 2022 https://opb.georgia.gov/budget-information/budget-documents/governors-budget-reports.

[34] Alexander, M. David, Mary Jane Connelly, and Richard G. Salmon. "An update in public school finance litigation." journal of education finance 10, no. 2 (1984): 135-149.

[35] Shuls, James V. "Financing school choice: How program design impacts issues regarding legality and equity." Kan. JL & Pub. Pol'y 27 (2017): 500.

[36] United States Department of Agriculture, "USDA Promotes Program Access, Combats Discrimination Against LGBTQI+ Community," access November 22, 2022 https://www.usda.gov/media/press-releases/2022/05/05/usda-promotes-program-access-combats-discrimination-against-lgbtqi.

[37] Dekalb Agriculture Technology & Environment, Inc. et al. v. DeKalb County School District et al. Civil Action File No.: 2020CV339543 . Access November 22, 2022, https://mcusercontent.

com/0bda5d5147ca0c51e1c30107f/files/a851f8d3-1f08-01b3-ddde-68131b01e403/Order.Baxter_signed102022_.pdf.

38 Governor's Office of Planning and Budget, "Governor's Budget Reports," access November 22, 2022 https://opb.georgia.gov/budget-information/budget-documents/governors-budget-reports.

39 Georgia Budget and Policy Institute, "Georgia Revenue Primer for State Fiscal Year 2022," access November 22, 2022 https://gbpi.org/georgia-revenue-primer-for-state-fiscal-year-2022/.

40 Georgia Constitution. Article VIII, Section VI, paragraph I. "Local taxation for education." Access November 22, 2022, https://law.justia.com/constitution/georgia/conart8.html.

41 Georgia Constitution. Article VIII, Section VI, paragraph IV. "Sales tax for educational purposes." Access November 22, 2022, https://law.justia.com/constitution/georgia/conart8.html.

42 Georgia General Assembly, "Quality Basic Education Act: Enacted," access November 22, 2022, https://readingroom.law.gsu.edu/cgi/viewcontent.cgi?article=2569&context=gsulr.

43 Georgia Budget and Policy Institute, "Georgia Revenue Primer for State Fiscal Year 2022," access November 22, 2022 https://gbpi.org/georgia-revenue-primer-for-state-fiscal-year-2022/.

44 Id.

45 Davis, Elton, and Isabel Ruthotto. "Financing Georgia's Schools." (2019).

46 Georgia Budget and Policy Institute, "Georgia Education Budget Primer for State Fiscal Year 2023," access November 22, 2022 https://gbpi.org/georgia-education-budget-primer-for-state-fiscal-year-2023/.

47 Georgia Budget and Policy Institute, "Overview of Georgia's 2023 Fiscal Year Budget," access November 22, 2022, https://gbpi.org/overview-of-georgias-2023-fiscal-year-budget/.

48 https://www.trsga.com

49 Rules and Regulations of the State of Georgia, "School Facilities and Capital Outlay Management," access November 22, https://rules.sos.ga.gov/gac/160-5-4.

50 Id.

51 Georgia Department of Education, "2020 Georgia's Charter School Program," accessed November 22, 2022 https://www.gadoe.org/External-Affairs-and-Policy/Charter-Schools/Documents/2020%20Charter%20Schools%20Annual%20Report%20-%20FINAL.pdf?csf=1&e=erlTkU.

52 House Bill 910, "Amended Fiscal Year 2022 State Budget," access November 22, 2022, https://www.legis.ga.gov/api/document/docs/default-source/house-budget-and-research-office-document-library/newsandhighlights/2022/amended_fy_2022_budget_highlights_house_version.pdf?sfvrsn=67c95538_2.

53 EdChoice, "Georgia Special Needs Scholarship Program," access November 22, 2022 https://www.edchoice.org/school-choice/programs/georgia-special-needs-scholarship-program/.

54 Office of Elementary and Secondary Education, "Awards," access November 22, 2022 https://oese.ed.gov/offices/office-of-discretionary-grants-support-services/charter-school-programs/state-entities/awards/.

55 State Charter Schools Commission of Georgia, "High-Quality Georgia Charter Schools to Receive Support to Serve More Students," access November 22, 2022 https://scsc.georgia.gov/press-releases/2022-09-09/high-quality-georgia-charter-schools-receive-support-serve-more-students.

56 House Bill 1215, "HB 1215 Education; provision that reduced the amount of certain funding to state charter schools that offer virtual instruction; remove," access November 22, 2022 https://www.legis.ga.gov/legislation/61771.

57 GeorgiaInsights, "Elementary and Secondary School Emergency Relief," access November 22, 2022, https://www.georgiainsights.com/cares-act.html.

58 GeorgiaInsights, "Dashboard," access November 22, 2022, https://www.georgiainsights.com/esser-budget.html.

59 Georgia Partnership for Excellence in Education (GPEE), "2022 CARES Impact Study Year One," access November 22, 2022, https://gpee.wpenginepowered.com/wp-content/uploads/2022/11/CARES-Impact-Study-Year-One-Report-Final.pdf.

60 Id.

CHAPTER 11

HAWAI'I

Brenda Mendiola
The University of Alabama

GENERAL BACKGROUND

Hawai'i's educational history and operation is unique among the 50 states. As the last state to join the Union in 1959, Hawai'i is the only state in the nation comprised of a single school district. After serving as the interim superintendent, Keith Hayashi, former principal, was recently appointed by the Board of Education to serve as the superintendent. Hayashi is tasked with helping "the school system out of the pandemic." [1]

The constitution[2] of the state of Hawai'i specifically provides for public education. Article 10 §1 says:

> The State shall provide for the establishment, support, and control of a statewide system of public schools free from sectarian control, a state university, public libraries, and such other educational institutions as may be deemed desirable, including physical facilities therefor.

Hawai'i is also unique in that property taxes form no part of its true school funding base, making funding for schools almost entirely reliant on the state legislature. As a result, the state's single school district has no independent tax au-

Funding Public Schools in the United States, Indian Country,
and US Territories (Second Edition), pages 187–198.
Copyright © 2023 by Information Age Publishing
www.infoagepub.com

thority. Fiscal support for public schools comes from the state's general fund—a source primarily characterizable as funded by general excise taxes, personal income taxes, corporate income taxes, and other special taxes on use and consumption. [3] Hawai'i's basic school fiscal support program entails a $2 billion budget that is expected to swell to more than $3 billion for FY 2023 funded by state, federal, trust fund, and special fund sources (see Table 11.1 later).

In total, Hawai'i's school funding system currently supports about 172,000 students across 294 schools (including 37 charters), 15 complex areas, and the state office.[4] Nearly all appropriated funds go to schools, with monies distributed by program categories known as EDNs.[5] In 2004, the state engaged in sweeping school system redesign. Act 51[6] provided reforms in 13 areas, chief among which was establishment of a new weighted student formula meant to reflect the costs of educational needs.

CURRENT POLITICAL CLIMATE

Legislative Makeup

Hawai'i State Legislature has 25 members in the Senate (1 Republican, 2 Democrats) each serving a four-year term and 51 members in the House of Representatives (4 Republicans, 47 Democrats) each serving a two-year term. The Senate is led by the Senate President, Democrat, Ron Kouchi, and the House of Representatives is led by the Speaker of the House, Democrat, Scott K. Saiki. Led by the Democratic Governor David Ige, Hawai'i is a solidly blue state.

Ige has served the state since 2014 and is nearing the end of his two-term limit.[7] The Governor presents the education budget to the legislature in January biannually with input received from the Board of Education in October. The Legislature works from January to May to finalize the budget with appropriations made in June and allocations in July. Hawai'i runs the entire state's budget on a biennium with a supplemental budget in the alternating years. The current biennium is comprised of the budgetary years July 1, 2021- June 30, 2023.

Union Representation and Engagement

Teachers are represented by the Hawai'i State Teachers Association (HSTA) formally incorporated in 1971. HSTA, a state affiliate of the National Education Association, serves the teachers as a collective bargaining agent working to improve not only pay and benefits for teachers, but working conditions and the professionalization of teaching.[8] The full agreement for the 2021-2023 biennium is more than 100 pages and covers in detail everything from duty free lunch period to fund raising.[9] A grassroots organization, Hawai'i Children's Action Network, is a non-profit group advocating for children by promoting access to affordable child-care and housing, paid family leave, and educational issues. [10]

School Finance Litigation

Hawai'i is among those rare states never having experienced school finance litigation. A major reason for such uniqueness is that Hawai'i is the only state in the nation to have only one school district within its borders, making inter-district fiscal equity a moot point. Since traditional school finance equity is not a topic for dispute in Hawai'i apart from intra-system equity, only issues of adequate funding remain as a point of contention.

Enrollment Trends

As was true of many schools in the United States, enrollment in Hawai'i public schools decreased during Covid. The estimate in September of 2021 was a decline of over 3,000 students or about 2%. Both public and charter schools experienced decreases. Enrollment has been steadily declining since 2013-2014 with losses estimated at close to 14,000.[11]

SOURCES OF REVENUE

With no property tax funds levied and with no option to levy taxes to fund education, public schools in Hawai'i rely on the general fund for support. Taxing sources include the General Excise Tax, Personal Income Tax, Corporate income Tax, Accommodation Tax, and a variety of special taxes as shown in Table 11.1. The state's general fund is the largest source of funding for Hawai'i schools with federal funds the second largest funding source. Federal funds are awarded through agencies including the US. Departments of Education, Agriculture, Defense and Health and Human Services.

TABLE 11.1. Sources of Funding FY 2022

Fund	Amount
General Fund	1,681,818,084
Special Fund	51,279,167
Federal Fund	283,849,620
Other Federal Fund	9,553,793
Private Contribution	150,000
Trust Fund	15,650,000
Interdepartmental Transfer	7,495,605
Revolving Fund	25,741,082
	$2,075,537,351

Source: https://www.hawaiipublicschools.org/DOE%20
Forms/budget/FY2022-Operating-Budget-Appropriation-
Summary.pdf

TABLE 11.2. Appropriation Summary FY 2022 Budget Summary of All Funds

EDN Fund	Amount
EDN 100: School Based Budgeting	$1,204,200,989
EDN 150: Special Education	$461,635,302
EDN 200: Instructional Support	$64,119,107
EDN 300: State Administration	$41,213,123
EDN 400: School Support	$274,060,744
EDN 500: School Community Services	$23,109,420
EDN 700: Early Learning	$7,198,665
Total Operating Budget	$2,075,537,351

Source: https://www.hawaiipublicschools.org/DOE%20Forms/budget/
FY2022-Operating-Budget-Appropriation-Summary.pdf

Special funds make up a small percentage of the overall budget with revenue derived from activities such as diver education, summer school programs, after-school program, school food services, and adult education. Trust fund allocations may come from gifts, donations, grants, foundations, athletic program activities and the like. State funds, along with federal funds, are appropriated by the state legislature. With so much of the funding coming from taxes, fluctuations in the economy—and in tourism which feeds the economy—lead to unpredictability.

Funds are appropriated by the Legislature by program category as shown in Table 11.2. The funds are distributed to the schools using the weighted school formula (WSF) detailed in Table 11.3. Most of the EDN 100 School Based Budgeting funds come from the WSF formula. Special education students with IEPs are supported through EDN150. School bills such as sewer, water, and electric are included in EDN 400 and EDN 500 pays for Adult Education programs offered through public schools. Public school Pre-K programs are under the jurisdiction of the Executive Office of Early Learning and paid through EDN 700. Other school supports such as the superintendent's office, Board of Education, testing, community programs, and other instructional supports, to name a few, are included in EDN 200 and 300.

TRENDS

After two years of decreases and shortfalls[12], Hawai'i is poised to more than double general fund operating appropriations from $1.61 billion in 2018 to $328.5 billion in 2023. This includes restoring $114.4 million in COVID-19 related reductions, $49 million to address budget shortfalls that existed before the pandemic, $165.5 million in additional resources for advancing education through the funding of new initiatives such as teacher salary compression, grow your own

TABLE 11.3.   FY 2022-23 Tentative WSF Allocations

WSF Tentative Allocation Calculation (based on FY2022-23 Preliminary Appropriation and Projected Enrollment)

	Total Projected Enrollment	Weighting Factor	Weighted Projected Enrollment	$ per Student	Total Allocation
Pe-K (SpEd)	1,549	1.000	1,549.00	$4,720.45	$ 7,311,977
K-2	36,620	1.000	36,620.00	$4,720.45	$ 172,862,873
Other Elem	43,370	1.000	43,370.00	$4,720.45	$ 204,725,910
Middle	29,138	1.000	29,138.00	$4,720.45	$ 137,544,468
High	50,534	1.000	50,534.00	$4,720.45	$ 238,543,213
Subtotal	161,211		161,211.00		$ 760,988,440
Student Characteristics					
Grade Level Adjustment					
Middle	29,138	0.032	925.91	$150.00	$ 4,370,700
K-2 Class Size	36,620	0.150	5,493.00	$708.87	$ 25,929,431
English Language Learners (Aggregate)	18,864	0.065	129.52	$305.89	$ 21,165,745
Fully English Proficient (FEP)	1,999	0.065	129.52	$305.89	$ 611,396
Limited English Proficiency (LEP)	11,332	0.194	2,202.88	$917.66	$ 10,398,582
Non-English Proficient (NEP)	5,534	0.389	2,151.44	$1,835.31	$ 10,155,767
Economically Disadvantaged	81,859	0.100	8,185.90	$472.04	$ 38,641,130
Gifted & Talented	4,766	0.265	1,263.00	$1,250.92	$ 5,961,931
Transiency	5,586	0.050	279.28	$236.02	$ 1,318,326
Subtotal			20,630.93		$ 97,387,264
School Characteristics					
Neighbor Island	52,241	0.008	417.93	$37.76	$1,972,808
Subtotal			417.93		$1,972,808
Total Weighted Allocation	161,211		182,259.86		$860,348,512

Non-Weighted School Characteristics Base Funding-per school based on school type

	#Schools				Total Allocation
					$ 94,233,300
Elem	167	$307,000			$ 51,269,000
Elem-Multi-Track	1	$402,000			$ 402,000
Middle	39	$461,000			$ 17,979,000
Middle-Multi-Track	0	$556,000			
High	34	$472,000			$ 16,048,000
Combination					
K-12	5	$750,000			$ 3,750,000
K-8	4	$525,000			$ 2,100,000
6-12	5	$537,000			$ 2,685,000
Subtotal	255				$ 94,233,000

TOTAL WSF FUNDS AVAILABLE FOR TENTATIVE ENROLLMENT ALLOCATION $ 954,581,512

Source: https://www.hawaiipublicschools.org/Reports/FY23WSFWeighting.pdf

teachers, menstrual products, hatchery program, Papahana 'o Kaiona, workforce development coordinators, and office facilities and operations.[13]

Weighted Student Formula

Most state funds are distributed to Hawai'i's individual schools through the Weighted Student Formula (WSF). The WSF was enacted for the first time in 2006-2007 to promote more equitable school funding. The WSF ties money to pupils' educational needs through a system of program weights. Weights are based on (1) student characteristics, (2) school characteristics, and (3) a non-weighted lump sum. Table 11.3 shows tentative WSF calculations for FY 2022-23. It is important to note that projected allocations are tentative and are subject to change based on the official enrollment count taken in August of 2022 and on the final appropriations to the WSF.

Committee on Weights

The actual weights applied in the WSF are established and evaluated by a Committee on Weights (COW) made up of educators, administrators and community members and is approved by the Board of Education. Pupil counts related to weights are conducted three times annually.

Student Characteristics

Student characteristics are those typically associated with vertical equity considerations in school finance, including primary grades (K-2); English Language Learner (including breakouts of Fully English Proficient, Limited English Proficient, and Non-English Proficient); Economically Disadvantaged; Transiency; Gifted and Talented, and Grade Levels. Dollars follow individual students.

School Characteristics

School characteristics relate to Multi-track and Neighbor Island variables.

Non-weighted Lump Sum

The non-weighted lump sum is based on school type such as elementary, middle/high, and combinations.[14]

CAPITAL OUTLAY AND DEBT SERVICE

Capital Improvements Program Budget

Capital improvements is part of the basic support program for public schools in Hawai'i. The state heavily supports the Capital Improvements Program (CIP), funding it at nearly 100%. The CIP budget is set by the state as part of a comprehensive program to manage all state facilities. The CIP includes development and improvements, renovation, repair and major maintenance to facilities, landscaping, new construction, land acquisition, and utility modifications.

- *Condition:* including maintenance and repair, technology infrastructure, hazardous materials, health, and safety, and structural improvements;
- *Program Support:* gender equity, restrooms, ADA compliance, support program spaces, and playgrounds;
- *Capacity:* new facilities and additions, temporary facilities, repurposing for capacity;
- *Equity:* science spaces, special education, energy, right-sizing, physical education, abatements.

Table 11.4 reveals the scope and amount of CIP support at the HIDOE as presented to the state legislature. As in all appropriations for entire state govern-

TABLE 11.4 CIP Budget Requests and Appropriations FY 2020 Biennium and FY 2021 Supplemental (in millions)

	FY 2020 (Biennium Budget)		FY 2021 (Supplemental Budget)	
	REQUESTED	**APPROVED**	**REQUESTED**	**APPROVED**
Capacity	$252	0	$252	$0
Repair & Maintenance	$175	$110.7	$175	$110.7
Health & Safety	$36.9	$10	$38	0
Compliance	$27.7	$5	$14.4	0
Instructional	$156.1	0	$156.1	0
Innovation	$1	0	$1	0
Support	$45.5	0	$45.5	0
Equipment	$4.2	0	$4.2	0
Project Completion	$30	$38	$30	$38
Technology Infrastructure	$9.1	$8.5	$3	$2.5
TOTAL	$737.5			
	$178.7	$719.2	$150.5	
Legislative Add-Ons	n/a	$294.7	n/a	$52.7
Mokapu Elementary	n/a	$92.5	n/a	
n/a				
Renovation of Pre-K Classrooms	$14.3	$6.5	n/a	n/a
TOTAL	$751.8	$565.9	$719.2	$203.2

Source: https://www.hawaiipublicschools.org/ConnectWithUs/Organization/Budget/Pages/cip-budget.aspx

ments' resource competition, Table 11.4 identifies the consonance and dissonance between agency requests and legislative enactment.[15]

EMPLOYEE BENEFITS

Healthcare

Employees are eligible for health benefits through the Employer-Union Health Benefits Trust Fund (EUTF). Group life insurance is provided at no charge for employees enrolled in the EUTF. The plan includes PPO and HMO medical options and options for drug, dental, and vision coverage. Both the employee and employer contribute to the cost of coverage. The Hawai'i State Teachers Association is active in negotiating health care costs and benefits for school employees.[16]

Retirement

Hawai'i operates the Employee Retirement System[17] (ERS) containing contributory, non-contributory, and hybrid plans. [18]

Contributory Plan

Employees hired after July 1, 1945, through June 30, 1984, are members of the Employee Retirement System (ERS) contributory plan. Employees in this group contribute 7.8% of gross monthly salary to the ERS. On resignation, employees with less than five years of service must within four years of date of resignation withdraw contributions made to the retirement fund. Employees in this plan may retire at age 55 with a minimum of five years' service or with 25 years of service regardless of age. Benefits calculation is expressed as 2% x *Service x Average Final Compensation* (AFC).

Non-Contributory Plan

Employees hired July 1, 1984, through June 30, 2006, are members of the ERS non-contributory plan. Employees make no contributions to the ERS. Employees in this plan are eligible to retire at age 62 with a minimum 10 years' service or at age 55 with a minimum 20 years of service. Normal retirement benefit is calculated as *1.25% x Years of Credited Service x AFC.*

Hybrid Plan

Employees hired on or after July 1, 2006, through June 30, 2012, are members of the ERS hybrid plan. Members of the contributory and noncontributory retirement plans were provided with the option to join the new hybrid plan or to remain in a current plan. Employees contribute 6% of gross monthly salary to the ERS. Normal retirement benefit is calculated as *2% x Years of Credited Hybrid Service x AFC.*

On June 23, 2011, the governor signed into law Act 163.[19] The new law provided for retirement benefit changes under the hybrid plan for employees who became members of the ERS after June 30, 2012. Employees hired on or after July 1, 2012, became eligible to retire at age 65 with a minimum of 10 years of service or at age 60 with a minimum 30 years of service.

Other Benefits

Hawai'i education employees may also participate in a 403(b) Tax Shelter Annuity program, a voluntary pre-tax retirement savings plan, flexible spending accounts (medical, dependent care), HI529 College Savings Program, and Flex Park for parking fee deduction from pre-tax earnings. Education employees receive along incentive awards for retirement and service. [20]

CHARTER SCHOOL FUNDING

Hawai'i's 37 public charter schools are run by independent governing boards operating under performance contracts with the State Public Charter School Commission.[21] Proposals for four additional charter schools will be heard in May of 2022. In Hawai'i, charter schools are public schools, funded on a per-pupil allocation separate from the Department of Education.

Funding for charter schools in Hawai'i should be carefully parsed to provide accurate comparison to traditional public schools. The best parsing explanation is found in statute as footnoted below.[22] In general, the Hawai'i Department of Education cautions that comparisons should be made based on recognizing that reporting differences in fiscal data can produce inaccurate comparisons that give the appearance of substantial differences in per-pupil funding between traditional and charter schools.

NONPUBLIC SCHOOL FUNDING

As is the case for any state education agency receiving federal funds, the Hawai'i Department of Education (HIDOE) has a process for ensuring that equitable services are provided for private school children, teachers, and other educational personnel. Equitable services apply to Title I Parts A and C, Title II Part C, Title III Part A, and Title IV Parts A and B. The Coronavirus Aid, Relief, and Economic Security (CARES) Act also required HIDOE to provide equitable emergency services to participating private schools.[23]

VIRTUAL EDUCATION

Online courses are offered in Hawai'i through the Hawai'i Virtual Learning Network (HVLN) implemented through the Office of Curriculum and Instruction. In addition to virtual courses, HVLN provides professional development to teachers, and provides schools with technology integration and consulting services.

TABLE 11.5 Federal COVID-19 Funding Allocated and Remaining

CARES ACT Grant Title	Allocated $ in millions	Remaining Balance $ in millions	Lapse Date
ESSER I *(CARES)	43.385,229	9,879,877	9/30/2022
ESSER II **(CRRSA)	183,595,211	73,060,264	9/30/2023
ESSER III ***(ARP)	412,530,212	136,537,943	9/30/2024
	639,510,652	153,723,844	

Source: https://www.hawaiipublicschools.org/DOE%20Forms/budget/CARES/CARES-budget-summary-may-2022.pdf
*Coronavirus Aid, Relief and Economics Security Act (CARES)
**Coronavirus Response and Relief Supplemental Appropriation (CRRSA)
***American Rescue Plan (ARP)

Courses offered through HVLN are considered as supplementary and enrollment in a regular education program (including charter schools) is required. Courses are taught by state-certified teachers and are aligned with state standards. Offered at no cost to students, enrollment is limited to two courses per semester for students in grades 6-12. Primary school students are enrolled by the School Site Facilitator. [24]

FEDERAL COVID-19 FUNDING

As shown in Table 11.5, more than $639,000,000 has been allocated to HIDOE with almost 25% of the funds remaining as unallocated. Not included in the table is the CARES Act Grant Coronavirus Relief (CR) award of $47,100,000 that lapsed December 31, 2021. All grants of the $47,100,000 allocated was spent— primarily on distance learning equipment. The largest award, ESSER III, over 400 million, includes appropriations for health and safety, social emotional learning, accelerated learning and a myriad of other appropriations to offset projected shortfalls and to keep programs going. Almost half of the unspent funds under ESSER III are in the category of accelerated learning. Schools also benefited from Governor's Emergency Education Relief (GEER) funding with $2.8 million budgeted for innovation grants in 2022.

CONCLUSION

The structure and governance of the Hawai'i education is unique due to its single school system structure and its reliance on tax revenues driven in part by the state's tourism industry—an industry that suffered severely during the peak of the COVID-19 pandemic. Other natural disasters such as storms, fires, and volcano eruptions also impact tourism. Regardless, the outlook for Hawai'i is good with a strong budget that is focused on recovery, making up for prior year deficits, and new programs. With a new superintendent, and soon a new governor yet to be elected, Hawai'i can expect new plans and initiatives aimed at advancing the five themes in the 2030 promise plan.[25] The themes focus on the Hawaiian culture, Equity, School Design, Empowerment, and Innovation. The challenge comes in making the strategic plan come to life in Hawai'i schools.

ENDNOTES

[1]   Interim schools Superintendent Keith Hayashi selected for the permanent job, May 19, 2022, Retrieved from https://www.hawaiinewsnow.com/2022/05/19/boe-plans-vote-new-schools-super-intendent-following-finalist-interviews/

[2]   Constitution, State of Hawaii. Retrieved from: http://lrbhawaii.org/con/

[3]   Deborah Verstegen, "A Quick Glance at School Finance: A 50 State Survey of School Finance Policies." (2019). Retrieved from: https://schoolfinancesdav.wordpress.com

[4]   Hayashi, K. Fiscal Year 2023 Budget Briefing Testimony. Retrieved from: https://www.capitol.hawaii.gov/session2022/testimony/Info_Testimony_WAM-EDU_01-13-22_EDN.pdf

[5]   EDN= acronym for "Education." A Budget Program Structure Designation for the Department of Education. Retrieved from: http://www.hawaiipublicschools.org/ConnectWithUs/FAQ/Pages/Acronyms.aspx#W

[6]   Act 51: Reinventing Education Act of 2004. SB3238, SD2, HD2, CD1. As amended. Retrieved from: http://www.hawaiipublicschools.org/DOE%20Forms/State%20Reports/Act51.pdf

[7]   Hawaii State Legislature https://www.capitol.hawaii.gov/members/legislators.aspx?chamber=S

[8]   Hawaii State Teachers Association hsta.org

[9]   For the complete HSTA/DOE agreement see https://www.hsta.org/wp-content/uploads/2021/08/HSTA-CBA-2021-2023-Final-2.pdf

[10] Hawaii Children's Action Network: Building a unified voice for Hawai'i's children. Retrieved from: https://www.hawaiican.org

[11] Enrollment at Hawaii's public schools declines for second year in a row as reported by Timothy Hurley, September 2, 2021, Retrieved from: https://www.staradvertiser.com/2021/09/02/hawaii-news/enrollment-at-hawaiis-public-schools-declines-for-second-year-in-a-row/Honolulu StarAdvertiserchoolfinancesdav.wordpress.com

[12] See State of the State report on Hawaii for reference https://www.nationaledfinance.com/docs/10_Jef_47.5_Hawaii.pdf

[13] The General Fund appropriations summary for 2022-2023 is available at https://www.hawaiipublicschools.org/DOE%20Forms/budget/BudgetSummaryFY2023.pdf

[14] State of Hawai'i, Department of Education. "Factsheet: WS/COW: Weighted Student Formula and the Committee on Weights." (2019). Retrieved from: http://www.hawaiipublicschools.org/DOE%20Forms/WSF/WSFCOW.pdf

[15] CIP Budget Information from https://www.hawaiipublicschools.org/ConnectWithUs/Organization/Budget/Pages/cip-budget.aspx

[16] Guidance for the provision of health care can be found in Legislative Rules and Statutes Chapter 87A (01.14.21). Retrieved from https://eutf.hawaii.gov/wp-content/uploads/2021/07/Chapter-87A-secured.pdf

[17] http://www.hawaiipublicschools.org/ConnectWithUs/Employment/WorkingInHawaii/Pages/ERS.aspx

[18] Employees' Retirement System Information Retrieved from https://www.hawaiipublicschools.org/ConnectWithUs/Employment/WorkingInHawaii/Pages/ERS.aspx

[19] 2011 Hawaii Code DIVISION 1. GOVERNMENT TITLE 7. PUBLIC OFFICERS AND EMPLOYEES 88. Pension and Retirement Systems CHAPTER 88 PENSION AND RETIREMENT SYSTEMS. Retrieved from: https://law.justia.com/codes/hawaii/2011/division1/title7/chapter88/.

[20] See the Benefits Brochure for new hires for more information Retrieved from https://www.hawaii-publicschools.org/DOE%20Forms/OTM/New%20Hire%20Resources/HIDOE%20Benefits%20Brochure.pdf

[21] Information about charter schools is available from the State Public Charter School Commission https://www.chartercommission.hawaii.gov/find-a-charter-schools

[22] §302D-28 Funding and Finance. Retrieved from: https://www.capitol.hawaii.gov/hrscurrent/Vol05_Ch0261-0319/HRS0302D/HRS_0302D-0028.htm

[23] Details about the provision of equitable services to private schools is available at https://www.hawaiipublicschools.org/ConnectWithUs/Equitable%20Services/Pages/home.aspx

[24] Visit the Hawaii Virtual Learning Network for more information about Hawaii's virtual learning program https://www.hawaiipublicschools.org/TeachingAndLearning/EducationInnovation/VirtualLearningNetwork/Pages/home.aspx

[25] https://www.hawaiipublicschools.org/VisionForSuccess/AdvancingEducation/StrategicPlan/Pages/Phase-I.aspx

CHAPTER 12

IDAHO

David C. Thompson
Kansas State University[1]

GENERAL BACKGROUND

Idaho's constitution was approved in 1890. Article IX, Section I contained the new state's education clause, placing a duty on the state legislature for the oversight of public education. Article IX has remained unchanged since adoption. The education provision requires the state legislature to establish a system of free schools, saying:

> The stability of a republican form of government depending mainly upon the intelligence of the people, it shall be the duty of the legislature of Idaho, to establish and maintain a general, uniform and thorough system of public, free common schools.[2]

In Fiscal Year 2021 (FY 2021), Idaho had 167 public school districts, 67 charter schools, and served nearly 305,000 schoolchildren[3] across school organizations that included a range from one-room schools to more urban settings. These children were served by 21,828 employees comprised of 18,643 teacher units statewide at a total salary cost for FY 2021 in the amount of $1,110,868,216.[4] Pupil characteristics were majority White (74.9%), Hispanic or Latino (18.5%), multiracial (2.9%), Asian (1.2%), Black/African-American (1.1%), Native Amer-

Funding Public Schools in the United States, Indian Country,
and US Territories (Second Edition), pages 199–212.
Copyright © 2023 by Information Age Publishing
www.infoagepub.com

ican or Alaskan Native (1.1%) and Native Hawaiian or Pacific Islander (0.3%). Pupils from low-income families made up 44% of the student population; 11% were identified as students with disabilities; 7% were students learning English; 2% were identified as homeless; 1% were militarily connected; and 1% were students from migrant families.[5]

POLITICAL CLIMATE AND REVENUE TRENDS

Like all states, Idaho has a distinct political profile and climate affecting all aspects of public education, including K-12 policy and related funding. The state legislature is made up of a Senate with 35 seats and a House of Representatives with 70 seats. The current legislative profile finds the Senate having 28 Republicans (80%) and 7 Democrats (20%), while the House currently seats 58 Republicans (83%) and 12 Democrats (17%). Relatedly, gender representation in the state legislature is 69% male with females holding 31% of seats. Legislative racial composition is predominantly Caucasian (94.29%), with minority groups totaling Hispanic (0.95%), Black (0.95%), along with a category of 'no data' (2.86%).[6] Idaho's fiscal year begins July 1 and operates on a 12-month basis.

Idaho has experienced variable fortunes related to economic and other conditions. Beginning in FY 2000 the state actively engaged reductions in the share of total state spending going to public schools, with reduction blamed on tax cuts and health and human services primarily in the form of Medicaid. It was additionally said that changes to tax structure also contributed to schools' fiscal losses. Tax changes included a reduction in the corporate income tax rate, indexing individual income tax brackets for inflation, increasing the income tax grocery credit, and trading a sales tax rate increase for an elimination of a public school maintenance and operations (M&O) property tax levy, resulting in tens of millions of dollars in lost net revenue to schools. Each of these changes reduced the state's capacity to fund public services and contributed to the slowing of state spending after FY 2000.

By 2018, the state legislature had begun to reverse this decline, with the state approving a 5.9% increase in state funding for schools in FY 2019. Monies in the new state budget reflected a long road over years to reach accord on a five-year plan for improvement, tied in part to full funding for the state career ladder plan; new monies for technology; increased funding for health insurance costs; increases for funding literacy, proficiency, professional development and more—in total, approximately $100 million in new funds for public schools.[7] The strategy had positive impact, as in 2021 one source judged Idaho's overall profile well ranked by national metrics. The 2021 data indicated overall state performance in the top 10% of the nation, with education ranked 29th and further identified as having 39.4% of the population holding college degrees. In 2021 the state ranked fourth in the nation for fiscal stability and third for its economy. Overall rating had increased dramatically since 2019 when the state was ranked sixteenth.[8]

Notwithstanding, Idaho has had its share of recent political turmoil, including common topics nationwide as well as unique to the Intermountain West. Mirroring those struggles, the Idaho legislature in 2021 passed a massive tax cut and declined to use any part of a $600 million state budget surplus for the benefit of public schools. Similarly, state legislative factions embraced nationally divisive social arguments in context of public schools. Simultaneously, other legislative bills intended to benefit schools were defeated.[9] How such struggles eventually will play out is unknown, including any effect on public school funding.[10] Table 12.1 illustrates a reasonable proxy of current climate and trends by comparing legislative appropriations in the most recent two years.

SOURCES OF REVENUE

Idaho's public schools are funded mostly from state general funds and are supplemented by dedicated state funds, federal funds, and local funds.[11] For FY 2021, appropriations totaled $2,862,199,600 from all sources as shown in Table 12.2. State general and dedicated funds are distributed to public schools according to statute and appropriation intent language (i.e., special distributions).[12]

SCHOOL FINANCE LITIGATION

Typical of most states, public school finance has been litigated in Idaho. A saga that began in 1975,[13] in 2005 the Idaho Supreme Court held in *ISSEO V*[14] that the current school funding system was simply not sufficient to carry out the legislature's duty under the state constitution. The state's highest court retained jurisdiction for a time, although it deferred to the state legislature for remedy. Additional claims were brought over the ensuing years. Of note to the present time has been a dispute over approximately $20 million in student fees which plaintiffs have alleged is the result of inadequately funding the state aid scheme for K-12 schools, thereby forcing local school districts to enact fees to offset revenue deficiency. Filed in both state and federal courts, *Zeyen*[15] had been stayed at the federal level pending a state ruling; however, in June 2020 the Idaho Supreme Court denied plaintiffs' due process claim for damages for past amounts, resulting in subsequent federal ruling wherein a U.S. District Court denied both plaintiffs' and defendants' motions in sum. The District Court did allow plaintiffs to submit another motion to specify fees sought for recovery.[16] Aside from these developments, however, there is no general equity or adequacy litigation working through the courts.

DISTRIBUTION FORMULA

Idaho funds K-12 schools through a resource-based funding formula. The state aid formula determines the cost of delivering education in types of school districts based on a calculated cost of resources such as staff salaries and course materials. As such, Idaho does not express state aid as a fixed per-pupil amount.

TABLE 12.1 Idaho Climate and Trends Proxy for School Funding Fiscal Years 2021-2022

FY 2022 Public School Appropriation (Revised)
(excludes IESDB)

1.	FY 2021 General Fund Original Appropriation	$1,974,146,800	
2.	**Expenditure Adjustments**		
	a. Freezing Instructional and Pupil Service Staff Career Ladder Movement	-$26,617,500	-1.35%
	b. Reversal of Freezing Instructional and Pupil Service Staff Career Ladder Movement	26,617,500	1.35%
	c. Adjustment for Increased FTE Support Units - Instructional and Pupil Service Staff Career Ladder Movement	14,764,300	0.75%
	d. Reducing Discretionary (Original)	-21,050,900	-1.07%
	e. Reducing Discretionary (CL Movement, Leadership Premiums, Restoration of 2% increase for Administrators and Classified Staff)	-51,056,400	-2.59%
	f. Reducing Discretionary (Adjustment for Increased FTE SU) (Instr/Pupil Serv, Admin/Classified Staff)	-18,268,000	-0.93%
	g. Suspending Leadership Premiums	-19,310,000	-0.98%
	h. Reversal of Suspending Leadership Premiums	19,310,000	0.98%
	i. Reducing Professional Development (including Gifted / Talented)	-10,000,000	-0.51%
	j. Reducing Technology	-10,000,000	-0.51%
	k. Eliminating 2% Base Salary Increase for Administrators and Classified Staff	-5,128,900	-0.26%
	l. Restoration of 2% Base Salary Increase for Administrators and Classified Staff	5,128,900	0.26%
	m. Adjustment for Increased FTE Support Units - Administrators and Classified Staff	3,503,700	0.18%
	n. Reducing IT Staffing	-4,000,000	-0.20%
	o. Reducing Content and Curriculum	-1,600,000	-0.08%
	p. Reducing Central Services Line Items	-1,000,000	-0.05%
	Total FY 2021 Expenditure Adjustments	**-$98,707,300**	**-5.00%**
3.	FY 2021 General Fund Appropriation (Revised)	$1,875,439,500	
4.	**Base Adjustments / Transfers**		
	a. Reducing Discretionary (Original)	21,050,900	1.07%
	b. Reducing Discretionary (CL Movement, Leadership Premiums, Restoration of 2% increase for Administrators and Classified Staff)	51,056,400	2.59%
	c. Reducing Discretionary (Adjustment for Increased FTE SU) (Instr/Pupil Serv, Admin/Classified Staff)	18,268,000	0.93%
	d. Reducing Adjustment for Increased FTE Support Units - Instructional and Pupil Service Staff Career Ladder Movement	-14,764,300	-0.75%
	e. Reducing Adjustment for Increased FTE Support Units - Administrators and Classified Staff	-3,503,700	-0.18%
	f. Reducing Professional Development (including Gifted / Talented)	10,000,000	0.51%
	g. Reducing Technology	10,000,000	0.51%
	h. Reducing IT Staffing	4,000,000	0.20%
	i. Reducing Content and Curriculum	1,600,000	0.08%
	j. Reducing Central Services Line Items	1,000,000	0.05%
	Total Base Adjustments / Transfers	**$98,707,300**	**5.00%**
5.	FY 2022 Base	$1,974,146,800	
6.	**Base Adjustments / Transfers**		
	a. Endowment / Lands Revenue (from $52,586,400 to $54,798,000)	-$2,211,600	-0.11%
	Total Base Adjustments / Transfers	**-$2,211,600**	**-0.11%**
7.	**Statutory / Maintenance**		
	a. Career Ladder - Increase of 285 mid-term support units (from 15,861 to 16,146)	$44,906,800	2.27%
	b. Advanced Opportunities (from $20,000,000 to $29,700,000)	9,700,000	0.49%
	c. Operational Increase - Increase of 325 Best 28 week support units (from 15,821 to 16,146)	9,388,300	0.48%
	d. Transportation (from $83,040,000 to $89,449,100)	6,409,100	0.32%
	e. Salary and Benefit Apportionment (Administrators, Classified) - Increase of 285 mid-term support units (from 15,861 to 16,146)	4,958,700	0.25%
	f. Charter School Facilities (from $10,372,600 to $13,204,900)	2,832,300	0.14%
	g. Master Educator Premiums (from $7,175,400 to $8,892,700)	1,717,300	0.09%
	h. Idaho Digital Learning Academy (IDLA) (from $12,078,400 to $14,034,500)	1,956,100	0.10%
	i. School Facilities Maintenance Match (from $1,972,200 to $3,477,800)	1,505,600	0.08%
	j. Bond Levy Equalization Support Program (from $8,796,600 to $9,524,200)	727,600	0.04%
	k. Border Contracts (from $1,484,100 to $2,139,100)	655,000	0.03%
	l. Leadership Awards / Premiums - Growth (FTE) (from $19,310,000 to $19,718,100; FTE from 18,996 to 19,398)	408,100	0.02%
	m. Math and Science Requirement (from $6,502,600 to $6,882,100)	379,500	0.02%
	n. Exceptional Contracts and Tuition Equivalents (from $5,833,400 to $6,204,900)	371,500	0.02%
	o. Teacher Incentive Award (National Board Certification) (from $90,000 to $40,000)	-50,000	0.00%
	Total Statutory / Maintenance	**$85,865,900**	**4.35%**
8.	**Line Items**		
	a. Discretionary Increase (Health Insurance, from $12,661 to $13,316, 5.17% increase)	10,575,100	0.54%
	b. Salary and Benefit Apportionment - 2% increase in Base Salaries (Administrators, Classified)	$5,564,400	0.28%
	c. Remediation (from $5,456,300 to $5,106,300)	-350,000	-0.02%
	d. Content and Curriculum (from $6,350,000 to $4,450,000)	-1,900,000	-0.10%
	e. IT Staffing (from $8,000,000 to $4,000,000)	-4,000,000	-0.20%
	f. Technology (from $36,500,000 to $26,500,000)	-10,000,000	-0.51%
	g. Professional Development (from $22,550,000 to $13,350,000)	-9,200,000	-0.47%
	Total Line Items	**-$9,310,500**	**-0.47%**
9.	FY 2022 General Fund Increase	$74,343,800	3.77%
10.	FY 2022 General Fund Total	$2,048,490,600	

Source: "Public School Finance: FY 2022 Appropriations Summary (2021)," Idaho State Department of Education, July 20, 2021, https://www.sde.idaho.gov/finance/files/budget/presentations/FY2022-Appropriations-Summary.pdf.
Note: IESDB refers to Idaho Educational Services for the Deaf and Blind.

The base unit for funding is Average Daily Attendance (ADA). There are two calculations for ADA: (1) from the first day of school through the first Friday of November; and (2) the best 28 weeks for ADA count of the school year. The at-

TABLE 12.2.   Idaho K-12 Revenue Sources FY 2021

Source	Public Schools	IESDB*	Total
General funds	$1,875,439,500	$10,739,000	$1,886,178,500
State dedicated Funds	105,408,700	308,900	105,717,600
Federal Funds	250,000,000	223,500	250,223,500
Total revenues appropriated	$2,230,848,200	$11,271,400	$2,242,119,600
Local funds (estimated property tax)	620,000,000	0	620,000,000
Total Revenues	$2,850,848,200	$11,271,400	$2,862,119,600

Source: "Idaho Public School Funding," Idaho State Department of Education, 2021, https://www. sde.idaho.gov/finance/files/general/manuals/Funding-Formula-FY21.docx
* IESDB refers to Idaho Educational Services for the Deaf and Blind.

tendance day is defined as a minimum 2.5 clock hours for kindergarten pupils and a minimum 4.0 clock hours for grades 1-12. ADA is then converted into Support Units as defined in statute.

The said support units are derived by converting ADA via divisors tied to attendance categories. The larger the ADA, the larger the divisor; and inversely the smaller the ADA, the smaller the divisor. The premise is that smaller programs require less ADA to generate a support unit, and larger programs require more ADA to generate a support unit. The net outcome is more funding per pupil for smaller programs by taking into consideration smaller class sizes that still require full-time staff. Table 12.3 identifies the nature and calculation of divisors for FY 2021.

The purpose of divisors is to represent costs by grade level and enrollment size defined as said support units. Support units are used to calculate cost elements that include salary and benefit apportionment, including career ladder and discretionary funds.

Annual operating costs may be conceptualized as the calculation of the support unit. As such, salary apportionment is the major driver, along with benefit costs described later in this chapter. Salary apportionment includes staff categories of (1) Instructional; (2) Pupil Services; (3) Administrative; and (4) Classified. Instructional and Pupil Service staff are placed in a career ladder cohort tied to experience and education. For administrative staff, an average experience and education multiplier index is generated and used to calculate salary benefit apportionment. These average indexes and career ladder average salaries are dominant variables in determining a school district's support unit value. Table 12.4 presents the ratio applied to each support unit's calculated value.

Operation of these ratios is illustrated in the following example where the effect of enrollment size is visible. A school district earning approval for 100 support units is permitted to calculate ratios as follows: 102.1 Instructional Staff Allowance (100 x 1.021); 7.9 Pupil Service Staff Allowance (100 x 0.079); 7.5 Administrative Staff Allowance (100 x 0.075); and 37.5 Classified Staff Allow-

TABLE 12.3 Idaho Calculation of School Support Units

PUBLIC SCHOOL SUPPORT UNIT (33-1002)
CALCULATION TABLES

COMPUTATION OF KINDERGARTEN SUPPORT UNITS

Average Daily Attendance	Attendance Divisor	Units Allowed
41 or more ...	... 40	1 or more as computed
31 - 40.99 ADA	... -	1
26 - 30.99 ADA	... -	0.85
21 - 25.99 ADA	... -	0.75
16 - 20.99 ADA	... -	0.6
8 - 15.99 ADA.	... -	0.5
1 - 7.99 ADA..	.. -	count as elementary

COMPUTATION OF ELEMENTARY SUPPORT UNITS

Average Daily Attendance	Attendance Divisor	Minimum Units Allowed
300 or more ADA		15
	23... grades 4,5 & 6....	
	20... grades 1,2 & 3....	
160 to 299.99 ADA.	20	8.4
110 to 159.99 ADA.	19	6.8
71.1 to 109.99 ADA	16	4.7
51.7 to 71.0 ADA..	15..	4
33.6 to 51.6 ADA..	13..	2.8
16.6 to 33.5 ADA..	12..	1.4
1.0 to 16.5 ADA...	n/a...	1

COMPUTATION OF SECONDARY SUPPORT UNITS

Average Daily Attendance	Attendance Divisor	Minimum Units Allowed
750 or more.....	18.5.............	47
400 - 749.99 ADA	16...................	28
300 - 399.99 ADA	14.5.............	22
200 - 299.99 ADA	13.5...............	17
100 - 199.99 ADA	12...................	9
99.99 or fewer .... Units allowed as follows:		
Grades 7-12		8
Grades 9-12		6
Grades 7-9		1 per 14 ADA
Grades 7-8		1 per 16 ADA

COMPUTATION OF EXCEPTIONAL EDUCATION SUPPORT UNITS

Average Daily Attendance	Attendance Divisor	Minimum Units Allowed
14 or more	14.5	1 or more as computed
12 -13.99	....	1
8 - 11.99.	....	0.75
4 - 7.99 .	....	0.5
1 - 3.99 .	....	0.25

COMPUTATION OF ALTERNATIVE SCHOOL SUPPORT UNITS

Pupils in Attendance	Attendance Divisor	Minimum Units Allowed
12 or more	.... 12	1 or more as computed

Source: "Public School Support Unit (33-1002) Calculation Template," Idaho State Department of Education, https://www.sde.idaho.gov/finance/files/budget/2021-2022/Unit-Table.pdf.

TABLE 12.4.   Idaho Staff Allowance Ratio Values FY 2021

Factor	Ratio
Staff Allowance per Support Unit	Instructional= 1.021
	Pupil Service= 0.079
	Administrative= 0.075
	Classified= 0.375

Source: Idaho Code § 33-1004, 2021, https://legislature.idaho.gov/statutesrules/idstat/title33/t33ch10/sect33-1004/.

TABLE 12.5.   School District Sample Calculation of Support Units FY 2021

Current Year Support Unit Calculation Through Midterm Reporting Period

	A.D.A	Special Education	Adjusted A.D.A		Unit Divisor		Support Units
Kindergarten Administrative	0		0	|	0	=	0
Elementary Administrative equals 300 or more:							
Grades 1-3		-	= 0.00	|	0	=	0
Grades 4-6		-	= 0.00	|	0	=	0
Elementary Administrative less than 300:							
Grades 1-6		-	= 0.00	|	0	=	0
Secondary Administrative		-	= 0.00	|	0	=	0
Exceptional Education							
Exceptional Preschool							
Exceptional Elementary							
Exceptional Secondary							
Juvenile Detention Center A.D.A							
Exceptional Education Total			0.00	|	0	=	0
SEPARATE ATTENDANCE UNITS							
1 Kindergarten				|	0	=	0
Grades 1-6				|	0	=	0
Secondary				|	0	=	0
2 Kindergarten				|	0	=	0
Grades 1-6				|	0	=	0
Secondary				|	0	=	0
3 Kindergarten				|	0	=	0
Grades 1-6				|	0	=	0
Secondary				|	0	=	0
4 Kindergarten				|	0	=	0
Grades 1-6				|	0	=	0
Secondary				|	0	=	0
5 Kindergarten				|	0	=	0
Grades 1-3				|	0	=	0
Grades 4-6				|	0	=	0
Secondary				|	0	=	0
ALTERNATIVE SCHOOL UNITS							
			0.00	|	0	=	0
			0.00	|	0	=	0
TOTAL Estimated Support Units (Round to nearest hundredth)					=		0.00

Source: "District Support Unit Calculation Template," Idaho State Department of Education, 2021, https://www.sde.idaho.gov/finance/files/budget/2021-2022/District-Support-Unit-Calculation-Template.xlsx.

ance (100 x 0.375). The enrollment sparsity weighting effect is also apparent in additional statutory authority for school districts having fewer than 40 support units to receive an additional 0.5 instructional FTE and an additional 0.5 administrative FTE. Further, school districts with fewer than 20 support units are granted an additional 0.5 instructional FTE, in addition to the above provisions for less than 40 support units.

Additional provisions weigh into the effect of calculated support units. The aforementioned career ladder factors into support unit value, as the state aid plan mandates that no full-time instructional or pupil service staff may be paid less than the minimum dollar amount on the career ladder residency compensation rung for the specified year.[17] In contrast, administrative and classified staff base salaries are set by the state legislature each year. Further, every school district must employ at least the allowed number of instructional and pupil service staff— i.e., a use it or lose it provision.[18] Table 12.5 illustrates how school districts calculate support units.

CATEGORICAL OR OTHER FUNDING

Idaho's basic K-12 school funding plan also results in other funding elements that include transportation, bond supports, technology, and professional development which are distributed separately.

The state of Idaho does not provide supplemental funding to cover the additional cost of educating other specific categories of pupils. However, Idaho considers specific grade levels as seen in staff ratios; students with disabilities; and school district size in the allocation of funding for staff costs. Services for English-language learners and pupils in career and technical education programs are funded through program-specific allocations.

Special Education

Idaho funds special education via a census-based system, anticipating that an average percentage of pupils in every school district will require special education services. Special education enrollment is assumed to be 6% of K-6 enrollment and 5.5% of 7-12 enrollment, excluding residential programs. Residential pupil counts are added to the assumed total for each district to create an aggregate service population. This count is divided by 14.5 to establish the number of exceptional child support units in the state. Importantly, funding allocated per special education unit is an appropriated amount rather than having a 1:1 correspondence to the base formula as is the case for regular education.

Additional special education funding is available through specific program allocations, including funding for school districts supporting pupils in residential facilities or districts that serve an outsized proportion of pupils with emotional disturbances.

Idaho does not currently provide increased funding for gifted and talented pupils. However, as recently as FY 2017, Idaho allocated $1 million for gifted and talented programs as a flat grant to school districts and through a flat allocation for each such child.

English Language Learners

Idaho provides additional funding for English-language learners (ELLs) through two program allocations. One program is distributed automatically to school districts based on the number of ELLs served. The other program offers grants through an application process.

Total funding for ELL is determined annually through the state's legislative appropriations process. Known as the State Limited English Proficiency (LEP) program, Idaho allocated about $3.8 million in FY 2018, $3.4 million of which was distributed based on ELL counts in each district, with the remainder supporting programs including professional development and digital content and curriculum. For FY 2021, this resulted in $205 per pupil. Districts qualify for LEP funding based on an annual assessment which determines each district's share of appropriations. Additional funding is available by grant application to the state's English Learners Enhancement Grants which may be used to support co-teaching, program enhancements, and regional coaches for ELLs.

All school districts are guaranteed ELL state funding if at least one eligible student is identified. Schools having reached a $10,000 threshold (i.e., 101 or more ELL students) of state funding are given access to Title III-A federal funding. The state requires first use of state funds and forbids supplantation of federal funds.

School districts having no documented ELL students are still required to create a language instruction educational program and to check assurances in case an ELL student is identified at any point in the school year.[19]

Other Compensatory Programs

The state of Idaho does not provide additional funding for pupils from low-income households or for school districts having concentrations of low-income students served.

Career and Technical Education

Idaho provides funding for career and technical education (CTE) programs through program-based allocations and by direct support for career technical magnet schools. School districts are eligible for funding related to additional costs for CTE programs, including materials, supplies, staff salaries, and travel. The state funds career technical magnet schools based on enrollment, whereby the number of pupils at each school is divided by 18.5 in order to yield class units, which are then multiplied by .33 to produce a support factor.

Technology

Funding for technology is a budget line item in legislative appropriation. For FY 2021, an appropriation of $26.5 million was made for classroom technology, technology infrastructure, and instructional learning management systems. A separate appropriation for technology staffing costs was made in the amount of $4 million. State statute directs the Idaho State Department of Education to devise a distribution formula.[20]

School Nurses and Other Student Support Services

Funding for an array of health and student support services is included in the instructional calculations in the state school aid distribution formula. The array includes school nurses, school psychologists, speech/ language/ audiology services, social workers, therapists, and media specialists. Salary support for technology services is included in the calculation. The full slate of formula-aided staffing is seen in Table 12.6.

TABLE 12.6. Budgeted K-12 Staffing FY 2021

Activity	Actual Employee Count	FTE Employee Total	Total Salaries	Total Base Salaries	Total Extra Pay	FTE Average Base Salary	FTE Average Base Salary + Extra Pay
Superintendent	114	95.98	$ 10,561,539	$ 10,481,435	$ 80,104	$ 109,204	$ 110,039
Asst. Superintendent	19	19	$ 2,275,529	$ 2,242,457	$ 33,072	$ 118,024	$ 119,765
Charter Administration	58	49.13	$ 4,494,721	$ 4,465,901	$ 28,820	$ 90,900	$ 91,486
Director	62	49.61	$ 4,113,846	$ 4,048,639	$ 65,207	$ 81,609	$ 82,924
Supervisor/Coordinator	140	120.55	$ 11,827,484	$ 11,666,292	$ 161,191	$ 96,776	$ 98,113
Principal	711	636.49	$ 53,081,555	$ 52,458,942	$ 622,613	$ 82,419	$ 83,397
Assistant Principal	301	282.47	$ 23,008,518	$ 22,691,466	$ 317,052	$ 80,332	$ 81,455
Head Teacher	5	1.66	$ 92,098	$ 87,198	$ 4,900	$ 52,529	$ 55,481
Teacher	18,643	17500.7	$ 906,831,922	$ 888,921,875	$ 17,910,047	$ 50,794	$ 51,817
Education Media Generalist	90	85.86	$ 5,379,549	$ 5,272,246	$ 107,303	$ 61,405	$ 62,655
Instructional Cordinator	238	191.42	$ 11,868,750	$ 11,644,647	$ 224,103	$ 60,833	$ 62,004
Counselor	765	730.14	$ 40,906,255	$ 39,746,544	$ 1,159,711	$ 54,437	$ 56,025
Psychological Examiner							
School Psychologist	187	167.42	$ 11,099,656	$ 10,616,637	$ 483,019	$ 63,413	$ 66,298
Speech/Language Pathologist	235	214.2	$ 12,674,084	$ 12,296,867	$ 377,217	$ 57,408	$ 59,169
Audiologist	4	3.2	$ 219,513	$ 216,813	$ 2,700	$ 67,754	$ 68,598
School Social Worker	52	50.46	$ 3,071,202	$ 3,035,960	$ 35,242	$ 60,166	$ 60,864
School Nurse	167	141.08	$ 7,305,819	$ 7,219,869	$ 85,950	$ 51,176	$ 51,785
Occupational Therapist	27	21.4	$ 1,475,253	$ 1,466,734	$ 8,519	$ 68,539	$ 68,937
Physical Therapist	10	8.91	$ 580,924	$ 576,599	$ 4,325	$ 64,714	$ 65,199
Technology Services							
	21,828	20,369.68	1,110,868,216	1,089,157,121	21,711,095	$ 1,372,432	$ 1,396,010
District Administrators	393	334.27	$ 33,273,118	$ 32,904,724	$ 368,394	$ 98,438	$ 99,540
School Administrators	1,017	920.62	$ 76,182,171	$ 75,237,606	$ 944,565	$ 81,725	$ 82,751
Pupil Services	1,447	1,336.81	$ 77,332,705	$ 75,176,023	$ 2,156,682	$ 56,235	$ 57,849
Instructional	18,971	17,777.98	$ 924,080,221	$ 905,838,768	$ 18,241,453	$ 50,953	$ 51,979
	21,828	20,369.68	$ 1,110,868,216	$ 1,089,157,121	$ 21,711,095	$ 53,470	$ 54,365

Source: "Statewide Certificated Staff Salary Report," Idaho State Department of Education, 2021, https://www.sde.idaho.gov/finance/files/staffing/salary-summaries/2020-2021/2020-2021-Statewide-Certificated-Staff-Salary-Report.xlsx.

Transportation

Idaho provides state funding for pupil transportation to qualifying school districts for the purpose of allowable costs for transporting pupils residing 1.5 miles or more from school; transporting pupils residing less than 1.5 miles from school by specific approval of the state board of education; transportation payments in lieu of bus service when approved; employer contributions to the state retirement system and to social security; and for providing transportation for approved school activities.

The state's share of transportation costs is set at 50% of reimbursable costs from the prior year, along with 85% cost-share for training and fee assessments and bus depreciation and maintenance. Provisions exist in statute for exceptions to the rate of reimbursement, such as hardship cases where ridership and/or terrain meet state-prescribed criteria. Transportation provisions relating to virtual learning also exist, along with provisions making charter schools eligible for state transportation aid as well as districts having undergone consolidation.[21]

Charter Schools

Charter schools in Idaho qualify for state aid on the same principle and process as traditional public schools. Charter schools are also eligible for most program-specific allocations, such as grant funding for ELLs. The primary difference is that charter schools in Idaho do not receive a share of local tax revenue.

Virtual charter schools in Idaho exist as well and are funded based on either actual hours of attendance or the percentage of coursework completed at the charter, whichever is more advantageous to the charter.

Capital Outlay and Debt Service

The General Maintenance and Operation (M&O) Fund includes the majority of revenues and expenditures of a school district. This fund accounts for the financial operation of districts' instructional programs supported by local tax revenues and state foundation support appropriations. Despite the M&O name, other funds account for retirement of debt and capital projects in Idaho.

The traditional bond mechanism is used to construct K-12 schools in Idaho. Referenda are required at the local level, wherein traditionally a 2/3 majority affirmative vote is required for passage. This supermajority requirement has resulted in various strategies for providing school facilities, namely (1) a bond election; (2) legislative aid; and (3) alternative financing. The traditional bond mechanism has been relatively successful, with an approximate 50% success rate over time. Partly in response, legislative aid has been made available, as the Idaho School Bond Guaranty Program pledges state sales tax and the state's bond rating to assist districts with voter initiatives. Additionally, the state has enacted a bond levy equalization program that uses a formula tied to local wealth factors to qualify districts for state assistance. Alternative financing options have included lease-to-own innovations.[22]

Beyond those measures, school districts may impose a levy of up to $2.00 for every $1,000 of assessed local property wealth for school facilities upon approval of 55% of eligible voters; between $2.00-$3.00 for every $1,000 of assessed local property wealth with approval of 60% of voters; and up to $4.00 for every $1,000 of assessed local property wealth with approval of two-thirds of voters.

Employee Benefits

All traditional benefits, including health care and retirement, are available to school district personnel in Idaho. On employment, all personnel are entered into the Public Employee Retirement System of Idaho (PERSI),[23] which currently serves nearly 40,000 retirees. New teachers are expected to choose between a defined benefit base plan and an optional choice plan that operates on 401(k) principles. At full retirement eligibility, the defined benefit plan utilizes a formula taking into account the retiree's average monthly salary multiplied by 2% multiplied by months of service credit divided by 12. For example, if a retiree presents a profile showing an average retirement age of 61 with 19 service years, the current anticipated benefit would be $1,370.

The Idaho Office of Group Insurance covers all public employees, offering health insurance and more. Local group experience at the school district level determines premiums and coverages.

Nonpublic School Funding

Private schools of any kind operate independently and without regulation or licensing in Idaho. Approximately 108 private schools were operating in Idaho in 2021.[24] In contrast, see earlier discussion of charter schools which are under state control.

Federal Covid-19 Funding

In late 2021, the U.S. Department of Education approved Idaho's plan for use of its share of the American Rescue Plan Elementary and Secondary School Emergency Relief (ARP ESSER) law and distributed remaining ARP ESSER funds to the state. The approved plan called for providing support to the most impacted students by providing school districts and charter schools with professional development resources on using attendance and absenteeism data, along with other achievement indicators, to identify students who missed the most instruction during the pandemic school years. Concomitantly, the state guaranteed support for districts in using a tiered system of support to improve student attendance and engagement. The approved plan also called for addressing lost instructional time impacts by using statewide data to identify evidence-based interventions for districts which could include high-dosage tutoring, extended learning time interventions, and acceleration academies. Finally, the approved plan called for the state of Idaho to use a portion of state reserve funds from the Emergency Fund to support rural districts and the Bureau of Educational Services for the Deaf and the Blind to implement accelerated learning strategies.[25]

Total ARP ESSER funds awarded to Idaho were $440,131,922.

SUMMARY

Between the years 2018–2021, improvement in the welfare of Idaho's public schools was noted. Discussion at the beginning of this chapter, however, found the Idaho legislature again passing massive tax cuts and refusing to use state budget surpluses for the benefit of public schools. The current moment also finds national arguments interjected into Idaho's public school climate and finds recent school increase-related legislative proposals having suffered defeat. As also noted at the chapter's outset, how such struggles eventually will play out is unknown—what can be eternally observed is that schools are a microcosm of society.

ENDNOTES

[1]   No state-based expert was available to author this chapter at time of second edition publication. The first edition chapter on Idaho was written by David C. Thompson, Kansas State University and lead editor for this book's first edition. The first edition chapter was made easier by Julie Oberle and Tim Hill in the Idaho Department of Education who helpfully provided data. This second edition chapter has been substantially rewritten by David C. Thompson, drawing from multiple sources as footnoted. For additional information and detail, contact the Idaho Department of Education.

[2]   Idaho Constitution, Article IX § 1.

[3]   "Data Dashboard," Idaho State Department of Education, 2021, https://idahoschools.org/state/ID

[4]   "Statewide Certificated Staff Salary Report," Idaho State Department of Education, 2021, https://www.sde.idaho.gov/finance/files/staffing/salary-summaries/2020-2021/2020-2021-State-wide-Certificated-Staff-Salary-Report.pdf.

[5]   "Data Dashboard," Idaho.

[6]   "Legislatures at a Glance," National Conference of State Legislatures, 2021, https://www.ncsl.org/research/about-state-legislatures/legislatures-at-a-glance.aspx.

[7]   Betsy Russell, "Idaho School Budget Set with 5.9 percent Increase for Next Year; No Rancor or Dissent," The Spokesman-Review, February 19, 2018, http://www.spokesman.com/stories/2018/feb/19/idaho-school-budget-set-with-59-increase-for-next-/.

[8]   "Best States: Idaho," U.S. News & World Report, (2021), https://www.usnews.com/news/best-states/idaho. However, various in-state sources such as parent advocacy groups may present a different view: see e.g., Reclaim Idaho, a 2021 grassroots initiative claiming that Idaho's state legislature ignores the will of the people—Reclaim Idaho is seeking $300 million in new funding for schools https://www.reclaimidaho.org.

[9]   "Worst Legislative Session Ever," Idaho Education Association, May 26, 2021, https://idahoea.org/reporter/worst-legislative-session-ever/. See other discussion such as Alexandra Duggan's "'Radical': Idaho's Far-Right Ramps Up Conversation Around Long-Established Learning Concept," KTVB7, updated November 15, 2021, https://www.ktvb.com/article/news/education/radical-idahos-far-right-ramps-up-conversation-around-long-established-learning-concept/277-ea13672f-a9c0-4e4e-9dda-51411b07cb33.

10 For a discussion of future trends, see e.g., Chapter 12 in R. Craig Wood, David C. Thompson, and Jeffrey Maiden, Money and Schools 8th Edition (2023), New York: Routledge.

11 School districts in Idaho are not required to levy local property taxes for education, but they may impose supplemental property taxes for operations and facilities costs. Districts may enact several supplemental levies, most of which require voter approval. School districts do not require voter approval to impose emergency levies to account for an increase in pupil count or to impose a tort levy to fund a liability plan.

12 Title 33, Chapter 10, Idaho Code.

13 Beginning with Thompson v. Engelking (1975), the Idaho Supreme Court denied education as a fundamental right; see also Idaho Schools for Equal Educ. Opportunity (ISEEO I) v. Evans (1993), wherein the Idaho Supreme Court held that while the term 'uniform' in the state constitution's education article did not require equality of spending, the term 'thorough' guaranteed students a certain level of education; see also ISEEO III (1998) holding that the thorough mandate required the state to provide a means for school districts to fund safe learning facilities. See additional compliance litigation in following footnotes.

14 Idaho Schools for Equal Educational Opportunity (ISEEO) v. State (ISEEO V), 129 P.3d 1199 (Idaho 2005).

15 See, e.g., Zeyen v. Boise Dist. #1, Case No. 1:18-cv-00207-BLW (D. Idaho Jul. 1, 2021) brought in federal court alleging illegal fees for supplies and elective courses.

16 Memorandum Decision and Order, Zeyen v. Boise Sch. Dist. No. 1, 522 F.3d 788 (2021).

17 §33-1004B, Idaho Code.

18 Charter schools are exempt from this provision.

19 Maria Puga, "2021-2022 CFSGA State English Learner Program & Title III-A," Idaho State Department of Education, Consolidated Federal and State Grant Application Workshop Tour presentation, May 2021, https://www.sde.idaho.gov/events/cfsga-workshop/files/presentations/2021-2022-CFSGA-Title-III-A-English-Learner-Presentation.pdf.

20 Julie Oberle, "FY 2021, FY 2022 Public Schools Appropriations," Idaho State Department of Education, Legislative Roadshow presentation, May 2021, https://www.sde.idaho.gov/events/leg-roadshow/files/presentations/Public-School-Finance.pdf

21 Idaho Statutes Title 33: Education § 33-1006, Transportation Support Program, FindLaw, 2021, https://codes.findlaw.com/id/title-33-education/id-st-sect-33-1006.html.

22 Nicholas G. Miller, "Commentary on Financing of Public School Buildings," Business Law blog, Hawley Troxell Attorneys and Counselors, October 23, 2017, https://hawleytroxell.com/2017/10/commentary-financing-public-school-buildings/.

23 Public Employee Retirement System of Idaho, 2021, https://www.persi.idaho.gov.

24 "Idaho Private Schools," Idaho State Department of Education, https://www.sde.idaho.gov/school-choice/private/

25 U.S. Department of Education, "U.S. Department of Education Approves Idaho's Plan for Use of American Rescue Plan Funds to Support K-12 Schools and Students, Distributes Remaining $146 Million to State," press release, September 13, 2021, https://www.ed.gov/news/press-releases/us-department-education-approves-idahos-plan-use-american-rescue-plan-funds-support-k-12-schools-and-students-distributes-remaining-146-million-state.

CHAPTER 13

ILLINOIS

Michael A. Jacoby

Illinois Association of School Business Officials

Benjamin Boer

Education Policy Expert

Melissa Figueira

Advance Illinois

GENERAL BACKGROUND

Article X, Section 1 of The Constitution of the State of Illinois[1], amended in 1970, sets forth the primary goals for the funding of public education. It simply states:

A fundamental goal of the People of the State is the educational development of all persons to the limits of their capacities. The State shall provide for an efficient system of high quality public educational institutions and services. Education in public schools through the secondary level shall be free. There may be such other free education as the General Assembly provides by law. The State has the primary responsibility for financing the system of public education.

Four key elements of Article X are:

Funding Public Schools in the United States, Indian Country, and US Territories (Second Edition), pages 213–229.
Copyright © 2023 by Information Age Publishing
www.infoagepub.com

TABLE 13.1.   Illinois Sources of Funding

	State		Local		Federal		Total
2019-20	$14,168.2	37.5%	$19,299.3	51.1%	$4,300.6	11.4%	$37,768.1

Note: State contribution includes the employer contributions (normal cost and unfunded liability payments) to the state teacher retirement systems.

1. The education development of all persons shall allow them to succeed to the "limits of their capacities."
2. The system of public education shall be "efficient."
3. The system of public education shall be "high quality."
4. The "primary responsibility for financing the system" lies with the state, not the local district.

While simple in concept, these key elements have been elusive for Illinois from the beginning, and legal attempts to challenge the state's funding of public education have been unsuccessful due to the opening phrase—"A fundamental goal…" Since a goal is something to reached in the future, courts have not considered a lawsuit that would mandate the legislature to accomplish the goal. Therefore, state spending on education in Illinois provided only 37.5% of all funds for public education in FY2020, thereby hindering the ability to achieve equitable or adequate educational opportunities for all children. Inequity is advanced with continuing dependence on local property taxes. "Illinois has the second highest property taxes in the nation." [2]

See Table 13.1 for sources of funding for Illinois schools[3] (dollars in millions):

CURRENT POLITICAL CLIMATE

The legislature in Illinois currently contains Democratic Party "veto proof" majorities in both the House and the Senate. Of the 59 seats in the Senate, 41 are Democrat and of the 118 seats in the House, 73 are Democrat. In addition, the Governor is a Democrat. This presents unique opportunities for one party to advance legislation. However, the various caucuses in the Democratic majority do not always agree, making certain types of legislation difficult to pass.

The budget process for the legislature is an annual cycle with a deadline of May 31. The fiscal year of the state is July through June. Extending beyond the May 31 deadline requires a super majority (3/5s or 60%) vs a simple majority resulting in annual pressure to agree on a budget within the Democratic caucus.

Two unions have presence in Illinois. The Illinois Education Association and the Illinois Federation of Teachers, which is also connected to the Chicago Teachers Union.

Beyond the unions, educational advocacy for management or administrators is generally conducted by the Statewide School Management Alliance (Illinois Association of School Administrators (IASA), Illinois Association of School

Business Officials (IASBO), Illinois Principals Association (IPA), and the Illinois Association of School Boards (IASB)) and other more specific associations or networks representing subsets of administrators. Some of the most active include ED-RED (primarily a Chicago metropolitan focus), Legislative Network of Du-Page (LEND), Large Unit District Association (LUDA), and the Illinois Alliance of Administors of Special Education (IAASE). Additionally, organizations such as Advance Illinois and the Center for Tax and Budget Accountability give primary focus to educational issues.

Enrollment in Illinois public schools has been declining since FY2007 from 2,118,692 to 1,957,018 in FY2020, which is a decrease of 7.63%. Contrary the decline in enrollment, low-income enrollment is increasing and is currently 48.5% and students of color now make up 52.5% of the total student enrollment. In addition, 12.5% of all students are considered English learners[4].

Students are housed in 852 districts (368 elementary, 96 high school, 388 unit) within 3,859 schools. Over the past ten years 16 districts have been consolidated.

SOURCES OF REVENUE

State Funding

The Illinois State Board of Education General Fund appropriations are summarized around the following categories. Table 13.2 presents FY22 allocations for each[5]:

Local School Revenue

There are two primary sources of local revenue for Illinois school districts:

- Property taxes have long been the most substantial source of funding and is initiated by an annual tax levy set by the local board of education. As noted above, 51.1% of all revenue comes from this source. Limits on property taxes come in two forms. 1. Statutory rate limits are set for each fund and can be increased by local referendum. 2. A Property Tax Extension Limitation Law (PTELL) was initiated in 1991 and applied to the five collar counties around Chicago. In 1994 it was applied to Cook County (Chicago). It limits the increase in property tax extensions to 5% or the Consumer Price Index, whichever is less. Other counties in Illinois are offered the option to adopt the limitation by referendum. As of FY2022, 6 counties were limited by statute, 33 counties have adopted the limit by referendum and 10 counties have rejected it by referendum. 53 counties have yet to initiate a PTELL referendum.[6]
- Local fees can also be assessed for textbooks, various elective course related or expendable supplies, student activities and transportation within 1 ½ miles of the school. Each district sets its own fees and there is significant variance across the state.

TABLE 13.2. Key Allocations for Illinois Education, FY22

Funding Highlights:	FY18 Appropriation ($000s)	% of Total Appropriation
Evidence Based Funding (EBF)	7,579,038.2	81.25%
Early Childhood, Transportation, Sp Ed, Illinois Lunch, Orphanage Tuition, Early Childhood, Transportation, Sp Ed, Illinois Lunch, Orphanage Tuition, CTE, Mentoring, SEL, Assessments, Advanced Placement, Ag Ed, National Board Cert, After-School, Truants, Consolidation, Autism, Safe Schools, Blind, Mental Health, STEM, Parent Education, Agency Capacity, State and District Tech Support	1,660,613.8	17.80%
Charter Schools, Teacher Cert, Drivers Ed, ROE Salaries, Bus Driver Training, Technology Loan Fund, Financial Assistance Fund	88,683.7	.95%
Total	9,328,335.7	100.00%

The focus of this chapter will be primarily on the Evidence Based Funding line above, which embraces 81.25% of state allocated spending for education.

DISTRIBUTION FORMULAS

Evidence Based Funding

In August of 2017, decades of advocacy efforts culminated in the passage of legislation that overhauled Illinois' historically regressive education funding system. Senate Bill 1947, was signed into law on August 31, 2017, becoming The Illinois Evidence Based Funding for Student Success Public Act, or Public Act 100-0465. The Act put in place a formula that prioritizes equity and allocates state funding to school districts based on student need.

The Evidence Based Model of adequacy (EBM), developed by national researchers, Allan Odden & Lawrence Picus, calculates the cost of an adequate and highly effective education comprised of interventions that have a proven impact on student progress. Illinois uses the EBM as the backbone for its funding formula providing a funding target that more accurately captures the necessary funding need from both state and local sources for each individual district.

Following is an overview of the components of the adequacy and distribution methodologies developed for Illinois based on the EBM and is now referred to as the Evidence Based Formula (EBF)

There are four major components to the formula:

1. A unique **adequacy target** for each district
2. A unique **local capacity** for each district
3. A unique **percent of adequacy** for each district

4. A **distribution method** that drives equity to the least funded districts

The following sections will explore each of these concepts in more depth.

The Adequacy Target

The Evidence Based Formula calculates a funding target for each district based on the overall cost of providing a set of research-based interventions, or "essential elements," proven to positively impact student learning. The costs of staffing and programming for these elements are applied to each district based on demographics to determine a district-specific Adequacy Target that reflects unique student needs[7]. This Adequacy Target provides the foundation for the way state funding is appropriated and distributed.

The list of essential elements is derived from the Evidence Based Adequacy Model developed by Odden & Picus. The responsibility for regularly tailoring these elements to Illinois and determining future costs of delivering programming lies with a Professional Review Panel composed of educators, the Illinois State Board of Education, and members of state educational associations and the general assembly. Table 13.3 presents the 34 essential elements for the Illinois formula currently include:

In the process of calculating each district's Adequacy Target, the model accounts for regional variation in cost through the application of a Regionalization Factor to each district's calculated raw costs for staffing and programming. This factor is based on the Comparable Wage Index[8] (CWI), which reflects systematic variations in the salaries of college-educated workers who are not educators. The application of such an index reflects the differences in competitive wages across geographical units and across time. The CWI for Illinois is normalized for each year using the average weighted index (weighted by average student enrollment or ASE) for the state.

To adjust for dramatic differences in wages between neighboring counties, the formula calculates the Regionalization Factor for each district using the greater of a county's actual CWI value and the weighted average of the county's CWI and those of its adjacent counties. Additionally, the Regionalization Factor has a floor of 0.9.

Percent of Adequacy

Once the Adequacy Target has been calculated for each district, the next step to distributing funds is to calculate how well funded each district currently is, including both the amount of revenue a district raises in local funds and the amount the district currently receives in state funding.

TABLE 13.3. Illinois Evidence-Based Funding Tiers, 2022

New Tier Funding	FY2018	FY2019	FY2020	FY2021	FY2022	Total	% of New Money
Tier 1	$326,630,217	$267,425,205	$279,548,555	$0	$260,762,838	$1,134,366,815	88.68%
Tier 2	36,313,680	29,596,928	29,818,112	0	36,237,158	131,965,879	10.32%
Tier 3	3,299,490	2,700,201	2,818,424	0	2,700,000	11,512,114	0.90%
Tier 4	366,609	300,022	312,491	0	299,999	1,279,121	0.10%
Total	$366,609,996	$300,022,356	$312,491,581	$0	$299,999,996	$1,279,123,929	100%

Determining Local Capacity

The calculation of Local Capacity in the EBF is intended to accurately account for the amount districts can and do contribute.

Additionally, in the face of budget crises, chronic underfunding, and years of proration, many districts have had to raise property tax rates to make up for the lack of reliable and sufficient education funding from the state. Exclusive of state teachers' pension contributions, the state of Illinois contributes 26% of education funding, while local taxes make up approximately 66% of education funding[9]. The national average for state contribution to education is closer to 50%. The formula aims to gradually shift the dynamic in Illinois over time to a greater reliance on state funding, to align Illinois more closely with the national average.

The EBF formula calculates local funding based on both an ideal for each district's local contribution, called the Local Capacity Target (LCT), and the actual amount each district currently collects in local tax revenues (Real Receipts)[10]. The goal of employing a target for calculating local contribution is to work to normalize local contribution across the state.

The Local Capacity Target for each district is calculated as follows:

- The formula first creates a Local Capacity Ratio, which is the ratio of a district's Adjusted Equalized Assessed Valuation (AEAV)[11] to the district's Adequacy Target. The Local Capacity Ratio acknowledges both local need and ability to pay, such that the higher a district's EAV, the higher its ratio, and conversely, the larger a district's adequacy target, the smaller its ratio will be.
- To standardize the Local Capacity Ratio across school district types[12], the ratio is adjusted to reflect the number of grades a district serves. Unit districts serve 13 grades (K-12), Elementary districts serve 9 grades (K-8), and High School districts serve 4 grades (9-12). To standardize across types, the ratio is therefore multiplied by 9/13 for elementary districts and 4/13 for high school districts.
- To translate the district's Local Capacity Ratio into the percent of adequacy to be funded locally, districts' ratios are then placed on a normal "cumulative distribution." The cumulative distribution is calculated based on the weighted average and weighted standard deviation of the adjusted Local Capacity Ratio for all districts.[13] Placing the Local Capacity Ratio on a cumulative distribution allows for the calculation of the percentile of the ratio for each district.
- The Local Capacity Percentage yielded by placing districts' ratio on the cumulative distribution is then multiplied by the district's Adequacy Target to produce the district's Local Capacity Target.

Using a calculated Local Capacity Target provides a goal for local contribution that works towards normalizing tax rates in the state. However, the primary goal of the formula is to ensure that funding flows to those districts that are *currently* the least adequately funded. For this reason, the Local Capacity Target is adjusted to consider the amount a district currently receives in local funding, and the Local Capacity Target is treated as exactly that: a target or goal that districts can work towards over time. For those that collect Real Receipts below their target, the formula uses their LCT. For those districts that collect Real Receipts above their LCT, their real receipts are adjusted downwards, towards their target, to create an Adjusted Local Capacity.

The implication of this adjustment of Local Capacity is that high tax, low spending districts would have the potential to lower their tax levy to more closely reflect the rates expected by the formula. This potential reduction in tax levy is enhanced through the inclusion of a property tax relief fund that provides grants to districts that lower their tax levy. At the same time, districts that tax below their LCT would be able to raise their taxes to the calculated amount without impacting their allocation of new state dollars.

The formula makes the adjustment to the Local Capacity Target in the following manner:

- Calculates the difference between each district's Real Receipts and their Local Capacity Target
- Multiplies gap between Real Receipts and Local Capacity Target by district's Local Capacity Percentage.
- Adds that product to district's Local Capacity Target to yield Adjusted Local Capacity

This dynamic approach to local capacity allows for a more realistic assessment of the ideal funds that could come from local property taxes, but at the same time, recognizes a portion of the receipts that are already available to fund a district's adequacy target.

Also included in the sum of a district's existing local resources is Corporate Personal Property Replacement Tax or CPPRT. CPPRT is considered local revenue and is based on the corporate personal property tax the district received prior to the elimination of the personal property tax in 1979. For purposes of the funding formula, the prior year CPPRT distribution from the Illinois Department of Revenue is utilized.

Establishing the Base Funding Minimum

The next calculation the formula requires is to determine the amount a district currently receives in state funding. Built into the proposed funding formula is a provision that no district will receive less state funding than it received in the immediately preceding fiscal year. This amount is referred to as a district's Base Funding Minimum. State revenues per district from the following sources comprised the initial Base Funding Minimum for each district: General State Aid (all

Evidence Based Elements: Core FTE		PK-5 *(per enrolled)*	6-8 *(per enrolled)*	9-12 *(per enroll*
Core Teachers K-3 (Low Income)	Class Size	15		
Core Teachers K-3	Class Size	20		
Core Teachers 4-8 (Low Income)	Class Size	20	20	
Core Teachers 4-8	Class Size	25	25	
Core Teachers 9-12 (Low Income)	Class Size			20
Core Teachers 9-12	Class Size			25
Specialist Teachers	% of Core	20.00%	20.00%	33.33%
		(per enrolled)	*(per enrolled)*	*(per enroll*
Instructional Facilitators (Coaches)	1 FTE per	200	200	200
Core Intervention Teachers	1 FTE per	450	450	600
Substitutes		33.33% of average salary		10 for @ F:
		(per enrolled)	*(per enrolled)*	*(per enrolle*
Core Guidance	1 FTE per	450	250	250
Nurse	1 FTE per	750	750	750
Supervisory Aides	1 FTE per	225	225	200
Librarian	1 FTE per	450	450	600
Library Aide/Media Tech	1 FTE per	300	300	300
Principal	1 FTE per	450	450	600
Asst Principal	1 FTE per	450	450	600
School Site Staff	1 FTE per	225	225	200
Per Student				
Gifted	$ per enrolled	$90		
Professional Development	$ per enrolled	$125		
Instructional Materials	$ per enrolled	$247		
Assessment	$ per enrolled	$27		
Computer Technology	$ per enrolled	$285.50	+ *$285.50 Tier 1 & 2*	
Student Activities	$ per enrolled	$104	$208	$717
Central Services				
Maintenance and Oper	$ per enrolled	$1,072	*Salary Portion* =	$366.96
Central Offics	$ per enrolled	$856	*Salary Portion* =	$445.73
Employee Benefits	30% of Salary	30%	+ Norm Cost if applicable	
Diverse Learners		*(per enrolled)*	*(per enrolled)*	*(per enrolle*
Intervention (Poverty) (DHS count)	1 FTE per	125	125	125
Intervention (EL) (EL count)	1 FTE per	125	125	125
Pupil Support (Poverty)	1 FTE per	125	125	125
Pupil Support (EL)	1 FTE per	125	125	125
Extended Day (Poverty)	1 FTE per	120	120	120
Extended Day (EL)	1 FTE per	120	120	120
Summer Sch (Poverty)	1 FTE per	120	120	120
Summer Sch (/EL)	1 FTE per	120	120	120
English Learners (EL)	1 FTE per	100	100	100
Special Ed Teachers	1 FTE per	141	141	141
Psychologist	1 FTE per	1000	1000	1000

(continues)

FIGURE 13.1.

To Recap, Local Capacity =

A. **Local Capacity Target (LCT)**, if Real Receipts < LCT
  or
B. **Adjusted Local Capacity (ALC)**, if Real Receipts > LCT

Local Capacity Target (LCT) = Adequacy Target * **Local Capacity Percentage**
  Local Capacity Percentage = Conversion of **Local Capacity Ratio** into "cumulative distribution"
    Local Capacity Ratio = (Adjusted EAV / Adequacy Target) * grade level adjustment
    Real Receipts Adjustment = (Real Receipts – LCT) * **Local Capacity Percentage**
Adjusted Local Capacity (ALC) = LCT + **Real Receipts Adjustment**

FIGURE 13.1. Continued

components), Bilingual or ELL, Special Ed Personnel, Funding for Pupils Requiring Special Ed Services (Child Funding), and Special Ed Summer School. The Base Funding Minimum acts as a guarantee that every district will receive at least the same amount in state funds as it received the preceding fiscal year. Additional state funding (beyond the Base Funding Minimum) is allocated from the formula in based on need. The next year, the same calculation is done, but the Base Funding Minimum for that year will also include the new funds distributed in the prior year. This means that no district will ever lose money from the state.

It is important to note that the Base Funding Minimum is per district, not a per pupil hold harmless based on enrollment. Declines in enrollment will still be considered in the calculation of a district's Adequacy Target and subsequent distribution, but a district level hold harmless protects districts with declining enrollment from seeing dramatic declines in state funding even if they are still far from reaching adequacy.

Accounting for Concentrated Poverty

In the Adequacy Calculation:

In the calculation of adequacy, a degree of recognition of the additional costs associated with concentrated poverty is included in the essential element of "class size." When calculating the cost of this element, the formula accounts for smaller class sizes based on a district's low-income percent (For K-3, 1 Full Time Equivalent per 15 low-income students and 1 FTE for every 20 non-low-income students; for 4-12, 1 FTE for every 20 LI students and 1 FTE for every 25 non-LI students).

In the Base Funding Minimum:

The calculation of prior year allocation of state funds used to determine a district's Base Funding Minimum includes funds previously distributed to districts through a poverty supplemental grant. To avoid penalizing low-income districts when the system was not adequately funded, the poverty supplemental was discounted when used in the formula by the degree to which the district was adequately funded. This reduced the amount of state funding recognized by the formula and therefore provided more dollars to low-income districts.

Percent of Adequacy

By summing a district's Local Capacity, CPPRT, and its Base Funding Minimum, (in other words, by adding together a district's expected local resources and current state funding to find its total amount of "Preliminary Resources") each district's distance from its Adequacy Target, or its "Percent of Adequacy" can be calculated. This is done by dividing the district's Preliminary Resources by its Adequacy Target. Districts with a low Percent of Adequacy are the least well-funded, or the farthest away from their Adequacy Target. The closer a district's Percent of Adequacy is to 100%, the more adequately funded a district is.

A Dynamic Distribution Methodology

The Percent of Adequacy forms the basis for the distribution methodology, which is designed to reduce the gap between current spending and adequacy for all districts over a period of several years. Those districts that are the least adequately funded (those that have the lowest Percent of Adequacy) receive the majority of new state funds. The amount of time it takes to bring all districts to adequate funding levels is dependent on the amount of new revenue appropriated for education each year.

Based on its Percent of Adequacy, each district is assigned to one of four Tiers for funding. A fixed percentage of all new state funds is allocated to each of these four funding tiers. According to the tier into which a district is placed, it then receives funding at a certain percent of its "Funding Gap." A district's funding gap is equal to the district's assigned Tier's Target Ratio times the district's Adequacy Target minus the district's Preliminary Resources. The percent of each Tier's funding gap that is to be filled through the distribution formula is referred to as the Tier's "allocation rate." The amount of new funding distributed to each Tier is equal to the Tier's Funding Gap multiplied by its Allocation Rate. It is important to note that the Funding Gap is different for each Tier. For example, a district in Tier 1 will have a Funding Gap based on the distance between its funding level and the Tier 1 Target Ratio and will have another gap between its funding level and 90% of its adequacy target (90% being the Target Ratio of Tier 2).

The criteria for placement into each of these tiers as well as the allocation methodology for each is described in Figure 13.2.

A Distribution Method that Prioritizes Equity

Under this formula education funding could be distributed in one of two ways: either each district could receive funding at a certain percent of their gap to reaching a funding target, or funding could be prioritized to those districts furthest from

	Placement Criteria	Allocation
TIER 1	Includes districts that are the least well-funded. These are all districts below the Tier 1 Target Ratio. This ratio is set dynamically and is based on expending all Tier 1 dollars to close the Funding Gap by each district by 30%. Since determining this value requires calculating the gap closing for each district, it uses an approach called Goal Seek which tries different values for the Target Ratio and then sets the Target Ratio based on that value that uses all the Tier 1 funds.	Tier 1 districts receive 50% of new state dollars. Since these districts are the least well-funded, they receive the greatest amount of new state funding.
TIER 2	Includes all districts with an Adequacy Level below 90% (which means it also includes all Tier 1 districts).	Tier 2 districts receive 49% of new state dollars.
TIER 3	Includes districts with an Adequacy Level between 90% and 100%	Tier 3 districts receive 0.9% of new state dollars.
TIER 4	Includes districts with an Adequacy Level above 100%	Tier 4 districts receive 0.1% of new state dollars.

FIGURE 13.2. Illinois District Allocation Tiers

their target amount by flowing dollars to those districts furthest from adequacy first (basically, "fill from the bottom"). The method in the Illinois Evidence Based Formula is actually a combination of these two approaches. Since the state bears the responsibility for ensuring that all districts are supported in progressing towards adequacy, Districts in Tiers 3 and 4 receive funding at a certain percent of their adequacy target, while districts in Tier 2 receive funding based on their gap to 90% of adequacy. But since Illinois is notorious for having the least equitable education funding system in the nation, the formula uses a "fill from the bottom" approach for districts in Tier 1, so that districts furthest from their Adequacy Target receive funding to fill a greater proportion of their gap.

Minimum Funding Level and Under-appropriation

The Minimum Funding Level serves as a mechanism to ensure that the least well-funded districts are receiving the most funding. In a scenario where there is only a small amount of new dollars appropriated, those dollars will be directed to the least well-funded districts. The Minimum Funding Level is set by the legislation at $300M per year. Failure on the part of the state to provide this minimum amount triggers an adaptation to the distribution formula which protects Tier 1 dollars and broadens the set of districts in Tier 1. The Tier 1 Allocation rate is adjusted, in this case, to 30% multiplied by the ratio calculated by dividing the New State Funds by the Minimum Funding Level.

The formula also adjusts if the appropriation made is less than the amount necessary to fund the Base Funding Minimum. In this case districts in Tier 3 and 4 have their funding reduced to the FY2017 level (if required). If funding needs to be reduced further, it is done on a dollar per-pupil basis across all districts.

Total Evidence Based Funding allocation for FY2022 is $7.6B. Below is a summary[14] of funding by Tier from the inception of the EBF in FY2018 (Note there was no new funding in FY2021):

CATEGORICAL FUNDING OUTSIDE OF THE EVIDENCE BASED FORMULA

Transportation

School boards of community consolidated districts, community unit districts, consolidated districts, consolidated high school districts, optional elementary unit districts, combined high school unit districts, combined school districts if the combined district includes any district which was previously required to provide transportation, and any newly created elementary or high school districts resulting from a high school unit conversion, a unit to dual conversion, or a multiunit conversion if the newly created district includes any area that was previously required to provide transportation shall provide free transportation for pupils residing at a distance of 1 1/2 (one and one half) miles or more from any school to which they are assigned for attendance maintained within the district, except for those pupils for whom the school board shall certify to the State Board of Education that adequate transportation for the public is available.

Each school board may provide free transportation for any pupil residing within 1 1/2 miles from the school attended where conditions are such that walking constitutes a serious hazard to the safety of the pupil due to vehicular traffic effective on the date that the Illinois Department of Transportation grants written approval.[15]

Reimbursement of regular and vocational transportation costs is based on the total cost of operation (adjusted for depreciation) minus local tax revenues (20% minimum threshold) and fees. Reimbursement is prorated if insufficient funds are allocated by the General Assembly. The proration for FY2021 was approximately 89% compared to 84% in FY2020. Total FY2022 Allocation is $281M

Special education transportation costs are reimbursed based on 80% of actual costs and prorated based on appropriation. The proration for FY2021 was approximately 85% compared to 83% in FY2020. Total FY2022 Allocation was $388M

Special Education

Previous special education funding lines for personnel reimbursement ($9,000 per FTE licensed special education teacher and $3,500 per FTE special education paraprofessional), per pupil funding for students receiving special education services and special education summer school, were absorbed into the Base Funding Minimum calculation under the EBF. Future distributions will be made based on student enrollment through the EBF.

Additional special education allocations include

- Orphanage Tuition: Reimburses school districts for per-pupil education cost and approved transportation costs to provide special education service to children residing in orphanages, children's homes, foster families, or other state-owned facilities. Total FY2022 allocation is $10M.
- Private Tuition: Tuition rates are managed by a Purchased Care Review Board and apply only if the approved cost to educate a student exceeds two times the general per capita cost for all students (calculated annually in the audited Annual Financial Report). This item was prorated at 78% for FY2021 compared to 80% in FY2020. Total FY2022 allocation is $152M
- Special Education Transportation: (see transportation section above).

English Learners

What was formerly referred to as the Bilingual Grant was folded into the Base Funding Minimum calculation under the EBF. Future distributions will be made based on the number of students designated as English Learners in each school district through the EBF. Programs are still required to file a grant application to retain and receive funding. It is noted that the General Assembly added $29M to this line prior to folding into the EBF. This was to eliminate proration prior to starting the new funding formula.

Early Childhood Education

The Early Childhood programs provide resource for early childhood and family education programs. These state and federally funded programs include Preschool for All, Prevention Initiative, and Preschool Development Expansion Programs. Local programs must apply to receive funding for Early Childhood programs. The total FY2022 allocation is $544M.

TEACHER RETIREMENT

There are three public school retirements systems in Illinois. All three are currently defined benefit programs; however, a new hybrid system (Tier 3) is under development and is likely to be implemented in FY2020.

- The Teacher Retirement System (TRS) qualifies for Social Security exemption and is for school district employees who are in positions requiring licensure. This includes teachers, local school administrators and central office administrators. There are two active tiers in this system, but for both tiers, the employee contributes 9.0% of salary. Tier 1 includes all applicable employees hired before January 1, 2011 and Tier 2 covers all that were hired on or after that date. Tier 2 is similar to a Social Security benefit and Tier 1 benefits include an annual compounded cost of living adjustment equal to 3% annually. The State of Illinois is responsible to pay the employer contribution (normal cost), which for FY2021 was 10.1%. Local school districts contribute 0.58%. In addition, the State of Illinois is responsible to pay any unfunded liability from prior years. This has grown to a significant amount and a 50-year ramp was approved in 1994 to address this issue. TRS reports that the unfunded liability at the close of FY2020 was $80.7 billion, resulting in significant state resources being allocated to address prior decisions to underfund the system. "For FY2020, approximately 84 percent of the state's $4.8 billion contribution to TRS was dedicated to paying off a portion of the unfunded liability, and only 16 percent dedicated to the year's pension obligation."[16]

- Chicago Teachers Pension Fund (CTPF) also qualifies for Social Security exemption and operates very similarly to TRS, however, it is applicable only to teachers and administrators in the Chicago Public Schools (CPS). Beginning with FY2018, the State of Illinois began paying the normal cost for this system, which was estimated at $221.3 million. This was a part of the final compromise around the Evidence Based Funding reform. CPS continues to be responsible for the unfunded liability (approximately $12.8 billion at the close of FY2019) of this system and receives a deduction to its local capacity target within the EBF to compensate for the annual use of its tax base to pay for the unfunded liability. There is also a statutory ramp for repayment of the CTPF unfunded liability. [17]

- Illinois Municipal Retirement Fund (IMRF) covers all non-licensed personnel who work in public education and other county and local governmental entities. This applies to all non-licensed employees who work for at least 600 hours annually. IMRF is not qualified for Social Security exemption and therefore is not connected directly to the State of Illinois. School districts pay the employer normal cost and employees pay a fixed rate of 4.5%. A school district's employer contribution is based on the actuarial analysis of its employees and can vary year to year. Since a school district is, and has always been, required to make its annual payments, IMRF has little to no unfunded liability.

CHARTER SCHOOL FUNDING

Charter schools in Illinois are established either by agreement with a local school district or by the Illinois State Board of Education. The funding for charters is driven by a Per Capita Tuition Charge (PCTC) which is calculated for each school district in an audited Annual Financial Report. Funding must be within a range of 97% to 103% of PCTC. If a charter is established by approval of a local school district board of education, the district submits payment to the charter based on the percent of PCTC required in the agreement. A charter school established by the Illinois State Board of Education will receive funding directly from the Illinois State Board of Education and deducted from state funding allocated to the district in which the charter resides. These charters were rejected by the local board of education but approved through appeal to the Illinois State Board of Education

TABLE 13.4.   Illinois ESSR Funding

Federal COVID Relief Programs	Total Allocation	LEA Allocation	State Set Aside
ESSER I	$569,467,218	$512,520,496	$56,946,722
ESSER II	$2,250,804,891	$2,025,724,402	225,080,489
ESSER III	$5,054,988,054	$4,549,486,249	$505,498,805
Total	$7,875,260,163	$7,087,731,147	$787,526,016

FEDERAL COVID-19 FUNDING

ESSER I, II and III funds provide grant opportunities that utilize Coronavirus Aid, Relief, and Economic Security (CARES) Act and Coronavirus Response and Relief Supplemental Appropriations (CRRSA) Act and The American Recuse Plan Act of 2021 dollars to assist districts in reducing barriers to prevent, prepare for, and respond to the COVID-19 pandemic. ESSER I funds are distributed through formula grants based on the percentage of Title I, Part A funds received in FY2020. ESSER II and III funds are distributed through formula grants based on the percentage of Title I, Part A funds received in FY2021. Below is a summary of ESSER grants available to local school districts: [18]

SUMMARY

Illinois is a very diverse state with 852 school districts. Approximately 70% of the 1.96 million students reside in and around the Chicago metropolitan area. There are many small rural school districts and several other large districts such as Peoria, Champaign/Urbana and the metro area east of St. Louis. This diversity offers many challenges to equity and adequacy of school funding.

The latest reform which replaced the general state aid formula with an evidence-based formula holds great promise for closing funding gaps across the state, both related to districts with large low-income populations and districts with little or diminishing local wealth. The goal to achieve adequacy for all districts by 2027 is now statutory but requires approximately $4.5 billion in additional funding now or a yearly increase of $797M starting in FY2023. This is much greater that the minimum funding level of $300M.

For a state that has struggled to balance its own budget over the last several decades, reaching this goal will be extremely difficult and will require diligent attention to future appropriations by the General Assembly. The outstanding pension liability will be a further hindrance to achieving fiscal health of the State of Illinois. However, now that the expectation for adequate funding for all students is set, there is hope for a much brighter future of revenue growth for Illinois schools.

ENDNOTES

1   Illinois General Assembly Website 2021: http://ilga.gov/commission/lrb/con10.htm
2   Benford, Alyssia. "Illinois." Journal of Education Finance 46, no. 3 (2021): 275-277. https://www.muse.jhu.edu/article/786662
3   Illinois State Board of Education 2020 Annual Report, pg 7.
4   Illinois State Board of Education Website 2021: https://www.isbe.net/Documents/2020-Annual-Report.pdf#search=annual%20report
5   Illinois State Board of Education Website 2021: https://www.isbe.net/Documents/FY2022-Budget-SB2800-HAM3.pdf#search=2022%20Budget
6   Illinois Department of Revenue website 2021: https://www2.illinois.gov/rev/localgovernments/property/Documents/ptellcounties.pdf
7   Michelle Turner Mangan, Ted Purinton, Anabel Aportela, "Illinois School Finance Adequacy Study—Part I: A Comparison of Statewide Simulation of Adequate Funds to Current Revenues," (March, 2010)
8   Taylor, L.L., and Fowler W.J., Jr. (2006). A Comparable Wage Approach to Geographic Cost Adjustment (NCES 2006-321). U.S. Department of Education. Washington, DC: National Center for Education Statistics.
9   NCES, Digest of Education Statistics 2016: "Revenues for public elementary and secondary schools, by source of funds and state or jurisdiction: 2013-14," https://nces.ed.gov/programs/digest/d16/tables/dt16_235.20.asp
10 Real Receipts = Applicable Tax Rate (ATR) * AEAV, ATR = Operating Tax Rate (OTR) where OTR is prior year OTR, less transportation
11 AEAV = 3-year average EAV, or prior EAV if prior has declined by 10% or more compared to 3-year average
12 Illinois has three different types of school districts, elementary, high school, and unit, which serve different grade configurations. Elementary district means a school district organized and established for purposes of providing instruction up to and including grade 8; High school district means a school district organized and established for purposes of providing instruction in grades 9 through 12; Unit districts serve grades K-12.
13 Both the weighted average and weighted standard deviation are calculated by weighting the districts' Effort Index by enrollment.
14 CTBA Analysis of ISB EBF Calculations
15 Illinois State Board of Education website 2021: https://www.isbe.net/Pages/Funding-and-Disbursements-Transportation-Programs.aspx
16 Teachers' Retirement System website 2021: https://www.trsil.org/news-and-events/pension-issues/unfunded-liabilities
17 Chicago Teachers' Pension Fund website 2021: https://www.ctpf.org/sites/files/2021-05/FY%202020%20Financial%20Annual%20Report%20-%20FINAL.pdf
18 NCLS website 2021: https://www.ncsl.org/ncsl-in-dc/standing-committees/education/cares-act-elementary-and-secondary-school-emergency-relief-fund-tracker.aspx

CHAPTER 14

INDIANA

Marilyn A. Hirth
Purdue University

Daniel Hile
Smith Green Community Schools

GENERAL BACKGROUND

Before 1930, Indiana schools relied primarily upon local revenues from property taxes, supplemented by state distributions from a dedicated common school fund and a state tax levy for special relief to districts with low taxable wealth.[1] In 1933, in order to provide poorer school districts with a proportionately greater share of state funds than wealthier districts, the state began to assume a substantial share of local school costs, distributing funds raised through a new gross income tax as tuition support on a per teaching unit basis.[2] In 1949 the Indiana legislature adopted a traditional minimum foundation type formula to fund public schools. From 1949-1973 districts were given a guaranteed minimum grant (foundation) for imposing a minimum property tax rate (called the qualifying rate) and if they did so, the state guaranteed them a specified number of dollars per pupil to spend (called the foundation).[3] Regardless of property tax wealth each district was guaranteed at least a minimum number of dollars to spend. Consequently, wealthy

Funding Public Schools in the United States, Indian Country,
and US Territories (Second Edition), pages 231–248.
Copyright © 2023 by Information Age Publishing
www.infoagepub.com
All rights of reproduction in any form reserved.

districts with higher assessed valuation per pupil raised more money per pupil than poor districts.[4]

Major reform occurred in 1973 when legislation was passed to reduce property tax rates and levies and slow their increase.[5] The tax reform program not only froze the property tax but also effectively dictated to each school district the number dollars it could raise and spend each year from its general fund.[6] Districts could request an excess levy only through approval by a referendum.

In 1993 the Indiana General Assembly made several changes to the foundation program. The formula revisions were the result of school finance litigation initiated in 1987 by Lake Central School District based on the inequities in funding being unconstitutional.[7] In 1993, an agreement was reached between the plaintiffs and the governor who promised to have the state legislature make changes to the funding formula if they dropped the litigation. A "reward-for-effort formula was phased in over a six year period.[8]

In 2006, the legislature adopted a "money follows the child" formula. This meant the amount of state money available for each regular education student would be the same, and the school corporation educating the student would receive the money for that student. Prior to 2006, the formula had contained a minimum guarantee, where a school district was assured of receiving at least the amount of money distributed through the formula the previous year, plus a fixed percentage increase of that amount. The minimum guarantee was eliminated from the formula.[9]

Another major change in school funding occurred again in 2008 when the Indiana legislature passed Public Law 146. P.L. 146 eliminated property tax levies as a general fund revenue source for school districts. P.L. 146 also capped Indiana school districts' ability to raise revenues from the local property tax without voter approval.[10] To phase in the impact of the law, the state provided school districts with levy replacement grants in 2009 and 2010 that offset losses of greater than 2% of their property tax revenues. In 2011, the levy replacement grant program expired, and schools districts experienced the full impact of the law. As a result, property taxes for homesteads were capped at 1%, agricultural land at 2%, and nonresidential real property at 3% of total assessed value.[11]

In 2010, due to the economic recession and lower-than-projected sales tax revenues, the state cut $300 million from public education, and school corporations were forced to make significant reductions in force and cuts in other areas of their budgets[12]. As a consequence of this series of formula revisions legal challenges to the constitutionality of the state's system of funding schools ensued.[13] In *Bonner v. Daniels* the Indiana Supreme Court ruled the constitutional claims of the case without merit. In *Hamilton Southeastern et al, v. Daniels* case the plaintiffs dropped the case before the judge issued a ruling. Their decision was due to changes the state legislature made to the funding formula paying school corporations for students actually enrolled and phasing out funding to corporations with declining enrollments.[14]

In 2015 the Indiana legislature made two significant changes to the school funding formula. Full-day kindergarten was funded through Basic Tuition Support rather than a categorical grant. Starting in 2016, full-day kindergarten students counted as a full (1.0) ADM and received the full foundation amount in the Basic Tuition Support calculation.[15] Changes to the complexity index was the second change. It transitioned from free or reduced lunch to textbook assistance in 2015, but the programs had the same eligibility criteria.[16] In 2016 and 2017 the Complexity Index was changed to being based on the percent of students in Supplemental Nutrition Assistance Program (SNAP). Temporary Assistance for Needy Families (TANF), or receiving foster care assistance.[17]

The 2017 Indiana legislature passed HEA 1009-2017 overhauling school corporation finance reporting and budgeting, effective January 1, 2019. It eliminated the General Fund, Transportation Fund, Bus Replacement, and Capital Project Funds, Art Association, Historical Society, Public Playground, and Racial Balance funds. The governing body of each school corporation was required to establish an **Education Fund** for the payment of expenses that are allocated to student instruction and learning under IC 20-42.5. Distributions of tuition support are received in the education fund under IC 20-40-2-3. The governing body of each school corporation was also required to create an **Operations Fund** to be used by the school corporation after December 31, 2018 under IC 20-40-18-1. The operations fund is generally used to pay non-academic expenses and consolidates the Transportation, Bus Replacement, Capital Projects, Art Association, Historical Society, Public Playground, and Racial Balance funds and levies. The legislature also passed HEA 1167. Section 29 permits a school corporation, by resolution, to transfer to its education fund or operations fund money that has been deposited in its rainy day fund.[18]

In fiscal year 2017 through fiscal year 2019, all school corporations received the foundation amount for each student as part of the Basic Tuition Support Grant. Virtual charter schools received 90% of the foundation amount. Beginning in fiscal year 2020, school corporations received the foundation amount for each non-virtual student and 85% of foundation for each virtual student. The complexity index and English language learner calculations were incorporated into the calculation of the Basic Grant.[19]

BASIC SUPPORT PROGRAM

School funding follows a statutory formula created and revised by the Indiana General Assembly as part of the biennium budget process, located at Indiana Code 20-43. The Indiana General Assembly appropriates funds for state tuition support. The appropriation supports three different programs: 1) state tuition support; 2) Choice Scholarship program; and 3) the Mitch Daniels Early Graduation Scholarship program. The school funding formula only applies to state tuition support while the other two programs operate under different parameters.[20]

State Tuition Support

The Tuition Support program is the primary source of funding. Referenda levies and other miscellaneous sources provide additional revenue. In the current funding formula State Tuition Support represents the total of Basic Tuition Support (which provides foundation funds) and four categorical grants.[21] The base amount of funding a school corporation receives reflects the Foundation Funding Amount (adjusted for the Transition to Foundation) multiplied by ADM (derived from the number of students) attending the school corporation[22]. This amount is referred to as *Basic Tuition Support*. Basic Tuition Support amounts are reported on a per-pupil basis, unless otherwise noted.[23] The Basic Grant aims to operationalize the state's foundation program. The foundation program amount grew from $4,569 per pupil in FY 2014 to $5,352 per pupil in FY 2019.[24] When the amount of Basic Tuition Support is added to the state's current categorical grants, this amount is referred to as *State Tuition Support*. The state's categorical grants include the *Honors Grant, Special Education Grant, Career & Technical Education Grant*, and *Complexity Grant*. This value represents total state funding provided for educational purposes.[25]

A simplified version of the funding process is illustrated in Figure 14.1.

Table 14.1 shows statewide membership (ADM) counts for FY 2016-2020.

Figure 14.2 provides an overview of the average fall and spring ADM and scholarship accounts.

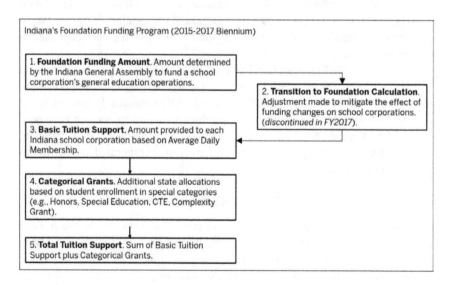

FIGURE 14.1.   Source: Center for Evaluation and Educational Policy. Indiana Department of Education (n.d.). ESSER II and III. Retrieved December 2, 2021 from https://in.gov/doe/grants/esser-ii-and-iii/

TABLE 14.1. Statewide Membership Counts for FY 2016-2020

	FY 2016	FY 2017	FY 2018	FY 2019	FY 2020
School Corp. Fall ADM	1,024,916	1,027,135	1,030,851	1,028,177	1,023,851
School Corp. Spring ADM	1,020,006	1,022,221	1,022,337	1,019,849	1,017,027
School Corp. Average ADM	1,022,461	1,024,678	1,026,594	1,024,013	1,020,439
Choice Scholarships	32,686	34,299	35,458	36,290	36,707
Mitch Daniels Early Graduation Scholarship	252	249	277	263	340
TOTAL	1,055,399	1,059,226	1,062,329	1,060,566	1,057,486

Source: Indiana Department of Education Office of School Finance, December 2020.

State Tuition Support was the sum of all of the grants: the Basic Grant, the Complexity Grant through fiscal year 2019, the Honors Diploma Grant, the Career and Technical Education Grant, and the Special Education Grant. As percentages of State Tuition Support, the three largest grants provided in FY 2019 were

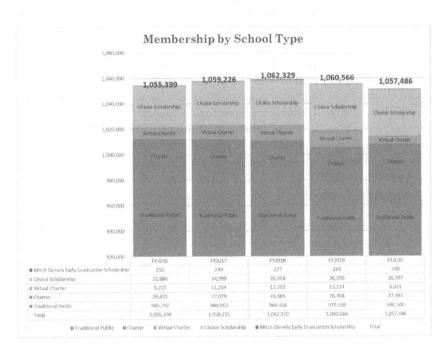

FIGURE 14.2 – Average of fall and spring ADM and the scholarship accounts.
Source: Indiana Department of Education Office of School Finance, December 2020.

TABLE 14.2. State Tuition Support Appropriations

FY 2016	FY 2017	FY 2018	FY 2019	FY 2020
$6,820,300,000	$6,980,500,000	$7,041,000,000	$7,160,000,000	$7,331,500,000

the Basic Grant (76.83 percent), Complexity Grant (10.67 percent), and Special Education Grant (8.14 percent).[26] State Tuition Support was not a predetermined amount but varied by a school corporation's formula results based on actual data counts.[27]

The fiscal year appropriations for state tuition support are shown in Table 14.2.

Information about each of the state tuition support grants is outlined below. The source of the information the *Indiana K-12 State Tuition Support Annual Report* (December 2020) provided by the Indiana Department of Education Office of School Finance.

Basic Grant.[28] The Basic Grant for fiscal year 2016 to fiscal year 2017 was comprised of a base amount per student, which consisted of the foundation amount plus a transition to foundation amount. The base amount per student was multiplied by the number of students to calculate the Basic Grant, based on the fall and spring ADM counts. In fiscal years 2018 and 2019, only the September count was used to calculate the Basic Grant. Beginning with fiscal year 2020, both the fall and the spring counts were again used to calculate the Basic Grant. Up until 2019, virtual charter schools received 90 percent of the foundation amount per student without a transition to foundation as part of the calculation. Charter schools were funded identically to traditional public schools with the exception of new charter schools. New charter schools were funded at the foundation amount per student beginning fiscal year 2016. The fiscal year 2017 Basic Grant was the same for all school corporations and was set at the foundation amount with the exception of virtual charter schools who received 90 percent of the foundation amount. Beginning in fiscal year 2020, the Basic Grant was comprised of several calculations, including the following

a. The foundation amount multiplied by the number of nonvirtual students;
b. 85% of the foundation amount multiplied by the number of virtual students, including those virtual students attending virtual charter schools;
c. A complexity multiplier of $3650 multiplied by the complexity percentage and multiplied by the number of students, regardless of whether the student was virtual or non-virtual;
  i. The complexity percentage is the larger of 1) the 2019 percentage of students who qualified for Supplemental Nutrition Assistance Program (SNAP), Temporary Assistance for Needy Families (TANF), or who received foster care services percentage or 2) the previous year complexity percentage reduced by .025.

TABLE 14.3. Foundation Amounts

FY 2016	FY 2017	FY 2018	FY 2019	FY 2020
$4,967	$5,088	$5,273	$5,352	$5,548

Source: Indiana Department of Education Office of School Finance, December 2020

d.   An augmentation for school corporations whose complexity percentage decreased by more 45% from the fiscal year 2017 complexity percentage and whose fiscal year 2017 percentage of English Language Learners was at least 18 percent.

Table 14.3 shows the foundation amount for fiscal years 2016 to 2020.

Complexity Grant.[29] The Complexity Grant utilizes demographic factors to provide additional funding based on the school corporation's percentage of students who met certain criteria as described for fiscal years 2014-2017. In fiscal year 2014, additional funding was based on the school corporation percentages of students who qualified for a free or reduced lunch in fiscal year 2013, with an additional augmentation for those school corporations with a percentage of at least 33%. In fiscal year 2015, complexity funding was based on the percentage of students eligible for free textbooks in 2014, with an additional augmentation for those school corporations with a percentage of at least 25%. The complexity index for fiscal years 2016 and 2017 used the sum of the following data based on October 1, 2014 data while fiscal years 2018 and 2019 use October 1, 2016 data based on the following:

a.   The percentage of students who qualified for Supplemental Nutrition Assistance Program (SNAP), Temporary Assistance for Needy Families (TANF), or who received foster care services in fiscal year 2017; plus

b.   An augmentation for traditional public school corporations whose complexity percentage decreased by more 45%from the fiscal year 2017 complexity index and whose fiscal year 2017 percentage of English Language Learners was at least 18 percent.

The calculation results were multiplied by $3,489 to determine the fiscal year 2016 complexity grant and by $3,539 to determine the fiscal year 2017 through 2019 complexity grant. Table 14.4 shows the amounts distributed for the Complexity Grant for fiscal years 2016 to 2019.

Honors Diploma Grant[30]. The Honors Diploma Grant was based on the number of students in the previous school year who received an Academic Honors diploma or a Core 40 diploma with Technical Honors. For fiscal years 2016 and 2017, the grant provided $1,400 for each student who, in the previous school year, received an Academic Honors diploma or a Core 40 diploma with Technical Honors and who also qualified for Supplemental Nutrition Assistance Program

TABLE 14.4.　Complexity Grant Totals

FY 2016	FY 2017	FY 2018	FY 2019	FY 2020
$891,554,291	$887,063,363	$768,522,710	$763,399,098	Part of Tuition Support

Source: Indiana Department of Education Office of School Finance, December 2020

(SNAP), Temporary Assistance for Needy Families (TANF), or who received foster care services. The fiscal year 2017 Honors Grant also provided $1,000 for students who received an honors diploma and did not qualify for SNAP, TANF, or receive foster care services. Indiana Code 20-43-10-2 limited use of Honors Diploma Award monies for:(1) staff training, program development, equipment and supply expenditures or other expenses related to the school's honors diploma program; or (2) programs for high ability students.

In fiscal year 2018, the grants referenced above increased to $1,500 for each student who, in in the previous school year, received an academic honors diploma or a Core 40 diploma with Technical Honors and who also qualified for Supplemental Nutrition Assistance Program (SNAP), Temporary Assistance for Needy Families (TANF), or who received foster care services. Funding for fiscal year 2019 forward also included an Honors Grant of $1,100 for students who received an honors diploma and did not receive SNAP, TANF, or Foster Care Services.

Table 14.5 shows the amounts distributed for the Honors Grant for fiscal years 2016 to 2020.

Special Education Grant.[31] The Special Education Grant was based on the number of special education students being served on December 1. The special education data collection was used to gather information on students receiving special education services on December 1 for the first required collection window and in April for the second required collection window for the school year.

In fiscal years 2016 and 2017, the Special Education Grant provided:

- $8,800 for students in programs for severe disabilities
- $2,300 for students in programs for mild and moderate disabilities
- $500 for students in programs for communication disorders or in homebound programs
- $2,750 for students in special education preschool programs

In fiscal year 2018, funding for a student with severe disabilities increased to $8,976 and in fiscal year 2019, the amount increased to $9,156 per student. In fiscal year 2020, funding for students in special education preschool programs increased to $2,875.

Table 14.6 shows the amounts distributed for the Special Education Grant for fiscal years 2016 to 2020.

Career and Technical Education Grant.[32] The Career and Technical Education Grant provided additional funding for career and technical courses. Grant

TABLE 14.5.   Honors Grant Totals

FY 2016	FY 2017	FY 2018	FY 2019	FY 2020
$24,234,800	$24,711,200	$28,673,200	$29,412,400	$30,320,900

Source: Indiana Department of Education Office of School Finance, December 2020

TABLE 14.6.   Special Education Grant Totals

FY 2016	FY 2017	FY 2018	FY 2019	FY 2020
$544,217,100	$550,956,483	$566,487,796	$582,207,430	$595,303,817

Source: Indiana Department of Education Office of School Finance, December 2020.

TABLE 14.7.   Career and Technical Education Grant Totals

FY 2016	FY 2017	FY 2018	FY 2019	FY 2020
$105,821,750	$109,641,000	$113,863,650	$120,936,610	$137,601,790

Source: Indiana Department of Education Office of School Finance, December 2020

amounts were based on the number of students, number of credit hours, and the rating given to the courses. The ratings consisted of high/moderate/low need and high/moderate/low wage. In fiscal years 2016, and 2017, the "other vocational programs" category of funding was divided into three categories: the number of students enrolled in an introductory career and technical course, the number of students enrolled in a foundational career and technical course, and the number of students enrolled in: an apprenticeship, a cooperative education program, or a work-based learning course.

Table 14.7 shows the amounts distributed for the Career and Technical Grant for fiscal years 2016 to 2020.

The **Choice Scholarship Program** is Indiana's mechanism to provide state aid for students attending private schools. Shortly after the program was started in 2011 a group of teachers, school officials and parents who opposed the vouchers sued the state on the grounds the program was unconstitutional. In March 2013 the Indiana Supreme Court ruled that under the state's voucher program Indiana tax dollars can be used to finance private school tuition. The vote was unanimous.[33]

Choice Scholarship Program[34]

Pursuant to Public Law 108-2019, I.C. 20-51, and 512 I.A.C. 4-1 The Choice Scholarship Program was passed as part of House Enrolled Act 1003-2011(Public Law 92-2011) and provides Choice Scholarships to students in households that meet eligibility and income requirements. The program provides funds to assist with the payment of tuition and fees at a participating Choice school.

For the 2011-2012 school year, Choice Scholarships were limited to 7,500 students. For the 2012-2013 school year, Choice Scholarships were limited to 15,000 students. Beginning with the 2013-2014 school year, the student cap was removed and Choice Scholarships were available to any student that met eligibility and income requirements. During the 2013 Session of the Indiana General Assembly, the program was further expanded to include eligibility components related to special education, siblings, and failing schools. During the 2017 Session, the Pre-K Track was added. During the 2019 Session, an additional income threshold and award amount was added and a second application window was established.

To participate in the Choice Scholarship Program a student must satisfy income and eligibility requirements.

Mitch Daniels Early Graduation Scholarship Program[35]

Pursuant to Public Law **108-2019, I.C. 21-12-10** Indiana Code 21-12-10 allows eligible students to receive a $4,000 Mitch Daniels Early Graduation Scholarship upon meeting all graduation requirements by the end of grade 11.

For FY 2019, scholarships totaling $1,052,000.00 were distributed to 263 students.

CURRENT POLITICAL CLIMATE

In Indiana, the state legislature is comprised of a House of Representatives with 100 members, and a Senate with 50 members. The legislature is only in session part-time, allowing members to live and work in the communities they serve for most of the year. The legislative session begins annually on the next Tuesday after the second Monday in January[36]. In even-numbered years, the legislature is required to adjourn no later than March 14; in odd-numbered years, the legislature must adjourn no later than April 29[37]. The state biennium budget is approved in odd-numbered years, and the fiscal calendar runs from July 1 through June 30.

At the start of 2022, the Indiana state government is controlled by a supermajority of Republican officials. The Governor is a member of the Republican party, and the Republican caucus has 39 Senators and 71 Representatives in the legislature[38]. Historically, the Indiana Department of Education has been led by the Superintendent of Public Instruction, which was a position elected by Indiana voters every four years. However, starting in 2021, the top educational leader for the state is now the Secretary of Education, which is appointed by the Governor[39].

In Indiana, the primary union that is actively engaged in education lobbying and advocacy is the Indiana State Teachers Association. ISTA is a state affiliate of the National Education Association, and in 2021 had an active membership of approximately 40,000 educators[40]. Notably, ISTA organized a Red for Ed rally at the Indiana statehouse in 2019, drawing thousands of teachers and supporters to highlight the issue of teacher pay[41].

There are several other associations and organizations that are actively engaged in education advocacy, often representing a specific group or sector of the profession. Several of the most engaged associations include the Indiana Association of Public-School Superintendents, Indiana Association of School Business Officials, Indiana School Boards Association, and the Indiana Small and Rural Schools Association. Representatives from these organizations regularly testify at the statehouse, meet with legislators, and work collaboratively to help influence and shape education policy.

The total number of students enrolled in Indiana's traditional and public charter schools has remained relatively constant over the past decade, with minimal variation between the 2009-10 and 2019-20 school years[42]. While school district consolidation is not currently a focus in the Indiana legislature, it is a topic that resurfaces periodically. The most recent school corporation consolidation in Indiana occurred in 2013. More recently, a district chose to de-consolidate in 2020, creating two new school corporations. However, the practice of school district consolidation or de-consolidation is rare in Indiana and is often met with community resistance due to a variety of local factors.

SOURCES OF REVENUE[43]

Practically all Indiana public school revenues are derived directly or indirectly from some taxing vehicle. State support to local public-school corporations is appropriated by the Indiana General Assembly from the Education Fund or dedicated State funds. Revenues to the State's General Fund include monies generated by sales and use taxes, the individual income tax, and corporate income taxes. Dedicated State funds include monies from the Hoosier Lottery.[44]

Locally, various forms of taxation are used to generate monies for schools and for civil units of government. The local taxes are charged, collected, and provided to the governmental units in a more direct way than State revenues. Examples of local taxes charged include the property tax, license excise tax, commercial vehicle excise tax, financial institutions tax, and special county equalizing school taxes in Lake and Dearborn counties. Other sources of income are non-tax items including receipts from transfer tuition, property sales, gifts, contributions, and earnings from investments.[45]

House Enrolled Act 1009-2017 created a significant series of changes to the fund structure for school corporations. Beginning January 1, 2019, all school corporations have two primary funds:

Education Fund: The Education Fund is the primary fund through which school corporations pay for classroom expenditures. It is analogous to the general fund.

School corporations do not impose a levy for the Education Fund; instead, funding for the education fund is derived from state and federal revenues. Specifically, IC 20-40-2-2 states that the governing body of each school corporation shall establish an education fund for the payment of expenses that are allocated to student instruction and learning. As statute is currently written, the education fund is the exclusive fund to pay for expenses allocated to student instruction and learning. [46]

Operations Fund: The Operations Fund is broadly used to pay for a school corporation's non-classroom expenditures. It is a combination of the former Transportation, Bus Replacement, Capital Projects, Art Association, Historical Society, and Public Playground funds.[47]

REFERENDUM TAX LEVY FUND[48]

The **Referendum Tax Levy Fund** was established by the 2002 Indiana General Assembly as a separate fund. The governing body of each school corporation for which a referendum tax levy is approved under I.C. 6-1.1-19-4.5 (before its repeal) establishes this fund and receipt proceeds from a referendum tax levy into this fund. Specific statutory language pertaining to the establishment of the referendum tax levy is in I.C. 20-46-1. The referendum tax levy fund law, I.C. 20-40-3, provides that money in this fund may be used for any lawful school expense.

Reasons for a referendum tax levy include 1) the governing body determines that it cannot, in a calendar year, carry out its public educational duty unless it imposes a referendum tax levy; 2) the governing body determines that a referendum tax levy should be imposed to replace property tax revenues that the school corporation will not receive because of the application of the circuit breaker credit under IC 6-1.1-20.6.

Approved referendum levies are outside the circuit breaker credit calculations. In other words, schools should receive all the taxes generated by the referendum tax levy. Additionally, schools may pursue a Referendum Capital Projects Debt Levy.

RAINY DAY FUND[49]

I.C. 36-1-8-5.1 permits a political subdivision, including public school corporations, to establish a **Rainy-Day Fund** to receive transfers of unused and unencumbered funds. Excluding debt service funds, and assuming the transfer is authorized by ordinance or resolution, in any year, the school corporation may transfer not more than ten percent (10%) of the school corporation's total annual budget for that fiscal year to the rainy-day fund. The DLGF may not reduce the actual or maximum permissible levy of a school corporation as a result of a balance in the school corporation's rainy-day fund.

The General Assembly created the **School Safety Referendum Tax Levy Fund** and **School Safety Referendum Debt Service Fund** in 2019. Specific statutory language for the fund is in I.C. 20-40-20. A school corporation for which the voters approved a school safety referendum tax levy under I.C. 20-46-9 shall establish both funds. Money in the School Safety Referendum Tax Levy Fund shall be used for school safety purposes, but may be transferred to the Education,

Operations, or School Safety Referendum Debt Service Fund to pay for school safety.[50]

OTHER FUNDING

In addition to the Basic Tuition Support additional funding is provided to supplement state support of the regular education program.

Gifted and Talented Education[51]

Pursuant to P.L. 108-2019, The purpose of this program is to support school corporation high ability programs. The High Ability Education program includes:

1. Funding to assist local schools in the development and implementation of their programs and services for high ability students, K-12.
2. Organizing and developing a State infrastructure of resources and communication for high ability programs.

Extent of Participation: Grants were awarded to 349 local education agencies for the 2019-2020 school year.

Non-English Speaking Program[52]

Pursuant to P.L. 108-2019, The 1999 Indiana General Assembly enacted the Non-English-Speaking Program. This program is to provide funds to local public-school corporations having a concentration of students who have a primary language other than English and limited English proficiency, as determined by WIDA ACCESS assessments.

The Indiana General Assembly increased funding for the NESP during the 2019 Legislative Session and revised the structure of the NESP funding formula. The new legislation removes the previously provided funding bonuses for local education agencies with an EL population above 5%. It allots $487 per each English learner in the LEA who received a Level 1 or 2 on the WIDA ACCESS or participated in the Alternate ACCESS for ELs with significant disabilities and allots $300 per each EL who received a Level 3 or 4 or who received a Level 5 on the Tier A form of the WIDA ACCESS assessment only. Initial allocations for the 2019-2020 grant are based on the 2018-2019 EL student count collected through the Language Minority (LM) data collection. All program funds are allocated to school corporations with no funds remaining at the State level for administration.

Early Intervention Program and Reading Diagnostic Assessment[53]

Pursuant to P.L. 108-2019, The $3,255,130 Early Intervention Program focuses on early grade level intervention (first and second grades) to improve the reading readiness and reading skills of students who are at risk of not learning to read.

TABLE 14.8.   Total Grant Awards, 2020

Number Grants Awarded	Individual Amounts Available	Total
349	$11,500 - $165,000	$12,889,958

Source: Indiana Department of Education Office of School Finance,

Adult Learners Fund[54]

Pursuant to Public Law 108-2019, I.C. 20-24-7-13.5

The Adult Learners fund is for a charter school that serves students, who are at least twenty-two (22) years of age and who have dropped out of high school before receiving a diploma. State law provides a listing of charter schools eligible to receive Adult Learner funds. The appropriation funds a full-time equivalency count of students at $6,750 per student for the fiscal year. The charter schools specified are removed from the state tuition support formula and funded through this appropriation.

National School Lunch Program[55]

Pursuant to P.L. P.L. 108-2019 and I.C. 20-26-9-1 thru I.C. 20-26-9-17, Each school district's grant is a pro-rata share of the appropriated amount based on that district's percentage of the total paid meals served in the State during the previous school year. The amount appropriated is the required State match for participation in the National School Lunch Program. Funds are distributed annually, usually in the month of October, for the previous school year. The October 2018 distribution was $4,943,923 for the 2018-2019 school year.

Teacher Appreciation Grant[56]

Pursuant to P.L. 108-2019 and I.C. 20-43-10-3.5, The Teacher Appreciation Grant, formerly known as the Annual Performance Grant, was appropriated by HEA 1001 (the Biennial Budget) during the 2019 Legislative Session of the General Assembly. It awards stipends to highly effective and effective teachers in their annual evaluations. Both school corporations and charter schools are eligible for the grant as well as entities participating in inter-local cooperatives. These stipends are based on a formula described in I.C. 20-43-10-3.5.

Curricular Material Reimbursement[57]

Pursuant to P.L. 108-2019 and I.C. 20-33-5, The purpose of Curricular Material Reimbursement funding is to provide reimbursement to school corporations, charter schools, and accredited nonpublic schools for a portion of the costs incurred during a school year in providing classroom instruction to children who meet the federal free and reduced lunch standards. Previous to 1999-2000 the program only provided assistance on behalf of students meeting free lunch standards.

CHARTER SCHOOLS

A charter school is a public school that operates under a contract, or charter, entered into between the school's organizer and a charter school authorizer (sometimes referred to as a charter school "sponsor"). Under I.C. 20-24, charter schools are established to serve the different learning styles and needs of public school students, to offer them appropriate and innovative choices, to afford varied opportunities for professional educators, to allow freedom and flexibility in exchange for exceptional levels of accountability, and to provide parents, students, community members, and local entities with an expanded opportunity for involvement in the public school system.[58] Charter schools in Indiana can be authorized by one of the following: (1) a governing body, (2) a state educational institution that offers a four year baccalaureate degree, (3) the executive (as defined in I.C. 36-1-2-5 IC of a consolidated city, (4) the Indiana Charter School Board, or (5) a nonprofit college or university that provides a four year educational program for which it awards a baccalaureate or more advanced degree. Unlike many states, Indiana's legislation does not place a limit on the number of charter schools that can open in the State.[59]

Charter schools receive basic tuition support from the state but do not have the authority to levy local taxes. In Indiana, funding follows the student. This means that, if a student chooses to enroll in a charter school, the charter school will receive state funding on a per-pupil basis in order to provide an education for that student. Similarly, if a student chooses instead to enroll in a traditional district school, the district school will receive state funding associated with that student. In this manner, the school that is providing an education to a student is the school that receives the state funding associated with that student.[60]

TEACHER RETIREMENT

In 1995 the Indiana General Assembly shifted the teacher retirement pension responsibility from the state to local school districts. Prior to 1995, the state paid 8.5% of certified employees' salary and the school district paid 3% of certified employees' salary. Effective July 1, 1995, two funds were established: pre-1995 and post-1995. The pre-1995 fund included any certified employee currently on the payroll, and the school district contributed 3% of the certified employees' salaries to the TRF. The state paid another 8% of the certified employees' salary into the TRF. The post-1995 fund included all new certified employees hired after July 1, 1995, and the school district contributed the 11.5% of certified employees' salary to the TRF. The state made no reimbursement to the school district. In 2001 the General Assembly increased the school district contribution level of the post-1995 fund to 12%.[61]

TAX CREDITS, DEDUCTIONS, AND EXEMPTIONS

Circuit Breaker Credits[62]

The Indiana General Assembly made significant changes in school finance in 2008, affecting property tax collections in 2008 and beyond. I.C. 6-1.1-20.6-7.5 allows a person a credit against the person's property tax liability for property taxes first due and payable after 2009. The amount of the credit is the amount by which the person's property tax liability attributable to the person's homestead exceeds one percent (1%); residential, agricultural, and long-term care property exceeds two percent (2%); and nonresidential real and personal property exceeds three percent (3%) of the gross assessed value of the property that is the basis for taxes for that calendar year. The exception to this limit is when the limits to property tax liability were expected to reduce in 2010 the aggregate property tax revenue that would otherwise be collected by all units of local government and school corporations in the county by at least twenty percent (20%) or property taxes imposed in an eligible county to pay debt service or make lease payments for bonds or leases issued or entered into before July 1, 2008 are not considered for purposes of calculating the credit. If a school corporation pursues a referendum for operating and/or debt service, the tax rate is outside the circuit breaker calculation. Debt service funds are "protected funds" for circuit breaker purposes, meaning non-debt funds receive the impact of circuit breaker credits prior to debt service funds. Units are required to fully fund debt service obligations in an amount sufficient to pay any debt service or lease rentals on outstanding obligations, regardless of any reduction in property taxes due to circuit breaker credits.

FEDERAL COVID-19 FUNDING

In response to the global pandemic caused by COVID-19, the United States federal government provided three rounds of funding to each state. These funds were intended to provide financial support to school corporations as they responded to the unprecedented needs created by the pandemic. Indiana received $214,472,770 for the first round, $888,183,537 for the second round, and $1,996,145,076 for the third round of funding[63]. Each school corporation received a proportionate share of these funds following the federal Title I allocation formula, resulting in a wide range of financial support between school corporations[64].

Each round of federal funding provided through this program followed a specific list of allowable expenses, all of which were related to the pandemic in some way. Some examples include indoor air quality, student learning loss, student instruction technology, and others[65]. As a condition of accepting this funding, each school corporation was required to develop a spending plan. Additionally, in order to qualify for the third and largest round of funding, school districts were also required to develop a plan to reopen schools for in-person instruction. Both of these plans were required to be shared publicly on the school corporation website[66].

ENDNOTES

1   Marilyn R. Holscher, "Funding Indiana's Public Schools: A Question of Equal and Adequate Educational Opportunity," Val. U. L. Rev. 25, no. 2 (1991): 288.

2   Ibid., 288.

3   Robert Lehnen & Carlyn Johnson, "Financing Indiana's Public Schools: Update 1989," Indianapolis, IN: School of Public and Environmental Affairs, (1989): 1

4   Ibid., 2

5   Carlyn Johnson & Robert Lehnen, "Reforming Indiana's School Finance Formula, 1973-1990: A Case of Unanticipated Outcomes" Journal of Education Finance 18, no. 3 (1993): 266.

6   Ibid., 266.

7   Lake Central School District et al. v. State of Indiana et al., Newton County Circuit Court, Indiana Cause No. 56 Col-8703- CP-81

8   Marilyn Hirth & Edward Eiler," Indiana's Formula Revisions and Bonner v. Daniels: An Analysis of Equity and Implications for School Funding," Educational Considerations 39, no. 2(2012): 38.

9   Ibid., 39.

10 Marilyn Hirth & Christopher Lagoni, "A Demographic Analysis of the Impact of Property Tax Caps on Indiana School Districts," Educational Considerations 41, no. 2 (2014): 8.

11 Indiana Department of Local Government Finance, Circuit Breaker Fact Sheet, 2008.

12 Hirth & Eiler, "Indiana's Formula Revisions and Bonner v. Daniels: An Analysis of Equity and Implications for School Funding"39.

13 See Bonner ex. Rel. Bonner v. Daniels 907 N.E. 2d 516 (Ind. 2009), and Hamilton Southeastern Schools et al. v. Daniels, Hamilton Superior Court. Cause No. 29 D01 1002 PL 198, filed February 10, 2010.

14 National Access Network, "Indiana: Recent Events," January 2011, http://www.schoolfunding.info/states/in/lit_in.php3.

15 Thomas J. Sugimoto, "Equity Analysis of the 2015-2017 Indiana School Funding Formula," Bloomington, IN: Center for Evaluation and Educational Policy, (2016): 9.

16 Ibid., p. 9

17 Ibid., p. 10

18 This section is from Digest of Public School Finance in Indiana 2017-2019 Biennium, Indianapolis, IN: Indiana Department of Education: 1.

19 Indiana Department of Education Office of School Finance, Indiana K-12 State Tuition Support Annual Report, December 2020: 2.

20 Ibid., p.1.

21 Sugimoto, Equity Analysis of the 2015-2017 Indiana School Funding Formula," 1.

22 Ibid., 5

23 Ibid., 5

24 Scott Sweetland, "Indiana," Journal of Education Finance, 46, no.3 (2021): 278.

25 Sugimoto, Equity Analysis of the 2015-2017 Indiana School Funding Formula," 6.

26 Scott Sweetland, "Indiana," Journal of Education Finance, 46, no.3 (2021): 278.

27 Indiana Department of Education Office of School Finance, Indiana K-12 State Tuition Support Annual Report, 2

28 Ibid., 5.

29 Ibid., 7.

30 Ibid., 8.

31 Ibid., 9

32 Ibid., 10

33 Scott Elliott and Tim Evans, The Indianapolis Star, March 26, 2013. Available at: https://www.usatoday.com/story/news/nation/2013/03/26/indiana-school-voucher-ruling/2021021/

34 This section is from Digest of Public School Finance in Indiana 2019-2021 Biennium, 24.

35 Ibid., 29.

36 Indiana Constitution, Article 4, Section 9.
37 Indiana Code 2-2.
38 Indiana General Assembly. (n.d.) Retrieved November 30, 2021, from https://iga.in.gov
39 Indiana Code 20-19-1-1.1.
40 Indiana State Teachers Association (n.d.). Retrieved December 2, 2021, from https://ista-in.org
41 Fittes, E. K. (2019, November 15). 'This is a warning shot': Indiana's red for ed rally isn't a strike, but it's closing schools anyway. Chalkbeat Indiana. https://in.chalkbeat.org/2019/11/15/21109268/this-is-a-warning-shot-indiana-s-red-for-ed-rally-isn-t-a-strike-but-it-s-closing-schools-anyway
42 Indiana Department of Education. (n.d.). School enrollment by grade 2006-2021 [Data set]. Indiana Department of Education. https://www.in.gov/doe/files/school-enrollment-grade-2006-21.xlsx
43 This section is from Digest of Public School Finance in Indiana 2019-2021 Biennium: 1.
44 Ibid., 1.
45 Ibid., 1.
46 Ibid., 3.
47 Ibid., 3.
48 Ibid., 6-7.
49 Ibid., 4.
50 Ibid., 5.
51 Ibid., 32.
52 Ibid., 34.
53 Ibid., 29.
54 Ibid., 30.
55 Ibid., 33.
56 Ibid., 35.
57 Ibid., 36.
58 Indiana Charter School Board, https://secure.in.gov/icsb/2447.htm
59 Ibid.
60 Ibid.
61 Denise Seger (2003). The Impact of an Unfunded Teacher Retirement Mandate on Two Midwestern Metropolitan School Districts (Order No. 3113869). Available from Dissertations & Theses @ CIC Institutions; ProQuest Dissertations & Theses Global. (305313941). Retrieved from https://search.proquest.com/docview/305313941?accountid=13360
62 Digest of Public School Finance in Indiana 2019-2021 Biennium, 4-5.
63 United States Department of Education. (n.d.). Elementary and secondary emergency relief fund. Office of Elementary & Secondary Education. https://oese.ed.gov/offices/education-stabilization-fund/elementary-secondary-school-emergency-relief-fund/
64 Indiana Department of Education (n.d.). ESSER I. Retrieved December 2, 2021, from https://in.gov/doe/grants/esser-i/
65 Indiana Department of Education (n.d.). ESSER II and III. Retrieved December 2, 2021 from https://in.gov/doe/grants/esser-ii-and-iii/
66 Ibid.

CHAPTER 15

IOWA

Ain A. Grooms

University of Wisconsin-Madison

GENERAL BACKGROUND[1]

Iowa's schools were originally created by each community's members when enough money had been raised to pay a teacher, provide a school, and purchase essential books and supplies. In 1864, a new state governance system was established by the legislature, creating local school boards and defining local board methods of operation. In 1868, Iowa Judge Dillon determined that school districts have only those powers which are expressly granted or necessarily implied in governing statutes, also known as Dillon's Rule.[2]

At one time there were over 5,000 school districts in Iowa. In the 1950s, the legislature adopted a reorganization law that required all areas of the state to be in a school district offering a kindergarten through grade 12 (K-12) education program, and reorganizing school districts so that no district had fewer than 300 pupils. School districts continued to be governed by local school boards, and operations of school districts were supported by property taxes. The method of fully financing school districts through property taxes remained in place until the mid-1960s. At that time, Iowa taxpayers sought the state's assistance in reducing the local property tax burden.

Funding Public Schools in the United States, Indian Country,
and US Territories (Second Edition), pages 249–261.
Copyright © 2023 by Information Age Publishing
www.infoagepub.com
All rights of reproduction in any form reserved.

In 1967, the state adopted a new way to fund Iowa's school districts by equalizing the property tax burden by county on a per-pupil basis. In 1971, the first state foundation program was adopted. This formula, (also known as the school finance formula), substantially increased state aid to school districts. The goals of the state foundation formula were "to equalize educational opportunity, to provide a good education for all the children of Iowa, to provide property tax relief, to decrease the percentage of school costs paid from property taxes, and to provide reasonable control of school costs."[3] Over the years, other components were added to the school finance formula.

Iowa is one of the few states where the school finance formula has not been successfully challenged through the court system. This is primarily because Iowa law establishes a *maximum* cost per pupil that, when multiplied by a district's enrollment, largely represents the maximum amount (ceiling) or spending authority a district can spend to educate students in the district. In this way, the Iowa school foundation formula has generally been considered equitable on a per-pupil basis across the state.

In FY22, Iowa enrolled 481,248 students in grades K-12 across 332 school districts. While the public school system remains overwhelmingly white (78%)[4], the student population is becoming increasingly more racially diverse. Almost 7% of the state's students are English Language Learners[5], and attend schools in both urban and rural communities. Across the state, 41% of students are eligible for free and/or reduced priced lunch[6] and 13% of K-12 students have Individualized Education Plans[7].

CURRENT POLITICAL CLIMATE

Iowa Republicans currently control the governor's office and both the State Senate and House. Thirty-two of the 50 State Senators and 60 of the 100 State Representatives belong to the Republican party. Additionally, both of Iowa's US Senators as well as three of four U.S. Representatives are members of the Republican Party. The seats of Governor Kim Reynolds, U.S. Senator Chuck Grassley (who has served since 1981), U.S. Representatives Cindy Axne, Randy Feenstra, Ashley Hinson, and Mariannette Miller-Meeks, and many state legislators are up for re-election in 2022. U.S. Senator Joni Ernst is up for re-election in 2026.

Iowa's fiscal year begins on July 1 and ends on June 30. Budget requests must be submitted by October 1 for the following fiscal year. The Governor reviews budget requests, holds public hearings, and submits recommendations every January. Iowa had one of the lowest unemployment rates in the country in December 2020 while simultaneously the state's GDP grew by almost 40%. The state ended FY20 with a budget surplus[8].

Iowa code's "Chapter 20[9]," or the Public Employment Relations Act, governs collective bargaining for state employees and was signed into law in 1974. It outlines what public employees are allowed to negotiate in their contracts (including wages, hours, vacation time, and health insurance) and offers a third party when the state and employees fail to reach an agreement. Chapter 20 also prohibits public employees from going on strike. In 2017, the state Legislature passed new Chapter 20 legislation. Under this new legislation, wages are the only mandatory category of negotiation, while hours, vacation time, holidays and other categories are permitted to be negotiated only if the employer and bargaining unit agree. Previously, bargaining units were able to negotiate insurance, retirement, leaves of absence, grievance procedures, and evaluation procedures, but under the new law, those items are prohibited from negotiations. Importantly, public safety employees (including police officers, sheriffs, and firefighters) are exempt from these legislative changes. Many public school districts rushed to sign employees to new employment contracts before the new Chapter 20 legislation when into effect in February 2017.

SOURCES OF REVENUE

The primary funding components include the uniform tax levy (property tax), state foundation aid, and additional levies and taxes:

- *Uniform Levy:* The uniform levy is a property tax levied equally against the taxable property valuation in each school district in the state. The uniform levy is $5.40 per $1,000 of taxable valuation. Because taxable valuation per pupil is different from one district to the next, the amount of funding raised in this manner differs significantly between districts.
- *State Aid:* Under the Iowa school finance formula, funding is equalized at 87.5% of the regular program cost per-pupil amount for each district. It is state money, or state foundation aid, that funds the difference between the amount received by the district from the uniform levy up to the foundation percentage of 87.5% of the state cost per pupil.[10] In addition to the regular program foundation, state foundation aid also includes state aid for the state categorical supplements (teacher salary, professional development, early intervention, and teacher leadership), and AEA special education support services. The difference between the equalization at 87.5% and 100% is then funded by an additional property levy, beyond the uniform levy.
- *Property Tax Replacement Payments:* There are several calculations that have been added to the formula over time to provide additional property tax relief: i.e., allowing state aid to fund parts of the formula that before were funded with property taxes. These property tax relief efforts have kept down the use of local property taxes in funding schools and have significantly increased state aid, but are a wash to school districts, as state aid replaces property taxes.
- *Additional Levy:* To fully fund a district's cost per pupil, the school foundation aid formula charges an additional property tax levy to bring the overall mix of property taxes and state aid to 100% of the value calculated by the cost per pupil times enrollment.[11] Under the formula, variances in property

tax rates among school districts are partially due to the additional levy. A larger property tax rate is needed for a lower taxable valuation per-pupil school district to fully fund its district cost per pupil than the property tax rate needed in a higher taxable valuation per-pupil district. Also, the additional levy provides the revenue to fund a portion of the AEAs, dropout prevention, and if a district is eligible, a budget adjustment (also referred to as budget guarantee) provision.

- *State Percent of Growth and Supplemental State Aid:* These are terms used in Iowa to describe the amount the state legislature allows the cost per pupil to grow from one year to the next. Prior to FY 2014 the state percent of growth was funded with a mix of property taxes and state aid. However, since FY 2014 the increase has been entirely funded with state aid as another method to hold down property tax growth in school districts. Each categorical supplement is also allowed to grow by the state percent of growth established each year.

- *Budget Adjustment* (also known as Budget Guarantee): This is a unique feature of the Iowa Foundation Aid formula. If a district has a budgeted regular program cost that is less than 101% of the previous year's regular program cost, the district (with board approval through resolution) may receive a budget adjustment to increase the total regular program funding to an amount that is 101% of the prior year's regular program funding. A district may be in this situation and be eligible if district enrollment decreases are greater than the impact of the state percent of growth or increase from one year to the next. The budget adjustment is funded entirely through local property taxes.[12]

In addition to the School Foundation Formula and the General Fund, there are other levies and revenue sources that can be approved by a school district or by the voters of the district:

- *Management Levy:* The management levy is a tax that can be levied annually by a school board. There is no maximum rate limit or dollar limit on the amount levied. However, the management levy may only be used to fund an early retirement program, unemployment compensation, judgements, costs of mediation and arbitration, tort liability, and property insurance.[13]

- *Physical Plant and Equipment Levy (PPEL):* The PPEL is a property tax levy comprised of two levies—the regular physical plant and equipment levy (up to $0.33), and the voter-approved physical plant and equipment levy (up to $1.34). The maximum amount of the joint levies may not exceed $1.67 per $1,000 of taxable valuation. This funding may be used for such stated purposes as purchase of grounds, construction of schoolhouses, technology hardware, non-instructional software, asbestos removal, and bus purchases.[14]

- *Public Education and Recreation Levy (PERL):* The PERL may be levied at 13.5 cents per $1,000 taxable valuation by a simple majority vote of the voters residing in the school district to establish and maintain public recreation places and playgrounds in district school buildings or on the grounds, and to support adult and community education. Once PERL is in place, the levy continues until the school board or the voters vote to discontinue the levy by a simple majority.[15]
- *General Obligation (GO) Bond Indebtedness Levy:* A school district may issue bonds, contract indebtedness, and levy property tax to pay the principal and interest on bonded indebtedness for a period not to exceed 20 years. The levy is made against all property in the school district. The proposition to issue bonds, contract indebtedness, and levy property tax to pay the principal and interest on the bonded indebtedness may be submitted to voters on specified school election dates. The proposition must be approved by 60% of those voting. The levy may not exceed $2.70 per $1,000 taxable valuation in any one year unless the voters approve a one-time election to set the maximum at $4.05 per $1,000 taxable valuation in a year. This additional levy must be approved by 60% of the total votes cast in favor of a $4.05 levy. If either election fails, a school board must wait six months from the date of the election before holding another election. [16]
- *Secure an Advanced Vision for Education (SAVE) Funds:* Another unique and desirable feature of Iowa school finance is a dedicated one-cent statewide sales tax for school infrastructure. The state increased sales tax from 5.0% to 6.0%, designating that the increase be used for school infrastructure or district property tax relief. The statewide penny is slated to be repealed at the end of 2029. However, legislation has been introduced to extend this funding through 2049. Most of the revenue from the penny tax is deposited in the Secure an Advanced Vision for Education (SAVE) Fund. All school districts receive the same per-pupil amount multiplied by its district enrollment. By law, these funds can be used for infrastructure needs, such as construction, reconstruction, remodeling, repair or purchasing schoolhouses, land, stadiums, or gyms. Funds can also be used to purchase revenue bonds for infrastructure needs as approved by a district's local school board, to be paid back with sales taxes over a limited period. Each school district's revenue purpose statement is approved by voters and provides further details on how SAVE funds can be used by the district.[17] SAVE funds can also be used for any PPEL or PERL purpose or to reduce the property tax levies of PPEL or PERL. If a district does not have an approved revenue purpose statement, then proceeds from SAVE are required to be used to reduce any debt levy, regular or voter approved PPEL, PERL, payment for principal and interest of revenue bonds, and for the payment or retirement of bonds issued for school infrastructure purposes.[18]

In February 2022, Governor Reynolds signed a law increasing state aid to schools by 2.5% (or $172 million) for FY23. State costs per pupil (SCPP) will increase to $7,413 from $7,227. With this increase, supplemental state aid (SSA) will total $181 per student, plus an additional $5 per student separate from SSA. Additional levies would be frozen at $683 per student regardless of increasing per pupil costs.[19]

DISTRIBUTION FORMULAS

The Iowa School Foundation Formula calculates the maximum spending authority (ceiling), as well as the mix of property tax and state aid that go into funding spending authority. The state foundation formula is pupil-driven: i.e., most elements of spending authority, as well as funding levels, are based on district enrollment or subsets of enrollment multiplied by a cost per-pupil amount or by enrollment multiplied by a weighting factor applied to either enrollment or cost per-pupil amount. The state foundation formula calculates a maximum school district spending amount (ceiling) which is referred to as maximum spending authority (MSA). MSA is the sum of the Combined District Cost, preschool formula funds, the instructional support levy program (ISL), any modified supplemental amount approved by the school budget review committee (SBRC), miscellaneous income, and unspent balance from the prior fiscal year.

Combined District Cost

Combined District Cost is a term at the core of the spending authority calculation, and it equals the sum of the Regular Program District Cost, Supplementary Weighting District Cost, Special Education District Cost, categorical supplements (Teacher Salary Supplement, Professional Development, Early Intervention Supplement, and Teacher Leadership Supplement), funds for supplemental weighting, Area Education Agency (AEA) Media, Education Services, Special Education Support, and Dropout Prevention funding. Several of these components are defined next:

- *Regular Program District Cost:* equals the district cost per-pupil (DCPP) amount times the district's budget enrollment and represents the majority of spending authority (about 74%), as well as the majority of the funding a district receives. The DCPP and any increase in the cost per pupil from year to year is set by the legislature. Budget enrollment is the number of school-aged children residing in a school district on October 1 of the year prior to the year being budgeted;
- *State Foundation Aid:* equals Regular Program State Foundation Cost Per Pupil (SCPP) times Weighted Enrollment (the sum of the Budget Enrollment, Supplementary Weighting, and Special Education Weighting). This determines the level of state aid and property taxes for funding purposes.

TABLE 15.1, Special Education Weighting Factors

Level	Weighting	Regular Program Weighting	Total Weighting (in per-pupil terms)
I	0.72	1.0	1.72
II	1.21	1.0	2.21
III	2.74	1.0	3.74

- *State Categorical Supplements:* include funding for:
  - Teacher Salary Supplement—additional funding for teachers' salaries;
  - Professional Development—additional funding for district level professional development;
  - Early Intervention Supplement—additional funding for more teachers at the early elementary level to reduce class size;
  - Teacher Leadership Supplement—additional funding to provide teacher leaders and mentors to improve teaching effectiveness.
- *Special Education District Cost* (Table 15.1) equals the Regular Program District Cost Per Pupil times the Special Education Weighting times the number of special education pupils identified at a given level. The greater the resources needed to support a child that qualifies for special education services, the higher the weighting:

Other Components of Combined District Cost

There are other components of Combined District Cost. The most significant ones from a funding aspect are highlighted below.

- *Area Education Agency (AEA) Flow-through Funding:* AEAs and regional educational resource centers cannot levy property taxes, so for budgetary purposes AEA funding flows through each school district's budget that is within an AEA boundary. AEAs receive regular program, special education, media, educational services and categorical supplements cost per-pupil amounts which, when multiplied by the district's enrollments within an AEA, make up the spending authority and funding for that AEA. In the past few years, the legislature has reduced AEAs funding by $7.5 million (permanent reduction) and up to an additional $15.0 million per year.
- *Dropout Prevention Funding:* Local Iowa school boards can approve additional funding, financed solely with local property taxes, for services for potential and returning dropouts to aid this group of students in staying, progressing, and graduating from high school. The maximum a local board can approve is subject to legislative limitation and a 25% match of other funds from the district.

- *English as a Second Language (ESL):* Iowa provides additional funding for the specific needs of students who speak English as their second language. The funding level is based on the number of English language learners identified by the district multiplied by a weighting factor of 0.22 times the cost per student amount for that district. This is included as part of supplementary weighting.
- *Gifted and Talented Funding:* Iowa also provides funding to help with the educational needs of gifted and talented students. The funding level is based on the number of identified gifted and talented students multiplied by a dollar per-pupil amount which was set at $38 per identified pupil in FY 2000 but has been allowed to grow and is currently at $62 per identified pupil. A district is required to provide a 25% match to these funds.
- *Home Schooling Assistance Program Funding:* Iowa provides funding to help with instruction and support services for home-schooled students and their parents. The funding is based on a weighting factor of .3 of 1% multiplied by the number of home-schooled children in a district times the cost per-pupil amount for that district.

Other Components of Spending Authority Beyond Combined District Cost

There are other components not included in the Combined District Cost that, when added together, help make up the maximum spending authority for a district:

- *Preschool Funding:* The legislature created a statewide voluntary four-year-old preschool program, offering free preschool to four-year-olds and funding it with state resources. Spending authority and funding is at half the cost per pupil times the number of four-year-olds enrolled in preschool.
- *Instructional Support Levy Program (ISL):* Districts can receive spending authority and funding up to 10% of their regular program funding level for additional instructional support. Since ISL is funded locally through either property taxes or a mix of property and income surtaxes, it requires board approval and must be reapproved every five years by the board, or every ten years through local election. There is a state aid component to this funding, but it has not been funded in recent years.
- *Modified Supplemental Amount:* School districts may be provided additional spending authority that is beyond the funding generated through the school foundation formula. This is called modified supplemental amount because the school district's spending authority may be modified and approved by the Iowa School Budget Review Committee (SBRC) to reflect factors specific to the individual school district for such things as opening new school buildings, asbestos removal, or negative special education balances, among other reasons. While modified supplemental amount increas-

es spending authority, it does not increase funding. Funding only comes if the district is willing and can, within limitations set by the legislature, increase its property taxes for cash reserves.

- *Negative special education balances:* A unique and desirable aspect of Iowa school finance is that the SBRC must grant a modified supplemental amount to school districts that certify they have negative special education balances. Federal law requires that school districts spend whatever is necessary to provide for the educational needs of special education students. Special education funding calculated in the school foundation formula is generally not sufficient to fully pay for a school district's special education programming, and districts must use other general fund resources to make up the difference. To receive additional spending authority for its negative special education balances, a school district must certify after year-end to the SBRC that the district does have a negative special education balance, and that it will fund the modified supplemental amount with unexpended cash balance or cash reserve levy. Based on this certification, the SBRC grants additional spending authority. Thus, districts may be able to recoup the funds from a negative special education balance in the succeeding year if the district board approves the use of property taxes to do so.[20]

- *Miscellaneous Income:* This is any general fund revenue that is not part of the combined district cost. In other words, if general fund revenue received by a school district is not from the uniform levy, state foundation aid or the additional levy, it is miscellaneous income.[21] These funding sources are also a component of spending authority. Examples include revenue received from other districts for open enrollment into the district, federal, state and local grants received outside the school foundation formula, and investment income.

- *Unspent Balance:* The last element of a school district's total spending authority is the unspent balance. The title 'unspent balance' is somewhat misleading since it seems to indicate that funds in hand were not spent when, in fact, it may only mean that total spending authority was unspent. Unspent balance is the difference between spending authority and *actual* expenditures. To the extent funds are available, unspent balance can be used for onetime expenditures. It is against the law for a district to have a negative unspent balance; if negative, a district is required to develop, gain SBRC approval, and implement a corrective action plan. While the unspent balance may not be backed by cash on hand, a school district can generate funds for spending its unspent balance by levying for cash reserve. This is called the cash reserve levy.

- *Cash Reserve Levy:* Within legislative limitations, a district can approve a property tax rate to provide working capital or cash for unforeseen events. However, it is important to note that while this levy brings in cash, it does not bring in spending authority.

CHARTER SCHOOL FUNDING

There are currently four charter schools in the state of Iowa, all of which are high schools. In May 2021, Governor Reynolds signed House File 813 into law expanding charter school authorization. This new bill allows interested groups to apply directly to the state rather than only to the local school board as instructed by previous legislation. Charter schools receive funding from students' school district of residence equal to the previous year's state cost per pupil, teacher leadership supplement, and any other additional monies including weighted funds associated with English Language Learners. School districts of residence must pay actual costs associated with the provision of special education supports.[22]

NONPUBLIC SCHOOL FUNDING

Approximately 6% of the state's school age children (or 33,000 students) were enrolled in nonpublic schools in FY20. Funds for nonpublic schools are provided through state aid appropriations. Students attending nonpublic schools are entitled to transportation provided by the school district of residence or parents can be reimbursed by the state[23]. Iowa spends approximately $8 million per year on nonpublic transportation. School districts must also make textbooks and curricular materials available to students attending nonpublic schools and are reimbursed for those costs at approximately $650,000 per year. School districts that participate in the Home School Assistance Program (HSAP) receive state funding (30% of per pupil funding) for each homeschooled student that voluntarily enrolls. Through this program, homeschooled students are assigned a supervising teacher. In 2019, the state spent almost $10 million on HSAPs[24]. Nonpublic schools are also able to use state funding to support the provision of school breakfast and lunch programs[25].

In early 2022, Governor Reynolds put forth the Students First legislation that would allow students who leave public schools to use public funds for tuition and fees at nonpublic schools. These funds—consisting of the student's weighted enrollment, teacher salary supplements, and professional development supplements—would be deposited into a savings account. The remaining per pupil monies from state appropriations would be deposited into a statewide fund and would be redistributed to public school districts. Students eligible for these scholarships include those with Individualized Education Plans and students from families earning less than 400% of the federal poverty levels, capping the number of scholarships at 10,000 per year[26]. These scholarships would cost an estimated $55 million in state funds[27]. The bill passed the Iowa Senate but did not pass the House. This is the second time that the governor's bill has failed to advance into legislation.

FEDERAL COVID-19 FUNDING

The Coronavirus Aid, Relief, and Economic Security (CARES) Act was signed into law in late March 2020 providing $30.7 billion in relief to states. Monies designated for schools fell under the Elementary and Secondary School Emergency Relief (ESSER) Fund program. Almost 10% of the CARES Act funds was allocated into the Governor's Emergency Education Relief (GEER) Fund to provide discretionary support for school districts and higher education institutions. Iowa allocated $72.5 million in ESSER funds and another $20.4 million in GEER funds[28] to both public school districts and nonpublic schools.

In December 2020, the Coronavirus Response and Relief Supplemental Appropriations (CRRSA) Act was signed into law, providing another $82 billion to support schools, districts, and states. Iowa distributed $310.4 million through the second round of ESSER (ESSER II) funds[29] to local districts, with particular attention to the needs of historically marginalized students as well as offering resources to school leaders. The CRRSA Act also allocated monies into a second round of GEER (GEER II) funds. Iowa received almost $38 million in GEER II funds, with the majority ($26 million[30]) earmarked for Emergency Assistance to Nonpublic Schools (EANS) and the remainder distributed to public school districts through a competitive grant program. Through this competitive process, 64 public school districts received $8.7 million total in GEER II funds to support mental health programming[31].

In March 2021, the American Rescue Plan (ARP) provided more emergency COVID relief. Under ARP, the third round of ESSER funds (ESSER III) totaled over $120 billion. ESSER III funds were distributed in two awards per state, with each state creating a plan to safely resume in-person instruction. School districts were required to utilize at least 20% of ESSER III funds to address learning loss through evidence-based interventions while also addressing the disproportionate impact of COVID on students from historically marginalized backgrounds. Iowa's public districts received $697.5 million in ESSER III funds, with $139.5 million reserved to address learning loss[32]. Nonpublic schools received $23.5 million in a second round of EANS (EANS II) funds[33]. Teachers and childcare workers were also offered a $1,000 retention bonus.

SUMMARY

The Iowa School Foundation Formula (also known as the School Finance Formula) creates a maximum spending authority (ceiling), as well as a method to calculate the mix of property taxes and state aid to fund the authority. Funding is equalized so that districts with lower taxable valuation per pupil and therefore less ability to generate property taxes are made whole to the 87.5% level by state aid, while districts with higher taxable valuation generating more property taxes receive less state aid. The formula is pupil-driven, that is, most components of the formula are based on district enrollment or subsets of district enrollment multiplied by a cost per-pupil amount or by multiplying enrollment by a weighting factor applied to the enrollment or cost per pupil. The formula is designed to provide equitable funding to address each student's needs, no matter where in Iowa that student resides. The state General Fund appropriation for K-12 in Iowa accounts for about half the monies appropriated by the State of Iowa and is augmented by property taxes at the local level. Over the past several years, Iowa has invested millions of dollars of federal COVID relief funds into its public and nonpublic schools to strengthen teaching and learning and reduce disparities. Select categories of resource allocation from FY21 are highlighted in Table 15.2.

TABLE 15.2.   2020-21 Allocation Summary (select categories)(in millions)

Category	Subcategory	FY21 Total
Enrollment	Student Enrollment	490,094 (FY20)
Program Funding	Regular Program Costs	$3,461.49
	Talented and Gifted Allocations	$31.86
	Budget Adjustment	$8.25
	District Cost for Supplemental Weighting	$108.23
	Special Education Instruction – Direct Cost	$478.59
Categorical	Teacher Salary Supplement	$296.59
	Professional Development Supplement	$33.60
	Early Intervention Supplement	$36.56
	Teacher Leadership Supplement on Aid and Levy	$167.28
	Preschool	$88.32
Taxes/Surtaxes	Instructional Support Income Surtax	$93.08
	Instructional Support Property Tax	$153.07
	Educational Improvement	$0.93
	Management Levy	$173.90
	Regular PPEL	$64.22
	Voter approved PPEL – Income surtax	$10.79
	Voter approved PPEL – Property tax	$174.06
	PERL	$3.53
CARES Act	ESSER – Federal formula (includes nonpublic)	$64.46
	ESSER – State grant (includes nonpublic)	$4.85
	GEER (includes nonpublic)	$20.37
TOTAL		$5,474.03

Iowa Department of Education, 2020-2021 state allocations and selected federal allocations, 2021.

ENDNOTES

[1] The author thanks Patti Schroeder and Shawn Snyder for an earlier edition of this chapter.

[2] An impactful ruling with broad application, originating in City of Clinton v. Cedar Rapids and Missouri River R.R., 24 Iowa 455 (1868).

[3] Iowa Code § 257.31(10).

[4] Iowa Department of Education, 2021-2022 Iowa public school district preK-12 enrollments by district, grade, race, and gender, 2021

[5] Iowa Department of Education, 2021-2022 Iowa public school K-12 English Learners (EL) by district and grade, 2021.

[6] Iowa Department of Education, 2021-2022 Iowa public school K-12 students eligible for free or reduced-priced lunch by district, 2021.

[7] Iowa Department of Education, 2021-2022 Iowa public school district K-12 and PK-12 all student enrollment, special education (IEP) enrollment by district, age group, grade, race and gender, 2021.

[8] Jeffrey A. Fletcher and Jan Friedel, "Iowa," Journal of Education Finance, 47(5), https://www.nationaledfinance.com/journal_of_ed_finance_475.php

[9] Iowa Code § 20.1

[10] Iowa Code § 257.1(2).

[11] Iowa Code § 257.4.

[12] Iowa Code §257.14.

[13] Iowa Code § 298.4.

[14] Iowa Code § 298.2.

[15] Iowa Code § 300.

[16] Iowa Code § 298.18.

[17] Iowa Code § 423f.

[18] Iowa Code § 423f.3.

[19] House File 2316

[20] Iowa Code § 257.31(14).

[21] Iowa Code § 257.2(9).

[22] Iowa Code § 256E.8

[23] Iowa Code § 285.1(14)

[24] Nonpublic School Funding History. Fiscal Services Division, Legislative Services Agency, October 29, 2019 https://www.legis.iowa.gov/docs/publications/IR/1050394.pdf

[25] Iowa Code § 283A.10

[26] Senate File 2369.

[27] Executive Summary, Education Omnibus Bill, Senate File 2369 https://www.legis.iowa.gov/docs/publications/NOBA/1288164.pdf

[28] Iowa Department of Education, CARES/CRSSA Funding, February 2021

[29] Iowa Department of Education, CRRSA Act: Final Elementary and Secondary School Emergency Relief (ESSER II) Allocations, April 2021

[30] Iowa Department of Education, CRRSA Act: EANS Allocations, April 2021

[31] Iowa Department of Education, GEER II—Mental Health Supports for Public PK-12 Schools Grant Awards, December 2021

[32] Iowa Department of Education, ARP Act: ESSER III Allocations, December 2021

[33] Iowa Department of Education, ARP Act: EANS II Allocations, July 2022

CHAPTER 16

KANSAS

Kellen J. Adams
Kansas State University

S. Craig Neuenswander
Kansas State University

David C. Thompson
Kansas State University

GENERAL BACKGROUND[1]

History[2]

The Kansas Legislature began providing funding for public schools in 1937 when it established aid for elementary schools.[3] Secondary schools were aided beginning in 1955.[4] Additional emergency aid was added in 1959.[5] Sweeping school consolidation occurred beginning in 1963, dramatically reducing the state's approximately 2,800 school districts to only 311 by 1969.[6] Legislative enactment of the state's first true school finance formula likewise followed in this same timeframe, known as the School Foundation Act (SFA) of 1965.[7] This formula broke conceptual ground in Kansas by creating a mindset supporting general state aid. Unique features were an adjustment per school district for teacher training and experience, along with a pupil-teacher ratio multiplier tied to each district's position relative to the state average. These elements combined to establish a state

Funding Public Schools in the United States, Indian Country, and US Territories (Second Edition), pages 263–282.
Copyright © 2023 by Information Age Publishing
www.infoagepub.com

duty to fund schools and acknowledged the need to better equalize educational opportunity among districts.

Major reform occurred again in 1973 as the state enacted the School District Equalization Act.[8] Known as SDEA, it was essentially a reward-for-effort formula. Reform occurred again in 1992 with enactment of the School District Finance and Quality Performance Act[9] (SDFQPA) which established a floor and caps on revenue and expenditure via a strongly structured foundation aid plan. Responding to economic distress tied to steep state tax reductions and political change, in 2015 the state abandoned the SDFQPA, substituting a system of block grants known as Classroom Learning Assuring Student Success Act[10] (CLASS) which froze school aid at prior year levels extending through Fiscal Year 2017 when a new aid formula was expected. In 2017, the state enacted the School Equity and Enhancement Act[11] (SEEA), which again in response to political change restored in most ways the key elements of the former SDFQPA foundation aid plan. Long-term effects of the recent intervening years and restorations are yet to be determined.[12]

All these state aid plans were vigorously litigated. The SFA (1965) failed under state court scrutiny,[13] leading to enactment of SDEA (1973) which in turn was litigated[14] and led to the SDFQPA (1992). The state remained embroiled in court battles over equitable and adequate funding levels and aid distribution methods as plaintiffs repeatedly challenged amendments to the SDFQPA[15] and nearby tax cuts, in part leading to enactment of the SEEA (2017). The state supreme court continues to retain jurisdiction primarily on adequacy grounds, recently adding a requirement for an inflation factor in an effort to provide certainty of the state's commitment and to avoid additional litigation. Some proponents within the state legislature continue to promote a constitutional amendment to limit or bar judicial interference in school funding matters.[16]

NOTABLE CONSTITUTIONAL LANGUAGE

Equity

The latest series of school finance legislation, referenced as the *Gannon* lawsuits, began in 2014 with *Gannon I*. This legislation ushered in an additional $126 million to the general aid formula.[17] However, in the 2015 legislative session block grants were enacted, providing for a gross reduction of $54 million.[18] The 2016 regular session then provided for *Gannon II*, providing for a fiscal impact of $4 million in new monies.[19] Later in 2016, a special session allowed for the enactment of *Gannon III*, netting a result of $38 million in new funding.[20]

Adequacy

The 2017 legislative session began with a shift in focus from equity, which had dominated the previous three sessions, to adequacy for Kansas' school districts. The first piece of legislation that made significant progress was the passage of *Gannon IV*, providing $293 million in new funding.[21] The 2018 legislative session subsequently provided significant sums of new monies with two separate pieces of legislation, as *Gannon V* added $454 million[22] and *Gannon VI* provided $92 million[23] more for Kansas schools. In the 2019 legislative session *Gannon VI* and *VII* provided an increased net sum of $85 million, forming the final piece of legislation providing new dollars to schools resulting from the *Gannon* lawsuit.[24]

Descriptive Statistics

The state of Kansas is currently divided into 286 school districts across 105 counties. These districts range in size from 42 students in USD 468-Healy to 46,987 students in USD 259-Wichita (2020-21 PreK headcount). The total PreK-12 headcount for public schools in the 2020-21 school year was 476,987.[25] Approximately one third of all students in Kansas classrooms are located in the state's largest six school districts. The total number of certified personnel for the same school year registered at 43,516 FTE, with 35,033 FTE serving as a teacher (PreK, Kindergarten, Special Education, Career Tech Ed, or classroom).[26] The remaining balance of educators were those in other certificated positions such as principals, counselors, and reading specialists.

As of the 2020-21 school year, there were 3,022 buildings registered for educational purposes across the 286 school districts. Included within this aggregate were 376 high schools, 219 junior high/middle schools, 733 elementary schools, and 323 sites for early childhood programs.[27]

Currently within the state's nearly half-million PreK-12 children, the gender breakdown is approximately 51.41% males and 48.59% females.[28] Ethnicity of school pupils breaks down by 63.27% White, 20.47% Hispanic, 6.84% African-American, and 9.41% Other.[29] With regard to economic status, 47.12% of students are identified as economically disadvantaged, while 52.88% of students are non-economically disadvantaged. Within the state's student population, 9.76% receive ELL services, while 15.68% are identified as students with disabilities.[30]

Across the student population, the attendance rate for the 2019-20 school year was reported at 94.5%. Within the same school year, 13.9% of students were considered chronically absent (missing 10% or more of the academic year), with 1.3% of students dropping out prior to graduation. Finally, the graduation rate for the same school year boasted a total of 88.3%, up from the previous school year.[31]

CURRENT POLITICAL CLIMATE

Legislative Makeup

The Kansas legislative branch is divided into two distinct houses of government-the Senate and House of Representatives. The Kansas Senate is composed of 40 districts across the state, while the House of Representatives is composed of 125 districts. Kansas senators currently serve four-year terms, while House representatives serve two-year terms. Both the Senate and House leadership consists of a majority and minority party leader. Additionally, there is an appointed Speaker of the House of Representatives.

Structural

The fiscal year for Kansas school districts begins on July 1 of each year, ending June 30. Beginning with the 2021-22 school year, school districts budget time-lines are determined by whether or not the district will exceed the Revenue Neutral Rate (RNR) for ad valorem tax amounts raised within their local jurisdiction. The RNR is a mechanism that creates minimum allowable thresholds for mill rate increases for school districts as each new fiscal year approaches. Any districts exceeding this rate have until September 20 to complete the necessary processes for filing their budgets with the local county treasurer and the Kansas State Department of Education. On the contrary, districts not exceeding this rate are bound by the previous timeline of August 25 to file these necessary budget documents.

Spending authority for school districts within the General Fund and Supplementary General Fund is finally calculated in late May each year, with final budget transfers to various restricted funds occurring on/near the end of the fiscal year in June. These monetary limits are first estimated following the September 20 headcount date, on which a physical headcount of all funding-eligible pupils, as well as their respective weightings, is obtained. This spending authority, known as the Legal Maximum Budget, has a few more revisions during the fiscal year calendar as final mill rates from the county(s) are established in November, as well as the final calculation made for Categorical Aid (Special Education) - a flowthrough mechanism that is largely dependent upon the number of teachers and paraprofessionals employed across the state throughout the year. Finally, a secondary enrollment count date of February 20 is used for four districts that are affected by military installations to reflect the mobility of those student populations.

Party Control of Branches and Legislative Bodies

The current legislative makeup heading into the 2022 session leaves both legislative bodies under a Republican majority. The current makeup of the House of Representatives as of the 2022 session is 86 Republicans and 39 Democrats, representing a supermajority. The current makeup of the Senate heading into the 2022 session is 29 Republicans and 11 Democrats, also a supermajority. The governor's office is currently held by Laura Kelly, a Democrat, with a term expiring in January 2023. The Kansas Supreme Court is composed of seven justices, with Justice Marla Luckert serving as chief of the court. As of December 2020, the current makeup is two justices appointed by a Republican governor and five justices appointed by a Democratic governor.

Union Representation and Engagement

While there is no required advocacy voice for teachers in the state of Kansas, local teachers are supported in virtually every school district via the Kansas National Education Association (KNEA), the American Federation of Teachers-Kansas (AFT-Kansas), or independent local bargaining groups.

Other Advocacy and Interest Groups

The primary citizen advocacy group that maintains a consistent presence and advocacy related to school districts is the Kansas Policy Institute (KPI). KPI is a 501(c)3 non-profit and research institution that was founded in 1996. The primary focus of KPI is promotion of public policy solutions, allowing citizens to keep more of what they earn (i.e., a mission of lowering taxes). This mission and vision have led KPI to frequently advocate against policies that raise taxes. Additionally, their focus has been the promotion of information regarding school district spending, with primary messaging geared toward perceived over-spending and expenditures recorded within alleged incorrect functions of the district.

Current School Finance Litigation

The School Equity and Enhancement Act (SEEA) was enacted in 2017 in response to the latest round of litigation, commonly referred to as the Gannon court case.[32] Throughout the life of this legislation, the litigation has been revisited twice for constitutionality, in both instances being upheld by the Kansas Supreme Court. The resulting effect is the state's highest court retaining jurisdiction throughout the initial five-year promissory period set to end in FY 2023.

Enrollment Trends

Statewide Kindergarten-12th grade enrollment in the 1992-93 school year was 480,269. Enrollment has expanded to 503,253 with the 2020-21 school year headcounts. The state enjoyed a modest increase in enrollment each year until a plateau in the 1999-2000 (501,441) school year that was followed by seven years of steady decline, ending with a low for this period at 496,143. Beginning in 2007-08, the state began a long run of nearly uninterrupted enrollment gains, topping out at 521,208 in 2014-15. The largest single-year decline occurred in the 2020-21 school year, with a decrease of 15,686 (3%).[33] At the time of this writing, the 2021-22 enrollment numbers were not yet audited, but are expected to be a slight increase from the low of 2020-21.

Throughout its history, Kansas has seen a decline in the number of school districts, most rapidly occurring in the late 1960s as a result of legislation that specifically addressed unification. Between the years 1963 and 1967, the state went from 1,840 districts to 339 districts. By 1976, this number had again decreased to 306. Beginning in the 2002-03 school year, legislation was again enacted, incentivizing consolidation through provisions that aided districts financially if they chose to pursue this structure. The district count at this time was 303 and fell to 286 by the 2011-12 school year, a count that has remained unchanged. Within this same ten year period, a total of 11 new unified districts were formed, often representing a consolidation of at least two previous districts.[34]

SOURCES OF REVENUE

Taxes

State revenue for aid payments to local school districts is primarily derived from income, sales, and property taxes as well as a variety of small fee funds and assessments. State revenue receipts have been volatile in recent years as the state legislature significantly reduced income taxes in 2012, forcing reliance on other revenue sources and cash balances. The 2017 legislature restored many of the income tax reductions. For FY 2021 total state aid to school districts was approximately $4,903,264,000.

Federal revenue primarily funds Title programs, including special education, and food service. Smaller amounts of federal revenue help fund career and technical education, capital improvement, and grants. For 2021 total federal revenue to school districts was approximately $717,469,00. Of this amount, approximately $208,700,000 was federal ESSER funds allowing school districts to respond to the COVID-19 pandemic.

Local revenue is calculated after state and federal revenues are known. School districts apply the state aid formula for each specific fund, subtract that amount and any federal funds from the budget, and levy the difference locally. Local school board revenue authority is limited to the property tax and a few miscellaneous fees. For FY 2021 local revenue was approximately $1,722,604,000.

The exception to this practice is the school district general fund budget. Every school district is statutorily required to levy 20 mills of property tax for the general fund. Prior to 2015 the 20 mill levy was collected by counties, distributed directly to school districts, and treated as local revenue. In 2014 the state legislature determined that counties should send that tax to the state, with the state distributing it back to local districts as state aid. For FY 2021 total state aid included approximately $736,318,000 from the 20-mill general fund levy.

Trends Over Time

With enactment by the 1992 Kansas Legislature of the School District Finance Quality Performance Act (SDFQPA), the state of Kansas began committing $3,600 per pupil for base funding. This resulted in a commitment of approximately $934,371,000 from the state general fund. Base aid per pupil then increased to $3,863 in FY 2004 before a substantial increase resulting from the *Montoy* case that caused the base aid per pupil to increase to $4,257 in FY 2006, resulting in approximately $1,920,529,000 from the state general fund. FY 2009 represented a 25-year peak when base aid topped out at $4,400 before suffering several years of sharp decreases and flat funding, reaching a low of $3,780 per pupil in FY 2012. This number finally rebounded as of FY 2021, with a state general fund commitment of approximately $3,113,681,000, including the 20 mill property tax mentioned above. This resulted in a base aid per pupil of $4,569.[35]

Across the same time period beginning in FY 1992, local spending funded primarily through locally raised property taxes varied widely as well. Beginning with enactment of the SDFQPA, local property taxes and other revenues generated $1,011,858,000 in FY 1994. Local revenue then peaked in FY 2014, generating $2,230,663,000. As of FY 2021, local revenues were generating $1,722,604,000.

At the federal level, funding has seen only a modest increase over the time period 1995-2015. Beginning in FY 1995, federal funding was $566 per pupil in the state of Kansas, compared to $637 per pupil at the national average.[36] This funding reached a 30-year high in 2010, with Kansas spending per pupil increasing to $1,880 compared to the national average of $1,623.[37] As of FY 2015, spending had decreased to $1,142 per pupil in the state of Kansas, while the national average plummeted to $1,076 per pupil. [38]

DISTRIBUTION FORMULAS

Regular Education Program

General Fund

The School Equity and Enhancement Act of 2017 essentially reinstated and renamed the former SDFQPA general fund foundation aid plan that operated from 1992-2015. Key changes were elimination of the block grant philosophy, a return to floors and caps on per-pupil revenue and expenditure levels, and restoration of the weighted enrollment concept, with per-pupil weightings added to a uniform base amount per pupil. Weightings are meant to adjust for at-risk, high-density at-risk, bilingual, special education, career technical education, high enrollment, low enrollment, declining enrollment, new school facilities, ancillary school facilities, cost of living, virtual enrollment, and transportation differences among the state's 286 school districts. These weightings are based on the principle of vertical equity meant to adjust for differences in pupils' educational needs. Weightings function as multipliers against base aid for student excellence (a legislatively established uniform budget per pupil amount), with base state aid serving horizontal equity by setting an expenditure floor/cap adjusted by these vertical weights. While essentially restoring the old SDFQPA, the new SEEA formula also made several refinements involving certain weights, enrollment count dates, at-risk funding, all-day kindergarten, early childhood education, and the local option budget.

Operationally, the general fund state aid formula is expressed as two parts as illustrated in Figure 16.1.

Base Aid for Student Excellence (BASE) is the foundation uniform per pupil amount. BASE is a legislatively determined amount, derived partly from histori-

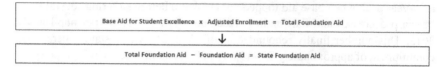

FIGURE 16.1. Kansas Basic Support Formula. Source: Kansas Legislative Research Department. 2014-2015 School Year School District Finance & Quality Performance Act & Bond & Interest State Aid Program – July 1, 2014. Modified by KSDE to reflect SEEA January 2018.

cal expenditure levels, partly from legislative quantification of educational need as determined by either cost studies or legislative preference, and ultimately is reconciled to match the legislatively appropriated amount assigned to public schools once the entire state's budget for the next fiscal year is passed into law. All districts receive the BASE amount per full-time equivalent (FTE) pupil or a proration thereof for part-time pupils. Once the BASE amount is set, enrollment adjustments are applied via total weighting factors indicated earlier using the process shown in Form 150[39] in the Kansas budget software. The result is Total Financial Aid (TFA). The final step is to calculate the local district's share which is then subtracted from TFA to result in State Financial Aid as shown in Form 148.[40] The outcome is a foundation aid plan built on a statewide uniform base budget per pupil adjusted by pupil weights tied to educational need under a uniform general fund tax rate.[41] The aid formula is reviewed and appropriated in each annual legislative session. However, since Kansas is a cash basis law state, if state revenues falter, aid reductions may occur since the state constitution does not permit deficit-spending.

Under the new 2017 general fund state aid formula, the per-pupil BASE amount was set at $4,706 for FY 2022. Pupil weighting adjustments are shown in Table 16.1.

The new 2017 SEEA made changes and improvements to the restored foundation aid plan. New highlights for 2017 were:

- Base aid increased to $4,006 in 2017-18, $4,165 in 2018-19, $4,436 in 2019-20; $4,569 in 2020-21, $4,706 in 2021-22, and $4,846 in 2022-23. Beginning in 2023-24, estimates are to be based on a three year average of the Midwest consumer price index.[42]
- Ancillary facilities and cost of living were continued.
- Declining enrollment weighting was reduced 50% in the 2017-18 school year and was eliminated beginning 2018-19.
- At-risk funding remained based on free lunch count; the at-risk weighting was increased from .456 to .484.

TABLE 16.1. Pupil Weighting Adjustments

Weight	Factor
Low Enrollment	Enrollment 0-99.9 = 1.014331
	Enrollment 100-299.9 = {[7337-9.655(E-100)]/3642.4} - 1
	Enrollment 300-1621.9 = {[5406-1.2375(E-300)]/3642.4}-1
High Enrollment	Enrollment 1622 and over = 0.035040
Bilingual	0.395 or .185 headcount, whichever is higher
K-12 At-Risk (free lunch)	0.484
High Density At-Risk	
50% or more free lunch; or	0.105
35%-49% free lunch	0.7 multiplier after subtracting 35% from total at-risk count
Preschool Aged At Risk	0.5 FTE
Career and Technical Education	0.5
Facilities	0.25 multiplier to FTE in new facility*
Ancillary Facilities	Weight calculated after approved tax appeal ÷ BASE = weight*
Special Education	Weight calculated by SPED aid ÷ BASE = weight*
Declining Enrollment	Weight calculated after special tax levy ÷ BASE= weight*
Cost of Living	Weight calculated after special tax levy ÷ BASE= weight*
Transportation	Weight calculated from density graph ÷ BASE= factor*
Virtual Enrollment	Separate formula: Full-time students = $5,000
	Part-time students = $1,700/FTE
	Students over 19 = $709 per credit earned
	*Additional conditions and restrictions apply

Source: Kansas Legislative Research Department. 2014-2015 School Year School District Finance & Quality Performance Act & Bond & Interest State Aid Program—July 1, 2014. Adjusted for 2017 legislative changes.

- High-density at-risk computation was changed to permit districts to choose between computing by attendance center or school district to account for local disparities in wealth among buildings.
- All-day kindergarten funding at 1.0 FTE was enacted for all pupils.
- New facilities funding was changed to include all bond elections held prior to July 1, 2015 with a .25 weighting.
- Bilingual education was changed to use the higher of .395 of contact hours or .185 of bilingual headcount.
- Low and high enrollment weighting was reinstated as in law prior to 2014-15.
- Early childhood funding was expanded by increasing state aid for four-year-old at-risk programs and provisions were made to fund three-year-old at-risk students.

- Mentoring and professional development were provided partial funding.
- Utilities, property and casualty insurance were added as options for payment from the capital outlay fund.
- Nonresident out-of-state pupil counts were changed for state aid purposes. Pupils count as 1.0 FTE for 2017-18 and 2018-19, reducing to .75 for 2019-20 and 2020-21, and .5 in 2021-22 and thereafter.

These changes were accompanied by increased appropriations to fund programs and to at least partially address the state supreme court's judicial monitoring where estimates of new required monies have ranged as high as $800 million. Total state aid appropriated to all 286 school districts for General Fund purposes, including the required 20 mill property tax, was $3,113,681,000 for FY 2021, and total General Fund budgets in all districts reached $3,625,672,000. State aid was 85.8% of total general fund budgets.

Supplemental General Fund

The 1992 SDFQPA scheme allowed school districts to engage additional local leeway spending within limits. Earlier reference to revenue and expenditure floors and caps in Kansas originated with SDFQPA, as all previous aid formulas were either unregulated local control or were built on reward-for-effort equalization as in the case of the SDEA of 1973. The initial SDFQPA created a base budget per pupil adjusted by program weights which resulted in the base budget amount serving as a uniform horizontal equity measure as well as an expression of vertical equity. However, the SDFQPA also provided school districts with additional local option spending leeway known at the time as the Local Enhancement Budget (LEB) which later was restyled as the Local Option Budget (LOB). At inception, the LEB was rightly named since it was meant to provide local choice for program enhancement. Over time, districts came to rely on it for funding basic services in the absence of state aid increases. Districts continue to rely on the LOB for basic supports, and its optional nature today is predicated by the minimum 15% of the total foundation aid that districts must now adopt, with a maximum of 33%. LOB adoption beyond the minimum is universal statewide for the reasons indicated.

The SEEA of 2017 preserved the LOB (named Supplemental General Fund in statute) and granted new local authority to increase this funding stream. Any district may now choose to levy up to an additional 33% of its Total Financial Aid entitlement (see SFA earlier in Table 18.1). To help offset this induced horizontal inequality, the state of Kansas provides equalized aid to the LOB, although at a different ratio than for TFA. The state currently equalizes the LOB in each district to the 81.2 percentile of assessed valuation per pupil, meaning that any district below that percentile is aided as if it were at that benchmark, while any district having an assessed valuation above the 81.2 percentile receives no LOB aid.

The LOB follows the formula shown in Figure 16.2. Calculation of each district's LOB authority follows Form 155[43] in the Kansas budget software. Total state

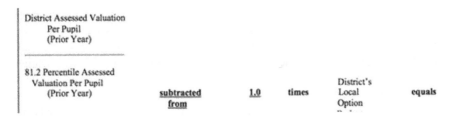

FIGURE 16.2. Local Option Budget Calculation FY 2021. Source: Kansas Legislative Research Department. 2014-2015 School Year School District Finance & Quality Performance Act & Bond & Interest State Aid Program—July 1, 2014.

aid appropriated to all 286 school districts for LOB purposes was $518,639,000 for FY 2021, and total LOB budgets in all districts reached $1,149,761,000. State aid was 45.1% of total LOB budgets.

Categorical or Other Funding

Special Education

Although special education was included in the earlier description of general fund pupil weightings in Kansas, the actual program operates as a separate fund. Inclusion in the general fund in Kansas is an artifice designed to temporarily inflate a school district's general fund for purposes of levying local option budget authority. The effect is to increase the budget for the supplemental general fund (LOB) since the LOB is calculated as a percentage of the general fund. Special education services state aid is therefore first deposited to the district's general fund and then transferred to its own special education fund.

Kansas school finance is characterized as intensely enrollment-driven, as the foundation aid formula relies on pupil counts expressed as FTE for all calculations and distribution of revenues. Special education is the exception to this principle by being tied primarily to the classroom unit. Consequently, the funded unit for special education is the classroom teacher.

Organization and operation of special education services in Kansas conform to any of three models: district-provided, interlocal agreements, and cooperatives. District-provided services are self-descriptive as single district budgets, directs, and controls services. Interlocals are multi-district entities organized as quasi-districts with separate budget authority. Cooperatives are also multi-district entities hosted by a member district, but with different legal structure wherein the host district carries the cooperative's special education budget on its books. In both interlocals and cooperatives, member districts share costs through member assessments. The choice of organization is often dictated by district size and cost-efficiency considerations perceived by the membership.

Calculation of special education services aid follows Form 118 of the Kansas budget software.[44] Key elements are the number of certified special education teachers, number of paraprofessionals, and teacher and pupil costs related to travel. The model recognizes that itinerant services are inherent to special education. Special education in Kansas is a reimbursement model, wherein costs are incurred locally and reimbursed by the state. However, state aid is not intended to fully cover the cost of special education, leaving school districts to fund the shortfall by budgeting general fund monies for transfer to the special education fund. The state is statutorily required to provide 92% of the excess cost of special education.[45] In practice, for FY 2021 state aid was approximately 73.2% of excess cost.

Special education aid in Kansas is based on a projected cost per teacher, set annually by the state department of education. Special education teachers are employees of each district or interlocal. The local district bears any cost difference if it provides a higher salary for its local teachers; in an interlocal agreement, member assessments are adjusted to cover any of these unfunded salary costs as the interlocal has its own salary schedule. The state further provides .4 funding for paraprofessionals hired by the district/interlocal/cooperative. State aid is therefore the product of 1.0 FTE teachers plus .4 FTE paraprofessionals multiplied by the allowable state per-teacher amount. For FY 2021, the state amount was $31,465. The resultant calculation yields the following procedure: [Estimated State Aid = (xFTE teachers + yFTE paras) * $31,465]. Special education service units can affect these costs via salary schedules and by balancing licensed teacher and paraprofessional positions.

Transportation services form the other major cost calculation in Kansas special education. Costs are reimbursed by the state in a cost-share ratio. Form 118 permits transportation salaries and benefits, insurance, equipment and maintenance, along with mileage costs for service delivery. Transportation costs are reimbursed at an 80% cost share with the district. A provision is made for maintenance in lieu of services for certain educational needs. Provision is also available for catastrophic services. The state and special education service providers also have access to all federal special education monies according to the state plan.

Total state aid to all 286 school districts for special education was $505,416,000 for FY 2021, and total special education budgets in all districts reached $1,017,356,000.

Transportation

Pupil transportation is a significant expense in Kansas given a largely rural and vast geography, and state aid for transportation is a weighting in every district's general fund calculation. Funding is provided for pupils residing at least 2.5 miles from school via a cost reimbursement formula, although others may ride at district expense. The state calculates a per-pupil cost using a complex density-cost graph that takes into account pupil sparsity. Operationally, the formula plots a curve of best fit for each district to yield a cost per pupil which is then multiplied against the number of transported pupils. This cost is tied to base state aid, thereby including it as a weighting to the general fund. In addition, transportation state aid for any school district is limited to no more than 110% of the prior year's actual expenditures. Calculation of transportation weighting is seen in Form 150 (Table III located inside Form 150).[46]

Total state aid to all 286 school districts for general transportation was $101,822,000 for FY 2021, and total student transportation expenditures in all districts reached $143,499,000. State aid was 71.0% of total regular route transportation budgets. No state aid is provided for activity trips and routes.

Technology

Currently, there is not any type of specific funding mechanism within the state aid formula for technology services. Rather, districts are able to provide these services through one of two mechanisms: localized expenditures from operational funds, or through the usage of the E-RATE program. The E-RATE program provides for federal dollars to discount local spending within various spending categories. Discounts range from 20% to 90% based upon the poverty level of the school district, with rural areas often receiving an even higher percentage.[47] These funds are dependent upon the expenditure of at least some local dollars.

Career and Technical Education

Kansas provides an additional 0.5 weighting for each FTE pupil enrolled in approved vocational courses. This weighting is added to the district enrollment and multiplied by the BASE.[48] Total state aid to all 286 school districts for career and technical education was $41,724,000 for FY 2021. Career and technical state aid was 36% of the total expenditures in the Career and Postsecondary Education fund.

School Nurses

Currently, there is not a specific funding mechanism for school nurses. Districts that have employed nurses for a number of years have made these positions possible through operational fund expenditures. With the infusion of funds made possible by pandemic relief (ESSER I-III) from the federal government, a number of districts have added nursing staff to assist with pandemic responses.

Textbooks and Classroom Supplies

While district budget documents contain a reserved fund for Textbook and Student Material Revolving expenditures, the availability of resources within this fund are all determined by local budget transfers (General or Supplemental General fund), locally assessed fees, or a combination thereof. The fund balance within this restricted fund often represents high peaks and low valleys as the cycle for purchases does not follow the same consistency of the revenue source(s) provided to it.

Student Support Services (Food Service)

All Kansas school districts are expected to operate a food service program in full compliance with federal and state regulations. Districts are free to structure food services in-house or to contract with outside vendors.

Virtually all districts engage in a four-way cost sharing in accord with local funding preferences. Reimbursement rates by the federal and state government carry the first part of costs, with the remainder shared by local districts and pupils. Each district is free to determine food service costs and to set the local prices and cost-shares. Each school board determines its participation, generally by scheduled transfers from the general fund to the food service fund. Any unfunded difference represents the cost to the pupil. The process is seen in Form 162[49] of the state budget software.

Total state aid appropriated to all 286 school districts for food service was $2,510,000 for FY 2021, and total food service expenditures in all districts reached $236,573,000. State aid was 1.1% of total food service budgets.

Other Topics as Addressed by the State

School districts may levy additional local property tax to provide funding for three specific areas of additional costs in some districts. Ancillary school facilities weighting allows districts with extraordinary enrollment growth to petition the State Board of Tax Appeals for authority to levy an additional property tax for up to two years to defray new facility start-up costs that arise beyond the costs financed in a bond election. After the initial two years, the levy amount phases out over a six-year period. A second option exists for districts experiencing enrollment decline. Such districts can appeal to the State Board of Tax Appeals for authority to levy an additional property tax for up to two years in an amount not greater than the revenue lost due to declining enrollment. This provision expired on June 30, 2018. The third levy is available to districts with average appraised home values greater than 125% of the state average. This cost-of-living weighting may not exceed 5% of a district's general fund budget and is subject to protest petition by local district voters.

Financing for these three funds is converted to a pupil weighting and becomes part of the state finance formula.[50] Revenue is generated entirely by local property tax in the districts utilizing these funds, with no state aid provision. Total funding for 2021 was $58,401,000.

The state provides various other aid to public schools including driver education, motorcycle safety, professional development, and mentor teacher programs. See Form 195 in the Kansas budget software for additional information on how these funds are distributed.

CAPITAL OUTLAY AND DEBT SERVICE

Capital Outlay

The state of Kansas provides considerable latitude to school districts in the use of their separate capital outlay funds. This fund is generally used for maintenance and upkeep and cash projects involving school facilities and equipment. Many school districts use this fund to accumulate cash reserves with an authorized tax levy, or occasionally utilizing scheduled transfers from the general fund. The 2017 SEEA expanded uses of the capital outlay fund to include utilities and property and casualty insurance. These options were eliminated in 2018.

School districts currently may locally levy up to 8 mills of property tax to fund the capital outlay. State aid for capital outlay was not provided from 2009 through 2014. The Kansas Legislature began funding state aid again in 2015, and implemented the current state aid formula in 2017, in response to a state supreme court ruling. The formula is equalized with the median assessed valuation per pupil (AVPP) receiving 25% state aid. Each $1,000 in AVPP above the median receives 1% less state aid. Each $1,000 below the median receives 1% additional state aid.

Total state aid to all 286 school districts for capital outlay was $72,726,000 for FY 2021, and total capital outlay revenue in all districts reached $508,054,000. State aid was 14.3% of total revenue.

Capital Improvement

The state provides capital improvement aid for school districts' facilities following successful local bond elections. State aid rates are based on assessed valuation per pupil (AVPP), with two separate formulas. Bond elections passed prior to July 1, 2015 generate state aid based on the median AVPP district receiving 25% state aid. Each $1,000 in AVPP above the median receives 1% less state aid. Inversely, each $1,000 below the median receives 1% additional state aid. For elections held after July 1, 2015 the district with the lowest AVPP receives 75% state aid. Every $1,000 increase in AVPP decreases state aid by 1%. This formula change currently reduces state aid to districts by approximately 36% from the prior formula.

Total capital improvement expenditures for FY 2021 were $605,952,000. Capital improvement state aid was $194,457,000 of that amount, or 32.1%.

School Facilities

The state of Kansas provides a general fund weighting for school districts that commence operation of new classroom facilities. The enrollment of the new school is multiplied by a factor of .25 provided other conditions are met. The weighting is calculated in Form 150[51] and is available only to districts exercising a minimum 25% LOB authority and which held a bond election prior to July 1, 2015 using bond money for new schools or classroom additions. The weighting is available upon commencing operation of the new facilities and is limited to two years thereafter. No school districts will qualify for this funding after 2020-21.

Total state aid to all 286 school districts for school facilities was $971,000 for FY 2021. State aid was less than one-tenth of 1% of total general fund budgets, excluding special education.

EMPLOYEE BENEFITS

Healthcare

Healthcare for school district employees is funded by General or Supplemental General fund monies. Currently, there does not exist a funding mechanism at the local, state, or federal level to specifically assist districts with this expenditure. The total premiums paid, both in dollars and percentages, varies widely across the 286 districts in Kansas. Additionally, districts offer a vast array of benefit packages across employee classifications, often using health care benefits as a primary driver for recruitment and retention purposes.

School districts currently fall under the jurisdiction of the Affordable Care Act (ACA) and as such, must either provide employee benefits as required or be subject to the employer penalty. There is currently one statewide health plan that districts may join, as well as a number of other employee trusts that are commonly associated with the same geographical area of member districts. Outside these options, districts may also sponsor their own plan, as well as provide for a self-funded mechanism for their employees. Aside from standards set by the Department of Labor (DOL), there is no statutory language providing for minimum coverage to employees, leaving room for a diverse set of offerings across the state.

Retirement

The Kansas Public Employees Retirement System (KPERS) applies to all public schools in Kansas. KPERS administers three defined-benefit retirement systems: the Kansas Public Employees Retirement System, the Kansas Police and Firemen's Retirement System, and the Kansas Retirement System for Judges. Schools are included under the public employee system.

School employees contribute to KPERS through payroll deduction. There is no school district contribution, as the state considers itself to be the payor for the employer share. The state's contribution for public school districts in 2020-21 was $485,620,000.

CHARTER SCHOOL FUNDING

The state currently has nine charter schools under the direct supervision of their local board of education. Charter schools in Kansas are independent public schools operating within a school district and are free of charge to parents and may be open to all pupils. These charter schools are subject to all rules and regulations pertaining to accreditation and other accountability within the state's charter guidelines.

NONPUBLIC SCHOOL FUNDING

Kansas has only minimally engaged in public funding for non-public schools, and typically has done so through mandated provision of certain shared services or by in-kind contributions. As a broad characterization, the state does not make provision for direct payment of state resources to private or parochial schools. The state does provide transportation for both public and nonpublic schoolchildren. Other sharing of services as mandated in federal law is observed.

The most direct involvement of Kansas public monies in non-public schools is by a tax credit provision initially adopted by the state legislature in 2014 and amended in the new SEEA of 2017. Under the SEEA, low-income pupils from the 100 lowest performing schools were granted tax credit scholarship options. Low income is defined as qualifying for free lunch programs. Qualified donors may make contributions and receive a 70% tax credit. A $500,000 per year contribution cap applies to donors. Qualified donors include corporations, insurance companies, or individuals. In 2021, $1,995,000 in scholarships were awarded to 632 students. A total of $3,535,000 were contributed to the program, resulting in tax credits of $2,475,000.

VIRTUAL EDUCATION

Local Kansas school districts may offer virtual courses, with funding for virtual pupils included in the general fund, but under a different formula than traditional pupils. Full-time virtual pupils are funded at $5,000 per FTE and part-time pupils are funded at $1,700 per FTE. Virtual pupils over the age of 19 are funded at $709 per credit earned up to a maximum of six credits.[52]

Enrollment in virtual schools increased significantly in 2020-21 due to families concerns about the COVID-19 pandemic. Total state aid to all 286 school districts for virtual education was $55,860,000 for FY 2021. Virtual education state aid was 1.8% of total general fund budgets, excluding special education.

FEDERAL COVID-19 FUNDING
(AMOUNTS RECEIVED & SPENDING PLANS)

The Coronavirus Aid, Relief, and Economic Security Act (CARES) was enacted on March 27, 2020. Embedded in the legislation was relief for K-12 schools under the Elementary and Secondary School Emergency Relief (ESSER I) fund. In total, the state of Kansas was awarded $84,106,416. Of that amount, $76,066,155 was designated to be distributed directly to school districts using the Title I formula.[53] The state board of education had authority to designate $8,031,261 which was designated to be used by school districts for special education expenditures related to the pandemic.[54]

The second piece of federal legislation enacted during the pandemic, the Emergency Coronavirus Relief Act, gave way to the ESSER II allocation. This provided funding in the amount of $332,846,815 for Kansas' 286 school districts.[55] The special education set-aside, designated for school districts, totaled $24,114,176, with half distributed in FY 2022 and half to be distributed in FY 2023.[56] In addition to the amounts awarded per district based upon the traditional Title formula, the Kansas State Board of Education (KSBE) enacted provisions for equality, ensuring a minimum funding per student (headcount) to shore up some of the large differences in awards to districts with lower poverty levels. These provisions, referred to as the True-Up Allocation, allowed for each district to be awarded up to a minimum of $300 per pupil if the previous award did not meet that threshold.

The final act of legislation as of the time of this writing was the American Rescue Plan (ARP), providing for the largest of the three awards within these pandemic-inspired legislative acts. Funds flowing directly to Kansas school districts were $747,526,664,.[57] The same provisions set forth by the state board of education for minimum dollars per pupil were applied to these awards as well, setting the threshold at $625 per pupil where applicable. Special education funds for ESSER III were a direct federal appropriation through the Title VI-B formula totaling approximately $28 million in Kansas.

Outside of the federal funding packages provided for the public school sector, the Emergency Assistance for Non-Public Schools (EANS) provided for two additional sums of money, targeted toward 75 of the state's eligible non-public schools. The EANS I package provided for approximately $27 million[58] in federal relief funds, while the EANS II package ushered in an additional $16 million.[59]

ENDNOTES

[1] We would like to acknowledge the work of John M. Heim and Randy D. Watson in coauthoring the chapter for the first edition of this work.

[2] David C. Thompson, S. Craig Neuenswander, John M. Heim, and Randy D. Watson. "Kansas." In Funding Public Schools in the United States and Indian Country, eds. David C. Thompson, S. Craig Neuenswander, John M. Heim, and Randy D. Watson (Charlotte, NC: IAP 2019), pp. 265-266.

[3] K.S.A. 72-5009, n.d.

[4] K.S.A. 72-5702, n.d.

[5] K.S.A. 72-6403, n.d.

[6] School Finance Overview-November 7, 2016

[7] K.S.A. 72-7001, n.d.

[8] K.S.A. 72-7030 et seq, n.d.

[9] K.S.A. 72-6410, n.d.

[10] K.S.A. 72-6463 et seq, n.d.

[11] K.S.A. 72-5131 et seq, n.d.

[12] Early analysis has begun. See, e.g., Shiloh J. Vincent, A Longitudinal Study of Selected State School Aid Formula Changes in Kansas 1992-2017, with Emphasis on the Classroom Learning Assuring Student Success (CLASS) Act of 2015. Unpublished doctoral dissertation, Kansas State University (2018); see also Kellen J. Adams, An Overview of Selected Impacts and Reconcep-

tualization of State Aid to Public School Infrastructure in Three Representative Kansas School Districts. Unpublished doctoral dissertation, Kansas State University (2018).

13 Caldwell v. State No. 50616 (Kan. Dist. Ct. Aug. 30, 1972).

14 Knowles v. State Bd. of Educ., 547 P.2d 699 (Kan. 1976).

15 Among others see Mock v. State (1991); numerous iterations of Montoy v. State (1999-2006); likewise Gannon v. State (2010-2017, citations omitted).

16 http://www.kslegresearch.org/KLRD-web/Publications/Education/2017-Article6-ProposedConstitutnlAmndmnts.pdf

17 HB 2506 (2014)

18 SB 7 (2015)

19 HB 2655 (2016)

20 HB 2001 (2016)

21 SB 19 (2018)

22 SB 423 (2018)

23 SB 61 (2018)

24 SB 16 (2019)

25 KSDE Data Central (Headcount Enrollment by Grade, Race, & Gender)

26 KSDE Data Central (Certified Personnel by Personnel Type)

27 KSDE Data Central (Number of Schools, Other Buildings, & Programs)

28 KSDE Report Card

29 KSDE Report Card

30 KSDE Report Card

31 KSDE Report Card

32 Gannon VII Litigation

33 KSDE Report Card (Headcount Enrollment by Grade, Race, & Gender)

34 History of School District Consolidations (KSDE)

35 Schools for Fair Funding (Funding over Time)

36 "How Has Education Funding Changed Over Time?" 2017

37 "How Has Education Funding Changed Over Time?" 2017

38 "How Has Education Funding Changed Over Time?" 2017

39 Tab F150. Retrieved from: http://www.ksde.org/Agency/Fiscal-and-Administrative-Services/School-Finance/Budget-Information/USD-Budget-Software

40 Tab F148. Retrieved from: http://www.ksde.org/Agency/Fiscal-and-Administrative-Services/School-Finance/Budget-Information/USD-Budget-Software

41 Not discussed here is the concept of taxpayer equity, wherein the state partly derives revenue to fund the school aid formula from a statewide uniform property tax rate for schools. This element completes the underlying philosophy of pupil/taxpayer equity via a uniform base per pupil budget (horizontal pupil equity), weightings (vertical pupil equity), uniform tax levy (horizontal taxpayer equity), and state aid making up the difference between tax yield and budget authority (vertical taxpayer equity). The concept of adequacy is not addressed here.

42 BASE (Base Aid for Student Excellence) https://www.ksde.org/Portals/0/School%20Finance/Base%20State%20Aid%20for%20Excellence.pdf?ver=2021-09-23-104644-393

43 Tab F155. Retrieved from: http://www.ksde.org/Agency/Fiscal-and-Administrative-Services/School-Finance/Budget-Information/USD-Budget-Software

44 Tab F118. Retrieved from: http://www.ksde.org/Agency/Fiscal-and-Administrative-Services/School-Finance/Budget-Information/USD-Budget-Software

45 K.S.A. 72-3422

46 Tab F150. Retrieved from: http://www.ksde.org/Agency/Fiscal-and-Administrative-Services/School-Finance/Budget-Information/USD-Budget-Software

47 Federal Communications Commission E-Rate https://www.fcc.gov/consumers/guides/universal-service-program-schools-and-libraries-e-rate

[48] Tab F150. Retrieved from: http://www.ksde.org/Agency/Fiscal-and-Administrative-Services/School-Finance/Budget-Information/USD-Budget-Software

[49] Tab F162. Retrieved from: http://www.ksde.org/Agency/Fiscal-and-Administrative-Services/School-Finance/Budget-Information/USD-Budget-Software

[50] Tab F242. Retrieved from: http://www.ksde.org/Agency/Fiscal-and-Administrative-Services/School-Finance/Budget-Information/USD-Budget-Software

[51] Tab F150. Retrieved from: http://www.ksde.org/Agency/Fiscal-and-Administrative-Services/School-Finance/Budget-Information/USD-Budget-Software

[52] Tab F150. Retrieved from: http://www.ksde.org/Agency/Fiscal-and-Administrative-Services/School-Finance/Budget-Information/USD-Budget-Software

[53] ESSER I Allocations (KSDE)

[54] ESSER I SPED Allocations (KSDE)

[55] ESSER II Allocations (KSDE)

[56] ESSER II SPED Allocations (KSDE)

[57] ESSER III Allocations (KSDE)

[58] EANS I (KSDE)

[59] EANS II (KSDE)

CHAPTER 17

KENTUCKY

William E. Thro[1]
University of Kentucky

Any discussion of school finance in the Commonwealth of Kentucky must deal with two realities. First, there are great disparities between Appalachia and the rest of the State. Henry Caudill's 1963 classic, "Night Comes to the Cumberlands,"[2] inspired President Johnson's War on Poverty,[3] but that War was lost in Eastern Kentucky.[4] By any objective measure, the fifty-four Kentucky counties[5] served by the Appalachian Regional Commission lag behind the rest of the Commonwealth and the Nation.[6] Indeed, in terms of per capita income, poverty rate, percentage of adults with a high school diploma, percentage of adults with a college degree, and homes with broadband access, the non-Appalachian counties of Kentucky (population 3.2 million) closely track the national average,[7] but the Appalachian counties (population 1.1 million) represent the worst of American poverty.[8]

Second, Kentucky believes in local government and local control.[9] Despite a population of only 4.3 million and a relatively small geographic area, Kentucky has 120 counties, more than any State except Texas, Georgia, and Virginia. [10] Each of those 120 counties has a school district and there are an additional fifty-three independent school districts or a total of 173 school districts.[11] Consequently, Kentucky does not and cannot take advantage of the efficiencies associated with economies of scale.

Funding Public Schools in the United States, Indian Country,
and US Territories (Second Edition), pages 283–295.
Copyright © 2023 by Information Age Publishing
www.infoagepub.com

This Chapter on school finance in Kentucky has seven distinct Sections. Section I reviews the school finance litigation that is the foundation of Kentucky school finance in the twenty-first century. Section II discusses the current political climate. Section III examines the current distribution formula. Section IV explores the current provisions concerning revenue. Section V details employee benefits with an emphasis on Kentucky's troubled pension system. Section VI describes funding for non-public schools. Finally, Section VII explores how the Covid Pandemic lead to a clash between the Governor and the Legislature that may well shape the future of school finance.

GENERAL BACKGROUND

The foundation of Kentucky's School Finance System is *Rose v. Council for Better Education*,[12] a 1989 decision where the Supreme Court of Kentucky invalidated *every* statute dealing with K-12 Education.[13] In doing so, *Rose* recognized that educational equality depends not on money or racial desegregation, but involves the complex interaction of multiple factors.[14] Twenty years later, in *Horne v. Flores*,[15] the U.S. Supreme Court reached a similar conclusion.[16] Both the courts in other State and the academy generally ignore this aspect of *Rose*, but it represents a profound truth. [17]

Three aspects of Rose are particularly important. First, it is faithful to the constitutional text. Second, it acknowledged local control as an implicit constitutional value. Third, it recognized the need for the legislature, not the judiciary, to solve the constitutional problem.

Faithful to the Constitutional Text

Rose was faithful to the constitutional text. Kentucky's education clause provides, "[t]he General Assembly shall, by appropriate legislation, provide for an efficient system of common schools throughout the state."[18] In describing how these "few simple, but direct words" establish "the will of the people with regard to the importance of providing public education in the Commonwealth,"[19] the Court explained:

> Several conclusions readily appear from a reading of this section. First, it is the obligation, the sole obligation, of the General Assembly to provide for a system of common schools in Kentucky. The obligation to so provide is clear and unequivocal and is, in effect, a constitutional mandate. Next, the school system must be provided throughout the entire state, with no area (or its children) being omitted. The creation, implementation and maintenance of the school system must be achieved by appropriate legislation. Finally, the system must be an efficient one.[20]

In resolving the critical issue—the meaning of "efficient"—*Rose* considered "foreign cases, along with our constitutional debates, Kentucky precedents and the opinion of experts in formulating the definition of 'efficient' as it appears in our Constitution."[21]

However, instead of adopting a quality standard adopted by another branch of government, *Rose* developed its own standard. Not surprisingly, it failed. The Court declared that:

> an efficient system of education must have as its goal to provide each and every child with at least the seven following capacities: (i) sufficient oral and written communication skills to enable students to function in a complex and rapidly changing civilization; (ii) sufficient knowledge of economic, social, and political systems to enable the student to make informed choices; (iii) sufficient understanding of governmental processes to enable the student to understand the issues that affect his or her community, state, and nation; (iv) sufficient self-knowledge and knowledge of his or her mental and physical wellness; (v) sufficient grounding in the arts to enable each student to appreciate his or her cultural and historical heritage; (vi) sufficient training or preparation for advanced training in either academic or vocational fields so as to enable each child to choose and pursue life work intelligently; and (vii) sufficient levels of academic or vocational skills to enable public school students to compete favorably with their counterparts in surrounding states, in academics or in the job market.[22]

As I noted in 1998, "[i]f this standard is taken literally, there is not a public school system in America that meets it."[23] A standard that is extraordinarily difficult to meet and is so substantively vague is inappropriate. While that criticism is still valid, the Kentucky courts' refusal to enforce the standard tempers the criticism. After almost three decades, the *Rose* standard is not substantive, but merely aspirational.

Acknowledged Local Control as a Constitutional Value

Second, while Kentucky does not have an explicit constitutional provision concerning local control, *Rose* implicitly recognized local control as a structural constitutional value. The Court seemed aware that the General Assembly would never contemplate abandoning local school districts when it observed:

> In no way does this constitutional requirement act as a limitation on the General Assembly's power to create local school entities and to grant to those entities the authority to supplement the state system. Therefore, if the General Assembly decides to establish local school entities, it may also empower them to enact local revenue initiatives to supplement the uniform, equal educational effort that the General Assembly must provide. This includes not only revenue measures similar to the special taxes previously discussed, but also the power to assess local ad valorem taxes on real property and personal property at a rate over and above that set by the General Assembly to fund the statewide system of com-

mon schools. Such local efforts may not be used by the General Assembly as a substitute for providing an adequate, equal, and substantially uniform educational system throughout this state.[24]

In effect, the Court seems to be harmonizing the structural constitutional value of local control with the textual constitutional value of federalism.

The Legislature Must Solve the Constitutional Problem

Third, *Rose* recognized the need for the legislative branch, not the judiciary, to solve the constitutional problem. *Rose* invalidated the entire educational *system*,[25] but emphasized "the *sole responsibility*... lies with the General Assembly."[26] The Court was careful "not to instruct the General Assembly to enact any specific legislation" or "direct the members of the General Assembly to raise taxes."[27] The Court's role was to "only decide the nature of the constitutional mandate."[28] Instead of creating a judicial solution,[29] the Court "directed the General Assembly to recreate and redesign a new system" that will guarantee to all children the opportunity for an adequate education, through a *state* system."[30]

CURRENT POLITICAL CLIMATE

In November 2019, Democrat Attorney General Andy Beshear, emphasizing his support for the dignity of classroom teachers and promising a $2,000 bonus for all teachers, narrowly defeated incumbent Republican Governor Matt Bevin. However, the Republicans swept all other statewide offices. For the first time in the State's history, a Democratic Governor faces a Republican Legislature and a Republican Attorney General, Secretary of State, Treasurer, Agriculture Commissioner, and Auditor.

In 2020, opposition to the Governor's Covid Policies as well as other issues led to further Republican gains. At present, the Republicans have more than seventy percent of the seats in both the House and Senate. While the Governor can veto any legislation, the legislature can override a veto with a simple majority. Thus, dominant Republican majority can easily override any veto.

In 2021, the Republican majority substantially limited the Governor's emergency powers during the thirty-day (non-budget) legislative session. In 2022, the Republican majority broke with tradition by introducing a budget before the Governor gave his budget address. The 2022-24 two-year budget reflects the Republican majority's priorities. It seems that Kentucky has entered an era of legislative dominance.

DISTRIBUTION FORMULAS

In 1990, immediately after *Rose*, The General Assembly—implicitly acknowledging both political reality and the constitutional limitation of local control—chose to enact reform rather than a revolution. Instead of dividing and consolidating school districts, moving to a system of centralized financing or radically altering teacher compensation, the legislature chose a path that retained the present school districts, continued a significant degree of local financing, and devoted additional resources to the current teacher compensation scheme.[31]

Specifically, the legislature passed the Support Educational Excellence in Kentucky ("SEEK") program, which provides the foundation for school finance in Kentucky.[32] Administered by the Kentucky Department of Education, SEEK attempts to ensure that each school district has sufficient funds to provide a constitutionally sufficient education to every student. Essentially, the State, guarantees to each district a certain amount of funding per pupil ("Guaranteed Base Funding"), and enhances this amount for certain children with unique circumstances ("Adjustments" or "Add-Ons").[33] The sum of the Guaranteed Base Funding and the Adjustments is the "Adjusted SEEK Base Funding."[34]

Local school districts are required to make a "Local Effort" by imposing real and personal property taxes.[35] To the extent the "Local Effort" fails to generate the amount of the "Adjusted Seek Base Funding," the State makes up the difference ("Calculated State SEEK Funding").[36] Additionally, local school districts have the option of raising additional revenue, some of which the State will match. Finally, the State provides a set amount of capital funding ($100) for each pupil. The remainder of this Section discusses each of these components in more detail.

GUARANTEED BASE FUNDING

During each two-year budget cycle, the Kentucky General Assembly establishes a per-pupil amount of funding.[37] Each school district receives a "Guaranteed Base Funding" amount, which is calculated by multiplying the per pupil funding amount by the prior year average daily attendance[38] with an adjustment for growth in enrollment. [39] If a district experiences a dramatic decline in enrollment, there are statutory provisions to minimize the impact.[40]

Adjustments to the SEEK Guaranteed Base

Because it costs more to educate certain children, there are "add-on" adjustments for: (1) at risk children; (2) children who receive instruction in a home or hospital setting; (3) exceptional children (those with disabilities); and (4) limited English proficiency children.[41] In addition, because transportation costs vary widely, school districts with greater transportation costs receive an adjustment.[42] Each of these "add-ons" is discussed in more detail below.

At-Risk Funding

Local school districts receive an additional fifteen percent of Guarantee Base Per Pupil Funding Amount for every child who receives free lunch under the federal government's school lunch program.[43]

Home and Hospital Funding

If a child is receiving instruction in a home or hospital funding under the provisions of state law, then the school district receives an additional sum of money equal to the Guaranteed Base Funding amount per pupil less $100.[44]

Exceptional Child Funding (Individuals with Disabilities)

Local school districts receive additional funds for any student who receives services under the Individuals with Disabilities Education Act. State law divides these students into three categories: (1) low incidence disabilities; (2) moderate incident disabilities; and (3) high incidence disabilities.[45] A school district receives an additional 24% of base funding for each child with low incidence disabilities; an additional 117% of base funding for each child with moderate incidence disabilities; and an additional 235% of base funding for each child with high incidence disabilities.[46]

Limited English Proficiency Funding

School districts receive an additional 9.6% of the Guaranteed Based Per Pupil Funding for each Limited English Proficiency student.[47] Federal law determines whether a child qualifies as Limited English Proficiency.

Transportation Funding

Kentucky law establishes a complex formula for calculating transportation costs.[48] The State's school districts are divided into density groups based on frequency, length, and type of transportation provided by the district.[49] Each density group then receives a set amount of money per pupil being transported by the district.[50] To the extent the school district transports students to local vocational schools or to the Kentucky School for the Deaf or the Kentucky School for the Blind, it will receive additional transportation money.[51]

Capital Outlay and Debt Service

With respect to capital funding, the State guarantees that each school district will receive $100 per pupil per year.[52] Local districts are required to generate a portion of this $100 through a local property tax.[53]

SOURCES OF REVENUE

Required Local Effort

As a condition of receiving any SEEK funding, Kentucky law requires each local school district to levy a minimum equivalent tax rate of 30 cents per $100 in assessed value of property and motor vehicles.[54] As noted above, to the extent the required local efforts fail to generate the amount required for the school district's Adjusted SEEK Base Funding, the State makes up the difference through Calculated State SEEK Funding.[55]

Optional Local Effort

In addition to the required local effort, school districts have two options to raise additional revenues.

First, under "Tier One Funding," school districts are permitted to raise up to fifteen percent of the district's Adjusted SEEK Base Funding (Guaranteed Base Funding + Adjustments).[56] If a district pursues this option, then the State will equalize the additional revenue. The level of equalization is set during each two-year budget cycle and generally helps property poor districts more than property rich districts.[57]

Second, under "Tier Two Funding," school districts—with the approval of the voters—may impose additional taxes and raise up to thirty percent of the district's Adjusted SEEK Base Funding plus the revenue raised in Tier One. The State does not match Tier Two Funds.[58]

EMPLOYEE BENEFITS

A generation after it was first established, the SEEK plan remains in place. Although the State has managed to maintain and even slightly increase the amount of per pupil funding in the SEEK program, the State has steadily shifted responsibilities to the local school districts.[59] This decrease reflects the ever-increasing financial pressures on Kentucky's school finance system. Two factors are particularly relevant—the costs of funding of the Kentucky Teacher Retirement and the dramatic increase in the costs of other governmental programs. The remainder of this Section discusses both factors.

Funding of the Kentucky's Public Employment Retirement System

Kentucky's defined benefit pension system for teachers and other public employees is both generous and ultimately unsustainable. To calculate the pension benefit, the State multiplies the teacher's years of service by the average of the three highest years' salary and then multiplying that total by a benefit factor (2.5%).[60] Teachers are generally able to retire with unreduced benefits after twenty-seven years of service, or the age of sixty, whichever comes first.[61] Conceivably, a teacher can retire before the age of fifty and receive two-thirds of his or her pay for the rest of their lives. Those who work until the age of sixty-five generally will receive up to one hundred percent of their pay.

For a variety of reasons, Kentucky's public pension systems are unable to meet future obligations.[62] Estimates of unfunded liability range for $33 to $84 billion. Moreover, the substantial amount of unfunded liability has led national bond rating agencies to downgrade Kentucky's credit rating and, thus, increase the costs of debt funding for roads and other infrastructure projects.

To solve the pension crisis, the legislature will have to reduce benefits substantially, increase expenditures on pensions, or some combination. Given the state constitutional constraints on reducing benefits, solving the pension crisis likely will involve increased expenditures on pensions. If expenditures on pensions are increased, it is virtually inevitable that the State will reduce expenditures on K-12 education.

CHARTER SCHOOL FUNDING

Although Kentucky has a charter school statute, there is no formal funding mechanism and, thus, there are no charter schools. Many Republicans in the General Assembly are eager to establish a funding mechanism. With Republican super-majorities in both chambers, it seems likely there will be a funding mechanism.

NONPUBLIC SCHOOL FUNDING

In 2021, the General Assembly overrode the Governor's veto and enacted legislation to supply $25 million in tax credits for students to attend private schools in the State's eight largest counties or to attend a public school in another district.

The Council for Better Education, the same group that brought the landmark school finance case, immediately challenged the state constitutionality of the legislation. In October of 2021, the Franklin Circuit Court, the trial court for the state capital of Frankfort, declared the statute unconstitutional.[63] The case is on appeal as of March 2022.

COVID ISSUES

In much of America, the Covid Pandemic led to disputes over in-person instruction, mask mandates, and educational funding. Yet, in Kentucky, the weakness of the teachers' unions and strong conservative sentiment outside of Louisville and Lexington largely diminished disputes over in person instruction and mask mandates. Most districts returned to in-person instruction in the Fall of 2020 and most dropped the mask mandates when the local school boards felt it was safe. As to funding, the Kentucky Department of Education effectively dispersed federal funds to local school districts to cover increased costs.[64]

However, Kentucky did experience a constitutional crisis—on both the state and federal levels—over the scope of the Governor's authority to deal with the Covid Pandemic. This constitutional crisis had two stages.

First, while Kentucky's Governor has a statutory—and arguably constitutional, "emergency power" of limited scope and duration, he lacks "*carte blanche* to disregard the Constitution for as long as the . . . problem persists."[65] At one point, the Governor prohibited "any event or convening that brings together groups of individuals."[66] His Orders often focused on *why* people were gathering rather than *how* people were gathering.[67] On occasion, he explicitly targeted religious services.[68] When a church held a drive-in Easter service where congregants parked their cars in the church's parking lot and listened to a sermon over a loudspeaker, the state police issued citations.[69]

Although the Governor generally lost the religious liberty challenges in federal court, in the Fall of 2020, the Supreme Court of Kentucky held his overall actions did not violate the state statute granting him emergency powers.[70] In doing so, the Court observed, "[w]hile the authority exercised by the Governor in accordance with [the statute] is necessarily broad," there are "checks on that authority," including "legislative amendment or revocation of the emergency powers granted the Governor."[71]

Second, when the General Assembly convened in January 2021, it immediately passed "H.B. 1, S.B. 1, and S.B. 2 which restrict the Governor's ability to take unilateral action during declared emergencies. The Governor vetoed those bills, and the General Assembly overrode his vetoes. The bills became effective on February 2, 2021."[72] The Governor then immediately challenged the constitutionality of the statutes, and a local trial court issued an injunction. Thus, the Court was confronted with the issue of whether the General Assembly could do what the Court implied it could do.

On August 10, 2021, while the Supreme Court of Kentucky was considering the appeal, the Governor, responding to the Delta Variant surge, issued a new Executive Order requiring "[a]ll individuals—all teachers, staff, students, and visitors—must cover their nose and mouth with a face covering when indoors in all" public and private schools.[73] On August 19, 2021, recognizing the conflict between this unilateral action and the statutes passed by the General Assembly, a federal trial court enjoined the Governor's Executive Order. In doing so, the federal court observed, the "Executive Branch cannot simply ignore laws passed by the duly elected representatives of the citizens of the Commonwealth of Kentucky. Therein lies tyranny. If the citizens dislike the laws passed, the remedy lies with them, at the polls."[74]

Two days later, the Supreme Court of Kentucky, meeting on Saturday for the first time in its history, upheld the statutes and dissolved the injunction.[75] In doing so, the Court declared the "General Assembly is the policy-making body for the Commonwealth, not the Governor or the courts, equitable considerations support enforcing a legislative body's policy choices." [76] Thus, the constitutional crisis ended with a clear legislative victory and a repudiation of the Governor's assertions of a broad executive power.

CONCLUSION

Thirty years after *Rose* prompted a significant reform of all aspects of education, Kentucky's SEEK system of school financing remains in place. However, the recently elected Republican super-majorities in both chambers of the Legislature have a quite different paradigm of educational policy and are less deferential to public education leaders. Having prevailed over the Governor in a constitutional battle over the response to the Covid Pandemic, the General Assembly is beginning to assert its powers. Assuming the Legislature's policy choices are contrary to the wishes of public education leaders—an assumption that seems almost inevitable—then another school finance case seems likely.

ENDNOTES

[1] General Counsel of the University of Kentucky, former Solicitor General of Virginia, and recipient of the McGhehey Award for Education Law and the Kaplin Award for Higher Education Law & Policy Scholarship. Mr. Thro is also a Fellow of the National Association of College & University Attorneys, and Distinguished Research Fellow of the National Education Finance Academy. Mr. Thro writes in his personal capacity and his views do not constitute the views of the University of Kentucky. Mr. Thro thanks Linda Speakman for her editorial assistance.

[2] See Henry M. Caudill, Night Comes To the Cumberlands (1963).

[3] See John Cheves, Bill Estep, & Linda Blackford, Fifty Years of Night 74 (2014) (Kindle Edition) (chronicling the current conditions of Appalachian Kentucky on the fiftieth anniversary of Caudill's work).

[4] See Kevin D. Williamson, Left Behind: An Elegy for Appalachia, National Review December 16, 2013, at 28.

[5] Those counties are Adair, Bath, Bell, Boyd, Breathitt, Carter, Casey, Clark, Clay, Clinton, Cumberland, Edmonson, Elliott, Estill, Fleming, Floyd, Garrard, Green, Greenup, Harlan, Hart, Jackson, Johnson, Knott, Knox, Laurel, Lawrence, Lee, Leslie, Letcher, Lewis, Lincoln, McCreary, Madison, Magoffin, Martin, Menifee, Metcalfe, Monroe, Montgomery, Morgan, Nicholas, Owsley, Perry, Pike, Powell, Pulaski, Robertson, Rockcastle, Rowan, Russell, Wayne, Whitley, and Wolfe.

[6] See Chives, Estep, & Blackford, supra note 2, at 3320 (chart comparing Appalachian Counties, non-Appalachian Counties, and nation as a whole).

[7] Id. For example, non-Appalachia Kentucky has a per capita income of $25,130 and the Nation has a per capita income of $28,501. The poverty rate is 16% for non-Appalachia Kentucky and 14% for the Nation. The percentage of adults without a high school diploma is identical (14%). Non-Appalachia Kentucky is slightly below the United States in terms of adult college graduates (28%-24%) and has an identical broadband rate (98%).

[8] Id. To illustrate, Appalachia Kentucky has a per capita income of $18,158 and the Nation has a per capita income of $28,501. The poverty rate is 25% for Appalachia Kentucky and 14% for the Nation. The percentage of adults without a high school diploma is 26%; almost double the national norm of 14%. Appalachia Kentucky is far below the United States in terms of adult college graduates (28%-12%) and substantially trails broadband rate (98%-87%).

[9] This commitment to local control is accentuated by the current political climate. For a discussion of the impact of political events on school finance, see generally William E. Thro & Angela S. Martin, State of the States—Kentucky, 47 Journal of Education Finance issue 5, (2022)(online only); William E. Thro, State of the States—Kentucky, 46 Journal of Education Finance 285 (2021); William E. Thro, State of the States—Kentucky, 45 Journal of Education Finance 303 (2020); William E. Thro, State of the States—Kentucky, 44 Journal of Education Finance 274 (2019),

[10] See United States Census Bureau, Geographic Areas Reference Manual (2018) (available at https://www.census.gov/geo/reference/garm.html)

[11] See Kentucky Department of Education, Kentucky Education Facts (2018) (available at https://education.ky.gov/comm/edfacts/Pages/default.aspx).

[12] 790 S.W.2d 186 (Ky. 1989).

[13] For a discussion of the long-term significance of Rose, see Scott R. Bauries, Forward: Rights, Remedies, and Rose, 98 Ky. L.J. 703 (2010); William E. Thro, Judicial Humility: The Enduring Legacy of Rose v. Council for Better Education, 98 Ky. L.J. 717 (2010); R. Craig Wood, Justiciability, Adequacy, Advocacy, and the "American Dream," 92 Ky. L.J. 739 (2010).

[14] Some scholars call for a renewed emphasis on financial resources. See William S. Koski & Rob Reich, When "Adequate" Isn't: The Retreat from Equity in Educational Law and Policy and Why It Matters, 56 Emory L.J. 545, 547 (2006)

15 Horne v. Flores, 557 U.S. 443 (2009). For some early observations about the impact of Horne, see William E. Thro, The Many Faces of Compliance: The Supreme Court's Decision in Horne v. Flores, 75 School Business Affairs 14 (October 2009).

16 Horne, 557 U.S. at 459-71.

17 But see D. Frank Vinik, The Contrasting Politics of Remedy: The Alabama and Kentucky School Equity Funding Suits, 22 Journal of Education Finance 60 (1996).

18 Ky. Const. § 183.

19 Rose, 790 S.W.2d at 205.

20 Id.

21 Id. at 210.

22 Rose, 790 S.W.2d at 212.

23 William E. Thro, A New Approach to State Constitutional Analysis in School Finance Litigation, 14 J. L. & Pol. 525, 548 (1998).

24 Rose, 790 S.W.2d at 211-12 (footnotes omitted)

25 The court declared that:

Lest there be any doubt, the result of our decision is that Kentucky's *entire system* of common schools is unconstitutional. There is no allegation that only part of the common school system is invalid, and we find no such circumstance. This decision applies to the entire sweep of the system-all its parts and parcels. This decision applies to the statutes creating, implementing and financing the *system* and to all regulations, etc., pertaining thereto. This decision covers the creation of local school districts, school boards, and the Kentucky Department of Education to the Minimum Foundation Program and Power Equalization Program. It covers school construction and maintenance, teacher certification-the whole gamut of the common school system in Kentucky.

While individual statutes are not herein addressed specifically or considered and declared to be facially unconstitutional, the statutory system as a whole and the interrelationship of the parts therein are hereby declared to be in violation of Section 183 of the Kentucky Constitution. Just as the bricks and mortar used in the construction of a schoolhouse, while contributing to the building's facade, do not ensure the overall structural adequacy of the schoolhouse, particular statutes drafted by the legislature in crafting and designing the current school system are not unconstitutional in and of themselves. Like the crumbling schoolhouse which must be redesigned and revitalized for more efficient use, with some component parts found to be adequate, some found to be less than adequate, statutes relating to education may be reenacted as components of a constitutional system if they combine with other component statutes to form an efficient and thereby constitutional system. *Rose*, 790 S.W.2d at 215.

26 Rose, 790 S.W.2d at 216.

27 Id. at 212.

28 Id.

29 For example, the Court could have ordered specific reforms such as a finance system that did not utilize local property taxes, a system of public-school vouchers, a transformation of the teacher certification process, the consolidation or division of school districts, or the centralized administration of education.

30 Rose, 790 S.W.2d at 212.

31 This is not a criticism of the profound and significant reforms undertaken by the Kentucky Education Reform Act. Rather, it is an acknowledgement that the pre-Rose and post-Rose educational systems are structurally the same.

32 Kentucky Department of Education, Support Education Excellence in Kentucky (SEEK) Executive Summary (2021) (available at https://education.ky.gov/districts/SEEK/Pages/default.aspx).

33 If enrollment rises dramatically during the academic year, the State may provide additional funds. See Ky. Rev. Stat. § 158.060(1).

34 SEEK Executive Summary, supra note 31, at 3.

35 See Ky. Rev. Stat. § 160.470(9)(a). Currently, the tax rate is 30 cents per $100 in assessed value.

36 SEEK Executive Summary, supra note 31, at 3.

[37] Id. at 1.

[38] The statute provides that average daily attendance is:

the aggregate days attended by pupils in a public school, adjusted for weather-related low attendance days if applicable, divided by the actual number of days school is in session, after the five (5) days with the lowest attendance have been deducted.

Ky Rev. Stat § 157.320(1). In addition, there are adjustments "for virtual and performance-based attendance, students under or over the funding age, and students residing in one district who attend in another district without a properly executed transfer agreement." *SEEK Executive Summary, supra* note 31, at 1.

[39] Id.

[40] Ky Rev. Stat. § 157.360(9) and (10).

[41] SEEK Executive Summary, supra note 31, at 1.

[42] Id. at 2.

[43] SEEK Executive Summary, supra note 31, at 1.

[44] See Ky. Rev. Stat. 157.270. The $100 reduction is intended to prevent capital outlay funding from being used for students who do not actually attend pubic schools. SEEK Executive Summary, supra note 31, at 2.

[45] See Ky. Rev. Stat. § 157.200.

[46] SEEK Executive Summary, supra note 31, at 2.

[47] Id. at 3.

[48] See Ky. Rev. Stat. § 157.370.

[49] Specifically, the statute:

requires a graph to be constructed utilizing the district's gross transported pupil density. At least nine different density groups must be identified by analyzing the results of the gross transported pupil density calculations. A smoothed graph of cost is then developed for each density group to determine the average cost per pupil per day.

Costs shall be determined separately for county school districts and independent school districts. The cost of transportation includes all costs recorded for the transportation to and from schools in the general current expense fund and function 2700 (student transportation). Each district in an identified density group receives funding based on the average cost per pupil per day for that group as determined by the smoothed graph which provides an incentive for districts to supply transportation services efficiently. In addition, independent districts are limited to the lowest average cost per pupil per day for their district or the lowest average cost per pupil per day for a county school district.

SEEK Executive Summary, supra note 31, at 2.

[50] As the Kentucky Department of Education explained:

The cost of transportation includes amounts representing depreciation of district-owned buses. A district will theoretically receive 100% of the state bid price or actual purchase price of a bus after year 10 and 124% of the state bid price or actual purchase price of a bus at the end of the funding cycle after year 14.

SEEK Executive Summary, supra note 31, at 2.

[51] Id. at 3.

[52] Id.

[53] Id.

[54] See Ky. Rev. Stat. § 160.470(9)(a).

[55] SEEK Executive Summary, supra note 31, at 4. Additionally, "[i]f local share using the prior year assessment increased by four percent (4%) plus the value of current year new property is less than local share using the current year assessment, that difference is the amount of additional funding to be provided." Id.

[56] Id.

[57] Id.

[58] Id.

[59] See Kentucky Center for Economic Policy, State Funding for Education Has Been Stagnant, But the 2022-24 Budget Presents a Unique Opportunity to Begin Reinvesting (2022) (available at https://kypolicy.org/state-education-funding-2022-2024-opportunity-for-reinvestment/)

[60] Ky. Rev. Stat. §§ 161.220(9); 161.620.

[61] See Ky Rev. Stat. § 161.600.

[62] By one measure, Kentucky's public pension systems are the worst funded among the fifty States. See Standard & Poor's, U.S. State Pensions Weak Market Returns Will Contribute to Rise in Expense, (2016).

[63] Council for Better Education, Inc. v. Johnson, No. 21-CI-461 (Ky. Franklin Cir. Ct. Oct. 8, 2021).

[64] Kentucky Department of Education, Covid 19 Resources for School Districts Grant Information (2022) (available at https://education.ky.gov/districts/fin/Pages/COVID-19.aspx).

[65] Calvary Chapel Dayton Valley v. Sisolak, 140 S. Ct. 2603, 2605 (2020) (Alito, J., joined by Thomas & Kavanaugh, JJ., dissenting),

[66] Ramsek v. Beshear, 989 F.3d 494, 496 (6th Cir. 2021)

[67] As the Sixth Circuit noted, "How can the same person be trusted to comply with social-distancing and other health guidelines in secular settings but not be trusted to do the same in religious settings?" Roberts v. Neace, 958 F.3d 409, 414 (6th Cir. 2020).

[68] Charles J. Russo, Even In A Pandemic, The Constitution Cannot Be Put Away and Forgotten: Emory University Canopy Forum on the Interactions of Law & Religion (April 2021) (available at https://canopyforum.org/2021/04/02/even-in-a-pandemic-the-constitution-cannot-be-put-away-and-forgotten/).

[69] Maryville Baptist Church, Inc. v. Beshear, 957 F.3d 610, 611–12 (6th Cir. 2020).

[70] Beshear v. Acree, 615 S.W.3d 780, 786 (Ky. 2020).

[71] Id. at 812-13.

[72] Cameron v. Beshear, 628 S.W.3d 61, 66–67 (Ky. 2021)

[73] Oswald v. Beshear, No. 2:21CV96 (WOB-CJS), 2021 WL 3698383, at *2 (E.D. Ky. Aug. 19, 2021)

[74] Id. at *3.

[75] Cameron v. Beshear, 628 S.W.3d 61, 67–68 (Ky. 2021)

[76] Id. at 73.

CHAPTER 18

LOUISIANA

Janet M. Pope
Louisiana School Boards Association

Dannie P. Garrett, III
Attorney at Law, LLC

Markey W. Pierré'
Southern Strategy Group of North LA

Wendy Baudoin
Louisiana School Boards Association

GENERAL BACKGROUND

The Louisiana Constitution provides that "the legislature shall provide for the education of the people of the state and shall establish and maintain a public educational system."[1] The state legislature is also tasked with establishing and providing for a public education system in Section I of Article VIII. In Section 13(B) of Article VIII, the Louisiana Constitution gives the State Board of Elementary and Secondary Education (BESE) responsibility for annually developing and adopting "...a formula which shall be used to determine the cost of a minimum foundation program of education in all public elementary and secondary schools

Funding Public Schools in the United States, Indian Country,
and US Territories (Second Edition), pages 297–313.
Copyright © 2023 by Information Age Publishing
www.infoagepub.com
All rights of reproduction in any form reserved.

as well as to equitably allocate the funds to parish and city school systems." The constitution tasks the Louisiana legislature with annually setting aside funds "… sufficient to fully fund the current cost to the state of such a program as determined by applying the approved formula in order to ensure a minimum foundation of education in all public elementary and secondary schools." These sections of the state constitution establish the legislative basis for the Minimum Foundation Program (MFP).[2]

The MFP is the process used by Louisiana to determine how local and state dollars are distributed across local school districts. The MFP is approved annually by the BESE and the legislature. The MFP determines the minimum district funding requirements, or the cost of education, for all public schools. This cost is calculated by adding together the base per-pupil amount, determined in legislation, and special allocations for at-risk and special education pupils and others.

The MFP helps to equitably distribute funds to all school systems, including local school districts and the Recovery School District. The state contributes the difference between the local contribution to the MFP and the minimum district funding requirement. The MFP provides incentives for local support. The state provides extra funds to local districts that exceed the required contribution of approximately 35%. Thus, districts with a greater local contribution can receive extra money from the state. This is in addition to the minimum district funding requirement. The state provides more money to districts that provide a greater percentage of their minimum district funding requirement. Thus, the amount of local funding is important because it directly contributes to the district's funding and also indirectly contributes by encouraging additional state-level funding.

Descriptive Statistics

In the 2021-2022 school year, there were 69 traditional public school districts and a Recovery School District (Baton Rouge and New Orleans) in the state of Louisiana.[3] Elementary and secondary education sites serve grades Pre-Kindergarten through 12, with the inclusion of a Transitional Grade 9 which provides students an opportunity to proceed to high school while taking remedial courses.[4] In 2021, the Louisiana legislature adjusted its compulsory attendance requirements to include individuals aged five and older and to include Kindergarten as a prerequisite to entering Grade 1 in public school. The law changed the previous requirement of compulsory attendance at age seven and optional enrollment into Kindergarten.[5]

In 2021-2022, the total population of students served in Louisiana public school districts, including non-traditional (charters, laboratory, special districts, etc.) was 690,092, a decline from previous years, and those students were served across 1,393 sites. Despite enrollment declines, the population of students in Louisiana remains diverse. The racial makeup of the student population identified as 53.71% Asian, American Indian, Black, Hispanic, Hawaiian/Pacific or Islander, 42.99% Caucasian, and 3.28% Multi-Race (Non-Hispanic). Male students account for

51.15% of the populations and female students account for 48.85%. Limited English Proficient students make up 4.19% of the student population. Economic status continues to be a demographic that is shared amongst the majority of Louisiana students, with 71.16% being identified as economically disadvantaged.[6]

There were 45,481 teachers reported to the Louisiana Department of Education during the 2020-2021 school year.[7]

CURRENT POLITICAL CLIMATE

Legislative Makeup

The Louisiana Legislature is comprised of single-member district elected officials. The number of Senators in Louisiana is 39. The number of Representatives is 105.[8] Members of the Legislature serve in a four-year term.[9]

Structural Makeup

Louisiana's legislature and all traditional public-school districts operate under a July 1 through June 30 fiscal year calendar. State law provides that school boards operate under the State fiscal year (July 1—June 30) and budget accordingly. Other local governmental bodies, such as parish and municipal governments have the authority to alternatively adopt a calendar year as their fiscal year.

Pursuant to the Louisiana Constitution, the legislative sessions in even numbered years allow for 60 legislative days in a 90-day period, from the early spring to early June. This session is termed a General Session and legislators are authorized to file legislation on a wide variety of subject matters, exclusive of levying or increasing a tax or fee. The legislative session in odd-numbered years allows for 45 legislative days in a 60-day period from late spring to early June. This session is termed a Fiscal Session and legislators are authorized to file legislation on fiscal matters, such as levying or increasing a tax or a fee. Additionally, each Legislator may also pre-file up to 5 bills on other subject matters. [10]

Party Control of Branches and Legislative Bodies

Over the past several election cycles, the Louisiana Legislature has become majority Republican. The Governor of Louisiana, elected in 2019 to a second term, is the sole Democrat elected to statewide office. The Board of Elementary and Secondary Education (BESE) is comprised of eleven members, three of whom are appointed by the Governor and eight of whom are elected from single member districts. Six of the eight elected BESE members, as of the 2019 regular elections, are Republicans and 2 are Democrats. As such, Republicans hold a majority of the seats on BESE.

Union Representation and Engagement

Three teacher unions operate within the state of Louisiana; (1) Louisiana Federation of Teachers, (2) Louisiana Association of Educators, and (3) Associated Professional Educators of Louisiana. All three are active advocates at all levels of government on public education and related issues. They often serve as members of advisory and study commissions, committees, and taskforces.

Other Advocacy and Interest Groups

Louisiana has active involvement from several stakeholders on education topics. Public education stakeholders include the Louisiana School Boards Association, the Louisiana Association of School Superintendents, the Louisiana Association of Principals, and the Louisiana Association of Public Charter Schools.

Noneducational stakeholders include organizations such as Stand for Children, Louisiana Association of Business and Industry, the Council for a Better Louisiana, and the Public Affairs Research Council.

These organizations and groups are often seated as members on commissions, task forces, and committees regarding public education.

School Organizational Trends

In recent years there has been discussion at the state level to address the fiscal concerns being experienced by small, rural school districts with significant losses in aggregate student enrollment, such as mechanisms to share expenses and professional services to reduce costs. There has not been any legislation, policy, or administrative rule introduced.

There has been recent interest in, with a small number of small districts moving toward, non-traditional school calendars. One small rural district has adopted a balanced year calendar with periodic 4-to-6-week breaks, without a long multiple month summer break. A few school districts have adopted a 4-day school week for students with some having faculty and staff utilizing the fifth day for such things as continuing education and administrative duties.

SOURCES OF REVENUE

State Funding through Louisiana's Minimum Foundation Program

The Louisiana Constitution, Article VIII §13, establishes an obligation for the state to fund K-12 public education. Subsection A says, "The legislature shall appropriate funds to supply free school books and other materials of instruction prescribed by the State Board of Elementary and Secondary Education to the children of this state at the elementary and secondary levels." Subsection B goes beyond books and materials to institute a minimum foundation program for public education funding—the MFP. It further mandates that there is also a local contribution. The MFP is designed to be based on the cost of providing public education and to equitably allocate the funds to parish and city school systems and other local school systems such as the Recovery School District schools (RSD), Louisiana State University (LSU), and Southern Laboratory schools, Office of Juvenile Justice schools, New Orleans Center for Creative Arts, Louisiana School for Math, Science and the Arts, Thrive and Legacy Type 2 Charter schools."[11]

Prior to the 1987 Amendment to Article VIII §13, the legislature determined how much the state would fund the MFP. Since the 1987 amendment, the legislature is now obligated to fully fund the MFP, showing prioritization by the voters of Louisiana for K-12 public education.

Though anticipated that the Base Per Pupil funding in the MFP would be increased by 2.75%, annually, the reality is that since 2008, the Base Per Pupil has only been increased by the anticipated 2.75% once[12], and an additional 1.375% increase for the 2019-2020 school year.[13] There have also been two instances of dedicated teacher and staff pay raises, funded through the MFP, but unavailable for general use.

Locally Generate Education Funding

Local funds for public education come from three sources: a five-mill ad valorem tax levied without election, ad valorem taxes imposed after a local election, and sales taxes levied after a local election.

Ad valorem taxes levied by a school board are subject to the Homestead Exemption. The Homestead Exemption provides that the first $75,000 in value of a home is not subject to ad valorem tax. There are rural parishes where upward of 80% of homes are valued at less than $75,000, meaning there are some rural properties entirely exempt from school board ad valorem taxes. Louisiana also has several special ad valorem provisions that freeze a homeowner's property value, so that the Assessor cannot recognize appreciation of that home's value; thus, the homeowner does not owe property taxes on the appreciated value of the home, even if that home value is frozen below $75,000.

Additionally, the imposition of a sales tax by a school board, in addition to an election, may also require permission of the Louisiana Legislature.[14] The legislature has authority (and has exercised it in the past) to exempt specific sales transactions from the local sales taxes approved by local voters.

DISTRIBUTION FORMULAS

Prior to 1997, the MFP was crafted under the BESE by determining the cost of K-12 public education by line item, such as teacher salaries and state contributions to state retirement systems, in which school board employees are required to participate. Since 1997, the MFP has been constructed as a block grant based upon student count adjusted on an equity basis based upon fiscal status to local school systems and charter schools without line items to establish what costs are being funded and at what levels.

Important Factors in the Louisiana MFP Formula[15]

Adoption and Implementation Process:
- The formula for the upcoming fiscal year must be submitted by the BESE to the state legislature by March 15.
- The legislature considers the formula submitted by the BESE during the legislative session. If the legislature agrees with the formula filed in resolution, the resolution is adopted. If the resolution does not meet legislative approval, then the resolution is rejected and returned to the BESE.
- The BESE has the option to revise the formula contained in resolution; resubmit the same formula; or take no action. Louisiana law provides that if no resolution is adopted, the existing formula will remain in effect.

Basic Components of the Louisiana School Finance System:
- Determine the cost of a minimum program of education;
- Equitably distribute funds across all school systems;
- Provide incentives for local support.

Structure of the MFP Formula:
- The allocation for Fiscal Year 2021-2022 totaled over $3.9 billion in support of 69 school districts, 140+ charter schools, and designated special schools;
- The formula is designed with separate calculations to provide funding for varying educational needs and costs;
- The current formula has four components or 'levels.'

Level 1 Funding
- Level 1 calculations utilize pupil counts and special student characteristics as the basis for determining the basic cost of education in each community across the state;
- Upcoming fiscal year projections are funded based on pupil count taken in the previous year on February 1;
- Students must qualify to be counted, both for base and weighted counts as applicable, according to the Student Membership Definition set forth in BESE policy;

Student Count
The first step in the calculation is to determine the Weighted Student Membership Count as seen in Figures 18.1–18.2.

The second step in the calculation is to determine the Total MFP Educational Cost as seen in Figure 18.3:

FIGURE 18.1. Calculating Louisiana Weighted Student Membership Count

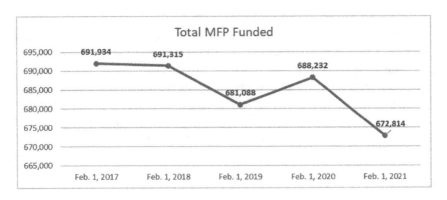

FIGURE 18.2. Calculating Louisiana Weighted Student Membership Count. Source: February 1 student count throughout the years found in the Louisiana Minimum Foundation Program (MFP) Reference Library under "MFP Budget Letter" a https://www.louisianabelieves.com/resources/library/minimum-foundation-program Year document. https://www.doa.la.gov/doa/opb/budget-documents/state-budgets/

Base Cost Per Pupil Amount

- The state and Local Base Cost Per-Pupil Amount is the amount utilized as the starting point for calculation of the cost of education in school districts and schools across Louisiana. This amount is used exclusively in the Level 1 cost calculation and is not the final pupil allocation that each district receives;

FIGURE 18.3 Calculating Louisiana Total MFP Educational Cost

- From 2000-01 to 2008-09, the MFP formula included a 2.75% increase to the Base Cost Per-Pupil Amount. The initial intent of the 2.75% was to address rising costs in delivering a quality education;
- From 2008-09 to 2013-14, the Base Cost Per Pupil remained the same;
- From 2014-15 to 2018-19, the Base Cost Per-Pupil amount remained at $3,961. During this time, the legislature appropriated additional funding for K-12 education outside the formula to address specific needs and priorities.
- From 2019-20, the Base Per Pupil amount increased by 1.375%, to $4,015. No further increase was included for fiscal years 2020-21 or 2021-22.

Sharing of Level 1 Total MFP Educational Cost
- The next step in the calculation is to determine the proportion of the total MFP educational cost to be shared between the state and the city and parish school systems.
- The proportion is based on the ability of the school systems to support education in their communities through local sales and property tax revenues. This calculation is often referred to as the 'wealth measurement.' This calculation utilizes data on local ad valorem, sales, and other revenue amounts.

The second step continues as follows:

- To determine the Local Cost Allocation in the MFP, the formula measures the potential of each city and parish school system to generate local revenue, rather than the actual amount collected. This method accounts for differences in the ability of city and parish school systems to raise local revenue;
- Ad valorem tax revenue and millage rates and sales tax revenue and rates are utilized in the calculation at a level appropriate to yield the 65/35 percent split;
- To determine districts' potential to generate revenue, the calculation multiplies statewide computed tax millages and rates against actual ad valorem tax assessments and sales tax bases;
- Each district will have a different allocation based on its unique situation. The percentage of cost funded by the state may range from a high of 89% to a low of 25%. Each year, as school systems are more or less able to support education costs through increases or decreases in local revenues, the formula adjusts the state and local allocations upward or downward as applicable;
- Overall, the formula attempts to ensure an average state contribution of 65% and an average local contribution of 35%, creating statewide equity in the formula.

FIGURE 18.4 Calculating Louisiana State Cost Allocation

State and Local Contributions

Once the Local Cost Allocation is determined, the next step is to calculate the State Cost Allocation as seen in Figure 18.4.

Level 2 Funding

- In the early years of the formula, some city and parish school systems did not have local revenue sufficient to meet the minimum local allocation required;
- Local school systems identified two obstacles to increasing local revenues at the time: (1) Taxpayers were not regularly willing to tax themselves more heavily; and (2) under the new formula, if a city or parish school system became more able to support education costs by becoming 'wealthier,' then the Level 1 allocations were decreased;
- As a result, a provision was added to the formula providing an incentive or reward to school systems taxing themselves above the minimum required level of financial support;
- To be eligible for the Level 2 Reward, a city or parish school system must generate local revenue above the local allocation required in Level 1. Any amount above the established minimum would be eligible for the reward calculation;
- The reward amount was about one-third of local revenues above the contribution required in Level 1;
- For some years, all city and parish school systems have met the required minimum local revenue level;
- The majority of city and parish school systems currently receive the reward, except for a few school systems which are not eligible because local revenues are above the cutoff point.

Level 3 Funding

- Level 3 contains allocations added to the formula over years due to requests from the Louisiana legislature to fund specific items;
- These allocations are determined on a per-pupil basis;
- This funding is in addition to the funding provided in Level 1 and Level 2;

- Categories of funding include a continuation of teacher pay raises provided by the legislature in 2001-02, 2006-07, 2007-08, and 2008-09 and support worker pay raises in 2002-03, 2006-07, 2007-08;[16]
- Support for increasing mandated costs of health insurance, retirement, and fuel allocation provides $100 per pupil to help defray the costs of these expenses.

Level 4 Funding
- Level 4 provides funding for specific programs and schools, each with a unique allocation method.
  - *Foreign Language Associates Allocation*– provides additional salary allocations of $21,000 per teacher to a school system or school employing foreign language teachers—statewide maximum of 300 teachers. The stipend allocation provides a $6,000 installation stipend for first-year foreign language associate teachers and a $4,000 retention stipend for second and third year teachers;
  - *Career Development Fund (CDF) Allocation*- provides approximately 6% MFP funding for specific courses providing career training for students;
  - *Supplemental Course (SCA) Allocation*- provides $59 per pupil for each student enrolled in grades 7 to 12 to support the cost of secondary course choices above and beyond the traditional classroom. Beginning in 2017-18, SCA allocation increased to $59 per pupil.[17]
  - *High-Cost Services (HCS) Allocation* - provides funding for pupils ages 3–21 with a current IEP who are currently receiving services with costs greater than three times the average per-pupil expenditure;
  - *Other Public Schools Allocation*- LSU and Southern Lab schools, Legacy Type 2 Charter schools, Office of Juvenile Justice (OJJ) schools, New Orleans Center for Creative Arts (NOCCA), Louisiana School for Math, Science, and the Arts (LSMA) and Thrive Academy of Baton Rouge (THRIVE).
- Dedicated teacher and staff pay raises of $1,000 and $500, respectively in 2019-20 ($99.4M).[18]
- Dedicated teacher and staff pay raises of $800 and $400, respectively in 2021-22 ($79.5M).[19]

Further, the definition of city, parish, or local public school systems and schools includes city or parish school systems, Recovery School District including operated and Type 5 charter schools, Louisiana School for Math, Science, and the Arts (LSMSA), New Orleans Center for Creative Arts (NOCCA), THRIVE, New Type 2 Charter schools, Legacy Type 2 Charter schools, Type 3B Charter schools, Office of Juvenile Justice (OJJ) schools, and Louisiana State University and Southern University Lab schools.[20]

Mid-Year Student Count Adjustments

The formula provides funding for mid-year adjustments for student gains and losses during the year. Two mid-year adjustments are provided using the following:

- October 1 Count: February 1 count compared to October 1 count; The State Cost Allocation per pupil multiplies increase/decrease in students.
- February 1 Count: October 1 count compared to February 1 count; Increase/decrease in students multiplied by one-half of the State Cost Allocation per-pupil.

Use of Funds

The MFP Resolution requires that state MFP funds shall only be expended for educational purposes:

- Expenditures are related to the operational and instructional activities of city, parish, or other public school systems or schools including:
  - Instruction, pupil support, instructional staff programs, school administration, general administration, business services, operations/maintenance of plant services, student transportation, food services, enterprise operations, community services, facility acquisition and construction services, and debt services;[21]
  - A significant portion of expenditures paid using MFP funds includes teacher salaries and benefits, including retirement since these expenses make up approximately 85% of all educational costs.

Expenditure Requirement

Expenditure requirements for the MFP are extensive and include the following principles and operations:

- The MFP is a block grant from the state to local school systems and schools;
- The block grant philosophy provides flexibility to school systems and schools in budgeting funds to spend as they see fit as long as program requirements outlined in the BESE are met;
- The MFP funds should be blended with other funds to support the total cost of education;
- To provide appropriate accountability for funds spent on K-12 education, the MFP Resolution requires an annual measurement and report on the manner in which general fund dollars, state and local funds combined, are spent;
- A 70% expenditure requirement requires public school systems and schools receiving MFP funds to spend 70% of general fund (state and local) dollars on the areas of instruction and school administration at the school building level;
- In the 2019-2022 fiscal year, 68 of the 69 traditional school districts met the 70% requirement and 52 of 53 schools/charters met the requirement;

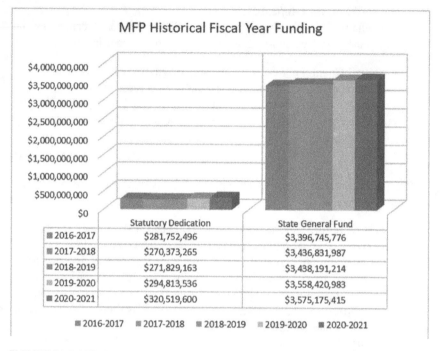

FIGURE 18.5 MFP Recent Appropriation History FY 2016 – 2020. Source: Data compiled from the Louisiana Division of Administrations annual State Budget Fiscal Year document. https://www.doa.la.gov/doa/opb/budget-documents/state-budgets/

> The 2 entities not meeting the 70% requirement were required to submit a plan to the LDOE detailing efforts over the next year to make budget and spending adjustments.[22]

MFP Appropriation History

The MFP's recent appropriation history is illustrated in Figure 18.5 across Fiscal Years 2016 through 2020. The total MFP allocation consists of State General Fund Appropriations as well as Statutory Dedications (FY 2016-17: $3,678,498,272, FY 2017-18: $3,707,203,252, FY 2018-19: $3,710,020,377, FY 2019-20: $3,853,234,519, FY 2020-21: $3,895,695,015).[23]

MFP Taskforce

In August 2013, the State Board of Elementary and Secondary Education convened the MFP Task Force to provide an advisory recommendation for the MFP. The Task Force represented a cross-section of education stakeholders. The Task Force met from September through December to discuss various issues relative to the formula including costs, local revenue availability, and funds distribution. The

MFP Task Force adopted a final recommendation in December, to be considered in March of the following year. The resolution annually recreated the MFP taskforce with the same goals and purpose. The MFP Taskforce has continued to be convened annually to make recommendations to the BESE as to the MFP for the coming year. The BESE is under no legal obligation to follow the recommendation.

MFP Formula Budgeting Cycle

The MFP follows a budget cycle calendarized as follows:

- August to December—Research and presentations;
- January to February—the BESE considers possible revisions to the MFP formula for the upcoming fiscal year;
- March—the BESE makes the final decision on the structure of the MFP formula and submits the proposed formula along with an estimated cost to the legislature via resolution for consideration;
- April to June—state legislature considers the MFP formula.

CAPITAL OUTLAY AND DEBT SERVICE

Louisiana does not provide a state capital outlay budget accessible to public school systems. The main source of capital outlay for local school districts is local ad valorem and/or sales taxes that may be bonded to generate funds available for capital projects, such as construction of schools and other educational facilities. Local bonded indebtedness must be approved by local voters as well as the State Bond Commission.

EMPLOYEE BENEFITS

Healthcare

Over half of the public school districts in Louisiana provide health insurance for their faculty and staff through the State Office of Group Benefits, the entity that provides health insurance to state employees. Others do so through the private insurance market.

Retirement

Title 11, the general retirement law, mandates that the legislature will appropriate the nonemployee portion of the actuarial cost of the state retirement system in which school employees have mandated membership. This obligation has been recognized by the courts,[24] as the state argued that it is meeting its obligation by embedding state retirement funding into the block grant, even though the discrete amount of that funding is indeterminable. The court accepted that argument that the MFP block grant includes funds dedicated to the state retirement systems, even though this ruling raises a charter school issue.

The system requires that the local school board then passes through retirement funds embedded in the MFP to the retirement system. For public school employees who are in the retirement system (including traditional public schools where employees are mandatory members and charter schools opting into the retirement system), the school governing body forwards between 19 and 22% of total payroll to the retirement system, ostensibly from those dollars embedded in the MFP. The Louisiana Legislative Auditor found that in 2020, $852.8M of the $3.9M MFP[25] went toward paying towards the Unfunded Accrued Liability (UAL) of the teachers and school employees retirement funds. For charter schools opting out of the retirement system, state dollars embedded in the MFP and dedicated to meeting the retirement obligation of the state are never provided to the retirement system; yet the charter school retains those dollars to use toward operating costs, including the hiring of for-profit charter operators in a number of schools. Traditional public schools and charter schools that participate in the retirement systems have an average retirement cost of 11.8% of total expenditures, whereas the non-participating charter school retirement cost is only 4.1% of total expenditures.[26]

CHARTER SCHOOL FUNDING

Charter school law[27] in Louisiana provides that such organizations be granted per-pupil funding in the same amount as both the state MFP and the de facto per-pupil local tax revenue levied by the local school board. Additionally, charter schools receive the second element of funding from the state that equals the amount of local tax levied by the local school board and the vote of the people—even taxes levied before the charter school was established and thus not considered at the time the voters approved the taxes. The state then withholds this additional charter school payment from the local school board's state MFP allocation, which has the effect of local school board taxes aiding the funding of charter schools over which the local school board has no authority, nor which were approved by local voters.

In several parishes, local school boards have been left in a circumstance of being obligated to fund a specific purpose, based on tax dedication approved by voters, yet those funds have been diverted to one or more local charter schools, resulting in the school board having to pay dedicated expenses without accompanying dedicated revenue. Additionally, charter schools are not obligated to use dedicated revenues per the dedication imposed by voters.

NONPUBLIC SCHOOL FUNDING

In Louisiana, nonpublic schools do get the benefit of some public funding, but courts have held that such funding cannot flow through the Minimum Foundation Program (MFP) as those funds are exclusively for public schools. The extent to which nonpublic schools are funded through State funds has decreased over a number of years.

The LA Constitution does however make an exception regarding "free school books" [28] which accounts for $2.9M in State General Fund funding in 2020-21.[29] Total non-public funding for 2020-21 was $20.7M, which was a reduction of $475K from the prior year.[30]

VOUCHER PROGRAM

Louisiana's voucher program is funded through a discrete line item, identified as student scholarships, for educational excellence in the subgrantee assistance category found in HB1 State General Fund.[31] The voucher program allows for payment of tuition at nonpublic schools, up to the value of the state MFP plus the local de facto per-pupil funding from local tax revenues. The total funding for the voucher program in 2020-21 was $41.96M.[32]

VIRTUAL EDUCATION

Louisiana has two wholly virtual public charter schools operating under its jurisdiction. Each local system has the option to provide virtual education, either partially, or wholly for its student population.

During the height of the COVID pandemic in the 2020-2021 school year, many districts opted for virtual education rather than opening campuses for in-person learning. A number of districts utilized federal funding to purchase computers for students to use to participate in virtual learning. While virtually all districts have moved back to 100% in person learning, some are still utilizing virtual instruction both for parents desiring to continue with that mode of education and to address COVID spikes or outbreaks at one or more schools within those districts. Early data from accountability testing indicates a marked decrease in student achievement among students with 50% or more of their instruction virtually.

FEDERAL COVID-19 FUNDING

During the COVID-19 pandemic, the state of Louisiana received a significant amount of funding. The funding allocation to the state from the Elementary and Secondary School Emergency Relief Fund (ESSER) was $ 4,052,561,878. The Governor's Emergency Education Relief Fund (GEER) provided the state with $ 73,262,119 for public schools and $ 111,240,434 under Emergency Assistance to Nonpublic Schools (EANS). The state also received $ 1,038,454,429 in funding from the Child Care and Development Fund (CCDF). Considering all the pandemic assistance received from these programs, Louisiana was allocated a total of $ 5,275,518,860 in federal pandemic dollars.[33]

SUMMARY

Each year the Louisiana Department of Education and the State Board of Elementary and Secondary Education convene the MFP Task Force meeting for the purpose of providing an up-to-date presentation regarding the history of the MFP. The Louisiana School Boards Association Executive Director reports to the Task Force that there continue to be various issues relative to the MFP, including costs, local revenue availability, and funds distribution. Other topics included an increase to the base level 1 per pupil in the MFP of 2.75%, state dedicated raises for certified teachers and uncertified personnel, and funding to offset the rising costs of health insurance for school systems. New interest in the over 20% of State MFP funding that is going directly to the UAL[34] has been highlighted by a report by the Louisiana Legislative Auditor and may find traction among legislators eager to see dollars going to classroom instruction.

ENDNOTES

1   Louisiana Constitution Article VIII, §1. Retrieved from: http://senate.la.gov/Documents/Constitution/Article8.htm.

2   Louisiana Constitution Article VIII, §13. Retrieved from: http://senate.la.gov/Documents/Constitution/Article8.htm.

3   Louisiana Department of Education. (n.d.) https://www.louisianabelieves.com/schools/public-schools.

4   Louisiana Department of Education. (n.d.) Transitional 9th Grade Guidance for Middle and High Schools. Retrieved from https://www.louisianabelieves.com/docs/default-source/links-for-newsletters/transitional-9th-grade-guidance-for-middle-and-high-schools.pdf?sfvrsn=2.

5   LA R.S. 17:151.3 (2021) http://legis.la.gov/Legis/Law.aspx?d=79863; LA R.S. 17:221 (2021) http://legis.la.gov/Legis/Law.aspx?d=80276.

6   Louisiana Department of Education. (n.d.) Oct 2021 Multi states (Total by Site and School System) https://www.louisianabelieves.com/resources/library/student-attributes.

7   Public School Staff Data: Classroom Teacher Actual Average Salaries for School Year 2020-2021, https://www.louisianabelieves.com/resources/library/workforce-attributes.

8   Louisiana Constitution Article III, §3. Retrieved from https://www.legis.la.gov/legis/Law.aspx?d=206418.

9   Louisiana Constitution Article III, §4. Retrieved from: https://www.legis.la.gov/legis/Law.aspx?p=y&d=206419.

10 Louisiana Constitution Article III, §2. Retrieved from: https://www.legis.la.gov/legis/Law.aspx?.d=206416.

11 Senate Concurrent Resolution No. 2, Senator Fields (2021). Retrieved from: https://www.legis.la.gov/legis/ViewDocument.aspx?d=1233764.

12 2014-2015 School Year increase of 2.75% increase in Base Per Pupil. Retrieved from: https://www.louisianabelieves.com/resources/library/minimum-foundation-program

13 2019-2020 School Year increase of 1.375% increase in Base Per Pupil. Retrieved from: https://www.louisianabelieves.com/resources/library/minimum-foundation-program

14 Louisiana Constitution Article VI §29. Retrieved from https://senate.la.gov/Documents/Constitution/Article6.htm.

15 Louisiana Department of Education. (n.d.) MFP Overview 2016-2017. Retrieved from: https://www.louisianabelieves.com/docs/default-source/minimum-foundation-program/2016-2017-overview-of-mfp-formula.pdf?sfvrsn=3.

16 Louisiana Department of Education. Minimum Foundation Program. MFP Library Each Year Table 3A for yearly comparisons. Retrieved from: https://www.louisianabelieves.com/resources/library/minimum-foundation-program.

17 House Concurrent Resolution, No. 7, Representative Landry (2017). http://www.legis.la.gov/legis/BillInfo.aspx?s=17RS&b=HCR 7&sbi=y.

18 Senate Concurrent Resolution No.3, Senator Morrish (2019), Retrieved from: https://legis.la.gov/legis/ViewDocument.aspx?d=1141941.

19 Senate Concurrent Resolution No. 2, Senator Fields (2021). Retrieved from: https://www.legis.la.gov/legis/ViewDocument.aspx?d=1233764.

20 Senate Concurrent Resolution No. 48, Senator Morrish (2018). Retrieved from: http://www.legis.la.gov/legis/ViewDocument.aspx?d=1098695.

21 The MFP has never included any funding for the costs of building public schools, making Louisiana only one of a few states that provide no such funding. Which States Fund Costs for Public School Buildings. Retrieved from: https://www.infrastructurereportcard.org/how-your-state-funds-school-construction/

22 Louisiana Department of Education (n.d.). FY2019-20 70% Instructional Requirement. Retrieved from: https://www.louisianabelieves.com/resources/library/minimum-foundation-program.

23 Louisiana Division of Administration (Sept. 30, 2020). State Budget Fiscal Year 2020-2021. Retrieved from: https://www.doa.la.gov/media/xvcnijzs/statebudgetfy21.pdf.

24 EBRPSS vs. LSERS (no citation, 2012).

25 Louisiana Legislative Auditor (Oct 13, 2021) Impact of Unfunded Accrued Liability Payments on Public Education Funding in Louisiana. Retrieved from: https://app.lla.state.la.us/publicreports.nsf/0/8d86cc09af17e0368625876d007c42be/$file/00024d0ed.pdf?openelement&.7773098.

26 Louisiana Legislative Auditor (Oct 13, 2021) Impact of Unfunded Accrued Liability Payments on Public Education Funding in Louisiana. Retrieved from: https://app.lla.state.la.us/publicreports.nsf/0/8d86cc09af17e0368625876d007c42be/$file/00024d0ed.pdf?openelement&.7773098.

27 LA R.S. 17:3991 (2021). Retrieved from: http://legis.la.gov/Legis/Law.aspx?d=80976.

28 Louisiana Constitution Article VIII §13. Retrieved from https://senate.la.gov/Documents/Constitution/Article8.htm.

29 Louisiana Division of Administration (Sept. 30, 2020). State Budget Fiscal Year 2020-2021. Retrieved from: https://www.doa.la.gov/media/xvcnijzs/statebudgetfy21.pdf.

30 Louisiana Division of Administration (Sept. 30, 2020). State Budget Fiscal Year 2020-2021. Retrieved from: https://www.doa.la.gov/media/xvcnijzs/statebudgetfy21.pdf.

31 2016-2017 MFP Budget Letter-HB1 p. 133. Retrieved from: http://www.legis.la.gov/Legis/ViewDocument.aspx?d=1013096.

32 Louisiana Division of Administration (Sept. 30, 2020). State Budget Fiscal Year 2020-2021. Retrieved from: https://www.doa.la.gov/media/xvcnijzs/statebudgetfy21.pdf.

33 Louisiana Department of Education. (n.d.) Pandemic relief Stimulus Funding Overview: Budget Hearings 2021. Retrieved from: https://www.louisianabelieves.com/docs/default-source/achieve/pandemic-relief-stimulus-funding-overview.pdf?sfvrsn=b5e26718_2.

34 Unfunded accrued liability of the teachers and staff retirement systems, LA Legislative Auditor. Retrieved from: https://www.lla.la.gov/reports-data/audit/Agency/index.shtml?key=T&agency=Teachers%27%20Retirement%20System%20of%20Louisiana

CHAPTER 19

MAINE[1]

Sharda Jackson Smith
University of South Carolina Upstate

GENERAL BACKGROUND[2]

Maine became a state in 1820, with its constitution established in the same year. Article VIII, governing educational provisions, declared:

> A general diffusion of the advantages of education being essential to the preservation of the rights and liberties of the people; to promote this important object, the Legislature are authorized, and it shall be their duty to require, the several towns to make suitable provision, at their own expense, for the support and maintenance of public schools; and it shall further be their duty to encourage and suitably endow, from time to time, as the circumstances of the people may authorize, all academies, colleges and seminaries of learning within the State.[3]

The state of Maine first began providing revenue for public schools in 1828. The earliest revenue came from public land sales and was granted to towns through a per-pupil formula. A banking tax was created in 1872, collecting a 1 mill property tax that was also distributed on a per-pupil basis, making it the first instance of the state engaging a statewide tax for school redistribution purposes. In 1974, Maine adopted a true statewide uniform property tax featuring a required

Funding Public Schools in the United States, Indian Country,
and US Territories (Second Edition), pages 315–327.
Copyright © 2023 by Information Age Publishing
www.infoagepub.com

tax rate, with matching state monies. Due to unpopularity given the tax's impact on wealthier towns, the provision was repealed and replaced in 1977. The revision refocused the tax away from the state as collector, but still provided aid based on local ability to pay as measured by tax capacity. State aid under the new plan was sourced from state income and sales taxes. In 2004, a statewide referendum set state aid at 55% of local costs.

The state aid plan was revised in 2005, with a new school funding formula known as the Essential Programs and Services (EPS) model. The EPS was designed to rely on research in best practices on student success. The EPS tied funding to state standards (i.e., the Maine Learning Results[4]) rather than being linked to either prior-year expenditures as the base for budgeting or to local school board budget preferences, although local boards had discretion to spend local dollars above the EPS. In 2016, voters approved a 3% income tax surcharge for high income earners; however, the state legislature subsequently repealed the surcharge while simultaneously increasing state school aid by $162 million.

CURRENT POLITICAL CLIMATE

The Governor and Legislature of Maine operate on a biennial budget that begins in even years and includes two fiscal year cycles. The 130th Legislative Session focused on a wide array of topics concerning education finance including directing the Maine Department of Education to report on charter school funding methods and reporting protocols, passing policy to permit the Maine State Housing Authority to examine and develop a program promoting home ownership by reducing education debt, and reestablishing the Commission to Study College Affordability and College Completion. The recent session also established protections for private student loan borrowers and passed a moderately partisan effort to manage dollars to private schools that enroll a particular percentage of publicly funded students meet certain requirement. Republican efforts to improve the Educational Opportunity Tax Credit failed and Democrat efforts to pass an act to increase the minimum grant amount under the Maine State Grant Program failed. The Education & Cultural Affairs joint standing committee is presently composed of 13 members (8 Democrats and 5 Republicans).

In 2022, the state of Maine financed a 10-year average of over 180,000 students enrolled in public schools, which included students that attended resident district schools, charter schools, another school district with tuition paid by a resident district, private schools with tuition paid by resident district, private schools with tuition paid by state or federal funds, non-resident school districts as a benefit to a parent who works at the attending unit, and/or non-resident school districts under a superintendent agreement; Over 37% of Maine students enrolled in 2022 were considered economically disadvantaged, defined as one who was directly certified by the Maine Department of Health and Human Services as having a family income below a defined threshold and being eligible for benefit programs, one whose parent or guardian has completed an Application for Free/Reduced

Lunch Meals and the family income falls with the program guidelines, one whose parent or guardian has completed a form providing economic status information and the family income falls within the program guidelines, or one who has been identified as homeless, in foster care, or a migratory student.

BASIC FUNDING PROGRAM

Essential Programs and Services Plan[5]

The Essential Programs and Services (EPS) plan serves as Maine's basic funding scheme. Using a complex set of cost factors, the state determines the amount, level, and cost of education components needed by school districts tied to the Maine Learning Results standards. The EPS allocation depends on student, staff, and school variables, resulting in individualized operating cost rates for each local school district.

As indicated, the state provides a 55% cost-share ratio for total EPS operating costs. The local share is based on property valuation. The state covers 100% of approved EPS special education costs for most school districts, and up to 33% for minimum subsidy receiving districts. The state provides added support for geographically isolated schools, and island schools are automatically included. Qualified school districts are adjusted for sparsity using grade-level enrollments, where qualification depends on threshold factors including K-8 <15 enrollment and minimum distance from the nearest school that could accept the headcount; and 9-12 <200 enrollment. The state also accounts for grade-level differences in the EPS through staffing ratios resulting in different supports based on grade span and district size.

Key EPS Elements[6]

The EPS is defined as those programs and resources deemed essential for students to meet the Learning Results standards. The EPS formula determines the state and local shares for each School Administrative Unit (SAU). As indicated, the formula is based on years of research on high performing cost-effective schools as judged by the state of Maine. Expressed as a formula, the EPS reads as:

EPS for the SAU—Required Local Share = State Share

Key State Share Components

The EPS takes into account a set of cost components in determining the aid formula's outcome. The EPS accounts for:

- *Student Demographics:* includes SAU pupil counts for PreK-K, grades 1-5, 6-8, 9-12, and specialized student populations;

- *EPS per-Pupil Rate for the SAU:* includes per-pupil amounts tailored to each SAU to reflect costs for personnel, administration, and instructional support;
- *Weighted Amounts:* includes additional per-pupil amounts for Limited English Proficiency (LEP) and economically disadvantaged pupils;
- *Target Amounts:* includes additional per-pupil amounts for four-year-old PreK pupils, K-2 pupils, student assessment, and technology resources;
- *Other Adjustments:* includes isolated small schools, adult education, and equivalent instruction variables.

Key Required Local Share Components

The EPS takes into account three variables in setting the local contribution to the EPS formula. The local share is defined as:

- *Valuation by town* as provided by the Maine Revenue Service. This variable annually defines local ability to pay;
- *Percent of students by town* within a combined school district. This variable is used to determine the distribution of the total allocation by town;
- *Mill expectation.* This variable is set by calculating the required funding level for each year.

Brief Results of EPS Rates

EPS dollars per pupil across Fiscal Years 2010-2022 are shown in Table 19.1. Table 19.2 next examines K-12 statewide total averages and growth in per-pupil operating costs as defined in the EPS across time (FY 2009 – 2019). Total state funds for the period FY 2012-2020 are then visually illustrated in Figure 19.1.

TABLE 19.1   State Average EPS Rates FY 2010-2022

School Year	Elementary	Secondary
FY 2021-22	$7,241	$7,746
FY 2020-21	$7,011	$7,519
FY 2019-20	$6,771	$7,274
FY 2018-19	$6,720	$7,211
FY 2017-18	$6,634	$7,117
FY 2016-17	$6,584	$7,078
FY 2015-16	$6,596	$7,064
FY 2014-15	$6,505	$6,963
FY 2013-14	$6,415	$6,859
FY 2012-13	$6,342	$6,784
FY 2011-12	$6,254	$6,705
FY 2010-11	$6,138	$6,566
FY 2009-10	$5,976	$6,405

Source: Maine Department of Education. (2022). https://www.maine.gov/doe/funding/gpa/eps

TABLE 19.2.   Statewide EPS Operating Costs Per-Pupil FY 2009 – 2019

Fiscal Year	Per-Pupil Operating Cost
2018-2019	$12,442.95
2017-2018	$12,197.95
2016-2017	$11,859.95
2015-2016	$11,348.78
2014-2015	$10,990.51
2013-2014	$10,545.58
2012-2013	$10,021.47
2011-2012	$9,726.80
2010-2011	$9,629.62
2009-2010	$9,662.93
2008-2009	$9,624.71

Source: Maine Department of Education. (2022). Operating costs refer to general fund and exclude major capital outlay, debt service, transportation, and tuition receipts.

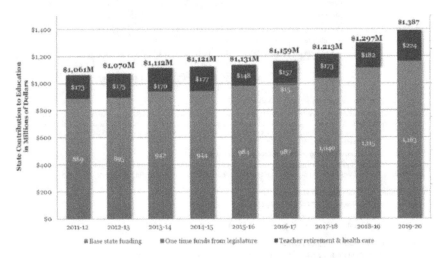

FIGURE 19.1. Total State EPS Dollars FY 2012 - 2020. Source: Maine Department of Education. (2022). https://www.maine.gov/doe/funding/gpa/eps

The EPS Calculation[7]

Figure 19.2 illustrates how Maine's Essential Programs and Services are calculated through state and local shares.

COVID-19

With the onset of the COVID-19 pandemic, the federal government allocated dollars towards education through a series of acts. In response, Maine submitted state

Maine's Funding Formula for Sharing the Costs of PreK-12 Education between State and Local:
- Determine the EPS Defined Cost for each Unit (Total Allocation)
- Determine the Required Local Share of those Costs (Local Contribution)
- The Difference Between the Two is the State Share (State Contribution)

Section 1 Attending Pupil Counts
- Uses average of October attending pupil counts for the school unit from the previous two years as reported in Synergy.

- Attending student counts are based on where students are educated. Public school district attending student counts include: (1) students from the local district attending schools in the district; plus (2) students from outside the district who are tuitioned in.

- Separated by PreK-K, 1-5, 6-8, and 9-12 for calculation of EPS determined ratios for each grade level.

Section 1 B1-8: Staff Positions Part 1 – Full Time Equivalent (FTE) Staff
- EPS has determined ratios of FTE Staff to Students necessary for each grade level and position.

- Current Staff to Student Ratios are shown in table; adjustment is made if the total number of PreK-12 students from Section 1 Line A3 is less than 1200:
    - EPS FTE Total is determined by dividing the Average Attending Pupils from Section 1 Line A3 for each Grade Level by the EPS Ratio; then adding the results for the four grade levels.
    - Actual FTE Totals are obtained from the NEO Staff module as entered by the SAU and downloaded each December 1.
    - Percentage of EPS is determined by dividing the EPS FTE Total by the Actual FTE Total.

Position		PreK – K		1 – 5		6 – 8		9 – 12	
			Under 1200		Under 1200		Under 1200		Under 1200
A.	Teachers	15:1	15:1	17:1	17:1	17:1	17:1	16:1	16:1
B.	Guidance	350:1	315:1	350:1	315:1	350:1	315:1	250:1	225:1
C.	Librarians	800:1	720:1	800:1	720:1	800:1	720:1	800:1	720:1
D.	Health	800:1	720:1	800:1	720:1	800:1	720:1	800:1	720:1
E.	Education Techs	114:1	103:1	114:1	103:1	312:1	281:1	316:1	285:1
F.	Library Techs	500:1	450:1	500:1	450:1	500:1	450:1	500:1	450:1
G.	Clerical	200:1	180:1	200:1	180:1	200:1	180:1	200:1	180:1
H.	School Admin	305:1	275:1	305:1	275:1	305:1	275:1	315:1	284:1

Section 1 B1-8: Staff Positions Part 2 – Adjusted EPS Salary
- The EPS Staff Salary is determined using a Salary Matrix. Years of Experience and Education Level Attained are important factors in determining the Minimum Teacher Salary for the EPS funding formula. The data entered by the SAU into the NEO Staff Module is used along with the Salary Matrix to determine the minimum teacher salary for each EPS Staff Position – the total of those positions is then used in this calculation.

- Actual salaries are ultimately determined by local contract agreements.

- Adjusted EPS Salary is calculated by multiplying the SAU data in EPS matrix salary amount by the % of EPS. That amount is then distributed to the Elementary and Secondary columns based on the percentage of attending pupils determined in Section 1A.

Section 1 Lines C1-4: Computation of Benefits
- Benefits are calculated using the EPS determined percentage for each category.

- The current EPS salary benefits percentage amounts for each of the following categories are (A) Teachers, Guidance, Librarians and Health (19%); Education and Library Technicians (36); Clerical (29%); School Administrators (14%).

Section 1 Lines D1-7: Other Support Per-Pupil Costs
- Other Support Per-Pupil Costs are calculated based on the EPS determined Per Pupil Amount.

- The most recent (FY 18) EPS Per Pupil amounts for each of the following support costs are shown in the table:

(continues)

FIGURE 19.2. Essential Programs & Services State Calculation for Funding Public Education (ED279). Source: Maine Department of Education. https://www.maine.gov/doe/sites/maine.gov.doe/files/inline-files/EPS%20Cost%20Component%20Calculations%20ED279%20Line%20by%20Line_updatedSeptember2017.pdf

	Other Support Costs	PreK – 8	9 – 12
1)	Substitute Teachers (½ Day)	42	42
2)	Supplies and Equipment	373	514
3)	Professional Development	64	64
4)	Instructional Leadership Support	28	28
5)	Co- and Extra-Curricular Student	39	123
6)	System Administration/Support	92	92
7)	Targeted System Admin/Support	46	46
8)	Operations and Maintenance	1,089	1,294

Section 1 Line E1: Regional Adjustment for Staff & Substitute Salaries
-The Regional Adjustment for Staff & Substitute Salaries is necessary due to variations in Income Levels and Housing Costs throughout the state of Maine.
-A fundamental premise of Essential Programs and Services is that there must be adequate resources to achieve desired outcomes and there must be *equity* in the distribution of adequate resources.
-The calculation of Personnel Costs in EPS is based on EPS Guiding Personnel Ratios and SAU Staff Profiles (Experience and Education level of staff); Regional Cost Differences. The EPS Regional Adjustment will either increase or decrease total salaries plus substitutes for a school unit based on the Labor Market Regional Cost Factor where the school is located.

Section 1 – Totals: Calculated EPS Per-Pupil Rates
-EPS Per-Pupil Rates are tailored for each individual SAU and reflect the costs for Personnel, Administration, and Instructional Support in that specific SAU.
-Rates are determined by dividing the Total Support Costs after the Regional Adjustment and Title I Revenues Adjustment have been applied by the Attending Pupil Count for both Elementary and Secondary.
-Per Pupil rates are then used to determine operating cost allocations on the subsequent pages of the ED279 report.
-If the SAU does not operate either an Elementary or Secondary School, or both, then the EPS Rate is determined using an average of the EPS rates for the SAU where the resident students attend school.

Section 2: (Operating Cost Allocations) – Lines A1-2: Subsidizable Pupils (Includes Superintendent Transfers)
-Public School Resident Subsidy Counts are the counts of students used in calculation of subsidy for school administrative units. These numbers are derived from the publicly funded resident enrollment counts reported in the State Student Information System. These numbers also include superintendent transfers. Resident subsidy counts are based on where the student's parent or legal guardian resides. Public school unit resident subsidizable counts include: resident students from the local school unit attending schools in the local school unit; resident students from the local school unit who are tuitioned to other public school units or private schools and who are paid for with public funds; resident students from other school units transferred by a Superintendent Transfer/Agreement. Resident Subsidy Counts do *NOT* include: students in the Maine Indian Education system (except for the Maine Indian Education Unit); students in State Operated schools; students in the Unorganized Territories; students in private schools (non-publicly funded); students free or paid for by the parents; students either below minimum age or over the maximum age for services.

Section 2: (Operating Cost Allocations) – Lines B1-7: Basic Counts

B1: 4YO/PreK Pupils Basic Count Operating Cost Allocation is determined by using the most recent October 1 4YO/PreK Pupils.

B2: K-8 Pupils Basic Count Operating Cost Allocation is determined by using the average of the two most recent October 1 K-8 Pupils times the Elementary SAU EPS Rate as determined in Section 1 of the ED279 report.

B3: 9-12 Pupils Basic Count Operating Cost Allocation is determined by using the average of the two most recent October 1 9-12 Pupils (using the average of the two most recent subsidizable pupil counts) times the Secondary SAU EPS Rate as determined in Section 1 of the ED279 report.

Section 2: (Operating Cost Allocations) – Lines B1-7: Basic Counts

B4: Adult Education Courses at .1 Operating Cost Allocation is determined by multiplying the adult education course count as reported by the SAU (on the EFM 39A and EFM 39B reports in NEO) by the Secondary SAU EPS Rate as determined in Section 1 of the ED279 report. (Note: for state subsidy purposes, school-aged adult education student courses are counted as .1 of a course for each semester-long course taken).

B5: 4YO/PreK Equivalent Instruction Pupils Basic Count Operating Cost Allocation is determined by using the most recent 'October Equivalent Instruction Pupils' count (as reported in the State Student Information System) times the Elementary SAU EPS Rate as determined in Section 1 of the ED279 report.

B6: K-8 Equivalent Instruction Pupils Basic Count Operating Cost Allocation is determined by using the average of the two most recent 'October Equivalent Instruction Pupils' count (as reported in the State Student Information System) times the Elementary SAU EPS Rate as determined in Section 1 of the ED279 report.

FIGURE 19.2. Continued

B7: 9-12 Equivalent Instruction Pupils Basic Count Operating Cost Allocation is determined by using the average of the two most recent 'October Equivalent Instruction Pupils' count (as reported in the State Student Information System) times the Secondary SAU EPS Rate as determined in Section 1 of the ED279 report.

Section 2: (Operating Cost Allocations) – Lines C1-6: Weighted Counts

4YO/PreK, K-8 and 9-12 Disadvantaged Percentage is calculated by dividing the PreK-8 Elementary Free & Reduced Lunch (FRL) Eligible most recent October 1 count by the Total PreK-8 Subsidy in the most recent October 1 count as reported in the State Student Information System. (Example: FRL PreK-8 Count 697 ÷ Total PreK-8 Subsidy Count 1,435 = 0.4857 disadvantaged percentage).

4YO/PreK, K-8 and 9-12 Disadvantaged Weighted Count Operating Cost Allocation is determined by multiplying the percentage of pupils eligible for free & reduced lunch by the most recent October 1 4YO/PreK Pupils (Line B1) and by the average K-8 (Line B2) or 9-12 (Line B3) pupils; then multiplying that number of disadvantaged pupils by the EPS determined weight (.15 at this time) and finally multiplying by the Elementary or Secondary SAU EPS Rate as determined on page 1 of the ED279 report. (Example: 0.4857 x 103.0 = 50.0 x 0.15 = 7.5 x 6,577 = $49,327.50).

4YO/PreK, K-8 and 9-12 Limited English Proficiency Weighted Count Operating Cost Allocation is determined by multiplying the number of limited English proficiency students that are provided services through programs approved by the Department of Education most recent October 1 count by the weight as determined depending on the total number of LEP students in the SAU and then multiplying that by the Elementary or Secondary SAU Rate as determined on page 1 of the ED279 report.

Section 2: (Operating Cost Allocations) – Lines D1-8: Targeted Funds

4YO/PreK, K-8 and 9-12 Student Assessment Targeted Funds Operating Cost Allocation is determined by multiplying the most recent 4YO/PreK October 1 pupils from line B1 basic counts; and the average K-8 or 9-12 pupils from line B2 & B3 basic counts respectively, by the EPS determined rate (currently 48.00).

4YO/PreK, K-8 and 9-12 Technology Resources Targeted Funds Operating Cost Allocation is determined by multiplying the 4YO/PreK October 1 pupils from line B1 basic counts; and the average calendar year K-8 or 9-12 pupils from line B2 & B3 basic counts respectively, by the EPS determined rate; currently 102.00 for Elementary and 308.00 for Secondary.

4YO/PreK and K-2 Pupils Targeted Funds Operating Cost Allocation is determined by multiplying the count of 4YO/PreK October 1 students and Kindergarten to grade 2 calendar year average students by the EPS determined weight, currently .10 and then by the EPS determined rate; currently set at the Elementary SAU Rate as determined on page 1 of the ED279 report.

4YO/PreK, K-8 and 9-12 Disadvantaged Students Targeted Funds Operating Cost Allocation is determined by multiplying the disadvantaged counts from lines C1, C2, & C3 by the EPS determined weight, currently .05 and then by the EPS Elementary and Secondary EPS rates as determined on page 1 of the ED 279 report.

Section 2: (Operating Cost Allocations) – Lines E1-2: Isolated Small School Adjustment

Isolated Small School Adjustment: A school administrative unit is eligible for an isolated small school adjustment when the unit meets the size and distance criteria established by the commissioner and outlined below. The isolated small school adjustment must be applied to discrete school buildings that meet the criteria for adjustment. The adjustment is not applicable to sections, wings or other parts of a building that are dedicated to certain grade spans.

Section 2: (Operating Cost Allocations) – Operating Allocation Totals

Operating Allocation Totals equals the sum of the Total Allocations from Section 2 lines B) Basic Counts, C) Weighted Counts, D) Targeted Funds and E) Isolated Small School Adjustments.

Percentage of EPS Transition Amount = 100.00%.

Adjusted Total Operating Allocation Amount = Operating Allocation Totals times EPS Transition Percentage.

Section 3: Other Allocations – A) Other Subsidizable Costs

Line A1: Gifted & Talented Expenditures from 2016-2017 – an allocation for Gifted & Talented Programs is determined using the most recent audited reported financial data of approved actual expenses or the approved budget, whichever is less, increased by an inflation adjustment, currently 1.5%.

Section 3: Other Allocations – A) Other Subsidizable Costs

Line A3: Special Education – EPS Allocation – weighted per pupil amounts for each special education student plus adjustments.

Base Component – Each identified special education student is weighted at 1.5 for up to 15% of the resident enrollment.

Prevalence Adjustment – Special education identified students above the 15% receive an additional .38 weight.

FIGURE 19.2. Continued

Special Education - EPS Allocation:
- Base Component Identified up to 15% (1.5 x EPS Rate x 295 Pupils) = $2,819,020.00
- Prevalence Adjustment Identified above 15% (.38 x EPS Rate x 0 Pupils) = $ 0.00
- Size Adjustment for <20 Pupils (.29 x EPS Rate x 0 Pupils) =
- High Cost In-District Adjustment =
- High Cost Out-of-District Adjustment =
- Federal Revenues Adjustment (to exclude Federal Revenues) =
- Maintenance of Effort Adjustment (to adjust 2013-14 actual expenses) = • Special Education – EPS Allocation Amount =
- Example: $ 0.00 $ 115,956.00 $ 319,043.00 $-470,810.00 $ 585,476.64 $3,368,685.64

Small Districts – Districts with fewer than 20 students with disabilities receive an adjustment to reflect lower student-staff ratios.

High Cost In-District – Students educated within the district estimated to cost more than three times the special education per-pupil base amount are identified as high cost in-district and an adjustment is made.

Maintenance of Effort – Districts are given a hold-harmless adjustment that is equal to at least the previous year's per-pupil expenditure minus adjustments for the loss of high cost students and shift in staff.

Line A4: Special Education – High-Cost Out-of-District Allocation

High Cost Out-of-District – Students educated outside the district estimated to cost four times the special education per-pupil base amount are identified as high cost out-of-district and an adjustment is made.

Special Education Model – FY2019
Special Education Allocation Calculation
– Step 1: Base Component
– Step 2: Prevalence Adjustment
– Step 3: Size Adjustment
– Step 4: High Cost In-District Adjustment
– Step 6: EPS Special Education Allocation
– EPS Maintenance of Effort Adjustment Calculation
High-cost Out-of-District Adjustment – Taken outside of the formula
– Separate allocation
Federal Revenues
– Removed from the formula completely
– No longer impacting the special education allocation

Section 3: Other Allocations – A) Other Subsidizable Costs

Line A5: Transportation Operating – EPS Allocation – an allocation for Transportation based on Pupil Density or Miles Driven; whichever is greater.

Section 3: Other Allocations – A) Other Subsidizable Costs

Line A6: Approved Bus Allocation – an allocation for bus purchases based on the amount approved for bus purchases made in the previous year.

Section 3: Other Allocations – B) Teacher Retirement Amount (Normalized Cost)

Line B: Teacher Retirement Amount (Normalized Cost) – an allocation for Teacher Retirement 'Normalized Costs' (Employer's Share) to be paid by the SAU to the Maine State Retirement System. The amount is an estimate provided for each SAU by MePERS.

Section 3: Other Allocations – Lines C1-5) Debt Service Allocations

Debt Service – Includes principal and interest costs for approved major capital projects in the allocation year. Major capital means school construction projects including onsite additions to existing schools; new schools; the cost of land acquired in conjunction with projects otherwise defined; the building of or acquisition of other facilities related to the operation of SAUs. Note: this is for approved State subsidizable debt service only – this does not include Local Only Debt Service.

Approved Leases & Lease Purchases – Lease costs for school buildings when the leases, including leases under which the school administrative unit may apply the lease payments to the purchase of portable, temporary classroom space, have been approved by the commissioner for the year prior to the allocation year.

Section 3: Other Allocations – Total Combined Allocation
Includes Section 2 Adjusted Total Operating Allocation, Other Subsidizable Costs, and Total Debt Service Allocation.

(continues)

FIGURE 19.2.   Continued

Section 4: Calculation of Required Local Contribution – Mill Expectation

Line A) Subsidizable Pupils by Member Municipality:

Distribution by Town of the Total EPS Allocation (Example):
The EPS Total Allocation is distributed to each member town based on their respective percent of the Average Calendar Year Subsidizable (Resident) Pupils.

Town A Operating Allocation Distribution = 974.5 ÷ 2,276.5 = 42.81% x 23,617,444.04 = $10,110,627.79
Town A Debt Allocation Distribution = 42.81% x 1,258,003.24 = $ 538,551.19
Total Municipal Allocation Distribution for Town A = $10,649,178.98

Line B) State Valuation by Member Municipality:

Required Local Contribution to the Town EPS Allocation:
The required local contribution (Ability to Pay) to the Town Allocation of EPS is equal to the two-year average of the Town's State Certified Valuation times the established mill expectation, but not to exceed the Total Town Allocation as determined in Section 4 Line A.

Town A = 827,766,667 x (8.48÷1,000=.00848) = $7,019,461.34

Line C) Required Local Contribution = the lesser of the previous two calculations:
The required local contribution is either the Distribution of the Total Allocation by Town amount as calculated in Section 4 Line A or the State Valuation two-year average of the Town times the mill expectation as calculated in Section 4 Line B – whichever is less. The State Contribution by Municipality (prior to adjustments) is the difference between the Total Allocation by Municipality and the Required Local Contribution by Municipality.

Section 5A provides the Total Allocation, Local Contribution and State Contribution amounts prior to any adjustments. Section 5B lists adjustments that may occur throughout the fiscal year to the State Contribution for those items listed above. Adjustments may add to the State Contribution or reduce the State Contribution depending on the type of adjustment.

Section 5: Totals and Adjustments	Total Allocation	Local Contribution	State Contribution
Total Allocation, Local Contribution, State Contribution	$20,433,467.21	$7,064,898.75	$13,368,58.46
Totals after adjustment to Local and State Contributions	$20,433,467.21	$7,064,898.75	$13,368,568.46
Other Adjustments to State Contribution			
1) Plus Audit Adjustment			$0.00
2) Less Audit Adjustments			$0.00
3) Less Adjustment for Unappropriated Local Contribution			$0.00
4) Less Adjustment for Unallocated Balance Excess of 3%			$0.00
5) Special Education Budgetary Hardship Adjustment			$0.00
6) Career & Technical Education Center Adjustment			$0.00
7) Plus Long-Term Drug Treatment Centers Adjustment			$0.00
8) Regionalization and efficiency assistance			$0.00
9) Bus Refurbishing Adjustment			$0.00
10) Less Maine Care Seed – Private			($13,88,68)
Adjusted State Contribution	$20,433,467.21	$7,064,898.75	$13,355,179.78
Local and State Percentages Prior to Adjustments:	Local Share %= 34.58%	State Share %= 65.42%	
Local and State Percentages After Adjustments:	Local Share %= 34.64%	State Share %= 65.36%	
FYI: 100% EPS Allocation			

Section 5F: Adjusted Local Contribution by Town for Warrant Article
Section 5F provides the Adjusted Local Contribution Amount by Town for use in the budget warrant articles.

FIGURE 19.2.   Continued

TABLE 19.3.　Maine Federal Relief Aid Packages

Federal Relief Aid Package	Coronavirus Aid, Relief, and Economic Security (CARES) Act	Coronavirus Response and Relief Supplemental Appropriations (CRRSA) Act	American Rescue Plan (ARP) Act
Focus and Allowable Uses	Address the impact that COVID-19 has had, and continues to have, on elementary and secondary school	Prevent, prepare for, and respond to COVID-19 related to addressing learning loss, preparing schools for reopening, and testing, repairing, and upgrading projects to improve air quality in school buildings	Safely reopen and sustain the safe operation of schools and address the impact of the coronavirus pandemic
Allocations	Elementary and Secondary School Emergency Relief Fund (ESSER) **$43,793,319** Coronavirus Relief Fund (CRF) **$342,000,000** Governor's Emergency Education Relief Fund (GEER) **$9,273,552** Rethinking Remote Education Venture (RREV) **$16,958,613** Child Nutrition CARES Grants to States **$27,701,541**	ESSER II **$183,138,601** GEER II **$4,082,345** Emergency Assistance for Non-public Schools (EANS) **$12,751,099**	ESSER III **$411,303,282** EANS II **$12,527,260** American Rescue Plan – Homeless Children and Youth (ARP-HCY) **$2,694,256**

Source: Maine Department of Education. (2021). https://www2.ed.gov/documents/press-releases/arp-esser-me-plan.pdf; Maine Department of Education. (2021). https://www.maine.gov/doe/sites/maine.gov.doe/files/inline-files/Federal%20Emergency%20Relief%20Fundsv2_0.pdf

plans to receive funding to support initiatives such as the return to in-person learning, safely reopen schools and sustain safe operations, address the academic impact of lost instructional time, staff to support students' time, invest in expanded afterschool care, and meeting emergency needs; some of the top priorities identified were to support social and emotional learning and mental and behavioral health for students, expanding restorative alternatives to exclusionary discipline, and student-centered learning through interdisciplinary, project-based instruction. As a result, the federal government granted billions of dollars to support about 172,000 students through the Coronavirus Aid, Relief, and Economic Security Act, Coronavirus Response and Relief Supplemental Appropriations Act, and the American Rescue Plan Elementary and Secondary School Emergency Relief Act.

SUMMARY

Through a cost-driven, adequacy-based funding model, Maine's school finance system is extensive and marked by change.[8] It is exhaustively analyzed at legislative and other levels.[9] One of its most recent changes was to stabilize student count in Maine's school funding formula by requiring its Department of Education to use a 3-year average for pupil counts, if that average is greater than the current 2-year average, when a SAU experiences a decrease of 10% or more of total SAU enrollment in the most recent year (PL 2021, c. 428).

SOURCES

"Constitution of the State of Maine." Maine State Constitution. https://www.maine.gov/legis/const/.

"How Is Public Education Funded in Maine?" Maine State Chamber of Commerce, 2018. https://www.educatemaine.org/docs/17-029_EDME-FundingPrimer-FNL-web.pdf.

"Legislation of Interest." Maine State Chamber of Commerce. https://www.mainechamber.org/legislation-of-interest.html.

"Maine Learning Results-Mathematics." Maine Learning Results-Mathematics | Department of Education. https://www.maine.gov/doe/learning/content/mathematics/learningresults.

"School Funding—General Purpose Aid (GPA)." Maine Department of Education. Accessed December 9, 2022. https://www.maine.gov/doe/sites/maine.gov.doe/files/inline-files/EPS%20Cost%20Component%20Calculations%20ED279%20Line%20by%20Line_updatedSeptember2017.pdf. Accessed May 2022.

Smith, Sharda Jackson. "Maine." *Journal of Education Finance* 47, no. 5 (2022).

"Student Enrollment Data." Student Enrollment Data | Department of Education. https://www.maine.gov/doe/data-reporting/reporting/warehouse/enrollment.

Thompson, David C., R. Craig Wood, S. Craig Neuenswander, John M. Heim, and Randy D. Watson. *Funding Public Schools in the United States and Indian Country*. Charlotte, NC: Information Age Publishing, Inc., 2019.

Verstegen, Deborah. "A Quick Glance at School Finance: A 50 State Survey of School Finance Policies." A Quick Glance at School Finance: 2018. https://schoolfinancesdav.wordpress.com/

ENDNOTES

[1] The first edition of this chapter was drawn from multiple sources and represented the editorial staff's interpretation of issues, trends and findings regarding the state of Maine(Thompson, David C., R. Craig Wood, S. Craig Neuenswander, John M. Heim, and Randy D. Watson. Funding Public Schools in the United States and Indian Country. Charlotte, NC: Information Age Publishing, Inc., 2019.). Although some items in this chapter reflect the first edition, this edition (2nd) updates information to reflect the most recent information available and to expand on particular nuances of Maine public education funding system.

[2] The first part of this section closely follows Maine State Chamber of Commerce, "How Is Public Education Funded in Maine?" (2018). Retrieved from: http://www.educatemaine.org/docs/17-029_EDME-FundingPrimer-FNL-web.pdf; Maine Department of Education. "Student Enrollment Data." Retrieved from: https://www.maine.gov/doe/data-reporting/reporting/warehouse/enrollment; This section mirrors the first edition of this chapter.

3   Constitution of the State of Maine. Retrieved from: https://www.maine.gov/legis/const/

4   Maine Department of Education. "Maine Learning Results." Retrieved from: https://www.maine. gov/doe/learning/content/mathematics/learningresults

5   Description of the EPS in the preceding two paragraphs partly relies on Deborah A. Verstegen, "A Quick Glance at School Finance: A 50 State Survey of School Finance Policies." Maine. (2018). Retrieved from: https://schoolfinancesdav.wordpress.com; This section mirrors the first edition of this chapter.

6   This section closely follows Maine Department of Education, "School Funding—General Purpose Aid (GPA). Retrieved from: https://www.maine.gov/ doe/sites/maine.gov.doe/files/inline-files/ EPS%20Cost%20Component%20Calculations%20ED279%20Line%20by%20Line_updated September 2017.pdf Retrieved May 22, 2022; This section mirrors the first edition of this chapter.

7   Ibid.

8   See "Maine." 2022. Journal of Education Finance 47 (5). https://www.nationaledfinance.com/ docs/18_Jef_47.5_Maine.pdf; See "Journal of Ed. Finance 47(5): 2022 State of States." Journal of Ed. Finance 47(5): 2022 State of States-National Education Finance Academy. Accessed May 31, 2022. https://www.nationaledfinance.com/journal_of_ed_finance_475.php.

9   See Maine State Chamber of Congress, "Legislation of Interest." Retrieved from: https://www. mainechamber.org/legislation-of-interest.html; Maine State Chamber of Commerce, "How Is Public Education Funded in Maine?" (2018). Retrieved from: http://www.educatemaine.org/docs/17-029_EDME-FundingPrimer-FNL-web.pdf

CHAPTER 20

MARYLAND

Chelsea E. Haines
Virginia Polytechnic Institute and State University

GENERAL BACKGROUND

Passed in 1978, the Education Article of the Maryland Code entrusted the supervision and administration of the public K-12 schools to the state's Board of Education and superintendent of schools. No longer used, the 1978 funding model established a per-pupil base level of annual spending to be shared by local and state taxes. Local contributions were based on a combination of a flat tax rate and the school district's wealth. State contributions filled the remaining base level, and provided supplemental funding "regardless of district wealth, based on the enrollment of children with special needs and the population density of a district."[1]

In 1981, the equity of the funding formula was challenged in *Hornbeck v. Somerset County Board of Education*. In 1983, the court agreed that the formula did not sufficiently provide for equitable funding across districts, thus violating the state constitution.[2] The court did not mandate equal per pupil funding, but rather "an adequate education measured by contemporary educational standards."[3]

Following the *Hornbeck* ruling, Maryland neglected to change the funding formula. In 1994, the American Civil Liberties Union (ACLU) and Baltimore City Public Schools filed separate lawsuits, later consolidated into *Bradford v. Maryland State Board of Education*, challenging asking for a definition of "adequacy"

Funding Public Schools in the United States, Indian Country, and US Territories (Second Edition), pages 329–344.
Copyright © 2023 by Information Age Publishing
www.infoagepub.com

329

of education in the state. In response to these and numerous other lawsuits, the state created the Commission on Education Finance, Equity, and Excellence, or the Thorton Commission, which was convened in 1999-2002.[4] The Thorton Commission was evaluating and making recommendations on how the state could, "ensure adequate school funding, reduce funding inequities among school districts; ensure excellence in school systems and student performance; and provide a smooth transition for recommended changes.on 1) ensuring adequate funding, 2) reducing inequities among districts, and 3) ensuring excellence in schools and student performance."[5]

In response to the Thornton Commission's recommendations, the *Bridge to Excellence in Public Schools Act* was passed in 2002, which "restructured Maryland's public school finance system and increased state aid through a new school finance formula that accounted for differences in local wealth and linked resources with students' needs."[6] The formula included per-pupil base funding, in addition to "a guaranteed tax base, a geographic cost adjustment, and weights to compensate districts for the additional cost of educating students from special needs groups," including at-risk, special education, and limited English proficiency students.[7] Full implementation of this funding model was reached in FY 2008.[8]

Approximately 10 years after it was enacted, in response to Chapter 288 of the *Bridge to Excellence in Public Schools Act,* a Study on Adequacy of Funding for Education in the State of Maryland was commissioned.[9] The study examined base funding levels, weights for students with special needs, and effects of poverty, as well as the impact of school size, supplemental grants program, measures of economic disadvantage, prekindergarten services, equity and wealth calculation, impact of moving school enrollments, and geographic index and produced a final report in 2016.[10]

The Commission on Innovation and Excellence in Education, or Kirwin Commission, was established in 2016 to review the 2002 funding formula in light of the commissioned adequacy study.[11] The Kirwin Commission released a report in 2019 with recommendations in five policy areas: 1) Early childhood education, 2) high-quality and diverse teachers and leaders, 3) college and career readiness pathways (including career and technical education), 4) more resources to ensure all students are successful, and 5) governance and accountability.[12] Hogan's response to the report was, "Unfortunately, the Kirwan Tax Hike Commission is hellbent on spending billions more than we can afford, and legislators are refusing to come clean about where the money is going to come from. Even after more than three years of meetings, there is still no clear plan whatsoever for how either the state or the counties will pay this massive price tag."[13] The *Blueprint for Maryland's Future Act* (HB 1300),[14] created to enact many of the Kirwin Commission's recommendations, was vetoed by Hogan in 2020, but overturned in the 2021 legislative session.[15] The Blueprint Act has been criticized for not increasing funding for "school basics," such as the number of classroom teachers and support personnel.[16]

Delayed reporting from the Kirwin Commission and the Covid-19 pandemic resulted in delayed enactment of funding formula changes until FY 2023. FY 2023 included implementation of funding formulas enacted by Chapter 36 (Blueprint of Maryland's Future-Implementation) and 55 of 2021.

DESCRIPTIVE STATISTICS

In 2021, Maryland had more than 1,400 public schools in 24 public school systems (or Local Education Agencies) with a student enrollment of 882,538.[17] The state employed 62,276 full time equivalent (FTE) teachers in FY 2021 for a pupil-teacher ratio of 14.17.[18] The total number of enrolled students, as well as enrolled students by gender for 2017-2021 are presented in Table 20.1. In 2021, female student enrollment totalled 430,667, and male enrollment totalled 451,833.

The total number of enrolled students by race and ethnicity for 2017-2021 are presented in Table 20.2.

TABLE 20.1.   Number of Enrolled Students by Gender 2017-2021

Year	All Students	Male Students	Female Students
2017	886,221	454,806	431,415
2018	893,689	458,327	435,362
2019	896,837	459,641	437,196
2020	909,414	466,525	442,889
2021	882,538	451,833	430,667

Source: Maryland State Department of Education. Report Card Demographics Filtered by Gender, Data Last Updated August 31, 2021, https://reportcard.msde.maryland.gov/Graphs/#/Demographics/Enrollment/3/17/6/99/XXXX/2021
Reporting categories are presented as they appear in the Maryland Report Card. Male and female are the classifications used to present gender.

TABLE 20.2.   Number of Enrolled Students by Race and Ethnicity, 2017-2021

Year	American Indian or Alaska Native	Asian	Black or African American	Hispanic/ Latino of Any Race	Two or More Races	White
2017	2,474	57,049	301,781	145,800	39,423	338,454
2018	2,387	58,823	301,542	155,346	40,739	333,552
2019	2,379	59,611	301,376	162,528	42,131	327,508
2020	2,369	60,148	301,303	176,838	43,628	323,824
2021	2,286	59,668	295,736	175,768	43,581	304,212

Source: Maryland State Department of Education. Report Card Demographics Filtered by Gender and Race and Ethnicity, Data Last Updated August 31, 2021, https://reportcard.msde.maryland.gov/Graphs/#/Demographics/Enrollment/3/17/6/99/XXXX/2021

CURRENT POLITICAL CLIMATE

Governor Larry Hogan was elected the 62nd governor of Maryland in 2015. Hogan became the second Republican governor to be reelected in history of the state, with a 2018 four-year term re-election.[19] In 2020, Hogan was named the most popular governor in the United States.[20] Throughout his tenure, Hogan's stated top priority has been education. Maryland is one of 12 states where the governor appoints the state board of education, who in turn appoint the chief state school officer, sometimes referred to as the state superintendent.[21]

In 2022, the Maryland General Assembly was under Democrat leadership in both the Senate and the House. For party affiliation of the general assembly, 131 (70%) were Democrat and 47 (30%) Republican. Senate party affiliation was 32 (68%) Democrat and 15 (32%) Republican, and House party affiliation was 99 (70%) Democrat and 42 (30%) Republican. In 2022, the general assembly had 188 members with 106 (56%) male and 82 (44%) female members. Senate membership was 47, with 32 (68%) male and 14 (32%) female members, and House membership was 141 with 74 (52%) male and 67 (48%) female members.[22]

Maryland has an annual operating budget cycle with the fiscal year beginning on July 1. The governor submits an operating budget to the General Assembly each January, and the General Assembly reviews the budget from January through April. According to the Maryland Constitution, the General Assembly must "enact a balanced budget by the 83rd day of the legislative session, or one week before the session ends" or the Governor must call for an extended session. Once the budget is enacted by the General Assembly, it becomes law.[23] Passed in 2020 under Chapter 645 and beginning in FY 2024, in order to enact a balanced budget, the Maryland General Assembly will have the authority to "increase, diminish, or add items, provided that the General Assembly may not exceed the total proposed budget as submitted by the Governor."[24] With this amendment, the Governor receives line-item veto power.[25]

In 2021, 11% (down from 13.1% in 2020) of Maryland's wage and salary workers were union members, slightly above the nationwide average of 10.3%.[26]

While not a comprehensive list, some relevant education advocacy groups include the American Civil Liberties Union of Maryland[27], Maryland Alliance of Public Charter Schools[28], Maryland Coalition of Families[29], Maryland Coalition for Inclusive Education[30], and Parent's Place of Maryland[31]. Special interest groups include the Maryland State Education Association[32] and a new state Parent Teacher Association[33].

CURRENT SCHOOL FINANCE LITIGATION

On January 16, 2020, a Maryland circuit court judge denied the state's motion to dismiss *Bradford v. Maryland State Board of Education*, even though it had not been actively litigated for 15 years.[34] The lawsuit aims to bring "adequate" and "equitable" education to students in Baltimore City.[35] Based on data from

2014-2015, Maryland was one of six states in the country where K-12 students in wealthy districts receive more funds than students from poor districts.[36]

Maryland is expected to appeal a federal ruling establishing "a contractual right to prescription drug benefits for State retirees who retired before January 1, 2019."[37] SB 578, effective July 2022, restored eligibility for prescription drug coverage for Medicare-eligible retirees.[38]

ENROLLMENT TRENDS

In FY 2021, Maryland's public school enrollments decreased by 19,704 students (2.3%) during the COVID-19 pandemic, which decreased foundation formula allocations.[39] Due to the COVID-19 Pandemic, Maryland did not publish report card results for 2019-2020 and 2020-2021, so data is based on the 2018-2019 school year.[40] Maryland public schools had a graduation rate of 87.1%.[41] Attendance rates for 2018-2019 were 94.8% in elementary schools, 94.4% in middle schools, and 91.1% in high schools.[42] Attendance rate is defined as the "percentage of students in school for at least half of the average school day during the school year" and a target rate of at least 94% was set following the 2013-2014 school year by the state. The adjusted cohort graduation rates defined by the U.S. Department of Education were 88.86% (4-year rate) and 88.88% (5-year rate), respectively.[43]

SOURCES OF REVENUE

Maryland's primary source of revenue are individual income taxes: "Approximately 37.6% of Maryland's total State and local tax revenues comes from the personal income tax, ranking Maryland second among all states in its reliance on the income tax."[44] The state also collects sales and use tax, transportation taxes, corporate income and other business taxes, property and taxes, tobacco and alcoholic beverage taxes, and estate and inheritance taxes, among other taxes.[45] Unlike some states, Maryland does not collect personal property taxes. In FY 2019, $9.9 billion in individual income taxes were anticipated, totalling 56% of general fund revenues. Local governments expected $5.9 billion in revenue in FY 2019. The second largest source of revenue, the sales and use tax, excludes most services and "exempts grocery food, residential utilities, and medicine from the sales tax base."[46] Maryland's typical sales tax rate is 6% and a local sales tax is not imposed.[47] Maryland's corporate income tax rate is 8.25%. The property tax rate in FY 2019 was "11.2 cents per $100 of assessable property."[48]

DISTRIBUTION FORMULAS

Following implementation of *Blueprint* legislation, Maryland's education formula includes thirteen categories: Foundation Aid, Transportation Aid, Compensatory Education Aid, English Learner Aid, Special Education Aid, Guaranteed Tax Base Aid, Comparable Wage Index Aid, Post College and Career Readiness Pathways

Aid, Concentration of Poverty Aid, Transitional Supplemental Instruction Aid, Prekindergarten Aid, and Career Ladder Aid.[49]

REGULAR EDUCATION PROGRAM

The regular education program in Maryland is known as the Foundation Program, and it accounts for "nearly half of direct State education aid."[50] The program establishes a minimum funding level per pupil and requires a local government match. This minimum funding level, or base amount, "assigns a cost to the education of a student with no special needs or services."[51] Multipliers are then applied to that base amount to generate supplemental funding for student categories of English Language learners, low-income students, and students with disabilities.[52]

The Foundation Program was $3.7 billion in FY 2023, a 15.4% increase from FY 2022.[53] FTE enrollment counts for 2020-2021 will not be used in determining the "3-year moving average enrollment" for calculating Foundation and other funding formulas.[54]

TECHNOLOGY

HB 1372 revised Chapter 36 (Blueprint-Implementation) by adding funding ($198 per pupil to be phased in by FY 2027) to the state's foundation program for educational technology and requiring additional reporting on technology usage.[55]

CATEGORICAL FUNDING

Compensatory Education Aid

Funding is provided to LEAs based on the number of students who meet Free and Reduced Priced Meal (FRPM) Eligibility requirements. A "hold harmless" grant was provided in FY 2023 to ensure funding doesn't decline based on enrollment declines due to the COVID-19 pandemic.[56] $1.3 billion is budgeted for the program in FY 2023, an $8.5 million (0.7%) increase from FY 2022.[57]

Concentration of Poverty Aid

Funding is provided to LEAs where at least 80% of students are eligible for FRPM in the form of a community school coordinator and per pupil grants.[58] HB1372 modified the phase-in concentration of poverty grants to accelerate funding for schools with higher poverty concentration rates. Schools with 80% of students who are eligible for free or reduced-price meals (FRPM) will reach 100% funding by FY 2028 with schools with 55% of students eligible for FRPM will reach 100% by FY 2030.[59] $190.3 million is budgeted for Concentration of Poverty Aid in FY 2023, a $73.3 million (62.8%) increase from $116.9 million in FY 2022.[60]

Comparable Wage Index Aid

The Geographic Cost of Education Index (GCEI) "is a mandated formula that accounts for the differences in the costs of educational resources among local school systems."[61] $157.9 million is budgeted for the GCEI in FY 2023, a 6.9% increase from $147.692 million in FY 2022.[62] As a result of Chapter 36 of 2021, the use of the GCEI will be replaced by the Comparable Wage Index (CWI) in FY 2024.[63] State aid will be distributed through CWI funding to LEAs where education delivery is more costly than in other LEAs due to local market and labor rates.[64]

Guaranteed Tax Base Aid

Under Guaranteed Tax Base Aid, funding is provided to LEAs "that 1) have less than 80 percent of the statewide average wealth per pupil, and 2) provide local education funding above the local share required by the Foundation Program. The program encourages less wealthy jurisdictions to maintain or increase local education tax effort."[65] Eight LEAs qualified for grants totaling $45.8 million in FY 2023, a $4.1 million decrease from FY 2022.[66]

Special Education Aid

Additional funding is provided for students with disabilities under the Special Education Formula, recognizing increased costs associated with educating these students. Students may receive services in public or nonpublic schools. The formula "is calculated based on a certain percentage of the annual per pupil foundation amount in each year and the number of special education students from the prior fiscal year. The State share of program cost is 50% statewide with a floor of 40% for each local school system."[67] Chapter 36 increased special education funding for public schools beginning in FY 2023, and the *Blueprint Act* provided an additional $65.5 million for special education in FY 2021 and FY 2022. Under the Special Education Formula, $311.1 million was allocated in FY 2022, and $401.3 million in FY 2023, a $90.2 million (29%) increase from FY 2022 to FY 2023. An additional $141.4 million is allocated for special education students in nonpublic placements for FY 2023, a $13.9 million increase (11%) from $127.5 million in FY 22.[68] An additional $27.2 million is allocated for special education student transportation, a $24.2 million increase (88%) from $3 million in FY 22.[69]

Transportation Aid

Funding is provided to LEAs for "public school transportation based on a formula that increases funding by the change in the Consumer Price Index for private transportation in the Washington-Baltimore area for the second preceding fiscal year."[70] $336 million is allocated for student transportation in FY 2023, a 16.6% increase from $288.1 million in FY 2022.[71]

Post College and Career Readiness Pathways Aid

The statutory allocation for the Post College and Career Readiness Pathways Aid program is described in Education Article §5–217,[72] and provides College and Career Readiness (CCR) grants to LEAS based on the number of students who meet college and career readiness standards outlined in Education Article §7–205.1.[73]

Additionally, by 2031, 45% of Maryland high school students must earn a Career and Technical Education (CTE) credential or complete an apprenticeship.[74] As outlined in Education Article §21–205, the governor must appropriate "at least $2 million annually for the Career and Technology Education Innovation Grant, which funds partnerships between county boards, community colleges, and industry partners to develop and implement high-quality CTE frameworks and pathways throughout the state."[75]

English Learner Aid

Funding is provided for English-language learners using a multiplier to the base per-pupil amount adjusted for local wealth levels. The base multiplier for FY 2022 was 2.00, but the multiplier will decrease over time to 1.85 in FY 2033.[76]

Guaranteed Tax Base Aid

The Blueprint Act established a program to provide additional grant funding to counties "with less than 80% of statewide per pupil wealth that contributed more than the minimum required local share under the foundation program in the prior year. The grant is based on local support for education relative to local wealth . . . [and] . . . cannot exceed 20% of the per pupil foundation amount."[77]

Additional Categorical Aid

Additional categorical funding is provided under Transitional Supplemental Instruction Aid, Prekindergarten Aid, and Career Ladder Aid. Transitional aid supports struggling learners in kindergarten through third grades.[78] Prekindergarten aid "includes (a) grants to expand access to free public prekindergarten programs throughout Maryland and (b) Publicly Funded Full-day Prekindergarten grants mandated in Education Article Section 5-229 under the Blueprint for Maryland's Future formulas."[79] Career Ladder Aid includes grants incentivizing teacher development and salary increases.[80]

School Health Services

While Maryland requires "mandated health coverage in schools by a school health services professional," a specified school nurse to student ratio is not specified and therefore not all schools employ a full-time school nurse. For example, "In some schools, trained unlicensed health staff are in each school working under the supervision of a registered nurse who may be responsible for one to three schools."[81]

In 2021, there were 89 School Based Health Centers (SBHC) in 14 Maryland counties. Administration will be moved from the MSDE to the Bureau of Maternal and Child Health at the Maryland Department of Health. Under the *Blueprint Act*, funding for SBHC will increase by $6.5 million to $9 million annually beginning in FY 2023.[82]

School Safety

Chapter 30 of the *Maryland Safe to Learn Act of 2018* reformed the Maryland Center for School Safety and moved under the administration of the Maryland State Department of Education.[83] $40.6 million was provided "in operating and capital funds to improve school safety and security in public schools, including local law enforcement enhancements."[84] $20.6 million was allocated for school safety grants in FY 2023 and FY 2022 respectively.[85]

CAPITAL OUTLAY AND DEBT SERVICE

Education represented nearly $1.3 billion in capital program uses in FY 2023 thanks to a budget surplus.[86] Maryland's K-12 school construction programs are administered by the Interagency Commission on School Construction. In 2020, the Maryland Stadium Authority (MSA) was authorized to issue up to $2.2 billion of revenue bonds through the Built to Learn Act (Chapter 20) for public school facilities.[87] In FY 2023, a total of $1.2 billion was budgeted for public school construction programs, "a historically high level": $459.2 million was authorized for general obligation (GO) bonds, $480.0 million for revenue bonds, $257.8 through general funds, $40.0 for federal funds.[88] Within debt affordability guidelines, HB 1229 (Chapter 32) increased statutory allocations for school construction from $400 million (Chapter 14 of the 21st Century School Facilities Act) to $450 million annually.[89]

EMPLOYEE BENEFITS

Healthcare

Health insurance plans for Maryland state employees, including public school teachers, are administered through the Maryland State Employees Health Benefits Program which falls under the Department of Budget and Management.[90] In FY 2017, state costs for health insurance for state employees totaled $1.2 million.[91] Medical, prescription, and dental health insurance plans are available to Maryland state employees and retirees through the State Employee and Retiree Health and Welfare Benefits Program.[92] An ever increasing percentage of the state budget, "retiree enrollment in the State health plan continues to grow faster than active employee enrollment."[93]

Retirement

Prior to 2012, 100% of teacher retirement costs were paid for by the state, but the *Budget Reconciliation and Financing Act* of 2012, "phased in a requirement that local school boards pay 100% of the employer normal cost for active members of the Teachers' Retirement and Pension Systems, while the State will continue to pay 100% of the amortized accrued liability for active and retired members. The employer normal cost represents the employer's share of the payment that is necessary to fund the benefits that currently employed members accrue in a given year."[94] This Act also "established the State Teacher Retirement Supplemental Grant as a mandatory general fund appropriation" beginning in FY 2015.

For FY 2023, a 7% decrease ($5.4 million) in public school teacher and personnel state retirement costs are expected from $779 million in FY 2022 to $724.6 million in FY 2023 due to "record investment returns (26.7%) in fiscal 2021 and the Board of Trustees of the State Retirement and Pension Systems electing to accelerate recognition of those gains, thereby substantially reducing the system's unfunded liabilities."[95]

Senate Bill 410/House Bill 743, both passed in FY 2022, authorize the hiring of "up to 25 retirees of each of the Teachers' Retirement System and the Teachers' Pension System as classroom teachers, substitute classroom teachers, teacher mentors, or principals without the retirees being subject to the statutory earnings limitation and offset."[96]

CHARTER SCHOOL FUNDING

The Maryland Public Charter School Program established the state's charter school law in 2003 and was subsequently amended in 2015 with Chapter 331, Acts of 215, which mandated a study of traditional and charter schools.[97] In 2022, Maryland had 50 public charter schools.[98] In Maryland, charter schools are subject to the same per-pupil funding as other public schools in their district. Whereas previously Maryland's charter schools did not receive any state funding for facilities,[99] Governor Hogan has supported public charter school construction projects through initiatives such as the Public Charter School Facility Fund Act of 2019.[100]

NONPUBLIC SCHOOL FUNDING

Vouchers are provided to free or reduced-price lunch program eligible students to attend nonpublic schools through the Broadening Options and Opportunities for Students Today (BOOST) Program. BOOST first received funding in FY 2017, and in FY 2019, $7.6 million was allocated for BOOST, a $1.6 million increase from FY 2018.[101] In FY 2022, funds were provided to 3,268 students to attend nonpublic schools, including 1,030 English language learners and 56% students of color.[102]

In FY 2023, special education funding for nonpublic schools was $141.4 million, a $13.9 million (10.9%) increase from FY 2022 funding. Local school systems are responsible for contributing "an amount equal to the local share of the basic cost of educating a child without disabilities plus two times the total basic cost. Any costs above this are split 70% State/30% local."[103]

VIRTUAL EDUCATION

SB 362 and HB 1163 established "what entities may operate or administer a virtual school, student applications, school accountability, teacher and education support personnel protections, required student services, and other general school policies, including class size, technology, and attendance."[104] Maryland's state law doesn't explicitly allow virtual charter schools.[105] Under HB 1372, beginning with the 2022-2023 school year, virtual schools will be required "to follow quality online education standards."[106]

FEDERAL COVID-19 FUNDING

Maryland was allocated $9.2 billion through the Federal Government for American Rescue Plan (ARP) State, and Local Fiscal Recovery Funds (SLFRF), including $3.7 billion in 2021.[107] In 2021-2024, $2.8 billion was earmarked through ARP for K-12 education, including $2.07 billion for LEAs and $39.2 million for nonpublic schools. From 2021-2023, $1 billion is allocated for Maryland, including $789.9 million for LEAs, through the Coronavirus Response & Relive Supplemental Appropriations (CRRSA) Act. From 2020-2022, $666.8 million was allocated to Maryland through the Coronavirus Adi, Relief, and Economic Security (CARES) Act, including $422.9 million for LEAs.[108]

In FY 2021, $10 million was dedicated to school reopening, $25 million to summer school, and $174.8 million to replace lost revenues due to shortfalls in gaming revenues.[109] $209.4 million in harmless grants helped offset decreased student enrollment due to the COVID-19 Pandemic in FY 2022[110] In FY 2022, $211.6 million was received in COVID-19 relief funding and the state provided $209.4 million in "hold harmless" grants to offset student enrollment decreases due to the pandemic.[111]

ACKNOWLEDGEMENT

Drs. Laura Checovich and Jennifer King Rice published the Maryland chapter in the first edition of *Funding Public Schools in the United States and Indian Country* (2019).

ENDNOTES

1   Laura Checovich, Financing Public Education in Maryland: A Brief History (2016).
2   Laura Checovich, Financing Public Education in Maryland: A Brief History (2016).
3   Molly Hunter, Maryland Enacts Modern, Standards-Based Education Finance System: Reforms Based on Adequacy Cost Studies (2002).
4   Laura Checovich & Jennifer Rice King, "Maryland," in Funding Public Schools in the United States and Indian Country, ed. Thompson et al. (Charlotte, NC: Information Age Publishing, Inc., 2019).
5   Molly Hunter, Maryland Enacts Modern, Standards-Based Education Finance System: Reforms Based on Adequacy Cost Studies (2002).
6   Laura Checovich & Jennifer Rice King, "Maryland," in Funding Public Schools in the United States and Indian Country, ed. Thompson et al. (Charlotte, NC: Information Age Publishing, Inc., 2019).
7   Ibid.
8   "Study of Adequacy of Funding for Education in the State Of Maryland" Maryland State Department of Education, Accessed August 31, 2022, https://www.marylandpublicschools.org/Pages/adequacystudy/index.aspx
9   Ibid.
10 "Final Report of the Study of Adequacy of Funding for Education in Maryland," APA Consulting, November 30, 2016, https://www.marylandpublicschools.org/Documents/adequacystudy/AdequacyStudyReportFinal112016.pdf
11 Chapter 701, Senate Bill 905, Commission on Innovation and Excellence in Education, https://mgaleg.maryland.gov/2016RS/Chapters_noln/CH_701_sb0905e.pdf
12 Maryland Commission on Innovation & Excellence in Education, "Interim Report," January 2019, https://dls.maryland.gov/pubs/prod/NoPblTabMtg/CmsnInnovEduc/2019-Interim-Report-of-the-Commission.pdf
13 The Office of Governor Larry Hogan, "Governor Hogan Statement on Education Funding," October 15, 2019, https://governor.maryland.gov/2019/10/15/governor-hogan-statement-on-education-funding/
14 House Bill 1300 Fiscal and Policy Note, https://mgaleg.maryland.gov/2020RS/fnotes/bil_0000/hb1300.pdf
15 Department of Legislative Services, Maryland General Assembly, "The 90 Day Report: A Review of the 2021 Legislative Session," http://dls.maryland.gov/pubs/prod/RecurRpt/2021rs-90-day-report.pdf, L-1
16 Kalman Hettleman, "Kalman Hettleman: The Foundation of the Blueprint for School Reform Could Collapse in the Years Ahead," December 14, 2021, https://www.marylandmatters.org/2021/12/14/kalman-hettleman-the-foundation-of-the-blueprint-for-school-reform-could-collapse-in-the-years-ahead/
17 Maryland State Department of Education, "2021 Maryland State Schools At A Glance," https://reportcard.msde.maryland.gov/Graphs/#/AtaGlance/Index/3/17/6/99/XXXX/2021
18 U.S. Department of Education, National Center for Education Statistics, Common Core of Data (CCD), "Local Education Agency (School District) Universe Survey," 2020-21 v.1a; "State Nonfiscal Public Elementary/Secondary Education Survey," 2020-21 v.1a.
19 The Office of Governor Larry Hogan, "Governor Larry Hogan," https://governor.maryland.gov/governor-larry-hogan/
20 Bruce DePuyt and Josh Kurtz, "And the Most Popular Governor in America Is . . . ," Maryland Matters, January 7, 2020, https://www.marylandmatters.org/2020/01/07/and-the-most-popular-governor-in-america-is/
21 Hunter Railey, "50-State Review," Education Commission of the States, August 2017, https://dls.maryland.gov/pubs/prod/NoPblTabMtg/CmsnInnovEduc/07_13_2018_StateEducationGovernanceStructures2017update.pdf#search=Vol.%209%20Education%20Handbook

22 "Membership Profile," Maryland General Assembly, January 13, 2022, https://mgaleg.maryland.gov/pubs-current/current-member-profile.pdf

23 "Citizen's Guide to the Budget: Maryland's Operating Budget Cycle," Department of Budget and Management, Accessed August 31, 2022, https://dbm.maryland.gov/budget/Pages/cycle-calendar.aspx

24 Maryland State Board of Elections, "Official 2020 Presidential General Election Question Text, The State Board of Elections, Updated December 4, 2020, https://elections.maryland.gov/elections/2020/results/General/gen_qtext_2020_4_S_00_4_01__.html

25 Kevin Kinnally, "Big Changes Ahead for Maryland's One-Of-A-Kind Budget Process," Conduit Street, August 3, 2022, https://conduitstreet.mdcounties.org/2022/08/03/big-changes-ahead-for-marylands-one-of-a-kind-budget-process/

26 U.S. Bureau of Labor Statistics, "Union Members in Maryland—2021," February 15, 2021, https://www.bls.gov/regions/mid-atlantic/news-release/unionmembership_maryland.htm

27 ACLU of Maryland, https://www.aclu-md.org/en

28 Maryland Alliance of Public School Charters, https://mdcharters.org/

29 Maryland Coalition of Families, https://www.mdcoalition.org/

30 Maryland Coalition for Inclusive Education, Inc. (MCIE), https://www.mcie.org/

31 The Parents' Place of Maryland, https://www.ppmd.org/

32 Maryland State Education Association, https://www.marylandeducators.org/

33 Scott MacFarlane, "New State PTA Created After Maryland PTA Shut Down," NBC Washington, May 26, 2021, https://www.nbcwashington.com/news/local/new-state-pta-created-after-maryland-pta-shut-down/2684085/

34 Bradford v. Maryland State Board of Education, (2020) https://www.naacpldf.org/wp-content/uploads/Bradford-ruling.pdf

35 Neydin Milián, "Statement On Today's Latest Victory In The Bradford Case Championing State Constitutional Right To Education," ACLU Maryland, January 21, 2020, https://www.aclu-md.org/en/press-releases/statement-todays-latest-victory-bradford-case-championing-state-constitutional-right

36 S. Q. Cornman, O. L. Ampadu, S. Wheeler, and L. Zhou, "Revenues and Expenditures for Public Elementary and Secondary School Districts: School Year 2014–15 (Fiscal Year 2015): First Look (NCES 2018-303)," U.S. Department of Education, (Washington, DC, National Center for Education Statistics, 2018). Retrieved from https://nces.ed.gov/pubs2018/2018303.pdf

37 SB 578 Fiscal and Policy Note, Department of Legislative Services Maryland General Assembly, https://mgaleg.maryland.gov/2022RS/fnotes/bil_0008/sb0578.pdf

38 Department of Legislative Services, "Maryland State Personnel, Pensions, and Procurement," Legislative Handbook Series, Vol. V, 2018, https://dls.maryland.gov/pubs/prod/RecurRpt/Handbook_Volume_5_Personnel_Pensions_Procurement.pdf

39 Department of Legislative Services, General Assembly of Maryland, "The 90 Day Report: A Review of the 2021 Legislative Session," (A-122, 2021). Retrieved from http://dls.maryland.gov/pubs/prod/RecurRpt/2021rs-90-day-report.pdf

40 Maryland State Department of Education, "Maryland State Data: 2018-2019 School Report Card," Retrieved from https://reportcard.msde.maryland.gov/Graphs/#/ReportCards/ReportCard-School/1/E/1/99/XXXX/2019

41 Ibid.

42 Ibid.

43 Ibid.

44 "Maryland's Revenue Structure," Legislative Handbook Series, (Vol. III, 2018), Retrieved from https://dls.maryland.gov/pubs/prod/RecurRpt/Handbook_Volume_3_MDs_Revenue_Structure.pdf

45 Ibid.

46 Ibid.

47 Ibid.

48 Ibid.

49 Maryland State Department of Education, "Maryland State Aid to Local Education Agencies," Retrieved from https://marylandpublicschools.org/about/Pages/OFPOS/StateAid/index.aspx

50 Department of Legislative Services Maryland General Assembly, "HB 1372 Fiscal and Policy Note," Retrieved from https://mgaleg.maryland.gov/2021RS/fnotes/bil_0002/hb1372.pdf

51 EdBuild, "Fund Ed: Formula Type Policies in Each State," Retrieved September 21, 2022 from http://funded.edbuild.org/reports/issue/formula-type

52 Ibid.

53 Department of Legislative Services, General Assembly of Maryland, "The 90 Day Report: A Review of the 2022 Legislative Session," (L-2, 2022). Retrieved from https://mgaleg.maryland.gov/Pubs/LegisLegal/2022rs-90-day-report.pdf

54 Department of Legislative Services Maryland General Assembly, "HB 1372 Fiscal and Policy Note," Retrieved from https://mgaleg.maryland.gov/2021RS/fnotes/bil_0002/hb1372.pdf

55 Ibid.

56 Maryland State Department of Education, "Maryland State Aid to Local Education Agencies," Retrieved from https://marylandpublicschools.org/about/Pages/OFPOS/StateAid/index.aspx

57 Department of Legislative Services, General Assembly of Maryland, "The 90 Day Report: A Review of the 2022 Legislative Session," (L-2, 2022). Retrieved from https://mgaleg.maryland.gov/Pubs/LegisLegal/2022rs-90-day-report.pdf

58 Maryland State Department of Education, "Maryland State Aid to Local Education Agencies," Retrieved from https://marylandpublicschools.org/about/Pages/OFPOS/StateAid/index.aspx

59 Department of Legislative Services Maryland General Assembly, "HB 1372 Fiscal and Policy Note," Retrieved from https://mgaleg.maryland.gov/2021RS/fnotes/bil_0002/hb1372.pdf

60 Department of Legislative Services, General Assembly of Maryland, "The 90 Day Report: A Review of the 2022 Legislative Session," (L-2, 2022). Retrieved from https://mgaleg.maryland.gov/Pubs/LegisLegal/2022rs-90-day-report.pdf

61 Ibid. A-75

62 Ibid. L-2

63 Deprtment of Legislative Services, "Effect of the 2022 Legislative Program on the Financial Condition of the State," (2022), Retrieved from https://dls.maryland.gov/pubs/prod/RecurRpt/Effect-of-the-2022-Legislative-Program-on-the-Financial-Condition-of-the-State.pdf

64 Maryland State Department of Education, "Maryland State Aid to Local Education Agencies," Retrieved from https://marylandpublicschools.org/about/Pages/OFPOS/StateAid/index.aspx

65 Ibid.

66 Deprtment of Legislative Services, "Effect of the 2022 Legislative Program on the Financial Condition of the State," (2022), Retrieved from https://dls.maryland.gov/pubs/prod/RecurRpt/Effect-of-the-2022-Legislative-Program-on-the-Financial-Condition-of-the-State.pdf

67 Department of Legislative Services, General Assembly of Maryland, "The 90 Day Report: A Review of the 2022 Legislative Session," (A-77, 2022). Retrieved from https://mgaleg.maryland.gov/Pubs/LegisLegal/2022rs-90-day-report.pdf

68 Ibid. L-2

69 Ibid. A-72

70 Maryland State Department of Education, "Maryland State Aid to Local Education Agencies," Retrieved from https://marylandpublicschools.org/about/Pages/OFPOS/StateAid/index.aspx

71 Department of Legislative Services, General Assembly of Maryland, "The 90 Day Report: A Review of the 2022 Legislative Session," (L-2, 2022). Retrieved from https://mgaleg.maryland.gov/Pubs/LegisLegal/2022rs-90-day-report.pdf

72 Maryland Code, Edu. §5–217

73 Md. Code, Edu. §7–205.1

74 Department of Legislative Services Maryland General Assembly, "HB 1372 Fiscal and Policy Note," Retrieved from https://mgaleg.maryland.gov/2021RS/fnotes/bil_0002/hb1372.pdf, p. 6

[75] EdBuild, "Fund Ed: Formula Type Policies in Each State," Retrieved September 21, 2022 from http://funded.edbuild.org/reports/issue/formula-type

[76] Ibid.

[77] Department of Legislative Services, General Assembly of Maryland, "The 90 Day Report: A Review of the 2022 Legislative Session," (A-75, 2022). Retrieved from https://mgaleg.maryland.gov/Pubs/LegisLegal/2022rs-90-day-report.pdf

[78] Maryland State Department of Education, "Maryland State Aid to Local Education Agencies," Retrieved from https://marylandpublicschools.org/about/Pages/OFPOS/StateAid/index.aspx

[79] EdBuild, "Fund Ed: Formula Type Policies in Each State," Retrieved September 21, 2022 from http://funded.edbuild.org/reports/issue/formula-type

[80] Md. Code, Edu. §6–1009

[81] Maryland State Department of Education, "School Health Services in Maryland: Fact Sheet," Retrieved September 21, 2022 from https://marylandpublicschools.org/about/Pages/DSFSS/SSSP/SHS/SHSMD.aspx

[82] Council on Advancement of School-Based Health Centers, "2021 Annual Report Health—General § 19-22A-05 HB 221, Ch. 199 (2017)," January 14, 2022, Retrieved from https://health.maryland.gov/mchrc/Documents/CASBHC%20Annual%20Report%202021%201.13.21%20to%20print.pdf

[83] SB 1265, Chapter 30, Retrieved from https://mgaleg.maryland.gov/2018RS/chapters_noln/Ch_30_sb1265E.pdf

[84] Chelsea Lyles, "Maryland," Journal of Education Finance 44, no. 3 (2019): 281.

[85] Department of Legislative Services, General Assembly of Maryland, "The 90 Day Report: A Review of the 2022 Legislative Session," (L-2, 2022). Retrieved from https://mgaleg.maryland.gov/Pubs/LegisLegal/2022rs-90-day-report.pdf

[86] Ibid. A-37.

[87] Department of Legislative Services, "Fiscal Briefing," January 2022, Retrieved from https://dls.maryland.gov/pubs/prod/OperBgt/2022_Fiscal-Briefing.pdf

[88] Department of Legislative Services, General Assembly of Maryland, "The 90 Day Report: A Review of the 2022 Legislative Session," (A-61, 2022). Retrieved from https://mgaleg.maryland.gov/Pubs/LegisLegal/2022rs-90-day-report.pdf

[89] Ibid. L-5.

[90] Department of Legislative Services, "Maryland State Personnel, Pensions, and Procurement," Legislative Handbook Series, Vol. V, 2018, https://dls.maryland.gov/pubs/prod/RecurRpt/Handbook_Volume_5_Personnel_Pensions_Procurement.pdf

[91] Department of Legislative Services, "Government Services in Maryland," Legislative Handbook Series, Vol. 2, 2018, https://dls.maryland.gov/pubs/prod/RecurRpt/Handbook_Volume_2_Government_Services.pdf

[92] Department of Legislative Services, General Assembly of Maryland, "The 90 Day Report: A Review of the 2022 Legislative Session," (C-22, 2022). Retrieved from https://mgaleg.maryland.gov/Pubs/LegisLegal/2022rs-90-day-report.pdf

[93] Department of Legislative Services, "Maryland State Personnel, Pensions, and Procurement," Legislative Handbook Series, Vol. V, 2018, https://dls.maryland.gov/pubs/prod/RecurRpt/Handbook_Volume_5_Personnel_Pensions_Procurement.pdf , p. 204

[94] Department of Legislative Services, "Education in Maryland," Legislative Handbook Series, Vol. IX, 2014, Retrieved form https://www.dllr.state.md.us/p20/p20legishandbook.pdf, p. 81

[95] Department of Legislative Services, General Assembly of Maryland, "The 90 Day Report: A Review of the 2022 Legislative Session," (L-2, 2022). Retrieved from https://mgaleg.maryland.gov/Pubs/LegisLegal/2022rs-90-day-report.pdf

[96] Ibid. C-26.

[97] Jesse Levin, Bruce Baker, Drew Atchison, Iliana Brodziak, Andrea Boyle, Adam Hall, and Jason Becker, "Study of Funding Provided to Public Schools and Public Charter Schools in Maryland, " American Institutes for Research, (December 2016), Retrieved from https://www.marylandpublic-

schools.org/programs/Documents/Charter-Schools/StudyFundingProvidedPublicSchoolsPublic-CharterSchoolsMD122016.pdf

[98] Maryland Alliance of Public Charter Schools, "About MAPCS," Retrieved September 22, 2022 from https://mdcharters.org/about

[99] Laura Checovich & Jennifer Rice King, "Maryland," in Funding Public Schools in the United States and Indian Country, ed. Thompson et al. (Charlotte, NC: Information Age Publishing, Inc., 2019).

[100] The Office of Governor Larry Hogan, "Governor Larry Hogan Announces Initiatives to Support Public Charter Schools," (January 23, 2019), Retrieved from https://governor.maryland.gov/2019/01/23/governor-larry-hogan-announces-initiatives-to-support-public-charter-schools/

[101] Department of Legislative Services, General Assembly of Maryland, "The 90 Day Report: A Review of the 2018 Legislative Session," (L-4, 2018). Retrieved from https://mgaleg.maryland.gov/pubs/legislegal/2018rs-90-day-report.pdf

[102] Maryland BOOST Scholarship Coalition, "Maryland BOOST: ScholarshipsThat Close the Achievement Gap," Retrieved September 23, 2022 from https://www.marylandboost.org/

[103] Department of Legislative Services, General Assembly of Maryland, "The 90 Day Report: A Review of the 2022 Legislative Session," (A-77, 2022). Retrieved from https://mgaleg.maryland.gov/Pubs/LegisLegal/2022rs-90-day-report.pdf

[104] Department of Legislative Services, General Assembly of Maryland, "The 90 Day Report: A Review of the 2022 Legislative Session," (L-9, 2022). Retrieved from https://mgaleg.maryland.gov/Pubs/LegisLegal/2022rs-90-day-report.pdf

[105] Education Commission of the States, "50-State Comparison," (January 2020), Retrieved from https://reports.ecs.org/comparisons/charter-school-policies-23

[106] Department of Legislative Services Maryland General Assembly, "HB 1372 Fiscal and Policy Note," Retrieved from https://mgaleg.maryland.gov/2021RS/fnotes/bil_0002/hb1372.pdf

[107] State of Maryland, "American Rescue Plan: State and Local Fiscal Recovery Funds: 2022 Annual Performance Report," Retrieved September 23, 2022 from https://dbm.maryland.gov/budget/Documents/operbudget/ARP-2022-SLFRF-Annual-Report.pdf

[108] Justin Dayhoff, Ary Amerikaner, & Krishna Tallur, "Federal P-12 COVID-19 Funding in Maryland," (March 29, 2022), Retrieved from https://www.marylandtaxes.gov/RELIEFAct/docs/03-29-2022-MSDE-Federal-COVID-Funding.pdf

[109] Department of Legislative Services, General Assembly of Maryland, "The 90 Day Report: A Review of the 2021 Legislative Session," (L-3, 2021). Retrieved from http://dls.maryland.gov/pubs/prod/RecurRpt/2021rs-90-day-report.pdf

[110] Ibid. L-1.

[111] Department of Legislative Services, General Assembly of Maryland, "The 90 Day Report: A Review of the 2022 Legislative Session," (A-67, 2022). Retrieved from https://mgaleg.maryland.gov/Pubs/LegisLegal/2022rs-90-day-report.pdf

CHAPTER 21

MASSACHUSETTS

David Danning[1]
Massachusetts Teachers Association (Retired)

GENERAL BACKGROUND

Public School Districts and Enrollment Totals

The current PK-12 public school funding system in Massachusetts has evolved into a multifaceted program of local property tax revenues, state appropriations, federal revenue, and a small element of private and fee-based revenue. As is the case in most, if not all, states, the bulk of funding is from local property taxes, and state appropriations are largely determined by the state's funding formula. State appropriations also include a number of grants and reimbursements.

Unlike public school finance in most of the nation, in which school districts are the appropriating and taxing authority, Massachusetts school districts are fiscally dependent on their underlying municipalities[2] and in effect are the departments of education of city or town government. In those municipalities, school committees (the Massachusetts term for local school boards) operate as the legislature for schools with authority to initiate the local education budget, set policy, hire the school superintendent, and negotiate collective bargaining agreements. In cities, the municipal chief executive officer is usually an ex officio member of the school

Funding Public Schools in the United States, Indian Country,
and US Territories (Second Edition), pages 345–364.
Copyright © 2023 by Information Age Publishing
www.infoagepub.com

committee and often, but not always, the chair. School budgets require, at some point prior to finality, the approval of the local appropriating authorities (generally, city councils in the state's 44 cities/town meetings in the Commonwealth's 307 towns). These 231 local school districts enrolled approximately 729,000 students in fiscal year (FY) 2022.[3]

In addition to these local districts, there are 84 public regional academic and regional vocational technical school districts serving almost some 130,000 students from two or more municipalities, again overseen by school committees (that are typically elected) whose budgets must be approved by a minimum of two-thirds of member municipalities.[4]

A set of 72 "Commonwealth" charter schools enrolling over 47,000 students in FY22 operate as largely independent entities whose applications are approved (or rejected) by the Massachusetts Board of Education and whose charter can be revoked or not renewed by the Board. These schools are funded by the diversion of state and local funds from regular districts that send students to them. Students in these schools must take the same state assessment examinations as students in regular school districts. However, Commonwealth charter schools are not under the authority of a local school committee. Therefore, whether these schools are public schools or essentially private schools funded with public dollars is open to debate.

In addition, six "Horace Mann" charter schools, which are approved by the local school committee (and, depending on the type of Horace Mann school, also by the local teachers' union) and are funded through the local budget process, enrolled about 2,700 students.

Two virtual school districts served a total of over 3,700 students, and six virtual schools within regular districts enrolled over 1,400 students. Finally, 25 special education collaboratives enroll over 4,100 students from two or more school districts.

In total, then, Massachusetts public school district enrollment (including charter schools, virtual schools, and collaboratives) was almost 916,000 in FY22. As a result of the direct and indirect effects of the COVID-19 pandemic, however, enrollment was most likely in the neighborhood of 30,000 lower than it otherwise would have been.

Student Demographics

Race and ethnicity: In FY22, white, Hispanic, African-American, Asian, and multi-race/non-Hispanic students accounted for 56 percent, 23 percent, 9 percent, 7 percent, and 4 percent, respectively, of total enrollment (including charter schools). Native American, Native Hawaiian, and Pacific Islander students comprised about 0.3 percent of enrollment.

Selected populations: Also in FY22, English language learner students accounted for 11 percent of total enrollment, while students with disabilities were 19 percent of enrollment. Low-income students—students from families with incomes below 185 percent of the federal poverty level—comprised 44 percent of enrollment.

Teachers

Including charter schools, there were roughly 75,000 public school teachers in FY21. Three-quarters of teachers are females, and one-quarter are males. (The data do not include a non-binary category.) Over 90 percent of teachers are white.

Local and regional district public school teachers are unionized; teachers in charter schools are typically not (although they have the right to unionize). The Massachusetts Teachers Association (affiliated with the National Education Association) represents the vast majority of teachers, primarily in the suburbs but also in some major cities such as Springfield and Worcester. With one or two exceptions, the remaining teachers (such as those in Boston, the state's largest school district) belong to the American Federation of Teachers Massachusetts (affiliated with the American Federation of Teachers).

History and Notable Constitutional Language

With respect to the state's PK-12 funding formula (outlined below), two key events took place in 1993. First, in *McDuffy v. Secretary of the Executive Office of Education*, the Massachusetts Supreme Judicial Court (SJC) found that the state had failed to meet its obligation under the Massachusetts Constitution to "provide an education for all its children, rich and poor, in every city and town of the Commonwealth at the public school level."[5] This obligation was in turn based on the SJC's interpretation of a provision in the education clause of the constitution that required the legislature and legal system to "to cherish . . . the public schools and grammar schools in the towns." In school finance terms, this was a finding primarily on "adequacy" grounds, although the SJC (and the plaintiffs) also made note of the funding disparities between "rich" and "poor" school districts. The Court left it to the Massachusetts legislature to devise a remedy for the constitutional violation.

Second, partially in anticipation of the SJC's finding, the legislature passed a comprehensive education reform measure, the Massachusetts Education Reform Act (MERA), which reorganized school district governance, accountability, assessment, and finance.[6] Among other things, it created a coordinated system consisting of a set of state-developed curriculum frameworks (which became the state's content standards) with a new system of accountability and assessment measures—including high-stakes testing—encompassing student, school district, and individual school performance. The law also clarified and expanded the role and authority of the school superintendent as chief executive with authority over personnel and daily operations and school principals as local educational leaders. The role of local school committees was clarified to include hiring superintendents, setting policy, preparing and implementing budgets, overseeing fiduciary responsibilities, and negotiating collective bargaining with unions.

The new school finance system for the first time in Massachusetts was a foundation program (the approach currently used by almost all states) designed to provide an adequate education to each student and thereby satisfy the constitutional requirement. The system was based largely on a proposal by the Massachusetts Business Alliance for Education (MBAE)—the most important private organization behind the general push for education reform—a couple of years earlier.

As part of the school finance system re-design, MERA provided for a Foundation Budget Review Commission to periodically review the components of the foundation budget—the centerpiece of the foundation program—and make recommendations for changes to the budget.

MERA also expanded a limited system of competition via inter-district school choice with tuition deducted from the funds of the sending district. In addition, it provided for a system of charter schools as outlined above.

CURRENT POLITICAL CLIMATE

Almost 60 percent of Massachusetts registered voters are independents. Democrats and Republicans account for about one-third and 10 percent, respectively, of registered voters. Both chambers of the state legislature, however, are overwhelmingly Democratic (over 80 percent in the House of Representatives, and 90 percent in the Senate). On the other hand, the current governor (Charles Baker) is a Republican (albeit a center-right version) and five the last six governors have been Republicans. All governors have supported keeping each school district at its foundation budget level of funding in the state's annual budget. Baker also supported (and signed) the 2018 Student Opportunity Act (SOA), which raised the foundation budget significantly (particularly in districts with high shares of low-income students) and committed the state to almost $2 billion in additional funding over a seven-year period.

Legislative sessions run for two years, while the state fiscal year is from July 1 through June 30 of the following year. The K-12 system is overseen by the Board of Elementary and Secondary Education, while the portion of pre-K that is outside the public system is under the Board of Early Education and Care.[7]

In addition to the governor, his or her administration, and the legislature, a number of non-profit think tanks and advocacy groups have weighed in on education finance matters. The major actors historically have included the following:

1. Massachusetts Association of School Committees (MASC).
2. Massachusetts Association of School Superintendents (MASS).
3. Massachusetts Association of School Business Officers.
4. Massachusetts Business Alliance for Education.
5. Massachusetts Budget and Policy Center.
6. Massachusetts Municipal Association (MMA).

7. Massachusetts Teachers Association (MTA).
8. American Federation of Teachers Massachusetts (AFT Massachusetts).

Each of these organizations has historically been a strong supporter of adequate state support for the funding formula and skeptical of and/or strongly opposed to choice (some would use the term "privatization") initiatives such as charter school expansion

At the time of this writing (fall, 2021), there is no pending school finance legislation. Litigation filed in 2018 arguing that the Commonwealth (notwithstanding MERA) had not met its constitutional obligation to fund public education adequately was withdrawn when the SOA was signed into law.

SOURCES OF REVENUE

According to data from the U.S. Census Bureau,[8] in FY19, local and state sources (the latter consist primarily of "general formula assistance") accounted for 56 percent and 39 percent, respectively, of total school district revenue.[9] Federal sources (mainly from IDEA, Title I, and school lunch funds) comprised only 4 percent of the total. Property taxes comprised the bulk of local revenues, while state revenues were financed largely by income and sales taxes.

In FY93 (the year prior to the implementation of MERA), local, state, and federal sources (again, according to the U.S. Census Bureau) accounted for 62 percent, 32 percent, and 5 percent, respectively, of total school district revenue. The decline in the local share, and increase in the state share, from FY93 to FY19 resulted largely from the $3.6 billion increase in general formula funding over the period associated with MERA (and, in particular, the period FY93 to FY00, when below-foundation districts were raised to foundation levels of spending).

It should be noted that the federal share of revenue in fiscal years 2021 and 2022 may have risen significantly as districts received funds through the major COVID-19-related funding laws (Coronavirus Aid, Relief, and Economic Security Act, Coronavirus Response and Relief Supplemental Appropriations Act, and American Rescue Plan Act). As noted, final Census data on the composition of revenue are available only through FY19 (although preliminary numbers are available for FY20[10]). Since these increases in federal revenues are most likely temporary, the composition of total revenue over the FY93 to FY19 period is the best indicator of underlying trends over time.

DISTRIBUTION FORMULAS

As noted, MERA created a foundation-based state school funding system (hereafter, the "Chapter 70 formula," as the components of the system were specified in Chapter 70 of the Massachusetts General Laws.[11]) The formula can perhaps best be portrayed as a "four-legged table":

- First leg: The foundation budget (the centerpiece of the Chapter 70 formula).
- Second leg: The minimum required district contribution in support of the foundation budget (hereafter, the "required contribution").
- Third leg: State school aid in support of the foundation budget (hereafter, "Chapter 70 aid").
- Fourth leg: Minimum required net school spending (hereafter, the "net school spending requirement").

As indicated, the foundation budget is funded through a combination of the required contribution and Chapter 70 aid.

Examining each of these components of the formula in some detail:

Foundation Budget

The foundation budget is the minimum district spending level required to provide an adequate education to all students (i.e., it is a standard of adequacy). It was originally derived from a costing of the educational inputs deemed necessary to deliver an adequate education (in school finance terms, it was a "resource cost" or "ingredients" model, and was based on a "professional judgment" approach to the determination of spending adequacy).

In the Massachusetts context, an adequate level of funding provides, at a minimum, the opportunity for all students to meet the state's content standards (the curriculum frameworks) and thereby satisfy the requirements of the education clause of the Massachusetts constitution.

Key features of the foundation budget include the following:

a. It establishes pupil:teacher ratios for grade levels and programs (e.g., vocational education, education for English learners).
b. It incorporates an average salary assumption for teachers and other staff.
c. It includes funds for employee benefits, books and equipment, technology, operations and maintenance, etc.
d. It adds resources for low-income, special education, and English learner students as increments over base funding.
e. It excludes transportation, capital equipment, school construction, and school lunches, which are funded largely outside of the foundation program.
f. The foundation budget is unique for each district. On a per-pupil basis, it varies primarily by three factors:
    1. The distribution of students among grade levels and programs.
    2. The geographic area in which a school district is located. (There is a "wage adjustment factor" which raises the foundation budgets of districts located in high-wage areas of the state.)

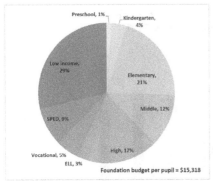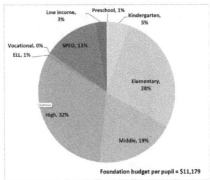

FIGURE 21.1. Foundation budget comparison, Holyoke and Weston Districts, FY22

3. The district's low-income enrollment as a share of total enrollment. For example, the FY22 foundation budget per pupil for Holyoke (low-income enrollment share of 80 percent) is $15,318, while that of Weston (low-income enrollment share of 7 percent) is $11,179.

g. Each district's foundation budget is adjusted annually for both inflation and enrollment changes (including the distribution of students across grade levels and programs). For example, the average per-pupil foundation budget in FY94 (the first year of the Chapter 70 formula under MERA) was $5,572, compared to $13,142 in FY22.

h. Like many states, the calculation special education (SPED) enrollment in the funding formula uses a "census-based" rather than a "population-based" approach, in which SPED enrollment is based on an assumed share of regular and vocational education students rather than the actual number of SPED students.

i. Districts are not required to allocate their actual spending in accordance with foundation budget categories. They only need to meet their formula-generated net school spending requirements (explained below).

The enrollment concept used in the foundation budget (and the overall Chapter 70 formula) is "foundation enrollment," the number of students (on an FTE basis[12]) for whom a district is financially responsible (including out-of-district choice, charter, and SPED students). The expenditure concept is "net school spending," which is education spending on both the school department and (in a non-regional district) municipal sides of a city or town budget. It is net of spending for transportation, capital equipment, school construction, and school lunches (i.e., the spending categories that are outside of the foundation budget). Therefore, to determine how a district's spending compares to its foundation budget, for

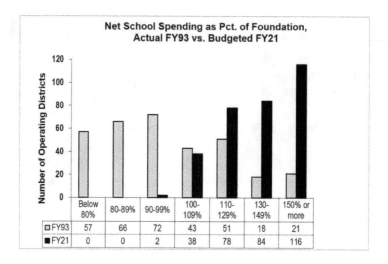

FIGURE 21.2. Historical Spending, Budgeted Versus Actual, FY93 to FY21

purposes of an "apples-to-apples" comparison, we use net school spending (rather than total education spending).

For calculation purposes, the components of the foundation budget were expressed as per-pupil rates for students in 13 enrollment categories (pre-school, kindergarten, high school, English learners, special education, etc.) and 11 functional categories (administration, classroom and specialist teachers, operations and maintenance, employee benefits and fixed charges, and so on). With the enactment in 2018 of the SOA (see below), these rates (which are adjusted over time for inflation) were incorporated directly into Chapter 70 of the Massachusetts General Laws.

Since its first year of operation in FY93 through FY18, the components of the foundation budget were enhanced only in relatively minor ways. The SOA, however, made four key changes to the foundation budget, based on recommendations by the 2015 Foundation Budget Review Commission (FBRC[13]), which increased the foundation budget significantly.

Special Education: The assumed enrollment percentages for in-district special education students were increased in response to evidence presented in the FBRC report that the previous percentages were too low. (The approach of basing SPED enrollment on assumed percentages rather than on the actual number of SPED students was maintained.) In addition, the per-pupil rate for SPED students in out-of-district placements (normally, in private SPED day or residential schools) was raised and integrated with the special education "circuit breaker" (which is explained later).

Health Insurance for education employees and retirees: The per-pupil foundation budget rate for health insurance for teachers and other education employees was increased and pegged to health insurance premiums for state employees covered under the state's Group Insurance Commission (GIC). In addition, health insurance for retired school employees—a cost borne by school districts or cities and towns which had been omitted when the foundation budget was originally developed—was expressly added to the foundation budget with the per-pupil rate also pegged to GIC rates. By linking health insurance foundation rates to GIC rates, these changes also improved the inflation adjustment process for health insurance, which had historically tended to understate actual health care inflation.

Perhaps counter-intuitively, the enhancements to the health insurance component of the foundation budget had the effect of increasing resources available for teaching and other areas outside of health insurance. Why? Because school districts and municipalities were already covering actual health insurance costs, which tended to exceed the foundation budget health insurance allocation. With health insurance underfunded in the foundation budget, this drew resources away from other parts of the foundation. The increase to health insurance in the foundation had the opposite effect of releasing resources and making them available to teaching, instructional materials, and so on.

English Learners: Based on national research findings, the SOA increased the per-pupil rates for English learners. For technical reasons, it also shifted the English learner enrollment category from a base to an incremental category.

Low-Income Students: The SOA made two key changes to the low income increment in the foundation budget: First, it increased the "low income" threshold to family income less than or equal to 185 percent of the federal poverty level from 130 percent, where it had been for several years.[14] Second, it established 12 low-income enrollment categories, based on the share of low-income students in total district foundation enrollment, with per-pupil rates increasing as low-income enrollment shares increase, based on the principle that higher degrees of poverty concentration require greater funding to offset the effects on students of poverty. These rates are in almost all cases higher than the low-income rates that had previously been in effect for several years, based on 10 low-income enrollment categories.

The SOA phases in these four increases to the foundation budget over the seven-year period from FY21 through FY27. Because of the pandemic-induced decline in state revenues, however, the first year of the phase-in was shifted to FY22, with the end date maintained at FY27.

Required Contribution

The required contribution is the minimum required expenditure for net school spending purposes from property taxes and other local resources. It is computed at the municipal level and allocated to each district to which a city or town sends students (where it becomes the "minimum required district contribution"), and is a function of both local fiscal capacity and local revenue growth. For each municipality, there is an annual "target contribution" (based on property wealth and residents' income) which is capped at 82.5 percent of its total foundation budget (the sum of its "pieces" of the foundation budgets of each of the districts—local and regional—to which it sends students). Cities and towns below the target must phase up toward (but not necessarily reach) the target over time, while municipalities above the target can phase down to the target.

At the statewide level, the goal is for 59 percent of the statewide foundation budget to be funded from the local contribution, and 41 percent from Chapter 70 aid. At the municipal level, cities and towns with relatively low fiscal capacity are expected to finance the foundation budgets of the districts to which they send students with relatively low contributions and relative high amounts of Chapter 70 aid. The reverse is true for municipalities with relatively high fiscal capacity.

It is important to note that municipalities are allowed to contribute more than their requirements, and almost all of them do. (There is no fiscal recapture provision in the Chapter 70 formula, so any above-required actual contribution stays with the city or town and its districts.) In FY21, the statewide actual contribution exceeded the required contribution by some $3.3 billion. The actual contributions of 314 districts (99 percent of the Commonwealth's 318 operating school districts) exceeded their required contributions, with the largest margins (not surprisingly) in those districts whose underlying cities and towns have relatively high property value and income.

Chapter 70 Aid

For each district, total Chapter 70 aid is comprised of several components[15]. Each of these components meets a specific objective of the Chapter 70 formula:

a. Component 1: Foundation aid ($5.1 billion in FY22/93% of total Chapter 70 aid). The objective: To provide sufficient aid to enable all districts to spend at foundation, given their required contributions.

b. Component 2: Hold harmless aid ($384 million/7%). The objective: To ensure that each district's total aid does not decline from its prior year level. Put simply—except during state fiscal crises in which revenues decline—no district incurs a reduction of its Chapter 70 aid from the previous year (irrespective of any changes to enrollment or its foundation budget).

c. Component 3: Minimum aid ($17 million/0.3%). The objective: To guarantee each operating district a Chapter 70 aid increase over the prior year of a certain amount per pupil. The minimum aid amount is set each year in the state budget. For FY22, minimum aid is $30/pupil.

d. Component 4: Minimum aid adjustment ($4 million/0.1%): The objective: To ensure that no district receives less in Chapter 70 aid that it would have had in the absence of the SOA.

There is a Chapter 70 aid floor target for each district of 17.5% of its foundation budget (the other side of the coin of the 82.5%-of-foundation cap on the required contribution). A district's total Chapter 70 aid is the sum of each of these components. The statewide total in FY22 is $5.5 billion.

Net School Spending Requirement

Each district has a net school spending requirement equal to the sum of its minimum required district contribution and its Chapter 70 aid, the intent of which is to ensure that funds intended for education are not redirected to other purposes. Largely because of years of prior year aid and minimum aid, combined with declining enrollments in most districts, the net school spending requirements of most districts in FY22 are above their foundation budgets. If a district's actual net school spending in any year is less than its net school spending requirement, the deficiency is added to the district's formula-generated minimum required net school spending in the following year. If the deficiency is large enough, the district may also incur a Chapter 70 aid penalty in the following year with no diminution in its net school spending requirement for that year (so that the aid reduction must be offset by additional district contribution).

Historical and Projected Outcomes

Since FY93 (the fiscal year prior to the implementation of the new funding formula under MERA):

Net school spending compared to the foundation budget: In FY93, almost 60 percent of school districts (accounting for roughly two-thirds of students) spent below their foundation budgets.[16] In FY21, only two districts, with 2 percent of total students, reported spending on a budgeted (rather than actual) basis below foundation.[17]

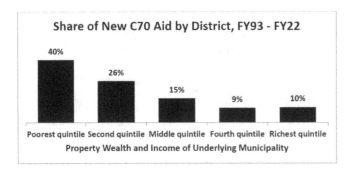

FIGURE 21.3.

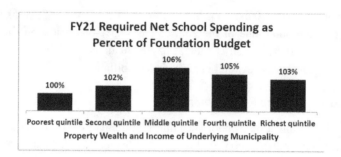

FIGURE 21.4.

Chapter 70 aid as a share of:

The foundation budget: On a statewide basis, Chapter 70 aid increased from 29 percent to 46 percent of the foundation budget over the FY93—FY22 period.

Required net school spending: Over the same period, Chapter 70 aid rose from 30 percent to 44 percent of required net school spending.

Actual net school spending: From FY93 to FY21 (on a budgeted basis), Chapter 70 aid went from 30 percent to only 35 percent of actual net school spending (after increasing to 41 percent in FY00).[18] The difference between Chapter 70 shares of required and actual net school spending results from almost all districts actually contributing more than their required district contributions.

Distribution Of New Chapter 70 Aid: Since FY93, Chapter 70 aid has increased by $4.2 billion (over 325 percent). Not surprisingly, the distribution of that aid has been progressive with respect to the property wealth and residents' income of districts' underlying cities and towns.

In FY21:

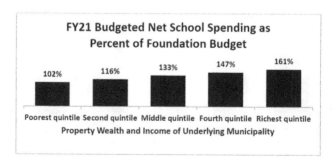

FIGURE 21.5.

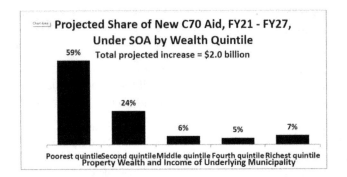

FIGURE 21.6.

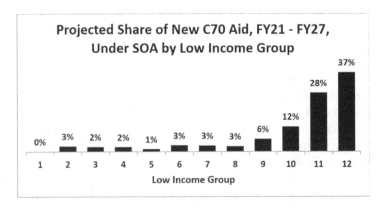

FIGURE 21.7.

Low Income	SOA
Enroll Shr.	Group
0 to 5.99%	1
6 to 11.99%	2
12 to 17.99%	3
18 to 23.99%	4
24 to 29.99%	5
30 to 35.99%	6
36 to 41.99%	7
42 to 47.99%	8
48 to 53.99%	9
54 to 69.99%	10
70 to 79.99%	11
≥ 80%	12

FIGURE 21.8.

Required net school spending as a share of the foundation budget varied only slightly by the property wealth and residents' income of districts' underlying cities and towns.

However, "rich" districts have a much greater capacity to contribute more than their required district contributions than "poor districts, leading to large disparities among districts regarding budgeted net school spending vs. foundation.[19]

Looking forward, according to one projection,[20] under the SOA, the $2.0 billion increase in Chapter 70 aid over the period FY21 to FY27 (the phase-in specified in the law) will be as follows regarding 1) the property wealth and residents' income of districts' associated cities and towns and 2) the low-income share of each district's foundation enrollment:

OTHER SOURCES OF STATE AND DISTRICT REVENUE

There are several additional sources of state financial aid to school districts. They include:

- *The Special Education Circuit Breaker* provides reimbursement to districts when the cost of individual student special education services (for both in-district and out-of-district students) exceeds four times the statewide average foundation budget per pupil. The FY22 threshold is roughly $52,500. Districts (irrespective of the property wealth and residents' income of their associated cities and towns) receive in the subsequent year reimbursement of 75% of the difference between total costs[21] and the threshold, subject to appropriation in the state budget. In FY21, circuit breaker expenditures were almost $322 million.
- *Regional Transportation Aid* is provided to regional school districts to defray costs of transporting students to regional school districts. The original intent of the legislation for this appropriation was for 100 percent reimbursement. Over time, funding had been reduced, but it rebounded to 96 percent FY21. In principle, transportation aid for local school districts is also provided for, but the state budget line item that finances this aid has not been funded since FY04.
- *Charter School Sending District Reimbursement* is provided to districts whose students enroll in Commonwealth Charter Schools. Details are provided below.
- *School Building Authority grants* are provided by the Massachusetts School Building Authority (MSBA) to underwrite the capital costs of new and renovated facilities. This program is funded by a dedicated 1 percent sales tax.
- *Grants to districts hosting inner-city students* in suburban schools under a Metropolitan Council for Educational Opportunity (METCO) program, an initiative of early desegregation programs in Boston and Springfield.

- *Grants to support students who are homeless* as provided in the McKinney/Vento Homeless Assistance Act.[22]
- *Grants to support the cost of school breakfast and lunches* as a local match to federal programs.[23]
- *Funds for temporary immigrant, migrant, and transient* students.
- *Additional funds* for underperforming districts;
- *Several earmarked funds* for special projects in cities, towns, and regions.

In addition:

- *Districts may retain certain revolving funds* into which are deposited such revenues as school lunch payments, athletic fees and gate receipts, and SPED circuit breaker reimbursement. There are more than a dozen permitted revolving funds that can be deployed strategically for authorized purposes.
- *School committees are authorized to accept* gifts, bequeaths, sponsorships, and other donations.

CAPITAL OUTLAY AND DEBT SERVICE

The major component of capital expenditures is spending on school building construction and renovation, which are generally funded by a combination of local revenues and grants from the MSBA (referenced previously). MSBA grants are largely determined by the income and wealth of a district's underlying municipality, as well the district's share of low-income students. There is also an "incentive factor" that plays a role.

Principal and interest payments on local borrowing for these purposes is also the major portion of school-related debt service. In some if not many cases, cities and towns may have to enact overrides to Proposition 2-1/2 (the state's property tax limitation law) to finance debt service.

Preliminary data from FY20 indicate that almost $679 million was spent by school districts on capital and other fixed assets, with over 90 percent for the purchase of land and buildings. Debt service was approximately $853 million, almost all of which was for debt service and debt retirement related to school construction.

EMPLOYEE BENEFITS

Teachers and administrators are provided with health insurance through their school districts or (less common) through the state's Group Insurance Commission. Employees pay a share of the premium, and that share has risen over the years. Retired teachers are usually also provided with health insurance.

In addition, retirement benefits are provided through the Massachusetts Teachers' Retirement System or, for teachers and administrators of the Boston school district, through the Boston Retirement System. Benefits are financed by both employees and the state; school districts and municipalities do not make a retirement contribution. Teachers and administrators do not receive Social Security benefits, and therefore do not make contributions to the Social Security system.

SCHOOL CHOICE FUNDING

Under the Massachusetts inter-district school choice program, each school district is by default a potential receiving district, and must affirmatively opt out of the program each year if it does not want to accept choice students. In FY22, over 17,000 students and 184 of the state's 318 operating districts are projected to participate in the program. Total tuition (including payments to two virtual schools) is projected at some $118 million.

The formal mechanism for financing choice tuition is the diversion of Chapter 70 aid from sending district to receiving district(s).[24] The tuition rate for a regular education student is capped at $5,000 (all sending districts are currently at the cap). For the two Massachusetts Commonwealth Virtual Schools (see below), the tuition rate, however, is almost $8,800 in FY22. To finance additional resources for special education choice students, an increment is added to the tuition rate.

CHARTER SCHOOL FUNDING

As noted previously, there are 73 Commonwealth (independent) and six Horace Mann (within-district) charter schools in Massachusetts, enrolling 46,000 and 2,600 students, respectively, in FY22 according to preliminary data. Commonwealth charter schools are subject to two caps: First, the total number of these schools cannot exceed 72 statewide (although charter schools in the lowest-performing 10 percent of school districts no longer count against this cap); and second, tuition payments are limited to 9 percent of a sending district's net school spending (18 percent for districts in the lowest-performing 10 percent of school districts). These two caps effectively also place a cap on statewide enrollment in Commonwealth charters. In addition, the number of Horace Mann charter schools is capped at 48.

Similar to school choice, the mechanism for financing Commonwealth charters is the diversion of Chapter 70 aid from sending districts to charter schools; the financial substance of the process is that a share of the sending district local contribution is reallocated to charter schools.[25] Horace Mann charters are financed as part of the host school district budget process.

The per-pupil tuition rate paid by sending districts to Commonwealth charters varies by district and charter school and consists of three components: 1) a foundation rate, determined by constructing a "mini foundation budget" for the specific students leaving the district for the school and then dividing by the number of students; 2) an above-foundation rate, determined by multiplying the foundation rate by the district's net school spending above its foundation budget; and 3) a per-pupil facilities rate that is set each year by the legislature. Multiplying the sum of these three components by the number of students yields the total tuition paid by the district to the school.[26]

Sending districts are fully reimbursed by the state for the facilities component of their tuition payments. Additional reimbursement is triggered any time a sending district's total payments to charter schools (excluding the facilities component) increases over its tuition in the prior year, and is implemented over three years at rates of 100 percent, 60 percent, and 40 percent of the increase in years one, two, and three, respectively. Reimbursement is subject to appropriation in the state budget, and has been underfunded for a number of years. (The SOA, however, phases in full reimbursement over a three-year period.)

Current projections for FY22 show 251 sending districts with 47,500 students (5 percent of statewide foundation enrollment) with total tuition of $839 million, reimbursement of $148 million, and district net cost (tuition minus reimbursement) of $691 million. Reimbursement is funded at only 75 percent of the calculated amount, a shortfall of over $51 million. (Under the SOA, full funding of reimbursement is phased in over several years.)

VIRTUAL SCHOOLS

Massachusetts provides for two types of public virtual schools: Massachusetts Commonwealth Virtual Schools (MCVS), which operate under a certificate granted by the Board of Elementary and Secondary Education and enroll students from anywhere in the state; and Single District Virtual Schools (SDVS), which are established by school districts and enroll only those students who reside in the school district in which the virtual school is located.

There are currently two schools of the MCVS variety (with a total of over 3,700 students), and seven SDVS schools serving OVER 1,400 students. MCVS schools are financed by tuition payments from the districts in which virtual students reside (see above), while SDVS schools are financed from the local school district budget. Total tuition paid to MCVS schools in FY22 is projected at almost $35 million.

FEDERAL COVID-19 FUNDING[27,28]

To date, Massachusetts has been allocated some $3.7 billion in K-12 education COVID-19 funding through a number of pieces of federal legislation, primarily the Coronavirus Aid, Relief, and Economic Security Act (CARES Act), the Coronavirus Response and Relief Supplemental Appropriations Act, 2021 (CRRSA), and the American Rescue Plan Act of 2021 (ARPA). Roughly $2.9 billion (over three-quarters) of the total has been from Elementary and Secondary School Emergency Relief Fund (ESSER), which was incorporated into the CARES Act, CRRSA, and ARPA; $215 million was provided through the CARES Act Coronavirus Relief Fund (CvRF); and $208 million was received from the ARPA CDC school testing program.

The allocation of ESSER funds to school districts is determined by the Title I, Part A formula, and is therefore progressive with respect to family income. Almost 85 percent of CvRF funds are provided to districts as School Reopening Grants, and distributed on a per-pupil ($225) basis. The balance is provided as Remote Learning Technology Essentials Grants, based on property wealth and income.

A small amount of funding (one to three percent of the total) was provided through the Governor's Emergency Education Relief Fund, which was part of the CARES Act, CRRSA, and ARPA, but data on the allocation of these funds to school districts are not available.

In addition to funds specifically designated for education, dollars from other elements of the COVID-19 legislation have been allocated for education. For example, Massachusetts has received $5.3 billion in ARPA state fiscal recovery funds. Through a supplemental appropriation to the state budget, Massachusetts has allocated $120 million from these funds to education. (Additional allocations may be forthcoming in a future supplemental appropriation.)

Data on the actual use of COVID-19 federal funds are currently quite limited. Anecdotal evidence suggests that they have been devoted to a wide range of allowable purposes.

NON-PUBLIC-SCHOOL FUNDING

In FY22, there were over 860 private schools (including day and residential special education schools) in Massachusetts serving over 128,000 students. Roughly one-third of these schools are religious schools.[29] Private schools are almost completely funded by tuition payments from the families of students attending these schools as well as local fund raising programs. Parochial schools may also receive some support from archdioceses and/or local parishes. Day and residential special education schools, however, are funded primarily by tuition payments from the school districts that SPED students would otherwise attend.

ENDNOTES

[1] The author wishes to thank and acknowledge the contribution of Glenn Koocher, Executive Director of the Massachusetts Association of School Committees and the author of the "Massachusetts" chapter in the first edition of this book. In a number of places in the current chapter, the language in Mr. Koocher's version is preserved verbatim. He would also like to thank Roger Hatch and Jeff Wulfson for helpful comments on an earlier version of this chapter,

[2] Prior to the passage of "Proposition 2-1/2" (Chapter 580 of the Acts of 1980), the Commonwealth's property tax limitation measure, Massachusetts school districts were fiscally autonomous and could levy property taxes.

[3] Unless noted otherwise, all of the data in this chapter are the most recent available as of the fall of 2021.

4   There is also one independent vocational school and two county agricultural school districts.

5   McDuffy was first filed in 1978 as Webby vs. Dukakis. Over the next 15 years, the case in its various iterations was supported by teachers' unions, other public education stakeholders, and legal and advocacy organizations.

6   MERA was passed by the legislature a few days before the McDuffy decision, and the governor signed the bill into law several days after the decision.

7   Only a minority of students in pre-K programs are in public school districts.

8   https://www.census.gov/data/tables/2019/econ/school-finances/secondary-education-finance.html.

9   A portion of general local aid to cities and towns (not reflected in these data) is also used to fund education.

10 These data, which to some extent take into account COVID-19-related federal funds, show a similar distribution.

11 General Laws, Commonwealth of Massachusetts, Chapter 70: School Funds and State Aid for Public Schools.

12 Pre-school and half-day kindergarten students are assigned an FTE value of 0.5. All other students are assigned a value of 1.0.

13 https://www.doe.mass.edu/finance/chapter70/FBRC-Report.docx. Through the state budget, to a large extent, the recommendations of the FBRC began to be implemented at various times and at various rates beginning in FY18.

14 Historically, Massachusetts had used the standard free/reduced-price lunch definition (family income < 185 percent of the poverty level) of student low-income status. With the implementation of the USDA Community Eligibility Provision for free meals, the necessary data were no longer available, and the Massachusetts Dept. of Elementary and Secondary Education (DESE) had to develop a new metric for low-income status based on student participation in Medicaid and several other state programs ("direct certification"). This effectively lowered the threshold to 133 percent of the poverty level. The Chapter 70 formula used this revised metric from FY16 through FY21, albeit with some modifications. DESE has now decided to supplement the state program data with information from forms similar in concept to those used in conjunction with the previous free/reduced-price-lunch metric.

15 Formally, the components are prior year (base) aid, foundation aid increase, minimum aid, and minimum aid adjustment. Functionally, the components are as outlined in the text. In addition, at various times, the formula has included other components. But what is presented here is the essence of the formula.

16 Although MERA was not implemented until FY94, for comparison purposes, DESE computed a foundation budget for each district for FY93.

17 It is possible that these two districts' actual (as opposed to budgeted) net school spending met or exceeded foundation in FY21. Actual FY21 net school spending data by district were not available at the time of this writing (fall, 2021).

18 For comparison purposes, DESE computed each district's actual net school spending for FY93 (and set required net school spending equal to actual net school spending).

19 Above-required district contributions could change in the future for above-foundation districts which receive significant increases in Chapter 70 aid under SOA, which would therefore change their net school spending compared to foundation.

20 By the Massachusetts Teachers Association.

21 The SOA added transportation to the special education costs eligible for reimbursement.

22 PL 100-77 (1987).

23 National School Lunch Act, 42 USC 1751.

24 In effect, however, a share of the tuition is paid from the local contribution.

25 Similar to the financial substance of choice tuition.

26 In addition, districts transport students or pay charter schools for transportation costs.

27 This section draws heavily on Colin Jones, ""The American Rescue Plan Act and Federal Relief Funds for K-12 Schools in Massachusetts," Massachusetts Budget and Policy Center, November 10, 2021.

28 The winter, 2021, issue of the Journal of Education Finance ("School Finance During the Pandemic: How are States Responding?") includes a chapter on Massachusetts.

29 https://www.privateschoolreview.com/massachusetts.

CHAPTER 22

MICHIGAN

Western Michigan University

Scott Sawyer

Saginaw Intermediate School District

GENERAL BACKGROUND

In 1993, the State of Michigan experienced an unprecedented conundrum related to financing its public schools. Kalkaska Public Schools, a district in northern Michigan, closed approximately two-thirds of the way through the school year due to insufficient funds. This travesty made headlines in many of the nation's most prominent media outlets—an entire school district had to close early because it lacked the financial resources to operate.[1] In 1994, Michigan took drastic action to change the method of funding public schools. Commonly known as Proposal A, this formula purported to provide stability, adequacy, and equity to the revenue allocated to schools. Debate remains strong after 27 years of Proposal A as to whether Michigan has provided adequate revenue streams for public education.

The crisis that enveloped Michigan was twofold. First, the pre-Proposal A funding system used a power equalization formula based primarily upon ad valorem taxable value for a local school district, which resulted in substantial horizontal

Funding Public Schools in the United States, Indian Country,
and US Territories (Second Edition), pages 365–380.
Copyright © 2023 by Information Age Publishing
www.infoagepub.com

inequity among local school districts.[2] Secondly, because the amount of revenue available to schools was dependent upon the local school district's home property values, ad valorem taxes among the various localities were unequal, and in some cases, it demonstrated significant discrepancies among these entities. During this time, approximately 80% of all school funding came from local sources, most notably ad valorem taxes.[3] Michigan property owners paid well over the average amount of their national counterparts. During 1993, Michigan residents' ad valorem tax was 35% higher than the national average. Any decrease in property tax would inevitably reduce the amount of revenue allocated for local public schools' operating budget. The majority of citizens recognized the need for quality schools and the reliance on the property owners to operate them. However, ad valorem taxes became incommensurate with other states and the school funding system did not represent equity among all property owners.

The authority for establishing public education in Michigan emanates from Article I, Section 8 of the Michigan Constitution. This article states, "The legislature shall maintain and support a system of free public elementary and secondary schools as defined by law. Every school district shall provide for the education of its pupils without discrimination as to religion, creed, race, color or national origin."

Noteworthy are the multitudes of contestations occurring throughout the nation regarding state legislatures appropriating public funds for parochial schools is the second part of Section 8, which declares, "No public monies or property shall be appropriated or paid or any public credit utilized, by the legislature or any other political subdivision or agency of the state directly or indirectly to aid or maintain any private, denominational or other nonpublic, pre-elementary, elementary, or secondary school. No payment, credit, tax benefit, exemption or deductions, tuition voucher, subsidy, grant or loan of public monies or property shall be provided, directly or indirectly, to support the attendance of any student or the employment of any person at any such nonpublic school or at any location or institution where instruction is offered in whole or in part to such nonpublic school students. The legislature may provide for the transportation of students to and from any school." This lucid clause, which proscribes public monies from supporting parochial schools, is coming under tremendous scrutiny because of legislative intent to circumvent the spirit of the clause and favorable judicial holdings by conservative justices to uphold legislation that financially supports parochial schools. Michigan is no different.

In 2020-2021, Michigan had the following demographic information:

Schools

- 56 Intermediate School Districts
- 537 Traditional Local School Districts
- 293 Public School Academies

Students

- 1,415,820   Total Students
- 6.00%   American Indian or Alaska Native
- 3.43%   Asian
- 17.72%   African American
- 8.44%   Hispanic/Latino
- .09%   Native Hawaiian/Pacific Islander
- 4.66%   Two or More
- 64.97%   White

Personnel

- 338,078 Teachers
- 11,169 Administrators

BASIC SUPPORT PROGRAM

The amended section of the Michigan Constitution in 1994 directed the legislature to establish the initial per-pupil foundation floor for each district. A majority of schools that could be characterized as "poor," or more specifically below the $4,200 threshold, saw a substantial increase in the per-pupil funding as a result of Proposal A. The per-pupil funding for schools in FY1994 provided an enhanced representation of the wealth disparities seen in Michigan prior to Proposal A's passage.

The state's first objective was to establish the minimum level of per-pupil funding. Multiple ideas were investigated yet rejected for various reasons. For example, some individuals suggested an averaging of allocations to bring immediate equity among all school districts. The averaging concept was unacceptable to parents in the high-revenue districts, as this would require a leveling down of the foundation grant, which would be politically unacceptable. A more enticing approach was to raise the lowest funded schools up, thereby "raising the floor." Out of this philosophy, the state decided to establish the foundation grant based upon three levels: the minimum grant, the basic grant, and the maximum grant.

The minimum grant established a floor so that all school districts would receive at least this minimum. For FY 1995 the amount was set at $4,200. The basic grant was the minimum amount the state mandated all schools to receive. In concert with this objective, the state decided to increase payments in various phases until all districts arrived at the basic grant. A sliding scale was employed, which allowed districts that were further away from the basic grant to receive larger allocations, ensuring they would reduce the gap more expeditiously. In FY 1995, the minimum grant was set at $4,200 and the basic was set at $5,000. A final objective regarding the foundation grant was to set a maximum amount the state would guarantee, which was $6,500. In contrast to the name, the maximum grant did not represent the highest per-pupil amount in the foundation program. The amount only dictated the level at which the state would provide funding as part of the foundational grant; local voter approval was required for districts that were raising more than that amount prior to Proposal A.

In FY 1995, 51 school districts exceeded the $6,500 maximum grant allocation. Districts that exceeded the maximum foundation grant were afforded the opportunity to retain the revenue above the maximum grant. Those districts were provided a safeguard against having to reduce their per-pupil allocation. The "hold-harmless" provision was enacted by voters in each respective district, which allowed a corresponding operating millage to be levied in order to secure the per-pupil allocation prior to Proposal A. The millage levied for the hold-harmless revenue is assessed separate from any other category.

Proposal A adjusted the authority for raising operating revenue from local school districts to the state. In FY 1994, local taxpayers were responsible for 63% of general operating revenue and the state 37%. Simply with the enactment of Proposal A, the percentages almost uniformly inverted with the state now responsible for 80% and the local district responsible for 20%.[4] The new law required that all homestead property[5] earmarked for school operation be taxed at a rate of 6 mills. This is defined as the State Education Tax (SET). Local school district constituents are required to approve the mills assessed on non-homestead[6] property.[7] The local non-homestead millage is a maximum of 18 mills. Therefore, a total of 24 mills may be levied on homestead and qualifying non-homestead properties for general operating revenue, unless a school district is considered a hold-harmless district, whereby the local voters must approve a separate millage rate separate from the non-homestead millage to meet the hold-harmless provision.

Various methods have been employed in the life of Proposal A to adjust the foundation grant on an annual basis. In concert with the executive branch, the legislature annually establishes the foundation grant based upon a number of variables and priorities, most notably the revenue forecasting for the following year. The mechanisms utilized by Michigan to determine foundation allowances are:

- The automatic foundation index to adjust the basic grant;
- The 2X formula sliding scale used for districts below the basic grant;
- Equal per-pupil adjustments for all districts and;
- Separate equity payments

The minimum per pupil foundation grant for FY 2021 was $8,111 and 134 of 829 school district above the minimum foundation. With the passage of the FY 2022 budget, the state established the minimum foundation at $8,700—effectively closing the gap between the minimum and basic foundation with only 43 of 829 school districts remaining above minimum/basic foundation. The changes for FY 2022 represent the largest increase in per pupil foundation grant since enactment of Proposal A, as well as the largest equalization effort, increasing the mean by 6.56% and decreasing the standard deviation by 13.4%.

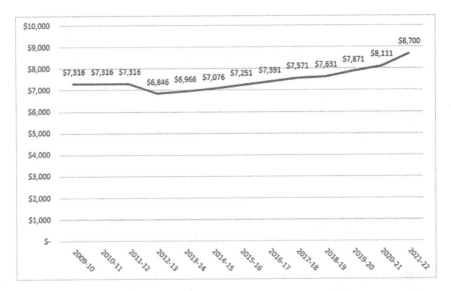

FIGURE 22.1.   Per Pupil Foundation Grant 2009-2010 through 2021-2022
Source: Kathryn Summers, Overview of K-12/School Aid [Michigan: Senate Fiscal
Agency, February 2019], 17.

Proposal A Funding Formula

Ironically, with the various components that are integrated to comprise the
foundation grant, the formula for determining the actual allocation for each local
district is abecedarian. The formula incorporates the foundation allowance with
the pupil enrollment for the local district. In addition, various categorical grants
are added to the total revenue to provide remediation for vertical inequity. The
formula for determining a local school district's revenue based on the per pupil
foundation is as follows:

Total Revenue = Foundation Grant
* Full Time Equivalency Student Enrollment (FTE)
+ Categoricals—Homestead Taxable Value

Student Enrollment—The Blended Count

The enrollment algorithm, which provides the total count for pupil enrollment,
has been fairly consistent since the inception of Proposal A. The state has occasionally modified the finer details of the formula for various reasons, which has
caused some school districts a loss of revenue or more recently a slight increase.
Figure 2 shows the general overall decline of student enrollment in Michigan with
charter schools slightly increasing.

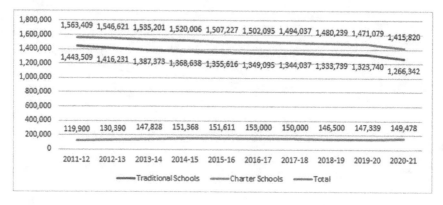

FIGURE 22.2. Pupil Enrollment Count. Source: Kathryn Summers, Overview of K-12/School Aid [Michigan: Senate Fiscal Agency, 2019], 17.

Determining student enrollment is completed with two count days during the calendar year. The spring count (February) is 10% of the FTE and the fall count (October) is worth 90%. The percentages have been adjusted several times since Proposal A's inception. The formula below shows how enrollment was calculated for the 2021-2022 school year:

[February 2021 FTE Count * (10%)]
+ [October 2021 FTE Count * (90%)]
= Total FTE for 2021-2022 School Year

To provide an example for examination, if XYZ school district had a student count of 1,000 for the winter count and 1,200 students in the fall count, the total FTE for this school is (1,000 x .10) + (1,200 x .90) = 1,180. The local school district will report 1,180 students as its total FTE and will use this number in the foundation grant formula.

Noteworthy, in 2020-2021 (the COVID year) this formula was modified to mitigate the impact of declining enrollment. Lawmakers shifted the weighting per-pupil funding for districts based on 75 percent of the 2019-2020 school year and 25 percent of the 2020-2021 school year. The funding formula was returned to normal in 2020-2021.[8]

TRANSPORTATION

Michigan does not provide financial resources for general transportation. Although, as highlighted by a legal holding in 1997 (see footnote 22), the State is responsible for approved costs associated with transporting special education students at a rate slightly over 70 percent. The state did allocate $3,814,500 in FY

2022 for bus driver safety instruction or evaluation and to reimburse for costs associated with the inspection of school buses.[9]

SPECIAL EDUCATION

Accounting for revenue allocated for students identified for special education services is difficult to ascertain in Michigan.[10] Michigan's funding of special education is a highly inequitable and inadequate.[11] Much of the responsibility for costs have shifted the funding responsibility to the local and county levels, yet Michigan's funding structure precludes local districts from levying taxes to cover additional special education costs. Under federal law, public school districts are required to provide a free appropriate public education (FAPE) to students with disabilities, in the least restrictive environment. Meeting the needs of students with disabilities is necessary, yet expensive.[12] A Michigan State University study found that, in order to fully fund special education costs, Michigan districts use more than $500 per pupil from general education funds, on average. This even exceeds $1,000 per pupil in some districts. This affects both special education and general education students because diverting general education dollars to cover the needs and requirements of special education dollars leaves fewer dollars for pupils overall.[13] In 2016, the state reported that local districts spent approximately $2.7 billion dollars for special education services.[14] School districts receive a foundation allowance on behalf of each special needs student they enroll, just as they do for general education students.[15] This foundation allowance provides a minimum, per pupil funding amount. Michigan has approximately 200,000 students who require these services and providing adequate funding is arduous.[16] Most of the funding for special education students comes from local property taxes levied by one of Michigan's 56 intermediate school districts (ISDs).[17] Each ISD levies a special education millage on local property owners to pay for services they provide directly or that they pay to other school districts to provide.[18] Intermediate school districts may not levy more than 1.75 times their 1993 special education millage rate approved by local residents.[19] Because these millages are a function of the total property value in their district, large disparities in special education per-pupil funding can occur from ISD to ISD.[20] The State assists in alleviating some of the disparity by providing a categorical that provides lower-funded ISDs with additional funds.[21] Larger payments are provided to ISDs that have lower property values.[22]

Additional payments are made to fund special education due to the Durant holding.[23] The Michigan Supreme Court ordered the State to reimburse local school districts and ISDs 28.6 percent of the total approved special education costs and 70.4 percent of the total approved transportation costs. For a small percentage of special education students who are placed in an institution by a court or state agency, the state reimburses those districts 100 percent of approved expenses. For a small group of school districts, another layer of funding is provided to ensure they are "held harmless" and their payment guarantee does not fall below 1997 levels. While state and local funds combine to provide the largest share of revenue for local school districts and ISDs, federal funds from the Individuals with Disabilities Education Act (IDEA) are provided. For many school districts, these revenues do not cover the entire expense for special education programs, thus, the district's general fund must pay for this gap.

GIFTED AND TALENTED EDUCATION

Michigan funds gifted and talented programs by creating line items in the budget for various initiatives established by the education community and enacted by the legislature. For example, for FY 22, $8,000,000 was allocated for dual enrollment incentive payments $1,200,000 for an advanced placement incentive program to increase the number of pupils who participate and succeed in advanced placement and International Baccalaureate programs, $4,723,000 for Robotics education ($600,000 to private schools) and $3,050,000 for STEM grants.[24]

BILINGUAL EDUCATION

In FY2022 the State allocated $25,200,000 to provide grants to districts offering programs of instruction for pupils of limited English-speaking ability.[25] Districts must administer the WIDA assessment and reimbursement is between $105 and $935 per full-time English language learner, based on WIDA scores. To be eligible to receive funding, districts must allow access for the Department to audit records and must provide a report on usage of funds.[26]

CAPITAL OUTLAY AND DEBT SERVICE

The primary financial responsibility for maintaining and constructing public school buildings in Michigan resides with the local school district. Michigan law allows for public schools to use up to 20 percent of its general operating revenue to finance capital projects, however, it is rare for public schools to use their main operating funds for this purpose. Local school districts are legally authorized to borrow money by taking out debt through unlimited tax or limited tax resolution bonds. Local school districts sell bonds, which raises a certain amount of revenue and pay off the principal and interest over time through tax levied on local property for unlimited tax bonds or through general operations budget for tax limited bonds. Unlimited tax bonds must be approved by a majority of local voters. More than 85 percent of Michigan's school districts charge taxpayers to pay down various outstanding debts.[27] At the end of calendar year 2020, Michigan school districts held combined outstanding bonded indebtedness of $14.8 billion.[28] Most states offer the local school districts some type of direct aid for facility expenses through reimbursements, matching grants, or other appropriations. Michigan does not afford school districts this service. Michigan does allow school districts to have their debt "qualified" by the state. A qualified loan is one that can use the state's credit rating, which is almost always more favorable than the rating an individual school district could get and usually translates to lower interest rates and borrowing costs. The state essentially guarantees its faith and credit that if the district fails to make its payments, the state will come in and assume the debt. Districts that do not want to abide by the state's terms for qualified borrowing can gain voter approval to issue "nonqualified" bonds for capital projects instead. However, the total debt for those voter-approved bonds is limited to 15 percent of SEV, or three times more than can be issued by a simple school board vote. The total debt limits do not apply to state-qualified bonds.

Qualified loans also allow districts to utilize Michigan's School Loan Revolving Fund, which is a pooled fund allowing districts to borrow from the state through a deferred loan to help repay bond amounts—effectively extending bond principal repayment schedules further and keeping millage rates low, provided the district meets minimum tax levy requirements. For these debt issues, after the regular bond repayment schedule is satisfied, the district begins repaying the state through the School Loan Revolving Fund by continuing the tax levy. Over 28 percent of schools with bonded debt utilize the School Loan Revolving Fund.[29]

A second financial method available to school districts in Michigan to fund capital projects is the "sinking fund." Sinking funds are established as separate savings accounts for certain projected facility costs. Sinking fund levies cannot exceed three mills or last more than ten years (prior to 2016, these limits were five mills and 20 years). These funds can be used to buy land, build or repair facilities, install infrastructure for technology and security as well as purchase computer equipment and software. About 30 percent of school districts use voter-approved sinking funds, most of them at a lower rate.[30]

EDUCATOR RETIREMENT

The Michigan Legislature enacted the Michigan Public School Employees Retirement Act (MPSERS) in 1945. This Act was originally designed to provide pension benefits, excluding health care, for retired school employees.[31] Article 9, Section 24 of the Michigan Constitution codified MPSERS in 1963. The health care benefits were not constitutionally embedded, but rather legislatively enacted in 1975. At that time, the State required all local school districts to bear partial costs of the program at the rate of 5% of salary for all public school employees. Substantial change occurred in 1994 with Proposal A, which placed most of the responsibility for the retirement program on the local school district. The per pupil foundation allowance increased for most districts in 1995, however, local districts became responsible for the amount defined by MPSERS, which was established at 14.56% the first year. This change transferred future obligations and a significant portion of the solvency of the retirement system to the local school districts.[32] The rate districts must pay has notably increased, intensifying the financial burden for all districts. Legislation enacted by the State in 2012 created multiple categories for employees to enter for retirement and provided a cap for local school districts. In addition, the State enacted legislation that established a payment to member schools, which is earmarked to be remitted to the state to pay for the unfunded actuarial accrued liability rate. For 2021-22, based on the teacher retirement program selected, districts paid from a low of 41.36% to a high of 45.21% of the teacher's salary. In this same cycle, the State pays 15.05% of those yearly totals to reduce a district's obligation. Infusing additional state dollars, modifying pension programs from defined benefit to defined contribution, and estimating lower return rates for state investments were enacted to mitigate the increasing financial burden on school districts, which will lower State funding obligations in the future.

The legislation enacted in 2012 was an effort to eliminate a growing unfunded accrued liability in the Michigan Public School Employees Retirement System (MPSERS). In FY2012, the actuarial accrued liability rose to $62.7 billion with actuarial value of assets of $38.4 billion for a fund ratio of 61.3%.[33] (Financial Services, 2013). The fund ratio amplified a downward trend in the financial health of the MSPERS program, as Michigan maintained a public educator retirement system that was 72% funded in FY2010.[34] For FY2019 (7 years after legislative reform), the actuarial accrued liability rose to $85.2 billion with actuarial value of assets of $51.4 billion for a fund ratio of 60.4%.[35] Over that same time period, active membership has decreased by 22 percent, while the retirement rolls have increased by 11%.[36] The goal of legislation enacted in 2012 to fully fund the pension system by 2038 remains a primary assumption in determining annual district contribution rates.[37]

The State budget allocated three line items in the FY 2022 budget to specifically address MPSERS costs. First, $277,400,000 was allocated to make payments to districts to offset a portion of the retirement contributions owed by the district. Second, $1,468,500,000 was allocated to pay the difference between the uncapped MPSERS contribution rate, and the capped rate that school employers paid. Lastly, $65,300,000 was provided to cover additional costs to MPSERS for a defined contribution costs for new hires.[38]

Enrollment in the majority of Michigan school districts has declined over the past decade, which is a requisite factor of the revenue allocated to local public schools. From 2004 through 2012, 425 of the 549 public school districts witnessed a decline in enrollment. Statewide enrollment over this period declined by 13.2%. A reason for the decrease in enrollment, outside of the flight due to the economy, is the increased allowance of charter schools. Since 2004, the number of charter schools increased from 199 to 293 in FY2021.[39] These schools enroll approximately 148,000 students, which equates to 11.4% of all public and charter school students in the state.[40] Very few of these charter schools participate in MPSERS. This drain of student enrollment decreases the number of teachers needed in traditional public schools, which reduces the number of workers per retiree.

EDUCATOR HEALTHCARE

The Michigan Legislature enacted Public Act 152 of 2011 to mandate cost controls on publicly funded health insurance contributions. This act set hard cap maximums on premium costs for single subscriber, 2-person subscriber, and full family coverages—mandating district cost-share health insurance premiums with employees or find health plans that cost less than the hard cap. The hard caps are increased annually based on the percentage change in the medical care component of the United States Consumer Price Index measured for the 12-month period from March—February. Individual districts may opt out the application of these hard caps by an annual majority vote of the board of education to implement an 80%/20% cost share between the district and employee, respectively. Additionally, the Michigan Legislature made the implementation of hard caps and the decision of a board of education to opt out of the hard caps into an 80%/20% cost-share a prohibited subject of bargaining under the Public Employment Relations Act.

OTHER CATEGORICAL FUNDS

While the majority of funding for public schools in Michigan comes from the per pupil foundation grant (approximately 70%), categorical aid provides a secondary method for funding schools.[41] The categorical aid allocated in Michigan frequently addresses vertical equity issues for students who require added costs above the per pupil foundation.[42] Two of the largest categorical allocations are for at-risk students and special education students. For the 2021-22 school year, the State allocated $522 million for at-risk students known as "Section 31a."[43] Students qualify for 31a monies by being documented as having two of six at-risk factors. For special education, the State allocated over $1.6 billion in this same period to provide payment for special education membership, special education transportation and other special education categorical programs.[44] These categorical allocations allow the State to identify any special interests and provide funding. For instance, over $37 million was allocated for career and technical education programs, almost $4 million for bus driver instruction and bus inspections, and almost $293.9 million for mental health services, counselors, and school nurses.[45]

FUNDING OF CHARTER SCHOOLS

Charter schools receive a district foundation allowance just as traditional local public school districts do. However, a charter school's foundation allowance is equal to the lesser of the foundation allowance of the surrounding conventional school district and the basic foundation allowance. FY 2022 was $8,700. Public Act 23 of 2018 extended a right to receive a portion of Intermediate School District (ISD) enhancement millages levied against ISD property owners to charter schools.[46]

EARLY CHILDHOOD EDUCATION

Over the past several budget cycles, the State has made improving the funding for early childhood programs a priority. In several categorical funds, the State has allocated funds for various uses for early childhood programs. In FY 2021-22, $431,870,000 million was provided in formulas to eligible intermediate school districts (ISDs) for comprehensive compensatory education programs to improve the school readiness of at-risk four- year-olds.[47] An approved school readiness program must include an age-appropriate educational curriculum, nutritional services, health screening, plan for parent involvement, and referrals for community social services.[48] At least 90% of the children participating in the program must be from families with income levels no more than 250 percent of the federal poverty level, with children from poorer families awarded slots before children from families with higher income levels.[49] Of the total appropriation, $10 million is earmarked for reimbursement of transportation costs at no more than the actual cost of transporting to the program.[50] An Early Childhood Block Grant Program ($13,400,000) has been established to provide an application detailing proposed uses of early childhood funding.[51] Of this total appropriation, $2.5 million is earmarked for home visits to at-risk children and their families, to improve school readiness, reduce the number of pupils retained in grade level, and reduce the number of pupils requiring special education.[52]

LOCAL SCHOOL REVENUE

A local obligation of tax revenue is required as part of the state per-pupil aid. Just as a 6-mill levy is placed on all homestead property in a local school district, an 18-mill tax is levied on all non-homestead property such as businesses, second homes, and qualifying farmland. An additional 6-mill tax must be levied on commercial personal property. The revenue raised from this levy can be calculated by multiplying the 18 mills by the total non-homestead taxable value of the school district.[53] This required levy is included as a portion of state aid per pupil foundation. Local revenue sources are a primary component for financing school building maintenance and construction. Please see Capital Outlay and Debt Service above.

FOOD SERVICES

The school lunch program in Michigan is made up of both a federal and state component, but the state distributes both payments. The federal program is calculated under the Richard B. Russell National School Lunch Act. Michigan's federal allocation in FY 2022 was $556,000,000.[54] The state payment, which is equal to 6.0127 percent of a district's costs for the school lunch program, was $23,838,400 in FY 2022.[55] The State reimbursement is a directive by the court in the Durant decision (see footnote 22). The State also allocated $4,500,000[56] to reimburse districts for the cost of providing breakfast, which is statutorily required under certain circumstances.[57]

STATE AID FOR PRIVATE SCHOOLS

Article VIII, Section 2 of the Michigan Constitution delineates that no public monies shall be allocated to pay for any private, non-public pre-elementary, elementary, or secondary school. The Michigan Legislature allocated $2.5 million dollars in two budget cycles ($5 million total), FY 2017 and FY 2018 to private schools to help them cover the cost of complying with state mandates. After a lengthy judicial process, the Michigan Supreme Court, in 2020, in a unique 3-3 decision, "affirmed by equal division" that the state may reimburse private schools for the costs of complying with state mandated tasks like employee background checks and immunizations.[58] Supporters of private schools in Michigan continue their covert and overt machinations to appropriate state monies to parochial schools.

EARMARKED STATE REVENUES

Michigan is somewhat unique from other states in that the majority of its public schools are funded through a special fund established by the State known as the State School Aid Fund (SSAF). The SSAF has earmarked funds that may only be used to support public education in Michigan.[59] In FY 21, the gross amount appropriated in the SSAF was $14,869,232,200, which was 87.6% of the $16.9 billion public school budget.[60] The following are sources of revenue statutorily or constitutionally allocated to the SSAF (the percentage of obligation varies):

- State Sales Tax
- State Use Tax
- State Income Tax
- State Education Tax
- Real Estate Transfer Tax
- Casino Gaming Tax
- State Lottery
- Cigarette Tax
- Liquor Tax[61]

FEDERAL CORONAVIRUS SCHOOL REVENUES

The Coronavirus Pandemic created new challenges for school districts, including deployment of new technology, acquisition of personal protective equipment, and facility care, cleaning, and improvement. Nationally, the federal government delivered $195 billion to school districts in three separate packages of revenue aid: Coronavirus Aid, Relief, and Economic Security Act ("CARES Act," Coronavirus Relief Fund ("CRF"), and American Rescue Plan ("ARP"). The majority of these funds came in three waves of Elementary and Secondary School Emergency

Relief funds, called ESSER I, ESSER II, and ESSER III. All ESSER funds from the federal government were allocated through state legislatures. In Michigan, ESSER I allocations were $350.8 million to public and charter schools to be expended by September 30, 2021. ESSER II quadrupled the first ESSER funding with a total allocation of $1.5 billion to Michigan schools to be fully expended by September 30, 2023. ESSER III, approved in March 2021, has an estimated allocation of $3.4 billion to Michigan schools to be fully expended by September 30, 2024. While the allowable expenditures for ESSERs I-III had slight variations, the core purpose remained consistent to prepare handle issues related to the current pandemic and to prepare infrastructure and training for future pandemics.

SUMMARY

For the fiscal year 2021—2022, Michigan allocated a total of $16,978,110,700 for education funding, which represents 24% of the state's total $69.9 billion budget for FY 2022. This budget expects to serve 1,434,500 students during this period.

ENDNOTES

[1] Isabel Wilkerson, "Tiring of Cuts, District Plans to Close Schools," New York Times, March 21, 1993.

[2] Citizens Research Council of Michigan, Distribution of State Aid to Michigan Schools, Report 3 17, August 2011. Per pupil revenue in Michigan had a range of $2,700 to $10,000.

[3] Joe Carrasco and Kathryn Summers-Coty, "K-12: A Moving Target" (Michigan Senate Fiscal Agency, 2002), http://www.senate.michigan.gov/sfa/publications/notes/2002notes/notesjulaug-02carrascosummers.pdf.

[4] House and Senate Fiscal Agencies, "School Finance in Michigan Before and After the Implementation of Proposal A: A Comparison of FY 1993-94 and FY 1994-95 Approaches to K-12 School Funding in Michigan," The Michigan School Aid Act Compiled and Appendicies (Lansing, MI: Senate Fiscal Agency, July/August 1994): 5.

[5] Homestead property is defined as a taxpayer's primary residence, including noncommercial agricultural property.

[6] Non-homestead property is defined as all other property such as business, rental property, vacation homes, and commercial agriculture.

[7] Kathryn Summers, The Basics of School Funding (Lansing, MI: Senate Fiscal Agency, 2012): 10.

[8] Brett A. Geier, "Michigan: State of the States," Journal of Education Finance, 46, no. 2 (Winter 2021): 299-301.

[9] Senate Fiscal Agency. FY 2021-2022 House Bill 4411, [Lansing, MI, 2021], 3.

[10] Ben DeGrow, How School Funding Works in Michigan [Michigan: Mackinac Center for Public Policy, 2017], 8

[11] Lori Higgins, "Michigan No Longer Ranks Near Bottom for Special Education, But That Doesn't Mean Students are Doing Better Academically." Chalkbeat (June 2019), https://michiganachieves.com/michigans-school-funding-crisis-opportunity/.

[12] The Education Trust—Midwest. 2020. Michigan's School Funding Crisis and Opportunity. Royal Oak, MI: The Education Trust—Midwest, https://michiganachieves.com/michigans-school-funding-crisis-opportunity/.

[13] David Arsen, Tanner Delpier, and Jesse Nagel. 2020. Michigan School Finance at the Crossroads: A Quarter Century of State Control. Lansing, MI: Michigan State University, https://education.msu.edu/ed-policy-phd/pdf/Michigan-School-Finance-at-the-Crossroads-A-Quarter-Center-of-State-Control.pdf.

14 Ben DeGrow, How School Funding Works in Michigan, 8

15 Ibid.

16 Ibid., 9.

17 Ibid.

18 Ibid.

19 Ibid.

20 Ibid.

21 Ibid.

22 Ibid.

23 Durant v. State of Michigan, 563 N.W.2d 646 (1997) (The Michigan Supreme Court held that special education, special education transportation, and the school lunch program are required by state law. It found that the state had been funding these programs at levels proportionally below those appropriated in 1978, when the Headlee Amendment was adopted and enacted. Through a different Special Master appointed by the Court of Appeals in 1995, state funding percentages from 1978 were determined for these services. The Supreme Court issued a monetary remedy for the amount of underfunding and a percentage the State must pay local school districts and ISDs for these services).

24 Senate Fiscal Agency. FY 2021-2022 House Bill 4411, [Lansing, MI, 2021], 3-4.

25 Mich. Rev. Sch. Code § 388.1641 (2021).

26 Ibid.

27 Michigan Department of Treasury, School Bond Qualification and Loan Program 2020 Annual Report, 3.

28 Ibid., 4.

29 Ibid., 8.

30 Ben DeGrow, How School Funding Works in Michigan, 11.

31 Tom Gantert. "Public School Pension System Totally Broken: Taxpayers on the hook," CAP-CON: Michigan Capitol Confidential (June 24, 2013), http://www.michigancapitolconfidential.com/18797.

32 Mich. Pub. Act 300 (2012).

33 Financial Services for Office of Retirement Services, Michigan Public School Employees Retirement Services: Comprehensive Annual Financial Report for the Fiscal Year Ended September 30, 2020 (Michigan: MPSERS, 2020), 104.

34 Ibid.

35 Ibid.

36 Ibid., 86.

37 Ibid., 56.

38 Mich. Rev. Sch. Code § 388.1747a-e (2021).

39 Michigan Student Data System, Number of Public School Districts in Michigan (Michigan: MSDS, 2021), https://www.michigan.gov/documents/numbsch_26940_7.pdf

40 Michigan House Fiscal Agency, Comparison of Proposed Pupil Membership Estimates (Michigan: 2021), https://www.house.mi.gov/hfa/PDF/RevenueForecast/Pupil_Handout_May2021.pdf

41 William J. Price, Michigan School Finance: A Handbook for Understanding State Funding Policy for Michigan Public Schools Districts [Houston, TX: National Council of Professors of Educational Administration, 2012], 37.

42 Ibid.

43 Senate Fiscal Agency. FY 2021-2022 House Bill 4411, 1-3.

44 William J. Price, Michigan School Finance, 14.

45 Senate Fiscal Agency. FY 2021-2022 House Bill 4411, 2.

46 Mich. Rev. Sch. Code § 380.705 (2021).

47 Senate Fiscal Agency. FY 2021-2022 House Bill 4411, 2.

48 Kathryn Summers, Appropriation Line Item, 11

49 Ibid.

50   Ibid.
51   Ibid., 12
52   Ibid.
53   Mich. Rev. Sch. Code § 380.1211 (2018).
54   Senate Fiscal Agency. FY 2021-2022 House Bill 4411, 2.
55   Ibid.
56   Ibid.
57   Kathryn Summers, Appropriation Line Item, 10-11.
58   Dave Boucher. "Divided Michigan Supreme Court Rules State Can Reimburse Private Schools," Detroit Free Press (December 28, 2020), https://www.freep.com/story/news/education/2020/12/28/michigan-supreme-court-state-can-reimburse-private-schools/4062193001/.
59   Price, Michigan School Finance, 9.
60   Jacqueline Mullen, Emily Hatch and Samuel Christensen."FY 2021-22: School Aid Summary: As Enrolled House Bill 4411 (S-1)," (Lansing, MI: Senate Fiscal Agency). (July 2021) https://www.msbo.org/wp-content/uploads/2021/07/schaid21-22HFA_Schoolaid_Enrolled-Summary.pdf.
61   Price, Michigan School Finance, 10-14.

CHAPTER 23

MINNESOTA

Nicola A. Alexander
University of Minnesota

GENERAL BACKGROUND

The Minnesota Constitution requires the state's legislature to provide for the operation of its public elementary and secondary schools. The education clause in Article XIII, Section I of the Minnesota Constitution, states:

> The stability of a republican form of government depending mainly upon the intelligence of the people, it is the duty of the legislature to establish a general and uniform system of public schools. The legislature shall make such provisions by taxation or otherwise as will secure a through and efficient system of public schools throughout the state.

The Minnesota school finance system is the method by which the legislature fulfills that responsibility.

Minnesota has a bicameral legislature and a biennial budget, where the governor makes proposals to the legislature regarding the state's operating budget in odd years, with proposed capital expenditures made in even years. As a result of state forecasts and other changes, it has become common for the Minnesota Legislature to enact annual revisions to the state's biennial budget. These revisions are

Funding Public Schools in the United States, Indian Country,
and US Territories (Second Edition), pages 381–399.
Copyright © 2023 by Information Age Publishing
www.infoagepub.com

referred to as supplemental budgets. The fiscal year (FY) runs from July 1 through June 30. The state's constitution requires Minnesota to maintain a balanced budget by the end of the budget cycle.[1] Minnesota enacted its FY 2022-23 biennial budget in June 2021. This chapter focuses on the upcoming biennium budget for fiscal years 2022-23 with references to the allocations in the previous fiscal year, FY 2021-2022. The analysis and description thus focuses on data encompassing July 1, 2021 through June 30, 2023. It reflects the summary of changes to the governor's original general fund recommendations and includes the incorporation of the federal COVID-19 aid, with special focus on Minnesota's American Rescue Plan in response to the federal American Rescue Plan Act.[2]

Schooling and School Finance

The first in the nation to operate public charter schools, Minnesota funded 325 traditional public school districts and 180 charter schools in school year (SY) 2021-2022. These public educational organizations employed 56,358 full-time equivalent teachers and served 872,759 public school students statewide in that year. The teaching population in Minnesota remains predominantly white at 96% of the teaching force, while the student population is more diverse, with 63.7% of students classified as white, 11.6% classified as black, 6.99% classified as Asian/Pacific Islander, 1.8% classified as Native Americans, and 10.1% classified as Hispanics. The percentage of English Language Learners accounted for 7.9% of the student population in SY2020-2021, and 32.19% of Minnesota's students were eligible for free or reduced price lunch. These averages mask large variations across the state, where rural school districts typically have less than 1% black students, and poverty rates are highest in inner city and rural communities.[3]

Up until the early 1900s, the local school boards contributed almost all of the funds used for operating public elementary and secondary school through the property taxes levied locally. In the early part of the 20th century, the state supplemented local contributions with limited amounts of state appropriations to school districts. Minnesota eventually developed a state aid program that provided all districts a flat grant for each pupil weighted for grade level and provided some districts with additional equalized amounts based on their district's property valuation, a measure of district wealth. These efforts on the part of the state, however, were not sufficient to stem the rapid and uneven rise in local property taxes that marked the late 1960s. In response, the 1971 Minnesota Legislature substantially increased the amount of equalized state foundation aid per weighted pupil and imposed a uniform statewide limit on the property tax rates that districts could establish. Just two years later, the 1973 Legislature eliminated flat grants and substantially increased the established foundational aid so that low-spending districts had per-pupil revenues that approximated the state average. For the next ten years, from 1973 to 1983, the legislature refined the foundation aid formula by modifying the foundational aid and required local tax effort without changing the basic structure of the program.

The 1983 Legislature enacted a new foundation aid program that became effective in the 1984-85 school year. The new program replaced the existing system with a five-tier foundation aid formula The main characteristics of the new program were equal access to revenues, recognition of specific cost differences, and more discretion on the part of school boards in choosing the necessary level of revenue.

By 1987, the Legislature replaced the foundation aid program with a modified funding formula called the general education revenue program, effective for the 1988-89 school year. In 1988, 52 outer ring suburban and rural school districts representing 25 percent of the state's K-12 enrollment filed a lawsuit against the Minnesota school finance system. The suit (*Skeen v. State of Minnesota*) claimed that Minnesota's school finance system was unconstitutional because the finance system was not uniform and school districts received disparate amounts of government aid. In 1989, a Minnesota trial court ruled that three parts of the finance mechanism were unconstitutional: (1) debt levy; (2) referendum levy; and (3) 302 revenue;[4] the state appealed the ruling. In 1993, the Minnesota Supreme Court reversed the earlier trial court decision and held the state's school finance system constitutionally permissible.

In 2021, former Supreme Court Justice Alan Page and Minneapolis Federal Reserve Bank President Neel Kashkari intensified their calls for Minnesota's Constitution to be amended to guarantee all children a "quality public education." Their proposed new language reads:

All children have a fundamental right to a quality public education that fully prepares them with the skills necessary for participation in the economy, our democracy, and society, as measured against uniform achievement standards set forth by the state. It is the paramount duty of the state to ensure quality public schools that fulfill this fundamental right.

While Minnesota House lawmakers have considered amending the state's constitution to reflect what has been termed the Page Amendment, there was no similar hearing in the state Senate.[5]

Summary of School Finance Trends, FY2016-FY2022

Table 23.1 provides data on Minnesota's E-12 and higher education general fund dollars for FY 2016 through FY 2022. Overall funding for E-12 education rose by 18.32% from FY 2016 to FY 2022, but annual increases have slowed somewhat from a 4.5% nominal increase from FY2016 to FY 2017 to a nominal increase of 1.6% from FY 2021 from FY 2022. If inflation is considered, the annual increase from FY2016 to FY 2017 was 2.5%, and the nominal increase from FY2021 to FY 2022 would actually reflect an inflation-adjusted decrease of 1.8%.[6]

State spending on E-12 schools has consistently accounted for about 85% of the over $10 billion spent on E-20+ education budgets in the last seven years.

TABLE 23.1. State General Fund Expenditures on Education, E-12 and Higher Education, FY 2016-FY 2022 (in thousands)

	Actual FY2016	Actual FY2017	Actual FY2018	Actual FY2019	Actual FY2020	Actual FY2021	Estimated FY2022
Total E-12 Education	8,516,938	8,901,333	9,233,048	9,587,811	9,835,739	9,919,135	10,077,280
Total Higher Education	1,529,168	1,555,720	1,651,198	1,642,451	1,693,377	1,714,340	1,756,101
Total Education	10,046,106	10,457,053	10,884,246	11,230,262	11,529,116	11,633,575	11,833,381
Total General Fund Spending	20,151,958	21,102,778	22,347,205	23,054,173	23,777,976	23,646,568	24,859,088

Source: Adapted from data obtained from Minnesota Department of Management and Budget, https://mn.gov/mmb-stat/documents/budget/operating-budget/enacted/2021/21eos-fba-detail.pdf

Overall, in FY2021 the latest year for which all fund amounts are publicly available, E-12 education represented 24.3% of the state's $82.8 billion expenditures from all funds and 41.9% of general funds, where most of the state's education's expenditures reside. These dollars funded programs for the state's 872,759 public school students.

The percentages of the total general fund expenditures devoted to elementary and secondary education has decreased over the seven-year period examined. In FY2016, 42.3% of general funds went to E-12 education; in FY2022, 40.5% of the general fund dollars is expected to go to E-12 education. If present trends continue, by FY2025, only 38.8% of the state's general fund dollars will go to funding K-12 education.[7] While the proportion of the general fund budget devoted to public elementary and secondary education is expected to decrease, the dollars devoted to this category is expected to increase. In the omnibus bills for 2020-2021 biennium, Minnesota devoted 19.84 billion of its general fund dollars to E-12 education; this amount is expected to increase to $20.99 billion in the 2022-23 biennium, and $21.8 billion in the 2024-25 biennium.

CURRENT POLITICAL CLIMATE

Minnesota has a divided government: the governor, Governor Tim Walz, belongs to the Democratic Farmer-Labor (DFL) party[8], the DFL holds the majority (70 Democrats, 59 Republicans, and 4 New Republicans) in the state House of Representatives and the Republicans have the majority in the state Senate (34 Republicans, 31 Democrats, and 2 Independents). In 2022, Minnesota was the only state legislature in the country to be split, and both parties have slim majorities in each of the legislative chambers, where the New Republicans caucus with the Republicans in the House and the two Independents caucus with the Democrats. Minnesota enacted new legislative district boundaries on February 15, 2022, when a special judicial redistricting panel issued an order adopting final maps.

The state constitution limits the Legislature to meeting 120 legislative days during each biennium. In addition, the Legislature may not meet in regular session after the first Monday following the third Saturday in May of any year. Thus, in 2022, the last day of regular session was on May 23, 2022. In the even numbered years, it convenes on a date set by joint agreement of both bodies. During this time, the House or the Senate may not adjourn for more than three days without the consent of the other body. In addition to its regular session, the legislature also meets when called by the governor to meet in special session.

Minnesota ended FY2022 with a budget surplus exceeding $9.2 billion.[9] With the discordant discourse on the national political landscape seeping into the state's political debates, it is not surprising that the legislative bodies were not able to reach agreement within the regular legislative session even with more funding available. Gov. Tim Walz has announced that he would meet with leaders from the Minnesota House and Senate to discuss calling a special session to finish major legislative proposals left undone after the Legislature missed the regular session deadline for completing its work.[10]

The governing parties started far apart on new education funding provisions for FY 2022-2023, where the House proposed $1.2 billion in new education revenues, the Senate proposed $31 million, and the governor proposed $709 million. Both the House and the Governor had provisions for reducing the amount that districts have to pay in cross-subsidies for special education and English language learner programs. They both expanded the minimum amount of funding for each district with special considerations for mental health support, and provide for grants for after school programs, culturally specific learning programs, and expanding rigorous coursework in schools for marginalized student groups, including Black students, Indigenous students, students of color and students in greater (rural) Minnesota. The only overlap in requests for new funding between the political parties was the proposal for grants for K-5 teachers to take the Language Essentials for Teachers of Reading and Spelling (LETRS) literacy training. While all three governing bodies agreed that this should be funded, the amounts proposed were very far apart, with the House proposing $3 million, the Senate proposing $30 million, and the governor proposing $3.3 million for this initiative.

SOURCES OF REVENUE

State revenue for aid payments to local school districts is primarily derived from income, sales, and property taxes as well as a variety of small fee funds and assessments. In FY 2021, school districts had $13.38 billion available from state and local sources (excluding local fees). Of that amount, $10 billion were in state appropriations, $79.4 million were in the form of state tax credits, $3.2 billion came from net levies, and $60.6 million were from dedicated funds. Net levies are certified levies minus tax relief aids. In FY2022, total non-dedicated revenues in the general fund budget amounted to $24.36 billion, of which 52.6% was from individual income tax, 6.1% came from corporate income tax, 25.6% came from sales tax, and 3.2% came from statewide property tax.

In the FY 2022/23 biennium budget, Minnesota raised more than $54.8 billion in general fund revenue, of which 52.5% came from individual income tax, 25.1% came from general sales tax revenues, 6.1% came from corporate taxes, and 3% came from revenue generated from the statewide property taxes. General fund revenues increased from close to $51.7 billion in the previous biennium, FY2020/ FY2021.

Most of the general education revenue is for the general operation of the school district and is not restricted by the state for a specific purpose. In addition to general education revenue, school districts also receive state appropriations through categorical aids, which are funds designated for specific purposes (such as special education and school integration/desegregation). General education revenue pays for operating expenses of the district including employee salaries, fringe benefits, and supply costs.

DISTRIBUTION FORMULAS

The components of Minnesota's school finance formula have remained relatively stable since 1989. In general, each component reflects the legislative perspective on school district funding needs. Components cover differential costs tied to economies of scale (e.g., small schools revenue, operating sparsity revenue, transportation sparsity revenue), differences in the needs of students served (e.g., English learner revenue, compensatory revenue, extended time revenue), programmatic costs (e.g., gifted and talented revenue) and the status of enrollment (e.g., declining pupil revenue).

In fiscal year 2003, Minnesota changed the way it calculated property taxes and brought some of these revenue streams under the auspices of the state. At this time, even though the bulk of the funding system was still structured as if it was foundational, it largely operated as a flat grant from 2003 through 2015, where the general education formula revenue was funded solely with state aid. The state established a Student Achievement Levy in FY2013 to generate an additional $20 million annually statewide in general education revenue, which was first effective in school year 2014-2015. It is a limited version of the local tax rate in place under the previous foundational formula, but this newest incarnation of the local levy was short lived. The 2015 Legislature passed legislation that phased out the levy over two years, beginning in FY 2018.

The latest embodiment of the school finance system, general education revenue, is the primary source of general operating funds for Minnesota's 325 traditional public school districts and 180 charter schools for the 2021-22 school year. Enrollment is the primary driver of Minnesota's school finance system, and the state distributes aid to each adjusted pupil unit. Adjusted pupil units reflect average daily membership weighted by the grade level of the student, where one voluntary pre-kindergarten student is weighted 0.6 pupil unit; a student in required

Kindergarten through grade 6 is weighted 1.0 pupil unit; and a student in grades 7 through 12 is counted as 1.2 pupil units. Prior to FY 2015, the state adjusted the pupil count to reflect organizational level in which the student is served as well as whether the student was in a district with stable, declining, or rising enrollments. In FY 2015, the enrollment status of the district was subsumed as one of the components in the general education aid formula and districts with declining enrollment from year to year are eligible for declining enrollment revenue. Thus, adjusted pupil units now reflect average daily membership weighted only by organizational level of the student served.

General Education Program

Minnesota finances its elementary and secondary schools through a combination of state-collected taxes and locally collected property taxes.[11] There are three categories of funding under this finance system: (1) State education finance appropriations; (2) state paid property tax credits; and (3) property tax levies. State education finance appropriations are funded with state-collected taxes and comprise general education aid and categorical aids. State paid property tax credits reflect the amounts paid by the state to compensate for reductions in local property tax revenues tied to state property tax credits. Property tax levies are largely made with voter approval but in some instances are at the discretion of individual school boards. Voter-approved levies usually authorize excess operating referenda and debt service levies. Operationally, the total general education program is expressed in Table 23.2 below:

The general education aid program has 13 subcomponents; revenue from this aid accounts for almost four-fifths of annual education finance appropriations, reflecting a majority of the financial support for Minnesota's school districts. This funding reflects flat grants, foundational aid, and equalized support and is grounded in principles of adequacy, horizontal equity, and vertical equity. These funding components reflect not only a minimum level of funding but also adjustments for a variety of district, pupil, and programmatic needs.

Total state aid appropriated to all school districts (traditional and charter) for the general education program amounted to $7.45 billion in FY 2021. An additional $2.55 billion was spent on categorical programs in that period. State educa-

TABLE 23.2.   Components of General Education Program Revenue

General Education Revenue = (Basic revenue + extended time revenue + gifted and talented revenue+ declining enrollment revenue+ small schools revenue+ basic skills revenue+ secondary sparsity revenue + elementary sparsity revenue + operating capital revenue + transportation sparsity revenue + equity revenue + transition revenue + referendum revenue (board approved) + referendum revenue (voter approved) + local optional revenue) * Pupil units.

Source: Fiscal Analysis Department of the Minnesota House of Representatives. (2021). Financing Education in Minnesota 2020-2021

tion finance appropriations totaled $10 billion in FY 2021, which accounted for 41.5% of the Minnesota's general fund dollars. State appropriations for programs are different from the revenues calculated based on the formula for those programs because of statutory requirements that the state pay most education aids over a two year period. Under this law, a majority percentage of the current year's entitlement must be paid in the current year, plus the adjusted balance of the previous year's entitlement. For FY 2021, state appropriations equaled 90% of the current year entitlement and the final 10% payment from the prior fiscal year, FY 2020.

Basic General Education Aid. The biggest subcategory of general education aid is the basic general education formula revenue, which establishes the minimum (or foundational) level of per pupil unit funding for school districts. This aid is set each year in legislation, and all school districts are eligible for this basic amount. This funding accounted for 70.3 percent of all general education revenue in FY 2021. Each district's share is determined by multiplying the formula allowance by the district's adjusted pupil units.[12] For FY 2021, the formula allowance is $6,567 per pupil unit. This portion of Minnesota's school finance system superficially resembles a standard foundation program comprised of a formula allowance and an established local tax rate. However, from FY 2003 through FY 2014, the established local tax rate was set at 0%, essentially causing this portion of the funding mechanism to operate as a flat grant.

As noted above, the legislature established the student achievement levy, effective FY 2015, to act as a limited version of the old general education levy that was in place prior to FY 2003. A district is not required to tax itself to the maximum level allowed. However, if a district chooses to tax itself less than the established levy rate, the district's share of total general education revenue state aid not subject to an aid/levy split is reduced proportionately. This levy is based on adjusted net tax capacity calculated for the prior year and was set at a rate of 0.35% in FY2015, 0.33% in FY2016, 0.30% in FY 2017 and 0.14% in FY 2018. After that year, the "required tax rate" reverted to 0%. Other levies for the general education program include the local portions of equity, transition, operating capital, referendum and local optional revenue. The local portions of general education revenue (excluding basic general education formula) are equalized.

Supplemental Components in the General Education Aid. There are 12 additional components to the general education program aid besides the basic general education revenue. These adjustments include aid to address differences among districts in four major areas:

1. *programmatic needs*: extended time revenue, gifted and talented revenue, learning and development revenue, revenue for staff developmen,t
2. *economies of scale and district structure*: declining enrollment revenue, secondary sparsity revenue, elementary sparsity revenue, transportation sparsity revenue, small school revenues, and operating capital revenue,

3. *needs of students served*: basic skills revenue (compensatory revenue and English learners)
4. *district wealth*: referendum revenue, equity revenue, local optional aid.

Table 23.3 provides data on each component of the general education program formula for FY 2021, the most recent year for which these details are available. It includes information on the number of districts (traditional and charter) that received aid from the specified program, the total aid appropriated for that formula component, the established formula amount for that revenue component, and whether or not that revenue stream is equalized.

Compensatory Education. Compensatory education programs are integrated in Minnesota's general education program as illustrated in Tables 23.2 and 23.3. Along with funding for English learners, compensatory revenue is a part of the basic skills revenue stream of that program. School sites generate the funding level based on the number and concentration of students eligible for free and reduced priced lunch (FRL) served at the site. The higher the concentration of eligible students, the higher the level of compensatory revenue that is generated. The level of concentration that influences the level of funding is capped. Even though compensatory education is included as part of the general education program, there are restrictions on how this money can be spent. Thus, compensatory revenue must be reserved in a separate account, and each district must produce an annual report describing how compensatory revenue has been spent at each site within the district.

The formula for this revenue stream is calculated for each site using multiple steps which are informed by the total number and relative concentration of students eligible for free or reduced price lunches in the subsidized federal program. Beginning in FY 2016, school boards may allocate up to 50 percent of the compensatory revenue on a district-wide basis. Prior to that, the district had to distribute these funds to the schools that generated them. All districts received some portion of the $542 million in compensatory revenue, which accounts for 6.2 percent of FY 2021 general education aid.

Categorical Programs

Special Education. Special education funding is a major portion of the categorical aid that the state appropriates to districts. State aid for this category amounted to $1.74 billion, which is 68.2% of all state categorical aid for FY 2021. There are four categories of special programs: (1) special education aid; (2) special education excess cost aid; (3) home based travel aid; and (4) special pupil aid.

All operating districts receive special education aid, but the amounts vary among districts. Prior to FY 2015, Minnesota used a partial cost reimbursement basis for funding special education, where districts received special education aid for the current year based on covering 69% of its certified special related expenditures in the previous fiscal year. The state has now adopted a census-based model,

TABLE 23.3. Detailed Description of the General Education Program for FY 2021

State Aid Component	Number of Traditional Districts Receiving	Number of charter school districts receiving	Total State Aid	Formula Amount Per Eligible Adjusted Pupil Unit	Equalized Aid[a]
Basic general education formula revenue	325[b]	180[c]	$6.2B	$6,567	No
Extended time revenue	145	36	$50.2M	$5,117	No
Gifted and talented revenue	325[b]	180[c]	$12.2M	$13	No
Declining enrollment	237	62	$39.8M	$1,839[d]	No
Small schools revenue	162	None	$16.4M	Up to $544[e]	No
Basic skills revenue (English Language Learner and Compensatory Aid)	325[b]	180[c]	$601M	Based on number and concentrations of eligible students	No
Sparsity (elementary and secondary sparsity revenue)	103	180[c]	$28.6M	Based on enrollment and geographic attendance area	No
Operating capital revenue	325[b]	180c	$213.6M	$188 - $243	Yes
Transportation sparsity revenue	307	69	$73.7M	Up to $1,026	No
Equity revenue[f]	325[b]	180[c]	$109.3M	$50 - $170	Yes
Transition revenue	199	36	$29.4M	Varies	Yes
Referendum revenue(board and voter approved)	230	n/a	$722.4M	capped by statute at $1,780 for FY2021	Yes
Local optional revenue	330	n/a	$628.6M	1st tier: $300 equalized at $880,000 2nd tier: $300-$760, equalized at $510,000	Yes

Source: Adapted from Fiscal Analysis Department of the Minnesota House of Representatives. (2021). Financing Education in Minnesota 2020-2021

Note: a Equalized aid refers to aid distributed using guaranteed tax base (also known as power equalization, guaranteed revenue, and guaranteed tax yield). b Table notes the total number of traditional public school districts in 2021-2022, the most recent data provided by the Minnesota Department of Education. The funding document noted that all districts were eligible without providing the count; the count noted in the table may vary from the numbers actually funded in the previous year. c Table notes the total number of charter school districts in 2021-2022, the most recent data provided by the Minnesota Department of Education. The funding document noted that all charter school districts were eligible without noting the count; the count noted in the table may vary from the numbers actually funded in the previous. d The declining enrollment formula is 28% of the current year formula allowance times the difference between the current year and previous year weighted pupil count. c Charter schools are ineligible for small schools revenue. f Excludes all districts in cities of the first class; i.e., Minneapolis, St. Paul, and Duluth for the equalized portion; however, all districts receive a flat rate of an additional $50 per pupil unit.

which takes into consideration overall district enrollment, poverty concentration, district size, and the average costs of educating students with different primary disabilities.[13]

There are three average cost categories for determining the special education aid needed:[14]

1. Category 1 includes those with the primary disability areas of autism spectrum disorder, developmental delay and severely multiply impaired: $10,400 times the December 1 child count;
2. Category 2 includes those with the primary disability areas of deaf and hard-of-hearing and emotional behavioral disorders: $18,000 times the December 1 child count;
3. Category 3: includes those with the primary disability areas of developmentally cognitive severe-profound, physically impaired, visually impaired, and deafblind.

Because the census-based approach is relatively new, Minnesota has included provisions which would essentially hold districts harmless. Thus, initial aid for the current year is calculated based on prior year fiscal calculations and includes the least of:

1. 62% of the district's old formula special education expenditures, excluding expenditures spent on transportation;
2. 50% of the district's nonfederal special education expenditures, excluding expenditures spent on transportation; or
3. 56% of the product of the sum of the census-based amounts.

Special education excess cost aid is intended to address vertical equity by compensating districts that have large unreimbursed special education costs relative to the district's general education revenue.[15] It is calculated based on the greatest of: (1) 56% of the difference between the district's unreimbursed nonfederal special education costs and 7% of the district's general education revenue; (2) 62% of the difference between the district's unreimbursed "old formula" special education costs and 2.5% of the district's general education revenue; or (3) zero.

In 2019, Minnesota Legislature enacted policy to reduce the amount of funds that districts must redirect in order to cover mandatory special education costs (often referred to as cross subsidies). Charter schools are not eligible for cross subsidy aid. The cross subsidy aid factor was 6.43% in FY2021.

General Transportation. Pupil transportation often is a huge expense, and the state largely addresses that cost as part of its general education revenue program. No categorical aid exists for transportation, which accounted for 5.21% of a district's budget on average.[16] While additional transportation needs are considered for rural districts via sparsity aid (including transportation sparsity revenue), there is no comparable funding for districts located in more densely populated areas. The formula to calculate transportation sparsity revenue employs a relatively complex density and sparsity index. The actual formula uses logarithms to calculate a revenue amount.[17]

School Facilities. Funding for facilities are part of both general education aid as well as in K-12 categorical aid programming. The operating capital revenue, which is part of the general education aid formula, is used for repair and betterment of facilities, acquisition of land, purchase or lease of equipment, and purchase of books. Even though operating capital revenue is part of the general education program, this revenue must be used for specified capital projects and may not be used for general operating purposes.[18] It is an equalized formula with an equalizing factor of $23,885 of districts' adjusted net tax capacity in FY 2021. The equalized amount increased to $22,912 in FY 2022.[19]

Beginning in FY 2017, all districts, charter school, intermediate districts, and cooperative units are eligible for the Long-Term Facilities Maintenance (LTFM) Revenue Program. This includes expenditures on deferred capital and necessary maintenance; approved health and safety capital projects; increased accessibility to school facilities; approved expenditures associated with remodeling. Charter schools are allowed to use this revenue for any purpose related to the school. All participants in the program must have a 0-year facilities plan. Districts must indicate if they plan to use a pay-as-you-go (issue annual levy) or pay-as-you-use (issue general obligation bonds); voter approval is not required for general obligation bonds for LTFM projects. For the purposes of these projects, the district's adjusted net tax capacity (the measure of district wealth) is reduced by 50% of the value of particular agricultural land within the district's borders. This increases the equalization aid available to those districts with large portions of agricultural land. The equalization factor is 123% of statewide average adjusted net tax capacity per adjusted pupil unit.

The LTMFR aid replaced the previous Health and Safety, Alternative facilities, and Deferred maintenance revenue programs. This revenue must not be used for "construction of new facilities, to remodel existing facilities, to purchase portable classrooms, nor to finance a lease purchase agreement, energy efficiency projects, facilities used for post-secondary instruction, violence prevention, security, ergonomics or emergency communication devices."[20]

Food Services. All Minnesota school districts are expected to operate a food service program in full compliance with federal and state regulations. Food service funds are part of the operating funds of districts but are separate from their general funds. Categorical aid for the districts include school breakfast and school lunch aid. Under the school breakfast aid, schools are eligible to receive 55 cents for each fully paid breakfast and 30 cents for each reduced price breakfast served to students in grades 1 through 12.[21] Districts that receive school breakfast aid must provide breakfast free of charge to those eligible for free and reduced price meals. All voluntary pre-kindergarten pupils and kindergarten students are eligible for school breakfast without charge regardless of the student's family income.

Schools are eligible to receive up to 12.5 cents of state funding for each lunch served. Districts receive 52.5 cents per reduced price lunch meal served.[22]

Other State Aids. The state provides various other categorical aid to public K-12 schools including American Indian Education Aid, Alternative Teacher Compensation Revenue (QComp), Achievement and Integration Revenue (AIM), Literacy Incentive Aid, Library Programs, Abatement Revenue, Advanced Placement and International Baccalaureate Programs, and Consolidation Transition Revenue. The AIM is relatively unique to Minnesota and is intended to pursue racial and economic integration, increase student achievement, and reduce economic disparities in Minnesota's public schools.[23]

Special Levies. School districts may levy additional local property tax to provide funding for their operating and capital expenditures. These levies are equalized and are part of the general education funding program. There are three primary categories of special levies: (1) referendum revenue; (2) local optional revenue; and (3) equity revenue.

Referendum revenues allow districts to increase the revenue available in the district's general fund and is generated with both voter approval and in more limited cases, approval of the board. Unlike other revenue streams that are based on adjusted net capacity of a school district (a small portion of the total market value), referendum revenue is based on market value. Minnesota provides three equalization tiers for referendum revenue, which is subject to an annual cap. The cap is adjusted annually for inflation based on the urban consumer price index. Only districts eligible for sparsity revenue can have district referendum revenue that exceeds this cap.

Minnesota's funding system also allows for equity revenue, which is aimed at reducing the disparity in revenues per pupil unit on a regional basis. There are two primary regions, the seven county metropolitan area and the rest of the state. Minnesota uses a set of three formulas to calculate equity revenue: (1) regular equity; (2) low-referendum equity; and (3) supplemental equity. Regular equity revenue is calculated by ranking all districts in each region based on their total and basic referendum revenue. If districts are below the 95th percentile, they are eligible for regular and low-referendum equity revenue unless they are districts in cities of the first class (i.e., Minneapolis, St. Paul, and Duluth). Low referendum equity was created to provide additional aid for districts with referendum amounts per pupil unit below 10 percent of the state average referendum amount. Prior to fiscal year 2005, a district's equity revenue was provided entirely in state aid.

CAPITAL OUTLAY AND DEBT SERVICE

School districts are responsible for financing their ongoing capital needs as well as major building construction projects. See discussion on school facilities for the financing of ongoing capital needs; this section focuses on major building projects.

To finance major building projects, districts often borrow money through the sale of bonds and levy an annual tax to repay the money over a period of years.

This "pay-as-you-use" strategy contrasts with the alternative of "pay-as-you-go," where districts build up money in their reserves to finance major capital projects. The amount of debt service revenue needed each year is equalized at varying rates depending on the ratio of the amount of debt service revenue to the district's total adjusted net tax capacity. Debt service for traditional general obligation bonds is calculated differently from use for long-term maintenance programs. As of FY 2018, debt service levels are equalized at the greater of $4,430 or 55.33% of the initial equalizing factor for the first tier; and the greater of $8,000 or 100% of the initial equalizing factor for the second tier. The initial equalizing factor is equal to the state average adjusted net tax capacity per adjusted pupil unit for the year before the levy is certified.[24] Debt service amounts that qualify for debt equalization are general debt service amounts for land acquisition, construction costs, and capital energy loans.

EMPLOYEE BENEFITS

Retirement and Other Postemployment Benefits. The Minnesota education finance system provides retirement benefits for teachers, administrators, nurses, librarians, social workers, counselors, and other professional personnel employed in Minnesota's public schools, including charter schools. There are two teacher retirement fund associations: (1) Teachers Retirement Association (TRA), which is statewide; and (2) a separate retirement fund association for teachers employed by the St. Paul district.

Since FY 1989, school districts have been required to make all employer contributions for teacher retirement and Social Security directly from their undesignated general fund revenue. No separate categorical aid for teacher retirement exists. However, special state aid is paid from the state to the statewide retirement fund for teachers employed by Minneapolis and Duluth and the St. Paul retirement fund, to reduce the unfunded liability in those funds.

Many Minnesota school districts have offered a number of postemployment benefits to their employees. These benefits are in addition to the employee pension benefits provided by the teacher retirement systems and the Public Employee Retirement Association (PERA). The largest share of these benefits consists of promises to pay certain health costs of retired employees. These benefits give rise to a liability under Statement No. 45 of the Governmental Accounting Standards Board (GASB), and in Minnesota, generally refers to retiree health benefits.

CHARTER SCHOOL FUNDING

Charter schools are public schools and are eligible for many of the state sources of revenue made available to traditional public school districts (see Table 23.3). They are eligible for general education revenue, special education aid, building lease aid, long-term facilities maintenance revenue, start-up grants, and other revenues that traditional public school districts receive. Charter schools are eligible to receive other aids, grants, and revenue like traditional public school unless a property tax levy is required to obtain the money.

Charter schools are exempt from many of the requirements governing traditional public schools, including the provision of transportation. If a charter school does not provide transportation services, the charter school receives $300 less per pupil and will not receive the transportation sparsity revenue portion of the general education revenue aid. If transportation services are not provided by the charter school, then the district in which the charter school is located must provide transportation to charter school students in the same way it provides transportation to students residing in or attending school in the traditional public school district. In that instance, the school district receives the $300 per pupil and the charter's transportation sparsity revenue to help pay for that transportation. While the basic skills, transportation sparsity, transition, and pension adjustment revenues are calculated for the charter school, the charter school receives the state average for all the other components of the general education revenue except for referendum revenue. Charter schools receive the state aid portion of referendum calculated based on the resident district of each charter school student. If a charter school operates an extended day, extended week or summer program, it is eligible for extended time revenue up to 25% of the statewide average extended time revenue per adjusted pupil unit. Charter schools with building leases qualify for aid equal to 90% of the approved cost of the lease or $1,341 per pupil, whichever is less.

STATE FUNDING FOR STUDENTS ATTENDING NON-PUBLIC SCHOOLS

Minnesota has two categories for funding nonpublic pupils—(1) nonpublic pupil aid[25] and (2) nonpublic pupil transportation.[26] Public school districts receive this aid for the benefit of their nonpublic school students.

Nonpublic pupil aid may be used for supplying secular textbooks and other instructional materials; it also includes provision of health services and secondary guidance and counseling services. The textbook funding level is based on the average amounts expended per pupil in public schools for similar materials two years prior; this amount is multiplied by a factor equal to the growth in the basic formula amount between the second prior year and the current year. Health services reimbursements are based on their actual costs per pupil or on the average costs of providing those services to public school students two years prior, whichever is less. Guidance and counseling services are reimbursed based on actual costs per secondary pupil or the average costs of providing those services to public secondary school students two years prior, whichever is less. State aid for nonpublic pupil transportation reimburses public school districts for the cost per pupil of providing transportation services. It is based on the costs of transportation two years prior and then adjusted for the change in the general education formula allowance between the current year and two years prior.

VIRTUAL EDUCATION

Minnesota offers categorical aid for telecommunications access revenue. This is a reimbursement program for eligible telecommunications and Internet access costs from the previous fiscal year. To access these funds, districts must apply for federal Internet funding, called "e-rate" funding. The revenue is calculated based on a district's eligible costs for the prior year minus any e-rate funding received that exceeds $16 per pupil. Eligible costs include ongoing costs for Internet access, data lines, and video links for certain purposes, recurring contractual costs for certain portions of a district's network, recurring costs for shared regional delivery of access between school districts, postsecondary institutions and public libraries as well as installation feeds for new lines or increased bandwidth.

FEDERAL COVID-19 FUNDING

The federal government passed three major relief packages in response to COVID-19: The Coronavirus Aid, Relief, and Economic Security Act (CARES), the Coronavirus Response and Relief Supplemental Appropriations Act (CRRSA), and the American Rescue Plan Act (ARP). They all included funding for education. These relief packages resulted in an infusion of nearly $73 billion into the state coffers, with most going to economic aid ($52.2 billion), about $3.34 billion going to education, and about $7.2 billion were unrestricted.[27] The Minnesota Department of Education (MDE) administers multiple grant opportunities from these three relief packages.

The CARES Act included an Education Stabilization Fund, which created two major sources of funding for schools: the Governor's Emergency Education Relief (GEER) Fund and the Elementary and Secondary School Emergency Relief (ESSER) Fund. It also contained section 5001, the Coronavirus Relief Fund (CRF), which established $150 billion in payments to state, local, and Tribal governments navigating the impact of the COVID-19 pandemic.

The CRRSA Act was signed into law on December 27, 2020. This includes additional ESSER and GEER funding and established the Emergency Assistance for Nonpublic School Fund (EANS Fund) as part of the GEER award. The EANS funds for the nonpublic schools are administered by the Minnesota Department of Education and have been distributed via an application in alignment with the federal guidance. This funding was intended to help nonpublic schools safely reopen or keep schools open.

The ARP Act was signed into law on March 11, 2021 and focuses on returning to, and maintaining, safe in-person learning for all students. The ARP includes $1.3 billion for E-12 education in additional ESSER funds for Minnesota to help schools returning to, and maintaining, safe in-person learning for all students. Per the federal law, 90% of these funds have been allocated to eligible districts and charter schools. The remaining funds are for use by each state education agency to create a plan to meet the needs of students based on community input.

Minnesota's ARP State Plan. The Minnesota Department of Education submitted a plan to the U.S. Department of Education in June 2021 on the use of flexible federal funds dedicated to education by the American Rescue Plan (ARP). The department's plan was informed through community engagement, and the MDE engaged in outreach efforts that included input sessions, public comment and direct conversations connected with a variety of Minnesotans impacted by the Department's work.

Per federal requirements, the MDE allotted at least 9.5% of its ARP funding for education to five areas: (1) addressing lost instruction time (learning recovery) which accounted for $66 million; (2) after-school programs, which accounted for $13.2 million; (3) summer enrichment, which accounted for $13.2 million; (4) school support, which accounted for $26 million; and (5) state support, which accounted for $13.6 million.

The bulk of the ARP funding went to supporting learning recovery. The MDE allocated funds directly to public schools using a formula based on the number of historically underserved students, focusing primarily on students receiving special education services. Historically underserved students include as students of color, American Indian students, students eligible for free or reduced-priced meals, students receiving special education services, students who are English learners and students experiencing homelessness. All public schools receiving funds must select evidence-based strategies from a list of programs identified by the Minnesota Department of Education. This allotment translates to 52.6% of the $132 million of available ARP funding.

The MDE will allocate 10% of its available funds to after school programs ($13.2 million). This includes allocations to Ignite Afterschool, an organization with expertise in evidence-based after school programing, for grant distribution. The MDE will direct 50% of these funds to community organizations and 50% of the funds to culturally specific community organizations.

The Minnesota Department of Education has committed 10% ($13.2 million) of its flexible ARP funds to summer enrichment. As with after school programs, the MDE will direct 50% of funds to community organizations and 50% of the funds to culturally specific organizations through a granting process.

MDE has allocated 19.7% ($26 million) of available ARP funds to school support initiatives that target systemic support for students. The bulk of that funding ($23 million) will be in other state activities funds while the remaining $3 million will reflect grant administration funds. Almost two-fifths of this funding will be dedicated to Multi-tiered systems of support ($5 million) and to full-service community schools ($5 million). The remaining funds are committed to expanding rigorous coursework ($4 million), employing trauma informed-anti-bias instructional practices training ($3 million), supporting Life Skills/Transition programs ($2 million), mentoring new staff in the teaching profession ($2 million), early learning programs ($1.5 million) and Tribal/State Relations training for public school leaders ($0.5 million).

The MDE committed $13.6 million for state supports to build and reinforce systems and structures within MDE to better support students, families and educators. Almost three-quarters of that funding address important strategies to address equity. This includes the Department's commitment to foster data disaggregation ($6 million); enhance public engagement by creating a public engagement division within MDE that will support public schools' efforts to provide translated materials for families, and resources for non-grant administrative support ($2 million), and the funding of non-grant administrative related supports ($2 million). The remaining $3.6 million of grant administration funds will be used to support MDE administration, monitoring, technical assistance and data gathering for ARP funds given to public schools and community organizations.[28]

ENDNOTES

1 Minnesota Office of Management and Budget. (n.d.). https://mn.gov/mmb/budget/state-budget-overview/current-estimates/

2 Nicola A. Alexander. (2021). Journal of Education Finance (Volume 47, Issue 5). Downloaded from https://www.nationaledfinance.com/docs/21_Jef_47.5_Minnesota.pdf.

3 Nicola A. Alexander & Sung Tae Jang (2019) 'Synonymization' threat and the implications for the funding of school districts with relatively high populations of black students, Race Ethnicity and Education, 22:2, 151-173, DOI: 10.1080/13613324.2018.1511533

4 https://law.justia.com/cases/minnesota/supreme-court/1993/c5-92-677-2.html

5 Minnesota House of Representatives. March 8, 2021. House lawmakers consider amending MN constitution to guarantee all kids a 'quality public education.' See, https://www.house.leg.state.mn.us/sessiondaily/SDView.aspx?StoryID=15745

6 Inflation was calculated using the CPI index provided by the US Bureau of Labor Statistics. See historical table of indices at http://www.usinflationcalculator.com/inflation/consumer-price-index-and-annual-percent-changes-from-1913-to-2022/. For the change from FY2016 to FY2022, I used the most recent index associated with calendar year 2022 (May 2022). For FY2016, I used the average index associated with all 12 months of CY2016.

7 Minnesota Management and Budget. (July 2017). See especially, https://mn.gov/mmb/assets/fba-nov17fcst-pie-charts_tcm1059-319765.pdf.

8 Hereafter, I will refer to the party and membership as Democratic and Democrats. Since 1944, the DFL has been a historical partnership between the Democratic party and the then Farmer-Labor party and is affiliated with the national Democratic party.

9 Minnesota House of Representatives. State's projected budget surplus swells to 9.25 billion. https://www.house.leg.state.mn.us/SessionDaily/Story/17164

10 Star Tribune. (May 23, 2022). Short special session possible after legislators leave work undone. https://mail.google.com/mail/u/0/?tab=cm#search/star+tribune/FMfcgzGpGBBltMXfZnsHctbF-DWLPSsWM.

11 The discussion of the elements of the Minnesota school finance program comes primarily from the annual publications of the Minnesota House of Representatives Fiscal Analysis Department; i.e., Financing Education in Minnesota (year).

12 Pupil unit reflects the average daily membership count weighted by grade level where one voluntary pre-kindergarten student is weighted 0.6 pupil unit; a student in required Kindergarten through grade 6 is weighted 1.0 pupil unit; students in grades 7 through 12 are counted as 1.2 pupil units.

13 See also, Fiscal Analysis Department. (2016). Financing Education in Minnesota 2020-2021, p. 36.

14 Ibid. See also Minn. Stat. §§ 126A.76.

15 Minn. Stat. §§ 125A.79.

16 See Minnesota Department of Education for statewide expenditure averages for major expenditure categories for FY 2021 at https://public.education.mn.gov/MDEAnalytics/DataTopic.jsp?TOPI-CID=79.

17 Fiscal Analysis Department. (2021). Financing Education in Minnesota 2020-2021, p. 22.

18 Minnesota House Research Department. (2016). Minnesota School Finance: A guide to legislators, p. 40.

19 Minn. Stat. §§ 126C.10, 13.

20 Fiscal Analysis Department. (2016). Financing Education in Minnesota 2016-2017, p. 44.

21 Minn. Stat. §§ 124D.1158.

22 Minn. Stat. §§ 124D.111.

23 Minn. Stat. §§ 124D.862

24 Minn. Stat. §§ 123B.53. See also Fiscal Analysis Department. (2016). Financing Education in Minnesota 2016-2017, p. 48.

25 Minn. Stat. §§ 123b.40-123b.48.

26 Minn. Stat. §§ 123b.92

27 Christopher Magan. (April 2022). Minnesota got $73 billion in pandemic aid. Where did it go? Star Tribune. https://www.twincities.com/2022/04/09/mn-73-billion-pandemic-aid-where-it-went/

28 For more detailed information about Minnesota's planned use of ARP funding, see State Plan for the American Rescue Plan Elementary and Secondary School Emergency Relief Fund. Downloaded on May 25 from file:///C:/Users/nalexand/Downloads/07.20.21%20-%20Minnesota%20ARP%20State%20Plan%20(2).pdf.

CHAPTER 24

MISSISSIPPI

Spencer D. Stone
Alabaster City Schools

GENERAL BACKGROUND

Mississippi became a state in 1817, and the first of four state constitutions was adopted in that same year. A fourth constitution was adopted in 1890; that adoption stands today, although it has been frequently amended and updated across the decades since its origin. The latest amendments came in 2020. The Mississippi constitution's education article places it among the barest of all 50 states, reading only:

The Legislature shall, by general law, provide for the establishment, maintenance and support of free public schools upon such conditions and limitations as the Legislature may prescribe.[1]

CURRENT CONTEXT

Education funding in Mississippi has been fraught with argument and revision.[2] Mississippi's schools are funding through property taxes "Each district is expected to contribute $28.00 of $1,000 dollars of assessed property wealth."[3] Recent history is generally regarded as beginning in 1997 when the state legislature

Funding Public Schools in the United States, Indian Country,
and US Territories (Second Edition), pages 401–408.
Copyright © 2023 by Information Age Publishing
www.infoagepub.com

passed the Mississippi Adequate Education Program (MAEP) in an effort to address two primary problems: low student achievement, and fiscal inequity among school districts. Background for the initiative was that Mississippi schoolchildren were being outperformed by other states. In contrast, almost every other state was spending more per pupil despite fewer challenges. Additionally, Mississippi districts with low tax bases were worse off than those in more prosperous communities because more affluent Mississippi communities were able to supplement state funding, making education's quality as defined by available resources a consequence of residence.

The Mississippi legislature subsequently engaged consultants, legislators, and other experts to study the situation. The outcome was two acts in legislation: the Mississippi Accountability System, and the Mississippi Adequate Education Program (MAEP). The Mississippi Accountability System significantly raised standards for teachers and students. The Mississippi Curriculum Test (MCT[1]), MCT[2], and the current MCT[3] were developed to measure student achievement, and schools were thereafter to be rated on test scores. The Children First Act of 2009 raised stakes, calling for removal of superintendents and school boards in chronically low performing schools.

The MAEP was a legislative commitment to provide resources to teachers and schools, tied to the new accountability system. The system was meant to hold districts and individual schools accountable for academic performance, with the MAEP providing a formula determining the necessary funding for each district to provide an adequate education. Importantly, the MAEP capped the portion of funding a local school district is required to provide.

The MAEP was intended to erase inequities by ensuring that children across Mississippi would be granted access to an adequate education without relationship to local wealth. In brief, the MAEP was meant to determine the per-pupil cost of a good education after accounting for the local district's responsibility. The MAEP's difference was meant to be the level of funding required from the state legislature.

A common defense of the Mississippi Education System from state politicians is that the state pays over 60% of the total state budget to education. This however is a misrepresentation of the facts. If only discussing the state monies spent on education, then the state actually spends about 22% of its state budget on K-12 education.

Mississippi received $1.6 billion dollars in COVID relief funds; $543 million dollars was earmarked for K-12 education. In their K-12 plan, Mississippi laid out their priorities for the funds: safely reopening schools and sustaining safe operations, addressing the academic impact of lost instructional time, supporting physical and mental health.[4]

TABLE 24.1.   Mississippi Adequate Education Program Detail 2018

What is the MAEP

MAEP is the state aid formula used to establish adequate current operation funding levels necessary for the programs of each school district to meet a successful level of student performance as established by the Mississippi State Board of Education using current statistically relevant state assessment data.

Purpose

To ensure that every Mississippi child, regardless of where he/she lives, is afforded an adequate educational opportunity as defined by the State Accountability System.

MAEP Funding Formula

ADA x Base Student Cost + At-Risk Component - Local Contribution + 8% Guarantee = MAEP Formula Allocation

MAEP Formula Allocation + Add-on Programs = Total MAEP District Funding

Base Student Cost Calculation

District Selection Process

Districts determined to be successful and efficient in four areas of school operations are selected for determining base student cost;

- Successful district: defined by the State Board of Education using current statistically relevant assessment data;
- Efficient school district: in each of the following Efficiency Components, a mean score for all districts is determined (only districts meeting successful status and above are selected for cost component calculations).
  - Instruction teachers per 1,000 students;
  - Administrator/staff ratio;
  - Maintenance and operations (M&O spending per 100,000 square feet); and (maintenance staff per 100,000 square feet);
  - Ancillary librarians and counselors per 1,000 students.
- Districts scoring one standard deviation above or two standard deviations below the mean for each component are ruled efficient;
- Districts meeting the successful and efficient standard are used to calculate the average cost for each component.
- By law, average cost for each component is calculated using expenditure data from the second preceding year.

 Average Costs of the Four Components are Added Together to Obtain the Base Student Cost. To provide stability for appropriation and budgeting, base student cost is calculated every four years rather than annually. An inflation adjustment is computed in the years between recalculation by multiplying 40% of base student cost times the current inflation rate as computed by the state's economist.

Example: FY 08 BSC x 40% x CPI = FY 09 Inflation

Component $4,574 x .40 x .03 (3% inflation rate) = $54

In this example, for FY 2009 $54 would be added to the FY 2008 BSC to arrive at FY 2009 BSC of $4,519.

Once Base Student Cost is determined, district allocations are calculated using the following formula:

ADA x Base Student Cost + At-Risk Component -

Local Contribution + 8 % Guarantee = MAEP District Allocation

(continues)

TABLE 24.1. Continued

Vocational Education:

One-half (1/2) teacher unit is added for each approved vocational program, with funding based on certification and experience of the approved teacher. Program approval criteria and vocational education teacher units are administered through the Office of Vocational-Technical Education and interfaced with the Office of Educational Accountability.

Alternative School Programs:

Three quarters of one percent (0.75%) of the district's ADA (grades 1-12, elementary and secondary special education self-contained and ungraded) or 12 students, whichever is greater, is multiplied by the statewide average per-pupil expenditure in public funds for the immediately preceding school year.

Source: Mississippi Adequate Education Program (MAEP). (2018). http://tpcref.org/wp-content/uploads/ MAEP_Explanation.pdf

Definitions of Program Elements

Average Daily Attendance (ADA):
- Grades K-12 months 2-3 of preceding year;
- Excludes self-contained special education ADA;
- High growth component: for any district having consistent growth in ADA in the three-year period prior to the appropriation, the average percent growth in ADA over those three years is added to the ADA for the district.

At-Risk Component:
5% of base student cost, multiplied by numbers of free lunch participants on October 31 of the preceding year;
As base student costs increase, the amount for At-Risk increases;
Added into total before calculation of the local contribution.

Local Contribution:
uses 2nd preceding year's data;
Reduced by ad valorem tax reduction grants;
Yield from 28 mills + ad valorem in lieu payments;
Capped at 27% of program costs, including the At-Risk component.

8% Guarantee:
Incorporated to ensure that a district receives a formula allocation of at least what was received in 2002 plus 8%.

Add-On Programs:

Transportation;
Special Education;
Gifted Education;
Vocational Education;
Alternative Education.

Transportation:
Determined by the ADA of transported students in a school district;
The allowable cost per student is calculated using a rate table approved by the State Board of Education which associates the rate allowed to the transported density of the district;
Density is determined by dividing transported ADA by total square miles in the district. The lower the density, the higher the rate. The higher the density, the lower the rate. The total amount of transportation funding allowed is dictated by the state legislature. The total of all district transportation funding cannot exceed amounts appropriated for such purposes;

Table 24.1.   Continued

Additional special education and vocational transportation allotment is administered by the Deputy Superintendent and the Office of School Building and Transportation and is interfaced with the Office of Educational Accountability and the Office of School Financial Services.

The 1993 legislature mandated that, beginning in 1993-94, each school district must have an intellectual gifted program. The mandate begins with grade 2 and increases by one grade each year until grade 6 is mandated in 1997-98. No other programs or grades are mandated, and the mandate applies to intellectual programs in grades 2-6 only.

Special Education:
A teacher unit is added for each approved program for exceptional students, with funding based on certification and experience. Program approval criteria and special education teacher units are administered through the Office of Instructional Programs and Services, Office of Special Services and is interfaced with the calculation.

Gifted Education:
A teacher unit is added for each approved program for gifted (artistic, intellectual, academic) students, with funding based on certification and experience of the approved teacher. Program approval criteria and gifted teacher units are administered through the Office of Instructional Programs and Services, Office of Academic Education and are interfaced with the Office of Educational Accountability, Office of School Financial Services.

**MAEP Formula Allocation + Add-on Programs
= Total MAEP District Funding**

MISSISSIPPI ADEQUATE EDUCATION PROGRAM OPERATION[3]

The Mississippi Adequate Education Program (MAEP) in place today, covering 162 independent school districts, is a formula that functions as a minimum foundation by producing a base student cost, i.e., an amount thought to be required in order to provide each student an adequate education. Each school district provides up to 27% of base student cost through a local contribution derived from local ad valorem taxes. The legislature is required to fund the difference between what local communities can provide and total base student cost. That amount is then multiplied by the district's average daily attendance (ADA) to determine the MAEP allocation.

The MAEP is scheduled for recalculation every four years, adjusted for inflation by multiplying 40% of base student cost by the current rate of inflation as computed by the state. The MAEP is meant to account for differences, including salaries and benefits, textbooks and materials, operational costs, transportation, special education, vocational education, gifted education, and alternative education. The MAEP is not meant to pay for administrative costs, leaving that expense to local shares. Other MAEP funding outside the formula relates to teacher supplies, National Board Certification, early childhood education initiatives, and costs for operating the Mississippi Department of Education.

Table 24.1 is taken from the Mississippi Department of Education's explanation for operation of the MAEP.

OTHER PROGRAMS[4]

District-Based Components

As observable in Table 24.1, the state of Mississippi provides almost none of the typical categorical supports common to many states. Namely:

Density or Sparsity for Small Schools Adjustment
None.

Grade Level Differences
None.

Declining Enrollment or Growth
If a school district has a consistent pattern of growth over the three-year period prior to the annual appropriation, the average percent of growth is added to the district's ADA.

Capital Outlay and Bond Debt Service
Bonded indebtedness for Mississippi school districts is limited to 15% of assessed property valuation. Additional authority for notes and certificates of indebtedness is limited to the amount a three mill tax levy can raise for ten years. No state support is evident.

Transportation
State aid to transportation in Mississippi is based on the ADA for transported pupils and a density formula and rate table. The result is the lower the density, the higher the rate. The rate table provides greater amounts per pupil to districts with fewer pupils per square mile. This is an add-on program amount.

Student-Based Components
As observable in Table 26.1, the state of Mississippi provides fiscal support for the areas of special education, low income, compensatory and at-risk education, gifted and talented education, career and technical education, and alternative education programs.

Special Education
Teacher units are added for each approved program for exceptional students. Funding is based on the certification and experience of the approved teacher. This is an add-on program amount. (CURRENT)

Low Income, Compensatory, and At-Risk Education
MAEP has an at-risk component based on 5% of Base Student Cost times the number of free lunch participants as of October 31 of the previous year.

English Language Learner and Bilingual Education
None.

Gifted and Talented Education
Teacher units are added for each approved program for gifted and talented students. Funding amounts are based on the certification and experience of each teacher. This is an add-on program amount. (CURRENT)

Career and Technical Education
One-half of a teacher unit is added for each approved program. Funding amounts are based on certification and experience of each teacher. This is an add-on program amount. (CURRENT)

Alternative Program Education
Based on three quarters of one percent (0.75%) of the school district's ADA for grades 1-12 or 12 students, whichever is greater, is multiplied by the state average per-pupil expenditure in the previous year. This is an add-on program amount. (CURRENT)

Preschool Education
Since 2013, Mississippi's Legislature has provided funds to local districts for Pre-k programs. The program started with a recommendation of $8 million annually, and had planned increases for spending over several years. For the 2022-2023 school year, the state appropriated $24 million for early learning collaboratives.

STEM Education
None.

State Support for Nonpublic Schools
Mississippi provides aid to distribute and loan books to nonpublic schools that maintain the same academic standards as public schools. The state regards such contributions as demonstrating nondiscriminatory practices.

Charter Schools
Charter schools in Mississippi must be approved by the Charter School Authorizer Board as defined in state statute. Four such charter schools were in place for 2018-2019. Charter schools are funded in the same manner as other public school districts. Projected charter enrollment is used for the initial funding calculation and is later reconciled with actual ADA.

SUMMARY

In 2021, the Mississippi legislature tried to pass House Bill 1439; this bill sought to lower the property tax owed by certain individuals. The plan was to make up these funds from sales taxes. Critics quickly pointed out that since education is funded through property taxes that the passage of this bill could lead to a major shortfall in education funding. MISSISSIPPI did pass HB 531 which will lower state income taxes—this could lead to a $1.5 billion shortfall in the general fund. The Legislature also tried to pass HB 31—which would allow for charter schools to determine their own formulas for how much funding the state local district had to send them. Overall, critics claimed Mississippi schools were underfunded by over $271 million in 2021 and have underfunded MEAP by $3 billion since 2008.[5] The same critics alleged that Mississippi's educational scene was riddled with challenges, including efforts to inject public funds into private schools while exempting those schools from standards, oversight, and accountability: initiatives accompanied by efforts to change funding laws in ways that would result in complete and total legislative deference.

ENDNOTES

[1] Mississippi Constitution, Article 8. Retrieved from: https://ballotpedia.org/Article_VIII,_Mississippi_Constitution

[2] This section borrows heavily from Parents Campaign for Better Schools, "Mississippi Adequate Education Program (MAEP)" (2020). Retrieved from: https://tpcref.org/mississippi-adequate-education-program-maep/

[3] https://www.nationaledfinance.com/docs/22_Jef_47.5_Mississippi.pdf

[4] Ibid. This section also relies on https://msparentscampaign.org/education-funding-2/

[5] https://www.ed.gov/news/press-releases/us-department-education-approves-mississippis-plan-use-american-rescue-plan-funds-support-k-12-schools-and-students-distributes-remaining-543-million-state

[6] This section partly relies on Deborah Verstegen, "A Quick Glance at School Finance: A 50 State Survey of School Finance Policies: Mississippi." (2018). Retrieved from: https://schoolfinancesdav.files.wordpress.com/2018/09/24-mississippi.pdf

[7] https://tpcref.org/wp-content/uploads/MAEP_Explanation_MDE.pdf

CHAPTER 25

MISSOURI

R. Craig Wood
University of Florida

Kai Cui
University of Florida

GENERAL BACKGROUND

Missouri, like every other state, funds public elementary and secondary education with a combination of local, state, and federal revenue sources. AS of FY2021, Missouri funds public elementary and secondary education primarily via 518 school districts. Of this number, seventy are elementary school districts, there are thirty-seven charter schools and three State Board of Education operated programs. The state has one virtual school. For the FY2021, there were approximately 879,845 students attending these schools. The state funds approximately $ 8.53 Billion toward education which represents 24 percent of the state budget. State revenues are from earmarked funds and general revenue funds. In recent years the total share of elementary and secondary education has shifted more to the local school districts given severe statutory and budget restraints placed on the legislature.

Funding Public Schools in the United States, Indian Country,
and US Territories (Second Edition), pages 409–419.
Copyright © 2023 by Information Age Publishing
www.infoagepub.com

The education clause of the Constitution of Missouri states, "A general diffu-
sion of knowledge and intelligence being essential to the preservation of the rights
and liberties of the people, the general assembly shall establish and maintain free
public schools.[1]

BASIC SUPPORT PROGRAM

The state education finance distribution formula consists of four main components as illustrated in Figure 25.1.

Weighted Average Daily Attendance (WADA): The WADA factor measures
attendance in each school district and adjusts state programs in the district is calculated by multiplying the average percentage of students on a particular program
in "Performance Districts" by the district's ADA. If this figure is higher than the
actual number in the district, every student above the adjusted number becomes a
weighted student for funding per student purposes. The total number of weighted
students a district serves is the WADA.[2]

"Weighted average daily attendance," is the average daily attendance plus the
product of twenty-five hundredths multiplied by the free and reduced price lunch
pupil count that exceeds the free and reduced price lunch threshold, plus the produce of seventy-five hundredths multiplied by the number of special education
pupil count that exceeds the special education threshold, plus the product of six-
tenths multiplied by the number of limited English proficiency pupil count that
exceeds the limited English proficiency threshold.

Currently, the finance distribution formula utilizes the following weights:

- FRL weight = .2
- IEP weight = .7
- LEP weight = .60[3]

State Adequacy Target: The WADA is then multiplied by the State Adequacy
Target to reach a projected amount of revenues for each school district. The state
calculates the minimum amount that will be spent on students in all school districts to ensure all students receive an adequate education, as defined by the statute. This factor is limited by a 5 percent cap on growth in state revenue received
by a district. The State Adequacy Target is the baseline amount given to each district per student, and is a measure of the average spending per student in schools
that meet state standards. These districts are identified as "performance districts."

WEIGHTED AV-ERAGE DAILY ATTENDANCE	×	STATE AD-EQUACY TARGET	×	DOLLAR VALUE MODIFIER	−	LOCAL EFFORT	=	STATE FUNDING

FIGURE 25. Missouri Distribution Formula

It is supposed to be recalculated every other year, but due to state budget deficits, the amount has not been recalculated every year.[4]

Dollar Value Modifier: The result of the WADA multiplied by the State Adequacy Target is then adjusted by the Dollar Value Modifier. This factor is a cost of providing educational services in areas of the state that have high costs of living. The factor adjusts for higher expenses (such as prevailing wages or costs of construction) in areas with a high cost of living. The Dollar Value Modifier is calculated in an attempt to account for the value of a dollar in a specific area. Thus, the Dollar Value Modifier increases funding in high cost of living areas. Importantly, all school districts are held constant in that low cost of living areas are not penalized as the legislature does not take moneys away from school districts. The Dollar Value Modifier formula compares the regional wage ratio for the school district, i.e., the average salary in the area, with the state median wage per job. The formula assumes that higher income areas will have proportionally higher costs of living.[5]

Local Effort: The local effort, is then deducted from the product of these collective calculations. That is, school districts with relatively low assessed valuations and resultant low districts' levy, receive more state moneys relative to other school districts. Thus, the lower the assessed value, the greater state aid with all other factors being equal, on a per student weighted basis. For purposes of determining the state contribution to a local school district the measure primarily reflects how much revenue a school district sets as the levy. The local tax revenue is calculated by multiplying the assessed property values by the property tax levy. The state utilizes a performance tax levy of $3.43 per $100 of assessed valuation for calculations of local effort.

Collector and assessor fees are subtracted from the levy to give the total local effort. Therefore, school districts with greater assessed valuations receive less state funding. Other revenue sources also contribute to the total for local effort. Proposition C, is a statewide 1 percent sales tax that is collected and redistributed to school districts based on the Weighted Average Daily Attendance factor, 50 percent of the Proposition C moneys go to school districts and is counted as local effort.[6] Additionally, local revenue comes from the state assessed railroad utility tax.

The bulk of the state portion of funding public elementary and secondary schools comes from general state revenues that are collected by state income taxes and sales taxes. Other state revenue is provided by gaming taxes, lottery proceeds, and other miscellaneous taxes. The local share comes primarily from local tax levy against the taxable assessed valuations of each school district,

It is critical to note that Missouri also utilizes a hold harmless provision that continues to exist wherein school districts are not affected under the current formula. Missouri's funding formula has several provisions built in that curtail a decrease of school district's state funding. For example, the highest WADA calculation from the current and the previous two years is used. This allows for quick increases in state aid, while allowing districts with declining enrollments to remain funded at a higher level from a previous year.

Additionally, barring legislation, the state adequacy target cannot decline. If a recalculation of the target yields a lower number, the target remains constant.

Even in the calculation of local effort, the system is designed to give school districts more state money, not less. By pegging local tax calculations to 2004 assessment levels and by allowing the assessed value to decrease, but not increase, the state has sheltered some districts from funding decreases.

Hold-Harmless School Districts

State aid may exist for a number of school districts under the previous formula. This provision allows school districts to decide if they will be on the current formula or if they will receive funds based on the old formula. Missouri shifted to the new funding formula during the 2006-07 school year. The hold-harmless provision in the new legislation guaranteed that school districts would not receive less state funding under the new formula. School districts can make this determination annually. Each year, approximately one-third of all Missouri school districts are categorized as "hold-harmless."[7]

SPECIAL EDUCATION

Special Education Grant funds are distributed to school districts in order to help alleviate the added costs of educating students with disabilities. These funds were projected to serve approximately 133,964 students with disabilities in FY 2021.

The Special Education High Need Fund provides additional funding to school districts serving high need students with disabilities whose educational costs exceeds three times the district's Current Expenditure per Average Daily Attendance (ADA). It was estimated by the that approximately 3,823 high needs students were to be served by this program in FY 2021.

Students With Severe Disabilities

State Board Operated Programs are schools and programs that are designed to serve students with severe disabilities who cannot be educated within the local school district. Three programs operate in Missouri:

- Missouri School for the Blind
- Missouri School for the Deaf
- Missouri Schools for the Severely Disabled[8]

GENERAL STUDENT TRANSPORTATION

Key Components of the Transportation Calculation include:

- Ridership

- Mileage
- Allowable Cost
- Eligible Cost
- Cost Factor
- Entitlement
- Appropriation Adjustment

Ridership Tracking is the tracking of all regular riders (both eligible and ineligible) from the beginning of the school year to the second Wednesday in October and from the beginning of the second semester to the second Wednesday in February.

Ridership

- Students living more than three and one-half miles from school must be provided transportation service.
- All students can be transported by local board decision[9]
- Funding is available for students who live one mile or more from school.
- No funding is available for students who live less than one mile from school (except when required by an IEP
- Ineligible riders are students who live less than one mile from school or are non-resident students.

Types of Ineligible Ridership

- Less Than One Mile–No Appreciable Cost
- Less Than One Mile—Parent Contract or District Expense
- Less Than One Mile[10]
- Non-Resident Students Transported

Allowable Costs

Allowable costs are costs for transporting students[11] administrative services, and costs paid to other school districts[12]

Eligible Costs

Eligible costs are the costs remaining after the allowable costs have been reduced by the costs associated with ineligible miles.

The cost factor is the efficiency rating in the school district's Calculation for State Transportation Aid used to measure the efficiency of the district's transportation program. The cost factor is calculated by comparing the school district's actual cost per pupil mile to a predicted cost per pupil mile (obtained through a simple curvilinear regression analysis).

Cost Factor (a.k.a. Efficiency Rating)

If the cost factor is 100 percent that means the district's cost per pupil mile equals the predicted cost per pupil mile and is efficient under the transportation formula. A 4 percent variance is built into the formula that allows the district's cost factor to be 104 percent or below and still be considered efficient.

Entitlement

Entitlement is 75 percent of the district's eligible costs after being reduced for inefficiency.

Appropriation Adjustment is a percent applied to the district's entitlement. The percent is calculated by adding all school districts' entitlements together and comparing the total to the appropriation available for payment. The appropriation adjustment changes each month a live payment is made as school districts make changes to the transportation data.

Order of Calculation

- Allowable Cost
- Cost for Eligible Miles
- Cost Adjusted for Ineligible Students Affecting the Calculation
- Cost Adjusted for Inefficiency
- Reimbursable Cost Reduced to 75 percent
- Entitlement Reduced by Appropriation[13]

CAREER AND TECHNICAL EDUCATION

Career Education provides funding for career and technical education. A range of programs and services provide training to assist students gain employment, continue their education, or to retrain in order to gain new industry skills. The state reported that approximately 96 percent of students who completed secondary career education programs in FY 21 were placed in employment, continuing education, or military service. These programs served approximately 179,825 secondary students in FY 21.[14]

SPECIAL LEVIES

School districts can have tax levies higher than the performance tax levy.

Each school district has statutory authority to establish its own tax rate, subject to the electorate. For purposes of state aid, the state funds based on a "performance tax levy" at $3.43 per $100 of assessed valuation, as of December 31, 2004 by 3.43 percent. "If a district's tax levy is lower than the state's performance tax levy, it will actually have less money locally than the estimated figure of the state. … if a district has a tax levy higher than the state's target, it will be able to raise additional funds with no penalty."[15]

CAPITAL OUTLAY

The state of Missouri does not have a capital outlay distribution formula. All expenditures and debt service are the responsibility of the school districts. Per state accounting rules and regulations, school district bond escrow accounts must be shown separately on a school districts' general ledger. Debt Service Funds must be held in a separate bank account. A school district Capital Project Fund must be used to account for all facility acquisition, construction, equipment, lease purchase principal and interest payments and other capital outlay expenditures. The Debt Service Fund is used to account for monies used to retire bond debt.

FOOD SERVICE

As in nearly every state, the largest portion of governmental revenue regarding food service is provided by the federal government under school nutrition services. Several federal programs provide funding to local schools for school breakfast, lunches, milk, and after school snacks. Students from low-income families are provided meals and after school snacks free or at a reduced rate. During FY 2021, on average, approximately 525,000 children per day received school lunch at an average cost of $3.55 per meal. During FY 2021, on average approximately 270,000 children received school breakfast at an average cost of $2.65 per meal.[16]

STATE FUNDING FOR OTHER PUBLIC SCHOOLS

At the time of this writing, the state of Missouri had thirty-six charter schools. Charter schools are free, public schools and are funded in exactly the same manner public school districts in Missouri with certain notable exceptions. The hold-harmless provision under the education finance distribution formula does not apply to charter schools in the state as they all, by definition, fall under the current formula and did not exist under the previous formula. Additionally, in that charter schools have no taxing authority, charter schools may not levy for purposes of capital projects and debt service. Thus, facility costs must be covered from the state and local general aid.

Charter schools may be organized as part of a local school district or as a separate local educational agency. Thus, they may be viewed as a charter school within a school district or viewed, for funding purposes, somewhat like a tractional public-school district.[17] If a charter school were part of a local school district, and does not have LEA status, the funds to the charter school are essentially flow through funds based on the same formula described previously. The charter school attendance and resultant weights are reported within the school district data. Within "...the district formula, local effort [is] subtracted. By not subtracting the local effort here, the district is paying the charter school the entirety of the funds calculated for the charter school by the WADA, adequacy target, and DVM.[18].In this situation, a school district also pays the charter school a portion of funds that exceeded the tax performance levy. A school district which exercises a tax rate above $3.45 must share those funds generated beyond this rate.[19]

If a charter school were granted LEA status, the Missouri Department of Elementary and Secondary Education funds the charter school within the foundation formula. "Additionally, DESE distributes the revenue to the charter school that the incidental and teacher funds raised in excess of the performance tax levy."[20]

OTHER STATE AIDS[21]

The state of Missouri has a number of other state aids for specific needs and purposes including:

- **The School Age Afterschool Program** provides funding to school districts and community -based organizations to improve academic achievement and individual development.
- **The Child Care Development Fund Program** provides funding to start new or expand existing afterschool programs. In FY2021, approximately 2,650 students were enrolled in CCDF programs.
- **21st Century Community Learning Center Program** provides funding for centers offering academic, artistic and cultural enrichment opportunities during non-school hours for students in high poverty areas and low-performing schools. In FY2021 approximately, 23,000 students were enrolled in CCLC programs.
- **The Virtual Schools Program** provides funds for a virtual public school. State funded slots are available for medically fragile students. This program was projected by the state to serve approximately 1,700 students in FY 17.
- **Small Schools Program** provides extra funding in the foundation formula for school districts with aver-age daily attendance of 350 or fewer students.
- **Title I** provides federal funding to schools to implement strategies for raising student achievement in schools with high numbers of children living in poverty who are costlier to educate.

RETIREMENT

The state of Missouri contributes 1.75 percent of teacher salaries toward retirement. Missouri has a five-year vesting period. All certificated employees are required to be a member of the Public School and Education Employee Retirement Systems of Missouri (St. Louis Public Schools and the Kansas City public school districts are under separate systems.) The state of Missouri allows individual school districts to decide whether or not they will offer Social Security coverage to teachers.

The Public Education Employee Retirement System of Missouri (PEERS) is primarily for non-Teacher School Employees. PEERS members participate in the

TABLE 25.1. All K-12 Programs Are Housed Within the Missouri Department of Elementary and Secondary Education Budget. Amounts shown are Appropriated and reflect Gubernatorial vetoes, but not any mid-year restrictions that may have been made[23]

Program	Budget Section	FY21 GR	FY21 Federal	FY21 Other	FY21 Total
Financial and Administrative Operations	2.005	$2,004,180	$2,705,959	$0	$4,710,139
Foundation—Equity Formula	2.015	$2,093,085,310	$0	$1,460,126,575	$3,553,211,885
Foundation—Small Schools Program	2.015	$15,000,000	$0	$0	$15,000,000
Foundation—Transportation	2.015	$21,174,611	$0	$72,773,102	$93,947,713
Foundation—Career Education	2.015	$50,069,028	$0	$0	$50,069,028
Foundation—State Board Operated Programs	2.015	$45,641,706	$7,763,465	$1,876,355	$55,281,526
Virtual Education	2.070	$700,000	$0	$389,778	$1,089,778
Urban Teaching	2.025	$1,700,000	$0	$0	$1,700,000
School Safety	2.065	$300,000	$0	$0	$300,000
K-3 Reading Assessment	2.030	$400,000	$0	$0	$400,000
STEM careers	2.035	$250,000	$0	$0	$250,000
School Nutrition Services	2.020	$3,412,151	$318,031,026	$0	$321,443,177
School Broadband	2.085	$0	$0	$3,000,000	$3,000,000
Missouri Scholars & Fine Arts Academies	2.060	$1	$0	$0	$1
Division of Learning Services	2.090	$4,120,580	$10,578,615	$0	$14,699,195
Adult Learning and Rehabilitation Services	2.090	$0	$34,203,951	$0	$34,203,951
School Age After- school Program	2.100	$0	$21,577,278	$0	$21,577,278
MAP (Missouri Assessment Program) Performance Based Assessment Program	2.105	$9,472,213	$7,800,000	$4,311,255	$21,583,468
Foundation—Career Education	2.015	$50,069,028	$0	$0	$50,069,028
Dyslexia Training Program	2.115	$400,000	$0	$0	$400,000
Title I	2.125	$0	$260,000,000	$0	$260,000,000
Education for Homeless Children	2.130	$0	$1,200,000	$0	$1,200,000
Title II (Improve Teacher Quality)	2.140	$0	$44,000,000	$0	$44,000,000
Title VI, Part B (Federal Rural and Low-Income Schools)	2.145	$0	$3,500,000	$0	$3,500,000
Title III, Part A (Language Acquisition)	2.150	$0	$5,800,000	$0	$5,800,000
Title IV, Part A (Student Support & Academic Enrichment)	2.155	$0	$21,000,000	$0	$21,000,000
Federal Refugee Program	2.120	$0	$300,000	$0	$300,000
Teacher of the Year program	2.165	$0	$40,000	$0	$40,000

TABLE 25.1. Continued

Program	Budget Section	FY21 GR	FY21 Federal	FY21 Other	FY21 Total
Character Education Initiatives	2.161	$1	$0	$0	$1
Adult Education & Literacy	2.185	$5,014,868	$9,999,155	$0	$15,014,023
Special Education Grant	2.200	$0	$244,873,391	$0	$244,873,391
Special Education High Need Fund	2.205	$39,946,351	$0	$19,590,000	$59,536,351
DFS/DMH Placements/Public Placement Fund	2.215	$625,000	$0	$5,000,000	$5,625,000
Readers for the Blind	2.225	$25,000	$0	$0	$25,000
Blind student literacy	2.230	$231,953	$0	$0	$231,953
Missouri Special Olympics Program	2.245	$100,000	$0	$0	$100,000
Missouri Charter Public School Commission	2.255	$0	$500,000	$3,083,085	$3,583,085
Missouri Commission for the Deaf and Hard of Hearing	2.260	$802,975	$0	$304,892	$1,107,867
Missouri Assistive Technology Council	2.275	$0	$787,528	$3,588,384	$4,375,912

Budget Basics: K-12 Education, 2021, Missouri Budget Project.

federal Social Security program, but most PSRS members do not. PSRS members contribute at a higher rate to their retirement system than do PEERS members, and the benefit factors used in retirement benefit calculations are different. PSRS members who participate in Social Security pay into PSRS at two-thirds the normal PSRS contribution rate.[22]

SUMMARY

The state of Missouri reflects a state that has two large urban areas, St. Louis and Kansas City, and numerous small rural communities with numerous school districts varying in size. Additionally, there are small relatively wealthy suburban school districts surrounding these large urban areas. The education finance distribution formula has particular strengths as well as weaknesses. Strengths include funding based on weighted students, cost of living adjustments, and performance targeting. Weaknesses include allowing school districts to essentially determine their own tax rates above certain levels as well as allowing school districts to determine which formula is to their advantage. Additional limitations include guaranteeing state aid based on assessed values of many years ago. An additional weakness is allowing very small school districts to exist which continues to create severe diseconomies of scale which the state continues to fund.

ENDNOTES

1 Mo. Const. art. IX, sec. (a).
2 *Missouri Education Funding Formula and Interactive Maps, School Funding General Overview*, Children's Education Alliance of Missouri.
3 RSMo §163.011.
4 *Missouri Education Funding Formula*, Children's Education Alliance of Missouri.
5 *Id.*
6 *Id.*
7 *A Primer on Missouri's Foundation Formula for K-12 Public Education, 2017 Update*, James. V. Shuls, Show Me Institute Policy Study, No. 10, March 2017.
8 *Budget Basics: K-12 Education, 2021, An Introduction to Missouri's K-12 Education and Funding*, Missouri Budget Project.
9 RSMo §167.231.
10 HB1180
11 RSMo §304.060.
12 5 CSR- 261.040.
13 *How Does the Transportation Calculation Work?* Debra Clink, Manager Student Transportation, Missouri Department of Elementary and Secondary Education, October, 2018.
14 *Budget Basics: K-12 Education, 2021*, Missouri Budget Project.
15 *A Primer on Missouri's Foundation Formula*, James. V. Shuls, Show Me Institute Policy Study.
16 *Budget Basics: K-12 Education, 2021*, Missouri Budget Project.
17 RSMo §160.41.
18 *A Primer on Missouri's Foundation Formula*, James. V. Shuls, Show Me Institute Policy Study.
19 *Id.* at 18.
20 *Id.*
21 *Budget Basics: K-12 Education, 2021*, Missouri Budget Project.
22 PSRS/PEERS Public School & Education Employee Retirement Systems of Missouri, psrs-peers.org.
23 *Budget Basics: K-12 Education, 2021*, Missouri Budget Project.

CHAPTER 26

MONTANA

Lou L. Sabina
Stetson University

Devon Viola
Stetson University

GENERAL BACKGROUND

The state of Montana took a much longer time than average to become a state, serving as a frontier territory until the mining boom of the late 1800s caused many to migrate to the state. The Montana territory was established in 1864, meaning that all governmental control was handled at the federal level, until Montana eventually became the 41st state in 1889.[1]

The first higher education institution established in Montana was known as Rocky Mountain College, a liberal arts/faith-based institution, which enrolled its first set of students in 1878.[2] The two largest and most prominent higher education institutions in Montana, the University of Montana and Montana State University, would be established a few years later. First, as part of the Morrill Land Grant Act of 1862, a large portion of land was set aside to establish higher education in Montana, which formed The Agricultural College of the State of Montana, which would later be known as Montana State University.[3] The University of Montana

Funding Public Schools in the United States, Indian Country,
and US Territories (Second Edition), pages 421–428.
Copyright © 2023 by Information Age Publishing
www.infoagepub.com

TABLE 26.1. State of Montana Population (in 20-year increments)

1870	1890	1910	1930	1950	1970	1990	2010	2021
20,595	142,924	376,053	537,606	591,024	694,409	799,065	989,415	1,104,271

was established two years later, coming from a federal congressional act in 1881 to use 46,000 acres to establish a higher education institution, which formally opened in 1895.[4] Today, there are 23 colleges and universities throughout the state, which include four-year, two-year, and tribal colleges.[5]

Because Montana began as a territory, it is important to note that the K-12 public school system did not begin as a state-controlled school system, but instead was a byproduct of the federal government and the federal system of education.[6] The first public school in Montana was established in 1866 in Virginia City, Montana, with the first public school term taking place from March 5th, 1866 to August 17th, 1866. The establishment of the Common Schools Act would continue to increase public school accessibility throughout the state, with eleven other organized school districts forming within the first year of Virginia City School District's tenure.[7]Due to the rurality and significant distance between major cities in Montana, much smaller school districts would form. As of the 2017-2018 school year, Montana had 429 school districts with 823 schools, of which, 435 were elementary schools, 217 middle schools, and 171 high schools.[8]

The population in Montana has continued to expand and grow around the major metropolitan cities of Billings, Missoula, Great Falls, and Bozeman. Historically, the first recorded population in Montana was 20,595,[9] with the current population estimate as of July 1st, 2021, according to the United States Census Bureau Report of 1,104,271.[10] Table 26.1 outlines the growth of population in Montana from 1870 to the current year.

CURRENT POLITICAL CLIMATE

On November 3rd, 2020, Montana elected Republican governor, Greg Gianforte.[11] This has led to a Republican-controlled Governor, Senate, and House of Representatives for the first time in 16 years. Governor Gianforte has prioritized raising minimum teacher pay to $34,000,[12] increasing opportunities for parents in school choice, and expanding programs through the use of the final American Rescue Plan for Elementary and Secondary School Emergency Relief payment.[13] Raising starting teacher pay is critical to incentivize teachers to remain in Montana and avoid brain drain, and although Montana had the 7th largest increase in average teacher salary between 1999 to 2018[14], Montana remains the lowest state in the country for starting teacher pay.

TABLE 26.2.   Montana General Fund for Schools FY 2016 through FY 2020

	FY 2016	FY 2017	FY 2018	FY 2019	FY 2020
Total General Revenue	$1.073 B	$1.097 B	$1.113 B	$1.134 B	$1.153 B
State Revenue	$685.3 M/63.9%	$703.5 M/64.1%	$739.5 M/66.4%	$775.9 M/68.4%	$787.5 M/68.3%
Local Revenue	$308.4M/28.8%	$313.6M/28.6%	$355.7M/32.0%	$340.8M/30.0%	$348.0 M/30.2%
Other Revenue	$78.9M/7.3%	$80.4M/7.3%	$17.9M/1.6%	17.6M/1.6%	$17.7M/1.5%

SOURCES OF REVENUE

The Montana Department of Public Instruction provided a breakdown of revenue for schools from FY 2016 through FY 2020. This information is provided in Table 26.2 .

State revenue consists of Direct State Aid, funding for Special Education, Guaranteed Tax Base Aid, funding for the American Indian Achievement Gap, Quality Educator funding, funding for at-risk students, Indian Education for All funding, and funding for Data Achievement. Local revenue consists solely from property tax levies. Other revenue includes non-levy revenues such as oil and gas, tuition, gross proceeds from coal, interest earnings, block grants, natural resources development, and fund balance reappropriations.

GENERAL DISTRIBUTION FORMULA
FOR MONTANA PUBLIC EDUCATION

Montana's general fund has a set minimum Base Amount of School Equity (BASE) and a set maximum level. There are three components to the BASE fund.

1. **Basic Entitlement**—this funding is driven by student enrollment. The minimum BASE amount is 80% of the enrollment-based entitlement, of which 44.7% comes from direct state aid[15] and the rest comes from local mills, guaranteed tax base aid, fund balance reappropriated, and non-levy revenue.
2. **Special Education**—this funding is based on special education's allowable costs.
3. **State-Funded Priorities**—this funding includes Quality Educator, At-Risk Student, Indian Education for All, American Indian Achievement Gap, Special Education, and Data for Achievement.[16] [17]

The largest component of BASE funding is determined by the state enrollment. This is the minimum funding each school district receives from the state if in operation. State entitlement differs between elementary schools, middle schools, and high schools. The Fiscal Year 2021 entitlements were as follows:

1. **Elementary K-6 Grades**—$53,541 for the first 250 or fewer pupils, plus an additional $2,678 for each additional 25 pupils over 250

2. **Middle School 7-8 Grades**—The elementary pupil calculation is included, and if the school is accredited, the rate is $107,084 for the first 450 pupils, plus an additional $5,354 for each additional 45 pupils over 450

3. **High School 9-12 Grades**—$321,254 for the first 800 or fewer pupils, plus an additional $16,063 for each additional 80 pupils over 800[18]

Specific funding for the six state-funded priorities for Fiscal Year 2021 is provided in Table 26.3.

TABLE 26.3.   Descriptions and Amounts for State-Funded Priorities

Category	Description	Amount
At-Risk Student	Addresses the needs of at-risk students. Once the legislature allocates an appropriation to the Office of Public Instruction, the appropriation is based on the Title I distributed amount.	Total amount of $5,641,973.
Data for Achievement	A school district receives a payment for each pupil in the district.	$21.41 per pupil.
Indian Education for All	A payment to assist with the implementation of the provisions of the Montana Constitution and the statutory requirements for recognition of American Indian cultural heritage.	$22.36 per pupil or $100 per district, whichever amount is greater.
Quality Educator	Each district and special education cooperative will receive a payment for each full-time equivalent licensed educator and for other licensed professionals employed by the school district, including registered nurses, licensed practical nurses, physical therapists, speech language professionals, psychologists, licensed social workers, counselors, occupational therapists, and nutritionists.	$3,335 per Quality Educator.
Special Education	Special education appropriation is allocated to schools and coops through four distributions. These include the Instructional Block Grant and Related Services Block Grant which are based on current year pupil enrollment, a reimbursement for disproportionate costs, and an additional distribution for special education cooperatives related to travel and administration.	No amount provided.
American Indian Achievement Gap	A payment for each American Indian student enrolled in the district on the fall enrollment count date.	$220.00 per American Indian pupil.

CATEGORICAL FUNDING FOR
MONTANA PUBLIC EDUCATION

Specific and noteworthy examples of categorical funding for Montana over the last 5 years include examples in (1) Special Education Categorical Funding, (2) Transportation Categorical Funding, (3) Technology Categorical Funding, and (4) English Language Learner Categorical Funding.

Special Education Categorical Funding

Based on the 2021 special education child count, approximately 17.5% of students in the K-12 system in Montana qualify for special education services under the Individuals with Disabilities Education Act (IDEA).[19] Special education revenues at the school level include IDEA, Part B Regulations (Assistance for Education of All Children with Disabilities Age 3-22), Children with Disabilities both ongoing and funding provided during the Great Recession and included in the American Recovery and Reinvestment Act (ARRA), Medicaid reimbursement for physical and occupational therapy, mental health services, other miscellaneous reimbursements, and transfers from other school districts or cooperatives.[20]

Funding for state special education includes the instructional block grant, related services block grant, reimbursement for disproportionate costs, and special education cooperatives. Table 26.4 documents historical special education appropriations from FY 2016 through FY 2020.

Transportation Categorical Funding

The transportation fund is used to pay for the costs associated with students getting to school and back from school to home. This includes bus purchases, construction of a bus barn, maintenance, driver salaries and benefits, costs associated with hiring a private contractor to run the transportation program, and transportation reimbursement contracts.[21] Montana also has a separate fund known as the

TABLE 26.4. Montana Special Education Funding Categories and Amounts FY 2016 - 2020

Special Education Category	FY 2016	FY 2017	FY 2018	FY 2019	FY 2020
Instructional Block Grant	$22,518,282	$22,518,282	$22,728,260	$22,728,260	$23,049,500
Related Services Block Grant	$7,506,094	$7,506,094	$7,576,087	$7,576,087	$7,683,100
Disproportionate Costs	$10,722,992	$10,722,992	$10,822,981	$10,822,981	$10,975,857
Special Education Cooperatives	$2,144,598	$2,144,598	$2,164,596	$2,164,596	$2,195,171
Totals	$42,891,966	$42,891,966	$43,291,924	$43,291,924	$43,903,428

Bus Depreciation Fund. This is used to accumulate funds for bus replacement and additional school buses. Revenues must come from non-levy revenues and a non-voted district tax levy which cannot exceed 20% of the original cost of a bus or communication systems and installed safety devices. The amount budgeted over time may not exceed 150% of the original cost.[22]

Two issues are impacting school transportation in the state of Montana. First, school bus drivers are in extremely short supply, which has forced local school districts to change starting times for schools, combine services offered to students to ensure adequate transportation, and increase combination for substitute bus drivers.[23] Second, buses have been required to upgrade their safety devices, as House Bill 267 notes that any school bus with route stops where children need to cross the road must be equipped with extended stop arms that partially obstruct the roadway.[24] The state will generally reimburse 50% of each district's transportation budget.

Technology Categorical Funding

Montana was already a state facing challenges with technology due to the rurality of many locations throughout the state, however, COVID-19 further exacerbated additional needs for technology support, specifically for public education. Montana Senator Jon Tester secured about $850,000 from the American Rescue Act to help 11 schools get better internet access through purchasing modems, routers, laptops, tablets, and Wi-Fi hotspots.[25] The Montana Office of Public Instruction also partnered with PBS during COVID-19 to provide a free Learn at Home Curriculum aligned with Montana State School Standards from 6:30 AM to 5:30 PM from September 8th, 2020 through December 18th, 2020.[26]

Student Services Funding—English Language Learners Funding

As of 2015, Montana was one of four states in the United States that did not provide ELL funding.[27] According to the National Center for Education Statistics, as of Fall 2018, Montana was 48th in the United States with percentage of ELL students, with only 2.4% of the total student population. The Montana Office of Public Instruction has designed their own resources so that ELL's can receive support from instructional personnel, which are readily available on their website.[28]

TEACHER SALARIES

At the time of this publication, Montana remains the lowest paying state in the United States for starting teacher salary at $33,000.[29] In an effort to boost teacher pay, Governor Greg Gianforte signed the TEACH Act, which provides additional funding to school districts in Montana that set the starting teacher pay at a minimum of $34,000, which would increase annually with inflation. Should a district have more than 6,500 students, beginning teachers would have to make 70% of the median teacher salary for the district to receive extra funding.[30] This program is set to go into effect for the 2022-2023 school year.

TABLE 26.5. ESSER Funding Summary for Montana K-12 Public Schools

	ESSER I	ESSER II/HB 630	ESSER III/HB 632	Total
Basic Allocation to School Districts	$37,165,707	$153,089,519	$343,817,312	$534,072,538
Special Education - Related Services	$3,000,000	$0	$0	$3,000,000
Supplemental Allocation to School Districts	$593,402	$3,400,000	$3,400,000	$7,393,402
Allocation to Other Educational Institutions	$30,000	$120,000	$120,000	$270,000
Special Needs Allocation	$0	$2,500,000	$0	$2,500,000
Targeted Support to School Districts	$0	$1,200,000	$0	$1,200,000
Education Leadership in Montana	$0	$939,449	$555,234	$1,494,683
OPI Database Modernization	$0	$8,000,000	$5,475,248	$13,475,248
Administration	$206,476	$850,497	$1,910,096	$2,967,069
State Learning Loss	$0	$0	$19,100,962	$19,100,962
State Summer Enrichment	$0	$0	$3,820,192	$3,820,192
State Afterschool Programs	$0	$0	$3,820,192	$3,820,192
Other	$299,645	$0	$0	$299,645
TOTAL	$41,295,230	$170,099,465	$382,019,236	$593,413,931

FEDERAL COVID-19 FUNDING

As part of the American Rescue Plan Elementary and Secondary School Emergency Relief (ESSER) Act, Montana received federal funds to combat learning loss during the pandemic and to reopen and sustain safe operation of schools.[31] Montana was one of the quicker states in the country to reopen schools, as more than 93% of the schools in the state have less than 500 students, and were able to reopen safely. Table 26.5 provides a funding summary for how the Montana Office of Public Instruction and Montana school districts plan to spend their ESSER funding.

ENDNOTES

[1] This is Montana. Montana Followed Meandering Path to Statehood. https://www.seeleylake.com/story/2016/08/04/news/part-1-of-2-montana-followed-meandering-path-to-statehood/1181.html.

[2] Rocky Mountain College. About RMC. https://www.rocky.edu/about-rmc.

[3] Montana State University. Montana State University: 125 Years of Excellence. https://www.montana.edu/marketing/about-msu/history/.

[4] University of Montana. Celebrate 125. https://www.umt.edu/125/history.php.

[5] Balletopedia. Higher Education in Montana, 1993-2016. https://ballotpedia.org/Higher_education_in_Montana,_1993-2016.

[6] Dale Raymond Tash. The Development of the Montana Common School System, 1864-1884. https://scholarworks.montana.edu/xmlui/bitstream/handle/1/4613/31762100115508.pdf?sequence=1&isAllowed=y.

7   Ibid, 6.

8   Montana Facts and Figures. Education Facts and Statistics. https://montanakids.com/facts_and_figures/education/Education_Facts_and_Statistics.htm#:~:text=For%20the%202017%2D2018%20academic,Altogether%20there%20were%20823%20schools.

9   Population.us. Population of Montana State. https://population.us/mt/.

10   United States Census Bureau. Quick Facts: Montana. https://www.census.gov/quickfacts/MT.

11   Keith Schubert. Gianforte Outlines Priorities in 'Montana Comeback' Speech. https://missoulacurrent.com/government/2021/01/gianforte-outlines-priorities/

12   Colter Anstaett. Governor Signs TEACH Act to Increase Pay for New Teachers in Montana. https://www.krtv.com/news/montana-politics/governor-signs-teach-act-to-increase-pay-for-new-teachers-in-montana.

13   Evelyn Pyburn. Feds Approve Montana's COVID Education Plan and Release $127 Million More to the State. https://www.yellowstonecountynews.com/202108200742/feds-approve-montanas-covid-education-plan-and-release-127-million-more-to-the-state/.

14   Alex Sakariassen. Raising Teacher Salaries. https://montanafreepress.org/2021/01/26/raising-teacher-salaries/.

15   Ibid, 15.

16   Ibid, 15.

17   David C. Thompson, R. Craig Wood, S. Craig Neuenswander, John M. Heim, and Randy D. Watson. Eds. Funding Public Schools in the United States and Indian Country. Information Age Press.

18   Ibid, 15.

19   Open Data Platform. IDEA Section 618 State Level Data Files Part B Child Count. https://data.ed.gov/dataset/idea-section-618-state-level-data-files-part-b-child-count/resources.

20   Kris Wilkinson. Special Education Funding including Special Education Cooperatives. https://leg.mt.gov/content/Publications/fiscal/2021-Interim/Dec-2019/Special-Education-Funding-Including-Cooperatives.pdf.

21   Ibid, 15.

22   Ibid, 15.

23   Jill Van Alstyne. Where Have All the Bus Drivers Gone? https://montanafreepress.org/2021/09/30/school-bus-drivers-in-short-supply-in-montana-and-nationwide/.

24   Hilary Matheson. Kalispell Schools to Buy More Stop Arms for Buses. https://dailyinterlake.com/news/2021/dec/18/kps-buy-additional-stop-arms-bus-fleet/.

25   Steve Fullerton. KLYQ: Montana Internet Speeds May Improve with These Changes. https://www.tester.senate.gov/?p=news&id=8650.

26   MSU News Service. MontanaPBS Programming to Support Students Learning at Home, Educators Return September 8. https://www.montana.edu/news/20316/montanapbs-programming-to-support-students-learning-at-home-educators-returns-sept-8.

27   Maria Millard. State Funding Mechanisms for English Language Learners. https://leg.mt.gov/content/Committees/Interim/2017-2018/Education/Meetings/Jan-2018/ECS%20on%20state%20funding%20for%20ELs.pdf.

28   Montana Office of Public Instruction School Support. Best Practices: Equitably Grading ELs Webinar. https://www.youtube.com/watch?v=193PVXGvF7w.

29   Iris Samuels. Montana Set to Raise Starting Pay for Public School Teachers. https://apnews.com/article/teacher-pay-greg-gianforte-elections-campaigns-montana-200da54cbb5fe4fa834d-2b53a080083a.

30   Ibid, 31.

31   U.S. Department of Education. U.S. Department of Education Approves Montana's Plan for Use of American Rescue Plan Funds to Support K-12 Schools and Students, Distributes Remaining $127 Million to State. https://www.ed.gov/news/press-releases/us-department-education-approves-montanas-plan-use-american-rescue-plan-funds-support-k-12-schools-and-students-distributes-remaining-127-million-state.

CHAPTER 27

NEBRASKA

Joel Applegate
Oberlin Public Schools

Bryce Wilson
Nebraska Department of Education

Kellen J. Adams
Chanute Public Schools and Kansas State University

David C. Thompson
Kansas State University

GENERAL BACKGROUND

Historically, funding for Nebraska's public schools was based on the local property tax. Property taxes were solely established to fund public education under the Common Schools Act, which was passed by the Nebraska Territorial Legislature in 1855. Until the mid-1960s, the general property tax was laid at both local and state levels. Indeed, the entirety of state government was financed primarily through property taxes until 1954 when voters approved a constitutional amendment adopting an income and/or sales tax meant to automatically eliminate the general property tax, although no enabling statutory action was taken. In 1965,

Funding Public Schools in the United States, Indian Country,
and US Territories (Second Edition), pages 429–440.
Copyright © 2023 by Information Age Publishing
www.infoagepub.com
All rights of reproduction in any form reserved.

the legislature developed the first income tax, triggering the 1954 amendment for the first time. As a result, until 1965 the property tax functioned as the principal funding source for all state governmental revenue in Nebraska.

As part of the 1966 statewide general election, opponents of the new income tax law launched a repeal referendum. At the same time, the Nebraska Farm Bureau developed a petition to completely erase property taxes from the state constitution. Voters, leaving the state with no real source of statewide revenue, approved both questions.

The 1967 Nebraska legislature consequently faced real issues. In response, the legislature approved the Nebraska Revenue Act of 1967, which included both sales tax and income tax provisions. The 1967 legislature also established the state's first comprehensive school funding reform law known as the School Foundation and Equalization Act. Three components key to school funding under the new law were:

- *Foundation aid*—Funding based on the number of students in attendance in a school district;
- *Equalization aid*—Funding based on property valuation in such a way meant to equalize funding between school districts with differing levels of property wealth; and
- *Incentive aid*—Funding provided to school districts that chose to offer summer school programs, employed teachers with advanced degrees, or both.

Unfortunately, the state legislature did not fully fund the new school finance plan. The main reluctance was a concern that property tax relief was less than expected. As a result, state aid under the School Foundation and Equalization Act only reached a maximum 13%, with much of the remaining share dependent upon local property taxes.

Not until the1980s did the Nebraska legislature begin to intensively focus on public education and its fiscal support issues. In 1985, the legislature passed Legislative Bill (LB) 662, which required elementary school districts to consolidate with K-12 districts because property owners in elementary districts were paying lower property taxes than K-12 districts, i.e., tax havens. LB 662 also increased sales taxes to generate more funding for schools. However, voters mounted a referendum to reject the new law because it forced school district consolidation. Voters repealed LB 662 during the 1986 referendum, once again leaving school tax issues unresolved until the 1990 legislative session.

In 1990, the Nebraska legislature passed LB 1059. LB 1059 was supported by the Nebraska School Financing Review Commission, which had been created in 1988 to review the state's school finance system. Recommendation from the Commission was that the tax burden on property owners was excessive, with inequities and an unsteady tax base for school districts. The Commission also stated that because of these inequities, there was no assurance that all students had equitable access to needed educational services.

Also in 1990 at the same time the Commission was making its recommendations, a group of landowners filed suit in *Gould v. Orr. Plaintiffs* argued that the funding system for Nebraska schools was inadequate and failed to provide equal educational opportunities because the state lacked a uniform tax system.

The combination of recommendations from the Commission and the lawsuit gave legislative impetus to LB 1059, which eventually replaced the School Foundation and Equalization Act of 1967. LB 1059 also survived a gubernatorial veto and ballot repeal initiative. As such, LB 1059 created inclusive funding reform for Nebraska schools and became known as the Tax Equity and Educational Opportunities Support Act (TEEOSA). TEESOSA had two main purposes: (1) to provide fiscal equity for both taxpayers and schools, and (2) to provide educational opportunities for all students. In the end analysis, LB 1059 sought to move away from reliance on property taxes toward reliance on sales and income taxes to fund K-12 schools. LB 1059 also amended school spending growth rates to a range of about 6.5%.

Another legislative bill introduced in 1990 sought to consolidate school districts. LB 259 addressed the need for school districts to offer all grades. There were three types of school districts in Nebraska at the time: (1) elementary only, (2) high school only, and (3) K-12 districts. LB 259 required elementary-only districts to merge with high school-only or K-12 districts. LB 259 was introduced due to concern that school districts with high schools were paying more property tax than elementary-only districts. From 1990 to 2007, reorganization and consolidation of schools reduced the number of districts from 845 to 271; as of Fiscal Year 2022, the state of Nebraska has only 244 operating school districts.

Although first introduced in 1990, TEEOSA is still the same formula in use today, though it has been slightly modified several times. Many changes made were due to budget constraints, including the stresses brought on by the recession in 2008. The recession reduced state funding by an estimated $189 million (2011-2012) and $222 million (2012-2013). Perennial issues continue to persist, as property tax relief—a concern in the 1960s—is still a top stressor for schools today. Nebraska's school funding profile in 2019 still finds the property tax and other local taxes providing a majority of monies for local school districts. The state's other major revenue sources (income and sales taxes) increasingly continue to be a point of contention, just as it was in the past despite evidence that a broader tax base better equalizes and relieves property tax burdens.

BASIC SUPPORT PROGRAM

Approximately three decades later, TEEOSA still serves as the funding formula for Nebraska's public schools. The main concept underlying TEEOSA is:

$$\text{Needs} - \text{Resources} = \text{Equalization Aid}$$

TEEOSA is structured to provide state aid to school districts in order to help supply the dollar difference between local districts' resource inadequacy and state-approved educational needs. The difference is called 'equalization aid.' Definitionally:

- *Needs*= what it costs a school district to educate students;
- *Resources*= local property taxes and other revenue sources;
- *Equalization Aid* = allocation from the state to offset the difference between needs and resources of a school district.

Local Sources

Nebraska's public school districts derive revenue from local, state and federal sources. Although local property taxes continue to be the largest proportion, many state attempts have been made to reduce reliance on the property tax for schools. In Fiscal Year 2017, approximately $2.1 billion (56%) in school funding came from local sources. Local funding includes residential and business taxes, with total property tax equating to $1.87 billion (89%) of total local funding (FY 2017). Other local revenue includes sales tax, motor vehicle tax, tuition/fees, and transportation. Figure 27.1 illustrates the role of local sources in fiscal resource proportions.

State Sources

The state share of Nebraska's P-12 school fiscal support in FY 2017 was roughly $1.41 billion (37%). State support is seen synonymously with TEEOSA, which is the largest state funding source. Almost $1 billion in state funding was distributed through TEEOSA in FY 2017.

TEEOSA offsets school districts' fiscal resource differences that stem from wealth variations that limit districts' ability to raise sufficient revenue through local taxation. Starting in FY 2018, every school district was entitled to receive some state aid through the formula due to 2016 legislative changes. However, even after recent changes, not all schools receive equalization aid, as only about 35% ultimately are equalization aid-eligible. Figure 27.1 illustrates the role of state sources in fiscal resource proportions.

Federal Sources

Nebraska's school districts participate in federal revenue eligibility through various school district entitlements and other programs. Almost $209 million in federal funds were received in FY 2017. Figure 27.1 illustrates the role of federal sources in fiscal resource proportions.

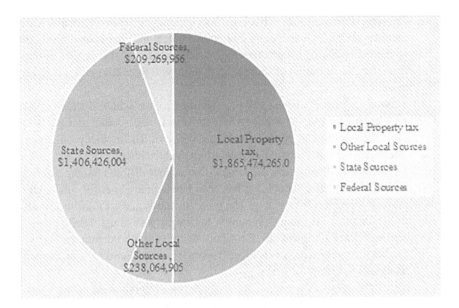

FIGURE 27.1. Federal, State, Local and Other Resource Shares for Nebraska Public Schools FY 2017. Source: Nebraska Department of Education. School Finance and Organizational Services, 2016/17.Statewide Annual Financial Report. (NDE, 2017).

TEEOSA Structure and Operation

Nebraska's state school aid formula known as TEEOSA is a complicated plan. Most revenue flows through TEEOSA in the form of equalization aid. The formula uses a four step process to establish the needs of school districts on dimensions of determining needs, calculating available resources, determining equalization aid, and adjusting for additional items to finally determine total state aid.

Step 1: Determining Needs

The first step in TEEOSA is to determine the needs of each school district. Needs are defined as the approved costs to educate students in a district. Calculation of needs includes 17 components. The largest component is basic funding (83% of total need). Basic funding is determined by creating a comparison group of school districts. Comparison groups are comprised of 10 schools larger and 10 schools smaller as measured by student count. These groups are used to help equalize spending among differently sized districts.

Components making up the needs calculations are as follows:

- *Basic Funding*—the major piece of TEEOSA's formula needs definition. Equalized spending is averaged using 10 schools larger and 10 schools smaller by student count;

- *Poverty Allowance*—for school districts completing a poverty plan which includes activities, curriculum and goals to meet the educational needs of students in poverty. Money received is calculated so that a district having a greater concentration of students in poverty will receive more funding up to a limit;

- *Limited English Proficiency (LEP) Allowance*—for school districts completing an LEP plan of activities which includes curriculum and goals to meet the educational needs of students with limited English proficiency. The district is funded based on a per-student calculation;

- *Focus School & Program Allowance*—for school districts having a focus school, defined as a school that has been labeled for a specific curriculum purpose—i.e., low performing. The program allowance is for those schools designated in a Learning Community for the purpose of a diversity plan;

- *Summer School Allowance*—for school districts that hold summer school for at least three hours per day for 12 summer weeks. Funding is calculated using a per-student factor;

- *Special Receipt Allowances*—the second largest component of the needs calculation. It includes special education, state wards, and accelerated or differentiated curriculum programs;

- *Transportation Allowance*—a district's amount is determined by the lesser dollar of two calculations on actual prior year transportation expenditures or route miles traveled. It is calculated as four times the state mileage rate;

- *Elementary Site Allowance*—for school districts having more than one elementary attendance center more than seven miles apart. It can also be a city or village having only one elementary school;

- *Distance Education & Telecommunications Allowance*—based on actual expenditures, the allowance is determined by transmission costs to provide distance learning classes;

- *System Averaging Adjustment*—for school districts with enrollments greater than 900 formula students that levy more than $1.00 per $100 of property tax valuation and whose basic funding per formula student is less than the average of all districts having enrollments greater than 900 formula students;

- *New School Adjustment*—for districts having constructed a new school building because of increasing enrollment. The amount of need calculated for this funding is based on the district's basic funding per formula student;

- *Student Growth Adjustment*—school districts with increased enrollment can apply and receive an amount based on the K-12 estimated year-end student count and the district's basic funding per formula student;

- *Community Achievement Plan Adjustment*—this adjustment applies to schools in the Learning Community that achieve standards based on written improvement plans;

- *Limited English Proficiency Allowance Correction*—a school district may receive a reduction to its needs based on actual expenditures and based on not meeting the requirements of its written plan;
- *Poverty Allowance Correction*—a school district may receive a reduction to its needs based on actual expenditures and having not met the requirements of its written plan;
- *Student Growth Adjustment Correction*—a school district will receive an increase in need if student growth is higher than the estimated student growth. Inversely, a decrease in need will follow if actual growth is lower than estimated student growth.

Step 2: Calculating Resources

The second step in TEEOSA is calculating resources by determining how much funding a school district has to fund its needs. There are four components to calculating resources:

- *Local effort rate*—the largest component. It is a hypothetical property tax rate that estimates how much funding a school district could raise locally. The local effort rate for 2016/17 was $1.00 per $100;
- *Allocated Income Tax*—a share of income taxes paid by taxpayers in the school district which is given back to districts;
- *Other Revenues*—includes interest earned on investments and tuition collected from other districts;
- *Net Option Funding*—applies when a school district receives funding for students who transfer to a school district from a home school district, meaning the net of more students optioning into the district than optioning out.

Step 3: Determining Equalization Aid

The third step in TEEOSA is determining state aid for equalization purposes. Equalization provides funding necessary to educate a student when a school district cannot generate enough local funding. "In 1990/91, nearly 90% of the state's K-12 schools (250 of 278) received equalization aid. About 31% of the state's school districts (75 of 245) received equalization aid in 2016/2017." The formula expressed earlier in text box is operational in Step 3.

Step 4: Additional Items in Determining Total State Aid

The last step in TEEOSA finds some components of resources (net option funding [10%], allocated income tax [4%], and other state aid [1%]) added back into the funding of equalization aid to determine total state aid to school districts. Table 27.1 illustrates the basic formula for calculating state aid, where:

Equalization Aid (85%) + Additional Components = Total State Aid

TABLE 27.1. TEEOSA Structure and Operation

Step 1	Step 2	Step 3	Step 4	Final Determination
Needs	- Resources	= Equalization aid	+ Additional items	= Total State Aid
Basic Funding (83%)	Local Effort Rate (79%)		Net Option Funding	
Special Receipts Allowance (6%)	Other Actual Receipts (16%)		Learning Community Transition Aid	
Poverty Allowance (4%)	Net Option Funding (3%)		Allocated Income Tax	
LEP Allowance (2%)	Allocated Income Tax		Community Achievement Plan Aid	
Transportation Allowance (2%)	Learning Community Transition Aid		Prior Year State Aid Correction	
Focus School & Program Allowance	Community Achievement Plan Aid			
Summer School Allowance				
Elementary Site Allowance				
Distance Education Adjustment				
Averaging Adjustment				
New School Adjustment				
Student Growth Adjustment				
Student Growth Adjustment Correction				
Community Achievement Plan Adjustment				
Poverty Allowance Adjustment				
LEP Allowance Adjustment				
Non-Qualified LEP Adjustment				

Source: Nebraska Department of Education (NDE), "Tax Equity and Educational Opportunities Support Act (TEEOSA) Certification of 2017/18 State" (Lincoln: NDE, 2017).

Table 27.2 provides a summary of system-calculated outcomes of TEEOSA, so that total contributions are revealed and detailed.

Other Provisions Affecting TEEOSA

In 1990, the Finance Review Commission believed that limits to school district budget growth were important to the new funding system. A major concern for the Commission was to ensure that a part of new state aid monies would be used to keep local property taxes low, rather than simply being added to the budget. In 1996, a property tax levy limit was added by the state legislature. This levy

TABLE 27.2. Nebraska 2018/19 State Aid Calculated by System

Formula Needs	$3,535,590,990
Yield from Local Effort Rate	$2,517,496,035
Net Option Funding	$102,541,643
Income Tax Rebate	$42,333,888
Other Receipts	$504,003,571
Community Achievement Plan	$6,197,049
Total Resources	$3,172,538,781
Equalization Aid	$848,435,395
Transition Aid	$906,222
Total State Aid Calculated	$1,000,414,197

Condensed from 2018/19 State Aid Certification (March 1, 2018). https://cdn.education.ne.gov/wp-content/uploads/2018/02/1819SA_SACalc-TEEOSA_A1.pdf

limitation placed a ceiling on the property tax rate that may be assessed against the taxable valuation of school districts (i.e., the same levy limit identified earlier as $1.05 for each $100 of property value). An example of the impact is provided in text box.

(Assessed Valuation)	X	(Property Tax Levy)	(divided by $100)	=	Property Tax Request
$ 800,000,000		$1.05	$ 840,000,000		$8,400,000

Source: Nebraska Department of Education School Finance and Organization. 2018/19 Budget Text for Nebraska Public School Districts. p. 17.

The net result was that school districts must keep within the taxing levy limit and spending limit (budget authority) when developing a budget.

Described next are three methods by which the state of Nebraska calculates school district budget authority: (1) the budget-based method; (2) the formula needs method; and (3) the student growth method. All three methods are calculated, with districts granted the greatest of the three results. Budget authority only applies to the General Fund.

Budget Based Calculation Method

The Budget Based Calculation uses information from the 2017/18 LC-2 (Lid Computation Form). The steps in the 2018/19 Budget Based Calculation are detailed below:

$$(GFBE - SGF - SPED - GFLE) \times 1.025$$

Step 1: The 2017/18 Total General Fund Budget of Disbursements and Transfers (GFBE) is reduced by 2017/18 Special Grant Funds (SGF), 2017/18 Special Education Budget of Disbursements and Transfers (SPED), and 2017/18 General Fund Lid Exclusions (GFLE). This calculation represents the adjusted general fund budget of expenditures on Line B-140 of the LC-2.

Step 2: The adjusted general fund expenditures from Step 1 are grown by the Basic Allowable Growth Rate of 2.5%.

Student Growth Adjustment Method

The Student Growth Adjustment calculation uses information from the 2017/18 Lid Computation Form (LC-2), the 2018/19 Student Growth Adjustment, and the 2018/19 Student Growth Correction from the 2017/18 State Aid Certification. The steps in the 2018/19 Student Growth Adjustment Calculation are as follows:

$$((GFBE - SGF - SPED - GFLE) + (SGA +/- SGACORR))$$

Step 1: The 2017/18 Total General Fund Budget of Disbursements and Transfers (GFBE) is reduced by 2017/18 Special Grant Funds (SGF), the 2017/18 Special Education Budget of Disbursements and Transfers (SPED), and the 2017/18 General Fund Lid Exclusions(GFLE). This calculation represents the adjusted general fund budget of expenditures on Line B-140 of the LC-2.

Step 2: The 2018/19 Student Growth Adjustment (SGA) is adjusted by the 2017/18 Student Growth Correction from the 2018/19 State Aid Certification is added/subtracted to the Adjusted General Fund Expenditures calculated in Step 1.

Formula Needs Based Calculation Method

The Formula Needs Based Calculation uses information from the 2018/19 State Aid Certification (TEEOSA Need) and the 2017/18 LC2. The steps in the 2018/19 Formula Needs Based Calculation are as follows:

$$((FN X 1.10)—(SPED X 1.025))$$

Step 1: The 2018/19 Formula Needs (FN) of the school district are increased by 110%.

Step 2: The increased 2018/19 Formula Needs are then reduced by the 2017/18 Special Education Budget of Disbursements and Transfers (SPED) that has been grown by the Basic Allowable Growth Rate (BAGR) of 2.5%.

OTHER STATE AID PROGRAMS

TEEOSA was designed to be comprehensive and consequently includes programs otherwise regarded as categorical in many states. Selected state aid programs are highlighted in the following headings—refer to Table 29.1 earlier for scope and detail of general financing involving typical categorical supports.

Special Education

Special education funding in Nebraska receives its largest dollar proportion from the federal government. In 2016-2017, the state received $67 million in federal revenue through the Individuals with Disabilities Education Act (IDEA) grants. IDEA directs how states provide services to children with disabilities.[1] Currently, the state of Nebraska provides $212 million in special education revenue. Federal funds for special education are passed through at the 100% level of allowed cost, while state funds for special education are reimbursed at the 50% level of allowed cost.[2]

Other Funds

The state of Nebraska maintains many funds that exceed the scope of this chapter. Consequently, selected funds are identified and briefly discussed here.

Depreciation Fund

A major fund used by Nebraska school districts is known as the Depreciation Fund. The Depreciation Fund was established to reserve monies for eventual capital outlay uses. Such monies are reserved and come from each school district's General Fund. Under these circumstances, a school district will show monies as an expense to the district's General Fund via transfer to the district's Depreciation Fund. The purpose is to spread costs for potential capital outlay projects over many years in order to avoid a disproportionate tax effort in a single year to pay for these projects.[3]

Activities Fund

The Activities Fund is widely used by Nebraska school districts for operations of quasi-independent student organizations, inter-school athletics, and other self-supporting or partially self-supporting school activities. Failing to have this account within the district's General Fund would misrepresent the financial position of school operations and would complicate adding of net expenses received or incurred by conducting school services. Under Nebraska law, the impact is important—if negative balances are incurred in the Activities Fund, the school district's General Fund must cover the deficit by transferring district funds to the Activities Fund.

Special Building Fund

A Special Building Fund is available for establishment in every Nebraska school district for the purpose of making improvements to capital assets. Examples of uses for the Special Building Fund include acquiring or improving sites and/or erecting, altering or improving school facilities. The tax levy for this fund is set at a maximum .014¢ per $100 assessed valuation.[4] Monies collected for construction and/or related costs and all other income associated with this fund must be accounted for through this fund structure. Importantly, general fund monies cannot be used for the purposes of this fund.

SUMMARY

In the long view, Nebraska has been struggling with reliance on property taxes to fund public schools since 1855—i.e., it is an issue as old as Nebraska's territorial legislation.[5] Throughout the 1960s, 1980s, 1990s and extending to today, heavy reliance on local property taxes to fund the state's public schools is still an unresolved issue. Significantly, Nebraska's school funding formula continues to rely heavily on local sources of revenue. Also significantly, Nebraska ranks 48th nationally in fiscal support for public schools.[6]

ENDNOTES

[1] Nebraska Department of Education. Rule 51: Regulations and Standards for Special Education programs. January 1, 2017 (Revised).

[2] Nebraska Department of Education. School Finance and Organizational Services. Retrieved from: www.education.ne.gov/fos/special-education-reporting-information/ (accessed January 26, 2018).

[3] Nebraska Department of Education. Program Budgeting, Accounting, and Reporting System for Nebraska School Districts: 2016 User's Manual (2016).

[4] Ibid.

[5] Ibid, Bergquist, p. 18.

[6] U.S. Census Bureau, Public Elementary-Secondary Education Finance Data (2016).

CHAPTER 28

NEVADA

Jacob D. Skousen
University of Nevada, Las Vegas

R. Karlene McCormick-Lee
University of Nevada, Las Vegas

GENERAL BACKGROUND[1]

The state of Nevada has 17 school districts and approximately 60 charter schools.[2] Of the 17 school districts, the Nevada Department of Education classifies 15 as rural school districts. The total number of students in K-12 public education in Nevada is approximately 487,000.[3] The student population has grown significantly over the last few decades. Since the 2006-2007 school year there has been an almost 15% growth in the student population.[4] Two school districts, Clark County School District and Washoe County School District, account for nearly 400,000 or 82% of the students in the state of Nevada. Additionally, the student population in Nevada has become more diverse. Of the student population the largest ethnic/racial group is Hispanic/Latino. The ethnic/racial student information for public schools in Nevada can be found in Figure 28.1.

In Table 28.1, the student ethnic/racial student information is differentiated by school district and ranked from the school district with the highest number of students to the school district with the lowest number of students.

Funding Public Schools in the United States, Indian Country,
and US Territories (Second Edition), pages 441–453.
Copyright © 2023 by Information Age Publishing
www.infoagepub.com
All rights of reproduction in any form reserved.

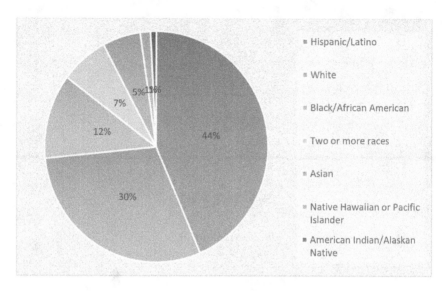

FIGURE 28.1.   Nevada Student Ethnic/Racial Percentages 2020-2021 School Year
Source: State of Nevada Department of Education, accessed September 1, 2021,
http://nevadareportcard.nv.gov/di/.

In the state of Nevada, a little over 72% of the students live in poverty, 12.5% receive special education services, and approximately 13% are identified as English language learners.[5]

Similar to all states in the United States, Nevada's State Constitution requires the state legislature to "…provide for a uniform system of common schools."[6] Since 1865 Nevada has had a system of public education.[7] While the demographics, enrollment numbers, and challenges of the Nevada educational system have changed over the years, the way the legislature has funded public schools remained under the same plan for a many decades.[8] For more than a half century, from 1967 to 2019, the state of Nevada utilized what was called the "Nevada Plan" for funding Nevada's schools.[9] School finance scholars have agreed that while the Nevada Plan had attempted to address the structural and fiscal differences across and within rural and urban local education agencies (LEAs), it was inadequate in addressing the unique needs of rapid growth and changing student population. In attempts to account for changes in federal guidelines and the drastic changes in the student population in Nevada's schools since 1967 when the Nevada Plan was adopted, the legislature instituted more than 80 different categorical grants and funding streams.[10]

In 2019, during the 80th biennial session of Nevada's Legislative Session, SB 543 was passed to create an 11-member Commission on School Funding to guide the work with the Nevada Department of Education to replace the 50-year-old

TABLE 28.1.   Nevada Student Ethnic/Racial Information 2020-2021 School Year

District Name	Total Students	Asian	Black	White	Hispanic	American Indian/ Alaska Native	Two or More	Pacific Islander
Clark County	319293	19077	49089	70995	150887	1101	22929	5215
Washoe County	64988	2911	1677	27550	27136	806	4017	891
Elko*	9609	67	82	5340	3268	582	237	33
Lyon*	8823	93	74	5410	2382	308	497	59
Carson City*	7836	138	54	3608	3467	173	374	22
Douglas*	5400	72	23	3543	1270	171	307	14
Nye*	5394	62	188	3008	1655	68	357	56
Humboldt*	3306	14	16	1813	1212	144	105	2
Churchill*	3247	53	56	1923	787	178	223	27
White Pine*	1228	3	13	864	232	45	69	2
Lander*	1027	6	3	607	341	34	35	1
Lincoln*	886	4	29	716	94	7	26	10
Pershing*	656	3	9	306	226	55	56	1
Mineral*	572	3	12	330	111	76	38	2
Storey*	448	4	5	371	47	2	18	1
Eureka*	324	0	0	251	42	14	16	1
Esmeralda*	101	0	1	52	36	6	6	0

* Indicates rural school district.
Source: State of Nevada Department of Education, accessed September 1, 2021, http://nevadareportcard.nv.gov/di/.

school funding formula.[11] While the commission had many responsibilities, its central charge was to provide recommendations to improve a pupil-centered funding formula, guide the implementation of the "Pupil-Centered Funding Plan," and define and identify revenue for optimal funding of Nevada education.[12] The results of the work of the Commission on School Funding are reported in the "Distribution Formula" section. The total allocation to the 17 school districts in Nevada during fiscal year (FY) 2021 was nearly $1.5 billion. Table 28.2 illustrates the total school district legislative allocation for FY 2021 with the percentage of the overall allocations.

The total budget for FY 2021 for K-12 education in Nevada was approximately $2.4 billion.

CURRENT POLITICAL CLIMATE

The state of Nevada has historically been known for a conservative republican political climate. Nevada's current governor and the majority in both legislative

TABLE 28.2. Nevada School District Allocations FY 2021

District Name	Total Students	Total Allocation	Per Pupil	Percentage of the Overall Allocation
Clark County	319,293	$949,035,464	$2,972	69.14%
Washoe County	64,988	$186,043,556	$2,863	13.55%
Elko*	9,609	$39,261,128	$4,086	2.86%
Lyon*	8,823	$58,589,262	$6,641	4.27%
Carson City*	7,836	$30,288,290	$3,865	2.21%
Douglas*	5,400	$16,958,789	$3,141	1.24%
Nye*	5,394	$30,658,549	$5,684	2.23%
Humboldt*	3,306	$12,010,227	$3,633	0.88%
Churchill*	3,247	$17,242,875	$5,310	1.26%
White Pine*	1,228	$7,125,493	$5,803	0.52%
Lander*	1,027	$982,359	$957	0.07%
Lincoln*	886	$10,654,388	$12,025	0.78%
Pershing*	656	$6,127,994	$9,341	0.45%
Mineral*	572	$5,083,297	$8,887	0.37%
Storey*	448	$726,971	$1,623	0.05%
Eureka*	324	$484,330	$1,495	0.04%
Esmeralda*	101	$1,288,846	$12,761	0.09%

* Indicates rural school district.
Source: State of Nevada Department of Education, accessed September 1, 2021, https://doe.nv.gov/StudentInvestmentDivision/Home/.

bodies, the Nevada State Assembly and the Nevada State Senate, are members of the Democratic party.[13] The current presence of political party affiliation in the governor's office and both legislative bodies has not always had been the case. This specific makeup of the state legislative bodies has been in place in the last few years.

The Nevada Legislature is one of only four US states to have biennial sessions and has regular sessions in odd-numbered years;[14] nevertheless, special legislative sessions have been called and most recently, two special sessions were called in 2020. It is notable to that the two special sessions were convened to address the fiscal circumstances due to the global pandemic, COVID-19.

There are two primary teacher associations in Nevada, 1) Nevada State Education Association, which is affiliated with the National Education Association, and 2) Clark County Education Association, which is "the largest education union in Nevada."[15] Both associations have been involved in legislation related to schools, especially school funding, school policy, and litigation.

Most notable in Nevada finance litigation is the lawsuit that was filed before the 2021 legislative session regarding inadequate funding. With the backing of Educate Nevada Now, an educational advocacy organization in Nevada, nine parents are the plaintiffs in the case, naming the state of Nevada, the Nevada Department of Education, State Superintendent of Public Instruction, and the Nevada State Board of Education as defendants.[16] Similar to other lawsuits in other states, the plaintiffs allege violation of the Nevada Constitution citing inadequate funding has led to the lack of "a basic right to a sufficient education."[17]

REVENUE SOURCES

The public education system in Nevada receives revenue from 12 sources.[18] Nearly 90% of the revenue comes from three sources: 1) Local School Support Tax, a 2.6% retail sales tax in the state and is the largest revenue source that is approximately 39%; 2) General fund, a revenue source making up approximately 32% of the revenue and is made up of many monies but largely comes from sales tax; and 3) Property tax, contributes 18% to the total revenue.[19] The other nine funding sources that provide the approximate 10% of the public education system funding in Nevada include the retail marijuana tax, the annual slot machine tax, the interest collected on the State Permanent School Fund, and a few other fees and proceeds.

Funding for P-12 education in Nevada has increased over the last decade. While the impact of the economic downturn in the late 2000s had lasting effects on public school funding in Nevada, the general trend for the last decade is an increase in funding. According to the legislatively approved budgets in Nevada, the Nevada Department of Education (NDE) funding during FY 2010 was approximately $1.6 billion and in FY 2019 NDE funding was nearly $2.4 billion.[20] It should also be noted that during FYs 2012, 2013, 2014, and 2015 NDE funding was nearly the same.

DISTRIBUTION FORMULA

After using the same funding formula for more than a half century, "The Nevada Plan," in 2019 the Nevada Legislature changed to the "Pupil-Centered Funding Plan" during the 80th biennial session. The education funding formula changed to provide equity within Nevada's complex system of schools, adjusting for the costs of providing education in urban and rural schools and in large and small school districts. This change to Nevada's funding formula reinforced equity and transparency by identified and allocated funding based on the cost of educating different students with different learning needs. This section will include a discussion of the 11-Member Commission that was charged with working with the Nevada Department of Education to recommend a replacement of the Nevada Plan, an outline the Pupil-Centered Funding Formula, a discussion about the regular education and other categorical programs, and charter school funding.

Nevada Senate Bill 543 established the creation of an 11-member Commission on School Funding to work with and guide the Nevada Department of education to overhaul the K-12 funding formula.[21] The commission was made up Senate representatives, individuals with school finance expertise, and the chief financial officers from four of the 17 school districts in Nevada. The six key responsibilities that the commission had related to the funding formula included: 1) Provide guidance on the implementation of the Pupil-Centered Funding Plan; 2) Review the per pupil funding amounts and the multiplier for weighted funding for each category of students; 3) Make recommendations to improve efficiency and effectiveness of public education; 4) Make Recommendations related to the Pupil-Centered Plan's equity and cost adjustment factors; 5) Provide ongoing recommendations for revisions as the state legislature approves the budge and the Nevada Department of Education provides reports of personnel and services; 6) Review the per pupil funding amounts and recommend revisions to create an optimal level of funding for public schools in Nevada.

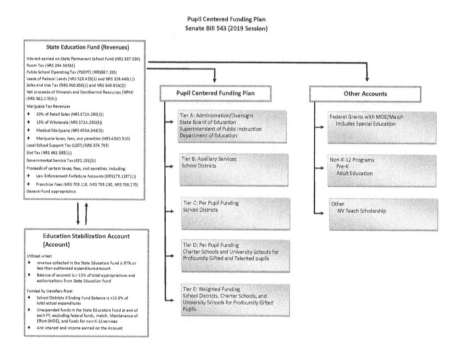

FIGURE 28.2: Nevada Pupil-Centered Funding Plan Chart.
Source: State of Nevada Department of Education, accessed September 1, 2021, https://doe.nv.gov/uploadedFiles/ndedoenvgov/content/Boards_Commissions_Councils/Commission_on_School_Funding/FinalPupil-CenteredFundingPlanSummary-Document2021.pdf.

The Nevada Pupil-Centered Funding Plan was designed to provide all students with a sufficient level of resources and to provide additional supports for students who need them. The funding formula is outlined in tiers. The Nevada Pupil-Centered Funding Plan Chart is provided in Figure 28.2.

Tier A "State Administration" consists of funding that is allocated to administration support of education programs. "School Operations," Tier B includes allocated funds for school districts' axillary services, including food services and transportation. Tiers C and D provide the "Per-Pupil Base Funding" that is guaranteed to all students regardless of the public school where the student attends. Tiers C and D also include an equity-based distribution of estimated attendance, zone enrollment, cost of living, labor, and geography. Finally, the "Weighted Funding" in Tier E provide weighted funding adjusted per-pupil for students identified as English language learners, at-risk, or gifted and talented. Nevada also made a noteworthy update to the definition of "at-risk" students that moves beyond students receiving free-or-reduced price lunch to a broader set of social and academic factors that could hinder student learning and graduation.

While the Nevada Legislature has made a recent overhaul to the school funding formula, Nevada remains one of the states with the lowest per pupil spending in the US. In fact, in a recent report Nevada ranked as 47th in per pupil spending when compared to the 50 US states.[22] The per pupil spending in the 17 school districts in Nevada are shown in Table 28.3.

CATEGORICAL FUNDING

Special Education

The Pupil-Centered Funding Plan removed special education from the weighted funding and provided this funding in a separate account. The Commission made this recommendation to allow school districts and schools to provide appropriate special education services to students according to the individualized education plans developed for each student and adherence to federal requirements for maintenance of effort. The total legislative allocation for special education in FY 2020 was $198,303,871.[23] The special education legislative appropriations for FY 2020 are provided in Table 28.4.

Transportation

It is important to understand the unique context of Nevada and its schools to understand the expenditures related to transportation. Nevada spans over 110,000 square miles and the school districts are representative in each of Nevada's 17 counties. Table 28.5 illustrates each school district and the total area of the county and the number of schools in the school district.

The average area of a school district in Nevada is 6,500 square miles, nearly six times the size of the state of Rhode Island. The combined transportation expenses during FY 2020 for school districts and charter schools in Nevada were

TABLE 28.3.   Nevada School District Per Pupil Spending FY 2020

District Name	Total Students	Total Per Pupil Spending
Clark County	319293	$9,571.73
Washoe County	64988	$9,652.62
Elko*	9609	$11,528.82
Lyon*	8823	$10,830.46
Carson City*	7836	$11,100.55
Douglas*	5400	$11,066.63
Nye*	5394	$12,096.37
Humboldt*	3306	$12,929.22
Churchill*	3247	$10,960.33
White Pine*	1228	$13,531.43
Lander*	1027	$12,708.84
Lincoln*	886	$17,387.33
Pershing*	656	$16,238.00
Mineral*	572	$16,416.10
Storey*	448	$16,653.51
Eureka*	324	$28,480.58
Esmeralda*	101	$36,914.72

* Indicates rural school district.
Source: State of Nevada Department of Education, accessed September 1, 2021, http://
nevadareportcard.nv.gov/di/.

TABLE 28.4.   Nevada Special Education Legislative Appropriations FY 2020

District Name	Total Special Education Allocation	Percentage of the Total Special Education Allocation
Clark County	$136,675,472	68.92%
Washoe County	$31,980,238	16.13%
Elko*	$4,757,225	2.40%
Lyon*	$4,012,938	2.02%
Carson City*	$4,434,258	2.24%
Douglas*	$3,791,120	1.91%
Nye*	$3,274,444	1.65%
Humboldt*	$1,853,448	0.93%
Churchill*	$2,545,194	1.28%
White Pine*	$1,136,219	0.57%
Lander*	$675,431	0.34%
Lincoln*	$1,083,409	0.55%
Pershing*	$849,384	0.43%
Mineral*	$468,555	0.24%
Storey*	$450,087	0.23%
Eureka*	$260,111	0.13%
Esmeralda*	$56,338	0.03%

* Indicates rural school district.
Source: State of Nevada Department of Education, accessed September 1, 2021, http://
nevadareportcard.nv.gov/di/.

TABLE 28.5.   Nevada School Districts, the Total Area, and Number of Schools

District Name	Total Area (In square miles)	Number of Schools
Carson City*	168	10
Churchill*	5,023	5
Clark	8,061	374
Douglas*	738	12
Elko*	17,203	19
Esmeralda*	3,589	3
Eureka*	4,180	3
Humboldt*	9,658	9
Lander*	5,519	6
Lincoln*	10,637	9
Lyon*	2,016	18
Mineral*	3,813	4
Nye*	18,159	13
Pershing*	6,068	4
Storey*	264	4
Washoe	6,542	89
White Pine*	8,897	11

* Indicates rural school district.

over $116 million. The transportation expenses during FY 2020 provided by the state special education fund were almost $80 million.[24] The total transportation expenditures for all school districts, charter schools, and special education during FYI 2020 were nearly $196 million.[25]

Technology

The Pupil Centered Funding Plan includes of funding for school technology. Additional funds, $50 million, were allocated from the Coronavirus Relief Funding during the 31st Special Session of the Nevada Legislature for internet connectivity to pupils.[26] These additional funds that were provided to school districts and charter schools are discussed in a subsequent section titled "Federal COVID-19 Funding."[27]

Career and Technical Education

During the 80th Nevada Legislative Session, the legislature authorized over $12.5 million for Career and Technical Education.[28] During the last few years this funding amount has changed very little and the requirement that 30% of the

TABLE 28.6. Nevada Fringe Benefit Rates FY 2020

Retirement	25.88%
Workers' Compensation	5.24%
Unemployment Compensation	1.45%
Medicare	1.54%
FICA	4.38%

Source: State of Nevada Department of Education, accessed September 10, 2021, https://doe.nv.gov/StudentInvestmentDivision/Home/.

funds must be distributed through competitive awards to school districts or charters schools also remains unchanged.

Textbooks and Classroom Supplies

The Pupil Centered Funding Plan is inclusive of funding textbooks and classroom supplies. Additional funds, $50 million, were allocated from the Coronavirus Relief Funding during the 31st Special Session of the Nevada Legislature to provide school districts and charter schools additional teaching resources and supplies.[29]

EMPLOYEE BENEFITS

There were 46,996 statewide school district employees who were eligible for health insurance and fringe benefits during FY 2020. The annual premium per employee was $6,699. Additionally, the rates related to fringe benefits, excluding health insurance paid by the school districts during fiscal year 2020 are found in the Table 28.6.

CHARTER SCHOOL FUNDING

Charter schools in Nevada are funded by the Nevada State Legislature. Approximately 49,000 students across Nevada attend charter schools.[30] Charter school student enrollment has trended in increasing enrollment for more than a decade and is projected to increase in the next FY, as there are an additional 10 charter school campuses to be added to the nearly 60 current charter schools currently being operated in Nevada.[31] Charter school funding was nearly $500 million in FY 2020 with the per pupil expenditure for charter schools being $7,305.98.

NONPUBLIC SCHOOL FUNDING

There are 19,427 students who attend private schools in Nevada.[32] While the Nevada Department of Education website has the following statement, "Private schools are not funded by the state" (para 1), there are some instances in which certain personnel in the local education agency (LEA) funded by public school monies are required to provide a service to private schools. For example, the federal Individuals with Disabilities Education (IDEA) Act requires public school districts to consult with private school personal regarding the identification and potentially providing services for students.[33]

DISTANCE EDUCATION

The growth of distance education has grown significantly in Nevada since the COVID-19 pandemic halted in-person schooling in March 2020. The Nevada State Department of Education has approved distance education programs in 15 of the 17 school districts in Nevada.[34] Additionally, there are 16 charter schools (of the 39 total) that have approved distance education programs in Nevada. Evidence of the growth of distance education can be found in the number of state approved distance education courses. Nevada requires approval of all distance learning courses through an application process found on the Nevada Department of Education website.[35] Prior to the closing of schools due to the COVID-19 pandemic there were less than 1,500 approved distance education courses in Nevada and currently are nearly 3,000, almost doubling the number of courses in just over a year.

FEDERAL COVID-19 FUNDING

During the 31st Special Session of the Nevada Legislature, Assembly Bill (AB) 3 authorized the transfer of $50 million provide through the Coronavirus Aid, Relief, and Economic Security (CARES) Act, to the Nevada Department of Education to provide monies for grant programs for school districts and charter schools.[36] While the grant programs' requirements included the targeting of specific student groups, such as English language learners, students eligible for free or reduced-price lunch, or students scoring below the 25th percentile on standardized assessments, AB 3 limited the funding and grant programs excluded students in special education programs.

Additionally, in September 2021 the US Department of Education approved the Nevada State Plan for the American Rescue Plan Elementary and Secondary School Emergency Relief (ARP ESSER) funds and the state of Nevada received $1.072 billion in additional federal funding. The Nevada State Plan identified the following priorities for which funds were allocated: 1) Support student social, emotional, and mental health and recruiting, supporting, and retaining effective educators and other school personnel, 2) Provide services and support for underserved student populations, including, students from low-income families, American Indian and Alaska Native students, Asian students, Hispanic/Latino students, Black/African American students, Pacific Islander students, students who identify with two or more races, English language learners, students with disabilities, students experiencing homelessness, migratory students, and students identified by the state as being involved in the criminal justice system, and 3) Safely reopening and sustaining safe operations in schools.[37]

SUMMARY

Nevada continues to increase student enrollment at a swift pace and in spite of concerted efforts, the changes seem to outpace the responses for adequate school funding. Even though the Nevada Legislature recently focused on and revamped the school funding formula, implementing the Pupil Centered Funding Formula, school finance continues to cause distress to many in Nevada. Among the changes to the funding formula were what many had suggested as revisions, including a formula that is flexible, responsive to changes in school district characteristics, weighted for students with additional needs, and equitable. Nevertheless, the recent litigation and report of Nevada being placed near the bottom of per pupil spending among the US provide evidence of the continued school finance concern.

ENDNOTES

[1]   We would like to acknowledge the work of David C. Thompson and R. Craig Wood in crafting the chapter for the first edition of this work.

[2]   "Nevada District Resources," State of Nevada Department of Education, accessed September 1, 2021, https://doe.nv.gov/home/DistrictResources/.

[3]   "Nevada Report Card," State of Nevada Department of Education, accessed September 5, 2021, http://nevadareportcard.nv.gov/di/.

[4]   State of Nevada Department of Education.

[5]   State of Nevada Department of Education.

[6]   Nevada, Const. ar. I, pt. II.

[7]   Verstegen, D. A. (2013). Leaving Equity Behind? A Quantitative Analysis of Fiscal Equity in Nevada's Public Education Finance System. Journal of Education Finance, 39(2), 132–149. https://www.jstor.org/stable/23597635.

[8]   Mary McKillip, and Danielle Farrie, "Nevada's New Formula is an Opportunity Not to Be Lost." Education Law Center, accessed September 10, 2021. https://edlawcenter.org/research/nevada/nevada-funding-formula.html.

[9]   Martinez, D. G. (2020). Nevada. Journal of Education Finance, 45(3), 336–338.

[10] Martinez, D. G. (2021). Nevada. Journal of Education Finance, 46(3), 316–318; Verstegen, D.A. (2013).

[11] Nevada Senate Bill 543, 80th Cong. (2019).

[12] "Commission on School Funding," State of Nevada Department of Education, accessed September 5, 2021, https://doe.nv.gov/Commission_on_School_Funding/.

[13] "Nevada State Senate," accessed September 10, 2021, https://ballotpedia.org/Nevada_State_Senate.

[14] Nevada Legislature, accessed September 8, 2021, https://www.leg.state.nv.us/Division/Research/Content/items/the-guide-to-the-nevada-legislature-current.

[15] Clark County Education Association (CCEA), accessed September 10, 2021, https://new.ccea-nv.org/whoweare/.

[16] Valley, J. (2020). Education funding lawsuit headed for Nevada Supreme Court after initial dismissal, The Nevada Independent, October 27, 2020, https://thenevadaindependent.com/article/education-funding-lawsuit-headed-for-nevada-supreme-court-after-initial-dismissal.

17 Shea v. State, No. 68253 (Nev. App. Feb. 18, 2016)

18 Kenny C. Guinn Center for Policy Priorities, Nevada K-12 Education Finance (Las Vegas, NV: Guinn Center, 2019), accessed September 10, 2021, https://guinncenter.org/wp-content/uploads/2019/04/Guinn-Center-K12-Ed-Finance-2019.pdf.

19 Kenny C. Guinn Center for Policy Priorities, Nevada K-12 Education Finance (Las Vegas, NV: Guinn Center, 2020), accessed September 10, 2021, https://guinncenter.org/wp-content/uploads/2020/09/Guinn-Center-Property-Taxes-Two-Pager.pdf.

20 Kenny C. Guinn Center for Policy Priorities.

21 Nevada Senate Bill 543, 80th Cong. (2019).

22 Melanie Hanson. "U.S. Public Education Spending Statistics" EducationData.org, August 2, 2021, https://educationdata.org/public-education-spending-statistics.

23 "Nevada Report Card," State of Nevada Department of Education, accessed September 5, 2021, http://nevadareportcard.nv.gov/di/.

24 "Coronavirus Relief Funding for School Districts and Charter Schools," Nevada Department of Education, (2020), https://doe.nv.gov/uploadedFiles/ndedoenvgov/content/Grants/CoronaFunding/SummaryofCRFGrantProgram.pdf.

25 State of Nevada Department of Education.

26 Nevada Legislature, accessed September 8, 2021, https://www.leg.state.nv.us/Session/31st-2020Special/.

27 "Nevada State Plan for the American Rescue Plan Elementary and Secondary School Emergency Relief Fund," Nevada Department of Education, (September 2021). https://doe.nv.gov/uploadedFiles/ndedoenvgov/content/FedReliefFund/Nevada-ARP-ESSER-State-Plan.pdf.

28 "State Funding for Career and Technical Education," Nevada Department of Education, (2021). https://doe.nv.gov/uploadedFiles/ndedoenvgov/content/Boards_Commissions_Councils/State_Board_of_Education/2021/March/FY20CompiledStateGrantsPerformanceReport.pdf.

29 "Nevada State Plan for the American Rescue Plan Elementary and Secondary School Emergency Relief Fund," Nevada Department of Education, (September 2021).

30 SPCCA Schools, State of Nevada Department of Education, accessed September 12, 2021. https://charterschools.nv.gov/ForParents/SPCSA_Schools/

31 State of Nevada Department of Education.

32 "Nevada Private Schools," State of Nevada Department of Education, accessed September 14, 2021. https://doe.nv.gov/Private_Schools/.

33 State of Nevada Department of Education, Private School Enrollment, accessed September 14, 2021. https://doe.nv.gov/uploadedFiles/ndedoenvgov/content/Private_Schools/Documents/NevadaPrivateSchoolEnrollmentDetails2020_2021.pdf.

34 State of Nevada Department of Education, accessed September 14, 2021. https://doe.nv.gov/Distance_Education/Home/

35 State of Nevada Department of Education.

36 "Nevada State Plan for the American Rescue Plan Elementary and Secondary School Emergency Relief Fund," Nevada Department of Education.

37 "Nevada State Plan for the American Rescue Plan Elementary and Secondary School Emergency Relief Fund," Nevada Department of Education, (September 2021).

CHAPTER 29

NEW HAMPSHIRE

Osnat Zaken

Touro University

GENERAL BACKGROUND

State Constitution

New Hampshire's State Constitution, was established October 31, 1783 to take Effect June 2, 1784 and subsequently amended and in force January 2019.[1]

The Republican Party controls the governorship and both chambers of the state legislature. The Republican Party controls the office of attorney general, while the Democratic Party controls the office of secretary of state. New Hampshire's state senators and representatives are elected to two-year terms.

As of December 3, 2021, Republicans controlled 54.22% of all state legislative seats nationally, while Democrats held 44.70%. Republicans held a majority in 61 chambers, and Democrats held the majority in 37 chambers. One chamber (Alaska House) was organized under a multi-partisan, power-sharing coalition.[2]

New Hampshire's primary education system recognizes that every student has their own path toward educational success. For the first time since 2012 funding for special education aid has increased to $26.5 million and tuition and transportation aid to $8.6 million to break down the barriers that prevent students from

Funding Public Schools in the United States, Indian Country,
and US Territories (Second Edition), pages 455–467.
Copyright © 2023 by Information Age Publishing
www.infoagepub.com

reaching their full potential. These measures continue the State's effort to deliver relief to local taxpayers. Property tax rates are largely controlled at the local level, and this Administration continues to provide municipalities with the opportunity to cut property taxes. The 2018-2019 State Budget returned $30 million to cities and towns for school safety upgrades. The current budget appropriated $63.7 million in one-time surplus monies to property-poor school districts, in a "pay as you go" manner, for Targeted School Building Aid grants which will ensure that the quality of New Hampshire's schools remains the best in the nation. Funding for Charter Schools also received expanding support and enabled a beneficial alternative learning environment for students.

New Hampshire's budget, made a strategic investments into higher education by expanding programs and pathways at community colleges and universities that will supply the workforce for the state's most in-demand fields such as health care and advanced manufacturing. With the State Government partnering with private business to provide funding, design curriculums, and create direct pathways to employment, this budget created a new model for state funding for higher education. Additionally, to ameliorate the burden that student debt places on college graduates, New Hampshire is taking the national lead and providing $32.5 million in student debt assistance over the biennium, and every biennium thereafter, without using taxpayer dollars.[3]

BASIC SUPPORT PROGRAM

Following the litigation history in New Hampshire, state education fiscal support is first conceptualized as Adequate Education Aid. Aid is further conceived as the 'Cost of an Opportunity for an Adequate Education' as determined in statute. These statutes specify how aid is calculated and distributed.

Adequacy Aid is calculated using the Average Daily Membership (ADM) of the students who reside within a municipality. Any full-time student K-12 enrolled in school for the entire year has an ADM of 1.00. If a student moves mid-year, they are counted as a fractional ADM in each municipality. Pursuant to statute, the previous school year ADM (2020-2021) is used in calculating the current fiscal year (FY 2022) adequacy aid. However, Section 51 of House Bill 2 of the 2021 State Budget Session requires the Department of Education to incorporate school year ADM prior to school year 2020-2021 into the calculation.

The total ADM for a municipality consists of:

- Students who attended a school operated by their resident district.
- Students tuitioned by the resident district to a district-operated school in NH or another State.
- Students tuitioned by the resident district to a non-public school, such as a special education program.
- Preschool students are not included.

- Charter schools students are not included, except as provided for in RSA 194-B:11.
- Home school students enrolled in high school academic courses at the rate of 0.15 ADM per course, only if excess adequacy aid appropriations exist at the end of the year.[4]

Cost of Adequacy

Every two years the base per pupil cost and additional costs for certain students are adjusted for inflation and used for both years of the State's biennium. RSA 198:40-d specifies that the US Bureau of Labor Statistics' Consumer Price Index for All Urban Consumers, Northeast Region, special aggregate index of "services less medical care services" will be used to make the adjustments. Starting July 1, 2021, this inflation adjustment is an increase of 2.1%.

For FY2022 and FY2023, the base per pupil rate is $3,786.66 per ADM. Adequacy includes an additional rate as follows:

- $1,893.32 for a free or reduced-price meal (F&R) eligible student. This eligibility determination is based on household income not participation in a lunch program. Students from households receiving TANF or SNAP are automatically eligible. Others need parental/guardian provided income information.
- $2,037.11 for a special education (SPED) student who has an individualized educational plan (IEP).
- $740.87 for an English Language Learner (ELL) receiving English Language instruction.
- $740.87 for each 3rd grade pupil whose achievement score on the state assessment for reading was below the proficient level. Students who did not take the test are not counted.

The cost of an opportunity for an adequate education for each municipality is calculated by applying the base rate and applicable additional rates to the ADM of each student.[5]

Calculating ADM for FY 2023

The ADM used for FY 2023 will be school year 2021-2022 with the exception of F&R ADM. The Governor authorized the Department to modify the F&R ADM being used in the formula. The modification was calculated by first determining the percent of F&R ADM relative to total ADM for school year 2019-2020. This percentage was applied to the total ADM for school year 2021-2022 to arrive at a modified F&R ADM for 2021-2022. The newly modified F&R ADM was compared with school year 2021-2022 actual F&R ADM, and the greater of the two numbers was used in the formula.

Determining Adequacy Grants

Statewide Education Property Tax Assessment

The Department of Revenue Administration determined the minimum tax rate needed to raise at least $363 million from the Statewide Education Property Tax (SWEPT) for the following school year. However, for FY 2023 the minimum amount needed to be raised is set to $263 million in State law. This reduction in the amount needed to be raised is set to only occur in FY 2023 under current law. The tax rate, rounded to the nearest one half cent, is applied to equalized valuations without utilities to achieve the minimum amount needed to be raised by the State. (RSA 76:3 and RSA 76:8.) Municipalities collect the SWEPT and send the total assessment amount directly to its school district(s) and the assessment amount is credited to the individual towns. While municipalities are responsible for collecting and distributing this tax revenue, SWEPT is a State tax, not a local tax. For FY2023, a tax rate of $1.230 per thousand will be applied to April 1, 2020 equalized values.

Relief Aid

The Relief Aid grant is an additional grant for municipalities based on the percentage of F&R eligible ADM relative to the total ADM. Eligibility starts at 12% F&R eligible with a grant equal to $150 per F&R student. The grant then increases by 12.5 cents (i.e., $0.125) for each additional .01% increase in F&R percentage (e.g., 12.01% has $150.125 grant). At 48 percent F&R eligible, the grant amount reaches a maximum of $600 per F&R ADM. The Relief Aid Grant is prorated to $17.5 million based on each municipality's percentage of the state-wide Relief Grant award as initially calculated.

Preliminary Grant Plus Relief Aid

When the SWEPT assessment is subtracted from the cost of adequacy, the balance is the preliminary Grant, and the Relief Aid grant is added. If SWEPT is more than the cost of adequacy, then the preliminary grant is zero.

SWEPT Reduction Hold Harmless Grant

A SWEPT Reduction Hold Harmless Grant is provided to municipalities that receive less of a total education grant when the new SWEPT amount raising $263 million statewide is compared to the SWEPT amount when $363 million is raised statewide. This is determined by first calculating the total education grant using the $263 million SWEPT grant. The total education grant is the preliminary grant, plus relief aid and SWEPT. The SWEPT reduction hold harmless grant is determined by comparing the calculated total education grant when $263 million is raised statewide to the total grant award if $363 million was raised statewide, the larger of the two calculations is used for determining the total education grant and the difference is considered the SWEPT Reduction Hold Harmless Grant.

Stabilization Grant

When a new funding formula was enacted for FY 2012, to ease the impact on municipalities facing a decrease in aid, the Legislature utilized a stabilization grant to cover the decreases. For FY 2023, the stabilization grant with be 100% of the 2012 amount. The stabilization grant is paid in addition to the total education grant.

Inclusion of Home-Schooled Course Credit

Prior to the final payment of adequacy grants in April, the Department of Education will determine if the appropriation allocated in the state budget for adequacy aid is sufficient to allow for inclusion of an ADM credit of 0.15 for each enrollment is an academic course by a home-schooled student.

Total Grant

A municipality's final grant is the sum of its preliminary and stabilization grants. For the final calculation in April 2023, the total grant will be no less than 95% of the November 15, 2021 estimate.[6]

COST PER PUPIL, 2020-2021

The Cost per Pupil represents, current expenditures from all funding sources (local, state and federal) associated with the daily operation of schools. Payments to other school districts and private schools have been subtracted. Revenues from the sales of lunches have also been excluded. Cost per Pupil is calculated by subtracting tuition and transportation from K-12 current operating expenditures, and then dividing by the average daily membership in attendance (ADM-A). The report "State Average Cost Per Pupil and Total Expenditures" identifies which expenditures have been included or excluded such as: operating, tuition, transportation, equipment, construction, interest and non-K-12 expenditures is $21,842.89.[7]

U.S. Public Education Spending

In the United States K-12 schools spend about $612.7 billion annually. This is about $12,612 per pupil. Federal, state, and local governments spend about $720.9 billion annually or $14,840 per pupil. The federal government provides 7.7% of funding, state governments provide 46.7%, and local governments provide 45.6%. On average, the U.S. spends $15,908 per pupil on postsecondary education and $33,063 per pupil on graduate and postgraduate education.

The United States allocates about 11.6% of public funding to education, below the international standard of 15%, and spends about 4.96% of its GDP on education, compared to the 5.59% average of other developed nations. The U.S. spends the fifth-highest amount per pupil compared to the 37 other OECD countries, behind Luxembourg, Switzerland, Austria, and Norway.[8]

Per Pupil Spending by State

Public school spending varies greatly in different states and depends on several factors. One factor is the money that the schools are allocated, which directly correlates with how much the schools spend on students. Higher teacher salaries and benefits also lead to higher per-pupil spending, among several other factors.

For most states, instructional employee salaries and benefits account for at least half of the total per-pupil spending. Administrative expenses and support staff also account for some of the spending.

New York has the highest per-pupil spending of all of the 50 states. New York currently spends $24,040 per pupil, approximately 90% above the national average. Utah has the lowest per-pupil spending of $7,628 per student.[9]

New Hampshire in 2019-20 spent per pupil $17,394 on public schools, ranking #10 in the nation, but in 2020-21 spending per pupil increased to $18,796 Most of this is paid for by local property taxes; in fact, New Hampshire relies more than any other state on local property taxes to foot the bill for public education.[10]

In spite of the high per-pupil spending, FY 2019-20 the state's average starting salary for teachers was $38,990, lower than all New England states except Maine. Average overall salary for teachers FY 2019-20 in New Hampshire was $59,622, and has FY 2020-21 increased to $61,789.[11]

SELECTED PROGRAM SUPPORTS

CARES Act and ESSER Funding responding to impacts of COVID-19

The CARES Act was signed into law on March 27, 2020. It includes the Elementary and Secondary Schools Emergency Relief (ESSER) funds to help K-12 educational entities prevent, prepare for, and respond to impacts of COVID-19.

Although ESSER funds are distributed to districts using a proportional distribution to the FY 2019-2020 Title I, Part A allocations, they are not Title I, Part A funds and are therefore not subject to the Title I, Part A requirements. ESSER funds may be used to support any school in a district regardless of its Title I status. Although ESSER funds are not subject to the Title I, Part A ESSER funds may take the place of State of Local funds for allowable activities, they are subject to equitable services and maintenance of effort requirements.

The purpose of the ESSER fund is to provide districts with emergency relief funds to address the impact COVID-19 has, and continues to have, on elementary and secondary schools that are providing educational services and attempting to return to normal operations. The ESSER grant provides districts considerable flexibility in determining how best to use ESSER funds. Districts are encouraged to target ESSER funding on activities that will support remote learning for all students, especially disadvantaged or at-risk students and their teachers.

ESSER is its own program intended to help with the COVID-19 response. As such, a district must submit a separate grant application to the New Hampshire Department of Education (NHDOE) in order to receive ESSER funds.[12]

Program Allocation Amounts in New Hampshire

New Hampshire provides aid to targeted priorities within and beyond the general aid scheme. Sections below outline the selected areas of special education, catastrophic aid, tuition, pupil transportation, school building aid, charter schools, and kindergarten.

Special Education

New Hampshire provides an allocation for special education on an ADM basis. This aid is intended to assist districts in complying with accounting for revenues that offset expenditures for special education programs and services. For FY 2021, state aid amounted to $ 58,607,614.97 which was distributed by formula to the school districts. Developmental Disabilities Funding Increased by $116.8 million in FY2020-21.[13]

The state also provided catastrophic aid to qualifying school districts. Catastrophic aid is based on the number of students. Districts are cost-eligible for 80% funding; provision is also made for 100% cost-eligible funding. The Sum of Entitlement for 2021 is 29,626,759.17.[14]

Kindergarten Aid

Aid is available to school districts operating full-day public kindergarten programs. For FY 2019, State kindergarten aid was $10,732,429.84 and served 9,756.75 ADM pupils.

Tables 29.1 and 29.2 illustrate supports for New Hampshire school districts for FY 2020-21. Table 31.1 provides a state summary of revenues and expenditures for the academic year 2020-21. Table 29.2 shows estimated expenditures for all school districts during the same time period and includes amounts by grade level and cost per pupil.

Tuition and Transportation Aid

New Hampshire provides school district reimbursement for Career and Technical Education tuition costs, along with aid for transportation for regular and alternative education. For FY 2021, CTE tuition and transportation aid to school districts totaled $8,491,634.27 for tuition and $508.365.73 for transportation, a total of $9.0 million. [17]

TABLE 29.1 Revenue and Expenditure Profile for New Hampshire School Districts FY 2021 STATE SUMMARY REVENUE AND EXPENDITURES OF SCHOOL DISTRICTS 2020-2021

REVENUE SOURCES		Percent
Local Taxation$	2,147,713,909	60.7%
Tuition, Food, & Other Local Revenue*	44,330,906	1.3%
Equitable Education Aid	1,011,796,605	28.6%
Other State Sources	82,116,322	2.3%
Federal Sources	252,513,392	7.1%
Other (Includes insurance settlements)	904,410	0.0%
Total Net Revenues	$3,539,375,544	100.0%
Sale of Bonds & Notes **	59,280,731	
DISTRIBUTION OF EXPENDITURES		
Regular Instruction*	$1,325,049,039	40.1%
Special Programs*	636,480,150	19.3%
Vocational Programs*	43,518,475	1.3%
Other Instructional Programs	47,341,631	1.4%
Student Support Services	262,114,902	7.9%
Instructional Staff Support	114,005,654	3.5%
General Administration and Business	149,495,895	4.5%
School Administration	180,393,572	5.5%
Business Services	23,231,070	0.7%
Plant Operations	285,682,623	8.7%
Pupil Transportation	132,011,073	4.0%
Non-Public Programs	884,303	0.0%
Community Programs	5,130,529	0.2%
Bond & Note Interest	39,591,564	1.2%
Charter Schools/Other Agencies	2,167,226	0.1%
Food Service	54,442,776	1.7%
Total Recurring Expenditures	$3,301,540,482	100.0%
Facility Construction	107,722,214	
TOTAL EXPENDITURES	$3,409,262,696	
Bond & Note Principal Payment	87,378,436	
* The following adjustments have been made to State Total DOE-25 data.		
Deducted from Revenues:		
Tuition from other NH school districts	103,512,050	
Transportation from other NH school districts	174,084	
Food service revenues except interest	4,709,821	
Services provided other NH school districts other than food	1,797,116	
Total Revenue Adjustments:	$110,193,071	
Deducted from Expenditures:		
Regular, Special and Voc Tuition from other NH school districts	$109,212,555	
Food service revenues except interest	4,709,821	
Total Expenditure Adjustments:	$113,922,376	

**Bonds & Notes must be repaid with revenues from other sources. To avoid double counting revenues, these amounts are shown below the total revenue line.[15]

TABLE 29.2. State Average Cost Per Pupil and Total Expenditures 2020-2021

	Elementary	Middle	High	Total
Part A - Expenditures				
Operating Expenses for Public Schools	$1,484,935,608	$535,582,021	$856,718,142	$2,877,235,771
Tuition (less interdistrict transfers)	25,630,886	19,085,026	129,391,727	174,107,639
Transportation	63,329,488	24,520,015	42,154,828	130,004,331
Elem and Secondary Current Expenses [1]	$1,573,895,982	$579,187,062	$1,028,264,697	$3,181,347,741
Capital Items (other than facilities reported below)				68,129,119
Bonds & Notes Interest				39,591,564
Total Recurring Elementary and Secondary Expenditures				$3,289,068,424
Facility Construction & Acquisition				107,722,214
Total Expenditures for Elementary and Secondary Education				$3,396,790,638
Current Expenditures Not Part of Public Elementary & Secondary				
Summer School	$2,245,636	$662,560	$1,381,802	$4,289,998
Non-public Programs				884,303
Adult Education				4,303,033
Community/Jr. College Ed. Program				28,901
Community Service				798,595
Allocation to Charter Schools/Other Agencies				2,167,226
Total Expenditures for 2020-2021 [2]				$3,409,262,694
Part B - Pupil Memberships				
Average daily membership in attendance [3]	76,813.02	31,024.90	48,243.36	156,081.28
Part C - Cost Per Pupil				
Operating Expenses for Public Schools	$19,331.82	$17,262.97	$17,758.26	$18,434.21
Tuition (less interdistrict transfers)	333.68	615.15	2,682.06	1,115.49
Transportation	824.46	790.33	873.80	832.93
Elem and Secondary Current Expenses	$20,489.96	$18,668.45	$21,314.12	$20,382.63
Capital Items (other than facilities reported below)				$436.50
Bonds & Notes Interest				253.66
Total Recurring Expenditures				$21,072.79
Facility Construction & Acquisition				690.17
Total Expenditures for Elementary and Secondary Education				$21,762.96
Current Expenditures Not Part of Public Elementary & Secondary				
Summer School	$29.24	$21.36	$28.64	$27.49
Non-public Programs				5.67
Adult Education				27.57
Community/Jr. College Ed. Program				0.19
Community Service				5.12
Allocation to Charter Schools/Other Agencies				13.89
Total Expenditures for 2020-2021				$21,842.89

(*continues*)

TABLE 29.2.   Continued

This State Average is based on district operated schools only.
[1]Inter-district tuition payments have been deducted. Inter-district transportation payments of $174,083.85 can not be attributed to a grade level and have not been deducted.
[2]Does not include Bond Principal repayment of: $87,378,436 Bond Principal repayments are not included because expenditures financed by bonds and notes have already been reported as expenditures in the current or a previous year.
[3]High school average daily membership (ADM) does not include ADM of 66.82 for students attending vocational programs out-of-state.
[1]This section follows closely from New Hampshire Department of Education, "FY2020 Adequate Education Aid: How the Cost of an Opportunity for an Adequate Education is Determined." Retrieved from: [16] https://www.education.nh.gov/sites/g/files/ehbemt326/files/inline-documents/sonh/state-avg-cpp-fy2021.pdf

Building Aid

New Hampshire provides support to school districts for infrastructure. District aid entitlement along with October and April payments are reported. For 2020-21 $ 26,972,727 and 2022-2023 24,960,075 aid was available to 82 school districts.[18]

Charter Schools

In the 2020-21 school year, New Hampshire had 28 public charter schools in operation. Charter schools are eligible for state aid paid by ADM. For FY 2020-21, a total 6509.0 ADM charter school students were recorded, with $43,603,474.54 in state aid paid. Another $1,692,000.27 was made available in the form of differentiated aid. Total special education differentiated aid to charter schools was paid in the amount of $1,234,293.95. [19]

State Support for Nonpublic Schools

Emergency Assistance to Non-Public Schools Programs provides emergency assistance to students and teachers in non-public schools through the Emergency Assistance to Non-public Schools (EANS) program.

As part of the Coronavirus Response and Relief Supplemental Appropriations Act, 2021, (CRRSA Act) Public Law 116-260, Congress set aside $2.75 billion of the Governor's Emergency Education Relief Fund specifically to provide emergency assistance to students and teachers in non-public schools through the Emergency Assistance to Non-public Schools (EANS) program. The purpose of the EANS program is to provide services or assistance to eligible non-public schools to address the impact that the Coronavirus Disease 2019 (COVID-19) has on non-public school students and teachers in the state. [20]

SUMMARY

- New Hampshire school funding per student spending FY 2019-20 was $17,394 which was #10 in the nation,
- FY 2020-21 funding per student spending saw an increase to $18,796.

TABLE 29.3.

2020-21 ADM	167,284.28
Base Adequacy Aid $3,786.66	$792,772,241.82
F&R ADM	38,848.41
F&R Differentiated Aid $1,818.02	$87,076,672.11
SPED ADM	30,185.64
ELL ADM	$5,068.02
SPED Differentiated Aid	61,493,509.53
ELL Differentiated Aid $740.87	3755481.83
Grade 3 Reading Below Proficient ADM	2,815.40
Grade 3 Reading Differentiated Aid	$2,086,582.62
Total Calculated Cost of an Adequate Education	$788,689,204.19
Statewide Education Property Tax (SWEPT)	$363,283,230
Preliminary Grants= Cost of Adequacy Less SWEPT plus relief	$467,459,889.67
FY 2012 Stabilization Grant	$158,480,276
Grant Eligibility: (1) Stabilization Received FY 12 (2) ADM > Zero (3) Cost of Adequacy > SWEPT	$157,467,805.00
FY 2021 Grants	$988,210,919.66

RSA 32:11-a.
See RSA 186-C:18 for legislation which describes the calculation and distribution of aid.
See RSA 198:48-c for legislation describing the calculation and distribution of aid.

- Teacher Average Salary FY 2019-20 was $59,622 which was #21 in the nation and FY 2020-21 saw an increase to $61,789.
- New Hampshire Public School Expenditures in 2019-20 Public School Expenditures were $3,211,565.
- FY 2020-21 there was an increase to $3,304,504
- Overall, New Hampshire Revenue and Non-Revenue Receipts in 2020-21 totaled $3,459,443. [21]

Table 29.3 provides a summary of estimated expenditures by major category relating to the state aid formula.

ENDNOTES

[1] NH AT-a-glance. State Constitution | NH.gov. (n.d.). Retrieved January 4, 2022, from https://www.nh.gov/glance/constitution.htm

[2] Party control of New Hampshire State Government. Ballotpedia. (n.d.). Retrieved January 4, 2022, from https://ballotpedia.org/Party_control_of_New_Hampshire_state_government

[3] Governor's executive budget summary - new hampshire. (n.d.). Retrieved January 4, 2022, from https://das.nh.gov/budget/Budget2020-2021/Executive%20Summary%20Final.pdf

[4] FY2022 explained - New Hampshire Department of Education. (n.d.). Retrieved January 4, 2022, from https://www.education.nh.gov/sites/g/files/ehbemt326/files/inline-documents/sonh/fy2022-explained.pdf

[5] FY2022 explained - New Hampshire Department of Education. (n.d.). Retrieved January 4, 2022, from https://www.education.nh.gov/sites/g/files/ehbemt326/files/inline-documents/sonh/fy2022-explained.pdf

[6] NH School Safe: Threat Assessment Micro-grant. (n.d.). Retrieved January 4, 2022, from https://www.education.nh.gov/sites/g/files/ehbemt326/files/inline-documents/sonh/nh-school-safe-threat-assessment_lea-application-.pdf

[7] Www.education.nh.gov. (n.d.). Retrieved January 4, 2022, from https://www.education.nh.gov/sites/g/files/ehbemt326/files/inline-documents/sonh/cpp-fy2021.xlsx

[8] Per pupil spending by state 2021. (n.d.). Retrieved January 4, 2022, from https://worldpopulationreview.com/state-rankings/per-pupil-spending-by-state

[9] Per pupil spending by state 2021. (n.d.). Retrieved January 4, 2022, from https://worldpopulationreview.com/state-rankings/per-pupil-spending-by-state

[10] Association, N. E. (n.d.). Teacher pay and student spending: How does your state rank? NEA. Retrieved January 4, 2022, from https://www.nea.org/resource-library/teacher-pay-and-student-spending-how-does-your-state-rank

[11] Association, N. E. (n.d.). Teacher pay and student spending: How does your state rank? NEA. Retrieved January 4, 2022, from https://www.nea.org/resource-library/teacher-pay-and-student-spending-how-does-your-state-rank

[12] Cares act and Esser Funding. Department of Education. (n.d.). Retrieved January 4, 2022, from https://www.education.nh.gov/who-we-are/division-of-learner-support/bureau-of-instructional-support/cares-act-funding

[13] NH School Safe: Threat Assessment Micro-grant. (n.d.). Retrieved January 5, 2022, from https://www.education.nh.gov/sites/g/files/ehbemt326/files/inline-documents/sonh/nh-school-safe-threat-assessment_lea-application-.pdf

[14] NH School Safe: Threat Assessment Micro-grant. (n.d.). Retrieved January 5, 2022, from https://www.education.nh.gov/sites/g/files/ehbemt326/files/inline-documents/sonh/nh-school-safe-threat-assessment_lea-application-.pdf

[15] NH School Safe: Threat Assessment Micro-grant. (n.d.). Retrieved January 5, 2022, from https://www.education.nh.gov/sites/g/files/ehbemt326/files/inline-documents/sonh/nh-school-safe-threat-assessment_lea-application-.pdf

[16] NH School Safe: Threat Assessment Micro-grant. (n.d.). Retrieved January 5, 2022, from https://www.education.nh.gov/sites/g/files/ehbemt326/files/inline-documents/sonh/nh-school-safe-threat-assessment_lea-application-.pdf

[17] NH School Safe: Threat Assessment Micro-grant. (n.d.). Retrieved January 5, 2022, from https://www.education.nh.gov/sites/g/files/ehbemt326/files/inline-documents/sonh/nh-school-safe-threat-assessment_lea-application-.pdf

[18] New Hampshire Department of Education Division of ... (n.d.). Retrieved January 5, 2022, from https://www.education.nh.gov/sites/g/files/ehbemt326/files/inline-documents/build-dist10-41.pdf

[19] NH School Safe: Threat Assessment Micro-grant. (n.d.). Retrieved January 5, 2022, from https://www.education.nh.gov/sites/g/files/ehbemt326/files/inline-documents/sonh/nh-school-safe-threat-assessment_lea-application-.pdf

[20] Emergency assistance to Non-Public Schools Program. Department of Education. (n.d.). Retrieved January 5, 2022, from https://www.education.nh.gov/who-we-are/division-of-learner-support/bureau-of-instructional-support/emergency-assistance-non

[21] Association, N. E. (n.d.). Teacher pay and student spending: How does your state rank? NEA. Retrieved January 5, 2022, from https://www.nea.org/resource-library/teacher-pay-and-student-spending-how-does-your-state-rank

[22] The Department of Education. Department of Education. (2022, January 4). Retrieved January 5, 2022, from https://www.education.nh.gov/

CHAPTER 30

NEW JERSEY

R. Craig Wood

University of Florida

Kai Cui

University of Florida

GENERAL BACKGROUND AND AID FORMULA BASIC DESIGN*

Since 1973, the New Jersey supreme court has handed down a series of decisions in an effort to uphold the state's constitutional requirement of a 'thorough and efficient' system of public education for all students. In *Robinson v. Cahill*[1] the court determined that the system of financing public education in New Jersey was unconstitutional. Since this original case, the state's high court has repeatedly imparted numerous rulings, variously known as the *Abbott*[2] decisions, to provide all students in New Jersey with equal access to quality public education. During that time, the court better defined what a thorough and efficient education really means.

These court decisions have also resulted in increased state aid for education and, importantly, more funds directed to poorer urban districts, also known as the *Abbott* districts.

Funding Public Schools in the United States, Indian Country, and US Territories (Second Edition), pages 469–483.
Copyright © 2023 by Information Age Publishing
www.infoagepub.com
All rights of reproduction in any form reserved.

Robinson v. Cahill

The New Jersey constitution was amended in 1875 to require the thorough and efficient system of education. In 1970, a suit was brought against the state of New Jersey and the cities of Jersey City, Paterson, Plainfield and East Orange, asserting that the state's funding formula for public schools discriminated against students from economically disadvantaged school districts. In 1973, the New Jersey supreme court deemed unconstitutional the state's system of primarily using property taxes to fund public schools and called for a new funding system. As a result of the court's decision in *Robinson*, the state legislature established the Public School Education Act of 1975 (also known as Chapter 212).[3] The act had three major goals.

- *Guarantee* that school districts of unequal property wealth would receive equal resources for equal tax rates;
- *Compensate* districts for the extra costs of educating students with extraordinary educational needs; and
- *Narrow* per-pupil expenditure disparities through a system of expenditure caps.

With the Act of 1975, New Jersey's legislators aimed to ensure that all students were able to receive a thorough and efficient education as required in the state constitution. Under the Act, school districts were able to raise funds as though the tax bases were equal to a guaranteed tax base (GTB). If school districts could not generate all necessary funds under the actual tax bases, the state would provide equalization aid to make up the difference.

Abbott I

Despite changes to the state's funding formula, a lawsuit was filed against the state of New Jersey on behalf of twenty children attending schools in Camden, East Orange, Irvington, and Jersey City. Plaintiffs asserted that the Public School Education Act of 1975 failed to provide a thorough and efficient education for all students.

Plaintiffs argued that under the then-current funding formula, the state provided roughly 40 percent of funds for all school operating costs, with the remainder of funds generated by the property tax. According to plaintiffs, due to vast property wealth differences among school districts, there were equally vast discrepancies in per-pupil expenditure. As a result of these disparities, plaintiffs argued that students in poorer school districts did not receive the same high-quality education as students in both average and economically advantaged school districts. In 1985, the New Jersey supreme court transferred the case to an administrative law judge for initial hearing. This decision, known as *Abbott I*,[4] was the first in a myriad of *Abbott* decisions that would be reached over the course of the next three decades. The series of *Abbott* decisions would profoundly shape education for students in New Jersey, aimed toward assisting economically disadvantaged students in the state.

Abbott II

The New Jersey supreme court handed down the second *Abbott*[5] decision, ruling that the Public School Education Act of 1975 was unconstitutional as applied to twenty-eight 'poorer urban' school districts (this number would later be increased to thirty-one districts, which would be known as the *Abbott* districts). The court found that schools in those poorer urban districts were unable to meet the needs of students under the state's funding formula. Furthermore, the court found that the then-current system of funding public schools was neither thorough nor efficient as applied to poorer urban districts. According to the court, "...the poorer the district and the greater its need, the less the money available and the worse the education."

Although the court acknowledged that simply fixing the funding disparity would not solve all of the educational inequalities that existed at that time between schools in low-income areas and schools in affluent areas, it also asserted that (if used wisely) it could help schools in low-income districts provide students with higher quality education. The current system under the Act enabled school districts to raise as much money as needed to provide a thorough and efficient education. If those school districts were unable to raise all necessary funds, the state would provide the difference. Despite this policy, the court found that schools in poorer urban areas were still failing, and under the current system had no "likelihood of achieving a decent education tomorrow, in the reasonable future, or ever."

Consequently, the court found the Act's funding formula to be flawed. Under the formula, local tax revenues were supplemented by state aid, known as equalization aid, to ensure that districts in poorer areas were able to reach the guaranteed tax base (GTB). The court found that the Act was only fully funded twice, once for the 1977-78 school year, and again for the 1978-79 school year. While the Act promised that all school districts would be funded at a 134 percent guaranteed base level, funding over the years had varied from 129 to 134 percent.

The court also noted several limitations with equalization aid, one of which greatly affected low-income school districts in New Jersey. The equalization aid that a district received under the Act was based on the budget for the previous year, not for the current school year. The court illustrated how a district with an equalization aid level of 80 percent of the district's budget could be impacted by the practice of using the previous year's budget. Thus, under the Act, there was tremendous potential that poorer urban school districts would be financially unable to meet the needs of the students and ultimately unable to provide them with the thorough and efficient education that they had a constitutional right to receive.

Quality Education Act

In response to the *Abbott II* decision, New Jersey's governor and state legislature passed the *Quality Education Act.*[6] (QEA) into law in July 1990. The QEA specifically was designed to comply with the New Jersey supreme court's ruling, which mandated that all students in the state of New Jersey would be supported by similar educational resources. The intent of the QEA was to "enhance educational opportunities for New Jersey's children by guaranteeing all school districts an adequate level of state aid."[7] The QEA identified thirty urban school districts as having special needs and aimed to provide those districts with increased financial support. Under the QEA, the Commissioner of Education was directed to determine an equity spending cap, permitting special needs districts to increase their spending budgets. In 1991, the QEA was amended to alleviate school districts' tax burdens, provide property intended to assist tax relief, and also impose spending limitations. Ultimately, the QEA aimed to achieve educational equity, improve the quality of education, and impose greater accountability regarding school spending.

Under the QEA's funding system, known as the 'foundation funding program,' the state department of education would determine a basic amount of money that would be spent for every child's education, regardless of socioeconomic status of the district. The QEA, which was funded primarily through taxes and the state education aid, determined how the various types of state aid would be distributed. Those types of state aid included: (1) state foundation aid; (2) categorical aid (including aid for special education, bilingual education, at-risk students, and county vocational schools); (3) other state aid for transportation, pension and social security costs, debt service; and (4) transition aid.

State foundation aid was a key component of the QEA. It was distributed to school districts to help finance operating costs such as teacher salaries, textbooks and supplies, administrative costs, maintenance, utilities, and out of district tuition. In order to calculate the amount of state foundation aid that a school district would receive, the state first determined the district's maximum foundation budget, or 'appropriate overall spending level.' The maximum foundation budget was based on the district's enrollment and the foundation amount, or the amount of money, determined by the state, to provide each student with a quality education. For the 1991-92 school year, the foundation amount was $6,640 per student. For the thirty high needs urban districts, the amount of foundation aid would increase by 5 percent; for the 1991-92 school year, this amounted to $332, resulting in a foundation amount of $6,972 per pupil. According to the rationale used in creating the formula, the additional state aid for those schools would help to address their special needs.

As various programs required different levels of funding, weights were assigned to grade and program categories to determine the amount of foundational funding required for each program. The foundation was multiplied by the foundation weight to determine the weighted foundational amount. For example, a student attending full-day kindergarten or pre-school was assigned a foundation weight of 1.00, and thus was entitled to a weighted foundation amount of $6,640 in 1991-92. A student attending a half-day kindergarten or pre-school program was assigned a weight of .5 and thus entitled to a foundation amount of $3,320.

Grades 1-5 were assigned a foundation weight of 1.00; grades 6-8 were assigned a foundation weight of 1.10; and grades 9-12 were assigned a weight of 1.33, thus a weighted foundation amount of $8,831 per pupil in 1991-92.

Once a foundation amount was established, the state then determined the school district's 'fair share,' or the amount of revenue the district should be able to generate through local taxes. In addition to the foundation amount, a facilities component was also used to determine the districts' maximum foundation budget.

Categorical aid was also provided to districts to cover the costs of additional programs such as special needs programs, bilingual programs, at-risk student programs and vocational programs. Other state aid was also provided under the QEA for districts to cover the costs of pension and social security, as well as transportation aid. Finally, transition aid was also provided for school districts that would be receiving less state aid under the QEA. Transition aid aimed to assist districts ease into the transition of a four-year period; after 1995-96 transition aid would be completely eliminated.

While the QEA was being implemented by the state legislature, the Education Law Center reactivated the *Abbott* case in 1992, asserting that the QEA violated the court's ruling.[8]

Abbott III

In 1994, the New Jersey supreme court upheld a superior court's decision that the QEA was unconstitutional based on its failure to assure parity of regular education expenditures between special needs districts and the more affluent districts.[9] Although under the QEA there was a significant increase in state aid (approximately $700 million) to the thirty special needs districts and no increase in aid to wealthier districts, the court ultimately determined that the QEA failed to achieve parity among poorer and wealthier school districts in the state. According to the court, while the QEA authorized the special needs districts to spend enough each year to achieve parity by the 1995-1996 school year, the Act did not guarantee funding sufficient to pay for the authorized level of spending. Under the QEA, the Commissioner of Education was directed to determine an equity-spending cap for the thirty special needs districts; this increase in spending would enable special needs districts to spend as much per pupil as wealthier school districts, also known as I and J districts.[10]

According to the court, while it was theoretically possible to use the equity-spending cap to achieve parity in terms of per-pupil spending among special needs districts and wealthier districts, the equity-spending cap was never exercised and there was no link between the equity-spending cap and the maximum foundation budget. In fact, at the time of the court's ruling, the equity-spending cap had not been calculated for the 1993-4 school year. The court ruled that because the QEA's design for achieving parity depended on the discretionary action of the executive and legislative branches, the state failed to guarantee funding for each district. The court also specified concerns regarding how special needs districts were using the additional state aid received under the QEA. According to the court, the state needed to monitor use of the increased state aid to ensure that the additional funding was being used for supplemental programs to meet the needs of students. Although each special needs district was required to develop an educational improvement plan under the QEA, the court found no evidence to suggest a correlation between the increased state aid and the educational improvement plan. Furthermore, the court asserted that the state failed to study which supplemental programs would best support students in the special needs schools, such as full-day kindergarten programs or health services. According to the court, simply providing increased funding to special needs schools would not improve the quality of education or ensure educational equity.

New Jersey Core Curriculum Content Standards

Following the *Abbott III* decision, the legislature worked to reform education funding to ensure that all students in the state of New Jersey would receive a thorough and efficient education as mandated by the state constitution. The reformation was implemented in 1995, when the governor executed the New Jersey Core Curriculum Content Standard[11] (NJCCCS).The standards provided an extensive outline of what all students should know and be able to do at each stage of their elementary, middle, and high school career. The standards were an effort to define the meaning of 'thorough' in the context of the 1875 state constitutional guarantee that students would be educated within a thorough and efficient system of free public schools.

The standards were designed to ensure that public education in New Jersey would prepare all students to compete in a competitive global workforce. Comprehensive standards were created for the following categories: Cross-Content Workplace Readiness, Visual and Performing Arts, Comprehensive Health and Physical Education, Language Arts and Literacy, Mathematics, Science, Social Studies, and World Language. The standards provided educators with a list of 'cumulative progress indicators' that indicated what all students should know and be able to do by the end of grades 4, 8, and 12. School districts had the autonomy to develop their own curriculums that would enable students to achieve the goals laid out in the NJCCCS.

Implementing the NJCCCS was the first step in complying with *Abbott III* and ensuring that New Jersey students would receive a thorough and efficient education. The second step was reforming how state aid was distributed to school districts across the state. In December 1996, the governor signed the Comprehensive Education Improvement and Financing Act[12] (CEIFA) into law, linking state standards to state aid.

Comprehensive Education Improvement and Financing Act

The CEIFA was designed to ensure that all students in the state of New Jersey, whether in regular or special needs school districts, would receive a thorough and efficient education. CEIFA was very different from the earlier Quality Education Act because it focused on providing students with both a thorough and efficient education by linking state standards to state aid. While the QEA used a complex formula to determine which schools required the most funding based on socio-economic status and enrollment, CEIFA linked state aid to the amount of funding schools would need in order to meet the specific goals of the new NJCCCS.[13]

Under CEIFA, a thorough education was defined as an education that met the NJCCCS. Efficient education was defined as a set of standards that were considered essential to meeting the NJCCCS such as class size, administrators/teachers per student, schools per district, and types and amounts of classroom supplies, services and materials, that are considered to be sufficient to achieve the state content standards. Local revenue would be used to fund all other school expenses, which were considered non-essential.

The CEIFA preserved the foundational funding structure established in the 1990 QEA. Under CEIFA, this foundation funding was referred to as the 'T & E' amount, defined as the amount of per-pupil funding needed to implement the NJCCCS.[14] In 1996, the T & E amount was set at $6,720. This number was based on a model education delivery system designed by the state as well as average salaries of school staff. The T & E level for the thirty special needs districts was set as 1.05 times that amount, thus $7,056 in 1996. Under CEIFA, school districts could generate additional revenue through local taxes, thus resulting in disparate per-pupil expenditures; however, the additional revenue was considered unnecessary in terms of providing students with a thorough and efficient education.

The CEIFA also addressed the court's concern in *Abbott III* that special needs school districts needed supplemental educational programs and support services. The act established Early Childhood Program Aid (ECPA) and Demonstrably Effective Programs Aid (DEPA). Through ECPA, special needs districts would receive additional funding for early childhood programs such as full day kindergarten, preschool programs, and other services. DEPA provided funding for special services such as health programs and social service programs for students in special needs districts.

Another important component of CEIFA was measuring performance indicators. Prior to the implementation of CEIFA, student performance was not evaluated until eighth grade. Under CEIFA, New Jersey students would be evaluated in fourth grade with the Elementary School Proficiency Assessment (ESPA), eighth grade through the Early Warning Test (EWT), and in high school through the High School Proficiency Assessment (HSPA). The purpose of the new evaluation system was to give educators and administrators an indication of whether students were meeting the performance goals of the NJCCCS, and what areas required improvement.

In January 1997, The Education Law Center returned to the New Jersey state supreme court to assert that the new funding act violated the *Abbott* rulings.

Abbott IV

In 1997, the New Jersey supreme court in *Abbott IV*[15] declared the CEIFA unconstitutional as applied to special needs districts. The court found that, like QEA, the CEIFA did not insure adequate funding for special needs districts. While CEIFA attempted to link standards to state aid, the court found that there was no concrete system in place to ensure that special needs districts had the resources to implement the NJCCCS, rendering it unconstitutional. The court also found that CEIFA failed to address school facilities in the special needs districts, which were in dire condition.

The court asserted that the 'model school district' used to determine the T & E or foundation amount was not representative of a successful school district in the state of New Jersey. The state argued that the additional funds that school districts were able to generate by local revenue under CEIFA were unnecessary to student achievement, and therefore wealthier school districts, although successful, were not used to develop the model school district used in the funding formula. The state claimed that wealthier districts frivolously spend excess capital and therefore should not be used in developing a model school district; however, the court disagreed, asserting that the level of spending for education in the wealthier districts was not attributable solely to inefficiency or directed to educational luxuries. Furthermore, the court found no evidence to support the assertion that all amounts spent by Livingston, Princeton, Millburn, and the other successful districts in excess of the T & E amount constituted educational inefficiency. According to the court, those additional funds that successful, wealthier districts were able to generate would only further the disparity between special needs districts and regular districts.

Ultimately, the court determined that one of the key problems with CEIFA was that it treated all school districts equally, rather than taking into account the additional needs of the special needs districts.

In response to *Abbott IV*, the state provided $246 million to the *Abbott* districts or thirty special needs districts for the 1997-98 school year in order to equalize spending.

Abbott V

In May 1998, the New Jersey supreme court issued its opinion in *Abbott V*,[16] requiring the Commissioner of Education to implement whole-school reform for the thirty special needs districts through Success for All,[17] a comprehensive initiative designed to increase student achievement. The Success for All program focused on reading, writing, and language arts and was designed to help at-risk students succeed in reading. In addition, the court directed the Commissioner to implement full-day kindergarten in the special needs districts. The court also ruled that the special needs districts could request additional funding to implement supplemental programs if the district were able to demonstrate need.

The decision in *Abbott V* required implementation of a comprehensive set of reforms for special needs districts, as well as a means for the districts to appeal for additional funding as needed.

The *Abbott* decisions enabled the state of New Jersey to assure funding parity; as a result, students in special needs districts would receive the same per-pupil funding as students in wealthier school districts.[18]

BASIC SUPPORT PROGRAM

New Jersey's basic support program for funding public schools was set in legislation in 2008 via the School Funding Reform Act[19] (SFRA). The formula incorporated both wealth equalization and categorical aid. Wealth-equalized aid sought fiscal equality by assuring that each school district would receive adequate funds based on local ability to generate tax revenue. The formula called for categorical aid to be disbursed based on a combination of student data and costs associated with pupil-driven performance categories. The SFRA was expressed formulaically as:

Adequacy Budget = (Base Cost + At-Risk Cost (Based on eligibility for free and reduced lunches)
+
Limited English Proficient Cost
+
Combination (of Limited English Proficient and At-Risk) Cost
+
Special Education Census)
×
Geographic Cost Adjustment

Although the SFRA has been modified over time,[20] categorical aid is still provided based on the following categories: (1) special education, (2) security, (3) transportation, (4) pre-school, (5) debt service aid/benefit payments, and (6) school choice aid.[21]

DEMOGRAPHIC, REVENUE, AND EXPENDITURE PROFILES

New Jersey ranks 47th in total land area compared to the other states; however, it is ranked second among densely populated states with approximately 1,260.11 people per square mile.[22] Although New Jersey is geographically small compared to the rest of the nation, this densely populated and diverse state is ranked among those states generating and spending the most money on public elementary and secondary education. For Fiscal Year 2019, New Jersey generated $31,772,613,000 in public school system revenue. It ranked fifth among the states that generate the most revenue.[23] New Jersey generated a per pupil current spending of $20,512 in

FY 2019, approximately 52 percent greater than the national median per-pupil revenue of $13,187.

Demographic Profile

Although New Jersey ranks fifth among the states that generate the most revenue for public education, it is not ranked among the top five states that have the largest populations or largest enrollments. For FY 2019, California had the highest state population with approximately 39,510,000 residents.[26] while New Jersey had a total of 8,880,000 inhabitants and 1,345,089 students enrolled in public schools.

Revenue Profile

For FY 2019, New Jersey reported $31,772,613,000 in public school revenue.[27] About 4.08 percent of total revenue ($1,299,343,000) was received from the federal government, 42.63 percent ($13,546,424,000) from state government, and 53.27 percent ($16,926,846,000) from local government.

Federal Revenue

In FY 2019, the fifty states and the District of Columbia reported $751.68 billion in total revenue, with 7.6 percent coming from the federal government ($57.8 billion), 46.68 percent from state government ($350.9 billion), and 45.61 percent ($342.90 billion) from local government. In comparison, New Jersey generated only 4.08 percent of total public school revenue from federal sources.

Sources of federal revenue included funding for Title I, IDEA, child nutrition, and vocational programs, as well as non-specified sources of funding and direct federal aid. Approximately 26 percent of federal funding to New Jersey ($359,030,000) was for special education. Title I funding accounted for 27.78 percent ($384,505,000). Federal child nutrition programs accounted for 27.6 percent ($382,064,000). Another 17.6 percent ($244,354,000) was received for other and non-specified programs distributed by the state for a variety of federal grant programs such as the Workforce Investment Act, Title V, the Safe and Drug-Free Schools and Community Act, and Mathematics, Science and Teacher Quality grants.[28] Finally, federal funding for vocational programs accounted for less than 1 percent ($10,521,000) of New Jersey's total federal revenue in FY 2019.

State Revenue

For FY 2019, 50 percent ($6,821,719,000) of all state revenue that New Jersey generated for public school education was through General Formula Assistance. General Formula Assistance includes revenue from income tax and sales tax, as well as non-categorical state assistance programs. Non-categorical programs include foundation funding, flat grants, and state public school fund distributions.

State payments on behalf of local educational agencies (LEAs) accounted for $22,467,013,000 (26.6 percent) of state revenue that New Jersey generated in FY 2019. This revenue was not bestowed directly on school districts; instead, the funds were used for benefits such as employee funds and health benefits. Additionally, revenues may be used to repay school districts for textbooks, telecommunications and school buses provided by the state.

Funding for compensatory programs amounted to $82,396,000 (0.6 percent) of public school revenue in 2019. Special education funding accounted for $1,165,941,000 (8 percent). Approximately 2 percent of state revenue in New Jersey was for transportation programs, with no state revenue generated for vocational programs.[29] Other and non-specified state aid amounted to $58,301,066,000 (11 percent); this revenue was used to support the central or school business office in data processing, staff services, and payments for fiscal services. Some revenue is included in this category because it was used for more than one of the programs mentioned in this section and therefore could not be placed in a distinct category.

Local Revenue

Nationally, local sources of revenue accounted for approximately 64.47 percent of total public elementary-secondary school system moneys in the fifty states and the District of Columbia in FY 2019. In New Jersey, local revenue accounted for a larger percentage of total revenue, as in FY 2019 fully 86 percent came from local governments.[30]

New Jersey's high taxation was born out as 86 percent ($14,575,138,000) of local revenue came from property taxes in 2019.[31] About 6 percent ($1,083,904,000) of local revenue came from parent government contributions which are tax receipts and other amounts appropriated by a parent government and transferred to its independent school system. Revenue from non-school local government amounted to 1.8 percent ($309,884,000) of total local revenue. School lunch charges amounted to another 1.4 percent ($246,705,000), while less than 1 percent came from tuition and transportation charges. Another 1.8 percent ($318,033,000) of New Jersey's total local revenue came from other charges. Finally, 4 percent, ($320,551,000) came from other local revenue.[32]

New Jersey is ranked among the states that generate the most revenue for public education. But the majority of New Jersey's public elementary and secondary education resources comes from local sources, with the bulk derived from property tax.

Expenditure Profile

The United States spent $752.29 billion in FY 2019 on public elementary and secondary education. Current spending accounted for $652.27 billion (86.7 percent) of the total expenditure; capital outlay accounted for $76.28 billion (10.13 percent); and other expenditures accounted for $23.74 billion (3 percent) of total spending. New Jersey's total spending amounted to $ 31,208,793,000 on public schools, earning it fifth place position among states spending the most on schools. About $29,488,400,000 (94.5%) of funds in New Jersey was used for current spending; another $1,404,067,000 (4.5 percent) was allocated to capital outlay; and $366,415,000 (1 percent) was assigned to other expenses.

Of the $652.27 billion current spending on public schools in the U.S. in FY 2019, approximately $394.16 billion (60 percent) was spent on instruction; $225.69 billion (34 percent) went to support services; and $32.42 billion (5 percent) went to other expenditures.

Of the $10,815,710,000 that New Jersey spent on support services, $3,222,374,000 (29 percent) went to pupil support services for recordkeeping, social work, student accounting, counseling, student appraisal, record maintenance, and placement services. It also included payments made for medical, dental, psychological, nursing and speech services. About $1,119,690,000 (10 percent) went to instructional staff support services which including expenditure for supervision of instruction service improvements, curriculum development, instructional staff training, and media, library audiovisual, television, and computer assisted services. About $531,156,000 (5 percent) was allocated to general administration to include spending for the board of education and office of the superintendent. Payments for school-level administration amounted to $1,375,199,000 (12.7 percent). Operation and maintenance of plant was $2,706,196,000 (25 percent) of total capital disbursement for support services. These funds were expended for building services such as electricity, heating, and air conditioning, as well as maintenance of grounds, property insurance, and security.[33]

New Jersey pupil transportation amounted to $1,154,375,000 (10.67 percent) of total expenditures for FY 2019. Other non-specified support services amounted to $706,7205,000 (6.5 percent), a category that included payments for business support such as in the areas of budgeting, payroll, auditing, and accounting as well as payments for central support such as in the areas planning, research and development.

Finally, school systems in the U.S. in 2019 spent $76,281,359,000 on capital outlay. Approximately 80 percent of those funds was allocated to construction, 5.3 percent to maintaining building and grounds, 3 percent to instructional equipment, and 11 percent to other equipment. Additionally, U.S. schools spent $20,127,198,000 in interest on debt and $3,601,694,000 to payments to other governments, which includes payments made to states, counties, cities, and special district school housing authorities including repayment of loans and debt service payments to entities that incur debt instead of the school system as well as payments made to other school systems. In comparison, New Jersey's school systems allocated $1,404,067,000 to capital outlay; these funds were distributed very similarly to national averages, with approximately 80 percent of total capital outlay allocated to construction, 5 percent to maintaining land and existing structures, 2.5 percent to instructional equipment, and 11.4 percent to other equipment. New

TABLE 30.1.   State Average All Operating Types of Expenditures in New Jersey
School Districts. Fiscal Years 2017-2019

Total Spending Per Pupil 2016-17 Costs Amount per Pupil: $20,852 2017-18 Costs Amount per Pupil: $21,866	**Total Legal Services Costs Per Pupil** Per Pupil Amount (2016-17 actual costs): $46 Per Pupil Amount (2017-18 actual costs): $44 Per Pupil Amount (2018-19 budget): $44
Budgetary Per Pupil Cost 2016-17 Actual Costs Amount per Pupil: $15,259 2017-18 Actual Costs Amount per Pupil: $15,809 2018-19 Budgeted Costs Amount Per Pupil: $16,599	**Administration Salaries and Benefits** Per Pupil Amount (2016-17 actual costs): $1,342 Per Pupil Amount (2017-18 actual costs): $1,403 Per Pupil Amount (2018-19 budget): $1,419
Total Classroom Instruction Per Pupil Amount (2016-17 actual costs): $9,001 Per Pupil Amount (2017-18 actual costs): $9,332 Per Pupil Amount (2018-19 budget): $9,724	**Total Operations and Maintenance of Plant** Per Pupil Amount (2016-17 actual costs): $1,812 Per Pupil Amount (2017-18 actual costs): $1,864 Per Pupil Amount (2018-19 budget): $1,985
Classroom Salaries and Benefits Per Pupil Amount (2016-17 actual costs): $8,466 Per Pupil Amount (2017-18 actual costs): $8,767 Per Pupil Amount (2018-19 budget): $9,095	**Salaries/Benefits—Operations of Maintenance of Plant** Per Pupil Amount (2016-17 actual costs): $906 Per Pupil Amount (2017-18 actual costs): $934 Per Pupil Amount (2018-19 budget): 997
Classroom General Supplies and Textbooks Per Pupil Amount (2016-17 actual costs): $288 Per Pupil Amount (2017-18 actual costs): $289 Per Pupil Amount (2018-19 budget): $324	**Board Contributions to the Food Service Program** Per Pupil Amount (2016-17 actual costs): $73 Per Pupil Amount (2017-18 actual costs): $53 Per Pupil Amount (2018-19 budget): $41
Classroom Purchased Services and Other Per Pupil Amount (2016-17 actual costs): $247 Per Pupil Amount (2017-18 actual costs): $276 Per Pupil Amount (2018-19 budget): $304	**Extracurricular Costs** Per Pupil Amount (2016-17 actual costs): $299 Per Pupil Amount (2017-18 actual costs): $308 Per Pupil Amount (2018-19 budget): $331
Total Support Services Per Pupil Amount (2016-17 actual costs): $2,437 Per Pupil Amount (2017-18 actual costs): $2,519 Per Pupil Amount (2018-19 budget): $2,701	**Personal Services—Employee Benefits** % of Total Salaries (2016-17): 30.1% % of Total Salaries (2017-18): 30.6% % of Total Salaries (2018-19): 33.3%
Support Services Salaries and Benefits Per Pupil Amount (2016-17 actual costs): $2,098 Per Pupil Amount (2017-18 actual costs): $2,168 Per Pupil Amount (2018-19 budget): $2,283	**Total Equipment Cost** Per Pupil Costs (2016-17): $88 Per Pupil Costs (2017-18): $92 Per Pupil Costs (2018-19): $82
Total Administrative Costs Per Pupil Per Pupil Amount (2016-17 actual costs): $1,675 Per Pupil Amount (2017-18 actual costs): $1,750 Per Pupil Amount (2018-19 budget): $1,774	

Source: State of New Jersey Department of Education (2019). https://www.nj.gov/cgi-bin

Jersey's public school systems also spent $264,843,000 in interest payments on debt and $51,483,000 was allocated to other governments.[34]

Per-Pupil Expenditure Profile
New Jersey ranked fourth among states with the highest per-pupil expenditure for Fiscal Year 2019.-The average per-pupil expenditure in the U.S. was $13,

187.[35] According to the National Education Association, New Jersey had the second highest starting teacher salary in the 2018-2019 school year, with an average of $52,854.[36]

Table 30.1 shows recent yearly amounts for New Jersey per-pupil expenditures for all operating types by major categories.

SUMMARY

Although geographically small, New Jersey is a densely populated and diverse state ranking among the top spenders in the nation on public education. The majority of school funding in New Jersey comes from local sources. In 2019, about 53.27 percent came from local revenue, 42.63 percent from state revenue, and 4.08 percent from federal revenue. Consequently, New Jersey is a state with high property taxes.

While New Jersey is ranked among the top state spenders, it is also one of the most diverse states. New Jersey finance data reflects that some districts show student poverty rates of 80 percent, while wealthier districts report 4 percent.[38] In light of need-based differences, it is important to keep in mind that some students need more financial support than others. The per-pupil expenditure is calculated by a simple mathematic equation—total spending divided by total students. This equation does not take into account the needs of students.

Per-pupil revenue and per-pupil spending are used to compare education funding within a state or among states. Assessing spending by pupil may not be the best indicator of funding and spending because all students across the state are treated equally regardless of need. The amount of funding per-pupil comparison is highly inappropriate and misleading, according to the former head of the Division of Finance for the New Jersey Department of Education, because it fails to take into account the differences in revenues and expenditures generated by the stark variations in concentrations of student poverty and other student needs.[39]

The Education Law Center recommends using a Funding Per Weighted Pupil calculation to assess per-pupil spending within a state. This calculation takes into account the needs of at risk students, limited English proficiency (LEP) students, and students who are both LEP and at-risk. If the Census Bureau used a weighted formula such as what the Education Law Center proposes, it would demonstrate a much clearer picture of how education funding is being distributed.[40]

New Jersey reflects a needs-based approach to financing public education. Decades of *Abbott* decisions have shaped New Jersey's school finance in an effort to ensure a 'thorough and efficient' education for all as outlined in the state constitution. Each *Abbott* decision has allowed the New Jersey supreme court to better define what constitutes a thorough and efficient education and how to provide children in the state of New Jersey with equal access to high quality education. According to the Education Law Center:

New Jersey has a high degree of "equity" in its school finance system, with small gaps between the poor and wealthiest districts. Many states do not spend enough on public education and have large funding gaps among districts, with low poverty districts far outspending higher poverty districts.[42]

New Jersey continues to make changes to its funding model in an attempt at increasing equity for students within the state.

ENDNOTES

*The authors wish to acknowledge that portions of this chapter were written for the first edition of this text by Luke J. Stedrak.

1   62 N.J. 473 (1973).

2   See, e.g., *Abbott v. Burke* (1985), 495 A. 2d 376 - NJ: Supreme Court; *Abbott v. Burke* (1990), 575 A. 2d 359 - NJ: Supreme Court; *Abbott v. Burke* (1994), 643 A. 2d 575 - NJ: Supreme Court; *Abbott v. Burke* (1997), 693 A. 2d 417 - NJ: Supreme Court; *Abbott v. Burke* (1998), 710 A. 2d 450 - NJ: Supreme Court.

3   Public School Education Act of 1975, N.J. STAT. ANN. 18A:4A,7A,1-33 (West 1989); Quality Education Act of 1990, ch. 52, §§ 1-33, 1990 N.J. Laws 587-613 (codified at N.J. STAT. ANN. §§ 18A:7D-1 (West Supp. 1994)).

4   *Abbott v. Burke*, 100 N.J. 269, 495 A.2d 376, N.J.,1985.

5   *Abbott v. Burke*, 119 N.J. 287 (June 1990)

6   1990 N.J. Laws 587 (codified as amended at N.J. STAT. ANN. §§ 18A:7D (West 1999)), *repealed by* 1991 N.J. Laws 200 & Comprehensive Educational Improvement and Financing Act of 1996, 1996 N.J. Laws 954.

7   J. Ellis and R.J. Swissler, Funding Education under the Quality Education Act of 1990. New Jersey Department of Education (1991). Retrieved from http://www.njleg.state.nj.us/PropertyTax-Session/OPI/FundingEducation.pdf

8   New Jersey Department of Education. (n.d.). Abbotts - History of Funding Equity. Retrieved from http://www.state.nj.us/education/archive/abbotts/chrono/

9   *Abbott III* 643 A. 2d 575 (1994).

10   New Jersey school districts are grouped into District Factor Groups which are a measure of the school districts' socioeconomic status. The categories are: A, B, CD, DE, FG, GH, I, and J. The lowest SES school districts are labeled as A or B, while the highest SES districts are labeled as I or J.

11   https://www.nj.gov/education/cccs/

12   ftp://www.njleg.state.nj.us/19961997/PL96/138_.htm

13   M.E. Goertz and M. Edwards. "In Search of Excellence for All: The Courts and New Jersey School Finance Reform." *Journal of Education Finance,* (1999) 25(1), 5-31.

14   State of New Jersey (1996). Comprehensive Educational Improvement and Financing Act. http://www.njleg.state.nj.us/PropertyTaxSession/OPI/BriefExplanationCEIFA.pdf

15   693 A. 2d 417 (1997).

16   710 A. 2d 450 (1998).

17   https://www.state.nj.us/education/archive/abbotts/wsr/shu/chap2.htm

18   Educ. Law Center. "The History of *Abbott v. Burke*." (n.d.). Retrieved from: http://www.edlaw-center.org/cases/abbott-v-burke/abbott-history.html

19   "School Funding Reform Act of 2008" (SFRA), P.L.2007, c.260.

20   As amended, NJ S2 (2018). Retrieved from: https://www.billtrack50.com/BillDetail/985333

21   New Jersey Department of Education. "A Formula for Success: All Children, All Communities." Retrieved from: http://nj.gov/education/sff/reports/AllChildrenAllCommunities.pdf.

22 States Ranked by Size and Population (2021). Retrieved from: http://www.ipl.org/div/stateknow/popchart.html

23 U.S. Census Bureau. (2021). *Public Education Finances: 2019.* Retrieved from: https://www.census.gov/data/tables/2019/econ/school-finances/secondary-education-finance.html.

26 Ibid.

27 Ibid.

28 Ibid.

29 Ibid.

30 Ibid.

31 Ibid.

32 Ibid.

33 Ibid.

34 Ibid.

35 Ibid.

36 National Education Association. "2018-2019 Average Starting Teacher Salaries by State." (n.d.). Retrieved from: https://www.nea.org/sites/default/files/2020-09/2018-2019%20Teacher%20Salary%20Benchmark%20Report.pdf

37 U.S. Census Bureau. (2021). *Public Education Finances: 2019.* Retrieved from: https://www.census.gov/data/tables/2019/econ/school-finances/secondary-education-finance.html

38 Ibid.

39 Ibid.

40 Ibid.

41 Education Week. (2019). *New Jersey Ranks First on Quality Counts Annual Report Card.* [Press Release]. Retrieved from: https://www.edweek.org/policy-politics/new-jersey-ranks-first-on-quality-counts-annual-report-card/2019/09

42 Educ. Law Center. The Right Way to Compare NJ Education Funding. (2010). Retrieved from: http://www.edlawcenter.org/news/archives/school-funding/the-right-way-to-compare-nj-education-funding.html

CHAPTER 31

NEW MEXICO

Marianna Olivares
Arizona State University

Cristóbal Rodríguez
Arizona State University

GENERAL BACKGROUND

New Mexico's public school system was established in 1891, after decades of debate among groups with differing religious and political beliefs.[1] The public school debate in New Mexico coincided with the transition from territory to statehood. Eventually in 1912, New Mexico became the 47th state to join the United States of America. The state's constitution includes Article XII,[2] which outlines the role the state takes for public education:

§1 provides "A uniform system of free public schools sufficient for the education of, and open to, all the children of school age in the state shall be established and maintained;"

§8 provides "The legislature shall provide for the training of teachers in the normal schools or otherwise so that they may become proficient in both the English and Spanish languages, to qualify them to teach Spanish-speaking pupils and students in the public schools and educational institutions of the state, and shall provide proper means and methods to facilitate the teaching of the English language and other branches of learning to such pupils and students;"

Funding Public Schools in the United States, Indian Country,
and US Territories (Second Edition), pages 485–495.
Copyright © 2023 by Information Age Publishing
www.infoagepub.com
All rights of reproduction in any form reserved.

§10 provides "Children of Spanish descent in the State of New Mexico shall never be denied the right and privilege of admission and attendance in or other public educational institutions of the state, and they shall never be classed in separate schools, but shall forever enjoy perfect equality with other children in all public schools and educational institutions of the state...."

While many changes have taken place over the course of the state's history, New Mexico's public system including, educators, advocates, policy makers, students, and communities, continue with the same dedication. The New Mexico Department of Education prides itself on providing the best possible education for all students. The "Vision and Mission"[3] is:

VISION- Rooted in our Strengths. Students in New Mexico are engaged in a culturally and linguistically responsive educational system that meets the social, emotional, and academic needs of ALL students.

MISSION- Equity, Excellence and Relevance. The New Mexico Public Education Department partners with educators, communities, and families to ensure that ALL students are healthy, secure in their identity, and holistically prepared for college, career, and life.

CURRENT CLIMATE

Most recently, New Mexico, like most states, is attempting to recover, reestablish, and move forward from the effects of the Covid-19 pandemic. With school closures, lack of access to instruction and materials, and health and safety concerns, New Mexico currently faces a daunting task that will require attention and efforts for years to come. A report released in August 2021 from the New Mexico Legislative Finance Committee, Public Education Subcommittee[4] has shed light of some of the results of school closures in March 2020. The report found that school closures reduced student engagement, posed a real risk for the mental health of students and families, as well as exacerbated summer loss of learning.

Even before the Covid-19 pandemic, significant concerns were being raised surrounding the equitable education and outcomes of low-income students. The graphs below show there is a noticeable gap in performance.

Also of note, one of the most notable and impactful recent litigation cases is that of Martinez and Yazzie v. New Mexico[5]. Of particular interest is the financial response to the rulings, after years of litigations in and out of the courts. The final ruling in 2019 stated that due to "dismal" outputs, inputs in funding and programming are insufficient. The Legislature increased recurring K-12 funding by $644.3 million. The details of which can be found in the Figure 31.2.

New Mexico K-12 school system consists of 89 regular school districts, 52 "other education agencies" (which include charter schools), and 6 state school districts (which include juvenile justice centers and schools for the deaf or visually impaired. Within regular school districts there are 315,372 students; 20,811

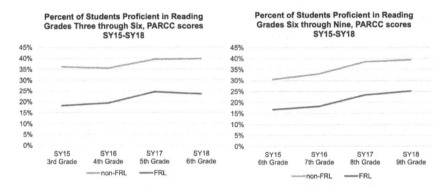

FIGURE 31.1.   Percent of Students Proficient in State Tests

teachers; and 814 schools. The total count of students in all types of districts amounts to 330,501 students. This is summarized in Table 31.1.

The latest report (school year 2017-2018) from the Civil Rights Data Collection shows a majority of students in New Mexico schools identify as Hispanic, 61.7%. Additionally, 22.9% of students identify as White; 10.3% identify as American Indian; 2% identify as Black; 1.9% identify as two or more races; 1.2% identify as Asian; .2% identify as Hawaiian or Pacific Islander. Special student populations include 15.1% of students receiving services under IDEA; 1% identified as 504; and 15% identified as English language learners.

As previously mentioned, New Mexico has not been immune to the effects of recent historical events taking place in the United States. The Covid-19 pandemic along with racial tensions and a recent change in presidential administration have all contributed to the political climate in New Mexico. However, this is being taken as an opportunity to evaluate and proceed with a clearer, more determined mission, in particular for the Public Education Department (PED). Under current

Legislative Appropriations and Laws	
At-risk funding: +$163.3 million	Instructional materials: +$27 million
Removed local and federal formula credits	PED operations: +$3 million
Sunset blanket class size waivers	Prekindergarten (ECECD): +$15.2 million
English learner funding through at-risk index	Educator and staff pay: +$200.5 million
Closed funding formula loopholes	Early literacy: +$8 million
Indian Ed. and BMEP initiatives: +$15 million	Transportation: +$21.8 million
K-5 Plus and ELTP: +$199.9 million	Wraparound and social support services reported through at-risk index expenditures

FIGURE 31.2.   Legislative appropriations from Martinez and Yazzie v. New Mexico

TABLE 31.1.   State Public Schools' Counts

	Schools	Students	Teachers
Regular	814	315,372	20,811
Other	53	14,775	947
State	19 (11 juvenile justice)	354	91
Totals:	886	330,501	21,849

Source: National Center of Educational Statistics (2021) Accessed September 2021. Retrieved from https://nces.ed.gov

leadership the PED is highly motivated to address some longstanding concerns within the public school system.

For context, the state legislature has 42 members in the Senate and 70 members in the House of Representatives. The executive branch is run by the governor. The governor holds power to veto, pardon, and appoint most of the state boards and departments, including the Department of Education. The current governor of New Mexico is Michelle Lujan Grisham. She has held that office since 2019. She is a member of the Democratic Party. The judicial branch of the state's government is made of the Supreme Court and a Court of Appeals. There are five Supreme Court Justices in New Mexico. From 1968-1988, New Mexico has voted for Republican presidential candidates. Since then, it is considered a swing state. New Mexico's sovereign Native American groups elect their own respective tribal councils to handle pertinent tribal affairs and represent their tribe in state and federal negotiations.

TABLE 31.2.   Student Demographics

Student Demographics	Percentage of Student Population
American Indian	10.3%
Asian	1.2%
Black	2%
Hawaiian Or Pacific Islander	.2%
Hispanic	61.7%
Two or More Races	1.9%
White	22.9%
Idea	15.1%
504	1%
ENGLISH LANGUAGE LEARNER	15%

Source: Civil Rights Data Collection (2021) Accessed September 2021. Retrieved from https://ocrdata.ed.gov

Other changes have also been seen in New Mexico's PED due largely to political leaders, active union representation and engagement, as well as advocacy groups. UnidosUS is the largest Latino civil rights and advocacy organization in the United States. It has played an active and pivotal role in improving the educational landscape of NM. Transform New Mexico is another advocacy group that seeks to address the inequalities and inadequacies the state has demonstrated. Both groups contributed greatly to the persistence and ultimate success of the *Martinez and Yazzie v. New Mexico*. Also, a historic 10% increase in teachers' salary was approved. Equally, proponents of education continue to advance the efforts towards a more justice oriented and equitable education for all children.

Before the pandemic and in response to mandates from the most recent passing of the Every Students Succeeds Act, New Mexico developed a plan for school years 2017-2020. This plan is known as New Mexico Rising: New Mexico's State Plan[6]. This includes *Strategic Plan 2017-2020: Kids First, New Mexico Wins*, which outlines student achievement goals, both short term and long term. It states, "A student's ethnic background, socio-economic status, primary home language, prior academic experience, or home community within the state is not an excuse to lower expectations for our students, our schools, or our educators that serve them."

The PED Goals for 2019-2020 are: more than 50% of students academically proficient in ELA and mathematics; more than 80% of students graduate high school; no more than 25% of college enrollees require remedial coursework. Long-term goals are: by 2020, New Mexico will be the fastest growing state in the nation when it comes to student outcomes; by 2022, 64.9% of students proficient on state ELA test and 61.2% of students proficient on state math test; by 2030, 66% of working-age New Mexicans will earn a college degree or post-secondary credential. Keeping in mind this plan and subsequent goals were made prior to the Covid-19 pandemic. Undoubtedly, there has been unforeseen circumstances and even a shift in priorities in response to the pandemic.

BASIC SUPPORT PROGRAM

The current public school funding formula in New Mexico was created in the Public School Finance Act of 1974. At the time, it was considered quite innovative in that it did not rely on local property taxes as a means to fund local schools.

The funding formula[7] starts with enrollment, which is referred to as "membership." Next, multipliers are used for the number of students in different grades, students in bilingual or special education, the education experience of teachers, the number of students at risk of having academic problems, and other factors. Ultimately, "units," or the resulting number is determined and multiplied by a unit dollar value. This dollar value is set annually by the Public Education Department, contingent on available funding. This determines a public school's "program cost." Lastly, adjustments are made for energy conservation credits; the re-

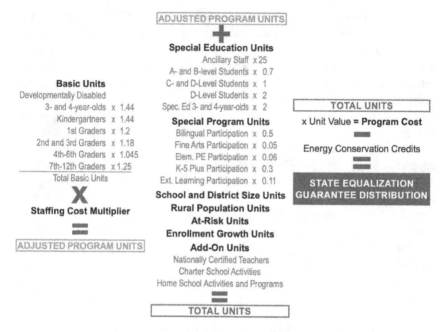

FIGURE 31.3   New Mexico Public School Funding Formula

sulting figure is called the "state equalization guarantee distribution." Figure 31.3 summarizes the funding formula.

The state's funding for school's operational costs comes from the state general fund. State funding also includes public schools' share of interest earned on the land grant permanent fund. Income from state trust land designated to contribute to public schools is also included. Separate from the funding formula are state and federal funds for transportation and other categorical school expenses. It is to be noted that charter schools are funded under the same funding formular. Charter schools are also able to apply for supplemental funds through the PED for special appropriations, specific to school needs and initiatives. Charter schools are typically largely funded by the state. While New Mexico has recently attempted to decrease the expansion of charter schools, lobbyists continue to push for school choice and promote charter schools.[8] Nonpublic schools may apply for instructional material allocations and are required to submit an annual report concerning the use of the funds.

Enacted by the Legislature of the State of New Mexico, the "General Appropriation Act of 2021"[9] details the fiscal allocations for the state. This includes Section I. OTHER EDUCATION, which outlines appropriations from the General Fund, Other State Funds, Internal Service Funds, and Federal Funds. All appropriations in the Act are in regards to Fiscal Year (FY) 2022. Noted in the Act, the

TABLE 31.3. Appropriations (in thousands of dollars)

Item	General Fund	Other State Funds	Internal Service Funds	Federal Funds	Total/Target
Personal services and employee benefits	12,486.2	3,056.6	45.0	7,475.9	23,063.7
Contractual services	890.3	720.4		19,631.9	21,242.6
Other	988.0	372.0		3,572.1	4,932.1
Performance Measures	a. Outcome: Number of local education agencies audited for funding formula components and program compliance (30)				
	b. Explanatory: Number of eligible children served in state-funded Prekindergarten				
	c. Explanatory: Number of eligible children served in K-5 plus				
	d. Outcome: Percent of students in K-5 plus meeting benchmark on early reading skills (75%)				
Subtotal					**49,238.4**

Public Education Department is focusing on "leadership and support, productivity, building capacity, accountability, communication and fiscal responsibility."

While all regional education cooperatives receive the same amount of money from the General Fund, school districts or charter schools may submit applications for additional funding from other funding sources. This accounts for the

TABLE 31.4. Regional Education Cooperatives Appropriations (in thousands of dollars)

	General Fund	Other State Funds	Internal Service Funds	Federal Funds	Total/Target
Northwest	103.4	5,196.0	17.9	284.0	5,601.3
Northeast	103.4	475.0		831.8	1,410.2
Lea county	103.4	1,649.3	347.4	5,019.0	7,119.1
Pecos valley	103.4	2,780.0	107.5		2,991.8
Southwest	103.4	975.0	38.0	800.0	1.916.4
Central	103.4	5,089.7	40.3	1,071.0	6,304.4
High Plains	103.4	4,444.5		1,398.7	5,946.6
Clovis	103.4	904.0		2,500.0	3,507.4
Ruidoso	103.4	5,441.1		2,219.0	7,763.5
Four corners	103.4				103.4
Subtotal					42,664.1

TABLE 31.5. Public Education Department Special Appropriations

	General Fund	Other State Funds	Internal Service Funds	Federal Funds	Total/ Target
Early literacy and reading support	1,661.0				1,661.0
Indigenous, multilingual, multicultural and special education	5,067.8				5,067.8
Principals' professional development	2,491.5				2,491.5
Teachers' professional development	2,869.5				2,869.5
Graduation, reality and dual-role skills program	415.3		200.0		615.3
National board certification assistance		500.0			500.0
Advanced placement test assistance	1,000.0				1,000.0
Student nutrition and wellness	2,342.0				2,342.0
Science, technology, engineering, arts and math initiatives	3,025.9				3,025.9
Subtotal					**19,573.0**

variation seen in Total funding. The Public Education Department prioritizes funding for those districts that show funds budgeted for certain actions and services such as new teacher mentorship, tutoring, data-guided instruction, or other evidence-based practices that improve student outcomes. FY 2022 saw a decrease in total funding for regional education cooperatives. FY 2021 had $55,804,000 in appropriations, compared to $42,664,100 in FY 2022. This was not the only category to see reduced funding.

The Public Education Department also prioritizes districts and charter schools that implement a K-5 plus program or extended learning time programs for

TABLE 31.6 Public Schools Facilities Authority Appropriations

	General Fund	Other State Funds	Internal Service Funds	Federal Funds	Total/Target
Personal services and employee benefits	4,394.0				4,394.0
Contractual services	110.9				110.9
Other	1,226.0				1,226.0
Performance Measures	a. Explanatory: Statewide public school facility condition index measured on December 31 of prior calendar year				
	b. Explanatory: Statewide public school facility maintenance assessment report score measured on December 31 of prior calendar year				
Subtotal					**5,730.9**

TABLE 31.7. Total Appropriations

	General Fund	Other State Funds	Internal Service Funds	Federal Funds	Total/Target
Total Other Education:	34,271.5	37,335.4	796.1	44,803	117,206.4

TABLE 31.8 Use of CARES Act Aid to New Mexico

Funding Category	Amount in Dollars	Percentage of Total Budget
Educational technology	30,074,741.61	30.96
Preparedness activities	28,565,533.30	29.41
Other student and school supports	17,631,013.92	18.15
Student supports and interventions	13,403,705.95	13.8
Other student and school supports	7,394,497.56	7.61

eligible students. Special appropriations also saw a decrease in funding. When compared to the previous years, FY 2022 appropriations were significantly lower at $19,573,000. FY 2021 included a total of $32,400,000 in special appropriations. Specifically, funds for principal and teacher professional development decreased. Several areas of special allocations were eliminated altogether from the previous year. Community school initiatives, school lunch copayments, teacher pathways coordinator, and math, engineering, and science achievement program, among others, were cut from the budget in FY 2022.

The purpose of the Public Schools Facilities Authority is to oversee all public school facilities in the eighty-nine districts across the state. They ensure the proper and adequate planning, building, and maintenance of facilities, as well as manage the state funding. Their oversight is in accordance with approved educational programs.

Overall, Table 31.7 shows a total of $117,206,400 in Section I of the General Appropriation Act of 2021. This is less than the prior year which had a total of $143,664,300. Budget cuts were seen across many categories. Some increases in special appropriation funds were also noted, due to increases in federal funding.

In response to the Covid-19 pandemic, the federal government passed the Coronavirus Aid Relief, and Economic Security (CARES) Act for the Elementary and Secondary School Emergency Relief Fund (ESSER)[10]. Roughly, $13.2 billion was allocated to states to aid in the costly efforts of providing a safe and accessible learning environment for school children. New Mexico was awarded $108 million. Ninety percent of the total amount was awarded as subgrants based on Local Education Agencies' proportional share of final 2019-2020 Title I, Part A allocations. Latest reports show, of the $97.72 million total budget, $86.2 million have been spent, leaving approximately 11.78% of unspent funds.

The largest expense was the allocation for educational technology. One hundred percent of these funds went towards purchasing technology devices. Preparedness activities, which accounted for another third of the total supplemental budget included funds (about $20 million) to sanitize facilities, as well as for planning during long-term closures. The larger portion of "other student and school supports" included funds for principals and school leaders, as well as money to continue previous activities and services offered at schools. The smaller allotment for "other student and school supports" spent $2.6 million on indirect costs. Overall, the federal funds were greatly needed in the state to address access and equity concerns among minority and low-income populations. The PED allocated money to LEAs in a way they saw fit and appropriate.

SUMMARY

While New Mexico's funding formula has strived to be equitable and account for unique funding needs of some subpopulations, there are still concerns over funding and appropriations. Truly, Covid-19 has placed an additional burden on the state's financial system. Nonetheless, long standing inadequacies in funding remain to be addressed. Steps to correct these shortcomings are found in the court mandated additional funds resulting from the Martinez and Yazzie v. New Mexico case. The effects of this increase in funds is yet to be seen and will surely be monitored for effectiveness. Additional federal support is also welcomed to help alleviate some of the extra costs associated with the pandemic. Lastly, advocates, educators, policymakers, students and community members continue to demand and progress towards a more equitable finance system with equitable allocations. Ultimately, this will lead to the much sought after academic gains for all students of New Mexico.

We would like to acknowledge the work of David Thompson and Craig Wood in crafting the chapter for the first edition[11] of this work. Previous editions of this chapter have contributed to this edition and provided valuable information to the field of education finance.

ENDNOTES

[1]   Everett, Dianna. "The Public School Debate in New Mexico: 1850-1891." Arizona and the West 26, no. 2 (1984): 107–34. http://www.jstor.org/stable/40169273.

[2]   New Mexico Constitution, As adopted January 21, 1911, and as Subsequently Amended by the People in General and Special Elections 1911through 2021. New Mexico Compilation Commission (2021). Retrieved from: http://www.sos.state.nm.us/nmconst2021.pdf

[3]   New Mexico Department of Education (2021). New Mexico Rising: New Mexico's State Plan for the Every Student Succeeds Act. Retrieved from https://www2.ed.gov/admins/lead/account/stateplan17/nmconsolidatedstateplan.pdf

[4]   New Mexico Legislature. "Legislative Finance Committee, Early Childhood & Education" Subcommittee Brief. Updated August 2021. Accessed October 1, 2021. Retrieved from https://www.nmlegis.gov/Entity/LFC/Early_Childhood_And_Education

5   Martínez and Yazzie v. New Mexico. (2019). Final Judgment, Nos. D-101-CV-2014-00793 & D-101-CV-2014-02224. Retrieved from http://nmpovertylaw.org/wp- content/uploads/2019/02/D-101-CV-2014-00793-Final-Judgment-and-Order-NCJ-1.pdf.

6   New Mexico Department of Education (2021). New Mexico Rising: New Mexico's State Plan for the Every Student Succeeds Act

7   Formula descriptions and interpretations hereafter rely in significant part on data found at the New Mexico Legislature's site https://www.nmlegis.gov; also, related links including https://webnew. ped.state.nm.us/bureaus/school-budget-finance-analysis/(2021), as well as https://www.nmlegis. gov/Handouts/ALFC%20082421%20Item%201%20TAB%20-%20A.pdf. Legislative Finance Committee, Public School Funding Formula. Updated April 2021. Accessed September 16, 2021. Retrieved from www.nmlegis.gov/Entity/LFC/Default

8   Martínez, Davíd G. "New Mexico." Journal of Education Finance 46, no. 3 (2021): 325-327. muse.jhu.edu/article/786680.

9   New Mexico Legislation. 2021 Regular Session- HB2 "General Appropriation Act." Retrieved from https://www.nmlegis.gov/Sessions/21%20Regular/final/HB0002.pdf

10 New Mexico Public Education Department. "ESSER I (CARES Act) Funding Report" Updated September 2021. Accessed October 2021. Retrieved from https://webnew.ped.state.nm.us/bureaus/title-i/cares-act-esser/esser-i-cares-act-funding-report/

11 Wood, C. R. et al (Eds) (2019). Funding Public Schools in the United States and Indian Country. Charlotte: Information Age Publishing.

CHAPTER 32

NEW YORK

Brian O. Brent
University of Rochester

Karen J. DeAngelis
University of Rochester

GENERAL BACKGROUND[1]

Enacted in 1894, Article 11 §1 of the New York State Constitution states the Legislature "shall provide for the maintenance and support of a system of free common schools, wherein all the children of this state may be educated." The State currently operates 731 school districts.[2] The five largest urban districts, commonly referred to as the "Big Five," are fiscally dependent on city government for local funding (New York City, Yonkers, Buffalo, Syracuse, and Rochester). All other districts are fiscally independent (i.e., have independent taxing and borrowing authority). The State also has 37 Boards of Cooperative Educational Services (BOCES) that provide shared services to component districts.[3]

Students

There are approximately 2.6 million public school students in New York State (NYS), with total K-12 enrollment ranging from slightly more than 1.0 million

Funding Public Schools in the United States, Indian Country,
and US Territories (Second Edition), pages 497–516.
Copyright © 2023 by Information Age Publishing
www.infoagepub.com

TABLE 32.1. NY Public School Students

Ethnicity	NY Percent of Total Enrollment[6]	US Percent of Total Enrollment[7]
American Indian or Alaska Native	1%	1%
Black or African American	17%	15%
Asian or Native Hawaiian/Other Pacific Islander	10%	5%
Hispanic or Latino	27%	27%
White	42%	47%
Multiracial	3%	4%
Other Groups		
English Language Learners	9%	10%
Students with Disabilities	18%	14%
Economically Disadvantaged	52%	51%
Academic Performance		
Adjusted Cohort Graduation Rate	83%	86%
Percent Taking Scholastic Aptitude Test (SAT)	79%	60%

students in the New York City (NYC) district to less than 20 students in a few districts. In addition, 443,000 students attend private K-12 schools throughout the State, with approximately 60% of this number attending schools within the NYC school district catchment area.[4] Overall student enrollment is predicted to decline 3% by 2028.[5] Table 32.1 presents select indicators of NY public school students compared to all US public school students.

Teachers

NY has among the most stringent requirements for becoming and maintaining a teaching certificate, including earning a bachelor's and a master's degree, completing a mentored teaching experience, having at least three years of teaching experience, passing licensing exams, and completing continuing education while employed.[8] Table 32.2 provides a profile of NY's 212,000 public school teachers compared to all US public school teachers.[9]

Total Revenues and Expenditures

NY public schools consistently have among the highest average revenues per pupil compared to other states, and nearly twice the national figure.[10] Notwithstanding the State's high comparative per pupil revenue, there is great disparity in spending among the State's districts. In 2018-19, per pupil spending for the district at the 10th percentile was $12,408 per pupil compared to $22,926 for the district at the 90th percentile. Although state aid does equalize spending to some

TABLE 32.2.   NY Public School Teachers

	New York	US
Estimated Average Annual Salary	$87,543	$63,645
Highest Degree Earned		
Less Than Bachelor's	3%	4%
Bachelor's	4%	40%
Master's	84%	48%
Education Specialist or Doctor's	9%	8%
Teaching Experience		
Less than 3 years	9%	5%
3 to 9 years	33%	30%
10 to 20 years	37%	46%
Over 20 years	21%	19%

extent, the disparities follow from the State's substantial reliance on local property taxes to fund schools, and the attendant variation in property wealth among districts. To illustrate, the average property value for the highest spending decile of districts was 568% greater than that of the lowest spending decile. Moreover, the average full value property tax rate between the highest and lowest spending deciles was nearly $3 per $1,000 of full value.[11]

Table 32.3 provides a snapshot of how NY public schools spend their dollars compared to all US public schools.

The table masks the high and growing percentage of NY's education dollars dedicated to fringe benefits. In 2019-20, fringe benefits accounted for 22% of NY

TABLE 32.3.   NY Public School Spending by Function[12]

Function	New York	US
Instruction	65%	54%
Student Support	3%	5%
Instructional Staff	2%	4%
General Administration	2%	2%
School Administration	4%	5%
Operation and Maintenance	9%	8%
Student Transportation	5%	4%
Other Support Services	3%	3%
Food Services	2%	3%
Capital Outlay	4%	9%
Interest on School Debt	2%	3%

districts' average total expenditures, up from 15% of total expenditures in 1999-2000.[13]

CURRENT POLITICAL CLIMATE

For decades, observers have referred derisively to the way NYS government conducts business as "three men in a room"—the Governor, the Senate Leader, and the Assembly Speaker.[14] Put simply, the phrase denotes three individuals effectively control the fiscal policy levers of the second largest state budget in the nation. Although the individual players have changed in recent years, many because of scandal, the Democrats now have firm control of both chambers of the legislature (~70%) and the governorship.

By mid-January, the Governor submits an Executive Budget proposal to the Senate and Assembly for review. The Senate Finance and Assembly Ways and Means committees analyze the Governor's priorities, revenue and expenditure estimates, and hold public hearings. Based on their independent and joint reviews, the two chambers ultimately agree on a revised budget. The Governor may use a line-item veto of specific items in the proposed budget, but the Legislature can override the Governor's vetoes by a two-thirds vote in each chamber.[15] The State's Constitution mandates the budget be approved by April 1, though the deadline is often not met. On April 7, 2021, the Legislature passed a $212 billion budget for fiscal year 2022, which includes about $30 billion in aid to schools.[16]

Board of Regents and State Education Department

New York's legislature elects and delegates to the Board of Regents stewardship of all educational activities in the State. The Board is comprised of 17 unsalaried members, one from each of the State's 13 judicial districts and four who serve at-large.[17] The Board governs the New York State Department of Education (NYSED) and appoints a Commissioner of Education. New York State Education Law (NYSEL), rules adopted by the Board of Regents, and regulations of the Commissioner provide legal and policy directives to operate regular public, charter, and private schools in the state.[18]

Union Representation and Engagement

Two major unions represent educators in NYS. New York State United Teachers (NYSUT) is a "federation" of more than 1,200 local unions representing 600,000 professionals who work in New York, including current and retired school personnel.[19] The United Federation of Teachers (UFT) is the sole bargaining agent for about 200,000 "non-supervisory" educators in the NYC School District.[20] Both unions are very active in increasing their members' wages and benefits, and improving working conditions.

Other Advocacy and Interest Groups

There are countless educational advocacy groups in NYS. In fact, the New York State Council of Education Associations (NYSCEA) was formed 50 years ago to serve as an "umbrella" organization for the State's many advocacy groups.[21] The NYS Council for Exceptional Children, NYS Council of School Superintendents, and NYS School Boards Association are among the State's most visible advocacy groups.

Current School Finance Litigation

NYS has been embroiled in school finance litigation for more than four decades. The first substantive challenge to its school finance system was *Board of Education, Levittown Union Free School District v. Nyquist,* brought by a set of "property poor" districts (57 N.Y.2d, 453 N.Y.S.2d 643, 1982). The plaintiffs alleged the State's school finance system, which was highly dependent on district property taxes and resulted in per pupil spending disparities, violated the State Constitution. NY's highest court, the Court of Appeals, ruled in favor of the State. The Court held although there were large spending disparities among districts, the Constitution did not require "equal" spending. The Court, however, ruled the State is constitutionally required to provide a "sound basic education."

In 1993, the Campaign for Fiscal Equity (CFE) filed suit alleging the State's school finance system denied NYC's schoolchildren their constitutional right to a "sound basic education." After intermediary courts bandied the case about, in 2003, the New York Court of Appeals ruled against the State. The Court determined a "sound basic education…consisted of at least the basic literacy, calculating and verbal skills necessary for productive civic engagement." Further, to develop these skills students need "minimally adequate physical facilities, and basic learning resources, as well as being taught up-to-date curricula by adequately trained teachers."[22] In 2007, the Legislature sought to meet the demands of the CFE ruling statewide by enacting the NYS Budget and Reform Act, which established a new general state aid program for schools—Foundation Aid (see below). Spurred by the Great Recession of 2008, the State did not fully fund Foundation Aid for the next 13 years.[23] Beginning with the 2021-22 NYS budget, the Legislature pledged to fund fully the Foundation Aid formula (phased in over three years).

Despite the State's recent promise to meet the CFE mandate, two other noteworthy school finance cases continue to wind their way through New York's court system. In *Maisto v. State,* originally filed in 2008, eight small city districts alleged the State denied their students a "sound basic education." In May 2021, an Appellate court ruled unanimously in favor of the plaintiffs.[24] In *New York for Students' Educational Rights (NYSER) v. State of New York,* filed in 2014, the plaintiffs similarly alleged the State failed to allocate funds sufficient to provide all students with "a meaningful educational opportunity."[25] It is not clear what the

State's recent commitment to fully fund Foundation Aid will have on the continuation of these cases.

SOURCES OF REVENUE

On average, NY school districts secure approximately 5% of total revenues from Federal sources, 40% from State formulae aids and grants, and 55% from local sources.[26] As with the total per pupil revenue figures, the distribution among the three revenue sources varies considerably across districts. Districts that are comparatively low wealth (i.e., income and property) and high poverty receive more Federal and State aid than high wealth, low poverty districts.[27] Correspondingly, local revenues account for a greater proportion of total revenues in higher than lower wealth districts.

Federal Revenues

NY school districts receive funds from a number a Federal categorical aids and grants. Title I of the Every Student Succeeds Act (ESSA) and the Individuals with Disabilities Education Act (IDEA) are the two most expansive U.S. Department of Education programs. Title I provides supplemental funds to districts through formulae and competitive grants to support schools with high concentrations of students in poverty.[28] The IDEA is the primary federal funding source for districts to support services for students with disabilities. In 2019, NY reported 500,000 school-aged students with disabilities received special education services.[29] In the same year, the U.S Department of Agriculture reported 54% of NY's students were eligible for free or reduced-price lunch.[30]

State Revenues

Over the decades, state aid as a percent of total expenditures has varied considerably depending on the economic and political landscape. State aid as a percent of local expenditures was about 31% percent in 1944-45, 48% in 1968-69, and 40% in 2020-21.[31] The State's General Fund provides approximately 79% of the funds supporting state aid, where the principal sources of revenue are state income and sales taxes. About 8% of state aid for public schools comes from the School Tax Relief program (STAR) (see below), and the balance of support, approximately 13%, derives from a Special Revenue Fund that accrues state lottery, video lottery terminal, and commercial gaming receipts.[32] The State earmarks all lottery and gaming proceeds for K12 public schools.[33]

Local Revenues

Property Taxes

Real property taxes constitute the primary source of local revenue for schools (approximately 89%).[34] Personal property, such as automobiles, is not subject to school taxes.

Property Tax Credits and Exemptions

Enacted in 1997, the STAR program provides state-funded, partial exemptions to homeowners for their primary residences (Section 425 of the Real Property Tax Law). The Basic STAR exemption exempts $30,000 of property value for homeowners who earn less than $250,000 annually. The Enhanced STAR exemption exempts $70,700 of property value for senior citizens (aged 65 and older) who earn less than $90,550 annually. In 2016, the law changed so that instead of applying to a local assessor for an exemption, new homeowners now register with the State and receive a STAR credit in the form of a check.[35] The State makes payments to school districts to compensate them for lost property tax revenues from STAR. In addition, school districts can opt to reduce, in part, the property tax liability of income poor, senior citizens (Section 467 of the Real Property Tax Law) and qualifying disabled persons (Section 459 of the Real Property Tax Law).[36] NY also provides a Farmer's School Property Tax Credit for farmers who meet income limitations and hold "qualified agricultural property."[37]

Property Tax and Spending Limits

Chapter 97 of the Laws of 2011 established a tax levy limit (commonly referred to as the property tax cap) on all local governments and independent school districts.[38] The property tax cap does not apply to NYC. The other Big Five dependent school districts are subject to the cap as components of their city governments.

The law establishes a limit on the annual growth of property taxes levied to 2% or the rate of inflation, whichever is lower. The property tax cap cannot be less than zero. There are a few exclusions to the cap, including "certain costs of significant judgments arising out of tort actions" and "unusually large year-to-year increases in pension contribution rates."[39] The cap also excludes the tax levy needed to support the local share of capital expenditures.

A proposed levy that does not exceed the property tax cap requires the approval of a simple majority of voters. A proposed levy that exceeds the property tax cap requires approval of 60% of voters. If the district does not obtain a supermajority, the levy remains at the previous year's levy.

Non-Property Taxes

NYS sales tax laws reserve 4% for the State and permit counties the option of supplementing this amount up to an additional 4.75%.[40] Five counties (out of 57 statewide) share a portion of their local sales taxes with approximately 153 school districts, amounting to $308 million in 2019-20.[41] In these counties, the county portion of the sales tax is prorated among districts based on enrollment. In addition, State law requires school districts receive a portion of payments in lieu of taxes (PILOTS) in areas where Industrial Development Agencies have granted tax exemptions.[42] Small city school districts can also levy a utility tax. New York City levies a residential income tax, commercial rent tax, and business and financial tax, portions of which flow to the NYC school district. Yonkers levies an income tax on non-resident commuters.[43]

DISTRIBUTION FORMULAS

NYS distributes funds to school districts using about 40 aid programs. Here we highlight the most consequential aids to school districts.

Foundation Aid [NYSEL §3602 (2 and 4) and §211-d]

NY employs a foundation aid formula to allocate general (unrestricted) aid to public school districts. In 2021, the Legislature committed to comply with the *Campaign for Fiscal Equity* ruling (see above) and increase foundation aid by $4.2 billion, phased in over three years. In 2021-2022, the State increased foundation aid by $1.8 billion and distributed an estimated $19.8 billion, representing 68% of the total State aid distributed.[44]

The State bases the foundation formula on four components, each dependent on a series of complex formulae that, taken together, seek to account for a district's relative educational need and local fiscal capacity. Here we offer a brief overview of key elements of each component:[45]

1. **Adjusted Foundation Amount (AFA).** The State holds the AFA "reflects the average per pupil cost of general education instruction in successful school districts… adjusted annually to reflect change in the consumer price index" (CPI):[46] For the 2021-22 school year, AFA was $6,917 per pupil, before the Regional Cost Index (RCI) and Pupil Needs Index (PNI) were factored in. Table 32.4 reports the RCIs of New York's nine regions:

    The PNI adjusts a district's AFA further by accounting for the number of students who are eligible for FRPL and English language learners, as well as Census poverty counts and student sparsity.

2. **Expected Minimum Local Contribution.** The State requires districts to contribute to its AFA per pupil an amount based on its relative wealth. The most noteworthy factor in the complex, multistep calculation is the Foundation Aid Combined Wealth Ratio (FACWR). The FACWR balances equally a district's income per pupil and property wealth per pupil relative to statewide averages. A district with a FACWR below 1.0 is a district of below average wealth and a district with a FACWR above 1.0

TABLE 32.4.   Regional Cost Indices

Region	Cost Index
Long Island/NYC	1.425
Hudson Valley	1.314
Finger Lakes	1.141
Capital District	1.124
Central New York	1.103
Western New York	1.091
Southern Tier	1.045
Mohawk Valley	1.000
North Country	1.000

is a district of above average wealth. The higher a district's FACWR, the higher their Expected Minimum Local Contribution and, accordingly, the lower their Foundation per pupil, all else equal.

3. **Selected Total Aidable Foundation Pupil Units.** The State applies a set of adjustments to districts' student head count for aid purposes. First, the State determines a district's Average Daily Membership (ADM), which is the total number of students enrolled during a session divided by the number of days in the session (e.g., 180).[47] Second, the State assigns additional "weights" to students if they have a disability and are receiving services (i.e., 1.41) or have been declassified and are in their first year of regular instruction (i.e., 0.5). Students who attend summer school are also assigned an additional weight (0.12).

4. **Foundation Aid Payable (FAP).** The FAP follows from the calculations highlighted above, as well as phase-in factors and minimum/maximum aid increases. For example, in 2021-22, the minimum aid increase was 2% over the 2020-21 Foundation Aid base.[48]

The 2021-22 budget also provides for a number of Foundation Aid set-asides, including $150 million to support school-based academic, health, mental health, nutrition, counseling, legal and other services to students and their families.[49]

Special Education

The State provides aid to students with disabilities through several programs. Here we highlight the most noteworthy.

Public Excess Cost Foundation Aid Set-Aside [NYSEL §3602(4.c)]

New York's Foundation Aid formula provides additional weighting to students with disabilities. To ensure that school districts meet federal maintenance of effort provisions for students with disabilities, each district must "set aside" a portion of its current year Foundation Aid.[50] Public Excess Cost Set-Aside provided for an estimated $2.9 billion in 2021-22.

Private Excess Cost Aid for Pupils in Approved Private School Placements or in State Operated Schools [NYSEL §4405(3]

The State provides wealth equalized aid for students with disabilities who attend approved private schools, Special Act School Districts, the New York State School for the Blind or the New York State School for the Deaf. The Department of Education and the Division of Budget must approve tuition charges of each private school annually.[51] In 2021-22, the State allocated an estimated $434 million to Private Excess Cost Aid.

Public High Cost Excess Cost Aid [NYSEL §3602(5)]

A school district can receive this aid for pupils with disabilities enrolled in resource intensive programs operated by public schools or BOCES. In 2021-22, the State allocated an estimated $664 million to Public High Cost Excess Cost Aid using a wealth equalized formula.[52]

Summer Component of 12-Month Programs for Students with Disabilities Public Excess Cost Set-Aside [NYSEL §4408]

The State uses this aid to support school aged children with severe disabilities who warrant a 12-month program. The State reimburses districts for 80% of education, maintenance, and transportation costs incurred during July and August. The balance (20%) is paid by the district from its General Fund. The student's county of residence later reimburses the NYSED for 10% of eligible costs. The State allocated an estimated $364 million to this aid in 2021-22.

Transportation

Transportation Aid (non-capital only) [NYSEL §3602(7)] supports districts' cost of transporting students to school, BOCES, shared programs at other schools, and occupational programs within the district.[53] Approved expenditures include operational costs associated with a school district's transportation supervisor's office and for the operation of district owned buses, contracted buses, and public service vehicles (subway included). Non-allowable transportation expenditures include the cost of transporting non-disabled pupils who live 1.5 miles or less from school and field trips. Transportation aid is property wealth equalized and adjusted for district pupil sparsity. In 2021-22, the state distributed an estimated $2.1 billion in transportation aid.

Technology

The State provides aid to support the acquisition and maintenance of educational technology through several programs. Most noteworthy is the Smart Schools Bond Act, which authorized the State to issue $2 billion in general obligation bonds to support districts' acquisition of technology equipment, as well as renovate/construct facilities to support technology. Districts can also use funds to construct/renovate facilities to accommodate prekindergarten programs. As of this writing, the State has approved over 1,303 Smart School Investment Plans totaling over $1.7 billion.[54] For 2021-22, the State also allocated $44 million to reimburse districts for computer software expenses up to $15 per pupil based on public and nonpublic school enrollments [NYSEL §751 and §752] and provided $36 million in Instructional Computer Hardware and Technology Equipment Aid [NYSEL §753 and §754] to reimburse districts for hardware expenses up to a wealth adjusted $24.20 per pupil.[55]

Career and Technical Education

BOCES Aid [NYSEL §1950(5)]

Districts other than the Big Five city districts are eligible to receive BOCES aid. The State's 37 BOCES provide services to two or more component school districts upon request, including career and technical education, special education, summer school general instruction, itinerant teacher services, technology services, and staff development.[56] Approved service costs are distributed among component districts in proportion to their level of participation.[57] BOCES aid is equalized by either a district's property tax rate or its relative property value per pupil. In 2021-22, the State allocated an estimated $1.1 billion in BOCES Aid.

Special Services Aid for Five Large City School Districts and Non-Components of BOCES [NYSEL §3602(10)]

The State provides Special Services aid to the Big Five city school districts and any district that is not part of a BOCES for career education, computer administration, and academic improvement. In 2021-22, the State allocated an estimated $281 million in Special Services Aid.[58]

Textbook Aid

Districts receive Textbook Aid [NYSEL §701] equal to the district's actual expenditures for eligible materials up to a maximum of $58.25 per public and nonpublic school pupils (i.e., flat grant per pupil). Districts loan textbooks aided under this program to nonpublic school students. Districts that spend more than the maximum allowable for Textbook Aid and Technology Aids (see above) can apply the excess to the other aids provided the total does not exceed the maximum amount allowable for the combined aids. In 2021-22, the State allocated an estimated $169 million in Textbook Aid.[59]

Library Materials Aid

Districts are eligible to receive Library Materials Aid [NYSEL §701] equal to $6.25 per pupil based on the number of students enrolled in public and nonpublic schools within the district's boundaries (i.e., flat grant per pupil). Districts are required to loan library materials equitably among public and nonpublic school students. In 2021-22, the State allocated an estimated $18 million in Library Materials Aid.[60]

Early Childhood Education (Prekindergarten Programs)

In 2014-15, the State committed $1.5 billion over several years to build a statewide universal full-day prekindergarten program (UPK) [NYSEL §3602-ee]. Beginning in 2019-20, funding was to be divided between two subgroups, three-year-olds and four-year-olds. An estimated $605 million, including $90 million to expand access for four-year-olds using Federal funds, was allocated in UPK Aid to districts in the 2020-21school year. Aid is provided at a per pupil funding rate with a maintenance of effort factor. An additional $340 million ($300 million of which was designated for New York City) was budgeted in 2021-22 for a competitive grant program to support eligible programs offered by schools, non-profit organizations, community-based organizations, charter schools, libraries, and/or museums.[61]

Pursuant to NYSEL §4410 the State allocated an estimated $1.0 billion in 2021-22 to support preschool special education programs and related services (i.e., itinerant services, transportation, evaluations, and administrative costs) for three- and four-year-olds with disabilities. While counties contract with and pay NYSED- and county-approved service providers, the State reimburses the counties approximately 59.5% of the costs of services. In addition, the State provides $75 per child for administrative costs.[62]

Bilingual Education

Part 154-2 of the Commissioner's Regulations [CR Part 154-2] established the standards for English Language Learners (ELLs)/Multilingual Learners (MLLs) that New York public school districts are required to meet. To assist districts in meeting the standards, NYSED operates seven Regional Bilingual Education Resource Network (RBERN) centers at regional BOCES as well as one statewide RBERN. These centers provide training and technical assistance to improve districts' ELLs/MLL programs.[63] In 2021-22, an estimated $18 million in Bilingual Education Grants [Chapter 53 of the Laws of 2020] was allocated to support regional bilingual education programs at RBERN centers and innovative programming.[64]

Other Categorical Programs and Topics Addressed by the State

The State allocates additional aid to districts for a variety of educational purposes. Above we highlighted the most noteworthy categorical aids. Those interested in descriptions of the full set of available aids can turn to the *2021-22 State Aid Handbook*. Here we draw attention to how New York addresses funding for two activities that often have categorical aids in other states.

Gifted and Talented Education

NY does not provide direct state aid to districts for gifted and talented education. However, it funds other programs to advance high school students' academic achievement. For example, in 2017 the State began funding AP exam fees for low-income students who qualify for the College Board's fee reduction.[65] In addition, the State provides funding for early college high school programs, which support public school students to earn college credits while still in high school.[66]

Compensatory Education

NY supports compensatory education needs and services by including a Pupil Needs Index (PNI) in the calculation of Foundation Aid. The PNI drives more resources to those districts with higher percentages of students eligible for free and reduced-price lunch, in poverty, and English Language Learners. In addition, Foundation Aid is dependent on pupil count weightings (e.g., students with disabilities).

CAPITAL OUTLAY AND DEBT SERVICE

Building Aid

School districts can receive Building Aid [NYSEL §3602(6)] for expenditures and financing (i.e., debt service) incurred to construct, renovate, purchase, or lease school buildings. Building Aid is also available to remediate lead contaminated drinking water (Chapter 296 of the Laws of 2016) and improve school safety systems (NY Safe Act, Chapter 1 of the Laws of 2013). Building aid is wealth adjusted, providing higher levels of aid to lower property value districts. In 2021-22, the State allocated $3.2 billion in Building Aid.[67]

Expanding Our Children's Education and Learning (EXCEL)

EXCEL [NYSEL §3641(14)] provides supplemental funding for selected types of construction projects, including education technology, health and safety, accessibility, physical capacity expansion, and energy. The State is authorized to issue a maximum of $2.6 billion in bonds and notes (a maximum of $1.8 billion for NYC). NYC has received its full allocation and, as of May 2021, other districts have received $769 million in funding, supporting approximately 3,100 projects.[68]

EMPLOYEE BENEFITS

Health Care

Educators' health care benefits are negotiated at the district level with health care providers and local collective bargaining units. In the early 2000s, districts outside of NYC began working with others in their geographic regions to form health care consortia to enlarge their risk pools in an effort to maintain quality and contain costs. The Rochester Area School Health Plan II, for example, serves more than 15,000 employees from all of the districts and two BOCES in Monroe County, NY.[69] By 2009, more than half of the districts and BOCES belonged to one of 31 consortia created throughout the State.[70] Teachers in NYC public schools have a choice of health plans through the City's Health Benefits Program.[71] Supplemental benefits, such as dental, vision, and prescription drug coverage, are provided through the United Federation of Teachers Welfare Fund.[72]

Teacher Retirement

The New York State Teachers' Retirement System (NYSTRS) was established in 1921 by the Legislature to administer retirement, disability and death benefits to eligible public school teachers, teaching assistants, counselors, and administrators in the State excluding those in NYC, which has its own retirement system (see below). As of June 30, 2020, NYSTRS served 822 employers, including public school districts, BOCES, higher education institutions, and charter schools, and 433,801 active and retired members, including beneficiaries.[73] The NYSTRS is funded through employer and member contributions and investment income. The employer contribution rate (ECR) is a uniform percentage of member payroll set annually at a level needed to cover benefits. The ECR for the 2020-21 school year was 9.53%.[74] Benefit structures and eligibility rules are based on a tier structure according to date of initial membership, with the most recent tier 6 applying to those who entered the system on or after April 1, 2012. Member contributions vary by tier and range from no annual contribution for tier 1 and 2 members to a variable rate contribution based on annual gross salary for tier 6 members. Members in tiers 1 through 4 are vested with five years of credited service, whereas 10 years are required for those in tiers 5 and 6.[75]

The Teachers' Retirement System of the City of New York (TRS) was established in 1917 under Chapter 303 of the Laws of 1917 and administers retirement, disability and death benefits to teachers and administrative personnel employed by the City's Department of Education as well as some employees of NYC charter schools (if school opts to participate) and the City University of New York (open to full-time faculty and adjunct instructors who opt to participate). As of June 30, 2020, the TRS served 215,000 members, 90,000 of whom were retired members and beneficiaries. Like the NYSTRS, the TRS is funded through member and employer contributions and investment earnings.[76] Employer contributions are adjusted annually based on actuarial valuation of liabilities and totaled $3.7

billion for fiscal year 2020.[77] The TRS also bases its benefits and eligibility rules using a tiered structure and has five tiers (I, II, III, IV, and VI) with the most recent tier VI applying to members who entered after March 31, 2012.[78] Members in tier VI have the highest contribution requirements, ranging from 3%-6% annually depending on their earnings.[79]

CHARTER SCHOOL FUNDING

Charter schools are authorized by the New York State Charter Schools Act of 1998 (NYSEL §2851[3]). Amendments to the law in 2007 and 2010 increased the cap on the number of charters from 100 to 200 in 2007 and then to 460 in 2010. As of September 2021, 331 charter schools were operating in the State, serving over 150,000 students.[80] Districts in the state pay a per pupil tuition rate to charter schools for each district resident student enrolled in a charter school, including any Federal or State aid for students with a disability in proportion to the level of services provided by the charter school. The annual per pupil rate had been the base amount provided by the district plus supplemental increases provided by the State. Starting in 2018-19, the base amount increases by a district-specific inflator equivalent to the annual change in the district's operating expenditures averaged over the three prior years.[81]

To lessen the fiscal impact of charter school transfers on districts, the State provides transitional aid and/or an apportionment for Supplemental Basic Tuition paid to charter schools. The transitional aid is targeted to districts outside of New York City that experience a substantial impact as determined by the effect on the districts' enrollments or budgets (more than 2%) [NYSEL §3602(41)]. In 2020-21, the estimated State allocation of transitional aid was $50 million. As of 2017-18, districts receive an apportionment equal to the amount of Supplemental Basic Tuition paid to charter schools in the prior school year [NYSEL §2856 (1)(d)]. The estimated allocation for 2021-22 was $155 million.[82]

NONPUBLIC SCHOOL FUNDING

Pursuant to Chapters 507 and 508 of the Laws of 1974, New York provides aid to private schools for costs associated with State-mandated efforts, including data collection and reporting, taking attendance, and testing. The 2021-22 state budget allocations for these activities totaled $189 million. Additional private school aid was allocated in the 2021-22 budget for academic intervention services ($904,000), health and safety equipment ($15.0 million), and STEM programs ($29.4 million), and support for public school students placed in special education programs in other settings; these settings include private schools, Special Act school districts, and State-operated schools in Rome and Batavia ($440.8 million).[83]

VIRTUAL EDUCATION

New York State awards up to $1.75 million annually in grant funds to provide public high school students without access to advanced coursework, such as Advanced Placement, International Baccalaureate, and dual-credit courses, with access via online or distance learning. BOCES-led consortia (comprised of at least one BOCES and seven districts) and the Big Five districts are eligible to apply for the two-year grants.[84] The State's Home Instruction regulations [Part 100.10 of the Commissioner's Regulations] apply to students who opt to enroll in an online school.

FEDERAL COVID RELIEF FUNDING

In 2020-21, New York State received approximately $13.1 billion in federal funds through the Coronavirus Response and Relief Supplemental Appropriations (CRRSA) and American Rescue Plan (ARP) Acts. This was in addition to approximately $1.2 billion received in 2020 through the Coronavirus Aid, Relief, and Economic Security (CARES) Act. These federal acts provided Elementary and Secondary School Emergency Relief (ESSER) and Governor's Emergency Education Relief (GEER) funds to enable states to provide local educational agencies (LEAs) with emergency assistance and relief funds to respond to the Covid-19 pandemic.[85]

Under the CARES Act, all of New York State's GEER funds ($164.2 million) were applied as a "pandemic adjustment" to the 2020-21 enacted budget to partially offset the State's share of state aid to its 673 "major" school districts (LEAs that are charter schools, Special Act school districts, and districts employing less than eight teachers were excluded). The funds were distributed based on relative shares of grants awarded to districts under Title I, Part A of the ESEA for the 2019-20 school year. The $1.037 billion in ESSER funds also were applied as a pandemic adjustment to the enacted budget and allocated similarly, although all LEAs, including charter schools and Special Act school districts, could receive funds. LEAs that received ESSER funds were required to provide equitable services to non-public schools serving resident students using a proportional share calculation based on the percentage of low-income students residing in the Title I attendance area who attend non-public schools.[86]

Under the CRRSA Act, the State was awarded just over $4 billion in ESSER2 (second round ESSER) funds, of which at least 90% needed to be allocated to LEAs, including charter schools and Special Act districts. An additional $322.9 million was received in GEER2 funds, of which $250.1 million was allocated for new Emergency Assistance to Non-Public Schools (EANS) grants. The remaining $72.8 million in GEER2 funds as well as the remaining 10% ($395 million) in ESSER2 funds were used to provide lower wealth districts with a minimum per pupil allocation.[87]

The ARP Act provided another approximately $9 billion in ESSER3 (third round ESSER) funds. Similar to the CRRSA Act, at least 90% of the ESSER3 funds were to be allocated to LEAs with allocations based on the relative shares of grants awarded to districts under Title I, Part A of the ESEA for the 2020 federal fiscal year. The 2021-22 enacted budget allocated the ESSER3 funds as grants in aid as follows: $8.09 billion to LEAs; $692.2 million for learning loss, summer, and afterschool program grants to LEAs; $195 million to support a $90 million allocation for full-day four-year-old prekindergarten expansion; $15 million for new full-day four-year-old prekindergarten competitive grants; $35 million to supplant State grant funds for NYC charter facilities; and $24.7 million for NYSED costs to administer the funds over three years.[88]

ENDNOTES

1   This chapter highlights New York's school finance system pursuant to the Laws of 2021. Also refer to: Osnat Zaken. 2021. "New York." *Journal of Education Finance* 46, no. 3: 328-330.

2   The University of the State of New York, The State Education Department. n.d. *New York Education at a Glance*. Albany, NY. https://data.nysed.gov/

3   The University of the State of New York, The State Education Department, Fiscal Analysis and Research Unit. 2021. *State Aid to Schools—A Primer: Pursuant to the Laws of 2020*: 13. Albany, NY. http://www.oms.nysed.gov/faru/PDFDocuments/2020-21Primer.pdf

4   Ray Domanico. 2020. *A Statistical Profile of New York's K-12 Educational Sector: Race, Income, and Religion*. New York, Manhattan Institute. https://media4.manhattan-institute.org/sites/default/files/statistical-profile-nyc-educational-sector-RD2.pdf

5   National Center for Education Statistics (NCES). 2020. *Projections of Education Statistics to 2028*. Washington, DC: 35. https://nces.ed.gov/pubs2020/2020024.pdf

6   *New York Education at a Glance*

7   National Center for Education Statistics (NCES). 2021. *Digest of Education Statistics: 2019*. Washington, DC. https://nces.ed.gov/programs/digest/d19/.

8   New York State United Teachers, NYSUT Research and Educational Services. 2021. *Fact Sheet 21-13 Teacher Certification in New York State*. Albany, New York. https://www.nysut.org/resources/all-listing/research/fact-sheets/fact-sheet-teacher-certification-in-new-york-state; Education Commission of the States. 2020. *50-State Comparison: Teacher Leadership and Licensure Advancement*. Denver, Colorado. https://www.ecs.org/50-state-comparison-teacher-license-reciprocity/

9   NCES. 2021.

10 National Center for Education Statistics (NCES). 2020. *Revenues and Expenditures for Public Elementary and Secondary Education: FY18*. Washington, DC: 9. https://nces.ed.gov/pubs2020/2020306.pdf

11 *State Aid to Schools*, 5.

12 NCES. 2021.

13 *State Aid to Schools*, 16.

14 Seymour P. Lachman with Robert Polner. 2006. *Three Men in a Room: The Inside Story of Power and Betrayal in an American Statehouse*. New York: New Press.

15 New York State, Division of the Budget. n.d. *Legislative Action (January-March)* Albany, New York. https://www.budget.ny.gov/citizen/process/process-legislature.html

16 NEWS10. 2021. *NYS Passes $212B Budget*. Albany, NY. https://www.news10.com/news/ny-capitol-news/new-york-state-fy-2022-budget/nys-passes-212b-budget/

17 The University of the State of New York. n.d. *The State Education Department, Board of Regents, Leadership*. Albany, NY. https://www.regents.nysed.gov/

18 New York State Education Department (NYSED). 2021. *Policy & Guidance*. Albany, NY. http://www.nysed.gov/policy-guidance

19 New York State United Teachers. n.d. *About Us*. Latham, New York. https://www.nysut.org/about.

20 United Federation of Teachers. n.d. *About the UFT.* New York City, New York. https://www.uft.org/your-union/about-uft

21 New York State Council of Education Associations. n.d. *About NYSCEA.* http://www.nyscea.org/about-nyscea/

22 ESCR-Net. 2015. *Campaign for Fiscal Equity et al. v. State of New York et al 719 N.Y.S.2d 475.* https://www.escr-net.org/caselaw/2006/campaign-fiscal-equity-et-al-v-state-new-york-et-al-719-nys2d-475

23 Education Law Center. 2021. *After Years of Sustained Advocacy, NY Takes a Big Step Toward Full School Funding.* July 8, 2021. https://edlawcenter.org/news/archives/new-york/after-years-of-sustained-advocacy,-ny-takes-big-step-towards-full-school-funding.html

24 Justia US Law. 2021. *Maisto v. State of New York.* https://law.justia.com/cases/new-york/appellate-division-third-department/2021/528550.html

25 NYSER is a coalition of individuals and many prominent educational advocacy groups, including the New York State School Boards Association, the New York State Council of School Superintendents, and the New York Rural Schools Association.

26 The University of the State of New York, The State Education Department, Office of State Aid. 2021. *2021-2022 State Aid Handbook: State Formula Aids and Entitlements for Schools In New York State.* Albany, NY: 4. https:// https://stateaid.nysed.gov/publications/handbooks/handbook_2021.pdf

27 The University of the State of New York, The State Education Department, Fiscal Analysis and Research Unit. 2021. *Analysis of School Finances in New York State School Districts 2018-19.* Albany, NY. http://www.oms.nysed.gov/faru/PDFDocuments/FinalDraft_2018-19_Analysis.pdf

28 The University of the State of New York, The State Education Department. n.d. *Every Student Succeeds Act (ESSA).* Albany, NY. http://www.nysed.gov/essa

29 The University of the State of New York, The State Education Department, Information and Reporting Services. n.d. *Number of Children and Youth with Disabilities Receiving Special Education Programs and Services.* Albany, NY. http://www.p12.nysed.gov/sedcar/goal2data.htm

30 NCES. 2021.

31 *Analysis of School Finances in New York State School Districts 2018-19.* 2021.

32 *State Aid to Schools*, 14.

33 Ibid.

34 Ibid., 2.

35 New York Department of Taxation and Finance, STAR Resource Center. n.d. Albany, NY. https://www.tax.ny.gov/star/

36 New York State Department of Taxation and Finance. n.d. *Senior Citizen Exemption.* Albany, NY. https://www.tax.ny.gov/pit/property/exemption/seniorexempt.htm; New York State Department of Taxation and Finance. n.d. *Exemption for Persons with Disabilities.* Albany, NY. htttps://www.tax.ny.gov/pit/property/exemption/disablexempt.htm

37 New York State Department of Agriculture and Markets. n.d. *Tax Credits and Agricultural Assessments.* Albany, NY. https://agriculture.ny.gov/land-and-water/tax-credits-and-agricultural-assessments

38 Office of the New York State Comptroller, Division of Local Government and School Accountability. n.d. *Property Tax Cap: Summary of Legislation.* Albany, NY. https://www.osc.state.ny.us/files/local-government/property-tax-cap/pdf/legislationsummary.pdf.

39 New York State Department of Taxation and Finance and the New York State Department of State. n.d. *The Property Tax Cap: Guidelines for Implementation.* Albany, NY. https://www.tax.ny.gov/pdf/publications/orpts/capguidelines.pdf

40 Ibid.

41 *State Aid to Schools*, 2-3.

42 Ibid., 3.

43 Ibid.

44   *2021-2022 State Aid Handbook*, 8.

45   Ibid.

46   Ibid., 9.

47   Ibid., 13.

48   Ibid., 13-14.

49   Ibid., 16.

50   Ibid., 45.

51   The University of the State of New York, The State Education Department, Office of State Aid. 2017. *2017-2018 State Aid Handbook: State Formula Aids and Entitlements for Schools In New York State as Amended by Chapters of the Laws of 2017.* Albany, NY: 41. https://stateaid.nysed. gov/publications/handbooks/handbook_2017.pdf

52   Ibid., 42.

53   *2021-2022 State Aid Handbook*, 30.

54   Ibid., 40.

55   Ibid., 37.

56   Ibid., 47.

57   Ibid., 48.

58   Ibid., 35.

59   Ibid., 50-51.

60   Ibid., 51.

61   Ibid., 52-55.

62   Ibid., 52.

63   New York State Education Department, Bilingual Education & English as a New Language. 2019. *Regional Support/RBERNS.* Albany, NY. http://www.nysed.gov/bilingual-ed/regional-sup-portrberns

64   *Description of 2017-18 New York State School Aid Programs*, 13.

65   The University of the State of New York, The State Education Department, Curriculum and Instruction. n.d. *Advanced Placement Fee Waivers.* Albany, NY. http://www.nysed.gov/curriculum-instruction/advanced-placement-fee-waivers

66   The University of the State of New York, The State Education Department, Access, Equity and Community Engagement Services. n.d. *Smart College Early High Schools.* Albany, NY. http:// www.nysed.gov/postsecondary-services/smart-scholars-early-college-high-school

67   *2021-2022 State Aid Handbook*, 19-28.

68   Ibid., 28-29.

69   See https://www.monroe2boces.org/RASHPII.aspx

70   New York State School Boards Association. 2009. *Can health insurance consortiums rein in school district health care costs?* https://www.nyssba.org/clientuploads/nyssba_pdf/Consortium-ReportFinal.pdf

71   See https://www1.nyc.gov/site/olr/health/active/health-active-responsibilities.page

72   See https://www.uft.org/your-benefits/health-benefits/about-welfare-fund

73   New York State Teachers' Retirement System. 2020. *Comprehensive Annual Financial Report Fiscal Years Ended June 30, 2020 and 2019.* Albany, NY: 10. https://www.nystrs.org/Library/ Publications/Annual-Reports

74   *2020 Annual Financial Report*, 13.

75   Ibid., 16.

76   Teachers' Retirement System of the City of New York (TRS). 2020. *Comprehensive Annual Financial Report Fiscal Years Ended June 30, 2020 and June 30, 2019.* New York: 6-7. https://www. trsnyc.org/memberportal/Publications/finance

77   Ibid., 27.

78   See https://www.trsnyc.org/memberportal/Resources/resources

79   *2020 TRS Annual Financial Report*, 11.

80 New York State Education Department. n.d. *Facts about Charter Schools in New York State*. Albany, NY. http://www.nysed.gov/charter-schools/about-us

81 New York State Education Department. 2020. *Charter School Basic Tuition*. Albany, NY. https://stateaid.nysed.gov/charter/

82 *2021-22 State Aid Handbook*, 41-43.

83 New York State Division of the Budget, Education Unit. 2021. *Description of 2021-22 New York Executive Budget Recommendations for Elementary and Secondary Education*. Albany, NY. https://www.budget.ny.gov/pubs/schoolPrograms.html

84 New York State Education Department. 2020. *Advanced Course Access (ACA) Program*. Albany, NY. http://www.p12.nysed.gov/funding/nysed-rfp-gc-19-015-aca-grant/home.html

85 New York State Education Department. n.d. *Federal Education COVID Response Funding*. Albany, NY. http://www.nysed.gov/federal-education-covid-response-funding

86 New York State Education Department. 2020. *2020 Coronavirus Aid, Relief, and Economic Security (CARES) Act: Administration of Governor's Emergency Education Relief (GEER) Funds and Elementary and Secondary School Emergency Relief (ESSER) Funds*. Albany, NY. http://www.nysed.gov/common/nysed/files/programs/federal-education-covid-response-funding/cares-act-faq.pdf

87 New York State Education Department. 2021. *Local Educational Agency Allocations of Federal Coronavirus Response and Relief Supplemental Appropriations Act, 2021 (CRRSA Act) and American Rescue Plan (ARP) Act Funding*. Albany, NY. http://www.nysed.gov/common/nysed/files/programs/coronavirus/crrsa-arpa-lea-allocations-5-4-21.pdf

88 *2021-22 State Aid Handbook*, 6.

CHAPTER 33

NORTH CAROLINA[1]

Eric A. Houck
University of North Carolina at Chapel Hill

Walter Hart
University of North Carolina at Charlotte

Jim R. Watson
University of North Carolina at Charlotte

GENERAL BACKGROUND

North Carolina educated approximately 1.4 million pupils in traditional public schools at about 10,600 dollars per pupil in the 2021-2022 academic year. This represents a 6% decrease in real-dollar, inflation-adjusted per pupil investment since 2018 and ranks the state at 39 in per pupil expenditures in the country.[2] In addition, another 131,000 students attend NC charter schools.[3] Demographically, the NC student population is approximately 52% White, 22% African American, 16% Hispanic, with 43% of children under 18 living in homes that are 200% above the poverty threshold.[4] Independent of charter schools (which will be discussed below) the state oversees 115 fiscally dependent school districts, of which 100 are county-wide and 15 are city-based.

Funding Public Schools in the United States, Indian Country,
and US Territories (Second Edition), pages 517–528.
Copyright © 2023 by Information Age Publishing
www.infoagepub.com
All rights of reproduction in any form reserved.

Policy Background

The state of North Carolina passed its first public school law in 1839, which established a funding system combining state and local funds. The state provided two dollars for every dollar local governments collected from taxes, an early form of matching fund with required local effort. The law further divided the state into districts with five schools per district and established a board of 'superintendents' to oversee each county's schools. In 1852, the General Assembly established the Office of General Superintendent of Common Schools, the precursor to the Department of Public Instruction. After the Civil War, the 1868 state constitution provided for free education for all children. Despite the efforts of activists and reformers of the day, this free education continued to be racially segregated into the 20th century. The Constitution also established the State Board of Education, which had the authority to set state standards and regulate teacher licensure, among other duties.[5]

In the 20th century, North Carolina's system of school funding evolved into something more recognizable to modern scholars. The General Assembly passed the Compulsory Attendance Act in 1913, established city school districts in 1921, and set a minimum funding level in 1931 through the School Machinery Act. The School Machinery Act was a mechanism to provide resources to meet the constitutional mandate of a free and uniform education for all students in the state. The School Machinery Act also repealed earlier provisions that required local effort in order to receive a state match and provided for local bonding authority for construction of schools; thereby establishing a tradition of local responsibility for capital costs and state responsibility for current costs.[6] With some modification, the logic of the School Machinery Act motivates North Carolina's current funding mechanism.

The U.S. Supreme Court's landmark ruling in *Brown v. Topeka Board of Education*[7] in 1954 brought the challenge of integration to North Carolina schools. Throughout the late 1950s and into the 1960s and 1970s, the state slowly integrated its all-Black and all-White systems.[8] Thomas J. Pearsall, then chairman of the state's Special Advisory Committee on Education, proposed an early version of a funding voucher, whereby students could use state dollars to go to a private school if their parents did not want them to attend an integrated school. However, the 1964 U.S. Civil Rights Act ended the effort by disallowing federal funds to go to any segregated school district.[9]

Post-integration, the legislature accelerated the rate of modernization. The General Assembly passed all-day kindergarten for all students in 1977, followed by the Basic Education Program (BEP) in 1985. The BEP is the cornerstone of North Carolina's policy and finance régime built on a systemic reform framework of defining standards, assessing performance, and holding schools and leaders accountable for school performance.[10] The BEP established statewide standards across all subject areas and gave the state board the authority to "describe the education program to be offered to every child in the public schools."[11] This authority also included "funds appropriated for that purpose."[12] In 1990, the state began issuing report cards for each school, reporting student outcomes.

Legal History

The North Carolina funding mechanism has been challenged on the basis of both equity and adequacy concerns. In 1987, the North Carolina Court of Appeals dismissed a case arguing for increased vertical equity in the state funding mechanism in *Britt v. North Carolina*.[13] The Court of Appeals had held that local supplemental funding could stand even though it contributed to glaring fiscal inequities across school districts. The North Carolina supreme court refused to hear the case.

The 1997 *Leandro v. North Carolina*[14] was a landmark case in school finance, establishing adequacy as a principle of a constitutional funding formula. Low-wealth rural districts, as well as high-poverty urban districts, cited the inability to raise sufficient local revenue as a disequalizing force in school funding. The court upheld the funding structure as constitutional, but also ruled unanimously that all students have a right to 'a sound, basic education' as evidenced by performance on state standardized tests. Just as importantly, the court placed the burden of education provision on the state instead of on local districts. Efforts to hold the state accountable to this decision from the bench have continued to the present day, although the legislature has taken little heed of the court's pronouncements.[15]

CURRENT POLITICAL CLIMATE

North Carolina is funded by a bi-cameral state legislature which creates biannual budgets when in session to be signed by the governor. Currently, both houses of the NC General Assembly are Republican controlled with a Democratic governor. Since North Carolina is a right-to-work state, the largest teacher's organization is the North Carolina Association of Educators (NCAE). Statewide, impetus for education reform is sustained by broad based organizations such as the North Carolina Public School Form and the business supported BEST-NC, along with left and right leaning policy advocacy groups. School enrollment has surged in the charter and homeschool sectors, while enrollment in public and independent sectors has remained relatively stable.

STATE AID FORMULA

The Basic Education Program (BEP) rests on a system of allotments based on pupil counts, making North Carolina's system a distinct minority among state finance mechanisms. Only seven states still use a resource-allocation system instead of a weighted-student model.[16] The state currently uses 37 different allotments, or a specific amount of resources determined by the funding mechanism. Allotments are largely dependent on each district's average daily membership (ADM). The 37 allotments are divided into two major categories: *position-based allotments* allocate personnel positions and *categorical allotments* allocate dollar grants. They can be further divided by function. Base Allotments are used to provide materials, staffing, and services necessary for district activities. Grant/Application Allotments are used for acquiring improvement funds through a competitive grant process. Local Education Agencies (LEAs) are allotted dollar amounts based on student counts. LEAs with low wealth or enrollment are given allotments to account for economic capacity and effort. Table 33.1 lists allotments by category and includes each allotment's name and Program Report Code (PRC). Employee allotments take a majority of resources. The sections that follow outline these components of the funding mechanism.

TABLE 33.1.   Allotments by Category and Program Report Code (PRC)

Base Allotments (position based)			
PRC 001: Classroom Teachers	PRC 002: Central Administration	PRC 005: School Building Administration	PRC 007: Instructional Support
PRC 012: Driver Training	PRC 013: Career & Technical Education (Employment)	PRC 014: Career & Technical Education (Program Support)	PRC 015: School Technology Fund
PRC 016: Summer Reading Camps	PRC 025: Indian Gaming Fund	PRC 027: Teacher Assistants	PRC 034: Academically and Intellectually Gifted
PRC 036: Charter Schools	PRC 056: Transportation	PRC 061: Classroom Materials and Instructional Supplies	PRC 073: School Connectivity
PRC 085: Class Reading 3D	PRC 120: LEA Financed Purchase of School Buses	PRC 130: Textbooks	
Grant/Application (dollar based)			
PRC 029: Behavioral Support	PRC 030: Digital Learning	PRC 039: School Resource Officer	PRC 040: After School Quality Improvement Grant
PRC 041: Panic Alarms Improvement Grant	PRC 042: Child and Family Support Teams: Nurses	PRC 043: Child and Family Support Teams: Social Workers	PRC 055: Learn and Earn
PRC 066: Assistant Principal Interns: Principal Fellows	PRC 067: Assistant Principal Interns: MSA Students	PRC 042: Child and Family Support Teams: Nurses	
Student Characteristics (dollar based)			
PRC 032: Children with Special Needs	PRC 054: Limited English Proficiency	PRC 063: Children with Special Needs: Special Funds	PRC 069: At Risk Student Services/ Alternative Schools
LEA Characteristics (dollar based)			
PRC 019: Small County Supplemental Funding	PRC 031: Low Wealth	PRC 024: Disadvantaged Student Supplemental Funding	

Source: http://www.ncpublicschools.org/docs/fbs/finance/reporting/coa/2012/programreportcodes. pdf. Categorization by authors (2022).

Position-Based Funding

Table 33.2 presents ratios and bases for position-based funding allocations for the 2017-2018 academic year. North Carolina uses the number of students in ADM to allocate teaching, support, and administrative positions. The state guarantees the position's salary and associated benefits relative to the average salary in that district. While LEAs were able to present estimated counts projections for funding, the ADM amount is now based on real counts from the previous year to estimate initial allocations in the current year. The differentiated student counts for ranges of grade levels represents an implicit weighting in the allocation of teacher positions. Also, the basis for salary allocation is the average school district salary

TABLE 33.2. Funding Ratios for Positions 2021-22

Category	Formula	Salary Basis
Classroom Teachers		
Kindergarten	1 per 18 in ADM.	
Grade 1	1 per 16 in ADM.	
Grades 2 - 3	1 per 17 in ADM.	
Grades 4 - 6	1 per 24 in ADM.	LEA Average
Grades 7 - 8	1 per 23 in ADM.	
Grade 9	1 per 26.5 in ADM.	
Grades 10 – 12	1 per 29 in ADM.	
Math/Science/Computer Teachers	1 per county or based on sub agreements	
Teacher Assistants	The number of classes is determined by a ratio of 1:21. • K - 2 TAs per every 3 classes • Grades 1-2 - 1 TA for every 2 classes • Grade 3 - 1 TA for every 3 classes	$42,760
Instructional Support	1 per 222.36 in ADM. Includes Mental Health Positions.	LEA Average
Administration		
Principals	1 per school with at least 100 ADM or at least seven state-paid teachers or instructional support personnel. Schools opening after 7/1/2011 are eligible based on at least 100 ADM only.	LEA Average
Assistant Principals	1 month per 98.53 in ADM.	LEA Average
Career Technical Ed. (CTE)	Base of 50 Months of Employment per LEA with remainder distributed based on ADM in grades 8-12.	LEA Average

Source: FY 2022-23 Planning Allotments worksheet, https://www.dpi.nc.gov/districts-schools/district-operations/financial-and-business-services.

of a given LEA in the previous academic year, which due to variation in teacher qualifications across LEAs, can also create distributional inequities.[17] That is, the state provides different salary amounts for each district based on the salary pool of its individual teaching corps. There is an exception for teacher assistants, who are allocated with a straight standard salary. This practice has implications for charter school funding, as will be described below.

Student Categorical Funding

Table 33.3 presents dollar allocations based on student characteristics, along with additional regulatory guidance in the funding mechanism. For example, academically gifted and special education funding is capped at a percentage of students in ADM. Of particular interest is the dollar allocation for gifted and for special education which are capped at 4% and 12.75% of the district ADM, respectively. Additional gifted or special education identified students are funded from local revenue sources. In addition, funding for students with disabilities is

TABLE 33.3. Dollar-based Allocation Based on Student Characteristics

Category	Basis of Allotment
Supplies	$ 30.17 per ADM plus $2.69 per ADM in grades 8 and 9 for PSAT Testing
Noninstructional Support Personnel	$308.29 per ADM.
Academically Gifted Students	$1,322.28 per child for 4% of ADM.
At-Risk Student Services	• Each LEA receives the dollar equivalent of one resource officer ($37,838) per high school. • Of the remaining funds, 50% is distributed based on ADM ($89.10 per ADM) and 50% is distributed based on number of poor children, per the federal Title 1 Low-Income poverty data ($358.14 per poor child). • Each LEA receives a minimum of the dollar equivalent of two teachers and two instructional support personnel ($272,812).
Children with Disabilities	
School Aged	• $5248.39 per funded child count. Child count is comprised of the lesser of the Dec 1 handicapped child count or 13.00% of the allotted ADM.
Preschool	• Base of $72,902.00 per LEA; • Remainder distributed based on December 1 child count of ages3, 4, and PreK- 5, ($4,954.49) per child.
Limited English Proficiency	Base of a teacher asst. ($39,216; remainder based 50% on number of funded LEP students ($504.61) and 50% on an LEA's concentration of LEP students ($3,893.85).

Source: FY 2022-23 Planning Allotments worksheet, https://www.dpi.nc.gov/districts-schools/district-operations/financial-and-business-services.

undifferentiated—every identified student in the state receives the same dollar allocation regardless of the severity or nature of the identified disability. This category was identified for further study in the 2018-2019 legislative session.[18]

District Categorical Funding

Table 33.4 presents funding categories that are dollar allocations based on district characteristics. There is a dollar allocation to LEAs based on size through the small county supplemental funding stream in graduated amounts for districts with ADMs less than 3,200 students. Support for career and technical education is a dollar-based grant that is then graduated based on student counts. Transportation funding is a dollar grant based on formula inputs which include total miles traveled.

Perhaps the most important and controversial dollar-based grants based on district characteristics are two funding streams to support disadvantaged students within districts and districts with low fiscal capacity. These allocations are discussed separately, below.

Low Wealth Supplemental Funding

Counties having below-average wealth, as measured by a formula, are eligible for supplemental funding. The formula includes three factors: anticipated total county revenue, tax base per square mile, and per capita income. Anticipated rev-

TABLE 33.4. Dollar-based Allocation Based on District (LEA) Characteristics

Category	Basis of Allotment	
Small County Supplemental Funding	ADM <	Allotment
	600	$1,710,000
	1,300	$1,820,000
	1,700	$1,548,700
	2,000	$1,600,000
	2,300	$1,560,000
	2,600	$1,470,000
	2,800	$1,498,000
	3,200	$1,548,000
CTE Program Support	$10,000 per LEA with remainder distributed based on ADM in grades 8-12 ($33.54).	
Disadvantaged Student Supplemental Funding	Formula based	
Low Wealth Supplemental Funding	Formula based.	
Transportation	Formula based	

Source: FY 2022-23 Planning Allotments worksheet, https://www.dpi.nc.gov/districts-schools/district-operations/financial-and-business-services.

enue is calculated by estimating the property value in the county plus the revenue the county receives from sales taxes, fines, and forfeitures. The tax base per square mile compares each county's property value per square mile to the state average. Many low-wealth counties have significant areas of swampland, which has zero value. This is meant to equalize counties with different topographies. Per capita income is a three-year average of income in the county compared to the state.[19]

Each factor is weighted to determine eligibility: 40% is anticipated revenue, 10% is density, and 50% is per capita income. These percentages are multiplied by each county's value (e.g. 50% multiplied by 90% of the state average in per capita income). If the total of these percentages is less than 100, the county is considered low wealth. Counties must maintain effort to receive this funding. Each must either have effective tax rates at or above the state average or contribute more dollars to the LEA's per pupil amount than the state average when accounting for wealth. If the county meets neither of these criteria, it receives funding equal to the percentage actually contributed relative to what it is able to contribute.[20]

Low-wealth supplemental funding is more restricted than other allotments. These funds are expendable only for instructional staffing and materials. They are meant to supplement, not supplant, local dollars. The state can sanction the county if it is found to be spending less than 95% of the average local effort per student for the past three fiscal years. LEAs can apply for waivers from this requirement in the event of school closures, loss of federal funds, or some other emergency such as a natural disaster.[21] Most LEAs are eligible for this supplemental funding.

Disadvantaged Students Supplemental Funding

North Carolina has adapted its allotment system to account for disadvantaged pupils in both high-wealth and low-wealth districts by providing dollar funding equivalents of additional teacher positions based on the count of disadvantaged students pegged to the formula ratios in the broader funding mechanism. North Carolina accounts for disadvantaged pupils in LEAs using a three-step process. First, the fundable disadvantaged population is used to generate additional positions based on a standard teacher-to-student ratio of 1:21. Second, this ratio is adjusted to account for district wealth. If the district is over 90% of the state wealth average (calculated using the Low Wealth Supplemental Funding formula), the teacher-to-student ratio falls to 1:19.9. If the district is between 80% and 90% of the state wealth average, the teacher-to-student ratio falls to 1:19.4. If the district is under 80% of the state wealth average, the teacher-to-student ratio becomes 1:19.1. However, 16 LEAs receiving funds during the FY 2006 program pilot year are still funded at a teacher-to-student ratio of 1:16 due to a hold-harmless provision passed by the General Assembly. Third and finally, these additional teaching positions are converted to dollars using the state average teacher salary and provided as a categorical dollar-based grant.[22]

The state imposes restrictions on this funding. LEAs must use these funds for classroom instruction, intensive in-school and/or after school remediation, purchase of diagnostic software and progress monitoring tools, and providing teacher bonuses and salary supplements. Only 35% of funds may be used for salary enhancements. These funds also have a non-supplant clause similar to Low Wealth Supplemental Funding.[23] In FY 2022, all 115 LEAs received this supplement.

Inferred Funding Weights

North Carolina allocates positions and dollars, but it does so differentially based on student, school, and district characteristics. In this sense, the funding mechanism can be considered a weighted model, and state-level administrators have made this argument in response to recent efforts to alter the basics of the funding mechanism.

One of the challenges of the resource-based funding model North Carolina uses lies in determining structural components that support and provide equitable resource provisions, especially in comparison to other states. Many states use some form of pupil weighting as a driver for their state funding mechanisms; to compare states with these types of mechanisms consists of the relatively simple step of comparing the funding weights for students identified in similar categories. This type of comparison is difficult when seeking to understand the structural equity of the North Carolina mechanism.

To facilitate these comparisons, Table 35.5 takes funding levels reported by the North Carolina School Business Office in testimony before the Joint Legislative Task Force on Education Finance Reform in 2018 and converts them into pupil weights to demonstrate the relative value the state places on different student, school, and district characteristics. As in other states with student weighting com-

TABLE 33.5.   Inferred Weights of Critical Funding Categories

Illustration of how funding is weighted for students in Kindergarten through Grade 3 (2018)		
Funding for Different Students	**State Dollars**	**Weight**
Every student	$5,410.53	1.00
Student from a Low-Income Family	$347.68	0.06
Special Learning Issues (IEPs)	$4,093.14	0.76
Small County	$754.40	0.14
Students Below Grade Level	$105.51	0.02
Disadvantaged Student Supplemental Fund	$263.13	0.05
Low Wealth County	$301.42	0.06
Limited English Proficiency	$839.54	0.16
Intellectually and Academically Gifted	$425.24	0.08
Career and Technical Ed	$0.00	0.00
Cooperative Innovative HS	$0.00	0.00

Source: Levinson, (2018) https://goo.gl/cu2dnT Weights calculated by author.

ponents in their mechanisms, these weights can be 'stacked' for students who exist and are counted within multiple categories. While the state has not reported their calculations to update these state dollars since 2018, Table 33.5 provides a rough snapshot of what the North Carolina mechanism would look like if expressed as a weighted system, for comparison to other states.

CHARTER SCHOOL FUNDING

North Carolina educates approximately 131,000 students in 204 charter schools. Charter schools are treated as independent districts by North Carolina. Charter schools are funded based on the same basic structure as traditional public school districts.[24] After their first year, each charter school receives the average per pupil expenditure for the LEA in which the charter school is physically located. To promote flexibility, this LEA-based, per pupil amount is calculated to include all categorical funds that the LEA would receive. These are averaged in on a per pupil basis, even if the demographics of the charter school does not match the demographics of the LEA in which it is physically located. The exceptions to this policy are the funds for student language learning and special education status, which are removed from the averaged LEA per pupil amount and then reallocated to the charter school per eligible pupil.

Unlike state funding, which is tied to the geographic location of the charter school, local supplemental funding is allocated to charter schools based upon the LEA in which the attending student resides. LEAs collect these funds and then apportion them out to all charter schools to which students living in the district attend. Therefore, it is the case that students enrolled in any given charter school may represent very different amounts of local funding based on their residence. This quirk in the funding system has real implications; recent work has determined that 20% of all charter school students attend a charter school in a different school district from the one in which they live.[25]

VIRTUAL EDUCATION

North Carolina operates two virtual schools—a virtual public school and a virtual charter school, both of which are publicly funded and serve students across all schooling sectors.

FEDERAL COVID-19 FUNDING

In addition to federal Elementary and Secondary Schools Relief (ESSR) I, II, and III funds as well as a distribution from the federal Governor's Emergency Education Relief funds, the state of North Carolina allocated 49.3 million dollars in state COVID-19 funding. In addition, the state used funds from the State Fiscal Recovery Funds to allocate salary bonuses to educators and other state workers.

Table 33.6 presents per pupil expenditures by object for all combined federal funds supporting COVID relief in the state for the 2020, 2021, and 2022 academic

TABLE 33.6.   Combined federal COVID funding per pupil expenditures, by Object, 2020-2022

Object	2019-20	2020-21	2021-22
Salary/Benefits	27.63	148.15	734.76
Supplies/Materials	16.16	223.52	210.92
Purchased Services	5.22	36.82	79.10
Capital Outlay	0.15	7.14	46.90
Other	7.92	5.09	50.54
Grand Total	57.08	420.73	1,122.21

Source: North Carolina Department of Public Instruction: https://bi.nc.gov/t/DPI-FinancialBusinessServices/views/COVID-19AllotmentExpendituresandDetailedExpenditures/Story1?%3Aembed=y&%3AisGuestRedirectFromVizportal=y&%3Aorigin=card_share_link and http://apps.schools.nc.gov/ords/f?p=145:10; author's calculations.

years. There were large increases over time in both salary and capital outlay expenditures per pupil, respectively. All told, combined funding across these three years amounted to approximately 534 dollars per pupil, or about an addition 5% of the average state investment per pupil over this timeframe.

ENDNOTES

[1] This chapter presents information on the basics of the North Carolina funding mechanism. For more up-to-date notes on current funding levels and micropolitical developments, the Journal of Education Finance's annual State of the State reports will be a helpful supplement. In the case of North Carolina, see Houck, Hart, & Watson (2022); available here: https://www.nationaledfinance.com/journal_of_ed_finance_475.php.

[2] See https://www.publicschoolsfirstnc.org/resources/fact-sheets/nc-public-ed-at-a-glance/.

[3] See https://www.dpi.nc.gov/media/13053/download?attachment.

[4] See https://www.bestnc.org/wp-content/uploads/2020/05/2020-Facts-Figures-Final-as-of-May-29-2020-12-PM.pdf.

[5] NC State Board of Education, "Chapter One," History of SBE. https://stateboard.ncpublicschools.gov/about-sbe/history/chapter-one

[6] Ibid.

[7] 347 U.S. 483 (1954).

[8] See Walker (1996) and Cecelski (1994) for powerful counternarratives of Black empowerment in the face of pressures to integrate all-White systems.

[9] Benjamin R. Justesen and Scott Matthews, "Part 5: Desegregation and Equality in Public Education," Public Education (NCpedia. January 1, 2006). Retrieved from: https://www.ncpedia.org/public-education-part-5.

[10] Anthony R. Rolle, Eric A. Houck, and Ann McColl, "And Poor Children Continue to Wait: An Analysis of Horizontal and Vertical Equity among North Carolina School Districts in the Face of Judicially Mandated Policy Restraints 1996-2006," Journal of Education Finance 34 no. 1 (2008): 75-102; Marshall S. Smith and Jennifer O'Day, "Systemic School Reform," Journal of Education Policy 5 no. 5 (1990): 233-267, DOI: 10.1080/02680939008549074

[11] N.C. Gen. Stat. § 115C-81.5 (2017).

[12] Ibid.

[13] Britt v. State of North Carolina 357 S.E.2d 432 (1987).

[14] Leandro v. State, 488 SE.2d 249 (1997). Retrieved from: https://law.duke.edu/childedlaw/school-discipline/attorneys/casesummaries/leandrov state/

[15] George Lange and R. Craig Wood. Education Finance Litigation in North Carolina; Distinguishing Leandro. Journal of Education Finance 32(1), p. 36-70.

[16] Allotment-Specific and System-Level Issues Adversely Affect North Carolina's Distribution of K-12 Resources. Report no. 2016-11. June 4, 2017. Retrieved from: https://www.ncleg.net/PED/Reports/documents/K12/K12_Report.pdf

[17] Christopher Needham & Eric A. Houck (2021). Allotting Inequity: Evaluating North Carolina's classroom teacher funding mechanism. Journal of Educational Human Resources. https://doi.org/10.3138/jehr-2020-0034.

[18] See finding 7 here: https://www.ncleg.net/documentsites/committees/bcci6701/Final%20Report%20of%20the%20Jt%20Leg%20Study%20Committee%20on%20Division%20of%20Local%20School%20Admin%20Units.pdf

[19] North Carolina Department of Public Instruction. North Carolina Public Schools Allotment Policy Manual. Retrieved from: http://www.ncpublicschools.org/docs/fbs/allotments/general/newpolicies17-18.pdf

[20] Ibid.

[21] Ibid.

[22] North Carolina Department of Public Instruction. North Carolina Public Schools Allotment Policy Manual. Retrieved from: http://www.ncpublicschools.org/docs/fbs/allotments/general/newpolicies17-18.pdf

[23] Ibid.

[24] See NCGS 115C-218.105.

[25] Kyle Abbot, K, Eric A. Houck & Doug L. Lauen, "Out of Bounds: The implications of non-resident charter attendees for North Carolina educational policy and finance." In Downs, T. & Killeen, K. M., eds.: Recent Advancements in Education Finance and Policy. Information Age Publishing.

CHAPTER 34

NORTH DAKOTA

Eric A. Houck

University of North Carolina at Chapel Hill

GENERAL BACKGROUND[1]

A foundation aid program designed to provide financial assistance to local school districts has been in effect in North Dakota since 1959. This initial program was adopted in part because the legislature recognized that property valuations, demographics and educational needs varied from school district to school district. The following is a condensed version of the evolution of the program.[2]

- Major changes began in the 1970s, introducing equity adjustments and recognizing economies of scale;
- In the early 1980s the state tapped into mineral taxes to supplement the common schools trust fund with the goal of providing 60% of the cost of education from state sources;
- A subsequent bust economy eroded state aid and pushed the funding burden onto local property taxes throughout the 1980s;
- During this time, legal action on the national level informed many changes the state began to undertake;

Funding Public Schools in the United States, Indian Country,
and US Territories (Second Edition), pages 529–539.
Copyright © 2023 by Information Age Publishing
www.infoagepub.com
All rights of reproduction in any form reserved.

- Two equity and adequacy lawsuits[3] provided impetus for structural changes to the major funding formulas. As a condition to staying the second lawsuit, the governor created a commission made up of school leaders, legislators and agency heads with heavy involvement of stakeholder groups. Largely due to the chemistry of its members, this commission performed much of the heavy lifting in creating and selling an acceptable solution;
- A new formula adopted by the 2007 legislature combined several funding line items with different allocation bases into one comprehensive formula. This was enabled in large part by an improving economy;
- Higher tax revenue aided efforts to further reform the K-12 funding formula and provide tax relief;
- The state took the next major step in 2013, as significant property tax relief was integrated into the formula.[4] School district levy authority was dramatically reduced and a per-student payment rate based on the cost of providing an adequate education was adopted. The changes shifted state/local support percentages from roughly 50/50 to 75/25.

BASIC SUPPORT PROGRAM[5]

The main school aid funding formula in North Dakota distributes well over 90% of total state K-12 funding. Transportation and special education excess cost funding have separate appropriations. The formula is driven by average daily membership (ADM) and uses various weights to account for the increased costs associated with school district size and serving students with special needs. In addition, there are adjustments to minimize budget impacts as districts transition to the new formula.

The base per-student rate was set by the legislature at $9,646 for each year of the 2017-19 biennium. The base level funding addresses education and operational costs for school districts. This includes core staffing, administration, operation, professional development, technology and instruction materials.[6]

Table 34.1 describes the basic components of the formula.[7] Part One calculates the base funding level by multiplying weighted student units by the base per-student rate set by the legislature and applies transition adjustments. Part Two determines the funding sources. The local share is 60 mills from local property taxes, plus a designated percentage of other local in-lieu-of property tax sources. The state aid payment provides the amount not funded by local sources.

Student Membership (ADM)

The main driver for the formula is student enrollment, as determined by the ADA of the most recently completed school year. A student's ADA is calculated by dividing the number of days a student was enrolled in the school district by the number of days in the regular school calendar (the minimum required in North

TABLE 34.1.   North Dakota K-12 School Funding Formula

	Part One: Calculate Base Funding Amount	
	Student Membership (ADM)	300
+	Other Program Weighted ADM	30
=	Weighted AMD	30
X	C. School District Size Factor	1.13
=	Weighted Student Units	373
X	Per Student Rate	$9,646
=	Total Formula Amount	$3,600,000
	Part Two: Determine State Aid Payment	
Local Share	60 mills times taxable valuation	$600,000
	75%-100% of local in-lieu revenue	$6,000
State Share	Difference is State Aid Payment	$2,940,000

Dakota is 182 days). Membership in less than a full day program is prorated based on hours.

Other Program Weighted ADM

Table 34.2 identifies the weighting factors used to reflect the differential costs of educating students based on factors such school size, special education and limited English proficiency (ELL). The state provides funding for regional education associations (REAs) through a factor in the main funding formula. REAs provide educational support services to member school districts. The funding generated by the factor is forwarded directly to the REA to which the district belongs. The state also provides each REA a $31,250 annual base operating grant.

School District Size Factor[8]

Weighting factors are established for three broad size categories based on school district ADM. Districts with ADM less than 110 receive a factor of 1.36. Districts with ADM between 110 and 900 are assigned a factor ranging from 1.35 down to 1.00. Districts at or over 900 ADM are not adjusted; e.g., their factor is 1.00.[9]

Transition Adjustments

When the new funding formula was enacted, consideration was given to minimizing disruption in local budgets due to the changes. This was addressed through transition adjustments based on funding levels in the 2012-13 payment year (the year preceding the formula change). An effective funding rate was established for

TABLE 34.2. North Dakota Weighting Factor Estimates

Student Based		Weight	ADM Added	Amount Generated
	Alt High School	0.250	201	$1,941,740
	Alt Middle School	0.150	2	$21,740
	Special Ed ADM (based on district ADM)	0.083	8,858	$85,446,294
	PK Special Ed ADM	0.170	194	$1,875,858
	ELL Level 1	0.400	143	$1,875,858
	ELL Level 2	0.280	188	$1,814,413
	At Risk	0.025	1,009	$9,734,357
	Home-Education (district supervised)	0.200	11	$106,974
Summer Program				
	Summer School	0.600	1,261	$12,164,378
	Special Ed ESY	1.000	49	$472,847
Isolated School District				
	>275 sq miles and <100 ADM	0.100	116	$1,114,499
	>600 sq miles and <50 ADM	1.100	-	-
Other				
	Regional Education Association	0.002	209	$2,016,207

each school district based on the revenue sources considered in the formula (state aid, property taxes and identified in-lieu of property tax revenue).

- Districts were guaranteed at least the effective rate per weighted student unit received in 2012-13. This rate has been increased periodically by the legislature;
- Districts were limited to a maximum effective rate per weighted student unit received in 2012-13. This limit was put in place to avoid windfalls certain districts would receive due to other unrestricted income not addressed in the formula. This rate has been increased periodically by the legislature;
- In addition, districts were guaranteed the same base level amount in dollars they received in 2012-13. This provided a floor in dollars not tied to enrollment changes.

SUPPLEMENTAL GENERAL FUND

North Dakota provides no supplemental state funds to school districts to reward or equalize for higher local levy effort.

COMPENSATORY EDUCATION

State/local funding generated for compensatory programs is done through weighting factors in the general state aid formula. The following weighting factors were effective for 2022-23:

- *Alternative education*: A weighting factor of .25 times alternative education ADM generated $2 million for districts operating approved alternative education programs;
- *English language learners:* A weighting factor times English language learner ADM generated $4 million for districts providing programs to students assessed eligible in one of the three highest need categories. The level I factor is .40, the level II factor is .28 and the level III factor is .07;
- *At-risk:* A weighting factor of .025 times the district's free and reduced price lunch percentage times the district's ADM generated $10 million. The free and reduced price lunch percentage is based on a rolling three-year average of eligible students in grades 3-8;
- *Summer programs:* A weighting factor of .60 times extended school year ADM generated $12 million for districts providing approved high school, migrant and remedial elementary summer programs.

Federal title programs provide significant funding to improve education for disadvantaged students. These programs are operated under the rules and regulations of the agency granting the funding. Expenditures for Title I and bilingual programs were $40 million in 2016-17.

SPECIAL EDUCATION

Additional formula funding identified for special education programs is generated through a weighting factor in the state aid formula, applied to the total ADA of the school district. Weights are added for preschool and extended year summer programs required by a student's individual education plan.

Separate funding is set aside at the state level to cover excessive costs of special education and agency placed students. School districts can claim reimbursement for costs over established liability limits depending upon the reason for the student's placement. Generally speaking, students placed by a school district for educational purposes are reimbursed for educational costs exceeding 4.0 times the state average cost of education. Student placements by external agencies for purposes other than education are reimbursed for educational costs exceeding 1.0 times the state average cost of education.

Special education services are provided through 32 special education units. Ten larger school districts operate as single district units, with the remainder organized into multi-district cooperatives. The units are approved by the state and share costs as governed by their by-laws.

The special education weighting factor added approximately $88 million to state aid payments, and the state separately reimbursed school districts $16 million in excess costs for high cost special education and agency placed students.

CAREER AND TECHNICAL EDUCATION

Approved career and technical education programs are funded in part through the State Board for Career and Technical Education,[10] an agency that is also involved in funding programs at designated post-secondary institutions. Local school districts are expected to provide a major portion of funding, and career and technical education programs are augmented by federal aid.

VIRTUAL EDUCATION

The North Dakota Center for Distance Education[11] (NDCDE) provides online courses that students can use for credit recovery, advanced placement, or courses not otherwise available in their school districts. The Center operates primarily on a fee basis. It is hosted within the state's Information Technology Division.

GENERAL TRANSPORTATION

State funding for transportation is provided to a maximum of 90% of actual expenditures under a rate schedule that uses the number of miles transported, the number of rides provided, and the type of vehicle used for transporting students to and from school. The following rates were effective for the 2017-19 biennium.

- School buses having a rated capacity of ten or more students are reimbursed at $1.11 per mile plus 30¢ per student ride provided;
- Vehicles with rated capacities of less than ten students are reimbursed at 52¢ per mile;
- Students transported by parents are reimbursed 25¢ per mile where school bus transportation is unavailable.

Total transportation expenditures were at $29 million coming from state sources in 2022.

SPECIAL LEVIES

School districts may levy local property tax in several ways. Some levies are under the general authority of the school board, while others require voter approval. School district levy authority was rewritten in 2013 with the implementation of the new integrated funding formula. Numerous special purpose levies were eliminated or combined. The following describes the school district levy authority as it exists today.

Fund Group 1—General Fund

- *General.* The general fund levy may not increase more than 12% in dollars over the previous year, up to a levy of 70 mills on the taxable valuation of property in the school district.[12] Local share in the state aid formula considers 60 of the 70 mills.[13] Voters can override levy restrictions by approving a specified mill levy rate. The approval can be for a period no longer than ten years at a time;
- *Miscellaneous.* Each district can levy up to 12 mills for any school district purpose without restriction;
- *Tuition.* A school district may levy the amount necessary to pay tuition for its students required to be educated in another school.

Fund Group 2—Special Reserve

- *Special Reserve.* Districts may levy up to three mills annually to build a special reserve fund to cover budget shortfalls. The fund cannot exceed an amount raised by a levy of 15 mills. Any excess funds are transferred to the general fund at the end of the year.

Fund Group 3—Capital Projects

- *Building.* Voters can approve up to 20 mills for a building fund dedicated to building maintenance and capital projects;
- *Special Assessment.* The school board has authority to levy the amount necessary to pay special assessments.

Fund Group 4—Debt Service

- *Sinking and Interest.* Voters can approve a levy to service bonded debt. A 60% majority vote is required;
- *Bond Judgment.* The school board may levy to pay any final judgment obtained against the school district.

SCHOOL FACILITIES

Plant operation and maintenance costs are included in the base per-student funding rate used for the state aid formula.

CAPITAL IMPROVEMENT

The state does not provide direct funding for capital improvements. School districts may pay for infrastructure purchases through existing levy authority, building fund levies and bond levies. All construction projects over $150,000 must have approval from the North Dakota Department of Public Instruction.

The state has set up a school construction assistance revolving loan fund to provide low interest loans to school districts. The fund is capitalized at $225 million and is authorized to make 2% loans to school districts that have approval for a bond issue.[14] Low interest loans for emergency purposes are also made available through the North Dakota Department of Trust Lands.

CAPITAL OUTLAY

Projects for North Dakota school districts are funded by local property taxes. For major projects, the local school board may request authority from the voters to issue bonds. A supermajority (60%) of qualified voters voting on the proposed project is necessary for approval.

Total outstanding bonds cannot exceed 10% of the total assessed valuation in the district. The voters confer authority to incur indebtedness at a specified amount, to then sell bonds to raise funding for the proposed project, and finally to establish a sinking and interest fund and associated levy to raise revenue to pay interest and amortize the outstanding principal.[15] School boards may also secure authority from voters to establish and maintain a building fund.[16] This authority may be approved for a maximum of 20 mills per year. Since 1985, school boards have had authority on their own initiative to sell bonds and then pay interest and amortize the principal from the proceeds of the building fund levy. A number of restrictions and requirements apply to such action. Capital project expenditures for 2016-2017 were $225 million.

FOOD SERVICES

The Child Nutrition and Food Distribution[17] office within the North Dakota Department of Public Instruction administers USDA child nutrition programs, nutrition education and training programs, and commodity assistance for schools, institutions and low-income individuals. The state participates through a required match. School districts are expected to operate food services in full compliance with federal and state regulations. Total spending for school food service was reported at $68 million in FY 2017. State receipts were $1.6 million and federal receipts totaled $24 million.

STATE FUNDING FOR NON-PUBLIC SCHOOLS

There are no provisions for direct aid to private schools in North Dakota. Sharing of services mandated by federal law is provided through school districts or special education units. The state has no provisions authorizing charter schools.

OTHER STATE AIDS

The state hosts PowerSchool, a student management information system, and requires school districts to use it. This system provides substantial amounts of data for state reporting and longitudinal data systems. It is funded by a direct state appropriation to the Information Technology Division at a cost of roughly $25 per student annually. K-12 schools connect to the state's communication backbone for broadband, Internet and networking services.

From time to time the legislature provides supplemental grants to school districts to address specific initiatives. These grants do not make up a significant part of school funding. Programs are almost always considered one-time funding but can and have been continued over several biennia. Grants have addressed teacher compensation, declining enrollment, rapid enrollment, supplemental English language learner programs, deferred maintenance, and school safety grants.

Special grant programs authorized for 2017-2019 were supplemental English language learner programs ($500,000) and rapid enrollment grants ($6 million). Supplemental flat grants ($500,000) were awarded to Regional Education Associations in addition to the funding generated through the funding formula. The 2017-2019 state aid appropriation included $800,000 for gifted and talented grants to school districts.

RETIREMENT

The Teachers' Fund for Retirement[18] (TFFR) is a qualified defined benefit public pension plan that is administered through the state's Retirement and Investment Office. The state does not provide direct contributions to the teacher retirement fund. The Legislative Assembly specifies the level of contribution required of both school districts and individual teachers. Employer contribution was 12.75% and member contribution was 11.75% as of July 1, 2014.

REVENUE

State general fund revenue for aid payments to local school districts is primarily derived from income, sales and mineral taxes as well as earnings from trust funds, the state owned bank, and the state owned mill and elevator. An increasingly significant source of K-12 formula funding comes from the common schools trust fund[19] and the foundation aid stabilization fund.[20] These two special funding sources were expected to provide $300 million of the $1 billion state aid distribution for K-12 in the first year of the 2017-2019 biennium.

The federal government provided $127 million in restricted funding in FY 2017, primarily for title, special education and food service programs. Districts received another $41 million in unrestricted federal revenue to compensate for the impact of reservations, military bases and national grasslands.

Local revenue is determined after state, federal and other revenue sources are identified. School districts prepare annual budget certifications, subtract projected state, federal and other sources, and levy the remainder in property taxes within statutory limits. Districts levied taxes of $320 million for general fund purposes in FY 2017. Another $108 million was levied for building funds and debt service.

TABLE 34.3 North Dakota Legislative Appropriations—Education 2022-23

Category	Weighted ADM	Entitlement
Pk special education	1,259.17	12,890,123
Kindergarten	9,521.09	97,467,398
Grades 1-6	55,095.07	564,008,232
Grades 7-8	18,121.39	185,508,669
Grades 9-12	32,209.94	329,733,156
Alternate high schools	691.23	7,076,122
Total ADM	116,897.89	1,196,683,700
Total weighted Adm		
School size adjustment		
Total weighted students		
	Weight	**Amount**
Total Formula amount	—	1,363,553,914
Transition max. weight	1.10	(10,497,075)
Transition min. weight	1.02	36,886,426
Adjusted formula amount		1,389,943,265
Property tax contribution	60%	(296,455,287)
In-lieu contribution	75%	(48,052,697)
State aid payments	—	1,045,435,281

Source: Education Funding Interim Committee, 2022

SUMMARY

Table 34.3 summarizes the state agency appropriations supporting North Dakota public education for the 2017-2019 biennium.[21] Appropriations to support K-12 schools represented 33.3% of total state general fund appropriations. Higher education was 14.5% of total state general fund appropriations. Fall 2022 enrollment in North Dakota public elementary and secondary schools was 116,898.

ENDNOTES

[1] The chapter in this second edition draws heavily from and owes a debt of gratitude to Jerry Coleman, former director of the School Finance unit at the North Dakota Department of Public Instruction (Coleman 2019).

[2] A more complete narrative on the legislative history relative to state school funding can be found in the background memorandums prepared by Legislative Council staff for interim education committees. See "Elementary and Secondary Education State Aid and Funding Formula Study – Background Memorandum", Legislative Council. Retrieved from: http://www.legis.nd.gov/files/resource/committee-memorandum/19.9030.01000.pdf

[3] *Bismarck Public School District No. 1 v. North Dakota*, 511 N.W.2d 247 (N.D. 1994); *Williston Public School District No. 1 et al. v. State of North Dakota, et al.,* Civil No. 03-C-507 (Dist. Ct. Northwestern Judicial Circuit, N.D. (2003); Agreement to Stay Litigation, *Willison Public School District No. 1 v. State,* No. 03-C-507 (N.D. Dist. Ct. 2006).

[4] The term 'state school aid integrated formula' is often used for the foundation aid formula because of the significant amount of property tax relief provided through the formula.

5   Anna Peters (2022). North Dakota. National Education Finance Academy. Available: https://www.nationaledfinance.com/docs/30_Jef_47.5_North_Dakota.pdf

6   The legislature, through the interim education funding committee, contracted with Picus, Odden and Associates to study the adequacy of the base level of support. The report can be found in the meeting minutes. See "Minutes of the EDUCATION FUNDING COMMITTEE Monday, June 2, 2014", North Dakota Legislative Branch. Retrieved from: http://www.legis.nd.gov/assembly/63-2013/interim/15-5088-03000-meeting-minutes.pdf?20141016152129.

7   The School Finance and Organization Office of the North Dakota Department of Public Instruction publishes an Excel worksheet on its web page that fully implements the actual formula computation. See "Worksheet for Estimating School District Revenue", School Finance and Organization, North Dakota Department of Public Instruction. Retrieved from: https:/www.nd.gov/dpi/SchoolStaff/SchoolFinance/SchoolDistrictFinance/SchoolDistrictBudgeting/

8   See https://www.ndlegis.gov/files/resource/committee-memorandum/effr-2019-final-report.pdf.

9   "North Dakota Century Code, Title 15.1-27-03.2 – School District Weighting Size Factor", North Dakota Legislative Branch. Retrieved from: http://www.legis.nd.gov/cencode/t15-1c27.html, accessed April 4, 2018.

10   https://www.nd.gov/cte/

11   https://www.ndcde.org

12   Districts may levy an amount in dollars using the alternative levy authority under North Dakota Century Code 57-15-01.1. The conditions necessary to use this authority are rarely met. See "North Dakota Century Code, Title 57-15-01.1 – Protection of Taxpayers and Taxing Districts", North Dakota Legislative Branch. Retrieved from: http://www.legis.nd.gov/cencode/t57c15.html

13   The amount considered in the state aid formula cannot increase 12% over the prior year to protect school districts that are unable to levy 60 mills because of the 12% limit on general fund levy increases.

14   "North Dakota Century Code, Title 15.1-36 – School Construction", North Dakota Legislative Branch. Retrieved from: http://www.legis.nd.gov/cencode/t15-1c36.html.

15   "North Dakota Century Code, Title 21-03 - Bonds", North Dakota Legislative Branch. Retrieved from: http://www.legis.nd.gov/cencode/t21c03.html.

16   "North Dakota Century Code, Title 57-15-16 – Tax levy for building fund in school districts", North Dakota Legislative Branch. Retrieved from: http://www.legis.nd.gov/cencode/t57c15.html

17   https://www.nd.gov/dpi/SchoolStaff/ChildNutritionFoodDistribution/

18   https://www.nd.gov/rio/tffr/default.htm

19   The common schools trust fund is provided for in Article IX of the Constitution of North Dakota, which provides that the fund is to be used to support the common schools of the state. The fund consists of income from state lands dedicated for the support of schools as well as 10% of oil extraction tax revenue and 45% of tobacco settlement money received by the state. The fund balance is approaching $4 billion dollars and income provided $300 million toward the $2 billion 2017-2019 state aid appropriation.

20   The foundation aid stabilization fund, provided for in Article X of the Constitution of North Dakota, was created by the voters to protect school districts from reductions due to state revenue shortfalls. This fund receives 10% of the oil extraction tax revenue. Once the fund reaches 15% of the general fund appropriation for K-12, the excess may be used for educational purposes. The legislature used $300 million from this fund to support the 2017-2019 appropriation, with $185 million considered one-time funding.

21   Source: "Agency Budget Information – 200 Education", North Dakota Legislative Branch. Retrieved rom: http://www.legis.nd.gov/fiscal/agency#agency-200, accessed April 4, 2018.

CHAPTER 35

OHIO[1]

Barbara M. De Luca

University of Dayton

Steven A. Hinshaw

Dayton Early College Academy

GENERAL BACKGROUND

A total of 1,736,847 students attended one of the 609 public school districts in Ohio in FY2021 while 115,419 students were enrolled in Ohio's 315 charter schools during the same year.[2] Of the 609 public school districts, 231 districts (with 280,00 students) are categorized as rural (high/average poverty, small/very small student population). Two hundred districts (with 385,000 students) are designated as small town (low/high poverty, small/average student population). A total of 123 districts (with 560,000 students) are suburban (low/very low poverty, average/large student population). Fifty-five districts (with 210,000 students) are high poverty urban while 8 (with 200,000 students) are very high poverty. Approximately 272 districts have under 100 students.[3]

Funding Public Schools in the United States, Indian Country,
and US Territories (Second Edition), pages 541–553.
Copyright © 2023 by Information Age Publishing
www.infoagepub.com

HISTORICAL OVERVIEW

In 1803, the year Ohio became a state, funding for public schools consisted of money provided directly by the parents of the children attending the schools[4] and dollars from the lease of School Lands granted by the Federal government.[5] It was not until 1825 that the legislature established common schools to be financed with one-half mill real property tax[6] increased to one mill in 1873, then 1.8 mills in 1920, and 2.65 mills shortly thereafter in 1921. A constitutional change by voters limited the state's ability to impose property taxes and placed it in the hands of local voters in 1933, but limited the district voted millage to 15. Because of this, some districts received less money than when the tax was state imposed and distributed. By this time, taxes on cigarettes and gasoline also provided revenue for schools.

The Ohio legislature approved a state lottery in 1975 with the promise that the lottery money would help schools. However, much, if not most of the lottery money distributed to schools has supplanted money previously allocated through the state budget; it does not add to the amount provided prior to existence of the lottery.

In 1976, the legislature enacted House Bill 920 (HB 920). This law limits taxes received on real property to the amount collected in the first year of a new operating levy. This means that when property values increase due to inflationary increases in market value, not because of improvements to the property, the value of the increase does not generate additional property tax. Additional property tax is only realized when additional mills are approved by voters on the new appraised property value or for new construction. After the passage of a new levy, the additional dollars generated are limited to those raised by the new mills on the current property value, not those already in place on the previous property value (known as existing mills). That is, the new mills are applied only to the new property value, not the old value. This results in fewer dollars going to school districts than expected with additional levy passage. This essentially creates a reduction in total mills. The percent by which the mills are reduced is referred to as the Reduction Factor (RF). HB 920 remains in place at the time of this writing.[7]

In 1980, a statewide referendum created a constitutional change that created two classifications of property: Class 1 residential and agricultural and Class 2 commercial, industrial, mineral, and utility property. The RF is computed separately for the two classifications. This statewide referendum also included the legislation in House Bill 920 and added it to the state constitution; therefore, any proposed changes to House Bill 920 would require another statewide vote.[8]

OPERATING REVENUE

Funding of P-12 public school districts in Ohio comes from primarily three revenue sources: Federal, State, and local governments. The percent of revenue from the Federal government has fluctuated from a low of 5.2% in 1997 and 1998 to a high of 9.8% in 2013. In 2019, 7.0% of the revenue came from the Federal government. State revenue fluctuated from a low of 41.9% in 2005 and 2006 to

48.9% in 2019. Local districts contributed a high of 50.52% in 1999 and 2000 to a low of 42.0% in 2019.[9]

Federal Revenue

Table 35.1 identifies some Federal aid programs and the estimated dollar value of the award in FY2021 and FY2022.[10]

State Revenue

Every two years, the Ohio legislature approves a biennial budget. For 87 years, from 1935 to 2021, state funding in Ohio followed a traditional foundation funding model, whereby a per-student amount was determined by Ohio's legislature

TABLE 35.1.*

Federal Grant Funds (Elementary and Secondary)	Estimated Ohio Award FY2021	Estimated Ohio Award FY2022
Grants to Local Education Agencies	$593,748,975	$597,766,150
State Agency Program—Migrant Education	1,422,900	1,422,900
State Agency Program—Neglected and Delinquent State Agencies	1,841,992	1,841,992
Impact Aid Basic Support Payments	2,272,110	2,604,555
Impact Aid Children with Disabilities	132,534	132,534
Impact Aid Construction	0	0
Supporting Effective Instruction State Grants	75,057,890	74,120,606
21st Century Community Learning Centers	44,059,069	45,840,207
State Assessments	10,329,591	10,329,591
Rural and Low-Income Schools Program School	3,112,817	3,195,675
Small, Rural School Achievement Program	3,114.805	3,197,716
Student Support and Academic Enrichment State Grants	42,894,730	42,800,213
Indian Education—Grants to Local Education Agencies	0	0
English Language Acquisition	11,625,929	13,095,362
Homeless Children and Youth Education	3,787,527	3,783,577
Special Education—Grants to States	572,901,396	573,061,373
Special Education—Preschool Grants	19,682,828	16,589,532
Grants for Infants and Families	23,029,913	23,029,913
Career and Technical Education State Grants	48,949,858	49,680,182

* U.S. Department of Education, Fiscal Years 2021-2022 State Tables for the U.S. Department of Education, State Tables by State. https://www2.ed.gov/about/overview/budget/ statetables/index.html

for a basic, adequate education. This was multiplied by the number of students to determine the base funding of the school districts. After the local share of the foundation formula was calculated using school district's property values (and an income factor added in FY2022), the difference between the state base calculation and the local calculation was the state share of the base cost. Additional categorical funding such as special education, gifted education, and transportation were added over time.

Prior to the 2010-2011 fiscal year the State implemented a residual funding model to determine the foundation level of funding. That is, after the cost of other state programs was determined, the leftover dollars (the residual) were allocated to education. The amount allotted to P-12 was then divided by the total number of students to determine the foundation level of funding per pupil. Beginning with the 2010-2011 fiscal year, the State implemented a new model called the PASS (Pathway to Student Success) that was an evidenced-based model to determine a base amount of expenditure using indicators such as number of teachers, number of administrators, operations, maintenance, and technology. The PASS local share was still calculated using a school district's property values. The State abandoned the PASS in 2013 due to its cost and complexity and implemented a new model called the Bridge that used 2011 funding levels to give the State time to devise a new formula. The State returned to the more traditional foundation funding model beginning in 2014-2015 with a base amount of expenditure determined by the State and a local share calculated on school district's property values. The changes in the 2014-2015 model included the addition of a local income level to determine the local share and the addition of categorical funding items for economically disadvantaged students and limited English proficient students.

In June 2021, the Ohio Legislature approved the FY2022-2023 education budget. However, as of the time of this writing the details of its implementation are still in the planning stage. Consequently, the explanation of how state revenue is distributed to each of the 609 school districts in the State is limited.

The FY2022 and FY2023 funding formula is dubbed "The Fair School Funding Plan," designed to address the three unconstitutional rulings of the *DeRolph* legal case since 1997. The first component of the formula is the base cost, the equivalent of the opportunity grant or foundation-level funding of previous years. The difference is that the new formula determines the base cost for each district separately using district teacher salaries and benefits, transportation costs, technology needs, number of building administrators, and athletic co-curricular activities.[11] The estimated average base cost per pupil is $7,200. The State estimates the base cost to be between $7,000 and $8,000 for over 80% of the 609 districts. The base cost will be shared between the State and each local district. The local share of the calculated base cost for each district will be determined using the local property value and the income of district residents. This state and local share calculation, referred to as the state share percent and local share percent, is the second component of the formula.[12, 13]

The third component of the Fair School Funding Plan is categorical aid. This component includes additional funding for low-income (Disadvantaged Pupil Impact Aid or DPIA), gifted, special needs, and career-tech programs. Each component, except low income, will be funded as part of the state share percent. Currently, low-income funding is distributed on a per pupil basis at $422 per low-income student, with the intention of making it a percent of the base cost in the future.[14] The percent will depend on the state share percent described above. See Table 1.2 for total expenditures for each category in this component.

A formula transition supplement amount of $112.5 million in FY2022 and $82.2 million in FY2023 is planned during the phase-in of the new formula.[15] The estimated total State expenditure for each fiscal year (2022 and 2023) is between $10.9[16] and $12.6 billion.[17]

Local Revenue

Local revenue is generated by a popular vote via levies on both real local property and school district income. In FY2020 local revenue constituted 43.7% of total revenue. The average number of operating mills per school district was 50.03. In FY2021, residential and agricultural real property valuation accounted for 71.44% of total real property value. The average district income tax per pupil for FY2020 was $1,539.93.[18, 19]

Levy options are extensive in Ohio. Table 1.2 identifies and briefly describes the most common levies available to local districts. Aside from the levies voted on by the public in Table 1.2, each political district (not school district) may impose 10 mills without a vote (called inside mills). On average, school districts receive about half of these 10 mills; other political district entities receive the remainder. Anything above the 10 mills must be voted on by the public via one of the levies in Table 1.2. Voted mills are referred to as outside mills, that is, outside the 10-mill limit. The 1980 statewide referendum also specifies that the RF cannot cause a school district's effective current expense millage rate (inside and outside combined) to fall below 20 mills (referred to as the 20-mill floor).[20]

The basic formula for generating local revenue from real property tax is:

Assessed Property Valuation x Number of Mills = Gross Tax

Assessed property value is 35% of appraised property value, appraisal updates being completed every three years. Because of the reduction factor (RF) (HB 920) explained above, the number of mills used for calculating property tax, referred to as effective mills, is the total number of voted mills (outside mills) multiplied by the RF plus the inside mills (nonvoted mills). See example in Table 35.3.

A tax credit, for residential and agricultural property of 12.5% is in effect for owner-occupied properties; the credit is 10% for properties owned, but not occupied by the owner. Finally, there is a credit for senior homeowners dubbed the Homestead Exemption.

TABLE 35.2*

Levy	Features	Term
Regular Operating Levy	Vote on mills, not dollars; for any district education purpose	1-5 years or continuous
Emergency Levy	Vote on dollars, not mills; mills adjusted each year to maintain levy dollar value	1-10 years
Substitute Levy**	Replaces Emergency Levy allowing for increased revenue based on new construction	1-10 years
Millage Incremental Tax Levy	Millage phased-in on a regular schedule; maximum of 5 increments	1-10 years
Dollar Incremental Tax Levy	Vote on dollars or percentage increases; maximum of 5 increments	1-10 years
Replacement Levy	For expiring operating levy; original number of mills on new (current) property value	1-5 years
Renewal Levy	For expiring operating levy; original number of mills on old (original) property value	1-5 years
Permanent Improvement Levy	Vote on dollars, not mills; for improvement of school property or purchase of assets lasting at least 5 years	1-5 years or continuous
School Safety and Security Levy	Vote on mills, not dollars; for school safety and security	1-10 years or continuous
Combination Levy	Combination of any two of the above, plus bond issue	Term varies on request
School District Income Tax Levy	Levied in increments of .25% only; for any district education purpose	Any specified number of years or continuous

* Stabile, R.G. & Rock, M.A. (2021). *Ohio School Finance Blue Book 2022-2023 Edition,* Powerhouse Press, LLC, Cleveland, Ohio. powerhousepress.com

** Legislative Services Commission (July 2, 2010). Ohio Laws & Administrative Rules, Ohio Revised Code, Section 5705.199. https://codes.ohio.gov/ohio-revised-code/section-5705.199

TABLE 35.3. Sample Tax Calculation for Ohio School District Real Property Tax

Assessed value of property	$100,000 market (appraised) value x .35 = $35,000 assessed value
Apply RF to outside (voted) mills (HB920)	30 outside (voted mills)
Reduction Factor of 25%	30 outside mills x .25 reduction factor = 22.5 outside mills
Plus inside (nonvoted) mills	22.5 outside mills + 5 inside mills (nonvoted) =
27.5 effective mills	
Determine Tax Liability before credits	.0275 x $35,000 = $962.50 Gross Taxes Owed
Determine Net Tax Owed	$962.50 - $120.31 (12.5% owner-occupied tax credit) = **$842.19**

A 1981 law permitted local school districts voters to vote on a school district income tax in 0.25% increments. This law was repealed in 1983 but reenacted in 1989. Described in Table 35.2, the tax generally applies to the same income as Federal and State income taxes. Income not taxable includes, but is not limited to, Social Security, child support, and public assistance payments.[21]

FACILITIES

In 1997, as a result of the *DeRolph vs. State of Ohio* case,[22] the State created the Ohio School Facilities Committee (OSFC) to institute and monitor a program to address the K-12 facility issues addressed in the lawsuit. In 2012, the OSFC and the Office of State Architect were combined to create the Ohio Facilities Construction Commission (OFCC), responsible for renovation and construction of state public K-12 buildings and state-supported universities, as well as cultural facilities, state agencies, and charter schools. All OSFC responsibilities were merged into those of the OFCC in 2017.[23]

The OFCC directs several programs for the construction and renovation of K-12 school buildings. One of the major K-12 programs for traditional public schools is the Classroom Facilities Assistance Program (CFAP), in place since 1997.[24] This is a shared program between each school district and the State. Each year the Ohio Department of Education ranks all public school districts on a three-year average income-adjusted property valuation per pupil. The rank determines the order in which each district's facility needs are addressed by the OFCC. The ranks are converted to percentiles. Each district's percentile rank identifies the portion of the construction cost that will be paid by the State. The remaining cost is the responsibility of the district. Two options are in place for districts to pay their share of the construction: pay for the project as it is being constructed (pay-as-you-go) or bond indebtedness paid via a local levy.

The Expedited Local Partnership Program (ELPP) allows a district to move ahead of its ranked position in the CFAP to implement a portion of its construction project. There are several other facilities construction programs including one for exceptional needs, two for vocational facilities, one for Regional STEM schools, and one for College Prep Boarding Schools.[25]

A school district can ask its community to vote on capital levies including a bond issue levy, a permanent improvement levy, and a county sales tax levy. The bond issue levy is a formal certificate of indebtedness in return for a loan to finance major construction or renovations. The lender is a financial institution, and the borrower is the school district via the property owners. In 2021, 473 school districts had at least one approved bond issue levy. The average tax rate was 4.28 mills. The permanent improvement levy is a restricted tax to be used only for any permanent improvement including sidewalks, parking lots, buses, computers – typically a capital expense that has at least a five-year life expectancy. In 2021, 536 school districts had this type of tax. The average gross tax rate was 2.0 mills. The county sales tax levy is similar to the permanent improvement levy with its restrictions; however, it is presented as a sales tax instead of a property tax. The County Commissioners would place the sales tax issue on the ballot, collect the tax, and remit the proceeds to the school districts according to an allocation plan that is negotiable and must be agreed upon by all school districts in the county. In 2021, there was one county with this type of tax.[26]

In Ohio Revised Code (ORC) Section 3315.18 and 3315.19, a requirement exists for school districts to spend or set aside funds for capital improvements and maintenance. The school districts must deposit into this fund an amount equal to 3% of the preceding year's formula as defined in ORC 3317.02 multiplied by their previous year's student population. This money must come from the school districts' revenues. The money deposited into this fund is restricted for acquisition, replacement, enhancement, and maintenance or repair of permanent improvements. However, a school district can satisfy this requirement by passing a permanent improvement levy specifically designed for this purpose. According to the Ohio Department of Education, as school district may apply once every three consecutive years "for a waiver from the requirements of this section if it can be demonstrated that the requirements of the law will result in reduction or elimination of important academic programs in the district."[27]

TRANSPORTATION

In FY2020, total staff costs for transportation were approximately $593.8 million, $265.33 million of which was for bus drivers, both regular and substitute. Total expenses for district owned buses were $731.05 million and $97.48 million for contractor-owned and leased buses.[28]

Although details of the new FY2022 funding are not known due to newly implemented funding formulas, current funding is based on the greater of the average cost per mile or the average cost per rider for the State. Resident students in each district from preschool through grade 12 are eligible to ride the school bus.

A total of $50 million is allocated to replace the oldest and highest mileage buses in FY2022. The minimum for each school district is $45,000. To encourage traditional districts to collaborate and share resources, the budget also provides $250,000 each fiscal year (maximum of $10,000 per year) to engage in activities that could result in a reduction of transportation operating costs.

School districts of residence are required to transport both community school (charter schools) and Ohio scholarship (voucher) students to their schools of choice providing the time to transport one way does not exceed 30 minutes.[29] STEM, scholarship, and community school students are weighted for the funding formula.[30] Special permission from the charter or scholarship school accepting a student is required in order to use mass transportation for students in grades K-8. Only one transfer is permitted for 9-12 charter or scholarship students in districts permitting mass transit. Conditions for allowing payment in lieu of services are also provided in the FY2022-FY2023 budget.[31]

COMMUNITY (CHARTER) SCHOOLS

According to the September 2021 (FY2022) Funding Report for charter schools (called community schools in Ohio), slightly more than 117,600 FTE students attended charter schools, 91,394 of whom were economically disadvantaged. Total State funding for these students including base funding, categorical funding, and transportation was slightly over $952.9 million.[32]

Under the prior law, charter school money went to the home school district of each student and that district sent the money to the charter school of attendance. Under the current law, the State money due to the charter school flows directly from the State to the school.[33] Community school funding is equal to the amount of money per resident pupil the traditional public school district would have received for each individual student, including base and categorical funding. Slightly more than 300 community schools operate in Ohio.

In June 2015, the State approved $25 million for a Community Schools Classroom Facilities Grant Program. In 2016, $17 million were awarded. Eight high-performing schools received this money. Of the remaining $8 million, four schools were award a total of $4 million in Round 2 in 2018.[34]

The FY2022-FY2023 budget legislation removes the restriction of where new start-up charter schools are permitted. Prior to the new law, new start-ups primarily were permitted only in the large urban districts and in academic distress districts.

SCHOLARSHIPS (VOUCHERS)

Ohio has an extensive voucher (called scholarship in Ohio) program. Table 35.4 identifies each program, general eligibility criteria, and the dollar value of the scholarship if available. Scholarships may be used for tuition only. The State provides an unlimited number of EdChoice scholarships per year for students attending failing public schools (traditional EdChoice Scholarship) and children in low-income households (at or below 250% of the Federal Poverty Guidelines) (referred to as EdChoice Expansion Scholarship) to attend private schools. Student from about 173 school buildings in 87 school districts are eligible for the EdChoice scholarship in FY2022. About 530 schools are providers for EdChoice and EdChoice Expansion Scholarship programs.[35]

Parents may choose from approximately 448 schools for the Jon Peterson Scholarship (children with special needs) and approximately 300 for the Autism Scholarship (children with autism). Fifty-seven schools are providers for Cleveland Scholarship students (original Ohio pilot project).[36]

Since the time of their inception, both community schools and scholarships have been highly controversial in Ohio. A majority of students in the scholarship programs attend private religious schools. There is a concern that public money is being used for private religious education. At the time of this writing, no court

TABLE 35.4*

Scholarship	General Criteria**	Dollar Value
Education Choice (EdChoice)	Student attends failing public school building in FY 2018 and FY 2019 or 20% of students Title I in FY 2019 and FY 2020 and FY 2021	K-8: $5,500 9-12: $7,500
EdChoice Expansion	Household at or within 250% of Federal Poverty Guidelines	K-5: $5,500 9-12: $7,500
Jon Peterson Scholarship	K-12 student on an IEP in home district	Based on disability; $7,588-$27,000 max
Autism Scholarship	Child identified with autism and has an IEP from home district (eligibility at age 3)	Lesser of fee for spec-ed program or $27,000
Cleveland Scholarship	Cleveland Municipal School District student may attend private school in Cleveland	K-8: $5,500 9-12: $7,500

*http://education.ohio.gov/Topics/Other-Resources/Scholarships

finding has supported this contention as a violation of church and state, but the controversy continues.

CORONAVIRUS DOLLARS

Ohio education programs received money from several different Federal sources. The Coronavirus Aid, Relief and Economic Security Act (CARES) provided $657.7 million to Ohio schools. School districts are reimbursed for money actually spent for projects approved in the CARES Act. The first round of the Elementary & Secondary School Emergency Relief Act (ESSER1) granted $489.2 million to Ohio schools. Funding for each district was dependent on the amount of Title 1

TABLE 35.5.* Ohio K-12 School Expenditures FY2020**

Expenditure (Mean)	TP (n=606**)	Charter (n=302)
Classroom Instruction Per Pupil	$7,276.52	$6,816.72
Range	$5,514.99-$14,474.07	-$2,706.34-$29,619.39
Administration Per Pupil	$1,27.35	$2,890.42
Range	$1,076.08-$3,476.23	$64.70-$13,593.53
Operating Per Pupil	$2,293.01	$1,586.62
Range	$8,425.91-$24,853.72	$0.00-$7,853.49
Classroom Instruction Percent	64.5%	60.25%
Nonclassroom Instruction Percent	35.5%	39.75%

*EFM Data 2019-2020. https://reportcard.education.ohio.gov/download
**Five micro districts excluded from analysis.

monies received.[37] The second round granted $1.99 billion to Ohio schools.[38] The third round granted $4.47 billion to Ohio schools.[39]

SUMMARY

In summary, Ohio's public schools receive Federal, State, and local money for traditional public schools and community schools. Federal government money makes up less than 10% of the total while State and local money make up the remainder, each contributing close to half on average.

Federal money comes primarily in the form of categorical grants promoting equity. Likewise, the goal of some state money is to promote equity, while some promotes adequacy, and some is directed to stimulate high quality education. Local money is based completely on wealth and/or income and the local voters' willingness to pay.

Charter schools and voucher programs are major controversial issues in the State. Another issue often raised is the effect of HB920 and the Reduction Factor. This causes Ohio voters to return to the ballot box on a relatively frequent basis. The *DeRolph vs. State of Ohio* case,[40] filed based on inequity and inadequacy, claimed that the State did not provide a "thorough and efficient system of common schools" as mandated by the Ohio Constitution, due to the inequities from district-to-district. Each biennial budget passed by the Legislature attempts to address these inequities in a variety of ways, many, such as those mentioned above, have become very controversial. Equity and adequacy continue to be funding goals.

ENDNOTES

1   The authors acknowledge reliance on the work on Ohio in the first edition/volume of this book. David C. Thompson, R. Craig Wood, S. Craig Neuenswander, John M. Heim, and Randy D. Watson (eds.). Funding Public Schools in the United States and Indian Country (Charlotte, NC: Information Age Publishing, Inc., 2019). In addition, the reader can refer to Vesely, Randall, "State of the States: Ohio," Journal of Education Finance 46, no. 3 (Winter, 2021): 337-339.

2   Because as of the time of this writing FY2021 expenditures were not available, FY2020 totals are reported here. Table 1.5 shows actual expenditures as a percent of total expenditures for both traditional public school districts (TP) and charter schools.

3   Ohio Department of Education, "Enrollment Data | Current Year Data," Ohio Department of Education, July 30, 2021, https://education.ohio.gov/Topics/Data/Frequently-Requested-Data/Enrollment-Data.

4   Richard E. Maxwell and Scott R. Sweetland, Ohio School Finance: A Practitioner's Guide (Newark, NJ: Matthew Bender and Company, 2008).

5   Burke, Thomas Aquinas. Ohio Lands-A Short History. "Part 5." Ohio Auditor of State. 1994. http://freepages.rootsweb.com/~maggie/history/ohio-lands/ohl5.html.

6   Ohio History Connection, "DeRolph vs. State of Ohio," Ohio History Central, https://ohiohistory-central.org/w/DeRolph_v._State_of_Ohio.

7   Maxwell and Sweetland.

8   Howard R. Fleeter, "An Analysis of the Impact of Property Tax Limitation in Ohio On Local Revenue for Public Schools," Journal of Education Finance 21, no. 3 (Winter, 1996): 343-365.

9   Roger G. Stabile and Michael Rock, Ohio Finance Blue Book, 2022-2023 edition (Cleveland: Powerhouse Press, 2021).

10 U.S. Department of Education, "Fiscal Years 2020-2022 State Tables for the U.S. Department of Education," U.S. Department of Education, updated: October 26, 2021, https://www2.ed.gov/about/overview/budget/statetables/index.html.

11 Smith, Raymond. "School Funding Formula in Ohio Reworked." Tribune Chronicle (Warren, Ohio), June 30, 2021. https://www.tribtoday.com/news/local-news/2021/06/school-funding-formula-in-ohio-reworked/.

12 Koppitch, Slagle, Lestini, Miskimen, & Mains, July 14, 2021. Welsh-Huggins, July 14, 2021.

13 Andrew Welsh-Huggins, "What Changes under Ohio's New Fair School Funding Plan?" AP News, July 14, 2021, https://owl.purdue.edu/owl/research_and_citation/chicago_manual_17th_edition/cmos_formatting_and_style_guide/periodicals.html.

14 Welsh-Huggins.

15 Stabile and Rock.

16 Smith.

17 Welsh-Huggins.

18 Ohio Department of Education. "FY2020 District Profile Report," Ohio Department of Education, https://education.ohio.gov/Topics/Finance-and-Funding/School-Payment-Reports/District-Profile-Reports/FY-2020-District-Profile.

19 Ohio School Boards Association, "Understanding school levies," Ohio School Boards Association, February 2018, https://www.ohioschoolboards.org/sites/default/files/OSBAUnderstanding-LeviesFactSheet.pdf.

20 Meghan Sullivan and Mike Sobul, "Property Tax and School Funding," Ohio Department of Taxation, Ohio.gov, updated: February 2010, https://tax.ohio.gov/static/research/property_taxation_school_funding_2012c.pdf.

21 Stabile and Rock.

22 Ohio History Connection, "DeRolph."

23 Ohio Facilities Construction Commission, "About OFCC | A History of the Commission," Ohio Facilities Construction Commission, https://ofcc.ohio.gov/Home/About-OFCC.

24 Ohio Facilities Construction Commission, "K-12 Schools," Ohio Facilities Construction Commission, https://ofcc.ohio.gov/Services-Programs/K-12-Schools.

25 Ibid.

26 Stabile and Rock.

27 Ohio Department of Education, "FY2022 Set-Aside," Section 3315.18(D), Item 4, Ohio Department of Education, August 17, 2021, https://education.ohio.gov/Topics/Finance-and-Funding/Finance-Related-Data/Set-asides/FY2022-Set-aside.

28 Ohio Department of Education, Office of Budget and School Funding, "F2020 Yellow Bus Cost Analysis, Fiscal Year 2019-2020," Ohio Department of Education, April 3, 2020, http://odevax.ode.state.oh.us/htbin/%20f2020-type1-cost-analysis.com?irn=999999.

29 Legislative Services Commission (September 30, 2021). Ohio Laws & Administrative Rules, Ohio Revised Code, Section 3327.01 "Transportation of pupils." https://codes.ohio.gov/ohio-revised-code/section-3327.01.

30 Ohio School Boards Association, "Budget Analysis and Discussion (BAD) Seminar," Ohio Department Funding Update, August 4, 2021, https://www.ohioschoolboards.org/events/view/budget-analysis-and-discussion-bad-seminar-virtual.

31 Legislative Service Commission, Ohio Revised Code, Section 3327.01 (Transportation of pupils), Ohio Laws and Administrative Rules. September 30, 2021. https://codes.ohio.gov/ohio-revised-code/section-3327.01.

32 Ohio Department of Education, "Community School Payment Reports FY2022," "Community Schools Funding," Ohio Department of Education, September 14, 2021, https://webapp1.ode.state.oh.us/school_options/F2022/Default.asp.

33 Ohio Education Association, House Bill 110 (State Budget FY 2022-2023): As Enacted, Ohio Education Association, July 2021, https://www.ohea.org/cms/assets/uploads/2021/07/OEA-analysis-of-HB-110-as-enacted-FINAL.pdf.

34 Ohio Department of Education, "Annual Report on Ohio Community Schools: July 1, 2019 – June 30, 2020," Ohio Department of Education, December 31, 2020, https://education.ohio.gov/getattachment/About/Annual-Reports/19-20-Community-Schools.pdf.aspx?lang=en-US.

35 Ohio Department of Education (ODE), February 3, 2021. "What Schools Can I Choose?" https://education.ohio.gov/Topics/Other-Resources/Scholarships/EdChoice-Scholarship-Program/Ed-Choice-Scholarship-Information-for-Parents/What-School-Can-I-Choose

36 Ohio Department of Education, "EdChoice Scholarship: What School Can I Choose?" Ohio Department of Education, February 3, 2021. https://education.ohio.gov/Topics/Other-Resources/Scholarships/EdChoice-Scholarship-Program/EdChoice-Scholarship-Information-for-Parents/What-School-Can-I-Choose.

37 Ohio Department of Education, "CARES Act Funding," Ohio Department of Education, August 16, 2021, https://education.ohio.gov/Topics/Reset-and-Restart/CARES-Act-Funding.

38 Ohio Department of Education, ESERII." https://ccip.ode.state.oh.us/documentlibrary/ViewDocument.aspx? DocumentKey=86411.

39 Ohio Department of Education, "American Rescue Plan Elementary and Secondary School Emergency Relief Fund (ARP ESSER)," Ohio Department of Education, May 2021, https://oese.ed.gov/files/2021/07/Ohio-ARP-ESSER-State-Plan-Final.pdf.

40 Ohio History Connection, "DeRolph."

CHAPTER 36

OKLAHOMA

Jeffrey Maiden
University of Oklahoma

Shawn Hime
Oklahoma State School Boards Association

GENERAL BACKGROUND

Though equalization of funding among districts is not required by the Oklahoma Constitution, the Oklahoma Legislature has established as a goal the maintenance of a degree of inter district funding equity, as specified in state statute.[1] Accordingly, Oklahoma has utilized a two-tiered equalization education funding formula since 1981. The Legislature annually appropriates state aid to flow through both 'halves' of the formula in a single line item.[2] The state provides the largest share of funding for common school annually, and education represents the largest single item in the annual state budget. The local portion of the formula includes yields based on a total of 39 local district mills plus other chargeable local district income.

State funding increased dramatically during the 1990s (mostly during the first half of the decade) due largely to implementation of the Oklahoma Reform and Funding Act of 1990[3] (more commonly known as HB1017). However, the Okla-

Funding Public Schools in the United States, Indian Country,
and US Territories (Second Edition), pages 555–565.
Copyright © 2023 by Information Age Publishing
www.infoagepub.com

homa economy suffered dramatically from the recession of the early 2000s and the Great Recession of the late 2000s and into the 2010s. These downturns have affected state funding for education.

Oklahoma is currently divided into 540 school districts, 31 of which are charters. These include both 'independent' K-12 districts and 'dependent' districts serving students in grades pk-8. Most local revenues are derived through ad valorem taxation (the 39 mill local levies through a variety of sources). Districts may levy by a maximum 5 mill building levy and a sinking fund levy to service debt. the state will distribute revenues to support local district capital outlay for the first time beginning fiscal year 2022. Local districts additionally derive miscellaneous revenues from interest income, gifts, student fees, property sales, transfer fees, tuition, rental and refunds.

CURRENT POLITICAL CLIMATE

The bicameral Oklahoma legislature includes a State Senate, consisting of 48 members elected for four-year terms. Half of the Senate membership is elected each two-year cycle. The Oklahoma House of Representatives consists of 101 members elected for two-year terms. These chambers are led by a Senate President Pro Tempore (in lieu of the Lieutenant Governor, who holds the position of President of the Senate according to the Constitution) and the Speaker of the House of Representatives.[4] Members are term limited to 12 years' service. The Oklahoma Legislature meets annually for regular sessions, from early February to late May.

The executive branch is led by a Governor who is elected for a four-year term (the next regular gubernatorial election is scheduled for November 2022). Governors are limited to two terms of office.[5] The Oklahoma Department of Education is led by a State Superintendent of Public Instruction, who is elected to a four-year term in the same year as the Governor and is also limited to two terms in office.[6]

Oklahoma is considered a 'ruby red' state. The majority of voters in each of Oklahoma's 77 counties has voted for the Republican presidential candidate since 2000. Nearly all statewide elected officials belong to the Republican party, including the Governor and State Superintendent. Oklahoma is currently a Republican 'trifecta' state, with a Republican Governor and with both houses of the Legislature maintaining Republican supermajorities. In effect, the Republican caucuses of the two houses drive legislation in the state. The political climate most certainly affects common and higher education funding.[7]

BASIC SUPPORT PROGRAM

The state of Oklahoma appropriated nearly $3 billion for general funding support to local districts during FY 2020-21. The basic state support mechanism for Oklahoma school district general funding includes a two-tiered equalization formula. The 'top half' includes a foundation formula coupled with a transportation

TABLE 36.1. Fiscal Year 2021 Oklahoma Common School Appropriations

Purpose	FY 21 Appropriation
Financial Support of Public Schools	**2,300,970,699**
General Revenue (GR)	953,338,319
Education Reform Revolving Fund (1017 funds)	1,015,074,419
Common Education Technology Fund	46,938,566
Oklahoma Lottery Trust Fund	32,739,428
Mineral Leasing Fund	9,211,258
Constitutional Reserve Fund	243,668,709
Amount appropriated from Constitutional Reserve Fund (Rainy Day)	51,000,000.00
Instructional Materials (70 O.S. 16-114a)	**33,000,000**
Flexible Benefit Allowance (appropriated from GR)	**535,537,021**
Certified Personnel	322,414,199
Support Personnel	180,277,721
Support of Public School Activities (appropriated from GR)	**100,919,026**
Administrative and Support Functions (appropriated from GR)	**15,027,640**
Lottery Trust Fund Transfer to TRS Revolving Fund	**3,637,714**
Lottery Trust Fund—Transfer to School Consolidation Assistance Fund	**3,637,714**
TOTAL APPROPRIATION	**2,992,729,814**

Source: Oklahoma State Department of Education, Oklahoma School Finance Technical Assistance Document, October 2020.

supplement. The 'bottom half,' the salary incentive aid, is a modified guaranteed yield formula.[8]

State formula aid is enrollment driven, with weighted average daily membership (ADM) used as the formula unit of funding through the foundation and salary incentive formulas (the transportation supplement uses ADH – average daily haul). Currently, ADM are weighted across three categories. The first is grade level weight[9] and the second weighting category is special education classification.[10] For districts that qualify, ADM may also be adjusted per a small school weight. Districts that do not qualify for the small school weight may qualify for additional isolation funding, which is a grant in aid rather than an ADM weight.[11] The teacher index weight, which is applied only to the salary incentive aid is provided to give districts the fiscal incentive to hire more experienced teachers with graduate degrees.[12]

The foundation program (known locally as the 'top half' of the formula) for a given local district includes a base support factor ($1,764.77for FY 21) multiplied by the district's weighted ADM. The local foundation program income for the district is subtracted from this product. This income includes district 15 mill tax levy, 75 percent of the 4-mill countywide levy, and collections from the state dedicated revenue sources (motor vehicle collections, gross production tax revenues, rural electrification tax revenues, and school land earnings). State foundation aid for a given district is the difference between the total foundation program and local foundation program income. State appropriated aid to school districts is therefore disbursed in inverse proportion to local ability to raise revenue.

The salary incentive aid formula (known locally as the 'bottom half' of the formula), fundamentally a guaranteed yield formula, constituted a second-tier resource equalization program. The local portion of the program were derived from an annual levy of a maximum 20 mills for each local district across three separate levies (the local support, emergency, and county levies). For FY 2020-21, the state guarantees $85.12 per weighted ADM for every mill levied up to 20. Both the base support factor and the weighted ADM factor of the bottom half of the formula decreased from FY 2019-20.[13]

District aid is calculated semiannually, in July and January. Aid is distributed through 11 monthly electronic transfers to local school districts. August through December disbursements are based on the July calculation, while January through June disbursements are based on a January calculation. The number of 'out of formula' districts, those who are ineligible for foundation and/or salary incentive aid because of substantial amounts of local revenue, have increased to 90 by FY 2021 (just under 18% of all districts). This increase is likely due in large part to the general increase in local wealth statewide coupled with decreases in state support dollars since the Great Recession.

VERTICAL EQUITY

The weighted average daily membership is comprised of the average daily enrollment plus the sum of nine additional possible weights delineated in Title 70 Section 18 of Oklahoma State Statutes. The funding formula uses student- and district-level weights to create vertical equity. The Oklahoma funding formula weights are allocated based on identified differences in students, teachers, and district factors that affect the cost to educate students.

ECONOMICALLY DISADVANTAGED

A student add-on weight of .25 is provided in both halves of the formula to assist local school district in defraying education costs for students from poverty as indicated by qualification for free or reduced lunches. Additional costs must be borne by districts, supplemented with federal funds. The total state aid formula revenue dedicated to students identified as economically disadvantaged was $378.8 million in FY 2021, representing 9.2% of state aid formula revenue.

SPECIAL EDUCATION

Special education weights are used in calculating weighted ADM in both 'halves' of the formula. The additional weights for special education students are as follows:[14]

Specific Learning Disability LD	0.40
Hearing Impaired	2.90
Visually Impaired	3.80
Multiple Disability	2.40
Speech or Language Impairment	0.05
Intellectual Disability	1.30
Traumatic Brain Injury	2.40
Autism	2.40
Emotionally Disturbed	2.50
Orthopedically Impaired	1.20
Other Health Impairment	1.20
Deaf - Blind	3.80
Spec Ed Summer Program	1.20

These weights have undergone minor modifications but no substantive revision since the implementation of the current formula in 1981. Revenues are not tracked to expenditures. Any additional costs are borne by the local school districts, supplemented by federal funding. Special education funding from the state aid formula was $459.6million in FY 2021, representing 11.2% of state aid revenue.

TRANSPORTATION

State transportation aid is provided as a supplement to the foundation formula. The transportation supplement is calculated by multiplying average daily haul (ADH) by a per-capita transportation allowance and then multiplying this product by a transportation factor (1.39 for FY 2021).[15] The ADH for a district represents the number of students legally transported who live at least one and a half miles from school. Transportation supplement proceeds are fully fungible, not tracked to specific transportation costs. Additional transportation costs are borne by local school districts. Transportation aid was $31.6 million from the state in FY 2021, representing less than 1% of total state aid revenue.

FACILITIES AND CAPITAL OUTLAY

The Oklahoma Constitution provides a State Public Common School Building Fund to assist school districts with capital outlay costs.[16] Historically, the Oklahoma Legislature had never appropriated monies into the fund, and there had been no state funding mechanism to support district capital outlay needs. However, The Redbud School Funding Act, (SB 229), which passed the Oklahoma Legislature in 2021, will provide facilities aid to certain districts in Oklahoma beginning in FY 2022

Local school districts may annually levy a maximum 5 mills to support a building fund. Building fund proceeds, with few exceptions as noted below, may not be mixed with the general fund. Most of the funding for capital outlay is derived through the sale of general obligation bonds. School districts must pass bond issues only after the approval of at least 60 percent of the voters voting in an election[17] (bonded indebtedness is the only vote requiring a supermajority). With a bond issue, a debt service levy is passed to service the debt. Though there is no limit on the number of debt service mills for a school district, no district may incur debt above a ceiling 10 percent of net assessed valuation.

Although the Oklahoma formula has demonstrated a degree of fiscal equity, capital outlay revenues among Oklahoma school districts are largely inequitable. Building fund proceeds generally cannot support general operations and vice versa. However, there are a few 'crossover' areas that may be supported by either the general fund, building fund, or bond funds.[18] crossover expenditures from the building fund include a school's utility bills, custodial, maintenance and security salaries, furniture, and insurance premiums. Bond fund expenditures that are also allowable from the general fund include equipment, textbooks and library books. Therefore, the inherent inequities in capital outlays appear to mitigate equities in general funding across Oklahoma districts, as wealthier districts are able to meet crossover funding costs more readily with building or bond fund proceeds, whereas less wealthy districts are more prone to rely more heavily on general fund proceeds to fund these crossover areas.[19]

CHARTER SCHOOLS

Charter schools are authorized by the Oklahoma Charter School Act of 2010.[20] According to statute, the following organizations may sponsor charters, each eligible if conditions outlined in the statute are met:

1. School districts;
2. Oklahoma State System of Higher Education member institutions;
3. Federally recognized Indian Tribes;
4. The State Board of Education.

The Oklahoma State Department of Education lists 24 current charter schools operating in the state.[21] Charter schools receive state aid through the funding formula, based on district location. Statute provides that a maximum five percent of the state allocation to a charter school may be retained by its sponsor for administrative costs.[22]

CAREER AND TECHNICAL EDUCATION

Career and technical education is governed by the Oklahoma Department of Career and Technology Education, with both governance and funding independent from Oklahoma common schools. The system includes 29 technology centers across 58 campuses statewide.[23]

VIRTUAL EDUCATION

Four virtual charter schools operate in Oklahoma. Virtual charter schools are governed by the Statewide Virtual Charter School Board,[24] which has the authority to oversee all virtual charter schools in the state, for regulating virtual charter school applications, and to sponsor virtual charter schools.[25]

STATE FUNDING FOR NON-PUBLIC SCHOOLS

The state does not provide financial support for private schools, though local districts are subject to support provisions encapsulated in federal law.[26]

TAX AND SPENDING LIMITS

Districts administrative costs are statutorily limited according to district average daily attendance (ADA), as follows:[27]

ADA > 1,500	5 percent
500 < ADA < 1,500	7 percent
ADA < 500	8 percent

Districts exceeding these limits are subject to a state aid penalty as well as a performance review of budgeting effectiveness and efficiency.[28]

GIFTED AND TALENTED EDUCATION

A student add-on weight of .34 is provided in both halves of the funding formula to assist local school district in maintaining programs for gifted students. Additional costs must be borne by districts. State aid generated by the gifted weight was $97.3 million from the state in FY 2021, representing 2.4% of state aid formula revenue.

BILINGUAL EDUCATION

A student add-on weight of .25 is provided for both funding formulas to assist local school district in defraying bilingual education costs. Additional cost must be borne by districts, supplemented with federal funds. State aid derived from the bilingual weight was $79.1million in FY 2021, representing 1.9 % of state aid formula revenue.

EARLY CHILDHOOD EDUCATION

Students in early childhood programs are weighted at 0.7 (half-day students) or 1.3 (full day students) as part of the pupil grade level weight in both halves of the formula. Additional costs are borne by local districts, supplemented by federal funds.

CATEGORICAL PROGRAMS

Numerous categorical programs were historically included as supplementary state support outside the formula in Oklahoma. Examples include driver's education, funding for textbooks, and compensatory education (among other areas). However, most of these categorical programs have been eliminated and proceeds have instead been appropriated through the state aid formula.

TEACHER RETIREMENT AND BENEFITS

Public school teachers, administrators and staff are members of the Oklahoma Teachers Retirement System (OTRS), a separate entity from the Oklahoma Public Employees Retirement System.[29] The OTRS is based on member contributions through payroll deduction, and districts are not required to fund employee contributions. The employer contribution is 9.5% of the employee's salary. While the employee must pay 7% of their salary toward the statutorily created defined benefit plan.

TECHNOLOGY

The Common Education Technology Revolving Fund was established by statute in 2014.[30] Funds are derived through tax revenue from the gross production of oil and are used as part of the state aid formula.

REVENUE

Local Revenue

The largest source of local revenue is ad valorem tax collections. Assessment ratios are constitutionally capped at 35%. Local boards of education are authorized by the Oklahoma Constitution to annually levy 15 mills for general fund education support.[31] The levy resulting from the 15 mills constitutes part of the local district contribution to the state foundation formula.

Districts are constitutionally guaranteed proceeds from a 4-mill county wide levy.[32] These revenues are distributed to local districts based on ADA. Part of these revenues constitute a portion of the local contribution to the state foundation program.

District voters decide an additional 20 mills for general fund support. These are derived from three separate levies: A 10-mill local support levy, a 5-mill emergency levy, and a 5-mill county levy.[33] The county levy is approved by a majority countywide vote and distributed to local districts based on ADA. Proceeds from these 20 mills are equalized by the state through the salary incentive aid formula.

Districts may, with approval of a majority of voters, pass a 5-mill building fund levy to support capital costs. Proceeds are not equalized by the state. Further, districts may, with the approval of a 60% supermajority of voters, pass a sinking fund levy to service debt.

School districts do not generate revenue through either income or sales tax. In fact, local income taxation is prohibited by the Oklahoma Constitution.[34]

Oklahoma school districts are limited in the amount of ad valorem taxes annually levied for the support of local school districts. Districts are authorized to levy a maximum 39 mills for the support of the general educational program. An additional 5 mill building fund is authorized, while districts may pass millage to service debt not to exceed 10 percent of total aggregate district net assessed valuation. Fair cash value of real property for tax purposes to may be increased no more than 5 percent per taxable year.

The state Legislature, based on State Question 340 passed in 1992, may not increase state taxation rate without the approval of a majority of voters participating in a statewide election.

State Revenue

The Oklahoma Legislature annually appropriates dollars to support public education, with revenues primarily flowing through the state aid formula. State general fund revenues are derived mostly through the income tax and state sales tax. Oklahoma also includes a state lottery, with 45% of lottery proceeds dedicated to common school funding. The Legislature is constitutionally prohibited from using lottery trust fund proceeds to supplant other state funds used to support education.[35]

Certain revenue sources are earmarked for the support of public education. The proceeds from these sources constitute part of state foundation aid to school districts. School land revenues are derived from the Permanent School Fund are earmarked for local districts. The fund is administered by the Commissioners of the Land Office.

Rural Electrification Association Cooperative Tax (R.E.A. Tax) revenues are in lieu of property tax collections, and are distributed in proportion to the number of miles of transmission lines with each district. Motor Vehicle Collections

Thirty-five percent of all motor vehicle fees collected are allocated to local school district from a separate motor vehicle fund. Proceeds are distributed through each county to school districts based on ADA.

Extractive industries provide a major source of revenue for Oklahoma, an energy producing state. Ten percent of Gross Production Tax revenues are earmarked for school districts, based on an ADA allocation.

REWARDS/SANCTIONS

Penalties are in the form of noncompliance with certain elements of reform. For example, districts that do not comply with state mandated class size restrictions may be penalized accordingly by having commensurate state aid withheld. Districts that employ too many noncertified teachers or do not maintain state minimum salary requirements likewise will have a measure of state aid reduced.

RECENT/PENDING LITIGATION

No case has been decided since the Oklahoma Supreme Court upheld the Oklahoma state support system in *Fair School Finance Council of Oklahoma, Inc. v. Oklahoma* in 1987.[36] *Fair II* in 1990[37] was filed but never adjudicated.

SPECIAL TOPICS

Oklahoma has led the nation in state funding cuts per pupil as a percentage over the past decade, at nearly 25%,[38] a fact that exacerbates relatively poor funding levels in the state given that Oklahoma is regularly among the lowest in per pupil support for education among the states.[39] Additionally, average teacher salaries have historically been among the lowest in the nation,[40] and Oklahoma school districts are prone to losing teachers to other states, particularly border states (each of which includes higher average teacher salaries).

ENDNOTES

[1]   70 O.S. sec. 18-101.

[2]   70 O.S. sec. 18-117.

[3]   Ok. Laws 1989, 1st Ex. Sess., c. 2. The official title was the Oklahoma Educational Reform Act, though it is more commonly known as HB 1017. Most of the provisions, with some slight modifications, have been incorporated into Oklahoma Statutes. The exceptions included some of the provisions for increased funding for education, primarily through state dedicated sources. These increases failed a statewide vote for constitutional amendment on June 26, 1990 (H.J.R. No. 1005, State Questions 634, 635, and 636).

[4]   Ok. Const. Art. V.

[5]   Ok. Const. Art. VI.

[6] Ok. Const. Art. XIII.

[7] See Wall, Rex and Jeffrey Maiden, "State of the States 2020: Oklahoma," Journal of Education Finance, vol. 46 no. 3 (Winter 2021), 340-341.

[8] 70 O.S. 18-200.1.

[9] 70 O.S. sec. 18-201.1(B)(1).

[10] 70 O.S. sec. 18-201.1(B)(2).

[11] 70 O.S. sec. 18-201.1(B)(3).

[12] 70 O.S. sec. 18-201.1(B)(4).

[13] Oklahoma State Department of Education, Oklahoma School Finance Technical Assistance Document, October 2020.

[14] 70 O.S. sec. 18-201.1(B)(2).

[15] 70 O.S. sec. 18-200.1(D)(2).

[16] Ok. Const. Art. X Sec. 32.

[17] 70 O.S. sec. 18-201.1(B)(4).

[18] Examples of crossover areas include building utilities, salaries of maintenance staff, and certain technology purposes.

[19] Hime, Shawn and Jeffrey Maiden, An Examination of the Fiscal Equity of Current, Capital, and Crossover Educational Expenditures in Oklahoma School Districts, Institute for the Study of Education Finance (ISEF-01FR, July 2017).

[20] Ok Stat 70-3-130.

[21] See http://www.sde.ok.gov/sde/current-charter.

[22] 70 O.S. sec. 3-130.

[23] Oklahoma Department of Career and Technical education, https://www.okcareertech.org/

[24] 70 O.S. sec. 3-145.

[25] See Statewide Virtual Charter School Board, 'Virtual Charter School Authorization and Oversight Process,' November 2017. Available online at http://svcsb.ok.gov/Websites/svcsb/images/Virtual%20Charter%20School%20Authorization%20and%20Oversight%20Process%20Manual.pdf.

[26] Every Student Succeeds Act, 20 U.S.C. ch. 28 § 1001 et seq.

[27] 70 O.S. Sec. 18-124.

[28] 70 O.S. Sec. 3-118.1.

[29] See https://www.ok.gov/TRS/

[30] 62 O.S. Sec. 62-34.90.

[31] Ok Const Art X Sec. 9(c).

[32] Ok Const Art X Sec. 9(b).

[33] Ok Const Art X Sec. 9(a,d).

[34] Ok Const Art X Sec. 5.

[35] Ok Const Art X Sec. 41.

[36] Fair School Finance Council of Oklahoma, Inc. v. Oklahoma, 746 P. 2d 1135 (1987).

[37] Fair School Finance II, CJ90 7165 (Okl. 1990).

[38] Data from the Center on Budget and Funding Priorities, State General Funding Per Student Still Lower than 2008 in 25 States. Available online at https://www.cbpp.org/state-general-funding-per-student-still-lower-than-2008-in-25-states .

[39] National Center for Education Statistics, Table 236.70 Current expenditure per pupil in average daily attendance in public elementary and secondary schools, by state or jurisdiction: Selected years, 1969-70 through 2014-15. Available online at https://nces.ed.gov/programs/digest/d17/tables/dt17_236.70.asp?current=yes .

[40] National Center for Education Statistics, Table 211.60 Estimated average annual salary of teachers in public elementary and secondary schools, by state: Selected years, 1969-70 through 2016-17. Available online at https://nces.ed.gov/programs/digest/d17/tables/dt17_211.60.asp?current=yes .

CHAPTER 37

OREGON

Andy Saultz
Pacific University

Alyssa Nestler
Pacific University

GENERAL BACKGROUND

Historically, school funding in Oregon was heavily reliant on local taxation. In fact, the first public education in Oregon pre-dated statehood. In the 1830s, New Englander John Ball opened the first public school, which largely served the children of fur trappers and explorers (Peterman, 2019). In 1859, Oregon became a state, and included Common schools, a statewide superintendent, and a school fund from the income of sales of land given to the federal government (Peterman, 2019). The initial distribution of these funds was based on counties. Much of the 20th Century was defined by a reliance on local property taxes to fund public schools. Equity concerns mounted as the variation in school funding was directly tied to racial and economic factors. Pressure mounted to address these inequities. From the political left, Civil Rights advocates pushed for a more equitable funding of schools. Meanwhile, those on the political right became increasingly frustrated with ever-growing property taxes. According to Peterman (p. 1, 2019), "per-pupil spending varied $675 to $1795" across the state. In 1976, the Oregon

Funding Public Schools in the United States, Indian Country,
and US Territories (Second Edition), pages 567–576.
Copyright © 2023 by Information Age Publishing
www.infoagepub.com
All rights of reproduction in any form reserved.

Supreme Court recognized equity concerns, but found in favor of the state because it stated that the constitutional duty relied on local control of school funding in the *Olsen v. State* decision.

Oregon had a levy-based property tax system until 1991 where each taxing district was able to calculate its own tax levy based on the wants and needs of the community with little to no regulation[1]. Counties could assess the value of property, and the full market value of the property was taxable.

In 1990, voters passed Measure 5 through a statewide referendum. This constitutional amendment, which became law in 1991, placed restrictions on the total amount and the percentage increase of local property taxes. More specifically, the Measure paced a limit of $5 per $1,000 real market value for school taxes and $10 per $1,000 real market value for general government taxes. This applied only to operating taxes, not bonds. If either the school or general government exceeded these thresholds, then the taxing district would have its tax rate reduced proportionally until the tax limit was reached, which is known as compression. As a result, the state legislature was tasked with a much larger role in public school funding. The legislature created a new funding formula to equalize funding across districts. Following the implementation of Measure 5 in 1991, the Supreme Court was once again tasked with claims of inequitable school funding in the *Coalition for Equitable School Funding v. State*. This Court, in a decision similar to the earlier Olsen case, found in favor of the state. This pattern continued in 1995 with the *Withers v. State,* when the Court denied the appeal from an appeals court stating that funding was inequitable across geographic regions of the state.

The State Legislature passed Measure 50 in 1997 to reduce property taxes, and to control the future growth of taxes[2]. Measure 50 significantly changed a number of components of taxation in the state of Oregon. First, it changed the assessed value to no longer equate to real market value. For 19979-1998, the assessed value of every property was reduced to 90 percent of its 1995-1996 assessed value. For existing property, Measure 50 limited the annual growth in assessed value to 3 percent. Measure 50 also made it so that assessed value could not exceed real market value. It also created a voter participation requirement for any bond levy if the bond is not in a general election. Combined, Measures 50 and 5 placed limits on the expansion and rate of local property taxes, which has led to a continual shift from local property taxes to state income taxes as the primary revenue for public education.

With the Courts seemingly set on the constitutionality of inequitable funding claims, advocates turned to voters. In 2000, voters passed a constitutional amendment that codified language around Adequate and Equitable Funding. The new language, embedded within Article VIII §8

> The Legislative Assembly shall appropriate in each biennium a sum of money sufficient to ensure that the state's system of public education meets quality goals established by law, and publish a report that either demonstrates the appropriation is sufficient or identifies the reasons for the insufficiency, its extent, and its impact on the ability of the state's system of public education to meet those goals.

TABLE 37.1. Statewide Student Enrollment

Measures of Student Enrollment	2015-16	2016-17	2017-18	2018-19	2019-20
Average Daily Membership-ADMr	568,642	571,775	572,856	573,825	572,585
Weighted Daily Membership-ADMw	701,613	707,233	706,296	703,747	704,285
Fall Membership (Enrollment on October 1)**	576,407	578,947	580,690	581,730	582,662
Average Daily Attendance (ADA)*	531,055	532,613	531,850	532,671	542,083

*ADA includes students who are counted based on instructional hours. ADA for those students is estimated by multiplying the ADM of those students by the ratio of ADA to ADM for "regular" students (Type 1 records in the ADM collection. Kindergarteners are counted as .5 in ADM and ADA through 2014-15 and then 1.0.
**Fall membership reported here includes some PK students.
Source: Oregon Department of Education. "Statewide Report Card 2019-2020." An Annual Report to the Legislature on Oregon Public Schools. (2020), p.15. https://www.oregon.gov/ode/schools-and-districts/reportcards/Documents/rptcard2020.pdf

Once again, the state created a new funding formula to attempt to equalize funding across the state. In 2001, the state legislature passed a Quality Education Model (QEM) statute which tied school funding to education performance indicators instead of basing funding on historic levels and enrollment exclusively[3]. The QEM also set a formula for the Legislature to use as a standard of what 'fully

TABLE 37.2. Gap Between QEM and Actual State Funding

Biennium	State School Fund for QEM Full Implementation	State School Fund Legislative Appropriation	Gap	Percent Gap
1999-01	$5,654.20	$4,562.00	$1,092.20	23.90%
2001-03	$6,215.60	$4,573.90	$1,641.70	35.90%
2003-05	$6,659.20	$4,907.60	$1,751.60	35.70%
2005-07	$7,096.70	$5,305.20	$1,791.50	33.80%
2007-09	$7,766.20	$6,131.00	$1,635.20	26.70%
2009-11	$7,872.80	$5,756.90	$2,115.90	36.80%
2011-13	$8,004.90	$5,799.00	$2,205.90	38.00%
2013-15	$8,775.00	$6,650.40	$2,124.60	31.90%
2015-17	$9,158.40	$7,376.30	$1,782.10	24.60%
2017-19	$9,971.00	$8,200.00	$1,771.00	21.60%
2019-21	$10,773.90	$9,000.00	$1,773.90	19.70%
2021-23	$9,994.00	$9,160.50	$833.60	9.10%

For 2021-23 the amount is the estimated Current Service Level since the legislative appropriation has not been made at this time.
Source: Quality Education Commission Report 2020. "Exhibit 2." (August 2020), p.9. https://www.oregon.gov/ode/reports-and-data/taskcomm/Documents/66421_ODE_Quality%20Education%20Model%20Report_2020%20v7.pdf

funding' public education equates to. As of 2021, the Legislature has never funded public education at the recommended QEM level. See Table 37.2 for an overview of the history of state allocation relative to QEM.

And, once again there was litigation around whether the new formula met the requirements described in the Oregon Constitution. In 2006, the *Pendleton School District v. State* argued that state's funding did not meet the QEM's adequacy requirement[4]. The Oregon Supreme Court agreed, stating that the legislature was deficient in supporting the QEM's quality standard. However, despite this ruling the court did not intervene further.

Student enrollment has increased a small amount in the last few years. Table 37.1 shows a total state enrollment of approximately 568,000 in the 2015-2016 school year, and an estimated 572,000 in the 2019-2020 school year. ODE officials note that enrollment for the 20-21 and 21-22 school years will see declines due to the pandemic and to an increase in homeschooling. It is unclear how big those declines are at this time.

POLITICAL CLIMATE

Since 2016, Democrats have dominated state-level legislative and executive leadership. As a result, the Democrats have been able to pass the majority of their agenda. However, Republicans in the Senate organized legislative walk outs in protest in the 2019, 2020, and 2021 legislative sessions. This has highlighted the urban/rural divide in the state, and led some in Eastern Oregon to support joining Idaho.

Oregon's Legislature works on a biennial budget cycle, and used to convene only in odd numbered years. This created fiscal challenges, and the Legislature relied heavily on an emergency board to amend budget items. Over time, the Legislative leadership has shifted to having a long, six month session in the odd years and a short, six week session in the even years. The part time legislative model relies heavily on the executive branch to update, recommend, and adjust policy.

Oregon's budget covers two fiscal years, referred to as a biennium, and spans from July 1 of an odd-numbered year to June 30 of the next odd-numbered year[5]. The 2021 Legislature approved the budget for July 1, 2021 to June 30, 2023. The budget cycle starts with agency requests, which are due to the Chief Financial Office (CFO) by September 1 of even years.

Next, the Governor and CFO review the budget request and present a Recommended Budget to the Legislature in January of odd years, for the upcoming biennium that starts in July of that same year. The Governor's Recommended Budget is submitted with the Tax Expenditure Report, which outlines the projected revenue and expenditures[6].

The Legislature uses the Governor's Recommended Budget as a starting point, and holds legislative hearings to get feedback from the public and agencies. The committee then creates a budget for that area (i.e. education) and that is drafted into an individual bill. Once all the budget bills are passed by each chamber, they collectively make up the Legislatively Adopted Budget. State agencies are then tasked with implementing the budget.

The Oregon Education Association (OEA) is one of the most powerful advocacy groups in Oregon. One measure of union strength ranked the OEA as one of the most powerful unions in the country[7]. The group spends heavily on elections and lobbying and is involved in nearly all educational policy in the state. Stand for Children is another powerful interest group in the state. The national office for Stand for Children is located in Portland, and the Oregon chapter is involved in most educational policy legislative efforts. Stand for Children also funds campaigns and has a considerable lobbying presence.

Enrollment in Oregon public schools increased from 576.407 to 582,661 (1.1%) from 2015-2020. While the enrollment of many racial/ethnic groups kept relatively constant, multi-racial student enrollment increased 17.5% and American Indian/Alaskan Native student enrollment declined 15.59%[8]. 3.62% of total enrollment were identified as homeless students in k-12 schools in 2019-2020.

SOURCES OF REVENUE

Oregon school funding comes from state, local, and federal taxes. For the 2019-2021 biennium, 32.2% of money, approximately $4.3 billion, came from local revenue[9]. This money comes via permanent district property taxes. Second, the Common School Fund, also known as the County School Fund, provided $21.9 million in revenue from state-managed timber trust land including state forest timber, Federal Forest Fees, and State Timber. Table 37.3 outlines the changes to total revenue from different sources, over time.

The Legislature sets the state appropriation, which comes from the state General Fund and Lottery Funds. Approximately 35% of the General Fund went to the State School Fund (SSF) for the 2019-2021 budget. The percentage of overall school funding coming from the state has increased from 50% in the 93-95 biennium to 68% in the 19-21 budget[10]. The State General Fund is primarily drawn from a state income tax, which includes a personal income tax and a corporate income tax. Oregon personal income tax rates range from 4.75% to 9.9% of taxable income. In 2019-21, personal income taxes comprised approximately 88% of the General Fund[11]. Oregon does not have a state sales tax, and property taxes are levied at the local and county levels. Lottery funds also go to the State General Fund, and are allocated specifically for k-12 education. Lottery funds funded about 1.5% of k-12 funding in the 2019-21 budget.

In 2019, the Legislature passed the Student Success Act (SSA), which created a corporate activities tax (CAT) and allocated that tax revenue to the programs initiated by the SSA. The SSA did this by establishing three new funds: the Student Investment Account, the Statewide Education Initiatives Account, and the Early Learning Account. The new CAT is estimated to bring in approximately $1 billion of revenue per year. The intent of this fund is to supplement the SSF, and to pay for new services/initiatives.

TABLE 37.3.   K-12 and ESD Revenue History (Dollars in Millions)

Revenue Source	2005-06	2006-07	2007-08	2008-09	2009-10	2010-11	2011-12	2012-13	2013-14	2014-15	2015-16	2016-17	2017-18	2018-19	2019-20	2019-20	2020-21
State (A)																	
State School Fund	$2,566.6	$2,737.7	$2,917.6	$2,911.2	$2,940.1	$2,797.7	$2,754.3	$2,856.80	$3,209.7	$3,440.7	$3,627.5	$3,745.50	$4,101.9	$4,101.9	$4,500.00	$4,500.0	$4,500.0
Local K-12 (B)																	
Property and Timber Taxes	1,093.60	1,167.20	1,223.70	1,278.00	1,331.30	1,368.40	1,400.10	1,421.30	1,466.50	1,541.60	1,616.60	1,685.8	1,753.30	1,819.00	1,904.50	1,904.50	1975.9
Other Local	112.2	120.2	127.5	102.1	97.9	97.6	86.6	95.8	86.8	92.6	99.2	90.5	98.9	100.5	93.7	93.7	95.9
Excluded from Formula	0	-15.5	-16.5	-17.3	-17.9	-18.1	-18.7	-19.3	-19.9	-20.5	-22.6	-23.6	-24.5	-25.4	-31.5	-31.5	-32.5
	1,205.80	1,271.90	1,334.70	1,362.90	1,411.30	1,447.90	1,467.90	1,497.80	1533.5	1,613.70	1,693.20	1,752.80	1,827.60	1,894.10	1,966.70	1,966.70	2,039.20
Local ESD (C)																	
Property Tax and other Local																	
Shared with K-12	79.4	83.3	87.1	90.5	94.9	98	100.9	102.3	103.3	108.6	113.8	118.6	121.3	125.9	135.7	135.7	140.7
	0	0	0	0	0	0	0	0	0	0	0	0	-4	-4	-4	-4	-4
	79.4	83.3	87.1	90.5	94.9	98	100.9	102.3	103.3	108.6	113.8	118.6	117.3	121.9	131.7	131.7	136.7
Total Sources (A+B+C)	3,851.7	4,082.8	4,339.3	4,446.0	4,446.3	4,343.6	4,323.2	4,456.9	4,846.5	5,163.0	5,434.5	5,616.9	6,046.8	6,117.9	6598.4	6,598.4	6,675.9

Notes: Dollars in millions Due to timing of data collection, local revenues here may be different from audited figures.
Forecast as of February 2019
Source: Legislative Revenue Office, "2021 Oregon Public Finance Basic Facts: Research Report #1-21. (2021), p. G10.

Oregon also has an Education Stability Fund (SSF). This fund, which was approved by voters in 2002, receives 18% of lottery net proceeds, and is limited to 5% of the General Fund from the prior biennium. The SSF may be used with economic, political, and budgetary mechanisms. The economic trigger is tied to the final quarterly forecast showing that the General Fund will be at least 3% less than the appropriations in the current biennium. The second way the SSF can be accessed is through a three-fifths vote of each chamber of the Legislature. Lastly, the Governor may declare a state of emergency, but three-fifths of each chamber is still required to use the money. The use of these funds is restricted to public, k-12 education. Oregon also has a Rainy Day Fund. Established in 2007, this fund draws from the corporate income tax. This fund has the same triggers as the aforementioned SSF.

DISTRIBUTION FORMULAS

There are 197 school districts and approximately 580,000 students in Oregon k-12 public schools. In sum, local revenue is 32% of the state and local formula operating revenue. State support from the SSF provides the other 68%.

The SSF equalization formula calculates the per student allocation, and recognizes that some student populations need more school services than others. For example, special education students count as 2.0 students, and additional weights are included for English as a second language programs, students from families living in poverty, and remote small schools. For details on changes to the equalization rates per student over time, see Table 37.4. State law stipulates that the state will only reimburse up to 11 percent of total student population of a district for special education costs[12]. The formula also funds 70-90% of eligible transportation costs. Districts are ranked by costs per student. Districts in the top 10% of costs get 90% of the transportation covered. Districts ranked in the next decile receive 80% of the transportation costs. The bottom 80% of districts in terms of transportation costs are funded at 70% of the transportation costs[13]. Table 37.6 shows the student weights for each category.

OTHER STATE EXPENDITURES

There are a host of other expenditures on public education at the state level. For example, the state allocated $1.6 mil for the Oregon virtual school district.

EMPLOYEE BENEFITS

The Oregon Public Employee Retirement System (PERS) is a hybrid plan. Prior to 2011, all teachers were included in a defined benefit plan. Teachers contributed zero to this fund, and the vesting period was five years. The amortization cost of the defined benefit plan was 6.4%, and the overall state funding of this system was 78.6%[14]. For the new employees, defined as hired after 2011, there is a hybrid defined contribution plan where teachers contribute 5.3% and the vesting period

TABLE 37.4. School Equalization Formula Revenue Per Student

	Average Daily Membership				State School Fund and Local Revenue			
	Unweighted (ADM)		Weighted (ADMw)		$ per ADM		$ per ADMw	
	#	Growth	#	Growth	$	Change	$	Change
1992-93	487,075		566,149		5,117		4,403	
1993-94	491,982	1.01%	578,502	2.02%	4,834	-5.50%	4,110	-6.60%
1994-95	495,315	0.68%	586,859	1.43%	5,041	4.30%	4,255	3.50%
1995-96	501,929	1.34%	595,070	1.40%	5,064	0.50%	4,272	0.40%
1996-97	508,819	1.37%	605,675	1.78%	5,107	0.80%	4,290	0.40%
1997-98	514,094	1.04%	616,035	1.71%	5,371	5.20%	4,482	4.50%
1998-99	517,348	0.63%	623,169	1.16%	5,502	2.40%	4,567	1.90%
1999-00	519,545	0.42%	632,895	1.56%	5,876	6.80%	4,823	5.60%
2000-01	522,752	0.62%	638,007	0.81%	6,072	3.30%	4,975	3.10%
2001-02	528,346	1.07%	647,959	1.56%	6,232	2.60%	5,082	2.10%
2002-03	530,694	0.44%	654,862	1.07%	5,779	-7.30%	4,683	-7.80%
2003-04	528,139	-0.47	657,110	0.34%	6,330	9.50%	5,088	8.60%
2004-05	538,139	-0.01%	657,820	0.11%	6,291	-0.60%	5,051	-0.70%
2005-06	533,311	0.98%	658,860	0.16%	6,792	7.90%	5,497	8.80%
2006-07	533,216	-0.02%	662,736	0.59%	7,240	6.60%	5,825	6.00%
2007-08	533,405	0.04%	660,918	-0.27%	7,671	6.00%	6,191	6.30%
2008-09	535,089	0.32%	661,507	0.09%	7,656	-0.20%	6,193	0.00%
2009-10	534,217	-0.16%	662,867	0.21%	7,869	2.80%	6,342	2.40%
2010-11	533,160	-0.21%	659,846	0%	7,862	3.00%	6,360	3.20%
2011-12	534,886	0.32%	662,303	0.32%	7,633	1.70%	6,165	1.70%
2012-13	533,787	-0.21%	659,846	-0.37	7,862	3.00%	6,360	3.20%
2013-14	538,234	0.83%	663,123	0.50%	8,520	8.40%	6,916	8.70%
2014-15	541,419	0.59%	671,863	1.32%	9,018	5.80%	7,267	5.10%
2015-16	568,642	5.03%	701,204	4.38%	9,003	-0.20%	7,300	0.50%
2016-17	571,578	0.52%	707,233	0.85%	9,262	2.90%	7,486	2.50%
2017-18	572,677	0.19%	706,296	-0.13%	9,992	7.90%	8,102	8.20%
2018-19	573,825	0.20%	704,229	-0.17%	10,071	0.80%	8,202	1.20%
2019-20	572,876	-0.17%	704,229	-0.17%	10,696	6.20%	8,701	6.10%
2020-21	566,265	-1.15%	708,687	-1.15%	11,192	4.60%	8,943	2.80%

Green=estimate from SSF formula
Yellow=forecast
Source: Legislative Revenue Office, "2021 Oregon Public Finance Basic Facts: Research Report #1-21. (2021), p. G8.

TABLE 37.5.   Biennial Formula Revenue

	2011-13	2013-15	2015-17	2017-19	2019-21*
Local	$2.96	$3.38	$3.67	$4.03	$4.03
State	$5.71	$6.65	$7.38	$8.20	$9.00
Total	$8.67	$10.03	$11.05	$12.23	$13.03

*Projected
Source: Oregon Department of Education. "Statewide Report Card 2019-2020." An Annual Report to the Legislature on Oregon Public Schools. (2020), p.16. https://www.oregon.gov/ode/schools-and-districts/reportcards/Documents/rptcard2020.pdf

is only six months. Overall, the retirement system is funded at 76.3% of total debt obligation. Statewide, base employer contribution rates as a percentage of covered salary was 25.2% in 2019-2021[15]. However, the majority of school districts have side accounts to offset these costs. The net rate for districts with side accounts was 18.3% in 19-21[16].

COVID-19 FEDERAL FUNDING

Oregon received substantial funding from the federal government to address the COVID-19 pandemic. In 2020, the CARES Act provided funding for the Elementary and Secondary School Emergency Relief Fund 1 (ESSER 1 Fund). The US Department of Education awarded these funds to the Oregon Department of Education (ODE), to route to local education agencies (LEAs) to address the impact COVID-19 had on districts. Oregon was awarded $121.1 million, 90% of which ($108.9 mil) were awarded to LEAs in the proportion they received under ESEA in the 2019 fiscal year[17]. The remaining funds were allocated by ODE. These funds were used to reimburse eligible expenses between March 13, 2020 and September 30, 2022.

SUMMARY

Oregon school funding can be divided into the pre-property tax reform, the property tax reform, and the Student Success Act eras. The pre-property tax reform

TABLE 37.6

Category	Additional Weight	Total Weight
Special Education Program	1.0	2.0
English Language Learner	0.5	1.50
Pregnant and Parenting	1.0	2.0
Students in Poverty Adjusted	0.25	1.25
Neglected and Delinquent	0.25	1.25
Students in Foster Care	0.25	1.25

era, approximately 1859-1990, was defined as an era where local control led to huge inequities, and school funding was overwhelmingly reliant on property tax revenue. This era led to large racial and socio-economic inequities across the state. From 1990-2019 could be defined as the property tax reform era. In large part due to Measures 5 and 50, Oregon shifted funding from local property taxes to state income taxes. In this era, public financing overall declined, as more regulations prevented, or limited, tax increases. In 2019, the state legislature passed the Student Success Act, which was the largest one time increase in school funding in the state's history. This new era is defined by the state coming closer to meeting the QEM for the first time.

ENDNOTES

[1] https://www.oregon.gov/DOR/programs/gov-research/Documents/303-405-1.pdf

[2] https://www.oregon.gov/DOR/programs/gov-research/Documents/303-405-1.pdf

[3] Oregon Legislative Committee Services. "Background Brief on Quality Education Model." (May 2004). Retrieved from: https://www.oregonlegislature.gov/lpro/Publications/2004DI_Quality_Education_Model.pdf

[4] Oregon Department of Education, Quality Education Commission. "Quality Education Model Final Report." (August 2018). Retrieved from: https://www.oregon.gov/ode/reports-and-data/task-comm/Documents/QEMReports/2018QEMReport.pdf

[5] https://www.oregon.gov/das/Financial/pages/Budgetprocess.aspx

[6] https://www.oregon.gov/das/Financial/pages/Budgetprocess.aspx

[7] Winkler, A., Scull, J., & Zeehandelaar, D. (2012). How strong are U.S. teacher unions? A state by state comparison. Thomas Fordham Institute Advancing Educational Excellence.

[8] https://www.oregon.gov/ode/schools-and-districts/reportcards/Documents/rptcard2020.pdf

[9] https://www.oregonlegislature.gov/lpro/Publications/Background-Brief-Education-Funding.pdf

[10] https://www.oregonlegislature.gov/lpro/Publications/Background-Brief-Education-Funding.pdf

[11] https://www.oregonlegislature.gov/lro/Documents/Basic%20Facts%202021.pdf

[12] https://oregon.public.law/statutes/ors_327.013

[13] https://www.oregonlegislature.gov/lpro/Publications/Background-Brief-Education-Funding.pdf

[14] Marchitello, M., Rotherham, A.J., & Squire, J. (2021). Teacher retirement systems: A ranking of the states. Bellwether Education Partners.

[15] https://www.oregon.gov/pers/Documents/General-Information/PERS-by-the-Numbers.pdf

[16] https://www.oregon.gov/pers/Documents/General-Information/PERS-by-the-Numbers.pdf

[17] https://www.oregon.gov/ode/schools-and-districts/grants/Pages/ESSER-Fund.aspx

CHAPTER 38

PENNSYLVANIA

Andrew L. Armagost
Pennsylvania Association of School Business Officials

Timothy J. Shrom
Pennsylvania Association of School Business Officials

GENERAL BACKGROUND

The education clause of the Pennsylvania constitution declares "the General Assembly shall provide for the maintenance and support of a thorough and efficient system of public education to serve the needs of the Commonwealth."[1] This system of public education in Pennsylvania was formally established in the 1830s through passage of the Common School Fund Act of 1831 and the Free Schools Act of 1834. The Act of 1831 established the first common school fund, with a revenue source directed from the sale of unpatented lands and fees collected from the land office. However, the Act of 1834 formally established a system of public schools throughout the Commonwealth by requiring counties to form school divisions which were made up of the school districts from every ward, township and borough in the several counties. The Act also provided for distribution of state support to fund common schools, providing funds to any county that voted affirmatively to impose a county school tax of not less than twice the amount received from the state. Funding distribution under the Act was calculated using the

Funding Public Schools in the United States, Indian Country,
and US Territories (Second Edition), pages 577–602.
Copyright © 2023 by Information Age Publishing
www.infoagepub.com

number of taxable inhabitants in the county. Disbursements went to the counties, which then distributed funds to the school districts. According to Walsh, while the law fixed the appropriation to one dollar for each taxable inhabitant, the General Assembly did not meet this requirement and from 1845 to 1872 the actual amount distributed varied between thirty-eight cents in 1865 and sixty-two cents in 1872.[2]

In the following years, the state formula for distributing general basic education funding remained mostly unchanged with some few minor attempts at change in 1863, 1897, 1911 and 1919.[3] In 1863, the state attempted to adopt a new distribution of funds based on the number of children attending a school. This calculation, formally enacted through the Appropriations Act of 1863, was found too difficult and was repealed the following year.[4] In 1876, the Commonwealth continued to appropriate funds based on the number of taxable inhabitants in each county and school district.[5] In 1897 the General Assembly attempted to improve distribution of funding on the basis of the number of children, number of teachers, and the number of taxable residents, providing for "one-third of the money annually appropriated for common schools in this Commonwealth to be distributed to each of these categories and for each category to be based upon the counts within the category. [6]

In 1911,[7] the General Assembly consolidated laws existing at the time pertaining to public education into a single omnibus statute and provided the following distribution of state subsidies:

> *Section 2504.* One-half on the basis of the number of paid teachers regularly employed for the full annual term of the school district, not including substitute teachers or teachers employed to fill vacancies which may occur during the school year; such number of teachers to be certified as herein provided;

> *Section 2305.* One-half on the basis of the number of children between the ages of six and sixteen residing in the respective school districts of the several counties of this Commonwealth, as reported to the Superintendent of Public Instruction under the provisions of this act.[8]

By Fiscal Year 1921, total state appropriation for the basic subsidy to school districts reached $8.85 million.[9] The Act of 1921, known as the Edmunds Act, made significant structural changes to the system of public education.[10] In 1927, a major report from a commission established by the state studied school funding throughout Pennsylvania and recommended that the state adopt a form of power equalization to equalize wealth among all school districts, as the report found that assessed value per teacher unit was not equitable across counties as a result of non-uniform assessments. Twenty years later, Act 447 of 1947 established the State Tax Equalization Board (STEB) with a purpose to provide for equalization throughout the state.

Act 14 of 1949, also known as the Public School Code, distributed basic education funding based on school district teaching units multiplied by a base factor enacted into law and the district's standard reimbursement fraction. During FY 1949-50, the base factor was $2,400 and state appropriation for basic education funding was $173 million. It is important to note that while Act 14 was never codified into Pennsylvania's consolidated statutes, the Act served as the single authoritative law on the system of public education and has been amended several times, with updates to the funding formula distributing basic education funding. From 1949 to 2008, dozens of enacted statutes have amended Act 14 to change the funding distribution for numerous types of grants and subsidies for public schools.[11]

During the 2008 fiscal year, Act 61 enacted recommendations of a study commissioned by the governor in 2006. The Act added Section 2502.48 providing for a student-based adequacy target for school districts and distributing funds for FY 2007-08. Funding for adequacy targets in the subsequent two fiscal years primarily came from federal recovery funding that was provided to states in response to the 2008 economic recession. Distribution of funds through the student-based adequacy targets for the 2010 and 2011 fiscal years came through omnibus amendments to the Fiscal Code enacted those years. Act 24 of 2011 ceased using the student-based adequacy target formula and prescribed for FY 2011-12 a formula based on factors used prior to Act 61. In the following years, Act 82 of 2012, Act 59 of 2013, Act 126 of 2014 (Fiscal Code) provided for the funding distribution formula.

Act 35 of 2016 was the most recent update to the basic education funding formula. As illustrated later in this chapter, the Act 35 weighted student formula distributes additional funding appropriated beyond the FY 2014-15 funding level to school districts based on recommendations of the legislative Basic Education Funding Commission established under Section 123 by Act 51 of 2014.

As this overview suggests, the Commonwealth of Pennsylvania's long history regarding public education dates back to the earliest days in the founding of the nation.[12] Since passage of the 1831 and 1834 acts establishing the system of public education, Pennsylvania's support and funding for public education has developed into a broader funding system covering basic and special education, career and technical education, school construction, employee retirement, pupil transportation and numerous other categories. However, studies have shown Pennsylvania school districts are enduring substantial fiscal stress,[13] and growing financial pressures continue to place funding of the system of public education at the forefront in much of today's state-level policy decisions. Table 38.4 through 38.7 illustrate the overall state appropriation of grants and subsidies supporting public schools, school district revenues by source and expenditures.

Currently, Pennsylvania's courts have moved forward by hearing a lawsuit[14] challenging the constitutionality of the current funding scheme in regard to the General Assembly's duty to provide for the maintenance and support of a thorough and efficient system of public education to serve the needs of the Commonwealth. In 2017, the Pennsylvania supreme court overturned precedent and struck down the longstanding political question doctrine[15] in the state and remanded the case back to the lower courts. At the time of this writing, the Commonwealth trial court has moved forward after months of postponements due to the COVID-19 pandemic. Witnesses for the petitioners began to take the stand on November 15, 2021 and concluded arguments January 26, 2022. As of mid-February, Respondents are nearing concluding their witnesses and final arguments in the case. A decision in the trial court is anticipated sometime before the end of the year.[16]

Statutory language can be found for almost all major aspects of education funding in Pennsylvania's Act 14 of 1949, also known as the Public School Code.[17] Regulations established by the Pennsylvania State Board of Education are located in Title 22 of the Pennsylvania Code,[18] and source data on school finance can be found on the Department of Education website.[19]

BASIC EDUCATION

Pennsylvania Act 35 of 2016 added Section 2502.53 of the Public School Code[20] to provide for a student-weighted formula that distributes any additional state dollars to support basic education funding beyond the amount allocated during FY 2014-15. The new basic education funding formula distributes support to a school district based on the following methodology. First, the district will receive a base amount equal to its 2014-2015 Basic Education Funding allocation with a handful of districts receiving additional targeted funds to their base allocation. The total base of all Pennsylvania school districts is approximately $5.66 billion. For the 2022-23 fiscal year, the base allocation includes more than $100 Million allocated by a 'Level Up Supplement' passed in the 2021-22 state budget[21]. These targeted funds are distributed to 100 school districts identified as those spending the least amount relative to their student needs. Each district will then receive a pro-rata share of the total allocation (approximately $898 million in fiscal year 2021-22) based on the district's weighted student count (WSC) multiplied by its median household income index (MHI) and its local effort capacity index (LECI). Additionally, the General Assembly consolidated the previously separate funding for social security reimbursements to school districts within the Base Education Funding appropriation which totals approximately $515 million during the 2021-22 fiscal year.

The weighted student count equals the sum of the following: (1) the three-year average daily membership; (2) three poverty weights based on the number of students living in poverty, acute poverty, and concentrated acute poverty; (3) an English language learner weight based on the number of students designated as English language learners; (4) a charter school weight based on the number of students who withdrew from the traditional public school and enrolled in a public charter school; and (5) the sparsity-size adjustment for qualifying school districts.

The three-year ADM is calculated by averaging the school district's three most recent years' ADM. The poverty factor is the sum of the three poverty weights: poverty weight, acute poverty weight, and the concentrated poverty weight. The three poverty weights are calculated as follows:

- the acute poverty average daily membership calculated by multiplying the school district's average daily membership by its acute poverty percentage and 0.6
- the poverty average daily membership calculated by multiplying the school district's average daily membership by its poverty percentage and 0.3
- the concentrated poverty average daily membership for qualifying school districts with an acute poverty percentage equal to or greater than 30% calculated by multiplying the school district's average daily membership by its acute poverty percentage by 0.3.

The English language learner (ELL) weight is calculated by multiplying the number of the school district's limited English-proficient students by 0.6. The charter school (CS) weight is calculated by multiplying 0.2 by the ADM for the district's students enrolled in charter schools and cyber charter schools.

A sparsity/size adjustment (SSA) is calculated for qualifying school districts with a sparsity size ratio greater than the 70th percentile of all districts. The sparsity/size adjustment is calculated by dividing the district's sparsity/size ratio by the ratio at the 70th percentile; subtracting 1; multiplying by the sum of (a) through (f); multiplying by 0.7. The sparsity-size ratio is calculated as follows:

- Calculate the sparsity ratio: divide the school district's ADM per square mile by the state total ADM per square mile; multiply by 0.5; subtract from 1;
- Calculate the size ratio: divide the district's ADM by the average of the ADM for all districts; multiply by 0.5; subtract from 1;
- Calculate the combined sparsity-size ratio by weighting the sparsity ratio at 40% and the size ratio at 60%.

The sum of these weights and the three-year ADM provides the weighted student count. Next, calculate the adjusted weighted student count (AWSC) by multiplying the weighted student count by the district's median household income index and the district's local effort capacity index. The median household income index (MHI) is calculated for each district by dividing 1 by the quotient of the district's median household income divided by the state median household income. The local effort capacity index (LECI) equals the sum of the local effort index and the local capacity index.

The local effort index equals the local effort factor multiplied by the lesser of 1 or the excess spending factor.

- The local effort factor is calculated for each school district as follows: divide its local tax-related revenue by its median household income multiplied by its number of households; multiply by 1,000; divide by the state-wide median;

- The excess spending factor is calculated for each district as follows: divide 1 by its net current expenditures per student-weighted average daily membership divided by the statewide median.

The local capacity index is calculated as follows: if the school district's local capacity per student-weighted ADM is less than the statewide median, divide its local capacity per student-weighted ADM by the statewide median; if the district's local capacity per student-weighted ADM is equal to or greater than the statewide median, the local capacity index is zero.

- The local capacity per student-weighted ADM for each school district is calculated as follows: multiply the sum of its market value and personal income by the statewide median local effort rate; divide by its student-weighted ADM;
- The local effort rate for each district is calculated as follows: divide its local tax-related income by the sum of its market value and personal income.

The result of multiplying weighted student count, median household income index, and local effort capacity index is the school district's adjusted weighted student count. The amount a district receives through this formula is determined by calculating the district's share of the state total adjusted weighted student count. That share is then distributed through the total state allocation. In Table 38.4, the state appropriation for basic education funding is line 1.

The Pennsylvania basic education funding formula is expressed as follows:

ADM + PVW + ELL + CS + SSA = Weighted Student Count (WSC)

WSC x MHII x LECI = Adjusted Weighted Student Count (AWSC)

AWSC x Total Student-Weighted Distribution / State Total AWSC

= Prorated Share to District

After more than five years funding this formula, the new student-weighted funding formula has been noticeably dynamic with annual changes or swings in a school district's share of the funding. As the amount re-distributed each year increases, the changing share dynamics have greater significance. Post COVID-19, early indications suggest that the dynamic nature of share changes will reflect the significant disparate impact the pandemic has had across the state on district demographics and economic factors. Since a school district's change in formula metrics are relative to all other school districts changes, policymakers will have difficulty discerning exactly how post COVID-19 metric factors will deviate from prior trends in school districts' share of future basic education funding allocations beyond FY 2021-22.

In addition to basic education funding, Pennsylvania provides another general education funding appropriation to school districts and charter schools. Currently, the state distributes $268 million annually through the Ready to Learn Block Grant, with the prescribed mission to (1) enhance learning opportunities for students and provide resources to innovate at the local level and (2) fund single-year or multi-year appropriation to specific districts to support education programs. Section 2599.6 of the Public School Code[22] provides funding for these grants. In Table 38.4, the state appropriation for this program is line 2.

SPECIAL EDUCATION

The state special education funding formula was last amended by Act 86 of 2016 and is distributed pursuant to Section 2509.5 of the Public School Code.[23] The new special education funding formula establishes three categories of student costs. The three cost categories and their corresponding weights are as follows: Category 1 includes students with costs ranging from $1 to $24,999 and has a formula weight of 1.51; Category 2 includes students with costs ranging from $25,000 to $49,999 and has a formula weight of 3.77; and Category 3 includes students with costs equal to $50,000 or more and has a formula weight of 7.46.

School districts receive allocations through two parts. First, the district receives an amount equal to its 2013-2014 Special Education Funding allocation. The total base of all Pennsylvania districts is approximately $948 million. Second, the district receives a pro-rata share of the allocated amount (approximately $196.4 million in FY 2021-22) based on the district's weighted student count (WSC) multiplied by its market value/personal income aid ratio (MVPI) and its equalized mills multiplier (EQM). Additionally, the state appropriates approximately $92.9 million in special contingency grants for specific programs and services for students with an Individualized Education Plan (IEP). In total, state funding for special education is $1.25 billion for FY 2021-22.

In calculating a school district's share of allocated funding, the WSC equals the sum of the special education student count and the sparsity-size adjustment for qualifying school districts. The special education student count is calculated by multiplying the number of students in each student category by its weighting. A sparsity-size adjustment is calculated by first calculating the sparsity-size ratio as follows:

- Calculate the sparsity ratio: divide the school district's ADM per square mile by the state total ADM per square mile; multiply by 0.5; subtract from 1;
- Calculate the size ratio: divide the district's ADM by the average of the ADM for all districts; multiply by 0.5; subtract from 1'
- Calculate the combined sparsity-size ratio by weighting the sparsity ratio at 40% and the size ratio at 60%.

If the school district's sparsity-size ratio is greater than the 70th percentile sparsity-size ratio, divide the district ratio by the 70th percentile ratio; subtract 1; multiply by 0.5; multiply by the weighted-student count. If the district's sparsity-size ratio is less than or equal to the 70th percentile sparsity-size ratio, the sparsity-size adjustment is 0.

After calculating the weighted student count, calculate the adjusted weighted student count by multiplying the weighted student count by the district's market value/personal income aid ratio and the district's equalized mills multiplier. The equalized mills multiplier is calculated as follows:

- Calculate the average of the most recent three years of equalized mills;
- If the school district's three-year average equalized mills is greater than the 70th percentile equalized mills, its equalized mills multiplier equals 1;
- If the district's three-year average equalized mills is less than or equal to the 70th percentile equalized mills, divide the school district's equalized mills by the 70th percentile equalized mills.

The product of these factors is the school district's adjusted weighted student count. The amount a district receives through the formula is determined by calculating the district share of state total adjusted weighted student count. That share is distributed through the total state allocation. In Table 38.4, the state appropriation for special education funding was line 5. Operation of the formula appears next.

$$[C1_n \times 1.51] + [C2_n \times 3.77] + [C3_n \times 7.46] + SSA = \text{Weighted Student Count}$$

$$WSC \times EQM \times MVPI = \text{Adjusted Weighted Student Count (AWSC)}$$

$$[AWSC \times \text{Total State Allocation}] / [\text{State Total AWCS}]$$

$$= \text{Prorated Share of New Special Education Funding}$$

EARLY CHILDHOOD EDUCATION AND EARLY INTERVENTION

During FY 2021-22, Pennsylvania will distribute approximately $242.3 million for high-quality early childhood education, $336.5 million to Early Intervention programs and $69.2 million to supplement funds for federal Head Start programs. The state program supporting early childhood education, known as Pre-K Counts, provided grant funding to providers, including school districts, serving high-need populations in underserved communities. The competitive grant program currently provides approximately 25,540 children access to early learning programs. Act 45 of 2007 established the Pre-K Counts program, and grant distributions are prescribed under Section 1514-D of the Public School Code.[24] In Table 38.4, state appropriation for the Pre-K Counts program is line 6. Additionally, the state Head Start supplemental program distributes grant funding pursuant to Sections

1502-D and 1503-D of the Public School Code[25] to supplement federal Head Start programs. The program provides a high-quality, standards-based educational program in addition to health, nutritional and social services. In Table 38.4, the state appropriation for the Head Start Supplement is line 7.

Pennsylvania's Early Intervention program aims to identify and support students who display needs for special services before entering the elementary grades. Working with early childcare providers such as Head Start, the program provides special instruction, family training, psychological services, physical therapy, speech therapy, family counseling and support services. In Table 38.4 earlier, the state appropriation for this program is line 4.

CAREER AND TECHNICAL EDUCATION

State reimbursement is provided to school districts for vocational programs focusing on agriculture education, distributive education, health occupations education, home economics education (gainful), business education, technical education, trade and industrial education, or any other occupational-oriented program approved by the Secretary of Education. Pennsylvania's statute regarding reimbursement to districts for career and technical education is distributed pursuant to Section 2502.8 of the Public School Code[26] and was last amended by Act 97 of 1979.

The career and technical education funding formula distributes support to a school district based on the following. The formula calculates the vocational average daily membership (VADM). The VADM is the ADM of students in vocational programs in a school district or charter school multiplied by 0.17. For career and technical centers, the vocational ADM is the ADM of students in vocational programs in a career and technology center multiplied by 0.21.

The formula then calculates the base earned for reimbursement. The formula calculates a school district's equalized mills ratio by first computing the difference between the highest equalized mill rate in the state and the district's equalized mill rate. This difference is divided by the difference between the highest equalized millage rate in the state and the lowest equalized millage rate in the state, resulting in an equalized mills ratio. The base earned for reimbursement is calculated by multiplying the equalized mills ratio by $200 and subtracting that product from the state median actual instruction expense per weighted ADM.

Under these conditions:

- The fully funded amount equals the lesser of the AIE/WADM or the BER multiplied by the greater of the market value/personal income aid ratio or 0.3750 multiplied by the VADM;
- For the 2000-2001 school year and each school year thereafter, any additional funding provided by the Commonwealth over the amount provided for the 1998-1999 school year would be distributed to area vocational-technical schools, school districts and charter schools with eight or more

vocational programs, and to school districts and charter schools offering a vocational agriculture education program;

- Based on Section 2502.6 of the School Code, the actual allocation is proportionately reduced so that the total does not exceed the amount appropriated.

In Table 38.4, the state appropriation for career and technical education funding was line 8. Additionally, Pennsylvania provides grants for career and technical education equipment and job training programs. Equipment grants are awarded to school districts and area vocational and technical schools; in Table 38.4, the state appropriation for the equipment grant program was line 9. The Job Training Program appropriation provides support to educational programs providing job training for economically disadvantaged youth and adults. The appropriation supports programs promoting economic development in regions where there is higher than average unemployment; assisting youth and adults in increasing technical work skills in order to become economically self-sufficient; and supporting collaboration among coordinating agencies. In Table 38.4, the state appropriation for the job training program is a part of line 18, representing $31.0 million.

PUPIL TRANSPORTATION

Pennsylvania's statute regarding reimbursement to school districts for pupil transportation was last amended by Act 97 in 1979 and is distributed pursuant to Section 2541 of the Public School Code.[27] Each school district is required to submit data to the Pennsylvania Department of Education on each vehicle used by the district to provide pupil transportation. A total cost allowance is calculated for each vehicle eligible for subsidy reimbursement by calculating the following: vehicle allowance, mileage allowance, utilized passenger capacity miles allowance, and layover or congested hours allowance. The allowance for each vehicle is a calculation of the age of the vehicle, size of the vehicle, number of students assigned to the vehicle and number of miles the vehicle travels with students. The resulting calculation is multiplied by the annual cost index, resulting in the maximum approved cost for the vehicle. The sum of each vehicles' maximum approved vehicle cost is then multiplied by the school district's market value aid ratio to determine the amount of state subsidy.

The vehicle allowance (Vehicle) is calculated by multiplying the final fraction by the sum of the basic and additional allowances. The basic allowance is calculated using the pupil seating capacity. If pupil seating capacity is 10 or less, the basic allowance is $360. If the pupil seating capacity is greater than ten, the basic allowance is $540. The additional allowance (ADD) is calculated using the age of the bus and pupil seating capacity. If the bus is ten years or less, the pupil seating capacity is multiplied by $15; if the vehicle's age is 11 years or more, the pupil seating capacity is multiplied by $12. The resulting additional allowance is added to the basic allowance and then multiplied by the final fraction. The product is the vehicle allowance.

The mileage allowance (Mileage) is calculated by multiplying the approved annual miles by $0.23. The approved annual miles are calculated by multiplying the approved daily miles by the number of days the vehicle is in use. The utilized passenger capacity miles allowance (UPCM) is determined by calculating the approved annual miles and multiplying that figure by the greatest number of assigned pupils at any one time. The result is the utilized passenger capacity miles and that result is then multiplied by $0.003. The result is the utilized passenger capacity miles allowance. The layover or congested hours allowance (LCH) is calculated by multiplying the approved annual excess hours by $3. The total vehicle allowance is determined by calculating the sum of the four allowances multiplied by a cost index. The cost index for operations in FY 2022-23, reimbursable in FY 2023-24, will reach 6.56 or 7% increase over the prior year. In Table 38.4, the state appropriation for pupil transportation funding is line 10. An illustration of the pupil transportation formula appears next.

[Vehicle + Mileage + UPCM + LCH] x Cost Index = Total Allowance

The state also provides reimbursement to school districts for a share of pupil transportation costs for non-public and charter school students. The reimbursement rate, last amended by Act 88 of 2002, is prescribed under Section 2509.3 of the Public School Code.[28] Reimbursement requirements for charter schools are prescribed in Section 1726-A as amended by Act 61 of 2008. Each school district is reimbursed $385 for each nonpublic and charter school pupil transported by the school district. In Table 38.4, state appropriation for nonpublic and charter school pupil transportation funding is line 11.

SCHOOL EMPLOYEE BENEFITS

School district spending on employee benefits include retirement contributions to the pension system, healthcare and social security payments. For FY 2019-20, total district spending on employee benefits ($7.92 billion) represented 64.9% of total employee salaries ($12.2 billion) and 24.2% of total spending ($32.8 billion).[29]

Most school employees in Pennsylvania are members of the Public School Employees' Retirement System (PSERS). Like other states, the system requires employer contributions and the Commonwealth. Pursuant to statute,[30] both the employer district and the Commonwealth are responsible for paying a portion of employer contribution rates. Employers are divided into two groups: school entities and non-school entities. School entities are responsible for paying 100% of the employer share. The Commonwealth reimburses school entities for approximately 50% of payments for employees hired on or before June 30, 1994; employees hired after June 30, 1994 face a statutory formula, although not less than one-half of the payment. Non-school entities and the Commonwealth each contribute 50% of the total employer rate.

Total employer contributions (all educational agencies within system) for FY 2022-23 are projected to exceed $5.1 billion.[31] The employer contribution rate-setting methodology is set in statute.[32] Table 38.1 shows the employer contribution rate history beginning with Fiscal Year 2012 and the certified projected rates for fiscal years 2019 through 2023. The table also shows projected rates for employers presuming a 7.25% annual return on pension fund investments. While employee contributions vary, most school employees contribute 7.5% of earnings along with social security/Medicare employee contributions.

In Pennsylvania, pension legacy cost issues remain[33] and pension reform legislation has been the focus of lawmakers for several years.[34] The General Assembly has enacted two distinct forms of remedy through Act 120 of 2010 and Act 5 of 2017. Act 120 of 2010 was the first successful effort at curbing rising pension costs to school districts and the Commonwealth. A key milestone in reform, Act 120 began to slow cost growth and instituted a number of important changes to reduce the costs of Pennsylvania's public pension systems. The reforms implemented by Act 120 included:

- Creating short-term funding relief through a series of annual rate collars that artificially limit the amount the employer contribution rate could increase over the prior year's rate to not more than 3% for FY 2011-12, not more than 3.5% for FY 2012-13, and not more than 4.5% for FY 2013-14;
- Reducing pension benefits for new employees by lowering the multiplier used to calculate retirement benefits from 2.5% to 2%, returning it to pre-2001 levels;
- Increasing the retirement age to 65 for new employees, extending the period for employees to vest from 5 to 10 years, and eliminating the lump sum withdrawal of contributions at retirement; and
- Implementing a shared risk provision for new employees, allowing for increased employee contributions if actual investment returns fall below assumed returns.

In 2017 the governor signed into law Act 5 of 2017, fundamentally changing retirement options for new hires beginning January 1, 2019. In addition, the legislation allows current members to opt in to one of three new options. The choice

TABLE 38.1 Pennsylvania School Employer Retirement Contribution 2018 ($ in thousands)

	2010-11	2011-12	2012-13	2013-14	2014-15	2015-16	2016-17
Employer Contribution Rate	5.64%	8.65%	12.36%	16.93%	21.40%	25.84%	30.03%
Actual District $ Contributions	$418,448	$939,909	$1,333,490	$1,819,028	$2,326,279	$2,847,895	$3,376,828

is irrevocable. This legislation introduced two new hybrid defined benefit (DB)/ defined contribution (DC) options and a straight DC option for members in the larger State Employee Retirement System (SERS) as well as PSERS. The new classes of service apply to all employees with the exemption of most hazardous duty employees who first become members in the new fiscal year beginning July 1 2019. In Table 38.4, the state appropriation for state's share of pension contributions is line 13.

In addition to pension eligibility, Pennsylvania school employees also participate in the Social Security and Medicare systems. Various public school entities within the Commonwealth (including school districts, intermediate units, and career and technology centers) are eligible for the School Employees' Social Security (state) subsidy. Reimbursement is available to these local education agencies for Social Security and Medicare tax contributions paid on behalf of their employees. This amount is equal to the sum of 0.5 multiplied by the contributions for existing employees and the greater value between 0.5 and the market value/ personal income aid ratio for new» employees. The appropriation is paid to school districts quarterly following receipt of data from each school district. In Table 39.4, the state appropriation for social security funding is line 12.

SCHOOL CONSTRUCTION

Currently, reimbursement to Pennsylvania school districts for the state share of school construction is prescribed by Sections 2571 - 2580 of the Public School Code.[35] The funding formula has been under review by the Pennsylvania Public School Building Construction and Reconstruction Advisory Committee pursuant to Act 25 of 2016.

In 2012, Act 82 directed the Pennsylvania Department of Education (PDE) to conduct a review of the process by which public school building projects are reviewed and approved for Commonwealth reimbursement. The report found considerable concerns regarding the outdated program and recommended initiating a thorough analysis of the program with the General Assembly. As a result, a committee was formed following passage of Act 25. Among the recommendations for substantial redesign of the construction reimbursement process, the committee released a new recommended reimbursement formula in the spring of 2018. However, no update to the state law has been enacted and only those projects submitted prior to the Act 25 timeline are receiving state reimbursement.

The total reimbursable subsidy is calculated by multiplying the base per full-time equivalent by an adjustment factor, a full-time equivalent factor, and a wealth factor. The product is divided by the number of years to calculate the annual subsidy the state would provide. The base per full-time equivalent (BASE) is the five-year statewide median structural cost per student determined from past completed projects. At the time the report was released, the amount was $18,251 and it was recommended the amount be updated every five years. An adjustment

TABLE 38.2.   Proposed PlanCON Room Schedule for Weighted FTE Capacity

Room Type	Unit FTE Capacity	Weight	Weighted FTE Capacity
Pre-K/Kindergarten Classroom	25	1.0	25
Special Education Classroom	15	1.0	15
Special Education Resource Room	10	1.0	10
Alternative Education Classroom	20	1.0	20
Regular Classroom	25	1.0	25
Art/Music Classroom	25	1.1	28
Career/Tech-Ed/TV Studio	20	1.6	32
Laboratory	25	1.3	33
Library/Gym	50	1.4	70

factor (ADJ) would be determined by the governor and General Assembly representing the state share of the base per full-time equivalent from 0 to 1.

The full-time equivalent factor (FTE) is the lesser of the school building enrollment or the full-time equivalent building capacity. The FTE building capacity is calculated using weighted FTE capacity room schedule based upon the following proposed room types, capacities and weights—see Table 38.2.

The wealth factor (WEALTH) proposed in the report was based on similar factors used in the basic education funding formula. To calculate the wealth factor, first multiply the school district's median household income index (MHI) by the district's local effort capacity index (LECI). Next, calculate the statewide median product of this calculation (SDMed). A ratio (RATIO) is determined by dividing the statewide median product by the school district's product. The ratio is multiplied by 0.5 and then that product is subtracted from 1 to calculate the initial wealth factor (FACTOR). If the result is less than 0.1500, then the district's initial wealth factor is set at 0.1500. The initial wealth factor is then adjusted by adding the district's sparsity size adjustment and concentrated poverty weight. The result is the district's calculated wealth factor.

The state distributes a reimbursement to school districts by an annual subsidy made over a set number of years (YEARS). Equal payments across years with a maximum ratio to structural cost is set at 65%. The school construction formula is illustrated next.

$$[[SDMed] / [MHI \times LECI]] = RATIO$$

$$[1 - [0.5 \times RATIO]] = FACTOR$$

$$[FACTOR + SSA + POV] = WEALTH$$

$$[BASE \times ADJ \times FTE \times WEALTH] / YEARS = Annual\ Subsidy$$

During the advisory commission's study recommending updates, Pennsylvania placed a moratorium on building projects eligible for reimbursement. The state typically appropriates funding for construction reimbursement through the Authority Rentals and Sinking Fund Requirements budget line item. In Table 38.4, the state appropriation for school construction reimbursement is line 14.

CHARTER SCHOOLS

Pennsylvania's charter schools are independently run public schools that are paid by public tax dollars, authorized and primarily funded by the school districts from which their students come. According to the state courts, "the relationship between a school district and a charter school is not contractual, but regulatory."[36]

Prior to FY 2011-12, Pennsylvania allocated state funding to school districts for reimbursement for a share of charter school tuition. However, on elimination of several state appropriations after the financial recession, Pennsylvania ceased providing state reimbursement to school districts. Table 38.3 illustrates growth in total tuition paid by school districts to charter schools and the approximate reimbursement from the state to school districts.

Currently, school districts send charter schools a per-pupil payment based on a state-established formula prescribed under Section 1725-A of the Public School Code.[37] Section 1725-A provides that for non-special education students, the charter school shall receive for each student enrolled no less than the budgeted total expenditure per average daily membership of the prior school year, as defined in Section 2501(20), minus the budgeted expenditures of the district of residence for nonpublic school programs; adult education programs; community/junior college programs; student transportation services; for special education programs; facilities acquisition, construction and improvement services; and other financing uses, including debt service and fund transfers as provided in the Manual of Accounting and Related Financial Procedures for Pennsylvania School Systems established by the department. This amount shall be paid by the district of residence of each student.[38]

Additionally, Section 1725-A provides that:

> For special education students, the charter school shall receive for each student enrolled the same funding as for each non-special education student as provided in clause (2), plus an additional amount determined by dividing the district of resi-

TABLE 38.3. Tuition Paid to Charters and State Charter School Reimbursement ($ in millions)

	2010-11	2011-12	2012-13	2013-14	2014-15	2015-16	2016-17	2017-18	2018-19	2019-20	2020-21
Total Tuition	$960	$1,145	$1,268	$1,436	$1,486	$1,549	$1,655	$1,823	$2,046	$2,194	$2,644
State Funds	$219	$0	$0	$0	$0	$0	$0	$0	$0	$0	$0

dence's total special education expenditure by the product of multiplying the combined percentage of Section 2509.5(k) times the district of residence's total average daily membership for the prior school year. This amount shall be paid by the district of residence of each student.[39]

Pennsylvania's charter school law was enacted by Act 22 of 1997. Since then, Pennsylvania's funding formula has caused significant debate and concern. Legislation was introduced in 2017[40] to provide for a charter school funding commission to study the current funding system, much like prior funding commissions established for basic education funding, special education, and school construction.

NON-PUBLIC (PRIVATE) K-12 SCHOOLS

In addition to funding for nonpublic school transportation detailed earlier, Pennsylvania also provides funding and services toward non-public (private) schools across several other support categories such as special education, instructional materials, and support services. For example, Pennsylvania appropriates funding annually to acquire and provide nonsectarian textbooks, instructional materials and equipment that are loaned free of charge to nonpublic school students. In 2018, the Department of Education reported an estimated 225,000 students were enrolled across 2,270 eligible schools. In Table 38.4, the state appropriation for this program is a part of line 18, representing $26.75 million in FY 2021-22.

Additionally, the state appropriates funding for services to students enrolled in a nonprofit, nonpublic school through disbursements to its 29 regional Intermediate Units. Services provided to eligible students include remedial reading and math, services for exceptional children, guidance counseling, psychological services, testing, and speech and hearing services. In 2018, the Department of Education reported an estimated 205,000 students enrolled across 1,940 schools were eligible for services. In Table 38.4, the state appropriation for this program is a part of line 18, representing $87.95 million for FY 2021-22.

Approximately 3,242 public school children receive special education services through one of the 34 designated private schools approved by the Department of Education. These students are specially assigned to one of these schools because appropriate education is not available in the public schools. The resident district must provide funding for at least 40% of the approved tuition rate and the remaining covered by the state. In Table 38.4, state appropriation for this program is line 5, representing $122.7 million for FY 2021-22.

Four chartered schools[41] in Pennsylvania provide special education services to low incidence blind and deaf students. The schools include the Overbrook School for the Blind, Western Pennsylvania School for the Blind, Pennsylvania School for the Deaf, and Western Pennsylvania School for the Deaf. The resident school district must provide funding for at least 40% of the approved tuition rate and the remaining is covered by the state. In Table 38.4, the state appropriation for this program is a part of line 16, representing $62.22 million in FY 2021-22.

OTHER GRANTS AND SUBSIDIES

The Commonwealth of Pennsylvania provides state funding for targeted and innovative professional development through the statewide Act 82 teacher evaluation system, Act 45 leadership training program, multi-measure evaluation system for professional development, and the Standards Aligned System (SAS). The SAS provides accessible information to schools and educators through its web-based resources to deliver standards-aligned instructional support. In Table 38.4, the state appropriation for teacher professional development funding is line 15.

Pennsylvania currently provides competitive grants to school districts and offers support related to school safety services. Distributed through the Office of Safe Schools in the Pennsylvania Department of Education, state grants are awarded pursuant to Section 1302-A of the Public School Code[42] and are targeted toward programs addressing school violence and improvements in school security. In Table 38.4, state appropriation for the Safe Schools Initiative is line 17.

Other grants and subsidies to school districts include the school food service reimbursement subsidy which provides funding for the School Breakfast Program and the National School Lunch Program. Distribution of funding for school food services is prescribed under Section 1337.1 of the Public School Code.[43] In Table 38.4, state appropriation for school food services is a part of line 16, representing $30 million in FY 2021-22. Pennsylvania also provides funding to support library access to educational materials through the Public Library Subsidy, Library Services for Visually Impaired and Disabled, and Library Access appropriations. In Table 38.4, state appropriations for these library programs are a part of line 18, representing $65.11 million in FY 2021-22.

REVENUES

For FY 2019-20, total local revenues ($18.41 billion) in the Commonwealth represented 55.8% of total revenue ($33.01 billion), while property taxes ($14.29 billion) represented 42.4%. Property taxes comprised 77.6% of total local revenues while the remaining share primarily came from local earned income taxes ($1.67 billion). State revenue to school districts totaled $12.14 billion for FY 2019-20, representing 36.8% of total revenue ($33.01 billion). State basic education funding ($6.65 billion) is the largest component of state revenue, representing 54.8% of total state revenue and 20.2% of total revenues during FY 2019-20. Summary Tables 38.5 and 38.6 later in this chapter provide further detail including prior years.[44]

LOCAL REAL ESTATE TAXES

Special Session Act 1 of 2006, known as the Tax Payer Relief Act[45] as amended by Act 25 of 2011, impacted local revenues for school districts. The law first generated state revenues from casino gaming to provide allocations for property tax relief on homesteads throughout Pennsylvania. Additionally, Act 1, which created annual indices linked to inflation and adjusted for each school district by the wealth aid ratio, limited districts' ability to increase local property taxes by subjecting increases above the district's index to a public referendum. However, increases for certain expenditures specific under statute could be exempted from referendum if approved by the Pennsylvania Department of Education. Tax limitations on local property taxes were made pursuant to Section 333 of the Tax Payer Relief Act.[46]

In 2015, the median property tax levied in Pennsylvania was $1,960 for a home having a median assessed value of $78,545. Tax rates are expressed in mills or $1 for each $1,000 of assessed property value. Each county in the state has its own method for determining assessed property value that includes county, municipal and school taxes. Therefore, a fair comparison for taxation among all counties is based on the effective tax rate or what percentage of a home›s median value is spent annually on property taxes. Essentially, a $3,000 tax levied on a home with an assessed value of $200,000 produces an effective tax rate of 1.5%, or the property tax/assessed property value multiplied by 100. The average tax collection rate estimated by school districts was 93.1%, meaning 6.9% of taxes levied were turned over to the county collections office for further collection efforts. Overall delinquent tax collection revenue represented an additional 3.3% of the $16.9 billion in current year taxes collected in FY 2019-20.

Pennsylvania has the 39th highest effective tax rate in the U.S. at 1.51% of median assessed home value. The national average rate in 2014 was 1.29%, which was 22 basis points lower than Pennsylvania and higher than the average annual rates of 35 of the 50 states and the District of Columbia.

TAX CREDITS, DEDUCTIONS, AND EXEMPTIONS

Pennsylvania has created two education tax credit programs known as the Educational Improvement Tax Credit (EITC)[47] and Opportunity Scholarship Tax Credit (OSTC)[48] programs. Tax credits under the EITC may be awarded to business firms making contributions to organizations certified by the Department of Community and Economic Development (DCED). A qualified scholarship organization provides tuition assistance in the form of scholarships to eligible students residing within the boundaries of a 'low-achieving school' to attend another public school outside the district or nonpublic school. A qualified educational improvement organization must contribute at least 80% of its annual EITC receipts as grants for innovative educational programs at a public school, charter school or a private school approved under Section 1376 of the Public School Code.[49] A business firm making a one-time contribution is eligible for a tax credit of 75% of the contribution while two consecutive year contributions make the business firm eligible for a tax credit of 90% of the contribution. A statutory limit provides a maximum of $135 million in tax credits between the EITC and OSTC programs.

FEDERAL COVID-19 STIMULUS FUNDING

Pennsylvania students and schools have been appropriated federal stimulus funds through three separate federal Acts under two separate administrations, providing one-time infusions of resources to ensure that critical services are provided, operations are maintained, and the effects of the pandemic are overcome.

First, the Coronavirus Aid, Relief, and Economic Security Act (CARES), passed in March 2020, which provided Pennsylvania schools with $525 million in federal funds through the Elementary and Secondary School Emergency Relief (ESSER) Fund. In December 2020, the Coronavirus Response and Relief Supplemental Appropriations Act (CRRSA) was approved, sending another $2 billion to Pennsylvania schools via the ESSER Fund. Finally, in March 2021, the American Rescue Plan Act (ARP) was passed, sending nearly $5 billion to Pennsylvania schools through the ESSER Fund and set-asides. The amount of ESSER funding a school district or charter school receives is dependent on its share of federal Title I-A funding, which, generally, is dependent on the LEA's population of economically disadvantaged students.

Within the total allocation of federal education stimulus funds provided through ESSER, the state was authorized to set-aside up to 10% of the total allocation for various targeted purposes and subject to respective requirements and provisions. In Pennsylvania, the state legislature enacted two separate appropriations and accompanying school code bills that allocated the set-aside funds. Act 24 of 2021 allocated funding to school districts and charter schools with $250 million (or 5% of total ESSER III) for learning-loss targeted, $50 million (or 1% of ESSER III) for summer enrichment programs and $50 million (or 1% of ESSER III) for after-school programs. This state law provided for a timeline for local education agencies to apply and a deadline for the Pennsylvania Department of Education to review submitted applications.

Additionally, Act 24 allocated funding with $43.5 million for Career and Technical Centers (CTC) based on share of the state's career and technical education subsidy formula; $15 million for Private Residential Rehabilitative Institutions (PRRI), Approved Private Schools (APS), and Pennsylvania Chartered Schools for the Deaf and Blind (CSDB) based on share of ADMs; $43.5 million for Intermediate Units (IU) based on MV/PI and ADMs; $14 million for A-TSI designated schools under the ESSA state plan based on economically disadvantaged enrollment; $19.9 million for programs for delinquent, neglected, and at-risk youth (as defined by Act 24 of 2021) based on Title I-D shares.

Furthermore, the CARES Act authorized the Governor through the Pennsylvania Department of Education to determine the educational use of Governor's Emergency Education Relief (GEER) funds. Funding allocations were distributed to support preschool and early intervention, postsecondary institutions and adult basic education providers, career and technical education centers (CTCs), students with special needs, historically underserved students, high-speed internet connection, and continuing education and equity grants. Table 38.4 illustrates the

TABLE 38.4. Summary of Federal Stimulus Distributions for GEER I and II Funding

GEER I	Amount $ in Thousands
Early Intervention	$3,000
Early Intervention Compensatory Education	$5,000
Compensatory Education (Special Education COVID-19 Impact Mitigation Grant (SECIM))	$10,000
Continuity of Education Equity Grants	$14,000
Connectivity and Technology	$15,000
Foundational support for CTCs	$10,500
A-TSI Foundational Support	$15,000
Other Foundational Support for Schools Designated for Improvement	$3,918
Safe Reopening Equity Grants for Postsecondary Institutions	$24,500
Equity Grants for Adult Basic Education Providers	$500
Emergency Support for Historically Black Colleges and Universities in PA	$3,000
Total	**$104,418**
GEER II	**Amount $ in Thousands**
Career and Technical Education Centers	$20,000
PRRI, APS, CSDB	$8,075
Community Colleges	$14,000
Pennsylvania State System of Higher Education	$5,000
Total	**$47,075**

distribution of $104.4 million in GEER I funds and $47.1 million in GEER II funds.

Table 38.5 illustrates the main federal tranches by fund name and by type of school entity or program. All funds can be utilized retrospective to March 2020 for supplementing or supplanting school expenditures but must be fully committed by September 2022, September 2023, and September 2024 for the Cares, CRRSA, and ARP funds respectively. School officials have indicated ESSER II and III amounts are substantial and will generally impact school budgets heavily in FY 2021-22 through 2023-24.

The Pennsylvania Department of Education website links provide significantly detailed information and allocations by fund.[50] Furthermore, additional information can be found.[51] It is fully expected that both state and federal reporting of spending use and outcomes will be rigorously detailed as every school has its own set of unique needs and challenges to address needs of students and educational programs. Presently, the Pennsylvania Association of School Business Officials (PASBO) along with other education associations have collaborated to collect qualitative and quantitative data to report on behalf of school leaders their implementation of federal funds and programs and the challenges they have overserved

TABLE 38.5.   Summary of Federal Stimulus Funds to Selected School Entities

| $ in Thousands | CARES Act | | CRRSA | | ARP | | Total Allocations |
	ESSER I	GEER I	ESSER II	GEER II	ESSER III	Act 24 Set-Aside	
Local Education Agencies	$400,120	$14,800	$ 2,224,964	$0	$4,500,458	$350,000	$7,125,542
Intermediate Units (IUs)	$0	$0	$0	$0	$0	$43,500	$43,500
Career and Technical Centers	$0	$10,500	$0	$20,000	$0	$43,500	$74,000
A-TSI Schools	$0	$15,000	$0	0	$0	$14,000	$29,000
APS, PRRI and CSDB	$0	$0	$0	$8,075	$0	$15,000	$23,075
Neglected, Delinquent, At-Risk	$0	$0	$0	$0	$0	$19,909	$19,909
	$400,120	**$40,300**	**$2,224,964**	**$28,075**	**$4,500,458**	**$485,909**	**$7,315,026**

so far and foresee moving forward. These annual budget reports can be found on the PASBO website.[52]

SUMMARY

Table 38.6 illustrates total state spending on K-12 education which is comprised of numerous programs and formula distributions. In total, Pennsylvania appropriated $13.63 billion in grants and subsidies to the system of public education for FY 2021-22, a $670 million increase over FY 2020-21. These figures did not include general government operations which are funds appropriated to the Pennsylvania Department of Education for general operations of the Department of Education.

Table 38.7 shows that total school district revenues over the past seven fiscal years increased from $26.2 billion to $33.0 billion. More importantly, the breakdown of total expenditures by accounting object for fiscal years 2018-19 and 2020-21, as illustrated in Table 38.8, shows which costs increased and decreased. Object 900, Other Uses of Funds, represents refinancing of old debt which comprised of 46.5% of the overall year over year increase in total expenditures. Finally, Tables 38.9 shows changes to school district expenditures by objects and functions across fiscal years 2010-11 through 2019-20.

TABLE 38.6. Summary of State Appropriations General Fund: K-12 Grants/Subsidies ($ in thousands)

	Support of Public SchoolS	Page	FY 2020-21	FY 2021-22
1	Basic Education Funding	3	$6,794,489	$7,074,736
2	Ready to Learn Block Grant	4	$268,000	$288,000
3	Special Education	4	$1,186,815	$1,236,815
4	Early Intervention	5	$325,500	$336,500
5	Special Education – Approved Private Schools	9	$122,656	$122,656
6	Pre-K Counts	5	$217,284	$242,284
7	Head Start Supplemental Assistance	5	$64,178	$69,178
8	Career and Technical Education	5	$99,000	$99,000
9	Career and Technical Education Equipment Grants	6	$5,550	$5,550
10	Pupil Transportation	6	$543,311	$597,408
11	Nonpublic and Charter School Pupil Transportation	6	$79,442	$79,442
12	School Employees' Social Security	7	$71,001	$67,229
13	School Employees' Retirement	7	$2,702,000	$2,734,000
14	Authority Rentals and Sinking Fund Requirements	8	$10,500	$201,303
15	Teacher Professional Development	10	$5,044	$5,044
16	Other Support Grants and Subsidies to Public Schools	--	$153,769	$157,308
	SUBTOTAL – SUPPORT OF PUBLIC SCHOOLS		$12,648,539	$13,316,453

OTHER GRANTS AND SUBSIDIES			FY 2020-21	FY 2021-22
17	Safe School Initiative	10	$11,000	$11,000
18	Other Grants and Subsidies	--	$216,968	$211,543
	SUBTOTAL – OTHER GRANTS AND SUBSIDIES		$227,968	$222,543
	TOTAL GRANTS & SUBSIDIES		$12,957,917	$13,628,753

TABLE 38.7. Total Revenues by Source for All 500 Pennsylvania School Districts (in thousands)

Source	2013-14	2014-15	2015-16	2016-17	2017-18	2018-19	2019-20
Local	$15,361,453	$15,886,606	$16,309,685	$16,838,909	$17,450,758	$18,155,673	$18,412,455
State	$9,582,677	$10,022,410	$10,475,164	$11,310,533	$11,494,982	$11,786,687	$12,138,335
Federal	$812,525	$814,577	$774,735	$842,702	$896,998	$926,417	$949,890
Other	$461,070	$854,694	$934,474	$1,758,691	$438,776	$546,457	$1,513,251
Total Revenue	$26,217,725	$27,578,287	$28,494,058	$30,750,835	$30,281,514	$31,415,234	$33,013,932
Total Expenses	$26,128,265	$27,386,591	$28,308,905	$30,495,436	$30,211,199	$31,396,049	$32,753,768

TABLE 38.8. Pennsylvania District Expenditures by Selected Objects FY 2019-2020 ($ in thousands)

Object Code and Description	2019-20 FY	2018-19 FY	Increase $	Increase %	Share of Increase
100 Personnel Services - Salaries	$12,204,078	$11,952,410	$251,668	2.11%	18.54%
200 Personnel Services - Employee Benefits	$7,922,316	$7,701,501	$220,815	2.87%	16.26%
Social Security Contributions	$908,835	$896,666	$12,169	1.36%	0.90%
Retirement Contributions	$4,121,586	$3,937,151	$184,435	4.68%	13.58%
300 Purchased Prof. and Technical Services	$1,871,203	$1,820,039	$51,164	2.81%	3.77%
400 Purchased Property Services	$528,984	$543,114	($14,130)	-2.60%	-1.04%
500 Other Purchased Services	$4,581,378	$4,572,162	$9,216	0.20%	0.68%
Charter School Tuition	$2,193,605	$2,045,818	$147,787	7.22%	10.88%
600 Supplies	$992,419	$1,012,160	($19,741)	-1.95%	-1.45%
700 Property	$264,235	$244,512	$19,723	8.07%	1.45%
800 Other Objects	$952,012	$925,770	$26,242	2.83%	1.93%
900 Other Uses of Funds	$3,437,143	$2,624,382	$812,761	30.97%	59.86%
Total Expenditures	$32,753,768	$31,396,049	$1,357,719	4.32%	100.00%

TABLE 38.9. Pennsylvania District Expenditures by Selected Functions FY 2019-2020 ($ in thousands)

Function Code and Description		2019-20 FY	2018-19 FY	Increase $	Increase %	Share of Increase
1000	**Instruction**	**$19,293,006**	**$18,792,259**	**$500,747**	**2.66%**	**36.88%**
	Regular Education Programs (1100)	$13,146,810	$12,835,175	$311,635	2.43%	22.95%
	Special Education Programs (1200)	$4,991,327	$4,800,807	$190,520	3.97%	14.03%
	Vocational Education Programs (1300)	$667,320	$664,254	$3,066	0.46%	0.23%
2000	**Support Services**	**$8,661,892**	**$8,621,787**	**$40,105**	**0.47%**	**2.95%**
	Instructional Support Staff (2200)	$904,657	$893,078	$11,579	1.30%	0.85%
	Administrative (2300)	$1,694,429	$1,643,648	$50,781	3.09%	3.74%
	O & M Facility Services (2600)	$2,316,020	$2,333,983	($17,963)	-0.77%	-1.32%
	Safety/Security (2660)	$187,163	$170,797	$16,366	9.58%	1.21%
	Student Transportation (2700)	$1,447,908	$1,557,757	($109,849)	-7.05%	-8.09%
3000	**Non- Instructional Services**	**$513,020**	**$541,402**	**($28,382)**	**-5.24%**	**-2.09%**
	Student Activities (3200)	$466,582	$493,722	($27,140)	-5.50%	-2.00%
4000	**Facilities Acquisition, Construction and Improvement Services**	**$83,528**	**$61,012**	**$22,516**	**36.90%**	**1.66%**
5000	**Other Exp. & Finance Uses**	**$4,202,323**	**$3,379,590**	**$822,733**	**24.34%**	**60.60%**
	Refunded Bonds (5120)	$1,153,632	$543,321	$610,311	112.33%	44.95%
	Capital Projects (5230)	$404,222	$307,258	$96,964	31.56%	7.14%
	Debt Service Fund Transfers (5240)	$670,134	$502,405	$167,729	33.39%	12.35%
	Total Expenditures	$32,753,768	$31,396,049	$1,357,719	4.32%	100.00%

ENDNOTES

[1] Pa. Const. Art. III, § 14.

[2] Louise Walsh and Matthew Walsh, History and Organization of Education in Pennsylvania (1930), https://hdl.handle.net/2027/mdp. 39015008840095 p. 228.

[3] The School Laws of Pennsylvania (Collection), available online at https://catalog.hathitrust.org/Record/007823490. https://catalog.hathitrust.org/Record/007823490

[4] Janice Bissett & Arnold Hillman, The History of School Funding in Pennsylvania 1682 – 2013 (2013), available online at https://slidex.tips/downloadFile/the-history-of-school-funding-in-pennsylvania.

[5] https://babel.hathitrust.org/cgi/pt?id=pst.000062684637;view=1up;seq=81

6   The School Laws of Pennsylvania (1899), available online at https://hdl.handle.net/2027/pst.000068060183?urlappend=%3Bseq=171

7   The School Laws of Pennsylvania (1913), available online at https://babel.hathitrust.org/cgi/pt?id=pst.000068060244;view=1up;seq=123.

8   Ibid p. 117.

9   Statistics of the Public Schools (1919), available online at https://babel.hathitrust.org/cgi/pt?id=pst.000011821519;view=1up;seq=5.

10   The School Laws of Pennsylvania (1923), available online at https://babel.hathitrust.org/cgi/pt?id=pst.000068060251.

11   For a complete legislative history of funding schools, see Janice Bissett & Arnold Hillman, The History of School Funding in Pennsylvania 1682 – 2013 (2013), available online at https://slidex.tips/downloadFile/the-history-of-school-funding-in-pennsylvania.

12   Janice Bissett & Arnold Hillman, The History of School Funding in Pennsylvania 1682 – 2013 (2013), available online at https://slidex.tips/downloadFile/the-history-of-school-funding-in-pennsylvania; Louise Walsh & Matthew Walsh, History and Organization of Education in Pennsylvania (1930), available online at https://hdl.handle.net/2027/mdp.39015008840095; and Michelle J. Atherton, How Pennsylvania Funds Public Schools: The Story Of The State Share (2014), available online at http://www.cla.temple.edu/corp/files/2012/12/State-Share-Issue-Memo.pdf.

13   William T. Hartman and Timothy J. Shrom, Hard Choices Still Ahead: The Financial Future of Pennsylvania School Districts (2017), available online at http://www.cla.temple.edu/corp/files/2017/03/Fiscal-Outlook-2017-Update-Policy-Brief.pdf.

14   William Penn School District v. Pennsylvania Department of Education, 170 A.3d 414 (Pa. 2017).

15   Christine Kiracofe and Andrew L. Armagost, Political Question Doctrine in the Keystone State: A Legal Analysis of Pennsylvania School Funding In Light of William Penn School District v. Pennsylvania Department of Education (2017).

16   William Penn School District, et al. v. Pennsylvania Department of Education et al. (587 M.D. 2014)

17   Act 14 of 1949 (March 10, P.L. 30).

18   22 Pa. Code § § 1--741.

19   Source data at http://www.education.pa.gov/Teachers%20-%20Administrators/School%20Finances/Finances/Pages/default.aspx.

20   24 P.S. § 25-2502.53.

21   Act 24 of 2021 amended 2522-E of the Fiscal Code Act of 1929

22   24 P.S. § 25-2599.6

23   24 P.S. § 25-2509.5

24   24 P.S. § 15-1514-D

25   24 P.S. § § 15-1502-D -- 15-1503-D

26   24 P.S. § 25-2502.8

27   24 P.S. § 25-2541

28   24 P.S. § 25-2509.3

29   Source data available online at http://www.education.pa.gov/Teachers%20-%20Administrators/School%20Finances/Finances/AFR%20Data%20Summary/Pages/AFR-Data-Detailed-.aspx#.VZwC6mXD-Uk

30   24 P.S. § 83-8326

31   Actual and projected calculations from PSERS Comprehensive Annual Financial Reports available online at http://www.psers.pa.gov/FPP/Publications/General/Pages/CAFR.aspx

32   24 P.S. § 83-8327

33   Keystone Pension Report, Fall 2012, available online at http://archive.pasbo.org/26Nov2012_Budget_PensionReport.pdf

34   Pennsylvania Association of School Business Officials Update on Pension Reform, https://www.pasbo.org/pension

35   24 P.S. § § 25-2571 -- 25-2580

[36] Foreman v. Chester-Upland School District, 941 A.2d 108 (Commonwealth Court of Pennsylvania, January 18, 2008).

[37] 24 P.S. § 17-1725-A

[38] 24 P.S. § 17-1725-A (a) (2)

[39] 24 P.S. § 17-1725-A (a) (3)

[40] Senate Bill 806

[41] Chartered schools are not the same as charter schools as established pursuant to the Article XVII of the Public School Code relating to cyber charter or brick and mortar charter schools.

[42] 24 P.S. § 13-1302-A (c)

[43] 24 P.S. § 13-1337.1

[44] Source data available online at http://www.education.pa.gov/Teachers%20-%20Administrators/School%20Finances/Finances/AFR%20Data%20Summary/Pages/AFR-Data-Detailed-.aspx#.VZwC6mXD-Uk

[45] Act 1 of 2006, Special Session 1 (June 27, P.L. 1873).

[46] § 333

[47] https://dced.pa.gov/programs/educational-improvement-tax-credit-program-eitc/

[48] https://dced.pa.gov/programs/opportunity-scholarship-tax-credit-program-ostc/

[49] 24 P.S. § 13-1326

[50] https://www.education.pa.gov/Schools/safeschools/emergencyplanning/COVID-19/Pages/default.aspx

[51] www.pasbo.org/esser

[52] https://www.pasbo.org/budget-reports

CHAPTER 39

RHODE ISLAND

Jacob D. Skousen
University of Nevada, Las Vegas

GENERAL BACKGROUND[1]

The smallest state in the United States, Rhode Island, became a state on May 29, 1790.[2] Rhode Island first adopted a state constitution in 1843.[3] In Article XII of Education in the Rhode Island State Constitution there are four specific sections that articulate the provision of public school. Section 1 pronounces the requirement of the state legislative body to "promote schools:"

> **Section 1.** Duty of general assembly to promote schools and libraries.—The diffusion of knowledge, as well as of virtue among the people, being essential to the preservation of their rights and liberties, it shall be the duty of the general assembly to promote public schools and public libraries, and to adopt all means which it may deem necessary and proper to secure to the people the advantages and opportunities of education and public library services.[4]

The next sections establish the "perpetual school fund" and communicate the use of "donations:"

Funding Public Schools in the United States, Indian Country,
and US Territories (Second Edition), pages 603–621.
Copyright © 2023 by Information Age Publishing
www.infoagepub.com

Section 2. Perpetual school fund.—The money which now is or which may hereafter be appropriated by law for the establishment of a permanent fund for the support of public schools, shall be securely invested and remain a perpetual fund for that purpose.[5]

Section 3. Donations.—All donations for the support of public schools, or for other purposes of education, which may be received by the general assembly, shall be applied according to the terms prescribed by the donors.[6]

Finally, Section 4 provides specific language about the "implementation" of Article XII:

Section 4. Implementation of article—Diversion of funds prohibited.—The general assembly shall make all necessary provisions by law for carrying this article into effect. It shall not divert said money or fund from the aforesaid uses, nor borrow, appropriate, or use the same, or any part thereof, for any other purpose, under any pretense whatsoever.[7]

It is of interest to note that in 1995 the Rhode Island Supreme Court decided on a case, *the City of Pawtucket v. Sundlun*, that challenged the state system of school finance. Specifically, the complaint stated that the system to finance schools violated the education and equal protection clauses of the State Constitution.[8] In this case the highest court in the state decided in favor of the state and the wrote, "The education clause leaves all such determinations to the General Assembly's broad discretion to adopt the means it deems 'necessary and proper' in complying with the constitutional directive." What some might see as contrasting the Sundlun ruling and adding an equal protection clause to the state's constitution, is Senate Bill S2095, "Rhode Island Right to an Adequate Education Amendment," that was passed in the Rhode Island Senate 36-0, with 2 members not voting, in March 2022. The same amendment was passed by the RI Senate during the 2021 General Assembly; however, the House of Representatives did not vote on it during the 2021 legislative session, and the 2022 session has not concluded as of the time this chapter was written. While there is not a decision regarding this bill that could change the state's constitution, the overwhelming support for this change may indicate change during this and/or the next legislative session. The currently drafted bill would amend Article XII of the state constitution with the additional language, "In furtherance of the duty to establish and maintain a system of free public schools, it shall be the additional duty of the general assembly and the state to guarantee an equitable, adequate and meaningful education to each child."[9]

The population of Rhode Island has had an average increase of 4.21% from the 1960 to the 2020 census, with the current population being 1,097,379.[10] During the 2020-2021 school year, the Rhode Island Department of Education (RIDE) identified 311 total schools, distributed across 32 regular school districts, four regional school districts, four state-operated schools, one regional collaborative LEA, and 23 charter schools.[11] There are 139,184 students who attend schools in

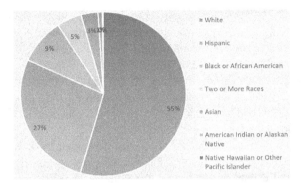

FIGURE 39.1. Rhode Island Student Ethnic/Racial Percentages 2020-2021 School Year. Source: RIDE, accessed May 2, 2022, https://www.ride.ri.gov/studentsfamilies/ ripublicschools/schooldistricts.aspx

Rhode Island.[12] The small majority of the students are white, and like the overall population of Rhode Island, there has been an increased racial and ethnic diversity over the last decade. The student racial and ethnic demographic information is found in Figure 39.1.

The percentage of male and female students in Rhode Island schools are 52% and 48% respectively. A little over 41% of the student population are economically disadvantaged and nearly 12% are identified as English language learners.[13]

RIDE reported that there are 13,902 educators in Rhode Island.[14] This number is disaggregated to 756 administrators (building- and district-level), 11,572 teachers, and 1,574 support professionals. The racial and ethnic demographics of the educators in Rhode Island can be found in Figure 39.2.

The Rhode Island General Assembly has made changes to school financing over the last 60 years. Most notable were the changes in the 1960s, when the state leg-

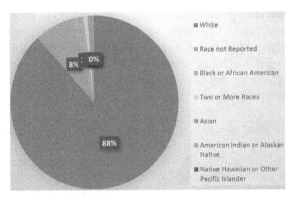

FIGURE 39.2. Rhode Island Educators Ethnic/Racial Percentages 2020-2021 School Year. Source: RIDE, accessed May 2, 2022, https://www.ride.ri.gov/students-families/ripublicschools/schooldistricts.aspx

islature provided a "minimum guarantee" of state aid to schools and the Thibeault Commission that utilized the median family income, instead of using local property tax values for funding equalization purposes. Later in the 1980s the state legislature sought to increase the state share of district revenue to 50% (an increase of 16% from the previously established percentage in 1964) through the passing of the Omnibus Property Tax Relief and Replacement Act. Following *The City of Pawtucket v. Sundlun* case in 1995 and recognizing a need to address education funding in Rhode Island, Governor Almond issued Executive Order 99-11 "to establish the Governor's Task Force on Elementary and Secondary Education Finance."[15] While no immediate changes were implemented, the task force was instrumental to the 2004 legislation of the Education and Property Tax Relief Act, which "recongnize[d] the need for an equitable distribution of resources among the state's school districts" and the 2006 legislated development of a committee to create a new school aid formula.[16] It should be noted that by 2009, every state in the United States was using a specific formula to determine and enact state aid except Rhode Island.[17]

The 2004 and 2006 legislated efforts may have impacted the development of an education funding formula, yet more significant in this process was the Governor's Task Force on Elementary and Secondary Education Finance to develop an education funding formula. The task force's efforts led to the 2010 Rhode Island General Assembly session and the passing of a funding formula that drastically changed school funding in Rhode Island. Due to "political tension" and that certain communities would not receive as much state aid as they had previously due to the redistribution of aid, the legislature created a 10-year gradual, or phase-in process, with an initial partial implementation during fiscal year (FY) 2012 and full implementation in FY 2020.[18] The significant change was a specific formula that would determine education aid and the provision that "the money should follow the student."[19] An executive order in 2015 established a "Funding Formula Working Group" that was charged to "review Rhode Island's education funding Formula."[20] The working group provided 20 recommendations, with 11 "Overarching Recommendations."[21] These recommendations may have influenced the changes to the funding formula that were made during the 2016 legislative session that allowed additional implementation flexibility, with full implementation enacted in FY 2021, and a formula was added to address the way the "funding follows the student" principle was executed.[22] The current funding formula will be described in the section "Distribution Formula."

The total amount spent on Rhode Island K-12 schools was just over $2.6 billion (FY 2021).[23] The total per pupil spending amount during FY 2020 was $18,438 and Rhode Island per pupil expenditure ranked ninth in the United States.[24] Table 39.1 shows the per pupil expenditure in Rhode Island from FY 2011 to FY 2020.

Figure 39.3 illustrates the amounts of state aid to Rhode Island school districts that were enacted in FY 2021. The majority share of the per-pupil spending, 52.37%, comes from local funding sources. Further descriptions of the funding sources are discussed in the "Sources of Revenue" section.

TABLE 39.1. Rhode Island Per Pupil Expenditure from FY 2011 to FY 2020

Fiscal Year (FY)	Total Per Pupil Expenditure	Total K-12 Spending (in billions)
FY 2020	$18,438	$2.621
FY 2019	$18,383	$2.619
FY 2018	$17,755	$2.529
FY 2017	$17,309	$2.445
FY 2016	$16,842	$2.366
FY 2015	$16,494	$2.319
FY 2014	$16,075	$2.255
FY 2013	$15,657	$2.205
FY 2012	$15,458	$2.175
FY 2011	$15,262	$2.177

Source: RIDE, accessed May 10, 2022, https://www.ride.ri.gov/FundingFinance/
SchoolDistrictFinancialData/UniformChartofAccounts.aspx#18211075-annual-per-pupil-
expenditure-reports

LEA	FY 2021 Total Aid	LEA	FY 2021 Total Aid	LEA	FY 2021 Total Aid
BARRINGTON	$6,148,515	NORTH KINGSTOWN	$11,867,847	BLACKSTONE ACADEMY	$4,087,723
BURRILLVILLE	$14,352,095	NORTH PROVIDENCE	$25,275,682	BLACKSTONE VALLEY PREP	$20,775,537
CENTRAL FALLS	$45,680,069	NORTH SMITHFIELD	$6,206,522	CHARETTE	$2,003,921
CHARIHO	$2,135,762	PAWTUCKET	$92,823,637	COMPASS	$612,659
CHARLESTOWN	$1,310,336	PORTSMOUTH	$3,833,800	GREENE SCHOOL	$1,367,227
COVENTRY	$23,564,535	PROVIDENCE	$272,263,071	HIGHLANDER	$7,048,284
CRANSTON	$69,762,285	RICHMOND	$4,693,797	HOPE ACADEMY	$2,671,156
CUMBERLAND	$20,799,151	SCITUATE	$2,727,973	INTERNATIONAL	$3,673,857
EAST GREENWICH	$3,490,911	SMITHFIELD	$6,227,712	KINGSTON HILL	$829,329
EAST PROVIDENCE	$36,377,563	SOUTH KINGSTOWN	$4,853,438	LEARNING COMM	$7,204,734
FOSTER	$1,065,648	TIVERTON	$7,475,572	NEW ENG LABORERS	$1,392,948
GLOCESTER	$2,218,174	WARWICK	$38,441,937	NOWELL ACADEMY	$1,875,016
HOPKINTON	$5,488,552	WEST WARWICK	$29,535,239	NURSES INSTITUTE	$3,078,471
JAMESTOWN	$405,580	WESTERLY	$8,255,191	PAUL CUFFEE	$9,414,866
JOHNSTON	$19,127,284	WOONSOCKET	$68,991,504	RISE MAYORAL	$3,119,604
LINCOLN	$15,198,686	BRISTOL-WARREN REGIONAL	$14,514,094	SEGUE INSTITUTE	$3,095,561
LITTLE COMPTON	$397,665	EXETER-W. GREEN REGIONAL	$5,696,331	SOUTHSIDE	$1,691,689
MIDDLETOWN	$7,894,209	FOSTER-GLOC	$5,207,656	TIMES2 ACADEMY	$8,311,236
NARRAGANSETT	$2,261,373	ACHIEVEMENT FIRST	$18,875,168	TRINITY	$2,421,787
NEW SHOREHAM	$178,491	BEACON	$3,346,066	VILLAGE GREEN	$2,391,718
NEWPORT	$14,034,125				

FIGURE 39.3. Source: RIDE, accessed May 2, 2022, https://www.ride.ri.gov/stu-
dentsfamilies/ripublicschools/schooldistricts.aspx

In addition to this introduction to Rhode Island, the population, and general information about education, there are eight sections in this chapter. Following the introduction, the "Current Political Climate" in Rhode Island is described generally. The "Revenue Sources" that fund the K-12 educational system in Rhode Island is the next section, followed by a description and explanation of the "Distribution Formula" utilized to fund schools in Rhode Island. The next sections, "Charter Schools" and "Nonpublic School Funding," provide an overview of the funding and trends of charter schools in the state and the public funding contributions that are expended for nonpublic schools. A general explanation of the state of "Virtual Education" is the next section, followed by the final section titled "Federal COVID-19 Funding" in which the federal funding provided to Rhode Island during the COVID-19 is discussed.

CURRENT POLITICAL CLIMATE

The state of Rhode Island has a General Assembly that convenes for a regular session annually.[25] The General Assembly consists of the Rhode Island House of Representatives and the Rhode Island State Senate. There are 75 representatives in the House, of which 66 are listed as being part of the Democratic Party and nine as members of the Republican Party. Of the 38 senators in the State Senate, 33 are democrats and 5 are republicans.[26] While over the last two decades Rhode Island voters have elected more Democratic Party affiliated candidates than Republican or unaffiliated candidates, the Rhode Island Department of State website as of May 2022 showed that the 708,273 registered voters are largely unaffiliated (45%), followed by democrat (41%), and finally republican (14%).[27]

There are two teacher associations in Rhode Island. The National Education Association Rhode Island (NEARI) has approximately 12,000 members, which equates to "one in every 100 Rhode Islanders."[28] NEARI is associated with the National Education Association (NEA). The Rhode Island Federation of Teacher and Health Professionals has approximately 10,000 members consisting of both teachers and those who work in the health profession.[29] Both associations focus on issues associated with teachers and students. For example, both organizations conduct work focused on the development of teachers and the well-being of students, academically, emotionally, and by meeting other needs like eye-care. It should also be noted that NEARI and Rhode Island Federation of Teacher and Health Professionals were engaged in the creation and implementation plans of the education funding formula passed by the Rhode Island General Assembly in 2010 and in the changes that were made during the 2012 and 2016 sessions.

There are no pending legal challenges regarding the state's education funding formula. The most notable cases regarding education finance in Rhode Island include *Pawtucket v. Sundlun* in 1995. Sundlun argued that the state's school finance system violated the equal protection clause. The Rhode Island Supreme Court ruled in favor of the state and provided clarification to the Rhode Island Constitution stating that it is the General Assembly, not the courts, that determine matters relating to education, "thereby foreclosing the possibility of significant judicial intervention into the state's education finance system."[30] This decision was further reinforced in 2014 in the case *Woonsocket v. Carieri,* where the plaintiffs argued that the state's funding system underfunded schools, especially those serving high poverty students and student learning English. The Rhode Island Supreme Court dismissed the case citing the 1995 ruling in *Pawtucket v. Sundlun.*[31]

As mentioned previously, Senate Bill S2095, "Rhode Island Right to an Adequate Education Amendment," is a legislatively referred constitutional amendment that could be put before voters if passed in the Senate and House during the General Assembly. This constitutional amendment would add the following language to Section 1: the heading, "Fundamental right to a public education and the duty to promote public libraries," and the final sentence in Section 1 would read, "In furtherance of the duty to establish and maintain a system of free public schools, it shall additionally be the duty of the general assembly and the state to guarantee an equitable, adequate and meaningful education to each child." Additionally, Section 2 would be changed in its entirety to the following, "This article shall be judicially enforceable. Any person or entity injured or threatened with any injury because of any noncompliance with its provisions shall be entitled to bring an action in Superior Court to enforce these provisions and to obtain declaratory and injunctive relief for any violation thereof." These constitutional amendments could put to question the precedent established in *Pawtucket v. Sundlun.*

REVENUE SOURCES

Rhode Island K-12 schools receive funding through three sources: 1) local funding, 2) state funding, and 3) federal government funding. The largest percentage of funding comes from local funding, which only comes from property taxes. During FY 2021, local funding amounted to approximately $1.35 billion, or about 52% of the overall education funding. Through state funding Rhode Island's K-12 schools received approximately $1.03 billion, equating to about 40%. Finally, the federal government allocated $197.8 million, or about 8% of the overall K-12 funding.

With the exception of FY 2012, funding for K-12 schools has increased over the last decade. Table 39.1 illustrates the total funding increase from $2.177 billion in FY 2011 to $2.621 billion in FY 202. From FY 2011 to FY 2020 there was an 18.5% increase in overall K-12 funding. Significant to the sources of revenue and the increasing education budget for Rhode Island schools is the increase in the state funding over the last decade. During FY 2012 state revenues made up 32% of the total education revenues and in FYI 202 state revenues was 37.3% of the total revenues. Figure 39.3 shows the revenue sources by school district during FY2020. To illustrate how the funding formula and the redistribution funding has impacted school districts, an example of two contrasting Rhode Island School Districts is provided. Central Falls School District (CFSD) is a high poverty and low property wealth district, and New Shoreham School District (NSSD) is a low poverty and high property wealth district. CFSD received the majority of rev-

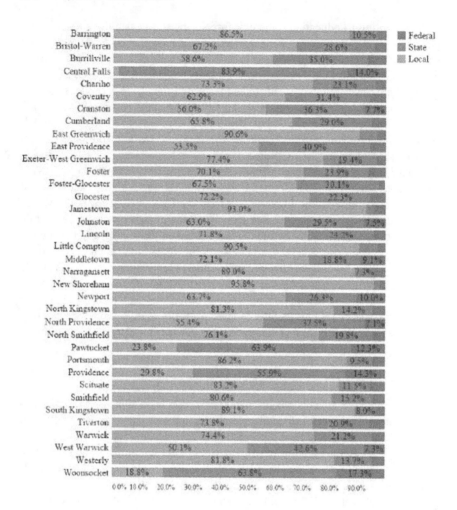

FIGURE 39.4. Rhode Island Revenue Sources in FY 2020. Source: Rhode Island Department of Education, accessed May 10, 2022, https://www.ride.ri.gov/Funding-Finance/FundingSources/StateEducationAid.aspx

enues from the state, nearly 84% of the total revenues. In contrast, NSSD received approximately 2% of the total revenues from state aid.

DISTRIBUTION FORMULA

In 2009 Rhode Island was the only state in the United States that did not have an education funding formula. The first funding formula in Rhode Island was approved in the Rhode Island General Assembly in 2010. While there were some modifications to the 2010 formula during the 2016 General Assembly, today the funding formula in generally the same as it was originally passed. The key principle upon which the formula is based in "the money follows the student."[32] This section will include a description of the funding formula, including the adjustments that were made in 2016, followed by explanations of the categorical and other funding that is provided to Rhode Island schools.

Core Instruction

The foundation of school funding in Rhode Island is the core instruction amount, which was based on studies from states that are considered by researchers to be among the "best practice financial models."[33] The core instruction amount is determined by a number of various costs and is compiled by the National Center for Education Statistics (NCES). In order to provide a context-based, informed amount, the NCES creates the core instruction amount annually, based on the average costs to provide a high-quality education in four New England States, Connecticut, Massachusetts, New Hampshire, and Rhode Island.[34]

The core instruction amount includes seven categories: 1) instructional staff, 2) other instructional services, 3) student support, 4) other student support, 5) general district administration, 6) school-level administration, and 7) staff benefits. Instructional staff includes the salaries for teachers and teacher aides. Other instructional services are expenses related to salaries and contracts for technical and professional services, supplies, and textbooks. The next two categories, student support and other student support, are inclusive of salaries for social workers, guidance counselors, school psychologists, speech pathologists, staff in health care or support staff for psychology and speech pathology, supervisors of instruction, library and media specialists, curriculum coordinators, supplies, textbooks, and other professional services. The general district administration are those expenses related to salaries for superintendent, central office staff, and the purchase of services and contracts at the district level. School-level administration includes salaries for principals, department chairs, administrative staff, and other purchased services. Finally, staff benefits are inclusive of all fringe benefits for instruction, administrative, and support staff.

State Share Formula

The formula to calculate the amount of State Share Ratio (SSR), or the education aid that is provided to LEAs that is covered by the state, was designed to provide equitable funding for school districts where property tax revenue is low and the proportion of students experiencing poverty is high. In the April 2022 report, "Rhode Island's Funding Formula After Ten Years," published by the Rhode Island Public Expenditure Council, the authors stated, "The state's education funding formula is designed in large part to direct greater state aid to those districts with less ability to raise money from property taxes and other local sources."[35] In order to determine the SSR, the State Share Ratio for the Community (SSRC) has to be calculated first. The purpose of the SSRC is to quantify the ability of a municipality to obtain local revenues and represents a weighted ratio of the wealth per student in a school district to the statewide wealth per student.[36] To calculate the SSRC the formula, the adjusted equalized weighted assessed value (AEWAV) and the resident average daily membership (RADM) data are utilized. The RADM is calculated by dividing the aggregate number of days of school enrollment by the number of school days. The SSRC formula is found in Figure 39.5.

The second step to calculate the SSR is the measure of students who experience poverty within the community. This component includes a quantity, by percent, of the pre-kindergarten through sixth grade students who qualify for free or reduce- price lunch (FRPL). It is important to note that it was purposeful to use this group, PK-6 grade, as the measure because their data had shown that these students were more likely to participate in the FRPL program.[37] Finally, the SSR is determined by using a root mean square, or quadradic mean, that gives greater weight to the larger of the two factors- SSRC or the percentage of poverty.

Funding Follows the Student

When the funding formula was passed by the Rhode Island General Assembly in 2010 the principle that funding follows the student was significant. The formula was designed in a way that would ensure funding for students who attended public school outside of the LEA where the student lives. Using yearly enrollment data, the state is able to confirm that per pupil funding is allocated to the LEA where the student was enrolled. When the formula was first implemented, the sending LEA, or the home school district where the student lived, was required to allocate to the receiving LEA, or the school district where the student was enrolled, the total local payment rate.

The Rhode Island General Assembly made changes to the funding formula in 2016, and one of those changes was an adjustment in the amount that the sending LEA would allocate to the receiving LEA. Because LEAs have financial obligations that are often based on student enrollment, a procedure was created to reduce

$$SSRC = 1 - \left(0.475 * \frac{\frac{DistrictEWAV}{DistrictRADM}}{\frac{StateEWAV}{StateRADM}}\right)$$

$$SSR = \sqrt{\frac{SSRC^2 + \%PKPOVERTY^2}{2}}$$

FIGURE 39.5. Rhode Island SSRC and SSR Formulas. Source: Rhode Island Department of Education, accessed May 10, 2022, https://www.ride.ri.gov/fundingfinance/fundingsources/stateeducationaid.aspx#32231124-funding-formula-distribution

TABLE 39.2. Total Per-pupil Expenditure Per Rhode Island by LEAs

LEA	Average Daily Membership	Total Per Pupil	LEA	Average Daily Membership	Total Per Pupil
Times 2 Academy	725	$14,541	North Kingstown	3,780	$18,573
Cumberland	4,627	$15,214	E Providence	5,045	$18,831
International Charter School	374	$15,241	Providence	22,919	$19,034
Barrington	3,403	$15,261	Johnston	3,192	$19,184
Southside Elementary Charter	143	$15,716	Chariho Regional	3,179	$19,233
Woonsocket	5,997	$15,816	Learning Community	576	$19,508
Blackstone Academy Charter	355	$15,890	Academy for Career Exploration	173	$19,575
The Hope Academy	213	$15,911	Middletown	2,144	$19,932
East Greenwich	2,563	$16,010	Tiverton	1,751	$19,963
Burrillville	2,230	$16,102	Foster	226	$20,127
Paul Cuffee Charter	818	$16,194	Davies Career & Technical Center	878	$20,162
Beacon Charter School	376	$16,248	Warwick	8,500	$20,591
N Providence	3,598	$16,470	Urban Collab Accelerated Prog	133	$20,815
North Smithfield	1,649	$16,507	Newport	2,139	$20,914
Pawtucket	8,718	$16,542	Nowell Leadership Academy	158	$20,982
N. E. Laborers Career & Const.	164	$16,625	Exeter-W. Greenwich Regional	1,620	$21,011
Coventry	4,501	$16,873	Metropolitan C&TC	786	$21,027
Highlander Charter School	605	$16,949	South Kingstown	2,853	$21,270
RIMA-Blackstone Valley	2,052	$17,013	Scituate	1,184	$21,549
Cranston	10,258	$17,040	Foster-Glocester Regional	1,347	$21,804
The Greene School	196	$17,070	Westerly	2,593	$22,655
Glocester	557	$17,196	Narragansett	1,276	$24,004
Segue Institute	234	$17,229	RISE Prep Mayoral Academy	280	$24,335
Smithfield	2,375	$17,244	Jamestown -Note 1	478	$28,477
Achievement First Mayoral	1,352	$17,266	Trinity Academy	212	$30,175
Portsmouth	2,413	$17,332	The Compass Charter School	197	$33,072
Charette Charter School	122	$17,734	Little Compton - Note 1	230	$35,905
Central Falls	2,836	$18,004	Kingston Hill Academy	239	$37,471
W Warwick	3,581	$18,254	New Shoreham	133	$40,292
Lincoln	3,189	$18,290	RI School for Deaf	79	$99,451
Village Green Virtual Charter	222	$18,444			
RI Nurses Middle Level College	270	$18,526			
Bristol-Warren Regional	3,130	$18,547			

Source: Rhode Island Department of Education, accessed May 10, 2022, Education, accessed May 10, 2022, https://www.ride.ri.gov/fundingfinance/fundingsources/stateeducationaid.aspx#32231124-funding-formula-distribution

the amount of local funding that was required to be sent to the receiving LEA. This procedure allowed funding to follow the student and allowed the sending LEAs to reduce their allocation by the greater of two amounts: 1) seven percent of the local payment rate, or 2) the per pupil value of certain expenses incurred by the sending LEA minus the average per pupil costs for such expenses incurred by all public charter schools.[38] In order to provide some understanding of the allocations, Table 39.2 shows the total per-pupil expenditures.

CATEGORICAL AND OTHER FUNDING

Rhode Island has state categorical education funding. While the categorical aid is only 2.9% of the overall PK-12 education aid provided, the $37.5 million allocated during FY 2022 is important for those programs that receive these funds.[39] There are seven spending categories that are included in the categorical education aid in Rhode Island: 1) early childhood, 2) English language learner, 3) high cost special education, 4) career and technical, 5) regional district transportation, 6) non-public transportation, and 7) school of choice density aid. Each of these categories will be briefly described in the subsequent sections, including the amounts allocated to each category. Figure 39.6 illustrates the Rhode Island categorical education funding during FY 2022. The final subsection is a discussion about funding that has been allocated in Rhode Island for school construction.

Early Childhood

Early childhood education has become of increasing importance in Rhode Island. During FY 2022 categorical funding was provided to create and expand free public pre-kindergarten options. The $14.9 million that was allocated for this specific category represents nearly 40% of the overall categorical funding. These funds were awarded on a three-year cycle, on a competitive basis, with a focus on high-quality pre-kindergarten programming. Additionally, at least 50% of the enrolled students must meet poverty status guidelines.

English Language Learner

The state of Rhode Island categorical education funding provides a portion of the per-pupil costs for English language learners (ELLs) who are in the beginning and intermediate levels of the English language acquisition. The second largest amount of categorical funding disbursed during FY 2022, $5 million, was to support ELLs. EL students are identified in and evaluated annually on the Assessing Comprehension and Communication in English State to State (ACCESS). ELLs who score in the entering, emerging, and developing categories are aid eligible. The amount the LEA receives for ELLs is 10% of the core instruction amount multiplied by the applicable LEA state share ratio.[40] In order for LEAs to receive this categorical funding they must submit a signed set of assurances, and where the amount exceeds $10,000, the state requires a detailed spending plan.

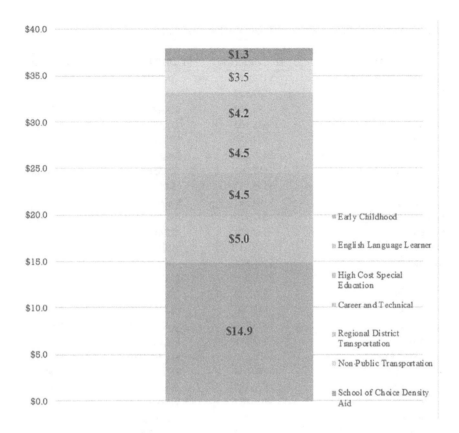

FIGURE 39.6.   State Categorical Education Aid FY 2022 (In millions). Source: Rhode Island Department of Education, accessed May 15, 2022, https://www.ride. ri.gov/fundingfinance/fundingsources/stateeducationaid.aspx#32231124-funding-formula-distribution

High-Cost Special Education

The categorical high-cost special education aid was $4.5 million during FY 2022. This categorical spending amount has remained $4.5 million since FY 2017. Table 39.3 shows the FY 2022 enacted aid for the high-cost special education categorical aid by LEA. There were several LEAs that did not receive any categorical funding in this category, and these were excluded from the table.

Transportation

Rhode Island provides categorical funding for regional district transportation and non-public transportation. The regional school district transportation funds provide 50% of the costs of transportation costs for regional school districts.[41] The

TABLE 39.3.   FY 2022 High-Cost Special Education Aid

LEA	High-Cost Special Ed.Categorical	FY 2022 Enacted Aid	Percentage of Enacted Aid
Barrington	$159,283	$8,232,393	1.69%
Burrillville	$82,527	$13,994,929	0.59%
Central Falls	$4,982	$48,422,397	0.01%
Chariho	$58,163	$1,847,937	3.15%
Coventry	$24,830	$24,191,219	0.10%
Cranston	$317,133	$69,876,885	0.45%
Cumberland	$17,393	$20,556,190	0.08%
East Greenwich	$145,133	$4,542,049	3.20%
East Providence	$304,592	$36,956,352	0.82%
Foster	$32,419	$1,106,412	2.93%
Glocester	$47,354	$2,481,208	1.91%
Jamestown	$47,241	$339,230	13.93%
Johnston	$198,886	$19,970,936	1.00%
Lincoln	$196,769	$16,231,922	1.21%
Middletown	$37,958	$8,185,474	0.46%
Narragansett	$18,364	$2,196,991	0.84%
New Shoreham	$25,178	$237,000	10.62%
Newport	$43,208	$15,005,286	0.29%
North Kingstown	$79,635	$11,302,964	0.70%
North Providence	$256,548	$27,298,296	0.94%
North Smithfield	$52,385	$6,372,462	0.82%
Pawtucket	$101,187	$96,013,908	0.11%
Portsmouth	$128,011	$3,800,556	3.37%
Providence	$348,934	$277,047,845	0.13%
Scituate	$123,423	$2,535,612	4.87%
Smithfield	$41,189	$7,085,403	0.58%
South Kingstown	$94,436	$4,969,168	1.90%
Tiverton	$120,762	$6,896,308	1.75%
Warwick	$730,676	$40,271,671	1.81%
West Warwick	$20,533	$30,945,717	0.07%
Westerly	$141,179	$8,083,721	1.75%
Woonsocket	$58,991	$70,423,976	0.08%
Bristol Warren Regional	$151,924	$13,130,078	1.16%
Exeter-W. Green Regional	$167,989	$5,468,643	3.07%
Foster-Glocester	$112,667	$5,763,335	1.95%
Blackstone Valley Prep	$232	$22,042,140	0.00%
Learning Community	$5,746	$7,552,355	0.08%
Paul Cuffee	$2,140	$9,880,237	0.02%

Source: Rhode Island Department of Education, accessed May 18, 2022, https://www.ride.ri.gov/fundingfinance/fundingsources/stateeducationaid.aspx

state also covers the costs for non-public transportation for out-of-district partici-pants in the statewide transportation system- special education transportation is excluded from these costs. The total amount for both categories of transportation was $7.7 million for FY 2022.

Career and Technical Education

There are state-run and charter-run career and technical schools in Rhode Is-land. These schools receive additional categorical education aid. During FY 2022 the state provided $4.5 million in categorical aid to career and technical programs. These categorical funds are utilized by LEAs to pay for a portion of the per-pupil costs of these high-cost programs, additionally this aid may also pay for the costs for the development of new career and technical programs.

In order for the career and technical education programs to receive Rhode Is-land state education funding the program must be approved through the state's application and approval process. The amount of funding is based on a per-pupil expenditure three-year average conducted by the Rhode Island Office of State-wide Efficiencies.

School of Choice Density Aid

The final and smallest amount of categorical education funding aid is called school of choice density aid. This funding is available for LEAs in which at least 5% of the student population is enrolled in a public school of choice.

SCHOOL CONSTRUCTION

In Rhode Island the significant costs of school construction are shared by the LEAs and the state government. Similar to the way the funding formula is equi-ty-centered, LEAs in communities with lower property wealth, receive a higher percentage of construction costs from the state. As an example, during FY 2021 reimbursement ratios in Rhode Island LEAs ranged from 35% for 18 municipali-ties to 96.7% in Central Falls where approximately 40% of the student population is identified as economically disadvantaged.

The need to make changes to funding school construction projects were identi-fied in the 2017 task force report. The report found that school construction spend-ing was insufficient to address the current and future deficiencies in Rhode Island schools. In 2018 the General Assembly authorized a $250 million general obliga-tion school construction bond, which voters approved. Since 2018 when the new system of school construction financing was implemented, over $1 billion in new construction projects have been approved by the RIDE. During FY 2022 LEAs received $80 million for completed school construction projects.

CHARTER SCHOOL FUNDING

There are 23 charter schools operating in Rhode Island. While the number of charter schools has remained relatively the same for more than a decade, student enrollment in charter schools over the same period has increased 170%.[42] As previously discussed, central to the Rhode Island funding formula is the principle that funding follows the student. Because charter schools do not have a municipality to provide direct support, the local funds those schools receive is determined by a local share calculation. The local share amount is calculated by the RIDE. Therefore, the per pupil funding amount for a student attending a charter school is the same as a student attending a district public school.[43]

NONPUBLIC SCHOOL FUNDING

Parents of students from pre-kindergarten to grade 12 students have two options for nonpublic school attendance: 1) private school, or 2) homeschool. There are 172 private schools serving approximately 22,000 students in Rhode Island.[44] The state of Rhode Island does not provide funding or reimbursement for private schools. In the document. "Rhode Island Non-Public School Requirements," it states, "There is no state policy at this time."[45] RIDE "does not directly supervise home instruction [home schooling]."[46] Those Rhode Island citizens who would like to homeschool their personal children must contact the LEA where they live to receive approval to provide home instruction.

VIRTUAL EDUCATION

The growth of virtual and distance education has grown significantly in Rhode Island since the COVID-19 pandemic halted in-person schooling in March 2020. Similar to what occurred in most states, during the pandemic Rhode Island schools shifted to online/virtual schooling. However, prior to the closing of schools in March 2020, the state of Rhode Island had a number of virtual public and private schools and a comprehensive statewide computer science initiative called, Computer Science for Rhode Island.

FEDERAL COVID-19 FUNDING

Federal funding is a relatively small portion of the overall education funding aid in Rhode Island. Over the last few decades, federal education funding in Rhode Island has declined, until the COVID-19 pandemic and the influx of $581.5 million in federal funding approved through the Elementary and Secondary School Emergency Relief (ESSER) fund. ESSER funds were allocated through three acts: 1) Coronavirus Aid, Relief, and Economic Security (CARES) Act, 2) the Coronavirus Response and Relief Supplemental Appropriations (CRRSA) Act, and 3) the American Rescue Plan (ARP) Act. Table 39.4 illustrates the funding received through CARES, CRRSA, and ARP.

TABLE 39.4. Federal ESSER Funds Allocated to Rhode Island

Source	Date	Funding Amount
CARES Act	March 2020	$41.7 million
CRRSA Act	December 2020	$166.3 million
ARPA Act	March 2021	$373.5 million

Source: Rhode Island Department of Education, accessed May 18, 2022, https://www.ride.ri.gov/InsideRIDE/AdditionalInformation/News/ViewArticle/tabid/408/ArticleId/742/RIDE-Submits-ARP-ESSER-State-Plan-Application-to-U-S-Department-of-Education.aspx

The first round of federal ESSER funding through the CARES Act was utilized "to purchase technology to support online learning, and administrative planning during long-term school closures."[47] As Rhode Island schools transitioned from online learning to returning to in school learning, the state plan articulated utilizing ESSER funding to realize the following priorities: 1) return to in-person learning, 2) safely reopen school and sustain safe operations, 3) support the students who were impacted the most by the pandemic, 4) attend to the academic impact, 5) invest in learning outside the regular school year, 6) expand the 21st Century Community Learning Center afterschool programming, and 7) support the mental health needs of staff and students.[48]

The disruptions in schools due to the COVID-19 pandemic were extreme. One severe outcome of the pandemic was a steep decline in student enrollment. From the student count in October 2019 to October 2021 student enrollment had declined nearly 4% in Rhode Island.[49] Because of this reality and the potential impact on school funding, the state enacted a "hold harmless" provision. This provision allowed the use of the greater RADM in calculating the total foundation costs and LEAs' SSF enrollment was calculated using the higher percentage of the overall RADM. Finally, Governor McKee proposed budget for FY 2023 extends the hold harmless provision to ensure that LEAs receive at least as much state aid as FY 2022.

ENDNOTES

[1] I would like to acknowledge the work of Ken Wagner in crafting the chapter for the first edition of this work.

[2] "Rhode Island," History.com, accessed May 1, 2022https://www.history.com/topics/us-states/rhode-island#:~:text=Despite%20its%20small%20area%2C%20Rhode,separation%20of%20church%20and%20state.

[3] Wagner, K. Rhode Island, in Funding Public Schools in the United States and Indian Country. Thompson, D., Wood, C.R, and Neuenswander., C.S., Eds. Charlotte, NC: Information Age Publishing, Incorporated, 2019.

[4] R.I. Const. art. XII, § 1

[5] R.I. Const. art. XII, § 2

[6] R.I. Const. art. XII, § 3

[7] R.I. Const. art. XII, § 4

8   City of Pawtucket v. Sundlun, Nos. 94-199-Appeal, Nos. 94-203-M.P., (Supreme Court of Rhode Island, 1995)

9   Ibid.

10 "Census: Rhode Island Profile," accessed May 4, 2022, https://www2.census.gov/geo/maps/dc10_thematic/2010_Profile/2010_Profile_Map_Rhode_Island.pdf

11 "RIDE Dashboard Stats," Rhode Island Department of Education, access May 2, 2022, https://www.ride.ri.gov/studentsfamilies/ripublicschools/schooldistricts.aspx

12 Ibid

13 Ibid.

14 Ibid

15 Wong, Kenneth K. "The Design of the Rhode Island School Funding Formula: Developing New Strategies on Equity and Accountability." Peabody Journal of Education 88, no. 1 (2013): 37–47. https://doi.org/10.1080/0161956X.2013.752638.

16 Ibid.

17 Ibid.

18 Ibid.

19 Ibid.

20 "Funding Formula Working Group," Accessed May 10, 2022, https://www.ride.ri.gov/Funding-Finance/FundingSources/StateEducationAid/FundingFormulaWorkingGroup.aspx#332360-meeting-materials

21 Ibid.

22 "Rhode Island's Funding Formula After Ten Years: Education Finance in the Ocean State," RIPEC, April 2022.

23 Hanson, M. "U.S. Public Education Spending Statistics" EducationData.org, accessed March 15, 2022, https://educationdata.org/public-education-spending-statistics

24 "Rhode Island Public Expenditure Council Releases Education Finance Report," April 27, 2022, Rhode Island Public Expenditure Council.

25 Rhode Island State Constitution, Article VI, Section 3.

26 "Rhode Island General Assembly," accessed May 10, 2022, https://ballotpedia.org/Rhode_Island_General_Assembly

27 "Rhode Island Voter Registration," Rhode Island Department of State, accessed May 10, 2022, https://datahub.sos.ri.gov/RegisteredVoter.aspx

28 National Education Association Rhode Island, accessed on May 10, 2022, https://www.neari.org/About/About-Overview

29 Rhode Island Federation of Teacher and Health Professionals, accessed on May 10, 2022, https://www.rifthp.org/home

30 Ibid.

31 Education Law Center, accessed May 15, 2022, https://edlawcenter.org/litigation/states/rhodeisland.html

32 Ibid.

33 Ibid.

34 Ibid.

35 Ibid.

36 Ibid.

37 R.I. Senate, "Special Legislative Task Force to Study Rhode Island's Education Funding Formula: Findings and Recommendations," January 28, 2020.

38 Ibid.

39 Ibid.

40 Ibid.

41 Ibid.

42 Skousen, Jacob D. "Rhode Island." Journal of Education Finance, 47, no. 5 (2022). https://www.nationaledfinance.com/docs/35_Jef_47.5_Rhode_Island.pdf

43 Infante-Green, A. "Funding Formula Reference Guide," Rhode Island Department of Education, 2018.

44 "Best Rhode Island Private Schools," accessed May 23, 2022, https://www.privateschoolreview.com/rhode-island

45 ""Rhode Island Non-Public School Requirements," accessed May 22, 2022, https://www.ride.ri.gov/Portals/0/Uploads/Documents/Students-and-Families-Great-Schools/Educational-Programming/Non-Public_Schools/NP%20Guidelines%20Website.pdf#PublicAid

46 "Home Schooling," accessed May 22, 2022, https://www.ride.ri.gov/studentsfamilies/education-programs/homeschooling.aspx#1722851-can-a-home-schooled-student-go-to-a-4-year-college-afterwards

47 Skousen, Jacob D. "Rhode Island." Journal of Education Finance 46, no. 3 (2021): 110.

48 "Learning, Equity, & Accelerated Pathways (LEAP) Task Force Report," Rhode Island Department of Education, July 2021, accessed May 23, 2022. https://www.ride.ri.gov/InsideRIDE/AdditionalInformation/LEAPTaskForce.aspx

49 Ibid.

CHAPTER 40

SOUTH CAROLINA

Mazen Aziz

University of South Carolina

Henry Tran

University of South Carolina

GENERAL BACKGROUND

The Colonial Period—Private and Voluntary Education

The early immigrants in South Carolina, who came from England, believed that education was a private and personal issue. The prosperous among them paid for their children's enrollment in private and church schools or employed private tutors to help them[1]. There was little public assistance for the colony's most fortunate children during this time. The Society for Propagation of the Gospel in Foreign Parts, a London-based organization created to convert indigenous and black people within the colonies to Christianity[2], began African slave education in 1701.

The 1800s—Free Schools

The South Carolina General Assembly passed approximately 750 Acts and Joint Resolutions throughout the 1800s, the most noteworthy of which was the new school legislation of 1811, which was the first statute to create "free schools"

Funding Public Schools in the United States, Indian Country,
and US Territories (Second Edition), pages 623–635.
Copyright © 2023 by Information Age Publishing
www.infoagepub.com

throughout the state[3]. Its goal was to put a public school in its forty-four electoral districts. The law allocated $300 per state representative to each district[4]. According to the Report and Resolutions of the General Assembly of the South Carolina legislature, the state had 869 free schools and 9187 pupils registered throughout several districts and parishes by 1841. The newly updated South Carolina State Constitution of 1868 established the Office of Superintendent of Education. It authorized the introduction of a new "school tax" and a "poll tax" to fund free public schools[5]. The South Carolina joint assembly approved a joint resolution authorizing $25,000 for public schools the following year, in 1869. These monies were allocated according to the number of students enrolled[6].

On February 3, 1870, the same general order passed another resolution, restoring back pay to teachers and settling a legal misunderstanding between teachers and county school commissioners (i.e., claim reimbursement due date leading instructors not to file claim reimbursements on time). A statewide comprehensive "School Law" was approved in the same year, establishing a State Board of Education with County Commissioners, Board of Examiners, and School Trustees, overseen by a State Superintendent of Education. The law defined tasks and responsibilities and set aside $50,000 for teacher salary, based on a daily rate of 5 cents per student's attendance[7].

The legislature appropriated $7000 for the establishment of a uniform system of school records and blank forms to be used by offices and teachers of the free common schools throughout the state, enacted a "school tax" on all taxable property[8] for the support and maintenance of all free common schools, amended acts to increase teacher salaries based on certification[9], and levied poll taxes on each man between the ages of 21 and 65 for the general public school fund across the state[10]. The legislature stated that there were 281,801 kids enrolled in public schools across the state by the turn of the century.

The 1900s—Addressing Race and Gender Disparities

In the 1900s, there was an increasing acknowledgment of race and gender disparities in both per-pupil expenditures and teacher pay. Average per-pupil expenditures in white schools stood at $14.94 compared to $1.86 for black ones. The annual average wage for black male teachers was $133 and $107 for black female teachers compared to $610 and $322 for their white counterparts in the 1913-14 academic year. Adult education classes were introduced in the 1920s as the state dealt with low reading test scores among its World War II military recruits. Reduced funding, pay cuts, divestment in capital initiatives, and shorter school semesters ushered in the 1930s economic downturn. In the 1940s, the inequities above persisted, with per-pupil funding for white schools being more than double that of black schools, at $111 compared to $50. The average compensation for white teachers was $643 greater than black teachers ($2,057 vs. $1,414).

Furthermore, the property values of white schools were more than five times higher than those of black schools, averaging $68.4 million vs. $12.9 million.

Finally, whites spent $2.4 million on transportation compared to $184,000 for blacks. The state of South Carolina spent $100 million in the 1950s and 1960s, around the time of the landmark U.S Supreme Court decision *Brown vs. Board of Education of Topeka*, to build 200 black and 70 white schools, improve 250 existing ones for both races, and provide school transportation for its black students, all to avoid desegregation. By the early 1970s, state spending on schools had risen to $300 million, with the sales tax taking on the majority of the revenue-generating burden compared to property taxes and federal desegregation assistance coming in through programs like the Elementary Secondary Education Act (ESEA) of 1965. The "Education Finance Act (EFA)" of 1977, which provided $100 million to the state's educational system over five years and tied spending to a predetermined standard, marked the end of this decade. The Education Improvement Act (EIA) of 1984, which included a one-cent sales tax increase, contributed an additional $217 million in financing during the decade.

The 2000s—Accountability, Efficiency, and Teacher Quality

Accountability, efficiency, and teacher quality marked a transition in the 1990s and 2000s. The federal No Child Left Behind Act (NCLB) of 2001, for example, was passed in 2001. To address the persistent teacher shortage problem in the state, the South Carolina Center for Teacher Recruitment (which began operations in 1980) evolved into CERRA, the Center for Education Recruitment, Retention, and Advancement. There was also a growing awareness of the injustice created by differences in conditions and educational possibilities experienced by pupils across the state, culminating in the state's school funding litigation, *Abbeville vs. the State of South Carolina*. The lawsuit was filed by the state's most rural, underperforming, and destitute districts, who claimed that the state was underfunding them[11].

BASIC SUPPORT PROGRAM

The Education Finance Act is South Carolina's primary educational support program (EFA). It was adopted in 1977 and represents the state's foundation education funding program, allocating $1.8 billion in state cash to school and local operations. According to the statute, the state will support an average of 70% of the foundation program's costs, with local school districts covering the remaining 30%. However, each district's contribution will differ, with state funding adjusting accordingly because of what they are expected to leverage from their local property tax wealth (i.e., defined by their "index of taxpaying ability") and their weighted pupil units. Districts with lesser tax-generating capacity receive more state assistance, whereas districts with higher tax-generating capacity receive less than.[12]

For the current fiscal year (i.e., 2021), the base student cost is $2,489 per pupil, with the total pupil count projected to be 764,037. The average state per-pupil funding is projected to be $6,902, $1,202 from federal, and $7,423 local. This is an average total funding level of $15,527, excluding revenues of local bond is-

TABLE 40.1. Revenue Codes, Classifications, and Weighting of Non-Special Needs Children*

Revenue Code	Program Code	Classification	Weighting Factor (WF)
3311	K	Kindergarten	1.00
3312	P	Primary	1.00
3313	EL	Elementary	1.00
3314	HS	High School	1.00
3332	HIAC	High Achieving	.15
3334	LEP	Limited English Proficiency	.20
3351	ACAS	Academic Assistance	.15
3352	PIP	Pupils in Poverty	.20
3353	DUAL	Dual Credit Enrollment	.15

https://ed.sc.gov/finance/financial-services/manual-handbooks-and-guidelines/funding-manuals/fiscal-year-2020-2021-funding-manual/

sues[13]. Beyond the EFA, districts also receive funding from other sources, including the Education Improvement Act (EIA) of 1984, which provides categorical funding for specific programs or initiatives designed to improve student achievement[14]. Table 40.1 lists the weights per non-special needs classification.

TRANSPORTATION

South Carolina Department of Education owned and operated one of the largest and oldest school transportation fleets (5621 buses) in the nation in the year 2021[15]. The S.C. Superintendent of Education announced a $24.54 Million investment in school buses and public transportation. $23,635,830 for 235 propane school buses[16].

CAPITAL OUTLAY AND DEBT SERVICE

The annual debt service on general obligation debt in South Carolina is normally limited to 5% of the preceding fiscal year's general state revenue, according to the state constitution. School bonds (for constructing, improving, equipping, renovating, and repairing school buildings or other school facilities and/or for the land to construct the facilities) and State's School Facilities bonds (to assist districts in providing educational facilities)[17] are two of the five types of bonds that are subject to this limit. The monies from the Public-School Facilities Assistance Act of 1996 are utilized to build permanent school teaching facilities and purchase fixed equipment (e.g., cost of construction, improvement, enlargement, and renovation of school facilities).

South Carolina's Capital Reserve Fund (CRF) equates to 2% of the state's general fund revenue ($176,095,044,for FY 2020-2021 and $183,584,490 for FY

2021-22) and can be used for capital improvements or nonrecurring projects if there is no year-end deficit[18][19]. The state allocates reimbursements to school districts for approved capital projects based on the needs and financial abilities of the school district. Funding can come from general funds, the Education Improvement Act (EIA), the Education Lottery, and funds from Children's Education Endowment Funds[20].

TEACHER RETIREMENT

The South Carolina Retirement System (SCRS) was established in July of 1945 as a defined benefits plan that provides retirement and other related benefits for teachers and state employees. In 1987, the state introduced its defined contribution plan, known as the State Optional Retirement System (PORS), for members not participating in SCRS. Funding for the retirement benefits derives from the balance of investment income as well as employee and employer contributions[21].

Beginning in the academic year 1998-99, school district employer contribution of the state retirement (as well as funds for group life insurance, social security, and health insurance) are allocated to school districts monthly in accordance with the Education Finance Act[22]. The retirement benefit amount is based on an individual's years of service, age, and compensation.

South Carolina politicians proactively implemented reforms to SCRS following the global stock market meltdown in 2008-2009 to ensure long-term sustainability. Employee contribution rates for SCRS were increased and capped in 2016 by the legislature. Employer contribution rates for SCRS have been increased to 13.56 percent, with annual increments of 1.0 percent scheduled through 7/1/22, resulting in employer rates of 18.56 percent[23].

In 2019, a national analysis of the incomes of K-12 public school teachers found a 19 percent pay difference when compared to comparable private-sector jobs[24]. At the same time, teacher benefits, such as pensions, help to close the gap, allowing states to attract and retain highly educated educators by reducing the overall pay disparity to 10%. When compared to other college graduates in employment in South Carolina, teachers earn 13.4 percent less[25].

Teacher turnover comes at a considerable cost to the school district, both financially and in terms of lost productivity. In comparison to individual defined contribution (DC) accounts, defined benefit (DB) pensions help to keep highly productive teachers on the job for longer. For example, 7.9% of South Carolina teachers on average leave the profession. However, 530 of the state's teachers are retained each year due to DB pension. This creates an average savings of $2.8 to $6.1 million saving in reduced teacher turnover across that states many districts[26]

SPECIAL EDUCATION

The South Carolina Department of Education (SCDE) is required by the Individuals with Disabilities Education Act (IDEA) (PL 108-446) and Education Department General Administration Regulation (EDGAR) to monitor local education agencies, charter schools, and state-operated programs to ensure fiscal compliance with state and federal laws, regulations policies and procedures that govern the provision of special education and related services to appropriately identified children[27]. Funding for special education is included in the state's primary funding formula, is weighted per pupil for students who are more expensive to educate, and is based on the cumulative 135-day average daily membership of each school district by program classification[28]. Table 40.2 lists the weights per special needs classification.

Funding formula for EFA appropriations:

District Allocation Formula =
(district WPU x BSC) – (state WPU x BSC x index x .3)

- *District WPU* is calculated by multiplying average daily membership (ADM) for each student classification by its' respective weighted factor (WF).
- *State WPU* is calculated by taking the difference between the districts' foundation program total cost and its' required local support.

TABLE 40.2. Revenue Codes, Classifications, and Weighting of special Needs Children

Revenue Code	Program Code	Classification	Weighting Factor (WF)
3331	AU	Autism	
3324	HH	Hearing Handicapped	2.57
3325	VH	Visually Handicapped	
3315	TM	Trainable Mentally Handicapped	
3321	EH	Emotionally Handicapped	2.04
3326	OH	Orthopedically Handicapped	
3322	EM	Educable Mentally Handicapped	
3323	LD	Learning Disabilities	1.74
3316	SP	Speech Handicap	1.90
3317	HO	Homebound	1.00

Method of Determining Student count: The cumulative 135-day ADM (average daily membership) of each school district by program classification
- ADM: Average daily membership
- WPU: Weighted pupil units
- BSC: Base student cost

https://ed.sc.gov/finance/financial-services/manual-handbooks-and-guidelines/funding-manuals/fiscal-year-2020-2021-funding-manual/

- *Index* The district's index of taxpaying ability is the district's relative fiscal capacity compared to that of all other districts in the State, based on the full market value of all taxable property of the district.

COMPENSATORY EDUCATION

The state of South Carolina defines compensatory education programs as those which "*serve the most severe cases of educational deprivation not classified as handicapped*" The state gives priority to students in grades 1-6 and those scoring below the 25th percentile on the Comprehensive Test of Basic Skills (CTBS) and prescribes an add-on weight for Compensatory education of 0.39. Each student in the state is counted in one of the main classifications and if deemed needing compensatory education, is counted additionally under the compensatory weight[29].

GIFTED AND TALENTED EDUCATION

Additional funding for personalized instruction for gifted and talented pupils is weighted at 0.15 in the state of South Carolina. The state classifieds gifted and talented students as "*students who are classified as academically or artistically gifted and talented or who are enrolled in Advanced Placement (AP) and International Baccalaureate (IB) courses in high school.*[30]" And specifies that districts should set aside 12 percent of their funds for the purpose of these students. The state also specifies that the department of education (SDE) could expend up to $500,000 of its' EIA funding for the support of gifted and talented teacher endorsements and professional developments[31].

BILINGUAL EDUCATION

Title III is part of the Elementary and Secondary Education Act of 1965 (ESEA) and its' purpose is to help English learners attain English language proficiency to meet academic standards. The state's department of education oversees language instruction for limited-English proficient and immigrant students through the Title III program. It does so by administering grants, recommending policy, promoting best practices, strengthening collaboration between federal, state, and local programs, and monitoring funded programs for accountability[32]. The state funds bilingual education through its primary funding formula[33]. The limited English proficiency classification is weighted at .20[34].

FUNDING OF CHARTER SCHOOLS

Charter Schools became an option for students in South Carolina in 1996 as a result of the South Carolina Charter Schools Act of 1996[35]. Charter schools can be authorized by a traditional school district, the South Carolina Public Charter School District (SCPCSD) that was created in 2006, or a higher education institute. Charter schools in the SCPCSD or an institute of higher education sponsored charter schools to receive state revenue from EFA and EIA funds, but not local tax revenue. For example, 13.7% of EIA funds (i.e., $ 126,461,481) in 2021-22 went to the SC public charter school district[36]. Because local money does not follow the child in SC, dollars are appropriated through an annual budget proviso for charter school funding. The charter schools chartered by SCPCSD and higher education institutions receive $3,870 per weighted pupil for students in physical schools and $2,043 per student for those enrolled in virtual charter schools[37]. They must make annual budget requests to the legislature to receive funding from the General Assembly. Locally sponsored charter schools are able to benefit from local funds and receive funding according to the same formula as local school districts. However, neither locally sponsored charters nor those sponsored by the SCPCSD receive transportation or facility funds (except for conversion charters and a few that negotiated with a district board). In contrast, traditional public schools receive the benefits of all the aforementioned funds.

Charter schools have access to tax-exempt financing of facilities through the South Carolina Jobs-Economic Development Authority. In addition, the state department of education must make available, upon request from an existing charter school or charter school applicant, a list of vacant and unused portions of buildings that are owned by school districts in the state and that may be suitable for the operation of a charter school. The owner of a building on the list is not required to sell or lease the building or a portion of the building to a charter school. However, if a school district declares a building surplus and chooses to sell or lease the building, a charter school's board of directors or a charter committee operating or applying within the district must be given the first refusal to purchase or lease the building under the same or better terms and conditions as it would be offered to the public. Charter schools are exempt from state and local taxation, except the sales tax, on their earnings and property whether owned or leased.

Charter schools also have access to low-interest loans through the Charter School Facility Revolving Loan Program for costs related to the construction, purchase, renovation, and maintenance of charter school facilities[38].

OTHER CATEGORICAL PROGRAMS

Categorical or unrestricted funds are allocated for specific purposes. These funds are both state and Federal government funded. The guiding principle in the generation of such funds is student average daily attendance (ADA)[39].

STATE AID FOR PRIVATE K-12 SCHOOLS

Although public funding of private schools is prohibited by South Carolina's constitution under *S.C Const. Art. 11, sec. 7,* and no financial assistance is available for private school attendance[40], private schools catering to the needs of high-poverty students are eligible to compete for the 21st Century Community Learning Centers Programs (Title IV, 21st Century Schools). These funds are assigned to state educational agencies which award the funds on a competitive basis to eligible organizations[41]. South Carolina's supreme court ruled against its governor proposing to use federal coronavirus relief funding in his attempt to create a private school grant program in 2020. The program would have given qualified students at participating private, parochial, or independent schools in South Carolina one-time, need-based awards of up to $6,500 to support or subsidize their tuition in 2020-21. $5,000 grants were expected to be funded[42].

EARLY CHILDHOOD EDUCATION

The Early Childhood Development and Academic Assistance Act of 1993 (Act 135) designates funds appropriated for half-day programs for four-year-olds and is based on the number of kindergarten children who are eligible for free and reduced lunch under the federal free lunch program, with a stipulation that no district receive less than 90 percent of the amount it received in the prior fiscal year. Early Childhood Assistance also receives a .26 add-on weight in the state's Education Finance Act appropriation formula.

In FY 2017-18, 6% of EIA funds (i.e., $ 59,208,178) were allocated to 4K public schools[43]. The state also appropriated $33.9 million to expand at-risk 4k programs to every school district in the state. The program was introduced as a pilot program in the annual budget proviso in 2006 for children in the plaintiff district of the *Abbeville County School District et al. vs. South Carolina* court case and the program was codified by law in 2014[44]. Funds are first provided for eligible children in the plaintiff trial districts, then to the remaining plaintiff districts in the lawsuit, and finally to eligible children in districts with poverty index > 90%[45].

According to the Education Oversight Committee, 4K enrollment jumped by 47%, or 4,600 children, with 50 new private, nonprofit, and faith-based providers opening 66 new 4K classrooms. There are 120 new 4K classrooms in public schools. Moreover, according to a poll conducted by First Steps, two out of every three parents reported that enrolling their kid in a First Steps 4K allowed them to work or further their education.

LOCAL SCHOOL REVENUE

Known as "State Aid to Subdivisions," the state of South Carolina collected eleven local taxes, ranging from income to alcohol, on behalf of local governments from the early to mid-1900s. These funds were collected locally but routed to the state treasurer to be processed to local governments on calculations for each tax. No uniform collection method existed for these 11 taxes as some would be diverted to the state's general fund when the state was in need while the rest would be redistributed based on statutory formulas.

Inconsistent tax formulas, flattening taxes, and revenue stagnation as compared to the overall economies in the 1980s greatly restricted local governments from effectively planning for expenditures and budgetary needs. Responding to this crisis the General Assembly relying on suggestions from the SC Advisory Commission on Intergovernmental Relations (SC ACIR), proposed the establishment of a "Local Government Fund."

Revenue from a simplified list of seven taxes, banks, beer, wine, gasoline, motor transport, alcohol (mini bottle), and income taxes, would directly go to the state general fund and instead of direct funding from these sources, local governments would receive 4.5% of the previous years (i.e., 1991) revenue from the same sources. Per the new law, these funds would be set aside before any other spending commitments are made to ensure consistent revenue streams for local governments.

The share was also split 83.278 for county and 16.722 for municipal governments and the funds would be distributed quarterly by the state treasurer to cities and counties. These distributions are based on a per capita basis based on the last census figures; each city/town would receive funds based on its percentage of municipal population[46]. The local per-pupil revenue for the state was $7,423 in the fiscal year 2021-22[47].

TAX CREDITS, DEDUCTIONS, AND EXEMPTIONS

Educational tax credits, deductions, and exemptions can be found in the South Carolina sales and use tax manual under the "Educational Exemptions Categories. Table 40.3 lists these exemptions code sections and descriptions.

TABLE 40.3. Revenue Codes, Classifications, and Weighting of Non-Special Needs Children

Code Section	Description
12-36-2120(3)	Textbooks, books, magazines, periodicals, newspapers and access to online information used in a course of study or for use in a school or public library. These items may be in printed form or in alternative forms such as microfilm or CD ROM. Certain communication services and equipment subject to tax under South Carolina Code §§12-36-910(B)(3) and 12-36-1310(B)(3) are not exempt.
12-36-2120(8)	Newspapers, newsprint paper and South Carolina Department of Agriculture Market Bulletin
12-36-2120(10)(a)	Meals or food used in furnishing meals to students in schools (not for profit)
12-36-2120(26)	Television, radio and cable TV supplies, equipment, machinery, and electricity
12-36-2120(27)	Zoo plants and animals
12-36-2120(27)	Zoo plants and animals

https://dor.sc.gov/resources-site/lawandpolicy/Documents/SC_Sales_and_Use_Tax_Manual_2017.pdf

EARMARKED STATE REVENUES

South Carolina allocated 47% of its general fund, just over $3.4 billion for education in the Fiscal year 2021-22. Specifically, the state appropriated $ $5,369,868,859 for K-12 educational expenditures. The budget also earmarked $ 13,900,000 in South Carolina Education Lottery certified surplus dollar, of the total $537,150,000, to create Education Savings Accounts[48].

FEDERAL COVID-19 FUNDING

On March 27, 2020, the Coronavirus Aid, Relief, and Economic Security Act (CARES Act) was signed into law. It delivers more than $2 trillion in direct economic aid to workers, families, small companies, state and local governments, and American industries while preserving employment. The CARES Act includes several financial sources, including the Coronavirus Relief Fund, the Governor's Emergency Education Relief Fund, the Elementary and Secondary School Emergency Relief Fund, and the Higher Education Emergency Relief Fund[49].

The Coronavirus Aid and Economic Security Act (CARES Act) provided significant relief to children and educators severely impacted by the Novel Coronavirus Disease (COVID-19). The US Department of Education (USED) awarded a grant to the South Carolina Department of Education (SCDE) under the Elementary and Secondary School Emergency Relief (ESSER) Fund to provide local educational agencies (LEAs) with emergency relief funds to address the impact that COVID–19 has had and continues to have on elementary and secondary schools in South Carolina. This entailed both continuing to provide educational services, such as remote learning, when schools and campuses are closed and formulating and implementing strategies for restoring normal operations[50].

Governor's Emergency Education Relief Fund

Funds for educational establishments included the Governor's Emergency Education Relief Fund, the Elementary and Secondary School Emergency Relief Fund, and the Higher Education Emergency Relief Fund. The Governor's Emergency Education Relief Fund provided $2.95 billion for governors to give emergency assistance through grants to local educational agencies and institutions of higher education most substantially impacted by COVID-19; funds were awarded at the Governor's discretion. South Carolina's contribution is $48 million[51].

Elementary and Secondary School Emergency Relief Fund

The Elementary and Secondary School Emergency Relief Fund included $13 billion for state educational agencies to meet COVID-19 expenditures; grants are provided at the discretion of the Superintendent of Education. The state contributed $216 million[52].

Higher Education Emergency Relief Fund

Higher education institutions received $13 billion from the Higher Education Emergency Relief Fund to cover costs incurred because of COVID-19-related changes in instructional delivery. Fifty percent had to be utilized to offer students emergency financial aid (food, housing, course materials, technology, childcare, and healthcare). Grants were granted to the institutions directly. South Carolina is responsible for $185 million of the total[53].

ENDNOTES

[1] http://www.carolana.com/SC/Education/History_of_South_Carolina_Schools_Virginia_B_Bartels.pdf

[2] Birnie, C. W. (1927). Education of the Negro in Charleston, South Carolina, Prior to the Civil War. The Journal of Negro History, 12(1), 13-21.

[3] http://www.carolana.com/SC/Education/sc_education_1800s.html

[4] The Statutes at Large of South Carolina—Volume V, Pages 639-641

[5] http://www.carolana.com/SC/Legislators/Documents/Reports_and_Resolutions_of_the_General_Assembly_of_South_Carolina_1841.pdf

[6] http://www.carolana.com/SC/Legislators/Documents/Acts_and_Joint_Resolutions_of_the_General_Assembly_of_the_State_of_South_Carolina_1868_1869.pdf

[7] http://www.carolana.com/SC/Legislators/Documents/Acts_and_Joint_Resolutions_of_the_General_Assembly_of_the_State_of_South_Carolina_1869_1870.pdf

[8] http://www.carolana.com/SC/Legislators/Documents/Acts_and_Joint_Resolutions_of_the_General_Assembly_of_the_State_of_South_Carolina_1871_1872.pdf

[9] http://www.carolana.com/SC/Legislators/Documents/Acts_and_Joint_Resolutions_of_the_General_Assembly_of_the_State_of_South_Carolina_1890.pdf

[10] http://www.carolana.com/SC/Legislators/Documents/Acts_and_Joint_Resolutions_of_the_General_Assembly_of_the_State_of_South_Carolina_1900.pdf

[11] http://www.carolana.com/SC/Education/History_of_South_Carolina_Schools_Virginia_B_Bartels.pdf

[12] SC Revenue and Fiscal Affairs Office, figure 189D, retrieved from http://rfa.sc.gov/files/Funding%20for%20Public%20Education%20-%20Trends%20and%20Observations%208-30-17.pdf).

[13] 13https://www.scstatehouse.gov/query.php?search=DOC&searchtext=per%20pupil&category=BUDGET&year=2021&version_id=7&return_page=&version_title=Appropriation%20Act&conid=36960838&result_pos=0&keyval=46335&numrows=10

[14] 14 Tran (2016). Taking the mystery out of South Carolina School Finance. NCPEA Press.

[15] https://www.wyff4.com/article/235-new-propane-fueled-school-buses-coming-to-south-carolina/36109560#

[16] https://governor.sc.gov/news/2021-04/gov-mcmaster-superintendent-spearman-scdoi-director-farmer-announce-2454-million

[17] South Carolina State Treasury, 2022, https://treasurer.sc.gov/media/82042/annual-state-debt-report-june-30-2020.pdf

[18] https://www.admin.sc.gov/budget/faq#:~:text=The%20Capital%20Reserve%20Fund%20(CRF,used%20to%20replenish%20the%20GRF.

[19] https://www.nationaledfinance.com/docs/36.1_Jef_47.5_SouthCarolina.pdf

[20] 2017-18 Appropriation Act—Department of Education. Proviso, 1A.14

[21] South Carolina Public Employee Benefit Authority; S.C. Code Ann. § 1-11-710(A)(2)

[22] SC Code § 59-21-160

[23] https://www.nirsonline.org/wp-content/uploads/2021/01/AARP-In-The-States-Snapshot-SC-Public-Employee-Retirement-System.pdf

24 https://www.epi.org/publication/teacher-pay-penalty-dips-but-persists-in-2019-public-school-teachers-earn-about-20-less-in-weekly-wages-than-nonteacher-college-graduates/#:~:text=Teacher%20pay%20penalty%20dips%20but,college%20graduates%20%7C%20Economic%20Policy%20Institute

25 https://www.nirsonline.org/wp-content/uploads/2021/01/AARP-In-The-States-Snapshot-SC-Public-Employee-Retirement-System.pdf

26 Boivie, I. 2017. "Revisiting the Three Rs of Teacher Retirement Systems: Recruitment, Retention, and Retirement." Washington, DC. NIRS.

27 https://ed.sc.gov/districts-schools/special-education-services/fiscal-and-grants-management-fgm/fiscal-monitoring/

28 http://ecs.force.com/mbdata/mbquest3D?rep=SD10

29 https://www.scstatehouse.gov/sess105_1983-1984/bills/eia.htm

30 https://www.scstatehouse.gov/query.php?search=DOC&searchtext=gifted%20and%20talented&category=BUDGET&year=2021&version_id=7&return_page=&version_title=Appropriation%20Act&conid=36962985&result_pos=0&keyval=46335&numrows=10

31 https://www.scstatehouse.gov/sess124_2021-2022/appropriations2021/tap1b.htm#s1

32 https://ed.sc.gov/policy/federal-education-programs/esea-title-iii/

33 http://www.ecs.org/clearinghouse/01/16/94/11694.pdf

34 https://www.scstatehouse.gov/sess124_2021-2022/appropriations2021/tap1b.htm#s1

35 S.C. Code Ann. § 59-40-10

36 https://www.scstatehouse.gov/sess124_2021-2022/appropriations2021/GOVPartIA.pdf

37 https://admin.sc.gov/sites/default/files/budget/FY22%20H610%20-%20SCPCSD.pdf

38 S.C. Code Ann. § 59-40-175

39 https://sites.google.com/a/acsd.k12.ca.us/categorical-state-federal-projects/home/funding-descriptions

40 https://www2.ed.gov/admins/comm/choice/regprivschl/regprivschl.pdf

41 https://ed.sc.gov/finance/financial-services/manual-handbooks-and-guidelines/funding-manuals/fy-2017-2018-funding-manual/

42 https://www.wltx.com/article/news/politics/south-carolina-supreme-court-blocks-money-private-schools/101-589d2be1-e662-44f5-86a0-8e60bd720aea

43 https://governor.sc.gov/sites/default/files/Documents/Executive-Budget/FY23%20Executive%20Budget%20Summary%2001102022.pdf

44 South Carolina Department of Education retrieved from https://ed.sc.gov/instruction/early-learning-and-literacy/cdep/cdep-resources-and-forms1/

45 Act 284, Read to Succeed, 59-156-110

46 http://www.masc.sc/pages/resources/history-of-the-local-government-fund.aspx

47 https://www.scstatehouse.gov/sess124_2021-2022/appropriations2021/wmp1b.htm#:~:text=The%20average%20per%20pupil%20funding,federal%2C%20and%20%246%2C406%20%247%2C423%20local.

48 https://www.scstatehouse.gov/sess124_2021-2022/appropriations2021/gbud2022.pdf

49 https://accelerate.sc.gov/cares-act-overview

50 https://www.ed.gov/news/press-releases/us-department-education-approves-south-carolinas-plan-use-american-rescue-plan-funds-support-k-12-schools-and-students-distributes-remaining-705-million-state

51 https://accelerate.sc.gov/cares-act/assistance-educational-entities

52 https://accelerate.sc.gov/cares-act

53 https://accelerate.sc.gov/cares-act/assistance-educational-entities

CHAPTER 41

SOUTH DAKOTA

Wade Pogany
Associated School Boards of South Dakota

Tyler Pickner
Associated School Boards of South Dakota

GENERAL BACKGROUND

South Dakota is a very rural state given its large land mass (77,115 sq. miles) and relatively small population. 2020 Census shows total residents of 884,659.[1] The education system has 149 public school districts, 47 non-public schools, and 19 tribal / Bureau of Indian Affairs schools. Student enrollments have grown in recent years to approximately 139,000 K-12 public school students, and 14,500 non-public school students.[2]

Other education demographics include a teaching pool of approximately 9700 teachers and ?? administrators. Total state and local expenditure for K-12 education of $612 million general funds, $36 million in Capital Outlay funds, $150 million in Special Education.[2] 2019 average teacher salary is $48,984 with average total teacher compensation of $63,454.[2]

South Dakota is also a politically conservative state. The State Legislature is comprised of 35 Senators and 70 members of the House of Representatives. Of

Funding Public Schools in the United States, Indian Country,
and US Territories (Second Edition), pages 637–649.
Copyright © 2023 by Information Age Publishing
www.infoagepub.com
637

the 105 members of the 2021 Legislature 90% are Republican 10% Democrat: Senate: 32 (R) 3 (D) House: 62 (R) 8 (D).[3]

The authority for educating stems from the SD Constitution, Article VIII. The Legislature is charged to " ...establish and maintain a general and uniform system of public schools wherein tuition shall be without charge, and equally open to all; and to adopt a suitable means to secure to the people the advantages and opportunities of education."[4]

EDUCATION FUNDING

In recent years the distribution of state funds in South Dakota's school finance system has evolved, but the funding sources have remained relatively consistent.

The two primary funding sources for the state's 149 public school districts are local property taxes and state general funds through the state aid formula. In addition, schools receive funding from federal sources, local bonds issues and other areas subsequently outlined.[5]

Prior to 1995, the South Dakota Legislature funded school districts through an expenditure driven formula. The more schools spent, the more state funding it received. The funding formula was revised by the state's legislature in 1995 and implemented in January, 1997.

The revised funding formula funded districts based on a calculation that included a per student allocation (PSA) funding model, a school district's enrollment and the amount of local property taxes levied within the district.[6] State law on school finance delineates the revised calculation which requires several steps in determining the PSA.[7] The formula establishes a school district's "local need" which is the amount required to fund the district with local property taxes and state aid. If a district is designated a small district – an enrollment under 600 students—a small school factor adjustment is also applied. The district's "local effort"—the total amount of local property taxes levied—is calculated, as well. Finally, the local effort is subtracted from the district's local need to arrive at the amount of state aid allocated to the district. [8]

The revised funding formula established a foundational system whereby some equity exists based on the ability of a district to raise property taxes (local effort) compared to their ability to fund the expenses of the district (local need). Districts with less property tax wealth receive more state funding because it has a diminished ability to raise necessary funding. Thus, a state aid foundational structure was established.

In the revised funding formula state aid is the largest source of revenue for local districts. Local property taxes are generally the next major source of revenue; other lessor sources of revenue for districts, includes county fines, federal grants, school district gross receipts and bank franchise taxes.[9] School districts also receive funds for education related purposes, such as capital outlay and pension funds collected through local revenue and special education funds from federal, state and local sources. A district may also be eligible for a sparsity factor benefit based on enrollment size and distance criteria.[10]

STATE AID STUDIED IN 2015

Growing Teacher Shortage

For decades, South Dakota teacher salaries ranked last in the nation.[11] Data gathered by the School Administrators of South Dakota and the Associated School Boards pointed to the fact low pay was a contributing factor to the growing teacher shortage in South Dakota.[12] Spurred by the increasing concern about teacher shortages in South Dakota,[13] Governor Dennis Daugaard established the Blue Ribbon Task Force in February, 2015 with the task of reevaluating the K-12 education funding system.[14]

The 26-member task force included legislators, school board members, administrators, teachers, members of the Governor's staff and state Department of Education staff, who were tasked with collecting and analyzing data, gathering input from stakeholders and the public and producing a recommendation of changes needed to address the issue.

The Task Force was led by two active legislators involved in education: Senator Deb Soholt and Representative Jacqueline Sly, who served as co-chairs. The goal was to operationalize recommendations from the task force during the 2016 Legislative Session. [15]

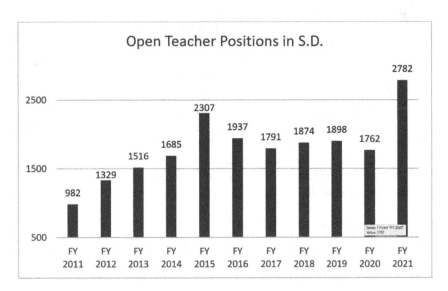

FIGURE 41.1. Open Teacher Positions in South Dakota. Source: South Dakota Teacher Placement Center.

Major Findings of the Task Force

As it related to the many aspects of the state's school funding system and the teacher shortage, the Task Force found:

- State funding priorities indicate a 149% increase in state dollars for K-12 education since FY96. However, other state funding needs have also increased, such as Medicaid which grew by 279%. The share of the State's general fund budget for education has decreased even though the amount of money given to schools through the current per student allocation has increased;
- South Dakota's average teacher salary in 2013 – 14 was $40,023. South Dakota's salary ranks last among the fifty states and the District of Columbia. Even adjusted by a comparable wage index, South Dakota's salaries lag behind the regional average (of Nebraska, North Dakota, Montana, Iowa, Minnesota, and Wyoming) by $11,888 and $8,643 behind our next lowest neighbor (North Dakota);
- Teacher turnover is not exclusively related to salaries, but in South Dakota, it is a significant factor;
- The incoming pipeline of teachers will not meet the projected needs of districts when looking ahead five years;
- The current funding formula is based on a per student allocation (PSA) that is derived from a set amount of money available and not the specific needs of a district;
- Capital outlay tax collections have increased by 116.6% or 9% a year from 2003 to 2015. At the same time, the PSA has increased by 25.4% or 2% a year. In actual dollars, the capital outlay increase has been $82.3 million to $178.3 million. In South Dakota, capital outlay per-student spending exceeds the national average by $405 per student;
- Administrator costs as a percentage of total expenditures are comparable to surrounding states. Slightly higher than the national average, South Dakota's percentage is lower than North Dakota and Montana and nearly the same as Iowa. The number of South Dakota school administrators per student is among the lowest in the region and in line with the national average;
- Reserve fund balances, on average, in South Dakota tend to be larger than is typical nationally;

Task Force Recommendations

Based on the data generated and findings of the Task Force recommendations were made to address the funding issues; most significant among the recommendations was the move to overhaul the state aid funding formula, based primarily on average teacher salaries rather a Per Student Allocation. Thus, creating a significantly different state funding model.

With an aim to improve teacher salaries, Governor Daugaard agreed with the recommendations and the recommendations for New Funding Formula for State Aid included: [16]

- Adopt a new formula based on a statewide target for statewide average teacher salary of $48,000 and maintain the average statewide student-to-teacher ratio at approximately 14:1;
- Replace current small school adjustment with a sliding scale, depending on school enrollment, for the target student-to-teacher ratio;
- Retain the current statutory minimum inflation factor of 3% or inflation, whichever is less in the new formula;
- Reevaluate teacher salaries every three years to assure South Dakota remains competitive with surrounding states;
- No change to the Limited English Proficiency Adjustment;
- No change to the Sparsity factor.

Recommendations for new funding for teacher salaries included:

- At least $75 million in new ongoing funding for teacher salaries;
- Use existing funds to the greatest extent possible;
- Increase the state sales and use tax for additional ongoing revenue.

Recommendations to ensure accountability in the school funding system included:

- Adopt mechanisms to monitor the implementation of the new formula;
- Develop benchmarks, in particular for average teacher salaries, to ensure goals are met.[17]

Other school finance mechanisms were also studied by the Task Force and changes were further recommended. The recommendations for additional adjustments included:

- Reinstate statutory caps on school district general fund reserves;
- Develop a tiered reserve caps system based on school enrollments;
- Dollar-by-dollar reduction in state aid payment for districts exceeding reserve fund cap;
- Phase in the caps over a three-year period;
- Establish an oversight committee to help districts with phase-in strategies for reserve caps, and assist when unique circumstances arise that may make the caps unrealistic;
- Eliminate the pension levy. The general education levies should be increased by 0.263 mills which would raise the same amount that the pension levy currently raises;
- Equalize "other revenue" to establish greater equity by equalizing future growth in other revenue sources.[18]

Recommendations for adjustments to the funding system on a phased-in approach included:

- Fully implement all recommendations at the end of three years;
- With a phased-in approach, two points must be considered:
  - $75 million in new funding for teacher salaries is intended as a supplement to the current appropriations for schools. If the new funding is phased-in over a period of years, it should be in addition to the inflationary increases required under current law;
  - Target teacher salary of $48,000 was chosen based on the most recent available data. If the reforms are phased-in over period of years, the target salary must be increased in order to remain competitive with surrounding states.[19]d

FUNDING FORMULA REVISED IN 2016

Based on the Blue Ribbon Task Force Recommendations, Governor Dennis Daugaard proposed to the legislature to implement the funding system adjustments; they included:

- House Bill 1182;
- Senate Bill 131; and
- Senate Bill 133.

These three bills were passed by the legislature during the 2016 session. Provisions from House Bill 1182, which included a half-cent increase in the state sales tax, took effect on June 1, 2016. The added half-cent provided an additional $67 million for K-12 education, $36 million for property tax relief, and $3 million for technical institutes. Provisions established in Senate Bill 131 and 133 took effect on July 1, 2016.[20]

With legislation passed the new State Aid Funding system for K-12 Education in South Dakota took shape.

GENERAL FUND

The revised funding formula is now based on a target teacher salary increased by CPI each year. For Fiscal Year 2021 to the formula set the target at $52,600). Here's how the state aid formula works:

- For each district, calculate a target student-to-teacher ratio, based on a sliding scale by student enrollment:
  - The district's target number of teachers is calculated by dividing the district's fall enrollment by the target student-to-teacher ratio;
  - The district's total instructional need is calculated by multiplying the district's target number of teachers by the statewide target for average teacher salary, and by increasing that total by 29% for benefits;

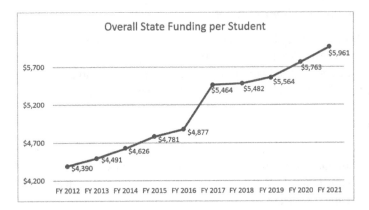

FIGURE 41.2.   Overall State Funding Per Student. Source: South Dakota Department of Education. 5 Year History of Per Student Allocations & Levies: https://doe.sd.gov/legislature/documents/5Yr-GFLevies-2021.pdf.

- The total instructional need is increased by a calculated overhead rate (FY2021 = 31.04%) to cover non-instructional costs. This category includes operating costs as well as salaries and benefits of non-instructional staff, such as administrators, guidance counselors, librarians, and school nurses;

- These steps calculate the district's total need for state aid. At this point, local effort is applied against total need, with the state providing any necessary funds to achieve the total need.

TARGET TEACHER RATIO FACTOR

The law provides the following sliding scale for the target ratio, based on student enrollments:

- Less than 200 – 12 students to 1 teacher;
- Between 200 & 600—Sliding scale between 12 to 1 and 15 to 1;
- Greater than 600—15 to 1.

The sliding scale retains the same enrollment thresholds as the small school factor of the previous funding formula (see page 2). The formula does not require school districts to strictly meet the target ratio or to use a certain level of funding for benefits and overhead costs; those standards are merely used to calculate total need, and districts retain local control on how to use the dollars they receive.

Calculating the Number of Students

South Dakota's state aid formula uses a fall enrollment count, which is essentially a school district's enrollment on the last Friday of September. This number includes students tuitioned out of the district and students who are enrolled less than full-time, but it does not include students for whom a district receives tuition.

Funding for Local Need

The money to pay for local need is raised through both local and state taxes. Taxes funding local need are divided between money raised through school district taxes, called "local effort," and money from the state's budget raised with state taxes, called "state aid."

Determining Local Effort

A school district's local effort is the amount of money raised by applying the maximum local property tax levies against the value of taxable property. The state Department of Revenue calculates the value of a school district's taxable property, upon which local effort is raised through local property taxes.

- For taxes payable in 2021, school districts can levy a maximum of: $1.41 per thousand for agricultural property;
- $3.16 per thousand for owner-occupied property; and
- $6.55 per thousand for non-agricultural property. Source (Bureau of Finance budget book)

The level of general education tax levy for school purposes is capped in law, but school boards may "opt out" of the maximums if two-thirds of the board supports it. This decision may be referred to a public vote, if 5 percent of the electorate signs a petition against the "opt out."

OTHER REVENUES COUNTED AS LOCAL EFFORT

Other revenues are funding sources that school districts receive that, in the past, were counted outside of the formula, and therefore not equalized across all districts. In FY18 a calculation of local effort based on the phase-in of "other revenue" equalization was implemented. These other revenues include:

- Utility taxes (rural electric & telephone);
- Revenue in Lieu of taxes (local and county);
- County apportionment;
- Bank Franchise tax; and
- Wind Farm taxes.

Each school district has been assigned a hold harmless base amount, based on the greatest of its previous three years of collections – Fiscal Years 2013, 2014 and 2015, that will be stepped down over five years at 20 percent per year.

Each year, any other revenue collected beyond the "hold harmless base" will be counted as local effort and therefore equalized across districts through the funding formula. At that point, these revenue sources will be treated in the same way as local property taxes.

This new money will not offset state or local funding and will not take any funds away from the state's education system. The state's share of funding ratio will be adjusted so that the state's dollar amount contribution is not reduced and local property taxes are not impacted.[21]

DETERMINING STATE AID

The amount of state aid provided to school districts is calculated by taking the total "local need" minus "local effort." A hypothetical school district example:

Local Need: $2,634,000

Local Effort – Prop Taxes: - $1,081,284

Local Effort – Other Revenue: - $52,000

State Aid = $1,500,716

For districts with very high levels of other revenue, the law allowed for an optional alternative to phase into the revised formula by permitting them to opt out of the revised formula, keep their current funding, which would remain frozen at the

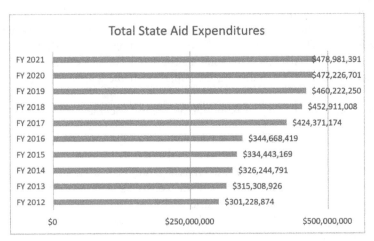

FIGURE 41.3. Total State Aid Expenditures. Source: South Dakota Department of Education. https://doe.sd.gov/ofm/statefunding.aspx.

Fiscal Year 2016 amount per student generated through the previous formula, plus revenues from the other identified revenues to be equalized. When the inflationary increases to the revised formula catch up with that school district, they may opt into the updated funding system.

GENERAL FUND CASH BALANCE CAPS

Included with the new funding formula legislation were other components with delayed implementation dates. Effective Fiscal Year 2019, districts may be penalized if they exceed an allowable percentage of cash, based on a monthly report of cash balances in their general fund in the prior fiscal year. The percentage general fund cash balance cap will be calculated by dividing the lowest monthly cash balance of the previous 12 months by the total general fund expenditures.

The purpose of this mechanism is to ascertain the general fund cash balance level that, over the course of a year, is never used. Districts' general fund cash balance allowances are based on student counts:

- Less than 200 students, cap at 40 percent;
- Between 200 and 600 students, cap at 30 percent;
- Greater than 600 students, cap at 25 percent.

Once in effect, a district in excess of the general fund cash balance cap would have its state aid reduced dollar-for-dollar. Gov. Daugaard appointed a five-member oversight board to consider districts' requests to waive their general fund cash balance cap in special circumstances.

SPARSITY FACTOR

Recognizing the unique challenges faced by extremely rural, isolated school districts, those meeting the definition of "sparse" receive additional money outside of the formula. These districts are eligible for additional state dollars not to exceed $110,000 per district. If the total appropriation for sparsity is less than the calculated amount for each district, the dollars available will be prorated to each district.

The criteria for meeting the definition of "sparse" include:

- State aid fall enrollment less than 500;
- State aid fall enrollment per square mile of 0.5 or less;
- School district area of 400 sq. miles or more;
- Distance of at least 15 miles between a district's secondary attendance center and that of an adjoining district;
- Must operate a secondary attendance center; and
- Levies at the maximum levy for general fund purposes.

Calculation of this additional aid is outlined in SDCL 13-13-79.[22]

SCHOOLS RECEIVE FUNDS THROUGH OTHER SOURCES

The state aid formula is not the only source of revenue for South Dakota schools. It is only one of more than 50 sources of revenue local schools can use for educating students. Some of the other revenue sources for general education include:

- Federal Grants;
- Rental Income;
- Investment Income;
- Admissions;
- Contributions/Donations;
- Schools also have other specialized funds to pay for certain education projects, including:
  - ○ Revenue collected from local taxpayers for capital outlay and bond redemption, over and above the per-student allocation;
  - ○ Federal, state, and local funds for special education, over and above the per-student allocation for special education students.

EMPLOYEE BENEFITS FACTOR

The "benefits factor" includes sufficient funds to cover all district benefit costs, regardless of current funding source, which means revenues currently collected by the pension levy can be utilized to cover the total benefits need.

CAPITAL OUTLAY FUNDS

The revised funding system made four changes to the state's capital outlay (CO) levy provisions:

- Repeals the sunset clause of Capital Outlay flexibility and makes it permanent. Broadens Capital Outlay flexibility so collections can be used for any general fund purpose at the current level of 45 percent of the Capital Outlay property tax revenue. It also requires funds used for flexibility be transferred to the general fund instead of expended out of the Capital Outlay fund;
- Requires districts make annual Capital Outlay requests in the form of a dollar amount, not a mill levy rate. Limits future growth in Capital Outlay collections by capping the maximum dollar amount that can be collected to increasing annually by 3 percent or inflation, whichever is less, plus new construction;
- Imposes an alternative maximum on Capital Outlay collections, on a per student basis, at $3,200. In future years this would inflate at the same rate as the formula CPI or 3 percent, whichever is less. This alternative maximum will take effect in Fiscal Year 2021, and a special provision will be made for districts with certain Capital Outlay debt obligations;

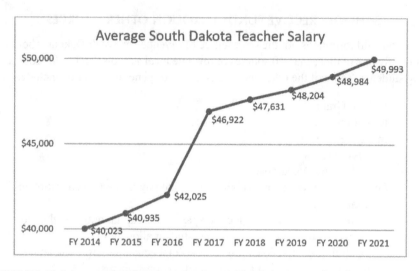

FIGURE 41.4 Average South Dakota Teacher Salary. Source: South Dakota Department of Education, South Dakota Legislative Research Council and National Education Association

- The revised funding system does not mandate that any current Capital Outlay funds be shifted to general education purposes and the adjustments have no effect on the general education levies.

CORONA VIRUS AND SCHOOL FUNDING

The US Congress provided several rounds of funding to South Dakota schools to assist with COVID expenses. Between the Coronavirus Aid Relief and Economic Security Act (CARES Act), American Rescue Plan (ARP), and Coronavirus Response and Relief Supplemental Appropriations Act (CRRSAS), South Dakota school districts and the State of South Dakota received over $550,000,000.[23] The State of SD was required to submit a state plan and every school district was required to submit their own spending plans for the use of these funds. Numerous projects to mitigate COVID were implemented including increased staffing, sanitation programs, increased meals provided during school closings, air purification systems installed, COVID testing, new and remodeling construction projects, etc. Schools continue to seek approval for their allocation requests as COVID.

On March 13, 2020, Governor Noem closed schools because of increased COVID infections and schools utilized distance learning to the extent possible. By the fall of 2020 most public school districts were reopened with face to face instruction while some provided distance learning options for parents and continued to remain open despite significant hardships to contain the spread and keep children safe. All school districts were open with little distance learning by fall of 2021.

CONCLUSION

The past several years have brought significant changes to how South Dakota funds school districts and the various changes have affected every school district differently. All the changes were balanced with the agreement that significant state aid funding would be provided with the increased sales tax, which was South Dakota's first permanent increase since 1968, making the debate and decision to increase state revenues through a half penny sales tax truly historic. The challenge for Legislators moving forward is continued funding for schools so they remain competitive in attracting and retaining quality teachers.

ENDNOTES

1   Census.gov
2   S.D. Department of Education Statistical Digest
3   S.D. Legislative Manual
4   S.D. Constitution Article VIII, Section 1
5   SC Davis vs. State of South Dakota 2011 (51)
6   SDCL 13-15-2 and 13-10-6; SC Davis vs. State of South Dakota 2011 (51)
7   SDCL 13-13-10.1
8   SDCL 13-13-10.1(6).
9   S.D. Constitution Article VII (3)
10 SDCL 13-13-78-79
11 NEA Teacher Salary Rankings: http://www.nea.org/assets/docs/2017_Rankings_and_Estimates_Report-FINAL-SECURED.pdf)
12 Low pay spells teacher shortage in South Dakota, Argus Leader, Sept. 17, 2014
13 Associated School Boards of SD online blog post, June, 28, 2015)
14 Associated School Boards SD online blog, Feb. 6, 2015. http://asbsd.org/index.php/gov-announces-task-force-for-k12/)
15 State of South Dakota Blue Ribbon Task Force Final Report online: http://blueribbon.sd.gov/
16 Associated School Boards of SD blog post Dec. 8, 2015.)
17 State of South Dakota Blue Ribbon Task Force Final Report. http://blueribbon.sd.gov/
18 16 State of South Dakota Blue Ribbon Task Force Final Report. http://blueribbon.sd.gov/
19 State of South Dakota Blue Ribbon Task Force Final Report. http://blueribbon.sd.gov/
20 South Dakota Legislative Research Council, archived bills, 2016: http://www.sdlegislature.gov/Legislative_Session/Bills/Bill.aspx?Session=2016
21 State of South Dakota Blue Ribbon Task Force Memo Explaining the New Funding Formula http://blueribbon.sd.gov/
22 20 South Dakota Department of Education—Issue Brief—March 2017 State Aid to K-12 General Education Funding Formula—http://doe.sd.gov/ofm/documents/17-SA-brief2.pdf
23 S.D. Department of Education—Federal COVID Funding: doe.sd.gov/coronavirus/caresact.aspx-#ARP
24 Journal of Education Finance (Volume 46, Issue 3): https://muse.jhu.edu/issue/44183
25 We would like to acknowledge the work of Matt Flett in crafting the chapter for the first edition of this work.

CHAPTER 42

TENNESSEE

Lisa G. Driscoll
The University of Tennessee, Knoxville

GENERAL BACKGROUND

In 1835 the first Tennessee constitution containing an education article was adopted and stated the necessity of educating the public by assigning a "duty" to the General Assembly for the establishment and appropriation of a perpetual common school fund.[1] After the Civil War ended, a new constitution was passed and ratified in 1870. New language has been interpreted by Tennessee courts as the state's intent to establish a "uniform" system of education, even though the same section was also amended to "no school established or aided under this section shall allow white and negro children to be received as scholars together in the same school."[2]

In 1885 the Tennessee General Assembly provided for "municipal corporations to levy additional taxes and to establish graded high schools."[3] Through the process allowed by the Tennessee Private Acts[4] private academies (which included high school grades) could establish themselves as special school districts with separate and established boundaries within from the county or municipality in which they were located. These special school districts could levy property taxes and receive local and state funding for their own schools. Over the next 40 years numerous special school districts were established through Private Acts. By

Funding Public Schools in the United States, Indian Country,
and US Territories (Second Edition), pages 651–661.
Copyright © 2023 by Information Age Publishing
www.infoagepub.com

1899 the General Assembly required each county to establish a high school and to levy special taxes (in lieu of the general fund) to fund these schools. To date four of the special school districts established during this period were still in operation.

Notable Constitutional Language

In 1954 the landmark U.S. Supreme Court decision, *Brown v. Board of Education*,[5] rendered unconstitutional the racially discriminatory language in the 1870 constitution. In 1977 the Tennessee constitutional convention approved a completely rewritten and abbreviated education clause that replaced detailed and operational language. The changes served to dilute the "duty" to establish and fund the common schools as noted in earlier constitutions. The new clause read:

> The state of Tennessee recognizes the inherent value of education and encourages its support. The General Assembly shall provide for the maintenance, support, and eligibility standards of a system of free public schools. The General Assembly may establish and support such postsecondary institutions, including public institutions of higher learning, as it determines.[6]

As of 2022, the 1977 the education clause in the Tennessee Constitution remains unchanged.

DESCRIPTIVE STATISTICS

In 2022 there were 141 regular public school districts organized by counties, and their cities, and towns within Tennessee. In addition, the state operates an Achievement School District, the Alvin C. York Institute, the Tennessee School for the Blind, the Tennessee School for the Deaf, and the West Tennessee School for the Deaf.

The number of students in average daily membership in the public schools has been steadily increasing, except for the academic year 2020-2021. In FY20 the percentages of students self-identified as white (62%), African American (24%), Hispanic (12%), and Asian (2%).[7] Since FY14 the percentage of students reporting their race-ethnicity as white or African American has decreased and the percentage of students reporting Hispanic has increased.

The number of licensed classroom teachers in Tennessee increased each year and reached a peak in FY17 and has remained within a range of plus or minus 1,000 teachers for the succeeding three years. In general, in rural school districts

TABLE 42.1. Average Daily Membership in Tennessee Public Schools

2014-15	2015-16	2016-17	2017-18	2018-19	2019-2020	2020-2021
959,536	960,959	963,294	965,549	966,285	973,632	957,423

Source: Tennessee Comptroller of the Treasury.

TABLE 42.2. Number of Licensed Personnel

	2014-15	2015-16	2016-17	2017-18	2018-19	2019-20
Classroom Teachers (Licensed)	64,094	64,928	65,091	62,525	61,583	62,879
Principals/ Asst. Principals	3,565	3,656	3,717	3,714	3,842	3,902
Instructional Support Only	8,221	8,536	9,071	10,728	12,279	12,584

Source: Tennessee Comptroller of the Treasury.

Note. Instructional Support category includes attendance personnel, supervisors, school psychologists & social workers, librarians, instructional coaches, special education paraprofessionals, guidance counselors, and technology personnel.

there was either no change or a decrease in the numbers of teachers, and in suburban and urban school districts there was an increase in numbers of teachers. The number of principals and assistant principals followed a similar trend as classroom teachers. The number of instructional support personnel increased each year in all districts, most likely due to increases in state funding for specific position types.

CURRENT POLITICAL CLIMATE

The Tennessee General Assembly is composed of the House of Representatives (99 representatives elected for 2-year terms) and the Senate (33 senators elected to four-year terms). In Tennessee all elected legislators assume office on the day they are elected in the general election. The legislature is limited to 90 days in session each year. The Governor may call a special or "extraordinary" session limited to a specified topic, as has been the case in recent years, and is limited to 20 session days.

Party Control of Branches and Legislative Bodies

The 112th General Assembly was elected in November 2020. The Republican political party comprises a majority in both the Senate (27 – R, 6 – D) and the House of Representatives (73 – R, 24 – D, 1 – Ind, 1—Vacancy).[8] All seats in the Tennessee House of Representatives and the seats in the Senate whose term ends in 2022 are on the ballot for the November 2022 election. Tennessee Governor Bill Lee (Republican) was elected in November 2018, is eligible to seek a second term, and has announced his intent to run for re-election.

Structural Aspects of the Tennessee Budget Process

Tennessee's fiscal year begins July 1 and ends June 30. Annual budget formulation by the executive branch occurs between July 1 and January 30 prior to the new fiscal year. The budget shall outline proposed expenditures for state government, proposed capital projects, and anticipated revenues. Typically, at the end of

January, the Governor presents a State of the State address to a joint session of the legislature held in the House Chamber of Tennessee State Capitol. In this address the recommended Budget that is based on the recurring budget from the previous year is presented. Tennessee's Constitution has a balanced budget requirement whereby expenditures cannot exceed revenues (and reserve funding) in a given fiscal year.

In Tennessee the governor's budget is based on conservative revenue predictions made earlier in the cycle. In the last three fiscal years revenues have exceeded budget amounts. In April 2022 the legislature passed a $52.8 billion state budget.[9] Funded initiatives from that budget include: a $1 billion investment in new, annual recurring education funding, $500 million for career and technical program improvements in all middle and high schools, $124.7 billion for teacher salary increases, and $16 million recurring with $16 million nonrecurring to the Charter Schools Facility Fund.[10]

UNION REPRESENTATION AND ENGAGEMENT

Tennessee has a right to work statute that states that it is unlawful for any employer or organization of any kind "...to deny or attempt to deny employment to any person by reason of the person's membership in, affiliation with, resignation from or refusal to join or affiliate with any labor union or employee organization of any kind."[11]

In 1978 Tennessee teachers were provided the right to bargain collectively with their local school boards with the passage of the Education Professional Negotiations Act (EPNA). Soon after the Tennessee Education Association (an affiliate of the National Education Association which claims to be an "association" of teachers, not a union) accepted a contract to be the sole representatives of teachers in the state of Tennessee. Over the following decade the Tennessee School Boards Association in their role representing local boards of education actively opposed collective bargaining and sought its repeal. In 2011 with a republican majority legislature and a governor of the same party, the law was repealed.

OTHER ADVOCACY AND INTEREST GROUPS

There are several education advocacy groups active in Tennessee. Some groups are affiliates of nationally based special interest groups (Tennessee Education Association, The Education Trust in Tennessee, the Tennessee Alliance for Equity in Education, and the Tennessee Federation of Teachers, and the Memphis Restorative Justice Coalition, among others). Other groups are exclusively state based (State Collaborative on Reforming Education (SCORE)). Finally, local groups including the Campaign for School Equity (Memphis), Johnson City Public Schools Foundation (Johnson City), Students, Parents Educators Across Knoxville (SPEAK)(Knoxville), and the Dollywood Foundation are just a few that focus on equitable and adequate funding and opportunities for students.

CURRENT SCHOOL FINANCE LITIGATION

In 1992 in response to the suit brought by the Tennessee Small School Systems (an unincorporated association of 77 rural, small school districts) against the state of Tennessee and Governor Ned McWherter,[12] the General Assembly passed the Education Improvement Act (EIA).[13] The Act was a major legislative effort that established a new funding formula entitled the Basic Education Formula (BEP).[14] The EIA was designed to address the issue of fiscal inequity among school districts by forcing sweeping changes to the finance and administration of public education. The most important of these changes was the value-added accountability system that used predicted student test scores to evaluate teachers, schools, and districts.

The BEP was a resource-based cost formula that employed an average of two fiscal capacity measures based on the county to determine need and ability to pay for the respective school district. Over the following two decades, districts claimed that the state shortchanged them by only paying for 10 months of benefits for employees, thus forcing districts to fund the other two months. Further, in most districts the slow-walk by the legislature in amending classroom level student to teacher ratios and the salary multiplier used in the annual calculation of instructional costs resulted with chronic underestimations of what it would take to fund schools. Districts in both urban schools having higher numbers of high-need students and districts rural areas having low fiscal capacity were both affected.

Twenty years later in March 2015, the school boards of seven school districts in the Chattanooga region of Tennessee filed a suit claiming that the BEP had shifted the cost of education to the locality which could not continue to fund the cost of students needing more resources for an adequate education.[15] Later that year in August, Shelby County, which includes Memphis and has an enrollment over 100,000, filed its own suit in Nashville chancery court against the State of Tennessee for failing to meet its obligation for free, adequate, and equitable educational opportunities.[16] In October 2017 Metropolitan Nashville Public School Board unanimously joined Shelby County as a co-plaintiff.[17]

Over the next 3 years, court dates were pushed back, and then back again, because of changes in the judges assigned to preside at the trial, and various recurring appropriations to fund health insurance, salaries, and required initiatives that were proffered to address pressing issues. In 2020 the original seven district plaintiff group dropped out of the suit. Soon after, in early 2021 a coalition of 84 small school districts, the Tennessee School Systems for Equity, joined the remaining plaintiffs. The court date which had been scheduled for October 2021 was moved forward to February 2022.

In November 2021 the Tennessee Governor initiated a series of funding subcommittees and public opinion opportunities across the state[18] that culminated with a proposal and legislation for a new funding formula entitled the Tennessee Investment in Student Achievement or TISA that was unveiled in February 2022.[19] This new funding formula applied weighted funding to the needs of individual student (student-based foundation formula) rather than to district and school level programmatic components as was done in the BEP. There were additional benefits in the plan touted by the governor such as facilities funding for charter schools.

House Bill 2143 and Senate Bill 2396 were filed stating its expressed purpose of replacing the BEP. In deference to the governor and legislature, the three-judge panel assigned to hear the case canceled the trial dates to observe how TISA will affect funding adequacy across the state. After much discussion and wrangling, the TISA bill was passed by the legislature on the final day of the 2022 session with several amendments designed to hold harmless some large, high fiscal capacity districts (including Metro Nashville and during the phase-in for full implementation scheduled for the 2023-24 school year. The governor signed the bill on May 2, 2022, and the new statute will proceed to the State Board of Education for the rulemaking process.

Since the TISA plan will not be implemented until the 2023-24 school year, it is unlikely that the adequacy trial will commence, if at all, until some years after that school year. As of May 2022, the equity and adequacy suit originally filed in 2015 by Shelby County Schools, joined in 2017 by Metro-Nashville Public Schools, and most recently in 2021 joined by the 84 school board plaintiffs organized under the umbrella of the Tennessee School Systems for Equity, is still active.

SOURCES OF REVENUE

Tennessee does not levy an individual income tax. The state authorizes 22 taxes, including local taxes. Tennessee has a 7.00 percent state sales tax and an optional local sales tax rate capped at 2.75%. The revenue from this tax comprises over 60% of all tax collections in the state.

Property taxes are levied by local jurisdictions (counties, cities, towns, and special districts) and apply to residential, agricultural, industrial/commercial property, and public utility property. These different categories of properties have different percentage multipliers applied to their appraised values, and the tax rate is set by the governing body of the jurisdiction(s) that the property is located in. Since school boards in Tennessee are dependent upon their county or city governing boards for the appropriation of local revenue to school districts, they are not authorized to directly collect tax revenue on behalf of their districts.

In recent years statewide tax revenue collections have increased each fiscal year. In the latter half of FY 21 revenues were expected to decline due to the COVID-19 pandemic, however, instead of declining revenues exceeded estimates.[20] For FY 22 state budget totaled $41.8 billion of which $20.9 Billion or 50% were state revenue dollars,[21] and $10.45 Billion or 25% comprised federal funds to the state.

For FY 22 K-12 education accounted for $5.6 billion in expenditures from state revenue. The required local match funding totaled $2.5 billion; however, most districts spend more than the minimum required. In FY23, a one-time appropriation of $750 million in state funds would apply.[22]

DISTRIBUTION FORMULAS

In May 2022 the Tennessee governor signed into law a new funding formula for the public schools. The new formula, the Tennessee Investment in Student Achievement (TISA), would go into effect with the 2023-24 academic year.[23] Beginning in 2024-25 it is planned that the state would provide $6.3 billion, and the initial required local match would be $2.5 billion which is level funded to the FY22 amount.

The TISA funding plan is a student-based foundation formula that applies four tiers of weighted funding to each individual student based on their needs, enrollment in specified programs, and progress toward goals.[24] The first tier encompasses a base level of funding for all students of $6,860. The second tier applies differentially weighted funding multipliers to the base amount according to existing student demographics or characteristics. These include whether the student lives in a sparsely populated area or a small community, whether the student is economically-\ disadvantaged or attends a school with a concentration of students in poverty, whether the student has unique learning needs including having a disability, whether the student is identified as gifted, whether the student is an English Learner, or whether the student is dyslexic. Also, individual students enrolled in a charter school would receive additional funding in this tier. Students possessing multiple eligibilities on these items may add the amounts to accumulate funding.

The third tier provides individual students that are members of groups of students identified for targeted goals to receive additional individual funding. For example, for students in kindergarten through the third grade, additional direct funding per student would be allocated to for literacy instructional enhancements. If by the fourth grade a student needs more support to reach literacy goals, the student would be eligible for literacy tutoring funding. Similarly, middle and high school students who enroll in career & technical programs would be eligible for an additional $5,000 on average to fund the costs of the program they enroll in. Finally, for college-bound students who need a retake of the ACT to be admitted or earn state scholarships, two ACT retakes would be directly funded so they may achieve a higher score. Finally, tier four directly incentivizes continued student progress toward a goal. As of this writing, the rules governing the administration of the TISA formula were being determined.

SPECIAL SCHOOL DISTRICTS

Special school districts are districts that have been created either by being granted a charter or by private acts by the General Assembly. In 2022 there were 14 special school districts in Tennessee. These school districts are funded through a prorated appropriation of the county calculated BEP, the county property and sales tax, and a special school tax levied across their attendance zone.

EMPLOYEE BENEFITS

The State of Tennessee offers group insurance plans for employees of school districts. These plans offer medical, dental, and vision coverage. The Tennessee Consolidated Retirement System (TCRS) administers a defined benefit retirement program for teachers and employees hired in public school districts hired prior to June 30, 2014. Teachers hired after that date are enrolled in the hybrid defined benefit program as a condition of their employment. The hybrid plan is a defined benefit plan coupled with a defined contribution plan. The plans are designed to provide retirement benefits, disability benefits, and death benefits. The plans are portable among eligible employers within the state, but not outside the state. This is a disadvantage for teachers who relocate to other states prior to reaching retirement age.

There is a five-year vesting requirement for both the defined benefit and the hybrid plans. The benefit calculation is based on an accrual factor, an average of the highest five years of compensation, and years of creditable service. School district employees in districts that pay lower salaries are likely to earn lifetime pensions that have lower dollar values for the same job compared with individuals working in districts with higher salaries. The state of Tennessee pays the Social Security portion of the FICA tax for its employees.

CHARTER SCHOOL FUNDING

Tennessee charter schools are public schools operated by independent, non-profit governing bodies (that must include parents) within school districts administered by local (elected) school boards. The Tennessee Public Charter Schools Act of 2002 stipulates that funding from the local school board shall be allocated to the charter school in an amount equal to the per student state and local funds received by the district.[25] Federal funds (Title I, IDEA, ESEA) may be appropriated as provided for as in federal law. For the academic year 2021-22 there were 116 charter schools operating in Tennessee.

Facilities costs are often an impediment to the operation of charter schools. Recent funding appropriated by the legislature may be used for facilities procurement and renovation.

Public charter school may purchase services such as transportation or food services from the authorizing school district. Some charter agreements include provisions whereby the authorizing school district provides employee benefits or retirement services. In those cases, the authorizing school district may withhold funds from the district allocation to cover the costs of such services.

NONPUBLIC SCHOOL FUNDING

As of the 2021-22 school year there were over 600 nonpublic schools which include private schools and home-schooling umbrella programs in operation in Tennessee. Currently, there is no provision in Tennessee that supports using public funding for nonpublic schools.

VIRTUAL EDUCATION

In 2011 the Tennessee Virtual Public Schools Act was passed. The statute allowed public school districts to create and fund virtual public schools. These schools are subject to the same accountability laws, rules, and regulations as other public schools, including regular assessments. For the academic year 2021-22 there were 57 virtual public schools operating in Tennessee. Twenty-five of these schools, accepted enrollment on a statewide basis.

COVID-19 FUNDING

The global COVID-19 health pandemic prompted the U.S. Congress to pass legislation to provide relief for the negative impacts. The three rounds of federal funding[25] appropriated $4.5 billion for K-12 education in Tennessee intended to be expended between March 2020 and 2024 in Tennessee to address essential academic supports including tutoring and early reading.[26] Since so many Tennessee students are low-income, reside in rural communities, and had no access to the internet, they were adversely impacted by remote learning during the pandemic. State funding initiatives in Tennessee to increase broadband access throughout the state were leveraged to complement the federal initiatives.

ENDNOTES

[1] Tenn. Const. of 1835, art. XI, §10. The fund was largely to receive its revenue from the sale of public lands and from interest on some state deposits.

[2] Tenn. Const. of 1870 art XI, § 12.

[3] The Annual Report of the State Superintendent of Public Instruction for Tennessee for the Scholastic Year Ending June 30, 1891, p. 37.

[4] A bill introduced and passed by the Tennessee General Assembly may be classified as either a Public Act or a Private Act. Private Acts do not amend the Tennessee Code and affect only one "locality." Private Acts need only approval of their local legislative delegation but may be referred to committee and the entire legislative body. Private Acts are published in bound volumes entitled Tennessee Private Acts. There are numerous Tennessee statutes that address the funding of special school districts. For an overview through March 2012, see, Office of Research and Education Accountability. Statutory Options for School District Mergers: Report Addressing House Resolution 30, 2011. (Tennessee Comptroller of the Treasury 2012). Retrieved from https://www.comptroller.tn.gov/Repository/RE/MemphisSchoolConsolidation.pdf

[5] Brown v. Board of Education, 347 U.S. 483 (1954).

[6] Tenn. Const. of 1977, art. XI, § 12.

[7] Cassie Stinson & Dana Brimm. K-12 Dashboard. December 2021.Office of Research and Education Accountability. Tennessee Comptroller of the Treasury. https://comptroller.tn.gov/office-functions/research-and-education-accountability/interactive-tools/k-12-dashboard.html

[8] Tennessee General Assembly. 112th General Assembly. https://www.capitol.tn.gov/

9   Tennessee Office of the Governor. Governor Lee Passes Full "America At Its Best" Agenda. April 29, 2022. https://www.tn.gov/governor/news/2022/4/29/gov--lee-passes-full--america-at-its-best--agenda.html#:~:text=NASHVILLE%2C%20Tenn.,the%20State%20address%20in%20February.

10   Tennessee Office of the Governor. Ibid.

11   Tenn. Code. Ann. §50-1-201 et seq. (2019).

12   Tennessee Small School Systems, et al. v. McWherter (I), 851 S.W. 2d 139 (Tenn. 1993).(Small Schools I)

13   Education Improvement Act, Tennessee Public Acts and Resolutions, chapter 535 (1992).

14   Tenn. Code Ann. § 49-3-351 (1992).

15   Hamilton County Board of Education v. Haslam was filed in March 2015. Seven school districts that allege the state has not fully funded the Basic Education Program by underestimating teacher salaries and benefits which with Average Daily Membership drives the total funding amount for k-12 education. In addition, the suit alleges that classroom costs are not fully funded either.

16   A second suit was filed against the state in September 2015, Shelby County Board of Education v. Haslam, which alleged the state failed to provide adequate funding to meet the needs of the large numbers of students in Memphis who are immigrants, students with disabilities and students from poverty backgrounds who have extensive needs for additional services, and thus, denied these students their rights to an adequate free public education and to an equal opportunity. The district claimed it lacked the necessary funds to offer prekindergarten services, to adequately fund CTE programs, extracurricular activities, music, art, and mandatory foreign language education. And that students must pay fees to access these programs.

17   After having its own lawsuit dismissed, Metro Nashville [Public Schools] Board of Education joined the Shelby County [Public Schools] Board of Education lawsuit in October 2017.

18   Tennessee Office of the Governor. Tennessee Education Funding Review Public Engagement. https://www.youtube.com/playlist?app=desktop&list=PLZTYHUY2zirHBiUkeVJxBd2TiN-TyTuMld See, also Tennessee Department of Education. TNDOE Announces Central Steering Committee; 18 Subcommittees to Explore Student-Centered Funding Strategy. October 12, 2021. https://www.tn.gov/education/news/2021/10/12/tdoe-announces-central-steering-commit-tee--18-subcommittees-focused-on-exploring-student-centered-funding-strategy-.html

19   Tennessee Department of Education. TISA Legislation Launches on Feb. 24 with Presentation from Gov. lee and Commissioner Schwinn. February 16, 2022. https://www.tn.gov/education/news/2022/2/16/tisa-legislation-launches-on-feb--24-with-presentation-from-gov--lee-and-com-missioner-schwinn.html

20   See, Lisa G. Driscoll. "Tennessee," Journal of Education Finance, vol. 46 no. 3 (2021).

21   Tennessee Department of Finance & Administration. Fiscal Year 2021-22 Budget Publications. https://www.tn.gov/finance/fa/fa-budget-information/fa-budget-archive/fiscal-year-2021-2022-budget-publications.html

22   Tennessee Department of Finance & Administration. Fiscal Year 2022-23 Budget Publications. https://www.tn.gov/finance/fa/fa-budget-information/fa-budget-archive/fiscal-year-2022-2023-budget-publications.html

23   Tennessee Department of Education. TDOE Releases Explainer Resources for TISA, the Tennessee Investment in Student Achievement. March 4, 2022. https://www.tn.gov/education/news/2022/3/4/---tdoe-releases-explainer-resources-for-tisa--the-tennessee-investment-in-stu-dent-achievement--.html

24   Tennessee Department of Education. See, the TISA Unique Learning Needs Crosswalk that shows the weights used in the calculation for an individual student. https://www.tn.gov/education/tnedu-funding.html

25   Tennessee Code Ann. §49-13-101-112(a). (2019)

25. The U.S. Congress funded education through three separate allocations to state agencies The first, passed in March 2020 through the Coronavirus Aid Relief and Economic Security (CARES) Act, awarded $13.3 billion to state educational agencies nationwide through the Elementary and Secondary School Emergency (ESSER I) Fund. Tennessee received $259 million (or about $239/

pupil at the district level). In December 2020, the Coronavirus Response and Relief Supplemental Appropriations Act (CRRSA) appropriated approximately $54 billion nationally for the Elementary and Secondary Relief Fund (ESSER II) with Tennessee receiving $1.1 billion dollars (or about $1,000/ pupil at the district level). During March 2021 the American Rescue Plan was signed into law and provided $122 billion for the ARP Elementary and Secondary School Emergency Relief (ARP ESSER III) Fund nationally. These funds were intended for schools to safely reopen and address learning impacts on students. Tennessee was allocated $2 billion in funding based on the approval of Tennessee's plan.

[26.] See TDOE Announces Approval of All Tennessee Districts' ESSR Plans (January 26, 2022) https://www.tn.gov/education/news/2022/1/26/tdoe--announces-approval-of--all-tennessee-districts---esser-plans--.html#:~:text=Nashville%2C%20TN%E2%80%94%20Today%2C%20the,12%20public%20school%20students%20in

CHAPTER 43

TEXAS

Catherine E. Knepp
Dripping Springs Independent School District

Mary P. McKeown-Moak
Moak, Casey & Associates

GENERAL BACKGROUND

"The history of public school finance in Texas has been one of slow development marked by periodic neglect, intermittent crisis, and sporadic reform."[1] Almost 200 years ago, Texas began providing support for schools in 1827 when the Mexican state of Coahuila y Texas provided land grants and municipal funds for educational purposes.[2] After Texas gained its independence from Mexico, the Education Act of 1839 furthered land grants that today form the basis of County Permanent School Funds, and the Constitution of 1845 provided the first state funding of free schools with a minimum of one-tenth of the revenue from a state property tax to fund the schools. The following year several cities obtained the right to establish local taxes to support schools.[3] The School Law of 1854 provided a permanent endowment fund distributed on a per capita basis, which operated as a voucher system with funds following the student to whatever school parents chose.[4] The Constitution of 1876 established the basic funding for schools: a flat, per capita

Funding Public Schools in the United States, Indian Country,
and US Territories (Second Edition), pages 663–681.
Copyright © 2023 by Information Age Publishing
www.infoagepub.com
All rights of reproduction in any form reserved.

amount from the Available School Fund consisting of income from the Permanent School Fund, a maximum of one-fourth of general revenue, and a poll tax of $1 on all males aged 21 to 60.[5] The Texas Constitution (Article VII, Section 1) states "A general diffusion of knowledge being essential to the preservation of the liberties and rights of the people, it shall be the duty of the Legislature of the State to establish and make suitable provision for the support and maintenance of an efficient system of public free schools."[6] Following the actions in the 1870s, funding issues were largely neglected until 1915. Between 1915 and 1949, funding for rural high schools, textbooks, and equity for rural schools were added. In 1949, the Legislature adopted a minimum foundation program that used a complicated economic index to determine the local share, with the State providing 80 percent of funds.[7]

For the last 50 years, Texas school funding has been challenged in court many times, and has gone from rulings that the system was constitutional but chaotic and unjust,[8] to unconstitutional,[9] to constitutional,[10] to unconstitutional,[11] and back to constitutional but flawed and imperfect.[12] In 1968 *Rodriguez v San Antonio ISD* was filed in federal court, asserting that the state's school finance system discriminated against students in poor districts. In late 1971, a U.S. District Court held the state's finance method unconstitutional, but in 1973 the U.S. Supreme Court reversed the lower court's findings, declaring the system constitutional but unjust,[13] since large differences in property wealth led to large differences in per pupil funding. After Rodriguez, all filings have been in the state's courts rather than federal courts. Between 1973 and 1984, when Edgewood ISD v Bynum was filed, many changes were made to the finance system including adding a second tier to the Foundation School Program (FSP), changes to the local share calculation, increases in total aid, adjusting equalization aid, including vocational and special education as components of the FSP, and adjustments for small schools.

In 1984, HB 72 made changes to the finance system, some of which are still in effect: a guaranteed yield program, a price differential index, a FTE count of students, and special equalization aid or a form of hold harmless for districts losing state funds. In 1989, increasing the basic allotment, changing special education weights, replacing the price differential index with a cost-of-education index, and adding a second tier based on tax effort and a guaranteed yield were added. In 1990 Senate Bill 1 made substantial changes to address the Court's findings in the Edgewood case, including: a 5-year phase-in of reform; 95% of students would be in a wealth-neutral system; added facilities and equipment rates; increased the local share of the FSP; increased the guaranteed yield in the power-equalized second tier system; raised the tax rate the state would match; and other efficiency reforms. In 1993, after voters rejected a constitutional amendment to authorize tax base sharing at the county level, SB 7 required that districts above a specified level of wealth per student[14] engage in tax rate reduction or recapture by choosing one of five options to limit access to property value above the equalized wealth level of $280,000 per weighted student.[15] At that time, 104 school districts had property wealth above $280,000 per WADA.[16] Those wealthy districts were given

5 years to choose one of the available options, and were protected by a hold harmless. By 2018, 191 school districts were subject to recapture, and over $2.07 billion was projected to be recaptured.[17] Only two options for the recaptured funds, both of which require voter approval, have been used in the last 25 years: pay the state, or pay another school district. SB 7 made other changes including adding a new special education weight for mainstreamed students[18], reducing the basic allotment, increasing the local fund requirement for Tier 1, and eliminating proration when state appropriations were insufficient to fund the formula by creating a "settle-up" process near the end of the year. SB 7 was challenged as unconstitutional by several groups, and the Court declared funding to be constitutional and further addressed the concept of adequacy by linking the constitutional provision for a general diffusion of knowledge to the goals for public education in Chapter 4 of the Texas Education Code.

Numerous changes to the finance system were made between 1995 and 2014. In 1999, the temporary hold harmless for wealthy districts was made permanent, and in 2017-18, 26 of the original districts are still held harmless. Among the most notable of other changes to the law were the addition of a facilities grant program and reduction or compression of tax rates to provide tax relief. School districts that lost property tax revenues due to the 2006 compression of tax rates have been held harmless through "Additional State Aid for Tax Reduction" (ASATR), which was in effect until 2017. For 2018 and 2019, financial hardship grants are being made to 127 school districts to continue the hold harmless under the tax compression hold harmless.

In 2014 in *Texas Taxpayer & Student Fairness Coalition et al. v Scott*,[19] the District Court ruled that the finance system was unconstitutional. On appeal, the Texas Supreme Court ruled in 2016 that the school finance system, although flawed and imperfect, was constitutional, and further that the Legislature was responsible for designing the system. Unless the Legislature made arbitrary or unreasonable choices, the Court would defer to the Legislature. In response, a School Finance Commission was established, which is studying the system, and will issue a report in time for the 2019 legislative session.

Not many changes were made during the 2017 session, as the legislature focused on bathrooms and voucher programs, and no bills related to either passed. One important change was that charter schools were made eligible for facilities funding. And, 15 percent or $236 million of the estimated $1.58 billion to be spent on pre-kindergarten programs must be spent for "high quality" prekindergarten programs as defined in the Texas Education Code (TEC) §29.167-29.171. Moreover, there are so many "fine tuning" adjustments or exceptions to the formulas or calculations that make intimate knowledge of the entire finance system a necessity for calculating the correct amount of a district's state funding.

To summarize the Texas court rulings on the school finance system, in 1989 and 1991 in Edgewood I and II, the system was ruled unconstitutional on equity grounds. In 1993, in Edgewood III, the system was ruled unconstitutional on statewide property tax grounds, but in 1995, in Edgewood IV, the supreme court ruled the system constitutional. In 2005, in West Orange Cove, the system was ruled unconstitutional again on statewide property tax grounds. In 2011, in Texas Taxpayers, the system was again ruled unconstitutional on equity grounds, but the court did not make a decision on adequacy. In 2016, the State Supreme Court determined that the legislature had failed to make the system "whole" but the legislature had not failed so badly that he system was unconstitutional, thereby taking the courts out of school finance.

In 2019, the 86th Legislature made changes to the school funding system after a year-long Texas School Public School Finance Commission in 2018. Gov. Greg Abbott signed into law HB 3, historic bill that directed more funding to Texas public schools. Notably, the bill increased teacher compensation, slowed the growth of recapture, and changed school district tax rate adoption laws in an effort to slow the growth of local property taxes. Together with the 87th legislature's HB 1525, which made tweaks to the changes initiated by HB 3, HB 3 was considered to be historic school finance reform.

CURRENT POLITICAL CLIMATE

Texas has a bicameral legislature that convenes its regular sessions on the second Tuesday in January of odd-numbered years for a session that may last up to 140 days. The governor is given authority under the state constitution to convene the legislature at other times during the biennium into a special session of up to 30 days. Special sessions are reserved for legislation that the governor deems critically important in the conduct of state affairs, and the legislature may consider only issues stated in the governor's call. In 2021, the legislature met in the regular session and three special sessions.

The House comprises 150 members, and elects a speaker who controls the agenda, while the Lieutenant Governor is the President of the Senate and sets the Senate agenda for its 31 members. For the last twenty years, republicans have held all of Texas' statewide offices, including governor and lieutenant governor. Republicans hold a majority in both the Senate and House, and in 2021 were able to pass bills without any Democrats voting for passage.

The 2021 legislative session was especially contentious. Democratic house members left Texas to block passage of what they considered restrictive voting laws, thereby ensuring that there was not a quorum in the House. The governor then called three special sessions to get passage of the voting bills, as well as bills impacting school districts such as critical race theory and transgender children in sports.

Texas has a biennial budget cycle with a fiscal year of September 1 to August 31. The Legislature appropriates funds for each year of the biennium. Budget bills may originate in either the House or the Senate.

The legislative process in Texas encourages open participation by advocacy groups through a structure that provides considerable access to legislators, staff, and other involved policy makers. There are numerous special advocacy groups that represent a variety of school district characteristics such as small districts, fast growth districts, large districts, etc. In addition, there are advocacy groups centered around personnel (such as teachers, counselors, superintendents, business officers), and groups centered around specific issues to influence legislative policy.

SOURCES OF REVENUE

Texas was not immune to general fluctuations in the U.S. economy. In 2011, declines in state revenues required deep cuts to state government funding, and state aid to school districts was reduced by about $4 billion. Some of those reductions were made up in the 2014-16 biennium, but total state appropriations remain below prior levels. This is in part due to increasing property values which reduce the amounts needed for state funding as calculated in the total Foundation School Program (FSP) Tier 1 and Tier 2 allotments, as will be explained later.

Increases in school funding brought by HB 3 (2019) brought funding back to 2011 levels, on average. However, challenges brought about by the COVID-19 pandemic in the 2019-20 and 2020-21 school years prevented Texas school districts and charter schools from experiencing that relief.

In the 2020-21 school year, total funding for traditional public schools and charter schools was estimated to be $66.8 billion, comprised of $37.0 billion (55%) of property taxes, $24 billion (36%) of state aid, and $5.8 billion (9%) of federal resources.[20] Public education educated 5,371,586 million students enrolled in 1,407 public school districts and charter schools. School districts varied in size from fewer than 10 students in ADA to nearly 197,000 students. Approximately 1,217 school districts and charter schools with about 20 percent of the state's total ADA enroll fewer than 5,000 students, and 999 of those districts enroll fewer than 1,600 students.

In total, Texas appropriated $34.9 billion in funding for K-12 public education.[21] This funding total includes money for the 20 Regional Education Service Centers, the State School for the Blind, State School for the Deaf, the Texas Education Agency operations, and state payments of about $2.7 billion to the Teacher Retirement System (TRS) on behalf of public education employees. Contributions to TRS are shared by the state, school districts, and the employee.

The majority of state funds are distributed to school districts and charter schools through the Foundation School Program (FSP). For 2020-21, public schools were entitled to over $22.5 billion of state aid for school operations and facilities from the FSP (about $1 billion of that funding was supplanted with federal ESSER II funding). The Foundation School Program, the Property Tax Relief Fund, the Technology and Instructional Materials Fund, the General Revenue Fund, and the Available School Fund combine to provide state aid, most of which is formula driven. In addition, the Permanent School Fund, which is an endowment fund created in the 1800s, provides investment income deposited in the Available School Fund.

Federal funds generally are used for the school lunch program, title programs, and special education. Some federal funding is received for career and technical education, migrant education, and special grants. For the 2020-21 biennium, federal funds (not including COVID-specific ESSER funding) were projected to total $10.7 billion, less than 10 percent of total school revenues.

Local tax revenues for schools are paid by individual and business property owners on the taxable value of their property, after adjustments and certain exemptions. School districts are authorized to tax up to $.17 above a base tax rate per $100 in property value for maintenance and operations. The maximum maintenance and operations tax rates vary based on statewide and local district property value growth. In 2020-21, M&O tax rates ranged from $.9920 to $1.0834 per $100 in property value. School districts may also levy interest and sinking tax rates up to $0.50 on voter-authorized bonds approved by the State's Attorney General. If property value declines after the bond issue, the rate is permitted to rise above $0.50 to make the debt service payments. In 2020-21, school districts levied $28.7 billion in property taxes for maintenance and operations, and $8.3 billion for facilities.

DISTRIBUTION FORMULAS

School districts and charter schools are funded by a two-tier funding system based on the average daily attendance of students. The basic funding formula is called the "Foundation School Program (FSP)" or Chapter 48, Texas Education Code (TEC). Legislatively adopted state policy calls for the system to provide both adequacy and equity for the public schools. Traditional school district funding is a shared responsibility between taxpayers and the state. The FSP has four basic variables: the number of students, the types of students, the property values in the district, and the tax rate that is applied to that property value. Each school district (and each open-enrollment charter school) is guaranteed a basic revenue level, with additional revenues allotted for students participating in special education, career and technology education, bilingual education, compensatory education, and/or gifted and talented programs, and for the size of the district, based on a series of weights or special allotments. Although funding is allocated based on the type of student, the State grants school districts the flexibility to expend dollars to best meet overall student needs, within the maintenance of effort provisions for federal funds and within the rules of §29 and §48 of the Texas Education Code.

Tier I

For public school districts, Tier 1 of the formula is a basic foundation program, with a "basic allotment" per pupil and a series of weights for student and district characteristics. Additional payments are supplied for various district needs like transportation, teacher incentive pay, and student exam reimbursements. The total cost is shared between the State and the school district. The district's share is determined by applying a maintenance and operations (M&O) tax rate to the district's taxable property value for the current year, and then the State pays any amounts between the total cost and the district share. More wealthy districts pay larger shares of their total entitlement. The wealthiest districts pay most of the full cost of Tier 1 and an additional amount to meet equity standards through the recapture provisions of Chapter 49, TEC.

The "basic allotment" is an amount that every school district is guaranteed to receive from the combination of state and local funds (as described above) for each student in Average Daily Attendance (ADA). "Average Daily Attendance" is defined clearly in TEA's Student Attendance Accounting Handbook; attendance records are turned in for every child by six-week period, with certain exceptions for migrant students. The count is taken at the same time every day. Local school districts have the option to choose the time for individual campuses or groups of students, as long as the time does not change once it is selected.[22] The basic allotment was $6,160 per ADA for 2021-22 for districts that levied their assigned maximum compressed maintenance and operations (M&O) tax rate (this rate varies by district based on property value growth) in TY2021 as certified by the Comptroller. Districts with lower tax effort are provided a reduced basic allotment.

To calculate the Tier I entitlement, the basic allotment is multiplied by the number of students in each category of the student population and by the weight for that category of students. These amounts are then summed, together with amounts for other allotments including a school safety allotment, an allotment for fast-growing districts, post-secondary readiness bonus payments, a mentor program allotment and teacher incentive pay. From that total is subtracted the school district's share for Tier I. The district share is determined by applying the district's compressed M&O rate to the taxable value for the prior year and dividing by 100. If the school district's share exceeds the total for tier I, the school district must remit the overage to the state as "Recapture" or "Robin Hood" funds.

Tier 2

Tier 2 is the guaranteed yield portion of funding and is used by districts to supplement revenue received in Tier 1. School districts may tax above the district's assigned maximum compressed tax rate, up to a statutory cap of $.17 above the district's maximum compressed rate. The first $0.05 may be levied without voter approval, but the remaining $0.12 requires voter approval. (In years following a natural disaster, pandemics and epidemics excluded, districts may adopt additional pennies without voter approval to regain funds spent on expenses incurred by the disaster.) In TY 2020, 421 school districts levied $.05 per $100 over their maximum compressed rate; 610 districts levied more than $.05 pennies per $100 over their maximum compressed rate, requiring voter approval in TY 2020 or before. The state equalizes revenue raised by each penny above a district's maxi-

TABLE 43.1. Weights and Allotments in the 2020-2021 School Finance Formulas (Including Charter Schools)

Type of Student/Program	Definition	Weight/Amount	Number of Students/Staff	Total Amount
Regular program	Students in attendance in a regular program, not including special ed or career/technology	1.00	4,538,642.402	$27,942,359,672
Small and Mid-Sized	Charter schools and schools with fewer than 5,000 students receive an allotment to help adjust for economies of scale			$1,209,735,807
Special Education	12 weights from 1.5 to 5.0	1.1 - 5.0	599,748.88	$4,013,009,447
Dyslexia	Students that receive services for dyslexia or a related disorder through instruction that meets applicable criteria established by the State Board of Education	.1 add on	279,715.029	$172,302,995
Career & Technology	FTE enrolled in gr. 7-12	1.35 (Beginning in 2021-22; will have 1.1 for FTE in CTE course not in an approved program of study; 1.28 for FTE in Levels 1 & 2 courses and 1.47 FTE in Levels 3 & 4 courses	311,979.735	$2,594,405,473
P-Tech & New Tech	Students in attendance in a P-Tech or New Tech School	$50 per ADA	20,962.71	1,048,140.00
Bilingual/Emerging Bilingual	Average Daily Attendance for students learning a second language: traditional bilingual students (.1), dual language students learning English (.15) and dual language students learning languages other than English (.05)	0.10 add on / .15 add on / .05 add on	730,263.774 / 215,571.090 / 35,560.619	$449,834,094 / $199,187,383 / $10,952,654
Early Education	Average daily attendance of students K-3 that are either (or both) economically Disadvantaged or are learning English	.1 add on	1,368,681.315	$843,096,919
College, Career and Military Readiness Outcomes Bonus	Graduates that exceed post-secondary benchmarks set by the Texas Education Agency each year	$5,000 Educationally Disadvantaged $3,000 Non Educationally Disadvantaged $2,000 (special education graduates)	21,743.000 / 35,295.000 / 881.000	$108,715,000 / $105,885,000 / $1,762,000

Compensatory Education	Economically disadvantaged students; each enrolled student is assigned a weight based on the census block in which the student lives. Census blocks that are identified as areas of economic disadvantage are ascribed one of five weights, increasing with the level of economic disadvantage.	0.2250 - 0.2750	3,213,052	$5,173,305,759
Compensatory Education—Pregnant	Pregnant students at risk of dropping out	2.41	575.718	$8,546,811
Compensatory Education-Residential Treatment	Students living in a residential treatment facility and whose parents do not reside in district (not applicable to economically disadvantaged or special education students)	.2 add on	371	$457,044
Fast Growth	Districts identified in statute to be fast-growth; prior to 2021-22, districts in top quartile of growth. Beginning in 2021-22, districts that grow over 250 students over 6 year period receive an allotment		1,294,369	$303,775,064
School Safety	Safety funding per student in ADA	$9.72 per ADA	4,991,071.055	$48,499,743
Gifted and Talented	Students performing at a high level. Capped at 5% of a district's ADA	0.07 add on (beginning in 2021-22)	237,420 (in 2018-19; last year before 2021-22 allotment was funded)	$162,135,150
New Instructional Facility	Students attending a newly built or renovated campus	Up to $1,000 per ADA in 1st year; $1,000 per new student in ADA in 2nd year; capped at $70 million beginning in 2021-22	65,882.012	$65,882.012
Transportation	$1.00 per regular program mile; more per mile for other types of transportation	$1.00 per mile	N/A	$300,121,990
Technology and Instructional Materials	Funding for instructional materials and technology	% of statewide enrollment	5,339,102	$1.03 billion for 2020-21 biennium
Available School Fund Earnings from Permanent School Fund based on prior year ADA		486.92 per ADA	4,905,301.24	$2,463,939,570.

Source: Texas Education Agency 2020-21 Statewide Summary of Finance updated November 16, 2021

mum compressed rate, so that every district is guaranteed a minimum amount of state and local revenue per WADA per penny of enrichment tax.

It is important to note that "WADA" is not "weighted average daily attendance" but a number calculated by dividing the total cost of Tier 1, with some deductions (transportation, New Instructional Facilities Allotment and funding related to early childhood intervention and college and career readiness exams and assessments), by the basic allotment. WADA is supposed to represent the number of students for which a district receives funding after adjusting for special needs. WADA calculated for charters is roughly equivalent of WADA calculated for small and mid-size ISDs, due to the fact that all charter schools are entitled to the small and mid-size school allotment. In 2020-21, there were 4.99 million students in ADA, and 7.02 million in WADA, including charter school students.

There are two parts to Tier 2: Level 1 "Golden Pennies" and Level 2 "Copper Pennies." Level 1 local funds are not subject to recapture, but Level 2 local funds are subject to recapture. In Level 1, for each of the first eight pennies above the compressed rate, the state ensures that each penny of tax effort yields a minimum dollar amount per WADA. This minimum funding level is achieved through a guaranteed yield, which is 160% of the basic allotment per penny of tax effort. In the General Appropriations Bill in 2020-21, the level was set at $98.56 in 2020-21. The remaining so-called "Copper Pennies," pennies up to the statutory cap of $.17 above the district's assigned maximum compressed rate, are equalized in Tier 2, Level 2, up to 80% of the basic allotment per penny of tax effort. In 2020-21, the General Appropriations Bill set the level at $49.28 per WADA. Revenues generated by local taxes in excess of $49.28 per WADA are subject to recapture.

Exhibit 43.1 displays the calculation of the Foundation School Program allocations for a property poor school district while Exhibit 43.2 displays the calculation for a property wealthy or Chapter 49 school district. In addition to the adjustments shown in these examples, there are many other adjustments that may be made in the calculation of a school district's allocation from the FSP, including hold harmless provisions that are in effect for certain school districts. Calculation of a district's entitlement is a very complicated process that requires extensive knowledge of the many different rules governing funding.

CAREER AND TECHNOLOGY

Districts receive an add-on weight for each student in a state-recognized program of study for career and technology courses (CTE). In 2020-21, schools received a 1.35 weight for each full-time equivalent student (FTE) in grades 7-12 participating in Career and Technical Education, where FTE is defined as 30 hours of contact per week between a student and school personnel. (Beginning in 2021-22, FTEs will earn one of three weights. Students in unapproved programs of study will receive a 1.0 weight, those in lower level CTE courses will receive a 1.28 weight, and those in higher level courses will receive a 1.47 weight.) In 2021-22 (and in the future), CTE students are not included in the regular program

EXHIBIT 43.1. Calculation of State and Local Revenues for a Property Poor District for 2020-2021

# Students		Type of Student	Weight	Total ($)
6,160	32,631.141	Regular Program ADA	1.00	201,007,829
6,160	2,150.791	Special Ed Mainstream FTE	1.15	15,236,203
6,160	.835	Special Ed Vocational Adj. Class FTE	2.30	11,830
6,160	.024	Special Ed Off Home Campus FTE	2.70	399
6,160	428.509	Special Ed Resource Room FTE	3.00	7,918,846
6,160	457.892	Special Ed Self Contained FTE	3.00	8,461,844
6,160	0	Special Ed Hospital Class FTE	3.00	-
6,160	3.142	Special Ed Residential Care FTE	4.00	77,419
6,160	84.355	Special Ed Speech Therapy FTE	5.00	2,598,134
6,160	6.081	Special Ed Homebound FTE	5.00	187,295
6,160	2,442.839	Career and Technology FTE	1.35	20,314,649
6,160	29,670	Compensatory Education ADA	0.225-.275	49,824,005
6,160	0	Compensatory Ed Pregnant ADA	2.41	-
6,160	1,286	Dyslexia	0.10	792,176
6,160	8,955.714	Bilingual ADA	0.05-.15	7,132,341
6,160	13,078.141	Early Education ADA	0.10	8,056,135
6,160	140.815	Dropout Recovery and Residential Placement		38,724
–	0	ADA attending new school		-
$ 50	55.21	ADA in P-Tech or New Tech High Schools		2,7612
$ 2,000 – 5,000	308	CCMR Outcomes Bonus		1,442,000
	0	Fast Growth Allotment		-
		Mentor Program Allotment		
$9.72	36,054.818	School Safety Allotment		350,453
		Teacher Incentive Allotment		-
		Transportation Allotment		888,597
		College Prep and Certification Exam Reimbursements		276,642
Tier 1 Guarantee				**324,386,926**
School District's Share Tier 1		$.9158 x 7,689,593,318/100		(70,421,296)
State Share, Tier 1				253,965,630
Available School Fund		$486.922 x 37,277.230		18,151,103
State Aid, Tier 1				**272,116,7339**
Tier 2				
M&O Rate = $1.0541		"Golden Pennies" = $0.08 "Copper Pennies" = $0.0583	WADA = 52,488.526	
		Tier 2 Level 1 DTR= $5,544,107*.08/100=.0721 Tier 2 Level 2 DTR = $4,040,269 *.0583/100 = .0525		
Tier 2 Guarantee		($98.56 x .0721 x 52,488.526) + ($49.28 x .0525 x 52,488.526)		50,892,478
Less Local Revenue				(9,581,233)
State Aid, Tier 2				**41,297,868**

EXHIBIT 42.2. Calculation of State and Local Revenues for a Property Wealthy District for 2020-2021

$	# Students	Type of Student	Weight	Total
6,160	28,736.893	Regular Program ADA	1.00	177,019,261
6,160	777.827	Special Ed mainstream FTE	1.15	5,510,126
6,160	44.107	Special Ed Vocational Adj. Class FTE	2.30	624,908
6,160	6.518	Special Ed Off Home Campus FTE	2.70	108,407
6,160	364.185	Special Ed Resource Room FTE	3.00	6,730,139
6,160	229.324	Special Ed Self Contained FTE	3.00	4,237,908
6,160	0	Special Ed Hospital Class FTE	3.00	-
6,160	.762	Special Ed Residential Care FTE	4.00	18,776
6,160	60.177	Special Ed Speech Therapy FTE	5.00	1,853,452
6,160	.546	Special Ed Homebound FTE	5.00	16,817
6,160	1,282.500	Career and Technology FTE	1.35	10,665,270
6,160	18,9500	Compensatory Education ADA	0.225-.275	32,971,708
6,160	4.461	Compensatory Ed Pregnant ADA	2.41	66,226
6,160	1,844	Dyslexia	0.10	1,135,904
6,160	11,216.922	Bilingual ADA	0.05-.15	8,024,035
6,160	10,552.140	Early Education ADA	0.10	6,500,118
6,160	.927	Dropout Recovery and Residential Placement		255
-	-	ADA attending new school		-
50	.823	ADA in P-Tech or New Tech High Schools		41
2,000 – 5,000	735	CCMR Outcomes Bonus		2,495,000
-	-	Fast Growth Allotment		-
	-	Mentor Program Allotment		
9.72	30,725.012	School Safety Allotment		298,647
		Teacher Incentive Allotment		66,421
		Transportation Allotment		931,301
		College Prep and Certification Exam Reimbursements		190,535

Tier 1 Guarantee			**259,393,563**
School District's Share Tier 1	$.9164 x $34,222,572,102/100		(313,615,651)
State Share, Tier 1			0
Available School Fund	$486.922 x 32,091.764		15,626,186
State Aid, Tier 1			**15,626,186**
Tier 2			
M&O Rate = $1.0541	"Golden Pennies" = $0.08 "Copper Pennies" = $0.064 Tier 2 Level 1 DTR= $26,548,793*.08/100=.0776 Tier 2 Level 2 DTR = $2,123,903 *.064/100 = .0062		WADA = 41,940.54
Tier 2 Guarantee	($98.56 x .0776 x 41,940.54) + ($49.28 x .0062 x 41,940.54)		5,520,483
Less Local Revenue			(28,678,515)
State Aid, Tier 2			5,520,483
Local Revenue in Excess of Entitlement			60,604,449

count. There were 311,979.735 FTEs in 2020-21 and a total program allotment of $2,594,405,473. In addition, for ADA who are enrolled in a P-Tech or New Tech campus, a district receives $50 additional dollars per ADA; 20,962.71 ADA in 2020-21 earned at a total allotment of $1,048,140. Expenditures of the funds must be made under the rules in §48.106 and Subchapter F of §29 of the TEC.

SPECIAL EDUCATION

Districts receive additional funding to provide services for special education students. Special education students are those students aged 3 to 21 with disabilities or a special condition. The allotment is based on a set of 12 different weights depending not on the special education condition but on the method of serving the student. The weights are multiplied by the number of full-time equivalent (FTE) student count, where FTE is defined as 30 hours of contact per week between a student and school personnel. Weights vary from 1.5 to 5.0; 599,748.88 FTE students were included in 2020-21, at a program amount of over $4 billion. Special education students are not included in the count of regular students. Uses of the funds must be made under the rules in §48.102 and Subchapter A of §29 of the TEC.

COMPENSATORY EDUCATION

Districts receive a .2250 to .2750 add on weight to the regular program funding for services to students who are performing below grade level or who are at risk of dropping out of school. Funding is based on the census blocks in which economically disadvantaged students live. Census blocks are assigned one of five funding tiers, ranging from Tier 1 to Tier 5. Tier 1 census blocks are the least economically disadvantaged, and Tier 5 are the most economically disadvantaged. Approximately 3.2 million students met the eligibility criteria for the 2020-21 school year, and more than $5.17 billion was allotted. School districts received an additional weight of 2.41 for the 575,718 students who are at risk of dropping out of school due to pregnancy, an allocation of $8.5 million. Expenditures of the funds must be made under the rules in §48.104 and Subchapter C of §29 of the TEC.

BILINGUAL

Districts receive one of three add-on weights for emergent bilingual students. Students in average daily attendance in a traditional bilingual programs garner a 0.10 add-on weight. These students have limited English proficiency, their primary language is not English, and their language skills are such that they have difficulty performing ordinary class work at an acceptable level in English. Students in average daily attendance in dual-language programs garner different weights. Students that are learning English garner a .15 add-on weight, and students that are proficient in English receive a .05 weight. In 2020-21, there were an estimated 981,000 students in attendance in traditional bilingual classes, 216,000 students learning English in dual language classrooms and 35,600 students proficient in English in dual language classrooms. In 2020-21, emergent bilingual students generated an allotment of $659,974,131 Expenditures of the funds must be made under the rules in §48.105 and Subchapter B of §29 of the TEC.

GIFTED AND TALENTED

In addition to regular program funding, districts receive a 0.07 add-on weight for students who perform at a high level of accomplishment or show the potential to achieve. The number of students is capped at 5 percent of a district's average daily attendance. The overall allotment is capped at $100 million annually. In 2018-19, 237,420 students were funded under the Gifted and Talented allotment, so the allotment is likely to be capped by the $100 million appropriation in the future. Expenditures of the funds must be made under the rules in §48.109 and Subchapter D of §29 of the TEC.

STUDENTS IN NEW INSTRUCTIONAL FACILITIES

Districts receive an additional $1,000 per student in ADA for every student attending a newly built campus, newly leased, or a repurposed instructional facility in its first year of operation, and for additional students attending in the second year. The total statewide appropriation for this purpose is limited by statute to $70 million per year. The state paid $65.8 million for the 2020-21 school year for the estimated 65,800 students in new instructional facilities.

TRANSPORTATION

Districts receive funding for school transportation. Regular education transportation is funded at $1.00 per mile. For 2020-21, the transportation allotment totals $300,121,990. Transportation for special education, career and technology education and, in limited cases, to private providers is also funded. Transportation for special education students is funded at the lesser of $1.08 per mile or the district/charter school's cost per mile. Some districts transport Career and Technical Education students during the day for various purposes. The districts are reimbursed for these costs according to the district's official extracurricular travel per mile rate as set by the board of trustees and approved by the agency. Districts may not receive state funding for transporting students that live within 2 miles of their school unless the area is deemed to be a hazardous traffic area by the school board.

TECHNOLOGY AND INSTRUCTIONAL MATERIALS

Since 2011, 50 percent of the distribution from the Permanent School Fund to the Available School Fund must be deposited into the Technology and Instructional Materials Fund to be distributed by the Commissioner to school districts in the form of a technology and instructional materials allotment. The Commissioner creates an account for each school district and charter school into which he deposits funds at the beginning of the biennium, allocated based on the percentage of statewide ADA in the district or charter school. Funds may be withdrawn as needed during the biennium, and some districts withdraw the funds at the beginning of the two-year period. For the 2020-21 biennium, school districts and charter schools have allocated about $1.03 billion. The Instructional Materials Allotment is added to the state revenue AFTER calculations of the amounts for Tier I and Tier 2.

In addition, to recognize that small or mid-sized districts cannot take advantage of economies of scale, a small size adjustment is added for districts with fewer than 1,600 ADA. For a district with fewer than 300 students in average daily attendance that is also the only school district operating in a county, the small-size adjustment is increased by 17.5%. A mid-size adjustment is made for districts with fewer than 5,000 students. This adjustment is 16 times smaller than the small-size adjustment. In 2020-21, there were 206 mid-sized schools and 840 small-sized schools.

AVAILABLE SCHOOL FUND

As mentioned earlier, the Texas Constitution requires that earnings from the Permanent School Fund be distributed to districts on a per student basis. For 2020-21 approximately $2.5 Billion from the Available School Fund (ASF) was distributed to school districts based on a rate of $486.922 for each of the 4.99 million students in ADA in the prior year. The Available School Fund distribution replaces FSP aid on a dollar for dollar basis.

CAPITAL OUTLAY AND DEBT SERVICE

Texas school districts may issue bonds to pay for the purchase of property, construction, acquisition, and equipment of a building or for purchase of school buses. Voters must approve the tax rate needed to re-pay the principal and interest on a bond before bonds are issued. Texas school districts can adopt interest and sinking (I&S) tax rates up to $0.50 cents to generate revenue used to fund the annual debt service payments associated with bonds. Districts may go beyond the 50 cent limit if the property tax base declines after the tax rate is approved by the voters. Almost all Texas school district debt is guaranteed under the Permanent School Fund, which impacts the bond rating favorably. The state assists school districts (charter schools are not eligible) to pay for facilities through two programs, the Instructional Facilities Allotment (IFA) and the Existing Debt Allotment (EDA). Funding formulas for facilities are similar to Tier II of the FSP because they work on a guaranteed yield per penny of tax effort per student. However, facilities funding formulas use ADA instead of the WADA used in Tier II.

Both of the formulas or allotments are guaranteed yield programs that assist school districts with debt payments on bonds. The IFA was authorized in 1997 to assist with instructional facilities. The state guarantees $35 per student in ADA for each penny levied for these facilities, and districts must apply to TEA for the funds. After TEA receives all requests, applying districts are ranked from lowest property wealth per ADA to the highest, and applications are funded in that order. State funding is limited to the lesser of the actual debt payment, or the greater of $250 per student or $100,000. Funding has not been sufficient to fully fund all requests, and only property-poor districts generally receive this aid.

The EDA was authorized in 1999 to assist districts with debt payments on bonds for which the district had made payments in the last year of the previous biennium and for which the district does not receive aid through the IFA. EDA funds may be used for both instructional and non-instructional facilities. The state guarantees the lesser of $40 per student in average daily attendance (ADA) per penny of I&S taxes levied by school districts to pay the principal of and interest on eligible bonds, or an amount that would result in a $60 million increase in state aid from the previous yield of $35. The yield was $39.40 in 2020-21.

Charter schools with an acceptable accountability rating became eligible in 2018-19 for EDA funding. Their EDA allotment is calculated using the state average debt service tax rate for school districts or a rate that will deliver $60 million in additional funding multiplied by the estimated EDA guaranteed yield multiplied by the charter school's ADA. The funding is allocated 50 percent to charter schools and 50 percent to traditional districts. Charter schools may seek to have bond debt guaranteed by the PSF. This is a very controversial provision because charter schools enroll about 10 percent of the state's ADA. In 2020-21, school districts and charter schools received $285 million in facilities aid.

EMPLOYEE BENEFITS

The Teacher Retirement System of Texas (TRS) manages pension funds for Texas public education. TRS health insurance programs for active members (TRS-ActiveCare) and retirees (TRS-Care). TRS is governed by a nine-member board of trustees, appointed by the governor and confirmed by the Texas Senate.

While districts are not required to provide health care through TRS, public education employees may be enrolled in TRS-Active Care. Those that are retired and are not yet Medicare eligible, may enroll in TRS-Care.

As for retirement pension funding, school district employees, the state and districts themselves are required to contribute a certain rate (based on the employee's salary) to TRS's pension fund. Districts must contribute funds that are at least 1.8% of the employee's salary and the state and employee both must contribute funds equal to 8% of the employee's salary.

CHARTER SCHOOL FUNDING

All charter schools have the same funding level based on state district average "basic allotment." For Tier 1 Funding purposes, all charter schools, regardless of the number of students, receive a stand-alone small & mid-sized district allotment based on an adjusted weighted average of the amounts provided to school districts under TEC, 48.101(b) or (c). For FY 2021 this amount was projected to average to be $1,058 per student in average daily attendance. Charter schools' tier two allotments are calculated using the state average M&O tax rates for the golden and copper pennies ($0.0613 and $0.0265, respectively in FY2021).[23]

The result of this formula is that charter schools benefit as more districts hold elections to increase their M&O tax rates. Also, use of unweighted averages for the charter schools effectively treats charters schools as if they were all small districts with less than 1,600 students.

NON-PUBLIC SCHOOL FUNDING

There is no state or locally appropriated funding for non-public school students in Texas.

VIRTUAL EDUCATION

Chapter 30 A of the Texas Education Code allows for the Texas Education Agency (TEA) to provide online courses to eligible students through the Texas Virtual School Network (TXVSN). The TXVSN is made up of two components—the course catalog and the full-time online schools. Only a handful of school districts are permitted to deliver full-time online instruction through the TXVSN, and students accrue funding for their district from completion of coursework (not average daily attendance). Before the COVID-19 pandemic necessitated greater access to state funded virtual education, the TXVSN was the only state-funded virtual education option.

During the 2020-21 school year, by commissioner waiver, the Texas Education Agency provided for students to learn remotely via two instructional methods that were not previously funded: synchronous and asynchronous instruction by the student's own classroom teacher. These students were counted as part of regular average daily attendance counts. In the second special session of the 87th Texas legislature, SB 15 permitted eligible public school students to receive instruction from their classroom teacher (like students did during 2020-21). The bill allowed for up to 10% of a district's enrollment to accrue funding through this local virtual education option.

FEDERAL COVID-19 FUNDING

The Elementary and Secondary School Emergency Relief (ESSER) provided $190 billion in federal aid from the three relief packages passed since March 2020. Texas used federal monies from ESSER I to supplant state aid to school districts instead of providing additional resources. However, some private schools (that do not receive state funding) were provided federal resources from ESSER I under the applicable federal law. Texas received $5.5 billion appropriated under ESSER II. Funds were allocated per federal statutory formula to school districts and charter schools. Under ESSER III, districts and open-enrollment charter schools applied to TEA to receive their allocation of the $11.2 billion appropriated to Texas for public education purposes under the ESSER III Fund. Funds under ESSER III could not supplant state funds. School systems were advised to use these new funds to respond to the pandemic and to address student learning loss as a result of COVID-19.

SUMMARY

In 2020-21, 1,407 public school districts and charter schools provided educational services to 5,371,586 enrolled students. School districts vary in size from fewer than 10 to 197,000 enrolled students, although approximately 1,217 school districts and charter schools with about 20 percent of the state's total enrollment enroll fewer than 5,000 students, and 999 districts or charter schools enroll fewer than 1,600 students. In 2020-21, school districts and charter schools were entitled to nearly $25 billion in state funds (the state supplanted some of these state dollars with federal ESSER II dollars). Local taxpayers paid over $37 billion in local property taxes to fund schools during the same time period. Most of the state funding was distributed by a two-tiered funding formula, the first tier of which is a foundation program with recapture, tier 2A is guaranteed yield funding with no recapture, and tier 2B is guaranteed yield funding with recapture.

ENDNOTES

[1] Thomas, Stephen B. and B.D. Walker. 1982. "Texas School Finance," Journal of Education Finance p. 223-24, Vol. 8, No. 2, pp. 223-281.

[2] Walker, Billy D. and W. Kirby. 1986. The Basics of Texas Public School Finance. Austin, TX: Texas Association of School Boards.

[3] Casey, Daniel T. The Basics of Texas Public School Finance, Sixth Edition. 1996. Austin, TX: Texas Association of School Boards.

[4] Thomas and Walker, op.cit, p. 228.

[5] Texas State Constitution of 1876, Article VII, Section 3.

[6] Texas State Constitution of 1876, Article VII, Section 1.

[7] Casey, op.cit. p. 11.

[8] San Antonio ISD v Rodriguez, 411 U.S. 1 (1973)

[9] Edgewood ISD v Bynum (1984); Edgewood v Kirby (1990); Carrolton Farmers Branch ISD v Edgewood ISD (1991)

[10] Edgewood ISD v Meno (1993)

[11] West Orange Cove v Neeley (2001); Texas Taxpayer & Student Fairness Coalition et.al. v Scott (2011)

[12] Ruling of the Texas Supreme Court in Texas Taxpayer & Student Fairness Coalition et.al. v Scott (2014)

[13] San Antonio ISD v Rodriguez, 411 U.S. 1 (1973)

14 Districts above the wealth level are called "Chapter 41" districts. In 2018, the Texas Education Agency report that there were 191 Chapter 41 districts, 26 of which are hold harmless districts.

15 Pace, Sheryl. 2018. An Introduction to School Finance in Texas, Fourth Edition. Austin, Texas: Texas Taxpayer and Research Foundation.

16 Ibid. p. 18.

17 Texas Education Agency, Cost of Recapture.

18 Texas funding for special education students is based on the method of service, not on the handicapping condition of the student.

19 Texas Taxpayer & Student Fairness Coalition et.al. v Scott (2014).

20 Federal fund numbers from the Texas Education Agency appropriations request.

21 Amounts from https://public.tableau.com/app/profile/state.of.texas.lbb/viz/FiscalSize-UpExpenditureandAppropriationDetail20_21a/FiscalSize-UpDetail

22 P. 54 Student Attendance Accounting Handbook, Texas Education Agency.

23 Texas Education Agency, School Finance Overview.

CHAPTER 44

UTAH

W. Bryan Bowles
Brigham Young University

Robert W. Smith
Alpine School District

GENERAL BACKGROUND

Utah's public school finance plan is a modified foundation program; Utah's official title for that program is The Minimum School Program. The foundation grant, which guarantees each student a minimum level of fiscal support, is only one component of the Minimum School Program. The value of the foundation grant, named the Weighted Pupil Unit (WPU) in Utah, is set each year by the legislature. School districts are required to tax local wealth (assessed valuation of local property) using the program's Basic Tax Rate, which is also set by the legislature. The difference between what can be raised locally by the Basic Tax Rate and the amount guaranteed between what can be raised locally by the Basic Tax Rate and the amount guaranteed by the state is paid by revenues generated from the State's Uniform School Fund, primarily personal income tax —- constitutionally earmarked for this purpose. Wealthy districts, using the Basic Tax Rate, capable of raising revenues greater than the value of the foundation grant are subject to

Funding Public Schools in the United States, Indian Country,
and US Territories (Second Edition), pages 683–701.
Copyright © 2023 by Information Age Publishing
www.infoagepub.com

683

recapture. Recaptured funds become revenue to the Uniform School Fund the following year. Finance of the foundation grant is heavily supported by the state, which pays about 80% of its total. On average, local school district revenues account for $776. of the $4,038 guarantee by the state per WPU. Such an active effort on the part of the state accounts for the high degree of fiscal equity evident in the state's school finance plan.

Consistent with the basic structure of a school finance foundation plan, Utah's 41 school districts are able to levy a number of additional taxes (5 primary levies in total) against the value of their local property, which varies from $170,665 to $2,860,931 per pupil (chart attached). Local tax rates are limited, and several are equalized to some minimal level by the state's finance formulas. Additionally, the state contributes significantly to support special services such as special education, applied technology, at-risk programs, class size reduction, and adult education programs. Indeed, the foundation grant, those funds that ensure each of Utah's 675,247 (projected FY2023—an increase of 1.18% over the prior year) students receive some minimum level of fiscal support, only account for about 14% of the state's Minimum School Programs, which are detailed in the sections following.

Utah current budget appropriated $9.7 billion to public schools, which is approximately 35% of Utah's $26. billion total operating budget.

- Clear principles guide Utah's public school finance statutes:
- All children are entitled to reasonably equal educational opportunities regardless of place of residence
- Establishment of a school system is primarily a state function—school district should pay a portion
- Each locality should be empowered to provide educational facilities and opportunities beyond the minimum program

HISTORICAL BACKGROUND TO UTAH'S CURRENT FINANCE PLAN

Prior to statehood in 1896, education was a local issue with "ward houses" of The Church of Jesus Christ of Latter-day Saints, often serving as both church and school. School revenues came in the form of charity, donations, and tuition.

Utah's constitution provided for a permanent state school fund and a uniform school fund (Article X, Section 5). Art XIII, Section 5(5) of Utah's constitution provides that "all revenue from...a tax on income shall be used to support the systems of public education and higher education..."

A "consolidation movement" began about 1890 and with it the move toward Utah's first real public school system. Utah's 224 school districts were legislatively consolidated into 40 by 1915. In 2009, the Jordan School District split into the Jordan School District and the Canyons School District. Utah now has 41 school districts that range from large urban districts to small rural districts.

The basic funding mechanism, a foundation program, was established in 1921: state participation based on state income taxes and local ad valorem property taxes. An equalization component was added in 1931, based upon weighted pupil counts and cost differentials.

Utah's new foundation plan was formalized by 1948 earmarking income taxes for funding public education and accounted for in the Uniform School Fund. Additionally, a uniform accounting system was established, uniform tax rates were set, and equalization of tax support was guaranteed. A system of weighted distribution units was introduced to distribute funds. State aid for building became part of the funding mechanism at the time. Finally, federal impact aid, an increased role for property taxes, and the voted leeway were all added to the funding plan. These components of the funding plan are still largely in place today.

A major school finance reform effort in 1973 resulted in a move toward improved statewide tax equalization (limited power equalization), the conversion to weighted pupil units (WPU) by which to promote vertical equalization. At this time, a number of categorical programs were introduced by the formula dealing with special services and programs not previously addressed in the funding formula.

A major review and reform of Utah's school finance program occurred in 1989. Many budgetary and formula changes were recommended and implement, including the establishment of a 1993 Capital Outlay Equalization Program and, finally, a Capital Foundation Program. In 2012, HB301 modified the tax rates each school district could levy and established two levels of board levy, depending on the current rates being assessed. This rate consolidation action created board levy equity issues among the 41 school districts until it was changed in 2018 by HB293, which established a single board levy cap of .002500.

In 2006, Utah Governor John Huntsman implemented large cuts to the state's individual income taxes. These tax cuts, combined with the effects of the Great Recession, have significantly reduced Utah's tax burden, but also decreased the amount of money generated for public schools. And, while the majority of other states raised taxes to make up for revenue declines caused by the recession, Utah avoided such a move by opting for further budget reductions. Additionally, Utah has made consistent cuts to the minimum property tax rate, a critical source of education funding, claiming "tax relief" for businesses and homeowners.

UTAH'S STATE ECONOMY

Utah's economic prosperity is described in the 1998 Economic Report of the Governor's Office of Planning and Budget as the longest sustained economic expansion in the state's economic history. Utah's economy, the Gross State Product, has grown, on average at a rate of over 8% per year after adjusting for inflation. The growth in new jobs has exceeded 3.0% for the last 10 consecutive years and during Utah's per capita income moved from the 49th ranking among states to 44th during this expansion period. Currently, Utah ranks 39th in per capita income.

These growth rates may have peaked, however, and legislative concern about the state's fiscal future is evident in the conservative proposed increases for state funding which increased less than expected.

During this expansion period the budget for public education grew by a 25% average, after adjusting for inflation. Considering the rapid growth of the state's budget, it is not surprising that education's percentage of the state's budget has declined steadily during the 1990s, from about 40% in 1989 to about 31% in 1998. That percentage (31%) continues to hold in 2018.

Utah's unique demographic makeup strongly influences public school financing. Utah's high birth rates and young population—31% of the state's population is under the age of 18 (U.S. Census)—presents clear education funding challenges. Utah has more children to educate and fewer working adults paying into the public education system. As a result, Utah spends just $8,968 per pupil per year, a number that is ranked 50th in the nation of 51 ranked entities and more than $4,000 below the national average.

MINIMUM SCHOOL PROGRAM

The structure for public school funding in Utah is known as the Minimum School Program (MSP) and was created in the early 1970s due to nationwide funding equity conversations. Following broad study and conversation, the MSP framework was put in place by the Utah Legislature, with the initial funding distributed in 1974. After the MSP had been in place for a period of time, a comprehensive review of the MSP was requested by the Utah Legislature and completed in 1990. Since that comprehensive review, significant changes have been made as follows: 1998—Utah Charter Schools Act (HB145S1); 2011—School District Property Tax Revisions (HB301); 2015—Property Tax Equalization Amendments (SB97S3); 2016—School Funding Amendments (SB38S4); and 2018 Tax Rebalancing Provisions (HB293S5).

Equitable funding for all children is one of the primary considerations in Utah's funding model. In Utah law, 53F-2-103, the legislature recognizes that "all children of the state are entitled to a reasonably equal educational opportunities regardless of their place of residence in the state and of the economic situation of their respective school districts or other agencies." In addition to equity of funding, statute requires a secondary consideration as it contemplates the reciprocal accountability between the State of Utah and each Local Education Agency (LEA) and the appropriate funding balance so each has "skin in the game." Finally, statute empowers each locality to "provide education facilities and opportunities beyond the minimum program." These three guiding principles have kept Utah in the forefront of equitable funding for students in the nation and influenced citizens and educations entities from legally challenging student funding.

Utah's MSP is comprised of the following four (4) core areas:

1. Basic School Program

2. Related to Basic Programs
3. Voted and Board Levy Programs
4. One-Time Programs

Basic School Program

The Basic School Program equalizes funding and distributes dollars to Local Education Agencies (LEA's) based on the number of Weighted Pupil Units (WPUs) the LEA generates and the dollar value of the WPU set by the Utah Legislature. The WPU value for fiscal year 2023 is $4,038, an increase of $223 or 5.0% over fiscal year 2022. A WPU is generated when a student is in membership for 180 days and 990 hours during the prior school year.

Utah law defines the WPUs for each program and are different between school districts and charter schools as follows:

District School Students	Charter School Students
Kindergarten—.55 WPUs	Kindergarten—.55 WPUs
Grades 1 - 12—1.0 WPUs	Grades 1-6—.90 WPUs
Special Education—1.53 WPUs	Grades 7-8 - .99 WPUs
	Grades 9-12 - 1.2 WPUs
	Special Education—1.53 WPUs

LEAs generate dollars in the Basic Program, based on their prior year WPUs plus growth in the current year, in the following areas:

*   Kindergarten WPUs
*   1-12 Student WPUs

These dollars are unrestricted and comprise a significant portion of most LEA budgets. As an example: when analyzing FY23 state revenue, unrestricted resources in the Basic Program account for 56.5% for the Alpine School District. Alpine School District is the largest LEA in Utah and serves ~80,000 students.

Also in the Basic program are revenues that are "restricted" for use in specific areas as follows:

*   Special Education WPUs
*   Career & Technical Education (CTE) WPUs
*   Class Size Reduction K-8 WPUs

The unrestricted and restricted portions of the Basic Program resources are primarily used for classroom instruction.

Related to Basic Programs

The related to basic programs are non-WPU driven and are often referred to in Utah as "below-the-line" programs. These programs are intended by the legislature to complement or enhance the basic program and are subject to annual appropriation. The following are a few of the major related to basic programs and their allocation methodology:

- Enhancement for At-Risk: Base amount + per student amount
- School Land Trust: Base amount + per student amount
- Flexible allocation: per student amount / WPU
- Charter school local replacement: per student amount / WPU
- Pupil transportation to and from school: qualification criteria comprised of number of miles and minutes driven
- Youth in Custody: qualification criteria
- Teacher Salary Supplement: grant based
- Critical languages and dual immersion: grant based

Voted and Board Local Levy Programs

As equalization is a primary tenet of Utah's Funding priorities, this funding source recognizes that regardless of where a student lives, the local tax generated will be vastly different and, therefore, additional state resources are provided to improve funding equity per student across the state. The state support for FY23 for voted and board local levy guarantee programs is estimated at $1.0 billion dollars statewide.

These guarantee programs establish a minimum revenue amount that is generated for each WPU a school district qualifies to receive multiplied by the tax increments the district levies, up to a maximum of 20 increments (HB293 - FY18 session) in the voted and board levy programs multiplied by a dollar value set by the legislature. The estimated guarantee value for FY23 is $55.37. As an example, district 15 levies 20 increments, has 1000 WPUs, and the guarantee is $55.37, their voted and board local levy program would guarantee $1,107,400 in revenue. If the local property tax only generated $707,400 in revenue, the state would contribute the additional $400,000 to the LEA.

One-Time Programs

The Legislature supports many one-time programs each year. These programs are used for specific or special needs and are not expected to continue long-term. Allocations may include resources for Teacher Supplies and Materials, Digital Teaching and Learning grants, etc.

PUPIL TRANSPORTATION

Utah provides funding to school districts to transport students to and from school if they meet the qualifying criteria for funding (discussed below) and in accordance with the prior year's eligible transportation as legally reported by LEA's. The prior year cost includes an allowance per mile for approved routes, an allowance per minute for approved routes and a minimum amount for each district. State law 53F-2-402 3(b), notes that the State will "contribute 85% of approved transportation costs, subject to budget constraints." Costs of equipment and administration of to and from transportation are also considered in the funding model. Spending on transportation among districts ranges from $277 per pupil to $1,500.

In order to qualify as an eligible student for transportation, the student must live at least 1.5 miles (elementary students) or 2.0 miles (secondary students) from their school. The qualifying distance must be calculated using the most direct route, road, trail or path to the nearest entrance on school property. The district must also have at least 10 qualifying students for a regular student route to be eligible or 5 qualifying special education students (a wheelchair student counts as 5). The state also provides a reimbursement or "fee in lieu of transportation" for parents of eligible students as an alternative for busing or when the cost of busing exceeds the reimbursement.

The funds received by LEAs in pupil transportation are restricted by program, thereby only used for transportation expenses. All school districts subsidize transportation costs with local resources. This funding reality is particularly challenging for rural districts who have significant geographic challenges and isolated student populations.

FOOD SERVICES

All Utah school provide full food service programs, following state and federal guidelines. Districts provide food services through private vendors, district cooperatives, and in-house departments. Individual districts, through local Board approval, set lunch prices without an expectation to be consistent throughout the state. Approximately 50-55% of the cost is borne through federal funding allocations. The State of Utah contributes between 15-20% of the cost on a reimbursement basis through revenue generated from taxes on alcohol. The remaining amount of revenue between 25-35% of revenue needed to fund this program is local revenue generated from lunch sales.

CAPITAL OUTLAY

Funding for capital projects, new school construction, renovation or replacement, including the maintenance and repair of facilities is primarily funded at the local level. Boards of Education approve the capital improvement plan and funding model to enact the plan subject to input from staff, constituents, and available resources.

Each school district may levy a tax for capital projects or technology projects up to a maximum of .003 (53F-8-303) per calendar year. As funds generated in each district vary due to the district's relative wealth and assessed property value per student, and with some districts experiencing more intense pressure for capital dollars due to rapid growth, the legislature has enacted two programs to mitigate the impact of growth and provide some equalization of revenue based on taxing effort.

The first capital outlay program is a foundational program and establishes an effort or floor of "at least .002400 per dollar of taxable value" to qualify for full funding. Should a district levy a combined rate less than the floor, the amount of funding is proportional to the floor. The guaranteed amount is based on the average daily membership (ADM) and assessed value per ADM and distributes the full amount in one lump sum payment to districts based on the legislative appropriation. These resources find their way to "low wealth" districts and those that have large student populations (ADM).

The second capital outlay program is the enrollment growth program and recognizes the additional pressure that fast growing districts and their taxpayers feel to keep up with the need for construction of new facilities. In order to receive funding in this program, districts must qualify for funding in the capital foundation program mentioned above and have enrollment growth in the past three years. The legislatively appropriated resources are distributed to those districts who have an average net increase of student enrollment over the prior three (3) years.

The final capital outlay funding mechanism is found in the statutory school building revolving account. This account was set up to allow short term loans for school districts and charter schools for construction and renovation of school buildings. The State Superintendent for Public Instruction administers this program, sets the amount of loans, the interest rate, and the term of repayment based on an appointed committee's recommendations. The repayment term is up to 5 years.

TEACHER RETIREMENT

The Utah Retirement System (URS) was created in 1986 as the State of Utah transitioned from a contributory program to a non-contributory program. Education employers who elected to participate may not withdraw from the system (UCA 49-13-202(1)). Employees who were participating in the contributory program prior to July 1, 1986, received the option to continue participation in the contributory system.

The URS non-contributory program provides defined benefits for eligible employees according to the framework of benefits outlined in state law. Education employees who meet the eligibility requirements outlined and were hired prior to July 1, 2011 are considered members of the Tier I benefits. A basic outline of Tier I non-contributory benefits are as follows:

- Unreduced retirement benefits at 30 years of service
- 2% benefit per year of service
- Retirement calculated on highest three years of salary average
- Continuation of service credit if disabled and employer has a qualifying plan

For example, if a teacher has 30 years of eligible service with a three-year average salary of $75,000, his retirement benefit would be ~$45,000 per year or 60% of his three-year average salary.

Responding to changes in governmental accounting standards and the impact of the "Great US Recession in 2009-11," the Utah legislature modified retirement benefits for eligible education employees hired after July 1, 2011, creating the Tier II benefit program. In the Tier II benefit program, eligible employee may choose to participate in a non-contributory program (with reduced benefits as compared to Tier I employees) or a contributory defined contribution program. If no election is made by the employee, the default election is the non-contributory program. A basic outline of Tier II non-contributory system benefits are as follows:

- Unreduced retirement benefits at 35 years of service
- 1.5% benefit per year of service
- Retirement calculated on highest five-year salary average
- Continuation of service credit if disabled and employer has qualifying plan

For example, if a teacher had 35 years of eligible service with a five-year average salary of $75,000, their retirement benefit would be ~$39,375 per year or 52.5% of their five-year average salary.

The contributory benefit option for Tier II employees is similar to a 401K program where the employer deposits the required contribution, currently 10% of the employee's salary, into a 401K.

Additional 401K contributions are made by education entities in Utah. Presently, employers contribute an additional 1.5% into an employee's 401K without requiring a match from the employee. Currently a few employers choose to contribute a higher percentage than the standard 1.5%.

Education entities also have the option to provide additional local retirement incentives, whether they are cash payment or insurance eligibility. With the accounting changes made by the Governmental Accounting Standards Board (GASB) in 2007, most retired insurance benefits were eliminated in lieu of complying with the accounting and trust requirements in the new standards.

SPECIAL EDUCATION

FY23 funding for students receiving special education services in Utah is slightly over $469 million. Funding is provided in the following major categories: Add-On—additional WPUs provided to "add-on" to the regular program; Self-Contained—additional WPUs provided based on the average daily membership of students in self-contained programs; and Pre-school—WPUs provided based on the actual enrollment of preschool students qualifying as SPED. Additional resources are provided for students who require intensive services and specialized care-giving.

GIFTED AND TALENTED

Funding for the state's Gifted and Talented programs has been subsumed under the category of Enhancement for Accelerated Learning programs. This funding category includes the traditional Gifted and Talented programs, the state's Advanced Placement program, its Concurrent Enrollment program, and its International Baccalaureate program.

Funding for the Gifted and Talented programs (about 20% of the Accelerated Learning budget) is distributed on a per pupil basis. Each district gets its share of the budget depending upon the district's proportional share of the state's total K–12 and Small Schools WPUs. Funding for the State's Advanced Placement is based on tests passed and hours completed. Funding for Concurrent Enrollment programs is based on the hours of higher education courses completed by students. The largest share of the budget in this category goes to Concurrent Enrollment (64%), which allows students to earn college credit concurrently while earning high school credit. The idea, wildly popular in the state, requires a certified teacher with a Masters degree to teach "college" content in what is otherwise a high school course. Funding for this program compensates the teachers, provides money for additional supplies and material, and reimburses some of the cost of the administrative work of both districts and colleges participating in the program.

Districts differ widely in their use of these funds to aid in educating gifted and talented students. Indeed, one of the growing concerns associated with these popular programs is that, with increased funding, the demand for more accountability also increases.

BILINGUAL EDUCATION

Funding for Bilingual Education is found within the related to basic program and part of the Enhancement for At-Risk Students program, which is allocated by formula to LEA's (53F-2-410). The composite of program funding is used to provide special help and instruction for students with limited knowledge of English among other program objectives. This is considered to be a special purpose district option program under the overall Minimum School Program. Funding may come from a combination of general discretionary state and local sources.

CHARTER SCHOOL FUNDING

Charter schools were initially authorized in Utah during the 1998 legislative session with a bill sponsored by Representative Brian Allen. The intended purpose of these new schools was to innovate, encourage more parental involvement, find ways to educate for less resources, and provide choice for students and parents. The first charter school was authorized in 2000 and began operation shortly thereafter. Nearly 20 years later, Utah has enrolled 78,000 students in its 138 Utah Charter Schools or 11.6% of the total students in Utah's public education system. The WPU generated for students in charter schools is slightly different than the allocation for students in district schools and was addressed earlier in this document. Legislators continue to look for ways to provide equitable opportunities for all students in Utah as shown in multiple pieces of legislation over the years like SB38 and HB293S5 in the last two legislative sessions.

STATE AID FOR PRIVATE K-12 SCHOOLS

Utah does not provide aid for private K-12 schools.

EARLY CHILDHOOD EDUCATION

Utah has not historically appropriated state dollars to support traditional preschool programs. In lieu of traditional preschool programs, the Utah State Legislature has supported an online program called UPSTART—Utah Preparing Students Today for a Rewarding Tomorrow (Utah Code 53F-4-402). That program has been administered by a private vendor, the Waterford Institute, a Utah-based nonprofit center. Parents who apply to participate are selected on a first come-first served basis until the appropriation runs out each fiscal year. UPSTART will serve up to 10,000 students in the FY23 school year. The program has grown quickly since its inception in 2008, bolstered by external evaluations that have shown early literacy gains among children who use it.

LOCAL SCHOOL REVENUE, PROPERTY TAXES, AND EXEMPTIONS

The Utah Legislature recognizes the importance of balancing taxation stewardship between the state and local level. As such, the legislature empowers local school board's with taxation in the following areas:

- **Basic State Levy**—53F-2-3-1 - rate set by the legislature is .001666 for FY19—This levy is a component of the fully equalized funding mechanism in Utah known as the Weighted Pupil Unit, which guarantees a fixed dollar amount per student, currently $4,038 for FY23, regardless of the local tax generated by this levy in each school district. In order to participate in the guarantee, each school district must levy this tax rate. The state adds income tax revenue to local revenue in order to guarantee the amount guaranteed per student.
- **Board Local Levy**—53F-2-602—statutory limit is .002500. This rate affords a local education entity to provide educational services "beyond the

minimum school program" as noted in statute. A local board has authority to set this rate annually, subject to the provisions of statute.

- **Voted Local Levy**—53F-2-601—statutory limit is .002000. LEA's may take to their voters a proposition to raise local property tax for specific purposes subject to the limits in statute. If approved by a majority of those voting in the local jurisdictions's election, the LEA may levy the tax the following fiscal year.
- **Capital Local Levy**—53F-8-303—statutory limit is .003000. LEA's may take a proposition to their voters to raise local property taxes for capital construction, maintenance of facilities, etc. Currently, no LEA's in Utah use this financing option.
- **Debt Service Levy**—53F-8-401, 405 and 11-14-19—The purpose of this levy is for payment of principal and interest on general obligation bonds. By a simple majority of voters, LEA's must pass a voter resolution authorizing the tax. If approved, the LEA may levy a tax sufficient to make the principal and interest payments on the outstanding debt. LEA's are subject to legal debt margin requirements in statute, which limits debt to 4% of the LEA's Fair Market Value, which is all taxable property within the LEA boundary.

When calculating property taxes in Utah, the Utah Legislature has provided an exemption to encourage primary home ownership and community stability. The primary home exemption is 45% of the primary home's assessed value. Property taxes are set as of the lien date, which is January 1st each year. Property taxes are due by November 30th each year.

Another factor to consider in Utah is the requirement for Truth in Taxation, which limits taxing entities to tax rate assessments that generate no more than the same budgeted revenue from one year to the next. Once the certified rate is set, new commercial or residential construction (growth) will yield additional marginal revenues for the LEA. In reaction to that growth, the certified rate reduces in order to maintain the same budgeted revenue. If an LEA wants to exceed their certified rate, they must follow the requirements found in 59-2-19, Notice and public hearing requirements for certain tax increases. The effect of this legislation causes tax rates to go down over time as property values increase. Statute intends that LEA's are accountable to the local taxpayers for any adjustments to tax rates that yield additional revenue.

OTHER CATEGORIES

Necessarily Existent Small Schools (NESS)

Several small schools are located in sparsely populated rural areas of the state where distance precludes the opportunity to combine students into larger schools. Because of their dis-economies of scale, they are compensated by the state through its Necessarily Existent Small Schools program. These funds are intended for specific schools that meet specific criteria. The law and board rules regulating this account are complicated and require schools to complete an annual funding application.

Beverly Taylor Sorenson Arts Learning Program

The Beverley Taylor Sorenson Arts Learning Program (BTSALP) provides arts-integrated instruction to elementary students. State funding provides matching funds for school-based arts specialists in participating schools and arts specialists in seven state universities. According to the BTSALP directors, the program currently resides in 300 Utah elementary schools in 31 (of 41) districts (including over 30 charter schools) and is serving approximately 202,800 students. The state allocation increased by $4,200,000 in FY2023 to $17,080,000 statewide.

K-3 Reading Improvement Program

The K-3 Reading Improvement Program was created during the 2004 General Legislative Session. The program was a project supported by late Governor Olene Walker who supported the goal of all Utah students reading at or above grade level by the time they complete the third grade. Monies have been appropriated annually since 2004. Three programs comprise the K-3 Reading Improvement Program: Base Level, Guarantee Program, and Low Income Students Program. School districts and charter schools "must submit a State Board approved plan for reading proficiency improvement prior to using the program funds" (USOE Finance & Statistics, MSP Descriptions, November 2006). The Utah State Office of Education has drafted a State framework for instruction and intervention to ensure all students progress at an appropriate and successful rate, mitigating the cycle of reading failure.

Formula—The formulas for each of the three funding programs include:

- Base Level—a base amount as determined by fall enrollment.
- Guarantee Program—"$21 per WPU minus the amount raised by a local tax levy of 0.000056," (USOE Finance & Statistics, MSP Descriptions, November 2006) or matching funds provided by the district or charter school.
- Low Income Program—"$21 per WPU minus the amount raised by a local tax levy of 0.000065," (USOE Finance & Statistics, MSP Descriptions) or matching funds provided by the district or charter school.

Statute allows the State Board of Education to use no more than $7.5 million for computer-assisted instructional learning and assessment programs. The 2022 legislature appropriated $14,550,000 for this program in FY23 school year.

Amendment G

During the 2020 Utah legislative session, Representative Robert Spendlove (co-sponsored by Senator Ann Millner) proposed Utah House Bill 357, titled *Public Education Funding Stabilization.* HB 357 required passage of a resolution to amend the Utah State Constitution, allowing more flexible use of income tax, previously held exclusively to support Public Education and Higher Education. HB 357 was established to provide for ongoing education funding and additional funding tied to growth in student enrollment and inflation.

Both chambers of the Utah state legislature were required to pass a resolution by a two-thirds vote during one legislative session to refer a constitutional amendment to a ballot for public vote.

The amendment was introduced into the legislature by Senator Dan McCay (R) and Representative Mike Schultz (R) as Senate Joint Resolution 9 on February 7, 2020. On March 6, 2020, the Senate approved the measure along party lines with all 27 Senate Republicans voting *yes* and all six Senate Democrats voting *no*. The House approved the measure with amendments by a vote of 67-5 and the Senate concurred with the House's amendments by a vote of 26-2.

After passage in both the House and the Senate, the constitutional amendment appeared on the November 2020 ballot as Amendment G. The ballot question read:

Shall the Utah Constitution be amended to expand the uses of money the state receives from income taxes and intangible property taxes to include supporting children and supporting people with a disability? The measure amended section 5 of Article XIII of the Utah Constitution by expanding the potential use of taxes on intangible property or from a tax on income. The amended Article XIII read:

(5) All revenue from taxes on intangible property or from a tax on income shall be used:
  a. to support the systems of public education and higher education as defined in Article X, Section 2; and
  b. to support children and to support individuals with a disability.

The constitutional amendment and House Bill 357 were supported by the Utah State Board of Education, Utah Education Association, Utah School Boards Association, Utah Association of Public Charter Schools, and other associations. The Utah Education Association wrote: "Senate Joint Resolution 9 allows income tax revenue to be used to provide services for children and the disabled in addition to education, all worthy of our tax support. House Bill 357 statutorily obligates legislators to invest in public education and provides a safety net to protect education funding from situations like we saw during the recession in 2008 when there was not enough revenue to even fund student enrollment growth."

On November 3, 2020, 1,413,260 voters weighed in on Amendment G, 54% (764,420) voted in favor, passing the amendment and changing the Utah constitution relative to the exclusive use of income tax for public education and higher education.

MSP LEGISLATIVE ESTIMATES

FY2023 allocations follow. The total MSP is $5.9 billion, with $3.7 billion in funding for various WPU categorical programs, $1.2 billion for below the line categorical programs, and $1.0 billion for the state guarantee and local funds for voted and board leeway programs. Details of FY23 estimates follow. Between local, state, and federal sources, Utah's public schools receive approximately $6 billion per year: 8% federal, 37% local, and 55% state.

Minimum School Program & School Building Program - Budget Detail Tables 2022 General Session FY 2022 Revised | FY 2023 Appropriated			
	Fiscal Year 2022 Revised		Fiscal Year 2023 Appropriated
Section 1: Minimum School Program - Summary of Total Revenue Sources and Expenditures by Program			
Total Revenue Sources	Amount		Amount
A. General State Revenue			
1. Uniform School Fund	3,633,458,900		3,874,091,600
a. Uniform School Fund, One-time	27,737,300		15,345,500
B. Restricted State Revenue			
1. USF Restricted - Trust Distribution Account	92,842,800		95,849,800
2. EF Restricted - Minimum Basic Growth Account[5]	56,250,000		56,250,000
3. EF Restricted - Charter School Levy Account[4]	29,837,600		31,273,900
4. EF Restricted - Teacher and Student Success Account[5]	115,734,800		140,686,800
5. EF Restricted - Local Levy Growth Account[5]	100,083,400		108,461,300
6. USF Restricted - Public Education Economic Stabilization, One-time[2]	0		168,600,000
Subtotal State Revenues:	**$4,055,944,800**		**$4,490,558,900**
C. Local Property Tax Revenue			
1. Minimum Basic Tax Rate			
a. Basic Levy	384,046,600		401,603,200
b. Basic Levy Increment Rate[5]	75,000,000		75,000,000
2. Equity Pupil Tax Rate[5]	100,083,400		108,461,300
3. WPU Value Rate[5]	69,234,800		94,186,800
4. Voted Local Levy	401,318,400		471,681,500
5. Board Local Levy	251,524,600		294,506,700
Subtotal Local Revenues:	**$1,281,207,800**		**$1,445,439,500**
D. Federal Sources			
1. Federal Funds - American Rescue Plan, One-time	10,000,000		0
E. Beginning Nonlapsing Balances	68,020,900		46,700,400
F. Closing Nonlapsing Balances	(46,727,700)		(46,700,400)
Total Revenues:	**$5,368,445,800**		**$5,935,998,400**
Total Expenditures by Program			
A. Basic School Program	3,482,094,900		3,712,060,400
B. Related to Basic School Program	982,124,000		1,193,478,000
C. Voted & Board Local Levy Programs	904,226,900		1,030,460,000
Total Expenditures:	**$5,368,445,800**		**$5,935,998,400**

Minimum School Program & School Building Program - Budget Detail Tables
2022 General Session
FY 2022 Revised | FY 2023 Appropriated

	Fiscal Year 2022 Revised		Fiscal Year 2023 Appropriated	
Section 2: Minimum School Program - Detail of Revenue Sources & Expenditures by Program				
Table A: Basic School Program (Weighted Pupil Unit Programs)				
WPU Value:		$3,809		$4,038
Basic Tax Rate:		0.001663		0.001661
Revenue Sources	Supplemental	Amount	Changes	Amount
A. State Revenue				
1. Uniform School Fund		2,826,030,100		3,014,113,600
a. Uniform School Fund, One-time		27,700,000		15,095,500
B. Restricted State Revenue				
1. USF Restricted - Public Education Economic Stabilization, One-time[2]				3,600,000
Subtotal - State Revenues:		*$2,853,730,100*		*$3,032,809,100*
C. Local Property Tax Revenue				
1. Minimum Basic Tax Rate				
a. Basic Levy		384,046,600		401,603,200
b. Basic Levy Increment Rate[5]		75,000,000		75,000,000
2. Equity Pupil Tax Rate[5]		100,083,400		108,461,300
3. WPU Value Rate[5]		69,234,800		94,186,800
Subtotal - Local Property Tax Revenues:		*$628,364,800*		*$679,251,300*
D. Beginning Nonlapsing Balances		20,505,800		20,505,800
E. Closing Nonlapsing Balances		(20,505,800)		(20,505,800)
Total Revenues:		**$3,482,094,900**		**$3,712,060,400**
Expenditures by Categorical Program	WPUs	Amount	WPUs	Amount
A. Regular Basic School Program				
1. Kindergarten	26,446	100,732,800	26,667	107,681,300
2. Grades 1-12 [2][1]	604,069	2,300,898,800	612,549	2,473,472,900
3. Foreign Exchange Students[6]	328	1,249,400	387	1,562,800
4. Necessarily Existent Small Schools[2]	10,708	44,387,800	10,708	46,838,900
5. Professional Staff	57,070	217,379,600	57,387	231,728,700
6. Enrollment Growth Contingency[2]	7,727	50,932,100	0	13,945,600
Subtotal - Regular Basic School Program:	*706,348*	*$2,715,580,500*	*707,698*	*$2,875,230,300*
B. Restricted Basic School Program				
1. Special Education - Regular - Add-on WPUs[1]	88,328	336,441,400	90,265	364,490,100
2. Special Education - Regular - Self-Contained	12,510	47,650,600	11,189	45,181,200
3. Special Education - Pre-School	11,311	43,083,600	11,372	45,920,100
4. Special Education - Extended Year Program	457	1,740,700	460	1,857,500
5. Special Education - Impact Aid[1]	2,060	7,846,500	2,072	8,366,600
6. Special Education - Extended Year for Special Educators	909	3,462,400	909	3,670,500
7. Students At-Risk - Add-on[1][2]	13,505	54,040,900	19,016	77,169,300
8. Career & Technical Education - District Add-on[1]	29,100	110,841,900	29,257	118,139,800
9. Class Size Reduction	42,375	161,406,400	42,604	172,035,000
Subtotal - Restricted Basic School Program:	*200,555*	*$766,514,400*	*207,144*	*$836,830,100*
Total Expenditures:	**906,903**	**$3,482,094,900**	**914,842**	**$3,712,060,400**

THE LINE

Minimum School Program & School Building Program - Budget Detail Tables 2022 General Session FY 2022 Revised | FY 2023 Appropriated				
		Fiscal Year 2022 Revised		**Fiscal Year 2023 Appropriated**
Table B: Related to Basic School Program (Below-the-Line)				
Charter School Local Replacement Rate:		*$2,701*		*$2,899*
Revenue Sources	Supplemental	Amount	Changes	Amount
A. State Revenue				
1. Uniform School Fund		712,378,300		760,417,500
a. Uniform School Fund, One-time		37,300		250,000
B. Restricted State Revenue				
1. USF Restricted - Trust Distribution Account		92,842,800		95,849,800
2. EF Restricted - Teacher and Student Success Account[3V]		115,734,800		140,686,800
3. EF Restricted - Charter School Levy Account[4K]		29,837,600		31,273,900
4. USF Restricted - Public Education Economic Stabilization, One-time[5L]		0		165,000,000
Subtotal - State Revenues:		*$950,830,800*		*$1,193,478,000*
C. Federal Sources				
1. Federal Funds - American Rescue Plan, One-time[3B]		10,000,000		
D. Beginning Nonlapsing Balances		47,515,100		26,194,600
E. Closing Nonlapsing Balances		(26,221,900)		(26,194,600)
Total Revenues:		**$982,124,000**		**$1,193,478,000**
Expenditures by Categorical Program	Supplemental	Funding	Changes	Amount
A. Related to Basic Programs				
1. Pupil Transportation - To & From School[2XX]	0	111,106,500	6,340,400	117,446,900
2. Pupil Transportation - Rural Transportation Grants	0	1,000,000	0	1,000,000
3. Pupil Transportation - Rural School Reimbursement	0	500,000	0	500,000
4. Charter School Local Replacement[3M]	0	218,178,700	19,071,900	237,250,600
5. Charter School Funding Base Program[3B]	0	8,100,000	(85,000)	8,015,000
Subtotal - Related to Basic Programs:		*$338,885,200*		*$364,212,500*
B. Focus Populations				
1. Students At-Risk - Gang Prevention and Intervention[6]	0	2,105,900	140,500	2,246,400
2. Youth-in-Custody[7E]	0	27,821,200	1,854,700	29,675,900
3. Adult Education[13]	0	15,635,900	1,042,300	16,678,200
4. Enhancement for Accelerated Students	0	6,048,300	403,200	6,451,500
5. Concurrent Enrollment	0	12,961,700	2,564,000	15,525,700
6. Title I Schools in Improvement - Paraeducators[2I]	0	300,000	250,000	550,000
7. Early Literacy Program[5]	0	14,550,000	0	14,550,000
8. Early Intervention[5]	0	24,455,000	12,200,000	36,655,000
9. Special Education Intensive Services[12]	0	1,000,000	0	0
10. English Language Learner Software Grants[20]	0	4,500,000	4,500,000	4,500,000
Subtotal - Focus Populations:		*$109,378,000*		*$126,832,700*
C. Educator Supports				
1. Educator Salary Adjustments[2]	3,630,500	191,584,700	3,630,500	191,584,700
2. Teacher Salary Supplement[1X]	0	22,266,100	0	22,266,100
3. Teacher Supplies & Materials	0	5,500,000	0	5,500,000
4. Effective Teachers in High Poverty Schools	0	688,000	113,000	801,000
5. Elementary School Counselor Program	0	2,100,000	0	2,100,000
6. Grants for Professional Learning	0	3,935,000	0	3,935,000
7. Grow Your Own Teacher and Counselor Program[2Y]	0	9,200,000	0	0
8. Educator Professional Time[2D]	0	0	64,000,000	64,000,000
9. Teacher Bonuses for Extra Assignments[2Z]	10,000,000	10,000,000	0	0
Subtotal - Educator Supports:		*$245,273,800*		*$290,186,800*
D. Statewide Initiatives				
1. School LAND Trust Program	0	92,842,800	3,007,000	95,849,800
2. Teacher and Student Success Program[3NN]	0	130,734,800	24,952,000	155,686,800
3. Student Health and Counseling Support Program[3X2]	0	25,480,000	0	25,480,000
4. School Library Books & Electronic Resources	0	765,000	0	765,000
5. Matching Fund for School Nurses	0	1,002,000	0	1,002,000
6. Dual Immersion[3J]	0	5,030,000	0	5,030,000
7. Beverley Taylor Sorenson Arts Learning Program[3XX]	0	12,880,000	4,200,000	17,080,000
8. Digital Teaching & Learning Program[4]	0	19,852,400	0	19,852,400
9. Public Education Capital and Technology[3J]	0	0	91,500,000	91,500,000
Subtotal - Other Programs:		*$288,587,000*		*$412,246,000*
Total Expenditures:		**$582,124,000**		**$1,193,478,000**

Minimum School Program & School Building Program - Budget Detail Tables				
2022 General Session				
FY 2022 Revised | FY 2023 Appropriated				
		Fiscal Year 2022 Revised		Fiscal Year 2023 Appropriated

Table C: Voted & Board Local Levy Programs

Guarantee Rate (per Tax Rate of 0.0001 per WPU):		$551.91		$555.37
Revenue Sources	Supplemental	Amount	Changes	Amount
A. State Revenue				
1. Uniform School Fund		95,050,500		99,560,500
B. Restricted State Revenue				
1. EFR - Minimum Basic Growth Account		56,250,000		56,250,000
2. EFR - Local Levy Growth Account		100,083,400		108,461,300
Subtotal - State Revenues:		251,283,900		264,271,800
C. Local Property Tax Revenue				
1. Voted Local Levy		401,318,400		471,681,500
2. Board Local Levy		251,524,600		294,506,700
Subtotal - Local Property Tax Revenues:		652,843,000		766,188,200
Total Revenues:		**$904,226,900**		**$1,030,460,000**
Expenditures by Categorical Program	Supplemental	Amount	Changes	Amount
A. Voted and Board Local Levy Programs				
1. Voted Local Levy Program	0	575,502,500	74,873,100	650,375,600
2. Board Local Levy Program	0	328,724,400	$1,360,000	380,084,400
Total Expenditures:		**$904,226,900**		**$1,030,460,000**
Total Minimum School Program Expenditures:		**$5,368,445,800**		**$5,935,998,400**
Balance :		*$0*		*$0*

Section 3: School Building Programs - Total Revenues & Expenditures (Not Included in MSP Totals Above)

Revenue Sources	Supplemental	Amount	Changes	Amount
A. State Revenue				
1. Education Fund		14,499,700		14,499,700
B. Restricted State Revenue				
1. EFR - Minimum Basic Growth Account		18,750,000		18,750,000
Total Revenues:		**$33,249,700**		**$33,249,700**
Expenditures by Categorical Program	Supplemental	Amount	Changes	Amount
A. Capital Outlay Programs				
1. Foundation Program	0	27,610,900	0	27,610,900
2. Enrollment Growth Program	0	5,638,800	0	5,638,800
Total Expenditures:		**$33,249,700**		**$33,249,700**

Office of the Legislative Fiscal Analyst

Date Modified: 2/18/2022
3/16/2022 14:07

Notes:

1. Administrative funding for certain MSP categorical programs can be found in this "MSP Categorical Program Administration" line item in the State Board of Education's budget. Adding program and administration funding will provide the full cost for the program.
2. One-time funding appropriated by the Legislature in FY 2022 or FY 2023, as follows:
   a. FY 2022: Small District Base (Part of NESS) - $3.6 m, Enrollment Growth Contingency - $23.5 m, Students At-Risk Add-on - $2.6 m, Pupil Transportation - $1.0 m, Charter School Funding Base - $5.0 m, Special Education Intensive Services - $1.0 m, ELL Software - $1.5 m (Transfer of funding balance remaining in old Initiatives Program), Grow Your Own Teacher and Counselor Program - $8.2 m (for 2 cohorts over 3 years).
   b. FY 2023: Enrollment Growth Contingency - $13.9 m, Students At-Risk Add-on - $3.1 m, Title I Paraeducators - $250,000.
   c. All appropriations from the Public Education Budget Stabilization Account are one-time and include the following: Public Education Capital and Technology - $91.5 m, Educator Professional Time - $64.0 m, Charter School Funding Base - $5.0 m, Small District Base Funding - $3.6 m, and English Language Learner Software - $4.5 m.
   d. The appropriation for Teacher Bonuses for Extra Assignments is funded one-time from federal American Rescue Plan state allocation.
3. Includes approximately $4.3 million in funding for student transportation at the Utah Schools for the Deaf and the Blind.
4. Local school districts levy a tax rate for their contribution to the Charter School Local Replacement program. The revenue generated from the tax is deposited into the Education Fund Restricted - Charter School Levy Account and appropriated to the program.
5. Education Fund Restricted (EFR) accounts created by the Legislature funded from state fund "savings" generated through increased property tax revenues collected by various tax rates that are part of the Basic Levy. When local school districts pay more of the cost of WPUs from the property tax, less state revenue is required. This state revenue is transferred to the restricted funds to support other education programs.
6. The Teacher and Student Success Program includes $15.0 million appropriated in FY 2020 from the Education Fund. This program is funded from two sources, the Education Fund as mentioned, and the remaining funding from the EFR-Teacher and Student Success Account.
7. The State Guarantee Rate was originally estimated at $55.37 for FY 2023. During the 2021 GS, the Legislature passed S.B. 142, "Public Education Funding Amendments", which allows the State Board of Education to increase the State Guarantee Rate to expend "excess" state funds when calculating the cost of the statutory rate indexing and growth produces an amount less than amount of state funds appropriated to the guarantee. The actual rate is set by the State Board of Education in their Legislative Estimates process.

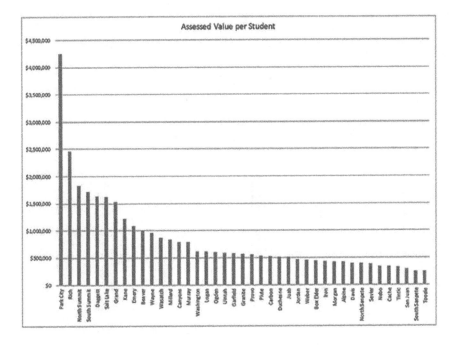

CHAPTER 45

VERMONT

Tammy Kolbe
University of Vermont

D. Akol Aguek
University of Vermont

A DESCRIPTIVE PROFILE OF SCHOOL FUNDING IN VERMONT

Vermont's constitution (1777) was the first in English-speaking North American to mandate public funding for universal education. Since that time, the "brave little state" has reaffirmed its commitment to public funding for education—consistently ranking among the top five states nationally for per pupil public elementary-secondary education spending.[1] The state is also noteworthy in its approach to raising revenues to pay for public education. Vermont's statewide property tax system is unique among states as is its approach to calibrating tax rates to reflect differences in educational costs among the state's school districts. However, in recent years, the state's education funding and governance systems have been challenged by a steady decline in student enrollments and strong preferences for local control over school district configurations and spending.

This chapter describes the history of Vermont's school funding system and the contemporary policy landscape. We begin with general background about the state's education funding and governance systems and political climate. This is followed

Funding Public Schools in the United States, Indian Country,
and US Territories (Second Edition), pages 703–720.
Copyright © 2023 by Information Age Publishing
www.infoagepub.com

703

by an overview of Vermont's Education Fund and the sources of revenue that contribute to this fund. We then describe how state funding is distributed to the state's local education agencies and how the state's public voucher system operates.

GENERAL BACKGROUND

Education Funding

Among states, Vermont operates a unique school funding system, relying on a statewide property tax system to generate revenues, local control over education spending, and an equalized pupil calculation that adjusts for differences in education costs among school districts. The current system was put in place in response to the 1997 Vermont Supreme Court decision *Brigham v. State of Vermont* and the resulting Equal Educational Opportunity Act of 1997.[2] The funding system went largely unchanged since Act 60s implementation, until recently when Vermont's General Assembly undertook two substantial initiatives to improve the system's efficiency and fairness: (1) Act 173 (2018), which substantially modified the state's special education funding formula; and (2) revisions to the pupil weights used to equalize spending among Vermont school districts in 2022.

Education Funding Prior to 1997. Between 1988 and 1997, the state provided funding to public schools according to a Foundation Plan that based state aid to schools on a set per pupil spending level that depended on the actual median per pupil expenditures for students. Education spending levels were locally determined by school districts (as approved by local voters) and paid for by taxes imposed on the value of real property within towns and cities that comprised the school district.

Under this system, towns with more real property wealth (larger grand lists) were able to raise more money for education spending at lower property tax rates than other jurisdictions with smaller grand lists. The State's Foundation Plan provided some funding to property-poor towns to offset this disadvantage, but this funding was limited and the state frequently underfunded its obligation. As a result, there were substantial disparities in education spending and tax burden among Vermont school districts. School districts in property rich towns on average spent more per pupil than districts with less property wealth and this translated into systematic differences in educational opportunities according to where Vermont students resided and attended school.

Brigham v. Vermont (1997). Vermont's Foundation Plan was challenged in Vermont courts in *Brigham v. State*. In 1997, the Vermont Supreme Court found the existing system unconstitutional. The parties in the case conceded that the Foundation Plan, as implemented, resulted in unequal opportunities for Vermont students; however, the State argued that this was justified by its interest in promoting local control over education decision making. The Court rejected this argument, and instead held that the current funding system "deprive[d] children of an equal educational opportunity in violation" of both Chapter I, Article 7 (Education Clause) and Chapter II Section 68 (Common Benefits clause) of the Vermont Constitution.

Specifically, the Court stated that education in Vermont is a "constitutionally mandated right" and that to "keep democracy competitive and thriving, students must be afforded equal access to all that our educational system has to offer." As a result, to "fulfill its constitutional obligation the [S]tate must ensure substantial equality of educational opportunity throughout Vermont" (*Brigham v. Vermont 1997*). The Court also asserted that the constitutional right to substantially equal educational opportunities is a responsibility held by the state that that cannot be delegated or overridden by local control.

Vermont Act 60. In response to the *Brigham* decision, the Vermont General Assembly passed Act 60—The Equal Educational Opportunity Act of 1997. Act 60 fundamentally changed how the state provides revenues to offset local education spending decisions.[3] In particular, Act 60 created a statewide property tax for local education that shifted the responsibility for paying for education from localities to the state, with the intent to eliminate the relationship between a school district's property wealth and education spending and a new Education Fund was established to redistribute revenues to offset education spending statewide. Additionally, to ensure taxpayer equity, Act 60 also included an adjustment to local education spending—the equalized pupil calculation—to account for differences in educational costs among school districts.

Vermont Act 173. In 2018, the Vermont General Assembly passed Act 173— "An act relating to enhancing the effectiveness, availability, and equity of services provided to students who require additional support." Act 173 established a new formula for allocating state funding for local special education programs, according to a census-based block grant. Specifically, the state will provide school districts with a fixed dollar grant amount for each student enrolled in a district, regardless of whether a student is identified for special education or not.

This new formula represents a fundamental shift from the current approach to allocating state aid for special education, where districts are currently reimbursed for 60% of their spending on students receiving special education. In making this shift, the General Assembly sought to break the link between state funding and special education identification as well as provide districts with more flexibility in how they use state aid to provide early intervening services for struggling students and group general and special education students who may benefit from similar interventions and supports to learn.[4] The law's implementation was delayed two years and is scheduled to phase in (over five years) starting FY2023.

Pupil Weighting. Act 173 (2018) the Vermont General Assembly also commissioned a study to evaluate the weights used to equalize costs among Vermont school districts in the state's existing funding formula. Not unlike other states, Vermont has been criticized for using persistently outdated pupil weights in their school funding formula.[5] The 2018 study responded to concerns about the extent to which the existing funding formula was effective in equalizing educational costs, and by extension, opportunities to learn for students across the state. The student need cost factors and weights used in the calculation have not been modified in more than 20 years, despite the significant changes in statewide demographics and student need that have transpired during that time.[6]

In Fall 2019, the University of Vermont, in partnership with the American Institutes for Research and a researcher at Rutgers University, published a comprehensive analysis of the state's approach to providing supplemental funding to districts and schools according to differences in student need or geographic location using pupil weights and categorical funding programs.[7] The study identified a comprehensive set of factors that are related to differences in educational costs among school districts, as well as changes to the weights for cost factors already contained in the formula (economically disadvantaged students, ELL, and secondary students).

In response, the General Assembly constituted a Task Force (Summer 2021) to consider how to implement the study's recommendations. The Task Force published its report in December 2021 and in May 2022 the General Assembly passed legislation that: (1) put in place a new universal income declaration that will be used to identify economically-disadvantaged students; (2) a supplemental program that provides fixed dollar grant to small and rural schools to cover fixed costs of operating high quality programs for ELL students; and (3) implemented the weights recommended by the 2019 UVM study. The provisions will go into effect for FY2025.

Education Governance

Vermont's education system is overseen by its Agency of Education (AOE) and State Board of Education (SBE). The state delegates a significant level of autonomy and authority to local communities and school districts. Vermont also has a well-established system of independent schools that receive public tuition dollars from towns that do not operate public schools.

State Oversight. In 2012, Vermont reorganized the state's governance and oversight for public and private education. Prior to this time, the State Board of Education (SBE) directed the work of the Vermont Department of Education and supervised the Commissioner of Education, who was responsible for implementing rules and regulations adopted by the Board. The Board was expected to direct the Department's policies, programs, and resources. Act 98 of 2012 shifted the roles between the SBE and AOE. It established the Vermont Agency of Education and elevated the prior Commissioner position to a cabinet-level Secretary of Education, appointed by, and reporting directly to, the Governor. In doing so, the SBE no longer has a supervisory disposition with respect to the AOE's work, and instead, is assigned specific responsibilities for the rulemaking process, determining school district boundaries and configurations, school approval, and establishing the vision for public education in the state.

Supervisory Unions & School Districts. Historically, Vermont's educational system has been highly decentralized, prioritizing small schools and strong local control over school governance and finances. More recently, however, there has been growing concern about the inefficiencies and threats to equal education opportunity posed by education unites that are too small, made worse by a declining school-aged population.[8] For AY 2012, there were 298 school districts in the state that served just about 85,000 students.

Amid concerns, the Vermont legislature enacted a series of laws intended to incentivize, and at times, require school district consolidation and school closure. Act 153 (2009) created a structure and incentives intended to stimulate voluntary school district mergers and requirements for consolidating special education programs at the supervisory union level. Two years later, Act 156 (2012) was passed, to provide additional funding and incentives for district-level mergers and Act 46 (2015) provided further incentives and requirements for school governance consolidation statewide. In response, there has been considerable realignment and reorganization of Vermont school districts.

Under Act 46, the preferred governance structure is a Supervisory District (SU/SD; also referred to a unified union school district). Under this structure, the unified school district has responsibility for educating all PK-12 students in a specific geographic catchment area. The SU/SD may be comprised of voters from a single town (e.g., Burlington) or multiple towns. The SU/SD elects a school board with representation from member towns. Act 46 also permits an "alternative governance structure" where two or more school districts, each governed by its own school board. Member school districts can include union high school and elementary districts (that cover multiple towns) and single town school districts Each districts send representatives to serve on a separate board that governs the supervisory union (SU).

By FY2020, through voter-approved and SBE-mandated mergers, the number of school districts in the state decreased to 120, and voters in 161 districts located in 146 towns formed 39 new SU/SD's (Vermont Agency of Education n.d.).

Tuition-only Districts. Vermont operates a tuition voucher system that allows towns without public school at all or a particular grade level to spend public tax dollars to send their students to public or approved private schools of the student's choice, if the schools are "approved under the laws of that state or country" (16 VSA §828). While all independent schools must be approved by the State, not all are approved to receive public tuition dollars. For the 2018-19 school year, 65 of the state's 130 independent schools were approved to receive public tuition dollars, accepting students from some 45 towns.

CURRENT POLITICAL CLIMATE

Vermont's fiscal year begins on July 1 and ends June 30. The state uses an annual budget. The General Assembly is not required to pass a balanced budget, the governor is not required to sign one, and deficits may be carried over into the following year. That said, state budget rules require lawmakers to balance revenues and expenditures. Like most states, each year, the Governor proposes a budget for the state for the following fiscal year, but only the legislature has the constitutional authority to appropriate funds and subsequently makes changes to the governor's proposed budget.

Vermont had a divided government for 2022, with. Republican as governor (Phil Scott) and Democrats in the majority in both the House and Senate. At the start of the 2022 session, neither party had a veto-proof supermajority in both chambers.

The General Assembly convenes for biennial sessions, the most recent being 2021-22. During this session, three education issues were at the forefront of legislative consideration:

1. Revisions to Vermont Act 46 to address challenges and inconsistencies with implementing the law's intent for education governance and school district consolidation.
2. The Governor's proposed substantial new investments in continuing and technical education. These investments are intended to widen the scope of alternative pathways for post-secondary training and workforce development in the state.
3. Revisions to the state's school funding formula, including the weights used to equalize costs among Vermont school districts.
4. Clarifying under what circumstances a school district is authorized to pay public tuition to a qualified school or program regardless of its religious status or affiliation; prohibited from paying public tuition to a school that does not comply with federal and State antidiscrimination laws; and must make dual enrollment available to students who attend a school with a religious mission.

Legislation revising Act 46 and the state's funding formula was passed and signed by the Governor and the approved budget included substantial new funding for career and technical education. Revisions to statute to clarify how public tuition dollars may and may not be used to pay for students attending religious schools was passed by the Senate, but not the House.

SOURCES OF REVENUE

Spending on K12 education in Vermont is largely paid for by revenues deposited into the state's Education Fund. Act 60 established the Education Fund as the recipient of revenues from: (a) a statewide education tax, (b) one-third of the state's sales tax collections, and (d) lottery funds (16 V.S.A.§ 4025). Table 45.1 summarizes the FY2021 contributions to the Education Fund from different sources.

Statewide Education Tax. With the passage of Act 60, the state shifted to a statewide education tax, where the state sets the tax rates and collects, and subse-

TABLE 45.1.   Revenue Sources Contributing to Vermont's Education Fund (FY2021)

Sources	FY2021 Contribution	
	$'s	%
Homestead education property tax	633.7	34.7
Property tax credit	(171.5)	
Non-homestead education property tax	735.2	40.2
Sales & use tax	507.6	27.8
Purchase & use tax (one-third of total)	44.7	2.5
Meals & rooms tax (one-quarter of total)	36.0	2.0
Lottery transfer	32.5	1.8
Medicaid transfer	7.4	0.4
Other sources (e.g., wind & solar, LUCT, fund interest)	2.9	0.2
Total	1,828.5	

quently disburses, revenues from localities. While property tax payments are still collected by towns, the tax is a state tax (i.e., towns collect the tax for the state, akin to businesses that collect sales taxes). Under current law, there are two classes of property subject to the statewide education tax, each with a different tax rate: (1) homestead property taxes and (2) non-homestead property taxes. For FY2021, $633.7 million of the Education Fund (32% of revenues) came from homestead property taxes and $735.2 (40.5% of revenues) came from non-homestead property taxes.[9]

The tax rate is the same for all non-homestead property but varies for homestead property according to local spending decisions. The minimum homestead tax rate is $1.00 on property and 2% on household income (property and income yields). The property yield can be thought of as the per pupil spending amount that the Education Fund can support with a uniform homestead tax rate of $1.00. In districts that spend more per pupil than the property yield, the tax is increased proportionally. Local spending is equalized using pupil weights to ensure that two towns with the same per-pupil education spending pay the same homestead tax rate.

An individual's homestead tax may be adjusted for household income. Taxpayers with income less than $90,000 can use the property tax adjustment on the first $40,000 of the house site value. For FY2021, almost 70% of Vermont resident households qualified for an income-based tax adjustment (Richter 2022). Resident homeowners with income under $47,000 are entitled to additional tax relief if their net education tax exceeds a fixed percentage of household income. About 30% of homesteads eligible for income sensitivity are also eligible for a homeowner rebate. The cost of the municipal homeowner rebate is paid for by the General Fund.

Non-homestead property includes all taxable real property that does not qualify as homestead, including commercial and industrial property, rental housing, second homes, and open land. Prior to Act 60, non-homestead tax revenue was retained by towns and cities where property was located to pay for local school budgets. After Act 60, these revenues are allocated to the Education Fund to be used statewide. Act 68 (2003) made the non-homestead property tax rate uniform for all taxpayers statewide (for FY2021 the rate was $1,628 per $100 of non-homestead property value).

The amount raised by the statewide education property tax is determined by subtracting non-property tax revenues from total uses and comparing this amount to total school district spending as indicated by locally approved school budgets. In this way, Vermont's education tax rates are set each year so that the Education Fund remains in "balance" (sufficient revenues are raised for education spending each year).

Other State Sources. The remaining revenues for the Education Fund come from a variety of sources unrelated to property taxes, including: 25% of the state's meals and room taxes; one-third of the revenues raised from the purchase and use tax; other revenues raised from the sales and use tax; Medicaid reimbursement funds; and state lottery receipts. For FY2021, approximately 35% of revenues to the Education Fund came from non-property sources ($631.1 million). Every dollar that is transferred to the Education Fund from other sources is one less dollar that does not need to be raised using the statewide education property tax.

DISTRIBUTION FORMULAS

Education Fund expenses have steadily increased over time. Projected spending for FY2022 is approximately $1.89 billion, an increase of 5.4% from FY2021 and 15.4% since FY2018. (Table 45.2)

School districts receive money from the Education Fund in two ways: (1) Education payments; and (2) categorical aid. For FY2021, education payments made up approximately 83% of Education Fund appropriations. (Table 45.3) This includes most of the costs of public schools, including tuition payments to other public, independent, and out-of-state schools; tuition payments to Career and Technical Education centers; and supervisory union costs.[10] Publicly funded pre-kindergarten is also included in the net education payment. The largest share of the remaining categorical aid is the state's special education reimbursement (12% of the Education Fund, FY2021).

Regular Education Program. School districts' education payment amounts are dependent on their *education spending per equalized pupil.* Spending is equivalent to a district's approved budget, less other revenues from federal and state categorical grants, deficit carryover spending from prior year, and tuition a district receives, for a given fiscal year.[11] Specifically:

Education Spending$_{district}$ = Approved School District Budget—Other Revenues

TABLE 45.2.   Education Fund Expenses (FY2018-FY2022)

	FY2018 (Final)	FY2019 (Final)	FY2020 (Final)	FY2021 (Anticipated)	FY2022 (Projected)
Education Expenses (in millions)	$1,635	$1,655	$1,726	$1,789	$1,886
% Change from Prior Year	-	1.22%	4.29%	3.65%	5.42%

Source: Agency of Education Budget Book: FY2022 Budget Recommendations & Annual Report (February 8, 2021); https://education.vermont.gov/sites/aoe/files/documents/edu-annual-report-budget-book-fy22.pdf

TABLE 45.3.   FY2020 Education Fund Spending per ADM

General Category	Education Fund per ADM	% of Total
Net education payment	$16,531.50	82.7%
Special education aid	$2,464.50	12.3%
State-placed students	$208.30	1.0%
Transportation aid	$229.10	1.1%
Technical education aid	$164.30	0.8%
Small school support	$97.20	0.5%
Essential early education aid	$78.70	0.4%
Flexible pathways	$89.10	0.4%
Teacher pensions	$78.70	0.4%
Other uses	$38.3	0.2%
Total	$19,980	

Source: Vermont Agency of Education. "Agency of Education Budget Book: FY2022 Budget Recommendations and Annual Report." Montpelier, VT, February, 8, 2021. https://education. vermont.gov/sites/aoe/files/documents/edu-annual-report-budget-book-fy22.pdf

Education spending is then adjusted for the number of equalized pupils in a school district.

$$\text{Education Spending Per Equalized Pupil}_{district} = \frac{\text{Education Spending}_{district}}{\text{Equalized Pupil Count}_{district}}$$

Education spending per equalized pupil is the key input in calculating a town's education tax rates (homestead and income-based). A town's homestead tax rate is calculated as:[12]

$$\text{Homestead Tax Rate}_{town} = (\text{Equalized PP Spending/Property Yield})$$

$$* \text{ Statewide Homestead Rate}$$

In this way, a district's equalized pupil count can serve to inflate or deflate a district's education spending per pupil, for the purposes of calculating local tax burden. For example, assuming no change in education spending per pupil, increasing the number of equalized pupils in a school district effectively lowers a district's per pupil education spending for the purposes of calculating a locality's property tax rate. Conversely, a decrease in the number of equalized pupils effectively raises a district's per pupil education spending for the purposes of this calculation. Put another way, the weighting used to calculate a school district's equalized pupil count affects local tax capacity to raise revenues to pay for education spending.

Pupil weights are used to calculate the number of equalized pupils in a school district. An equalized pupil can be thought of as an average pupil in terms of educational costs in a school district. That is, an equalized pupil in a school district will have the same cost as any other equalized pupil, even though the actual per pupil cost of individual students varies. The current formula recognizes four categories of students that are presumed to have higher or lower costs (current weighting in parentheses): (1) economically disadvantaged students (1.25); (2) English language learners (1.20); (3) secondary students (1.13); and (4) pre-kindergarten students (0.46). In May 2022, the Vermont General Assembly adopted new weights for the equalized pupil calculation, based on findings from the 2019 report by UVM, Rutgers University, and AIR. The new weights will go into effect for FY2025. (Table 45.4 compares the existing and new weights.)

TABLE 45.4. Summary of Existing & Future Weights for Vermont's Equalized Pupil Calculation

Cost Factor	Measure	Weight Value	
		Existing	Updated (Starting FY2025)
Student Needs	Poverty Rate (Vermont AOE)	0.25	
	Free- or Reduced-Price Lunch (FRPL) Rate		1.03
	% of ELLs	0.20	2.49
Context			
Enrollment	<100 Students		0.21
	101–250		0.07
Population Density	<36 Persons per Square Mile		0.23
	36 to <55		0.15
	55 to <100		0.12
Grade Range	% Middle Grades Enrollment		0.36
	% Secondary Grades Enrollment	1.13	0.39
	Pre-kindergarten	0.46	0.46

Categorical & Other Funding. Vermont's education funding system includes categorical grants that provide supplemental state aid to school districts and schools to offset specific types of educational costs. Most categorical funding programs have specific requirements that must be met to qualify for additional aid and have stand-alone state appropriations. Three funding programs make up the majority of the state's categorical aid to school districts: (1) special education; (2) transportation aid; and (3) small schools grants. (Table 45.5). The Education Fund also provides grants for technical education programs, state placed students, flexible pathways initiatives, and early essential education.

Special education. In Vermont, the bulk of funding for special education and related services for SWD comes from state and local sources, with just about 6%

TABLE 45.5.   Grant Programs Paid for by Vermont's Education Fund

Grants	Description	FY2021 Appropriation
Technical Education	The state provides funding to technical centers to reduce the tuition paid by school districts, based on three-year average enrollments; to defray the cost of salaries for technical center directors, guidance coordinators, and cooperative education coordinators; and to reimburse costs of transporting students to CTE centers.	$14,816,000
Special Education	The special education finance program administers the State's special education funding laws. The current state funding formula for K-12 services is a reimbursement system.	$223,718,575
State-placed Students	The state pays costs associated with educating children in state custody who are placed in schools near their foster programs.	$18,000,000
Flexible Pathways	Vermont's Flexible Pathways Initiative requires schools serving students grades 7-12 to offer flexible pathways to graduation, including work-based learning experiences, dual enrollment, early college, and virtual education.	$8,262,725
Essential Early Education	Essential Early Education (EEE) grants are provided to supervisory union/districts to fund preschool special education services for children ages 3-5.	$7,044,052
Transportation	Transportation aid is available to reimburse up to half of school district expenditures to transport students to and from school. Exact reimbursement percentages are limited by appropriated amounts and are determined by the amount of district expenditures.	$20,459,000
Small Schools	Small school districts operating at least one school are eligible for a small schools support grant if the two-year average enrollment is less than 100 or if the average grade size is 20 or fewer.	$8,200,000

Source: Vermont Agency of Education. "Agency of Education Budget Book: FY2022 Budget Recommendations and Annual Report." Montpelier, VT, February 8, 2021. https://education. vermont.gov/sites/aoe/files/documents/edu-annual-report-budget-book-fy22.pdf

of total funding coming from federal grants. In recent years, approximately 60% of a school district's remaining costs have been funded by the State, through a categorical grant that reimburses districts for allowable costs related to providing special education and related services as specified on a student's IEP. Beginning in FY2020, the state began reimbursing 95% of student-specific costs over an extraordinary threshold of $60,000. For FY2021, the total state appropriation was $223,718,575.

Starting in FY2024, Vermont will migrate to a census-based funding model, where state aid will be allocated to school districts on a per capita basis. This change was intended to break the link between student identification, service delivery, and state aid, and provide districts with new flexibility in how they develop systems of support for struggling students.

Transportation aid. The State also operates a transportation grant program, designed to offset spending by supervisory unions and school districts for the cost of transporting students to and from school for regular classroom services. Grantees are eligible to have up to 50% of their allowable expenditures reimbursed by the State.[13] For FY2021, total state aid was $20,459,000, equivalent to about 45% of allowable transportation expenditure statewide.

Small schools grant. Historically, Vermont has operated a grant program that provides supplemental funding to "small" districts and schools. This program is intended to offset the higher costs of operation due to limited economies of scale in small districts and schools. Specifically, the State provides formula grants to school districts operating schools with a two-year average combined enrollment of less than 100 students, or in instances where the average grade size is 20 or fewer students. Districts that receive a support grant are also been eligible for a supplemental stability grant in instances where there is at least a 10% decrease in its two-year average enrollment in any one year. In 2015, as part of the State's larger effort to encourage consolidation among Vermont's small districts and schools, Vermont's General Assembly put in place two additional criteria schools must meet to qualify for a Small Schools Grant (Act 26, Section 21)—specifically:

1. geographic-isolation; or
2. demonstrated academic excellence and operational efficiency.

The law defined geographic isolation in terms transportation routes—i.e., "lengthy driving times or inhospitable travel routes between the school and the nearest school in which there is capacity" (16 VSA §4015(B)(i)). A school's performance and efficiency were defined broadly as "measurable success in providing a variety of high-quality educational opportunities that meet or exceed" the State's Educational Quality Standards; the outcomes for students from economically-disadvantaged backgrounds; student-to-staff ratios; and participation in a merger study (16 VSA §4015(B)(I-IV).

The State Board of Education was charged with the task of adopting the metrics used to determine eligibility. In its efforts to do so, the Board noted that developing metrics that are "objective, comparable, and measurable" was a challenging task, especially measuring geographic isolation and the excess capacity of neighboring schools.[14] As an interim measure, the Board defined the metric for geographic isolation as a "school more than 15 miles from the nearest school in which there is capacity, or more than the 5% of the applicant school's students reside more than 15 miles from the nearest school in which there is capacity."[15] The Board also recommended a system for using data from the AOE's Annual Snapshot—Academic Proficiency category to evaluate school performance. For FY2019, $7,274,974 was allocated from the small school grants program to 25 school districts.

The state's Small Schools Grant program will sunset FY2025 when two new weights are added to the regular education formula's equalized pupil calculation—one for school size (<250 pupils) and the other for sparsity (population density).

CAREER AND TECHNICAL EDUCATION

Career and technical education is provided through at 15 regional technical education centers and 3 technical center school districts (aligned with comprehensive high schools). School districts pay tuition to the regional centers for their students to attend. Assessed tuition is based on the rolling six semester average of full time equivalent (FTE) students. Students included in the FTE count are those who report as present for at least 80 hours on or before October 15 and/or before March 15, and students who participate in CTE programs outside their regions or students approved for early college or CTE program. The headcount of students either through FTE for a CTE or ADM for a public school district, poses challenges in the field. A challenge with the current approach is the transfer of resources between sending school districts and CTE programs.

Out of state students and adults with diplomas, and those participating less than 80 hours, are not included in the FTE count and are not funded through FTE tuition assessed to sending school districts. These students are direct billed tuition. Additionally, annually, AOE makes nearly $300,000 in federal and state funds available to the regional CTE centers for program innovation. These funds are intended to incentivize regional CTE centers to modify existing or develop new programs to serve the needs of business and industry and to respond to student interest. Funds are awarded through a competitive grant process. Typically, there is also an equipment grant program to which CTEs can apply for reimbursement for investments in equipment replacement. The annual appropriation for this fund is $500,000. School districts that provide transportation for students to and from CTE centers are also eligible for transportation assistance funding (16 VSA §1563).

CAPITAL OUTLAY & DEBT SERVICE

Vermont's school construction was suspended by the General Assembly (Agency of Education n.d.). Rather, school districts assume the costs for facilities construction and maintenance, and their costs (including debt service) are reflected in local school budgets. Specifically, capital planning projects are paid for by school districts through bonds.

The state operates a separate Emergency Construction Aid program that provides reimbursement for school construction projects under $100,000 that are necessary to address immediate health and safety threats to students and employees, and that were created by unanticipated circumstances or events. Districts may be eligible for state reimbursement of up to 30% of their costs.

EMPLOYEE BENEFITS

Retirement

The Vermont Teacher Retirement System (VSTRS) is the public pension plan provided by the State of Vermont for the state's teachers. Both employees and employers contribute to the VSTRS. Most VSTRS active members pay between 5-6% of salaries (with the mount depending on years of service). The state is primarily responsible for paying the employer share of contributions to VSTRS. The employer (state) portion of pension costs is comprised of two components: (1) the normal cost;[16] and (2) an amortization payment toward unfunded liabilities. The Actuarially Determined Employer Contribution (ADEC), calculated annually, represents the total recommended amount the state should pay to fully fund both the normal costs and the amortization payment.

The VSTRS employer share of normal costs is charged to the Education Fund, and the unfunded liability amortization payment is paid from the state's General Fund. A smaller portion of costs are also paid for by LEAs for employees whose salaries are federally funded. For FY2022, the total ADEC for VSTRS was $196.2 million, with $37.6 million (19%) in normal costs paid for by the Education Fund, $152.1 million (78%) in unfunded liability paid for by the general fund, and $6.6 million (3%) paid for by LEAs.[17] There are serious concerns about the state's rapidly increasing pension liability. Pension costs have and are expected to continue to grow faster than General Fund revenues—e.g., VSTRS costs are expended to grow 69.7% between FY2021 and FY2026, whereas General Fund revenues are expected to be 14.7% higher in FY2026 (Pension Benefits, Design, and Funding Task Force 2022).

Between FY2019 and FY2020, there was a significant increase in the normal costs for VSTRS. However, employee contributions did not grow at the same rate and employee contributions as a share of total aggregate normal costs declined. This put additional pressure on the state to pay the remaining portion of the normal cost through the ADEC. In addition, the VSTRS has a substantial unfunded liability, largely driven by underfunding of the employer contribution between

1979 and 2006, and the subsequent dramatic economic downturn in 2008-2008 created a new hole in the VSTRS that has remained unfilled. Additionally, until FY2015, the state formerly paid VSTRS retiree health benefits from pension assets at an actuarial loss. This practice added about $138.5 million to the VSTRS unfunded liability (starting in FY2009). Altogether, VSTRS unfunded pension liability increased from $379.5 million in FY2008 to $1.950 billion for FY2021, and its funded ratio declined from 80.9% to 52.9%. There is also an underfunded liability for retiree health care benefits of $1.504 billion (Pension Benefits, Design, and Funding Task Force 2022).

In 2021, the General Assembly created the Pension Benefits, Design and Funding Task Force (Act 75). The Task Force was charged with making recommendations about benefits and funding sources that would reduce the underfunded pension and health care liabilities. The Task Force released its final report in January 2022, and the General Assembly was actively considering its recommendations and potential changes to statute during the most recent legislative session.

Healthcare

Act 11 of 2018 established the Statewide Commission on School Employee Healthcare Benefits, including a 10-person commission charged with negotiating healthcare benefits for all school employees (16 VSA §61). In 2021, House Bill 81 was passed by the General Assembly to make additional clarifications to Act 11.[18]

The first round of bargaining was completed in 2019, and starting January 1, 2021, Vermont implemented its first-ever statewide public-school employee healthcare package. The new statewide healthcare plan mandates how much public-school employees pay for premiums and out-of-pocket expenses, how out-of-pocket expenses are administered, who is eligible for healthcare, and how grievances are handled, and is binding on all Vermont school boards. Licensed educators and support professional working 17.5 hours or more a week are eligible for all tiers of coverage. Local school boards and local associations will bargain locally for premium proration for less-than-full-time employees. Premium shares for teachers and other licensed school employees will be 20%; school boards will pay the remaining 80% and any administrative charges required by third-party administrators. The current healthcare agreement expires December 31, 2022.

VSTRS retirees and beneficiaries are eligible to receive group medical insurance through VSTRS after retirement. Subsidy eligibility is based on years of service as of June 30, 2010.[19]

Charter School Funding

Vermont does not authorize charter schools.

Nonpublic School Funding

Vermont's Town Tuitioning Program was established in 1869, making it the oldest school choice program in the United States.[20] The tuitioning program provides educational options for students whose towns do not operate a public school at a student's grade level. Vermont towns that do not operate schools for some or all of the grades K-12, nor belong to a union school district for those grades, are required to pay tuition to another public or approved independent school (nonreligious private school inside or outside of Vermont) for students to attend school. Students must reside in the identified town. Most "sending" towns allow parents to choose which school their child will attend, but some towns send all their students to one school or school district. For AY2021, four percent of Vermont students were eligible to participate in the program.

Vermont law requires these schools to pay full tuition to public schools and tuition up the Average Announced Tuition for Union Schools to approved independent schools. Average tuition is calculated separately for grades K-6 and 7-12. For 2021-22, the upper limit for tuition paid to independent schools was $16,752 for students grades 7-12 and $15,295 for elementary schools. Approved independent schools are required to accept the average tuition amount as full payment, even if their tuition for students who do not come from sending town is higher. The intent is to ensure that districts without public schools pay no more than what they would pay if they operated a public school. Parents in sending towns who elect to send their children to other private schools, including out-of-state and international boarding schools, must make up the difference between the Vermont's average tuition and the school's full tuition amount.

Virtual Education

The Vermont Virtual Learning Collaborative (VTVLC) partners with the state to provide a range of online learning opportunities for Vermont students. VTVLC is operated by the River Valley Technical Center as a virtual program, as a cooperative model with partnering schools in offering both online and blended flexible learning pathways to students. VTVLC offers two full-time enrollment options for high school students: (1) full-time enrollment; and (2) a collaborative diploma program (CDP), which allows students who live in towns with non-operating schools the option of earning their high-school diploma from a geographically distant Vermont public high school. VTVLC also offers for Home Study students.

For AY2021, there were no fees to participate in the cooperative (as a partner school). That said, there are differences in the number of enrollments and options a partner school can offer to students at no cost, depending on whether the partnering school contributes teachers to the cooperative model. Teaching partner schools first use their earned partner seats, and then must pay $1,200 per student per semester. Non-teaching partner districts pay $2,500 per student per semester and home study students pay $3,000 per student per semester. There is no cost to the student if they reside in a "sending" town that pays tuition for a grade level.

Vermont's AOE also supports VTVLC with support for special education and its efforts to expanding a K-6 curriculum, in addition to its existing K-12 curriculum.

Federal COVID-19 Funding

Vermont has contended with how to effectively respond to the fallout from the COVID-19 pandemic, particularly with respect to prioritizing federal and state funding for pandemic response and recovery efforts in schools. Broadly, the state focused its efforts on three recovery strategies and goals, focused on addressing specific harms: (1) academic achievement; (2) social emotional learning and well-being; and (3) educator well-being. In 2021, AOE published the Education Recovery Framework and Toolkit to assist Vermont school districts when planning for and engaging in activities to address the educational impacts of COVID-19.

Like most states, Vermont received considerable federal funding to support these efforts and a key policy consideration has been how to best spend additional federal dollars. Specifically, the AOE is responsible for administering COVID-19 Emergency Federal Funding provided through: (1) the Coronavirus Aid, Relief, and Economic Security Act; (2) Coronavirus Response and Relief Supplemental Appropriations Act; and (3) the American Rescue Plan.[21] Altogether, Vermont received approximately $140 million in funding from the CARES Act, $133.2 million from CRRSA, and $287.7 million from ARPA.

ENDNOTES

[1] Coolidge, Calvin. (1928). "Vermont is a State I Love." Transcript of speech delivered at Bennington, Vermont, September 21, 1928. https://coolidgefoundation.org/resources/vermont-is-a-state-i-love/

[2] (Act 60)

[3] It is noteworthy that Act 60 did not address how education spending is determined in Vermont; rather, it maintained the ability for local voters to determine the amount spent on education in their local school district.

[4] Kolbe, Tammy & Kieran Killeen. Study of Vermont State Funding for Special Education. Burlington, VT: University of Vermont, 2017. https://legislature.vermont.gov/assets/Legislative-Reports/edu-legislative-report-special-education-funding-study-executive-summary-and-full-report.pdf

[5] Tran, H., Buckman, D., Bynoe, T. & Vesely, R. (2022). School finance during the COVID-19 pandemic: How are states responding in FY21? Journal of Education Finance, 47(5).

[6] Kolbe, Tammy, Bruce Baker, Drew Atchison, and Jesse Levin. Study of Pupil Weights in Vermont's Education Funding Formula. Burlington, VT: University of Vermont, 2019. https://education.vermont.gov/sites/aoe/files/documents/Executive-Summary-508.pdf

[7] Kolbe, et al

[8] Rogers, John, Talia Glesner, and Herman Meyers. "Early Experiences Implementing Voluntary School District Mergers in Vermont." Journal of Research in Rural Education, v.29 n8 (2014): 1-14.

[9] Richter, J. "Education Finance in Vermont." Testimony before Vermont House Committee on Education, February 24, 2022. https://ljfo.vermont.gov/assets/Subjects/Education-Finance-101/28f-dea5494/GENERAL-360592-v1-Introduction_to_Education_Finance_in_Vermont_V2.pdf

[10] Given the statewide property tax, education payments also include the 40% local share of special education costs and the local share of transportation costs (55%).

[11] As a result, tax rates that are calculated using on total statewide education spending do not reflect the total level of spending across districts (i.e., the full budgeted amount). Rather, what is included is: general payroll and operating costs that do not have specific funding sources; special education not covered by federal aid or state categorical grants; transportation costs not covered by state categorical aid; tuition owed by a district; and federal funding through its consolidated grant program.

[12] For FY2021, the yield was $10,998 and 1.00, respectively.

[13] It is important to note that not all Vermont school districts provide transportation, and some do so for only certain grade levels (e.g., students in the elementary grades).

[14] Huling, Krista. Determining Eligibility for Small School Grants. Barre, VT: Vermont State Board Education. https://education.vermont.gov/documents/sbe-determining-eligibility-small-school-grants

[15] Huling 2018

[16] The normal cost is the present value of the future retirement benefits accrued during the current year—i.e., the amount that should be paid into the pension fund every year to pay for a year's worth of future retirement benefits earned by the active workforce, based on the pension system's economic and demographic assumptions in place at the time.

[17] Pension Benefits, Design, and Funding Task Force. Final Report. Montpelier, VT: January 10, 2022. https://legislature.vermont.gov/Documents/2022/WorkGroups/PensionTaskForce/Highlights/Pension%20Task%20Force;%20Final%20Report%20and%20Recommendations;%20January%202022.pdf

[18] Scott, Phil. Letter to Ms. Wrask, April 8, 2021. https://governor.vermont.gov/sites/scott/files/Gov-Scott_H.81_Letter.pdf

[19] Office of the State Treasurer. "VSTRS Group C Plan Description" https://www.vermonttreasurer.gov/content/retirement/vstrs-plans/group-c#Other%20Retirement%20and%20Survivorship%20Benefits

[20] On June 11, 1999, the Vermont Supreme Court barred religious schools from participating in the state's Town Tuitioning program. The Court concluded that including religious schools in the program was a violation of the Vermont Constitution, which prohibits using public funding for religious worship. In 2021, a federal appeals court ruled that students in sending towns could use their town's tuition assistance at religious schools. The Vermont General Assembly debated legislation that would clarify how public dollars may be spent at private schools, including ensuring that dollars spent at religious schools are spent for non-sectarian purposes.

[21] Vermont Agency of Education. "COVID-19 Education Recovery Planning." https://education.vermont.gov/covid19/education-recovery

CHAPTER 46

VIRGINIA

William Owings

Old Dominion University

Leslie S. Kaplan

Education Researcher and Writer

GENERAL BACKGROUND

History

The evolution of education in the new American republic varied among the regions. Virginia, as Elwood Cubberley wrote, fell into the category of *pauper and parochial* school conditions.[1] In colonial times (excepting Governors Thomas Jefferson, James Monroe, George Cabell, and John Tyler), the Commonwealth of Virginia was slow to support free public schools. This was also true of many other southern states. In 1810, under Governor Tyler's leadership, the Virginia General Assembly established the Virginia Literary Fund to provide public education funding for the poor.[2] Although the Literary Loan funds were to be used only for public schools, government officials frequently redirected those resources to other purposes. One early diversion helped to establish the University of Virginia.[3]

Funding Public Schools in the United States, Indian Country,
and US Territories (Second Edition), pages 721–735.
Copyright © 2023 by Information Age Publishing
www.infoagepub.com

TABLE 46.1 – 2021-22 Student Enrollment Demographics by Race/Ethnicity*

American Indian or Alaska Native	Asian	Black – Not of Hispanic origin	Hispanic	Native Hawaiian or Pacific Islander	Non-Hispanic, 2 or more races	White
0.02%	7.4%	21.8%	18.1%	0.02%	6.5%	45.8%

*Total does not equal 100% due to rounding.
Source: https://p1pe.doe.virginia.gov/apex/f?p=180:1:103207564023982

Notable Constitutional Language

After the Civil War, in 1867, Virginia assembled a constitutional convention. Effective in 1870, the new constitution required a compulsory universal free system of public education to be funded by the Commonwealth by the Literary Fund and a state-wide property tax.[4] W. H. Ruffner was appointed as the first Superintendent of Public Instruction in the same year. Separate and unequally funded schools became available for Black and White students.

In 1902, Virginia enacted another new state constitution calling for the establishment and maintenance of an efficient system of free public schools. The new constitution reduced the distribution of funds based on the number of children in each school district from 5-21 to 7-20 years of age.

In 1972, Virginia legislators ratified an updated constitution which required a more comprehensive system for managing and funding public schools. Its name is still used today—Standards of Quality (SOQ). It required the General Assembly "shall provide for a system of free system of public elementary and secondary schools for all children throughout the Commonwealth, and shall seek to ensure[5] that an educational program of high quality is established and continually maintained."[6]

Descriptive Statistics

In the 2021-22 school year, 1,251,970 students enrolled in 132 school divisions. The largest, Fairfax County had 178,605 students and the smallest, Highland County, had 178 students.[7] The state-wide demographics by race and percentages are as presented in Table 46.1.

The latest Virginia Department of Education (VDOE, 2020-21) data available regarding number of teachers totaled 105,906.[8]

CURRENT POLITICAL CLIMATE

In 2019, for the first time in 21 years, the voters elected a Democratic House, Senate, and Governor. In a 2021 reversal, the voters elected a Republican Governor and majority to the House while the Senate maintained a slim Democratic majority. The new Governor's first Executive Order was to "begin the work of identifying and addressing inherently divisive concepts—including 'Critical Race Theory and its progeny'—in public education."[9] The Secretary of Education's report has "rescinded" all previous resources and publications on the Virginia Department of Education's website regarding equity, diversity, inclusion, and cultural responsiveness. Freedom of Information requests related to major changes have been refused and several newspapers have file suit.

As of this writing (May 3, 2022), the governor has vetoed 26 Democratic bills and the House and Senate are at loggerheads holding the budget as hostage.[10] One of the major issues is a 5% salary increase for public school teachers and state employees. So far, both sides are standing firm and school systems are uncertain how much funding will be allocated for salaries.

Legislative Makeup

Virginia's part-time House and Senate are responsible for passing legislation and a biennial budget. The budget is enacted into law in even-numbered years, and amendments are enacted on odd-numbered years. The fiscal calendar begins on July 1 and ends on June 30.

Union Representation and Engagement

Virginia has a long history as a right-to-work state. However, in 2020, the Code of Virginia (effective 2021) was changed to allow local government employees to bargain collectively.[11] State employees are not included in this legislation. The governing body has 120 days after receiving certification that a majority of public employees want to "adopt" or "not adopt" an ordinance to approve collective bargaining. As of this writing, only four northern Virginia localities, Alexandria, Arlington, Fairfax, and Loudoun, have approved such an ordinance.

Current School Finance Litigation

As of this writing, there is no new finance litigation in Virginia. Several newspapers, however, have filed suit over Governor Youngkin's refusal to make certain documents public and release them under the Virginia Freedom of Information Act.

Enrollment Trends

Towards the end of 2019, Virginia saw a drop in students once COVID manifested. Enrollment dropped by 45,327 pupils. By 2021-22, enrollment is down another 769 students. The state held harmless school divisions for funding due to enrollment decreases.

TABLE 46.2 – Total Virginia Student Public School Enrollment 2016-2017 through 2021-2022

Year	Total Enrollment	Change
2016-2017	1,284,114	na
2017-2018	1,292,706	8,592
2018-2019	1,290,513	(2,193)
2019-2020	1,298,083	7,570
2020-2021	1,252,756	(45,327)
2021-2022	1,251,987	(769)

https://p1pe.doe.virginia.gov/apex/f?p=180:1:103207564023982:SHOW_REPORT

SOURCES OF REVENUE

Revenue for Virginia's public schools mainly comes from local taxes, state sales tax, state taxes and federal funds. Table 46.1 shows the amount and percentage from each source. Local taxes are the primary source of revenue for Virginia's public schools. The major source of these funds comes from local property taxes on real estate and public service corporations. Other local taxes come from optional local sales, motel and hotel rooms, personal property, business licenses, utility, motor vehicle licenses, and others. State taxes account for the second largest source of revenue for education. In FY 2021, local funds accounted for 45.98% of total education funding.

The 2022-2024 proposed budget revenue forecast showed the sources and totals (Table 46.4.).[12]

DISTRIBUTION FORMULAS

Regular Education Programs

The Standards of Quality (SOQ) describe the foundation level of services and funding for local school divisions and covers eight budget categories: Instruction;

TABLE 46.3 – Revenue/Expenditure by Source and Percentage for Virginia Public Schools, FY2021

Source	Revenue/Expenditure	Percent
Local	$9,406,893,612	45.98
State	$6,186,190,156	30.24
Sales Tax	$1,650,161,513	8.07
Federal	$1,748,507,131	8.55
Total	$22,325,124,367	100.0

Source: Table 15 of the Superintendent's Annual Report for Virginia, FY 2017. Retrieved from: https://www.doe.virginia.gov/statistics_reports/supts_annual_report/2020-21/index.shtml

TABLE 46.4.   The Virginia Fund Forecast for FY 2022*

Total Revenues		Total Transfers	
Corporate income	$1,721.5	ABC profits	$161.4
Individual income	17,919.7	Sales tax (0.25%)	487.3
Insurance premiums	394.3	Transfers per the Appropriations Act	99.9
State sales and uses	4,427.8		
Wills, suits, deeds, and contract fees	593.7		
Miscellaneous	874.7		
Total Revenues	$25,931	Total Transfers	$748.6
Total General Fund		**$26,680.3**	

*Dollars in millions

Administration, Attendance, and Health; Transportation; Operations and Maintenance; Facilities; Debt and Fund Transfer; Food Services (which must be self-funding through sales); and Technology.

The SOQ also includes a calculation for determining a locality's wealth—or fiscal capacity. Using a mixture of true value of property (weighted at .5), local adjusted gross income (weighted at .4), and local taxable retail sales (weighted at .1), the state determines local fiscal capacity on a range from 0.1692 to 0.8000 in the 2021-22 year. This figure is referred to as the Local Composite Index (LCI) which determines the local required effort. This figure tends to equalize for variance in local fiscal capacity: less wealthy school districts (Virginia calls them *divisions*) receive more state aid, and wealthier school divisions receive less aid.

Using the formula, a school division with an LCI of .3511 would be responsible for funding 35.11% of the SOQ costs—or the school division's local required effort. In turn, Virginia would fund 64.89% of the SOQ costs. All school divisions in Virginia typically exceed their local required effort. In FY 2021, the average local expenditure in excess of LRE was 59.74%, with wealthy Loudoun County exceeding the LRE by 189.92%.[13]

SOQ funding is the largest category of Virginia's Direct Aid budget to school divisions, averaging about 90% of local funding.[14] Additional funding is appropriated in five other categories including: Incentive Programs, Categorical Programs, Lottery Proceeds Fund, Supplemental Education Programs, and Federal Funds.

Categorical or Other Funding

Incentive programs are not required; they are voluntary for the locality. Examples include Governor's Schools, special education programs, and compensation supplements in the Commonwealth's higher cost of living areas. School districts must agree to ensure they will offer the specific program and meet all the established requirements. This category generally accounts for 2-3% of total state funding.

Categorical programs provide funding beyond that required in the SOQ by state or federal regulations. These programs target specific student populations such as adult education and literacy, Virtual Virginia (on-line courses for students enrolled in public school), required services for students identified as eligible for special education services, and the school lunch program state match. This category generally accounts for approximately 1% of total state funding.

Lottery Proceed Funds are designed for 20 programs formerly funded with general funds. Virginia's lottery began in 1987 to aid public education. But rather than supplement state education funding, the lottery funds supplanted it. Lottery revenue funds four SOQ accounts: Textbooks, ESL (English Language Learners), Early Reading Intervention, and the Standards of Learning (SOL, academic competencies required for state accountability testing) for Algebra Readiness. Most funding requires a local match, and some funding is equalized based on students eligible for Free or Reduced-price lunch rates. The Virginia Preschool Initiative, Early Reading Intervention, and K-3 Class Size Reduction programs also receive funding and generally account for 7-8% of total state funding.

Supplemental Education Funds provide monies for specific purposes that the Act spells out. This small percentage of state funding (less than 1%) goes toward the Virginia Teaching Scholarship Loan program and National Board Certification teacher bonuses. Funding is not available to all school divisions in the Commonwealth—only according to language in the Act.

Typically, federal funding to Virginia comes from the Elementary and Secondary Education Act (ESEA), Individuals with Disabilities in Education Act (IDEA), Carl Perkins Act, Adult Education and Family Literacy Act, and the School Nutrition Act. Funds are paid on a reimbursement basis to school divisions based on a formula.

Special Education

Virginia allocates funds for special education using a staff-based formula. For each child counted in the school division's average daily membership (ADM), the state pays an amount—called the *special education add-on*—to assist in the cost of implementing the state's special education program standards. The state calculates the per-child special education add-on amount by determining the theoretical number of teachers and aides needed to meet the Standards of Quality for special education in each school. This theoretical number is based on information supplied on the December 1 Count of Children Receiving Special Education and Related Services. The state then decides its share of these theoretical costs according to the locality's composite index of local ability to pay. The state pays these funds into each local school board's the general fund.[15] All disbursements are subject to availability of funds.

The state of Virginia provides additional funds to support the cost of providing special education in local school divisions for homebound instruction, children with disabilities enrolled in public regional special education programs, children with disabilities receiving special education and related services in regional or local jails, and children with disabilities whose IEPs specify private day or private residential placement. The state also reimburses costs of education of children with disabilities who have been placed in Code of Virginia-licensed foster care or other custodial care, an orphanage or children's home, or child caring institution or group home. Tuition for these institutional placements is funded through an interagency pool which exists under the Comprehensive Services Act to pay the state's share of these costs. Payment is in the form of percentage reimbursement (based on a locality's ability to pay) for actual costs incurred for services purchased.[16] State and federal funds also support education of children with disabilities at state mental health facilities, state training centers for people with intellectual disabilities, and state specialized children's hospitals.

The local educational agency must also pay a proportionate share of its federal special education funds for the special education and related services costs for children ages 3 through 21 with disabilities whose parents place them in private elementary or secondary schools, including religious schools, located in the school division or who are homeschooled. These costs may include direct and consultative services, equipment or materials, and for training private school teachers and other private school personnel.[17] Local school boards determine how much local funding to request from the governing body (city council, town council or board of supervisors) by costing out all its programs and then subtracting out the anticipated revenues from state, federal and other sources.[18]

Likewise, federal funds are available both for preschool and K-12 special education programs to help LEAs with the excess costs of educating children with special needs. LEAs describe the use of these funds in their annual plans submitted to VDOE. These may include early intervention service—such as additional academic and behavioral supports—for children K-12 not currently identified as needing special education or related services to succeed in a general education environment. Eligibility for federal funds depends, in part, on the LEA's maintenance of their fiscal effort, using the federal funds to supplement but not supplant, state and local special education and related services expenditures.[19]

A formula considering historical federal funding, total school enrollment, and poverty level determines the amounts each school receives. In any given year, the Department of Education has the discretion to offer other federal grant opportunities designed for statewide program improvement. School divisions must apply annually for any federal funds and cannot commingle federal special education funds with other funds. Once the school division receives state approval, the school division spends the money, and the state reimburses approved expenditures. School divisions may also seek federal Medicaid reimbursement for certain students and services by applying to the Department of Medical Assistance Services to be an approved provider.[20]

For the school year 2018-2019, Virginia's state total for IDEA Part B (Section 611) special education flow-through funding was $264,258,325[21] and the state total for Part B (Section 619) preschool subgrants was $6,939,845.[22]

If the VDOE determines that an LEA is adequately providing a free and appropriate public education to all children with disabilities living in the areas the LEA serves with state and local funds, the VDOE may reallocate any part of the funds under Part B of the Act that the school division does not need to other school divisions in the state that are not adequately providing special education and related services to all children with disabilities living in areas they serve.

Transportation

Each school day, more than 15,000 school buses transport almost one million students in Virginia.[23] Virginia allows reimbursement for school division transportation expenses including allowed mileage and school bus purchases under the Direct Aid Budget. School divisions would be eligible for the percentage reimbursement of allowable charges based on the Local Composite Index.

Career and Technical Education

Career and Technical Education (CTE) is funding through state appropriations to school divisions by SOQ funding and supplemented by federal funds through the Carl D. Perkins Career and Technical Education Act.

CAPITAL OUTLAY AND DEBT SERVICE

The responsibility for constructing, furnishing, and equipping public schools in Virginia is the responsibility of the local school division. Facilities can be financed using 1) Cash, 2) Bonds, or 3) Bank Loans. Bonds are most frequently used. Virginia's Constitution limits cities and towns from issuing bonds or any other interest-bearing obligations to 10 percent of assessed real estate value.[24] Counties that wish to sell bonds are required to hold a referendum for voter approval.[25]

General obligation bonds are secured by the full faith and credit of the issuer with taxing power by one of four methods. First, direct local government borrowing, has the locality issue and sell bonds on the public or private market. Second, the Literary Fund Direct Loan program administered through the Virginia Department of Education, funds individual projects up to $7.5 million with a cap of $20 million to any locality. Third, the Virginia Public School Authority (VPSA), a pooled bond program administered by VSPA, can provide funds. Fourth, funding can come through Subject to Appropriation Bonds usually issued through a local industrial development authority (IDA) or a local economic development authority (EDA). The IDA or EDA borrows the funds to build the school and then leases the school back to the school division. This fourth method is usually more expensive than the first three methods.

After construction, building maintenance is funded through the SOQ funding through the state according to the local composite index. Additional information on school facility funding can be found at the following location.[26]

EMPLOYEE BENEFITS

Health Care Benefits

All health care benefits are arranged at the local level and vary across the Commonwealth. State employees have the a uniform state negotiated health care benefit.

Virginia Retirement System[27]

Virginia has three basic retirement plans for school employees, aptly named Plan 1, Plan 2, and the Hybrid plan. The plan to which employees belong depends on their hiring date. Plans 1 and 2 are defined benefit plans. The Hybrid plan is a mix of defined contribution and defined benefit. Each successive plan provides a lower retirement benefit for employees. Additionally, a supplemental defined contribution plan allows payroll deduction for a tax-deferred savings account.

Those in Plan 1 were hired or rehired before July 1, 2010, who had at least five years of creditable service as of January 1, 2013 and had not taken a refund. The account accrues 4% interest compounded annually. The retirement benefit is based on the average of the employee's 36 consecutive months of highest compensation, years of service, and a multiplier of 1.7. An unreduced benefit requires the employee to be at least 50 years of age with at least 30 years of creditable service or age 65 with at least 60 months of service credit. Employees contribute 5% of compensation on a pre-tax, salary-reduction basis.

A hypothetical retirement Plan 1 employee's benefit could calculate as follows. Let's assume the highest 3-year average salary of $100,000 (to keep the math simple) over a 30-year career with the multiplier of 1.7. Thirty years multiplied by 1.7 equals 51% of the average salary or $51,000. If another hypothetical employee had the same final average salary with 40 years of service, 40 multiplied by 1.7 equals 68% of the salary or $68,000 per year. A $4.00 per month health insurance credit is available for those with at least 15 years of service along with a benefit reducing life insurance benefit.

Those in Plan 2 were hired or rehired before July 1, 2010, did not have at least five years of creditable service as of January 1, 2013, and had not taken a refund. The account accrues 4% interest compounded annually. The retirement benefit is based on the average of the employee's 60 consecutive months of highest compensation, years of service, and a multiplier of 1.65. An unreduced benefit requires the employee to be of normal Social Security retirement age with at least 60 months of service credit or when the person's age in years and service in years equals 90. Employees contribute 5% of compensation on a pre-tax, salary-reduction basis.

A hypothetical retirement Plan 2 employee's benefit could calculate as follows. Let's assume the highest 5-year average salary of $100,000 (to keep the math simple and consistent) over a 30-year career at age 60 (30 + 60 = 90) with the multiplier of 1.65. Thirty years multiplied by 1.65 equals 49.5% of the average salary or $49,500. If another hypothetical employee had the same final average salary with 40 years of service, 40 multiplied by 1.7 equals 66% of the salary or $66,000 per year. A $4.00 per month health insurance credit is available for those with at least 15 years of service along with a benefit reducing life insurance benefit.

Those in the Hybrid Plan were hired on or after January 1, 2014. The employee contributes a mandatory 4% of creditable compensation to the plan. Employees contribute on a pre-tax salary reduction basis. The employer pays to the defined benefit component of the plan at the same rate (4%) less any employer contributions to the defined contribution component of the retirement plan. Employees contribute 1% of creditable compensation to the 401(a) (Hybrid Plan defined contribution) account with an employer match. Beginning January 1, 2016 school divisions could elect to offer Hybrid Plan employees an employer-sponsored 403(b) option for employee's voluntary contributions. Employees could contribute up to 4% of compensation with employers matching up to 2.5% of compensation.

A hypothetical retirement Hybrid Plan employee's benefit could calculate as follows. Let's assume the highest 5-year average salary of $100,000 (to keep the math simple and consistent) over a 30-year career at age 60 (30 + 60 = 90) with the multiplier of 1.0. Thirty years multiplied by 1.0 equals 30% of the average salary or $30,000. If another hypothetical employee had the same final average salary with 40 years of service, 40 multiplied by 1.0 equals 40% of the salary or $40,000 per year. On top of this benefit is the defined contribution plan. This component requires an employee/employer contribution of 1% with a voluntary employee contribution of 0-4% and an employer match of 0-2.5%. This portion of the calculation would vary from person to person. The same $4.00 per month health insurance credit is available for those with at least 15 years of service along with a benefit reducing life insurance benefit as for those in Plan 1 or Plan 2.

CHARTER SCHOOL FUNDING

Virginia has relatively clear and accountable public charter school laws. All charter schools in Virginia are nonsectarian alternative public schools located within a school division and under the authority of a local school board.[28] A public charter school may be created as a new public school or by converting all or part of an existing public school. No public charter can be established by converting a private school or a nonpublic home-based educational program. Enrollment is open to children who reside within the relevant school division (or divisions, for regional public charter schools) using a lottery process on a space-available basis. Public charter students are included in the LEA's average daily membership. Charters may be approved or renewed for a period not to exceed five years. At present, Virginia has eight public charter schools in operation located in Albemarle (2 schools), Loudoun County (2 schools), York County, Richmond (2 schools), and Virginia Beach. As such, funding trends are difficult to separate and obtain.[29]

Before a public charter application (or application for renewal) can be submitted for review, the state Board of Education must review, comment, and decide whether the proposed application meets the Board's approval criteria. The Board review examines the applications for feasibility, curriculum, financial soundness, and other objective Board-established criteria, consistent with existing state law. As part of the application, the public charter must report on its academic and other progress. It must also provide a financial statement, on the Board-prescribed forms, that disclose the costs of administration, instruction, and other spending categories that is concisely and clearly written to enable the school board or boards and the public to compare such costs to those of other schools or similar organization. Failure to meet or make reasonable progress towards achievement of the content standards or student performance and/or failure to meet generally accepted standards of fiscal management may lead to the charter's revocation.[30]

The local school board contracts with the public charter school for an agreement stating the conditions for funding the public charter, including funding for the educational program and services (i.e., food services, custodial and maintenance, curriculum, media and library services, and warehousing) to be provided. The per pupil funding provided to the charter school is negotiated in the charter agreement and must be commensurate with the average school-based costs of educating the students in the existing schools in the division (or divisions) unless the cost of operating the charter school is less than that average school-based cost. The funding and service agreements may not provide a financial incentive—or constitute a financial disincentive—to establish a public charter school. The public charter also receives a proportionate share of state and federal resources allocated for students with disabilities and school personnel assigned to special education programs and under other federal or state categorial aid for eligible students. Any educational and related fees collected from students enrolled at a public charter school are credited to the public charter's account established by the relevant local school board. Finally, the public charter school's management committee (composed of parents of students enrolled in the school, teachers, and administrators working in the school, and community sponsors' representatives) is authorized to accept gifts, donations, or grants of any kind made to the public charter and to spend such finds in accordance with the donor's prescribed conditions, as long as they are in accord with law or the charter agreement with the LEA.

A management committee administers and manages the school in a manner to which the public charter and the local school board agree. Public charters are subject to the Standards of Quality, Standards of Learning, and Standards of Accreditation requirements. Any services for which a public charter school contracts with a school division—such as for building and grounds, maintenance and operation, or performance any required service—shall not exceed the division's cost to provide such services. Under no circumstance may a public charter school charge tuition or be required to pay rent for space.

In 2007 (amended in 2016), the state created in the state treasury a special non-reverting fund, the Public Charter School Fund ("The Fund"), to be credited with any gifts, grants, bequests, or donations form public or private sources paid into the state treasury to support public charters. Any monies remaining in the fund, including interest, at the end of the year does not revert to the general fund but remains in the Fund for the purpose of supporting public charters schools. The state Comptroller, upon written request from the Superintendent of Public Instruction, is the only person who can expend and disburse funds. The State Board of Education was to establish criteria for making distributions from the Fund and guidelines governing it as deemed necessary and appropriate.[31]

Accountability is a watchword for Virginia's public charters. In 2016, the General Assembly passed a law amending the charter application, adding a section on the applicability of other laws, regulations, policies, and procedures for civil rights, health and safety, and student assessment and accountability as other public schools. The revision requires the charter contract to address the academic and operational performance expectations with annual performance targets. The performance framework must include indicators, measures, and metrics of student academic proficiency; student academic growth; achievement gaps in both proficiency and growth (disaggregated) between major student subgroups;[32] attendance; recurrent annual enrollment; postsecondary education readiness of high school students; finance performance and sustainability; and the management committee's performance and stewardship, including compliance with all applicable laws, regulations, and terms of the charter contract. Public charter management committees are subject to and must comply with the Virginia Freedom of Information Act.[33] An executed charter school contract must be approved in an open meeting of the local school board before a charter school can begin.

VIRTUAL EDUCATION

The Code of Virginia allows school divisions to offer online instruction to students in multiple divisions using a private organization, educational institution, or nonprofit virtual school organization that meets Board of Education-approval criteria to operate as a multidivision online provider. Approved providers contract with the local school divisions. Generally, local mentors may support student learning. A multidivision online provider must hold accreditation from a Board of education-approved agency and must meet Board of Education-approved criteria to operate.[34]

In 2015 - 2016, Virtual Virginia (VVa), a program of the Virginia Department of Education, offered 72 online Advanced Placement, World Language, core academic, and elective courses. Students receive instruction via the Internet through a secure, web-based environment; students may participate at school or at home.

Virtual Virginia teachers are highly qualified and hold Virginia licenses in their content area. Since its start in 2002, VVa has served over 72,000 students. During the 2015- 2016 academic year, 11,642 students enrolled, with 26,213 half-credit enrollments. Ninety-nine percent of VVa students are public school students.

Funding for full-time virtual charter schools tends to flow through the state's per -pupil funding formula. The funding, some or all, follows the student. Supplemental online, such as by the course, typically received funds through state appropriation and/or course fees that the district and/or student pays. Essentially, it is a fee for service.

Independent national studies suggest virtual schools funding should be about the same as those for a regular brick and mortar school. Costs for full-time virtual schools ranged form $7,200 to $8,300 per pupil as compared to $10,000 per pupil national average for K-12 education. Average funding for virtual charter schools in the United States is $6,500 per pupil (2010).[35] In Virginia, an annual legislative allotment to Virtual Virginia limits access to number of online courses available.[36] Local school districts may also support their own virtual program, such as in Fairfax County.

During the 2015-16 school year, 12 of the 20 approved online virtual education providers operate in Virginia offering 273 courses, 160 of which received approval. Student enrollment in the virtual education program in 2015-2016 totaled 7,123 students and ranged from 2,200 in Henrico County and 1,361 in Fairfax County to zero in Gloucester County. Seventy-eight percent of students taking courses from approved providers completed the courses; 75% both completed and passed the courses.[37]

Challenges to Virginia's virtual education program includes discrepancy in the enrollment data submitted by providers and the data reported by school divisions through the Student Record Collection.

FEDERAL COVID-19 FUNDING

Total Federal COVID-19 funding for Virginia totaled $238,599,192.

SUMMARY

As is much of the country, Virginia's schools are facing challenging times with a polarized public over issues of funding public schools, expanding charter schools, and what should be included in curricular matters. Sadly, students and school employees bear much of the burden.

ENDNOTES

[1] Cubberley, E. (1947). Public education in the United States: A study and interpretation of American educational history. Cambridge, MA: Houghton Mifflin, 97-105.

[2] Constitution of Virginia, (1971), Article VIII, §8 and Code of Virginia (1950), §§22.1-142 to 22.1-161.

3   Acts of Virginia Assembly of the Commonwealth of Virginia, (1818).

4   Constitution of Virginia, (1869), Article VIII, §§1-12.

5   Also known as "try to, but this is not required."

6   Constitution of Virginia (1971). Article VIII §1.

7   https://p1pe.doe.virginia.gov/apex/f?p=180:1:107989727065701

8   https://www.doe.virginia.gov/teaching/workforce_data/index.shtml

9   https://www.doe.virginia.gov/statistics_reports/interim-30-day-report-on-inherently-divisive-concepts.pdf

10 https://www.politico.com/news/2022/04/13/glenn-youngkin-vetoes-democratic-bills-00024927

11 https://law.lis.virginia.gov/vacode/title40.1/chapter4/section40.1-57.2/

12 https://dpb.virginia.gov/budget/buddoc22/BudgetDocument.pdf

13 https://rga.lis.virginia.gov/Published/2022/RD164/PDF

14 Virginia Education Association (2009, July). Funding K-12 education in the Commonwealth. School finance 101. Richmond VA: Author. Retrieved from http://www.veanea.org/assets/document/finance-2010-04.pdf

15 Virginia Department of Education (n.d.). How special education programs are funded in Virginia's schools. Richmond, VA: Author. Retrieved from http://www.doe.virginia.gov/special_ed/grants_funding/how_speced_funded.pdf

16 Virginia Department of Education (n.d.). How special education programs are funded in Virginia's schools. Richmond, VA: Author. Retrieved from http://www.doe.virginia.gov/special_ed/grants_funding/how_speced_funded.pdf

17 Superintendent's Memo 309-18, Superintendent's Memo 309-18, Attachment A, and Guidance document (2018). http://www.doe.virginia.gov/special_ed/grants_funding/index.shtml#fed

18 Virginia Department of Education (n.d.). How special education programs are funded in Virginia's schools. Richmond, VA: Author. Retrieved from http://www.doe.virginia.gov/special_ed/grants_funding/how_speced_funded.pdf

19 Virginia Department of Education, Division of Special Education and student Services (2010, January 25). Regulations governing special education programs for children with disabilities in Virginia. Part IV. Funding. Richmond, VA: Author. Retrieved from http://www.doe.virginia.gov/special_ed/regulations/state/regs_speced_disability_va.pdf

20 Virginia Department of Education (n.d.). How special education programs are funded in Virginia's schools. Richmond, VA: Author. Retrieved from http://www.doe.virginia.gov/special_ed/grants_funding/how_speced_funded.pdf

21 Virginia Department of Education (2021). Division of special education and student services Grants and funding. IDEA Part B (Section 611)—Flow-Through funding, 2019-2021. Retrieved from https://www.doe.virginia.gov/special_ed/grants_funding/index.shtml

22 Virginia Department of Education (2021). Division of special education and student services Grants and funding. IDEA Part B (Section 619), Preschool subgrants awards. Retrieved from https://www.doe.virginia.gov/special_ed/grants_funding/index.shtml

23 Virginia Department of Education (n.d.) Pupil transportation. Richmond, VA: Author. Retrieved from http://www.doe.virginia.gov/support/transportation/index.shtml

24 Virginia Constitution, Article VII, §10(a). Debt.

25 Code of Virginia, §15.2-2611. Holding of election; order authorizing bonds; authority of governing body.

26 http://www.doe.virginia.gov/support/facility_construction/literary_fund_loans/funding_options.pdf

27 All retirement plan information can be found at: https://www.varetire.org/members/index.asp

28 Virginia General Assembly (2016, July 1). Virginia's charter school laws. Code of Virginia. Retrieved from http://www.pen.k12.va.us/instruction/charter_schools/index.shtml

29 Owings, W., Kaplan, L., and Neal, H (2022). State of the States: Virginia. Journal of Education Finance, 47(5), 369-371. Retrieved from https://www.nationaledfinance.com/docs/39_Jef_47.5_Virginia.pdf

30   A public charter school applicant whose application was denied or a grantee whose charter was revoked or not renewed is entitled to petition the local school board for reconsideration. Before reconsideration, the applicant or grantee may seek technical assistance for the Superintendent of Public Instruction to address the reasons for the denial, revocation, or non-renewal.

31   Virginia Department of Education. (n.d.) Charter schools. Richmond, VA: Author. Retrieved from http://www.pen.k12.va.us/instruction/charter_schools/index.shtml

32   Student subgroups are based on gender, race, poverty status, special education status, English language learner status, and gifted status.

33   Virginia Department of Education. (n.d.) Charter schools. Richmond, VA: Author. Retrieved from http://www.pen.k12.va.us/instruction/charter_schools/index.shtml

34   Virginia Department of Education. (n.d.). Virtual school programs (Multidivision online providers). Retrieved from http://www.doe.virginia.gov/instruction/virtual_learning/virtual_schools/index.shtml

35   Powell, A. (n.d.) Costs and funding for virtual schools. International Association for K-12 Online Learning. Retrieved from http://sfc.virginia.gov/pdf/committee_meeting_presentations/2011%20Interim/September_22/092211_No2.pdf

36   Powell (n.d.)

37   Virginia Board of Education (2016, November). Virginia Board of Education's 2016 annual report on the condition and needs of public schools in Virginia. Appendices H, p. 115 – 143; Appendix I 144 – 148.Retrieved from http://www.pen.k12.va.us/boe/reports/annual_reports/2016.pdf

CHAPTER 47

WASHINGTON

David S. Knight
University of Washington

Pooya Almasi
University of Washington

JoLynn Berge
Northshore School District

This chapter explores the state school finance system of Washington State. We follow a similar outline as other chapters in this volume, starting with a general background, and then describing the current political climate, sources of revenue and trends over time, the distribution formula, and special consideration including capital outlay, employee benefits, charter schools, virtual education, and federal COVID-19 stimulus funding. We conclude with recommendations for future reading and research.

GENERAL BACKGROUND

History

Washington State's system of financing public education was initially established with the founding of the state in 1889[1] At that time, state responsibility over education was gaining in prominence nationally, particularly on the heels of failed efforts within the U.S. Congress to establish a national system of education.[2] African American community groups and other activist groups during the Reconstruction era prioritized strong constitutional commitments to education that included

Funding Public Schools in the United States, Indian Country,
and US Territories (Second Edition), pages 737–755.
Copyright © 2023 by Information Age Publishing
www.infoagepub.com

anti-discrimination language and encouraged broader fiscal support for education beyond localities.[3] Thus, during the state's first legislative session, lawmakers established the Common School Fund, which would generate revenues for public education primarily through sale of federal forest land.[4] The legislature determined that counties would also contribute a small portion of revenues and that districts would be permitted to raise revenues to support local schools. As in many states, education stakeholders have debated the balance of local and state support for public schools. Soon after the establishment of the Common School Fund, the state legislature passed a new state levy assessed on a per census child basis, in response to concerns that the Common School Fund did not provide ample provision for education.[5]

Despite these initial commitments to the equitable financing schools, the first legislative session also set in place a school finance system that marginalized or excluded Indigenous groups and relied on the expropriation of land inhabited by Native Americans. The process of settler colonialism, led by White settler missionaries and political and miliary institutions, embedded fundamental inequities in the state's cultural, economic, and political infrastructure.[6] That process continues to present day and many stakeholder groups have pushed for reforms with varying degrees of success.

During the 1960s and 70s, a growing number of districts around the country began challenging the constitutionality of their state's system for financing schools. In 1971, Washington legislators commissioned a study of how the *Serrano v. Priest* decision in California may impact Washington school finance.[7] The state's first more judicial challenge, *Northshore v. Kinnear* in 1973,[8] was decided in the State Supreme Court in favor of the state.[9] In the subsequent years, many districts were unsuccessful in passing local enrichment levies. In 1975, as many as 65 school districts, including Seattle Public Schools and several other large districts collectively representing 40 percent of students statewide, had levies fail twice in a row, placing education funding at severe risk. Seattle brought a new lawsuit and the state's Superior Court sided with plaintiffs in *Seattle v. Washington* (1977), ruling that the state legislature was responsible for "defining and giving substantive content to basic education" and funding basic education through a dependable tax source.[10] At that time, state legislators had commissioned a study of the state's school finance system, and educational organizations and citizen's groups were calling for major finance reforms.

In response to the Superior Court decision and ongoing efforts across the state to improve the finance system, the legislature passed the Basic Education Act of 1977, which established much of the state's current K-12 school finance policy structure. This act established the state's education goals, identified a specific number of hours of study required for each subject and grade level, and created a funding formula based primarily on student enrollment in each district. The purpose of the formula was to provide all students with equal educational opportunity to achieve common goals. The formula provided funding for specific staff and non-personnel resources and included separate funding strategies for remote schools, and other programs such as special education, bilingual education, and transportation. The legislature also passed the Levy Lid Act of 1977, which imposed limitations on the amount of local levy revenue districts can raise and prevented districts from spending levy funds on employee compensation.[11] Under these two acts, the state is responsible for funding the entire share of what the legislature deems "basic education," while local districts can add enrichments through local levies but are not expected to contribute funding for basic education. Since 1977, state legislators have altered levy lid policies, added an equalization program (Local Effort Assistance), and made changes to the definition of and resources provided under basic education, but the overall K-12 finance structure, including the lack of any "expected local share" for base funding has not changed substantially.

Notable Constitutional Language

As noted earlier, successful court challenges in Washington stem in part from the state's strong constitutional language regarding public education. Section 1 of Article IX of Washington's constitution states the following:

> It is the paramount duty of the state to make ample provisions for the education of all children residing within its boards, without distinction or preference on account of race, color, caste, or sex.[12]

The language is unique among states for two reasons. First, use of the phrase "paramount duty" implies the state must fund education before funding any other service.[13] When state constitutions describe a general duty or obligation to provide public education, courts have inferred that education funding is of equal priority to other state obligations. Second, the text specifically names that these resources are to be provided "without distinction" of student background. Other states make more broad reference to a "uniform" system of funding, and Section 2 of Article IX in Washington's constitution states that the "legislature shall provide for a general and uniform system of public schools." The text in Section 1 goes somewhat further in referring to a paramount duty and specifically naming groups for which the education finance system must not discriminate.[14] This portion of the constitution, Section 1 of Article IX, was the predominant basis for the state's most recent constitutional challenge in *McCleary v. Washington*, which was again decided in favor of plaintiffs.

DESCRIPTIVE STATISTICS

The state currently supports 295 school districts and 35 other local education agencies including tribal compact districts, independent charters, and other entities., which collectively operate 2,500 schools and serve approximately 1 million students. Table 47.1 provides some basic descriptive statistics for these school districts. The first column shows statewide averages, and the next three columns show averages disaggregated by school poverty rate. School and district counts

TABLE 47.1. School and Student Characteristics in Washington State, 2019-20 to 2021-22

	All	Lower-Poverty Schools	Middle-Poverty Schools	Higher-Poverty Schools
Students	1,110,233	425,505	364,339	320,389
Schools	2,468	823	823	822
Trad. Public	1,976	659	667	650
Alternative	237	80	83	74
Re-engagement	77	18	18	41
Special education	69	31	25	13
Tribal compact	7	0	1	6
Charter	16	2	7	7
Other	86	33	22	31
Trad. pub. sch. districts	295	—	—	—
Other districts	35	—	—	—
Student race/ethnicity				
Amer. Indian / Indigenous	1%	0%	1%	2%
Asian	8%	12%	6%	5%
Black / African American	5%	3%	5%	7%
Latinx	25%	13%	22%	44%
Pacific Islander / HI Native	1%	0%	1%	2%
Two or more races	9%	9%	9%	8%
White	51%	62%	56%	32%
Program classifications				
Gifted	6%	9%	5%	3%
Bilingual / MLL	12%	6%	9%	23%
Special Ed.	15%	13%	15%	16%
Sec. 504	4%	6%	4%	3%
Migrant	2%	0%	1%	5%
Mobile	4%	4%	5%	5%
Low-income	45%	21%	49%	75%
Homeless	3%	1%	3%	4%

Note: The first column shows statewide averages, and the next three columns shows averages disaggregated by school poverty rate, where lower-poverty schools enroll fewer than 36% of students classified as lower-poverty, high-poverty schools enroll greater than 61%, and middle-poverty schools lie within this range. Students classified as low-income are those eligible to receive free or reduced-price meals. All values reflect a three-year average from 2019-20 to 2021-22 except the count of schools and districts, which reflect just the 2021-22 school year.

correspond to the 2021-22 school year, but all other figures represent a three-year average from 2019-20 to 2021-22. Student racial/ethnic categories are somewhat reflective of national averages, except the state's public schools enroll a greater percent of students who identify as Asian and smaller percent of students who identify as Black, relative to national averages.[15]

The next three columns of Table 47.1 divide school into three groups based on student poverty rate (with an equal number of schools in each group). Disaggregating racial/ethnic categories by school poverty rate highlights how students in Washington are segregated across race and class. For example, Table 47.1 shows that among lower-poverty schools, students who identify as White represent 62% of students, whereas 3% and 13% identify as Black or Latinx, respectively. In higher-poverty schools, the average percent of students who identify as Black or Latinx is 7% and 44%, compared to 32% for White students. In other words, historically marginalized students of color are two to three time more likely to attend a high-poverty school than a low-poverty school, while White students are half as likely. Similar patterns emerge among the state's special enrollment classifications. Students placed in gifted programs are more likely to attend lower-poverty schools, while those receiving special education services and students classified as multi-language learners as well as migrant, mobile, and homeless students are all substantially more likely to attend higher-poverty schools.

In the next subsection, we discuss the current political climate, including legislative makeup, union representation, notable advocacy groups, and recent policy changes.

CURRENT POLITICAL CLIMATE

Legislative Makeup

The Washington State Legislature is made up of a House of Representatives including 98 members (two for each of the 49 legislative districts) and a State Senate, which includes 49 senators and the state's Lieutenant Governor who serves as Senate president. As of January 2021, Democrats control both houses, with a 57-41 majority in the House and a 28-21 majority in the Senate. Washington's legislative sessions run every year, but the state budget is debated only during odd-numbered years, during which sessions last 105 days. During even-number years, legislators meet for 60 days, and the Governor is permitted to call special 30-day sessions at any point during the year.

Most positions in the Executive Branch are elected positions including the Governor, Lieutenant Governor, Attorney General, the Superintendent of Public Instruction, and other positions. Democrats have held the Governor's office since 1985. Washington's judicial branch includes the State Supreme Court, Appeals, and Superior, with district and municipal courts addressing misdemeanor crimes and smaller claims. Judges at all three major levels are elected, while district and municipal judges can either be appointed or elected depending on local regulations.

Union Representation and Engagement

The state has strong teacher unions and wide participation that includes 98 percent of the state's teachers.[16] The Washington Education Association is a statewide union, affiliated with the National Education Association as well as regional and local district affiliates. An analysis of teacher union strength placed Washington 10th across all 50 states.[17] That study considered thirty-seven factors across five areas: resources and membership, political involvement, scope of bargaining, state policy context, and perceived influence based on an originally collected survey of stakeholders in each state. The state ranked third overall in resources and membership, behind only New York and New Jersey, but tied with Hawaii and Minnesota. Annual revenues and membership rates of WEA helped increase Washington's rank of union strength. The next two strongest areas are perceived influence and scope of bargaining. Key education stakeholders were surveyed about the extent to which (a) teacher unions influence education policy relative to other influential entities, (b) state politicians rely on teacher union support to get elected, and (c) state education policy aligns with union preference, among other issues. Survey respondents suggested that unions play an important role in guiding education policy in Washington, and the state ranked 9th overall based on these survey measures.[18] Washington teacher unions benefit from a relatively wide scope of bargaining; teacher strikes are legally permissible and collective bargaining with local districts is considered mandatory. The state's unions are less powerful with respect to involvement in politics, ranking 48th in union representation among Democrat and Republican convention delates and 29th in the percent of state political candidate campaign contributions donated by teacher unions.

The state union and local affiliates played a key role in the implementation of recent finance reforms, ensuring a greater share of funds were spent "in the classroom" on instructional resources including teacher compensation, supports, and materials. In 2018-19, school districts had access to a substantial infusion of funding as part of House Bill 2242 and Senate Bill 6362 (Sun et al., 2022).[19] These two bills were enacted in response to the *McCleary v. Washington*, the most recent school finance State Supreme Court case (discussed in greater detail below). While districts have some flexibility in how new funds were allocated, a substantial portion of new funds were targeted towards increases in teacher salaries, consistent with recent research linking patterns of educational spending following a state school finance reform to state teacher union strength (Brunner et al., 2020).

Other Advocacy and Interest Groups

In addition to strong local unions, Washington is home to a wide array of advocacy and interest groups. Several education philanthropic organizations are headquartered in the greater Seattle region, including the Bill and Melinda Gates Foundation, the Ballmer Group, and the Raikes Foundation. In recent years, the Gates Foundation has supported traditional public school initiatives as well as proposals to expand the number of charter schools in the state.[20] The Ballmer Group has made substantial investments in higher education scholarships to support the youth mental health and educator workforce,[21] while the Raikes Foundation supports a broad set of initiative around education and youth homelessness.

Several community activist groups also have influence over education policy in Washington, including Southeast Seattle Education Coalition, the Equity in Education Coalition, Supporting Partnerships in Education and Beyond, Black Education Strategy Roundtable, and local affiliates of the National Association for the Advancement of Colored People, among other groups.

Recent School Finance Litigation and Policy Reforms

As noted above, unions and community activist groups were critical during the recent state school finance litigation as well as during the implementation of the ensuing reforms. In 2007, school districts, local unions, and several families filed a lawsuit alleging the state's finance system was not meeting the state constitutional requirements quoted earlier. The *McCleary v. Washington* case was ultimately argued before the State Supreme Court and decided in favor of plaintiffs. The decision, reached in 2012, called on state legislators to expand the definition of basic education and provide funding to support the resources guaranteed through the new funding formula. Figure 47.1 presents a timeline of the court case and legislative reforms that followed. Two bills were passed prior to the final court decision. House Bill 2261 (passed in 2009) created the Prototypical School Funding Model in place today. The bill did not outline specific funding amounts or revenue sources, but these details were included and authorized in House Bill 2776 (passed in 2010). As part of the McCleary decision in 2012, the court determined

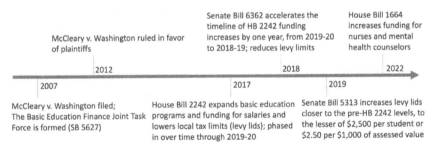

FIGURE 47.1. Timeline of legislative reforms and education resource enhancements. Note. Citations to bills are included in the reference section. This timeline draws on a previous version created by the Office of Superintendent for Public Instruction (2020).

that additional provisions were needed to meet the constitutional requirements for funding public education. Finally, House Bill 2242 further expanded resources embedded in the Prototypical School Funding Model and created a new educator salary allocation model that relied on a regionalization factor tied to local cost of living. The bill also increased state property tax and lowered local levy lids—a process sometimes referred to as the "levy swap" because for many households, the change simply exchanged local property taxes for state property taxes.[22]

When the Supreme Court determined that House Bill 2242 provisions were not on a fast enough timeline, legislators passed Senate Bill 6362 which accelerated by one year the full phasing in of House Bill 2242 from 2019-20 to 2018-19. After agreeing to large salaries increases in 2018-19, and under new local tax limitations, districts around the state faced substantial budget shortfalls by 2019. In response, the state increased levy lids up to $2.50 per $1,000 of assessed values through Senate Bill 5313, allowing districts to raise sufficient local enrichment funds to support ongoing initiatives. In response to the various ripple effects of the COVID-19 pandemic, the state expanded funding for nurses and counselors during the 2022 legislative session through House Bill 1664. Recent studies of these reforms show that all district experienced increases in overall funding; however, the regionalization factor and other adjustments targeted the largest increases to wealthier districts serving fewer shares of low-income students and students of color.[23]

SOURCES OF REVENUE

Tax Revenues

School districts receive tax revenues from local, state, and federal sources. Local school districts have flexibility to raise local funding to support either capital investment or current expenses. Washington school districts are permitted to run elections for long-term bonds to pay for major school construction and maintenance projects; enrichment levies to pay for additional staff members, salary increases, or materials; transportation levies to pay for school buses; or capital projects levies to pay for physical equipment and infrastructure. A capital project levy can be designated as technology levy if the district commits to purchasing technology with the funds generated. Local tax limitations, or "levy lids" were increased in 2010 to 28 percent of total funding (up from 24 percent). House Bill 2242 (2017) reduced levy lids to the lesser of $1.50 per $1,000 of assessed value or $1,500 per student, but levy lids were then increased (under SB 5313, 2019) to the lesser of $2.50 per $1,000 of assessed value or $2,550 per student.[24]

State tax revenues are generated primarily through property and sales tax revenues and a unique tax called the Business and Occupation tax, which taxes gross receipts rather than business profit or income.[25] Washington levies several other excise taxes on real estate, public utilities, alcohol, tobacco, marijuana, and other goods and services, but the state is one of seven that does not levy income tax. In 2019, The Tax Foundation ranked Washington's tax revenue system among the most regressive in the nation, resulting from a lack of any income tax and heavy reliance on sales tax. Lower-income households pay a higher percentage of annual income on goods subject to sales tax and are disproportionately impacted by sales taxes.[26] The state levies a 6.5% sales tax and localities levy an average of 2.79% sales tax rate, implying a statewide combined state and average local sales tax rate of 9.29% as of January 2021, the fourth highest among all other states.[27] The state collects an average of $2,118 per capita in sales tax (ranked 2nd) and Washington consistently ranks in the top five among states in terms of the percent of government revenues supported through sales tax, ranging from about to 35 to 45 percent, depending on the year. The state's property taxes are closer to national averages. Cammenga estimates the state collects $1,645 per capita in property tax rates (ranked 22nd among states).[28]

The state maintains several other tax revenue streams that support public education. The state recently added a capital gains tax that generates funding for early childhood education and subsidized childcare. That tax is currently being challenged through litigation, as the state's supreme court has generally interpreted Washington's constitution as prohibiting a progressive state income tax.[29] Among other taxes, local school districts and the state collect taxes on timber, although timber tax revenues are not substantial proportion of total district or state budgets. All together these taxes generate approximately $55 billion for the 2019-21 Biennium.[30] Public schools in Washington also receive federal funding, through Title programs outlined in the Every Student Succeeds Act. In the 2020-21 school year, federal, state, and local tax revenues generated approximately $1,000, $12,500 and $4,000 per student, for a total of $17,500 per student, on average statewide. Funding for school year 2020-21 was unique, given substantial federal stimulus funding, which we describe in a separate section later in this chapter. In the subsection below, we describe how local, state, and federal tax revenues in Washington have changed over time.

Tax Revenue Trends Over Time

As shown in Figure 47.2, local, state, and federal tax revenues in Washington were relatively flat from 1994-95 through 2012-13 after adjusting for inflation. State tax revenues increased slightly during the economic boom of 2005 to 2008 but declined during the Great Recession. State funding starts gradually increasing in 2013-14, when HB 2242 began providing funding for additional staffing and other resources. That bill is sometimes referred to as the "McCleary Fix," since it addressed much of the legislative mandates outlined in the *McCleary v Washington* State Supreme Court decisions. State funding increases at an even quicker pace in 2018-19, when the state passed SB 6362 to speed up the timeline of HB 2242. Local tax revenues were even more stable over this period, declining only once in a 27-year window, in 2018-19, when the state passed binding levy lids. Similarly, federal tax revenues are stable over time, with slight increases aligned

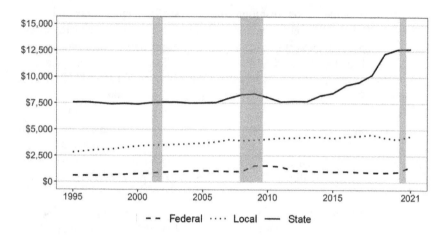

FIGURE 47.2. Federal, state, and local funding per student in Washington school districts, 1994-94 to 202-21. Note. Dollars are in real 2015 dollars, but not adjusted for other factors such as differences in local cost. Grey shaded regions represent economic recessions.

with the Great Recession and the COVID-19 pandemic. We next discuss how these funds are distributed across school districts.

DISTRIBUTION FORMULAS

Regular Education Program

Washington allocates funding to school districts through am enrollment-driven funding formula but is unique for at least two reasons. First, the state does not have any expected local share, meaning that base funding is provided completely by the state. All local tax revenues support capital and facilities projects or are considered enrichments on top of the base funding. The base level of funding, which supports what is formally defined in Washington as the "Program of Basic Education," is paid completely by the state (OSPI, 2021). This approach is used by only seven other states, including Delaware, Idaho, Indiana, Nevada, New Mexico, North Carolina, and Vermont.[31] In all other states, local districts are expected to contribute a portion of basic funding through local taxation, and wealthier districts typically contribute a greater percentage of the base allotment.[32]

Second, Washington uses a resource-based funding formula, where the amount of funding each district receives is based on a set of staffing ratios, multiplied by prespecified salary levels, with additional funding for special student populations, materials, and transportation. Only seven other states used a resource-based model as of 2021-22, Alabama, Delaware, Idaho, South Dakota, Tennessee, West Virginia, and Wyoming.[33] Most states use a dollar-based formula, where each dis-

TABLE 47.2. Staffing Ratios for Washington's Prototypical School Funding Model

	Elementary (K-6)	Middle (7-8)	High School (9-12)
Class size ratios for teacher staffing	17 (k-3); 27 (4-6)	28.53	28.74
Enrollment basis for all other staffing ratios	400	432	600
Staffing ratios			
Principals/Administrators	1.253	1.353	1.880
Librarian/Media Specialist	0.663	0.519	0.523
Guidance Counselors	0.493	1.216	2.539
School Nurses	0.076	0.060	0.096
Social Workers	0.042	0.006	0.015
Psychologists	0.017	0.002	0.007
Instructional Aides	0.936	0.700	0.652
Office Supp. & Non-inst. Support	2.012	2.325	3.269
Custodians	1.657	1.942	2.965
Student and Staff Safety	0.079	0.092	0.141
Parent Involvement Coordinators	0.083	0.000	0.000

trict receives a set dollar amount based on student enrollment and other factors, and legislators make changes to the base allotment dollar amount, rather than specific staffing ratios.[34] Under Washington's resource-based funding formula, staffing ratios are based on a prototypical school model which distributes funds based on characteristics of the district, in particular total student enrollment.

Table 47.2 shows the staffing ratios for teachers and all other staff categories. First, the number of funded full-time equivalent (FTE) teachers is based on each district enrolment divided by class size for each grade (row 1), multiplied by one plus a planning time factor. The planning time factor for school year 2020-21 is 15.5% for elementary grades (K-6) and 20% for secondary grades (7-12), as determined by the state legislature Thus a district with 170 grade K-3 students would receive funding for 10 teachers, plus an additional 15.5% planning time factor for a total of 11.55 teachers. Next, the number of all other FTE staff is determined through staffing ratios as shown in the bottom portion of Table 47.2. For example, a district with 600 high school students would receive funding to hire 2.539 guidance counselors and 0.096 nurses. To determine the specific funding amount for each district, the state multiples each FTE by a statewide salary amount for each staff type (e.g., $68,937 for all certificated instructional staff in 2021-22, OSPI, 2022). HB 2242 included a regionalization factor, that adjusted this funding upward by 6, 12, or 18 percent, for districts with above average property values. Finally, the funding formula for the Program of Basic Education includes districtwide support, including funding for 0.628 FTE technology specialists, 1.1813 facilities, maintenance, and groundskeepers, and 0.332 warehouse, laborers and mechanics for every 1,000 students. Districts also receive funding for central office administrators equal to 5.3% of the FTE units generated by the formula for K-12 teachers. While these staffing ratios determine district funding rates, districts have wide flexibility in the staff they choose to hire, subject to collective bargaining agreements.

TAX BASE EQUALIZATION THROUGH
THE LOCAL EFFORT ASSISTANCE PROGRAM

Property values vary widely across school districts, resulting from a long history of redlining and racist housing practices in every major U.S. city, especially from the 1920s to present day.[35] Thus, when districts pass local tax levies, the same level of taxation generates vastly different tax revenues, depending on the local property values for each district. Washington has a program called Local Effort Assistance (LEA) that provides tax base equalization funding for districts that pass local levies. In 2021, 284 out of 295 school districts in the state passed levies for enrichment programs, and 166 were eligible for LEA (down from 176 and 177 the prior two years). In calendar year 2021, districts received a total of $305 million, or about $300 per student.[36] LEA is designed such that any district assessing a tax rate of $1.50 per $1,000 of assessed value generate at least $1,550 per student. This equalization is still below the local revenues per student generated by the average district statewide, of $2,028, for districts with levies.[37]

COMPENSATORY FUNDING FOR STUDENTS IN POVERTY

The state's funding for basic education has only one program that distributes funding based on a student's household income, called the Learning Assistance Program (LAP). While the funding is based on the percent of a district's students eligible for free and reduced-price lunch, the purpose of LAP is to support students scoring below grade level in math, reading, and language arts. Specific funding amounts for LAP are tied to the prototypical school model. For the prototypical class size of 15 students, the formula allocates 2.3975 hours per week of additional instruction. This funding ultimately results in approximately $380 per student for the typical district, or about $600 per student for the typical high-poverty district and $250 per student for the typical low-poverty district.[38] As part of HB 2242, the state added a program within LAP that targets high-poverty schools, those with at least 50% of students who are eligible for free or reduced priced lunch. Under the change, districts receive an additional 1.1 hours per week of instruction hours each prototypical class size of 15 students, and district must target those funds to the schools from which they were generated.

Capital Outlay and Debt Service

As noted, in addition to enrichment levies to support ongoing operations expenditures, districts in Washington can levy capital projects levies, transportation vehicle levies, and longer-term bonds. However, school construction and other expenses outside ongoing maintenance are not considered part of the Basic Program of Education, and thus not part of the State's constitutional obligation, as determine in the *McCleary v. Washington* case. In other words, the state's provision of tax base equalization—to help put districts with lower property values on equal footing as wealthier districts—represents a policy decision of the state agency and legislators, is not required under the state constitution, and is thus subject to cuts in the event of economic uncertainties. To pass local levies, districts need a majority approval from local voters and a 65% approval rating to pass bonds.

Employee Benefits

All full-time state employees in Washington receive fringe benefits on top of compensation, which include support for healthcare and retirement. Healthcare procurement decisions are consolidated under the School Employees' Benefits Board, a nine-member board similar to the Public Employee Benefits Board for all state employees. The board determines employee eligibility and enrollment policies. Instead of local bargaining for medical, dental, vision, and other insurance benefits, bargaining over dollar amounts for health care benefits take places at the state level, between the Governor and a representative coalition of school employees.

Educators receive state funding for their retirement as part of the state's retirement plan. The state's pension program is supported in part by the Pension Funding Stabilization Account, part of the Washington State Near General Fund.

Charter School Funding

Washington's first charter schools were established through a voter initiative in 2012; however, a 2015 Supreme Court decision ruled charter schools were not common schools and thus could not accept state funding.[39] In 2016, the legislator authorized funding for charter schools through SB 6194, re-establishing a legal framework for charters in the state. The number of new charters is capped to 40 over a five-year period with no more than eight in a given year. Charters receive state funding through the Washington Opportunity Pathways Account, which receives funds from an in-state lottery that are not otherwise dedicated to debt service of two Seattle sports stadiums or the Exhibition Center. The state uses the same prototypical school funding model used in the traditional public school sector to determine the level of funds for charter schools.

Nonpublic School Funding

Private funding for public education comes from a variety of sources. The most public forms include large donations from private philanthropies and parent-teacher organizations and associations. Like other states, analyses have uncovered resource disparities resulting from the fundraising efforts of parent groups.[40] While some districts have experimented with redistribution plans, the state does not have a robust regulatory framework governing private donations of school funding.

Virtual Education

Virtual education in Washington is supported through OSPI's alternative learning experience (ALE) program and receives state funding on a per-student basis (RCW 28A.250.005). The ALE program is designed to provide education opportunities outside traditional settings, and many of these options are fully online or hybrid programs (Washington State Auditor's Office, 2018). The number of students enrolled has grown over time, particularly during the COVID-19 pandemic. The state estimates a 35% increase in enrollment from 2019-20 to the 2020-21, up to about 17,000 full-time students, representing about 2% of statewide enrollment.[41] A larger number of students, about 3-4% statewide, attend at least one online class.[42] An analysis reported in Furaro (2021) found much of this increase was driven by transfers to profit online learning companies. In 2011, the legislature expanded regulations pertaining to the quality of online courses though HB 2065. Further regulations including required audits were added in 2013 through SB 5946.

FEDERAL COVID-19 FUNDING

Washington received $2.9 billion in federal funds during the COVID-19 pandemic across the three major stimulus bills.[43] The Coronavirus Aid, Relief, and Economic Security Act (2020), the Coronavirus Response and Relief Supplemental Appropriations Act (2021), and the American Rescue Plan Act (2021) provided about $217 million, $825 million, and $1.9 billion, respectively, and these bills are commonly known as the Elementary and Secondary School Emergency Relief, or ESSER I, II, and III (NCSL, 2022). The state education agency, OPSI, keeps 10% of these funds and allocates the rest directly to school districts, providing $2.6 billion or about $2,300 per student. Districts have three years to spend funds, up until September 2024, so this figure translates to about $760 per student per year for the typical district, representing roughly a 4.5% increase in funding for three years. A May 2022 letter described a new timeline that allows districts to request additional time to spend funds.[44] The specific amount of funds each district receives varies widely because funds are distributed according to the Title I formula, which is tied to the number of low-income students attending each school district. Federal lawmakers distributed these funds progressively with respect to student poverty, in part, because during the last recession, higher-poverty district bore a disproportionate share of state budget cuts.[45]

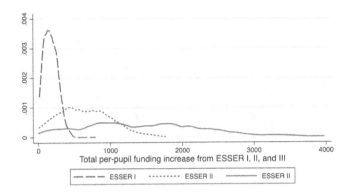

FIGURE 47.3. Distribution of federal stimulus funding across Washington school districts. Note: graph shows distribution of each of the three federal stimulus bills. ESSER = Elementary and Secondary School Emergency Relief Fund. ESSER I, II, and II refer to the CARES Act, CRCRCS Act, and the American Rescue Plan Act, respectively. ...

Figure 47.3 shows the distribution of the three stimulus bills, which provided on average $170, $650, and $1,460 per pupil, respectively. While each stimulus package followed a similar allocation strategy, using the Title I formula, the allocation of ESSER III funds appears more varied in part because there were simply more funds disturbed. Funding for ESSER I ranged from close to zero dollars up to about $500 per pupil, while ESSER III funding ranged from close to zero dollars up to about $4,000 per pupil. Figure 47.4 shows how the distribution of these funds correlates with student demographics. Each circle represents a school district, with size proportionate to district enrollment during the 2021-22 school year. We divide funding amounts by three, so the y-axis in Figure 47.4 is interpreted as the additional annual per-pupil funding districts receive through federal stimulus over three years, for school year 2021-22, 2022-23, and 2023-24. The first panel of Figure 47.4 shows a strong positive relationship between federal COVID-19 aid and student poverty rate across districts. Typical low-poverty districts, where low-income students represent about 20% of low-income students, receive about $250 per year over three years, while higher-poverty districts in which about 80% of students are classified as low-income revenge approximately $1,500 per year. The next three panels in Figure 47.4 show the relationship between annual per-pupil ESSER funds and the percent of students in each district who identify as Black, Latinx, and White. The allocation of ESSER funds is progressive with respect to both poverty rate and student race, allocating a greater amount of funds to higher-poverty districts and districts serving greater percentages of Black and Latinx students.

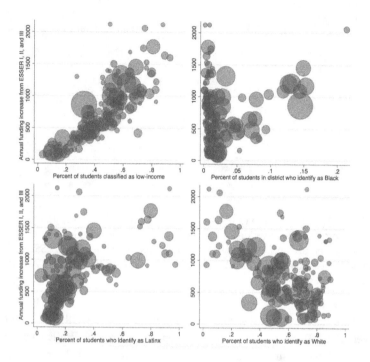

FIGURE 47.4.   Distribution of federal stimulus funds by student race/ethnicity and income, 2019-20. Note. Each circle represents a school district with size proportionate to enrollment. Graph shows annual per-student funding for all three federal stimulus bills (spread over three years).

CONCLUSIONS AND RECOMMENDATIONS FOR FUTURE READING AND RESEARCH

This chapter describes the major components of Washington State's public school finance system. While the state's strong constitutional language and political progressiveness provide conditions favorable to an adequate and equitable finance system, the system fall short in many areas.[46] First and foremost, Washington distributes a greater level of state and local funds to lower-poverty schools districts and those serving greater shares of White students The state would also benefit from reforms to special education funding and tax base equalization.[47] For additional background information, we direct readers to OSPI's guidance documents, especially the Citizen's Guide to K-12 (2022) and the Organization and Financing of Washington's Public Schools (2020). For recommendations for reforms, we guide readers to Varghese et al. (2021), the Washington State Institute for Public Policy, and studies conducted by the Center for Education Data and Research, including Goldhaber et al. (2021). Finally, we recommend additional research on

Washington's finance system, including (a) how different types of local tax levies are generated and spent; (b) the adequacy of the state's compensatory education program, the Learning Assistance Program; and (c) alternatives to the state's regionalization factor. Through incremental reforms that improve the state public school finance system, Washington can do a better job ensuring all students have equal educational opportunity to reach their potential.

ENDNOTES

[1] Beadie, N. (2016). The Federal Role in Education and the Rise of Social Science Research: Historical and Comparative Perspectives. Review of Research in Education, Centennial Volume, 40, 1-37; Thorpe, F. N. (Ed.) (1909). Constitutions, colonial charters, and other organic laws of the states, territories, and colonies now or heretofore forming the United States. Cambridge University Press.

[2] Beadie, 2016; Tyack et al., 1987.

[3] Smallwood, J. M. (1978). Early 'Freedom Schools': Black Self-Help and Education in Reconstruction-Texas, A Case Study. Negro History Bulletin, 41(1), 790-793; Tyack & Lowe, 1986).

[4] Plecki, M. L. (2000). Washington's school finance reform: Moderate success and the need for improvement. Journal of Education Finance, 25(4), 565-581.

[5] Theobald, N. D., & Hanna, F. (1991). Ample provision for whom?: The evolution of state control over school finance in Washington. Journal of Education Finance, 17(1), 7-32.

[6] Daza, S. L., & Tuck, E. (2014). De/colonizing,(post)(anti) colonial, and indigenous education, studies, and theories. Educational Studies, 50(4), 307-312

[7] Plecki, 2000

[8] Northshore School District v. Kinnear, 84 Wn2d at 725 (1974).

[9] Theobald & Hanna

[10] Seattle School District No. 1 v. State of Washington, 90 Wn2d 476 (1978).

[11] Gale, D. H. (1981). The politics of school financing in Washington State. Unpublished Doctoral Dissertation, University of Washington, Seattle, WA.

[12] Washington Constitution (1889), Article 9, Section 1.

[13] McCleary v. Washington, 269 P.3d 227 (2012).

[14] Beadie, 2020

[15] National Center for Education Statistics, 2020

[16] Corcoran, S. P., & Stoddard, C. (2011). Local demand for a school choice policy: Evidence from the Washington charter school referenda. Education Finance and Policy, 6(3), 323-353; Strunk, K. O., Cowen, J. M., Goldhaber, D., Marianno, B. D., Kilbride, T., & Theobald, R. (2018). It is in the contract: How the policies set in teachers' unions' collective bargaining agreements vary across states and districts. Educational Policy, 32(2), 280-312.

[17] Winkler & Zeehandelaar, 2010

[18] Winkler & Zeehandelaar, 2010

[19] Engrossed Second Substitute Senate Bill 6362 (Chapter 266, Laws of 2018, regular session) and Engrossed House Bill 2242 (Chapter 13, Laws of 2017, 3rd special session)

[20] Shaw, L. (2011). Gates Foundation pours funds into education advocacy groups. Seattle, WA: Seattle Times. Retrieved from: https://www.seattletimes.com/seattle-news/gates-foundation-pours-funds-into-education-advocacy-groups/

[S]haw, L. (2005). *Gates Foundation withholding grant from local schools*. Seattle, WA: Seattle Times. Retrieved from: https://www.seattletimes.com/seattle-news/education/gates-foundation-withholding-grant-from-local-schools/; Rosenthal, B. M. (2012, July 17). *Latest big gift to charter schools initiative: $600,000 from Walmart heiress*. Seattle Times. Retrieved from: http://blogs.

seattletimes.com/ politicsnorthwest/2012/07/17/latest-eye-popping-gift-to-charter-school-initia-tive-600k-from-wal-mart-heiress/.

[21] Balta, V. (2021). $38M set of gifts from Ballmer Group to address behavioral health crisis aims to bolster workforce, resources across Washington through UW-led programs. Seattle, WA: UW News. Retrieved from: https://www.washington.edu/news/2021/05/14/38-million-set-of-gifts-from-ballmer-group-to-address-behavioral-health-crisis-aims-to-bolster-workforce-resources-across-washington-through-uw-led-programs/

[22] Bazzaz, D. & Morton, N. (2019). Washington lawmakers made 11th-hour changes to school-levy policy, but who benefits? Seattle, WA: Seattle Times. Retrieved from: https://www.seattletimes.com/education-lab/washington-lawmakers-made-11th-hour-changes-to-school-levy-policy-but-who-benefits/

[23] See, for example, Knight, D. S., & Plecki, M. (2022). Establishing priorities for education finance under fiscal uncertainty: Recommendations for Washington State policymakers. Seattle, WA: University of Washington.

[24] Jackson, T. E. II, & Thomas, T. C. (2022). Washington. Journal of Education Finance, 47(5).

[25] Washington Department of Revenue. (2022). Funding education. Olympia, WA: Author. Retrieved from: https://dor.wa.gov/forms-publications/publications-subject/tax-topics/funding-education

[26] Brunori, D. (2016). State tax policy: A primer. Rowman & Littlefield.

[27] Cammenga, 2022). Cammenga, J. (2022). State and local sales tax rates, 2022. Retrieved from: https://taxfoundation.org/publications/state-and-local-sales-tax-rates/

[28] Cammenga 2022

[29] Blanford, S. (2022). Court puts profits of Washington's wealthiest over kids and families. Seattle, WA: Children's Alliance

[30] Senate Ways & Means Committee, 2021

[31] Verstegen, D. A. (2018). A 50-state survey of school finance policies and programs. https://school-financesdav.wordpress.com

[32] Houck, E. A., & DeBray, E. (2015). The shift from adequacy to equity in federal education poli-cymaking: A proposal for how ESEA could reshape the state role in education finance. RSF: The Russell Sage Foundation Journal of the Social Sciences, 1(3), 148-167; Martínez, D. G. (2021). Interrogating social justice paradigms in school finance research and litigation. Interchange, 52(2), 297-317; Martínez, D. G., & Heilig, J. V. (2022). An opportunity to learn: Engaging in the praxis of school finance policy and civil rights. Minnesota Journal of Law & Inequality, 40(2), 311; Needham, C., & Houck, E. A. (2019). The inequities of special education funding in North Carolina. Journal of Education Finance, 45(1), 1-22; Rolle, A., Houck, E. A., & McColl, A. (2008). And poor children continue to wait: An analysis of horizontal and vertical equity among North Carolina school districts in the face of judicially mandated policy restraints 1996-2006. Journal of Education Finance, 34(1), 75-102.

[33] EdBuild, 2020

[34] Verstegen, D. A. (2011) Public education finance systems in the United States and funding policies for populations with special educational needs. Education Policy Analysis Archives, 19(21). Re-trieved from http://epaa.asu.edu/ojs/article/view/769

[35] Gregory, J. (2020). Seattle's race and segregation story in maps 1920-2020. Seattle, WA: University of Washington. Retrieved from: https://depts.washington.edu/civilr/segregation_maps.htm; Lukes, D. & Cleveland, C. (2021). The lingering legacy of redlining on school funding, diversity, and performance. EdWorkingPapers, 21-363, The Lingering Legacy of Redlining on School Funding, Diversity, and Performance. (EdWorkingPaper: 21-363). Retrieved from: https://doi.org/10.26300/qeer-8c25; Rothstein, R. (2017). The color of law: A forgotten history of how our government segregated America. New York, NY: Liveright Publishing Corporation.

[36] Knight & Plecki, 2022

[37] OSPI, 2022.

[38] Knight & Plecki, 2022

[39] Washington State Board of Education. (2022). Charter schools. Olympia, WA: Author. Retrieved from: https://www.sbe.wa.gov/faqs/charter.

[40] Rowe, C. (2017). 'Stealth inequities': How Washington's education system hurts poor schools. Seattle, WA: Seattle Times. Retrieved from: https://www.seattletimes.com/education-lab/stealth-inequities-how-washington-education-system-hurts-poor-schools/

[41] Furaro, H. (2021). Washington state's for-profit online schools are expanding enrollment during the pandemic. Seattle, WA: Seattle Times. Retrieved from: https://www.seattletimes.com/education-lab/washingtons-for-profit-online-schools-attract-nearly-6000-more-students-this-school-year/

[42] Nelson, R. (2018). Update: Online learning. Olympia, WA: Office of Superintendent for Public Instruction. Retrieved from: https://www.k12.wa.us/sites/default/files/public/legisgov/2018documents/2018-01onlinelearning.pdf

[43] National Conference of State Legislators. (2022). Elementary and secondary school emergency relief fund tracker

[44] Lieberman, M. (2022). Schools can seek more time to spend ESSER funds on outside contracts. Washington, D.C.: Education Week. Retrieved from: https://www.edweek.org/policy-politics/schools-can-seek-more-time-to-spend-esser-funds-on-outside-contracts/2022/05; Rodríguez, R. (2022). Letter to Mr. Daniel Domenech, Executive Director, AASA. Washington, D.C.: U.S. Department of Education. Retrieved from: https://aasa.org/uploadedFiles/AASA_Blog_The_Total_Child(1)/AASA%20Response%20Letter%205_13_22.pdf

[45] King, J. B. (2020). Letter to Lamar Alexander and Patty Murray, chairman and ranking member of the Senate Help Committee. Washington, D.C.: The Education Trust; Knight, D. S. (2017). Are high-poverty school districts disproportionately impacted by state funding cuts? School finance equity following the Great Recession. Journal of Education Finance, 43(2), 169-194.

[46] Malin, 2016

[47] Knight & Plecki, 2022

CHAPTER 48

WEST VIRGINIA

Keith A. Butcher
University of Houston

GENERAL BACKGROUND

West Virginia became a state on June 20, 1863.[1] Article X (Education) of the state constitution stated, "The Legislature shall provide, as soon as practicable, for the establishment of a thorough and efficient system of free schools."[2] The first two sections of Article X of the West Virginia Constitution provided for the establishment and funding of a system of free schools stating:

ARTICLE X.
EDUCATION

1. All money accruing to this State, being the proceeds of forfeited, delinquent, waste and unappropriated lands; and of lands heretofore sold for taxes and purchased by the State of Virginia, if hereafter redeemed, or sold to others than this State; all grants, devises or bequests that may be made to this State for the purposes of education, or where the purposes of such grants, devises or bequests are not specified; this State's just share of the Literary fund of Virginia, whether paid over or otherwise liquidated, and any sums of money, stocks or property which this State shall have the right to claim from the State

Funding Public Schools in the United States, Indian Country,
and US Territories (Second Edition), pages 757–769.
Copyright © 2023 by Information Age Publishing
www.infoagepub.com

of Virginia for educational purposes; the proceeds of the estates of all persons who may die without leaving a will or heir, and of all escheated lands; the proceeds of any taxes that may be levied on the revenues of any corporation hereafter created; all monies that may be paid as an equivalent for exemption from military duty, and such sums as may from time to time be appropriated by the Legislature for the purpose, shall be set apart as a separate fund, to be called the School Fund, and invested under such regulations as may be prescribed by law, in the interest bearing securities of the United States, or of this State; and the interest thereof shall be annually applied to the support of free schools throughout the State, and to no other purpose whatever. By any portion of said interest remaining unexpended at the close of a fiscal year, shall be added to, and remain a part of, the capital of the School Fund.

2. The Legislature shall provide, as soon as practicable, for the establishment of a thorough and efficient system of free schools. They shall provide for the support of such schools by appropriating thereto the interest of the invested school fund; the net proceeds of all forfeitures, confiscations and fines accruing to this State under the laws thereof; and by general taxation on persons and property, or otherwise. They shall also provide for raising, in each township, by the authority of the people thereof, such a proportion of the amount required for the support of free schools therein as shall be prescribed by general laws.[2]

In 1933, the Legislature abolished the 398 original school districts and established the county unit of government. This action created 55 county school districts, each with a five-member board of education.[3] The tax limitation amendment of 1934 established the maximum tax rates on four classes or property (WVC, Article 10, Section 1).[4] The West Virginia Public School Support Plan (PSSP) was created in 1939. The PSSP was rewritten in 1971 and amended in 1973, 1981, 1982, and has been revised almost every year since 1982.[5] In aggregate, the PSSP, among other areas, computes funding for schools in the areas of professional educators, service personnel, fixed charges, transportation, administration, other current expenses, and instructional programs.

In 1982, the circuit court of Kanawha County (*Pauly v. Kelley,* CIVIL ACTION NO. 75-1268) found that the system of school finance in West Virginia was unconstitutional, stating that the system did not provide equitable and adequate funding for a thorough and efficient system of education.[6] In addition to other deficiencies in the school finance system, Special Judge Arthur M. Recht found that:

The inadequacies and inequalities in educational offerings in West Virginia are directly produced by the inadequacies and inequalities in the level of educational resources and expenditures among counties in West Virginia. The present system allocates funds according to factors such as the amount of a county's property wealth and its ability to pass excess and bond levies. These factors bear no relation to educational needs and costs of substantive educational offerings and results. Indeed, counties where children have the greatest educational needs attend school in counties which in most instances have the least taxable wealth per pupil and the fewest education resources.[6]

The court ordered the executive and legislative branches of government to develop a plan that would create an equitable and quality system of education. The West Virginia Supreme Court approved the Master Plan for Public Education on December 12, 1984.[7] As a result of the Recht decision, and implementation of The Master Plan, the school aid formula was revised to provide more of an equitable funding distribution to counties. In 2003, Judge Recht closed the decades-long *Pauley v. Kelley* case, relinquishing jurisdiction.

PUBLIC SCHOOL SUPPORT PROGRAM

The West Virginia Public School Support Plan (PSSP) is the established plan of financial support for public schools.[8] The PSSP defines the statutorily the responsibilities of both the State and the fifty-five county school districts. The State's responsibility is the total of the allocated funding calculated under Steps 1 through 7 of the PSSP, less the amount calculated as the school districts' local share. The basic foundation allowance of the PSSP provides funding to the local school districts for professional educator salaries (Step 1), service personnel salaries (Step 2), professional student support personnel salaries (step 5), employee benefit costs (Step 3), transportation operating costs (Step 4), general operating costs, substitute employee costs and allowances for faculty senates (Step 6), and instructional improvement programs, technology improvement funding, advanced placement programs, and teacher and leader induction and professional growth (Step 7). Additional allocations are provided for other programs such as alternative education programs and increased enrollment. Although not part of the PSSP, the State provides an appropriation for the education of exceptional children.

The total number of funded personnel (Steps 1, 2, and 5) for each district is determined by the net enrollment of each district.[8] In addition, each district's state aid allowance for personnel is dependent upon the salary degree classifications (pay grade for service personnel) and actual years of experience of the personnel employed by each district. In general, student transportation funding (Step 4) is determined by the actual transportation expenditures incurred by each district. Funding for technology (Step 7b) and instructional improvements to instructional programs (Step 7a) is based on the previous year's allocation plus 20% and 10% of the increase in local share for each purpose, respectively. Beginning with fiscal year 2020, additional funding is provided to support teacher and leader induction and professional growth (Step 7d) based on the previous year's allocation plus 20% of the increase in local share. The allocation of professional growth funding to county boards of education is based on a variety of factors with the greatest weight given to the number of teachers and school administrators employed with limited or no experience. District funding computations using enrollment and employment data are based on each district's second month reported data from the preceding school year.

For the purposes of determining PSSP funding, school districts are designated in four groups based on student net enrollment per square mile (see Table 48.1).

TABLE 48.1

District Type	Enrollment
Sparse	Less than 5 students per square mile
Low	5 to less than 10 students per square mile
Medium	10 to less than 20 students per square mile
High	20 or more students per square mile

Source: State of West Virginia Executive Summary of the Public-School Support Program Based on the Final Computations for the 2021-22 Year, p1.8

In addition, for districts with less than 1,400 students, the PSSP determines an additional number of students to be added to the county's actual enrollment based on the following formula. Determine the enrollment difference between the district's actual enrollment and 1,400; multiply the difference by the percent derived by dividing the district's student population density into the student population density of the district with the lowest density, and; restrict the total net enrollment for each eligible district so that it does not exceed 1,400. The amount derived from this calculation is then increased by an additional ten percent to be reduced to 1,400 students if the calculation were to exceed this amount.

The total basic foundation program allowance is the sum of the following seven allowances (Step 1 – Step 7), excluding the amounts for the West Virginia School Building Authority (SBA) and retirement, less the amount calculated for local share.

STEP 1. Foundation Allowance for Professional Educators

The PSSP provides to each public school district funding for the salaries of professional educators.[9] This allowance includes the annual state minimum salary per degree classification and years of experience (WVC §18A-4-2), the state salary increment paid to each principal and assistant principal (WVC §18A-4-3) and a state supplement amount established to assist the State in meeting its objective for establishing salary equity among the school districts (WVC §18A-4-5).

The State has established a funding ratio of allowable professional educators (PE) per 1,000 students (see Table 48.2).[10] Each district is required to maintain a minimum number of professional instructional personnel (PI) or suffer a reduction in the Step 1 allowance. Districts with a net enrollment increase are exempt from the PI reduction requirement. Effective with the 2018-19 school year, the PI requirement is based on a percentage of the lesser of the number of professional educators actually employed or the number funded (see Table 48.2).

TABLE 48.2.   West Virginia Allowance for Professional Educators

District Category	PE	PI
Sparse	72.75	91.07%
Low	72.60	91.18%
Medium	72.45	91.24%
High	72.30	91.29%

Source: State of West Virginia Executive Summary of the Public-School Support Program Based on the Final Computations for the 2021-22 Year, p. 2.

STEP 2. Foundation Allowance for Service Personnel

The PSSP provides to each public school district funding for the salaries of service personnel (secretaries, cooks, bus drivers, mechanics, etc.).[11] This allowance includes the annual state minimum salary per pay grade and years of experience (WVC §18A-4-8a) and a state supplement amount established to assist the State in meeting its objective for establishing salary equity among the school districts (WVC §18A-4-5). The State has established a funding ratio of allowable service personnel (SP) per 1,000 students (see Table 48.3).

STEP 3a. Foundation Allowance for Fixed Charges

The PSSP provides funding to each district to cover the employer's share of contributions for social security, unemployment compensation and workers' compensation.[12]

STEP 3b. Foundation Allowance for Retirement

Step 3 of the PSSP also provides an allowance to the teachers' retirement system, calculated as follows:

(1) The average retirement contribution rate of each county board multiplied by the sum of the basic foundation allowance for salaries; all salary equity appropriations;

TABLE 48.3.   West Virginia Allowance for Service Personnel

District Category		SP
Sparse		45.68
Low		45.10
Medium		44.53
High	43.97	

Source: State of West Virginia Executive Summary of the Public-School Support Program Based on the Final Computations for the 2021-22 Year, p. 2.

and such amounts as are paid by the school districts as salary supplements, to the extent that such county supplements are equal to the amount distributed for salary equity among the school districts; and (2) the additional amount estimated to be required to eliminate the unfunded liability by June 30, 2034, such amount to be based on an annual actuarial report to be provided to the Legislature.[13]

STEP 4. Foundation Allowance for Transportation Costs

The PSSP provides to each school district the following allowances for student transportation:

a. An allowance for the operations, maintenance and contracted services of student transportation services based on a percentage of each district's actual costs corresponding with their student population density (see Table 48.4), not inclusive of salaries.[14]

b. An allowance of 10% of actual expenditures for that portion of the bus fleet (12-year replacement cycle) that is using propane or compressed natural gas as an alternative fuel.

c. An allowance of 10% of actual expenditures for operations, maintenance, and contracted services, exclusive of salaries, for that portion of the bus fleet used to transport students to and from multi-county vocational centers.

d. An allowance equal to 100% of the insurance premium costs on buses, buildings and equipment used in transportation.

e. An allowance equal to 8.33% of the current replacement value of each school district's school bus fleet plus the remaining replacement value of buses purchased after July 1, 1999 that attain 180,000 miles.

f. Aid paid to students in lieu of transportation, based on the state average amount paid per pupil.

Each district's student transportation allowance is limited to 1/3 above the computed state average allowance per mile multiplied by the total mileage for the district. This amount does not include the allowance for the purchase of additional buses. Each School district is required to reserve one-half of one percent of its

TABLE 48.4. West Virginia Allowance for Transportation Costs

District Category	Percent of Actual Expenditures
Sparse	95.0%
Low	92.5%
Medium	90.0%
High	87.5%

Source: State of West Virginia Executive Summary of the Public-School Support Program Based on the Final Computations for the 2021-22 Year, p. 3.

total transportation allowance for expenditure for trips related to academic class-room curriculum.

STEP 5. Foundation Allowance for Professional Student Support Services

Prior to the passage of HB206 during the 2019 First Special Legislative Session, funding for Step 5 was based on the 2012-13 allowance and was limited to school nurses and school counselors. HB 206 expanded the definition of professional student support personnel to also include professional personnel providing social and emotional support to students and to professional personnel addressing chronic absenteeism. Beginning with the 2019-20 funding year, each district will be provided an allowance to pay the annual state minimum salary and the state supplement amount for professional student support personnel at a funding ratio of 5 positions per each 1,000 students in net enrollment.

STEP 6. Foundation Allowance for Other Current Expenses, Substitutes Salary Costs and Faculty Senates

Step 6 of the PSSP provides an allowance to each school district for other current expenses, substitute salary costs and faculty senates.[16]

- Step 6a. *School Operating Expenses.* The actual operations and maintenance expenditures reported by each county are divided by the total reported square footage of school buildings in each county to determine a state average expenditure per square foot for operations and maintenance. The total reported square footage for school buildings in each county is divided by the total net enrollment for each county to calculate a state average square footage per student. Each county's net enrollment is multiplied by the state average expenditure per square foot and the state average square footage per student. Each county's total is then multiplied by 71.25% to determine the Step 6a allowance.
- Step 6b. *Substitute Salary Costs of Professional Educators.* The allowance for professional educator substitute salary costs is 2.5% of the computed allowance for salaries under Steps 1 and 5; distribution is made to each district proportionally based on the number of professional educators respectively authorized.
- Step 6c. *Substitute Salary Costs of Service Personnel.* The allowance for service personnel substitute salary costs is 2.5% of the computed allowance for salaries under Step 2; distribution is made to each district proportionally based on the number of service personnel allowed.
- Step 6d. *Faculty Senate.* Each district receives an allowance of $400 multiplied by the number of professional instructional and student support personnel employed at each school. School districts are required to forward

the allowance to each school during the month of September of each year. Faculty Senate funds are to be used for academic materials, supplies, and equipment.

STEP 7. Foundation Allowance for the Improvement of the Instructional Program

Step 7 of the PSSP provides allowances for improvement of instructional programs; improvement of inst5uctional technology; advanced placement dual credit, and International Baccalaureate programs; teacher and leader induction programs, and funding to meet debt service requirements on revenue bonds issued by the West Virginia School Building Authority.[17]

- Step 7a. *Improvement of Instructional Programs.* The amount appropriated each year to districts for the improvement of instructional programs is the amount appropriated for the preceding year plus 10% of the growth in local share. Step 7a funds are to be used to improve instructional programs in accordance to a plan developed by each county board and submitted to the State Board for approval. The State distributes $150,000 to each school district as a base amount with the remaining funds allocated proportionally on the basis of the average of each district's average daily attendance for the preceding year and the district's second month enrollment.

- Step 7b. *Improvement of Instructional Technology.* The amount appropriated each year to districts for the improvement of instructional technology is the amount appropriated for the preceding year plus 20% of the growth in local share. Step 7b funds are designated to improve instructional technology according to the county and schools' strategic plans. The State distributes $30,000 to each school district as a base amount with the remaining funds allocated proportionally on the basis of the average of each district's average daily attendance for the preceding year and the district's second month enrollment.

- Step 7c. *Advance Placement, Dual Credit, and International Baccalaureate Programs.* PSSP provides an allowance for students enrolled in advance placement, dual credit, and international baccalaureate courses. This allocation is based on one percent (1%) of the state average per pupil state aid multiplied by the number of students enrolled in such courses in each district.

- Step 7d. *Comprehensive Systems for Teacher and Leader Induction and Professional Growth.* The amount appropriated through the PSSP for this teacher and leader induction and professional growth programs is the amount appropriated in the immediately preceding school year plus 20% of the growth in local share. The funds are distributed to the county boards of education in a manner established by the State Board of Education in accordance with factors outlined in statute.

- Step 7e. *Debt Service.* Step 7e provides to the West Virginia School Building Authority (SBA) the amount of funds required to meet debt service requirements on revenue bonds issued by the SBA prior to January 1, 1994.

LOCAL SHARE

West Virginia defines local share as a computation of each school district's projected regular levy property tax collections for the year: "the amount of revenue which the levies would produce if levied upon one hundred percent of the assessed value of each of the several classes of property contained in the report or revised report of the value made to it by the Tax Commissioner."[18] Projected excess levy tax collections are not included as part of local share. Local share for each year is computed by multiplying the taxable assessed valuation of all property in the district for the current fiscal year as certified by the county assessor by 85% of the regular levy rates for the year as set by the Legislature and then deducting four percent (4%) as an allowance for discounts, exonerations, delinquencies, and reducing the amount further by the amount that is to be paid to the Assessor's Valuation Fund. Table 48.5 provides the projected levy rates for calculating local share.

The total local share calculated for each school district is subtracted from the total basic foundation allowance to determine the State's share that is appropriated. It is noted that State code provides that the allocation for each school district is to be adjusted for certain circumstances where the calculated local share is not reflective of local funds available to the school district, errors by the county assessor or payments received in lieu or property taxes.[19]

OTHER ALLOWANCES

Other allowances are provided to school districts through the PSSP for county transfers, increased student enrollment, alternative education, Limited English Proficient students, and the Public Employees Insurance Fund.

- *County Transfers.* According to the PSSP, an allowance is provided for county school districts that agree to transfer students to another school district pursuant to an agreement approved by the State Board, if funds are

TABLE 48.5. Projected Tax Levy Rates for West Virginia Local Share

Property Class	Amount per $100 of Assessed Valuation
Class I Property	19.40¢
Class II Property	38.80¢
Class III Property	77.60¢
Class IV Property	77.60¢

Source: State of West Virginia Executive Summary of the Public-School Support Program Based on the Final Computations for the 2021-22 Year, p. 6.

TABLE 48.6. Public School Support Program Summary

PSSP Step	2019-20	2020-21	2021-22
Step 1. Professional Educators	911,031,520	897,576,715	869,082,617
Step 2. Service Personnel	305,981,816	301,789,240	291,835,429
Step 3. Fixed Charges	108,941,390	106,219,537	101,669,823
Step 4. Transportation	75,457,864	78,177,730	69,037,827
Step 5. Professional Student Support Services	63,144,004	62,148,699	59,608,039
Step 6. Other Current Expenses, Substitute Employee Salaries, and Faculty Senates	162,583,490	170,216,073	161,739,678
Step 7. Improvement of Instructional Programs	72,392,151	84,543,338	84,567,280
Total Basic Foundation Allowance	1,699,532,235	1,700,671,332	1,637,540,693
Local Share	(451,962,610)	(476,083,702)	(476,260,743)
Other Adjustments	(2,681,318)	(2,716,826)	(3,254,844)
State Aid Allowance for County School Districts	1,244,888,307	1,221,870,804	1,158,025,106
Teacher's Retirement System—PSSP	407,693,000	371,239,000	363,628,000
Public Employees Insurance Agency	228,267,791	222,461,499	206,938,256
School Building Authority (for debt service on bonds issues prior to January 1, 1994)	24,000,000	24,000,000	24,000,000
Other Allowances (increased enrollment, alternative education programs, ESL, county transfers)	10,726,812	12,844,968	29,881,761
Total Appropriation—PPSP	$1,915,575,910	$1,852,416,271	$1,782,473,123

Source: State of West Virginia Abbreviated Summary of the Public-School Support Program Based on the Final Computations for the Years of 2019-20, 2020-21, and 2021-22.

appropriated. The allowance for the year in which the transfer occurs is to be 100% of amount in the agreement, not to exceed the district's per pupil state aid allocation; the allowance in the first year after the transfer occurs is to be 50% of the agreed amount; and the allowance for the second year is to be 25%.[20] This allowance is to be reduced under certain circumstances.

- *Increased Enrollment.* Each school district, which has an increase in net enrollment, is to receive an allocation equal to the district's increase in net enrollment over the previous year multiplied by each district's average per pupil state aid.[21]
- *Alternative Education.* The allowance provide by the PSSP for alternative education programs is $18 per enrolled student.[22]
- *Limited English Proficient (LEP) Students.* State statute does not require any specific amount of funding be appropriated to districts for LEP stu-

dents through the PSSP. Districts are required to apply for the funds that are available in accordance with the provisions contained in State Board policy.[23]

- *Public Employees Insurance Fund.* The total allowance provided through the PSSP for the Public Employees Insurance Fund is based on an average premium rate for all school district employees, as established by the PEIA Finance Board, multiplied by the number of personnel allowed for funding under the Public-School Support Program.[24] The average premium rate includes a proportionate share of retires' subsidy established by the PEIA Finance Board.

SCHOOL BUILDING AUTHORITY

The West Virginia School Building Authority (SBA) was created in 1989 by the West Virginia Legislature to meet the educational planning and school construction needs of the state.[25] The Legislature created a state funding mechanism through the SBA that would assist local boards of education in the construction and renovation of new and existing facilities. A board made up of citizens, State Board of Education members and members of the construction trades industry governs the policies and procedures of the SBA. Each county school district in West Virginia must have a Comprehensive Educational Facilities Plan (CEFP) approved by the SBA and the State Board of Education. School projects from approved CEFPs are eligible for capital improvement funds from the SBA based on the needs of the facilities in each district. County school districts work with SBA staff to evaluate the needs of the facilities. The SBA is funded annually by the West Virginia Legislature using funding generated through the General State Revenue, Lottery Funds, and Excess Lottery Funds. Construction Funds are created through the annual sale of capital improvement bonds and General Revenue.[26]

PUBLIC EMPLOYEES INSURANCE AGENCY

The West Virginia Public Employees Insurance Agency (PEIA) was established in 1971 to provide insurance coverage to eligible employees. Benefits are available to all current employees of the State of West Virginia, including employees of various related State agencies and local governments. PEIA participants may elect health insurance coverage through a fully self-insured preferred provider benefit plan (PPB) or through external managed care organizations (MCO). Participants may also elect to purchase optional life insurance. PEIA relies almost solely on the premiums paid directly by its participating employers and employees.[27]

CONSOLIDATED PUBLIC RETIREMENT BOARD
TEACHERS' RETIREMEMENT SYSTEM

The State Teachers' Retirement System (TRS), a defined benefit plan, was established on July 1, 1941, to provide retirement benefits for teachers and school service personnel. In 2021, TRS had approximately 41,594 active members and 36,394 retired members. Active members contribute 6% of their gross monthly salary into the retirement plan. For members enrolled prior to July 1, 1991, the employer contributes an additional 15% of the member's gross monthly salary into the plan. For members hired for the first time on or after July 1, 2005, or for members who transferred from the Teachers' Defined Contribution (TDC) System, the employer contributes an additional 7.5% of the member's gross monthly salary into the plan. TRS members hired before July 1, 2015, are eligible for Tier I program benefits. Those hired for the first time and become a member of TRS on or after July 1, 2015 are under Tier II program benefits.[28]

COVID-19 RELIEF FUNDING

State and Federal Sources

The COVID-19 pandemic further emphasized the challenges faced by West Virginia public school students.[29] The CARES (Coronavirus Aid Relief and Economic Security) Act provided federal stimulus dollars to assist state agencies, local school districts, businesses, organizations, families and students, and other entities during the COVID-19 pandemic. As part of the recently passed federal Coronavirus Aid Relief and Economic Security (CARES) Act, West Virginia received more than $339 million. These dollars are a part of the Elementary and Secondary School Emergency Relief Fund (ESSERF) round two allocations can be used for, but not limited to:

- Continuity of operations,
- Pandemic learning loss activities, and
- Health and safety needs.[30]

In addition to ESSERF funding, federal funding was also received through the Higher Education Emergency Relief Fund (HEERF) and the American Recovery Plan (ARP). West Virginia provided additional funding through the WVDE Competitive Grant Allocation and the Extracurricular Equity Fund (ECEF).[30] West Virginia school districts received a total of $1,172,275,559.57 in COVID-19 relief funding. An additional amount of $8,318,511.11 was received by multi-county career and technical schools, the West Virginia School for the Deaf and Blind, and the West Virginia School for Diversion and Detention. Non-public schools received $21,219,973.50 in COVID-19 relief funding. The total amount received by West Virginia schools for COVID-19 relief funding to date is $1,201,818,044.18.[31]

NOTES

[1] https://www.history.com/this-day-in-history/west-virginia-enters-the-union
[2] http://www.wvculture.org/history/statehood/constitution.html
[3] WVC §18-1-3
[4] https://tax.wv.gov/Business/PropertyTax/Pages/PropertyTax.aspx

[5] https://nces.ed.gov/edfin/pdf/StFinance/WestVir.pdf

[6] http://www.wvculture.org/HiStory/education/recht01.html

[7] http://www.wvencyclopedia.org/articles/19

[8] State of West Virginia Executive Summary of the Public School Support Program Based on the Final Computations for the 2021-22 Year, p1.

[9] State of West Virginia Executive Summary of the Public School Support Program Based on the Final Computations for the 2021-22 Year, p1.

[10] State of West Virginia Executive Summary of the Public School Support Program Based on the Final Computations for the 2021-22 Year, p2.

[11] State of West Virginia Executive Summary of the Public School Support Program Based on the Final Computations for the 2021-22 Year, p2.

[12] State of West Virginia Executive Summary of the Public School Support Program Based on the Final Computations for the 2021-22 Year, p2.

[13] State of West Virginia Executive Summary of the Public School Support Program Based on the Final Computations for the 2021-22 Year, p3.

[14] State of West Virginia Executive Summary of the Public School Support Program Based on the Final Computations for the 2021-22 Year, p3-4.

[15] State of West Virginia Executive Summary of the Public School Support Program Based on the Final Computations for the 2021-22 Year, p4.

[16] State of West Virginia Executive Summary of the Public School Support Program Based on the Final Computations for the 2021-22 Year, p4-5.

[17] State of West Virginia Executive Summary of the Public School Support Program Based on the Final Computations for the 2021-22 Year, p5-6.

[18] WVC §18-9A-11(a)

[19] WVC §18-9A-12

[20] WVC §18-9A-14

[21] WVC §18-9A-15

[22] WVC §18-9A-21

[23] WVC §18-9A-22

[24] WVC §§5-16-18 and 18-9A-24

[25] WVC §18-9D

[26] https://sba.wv.gov/aboutus/Pages/default.aspx

[27] WVC §5-16-18

[28] http://www.wvretirement.com/TRS.html

[29] Ferris, R., Vesely, R. (2021). West Virginia. Journal of Education Finance. 46(3), 377-379.

[30] Federal Relief Funding—West Virginia Department of Education (wvde.us)

[31] WVSchoolsPandemicReliefFunding-071521-v1.pdf (wvde.us)

CHAPTER 49

WISCONSIN

Lisa Lambert Snodgrass
Purdue University

GENERAL BACKGROUND

The Wisconsin public education system has a rich, long history dating back to the founding of territorial Wisconsin in 1836. In 1840, the Wisconsin Territorial Legislature established a set of regulations for the establishment and administration of public schools. While the 1849 Act faced much opposition and has gone through many iterations, it served to establish a tax-supported funding system for free public education in the state that persists today.[1]

Presently, the Wisconsin public school system educates 854,959 elementary and secondary students via 421 public school districts, 236 charter schools (44,703 student enrollment), and 129 Statewide Parental Choice program voucher schools (28,770 2student enrollment). School districts can be identified by three configurations: (1) elementary and secondary grades combined (PK-12); (2) elementary grades only; and (3) high school grades only. Intermediate configurations include 12 regionally based cooperative educational service agencies (CESAs) and four county-based children with disabilities education boards (CCDEBs). All school districts are fiscally independent. In contrast, CESAs are fiscally dependent on their respective school district members while CCDEBs represent a mix, with three fiscally independent and one fiscally dependent.

Funding Public Schools in the United States, Indian Country,
and US Territories (Second Edition), pages 771–792.
Copyright © 2023 by Information Age Publishing
www.infoagepub.com

The state provides approximately 45% of school district revenues while local districts provide 43.8%. Federal aid represents 6.7%. In the 2021-2023 Biennial budget, the state allocated a 2021 base of $7,385,415,900 in state aid to K-12 education. Of that, the state classified $4,920,420,000 as general or basic aid and $1,374,995,900 as categorical aid. Total state aid represented approximately 32.4% of the state's general fund. While this is a decrease from the 2019-2021 Biennial budget, education spending continues to be the single largest appropriation to date. An additional $100 million was allocated to K-12 statewide education from Federal COVID-19 Relief funds.

In Wisconsin, 38% of public school students are considered economically disadvantaged, defined as eligible for the federal free or reduced price meal program. Approximately 14% are classified as having a disability, and 6% are identified as English language learners. Although the high school graduation rate was 89.5% in 2021, above the national average but down from 90.5 in 2020, proficiency in English language arts and mathematics fell to 32% and 31% respectively.

CURRENT POLITICAL CLIMATE

Legislative Make-up

There are three branches of government in Wisconsin: the executive branch, which includes the governor and state agencies and departments, the judicial branch or the court system, and the legislative branch. Wisconsin Legislature is composed of an upper house, the Wisconsin State Senate, and a lower house, the Wisconsin State Assembly. The Legislature has 132 total members with equal representation of constituent districts.[2]

Since 2011 the both the upper and lower houses of the Legislature have been held by Republican majority while the Executive Branch, including the offices of the governor, attorney general, and the secretary of state, has been controlled by the Democratic party, creating a Democratic triplex (when a single political party controls three offices in the state's governmental structure). Since 1992, there has been an uneven trifecta (when a single political party holds a majority in both houses of the state legislature and the governor's office) with the Republican Party holding 23 trifectas and the Democratic Party holding 14.[3]

Union Representation

While Unions have had a strong foundation in the Wisconsin labor force, union membership and thus representation has been declining in Wisconsin in recent years with just 7.9% of the labor force represented.[4] The decline of union membership may be linked to the Republican lead 2011 Wisconsin Act 10.[5] Act 10 restructured collective bargaining policies, limiting the ability of unions to only engage in wage and wage increases bargaining and disallowing employers to collect union due on paychecks. Union membership has declined slightly each year since its implementation.

Current School Litigation

Recent school litigation in Wisconsin has centered on three issues: school closings due to COVID-19, school choice vouchers, and distribution of CARES Act funding to private schools. Litigation regarding school closings due to COVID-19 included *School Choice Wisconsin Action (SCWA) v. Bowersox* and *WCRIS v. Heinrich* both of which challenged the authority of the local county health department to issue school closure orders. In both cases the Wisconsin Supreme Court ruled in favor of the plaintiffs indicating that the county health departments had overreached its authority in issuing closure orders for both public and private schools.[6]

Wisconsin's Parental Choice program has faced numerous legal challenges since inception. Currently, there are more than 10 lawsuits challenging the policy and its implementation restrictions. The majority of suits, including *Heritage Christian Schools v. the Wisconsin Department of Public Instruction (DPI)*, *School Choice Wisconsin v. Carolyn Stanford Taylor*, and *School Choice Wisconsin Action v. DPI*, center on issues of equity of access to Wisconsin's Parental choice program (voucher program), specifically for enrollment policies, data sharing, and digital access.

On behalf of private schools in the state, the Wisconsin Institute for Law and Liberty joined three amicus briefs, *Michigan v. Devos*; *Washington v. Devos*; and *NAACP v. Devos* over the equity of access of CARES Act funding for private schools. The case is currently moving through the judicial system.[6]

Enrollment Trends

Both public and private school enrollment in Wisconsin continues to trend downward. Between 2006 and 2021, public school enrollment has declined nearly 3% with overall education (public, private, and home schooling) enrollment declining 5%.[7] The U.S. Census Bureau data may provide some indication for the downward trend: 2021 data shows a decline in the 0-18 age group of 4%, compared to a growing percentage of people aged 65 and older of 17.9%.[8] Additionally, the state's demographic make-up is changing. The white population dropped by 3.4% while the Black population grew by 4.8% and the Hispanic population grew by 33.1%. These changing demographics will continue to impact enrollment trends well into the future.

The statewide enrollment decline has been fodder for the state politicians. The legislative discourse has concentrated on issues of rising educational costs and requested expenditures while enrollment is in decline. This discourse has led to contentious budget discussions between the Republican Legislative majority and the Democratic Executive Branch. The current Governor, Tony Evers, has had to use veto power to overturn Republican led fiscal cuts to public education each year since taking office.

SOURCES OF REVENUE

Taxes

In Wisconsin, public school districts receive funding from four sources: state aid, property tax, federal aid, and local non-property tax revenues (interest profits and local fees). General (basic) aid to public schools is dependent on state-imposed revenue limits. However, state categorical aid and federal aid are not limited. Revenue that a school district receives from local non-property tax sources, e.g., student fees, ticket sales, or interest income, is exempt from revenue limits. In addition, special provisions apply to the treatment of property tax levies for debt service and for community service activities.

Under Wisconsin law, there is a limit on the annual amount of revenue each school district can raise through the combination of general school aid, computer aid, and local property tax levy.[11] In addition to Equalization Aid, Integration Aid, Special Adjustment Aids, and High Poverty Aid are included in the calculation of a district's revenue limit. A school district can exceed its revenue limit only by local voter approval of a referendum.[11]

Trends Over Time

Since 2009, Wisconsin legislators along with the governor(s) have been focused on reducing the personal income and corporate income tax rates. In 2021, Wisconsin passed AB 68 that permanently lowered both personal and corporate income rates one income tax bracket for a projected savings of nearly $2 billion between 2021-2023.[12]

Taxes that support public education have fluctuated over the past ten years. In response to increasing the per-pupil spending state aid rose, with a 4.5% increase in 2019 and an additional 3.3% in 2020. However, due to COVID-19 and anticipation of plunging state revenues, in June 2020 Governor Evers cut 70% of the overall state budget, of which a disproportionate 59% came from cuts to public education. School districts have yet to recover from these deep cuts, even with funds from the federal HEROES and CARES Acts supplemental funding.[13]

Property taxes have risen steadily in many districts over the past decade, mainly due to successful referenda. However, in 2020, there was a substantial increase of 3.3% for statewide property tax. This increase was due to 43 of 51 school referendums passed through voter support.[14] While this does not necessarily indicate a trend, it is important to note here for future reference.

DISTRIBUTION FORMULAS

Regular Education Program

Equalization Aid

For general aid, Wisconsin continues the implementation of a guaranteed tax base formula, referred to as the 'equalization formula." The major purpose of a guaranteed tax base formula is to provide taxpayer, not student, equity. 'Equalization Aid' is calculated via a complex three-tier guaranteed tax base formula where the first tier acts like a flat grant and the second tier as a foundation without a required minimum local tax rate, while the third tier most resembles a true guaranteed tax base approach. In addition, the third tier includes a 'negative aid' feature, which, on paper, acts like a recapture provision.[11]

The five primary components of the computation of Equalization Aid include: (1) pupil membership; (2) shared cost; (3) equalized property valuation; (4) state-guaranteed property valuations; and (5) total amount of state funding available for distribution. Pupil membership (i.e., student enrollment), shared cost, and equalized property valuation are calculated on data from the previous year for each school district. Shared cost is defined as school district expenditures that the state has deemed aidable through the equalization formula. Equalized valuation is the full market value of taxable property in the school district, while guaranteed valuations are the amount of property tax base support that the state guarantees for each student.[11] There are three guaranteed property valuations used in the equalization formula that are applied to the three tiers.[16]

In Tier One, commonly known as the 'Primary Aid' tier, each school district whose equalized property valuation per pupil is below $1,930,000 receives Tier 1 or Primary Aid funding up to $1,000 per student. Because only a handful of school districts have per-pupil property wealth exceeding this figure, virtually all districts receive this type of aid. Notably, a district's Primary Aid cannot be reduced by negative aid. This feature is generally referred to as the Primary Aid hold harmless.[16]

Tier Two, also referred to as the 'Secondary Aid' Tier, computation provides Equalization Aid for shared cost between $1,000 per pupil and the state-determined secondary cost ceiling (also referred to as secondary shared cost) for those school districts having property values per pupil up to the secondary valuation.[16] For FY 2021-2022, the state set the secondary cost ceiling at $10,771 per pupil, and the secondary guaranteed property valuation at $1,563,771 per pupil.[11]

Tier Three or 'Tertiary Aid' considers shared costs per student above the secondary cost ceiling or $10,771. In FY 2021-22, state aid on tertiary-shared cost was calculated using the tertiary guaranteed property valuation per pupil of $715,267. The tertiary guarantee is set equal to the statewide average equalized property value per student. It is deliberately set at an amount lower than the secondary guarantee so that the state's share will be lower on costs above the secondary cost ceiling per pupil.[11] If a school district's tertiary aid is a negative number, this amount is deducted from its secondary aid. If the sum of a district's secondary and tertiary aid is a negative number, this amount is not deducted from its primary aid amount.[16]

Categorical or other funding

Per-Pupil Aid

In the Per-Pupil Aid program all school districts in the state, regardless of property wealth, receives the same amount per pupil. Between its origins in FY 2013 to the latest data, funding expanded from $50 per pupil to a budgeted amount of $742 per pupil in the 2021-2022 school year. Per Pupil Aid has grown drastically in less than ten years, from FY2013 allocation of $63,462,200 to the FY2021 total state Per Pupil Aid funding of $610,419,656. No other part of the state school funding system approximated this rate of growth during this time period. As a type of general purpose aid that acts as a flat grant,[11] it represents the most disequalizing form of state aid.[11]

Special Adjustment Aid

This additional aid is provided to school districts as: (1) hold-harmless aid due to declining enrollments; or (2) incentive aid for school district consolidation. In the former, the state guarantees districts with declining enrollments 85% of their prior year's general aid. In the latter, for the first five years after consolidation, the state guarantees the new school district at least as much general aid as the separate districts received in the year prior to consolidation. In the sixth and seventh years, the consolidated district receives a revenue limit adjustment equal to 75% of the consolidation aid it received in the fifth year.[11] No district received Special Adjustment Aid in 2021-2022.

Special Education

Wisconsin provides funding for students with disabilities through three categorical aid programs: *Special Education and School-Age Parents Aid*; *High Cost Special Education Aid*; and Additional Special Education Aid.

Special Education and School-Age Parents Aid

As the main state categorical aid program supporting special education in Wisconsin, these funds provide school districts with partial reimbursement for eligible costs, as defined by the state, which were incurred the prior school year.[17] In addition to school districts, CESAs, CCDEBs, some types of charter schools are eligible for this aid. The Wisconsin DPI estimates that this aid program covers about 25% of eligible special education expenses at the local level. In 2021-2022, the state distributed $468,091,800 in Special Education and School-Age Parents Aid. For the 2022-2023 fiscal year, the state allocated $517,890,000.[18]

High Cost Special Education Aid

This program provides state aid for students with disabilities who required more than $30,000 in expenditures on special education-related services in the prior school year, excluding certain reimbursements.[11,17] Like the Special Education aid above, school districts, CCDEBs, CESAs, and some types of charter schools are eligible to receive this aid. The average reimbursement rate is 90% of each student's cost above $30,000.[11] Allocation for 2020-2021 was 11,106,000. While not yet released, allocations for this aid are expected to increase for 2022-2023.

Additional Special Education Aid

This state aid program is targeted to small school districts with high special education costs and below average ability to raise property tax revenues. Eligibility is based on a formula defined in state law.[11,17] To be eligible, a school district must meet three criteria: (1) its per-pupil revenue authority must be below the state average; (2) special education comprises more than 16% of the district's total costs; and (3) student enrollment, defined as membership for Equalization Aid, is below 2,000. Prior school year data are used to assess whether a school district meets these criteria. Under Wisconsin law, a school district may not receive both Supplemental Special Education Aid and *High Cost Special Education Aid*.[11] In 2021-2022, the state allocated $11,106,000. State appropriations for the 2022-2023 year are allocated at $11,439,200. [18]

Special Education Transition Grants

This one-year program offers grants up to $1,000 per pupil to school districts or independent charter schools for students who met the following three criteria: (1) attended school in the district or charter school in the 2014-2015 or 2015-2016 school years; (2) had an individualized education program (IEP); and (3) was enrolled in a higher education program or another postsecondary education or training program, or was competitively employed for at least 90 days.[11] An appropriation of $1,500.000 was provided in for both the 2021-2022 and the 2022-2023 fiscal years.[18].

County Children with Disabilities Education Boards

CCDEBs that are fiscally independent and fund the local share of their educational programs through the county property tax levy are eligible to receive state aid for students enrolled solely in CCDEB-operated programs and for costs incurred by CCDEBs for students jointly enrolled in school district and CCDEB programs. Calculation of the level of state aid is somewhat complex and is dependent on a school district's level of Equalization Aid, shared costs, and/or net costs of the CCDEB's services.[11] This allocation has remained unchanged since the 2015-2016 school year, with the 2021-2022 and the 2022-2023 allocations set at $4,067,300.[18]

TRANSPORTATION

Pupil Transportation Aid

Wisconsin state aid, appropriated by the state legislature, partially reimburses school districts for the costs of transporting public and nonpublic school pupils.[17] Independent charter schools choosing to provide transportation are also eligible to receive aid, though Wisconsin DPI has contested this. Public school districts are not required to transport charter school students. Aid is calculated based on the distance each student is transported as shown in Table 49.1. Since 2016, the reimbursement formula now includes funding for summer school. Due to COVID-19, for the 2020-2021 school year, aid was based on 2019-2020 ridership data. The 2021-2022 and 2022-2023 Pupil Transportation Aid is allocated at $24,000,000 annually.[17]

High-Cost Transportation Aid

This aid is provided to school districts with higher than average per-pupil transportation costs for the previous school year. The 2021 Wisconsin Act 58 increased the High Cost Pupil Transportation aid funding to $19, 856.200 with $200,000 being earmarked for the stopgap measure.[11,17] Eligible districts receive funding based on the difference between the district's per-pupil transportation cost and the aid threshold of 150% of the statewide average. Eligibility rests on two criteria: (1) per-pupil transportation cost, based on audited information from the previous fiscal year exceeding 150% of the statewide average per-pupil cost; and (2) pupil population density is 50 pupils per square mile or less.[11]

Open Enrollment, Course Options, and Youth Options Aid for Transportation

Wisconsin's open enrollment program allows students to attend a public school outside the school district of residence within the state. Although parents are responsible for transporting their children to and from the school, exceptions are

Table 51.1 Wisconsin Reimbursement Formula for Pupil Transportation

Distance (in miles)	Reimbursement Per Pupil ($)	
	Regular School Year	Summer School
0-2*	$15	$0
2-5	$35	$10
5-8	$55	$20
8-12	$110	$20
12 and over	$375	$20

*Note: Limited to transportation in hazardous areas.

made for low-income students and those with disabilities. Low-income students, defined as those eligible for the federal free and reduced price lunch program, may apply to the state for reimbursement of transportation costs.[11] The state then determines the reimbursement amount, which may not exceed the parent's actual costs or three times the statewide average per-pupil transportation costs, whichever is less. For students with disabilities, defined as those with an IEP, the nonresident district must provide transportation.[11]

Under the state's Course Options program, any student in a public school may enroll in up to two courses at any time at other educational institutions, including public schools in a nonresident school district, the University of Wisconsin system, technical colleges, nonprofit institutions of higher education, tribal colleges, charter schools, and any state-approved nonprofit organization.[11,] Although parents are generally responsible for transportation, they may apply for state reimbursement of transportation costs if they are unable to afford them. The state then calculates the amount of the reimbursement, giving preference to low income students, defined as those eligible for the federal free and reduced price lunch program. For the 2021-2022 school year, state aid was $454,200 with a maximum per pupil reimbursement of $1,218.54.

In Wisconsin's Youth Options program, 11th and 12th grade public school students have the opportunity to enroll in one or more nonsectarian courses at a postsecondary institution for postsecondary credit. These include the University of Wisconsin campuses, Wisconsin technical colleges, participating private, nonprofit colleges, and tribal colleges. Funding is available to eligible families. Preference for reimbursement is given to low income students, defined as those who are eligible for the federal free and reduced price school lunch program. In order to be eligible for reimbursement of transportation costs, the postsecondary courses must be taken for high school credit. State aid for this program was combined with the Course Options program, set at $454,000 for 2021-2022 and 2022-2023.[18]

TECHNOLOGY

Digital Learning Funding and Grant Programs

In 2016 the Wisconsin Digital Learning Plan was developed with a focus on providing equitable, personalized, applied and engaged digital learning across all grades and all schools. Before ending in 2022, the WDLP featured two popular programs in the plan, one funded by the state and one funded through a private foundation: State of Wisconsin Division of Enterprise Technology: Technology for Education Achievement (TEACH) and the Wisconsin Technology Initiative (WTI).

TEACH began in 2016 and was overseen by the Wisconsin Department of Administration, Division of Enterprise Technology until due to state budget allocation changes, the program ended in 2022. The grant program provided subsidies to eligible schools, libraries, and other educational institutions to cover telecommunication access. From 2016–2022, TEACH also provided infrastructure grants totaling $15,000,000 annually to build technology capacity for rural school districts. As noted above, the both TEACH grant programs ended in 2022.[19]

The WTI was founded by the John and Tashia Morgridge Family Foundation in conjunction with CISCO to provide funding to K-12 schools who share four goals: to upgrade classrooms technology (interactive white boards, iPads, etc.), to provide professional development to teachers in technology usage, partner with schools of education to update technology curricula, to professionalize teaching. To date the program has provided more than $15 million in grants to Wisconsin schools.[19]

Technical Education Equipment Grants

Sponsored by the Wisconsin Department of Workforce Development as part of the Fast Forward initiative to match manufacturing employers with qualified employees, the grant program provides competitive funding to public schools grades 6-12, technical colleges, and public libraries. The purpose of the grant program is to furnish classrooms and labs with technology and equipment as well as provide professional training for educators to implement innovative technology curriculum. In 2021, 15 school districts were awarded $440,000 to create high tech labs that will train 2,800 students.[20] The state allocation for 2021-22 and 2022-2023 was $875,000 annually.[18]

CAREER AND TECHNICAL EDUCATION

The Wisconsin Career and Technical Education (CTE) program is overseen by the Department of Workforce Development and is organized into 16 career clusters with 79 career pathways.[21] Funding for CTE is a combination of Carl Perkins Act federal funds and state appropriations. For 2022, Wisconsin received $24,446,105 in Perkins funds. State fund allocations included $6,500,00 each year from 2021-2023 for Career and Technical Education incentive grants and an additional $51,500 annually for Career and Technical Education completion awards. The DWD also allocated $500,000 toward CTE teacher training each year from 2021-2023.[18]

SCHOOL NURSES AND MENTAL HEALTH SERVICES

While there is no funding allocation in the 2021-2023 Wisconsin Biennial budget specifically for school nurses, the Wisconsin Department of Health Services (DHS) and the DPI have joined together to provide a statewide funding opportunity for all CESAs for the recruitment and retention of school nurses and health services workers. Totaling $8,000,000, the funds are available to K-12 schools with social vulnerabilities and with student enrollment of 35 or more students.[22]

Mental Health Services

As mental health issues in K-12 schools is a growing concern, Wisconsin has responded by allotting both aid and grants in the 2021-2023 Biennial budget. Aid for school mental health programs was allocated $12,000,000 annually to help defray the costs of hire and retain social workers or the costs of contracting social work services. Additionally, $10,000,000 was set aside annually for school-based mental health services grants to aid in costs associated with collaborations with community health agencies to provide mental health services.[23]

STUDENT SUPPORT SERVICES

Achievement Gap Reduction

The Achievement Gap Reduction (AGR) is a grant program that began in 2015. AGR requires schools to implement one of three strategies as part of a five-year contract: one-to-one tutoring by a licensed teacher, professional development for teachers, and maintenance of 18:1 or 30:2 ratio in the classroom as well as professional development on small group instruction. Remaining unchanged since 2015, the 2021-2023 Biennial budget allocated $109,184,500 for grants.[18]

Bilingual-Bicultural Aid

Wisconsin's Bilingual-Bicultural Aid provides funding to school district programs to improve English language comprehension, speaking, reading, and writing ability of limited English speaking (LEP) students. School districts receive reimbursement at a specified percentage rate for eligible costs incurred the previous school year. The state requires special classes for LEP students at schools that enroll ten or more LEP students in a language group in grades K-3; or 20 or more in grades 4-8 or 9-12.[11] The 2021-2023 budget provided $8,589,800.

Early Childhood Education

Four-Year-Old Kindergarten (K4) Grants

Wisconsin provides two-year grants to school districts that implement a K4 program. Eligible districts receive up to $3,000 per pupil the first year of the grant and up to $1,500 per pupil in the second year. Districts continuing in the grant program in their second year have priority for funding over districts new to the program. In the 2015-2016 school year, eight school districts received $1,350,000 in grants.

Head Start Supplement

Head Start is a state-administered grant program whereby grants are awarded to local Head Start providers, including but not limited to school districts and CESAs, to supplement federal funds that provide educational, health, nutritional, social, and other services to economically disadvantaged preschool children and their families. The purpose of state funds is to enable expansion of Head Start and Early Head Start programs to serve more families. Grants may be used as a match for federal funds only if state funds are used to secure additional federal support.[11] In FYs 2021-23, the state allotted $6,264,100 to this grant program.

Gifted and Talented Education

In Wisconsin, gifted and talented education is a grant-based program to provide qualified students with services and activities to assist them in development of their full potential. Grants may be awarded to nonprofit organizations, CESAs, institutions within the University of Wisconsin system, and the Milwaukee Public Schools, either individually or as collaborative projects.[11] Funding for the 2021-2022 and 2022-2023 school years was $274,400 respectively.[18]

High Poverty Aid

High Poverty Aid is distributed to school districts where 50% or more of their student enrollment qualifies for the federal free and reduced price lunch program. High Poverty Aid is subject to revenue limits for all eligible school districts except the Milwaukee Public Schools (MPS). For MPS, High Poverty Aid must be used to reduce the school property tax levied for the purpose of offsetting any state aid reduction attributable to the Milwaukee Parental Choice program. Normally, one would consider the purpose of such an aid program as compensatory, but, in the case of the Milwaukee Public Schools, its effect is to reduce local property taxes.[11] In 2021-2022 and 2022-2023, the state provided $16,830,000 in High Poverty Aid annually.

Nutrition Programs

Student nutrition aid programs include school lunch, school breakfast, and school day milk. Wisconsin provides aid to school districts, charter schools, and private schools in order to: (1) partially match the federal contribution under the national school lunch program that provides free or reduced price meals to low income children; (2) provide a per-meal reimbursement of 15¢ for each school breakfast served under the federal program; and (3) fully reimburse the cost of milk for low income PK-5 students in schools that do not participate in the federal special milk program. For the each of the 2021-2022 and 2022-2023 school years, state aid for the school lunch program was $4,218,100. For the school breakfast program, it was $2,510,500; and, the school day milk program was funded at $1,000.000.[18]

Tribal Language Revitalization Grants

The Tribal Language Revitalization grants support instruction in one or more American Indian languages through grants to school districts and CESAs. Funding is provided from tribal gaming program revenue. To be eligible, a school district or CESA, in conjunction with a tribal authority, must apply for a grant annually.[11] State funding allocations have remained steady since 2017, with $222,800 budgeted for the 2021-2022 and 2022-2023 fiscal years.[18]

OTHER TOPICS

Alcohol and Other Drug Abuse (AODA)

Started in 1979, AODA is a block grant-funded program designed aid schools in preparing programs and curricula to address alcohol and other drug abuse among school-age children and young people. Emphasis is placed on prevention and intervention through K-12 curriculum development, family involvement, drug abuse resistance education, and student-designed prevention or intervention projects.[11] Revenue from the penalty assessment surcharge funds these grants. Funding in the amount of $1,284,700 was allotted for each school year in the 2021-2023 Biennial budget.[18]

Educator Effectiveness Evaluation Grants

These grants reimburse school districts and independent charter schools for costs associated with the state-mandated educator effectiveness evaluation system. Eligible costs include system development, training, software, support, resources, and refinement. Those using an approved alternative evaluation process are also eligible. An application is required on an annual basis to receive grant funding, which is set at $80 for each participating teacher, principal, or other licensed educator.[11] The state allocation has remained unchanged since 2016-2017 at $5,746,000 in the most recent Biennial budget.

Educational Telecommunications Access Support (ETAS)

This program is part of Digital Learning Plan designed and overseen by the State Superintendent and the Digital Learning Advisory Council (DLAC). Since its inception in 2011 and because of the impact of COVID-19, the focus of this grant support is on building a broadband infrastructure for schools and libraries, with particular attention to rural schools and communities. This support program is in addition to the TEACH funds noted earlier in this chapter. ETAS strives to support schools and libraries in having a broadband system that is affordable and available to all schools, libraries and homes for 24/7 access to learning. In the 2021-2023 budget, the state of Wisconsin allocated $15,984.200 for each fiscal year.[18]

Peer Review and Mentoring Grants

The Peer Review and Mentoring grants are awarded annually on a competitive basis. Under this program, CESAs, consortia of school districts, consortia of CESAs, or consortia of CESAs and school districts are eligible to apply for grants to provide peer review and mentoring for early career teachers. Grantees are required to provide matching funds, which may be in the form of money and/or in-kind services, and must be equivalent to at least 20% of the amount of the grant. Individual grants may not exceed $25,000 per applicant for the fiscal year.[11] For 2021-2023, $1,606,700 was budgeted for each fiscal year.

Robotics League Participation Grants

These grants provide funding for student participation in robotics competitions. In the 2021-2022 school year, grants of up to $5,000 were available to eligible teams consisting of students in grades 9-12 and at least one mentor. Grants may be awarded to public schools, independent charter schools, and home-based educational programs. Funds must be used to participate in a competition sponsored by a nonprofit organization that requires teams to design and operate robots. Eligible expenses include fees, kits, supplies, travel expenses, and a stipend for the team mentor. Teams must provide matching funds equal to the amount of the grant.[11] In 2021-2023, a total of $500,000 was budgeted each year for grant awards. [18]

School Library Aid

Wisconsin provides School Library aid to school districts for the purchase of library books, instructional materials, and library-related computers and software. The funding source is income generated from the state's common school fund. School districts receive a per-capita payment based on the share of the total number of children in the state between the ages of 4 - 20 residing in their respective districts. For the 2021-2023 school years, total state aid was $42,000,000 per year.[18]

Sparsity Aid

This program, created in 2007, provides unrestricted aid to small school districts with low pupil density. Eligible districts must have fewer than 1000 pupils, and fewer than ten pupils per square mile. In 2021-2022, two tiers of aid were created. Tier 1 eligibility is for school districts with fewer than 745 students and no more than ten students per square mile. Tier 2 eligibility is for school districts with 746 – 1000 students and less than 10 students per square mile. A stopgap measure of 50% of previous aid is in place for school districts that received funding support the previous year but no longer qualify the current year. Aid is calculated at $400 per pupil based on the previous school year's enrollment.[25] For the 2021-202 school year, total state aid was $27,962,400. $27983,800 has been allocated for the 2022-2023 school year.[18]

State Tuition Payments

These payments are provided to school districts that enroll students who reside in facilities as a result of action taken by a unit of local, state or federal government. To receive payments, school districts must apply for reimbursement for eligible students they enrolled in the prior school year.[11] For the 2021-2022 and 2022-2023 school years, appropriation was set at $8,242,900.[18]

Supplemental Aid

This aid program provides state fiscal assistance to school districts with several unique characteristics: large geographical size, small student population, and small tax base due to a high percentage of exempt property.[11] Specifically, a school district must meet three criteria: (1) enrollment below 500 pupils based on prior school year enrollment; (2) at least 200 square miles in area; and (3) at least 80% of real property in the school district exempt from property taxation, taxed as forest croplands, owned or held in trust by a federally recognized American Indian tribe, or owned by the federal government.[11] School districts that meet these criteria must apply annually for funding. In that sense, this type of funding more closely resembles a grant program although the state refers to it as categorical aid. The stated purpose is to supplement Equalization Aid.[11] Eligible school districts receive $350 per pupil based on prior year enrollment. For the 2021-2022 and 2022-2023 school years, $100,000 was budgeted respectively.[18]

CAPITAL OUTLAY AND DEBT SERVICE

Capital Expansion Funds and Long-Term Capital Improvement Trust Funds

Wisconsin state law authorizes school districts to create a Capital Expansion Fund (Fund 41) to finance current and future capital expenditures related to buildings and sites.[11,26] If a school district makes an expenditure from its Capital Expansion Fund, its shared cost is increased by an amount determined by dividing the expenditure by the number of years in which the district levied a property tax for the capital project. State law also gives school districts the option to create Long-Term Capital Improvement Trust Funds (Fund 46) to finance projects included in a long-term capital improvement plan.[11] The plan must be approved by the school board and cover at least a ten-year period. School districts may not make expenditures from the fund in the first five years after its creation. State law specifies that a school district's shared cost includes any amount deposited into the fund, but does not include any amount expended from the fund.[11]

Bond Debt Programs

In Wisconsin, financing of school infrastructure, with few exceptions, is a local responsibility; that is, the state provides no substantive aid. As a result, school districts must rely primarily on bonded indebtedness, subject to voter approval, to finance capital projects. State law prescribes how these referenda are to be conducted and limits a school district's total debt to 10% of its equalized property valuation.[11]

EMPLOYEE BENEFITS

Healthcare

Insurance for public school employees is provided through the Wisconsin Group Health Insurance program administered by the Department of Employee Trust Funds (ETF). Employees may select coverage from a variety of levels (subject to change annually) for health, dental, and pharmacy benefits.[27]

Retirement

The Wisconsin public school employee retirement system is part of the larger public employee retirement system known as the Wisconsin Retirement System (WRS), which is administered by the state's Department of Employee Trust Funds. The WRS is a defined benefit program where retiree annuities are adjusted annually based on investment returns to the trust funds.[11,28]

CHARTER SCHOOL FUNDING

Charter schools in Wisconsin are classified as public schools, although they may be managed by private entities. The method by which the state funds charter schools depends upon the charter authorizer.[29] Charter schools may be authorized by one of two methods. First, they may be authorized by the school district in which they reside. In Wisconsin, these are referred to as 'instrumentality' charter schools, and there is no statewide cap on the number of instrumentality charter schools that may be established by school districts. Charter schools may also be authorized by other state-approved entities where there may be state-imposed limits on their numbers.[11] These are referred to as 'independent' charter schools. A third variation is virtual charter schools.

For an instrumentality charter school, the contract between the school district and the charter school specifies the amount to be paid to the charter school. In contrast, independent charter schools receive state aid that, for the 2021-2022 school year was $83,154,500 in state aid and $83,304.600 for the 2022-2023 school year. It should be noted that, in some cases, the state might reduce school districts' Equalization Aid to generate sufficient revenues for state aid to independent charter schools. In addition, independent charter schools are eligible for state aid related to special education, transportation, and nutrition programs. Instrumentality charter schools are not eligible for such aid, but they may negotiate for the provision of such services in the contract with their authorizing school district.[11] In the 2021-2022 school year, student enrollment in Charter schools was 49,678 and 10,672 in Independent Charter Schools.

Virtual charter schools are a subtype of instrumentality charter schools. From their inception in Wisconsin in 2002, they have not been without controversy.[30] Virtual charter schools accept students from the school district within which they are chartered, students from other Wisconsin school districts, and out-of-state students. Funding for within-district students is negotiated with the school district, while funding for students from other school districts is provided through the Open Enrollment program described below.[11] For out-of-state students, virtual charter schools are required to charge tuition equivalent to the cost of an open-enrolled student: $8,161 per pupil in 2021-22 and estimated at $8,224 for 2022-2023. In the 2021-2022 school year, 13,395 students enrolled in Virtual Charter Schools.

Open Enrollment

Open enrollment represents a form of public K-12 inter-district school choice in Wisconsin. Authorized by the state in 1998, this program allows parents to apply for children to attend public school in a district other than the one in which they reside. In addition, students may attend prekindergarten, four-year-old kindergarten, early childhood or school-operated childcare programs outside their school district of residence if their school district of residence offers the same type of program that the student wishes to attend and the student is eligible to attend that program in his or her school district of residence.[11]

Under the open enrollment program, resident school districts are allowed to count students who have transferred to another district in their pupil membership for revenue limits and general support purposes. Then, for each open-enrolled student, a uniform state-set amount is transferred from the resident school district to the nonresident district in the final state aid payment at the end of the school year.[11] In 2021-2023 Biennial budget the state allocation of $8,242,900.[18]

NONPUBLIC SCHOOL FUNDING

Overview of Private School Choice

Wisconsin has a long history regarding the provision and funding of private school choice, beginning with the Milwaukee Parental Choice Program (MPCP) in 1989. Additions that are more recent include the Racine Parental Choice Program (RPCP) and the Wisconsin Parental Choice Program (WPCP), the latter a statewide expansion. All are voucher programs. Student eligibility, which is established by state law, varies for each program and is a combination of student residence, income, and prior year attendance. Choice school teachers and administrators, unlike their counterparts in public schools, are not required to hold a state educational license if they hold, at minimum, a bachelor degree.[11]

Participating private, nonprofit, religious, and nonsectarian schools receive a state aid payment determined through statutory formula for each eligible student on behalf of the parent or guardian. For the 2021-2022 school year, a voucher was valued at $8,336 for a K-8 pupil and $8,982 for a pupil enrolled in grades 9-12.[31] In addition, Wisconsin has a Special Needs Scholarship, which is also a voucher program. A fifth program, referred to as a 'Private School Tuition Deduction,' subsidizes parents, regardless of wealth, who choose to send their children to private schools through the ability to deduct the cost of tuition from reported income on their annual state tax return. Finally, the state also authorizes Home-Based Private Education, commonly referred to as homeschooling.[11]

Milwaukee Parental Choice Program (MPCP)

In the 2021-2022 school year, 28,770 students redeemed vouchers at 129 private schools in Milwaukee, for an estimated $237,712,600 in state aid.

Racine Parental Choice Program (RPCP)

The Racine Parental Choice Program was authorized by the state beginning in the 2011-2012 school year. It is available to students in the Racine Unified School District (RUSD). Located in southeastern Wisconsin, RUSD enrolls 19,455 K-12 students. In the 2021-2022 school year, 3,940 students redeemed vouchers at 27 private schools within the borders of RUSD for an estimated $32,700,00 in state aid.

Wisconsin Parental Choice Program (WPCP)

The Wisconsin Parental Choice Program is a statewide voucher program that began with the 2013-2014 school year.[11] In the 2021-2022 school year, 14,452 students redeemed vouchers at 301 private schools across the state, excluding Milwaukee and Racine, for an estimated $119,100,00 in state aid.

Special Needs Scholarships

Enacted in 2015, this Wisconsin program allows a student with a disability, who meets certain eligibility requirements, to receive a state-funded scholarship or voucher to attend a participating private school.[11,32] For the 2021-2022 school year, the maximum scholarship was $13,013 per student. 1,757 students received vouchers at 134 private schools participating in the SNSP program.

Private School Tuition Deduction

This Wisconsin state program allows parents of elementary and secondary students to deduct private school tuition from their taxable income as reported on their annual state tax return,[33] thus lowering their state tax liability. The maximum deduction is $4,000 per calendar year per K-8 student and $10,000 per student in grades 9-12. To qualify, a student must be claimed as a dependent for federal income tax purposes and be enrolled in kindergarten or grades 1-12 of a private school, as defined in state law.[11]

Home-Based Private Education

Home-based private education refers to a program of educational instruction provided to a child by a parent, guardian, or person designated by the parent or guardian.[34] While the state provides no direct aid to those who homeschool, school districts may incur costs related to homeschooled students. For example, under Wisconsin state law, a homeschooled student may attend at no cost a maximum of two courses per semester in two school districts.[34] Second, the child may participate in interscholastic athletics and extracurricular activities on the same basis and to the same extent as students enrolled in the school district, again at no cost unless the district charges fees to resident students. Third, although school districts are not required to provide special education services to homeschooled students, district are required to identify and evaluate all children in the district who may have a disability. In 2021-2022, a total of 31,878 students were home-schooled, representing a little over 3.25% of all students statewide.[35]

VIRTUAL EDUCATION

Virtual Charter Schools

See earlier full description in the Charter School Funding section.

FEDERAL COVID-19 FUNDING

As mentioned briefly in earlier sections, COVID-19 had a drastic impact on education funding in Wisconsin. Due to estimated plunging tax revenues, in June 2020 the governor cut $70 million from the overall state budget of which $41 million or 59% came from education allocations. Again in response to declining revenue, in July of 2020 and additional $250 million was cut from the budget and K-22 education bore the brunt of the cuts at approximately one third.[13]

Federal aid came in the form of the Coronavirus Aid, Relief, and Economic Security Act (CARES), a federal funding act passed in response to COVID-19. The $30.75 billion Education Stabilization Fund consisted of three allocations: the American Rescue Plan Elementary and Secondary School Emergency Relief (ARP ESSER), the Governor's Emergency Education Relief (GEER) fund, and the Higher Education Relief fund. As ARP ESSER and GEER affected K-12 education, each is detailed below.

For ARP ESSER support, Wisconsin was apportioned $1,540,784,854. The DPI allocated 90% of the funds directly to the local education agencies (LEAs) or $1,386,706,369. The remaining ten percent ($154,078,485) was reserved for programs and resources to address students' social-emotional as well as academic needs, with particular focus on the disproportionate impact of COVID-19 on un-

TABLE 49.2.   ARP ESSER III Allocation – Authorized Amount and DPI Plan

	Funding Amount		Percent of Allocation	
	Authorized	DPI Plan	Authorized	DPI Plan
Grants to LEAs (Title 1-A based allocations)	$1,386,706,369	$1,386,706,369	90.00%	90.00%
Earmark Funds				
Learning Loss Earmark	$77,039,242	$77,039,242	5.00%	5.00%
Summer Learning Earmark	$15,407,849	$15,407,849	1.00%	1.00%
Comprehensive Afterschool Earmark	$15,407,849	$15,407,849	1.00%	1.00%
Non-Earmark Funds (flexible use)	$38,519,621		2.50%	
Minimum LEA grant ($600,000)*		$39,361,356		2.55%
Administrative Costs (and focus on reading)	$7,703,924	$6,862,189	0.50%	0.45%
TOTAL	$1,540,784,854	$1,540,784,854		

*For LEAs with 25 or fewer pupils, and for the state's two residential schools (WCBVI hand WESP-DHH), the minimum LEA grant with be $200,000.

derserved and underrepresented student populations.[36] The plan for the ARP ES-SER funds included support for safely reopening schools, maintaining safe school operations during the pandemic, and implementing programming and services to address the mental health and the academic needs of students due to COVID-19. Table 49.2 explains allocations.

Wisconsin received $46.7 billion in funding for GEER. Funds from this program provided emergency support to LEAs to provide continuous educational services and safe operations and functionality. Priority of distribution of funds was based on economic need, technology access and needs, broadband needs, and students' scores on the English Language Arts Assessment. 39% of GEER funds supported broadband and educational technology infrastructure needs while 37% was distributed to LEAs to prepare and maintain safe school operations. Finally, nearly 23% was allocated to address long-term school closure issues, with particular focus related to learning loss.[37]

ENDNOTES

[1] Jorgenson, L.P. "The Origins of Public Education in Wisconsin." *The Wisconsin Magazine of History 33*, no. 1 (1949): 15-27.

[2] Wisconsin State Legislature, "What is the legislature?," accessed May 15, 2022, https://legis.wisconsin.gov/about/what

[3] BallotPedia, "Party control of Wisconsin state government," accessed May 15, 2022, https://ballotpedia.org/Party_control_of_Wisconsin_state_government

[4] U.S. Bureau of Labor Statistics, "Midwest Information Office," accessed 5 July 2022 https://www.bls.gov/regions/midwest/news-release/unionmembership_wisconsin.htm

[5] Wisconsin Legislative Council, "2011 Wisconsin Act 10," accessed 5 July, 2022, https://docs.legis.wisconsin.gov/2011/related/lcactmemo/act010.pdf

[6] Wisconsin Institute for Law & Liberty, "Education Reform," accessed 5 July 2022, https://will-law.org/education-reform/

[7] National Center for Education Statistics, Public School Enrollment, accessed 5 July 2022 https://nces.ed.gov/programs/coe/indicator/cga/public-school-enrollment

[8] United States Census Bureau, "Wisconsin," accessed 5 July 2022 https://www.census.gov/quickfacts/WI

[9] Computer Aid is state funding provided to local units of government, including school districts, equal to the amount of property tax that would otherwise have been paid on exempt equipment

[10] Wis. Stat. 120.90 (2017).

[11]. Crampton, F. E. "Wisconsin." In *Funding public schools in the United States and Indian Country*, ed. David C. Thompson, R. Craig Wood, S. Craig Neuenswander, John M. Heim, and Randy D. Watson, 777-796. Charlotte, NC: Information Age Publishing, 2019.

[12] Wis. Stat. §68 (2021)

[13] Snodgrass, Lisa Lambert. "Wisconsin." *Journal of Education Finance* 47, no. 5 (2021): 380-382.

[14] Fox, Madeline. "Wisconsin Voters Approved 84 Percent of School Referendums in Election." *Wisconsin Public Radio*. Nov. 6, 2020, https://www.wpr.org/wisconsin-voters-approved-84-percent-school-referendums-election

[15] Wis. Stat. §115.437 (2017).

[16] Lang, B. (2021). *2021-22 General School Aids Amounts for All School Districts*. Legislative Fiscal Bureau. Retrieved from https://docs.legis.wisconsin.gov/misc/lfb/misc/173_2021_22_general_school_aids_amounts_for_all_school_districts_12_3_21.pdf

[17] Wis. Stat. §121.59 (2017).

[18] Wis. Stat. §58.32 (2021).

[19] WDPI, "Digital Learning Funding and Grant Programs," accessed 6 July 2022, https://dpi.wi.gov/imt/grants/teach

[20] DWD, "DWD Announces Technical Education Equipment Grants," accessed 6 July 2022, https://dwd.wisconsin.gov/press/2022/220405-tech-ed-grants.htm

[21] WDPI, "CTE," accessed 6 July 2022, https://dpi.wi.gov/cte .

[22] WDHS, "K-12 School Nurse Workforce Recruitment & Retention," accessed 6 July 2022, https://www.dhs.wisconsin.gov/k-12-school-nurse-workforce-recruitment-retention

[23] WDPI, "Aid for school mental health programs,' accessed 6 July 2022, https://dpi.wi.gov/sspw/mental-health/aid-school-mental-health-programs

[24] WDPI, "State school-based mental health services grant program," accessed 6 July 2022, https://dpi.wi.gov/sspw/mental-health/school-based-grant-program

[25] Wis. Stat. §115.437 (2021).

[26] WDPI, "Capital Project Funds," accessed 7 July 2022, https://dpi.wi.gov/sfs/finances/fund-info/capital-projects-funds

[27] Wis. Stat. § 40.515 (2015 a. 55; 2017 a. 59).

[28] ETF, "Wisconsin Retirement System Fact Sheet," accessed 7 July 2022, https://etf.wi.gov/resource/wisconsin-retirement-system-fact-sheet

[29] Wis. Stat. **§118.40 (2021)**.

[30] Wis. Stat. §115.001(16) (2021).

[31] Wisconsin Department of Administration, "Fiscal Estimates," accessed 7 July 2022, https://docs.legis.wisconsin.gov/2021/related/fe/ab970/ab970_dpi.pdf

[32] Wis. Stat. **§**115.7915 (2017); Wis. Admin. Code PI 49 (2021).

[33] Wis. Stat. **§**71.05(6)(b)49 (2021).

[34] Wis. Stat. **§115.001 (2021)**.

[35] WDPI, "Home-based Enrollment Trands," accessed 7 July 2022, https://dpi.wi.gov/parental-education-options/home-based/statistics

[36] WDPI, "Wisconsin Department of Public Instruction Plan for Elementary and Secondary School Emergency Relief Fund III (American Rescue Plan Act, 2021)," accessed 7 July 2022, https://dpi.wi.gov/sites/default/files/imce/policy-budget/pdf/DPI_Plan_for_ESSER_III_4.1.2021_JCF.pdf

[37] Wisconsin Policy Forum, "Report: How are school districts spending their federal relief funds?" accessed 7 July 2022. https://wispolicyforum.org/wp-content/uploads/2022/05/Focus_22_11_ESSER_Update.pdf

CHAPTER 50

WYOMING

Neil Theobald
University of Wyoming

GENERAL BACKGROUND

The Wyoming Constitution, Article 7, Section 1 delegates to the Wyoming Legislature the task of delineating and financing the state's education system:

> The legislature shall provide for the establishment and maintenance of a complete and uniform system of public instruction, embracing free elementary schools of every needed kind and grade, a university with such technical and professional departments as the public good may require and the means of the state allow, and such other institutions as may be necessary.[1]

For its first century of statehood, beginning in 1890, local property taxes provided the majority of funding for Wyoming's K-12 school districts. Problems with this approach developed, though, beginning with the onset of World War II. From the 1940s onward, sustained high national demand for Wyoming coal and other in-place minerals created large disparities in per-pupil local property tax revenue across Wyoming school districts.

The current system of school finance stems from a series of four legal challenges started in 1971. The initial effort[2] focused on a state constitutional provision

Funding Public Schools in the United States, Indian Country, and US Territories (Second Edition), pages 793–802.
Copyright © 2023 by Information Age Publishing
www.infoagepub.com

(Article 1, Section 28) requiring that "all taxation shall be equal and uniform." In response, the Wyoming Supreme Court directed the legislature to provide each Wyoming school district with an equal per-pupil share of local property tax revenue derived from county-level ad valorem taxes.

The second legal challenge began less than a decade later, when Washakie County School District Number 1 (WCSD1), a small district in north central Wyoming, filed suit against the state seeking relief from "the inequities that are resulting from the financing system currently used in this state."[3] The local district court dismissed the complaint in 1979.

However, on appeal, the Wyoming Supreme Court found for WCSD1 in 1980 and declared

> The State's system of school financing, based principally on local property taxes, whereby property-richer school districts uniformly have more revenue per student than property-poorer ones, is unconstitutional in that it fails to afford equal protection in violation of the State Constitution.[4]

In response to the Court's decision, House Bill 212 (HB 212) was enacted in 1983. HB 212 created the Wyoming School Foundation Program, which provided a block grant to each school district with additional funding provided to districts for special education, vocational education, and pupil transportation.

The third legal challenge began another decade later with four of Wyoming's largest school districts (Campbell County Number 1, Uinta County Number 1, and Sweetwater County Numbers 1 and 2) contending that, even with the implementation of HB 212, the Wyoming system of school financing continued to be in violation of the Equal Protection Section of the Wyoming Constitution (Article 1, Section 34): "All laws of a general nature shall have a uniform operation."[5]

The state's largest school district (Laramie County School District Number 1) and the Wyoming Education Association (WEA) soon joined these four districts as plaintiffs. However, in a break from the previous coalitions, 23 of the smallest school districts sided with the State to defend HB 212. This separation among school districts on the basis of enrollment was explained as follows:

> The large district plaintiffs contended that the school finance system failed to fund their actual operating costs....From the perspective of the small districts, the funding formula was weighted appropriately in their favor since it recognized that it arguably costs more to educate each student in a less populated school district.[6]

In 1993, the local district court declared individual aspects of the state's K-12 school finance system unconstitutional because these components did not operate in a uniform manner across all school districts. However, the court found all other aspects of the system to be constitutional.

On appeal, in 1995, the Wyoming Supreme Court sided with the large school districts and the teachers' union in declaring the state's entire K-12 school finance system unconstitutional.[7] At the core of its decision, the court ruled that the state must fund a "quality" education for every Wyoming child:

> The legislature must first design the best educational system by identifying the "proper" educational package each Wyoming student is entitled to have whether she lives in Laramie or in Sundance. The cost of that educational package must then be determined and the legislature must then take the necessary action to fund that package. Because education is one of the state's most important functions, lack of financial resources will not be an acceptable reason for failure to provide the best educational system. All other financial considerations must yield until education is funded.[8]

The court gave the Wyoming legislature until July 1, 1997, to adopt and implement a new school finance system.

In national rankings, Wyoming has been judged the most conservative state in the Union.[9] Beginning with the Supreme Court's 1995 decision in *Campbell County Sch. Dist. No. 1 v. State of Wyoming* (known as *Campbell I*), this series of judicially-mandated school funding changes started to raise significant separation of power concerns across the state.[10] All 50 state constitutions say at least something about education. The Wyoming Supreme Court's application to K-12 school funding of Wyoming's requirement for "Equal Protection" was a contentious topic of statewide debate through the rest of the 1990s and into the 2000s.

The Wyoming Legislature passed House Bill 1001 (HB 1001) in 1997 in response to *Campbell I*. Almost immediately, though, this legislation was seen as unsatisfactory by the larger districts and the teachers' union. The plaintiffs charged that HB 1001 did not "comport with the Wyoming Constitution as interpreted by the court."[11] Specifically, critics charged that, instead of immediately operationalizing the court's mandates, HB 1001 "more closely resembles a good faith promise for future substantive action."[12]

The fourth and final legal challenge commenced immediately with the large school districts and the WEA challenging the constitutionality of HB 1001. The Wyoming Supreme Court initially provided the Wyoming Legislature additional time to address these concerns. In its 1998 session, the legislature created a state-funded school capital construction system that they believed would address the Court's major concerns.

In 2001 (in what is known as *Campbell II*), the Court invalidated the state's entire school finance system for the third time in 21 years:

> This court reluctantly concludes that, while great effort has been made by many and some improvement has been achieved, the constitutional mandate for a fair, complete, and equal education "appropriate for the times" in Wyoming has not been fully met.[13]

The Court ordered the State to take action to enact the needed school funding system modifications on or before July 1, 2002.

House Bill 45 (HB 45) was enacted in 2002 to develop a new school capital construction system in response to the Supreme Court's 2001 decision. HB 45 created a system in which construction funding was based on the wealth of the state, not on local wealth.

The plaintiffs in *Campbell I* and *Campbell II* again challenged the constitutionality of the school funding system. However, in 2008 (in what is known as *Campbell III*), the Wyoming Supreme Court affirmed that the state's actions were adequate and resulted in a constitutional system of school finance in Wyoming.[14] Thus, *Campbell III* closed a 30-year series of judicially-mandated school funding changes in the state.

BASIC SUPPORT PROGRAM

From 2017-2020, Wyoming earned the nation's highest score in Education Week's Quality Counts report, which evaluates states on overall spending and the degree to which that funding is equitably allocated across districts. In 2021, though, Wyoming fell to third place (behind New Jersey and New York) and declined on six of the eight graded indicators.[15] Yet, Wyoming remains the only state among Quality Counts' top 10 located outside of the Northeast or Mid-Atlantic regions. In addition, Wyoming is one of only five states in the U.S. in which per-pupil expenditures in every school district are above the U.S. average.

These funding levels are created by a 3-step process developed to implement the Wyoming Supreme Court's 2001 decision (*Campbell II*):

- Define the "basket of educational goods and services" constituting the proper education to which every Wyoming child is entitled and recalibrate this basket every five years;
- Annually monitor the actual cost of providing the basket in the various sizes and locations of school districts; and
- Fund the basket.

A total revenue amount in the form of a "block grant" is provided to each school district to facilitate provision of the basket. The actual dollar amount of each district's block grant is determined by seven formula-driven school district characteristics (number of employees, regional cost of living, inflation adjustments for salaries, materials, and energy, prior-year special education costs, pupil transportation costs, the number, size, and location of statutorily-defined "small schools," and qualification as a "small school district"). While the model calculates a formula-driven number of employees for each school district (the most important factor in determining the district's grant) each district chooses the actual number of employees.

If local revenue is less than the block grant, then the state funds the difference. If local revenue is more than the block grant, then the state "recaptures" the difference and allocates these funds as part of the funding provided to non-recapture districts.

Step 1: Define the Basket of Educational Goods and Services

This recalibration process is required "not less than once every five (5) years."[16] The purpose of recalibration is to ensure that Wyoming's school finance system provides an adequate level of funding. The most recent recalibration was conducted in 2020.

Step 2: Monitor Changes in Cost of Basket in School Districts Across State

Annual review of the impact of inflation on the funding model is required through a "monitoring process."[17] This process provides guidance on the annual inflation adjustment percentages for the state's K-12 funding model's prices (e.g., energy, educational supplies and materials). In addition, school districts with higher labor costs are provided additional salary funding to account for these regional cost differences.

Step 3: Fund the Basket of Goods and Services in Each School District

The state provides a salary allocation for each personnel category (e.g., superintendent, teacher) based on the district's prior year average experience, education, and responsibility of employees in that category. Each district's salary total is then adjusted for regional cost differences. The state funds employee benefits at 21.1% of this adjusted salary allocation and provides health insurance reimbursement.

The funding of the basket of goods and services is a block grant. Each district is allowed to allocate these resources based on its own specific needs and priorities. Thus, school districts are not required to pay their employees the salary or benefit amounts received from the state, nor are they required to employ the number of staff funded in each personnel category.

Recent Changes to Basic Support Formula

Due to eroding tax revenues in 2020 from coal, oil, and gas industries, the state cut $3.6 million from school spending in the 2021-22 school year. These decreases were achieved primarily by limiting health insurance reimbursements and reducing inflation adjustments for salaries, materials, and energy. Preliminary estimates had suggested much larger K-12 cuts in 2021-22, but Wyoming tapped the state's Legislative Stabilization Reserve Account, commonly known as the "rainy day fund," to maintain funding per pupil.

TABLE 50.1. Wyoming Total Basic Support Formula Funding Per ADM FY 2019-2023

2018-19	2019-20	2020-21	Est. 2021-22	Est. 2022-23
$16,050	$16,321	$16,507	$16,517	$16,666

Source: Wyoming Legislative Service Office, 2022

Thus, in the 2021-22 school year, per-pupil state funding is projected to be $16,517 per ADM. This projection is $10 per ADM higher than actual per-pupil funding in 2020-21 (see Table 50.1).

In March, 2022, the Wyoming Legislature passed a 2-year state budget that allocates $1.523 billion in State funding to the basic support formula for the 2022-2023 school year. Per-pupil state funding is projected to be $16,666 per ADM or $149 per ADM higher than projected per-pupil funding in 2021-22.

Funding Per ADM ranges from $14,209 in Sheridan #2 (a relatively wealthy district with 3,500 students, 6th largest of 48 Wyoming school district, located on the Wyoming-Montana border) to $34,898 in the neighboring Sheridan #3 (a rural district with 100 students, the smallest Wyoming school district).

K-12 CAPITAL CONSTRUCTION

As explained above, the K-12 capital construction funding process enacted in 2002 was the final court-mandated revision to Wyoming's school formula. The goal of the new process is that the level of each district's capital funding should be based on the wealth of the state, not on local wealth.

The 2022-2024 state budget allocates $245.4 million in State funding for K-12 capital construction ($86.4 million) and major maintenance ($159.0 million). The major maintenance allocation is formula-driven with 2022-23 school year amounts ranging $200,000 in Sheridan #3 (a rural district with 100 students, the smallest Wyoming school district) to $10,380,000 in Laramie #1 (the largest Wyoming school district, comprising Cheyenne, with 13,800 students).

The capital construction component is allocated by a School Facilities Commission (SFC). Each biennium, SFC updates the current school building con-

TABLE 50.2. Wyoming K-12 School Capital Construction Funding FY 2015-2024 (in Millions)

	2014-16	2016-18	2018-20	2020-22	2022-24
Major Maintenance	$115.4	$118.5	$145.0	$153.0	$159.0
Capital Construction	$307.4	$144.9	$52.7	$100.2	$86.4
Total	$422.8	$263.4	$197.7	$253.2	$245.4

Source: Wyoming Legislative Service Office, 2022

dition remediation schedule, which ranks Wyoming's K-12 school buildings in terms of need of replacement and capacity. In 2022-24, SFC will approve $86.4 million in funding to replace those buildings at the top of this priority list.

SCHOOL CHOICE[18]

Wyoming places the only four charter schools in the state under the jurisdiction of local school boards. The State provides about $400,000 per year for charter school lease payments. No private or religiously-affiliated schools are eligible to become charter schools.

A bill that failed by a significant margin in the 2021 Wyoming Legislature, and did not even receive a vote in the 2022 session, would have reimbursed parents for tuition or other expenses related to private school and homeschooling. The bill capped reimbursement at one-half of what the local school district receives in per-pupil funding.

COVID FUNDING

Following a recommendation by Governor Mark Gordon, 35 of Wyoming's 48 school districts closed on March 16, 2020. Governor Gordon closed all schools in the state on March 20, 2020. By the beginning of the 2020-21 school year, though, "most schools were in-person in Wyoming."[19] For the 2020-21 school year, Burbio, a school data aggregator, rated Wyoming as having the highest in-person school learning mode among the 50 states and the District of Columbia (DC).[20]

The three federal COVID-19 relief packages provided Wyoming school districts with Elementary and Secondary School Emergency Relief (ESSER) funds totaling $424.4 million. Federal rules allowed a state to ask LEAs (school districts) how they intend to use the funds, "as long as it does not limit how the LEAs use their funds."[21]

In addition, the Wyoming Department of Education (WDE) received $47.2 million in ESSER funds. About two-thirds of these ESSER funds were distributed to districts and communities through competitive grants. The other one-third was

> Used to support districts in formative assessment and progress monitoring of student performance in the light of interrupted learning due to COVID, professional development in the area of literacy instruction, best practices in building cleanliness.... providing high quality after-school opportunities to students on Wyoming reservations, strengthening the quality of virtual education offerings, improving educational practices through the understanding and use of student data, and increasing the health of students and educational staff through Social, Emotional, and Mental Health initiatives.[22]

Through July 21, 2022, COVID-19 related deaths among Wyoming residents totaled 1,850. This is the fifth lowest total nationally, trailing Vermont, Alaska, DC, and Hawaii.[23]

CONCLUSION

The 2022-24 state budget is $456 million lower than the 2020-22 budget, but uses $390 million in federal relief funds to backfill about 85% of the state budget decrease. As a result, total basic support formula funding in the 2022-23 school year is expected to be unchanged from 2021-22, even though Wyoming expects ADM enrollment to fall by nearly 1%.

Using one-time federal funds to pay on-going school finance expenses clearly isn't sustainable. The harsh reality is that the $2+ billion federal relief package the state received the last two years will almost certainly not recur. For the last 25 years, Wyoming has paid on-going school finance costs with extraction payments from Wyoming's coal, oil, and gas industries, which have allowed a truly remarkable "exporting" of Wyoming's public service costs to the other 49 states.

Tables 50.3 and 50.4 show the 2020 direct tax collections (Table 50.3) and 2020 public service costs (Table 50.4) for a 3-person Wyoming family earning

TABLE 50.3. Direct Tax Collections From a 3-Person Family in Wyoming with Income of $65,000 and Owning a Home Valued at $270,000

Tax	2020 Taxes Collected
Property Tax	$1,700
Retail Sales	$1,100
Vehicle Registration	$550
Gasoline	$200
Cigarettes	$110
Alcohol	$110
Total Taxes Collected to Fund Public Services	$3,770

Source: Wyoming Department of Administration & Information, Economic Analysis Division, 2021.

TABLE 50.4. Public Service Costs For a 3-Person Family in Wyoming with Income of $65,000 and Owning a Home Valued at $270,000

Public Service	2020 Public Services' Costs
State Services	$8,130
K-12 Education	$7,490
Special District	$5,730
County	$3,510
City/Town	$3,420
Total Cost of Public Services Received	$28,280

Source: Wyoming Department of Administration & Information, Economic Analysis Division, 2021.

the state's median household income of $65,000 and owning a home valued at $270,000. Wyoming does not levy a corporate income tax or individual income tax, but has traditionally collected a large amount of revenue from severance taxes, which are taxes on the extraction of natural resources (e.g., coal, oil, natural gas).

Total personal tax collections from a 3-person family in Wyoming in 2020 covered barely one-half the costs of the K-12 education services the family received. Overall, the family consumed 7.5 times the value of services it funded from its tax payments to the state. Coal, oil, and natural gas exported to other states made this possible.

Over the last year, oil prices have increased markedly, nearing $140 per barrel at one point, after falling to barely $11 per barrel at its nadir in Spring, 2020. This dramatic increase created very high extraction payments in 2021-22 and allowed the state to transfer about one-half of the federal relief funds it received to the state's "rainy day fund." The state has until the end of 2024 to obligate these federal funds and until the end of 2026 to spend this money.

The goal of this transfer is to generate investment returns on the federal funds for the 5+ years that the state holds the money before it is spent. The state hopes this investment income will provide a cushion against the boom-and-bust state revenue swings created by heavy support on fossil fuel extraction. Critics, though, argue that this strategy makes the state's future at least somewhat dependent on stock market returns.

Clearly, the pressing state issue affecting the state's school funding system, and every other aspect of life in Wyoming, is the future of the state's mineral-based economy. Will Wyoming continue to enjoy massive injections of mineral revenue?

In the absence of a continuing long-term boom in the fossil fuel energy sector, meeting its constitutional obligations requires that Wyoming

1. Begin to redirect rainy day funds to the state's school funding system, which will decrease future investment returns,
2. Raise taxes on non-mineral sources in one of the country's most tax-averse states (Wyoming has no personal or corporate income tax and comparatively low sales and property taxes), and/or
3. Reduce school spending in ways that are consistent with the *Campbell* decisions.

NOTES

[1] sos.wyo.gov/Forms/Publications/WYConstitution.pdf (2018).
[2] *Sweetwater County Planning Committee for Organization of School Districts v. Hinkle*, 491 P.2d 1234 (Wyo. 1971).
[3] *Washakie Co. Sch. Dist. No. One v. Herschler*, 606 P.2d 310, 1 (Wyo. 1980).
[4] *Washakie*, 606 P.2d at 2.
[5] sos.wyo.gov/Forms/Publications/WYConstitution.pdf (2018).

6   Sparkman, William E., Dayton, John, & Hartmeister, Fred (1996). Financing Wyoming's Public Schools: The Wyoming Legislature Gets to Try Again. *Land & Water Law Review*: 31(2), p. 471.

7   *Campbell County Sch. Dist. No. One v. State of Wyoming*, 907 P.2d 1238 (Wyo. 1995).

8   *Campbell*, 907 P.2d at 30.

9   https://oilcity.news/community/2020/01/10/wyoming-ranks-as-most-conservative-state-in-the-country-hawaii-the-most-liberal/

10 Heise, Michael (1998). Schoolhouses, Courthouses, and Statehouses: Educational Finance, Constitutional Structure, and the Separation of Powers Doctrine. *Land & Water Law Review*: 33(1), p. 301.

11 Heise, *Land & Water Law Review*: 33(1) at 283.

12 Heise, *Land & Water Law Review*: 33(1) at 299.

13 *Campbell County Sch. Dist. No. One v. State of Wyoming*, 19 P.3d 518 (Wyo. 2001) at 1.

14 *Campbell County Sch. Dist. No. One v. State of Wyoming*, 06-74, 06-75 (Wyo. 2008).

15 https://www.edweek.org/leadership/quality-counts-2021-educational-opportunities-and-performance-in-the-united-states/2021/01 (2021).

16 Wyoming Statutes Title 21. Education § 21-13-309(t).

17 Wyoming Statutes Title 21. Education § 21-13-309(u).

18 For a more fulsome overview of Wyoming's alternatives to traditional public schools, please see: Theobald, Neil (2022). Wyoming. *Journal of Education Finance*: 47(5), p. 384-385.

19 https://ballotpedia.org/School_responses_in_   Wyoming_to_the_coronavirus_(COVID-19)_pandemic#Timeline_by_school_year.

20 https://about.burbio.com/school-opening-tracker.

21 Memo from Wyoming Department of Education to Wyoming Legislator's Joint Education Committee, July 19-20, 2021, p. 2.

22 Memo from Wyoming Department of Education to Wyoming Legislator's Joint Education Committee, July 19-20, 2021, p. 2.

23 Https://usafacts.org/visualizations/coronavirus-covid-19-spread-map/0

PART II

SCHOOL FINANCE IN INDIAN COUNTRY,
US TERRITORIES, AND THE DISTRICT OF COLUMBIA

CHAPTER 51

DISTRICT OF COLUMBIA

Michael C. Petko

National Education Association

GENERAL BACKGROUND

Public Schools in The District of Columbia

Authorization for the District of Columbia's (DC) education system is derived from a clause in the Home Rule Act (HRA) of 1973.[1] Prior to the HRA, public schools in were governed by Congress with over 17 various government structures since 1804.[2]

DC has had a long history of problems with its education system. Part of the issue has been blamed for the lack of local governance. However, many parties have contributed to the problems facing education in DC, so it would be safe to place the blame is on everyone. In a 2008 study, Hannaway and Usdan provided a detailed list of guilty parties. They wrote:

> In recent years, the Board of Education (both appointed and elected), a number of U.S. Senate and U.S. House of Representative committees, the DC City Council, DC Financial Control Board, a state education office, the mayor, the DC Chief Financial Officer, two charter school boards, many superintendents (appointed by different authorities), and unions have all played key roles in education policy making and

Funding Public Schools in the United States, Indian Country,
and US Territories (Second Edition), pages 805–836.
Copyright © 2023 by Information Age Publishing
www.infoagepub.com

school management. At almost any point in time, overlapping areas of responsibility provided all players with reason to blame each other when things went wrong, and they left none of the players with sufficient power to demand quality performance.[3]

Other studies have documented DC's problematic school system throughout the 20th Century which eventually led to the presidential creation of the DC Financial Responsibility and Management Board (or Control Board), reducing the authority of the elected board and given authority to overhaul the entire system. The education system under the Board of Education had fallen apart to the extent that the HR department did not know how many students it had, how many teachers it had, or who had been paid.[4]

In 2007, DC created the Public Education Reform Amendment Act (PERAA), effectively eliminating the independence of the Board of Education from city government and moving control of public education to the mayor. PERAA created a new state department of education headed by a chancellor. It also required that an independent 5-year evaluation be completed to determine the effectiveness of PERAA.[5] Several new offices were created by the implementation of PERAA with a new Department of Education headed by the Deputy Mayor for Education, the establishment of the Office of the State Superintendent of Education (OSSE), the State Board of Education and the Public Charter School Board.[6]

Current Education System

The District of Columbia basically operates two public school districts. The D.C. Public School system (DCPS) operates what would be considered more traditional public schools, while the D.C. Public Charter School District (DCPCS) provides funding to public charter schools. Although charter schools are required to be managed by private non-profits, they are considered public for purposes of funding. Although both the DCPS and DCPCS are fiscally dependent on the District for their funding and both budgets are set by the Mayor and City Council, they function as two separate Local Education Agencies (LEA's) with separate budgets, boards, and accounting standards. The Deputy Mayor for Education's (DME) office contains the State Education Agency (SEA) and has a separate office of the State Superintendent. DCPCS was created with the enactment of the DC School Reform Act of 1995, which was later amended in 1996 to create the DCPCS School Board, acting as an independent school board and the sole authorizer of charter schools.[7] The School Reform Act also required that the District provide a "uniform dollar amount" per resident pupil for both the DCPS and DCPCS.[8]

Funding for DCPS and DCPCS comes from the Uniform Per Student Funding Formula (UPSFF), which was originally passed in 1998 and became effective in 1999.[9] The UPSFF provides for a minimum allocation per resident student and uses weightings to provide additional funding percentages for grade levels and special categories. The UPSFF also requires that the DCPS provide for tuition for special education students who are placed in non-public schools and for SEA functions for teacher certification and grant administration.[10]

Governance

The Mayor and DC City Council are ultimately responsible for the function of the two public school systems, and budgets are appropriated from the Mayor's annual budget. The Office of the Deputy Mayor for Education is charged with implementing the mayor's vision and it monitors the Office of the State Superintendent for Education (OSSE) and the DCPS. THE DCPCS's board is appointed by the mayor and charged with overseeing the charter schools. The DCPCS Board is also the sole authorizer of charter schools.

There are a total of six different entities that control public education funds in the District:[11]

1.   The Office of the State Superintendent manages the disbursement of federal funds to the two systems and also provides placement of special education system into non-public schools as well as any loan guarantees to charter schools.
2.   The Department of General Services (DGS) manages the maintenance and repairs for DCPS.
3.   DCPS is the public system for traditional public schools.
4.   DCPCS is considered a public school system, but all charter schools are required to be private, non-profit and manage their own budget with its own school board.
5.   DCPCS School Board (PCSB), created in 1996, acts as the sole authorizer for charter schools and also monitors legal compliance and fiscal management of all charter schools. It has oversight of all public schools, which are managed by independently run nonprofit organizations considered as LEAs.[12]
6.   District of Columbia Retirement Board (DCRB) is the teacher pension for DCPS staff and has a separate funding system outside of the DCPS budget. Teachers pay into the system in two tiers. The DC government provides additional funding to keep the fund sound when necessary. Currently, charter schools must provide for separate retirement plans.

Basic Facts for DCPS

Since DC runs two independent school districts, statistical information is presented here for both the DCPS and the DCPCS.

DCPS School Statistics[13]

For the school year (SY) 2020-21, DCPS enrolled 49,890 students. The demographic mix was 58% Black, 21% Hispanic, 3% multiracial, less than 1% Native

Hawaiian or other Pacific Islander, less than 1% American Indian or Alaska Native, and 16% White.

Over 75% of students were classified as economically disadvantaged, with 16% in some sort of Special Education program and 15% attending an ELL program. The At-Risk population accounted for 42% of DCPS. At-Risk students are those who qualify for Temporary Assistance for Needy Families, Supplemental Nutrition Assistance Programs, or are under the care and supervision of the Child and Family Services Agency. Students who are in high school and at least one year older than their expected grade were also classified as At-Risk.

There are approximately 117 schools within the DCPS system. The largest number of schools is elementary (66), with high schools next (15), and middle and education campuses both having 14. There are 2 primary schools, 3 Opportunity Academies, 1 special education school and 2 Youth Engagement schools.

Student Performance in DCPS[14]

The National Assessment of Educational Progress (NAEP) is usually a measure used by many states and districts to assess how students compare to peers in other states and LEAs. The DCPS reports that its students have seen progress in scores on the NEAEP over the last 10 years. Reading scores for 4th grade has grown by over 11 points since 2009, and 11 points for 8th grade in the same measure. For math, 4th grade scores have risen by 15 points, while 8th grade math scores have risen by 18 points. DCPS also reports that students scoring proficient in every grade and subject has increased. Special education students have also seem growth in proficiency during that same period, with 4th grade special education students seeing a 29-point growth in reading, and 8th grade special education students seeing a rise of 21 points in reading and 37 points in math. DCPS has a graduation rate of approximately 76%.

Basic Facts for DCPCS[15]

DCPCS School Statistics

DCPCS oversees 128 campuses, which are operated by 66 Local Education Agencies (LEAs). There are a total of 43,857 students who attend DCPCS for the 2020-21 SY. The total students in DCPCS schools is roughly 46.9% of the total eligible student population in DC. Of those students, 24,004 are in PK3 through 5, 8,296 are in middle school (grades 6 through 8), and 6,693 are in high school (grades 9 through 12). There are also 3,748 adult learners enrolled in DCPCS programs.

There is a large population of At-Risk students (50%) who attend DCPCS schools, which is a little higher than DCPS (42%). However, only 7.% of students are ELL and 18% are students with disabilities (similar to DCPS). For Special Education (SPED) students, DCPCS provides educational services to a slightly more severe needs group than the DCPS. SPED students are classified in 4 levels, with level 4 being the more severe need than levels 1-3. DCPCS SPED students (18% of the student body) are provided education services in the following percentages: Level 1—28%; Level 2—30%; Level 3—15%; and Level 4—27%. By contrast, DCPS provides more SPED services to Level 1—38% with other levels being slightly lower than DCPCS: Level 2—26%; Level 3—12%; and Level 4—24%. There is a similar graduation rate in DCPCS (76.6%) compared to DCPS, but that rate has increased since SY 2013-14 (68.9%).

The demographic breakdown of DCPCS students is 78% Black; 11% Hispanic/Latino; 7% White; 3% Two or more races; 1% Asian; and less than 1% for both American Indian/Alaskan and Hawaiian/Pacific Islander.

Student Performance at DCPCS

The main measurement for performance in the DCPCS is known as the Partnership for Assessment of Readiness for College and Careers (PARCC). This is the Districts' annual assessment of math and English language and arts literacy (ELA) and is based on the Common Core State Standards.[16] The DCPCS reports that students score very well against the DCPS students, and scores have improved over time, with over 31.5% scoring a 4+ on the PARCC in 2019. This was an increase of over 7.7% from 2015.

Between 2017-18 and 2018-19 SYs, DCPCS students improved slightly more in ELA (from 26% at level 4 [Met Expectations] to 28%). Math percentages stayed the same between those years, but there was a slight improvement in those reaching level 3 in math.[17] Graduation rates across all racial demographics are reported to be higher than those in DCPS (See Appendix C).

CURRENT POLITICAL CLIMATE

The District

Washington DC (herein DC) is a unique city by any standard. It is the home of the United States Federal government and was designated as a district under the jurisdiction of the federal government and not part of any state.[18] Until 1973 DC had no independent municipal government. It was the Home Rule Act[19] that granted DC a limited governmental authority.[20] The limitation allows DC some form of municipal government, but Congress still has authority over the budget. Although DC has a Representative in Congress, that person does not have a vote on legislation. The issue of limited independence has been a major political rallying cry for DC residents for decades.[21] Just recently, the House of Representatives just passed an act to allow self-rule in DC with full representation in Congress, but it has not passed the Senate.[22]

System of Government

The District of Columbia's government has three branches similar to other state governments: Executive, Legislative, and Judicial and was established by the Home Rule Act in 1973 (HRA). With the establishment of the HRA, a local form of government was created where local officials have authority to pass laws and govern local affairs, but the United States Congress maintains the power to overturn local laws.[23] Although DC is provided a position as an incorporated body under the HRA, the United States Congress still maintains power to overturn any local laws or to create laws to govern local affairs.[24] Since DC is not considered a state and still under the jurisdiction of Congress, it does not receive any voting members to represent it in Congress, although it has non-voting member in the House of Representatives to present DC interests.

The executive branch is governed by the Mayor who serves a 4-year term. The Mayor is given sole authority for the administration of the daily operations of the District. There is a City Administrator appointed by the Mayor to manage the various government agencies and to implement the legislative actions of the Mayor and DC Council. Deputy Mayors form an executive branch, reporting to the City Administrator.

Unique among municipal governments are three independent agencies, which are responsible for interacting with the Congressional Oversight Committee and preparing report for that committee and for the Executive and Legislative branches.[25] However, the chief position is appointed by the Mayor and Council, they run independently of their immediate control: The Offices of the Chief Financial Officer, the Inspector General, and the Attorney General (see, Appendix B).

The legislative branch consists of 13 members, which form the Council. DC is separated into 8 districts or "Wards," each with an elected Council member. There are four At-Large members and a Council Chairman. Each serve a 4-year term and the election cycle is staggered. The Council passes laws, approves DC's budget, and is responsible for the general oversight of the executive branch.[26] There is also a 41-member Advisory Neighborhood Commission (ANC), which represents smaller subsets of each Ward. The ANCs represent local issues to various DC agencies or to the Executive branch or Council.

The Judicial branch is established in Title IV, Part C of the HRA.[27] The Judiciary includes the court system and other boards and commissions. The trial court is known as the Superior Court with a chief judge and 61 associate judges. The Court of Appeals is the highest court, consisting of a chief judge and eight associate judges. All judges are appointed by the President of the United States and receive confirmation through the U.S. Senate like federal judges.

Within the District, there are four officially recognized political parties: Democrat, Republican, Libertarian, and D.C. Statehood Green parties.[28] The Mayor is affiliated with the Democrat party as well as 10 of the 13 city Council members. The other two are registered as Independent.

Budget Process

The District's fiscal year is from October 1st to September 30th. DC provides monthly updates to its budget through its Financial Status Report (FSR) and quarterly updates for the capital budget. The Office of the Chief Financial Officer (OFCO) is responsible for collecting budget information and creating reports for DC government and for Congress. The Mayor's office starts the budget process by creating a proposed budget that is then given to the Council for approval. The Council can adopt the Mayor's budget, present changes, or offer its own budget. The budget then returns to the Mayor for approval or veto. If vetoed, the Council can override the veto or work with the Mayor's office to finalize and acceptable budget. Once both parties have accepted the proposed budget, it is transmitted to the US Congress for approval, and Congress must approve the budget as one of the 12 annual federal appropriations bills. Once, approved, the OFCO provides direction to the various agencies regarding transfer, dissemination, collection and reporting of revenues and expenditures. The

The calendar is as follows:

- Budget Guidance: July—September
- Agency Budget Request Development: October - December
- Budget Analysis: November - January
- Budget Presentation: January - March
- Budget Request Act and Budget Support Act: March - June

Unionization

There are 15 international unions with 48 locals and 114 collective bargaining units within DC. They include the following:

- American Federation of Government Employees
- American Federation of State, County and Municipal Employees
- National Association of Government Employees
- The Committee of Interns and Residents
- The Council of School Officers
- District of Columbia Nurses Association
- Doctors Council of the District of Columbia
- Fraternal Order of Police
- International Association of Firefighters
- Alliance of Independent Workers Union
- National Union of Hospital and Healthcare Employees
- Service Employees International Union
- International Brotherhood of Teamsters
- Washington Area Metal Trades Council
- Washington Teacher's Union

These labor organizations are certified by the Public Employee Relations Board to represent District of Columbia government employee.[29] The Washington Teacher's Union is an affiliate of the American Federation of Teachers, AFL-CIO.[30]

There are four labor unions that represent DCPS employees.[31]

1. The Teamsters Local 639, an affiliate of the AFL-CIO, represents custodial employees and attendance counselors.

2. The Washington Teacher's Union (WTU) is an affiliate of the AFL-CIO. WTU has a membership that includes Athletic Trainers, Audio Visual Coordinators, Elementary and Secondary Counselors, Curriculum Development Specialist, Hearing Therapist, Instructional Coaches, Job Coordinators, Elementary and Secondary Librarians, Literacy Professional Developers, Numeracy Professional Developers, Placement Counselors, Psychiatric Social Workers, Reading Specialist, School Psychologists, School Social Workers, Speech Language Pathologist, Elementary and Secondary Teachers, Junior ROTC Instructors, Mentor Teaches, and Incarcerated Youth Workers. For collective bargaining purposes, all these positions are labeled as teachers. There are two pay grades ET and EG. ET is given to 10-month, contracted teachers (There are some 11- and 12-month positions), while EG refers to 12-month employees.

3. The Council of School Officers, Local #4 (CSO) covers Assistant Coordinators, Assistant Directors, Assistant Principals, Associate Principals, Athletic Directors, Audiologists, Coordinators, Dean of Students, Directors, Instructional Supervisors, Master Educators, Mentor Principals, Occupational Therapists, Physical Therapists, Principals, Psychologist, Senior Master Educators, Social Worker Specialist, Speech Pathologists, Speech Therapist, Supervisor, Administrative Officers, Business Managers, Coordinators, and Specialists. The CSO is also an affiliate of the AFL-CIO.

4. The American Federation of State, County and Municipal Employees, Local 2921 (AFSME), also an affiliate of the AFL-CIO, covers two broad classification of employees in DCPS schools:

   a. Instructional Program Assistants, which includes Computer Lab Assistants, Educational Therapy assistants, Family Service Workers, and Instructional Assistants; and Instructional Program Assistant Unit; and

   b. Secretarial/Clerical Workers, which includes Clerks, Administrative Assistants for Typing, or Receptionist, Braille Transcribers, Central Office Assistants (including Typing), Central Office Clerks (including both Clerks for Typing) Data Entry Clerks, Food Program Assistants, Guidance Clerks, Lead Payroll Technicians, Library Technicians, Mail Clerks and Supervisors and Assistants, Payroll Clerks and Supervisors and Technicians, Procurement

Technicians, Receptionists, Secretaries, Supply Clerks and Technicians, and Clerks in charge of Time and Leave.

SOURCES OF REVENUES

According to DC's 2020 annual financial report (See Appendix D), the District's overall financial status improved between 2019 and 2020. There was a loss to sales and use taxes of over $390 million, probably due to the COVID shutdown. Total revenue losses from sales and other revenues was slightly over $500 million. However, the total revenue increase between 2019 and 2020 was over $1.6 billion. This was due to the federal stimulus funds added to DC's federal appropriations.

The largest source of revenues for DC is the federal appropriation funds, which is reported as operation grants and contributions ($4.826 billion) in Table MDA-2 (See Appendix D). Property taxes ($3.061 billion) and Income ($3.021 billion) and sales and use taxes ($1.317 billion) also providing a main source of revenues. There are other types of taxes and non-tax revenues that provide an additional $1.5 billion to the budget. Overall, DC's budget generates close to $15 billion per year, and has grown steadily.

The Office of the Chief Financial Officer provides a quarterly revenue estimates and quarterly reports.[32] Appendix E provides a table for General Fund Trends from 2016 through 2022.[33] The District's main sources of local revenue are the individual income, property and sales taxes. In 2020, property taxes amounted to 30.15% ($2.836 billion) of the General Funds. Individual taxes represented

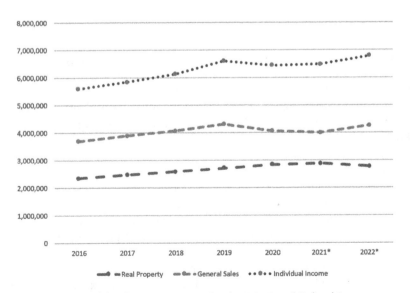

FIGURE 51.1. Trend for three Main Taxes for the District of Columbia

25.26% ($2.377 billion) in the same fiscal year, and sales taxes brought in 12.99% ($1.222 billion) during that same time.

Although the sales tax decreased from the previous year (FY 2019), where it generated over $1.597 billion (16.37% of the general fund budget), the loss was more than compensated by the influx of federal stimulus funds for COVID relief. Figure 51.1 illustrates the growth of the three main taxes from 2016 to the estimates for 2021 and 2022. It appears that while individual income and sales taxes fell during the COVID recession period, they are projected to rise while property taxes are expected to fall.

DISTRIBUTION FORMULA

General Fund

The UPSFF is contained in the DC Code and is updated every year as needed to reflect changes in the base and weights.[34] The UPSFF only provides funding for students who are considered residents of the District. Non-resident students are required to pay tuition to attend any District public school or charter school. The formula also does not apply to students enrolled in private institutions that provide special education services, which is paid by the District directly. The formula only applies to operating budget appropriations and does not consider funds from federal or other sources. Charter schools are funded equally by law from the UPSFF. The only limit to the UPSFF for charter schools occurs after the DCPS student enrollment count is verified by an independent contractor. Once a student count is verified, additional enrollment in a charter school will not count for that school year.[35]

Base Funding

Base funding is established in the code and updated periodically by need. For Fiscal Year 2022, the foundation level is $11,730 per student. According to the code, this amount is set for subsequent years with adjustments made for inflation, any potential revenue losses or revisions required by law.[36] Such revisions are adjusted by code and established into law. Previous years USPFF allocations are shown in Table 51.1:

Weighting

The Base funding amount is not the total amount provided to schools from the District. Additional weights are applied to the base according to grade level and need.[37] Weighting is applied to adjust for different educational services required at different grade levels. The chart below reflects the weights to be applied in the 2021 formula.[38]

The allocation for a three-year-old, pre-kindergarten student is 34 percent above the base, or $15,718 for the 2020-21 school year. The total foundation then is found by applying the additional percentage for grade level to the base. The

TABLE 51.1.

Fiscal Year	USPFF Base Funding	Law
2003	$6,419*	D.C. Law 14-307
2004	$6,551	D.C. Law 15-39
2005	$6,904	D.C. Law 13-205
2006	$7,307	D.C. Law 16-33
2007	$8,002	D.C. Law 16-192
2008	$8,322	D.C. Law 17-20
2009	$8,770	D.C. Law 17-219
2010	$8,945	D.C. Law 18-223
2011	$8,770	D.C. Law 18-370
2012	$8,945	D.C. Law 19-21
2013	$9,124	D.C. Law 19-168
2014	$9,306	D.C. Law 20-61
2015	$9,492	D.C. Law 20-155
2016	No Change	No Change
2017	$9,682	D.C. Law 21-36
2018	$9,972	D.C. Law 23-209
2019	$10,658	D.C. Law 38-2903
2020	$10,980	D.C. Law 38-2903
2021	$11,310	D.C. Law 38-901

*Numbers are rounded to the nearest dollar amount.

formula is as follows: Base x Weight = PPA (or the USPFF foundation for each student).[39]

As of the 2021-22 school year, the District has included three new UPSFF supplemental weights:

1. The At-risk High School Over-Age Supplement (provided for LEAs with high school students one year older or more than expected age for grade)
2. The Elementary EL" supplement (for students enrolled in pre-K 3 through 5th grade)
3. The Secondary EL supplement(for students who are LEP/NEP and enrolled in sixth through 12 grade or an alternative or adult education program).

Table 51.2 provides the schedule of weighting based on school level.

TABLE 51.2. General Education

Grade Level	Weighting	Per Pupil Allocation
Pre-Kindergarten 3	1.34	$15,718
Pre-Kindergarten 4	1.30	$15,249
Kindergarten	1.30	$15,249
Grades 1-5	1.00	$11,730
Grades 6-8	1.08	$12,668
Grades 9-12	1.22	$14,311
Alternative program	1.52	$17,830
Special education school	1.17	$13,724
Adult	0.89	$10,440

Per-School Totals

Appropriations for DCPS are based on the verified enrollment of the previous year.[40] Adjustments are then made after the current year's official count is completed during the fall of the new school year. For DCPCS, appropriations are derived from projected enrollment of resident students in all public charter schools plus the total estimated per pupil cost for facilities allotment.[41] Adjustments are also made after the verified count is completed. Budget planning for the DCPS and DCPCS is governed by the Office of the Chief Financial Officer (CFO) through the "Annual Operating Budget and Capital Plan.[42] The CFO provides guidance through its annual "Proposed Budget and Financial Plan."[43] Each department is presented with budget plan guidance for the following year. Also, the CFO requires that each department provide monthly financial reports and quarterly capital budget reports.

Supplemental General Funds

The UPSFF also provides supplemental allocations to the foundation level through additional weighting factors. These supplemental revenues are available in addition to the basis counts and are applied to students who are entitled or receiving special education, English as a second language or bilingual education services, and summer school instruction.[44] LEP/NEP, summer school, and residential school students.

Supplemental allocations are applied to four areas: 1) special education; 2) English as a second language or bilingual education services; 3) summer school instruction for students; and extended school days for at-risk students and full-time residence students.

Allocation of supplemental funding is calculated by applying weighting to the foundation level. Supplemental funding provides additional funding above the USPFF for four categories: 1) Special Education; 2) General Education (ELL and

TABLE 51.3.

Level/Program	Definition	Weighting	Per-Pupil Supplemental Allocation FY 2021
Special Education Add-ons			
Level 1: Special Education	Eight hours or less per week of specialized services	0.97	$11,378
Level 2: Special Education	More than 8 hours and less than or equal to 16 hours per school week of specialized services	1.20	$25,076
Level 3: Special Education	More than 16 hours and less than or equal to 24 hours per school week of specialized services	1.97	$23,108
Level 4: Special Education	More than 24 hours per week of specialized services which may include instruction in a self-contained (dedicated) special education school other than residential placement	3.49	$40,938
Special Education Compliance	Weighting provided in addition to special education level add-on weightings on a per-student basis for Special Education compliance.	0.099	$,161
Attorney's Fees Supplement	Weighting provided in addition to special education level add-on weightings on a per-student basis for attorney's fees.	0.089	$1,044
Residential Special Education	DCPS or DCPCS that provides special education students with room and board in a residential setting, in addition to their instructional program	1.67	$19,589
General Education Add-ons			
Elementary -- EL	Additional funding for English Language Learners at the Elementary grade level.	0.50	$5,865
Secondary -- EL	Additional funding for English Language Learners at the Secondary grade level.	0.75	$8,798
At-risk	Additional funding for students in foster care, who are homeless, on TANF or SNAP, or behind grade level.	0.24	$2,815
HS Over-Age Supplement	Additional funding for students who are at risk and are one year older than expected age at school grade.	0.06	$704

(*continues*)

TABLE 51.3. Continued

Level/Program	Definition	Weighting	Per-Pupil Supplemental Allocation FY 2021
SPED Residential Add-ons			
Level 1: Special Education - Residential	Additional funding to support the after-hours level 1 special education needs of students living in a D.C. Public School or public charter school that provides students with room and board in a residential setting	0.370	$4,340
Level 2: Special Education - Residential	Additional funding to support the after-hours level 2 special education needs of students living in a D.C. Public School or public charter school that provides students with room and board in a residential setting	1.340	$15,718
Level 3: Special Education - Residential	Additional funding to support the after-hours level 3 special education needs of students living in a D.C. Public School or public charter school that provides students with room and board in a residential setting	2.890	$33,900
Level 4: Special Education - Residential	Additional funding to support the after-hours level 4 special education needs of limited and non- English proficient students living in a D.C. Public School or public charter school that provides students with room and board in a residential setting	2.890	$33,900
LEP/NEP -Residential	Additional funding to support the after-hours limited and non-English proficiency needs of students living in a D.C. Public School or public charter school that provides students with room and board in a residential setting	0.668	$6,662
Special Education Add-ons for Students with Extended School Year ("ESY") Indicated in Their Individualized Education Programs ("IEPs")			
Special Education Level 1 ESY	Additional funding to support the summer school or program need for students who require extended school year (ESY) services in their IEPs.	0.063	$739
Special Education Level 2 ESY	Additional funding to support the summer school or program need for students who require extended school year (ESY) services in their IEPs	0.227	$2,663
Special Education Level 3 ESY	Additional funding to support the summer school or program need for students who require extended school year (ESY) services in their IEPs	0.491	$5,759
Special Education Level 4 ESY	Additional funding to support the summer school or program need for students who require extended school year (ESY) services in their IEPs	0.491	$5,759

Adjustment to the USPFF

There is a provision in the code to allow for an adjustment to the per-student allotment during years of economic downturn. However, the amount cannot go below 95% of the previous year's fiscal funding.[49]

Compensatory Education

Any compensatory education expenditures are covered outside of the normal DCPS and DCPCS budgets. The OSSE manages all compensatory education requests through its Special Education office. Disputes are handled through a special Dispute Resolution office. The expense is covered through OSSE, and the process is managed by the Office of Specialized Instruction. Expenses are covered by the OSSE budget.

General Transportation

Generally, transportation in the District for public and charter school students is not provided by the District. However, under special conditions, transportation may be provided through various District offices. Transportation would be provided to students for those who require Special Education Services, are temporarily moved to a different location (swing space), are attending extracurricular activities outside of the regular school day, or to attend a field trip.[50]

Students who are eligible for transportation due to special education needs can receive transportation services through the OSSE's Department of Transportation. The District will provide for transportation for students who are temporarily moved from their primary school and will plan with the individual school to provide transportation for students who require it. Field trips and outside activities are also provided for by the District and managed by the individual school through approved venders.

As part of the School Transit Subsidy Act of 1978,[51] The District Department of Transportation (DDOT) arranged an agreement with the Washington Metropolitan Area Transit Authority (WMATA) to provide free rides to students on city transportation services and discounted fares on the subway. The subsidy is managed and paid through the DDOT.[52]

CAPITAL OUTLAY AND DEBT SERVICE

Capital Outlay[53]

Capital outlay is covered under Title 38, Chapter 29B of the DC Code. The creation, purpose, and accountability of any capital spending is covered by three subchapters as follows:

- Subchapter I. Public School Capital Improvement Fund. §§ 38-2971.01 – 38-2971.04 This establishes a non-lapsing special revenue fund called the

At-risk); Residential (generally for special education students who are live on a school site); 4) Special Education Extended school year (summer school).

Table 51.3 shows the 2021 Code for supplemental weights for DCPS and DCPCS.[45]

The supplemental allocation is a full amount added to the USPFF. For example, if a student in grades 6-8, who is listed as a Special Education 2 would receive an allocation totaling $22,736.76. The formula would be applied as follows: (Base x Weight) + Level 2, Sped. So, for the school year 2021, that child's funding would be as follows:

$$(\$11,310 \text{ x } 1.08) + \$25,076 = \$37,291 \text{ (rounded)}$$

Special Weighting for At-Risk Students

There is an additional amount provided through the USPFF for student's considered at-risk. Weighting is determined by the Mayor and applied after other weights are considered. The additional amount is then added to the total. For example, a student who attends grades 6-8, and is classified as a Special Education 2 student, would receive the $33,291 plus the at-risk weighting. At-risk weighting is only applied to the Base but is added to the total. For example, if the at-risk weight is determined to be 0.24 of the Base, that would be an additional $2,815 added to the $33,291 for a total of $36,106 for that student.

Excluded Education Costs

Certain costs are excluded from the USPFF. Costs for transportation for students with disabilities (This is covered by the Office of the State Superintendent of Education's Division of Student Transportation[46] (OSSE DOT), tuition payments for private placements for students with disabilities and any costs associated with the performance of any function of the state education office of the District. Such costs are allocated by the Mayor and Council of the District directly to the Office of the State Superintendent of Education (OSSE) or to a credited agency that performs a special function.[47] Other functions such as school resource officers and nurses are covered outside of the DCPS and are funded through outside departments. Legal services arising from special education lawsuits are covered by the Office of Attorney General (OAG). Construction costs (just for DCPS, Charter schools are covered under another provision in the law) are covered by the Department of General Services (DGS). The Metropolitan Police Department (MPD) provides for school resource officers. The Departments of Health (DOH) and Behavioral Health (DBH) provide for nurses and mental health professionals. The Department of Transportation provides crossing guards.[48]

"Public School Capital Improvement Fund." The Fund is separate from the General Fund and is to be used for modernization of facilities.

- Subchapter II. Fiscal Effect. §§ 38-2972.01 – 38-2972.01 Deals with the impact of the Fund on the transferring of General Fund sources for school facilities expenditures. The purpose of this section is to be temporary until the Capital Fund is fully funded.
- Subchapter III. Public School Capital Improvement Expenditure Accountability. §§ 38-2973.01 – 38-2973.05 This section establishes the process of auditing the Capital Fund.

School Facilities

The District provides funding for DCPS and DCPCS schools, but that funding varies considerably. Funding for DCPS facilities comes directly from the District's budget as part of the Master Facilities Plan (MFP), which is required to be updated every year.[54] The MFP is a 10-year plan that covers all buildings and construction in the District. The Deputy Mayor for Education is responsible for providing the MFP for DCPS, which was originally managed by the Office of Public Education Facilities Planning (OPEFP) and was responsible for facilities maintenance and construction. Starting in 2012, the OPEFP's functions are being handled by the DGS.[55] Part of the OPEFP's original charge was to also establish a Public Charter School Registry to assist charter schools with planning and technical support, although charter schools do not get funded directly through the DME.

Capital Improvement

The MFP is connected to the District's budget process through the District's Capital Improvement Plan (CIP), a six-year plan for capital construction, which includes schools. The CIP includes information on specific projects' funding and construction schedule. It includes information on modernization and replacement of school facilities; small capital projects like upgrades, replacements for areas like roof, and any Federally required changes or improvements.[56]

Financing for the capital plan comes from general obligation municipal bonds issued by the District, which are paid in 20-to-30-year cycles.

For the FY 2022, the CIP[57] is allocating to education the following:

- $288.0 million for DC Public Schools, to include
- $161.9 million for the renovation of elementary and middle schools,
- $47.1 million for Bard High School Early College renovation,
- $41.7 million for renovation and capital maintenance of building components,
- $17.6 million for early childhood education centers, and
- $8.8 million for the swing space needed during construction.

Facilities Funding for Charter Schools

Charter schools do not receive direct funds for facilities from the District. Rather, funding is provided annually through the UPSFF on a per-student basis, with additional funding provided for residency programs.[58] The annual allotment provides charter schools with funds to rent or acquire school space. No additional money is provided through the District for charter facilities, but charters have complete discretion over how the additional allotted funds are spent. Charters also have access to additional Federal facilities programs through the OSSE's Office of Public Charter School Financing and Support.[59] In 2014, the District Council passed a law allowing the mayor to designate DCPS building that are considered surplus and allow charter schools to buy or lease them.

Debt Service

Debt service for education is handled through the Office of the Chief Financing Officer (OCFO). The OCFO publishes reports annually on the District's indebtedness and CIP operations. By legislation, the District limits to 12% of the total general budget in any year during the CIP period (currently from FY 2014 through FY 2019).

The District uses a debt service model to determine debt service costs. Calculations are based on the amount of the planned general fund expenditures, factoring actual cost of the type of service with projected out-year obligations and costs considered.

Currently, there are two School Modernization General Obligation Bonds (G.O.) being serviced. A 2007 Issuance of $60 million is being paid at a rate of $2,781,425 per year through 2025. A second G.O. Bond was issued in 2008 for $90 million and is being paid at a rate of $5,844,288 per year through 2025. All debt service payments are taken out of the District's CIP plan.

CAREER AND TECHNICAL TRAINING

Programs for career and technical education (CTE) are managed through the DCPS's Career and Technical Education Office (CTTO). The program is a three or four-year course, which supplements the high school core classes. The CTE programs include participation for certification exams and provides work-based learning experiences. There are approximately 17 schools providing over 19 CTE programs. There is no supplemental funding provided through the USPFF at this time.

FOOD SERVICES

The Food and Nutrition Services (FNS) of DCPS provides guidance to all DCPS schools. Currently, all DCPS students are provided a free breakfast. In 2020-21, 87 schools were certified for the Community Eligibility Provision (CEP), allowing students to receive lunch at no charge. All DCPS students are required to fill out a Free and Reduced-price Meal application regardless of eligibility.[60]

EMPLOYEE BENEFITS

Healthcare[61]

Current health benefits are provided to October 1, 1987.[62] DCPS contributes up to 72% of premiums for any plan chosen by the employee. Plans available include PPOs, HMOs, and CDHPs (basic indemnity plan). All full-time permanent employees, part-time over 20 hours, temporary (at least 13 months of employment or who work at least 90 days within a 12-month period) are eligible for health care. There is an optional dental and vision plan, but union employees are automatically enrolled in individual plans as part of their collective bargaining agreement. There is a basic life insurance plan with an option for supplemental insurance.

DCPS employees are also eligible to continue healthcare coverage in retirement.[63] There is a cost involved that is determined at the time of retirement, with a portion covered by DCPS as part of the retirement benefits. The school board is responsible for determining coverage and costs. Currently, retirement healthcare coverage is available for District coverage with a minimum of 10 years of service. Also, the retiree must have been enrolled in the District's health plan for at least 5 years. The initial cost to the employee is 75% of the current premium's coverage amount with a 2.5% reduction for every year of service greater than 10 years. The Federal coverage requires a minimum service of 5 years with a minimally enrolled period of 5 years. Cost is around 25% of premium coverage costs.

Retirement[64]

The Teachers' Retirement System is a separate entity from the District Public School System and resources are provided through a combination of teacher participation and the government of the District. In 1998, the federal government passed the Police Officers, Firefighters, and Teachers Retirement Benefit Replacement Plan Act of 1998 (Act 1998).[65] Under this act, the federal government assumed the District's unfunded pension liabilities for the pensions of teachers, police officers, firefighters and judges. Under Act 1998, the federal government pays the retirement, death benefits, and any disability benefits for employees for any service accrued prior to July 1, 19997. Any cost for benefits after that date fall on the District government. The plan is available to all DCPS teachers but not available to DCPCS teachers. Funding for the plan by the District government is governed by law.[66] Pursuant to law, the District is to contribute an amount equal to or greater than that certified by the District of Columbia Retirement Board (DCRB). The District projected contribution for 2021 was $70,478,000, a 19% increase from 2020 ($58,888).[67]

According to the DCPS website, eligible employees include all WTU members, Council of School Officers, and any member in ET-classified positions.[68] Eligible employees are enrolled automatically and pay a contribution toward the defined benefit plan. Those employees hired before December 1, 1996 pay 7% of pre-tax income into the plan. Those enrolled after December 1, 1996 pay 8%.

TABLE 51.4. Vesting Rates

Years of Creditable Service	Vested Percentage
Less Than 2	0%
2	20%
3	40%
4	60%
5 or more	100%

There are two separate individual defined contribution plans that all employees are eligible to use—403(b) and a 457 plan. Both of these are optional plans and an employee must choose only one.

Vesting occurs on a graded schedule. Table 51.4 illustrates the vesting schedule. Retirement benefits are based on a formula as follows:[69]

2% multiplier x Average salary over consecutive 36 months x Years of service.

A teacher making a 3-year average salary of $90,0000 with 30 years of experience, would expect to have an annual pension benefit worth $54,000 including a cost-of-living adjustment (capped at 3%) every year.

Eligibility for retirement depends on start date, age, and years of service. Eligibility under voluntary retirement is as follows:

- Age 55 and at least 30 years of service
- Age 60 and at least 20 years of service
- Age 62 and at least 5 years of service
- Any age with at least 30 years of service if hired on or after November 1, 1996.

DCPS also has available a deferred retirement option, a disability retirement option and an involuntary retirement. The disability and involuntary retirements are determined by DCPS. Both the deferred and disability retirements are determined by the School Board and require at least 5-years of DCPS service for eligibility. The involuntary retirement is available for employees removed from service for reason other than misconduct or delinquency with at least 25-years of service or 20-years and age 50. Participants also have the option of purchasing up to ten years of full-time prior public school teaching outside of DCPS.

CHARTER SCHOOL FUNDING

Funding for charter schools has been covered in this chapter in previous sections. Since DCPCS is considered a public charter system, it is provided student funding through the UPSFF with all weighting. [70] The only difference between the two school systems in the area of funding is with facilities. DCPS facilities is funded through other District agencies, while DCPCS is funded by the individual LEAs. However, each charter school is allocated funds by the District for facilities purposes on a per-student basis.

NON-PUBLIC SCHOOL FUNDING

The District does not provide funding for non-public schools through the USPFF except for authorized charter schools, which are considered public for USPFF purposes but are to be managed by private non-profit organizations. There is a provision in the Code for the District to provide funding to a private school which serves a special-needs student. Such funding is provided at cost. There is no provision for travel to such school for the student.

Appropriations to charter schools are paid directly to the charter school by the Mayor and sent to a bank selected by the charter school. Payments are made quarterly based on each charter schools' quarterly report. Payments are made on the 15th of July, October, January and April. Amounts are determined by the USPFF for all charter schools and appropriated based on student counts.[71]

ADDITIONAL REVENUES

Besides the funds provided through the USPFF, District schools receive additional funding from various sources. The DGS provides funding directly for school facilities, while the DOT provides resources for crossing guards. Additionally funding for school nurses is provided through the Department of Health, and mental health professionals are funded through the Department of Behavioral Health. The Metropolitan Police Department funds any school resource officer, and the District's Office of Attorney General provides support for any lawsuit the DCPS might face.[72]

The OSSE receives all federal funds for both the DCPS and DCPCS, and distributes the funds to each LEA, which then allocate them accordingly. In the event that a special needs child requires an outside placement, the LEA is required to provide for that funding. The OSSE also has a special source of funding for such placement. The monitoring of the child is still the responsibility of whichever school he or she is attached to for public funds.

Private Funding

Both the DCPS and DCPCS are allowed to seek private funding. The DC Public Education Fund connects the DCPS with philanthropic sources. Parent organizations also help raise additional resources, and there is currently no restrictions on how funds may be used.[73]

VIRTUAL EDUCTION

DCPS provides a Home and Hospital Instruction Program (HHIP) for students who have been diagnosed with a physical or psychiatric condition that prevents them from attending a traditional classroom. The HHIP program uses various methods to connect students to a classroom and a regular assigned classroom teacher as much as possible. The rationale for the program is to provide a temporary solution with the objective of transitioning the student back into the classroom, but also providing the student with the least restrictive environment.

During the COVID-19 pandemic, DCPS created virtual learning for all students in an effort to provide continuity of educational instruction. Along with every other state, the District was forced to create an ad hoc system of virtual learning. The outbreak of COVID-19 during the 2019-20 school year created a challenge to provide educational services to all students on an equitable basis. This challenge was addressed through many official correspondence letters and reports to the community. With the entire shut down of the school system in April 2020, DCPS struggled to provide any educational services at all, with final grades for students listed as an attendance grade rather than a letter grade for pass or fail purposes.

Through the summer of 2020, DCPS worked with teachers and parent groups to create a virtual learning environment for all students. The virtual program can be accessed online at the DCPS Instructional Continuity Plan (ICP).[74] The program is available to all students in DCPS and DCPCS if needed. For some students, access is a problem, so the DCPS schools created a hybrid model with what is called CARES classrooms. These are classrooms where students can come into to access the ICP program with an accompanying teacher to provide additional support.[75]

FEDERAL COVID-19 FUNDING[76]
(Amounts Received & Spending Plans)

COVID funds for the District are classified as Elementary and Secondary School Emergency Relief (ESSER)

The District will receive three rounds of funding through ESSER as follows:

- ESSER I – authorized by the Coronavirus Aid, Relief, and Economic Security (CARES) Act
- ESSER II – authorized by the Coronavirus Response and Relief Supplemental Appropriations (CRRSA) Act
- ESSER III – authorized by the American Recovery Plan (ARP) Act

The District will receive over $300 million in ESSER funds for the support of DCPS, DCPCS and private schools.

For FY 2020, DCPS received $22 million under ESSER I, of which $3 million was allocated to private schools and DCPCS. The ESSER I spending plan is as follows:

- $16 million: Technology.
- $3 million: Equitable services to private schools.
- $2 million: Summer Learning and Supplemental Programming.
- $1 million: Staffing.

The remaining $1 million is rolled over into the FY 2021 school year.

For FY 2021, DCPS received $86 million under ESSER II. The allocation of these funds are as follows:

- $26 million: School-based academic and social emotional acceleration.
- $15 million: Technology and Related Supports for Students.
- $12 million: Technology and Related Supports for Educators.
- $9 million: Teaching and learning and educator professional development.
- $9 million: Meal service, warehouse, and curricular support.
- $9 million: In-Person Learning Innovations.
- $6 million: Other investments in response to mid-year COVID- related needs, including family engagement and reopening.

Under ESSER III, which will cover FY 2022, DCPS will receive $191 million. Fund allocation is planned and will be finalized by June 30, 2022. DCPS has allocated $20.8 million to ensure schools open for the 2021-22 school year.

SUMMARY

Appendix F provides information on the approved budgets for DCPS and DCPCS for FY 2022. Total funds for DCPS have grown by 15.8% over FY 2021. The change can be attributed to the increase of Federal funds from the COVID-19 relief funds.

The increase in charter schools in the District has seen a change in the way the District allocates resources to public education and in the share of those resources to private entities. Since charter schools are governed by private non-profits, they are traditionally private schools. However, under the District's rule for funding, they are considered public and are beginning to receive a larger and larger share of public funding. For FY 2022, charter schools' budget is only 76% that of DCPS. In 2018, the budget for charter schools was 86%, and increased growth in charter opening seem to indicate that DCPCS' budget would exceed DCPS. However, the influx of COVID-19 federal money has temporarily raised DCPS' budget. DCPCS schools continue to open, and future share of UPSFF funding will continue to increase.

APPENDIX A: DISTRICT OF
COLUMBIA ORGANIZATION CHART

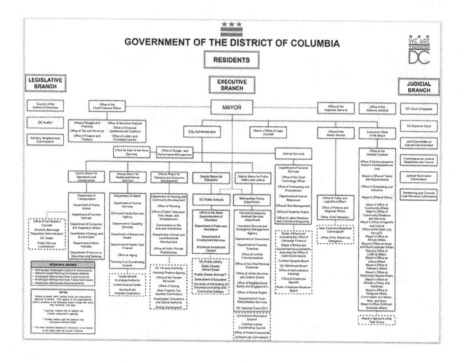

APPENDIX B: DCPS DESCRIPTIVE STATISTICS[77]

Enrollment by Grade

Grade	SY 11-12	SY 12-13	SY 13-14	SY 14-15	SY 15-16	SY 16-17	SY 17-18	SY 18-19	SY 19-20	SY 20-21
PK 3	2105	2161	2197	2276	2310	2362	2374	2498	2564	2134
PK 4	3294	3409	3368	3339	3522	3468	3423	3464	3524	3368
K	3790	4123	4182	4108	4208	4225	4201	4145	4225	4000
1	3687	3741	4113	4143	4163	4181	4093	4228	4160	4018
2	3205	3546	3688	4101	4109	3996	3939	4023	4194	3972
3	3233	3182	3460	3626	4085	4044	3862	3953	4008	3989
4	3162	3082	3059	3349	3596	3961	3882	3841	3988	3876
5	3016	2799	2846	2789	3106	3267	3595	3624	3638	3652
6	2348	2279	2242	2237	2077	2321	2313	2777	3017	2812
7	2203	2338	2364	2312	2279	2155	2375	2443	2999	2911
8	2357	2194	2412	2519	2318	2332	2176	2446	2580	2935
9	3706	3972	3959	4175	4123	3614	3362	3211	3992	3869
10	2682	2558	2558	2569	2717	2790	2774	2741	2698	3131
11	2424	2355	2363	2421	2512	2660	2612	2556	2349	2337
12	2114	2028	1935	2181	2326	2363	2524	2441	2370	2220
AO*	1394	1378	1381	1137	769	623	408	425	469	421
UN/CE**	474	412	266	266	219	193	231	240	261	245
DCPS Total	45191	45557	46393	47548	48439	48555	48144	49056	51036	49890

*AO= Adult: Includes students classified evening students

**UN= Ungraded; CE= Students classified as Certificate Option (CE) who are special education students on a certificate non-diploma track

Demographics

Category (% Student Population)	SY 11-12	SY 12-13	SY 13-14	SY 14-15	SY 15-16	SY 16-17	SY 17-18	SY 18-19	SY 19-20	SY 20-21
Black	71%	69%	68%	67%	64%	62%	60%	59%	58%	58%
Hispanic	15%	16%	16%	17%	18%	20%	21%	20%	21%	21%
Asian	2%	2%	2%	2%	2%	2%	2%	2%	2%	2%
Two or More Races	2%	2%	2%	2%	2%	2%	2%	3%	3%	3%
Native Hawaiian/Other Pacific Islander	<1%	<1%	<1%	<1%	<1%	<1%	<1%	<1%	<1%	<1%
American Indian/Alaska Native	<1%	<1%	<1%	<1%	<1%	<1%	<1%	<1%	<1%	<1%
White	10%	11%	12%	12%	13%	14%	15%	16%	16%	16%
In Special Education	18%	17%	15%	16%	15%	14%	14%	15%	15%	16%
ELL	10%	10%	10%	10%	10%	12%	14%	15%	16%	15%
Economically Disadvantaged*	N/A	N/A	N/A	N/A	78%	77%	77%	74%	73%	75%
At-Risk**	N/A	N/A	N/A	N/A	48%	44%	44%	44%	43%	42%

*Refers to students, identified by the Office of the State Superintendent of Education (OSSE), who possess one of the following characteristics at any point in the SY: Received Free or Reduced-Price Lunch (FRL); Received FRL through CEP (attending a school where the entire student population receives FRL); Eligible to receive TANF or SNAP benefits; Identified as homeless in available homeless data feeds; Under the care of CFSA.

** Students who are at-risk are those who qualify for Temporary Assistance for Needy Families (TANF), the Supplemental Nutrition Assistance Program (SNAP), have been identified as homeless during the academic year, who are under the care of the Child and Family Services Agency (CFSA or Foster Care), and who are high school students at least one year older than the expected age for their grade.

Y 20-21 Schools

Type of School	Number of Schools
Primary Schools	2
Elementary Schools	66
Middle Schools	14
High Schools*	15
Education Campuses**	14
Opportunity Academies***	3
Special Education Schools	1
Youth Engagement Schools****	2
Total	117

*The High Schools category includes application high schools (School Without Walls, Phelps ACE HS, Ellington School of the Arts, Banneker HS, McKinley Tech HS).

**The Education Campuses category includes schools serving grades PK-8 plus Cardozo EC and Columbia Heights EC which serve grades 6-12.

***Luke C. Moore HS, Washington Metropolitan HS, Ballou STAY HS, and Roosevelt STAY HS

****Youth Services Center and Inspiring Youth Program

APPENDIX C: COMPARISON OF GRADUATION RATES FOR DISTRICT OF COLUMBIA, DCPS AND DCPCS

DC 2019 4-year Adjusted Cohort Graduation Rates, by student group

			2019 4-year ACGR by student group								
		Gender			Race						
Sector	Overall	Female	Male	Black/ African-Ameri-can	His-panic Latino of any race	White	Asian	Two or more races	At-risk	English Learn-ers	Students with Disabili-ties
State	68.2%	75.2%	61.4%	67.8%	59.6%	92.8%	91.8%	76.7%	57.7%	50.7%	49.8%
	(3359)	(1818)	(1541)	(2435)	(546)	(271)	(67)	(33)	(1931)	(287)	(499)
DCPS	65.1%	72.6%	57.8%	63.9%	56.5%	92.3%	91.8%	77.8%	52.4%	47.2%	43.8%
	(2170)	(1189)	(981)	(1432)	(419)	(229)	(56)	(28)	(1160)	(224)	(271)
PCS	76.4%	81.0%	71.8%	75.9%	73.8%	95.5%	91.7%	n<10	70.0%	70.0%	62.6%
	(1189)	(629)	(560)	(1003)	(127)	(42)	(DS)	(n<10)	(771)	(63)	(228)

Notes: The number of four-year graduates in 2018-19 school year is included in the parenthesis (). Students in the 2019 4-year adjusted cohort include students who began ninth grade for the first time in the 2015-2016 school year. Student groups below the minimum n-size of 10 students are not reported. Some student groups above the minimum n-size of 10 are not reported (DS: data suppression) due to the ability to determine values for student groups below the minimum n-size from these data.

APPENDIX D: DISTRICT OF COLUMBIA OVERVIEW OF FINANCIAL POSITION AND OPERATIONS[78]

OVERVIEW OF THE DISTRICT'S FINANCIAL POSITION AND OPERATIONS

The District's overall financial position remained strong despite the economic and financial impacts of COVID-19. The District's financial position and operations for the past two fiscal years are summarized in **Tables MDA-1** and **MDA-2**. The information for fiscal years 2020 and 2019 is based on the government-wide financial statements presented on pages 52 and 53.

Table MDA-1
Net Position as of September 30, 2020 ($000s)

| | Governmental activities | | Business-type activities | | Totals | | |
	2020	2019	2020	2019	2020	2019	Variance
ASSETS							
Current and other assets	$ 7,784,964	$ 6,479,313	$ 317,801	$ 594,466	$ 8,102,765	$ 7,073,779	$ 1,028,986
Capital assets	15,315,706	14,534,439	70,136	68,849	15,385,842	14,603,288	782,554
Total assets	23,100,670	21,013,752	387,937	663,315	23,488,607	21,677,067	1,811,540
DEFERRED OUTFLOWS OF RESOURCES	286,527	251,997	-	-	286,527	251,997	34,530
LIABILITIES							
Long-term liabilities	14,491,829	12,910,442	10,458	9,885	14,502,287	12,920,327	1,581,960
Other liabilities	2,379,115	2,008,918	210,263	67,439	2,589,378	2,076,357	513,021
Total liabilities	16,870,944	14,919,360	220,721	77,324	17,091,665	14,996,684	2,094,981
DEFERRED INFLOWS OF RESOURCES	181,414	273,443	-	-	181,414	273,443	(92,029)
NET POSITION							
Net investment in capital assets	3,232,889	3,571,065	70,136	68,849	3,303,025	3,639,914	(336,889)
Restricted	1,891,026	1,803,748	90,550	503,431	1,981,576	2,307,179	(325,603)
Unrestricted	1,210,924	698,133	6,530	13,711	1,217,454	711,844	505,610
Total net position	$ 6,334,839	$ 6,072,946	$ 167,216	$ 585,991	$ 6,502,055	$ 6,658,937	$ (156,882)

Table MDA-2
Change in Net Position for the Year Ended September 30, 2020 ($000s)

| | Governmental activities | | Business-type activities | | Totals | | |
	2020	2019	2020	2019	2020	2019	Variance
REVENUES							
Program revenues							
Charges for services	$ 891,589	$ 869,744	$ 313,407	$ 323,407	$ 1,204,996	$ 1,193,151	$ 11,845
Operating grants and contributions	4,826,314	3,916,440	1,025,633	18,319	5,851,947	3,934,759	1,917,188
Capital grants and contributions	278,833	258,500	-	-	278,833	258,500	20,333
General revenues							
Property taxes	3,061,745	2,888,245	-	-	3,061,745	2,888,245	173,500
Sales and use taxes	1,317,113	1,707,745	-	-	1,317,113	1,707,745	(390,632)
Income and franchise taxes	3,021,673	2,969,289	-	-	3,021,673	2,969,289	52,384
Other taxes	864,100	981,113	139,833	142,877	1,003,933	1,123,990	(120,057)
Non-tax revenues	646,653	664,420	10,840	12,416	657,493	676,836	(19,343)
Total revenues	14,908,020	14,255,496	1,489,713	497,019	16,397,733	14,752,515	1,645,218
EXPENSES							
Governmental direction and support	1,269,743	1,157,810	-	-	1,269,743	1,157,810	111,933
Economic development and regulation	845,768	700,346	-	-	845,768	700,346	145,422
Public safety and justice	1,920,012	1,673,214	-	-	1,920,012	1,673,214	246,798
Public education system	3,132,645	2,949,935	-	-	3,132,645	2,949,935	182,710
Human support services	5,463,907	5,148,903	-	-	5,463,907	5,148,903	315,004
Public works	1,162,410	860,918	-	-	1,162,410	860,918	301,492
Public transportation	424,271	425,753	-	-	424,271	425,753	(1,482)
Interest on long-term debt	430,752	425,812	-	-	430,752	425,812	4,940
Office of lottery and gaming	-	-	176,987	168,454	176,987	168,454	8,533
Unemployment compensation	-	-	1,568,065	120,010	1,568,065	120,010	1,448,055
Not-for-profit hospital corporation	-	-	160,055	149,736	160,055	149,736	10,319
Total expenses	14,649,508	13,342,691	1,905,107	438,200	16,554,615	13,780,891	2,773,724
Increase in net position before transfers	258,512	912,805	(415,394)	58,819	(156,882)	971,624	(1,128,506)
Transfers in (out)	3,381	8,740	(3,381)	(8,740)	-	-	-
Change in net position	261,893	921,545	(418,775)	50,079	(156,882)	971,624	(1,128,506)
Net position - October 1	6,072,946	5,151,401	585,991	535,912	6,658,937	5,687,313	971,624
Net position - September 30	$ 6,334,839	$ 6,072,946	$ 167,216	$ 585,991	$ 6,502,055	$ 6,658,937	$ (156,882)

Refer to Note 1W - Reconciliation of Government-Wide and Fund Financial Statements, on page 86 for additional information on the differences between the two bases of accounting that the District used in this report.

APPENDIX E: DISTRICT GENERAL REVENUE FUNDS, 2016-2022

General Fund Revenue for District of Columbia

	2016	2017	2018	2019	2020	2021*	2022*
Real Property	2,357,503	2,473,328	2,588,414	2,710,080	2,836,733	2,883,966	2,774,303
Personal Property	59,101	63,305	62,580	78,997	77,698	70,193	69,990
Public Space Rental	40,386	32,468	33,507	38,680	39,662	35,323	35,676
General Sales	1,343,074	1,419,197	1,481,046	1,597,727	1,222,446	1,113,119	1,481,845
Alcoholic Beverages	6,468	6,641	6,758	7,042	6,009	6,006	6,199
Cigarette	30,451	29,530	29,750	28,546	24,934	23,103	22,479
Motor Vehicle	45,997	45,915	45,521	45,973	40,713	40,700	41,107
Motor Fuel Tax	25,331	26,099	25,761	27,935	22,472	25,774	26,706
Individual Income	1,907,862	1,958,277	2,065,530	2,299,326	2,377,236	2,486,961	2,527,636
Corporate Franchise	387,081	389,218	362,944	507,911	575,646	590,367	603,219
U.B. Franchise	169,387	165,027	155,000	134,745	152,051	164,979	165,037
Public Utility	135,568	138,124	143,234	156,274	136,813	124,837	148,157
Toll Telecommunications	50,930	49,543	41,743	41,899	40,891	36,314	34,898
Insurance Premiums	104,917	108,213	110,324	118,802	120,004	127,265	127,772
Healthcare Provider Tax	17,014	13,949	14,202	14,338	16,217	15,652	15,965
Private Sports Wagering	0	0	0		273	2,596	2,856
Games of skill	0	0	0		0	1,210	3,329
Ballpark Fee	32,764	31,107	33,900	45,096	37,248	34,902	37,400
Hospital Bed Tax and Hospital Provider Fee	16,806	15,928	14,307	13,797	12,846	15,127	15,127
ICF-IDD Assessment	4,860	4,913	4,792	4,864	6,831	5,539	5,539
Estate	53,967	41,215	43,482	22,311	37,249	35,021	37,143
Deed Recordation	250,028	250,740	261,417	299,512	261,211	265,076	293,990
Dee Transfer	174,640	188,781	198,485	228,249	179,403	213,483	227,115
Economic Interest	19,450	21,336	17,824	33,306	12,124	13,569	21,831
Total Taxes	7,233,585	7,472,856	7,740,519	8,455,407	8,236,710	8,331,082	8,725,319
Total Non-Tax	509,008	487,514	445,440	619,241	522,895	397,371	451,408
Other Sources	53,287	45,600	45,000	45,050	38,060	44,099	56,586
Special Purpose	533,557	548,367	632,182	644,828	612,092	705,496	740,330
Total General Fund	8,329,437	8,554,336	8,863,141	9,764,527	9,409,757	9,478,048	9,973,643

*FY numbers are estimates from D.C. Tax Facts 2021

Source: D.C. Tax Facts Annual Reports, 2007-2021

APPENDIX F: PROPOSED BUDGETS FOR DCPS AND DCPCS

FY 2022 Approved Gross Funds Operating Budget and FTEs, by Revenue Type

Table GA0-2 contains the approved FY 2022 budget by revenue type compared to the FY 2021 approved budget. It also provides FY 2019 and FY 2020 actual data.

Table GA0-2

(dollars in thousands)

	Dollars in Thousands						Full-Time Equivalents					
Appropriated Fund	Actual FY 2019	Actual FY 2020	Approved FY 2021	Approved FY 2022	Change from FY 2021	% Change*	Actual FY 2019	Actual FY 2020	Approved FY 2021	Approved FY 2022	Change from FY 2021	% Change
GENERAL FUND												
Local Funds	857,435	925,803	982,009	1,006,498	24,489	2.5	7,542.9	8,047.9	8,475.6	8,604.6	129.0	1.5
Special Purpose Revenue Funds	9,693	8,859	12,037	10,128	-1,909	-15.9	22.0	25.4	62.7	43.9	-18.7	-29.9
TOTAL FOR GENERAL FUND	867,128	934,662	994,046	1,016,625	22,580	2.3	7,564.8	8,073.3	8,538.2	8,648.5	110.3	1.3
FEDERAL RESOURCES												
Federal Payments	0	6,869	30,000	17,500	-12,500	-41.7	0.0	0.0	166.0	164.1	-1.9	-1.2
Federal Grant Funds	31,894	30,748	5,879	10,199	4,319	73.5	152.6	127.7	62.0	25.0	-37.0	-59.7
TOTAL FOR FEDERAL RESOURCES	31,894	37,617	35,879	27,699	-8,181	-22.8	152.6	127.7	228.0	189.1	-38.9	-17.1
PRIVATE FUNDS												
Private Grant Funds	1,745	2,472	308	2,650	2,341	759.2	14.0	17.8	0.0	20.0	20.0	N/A
Private Donations	112	1,093	0	0	0	N/A	0.0	0.0	0.0	0.0	0.0	N/A
TOTAL FOR PRIVATE FUNDS	1,857	3,566	308	2,650	2,341	759.2	14.0	17.8	0.0	20.0	20.0	N/A
INTRA-DISTRICT FUNDS												
Intra-District Funds	111,246	107,068	112,032	275,755	163,723	146.1	386.5	547.7	494.6	506.1	11.5	2.3
TOTAL FOR												

FY 2022 Approved Operating Budget and FTEs, by Division/Program and Activity

Table GC0-4 contains the approved FY 2022 budget by division/program and activity compared to the FY 2021 approved budget. It also provides FY 2019 and FY 2020 actual data. For a more comprehensive explanation of divisions/programs and activities, please see the Division/Program Description section, which follows the table.

Table GC0-4

(dollars in thousands)

	Dollars in Thousands					Full-Time Equivalents				
Division/Program and Activity	Actual FY 2019	Actual FY 2020	Approved FY 2021	Approved FY 2022	Change from FY 2021	Actual FY 2019	Actual FY 2020	Approved FY 2021	Approved FY 2022	Change from FY 2021
(1000) DC CHARTER SCHOOLS										
(1001) Administrative Expense	179	1,091	187	186	0	1.0	1.0	1.0	1.0	0.0
(1100) DC Charter Schools	887,284	921,462	934,713	1,011,148	76,435	0.0	0.0	0.0	0.0	0.0
SUBTOTAL (1000) DC CHARTER SCHOOLS	887,463	922,553	934,900	1,011,334	76,434	1.0	1.0	1.0	1.0	0.0
TOTAL APPROVED OPERATING BUDGET	887,463	922,553	934,900	1,011,334	76,434	1.0	1.0	1.0	1.0	0.0

(Change is calculated by whole numbers and numbers may not add up due to rounding.)

Note: For more detailed information regarding the approved funding for the activities within this agency's programs, please see **Schedule 30-PBB Program Summary by Activity** in the **FY 2022 Operating Appendices** located on the Office of the Chief Financial Officer's website. "No Activity Assigned" indicates budget or actuals that are recorded at the division/program level.

ENDNOTES

1. DC Code § 1-201.01 et seq. For a full reading of the Home Rule Act of 1977 (Amended through October 21, 1998) see online source at District of Columbia Home Rule Act—Contents (abfa.com).

2. National Research Council. A Plan for Evaluating the District of Columbia's Public Schools: From Impressions to Evidence. National Academies Press, 2011, p. 31.

3. Hannaway, J. and Usdan, M.D. (2008). Mayoral takeover in the District of Columbia. In W.I. Boyd, C.T. Kerchner, and M. Blyth (Eds.), The Transformation of Great American School Districts: How Big Cities are Reshaping Public Education (pp. 1130118). Cambridge, MA: Harvard Education Press. As cited in National Research Council. A Plan for Evaluating the District of Columbia's Public Schools: From Impressions to Evidence.

4. The author attended a presentation by a representative of the Control Board in 1998 at the University of Florida, where it was related by the presenter that one could simply go into the HR office and complain that he or she did not receive a salary check; whereby the HR staff would ask the person how much did he or she make and then simply write a check without any documentation necessary.

5. Ibid. p. 1.

6. Ibid. p. 3.

7. "About the District of Columbia Public Charter School Board;" Online http://dcpubliccharter.com/About-the-Board.aspx.

8. DC Code § 31-2853.41.

9. DC Code § 31-2901.

10. DC Code § 31-2907.

11. Soumya Bhat, "Investing in Our Kids: District of Columbia School Finance Primer." Fiscal Policy Institute. Online < https://www.dcfpi.org/wp-content/uploads/2015/03/Revised-School-Primer-March2015-FINAL.pdf>. See also, Appendix A for a comprehensive organizational chart of DC government.

12. For additional information on DCPCS, see DC Public Charter School Board 2021 Annual Report. Available online: https://dcpcsb.org/about-us/dc-pcsb-annual-reports.

13. See Appendix B for yearly charts on these statistics.

14. District of Columbia Public Schools/School Data/DCPS at a Glance: Performance. Online at https://dcps.dc.gov/page/dcps-glance-performance. Accessed on 11/2/2021.

15. Detailed information for DCPCS can be found in its 2021 Annual Report. See FT 12 for link. Additional information can be found at Charter Sector Facts and Figures. Online: https://dcpcsb.org/about-us/charter-sector-facts-and-figures.

16. Office of State Superintendent of Education. Online: https://osse.dc.gov/parcc.

17. There are 5 levels to the PARCC test. Level 1 are those who did not yet meet expectations; Level 2 are those who partially met expectations; Level 3 are those who approached expectations; Level 4 are those who met expectations, and Level 5 are those who exceeded expectations.

18. U.S. Const. art 1. , § 8.

19. For a full reading of the Home Rule Act of 1977 (Amended through October 21, 1998) see online source at http://www.abfa.com/ogc/hrtall.htm.

20. National Research Council. A Plan for Evaluating the District of Columbia's Public Schools: From Impressions to Evidence. National Academies Press, 2011, p. 12. The general purpose of the HRA was to create a local government to relieve the burden of Congress to manage the local affairs of the District (see, Section 102 of the HRA. Online: http://www.abfa.com/ogc/hrtall.htm.).

21. Ibid.

22. NBC12. "U.S. House passes D.C. statehood bill, [sic] but votes still lacking in Senate." Online: https://www.nbc12.com/2021/04/25/us-house-passes-dc-statehood-bill-votes-still-lacking-senate/. Accessed, 10/30/21.

23   D.C. Code 1-206.
24   D.C. Code 1-101(b).
25   D.C. Code 47-317.1.
26   D.C. Code 1-221.
27   D.C. Official Code 1-204.31.
28   Source BallotPedia.com. Political parties in Washington, D.C. Online: https://ballotpedia.org/Political_parties_in_Washington,_D.C.
29   Source found on DC.gov at Office of the City Administrator. Online: https://oca.dc.gov/page/labor-organizations. Accessed 11/4/2021.
30   The official title is "The Washington Teachers' Union, Local #6, American Federal of Teachers, AFL-CIO. Source: The Constitution and By-Laws of the Washington Teachers' Union, Local 6. Online Access: https://d3n8a8pro7vhmx.cloudfront.net/wtulocal6action/pages/55/attachments/original/1560536582/The_Constitution_and_Bylaws.pdf?1560536582. Admittedly, there is a little confusion as to the differences in the AFT's name on the title of the constitution and in Article 1. However, the correct name for the AFT is the American Federation of Teachers.
31   The source for the union representation can be found on DCPS website for DCPS-Union Collective Bargaining Agreements. Online: https://dcps.dc.gov/page/dcps-union-collective-bargaining-agreements.
32   Revenue and Quarterly Revenue Estimates reports can be located online at https://cfo.dc.gov/page/revenue-trends.
33   Source: D.C. Tax Facts 2021. Online: https://cfo.dc.gov/node/230872.
34   See, DC Code, Title 38, Chapter 29, Subchapter 1 §§ 38-2901 – 38-2914.
35   DC Code, § 38-2902.
36   DC Code § 38-2903 (see also, §§ 38-2909, 2910, and 2911).
37   D.C. Code § 38-2904.
38   Source: 2020-21 Uniform Per Student Funding Formula (UPSFF) Payment Letter provided through the Office of the State Superintendent of Education. Online: https://osse.dc.gov/page/grants-and-funding-0.
39   DC Code § 38-2904.
40   DC Code § 38-2906(a).
41   DC Code § 38-2906(b)(1)(2).
42   Available Online: https://cfo.dc.gov/node/289642.
43   Ibid.
44   DC Code § 38-2905.
45   Ibid.
46   See, OSSE, Special Education Transportation Services Policy. Online: ttps://osse.dc.gov/publication/special-education-transportation-services-policy.
47   DC Code § 38-2907.
48   Soumya Bhat, "Investing in Our Kids: District of Columbia School Finance Primer." Fiscal Policy Institute. Online < https://www.dcfpi.org/wp-content/uploads/2015/03/Revised-School-Primer-March2015-FINAL.pdf>.
49   DC Code § 38-2910.
50   Student Transportation Policy: Chancellor's Directive #301.November 2017.
51   D.C. Law 2-152.
52   Ibid. See also, Finance & Administration Committee, Action Item III-A, July 10, 2014, DC Student Transit Subsidy Agreement. Online: https://www.wmata.com/about/board/meetings/board-pdfs/upload/071014_3ADCStudentTransitSubsidyCOMBINED.pdf
53   D. C. Code §§ 38-2971.01 – 38-2971.04; §§ 38-2972.01 – 38-2972.01; §§ 38-2973.01 – 38-2973.05.
54   DC Code § 38-2803.

[55] Soumya Bhat, "Investing in Our Kids: District of Columbia School Finance Primer." Fiscal Policy Institute. Online < https://www.dcfpi.org/wp-content/uploads/2015/03/Revised-School-Primer-March2015-FINAL.pdf>.

[56] Ibid.

[57] DC FY 2022 Approved Budget and Financial Plan, Vol. 5. Online: https://dcgov.app.box.com/s/09xxasiudp45rhfsuwa3rl0gzx8zissq.

[58] D. C. Code § 38-2908.

[59] Soumya Bhat, "Investing in Our Kids: District of Columbia School Finance Primer." Fiscal Policy Institute. Online < https://www.dcfpi.org/wp-content/uploads/2015/03/Revised-School-Primer-March2015-FINAL.pdf>.

[60] About School Meals: https://dcps.dc.gov/food

[61] DCPS Health Benefits. Online: https://dcps.dc.gov/page/dcps-health-benefits.

[62] Any employee hired prior to September 30, 1987 would be eligible for Federal health benefits. For information on, see www.opm.gov.

[63] For specific information on the benefits and coverage, see "District of Columbia Teachers' Retirement Plan: Summary Plan Description 2017.

[64] Information provided by the District of Columbia's FY 2018 Proposed budget and Financial Plan, Vol. 3, Agency budget Chapters, Part II, Public Education system. P. D-21.

[65] DC Code § 1–901.01. See also, DC Law 12-152.

[66] DC Code § 1-907.03(b).

[67] Bolton Employee Benefits, Actuarial & Investment Consulting. "District of Columbia Retirement Board Teachers' Retirement Plan and Police Officers and Firefighters' Retirement Plan: Actuarial Valuations as of October 1, 2019 to Determine the District's Contribution for the Fiscal Year Ending September 30, 2021." Online: https://dcrb.dc.gov/sites/default/files/dc/sites/dcrb/publication/attachments/DCRB%202019%20Valuation%20FINAL-Oct%201%2C%202019-Bolton.pdf.

[68] DCPS Retirement FAQs. Online: https://dcps.dc.gov/page/retirement-faqs.

[69] DCPS. March 2020. "Retirement Workshop District of Columbia Teachers' Retirement Plan."

[70] DC Code § 31-2853.41.

[71] D. C. Code § 38-2906.02

[72] Soumya Bhat, "Investing in Our Kids: District of Columbia School Finance Primer." Fiscal Policy Institute. Online < https://www.dcfpi.org/wp-content/uploads/2015/03/Revised-School-Primer-March2015-FINAL.pdf>.

[73] Ibid.

[74] Site: https://dcps.instructure.com/courses/179580.

[75] For additional information on the program, see letter online from the Chancellor of DCPS. Online: https://dcps.dc.gov/sites/default/files/dc/sites/dcps/page_content/images/DCPS-Distance-Learning-Guide-English.pdf.

[76] For more detailed information on COVID-19 funds and expenditures, see DCPS' "ESSER Overview." Online: https://dcpsbudget.com/budget-data/central-office-budgets/covid-19-agency-budget-additions/.

[77] Data available on DCPS website: https://dcps.dc.gov/node/96629.

[78] Source: DC Annual Financial Report, 2020. Available online: https://cfo.dc.gov/sites/default/files/dc/sites/ocfo/publication/attachments/FY%202020%20DC%20CAFR_Full%20Report.pdf.

CHAPTER 52

INDIAN COUNTRY[1]

Alex RedCorn
Kansas State University

Meredith L. McCoy
Carleton College

Hollie J. Mackey
*White House Initiative on Advancing Equity, Excellence, and
Economic Opportunity for Native Americans and
Strengthening Tribal Colleges and Universities*

INTRODUCTION[2]

Approximately 660,000 American Indian, Alaska Native, and Native Hawaiian students attend schools every day in every state across the United States.[3] They attend public, private, charter, and federal schools in rural, urban, and suburban settings, placing the responsibility for educating Indigenous students on all educational institutions. Even as Native nations possess an inherent right to govern their peoples and territories, 93% of Native students attend public schools which are not under their direct administration, creating a complex tapestry of overlapping jurisdictions and interests that complicate contemporary Indian education.[4] Unfortunately, these interlocking legal and curricular structures are often inscrutable

*Funding Public Schools in the United States, Indian Country,
and US Territories (Second Edition)*, pages 837–866.
Copyright © 2023 by Information Age Publishing
www.infoagepub.com

to many policymakers and practitioners across federal, state, and local levels of education. This chapter introduces the complex financial and bureaucratic landscape that undergirds schooling for students across Indian Country. In doing so, it provides educational leaders, policymakers, and stakeholders a foundational understanding of American Indian education finance with the hope that a more thorough knowledge of these systems and their histories will facilitate more effective partnerships at all levels between stakeholders and Native nations.

Indian Country is vast, and each Native nation's and urban Native community's experience is distinct. Significant local factors shape the school experiences of students in each region and state, distinctions to which this brief introduction cannot attend. For example, Alaska Natives and Native Hawaiians have unique histories and legal standing that are specific to their educational contexts and sometimes differ from Native nations whose territories share geography with the contiguous 48 states. Anyone working toward developing a deeper understanding of the complex legal, political, and social contours of Indian education must take the additional steps to educate themselves on the specifics of their local context.

The chapter begins by offering historical context in American Indian education and showing the relationships between land dispossessions, attempts to erase and assimilate Indigenous peoples, and educational systems. These histories are important because they provide the legal foundation upon which today's complicated financial regulations rest. After acknowledging these important foundational perspectives, the chapter offers an overview of various bureaucracies associated with financing education across Indian Country. It concludes with a list of primary bureaucracies and funding streams associated with P–12 Indian education. By acknowledging the complicated and interwoven past of Indigenous peoples and the U.S., the chapter provides a foundation for practitioners navigating entangled relationships going into the future.

HISTORICAL CONTEXT

Native people have a unique position with legal roots unlike any other demographic group in the U.S. Though frequently listed alongside racial and ethnic categories on questionnaires, "American Indian" or "Native American" represents status within a sovereign Native nation, which operate in a government-to-government relationship alongside federal, state, and local governments.[5] This has significant ramifications for how education works for Native students. Conversations about Indian education in the U.S. must therefore begin by acknowledging that tribal sovereignty and treaty rights shape how Indigenous peoples participate in contemporary American education systems.

When contemporary Native nations exercise self-determination in education, they push back against 500 years of colonialism built on conquest and erasure. While this history has been well documented by historians, anthropologists, and legal scholars, non-Native education practitioners have historically paid less attention to the histories of displacement, dispossession, and deculturalization. With this in mind, it is important that those involved in education policy and practice understand the following: (1) American education finance is rooted in Indigenous land dispossessions and assimilation; (2) all stakeholders are responsible for Indian education; and (3) Indigenous people have always shaped the educational experiences of their children, and institutions of education must partner with Native nations, families, and communities moving forward.

Any explanation of this history must begin with treaties. As government-to-government agreements, treaties are living documents obligating the U.S. to uphold agreed-upon provisions for Indigenous peoples in perpetuity. U.S. treaty negotiators often used fraudulent and coercive negotiating tactics, resulting in treaties that disproportionately advantaged the U.S.[6] As a result, Henry M. Teller, Secretary of the U.S. Department of the Interior from 1882–1885, noted that education "is not a gratuity, but a debt due the Indians."[7] Today, all lands taxed for public education are Indigenous lands acquired through theft, warfare, and treaties. Land-tax-based school finance formulas are therefore inherently tied to Indigenous land dispossessions.

While a robust accounting of this history is beyond the scope of this chapter, a few key historical moments are necessary to understanding the stakes of Indian education today. First, corresponding to these land dispossessions, some of the earliest forms of federal education finance used contracts with religious missionary organizations to promote the assimilation of Indigenous people.[8] These contracts expected missionaries to provide agricultural and "moral" instruction, building on an already centuries-old legacy of forcing Indigenous people to convert to Christianity. In 1819, the U.S. Congress passed the Civilization Fund Act to contract with "capable persons of good moral character" to teach English reading and writing, math, and European-style agriculture.[9] The law, which had been passed thanks in part to the lobbying of religious organizations, formally set aside funds for such groups to assimilate Indigenous people.[10] In this way, assimilation to whiteness and to Christianity became the original foundation for Indian education, and much of what has occurred since aligns with this original mission. Despite federal assimilation efforts, many Native nations today are committing significant time and resources to teaching their own languages, histories, and cultures in their communities, both in the schools that serve their students and in community classes.

Within fifteen years of the Civilization Fund Act, the U.S. Supreme Court established two principles with significant impacts for tribal sovereignty and schools: first, that "tribes are under the protection of the federal government" and second, that "tribes hold sufficient powers of sovereignty to shield themselves from any intrusion by the states and it is the federal government's responsibility to ensure that this sovereignty is preserved."[11] These precedents are foundational to understanding the federal government's unique trust responsibility, which includes a fiduciary responsibility for Indian education. Early court rulings established that Native nations' legal authority is equal to, and not lesser than, that of the states.

In subsequent decades, settlers continued to utilize education as a powerful tool for conquest that worked alongside land dispossession to establish settler control over Indigenous lands. In the late 19th century, the federal government began to directly operate Indian schools to assimilate Native children.[12] Throughout the country, hundreds of boarding and day schools operated between the 1870s and 1970s, some of which continue today in modified form under the Bureau of Indian Education (BIE) (for more on the BIE's contemporary vision and practices, see BIE Strategic Direction 2018-2023).[13] These violent institutions prohibited Indigenous languages and cultural practices and used vocational courses to train Indigenous students to participate in the American economy at the lowest levels of the workforce.[14] Resources dedicated to this effort help paint a picture of this era—the $2,936,080 spent on the schools in 1900 when they served 21,568 students would be worth over $88 million today, or only about $4,086 per pupil for the year.[15]

School leaders and policy makers expected Native students in the schools to accept assimilation wholeheartedly, including settler practices around land and capitalism. For example, policy makers saw Native students in the schools as instruments in convincing their communities to accept the General Allotment Act of 1887 (also known as the Dawes Act), which forced many Native nations to partition their lands into individual ownership. This practice eroded tribal land bases and enabled settlers to overtake Indigenous lands. Today, the taxing of these same lands fuels education finance for public schools in communities across the U.S.

As Native nations were reckoning with the loss of land through the Dawes Act, some institutions of higher education were establishing endowments thanks to additional land tracts stolen from Indigenous people via the Morrill Act, as documented by the groundbreaking journalism of the *Land Grab Universities* project.[16] Approximately 250 Native nations lost a total of nearly 11 million acres of lands that went to fund early land grant institutions. This loss of land signified a vast financial boon for settlers (an equivalent of nearly $500 million in 2020 dollars), and it also meant the loss of homes, educational spaces, farms and hunting territories, religious spaces, and more for those dispossessed Native communities. This, too, is part of the legacy of education finance in Indian Country.

As early as the 1890s, Native students began to attend public schools (see table 52.1).[17] States protested, often on the basis that Native students were not their responsibility, resulting in multiple court challenges. As a result of these cases, states may not deny public education to Native students on the basis of race or political status as citizens of Native nations.[18] States and local school districts are therefore responsible for providing educational opportunities to Native youth, including identifying the financial resources to provide for that schooling.

Since most states rely primarily on property taxes for school revenues and may serve students living on reservation lands held in trust by the federal government (lands which cannot be taxed by the states in most cases), Congress passed the Johnson O'Malley (JOM) Act of 1934.[19] JOM initially allowed the federal

TABLE 52.1.   Landmarks in Indian Education Finance and Law for Native Students

1819   PL 15-85 Civilization Fund Act passed. The Act authorized the federal government to contract with "capable persons of good moral character" to teach European-style agriculture to adults and reading, writing, and math to children as part of the federal government's "civilization" program.

1879   The Carlisle Indian Boarding school was founded, marking federal expansion in the direct administration of Indian schools.

1924   *Piper v. Big Pine School District.* Alice Piper sued the Big Pine School District in California for denying her admission to school on the basis of being Native American. Though Big Pine School attorneys argued that serving Native students would be a financial burden to their district, the California Supreme Court held that the state must admit Native students to state-supported schools.

   PL 67-85 In the same year, the Snyder Act passed, making all Native people citizens of the United States. This later had implications for court cases about admitting Native students to state-funded public schools.

1933   *Grant v. Michaels et al.* The Montana Supreme Court ruled that states with constitutional mandates for a free public education must serve all students, including Native students, even in the presence of a nearby federal Indian school.

1934   PL 73-167 Johnson-O'Malley Act of 1934 passed. The law initially passed to allow the federal government to contract with states to provide for education, healthcare, and other needs of rural Native communities, conveying federal funds to states to compensate for the non-taxable trust lands on which many Native students live. Today, it provides funding for educational programs that meet the unique needs of Native students, including programs to revitalize Native languages and cultures. JOM funds cannot be used for a school's general infrastructural costs.[a]

1950   Impact Aid (PL 815 and PL 874) passed. It provided financial support to schools serving non-taxable federally impacted areas, including Indian trust lands, Alaska Native Settlement Claims Act lands, and lands utilized by branches of the U.S. military, as a way to compensate for the lack of property tax revenues for the school.[b]

1964   PL 88-452 The Economic Opportunity Act passed. Native students have also benefited from its programs, which include Head Start, Upward Bound, and the Indian Community Act Program.

1965   PL 89-10 Elementary and Secondary Education Act of 1965 passed. Though it did not create any grants specific to Native students, it extended Impact Aid to support local education agencies (LEAs) serving federally affected areas, including tribal lands.

1966   PL 89-750 Education Amendments of 1966 passed. The amendments addressed Native students in Bureau-operated schools. In addition, Impact Aid expanded coverage for certain previously uncovered Native students.

   In addition, the Rough Rock Demonstration School was founded on the Navajo Nation. An advancement in educational self-determination, this was the "first school to be overseen by a locally elected, all-Indian governing board, and the first to incorporate systematic instruction in the native language and culture."[c] Using funds from both the Office of Economic Opportunity (OEO) and the BIE, this school was supervised by the Demonstration in Navajo Education, Inc. board.

continues

TABLE 52.1. Continued

1967	PL 90-247 Education Amendments of 1967 passed. Its attention to disabled students included disabled Native students. These amendments also expanded operation costs for Bureau-operated schools and provided construction funds for LEAs whose students lived on federal Indian trust lands.
1970	PL 91-230 Education Amendments of 1970 passed. Under the Bilingual Act, it allowed tribal organizations to apply for grants. ESEA also created pathways for hiring teachers through the national Teacher Corps.
1972	PL 92-318 Education Amendments of 1972 passed. It included the Indian Education Act, which significantly expanded ESEA attention and funding for Native students, including through the creation of the Office of Indian Education and the National Advisory Council on Indian Education. It also included Alaska Natives under programs available to "Indians."
1974	PL 93-380 Education Amendments of 1974 passed. It allowed funding for professional development for teachers and project/program administrators working with Native youth. The amendments created fellowships for Native youth to pursue graduate and professional degrees.
	PL 93-644 Separately, the 1974 Native American Programs Act passed as part of a reauthorization of the Economic Opportunities Act, creating the Administration for Native Americans (ANA) within the Department of Health and Human Services (HHS). The ANA was authorized to advocate for Native peoples within federal programs and policies, as well as to provide funds and technical assistance for certain community projects.
1975	PL 93-638 Indian Self-Determination and Education Assistance Act of 1975 passed. Separate from ESEA, this law allowed the Department of the Interior, Department of Education, and Department of Health and Human Services to contract directly with or make grants directly to federally recognized tribes to provide services otherwise provided by these agencies.
1978	PL 95-471 The Tribally Controlled Community College Assistance Act of 1978 passed, securing stable funding for tribally controlled postsecondary educational institutions.
	PL 95-561 In addition, the Education Amendments of 1978 passed, creating funds for regional Indian education support centers. In keeping with the Indian Self-Determination and Education Assistance Act of 1975, the 1978 Amendments required that the Bureau of Indian education "facilitate Indian control for Indian affairs in all matters relating to education." It ordered a new policy for recruiting Native educators to teach in Bureau schools and expanded ESEA to cover not only the "special educational needs" of Native youth but also their "special educational or culturally related academic needs."
1980	PL 96-374 Education Amendments of 1980 passed. It created the Advisory Council on Native Hawaiian Education and ordered a study of the available federal and state funds for Native Hawaiian education programs.
1984	PL 98-511 Education Amendments of 1984 passed, including the Indian Education Amendments of 1984. These amendments required the Bureau of Indian Affairs schools to develop a fiscal accounting system for the Bureau, the Office of Indian Education, each BIA school, and any schools authorized under the Indian Self-Determination and Education Assistance Act.
1985	PL 99-89 Indian Education Technical Amendments Act of 1985 amended Title XI (Indian Education) of the Education Amendments of 1978

continues

TABLE 52.1.　Continued

1988　PL 100-297 The Augustus F. Hawkins-Robert T. Stafford Elementary and Secondary School Improvement Amendments of 1988 passed. It renewed Indian Education and Impact Aid, among other programs, and expanded grants available for serving Native students from the Department of Education. The amendments established a new title for the education of Native Hawaiians. They also created the Office of Indian Education within the Department of Education, which was ordered to establish an auditing system for at least 25% of the LEAs supported under the Indian Education Act of 1988 and to submit an annual report to Congress with its findings. The amendments authorized funds to develop tribal education departments to administer tribes' education programs. Included in the Amendments with the Tribally Controlled Schools Act of 1988, which authorized grants for operations and administrative costs associated with tribally controlled schools. "297 boards" provide oversight for the use of these funds. The amendments also authorized the convening of a White House Conference on Indian Education.

1991　PL 102-524 Native American Languages Act of 1991 passed. Separated from ESEA, it authorized the Department of Health and Human Services to administer grants to tribal governments and Native organizations for Native language revitalization programs.

1994　PL 103-382 Improving America's Schools Act (IASA) of 1994 passed, renewing ESEA. The IASA combined American Indian, Native Hawaiian, and Alaska Native education into Title IX of the ESEA. It also included the Native Hawaiian Education Act and the Alaska Native Education Equity, Support and Assistance Act.
　　　Meyers v. Board of Education. Meyers ruled that all stakeholders—federal, state, and tribal—have a responsibility to Native students and that Native students have a right to an equal educational opportunity.d

1999　PL 106-568 Omnibus Indian Advancement Act passed. Instead of authorizing new grants, it authorized the BIA to create an external non-profit organization called the American Indian Educational Foundation to raise money to support the educational advancement of students affiliated with Bureau schools.

2001　PL 107-110 No Child Left Behind Act of 2001 passed. American Indian, Native Hawaiian, and Alaska Native Education moved to Title VII.

2006　PL 109-394 Esther Martinez Native American Languages Act of 2006 passed, amended the Native American Programs Act of 1974. The Esther Martinez Act provided financial support for Native language revitalization. Esther Martinez grants are currently administered by the ANA.

2007　PL 110-134 The Improving Head Start for School Readiness Act passed, creating the National American Indian/Alaska Native Head Start Collaboration Office (NAIANHSCO). This office focused on building collaborations with stakeholders invested in early childhood programs administered by Native nations.

2014　The Obama Administration created the General Indigenous Initiative which included, among several other elements, a set of new Native Youth Community Project (NYCP) grants.e

2015　PL 114-95 Every Student Succeeds Act of 2015 passed. American Indian, Native Hawaiian, and Alaska Native education moved to Title VI, adding mandatory consultations with Native nations for the first time. Grants from 2001 were continued, and new grants provided support for programs related to sustaining language and culture.

continues

TABLE 52.1. Continued

2018	*Yazzie v. State of New Mexico* and *Martinez v. State of New Mexico* court rulings held that inadequate funding for education violated the New Mexico's constitutional mandate for a free public education as well as protections for English language learners, low-income students, and Native students. The court ordered the state legislature to create a funding and accountability plan to ensure that districts adequately prepare all students to be college and career ready.[f] PL 115-404 Johnson-O'Malley Supplemental Indian Education Modernization Act requires the Department of the Interior to annually update the number of Indian students eligible for the JOM program. the JOM program previously used student counts from 1995.[a]
2019	PL 116-101 Esther Martinez Native American Language Programs Reauthorization Act reduced the number of required enrollees for grants, and reauthorized the program through 2024.
2021	President Biden issued an Executive Order 14049 to establish the White House Initiative on Advancing Educational Equity, Excellence, and Economic Opportunity for Native Americans and Strengthening Tribal Colleges and Universities, updating the previous White House Initiative created in 2011 by Executive Order 13592.[g]

[a]Bureau of Indian Education (BIE). Johnson O'Malley. (Washington D.C., Bureau of Indian Education, 2018). Retrieved from https://www.bie.edu/JOM/
[b]US Department of Education. Office of Impact Aid Programs. (Washington D.C., US Department of Education, 2017) Retrieved from https://www2.ed.gov/about/offices/list/oese/impactaid/index.html
[c]Teresa L. McCarty, "School as Community: The Rough Rock Demonstration," *Harvard Educational Review* 59 (1989): 484–503.
[d]Baca, "Meyers v. Board of Education."
[e]More at https://obamawhitehouse.archives.gov/nativeamericans/generation-indigenous and https://genindigenous.com/
[f]Louise Martinez, et. al., v. Secretary-Designate of the New Mexico Public Education Department, No. D-101-CV-2014-00793 (State of New Mexico, County of Santa Fe, First Judicial District 2018); Wilhelmina Yazzie, et. al., v. State of New Mexico, Hannah Skandera, et. al., No. No. D-101-CV-2014-02224 (State of New Mexico, County of Santa Fe, First Judicial District 2018).
[g]The White House. Executive Order on the White House Initiative on Advancing Educational Equity, Excellence, and Economic Opportunity for Native Americans and Strengthening Tribal Colleges and Universities (Washington D.C., The White House, 2021). Retrieved from: https://www.whitehouse.gov/briefing-room/presidential-actions/2021/10/11/executive-order-on-the-white-house-initiative-on-advancing-educational-equity-excellence-and-economic-opportunity-for-native-americans-and-strengthening-tribal-colleges-and-universities/
Source: Meredith L. McCoy. Adapted from "Contextualizing ESSA: A Critical Race Theory Analysis of Settler Colonial Structures and Indigenous Agency in Federal Indian Education Policy, 1819-2018" (Dissertation, Chapel Hill, University of North Carolina at Chapel Hill, 2019). By permission.

government to contract with states to provide supplemental support for education and other services. According to the 1976 federal Task Force on Indian Education, JOM offered "federal recognition of a continuing unique responsibility for Indian education in spite of the states' legal obligation to educate Indians just as other citizens." Its major initial impact was "continuing tuition payments, which had been made to local school districts for decades by the federal government in lieu of property taxes for Indian education in public schools."[20] An amendment in 1936 broadened the parameters to allow the Secretary of the Interior to contract with "any state, school district, tribal organization, or Indian corporation." Still,

Native nations were rarely involved in decisions about how to use such funds during the early days of the JOM program.[21]

Initially, states contracting through JOM often moved the money into their general funds since regulations were unclear and there were no requirements to provide additional programming or services for Indian students. Once Impact Aid laws were introduced in the 1950s to offset the loss in property taxes for schools located near untaxable federal lands, JOM funds were supposed to support supplemental programming to meet the unique needs of Indian students. However, the practice of continuing to roll JOM monies into the general fund without supplemental services continued.[22] Native families protested throughout the 1970s to ensure the appropriate usage of federal funds.

While new regulations improved the alignment of JOM and Impact Aid funds with their stated missions, many still critique state education agencies (SEAs) and local education agencies (LEAs) for misusing money intended for Indian students. Taking money intended for Indian children without consulting tribal governments, families, or community members is a form of resource theft. In this form of neo-colonialism, educational leaders see money provided to Indians in a similar manner that settlers saw land a few generations before—free with no obligation. Adding insult to injury, this money represents what was promised to Native nations in exchange for that land.

As this historical context makes clear, educational leaders have too often pursued funding opportunities that exist to fulfill the federal trust responsibility for American Indian students without prioritizing the culturally relevant programming particular to American Indian students for which such funding was intended. Given the reality that Indigenous peoples are attending schools across all states and territories, all leaders have a responsibility to dedicate resources toward meeting the unique needs of American Indian students. Stakeholders must recognize that funding American Indian education is not simply about advocacy in multiculturalism; it is about countering historical assimilation and theft while upholding the United States' responsibilities to Native nations.

In the present moment, scholarship continues to document achievement gaps between American Indian and Alaska Native students (AI/AN) and their non-AI/AN peers, while also outlining how curricula and policy are inherently tied to power, privilege, colonialism, conquest, and cultural erasure.[23] This problem rests on all of us, whether we work in state governments, SEAs, LEAs, tribal governments, or tribal education departments and/or agencies (TEDs/ TEAs). And while many involved in education policy and practice outside of high Indian enrollment (HIE) schools may believe that Indigenous students are not 'their problem,' it is worth repeating that 93% of American Indian children attend public schools across the nation.[24] With over 600,000 Indigenous students in classrooms across the country, a figure which surpasses total enrollment numbers of many states, the vast majority of those students are attending rural, suburban, and urban public schools. Therefore, many policymakers and practitioners already serve Indigenous students without knowing it. Ignoring Indigenous students during financial decision making, even if they occupy a very small minority of enrollments, implicates leaders in the ongoing cultural erasure occurring through educational systems.

Landmarks in Indian Education Finance and Law for Native Students[25]

Table 52.1 provides an overview of select developments specifically related to law and policy changes that directly influenced tribal, federal, state, and local funding structures for serving Native students, both in terms of appropriations and in terms of admission to state schools. Table 52.1 is not exhaustive, and some politically visible landmarks related to Indian education are not included: e.g., the Indian Reorganization Act of 1934, the Problem of Indian Administration Report of 1928, the Indian Relocation program of the 1950s, and the Indian Education—A National Tragedy, A National Challenge of 1969. Table 52.1 focuses on specific education law, policy, and bureaucratic developments.

MAPPING THE CURRENT FINANCIAL LANDSCAPE ASSOCIATED WITH INDIAN EDUCATION

Having established a foundational understanding of Indian education historically, the chapter next outlines the primary funding streams, bureaucracies, and institutional perspectives in Indian Education today.

Bureau of Indian Education in the Department of the Interior

From a federal perspective, the Bureau of Indian Education (BIE) in the Department of the Interior (DOI) is the entity charged with managing federal Indian schools, and the mission of the institution has largely shifted away from its assimilationist past. The BIE is one of two federally funded school systems in the U.S., the other being in the Department of Defense (DOD). BIE serves approximately 48,000 students (7% of the Indian student population) through 183 elementary and secondary schools and/or dormitories across 23 states and 64 reservations. The states with the most schools or dorms are Arizona (54), New Mexico (44), South Dakota (22), and North Dakota (11). Of these schools, 53 are under the direct administration of the BIE; another 130 are tribally controlled under contracts through the Indian Self-Determination and Educational Assistance Act (sometimes called '638 schools' or '638 contracts') or Tribally Controlled Grant Schools Act (sometimes called '297 schools' or as having '297 grant boards'). The BIE also provides supplemental base operation funding to 33 post-secondary schools consisting of 29 Tribal Colleges and Universities (TCUs), two tribal technical colleges, and directly operates two post-secondary schools—Haskell Indian Nations University (HINU) and Southwestern Indian Polytechnic Institute (SIPI). While the BIE remains a primary institution of education across Indian Country, there persists a constant struggle for adequate funding via the federal government's upholding of its fiduciary responsibilities, particularly regarding resources and upkeep with facilities.[26] Overall, the BIE's enacted budget in 2021 was $1,237,369,000 with 2,769 FTEs.[27]

Funding for BIE elementary and secondary schools is determined by formulas, special needs, or specific appropriations. The Indian School Equalization Program (ISEP) provides base funding according to a formula that computes an average daily membership (ADM) and weighted student units (WSUs) for characteristics such as grade level, presence of dormitories, special education needs, small schools with enrollments of less than 100 students, and schools with gifted and talented and language development programs.[28] The U.S. Congress sets the total available amount, and in Fiscal Year 2021, the BIE's distribution through ISEP formula funds, including ISEP program adjustments, was $432,423,000 which per WSU was $6,084.21 based on 69,453.52 WSUs.[29]

Beyond ISEP in FY 2021, the BIE is responsible for administering other elementary and secondary school appropriated funds for early child and family development ($21,000,000), education program enhancements ($14,451,000), student transportation ($58,143,000), tribal grant support costs ($86,884,000), and some funding that goes to tribal education departments ($5,000,000). Additionally, Johnson-O'Malley (JOM) Assistance Grants ($21,140,000) are allocated by the BIA to tribes and the BIE to public schools, and the 2018 passage of the JOM Modernization Act (PL 115-404) unlocked a student count that drove JOM funding which had been frozen at 1995 levels.

Furthermore, the FY 2021 BIE budget also included funds for TCUs ($76,510,000), technical colleges ($8,151,000), HINU and SIPI ($26,258,000). Other higher education expenditures include funds to supplement six TCU budgets, various post-secondary scholarships and adult education programs totaling $42,495,000. BIE appropriations for facilities operations and maintenance was $131,784,000, an amount allocated to elementary and secondary schools, HINU, and SIPI per a facilities formula. In 2021, the BIE funded school facilities containing about 23.5 million gross square feet. Additionally, the BIE enacted $264,277,000 in FY 2021 towards education construction for new schools, facilities, employee housing, and affiliated repairs and improvements. Regarding COVID relief funding, the BIE received $665,819,923 in CARES Act funds, and $850,000,000 from the American Rescue Plan.

In addition to the BIE-appropriated funds, in FY 2021-22 the BIE received about $227,123,320 from the Department of Education's appropriations for elementary and secondary schools that BIE allocates to schools based on student ADM and special needs. The majority of funds are allocated to schools by formula. Overall, it is estimated that of the federal funding that feeds BIE-funded schools, the BIE provides about 76%, while the US Department of Education provides about 22%.[30]

The U.S. Department of Education and Department of Health and Human Services

Indian education financing can be found across several federal offices outside of the BIE. Most notably, the U.S. Department of Education (ED) and the Department of Health and Human Services (HHS) also provides financing and oversight for Indian education. Overall, a variety of ED funding mechanisms have unique associations with Indian education, most of which primarily go to state public schools, with less than a quarter going to the BIE through set-asides. According to a report by the Congressional Research Service, Indian education programming can be linked to the following:

- Titles I-A: Grants to LEAs
- Title I-B: State Assessment Grants
- Title II-A: Supporting Effective Instruction
- Title III-A: English Language Acquisition
- Title IV-B: 21st Century Community Learning Centers
- Title VI-A: Indian Education Programs
  - Part 1: Grants to local education agencies
  - Part 2: Special Programs for Indian Children
  - Part 3: National Activities
- Title VI-C: Alaska Native Education Equity
- Title VII: Impact Aid
- IDEA Part B: Special Education Grants to States
- IDEA Part C: Early Intervention for Infants and Toddlers with Disabilities
- MHVAA: Education for Homeless Children and Youths
- Perkins Native American Career and Technical Education Program (NACTEP).[31]

In FY 2020, ED spent almost $1.3 billion on Indian Elementary-Secondary Education Programs, which has seen an 18% increase from FY2011 to FY2020. Included in the FY 2020 budget were $247,960,000 in BIE set-asides, 19% of the $1.3 billion. Of this amount, Impact Aid is the largest single funding mechanism in ED related to Indian education which accounted for about 59% ($766,586,000).[32] However, as described by the Congressional Research Service, "there is no requirement that the funds be used specifically or preferentially for the education of Indian students" and "there is also a requirement that the LEA consult with the parents and tribes of children who reside on 'Indian lands' concerning their education and to ensure that these children receive equal education opportunities."[33] Overall, as described below, consultation is becoming increasingly important in our education landscape.

Within ED, the Office of Indian Education (OIE; found in the Office of Elementary and Secondary Education) administers various grant programs, the most visible being the Title VI-A formula grants that are often referenced generically as

'Indian Ed.' However, Title VI-A has three subparts for which the OIE is responsible (FY 2021, totaling $181,239,000)): 1) Grants to local education agencies ($105,381,000), 2) Special programs for Indian Children ($67,993,000), and 3) National Activities ($7,365,000).[34] These subparts and their affiliated programs offer a mixture of formula and demonstration grants which are outlined in Table 52.2 at the end of this chapter, but it should be noted that the OIE also responsible for paying for programs that do not necessarily go straight to students, and they do not necessarily have direct oversight. As an example in part 3, National Activities, they are responsible for supporting the National Advisory Council on Indian Education, as well as the National Indian Education Study (ancillary to NAEP). Additionally, as part of the American Rescue Plan Act of 2021 (Section 110066[1]), OIE was able to award one-time funds totaling $20 million directly to 15 Tribal Education Agencies (TEAs) for activities for their American Indian Resilience in Education (AIRE) program.[35] This was historic, considering it was a direct funding of TEAs in a quantity never done before (more on this below).

HHS also plays a role in financing Indian Education. The Administration for Native Americans (ANA), which is under the Administration for Children and Families (ACF), manages grants related to Indigenous language education and preservation, such as the Esther Martinez Immersion and Native Language Preservation and Maintenance (P&M) programs, among other programs.[36] HHS also administers Head Start and Early Head Start grants to through the Office of Head Start (OHS), also under ACF, which funds programs to Native nations for early childhood education. In OHS, Region XI is specifically associated with Head Start programming for federally recognized Native nations or tribal organizations, as well as some tribal colleges and Alaska corporations. Overall, they serves around 20,000 students through over 140 programs across 26 states, with the majority of the students being AI/AN.[37] The National American Indian and Alaska Native Head Start Collaboration Office supports these programs through a contract with OHS.[38] Additionally, as part of the COVID relief package, ANA awarded $20 million in funding to 210 recipients of the Native Language Preservation and Maintenance Emergency grant as part of the American Rescue Plan Act of 2021.[39]Table 52.2 later provides more detail related to these Indian education funding streams in HHS.

Tribal Education Departments/Agencies: A Growing Role

Tribal Education Departments (TEDs), also referred to as Tribal Education Agencies (TEAs), are the arms of tribal governments responsible for executing the educational agenda for Native nations. As Bowers outlined in a report for the Tribal Education Department's National Assembly (TEDNA), more than 200 of the 574 federally recognized tribes have TEDs, and 32 different states have TEDs operating within their borders.[40] The size and capacities of these institutions can vary widely, along with roles and responsibilities, with some TEDs taking on administrative oversight of schools (i.e., BIE schools under '638 contracts') and others running a few federally funded programs for their citizens.[41] Their responsibilities range from early childhood to adult education contexts. Furthermore, while some TEDs have sufficient funds acquired through economic enterprises and tribal LLCs which allow them to operate with a large staff of paid employees, many function with a singular employee or handful of staff members tasked with administering federal programs such as JOM, higher education scholarships, Head Start, and more.

To illustrate this diversity, preliminary data from a 2021 nationwide TEDNA survey completed by 34 TED leaders, while not generalizable and not representative of the majority of tribal governments, gives us a glimpse into TED operations. Of the 34 TEDs represented, their Native nations serve a total of 239,647 citizens ranging from 300 to 36,000, averaging 7,048 total enrollment per nation. Additionally, the sum of their 34 budgets totaled $95,748,000, with the highest being $26,000,000; yet, 25 of the 34 had a budget of $1,000,000 or less, indicating that smaller TED budgets are much more common that the larger multi-million dollar budgets. As an example, two small tribes who responded indicated that they did not have an official TED and/or recently dissolved their education programming. Additionally, these TEDs collectively employed 710 FTE (highest at 212, 20 of the 34 indicating 5 or fewer) and just under half of their budgets are derived from revenues generated by tribal enterprise, and the other half coming from federal programs, with some instances of unique funding through states or other sources.[42] Given this diversity, it would be illogical to make generalizations about TEDs across Native nations. Remembering that there are over 200 TEDs across the US out of 574 nations, a figure which has not been updated in over a decade; these figures are only a glimpse of education funding through Native nations. Furthermore, in the survey many of the TEDs indicated that while they were their nation's "Education Department" (or similar title), they did not represent other entities such as their nation's "language department," or "cultural center," which means those additional budgets, FTEs, and programs are not factored into these numbers.

While the U.S. Congress has authorized the direct funding of TEDs as a discretionary program since FY 1989, no appropriations were made until the Obama administration's STEP and TED programs in 2015, despite many requests from prominent organizations representing Indian Country.[43] The STEP program, administered through the U.S. Department of Education's Office of Indian Education, is designed to promote collaboration between TEDs/TEAs, SEAs, and LEAs, as well as to build capacity for TEDs/TEAs to conduct certain administrative functions.[44] This was first piloted in 2012–2015, and the first full round of funding ($1,766,232) was granted to five communities across Idaho, Montana and Oklahoma for 2015–2019. Four additional awards were granted starting in 2019 to communities in Massachusetts, Virginia, Alaska, and California.[45] The TED program, which is administered out of the BIE, is intended to also build TEDs' capacities to take on a more direct role in the education of their youth, particularly in communities with BIE schools. In 2015, the TED program provided $700,000 to four Native nations with BIE schools.[46]

While often left out of conversations about funding in Indian Education, TEDs are beginning to gain more attention as an active player in the field. New ESSA requirements mandate that certain LEAs and SEAs engage in consultations with Native nations to receive funding. TEDs can provide a formal institution to potentially address consultation requirements and assert the nation's views on how federal Indian Education dollars are spent with their students.[47] Since TEDs vary widely in their capacities to take on administrative responsibilities and programming, education practitioners will need to learn about the specific TED programming or other tribal government offices operating near their locales. In this new ESSA landscape, it is imperative that leaders recognize that TEDs are a manifestation of tribal sovereignty and even though current law and policy tends to still prioritize LEAs and SEAs, TEDs have an important role to play.[48] TEDs have an interest in advocating for their tribal citizens in whatever schools they attend, whether they be located in rural (66%) or urban and suburban school settings (33%) and whether they attend federal Bureau of Indian Education schools (7%) or general public schools (93%).[49]

Given the reality that over 90% of American Indian students attend public schools, TED partnerships have become an important part of the education landscape.[50] There are many cases in which TEDs have offered substantial resources to programs and employees that are of direct benefit to LEAs serving their citizens. For example, the Osage Nation of Oklahoma has no existing K–12 BIE school within the local community, and using dollars raised through Osage Nation enterprises they pay to run their own Birth-6th grade Immersion school, but also pay for language teachers, tribal education advocates, and tutors, among other initiatives, to work among the rural LEAs operating within reservation boundaries. Furthermore, they spearheaded a partnership with Tulsa Community College that allows Osage and non-Osage high school juniors and seniors across several rural LEAs to take college level coursework in Osage Nation facilities. This illustrates how fostering productive partnerships can help TEDs, LEAs, and SEAs work together to dedicate resources toward shared goals that benefit all students. Therefore, SEAs and LEAs would be wise to make sure they are building strong relationships with TEDs. Such relationships must respect the unique sociocultural needs of American Indian students and the voices of Native nations. For helpful guides on how to build such relationships, see the National Indian Education Association's *Building Relationships with Tribes* series.[51]

State-Tribal Relationships

Given the government-to-government relationship between states and Native nations, there are a variety of ways that partnerships are developed and formalized between these two political entities. For example, the STEP program mentioned above is an example of a grant program that enhances collaboration between

TED/TEAs, SEAs, and LEAs. Some broader considerations regarding state-tribal partnerships are outlined in the next paragraphs.

Native nations have legal authority that is equal to and not lesser than that of the states. As a result, these nations maintain rights to self-governance and economic development. One mechanism for economic development in Native communities is gaming, though gaming is also constrained by laws about what is permissible within a given state. After *California v. Cabazon Band of Mission Indians* affirmed Native nations' rights to engage in many types of gaming (referred to under the law as Class I and Class II gaming), the Indian Gaming Regulatory Act of 1988 (IGRA) created a regulatory structure for gaming in Indian Country.[52] This structure established pathways for state-tribal compacts for Class III gaming and statutorily protected Indian gaming as a way for Native nations to promote self-sufficiency through economic development. Native nations use gaming as a means for generating revenue for social services, including education. As mentioned previously, of the 34 TEAs/TEDs surveyed in the 2021 TEDNA report, just under half of their budgets were derived from funds generated by their respective enterprise efforts—with very few instances of state funding of Native themed programs in education. Since the 1990s, there have been hundreds of state-tribal gaming compacts and agreements signed across 27 states, many of which are tied to education financing for tribal governments and state governments alike.[53] Each of these compacts is generated in a specific sociocultural, economic, and political environment; given the diversity of compacts, this mechanism for generating revenue for states and Native nations does not operate uniformly across the country. Therefore, it is important to keep in mind that every state-tribal gaming context is different.

As one example, Native nations in Arizona contributed $48,384,939 to the Instructional Improvement Fund, which was established by A.R.S 15-979 to be used by school districts for classroom size reduction, teacher salary raises, dropout prevention, and instructional improvement. The cumulative contributions from Arizona's Native nations to the Instructional Improvement fund through FY 2021 is $759,289,122, with additional contributions going towards emergency services, wildlife conservation, state tourism, and support for local governments.[54]

As another example, the state of Oklahoma is unique because it has 39 Native nations within its boundaries, more than any other state in the Nation. Of those nations, 35 have signed gaming compacts with the state. Three-fourths of those nations engaged in gaming commit their revenue to governmental services such as education, as well as economic and community development, and only a quarter of those nations distribute per-capita payments (and those that do still pay federal income tax on those payments).[55] In FY 2021, Native nations in Oklahoma collected over $2.2 billion in gaming revenue, and as per state-tribal gaming compacts, $163 million went to the state of Oklahoma through exclusivity fees, and which are based on a sliding scale associated with Class III games and table games. This was a 32% increase over the previous year. Of that revenue,

$143.2 million went to the Education Reform Revolving Fund (1017 Fund). Note that this is over $90 million higher than that of Arizona, showing the disparate ways this unfolds in different states Overall, from 2005-2021 the 1017 fund has received $1.6 Billion from these exclusivity fees generated from tribal gaming.[56] While this money is intended to be a supplemental source of education funds, critics of Oklahoma's funding model claim the state uses this money to fill an ongoing shortfall to maintain funding levels without increasing revenues.

Education is one of many social services supported by Native nations, and just as state governments debate education finance and fiscal management, tribal governments also have to make hard decisions about what to do with limited resources. From the perspective of Native nations, gaming and other enterprises are potential mechanisms to help expand funding for education programming. Still, it is important to note that gaming remains controversial in many contexts, and not all tribal nations engage in gaming, nor is its sustainability certain. Of those that do, many do not turn a significant profit. For that reason, it would be inaccurate to think that the existence of a tribal casino equates to lucrative funding for education. It would also be inaccurate to think that just because a Native nation reaches a degree of self-sufficiency in the context of educational programming, that LEAs, SEAs, and the federal government shed their responsibility for providing appropriate educational funding to American Indians.

Among the hundreds of state-tribal gaming compacts that impact education financing, some Native nations and states have recently begun engaging in state-tribal compacts and singing memoranda of understanding (MOUs) specific to education outside the context of gaming. In 2013, the Washington state legislature passed the Engrossed Second Substitute House Bill (E2 SHB) 1154, which paved the way for state-tribal education compact schools (STECs), of which there are now seven in the state. The bill authorized state-tribal education compacts between the Superintendent of Public Instruction and Native nations, allowing schools covered by the compacts to work under modified regulations for staffing, standards, funding, admissions, and accountability.[57] As another example, the state of Wisconsin's Executive Order 39, issued in 2004, recognizes the sovereignty of the 11 Native nations within the state and laid a foundation for encouraging consultation and cooperation between tribes and the state.[58] This led to development of the Wisconsin State-Tribal Consultation Initiative, and now almost every department in Wisconsin's executive branch has created state-tribal consultation policies with input from local Native nations. Additionally, Wisconsin's independent agency overseeing education, the Department of Public Instruction (DPI) headed by an independently elected state constitutional officer, has begun the process of building MOUs with local Native nations that are specific to fostering collaboration and resource sharing for the purpose of improving the quality of educational services provided by both entities. According to DPI, the Lac du Flambeau Band of Lake Superior Chippewas was the first to formalize an MOU with the Wisconsin DPI, followed by the Bad River Band of Lake Superior Chippewas, the Oneida Nation, and the Red Cliff Band of Lake Superior Chippewas.[59] The DPI has also created a guide to help local school districts establish their own MOUs with Native nations.

Beyond compacts and MOUs, some states have mandated systemic changes for the improvement of education for and about American Indians. Wisconsin appropriated funding for the DPI American Indian Studies Program in its 1989–1991 biennial budget bill (referenced as Wisconsin Act 31). This program has also helped develop several state statutes that mandate more appropriate American Indian curricular content in schools and teacher training.[60] The act of developing MOUs between the Wisconsin DPI and Native nations are a way to help all parties work together to meet these state statutes, federal law, and be proactive in addressing the educational needs of school-aged students in Native nations. Furthermore, Washington's *Since Time Immemorial* initiative and Montana's *Indian Education for All* programming are also positive steps toward addressing the ongoing ways in which curricula across the country marginalize and erase American Indian worldviews.[61] It should be acknowledged that while these developments are applauded throughout Indian Country, they address such deep-seated systemic issues that additional resources are needed at all levels of systems to help support the transition in the form of professional development, institutional liaisons, educator training, travel, new positions, development of new coursework, new materials, and so on.

Regarding the different ways SEAs approach funding Indian education initiatives, a report from the National Congress of American Indians (NCAI) that surveyed states with federally recognized nations within their borders (37 surveyed with 28 respondents) showed that a third of the states that responded allocate resources for Native American education curricula. Additionally, 18 of the 28 respondents indicated they have full or part-time staff in their SEA dedicated to Indian education, with Hawaii having the most (16 FTE). Overall, seven states have at least 2 FTE, and the remaining states have 1.5 FTE or less.[62] However, it should be noted that some of these positions might be more of a reflection of federal grants for Indian education funneling through SEAs, rather than the state allocating the money.

All these developments demonstrate the importance of building strong relationships between states and Native nations.

Taxes and Indian Land Ownership

Understanding that many education finance systems are rooted in property taxes, the laws and policies surrounding Indian land ownership and taxing are relevant to education finance for public schools serving Native children on Indian land. The degree to which education financing is tied to the power of taxation impacts Indian education since current laws "prohibit tribal governments from taxing and limits bonding against Indian lands" which results in "inadequate buildings and facilities for schools that serve Native students."[63] The federal government's role in education services for Native students helps compensate for this lack of revenue, yet schools relying primarily on federal funds for operation are consistently underfunded. There are three primary types of ownership associated with Indian land—restricted fee land, trust land, and fee simple.[64] Even on Indian trust land, where the Native nation has jurisdiction, there are still restrictions related to taxation since the title is held by the Secretary of the Interior. Due to these regulations, as NCAI has observed, "tribal governments lack parity with states, local governments, and the federal government in exercising taxing authority. For example, tribes are unable to levy property taxes because of the trust status of their land, and they generally do not levy income taxes on tribal members."[65] In addition, many reservations face high rates of poverty and lack sufficient opportunities for employment, leaving tribes "unable to establish a strong tax base structured around the property taxes and income taxes typically found at the local state government level."[66] Where tribes are able to generate revenue through taxes, these are often inadequate to support the wide array of government services the tribe must provide.

The political consequences of tax systems vary widely across all Native nations, considering that each locale varies in terms of population size, poverty, wealth, economic development, and geographic footprint. It is therefore not realistic for some nations to aggressively pursue other forms of taxing for the purpose of education even if they have the power to do so.

These land and taxation laws play an important role in the financing of SEAs and LEAs located on or near tribal communities and serving American Indian students. While programs such as Impact Aid help offset the costs associated with educating Indian students attending these public schools (without requirements to spend on Indian education programming), this can generate political tensions, particularly when tribal nations pursue land buyback efforts to reclaim land lost during allotment. In these cases, such actions are seen as a threat to local education financing. Some communities use Payment in Lieu of Taxes (PILT) which can "help local governments carry out such vital services as firefighting and police protection, construction of public schools and roads, and search-and-rescue operations." These are payments made for tax exempt lands as "one of the ways the Federal Government can fulfill its role of being a good neighbor to local communities."[67]

It should also be noted there are 229 nations in Alaska and that the Alaska Native Claims and Settlement Act of 1971 (ANCSA) created a different framework than the land into trust process used for nations in the 'lower 48.' As the National Congress of American Indians describes, "Originally, ANCSA allotted 40 million acres of land, divided among 12 [now 13] for-profit regional Native corporations and 220 village corporations, established to manage Alaska Native lands and resources."[68] While Indigenous nations of Alaska operate in these frameworks, Native Hawaiians also operate in unique circumstances compared to Native nations found within the contiguous 48 states.[69] Additionally, there are several Native nations that operate under the status of state recognition, and this status also comes with unique circumstances regarding land ownership, jurisdiction, and taxation.

Primary Funding Streams for Education across Indian Country

Table 52.2 lists funding streams associated with Indian education. The list is not exhaustive, but these represent some of the most common programs and bureaucracies associated with funding education across Indian Country via SEAs, LEAs, TEDs/TEAs, and the federal government. When viewing the table, it is emphasized that with such a large percentage of American Indian students attending public schools (93%), state funding remains one of the primary funding streams for the education of Native students. With BIE schools then carrying approximately 7% of Native student enrollment, this firmly establishes public schools and federal BIE schools as the primary institutions of education for Indian Country. Furthermore, it is acknowledged that with over 570 federally recognized Native nations and the growth of TEAs/TEDs discussed previously, the Native Nations are beginning to take a more active role and should be regarded as an important part of the bureaucratic and financial landscape of Indian education; they are included here, though not all Native nations currently have TEAs/TEDs as part of their governance systems. The remainder of Table 52.2 highlights a variety of federal programs associated with Indian education, all of which have different policies and/or eligibilities. Education leaders should *always* be cognizant of their unique local contexts at the intersection of LEAs, SEAs, and Native nations.

Additionally, federal grants increasingly require input from Native nations as a way to support Indigenous rights to self-determination regarding Indian education funds. Depending on local capacities and geographies, there are also many programs that offer opportunities to engage in formal consortia partnerships to attain eligibility. A caution must be given to non-Indian educators exploring funding opportunities with Indian communities: Native communities often receive requests to partner with non-Indian institutions for grants, and this is completely acceptable. However, too often these institutions prioritize their reputation and acquisition of funds over the needs and voices of Indian institutions and stakeholders, which is not an ideal foundation on which to build collaborative and productive partnerships. Often, these kinds of partnerships create an illusion, on paper, that a productive two-way partnership is in place when in reality it is heavily one-sided. Not all partnerships operate this way, but given the long history of exploitative relationships, all stakeholders will need to demonstrate a commitment to long-term, meaningful partnerships. It is therefore recommended that non-Indian institutions explore ways to engage in ongoing and substantive partnership building with Indian institutions and their stakeholders beyond grants.

CONCLUSION

Indian education is a complex bureaucratic network of overlapping sovereignties, jurisdictions, and responsibilities that rests on an important legal foundation—the federal trust responsibility. This network places responsibility on all institutions of education that serve Indian students, even when enrollments are a small percentage of the student body. While current stakeholders are not personally responsible for the traumatic histories inflicted on Indigenous peoples through conquest, land dispossessions, and education, these are inherited legal systems and political histories whose legacies must be addressed. Positive change can be jointly achieved by ensuring that Native nations have a stronger voice in programming, curricula, and spending; by building ongoing collaborations that center on Indigenous perspectives; and by adequately funding educational systems that support Native nations and Native students.

TABLE 52.2. Primary Funding Streams and Bureaucracies Associated with P–12 Education Across Indian Country

Funding Stream	Details	Eligible Recipients
State Funding Formulas		
Funding formulas found across all 50 states	With over 90% of American Indian students attending public schools, state laws and policies associated with school funding are essential bureaucratic components to funding the education of American Indian education. Many of the grants found below are intended to supplement this funding.	LEAs and other institutions eligible for funding according to state laws and policies.
Native Nations and Tribal Education Departments/Agencies (TEDs/TEAs)		
Funding opportunities through and with Tribal Nations	With over 570 federally recognized Native nations, these governments are an essential piece of the bureaucratic landscape in terms of funding for Indian Education. While their make-up and capacities vary widely, many Native nations administer education programs with funds raised through local enterprise, or through federal grants (many listed below). Even when not administering programs directly, partnerships through consortia agreements and/or consultation with Native nations are requirements for various grants and policies found across ESSA.	Most likely recipients are citizens of each Native nation, although non-Natives and/or other enrolled Natives often benefit from programs administered through Native nations.
Bureau of Indian Education (BIE), U.S. Department of the Interior		
Indian School Equalization Program (ISEP)	Formula that distributes funds to BIE schools and dormitories for basic operation costs.	BIE operated schools, and tribally operated schools that are administered by tribes or tribal organizations under a PL 93-638 contract or PL 100-297 grant.
Johnson O'Malley (JOM)	The JOM program provides supplemental education funds to meet the unique needs of eligible Indian students; funding is on a formula-basis. A local Indian Education Committee must be involved in the administration of this program.	Any state, school district, tribal organization, Indian corporation, or previously private BIE funded school with eligible AI/AN children.
TED Program	A grant program to promote administrative capacity building for Native nations with BIE schools. Last issued in 2015a, with anticipated awards available again in 2022.	TEAs with BIE funded supply in their community may apply.
Office of Indian Education (OIE), Office of Elementary and Secondary Education in U.S. Department of Education		
	The JOM program provides supplemental education funds to meet the unique needs of eligible Indian students; funding is on a formula-basis. A local Indian Education Committee must be involved in the administration of this program.	

Note: There are more funding mechanisms associated with Indian Education across various title programs listed earlier in this chapter, but these represent what tends to be the most visible Indian education funding and programming in U.S. Department of Education

Program	Description	Eligibility
Title VI-A Part 1: Grant to Local Education Agencies (Formula Grants)	Formerly Title VII under No Child Left Behind Formula grant designed to help schools that serve American Indian students to meet their unique cultural, language, and education needs. New under ESSA: Mandatory consultations with Native nations or Indian organizations may apply depending on AI/AN enrollment percentages, size of program, and distance from Native nations.[b] As authorized by section 6116 of ESEA as amended by ESSA	LEAs with a threshold of Indian student enrollment are the primary recipients (with applicable exemptions), eligible BIE funded schools, Indian Tribes, Indian Organizations, or Indian Community Based Organizations (ICBOs).[c]
Title VI-A Part 2: Special Programs for Indian Children (Demonstration Grants)	Discretionary demonstration grant program with a focus on improving achievement for AI/AN students. Formerly known as Native Youth Community Projects, but for FY 2020 posted as Accessing Choice in Education (ACE). Awarded to projects that expand choice in education by enabling a tribe, or the grantee and it's tribal partner, to "to select a project focus that meets the needs of their students, and enabling parents of Indian students, or the students, to choose education services by selecting the specific service and provider desired."[d]	SEAs, LEAs, Indian tribes, Indian organizations, federally supported elementary and secondary schools for Indian students, and Indian institutions, including Indian IHEs, or a consortium of such institutions may apply.[d]
	Professional development grants for specialized American Indian educator training programs are also included under Title VI Part 2.	Institutions of Higher Education (IHEs) and Tribal Colleges and Universities (TCUs), and encourage consortium agreements with Native nations when appropriate.
Title VI-A Part 3: National Activities	Native American Language Program (NAL@ED): Discretionary grant program intended to support Indigenous language maintenance and revitalization in schools as envisioned by the Native American Languages Act of 1990.	Indian tribes, TCUs, TEAs, LEAs, BIE-funded schools, Alaska Native Regional Corporation, and non-profits (tribal, Alaska Native, Native Hawaiian, or other); a nontribal for-profit organization may apply.[e]
	State-Tribal Education Partnership Program (STEP): Discretionary/competitive grant program intended to promote collaboration among SEAs, LEAs, and TEAs and build capacity for TEAs to take on some administrative responsibilities.	TEAs, or a consortium of TEAs, in partnership with SEAs and LEAs may apply.f
	Support for the National Advisory Council on Indian Education and the National Indian Education Study	

(continues)

TABLE 52.2. Continued

Administration for Native Americans (ANA),[g] Office of the Administration for Children and Families in U.S. Department of Health and Human Services

Funding Stream	Details	Eligible Recipients
Native Languages Preservation and Maintenance (P&M)	Competitive grant program intended to support the development and implementation of curriculum and education projects that enhance Native languages preservation and restoration efforts in Native communities.[h]	Federally recognized tribes as recognized by the BIA; incorporated non-federally recognized tribes; incorporated state-recognized tribes; consortia of Indian tribes; incorporated non-profit multi- purpose community-based Indian organizations; Urban Indian centers; Alaska Native villages as defined in the ANCSA and/or non-profit village consortia; incorporated non-profit Alaska Native multipurpose, community-based organizations; non-profit Alaska Native Regional Corporations/ Associations in Alaska with village-specific projects; non-profit Alaska with village-specific projects; non-profit Alaska Native Regional Corporations/ Associations in Alaska with village-specific projects; non-profit Alaska native community entitles or tribal governing bodies (Indian Reorganization Act or Traditional Councils) as recognized by the BIA; Public and non-profit private agencies serving Native Hawaiians; national or regional incorporated non-profit Native American organizations with native American community-specific objectives; public and non-profit private agencies serving native peoples from Guam, American Samoa, or the Commonwealth of the Northern Mariana Islands; Tribal colleges and Universities, and colleges and universities located in Hawaii, Guam, American Samoa, and/or the Commonwealth of the Northern Mariana Islands that serve Native American Pacific Islanders.[i]
Esther Martinez Immersion	Competitive grant program focused on supporting community-driven Native American language revitalization projects. Funding supports three-year projects being implemented by Native American Language Nests and Survival Schools.[j]	
Native Youth Initiative for Leadership, Empowerment, and Development (I-LEAD)	Competitive grant program intended to "support local community projects that foster Native youth resiliency, and to empower Native youth across four broad domains of activity: (1) Native youth leading (leadership development), (2) Native youth connecting (building positive identity, community connection, and social-emotional health), (3) Native youth learning (education success), and (4) Native youth working (workforce readiness)."[k] While there are currently grantees operating these programs, there are no I-LEAD competitions for FY 2018.	

Office of Head Starts (OHS),I Office of the Administration for Children and Families (ACF) in U.S. Department of Health and Human Services (HHS)

Head Start and Early Head Start Programs	Provides early childhood services to low-income children through grants funded and administered through the Office of Head Start (OHS), which serves 156 federally recognized tribes with AI/AN Head Start and Early Head Start programs in 26 different states. Region XI funds Head Start grant programs to federally recognized tribal nations. The National American Indian and Alaska Native Head Start Collaboration Office (NAIANHSCO) supports this work across all 26 states, but it funded through OHS by contract.	Federally recognized tribal nations

Source: Original table from authors.

a Office of the Assistant Secretary–Indian Affairs, "Eight Tribes Receive Nearly $2.5 Million in Grants." (November 5, 2015).

b Generally, LEAs with 50% or more Native students in their student population or who have received more than $40,000 in Title VI Indian Education funds must consult with the Native nations of the students they serve. See National Indian Education Association, "Building Relationships with Tribes."

c U.S. Department of Education, "Indian Education Formula Grants (Formula Grants)," U.S. Department of Education, 2022, https://oese.ed.gov/offices/office-of-indian-education/indian-education-formula-grants/

d U.S. Department of Education, "Demonstration Grants for Indian Children," 2022, https://oese.ed.gov/offices/office-of-indian-education/demonstration-grants-for-indian-children/

e U.S. Department of Education, "Native American Language Grant (NAL@ED)," U.S. Department of Education, 2022, https://oese.ed.gov/offices/office-of-indian-education/native-american-language-program/

f U.S. Department of Education, "State Tribal Education Partnership (STEP)." U.S. Department of Education, 2022, https://oese.ed.gov/offices/office-of-indian-education/state-tribal-education-partnership-step/

g Carmelia Strickland (Director, Division of Program Operations, Administration for Native Americans) contributed to the content of this section (Personal Communication, Dec. 18, 2018) GETTING UPDATED CONFIRMATION

h Administration for Native Americans, "About Native Languages."

i 42 USC Sec 2991b and 45 CFR Sec 1336.33

j Ibid.

k Administration for Native Americans, "SEDS Special Program Areas."

I Angie Godfrey (Region XI Program Manager, Office of Head Start) contributed to the content of this section (Personal communication, Dec. 18, 2018)

ENDNOTES

[1] Following the National Congress of American Indians (NCAI), a national Indian advocacy organization, we use the term "Indian Country" in a broader sense to refer to "tribal governments, Native communities, cultures, and peoples," with an understanding that Indian education involves stakeholders both inside and outside of Native nations and reservations. "Indian Country" (both capitalized) differs from "Indian country," a legal term that describes "the area over which the federal government and tribes exercise primary jurisdiction" and refers narrowly to specific territories, lands, and governments. See National Congress of American Indians, "Tribal Nations and the United States: An Introduction" (Washington, D.C.: National Congress of American Indians, n.d.), http://www.ncai.org/resources/ncai_publications/tribal-nations-and-the-united-states-an-introduction. Throughout this chapter, we use Native and Indigenous interchangeably to refer to students and nations. We use Indian, American Indian, or tribal primarily where such terms are associated with formal laws, policies, and government offices. These general terms facilitate a discussion of policy and finance across multiple settings; where possible, however, it is important to use the specific names each individual or nation prefers.

[2] The authors want to thank those who provided insights for this chapter (1st and 2nd editions): Jacob Tsotigh, formerly with the National Indian Education Association; Cornel Pewewardy, Professor Emeritus, Portland State University; Joe Herrin and Vanda Cervantes, Bureau of Indian Education; Julian Guerrero, Office of Indian Education; David O'Connor, American Indian Studies Program, Wisconsin Department of Public Instruction; Carmelia Strickland, Administration for Native Americans; Angie Godfrey and Todd Lertjuntharangool, Office of Head Start.

[3] National Indian Education Association, "NIEA Federal Appropriations Priorities: The Federal Trust Responsibility to Native Education" (Washington, D.C., 2022), https://static1.squarespace.com/static/5cffbf319973d7000185377f/t/604c59df8c95fb7a4573f8cc/1615616482890/NIEA+-FY+2022+Budget+Request.pdf.

[4] National Indian Education Association, "Native Nations and American Schools: The History of Natives in the American Education System" (Washington, D.C.: National Indian Education Association, n.d.).

[5] National Congress of American Indians, "Tribal Nations and the United States: An Introduction."

[6] Martin Case, The Relentless Business of Treaties: How Indigenous Land Became U.S. Property (Minneapolis: Minnesota Historical Society Press, 2018); Vine Deloria and Clifford M. Lytle, American Indians, American Justice (Austin: University of Texas Press, 1983); Melody L. McCoy, The Evolution of Tribal Sovereignty over Education in Federal Law since 1965 (Boulder: Native American Rights Fund, 2005), http://www.narf.org/wordpress/wp-content/uploads/2015/01/gold.pdf.

[7] Helen Maynor Scheirbeck et al., "Report on Indian Education; Task Force Five: Indian Education; Final Report to the American Indian Policy Review Commission" (Washington, D.C.: Government Printing Office, 1976), 67.

[8] Margaret Connell Szasz, Education and the American Indian: The Road to Self-Determination since 1928, 3rd ed., rev.enl. (Albuquerque, N.M.: University of New Mexico Press, 1999).

[9] "Civilization Fund Act of 1819," Pub. L. No. 15–85, 3 Stat. 516 (1819).

[10] James E. Seelye, Jr. and Steven A. Littleton, eds., Voices of the American Indian Experience (Santa Barbara, California: Greenwood, 2013).

[11] Deloria and Lytle. American Indians, American Justice. 32. See also: Johnson v. M'Intosh, 21 U.S. 543 (Supreme Court of the United States 1823); Cherokee Nation v. Georgia, 30 U.S. 1 (1831); Worcester v. Georgia, 31 U.S. 515 (Supreme Court of the United States 1832).

[12] David Adams, Education for Extinction: American Indians and the Boarding School Experience, 1875-1928 (Lawrence: University Press of Kansas, 1995), 52.

[13] US Department of Interior, "Bureau of Indian Education Strategic Direction 2018-2023" (Washington D.C., 2018), https://www.bie.edu/sites/default/files/documents/idc2-086443.pdf.

[14] For more, see Brenda Child, Boarding School Seasons: American Indian Families, 1900-1940 (Lincoln: University of Nebraska Press, 1998); Clyde Ellis, To Change Them Forever: Indian Education at the Rainy Mountain Boarding School, 1893-1920 (Norman: University of Oklahoma Press, 1996); K. Tsianina Lomawaima, They Called It Prairie Light: The Story of Chilocco Indian School (Lincoln: University of Nebraska Press, 1994).

[15] Adams, Education for Extinction, 26–27.

[16] Robert Lee et al., "Land-Grab Universities: A High Country News Investigation," 2020, https://www.landgrabu.org/.

[17] Irving G. Hendrick, "The Federal Campaign for the Admission of Indian Children into Public Schools, 1890-1934," American Indian Culture and Research Journal 5, no. 3 (1981): 13–32.

[18] Lawrence R. Baca, "Meyers v. Board of Education: The Brown v. Board of Indian Country," University of Illinois Law Review 5 (2004): 1155–80.

[19] "Johnson-O'Malley Act," Pub. L. No. 73–167, 25 CFR 273 (1934).

[20] Scheirbeck et al., "Report on Indian Education," 73.

[21] Timothy LaFrance, Handbook of Federal Indian Education Laws (Boulder: Native American Rights Fund, 1982).

[22] LaFrance.

[23] For more, see: Vine Deloria and Daniel R. Wildcat, Power and Place: Indian Education in America (Golden, Colo.: American Indian Graduate Center, 2001); Gloria Ladson-Billings, Critical Race Theory Perspectives on the Social Studies: The Profession, Policies, and Curriculum (Greenwich: Information Age Publishing, 2003); K. Tsianina Lomawaima and Teresa L. McCarty, "When Tribal Sovereignty Challenges Democracy: American Indian Education and the Democratic Ideal," American Educational Research Journal 39, no. 2 (2002): 279–305; Hollie J. Mackey, "The ESSA in Indian Country: Problematizing Self-Determination Through the Relationships Between Federal, State, and Tribal Governments," Educational Administration Quarterly 53, no. 5 (2017): 782–808; Sarah B. Shear, "Cultural Genocide Masked as Education: U.S. History Textbooks Coverage of Indigenous Education Policies," in Doing Race in Social Studies: Critical Perspectives (Charlotte: Information Age Publishing, 2015), 13–40; Sarah B. Shear et al., "Manifesting Destiny: Re/Presentations of Indigenous Peoples in K-12 U.S. History Standards," Theory and Research in Social Education 43, no. 1 (2015): 68–101; Wayne Journell, "An Incomplete History: Representation of American Indians in State Social Studies Standards," Journal of American Indian Education 48, no. 2 (2009): 18–32; Sarah B. Shear et al., "Toward Responsibility: Social Studies Education That Respects and Affirms Indigenous Peoples and Nations" (National Council for the Social Studies, 2018), https://www.socialstudies.org/positions/indigenous-peoples-and-nations.

[24] National Indian Education Association, "Native Nations and American Schools."

[25] For additional histories of Indian Education, see Adams, Education for Extinction; K. Tsianina Lomawaima and Teresa L. McCarty, "To Remain an Indian": Lessons in Democracy from a Century of Native American Education (New York: Teachers College Press, 2006); Jon Reyhner and Jeanne Eder, American Indian Education: A History, 2nd Edition (Norman: University of Oklahoma Press, 2017); Szasz, Education and the American Indian; Margaret Connell Szasz, Indian Education in the American Colonies, 1607-1783, Bison Books ed. (Lincoln: University of Nebraska Press, 2007); Thomas Thompson, ed., The Schooling of Native America (Washington, D.C.: Office of Education, 1978)., among others.

[26] Cassandria Dortch, "Indian Elementary-Secondary Education: Programs, Background, and Issues" (Washington, D.C.: Congressional Research Service, June 16, 2017); Ahniwake Rose, "Testimony of the National Indian Education Association: Before the United States House of Representatives Committee on Appropriations Subcommittee on Interior, Environment, and Related Agencies. National Indian Education Association," 2018, http://www.niea.org/wp-content/uploads/2016/02/NIEAs-Testimony-Before-House-Appropriations-Subcommittee-on-Interior-Environment-for-the-FY-2019-Budget.pdf.

[27] Bureau of Indian Education, "The United States Department of Interior Budget Justifications and Performance Information: Fiscal Year 2022."

28 See 25 U.S.C. 13, 2008; P.L. 107-110, 115 Stat. 1425.

29 Bureau of Indian Education.

30 The dollar amounts listed above are from the BIE 2022 Justifications document. Further details in this section were provided by Joe Herrin and Vanda Cervantes, via personal communication February 4, 2022.)

31 Cassandria Dortch, "Indian Elementary-Secondary Education: Programs, Background, and Issues" (Congressional Research Service, July 28, 2020), www.crs.gov.

32 Dortch.

33 Dortch, 25.

34 US Department of Education, "Department of Education: Indian Education Fiscal Year 2022 Budget Request," Budget Request (Washington D.C., n.d.), https://www2.ed.gov/about/overview/budget/budget22/justifications/e-indianed.pdf.

35 US Department of Education, "American Rescue Plan—American Indian Resilience in Education (ARP-AIRE)," Office of Elementary and Secondary Education, n.d., https://oese.ed.gov/offices/american-rescue-plan/american-rescue-plan-american-indian-resilience-in-education-arp-aire/.

36 US Department of Health and Human Services, "Funding Opportunities," Adminstration for Native Americans, accessed January 15, 2022, https://www.acf.hhs.gov/ana/grants/funding-opportunities.

37 Meryl Yoches Barofsky, Laura Hoard, and AI/AN FACES Workgroup, "Region XI American Indian and Alaska Native Head Start: A Portrait of Children and Families," October 2018, https://www.acf.hhs.gov/sites/default/files/documents/opre/14007_acfopre_aian_brief_508_compliantb_2.pdf.

38 National American Indian and Alaska Native Head Start Collaboration Office (NAIANHSCO), "National American Indian/Alaska Native Head Start Collaboration Office: Strategic Plan 2015-2020" (Washington D.C., 2016), https://eclkc.ohs.acf.hhs.gov/sites/default/files/pdf/aian-strategic-plan-2015-2020.pdf.

39 US Department of Health and Human Services, "American Rescue Plan Award Recipients," Administration for Native Americans: An Office of the Administration for Children and Families, accessed February 4, 2022, https://www.acf.hhs.gov/ana/grants/2021americanrescueplanawardrecipients.

40 Amy Bowers, "Tribal Education Departments Report" (Boulder: Tribal Education Departments National Assembly, 2011), https://www.narf.org/nill/resources/education/reports/tednareport2011.pdf.

41 Dawn M. Mackety et al., "American Indian Education: The Role of Tribal Education Departments" (Denver: McRel, 2009).

42 Alex RedCorn et al., "TEDNA Report 2021 (Forthcoming)," n.d.

43 McCoy, "An Historical Analysis of Requests for Direct Federal Funding for Tribal Education Departments for Fiscal Years 1989-2004."

44 US Department of Education, "State Tribal Education Partnership (STEP)," Office of Elementary and Secondary Education, December 17, 2021, https://oese.ed.gov/offices/office-of-indian-education/state-tribal-education-partnership-step/.

45 US Department of Education, "Grants Awarded," Office of Elementary and Secondary Education, December 17, 2021, https://oese.ed.gov/offices/office-of-indian-education/state-tribal-education-partnership-step/awards-2/.

46 Office of the Assistant Secretary—Indian Affairs, "Eight Tribes Receive Nearly $2.5 Million in Grants: Funds Help Tribes Take Control of Own Educational Programs," 2015, https://www.bie.edu/cs/groups/xbie/documents/text/idc1-032163.pdf.

47 National Indian Education Association, "NIEA Consultation Guides," National Indian Education Association, accessed September 30, 2020, https://www.niea.org/niea-consultation-guides.

48 Mackey, "The ESSA in Indian Country."

49 The Education Trust, "The State of Education for Native Students" (Washington, D.C.: The Education Trust, 2013).

50   Andrea D. Beesley et al., "Profiles of Partnerships Between Tribal Education Departments and Local Education Agencies" (Washington, D.C.: Institute of Education Sciences, National Center for Education Evaluation and Regional Assistance, REL Central, 2012), https://ies.ed.gov/ncee/edlabs/regions/central/pdf/REL_2012137_sum.pdf.

51   National Indian Education Association, "NIEA Consultation Guides."

52   California v. Cabazon Band of Mission Indians, 480 U.S. 202 (Supreme Court of the United States 1987).

53   Office of Indian Gaming, "Indian Gaming Compacts," U.S. Department of the Interior—Indian Affairs, n.d., https://www.bia.gov/as-ia/oig/gaming-compacts.

54   Arizona Department of Gaming, "Arizona Department of Gaming Annual Report: Fiscal Year 2021" (Phoenix, AZ: Arizona Department of Gaming, 2021), https://gaming.az.gov/sites/default/files/2021%20ADG%20Annual%20Report.pdf.

55   Oklahoma Indian Gaming Association, "Facts about Indian Gaming," accessed January 15, 2021, https://oiga.org/about/#facts.

56   Oklahoma Office of Management and Enterprise Services, "Oklahoma Gaming Compliance Unit Annual Report: Fiscal Year 2021" (Oklahoma City, Oklahoma: Oklahoma Office of Management and Enterprise Services, 2021), https://oklahoma.gov/content/dam/ok/en/omes/documents/GameCompAnnReport2021.pdf.

57   State of Washington Office of Superintendent of Public Instruction, "State-Tribal Education Compact Schools (STECs)," Office of Native Education, 2018, http://www.k12.wa.us/IndianEd/STECs.aspx.

58   Wisconsin State Tribal Initiative, "Wisconsin State Tribal Relations Initiative," Wisconsin State Tribal Relations Initiative, n.d., http://witribes.wi.gov/.

59   An updated list can be found at Wisconsin Department of Public Instruction, "American Indian Studies: Memorandum of Understanding (MOU)," Wisconsin Department of Public Instruction, n.d., https://dpi.wi.gov/amind/mou.

60   Wisconsin Department of Public Instruction, "State Statutes for American Indian Studies in Wisconsin," Wisconsin Department of Public Instruction, n.d., https://dpi.wi.gov/amind/state-statues.

61   Washington Office of Superintendent of Public Instruction, "Since Time Immemorial: Tribal Sovereignty in Washington State," Since Time Immemorial, 2017, http://www.k12.wa.us/IndianEd/TribalSovereignty/default.aspx; Montana Office of Public Instruction, "Indian Education for All," Montana Office of Public Instruction, accessed July 13, 2020, https://opi.mt.gov/Educators/Teaching-Learning/Indian-Education-for-All.

62   National Congress of American Indians, "Becoming Visible: A Landscape Analysis of State Efforts to Provide Native American Education for All" (Washington D.C.: National Congress of American Indians, September 2019), https://www.ncai.org/policy-research-center/research-data/prc-publications/NCAI-Becoming_Visible_Report-Digital_FINAL_10_2019.pdf.

63   National Indian Education Association, "NIEA Federal Appropriations Priorities: The Federal Trust Responsibility to Native Education" (Washington, D.C., 2022), 7, https://static1.squarespace.com/static/5cffbf319973d7000185377f/t/604c59df8c95fb7a4573f8cc/1615616482890/NIEA+-FY+2022+Budget+Request.pdf.

64   Restricted Fee land is land held by Native individuals who must receive permission from the Department of Interior (DOI) in order to sell or pass land to heirs. This land is often associated with the allotment era through families that never relinquished ownership of this land, even under guardianship of non-Native people. Trust land is land that is held in trust under title of the Secretary of the Department of Interior for a Native nation or individual, and this land falls under the jurisdiction of the Native nation and federal government. Both restricted fee and trust land are exempt from state and local taxes. If a Native nation purchases land as fee simple, a deed purchase just like any other business or individual might do, it is taxable until it undergoes a fee-to-trust review process by the DOI and is taken under title of the Secretary. For more, see National Congress of American Indians, "Tribal Nations and the United States: An Introduction."

[65] National Congress of American Indians, "Taxation," National Congress of American Indians, n.d., http://www.ncai.org/policy-issues/tribal-governance/taxation.

[66] National Congress of American Indians.

[67] U.S. Department of the Interior, "Payments in Lieu of Taxes," U.S. Department of the Interior, 2018, https://www.doi.gov/pilt.

[68] National Congress of American Indians, "Tribal Nations and the United States: An Introduction," 26.

[69] For more on Alaska Native education, see Alaska Native Knowledge Network, "History of Alaska Native Education," Alaska Native Knowledge, 2011, http://ankn.uaf.edu/Curriculum/Articles/History/.For more on Native Hawaiian education, see Native Hawaiian Education Council, "History," Native Hawaiian Education Council, n.d., http://www.nhec.org/about-nhec/history/.

CHAPTER 53

U.S. TERRITORIES

Lou L. Sabina
Stetson University

Anna Peters
University of Florida

This chapter discusses the financial and bureaucratic considerations of five US Territories; American Samoa, Guam, the Northern Mariana Islands, the US Virgin Islands, and Puerto Rico. This is new with the current edition of the textbook and will continue to be included in future editions.

AMERICAN SAMOA

GENERAL BACKGROUND

The history of the United States' involvement in American Samoa can be traced back to 1878, when then U.S. Navy Commander Richard Meade negotiated a treaty to build a coal station on the eastern island of Tutulia in Pago Pago.[1] This led to the United States Navy eventually converting the coal station to a naval base, which was recognized by the Berlin Treaty in 1899.[2] World War I and the continued conflicts pre-World War II led to the construction of a United States Naval Air Base in 1940, which remained until 1951.[3] When the Deed of Cession

Funding Public Schools in the United States, Indian Country,
and US Territories (Second Edition), pages 867–891.
Copyright © 2023 by Information Age Publishing
www.infoagepub.com

was signed in 1929, American Samoa officially became an unincorporated United States Territory, and United States nationalization rights were granted thereafter in the 1930s.[4] In the 1960s, American Samoa established their own constitution under the approval of United States President Dwight D. Eisenhower[5] which included 16 specific Bills of Rights.[6] Section 3 promises that the protection of persons of Samoan ancestry by the Government of American Samoa, "against alienations of their lands and the destruction of the Samoan way of life and language, contrary to their best interests. Such legislation as may be necessary may be enacted to protect the lands, customs, culture, and traditional Samoan family organization of persons of Samoan ancestry, and to encourage business enterprises by such persons."[7] Currently there are three districts (Eastern, Western, and Manu'a) and two unincorporated tolls (Swains Island and Rose Atoll, which is uninhabited), which are divided into 15 counties.[8] The education system in American Samoa is run by one American Samoa Department of Education, which oversees 22 public elementary schools, 6 public high schools, and the American Samoa Community College (ASCC), in the village of Magusa, which is the only tertiary education institution in American Samoa.[9] [10] The most recent report on student demographics in American Samoa is from National Center of Education Statistics in SY 19-20, which reported 10,448 students between 29 elementary and high schools.[11] The most recent report on teacher units in American Samoa is from the American Samoa 5 Year Plan, which reported 1,063 teacher units in SY 15-16.[12]

CURRENT POLITICAL CLIMATE

As an unincorporated United States territory, American Samoa has its own government structure, which has been described as a presidential representative democratic dependency, of which the governor and lieutenant governor (limited to two terms each), elected on the same ticket, are the heads of the government for American Samoa.[13] American Samoa operates as non–partisan, however, candidates have what is called a "party alliance" (Republican and Democratic), with the current governor, Lemanu Peleti Mauga (party alliance, Democratic) being elected in the 2020 Gubernatorial election.[14] Additionally, long-standing tribal traditions are an informally enforced local control using the Matai System.[15]

American Samoa does not have a teacher's union, however, in 2007, teachers went on strike for the first time to protest the lack of a pay increase from the government.[16] It was noted by the then director of education that the teacher's strike had little impact and that personnel from the Department of Education filled in for teachers for the day, and only 18 teachers participated in the strike.[17] No attempts at union organization or even minor strikes have taken place since, and an additional strike in 2020 involving lack of summer pay for teachers who participated in summer workshops was eventually called off.[18]

An example of an advocacy group in American Samoa is the Orphaned Starfish Association (OSA), which is dedicated to providing technology and technology access to native island children. OSA commits resources including computers, curriculum, teachers, and other technology so that students do not have barriers to higher education or future employment. OSA commits these resources "for life" so that native students can be successful.[19] Public health issues are controlled by the American Samoan Government itself, however, American Samoa also receives support from the United States Department of Agriculture Rural Development Hawaii and Western Pacific Office and the Western Rural Development Center.[20]

Recent legislation for American Samoa and the Northern Mariana Islands was introduced by Northern Mariana Islands Delegate Gregorio Kilili Camacho Sablan, who proposed the Northern Mariana Islands and American Samoa College Access Act, which would grant residents of American Samoa and the Northern Mariana Islands funding to cover the difference between in-state and out-of-state tuition if they attend a public institution of higher education in a different state or territory.[21]

According to the American Samoa Department of Commerce website, there were a total of 13,309 students in SY 11-12,[22] contrasted from the report from the National Center of Education Statistics in SY 19-20,[23] which reported 10,448 students indicates a decline of enrollment of 21.5%. College enrollment at the American Samoa Community College for SY 11-12 was 2,042,[24] and in SY 19-20, according to the U.S. News and World Report was 1,034 students, indicating a decline in enrollment of 49.4%[25]

SOURCES OF REVENUE

American Samoa has a separate taxation system from the United States, however their system is modeled on U.S. Income Tax laws in the Internal Revenue Code.[26] Since 2001, residents of American Samoa that are considered to be bona fide residents for an entire calendar year are eligible for a "possession exclusion."[27] For individuals that qualify, they may exclude from their federal income taxes any wages, salaries, and other kinds of pay from non-U.S. government sources. All income from the U.S. government must be declared and is taxable.[28] Both the corporate and personal income tax rate is 27% (as of 2020), and the Sales Tax Rate is 15%.[29] The overall budget in American Samoa for both FY 19 and 20 was $439.58 million according to the Office of Program Planning and Budget.[30] Additionally, the Office of Program Planning and Budget director Catherine D. Saelua comments that of this budget, 35% comes from Local Sources in American Samoa, with the other 65% coming from the United States Federal Government.[31] For FY 20, of that $439.58 million, $72.75 million is earmarked for education and educational programs (16.5% of the total budget).[32]

DISTRIBUTION FORMULAS

Education in American Samoa relies on local and federal funding to support its programs. During the 2021-2022 budget address, Minister of Finance Afioga Mulipola Anarosa Ale Molio'o noted that the Ministry of Education, Sports, and Culture had earmarked $105,877,332 which would go to various education and social programs. This includes roughly $77 million which came from federal funding, and $10 million which came from local funding. Additionally, $11.95 million was provided to American Samoa from externally financed grants and projects.[33]

For FY 21, the U.S. Department of the Interior transmitted additional funding specifically for the American Samoa Community College of $1,558,000, part of which is going toward teachers to provide additional opportunities for training and increasing access to higher education.[34]

Specific and noteworthy examples of categorical funding for American Samoa over the last 5 years include examples in (1) Special Education Categorical Funding, (2) Transportation Categorical Funding, (3) Technology Categorical Funding, (4) Textbooks, Curriculum, or classroom Supplies Funding, and (5) Student Services Categorical Funding.

Special Education Categorical Funding

Due to a complaint from four separate parents and parent groups in 2013/2014 to the U.S. Department of Education's Office of Civil Rights, American Samoa began an overhaul of their special education system to ensure that all students receive a free and appropriate education as required by federal law.[35] The American Samoa Department of Education was required to conduct a review of all Individualized Education Programs (IEPs) to ensure students were receiving the services and evaluations they needed for the 2014-2015, 2015-2016, and 2016-2017 school years. This led to additional funding being earmarked specifically for special education, in efforts to recruit personnel that were certified and capable of assisting students with disabilities.[36] To help fund these efforts, American Samoa received $6.3 million under IDEA, and 600K toward early intervention services for infants and toddlers.[37]

Transportation Categorical Funding

The most recent categorical funding for transportation came in 2016, when American Samoa acquired six additional school buses. According to the Department of the Interior, $9.5 million was granted to American Samoa for infrastructure improvements, of which, $600,000 was granted to provide additional school buses due to overloading to help with scheduling of maintenance and to provide safer transportation for students.[38]

Technology Categorical Funding

Technology, internet, and general technological infrastructure were a priority in American Samoa even before the COVID-19 pandemic. In 2017, a five-year plan known as the Library Service and Technology Act (LSTA) was passed with specific outcome targets including increased computer training, increased computer class participation, and increased online database services to be in effect by 2018, with increasing access through 2022.[39] The LSTA did not only target school-aged children, but the adult population as well. Additionally, in 2019, telecommunications provider Blusky provided $20,000 to 7 high schools to improve and advance the learning of students and to promote interests in STEM Education.[40] Finally, and perhaps most important for the infrastructure of American Samoa, the Build Back Better Act will provide $100 million to American Samoa that will go toward transportation, roads, bridges, ports, airports, broadband, cyber security, sewer, and safe drinking water.[41]

Textbooks, Curriculum, or Classroom Supplies Categorical Funding

The most recent investment in textbooks, curriculum, and/or classroom supplies occurred in 2020 with the selection of IXL Learning, a mathematics curriculum aligned with Common Core standards. The ASDOE agreed to a three-year deal to make IXL the choice curriculum across all schools in American Samoa. This curriculum was selected due to its alignment with mathematics and use of technology as a driving force in instruction.[42]

Student Services Funding

As part of the $18.53 million budget for FY22, $500,000 has been designated for sports development, which is double the amount made available by the special programs budget in prior years. This amount is specifically designated for football, citing the number of talent scouted and drafted from American Samoa that are currently playing in the National Football League.[43]

CAPITAL OUTLAY AND DEBT SERVICES

As part of the $9.5 million budget for infrastructure in FY16, two school buildings received major upgrades and renovations. Samoana High School received a new two-story building equipped to hold 10 new classrooms, a customized workshop area, and a new band room, and Aua Elementary School received a new covered recreational area and assembly area for students. These were the most recent and largest capital projects in American Samoa to improve school buildings.[44]

TEACHER SALARIES

In August 2021, a bill was passed that will raise starting teacher salaries. Under the new bill, the starting salaries for teacher degree holders with an AA degree is at $20,635; BA at $31,560; MA at $41,074 and PhD at $50,233.[45]

VIRTUAL EDUCATION

Like many other states and territories, American Samoa did not have the infra-structure ready to support online learning immediately after COVID for the 2020-2021 school year. A challenge presented itself where laptops and distance learning technologies were not received across American Samoa until December 2020.[46] It is worth noting that despite fears of COVID, the enrollment at American Samoa Community College actually increased by 100 students during 2020-2021, with 67% of students being face-to-face with COVID protocols including masks and social distancing in place, and 33% of students participating in distance learning.[47]

FEDERAL COVID-19 FUNDING

The United States Department of Education awarded $45.59 million to American Samoa through the Coronavirus Aid, Relief and Economic Security (CARES) Act, with $38.32 million under the Elementary and Secondary School Education Relief Fund for State Education Agencies (ESSER), and $7.27 million under the Governor's Emergency Education Relief (GEER) fund.[48] As of March 3rd, 2021, only a small percentage of the funding had been spent ($7.2 million or 15.8% of total funding).[49]

GUAM

GENERAL BACKGROUND

Guam was initially settled by Spanish colonizers in 1521. In 1898, Spain signed the Treaty of Paris with the United States, establishing Guam as a U.S. territory. In 1941, the Japanese seized control of Guam during World War II, although the U.S. reclaimed Guam three years later.[50] Guam has no constitution, and their governing document is the "Organic Act of Guam."[51]

The Guam Department of Education is the sole district in the territory. Guam has 26 elementary schools, 8 middle schools, and 6 high schools, with one alter-native school.[52] The Guam Department of Education serves about 30,000 school children and 3,755 employees, including 2,362 teachers.[53] In recent years, Guam has struggled with retaining teachers. This is due to being geographically isolated (without a competitive salary to attract teachers from the mainland U.S.), im-migration restrictions preventing the Guam DOE from hiring staff from nearby countries, and the lack of personnel being trained on the island.[54]

CURRENT POLITICAL CLIMATE

Guam is an unincorporated territory of the United States. Guam's legislature is unicameral, with 15 senators elected for two year terms. Guam has one delegate to the U.S. House of Representatives, however, that representative cannot vote on the final passage of legislation.[55] Guam's Democrat governor, Lou Leon Guerrero, was elected in 2019. Guam is unionized through the Guam Federation of Teachers, which is a subdivision of the American Federation of Teachers.[56] The Guam Federation of Teachers engages in collective bargaining for their teachers, with the most recent teacher contract being ratified on September 25th, 2017. One superintendent oversees all public schools in Guam.

Enrollment in Guam public schools is in decline. Enrollment has fallen from 31,698 during the 2012-2013[57] academic year to 27,497 during the 2020-2021 academic year,[58] losing an average of 525 students annually. The Guam Department of Education states that the decline in enrollment between the 2017 and 2019 academic years may be linked to the B.A.M. scandal, where a former high school teacher opened a private high school that sold false diplomas.[59] Other explanations offered include the increase in private and charter schools and private and charter school enrollments.

SOURCES OF REVENUE

The majority of the funding for education in Guam comes from local sources according to the Guam Department of Education. Roughly 80% comes from local sources, and 20% comes from federal appropriations.

DISTRIBUTION FORMULAS

The Guam Department of Education is primarily funded through the General Fund of Guam.[60] As of 2019, GDOE is currently in the process of implementing a funding formula, however, this has not passed legislation as of yet.[61]

Special Education Categorical Funding

Guam has struggled to provide specific funding and support to special education students. This could be attributed to the historical lack of prioritization of special education in Guam, specifically at the University of Guam. According to Fee[62], from 1987 to 2007, only 12 teachers graduated from the Guam special education program, which forced a major program redesign. Since then, the program had increased their graduation rate by 1000%, which has improved the access of teachers that can teach special education. In order to receive additional funding for special education, not just in Guam, but in the other outlying territories, the IDEA Parity for Outlying Areas Act was proposed in the House to provide additional funding for special education.[63] As of this publication, this act has not been passed. For the 2021-2022 school year, there are 1,752 special education students in Guam, and it has been proposed that the $287 million funding from the federal government provided for the pandemic be used to provide additional support for these students.[64]

Transportation Categorical Funding

Using federal funding from the CARES Act, The Department of Public Works in Guam was able to secure an additional 27 buses for use for the 2021-2022 school year. This cost roughly $300,000, but was considered a major improvement over the 111 buses previously available. The Department of Public Works reported that ideally, Guam would have 188 buses for all schools, public, private, and charter, but this is a major step in improving the transportation for students in Guam.[65]

Technology Categorical Funding

In order to compensate for the lack of technology accessibility in Guam, the Department of Education opened up learning centers throughout the territory where students could receive support after school and on the weekends. In December 2021, 21 of the learning centers were closed due to lack of support and lack of participation.[66] In addition, Guam is using technology to fund accelerated learning programs to catch students up for learning lost during the pandemic. This has been met with some controversy, as there is no guarantee that students are receiving an equivalent education by completing online modules as opposed to direct face-to-face instruction.[67] Currently, funding is coming to Guam as part of the 6th Wave of the Emergency Connectivity Fund passed by the Federal Government, which is providing a little over $602 million to the states and all territories to increase internet access.[68] Guam will receive a proportional amount based on their student population.

Career and Technical Education Categorical Funding

One major initiative has recently passed in Guam that will increase support for Career and Technical Education throughout the territory. In December 2021, Guam's first and only Bachelor's Degree in Career and Technical Education from Guam Community College received teacher education certification.[69] This will allow individuals who have associate's degrees in popular CTE fields to apply those associate degrees to receive certification to teach while maintaining their practices. This is a major step in improving access to career and technical education to students in Guam.

School Nurses Categorical Funding

Not much direct support has been provided to school nurses in Guam, however, on December 29th, 2021, Guam provided $40,000 to support nursing programs and to educate young children on the dangers associated with diabetes.[70]

Curriculum, Textbooks, and Classroom Supplies Categorical Funding

Guam requires students to wear uniforms to attend any schools K-12. To support students who come from struggling families, are homeless, or in foster care, the Guam Department of Education set aside $2 million for the 2021-2022 school year from federal funding for students in need. It is expected that 5,000 students will need this service, up from 1,000 the previous school year. The students and their families need to request a voucher at their home school in order to receive this funding.[71]

Student Support Services Categorical Funding

In order to provide support for students to catch up for lost instructional time, Guam will be expanding after school programs and creating The Summer Academic Academy (K-8 Academy and High School Academy) which will go into effect for Summer 2022. The purpose of this funding is to ensure that students are reaching grade-level proficiency and catching up for lost time during the COVID pandemic. Funding for this program will come out of the federal funding provided from the CARES Act.[72]

CAPITAL OUTLAY AND DEBT SERVICES

The major capital project currently taking place in Guam is the reconstruction of Simon Sanchez High School. This ten-year plan will double the size of the high school, and eliminate facility sharing between the middle school and high school.[73] Another major construction project in Guam began in July 2021, with groundbreaking for a $32 million charter school. The iLearn Academy Charter School is receiving a $12 million loan to begin construction. This is Guam's first new school building in the last 10 years.[74]

EMPLOYEE BENEFITS

The Guam Department of Education offers medical and dental benefits to its employees, which is negotiated by the Guam Federation of Teachers as part of their collective bargaining agreement.[75] In FY 19, $11.5 million was allocated for retiree healthcare benefits.[76]

CHARTER AND NON-PUBLIC SCHOOL FUNDING

Guam recently separated charter school funding from public school funding.[77] There are 26 private schools operating in Guam. 22 are operated by religious organizations (14 Catholic, 8 Protestant), the remaining four are operated by other organizations. The Department of Defense Activity oversees the operations of one high school, two middle schools, and two elementary schools; these schools educate students living on military bases in Guam.

FEDERAL COVID-19 FUNDING

Guam received $287 million in funding from the American Rescue Plan Outlying Areas State Educational Agency.[78] Guam plans to use this funding for capital projects to meet health and safety standards to reopen schools, professional development to address lost instructional time, and summer learning programs to help students overcome missed learning gains.[79]

NORTHERN MARIANA ISLANDS

GENERAL BACKGROUND

The Northern Mariana Islands are made up of fourteen islands in the Pacific Ocean, north of Guam. The population of the Northern Mariana Islands is 47,329 as of the 2020 Census. The Northern Mariana Islands became a U.S. territory after World War II ended, when the United States acquired the territory from Japan. There are a total of 20 schools distributed throughout the commonwealth; 9 elementary schools, 5 middle schools, 2 combination junior and senior high schools, and 4 high schools. The territory has over 10,000 students enrolled.[80]

CURRENT POLITICAL CLIMATE

The Northern Mariana Islands is led by a Republican governor, Ralph Torres. The Commonwealth has a bicameral legislature. With a small population and insular community, residents have expressed concern over whether nepotism exists within the government.[81]

SOURCES OF REVENUE

Schools in the Northern Mariana Islands are funded through federal and local sources. According to the Northern Mariana Islands Office of Instruction, roughly 65% of funding comes from local sources and 35% of funding comes from federal funding.

CATEGORICAL FUNDING

Information on specific categorical funding for the Northern Mariana Islands is provided below.

Special Education Categorical Funding

In 2015, the Northern Mariana Islands faced criticism regarding their support of special education students, with Rep. Blas Jonathan "BJ" Attao noting the burden this was putting on the public school system, due to lack of qualified candidates in special education positions, and the district relying on outside recruiting in order to staff their hard-to-fill special education positions, most of which require a master's degree.[82] Steps began to remedy this situation, including providing scholarships to students pursuing special education, and funding to pay for student loans for teachers pursuing special education certification. Additionally, in 2019, the Northern Mariana Islands Office of Vocational Rehabilitation began offering services to assist special education students in finding employment or continuing on for higher education post-graduation. Over $900,000 has been invested up to this point in this program, with 22 students currently enrolled to receive services post-graduation.[83] Additionally, funding is reserved for online speech and occupational therapy, with 400 students receiving services currently during the 2021-2022 school year.[84]

Transportation Categorical Funding

New school buses have not been purchased since the 2014-2015 school year for the Northern Mariana Islands. For the 2015-2016 school year, two new buses were added to the current fleet of 29[85] at a total cost of $280,000.[86]

Technology Categorical Funding

Funding and support for technology has been a challenge and low priority for the Northern Mariana Islands. Prior to 2012, limited training existed for teachers to integrate educational technology into their classroom programs. In an effort to remedy this situation, the CNMI Public School System began an Educational Technology program for teachers consisting of five—45 hour certification courses revolving around how technology can support teaching and learning. The goal of the program is to empower both public and private school teachers to integrate technology into their classrooms to prepare students for the challenges of the 21st Century. The program recently celebrated its 9th anniversary.[87]

Career and Technical Education Categorical Funding

An immediate priority in the Northern Mariana Islands is Career and Technical Education. A grant was recently received to construct a vocational educational facility at Marianas High School. The U.S. Department of Commerce's Economic Development Administration awarded a $6 million grant, which will be matched with $6 million support for local funding. The facility is 50,000-square feet and will house hospitality, automotive technology, nursing, cosmetology, and other vocational training programs and construction of the facility is expected to bring 85 jobs to the islands. Additionally, both Northern Marianas College ($13 million) and Northern Marianas Technical Institute ($10 million) received U.S. Department of Commerce Economic Development Administration grant funding to support their existing vocational education programs in 2021.[88] The Commonwealth of the Northern Mariana Islands also advertises available scholarships to career and technical education programs for an undisclosed amount for those interested in pursuing careers in vocational fields.[89]

School Nurses Categorical Funding

School nurses are another area in which the Commonwealth struggles to recruit qualified individuals to serve in positions. During the 2020-2021 school year, funding was used from the Economic Stabilization Fund in order to hire 22 part-time student nurses or retired nurses to ensure a school nurse or nursing student was available in every school, which last occurred in 1991.[90] A total of $550,000 was allocated in order to fund this initiative.[91]

Student Support Services Categorical Funding

The Commonwealth has implemented two new student services programs in the schools this year, one focused on mental health and the other focused on providing new uniforms and equipment to athletic programs. The mental health program is geared exclusively toward middle schools, and features three curricular-based programs, "Making a Difference" (6th Grade), "Making Proud Choices" (7th Grade), and "Be Proud, Be Responsible" (8th Grade). The Commonwealth, through the Federal Grants Program, were able to procure uniforms for the entire system ($18,440) which can be loaned out to players and coaches for the duration of each sporting season.[92]

CAPITAL OUTLAY AND DEBT SERVICES

In addition to dealing with a global pandemic, the Northern Mariana Islands also faced the challenge of dealing with a weather-related disaster, following Super Typhoon Yutu in 2018. In many cases, new capital projects have stalled in order to rebuild previously existing structures. A total of $7.7 million was invested for rebuild and repair programs at three schools, Francisco Mendiola Sablan Middle School, Da'ok Academy, and William S. Reyes Elementary School. Nine additional school rebuilding projects are stalled, waiting for FEMA approval.[93] An additional repair from Super Typhoon Yutu was also approved; as $13 million was invested in Northern Marianas College to increase their capacity and support economic growth and development.[94]

CHARTER AND NON-PUBLIC SCHOOL FUNDING

No information is available from the Commonwealth or the Saipan Tribute (the largest newspaper in Northern Mariana Islands) related to charter or non-public school funding.

VIRTUAL EDUCATION

Pre-COVID, opportunities for digital learning were already investigated by the Office of Public Instruction in the Northern Mariana Islands. In 2019, approximately 2,000 students pursued digital learning options, which led to a major training program throughout the entire commonwealth related to digital learning.[95]

One of the justifications for this program was that many students end up pursuing higher education through distance learning, providing them with an option to experience distance learning before entering college or university. Effective on March 24th, 2020, the entire commonwealth moved online for school and finished out the remainder of the school year online.[96] Support was provided from the American Rescue Plan to improve upon virtual instruction.[97]

FEDERAL COVID-19 FUNDING

The Commonwealth of the Northern Mariana Islands received $160 million from the American Rescue Plans Outlying Areas State Educational Agency.[98] Northern Mariana Islands plans to use this funding to reopen schools, make capital improvements on infrastructure, and to protect teacher jobs. An additional $74.4 million was awarded in early 2021, which supplemented the initial funding. $61.7 million goes directly toward the public school system, and the additional $12.7 million goes toward the higher education system, with $4.8 million going directly to Northern Marianas College.[99]

VIRGIN ISLANDS

GENERAL BACKGROUND

The United States Virgin Islands were purchased from Denmark in 1917 for $25 million during World War I in an attempt to improve military positioning. St. Thomas, St. Croix, and St. John were considered the United States Virgin Islands. The Islands remained under military control until 1936. A fourth island, Water Island, was added in 1996. Today, the Virgin Islands are considered a United States territory led by an elected governor.[100]

The Virgin Islands Department of Education is made up of two school districts, the St. Thomas/St. John School District, with 7 elementary schools, three junior high schools, and two high schools, and the St. Croix School District, with 7 elementary schools, one junior high school, and three high schools. The largest governmental agency in the territory, functions as both a local and state agency. The agency has 3,124 employees.[101]

CURRENT POLITICAL CLIMATE

Democratic Governor Albert Bryan Jr. is the current governor, having been elected in 2019. The U.S. Virgin Islands has a unicameral legislature with 15 members who are elected by residents of the islands. The Organic Act of the Virgin Islands of 1954 serves as a constitution for the islands.[102] Public school enrollment over the last 3 school years has shown a continued decline. In the 2016-2017 school year, total enrollment was 13,194. Since that time, public school enrollment has decreased by 19% (2,476 students).[103]

SOURCES OF REVENUE

Gov. Bryan has recommended a General Fund appropriation of $184,438,881 for FY 2022. The Department is to also receive $3,145,654 from Other Funds and $29,740,728 in Federal Funds for a total funding level of $217,825,263.[104]

CATEGORICAL FUNDING

Information on specific categorical funding for the Virgin Islands is provided below.

Special Education Categorical Funding

The U.S. Virgin Islands has focused on early childhood education and has consistently applied for federal funding under IDEA in order to support the infant and toddler population. This focus has supported both districts in identifying students in need of exceptional student education services early on in their educational careers.[105]

Transportation Categorical Funding

The U.S. Virgin Islands Education Department contracts with Abrahamson Enterprises Inc. to provide bus transportation to students. The buses are owned by School Bus Inc., and Abrahamson Enterprises operates the buses. Starting in September 2021, students will transition to being transported in buses owned by the department.[106] The total cost for fifteen buses, which is the first wave of bus purchasing, is $1,736,633.[107]

Technology Categorical Funding

Two specific initiatives have allowed for additional funding for technology in the U.S. Virgin Islands. First, the Emergency Connectivity Fund to allow for families to have access to internet and technology was awarded in November 2021, with $33,000 going to the United States Virgin Islands. This money is specifically to improve speeds to allow for teleconferencing both locally and nationally.[108] Another initiative came from the United States Department of Agriculture who funded both distance learning and telemedicine. The United States Virgin Islands received a percentage of $42 million to support distance learning opportunities for students in high school to receive opportunities not readily available on the islands.[109]

Student Support Services Categorical Funding

In order to support recent high school dropouts and adults without a high school education, philanthropic donors, the Stephenson Family, have matched a one million dollar grant from My Brother's Workshop in order to build a 1,000 student campus in St. Thomas. This 15,000 square foot campus, due to finish in 3 to 4 years, will offer programming including vocational training, mentoring, mental health counseling, tutoring, online high school diplomas, job placement services, anger management, parenting classes, and access to art, music, and sports.[110] Construction of the campus officially began in December 2021.[111]

FEDERAL COVID-19 FUNDING

The U.S. Virgin Islands, along with three other outlying territories (American Samoa, Guam, and the Northern Mariana Islands) share $850 million in federal funding, of which $138,158,430 is allocated to the U.S. Virgin Islands.[112] The U.S. Virgin Islands Department of Education plans to use American Rescue Plan (ARP) funding for 26 different initiatives across both school districts.[113] Fifteen of these projects are to be implemented from October 2021 to September 2024, including projects pertaining to social/emotional wellness, hygiene, facilities, nutrition, supplies, transportation, community engagement, and mitigating lost instruction time. Seven of these projects are to be implemented by the end of the 2023-2024 academic year, including projects related to career and technical education, assisting students with disabilities, learning recovery, and enrichment programs. One project related to mitigating the effects of lost instructional time is to be implemented by the end of the 2022 - 2023 academic year. One project related to technology and innovation is to be implemented by December 2025. One project related to social and emotional wellness is to be implemented by December 2024. One project related to facilities is to be implemented by June 2024.

PUERTO RICO[114]

GENERAL BACKGROUND

On October 18th, 1898, the United States acquired Puerto Rico from Spain, as a condition of the Spanish-American War. In 1917, Puerto Rico became a United States territory, and all of its citizens became United States citizens.[115] According to the United States Census, Puerto Rico, as of 2021, has a population of approximately 3.3 million residents[116], which is a 10% decline post Hurricane Maria, which ravaged the Territory in 2017.[117] There are currently 847 schools in Puerto Rico, with a student population of 292,518.[118]

CURRENT POLITICAL CLIMATE

Puerto Rico, like the other United States territories, is led by a governor, which began in 1948. The current governor of Puerto Rico is Democrat Pedro Pierliusi, who became governor in 2021. Governor Pierliusi was the former Attorney General of Puerto Rico before becoming governor. The major crisis facing Puerto Rico is not the pandemic, but is post-Hurricane Maria bankruptcy, and rebuilding the island in a way that restores Puerto Rico to its prior conditions. Billions in federal funding allocated to Puerto Rico from Hurricane Maria have yet to arrive, which is further decimating the infrastructure and the capabilities of the Territory. Governor Pierliusi intends to focus his efforts on obtaining all federal funding promised from FEMA from Hurricane Maria and the funding from the American Rescue Act and direct finances toward public education, crime, mental health, the environment, and corruption.[119] Additionally, there is a roughly 50/50 split between citizens of Puerto Rico to become the 51st state. Although statehood has been supported by the United States House of Representatives in 2020, there are concerns among Puerto Ricans that culture could be lost and many citizens of Puerto Rico would migrate to the United States and abandon the territory.[120] However, it should be noted that since Gerald Ford, all nine United States Presidents openly supported Puerto Rico becoming a state, should the popular vote in Puerto Rico recommend approving statehood.[121]

SOURCES OF REVENUE

Revenue for schools in Puerto Rico is a highly contested subject that has faced significant scrutiny in terms of the use of federal and local funds for public education. The Puerto Rico Department of Education is the largest employer in the territory, and close to 30% of all revenues are allocated to public education.[122] However, due to lack of state funding, Puerto Rico must rely on federal funding in order to successfully fund schools, and perhaps most importantly, teacher salaries. An example of the federal funding dilemma in Puerto Rico was provided by PR51ST, an advocacy group campaigning for Puerto Rico to become the 51st U.S. State. They note that in 2017 (pre-Hurricane Maria), Puerto Rico "received $663,334,371 in federal funds for K-12 education. Connecticut, a state with a similar population size, received just $335,384,548. However, most funds for public education come from states and cities. Connecticut spends an average of $16,576 per pupil, while Puerto Rico spends $6,400 per pupil.[123]" The lack of state and local funding cripples Puerto Rico's opportunities, despite being the largest United States territory. Therefore, Puerto Rico must rely on special funding, such as funding from the American Rescue Act, and federal FEMA funding from Hurricane Maria to rebuild and revitalize the Territory's infrastructure and education system.

CATEGORICAL FUNDING

Information on specific categorical funding for Puerto Rico is provided below.

Special Education Categorical Funding

Puerto Rico has an abnormally large population of students who require services in exceptional student education. According to the National Center for Education Statistics report on Children and Youth with Disabilities, approximately 40% of students require and would qualify for ESE services.[124] With charter schools lacking both the personnel and infrastructure to provide resources to exceptional education students, this has led to pressure being placed on public education to provide appropriate education for identified and potentially identified students.[125] Even more troublesome is that in 2004, Puerto Rico received $38.1 million in IDEA grant money to specifically fund exceptional student education, and the funding lapsed without being used.[126] Puerto Rico has committed to use a significant amount of their American Rescue Act funding to fund special education for the territory, including $245,000 for Payment of Provisional Remedy Services for Students Participating in the Special Education Program, $41,000 for funding for School Psychologists, and $1.3 million for an automated software program which would autofill certain sections of a student's IEP (Individualized Education Plan). An additional part of the American Rescue Act funding would be used to provide services for special education students with maladaptive problem behavior (experiencing tantrums, spitting, scratching, pulling hair, getting outside the classroom, aggression, and self-harm), to avoid the use of suspension and other disciplinary techniques.[127]

Transportation Categorical Funding

The major funding for transportation in Puerto Rico came in the form of mobile classrooms that are portable from school to school as needed. $46,787,543 was provided from the American Rescue Act to fund portable school trailers and modules. This funding is set to impact 38 schools and 8,900 students predominantly in the southern municipalities which were seriously impacted by Hurricane Maria.[128] Additionally, the Bipartisan Infrastructure Law which was passed by the Biden/Harris administration will also contribute to the repair and rebuilding of roads damaged from Hurricane Maria. $1.1 billion is allocated to this project, which also includes purchasing new buses for public and school transportation and electric charging stations for electric buses and vehicles.[129]

Textbooks, Curriculum, or Classroom Supplies Categorical Funding

Curriculum is currently going through a major reform in Puerto Rico, with an emphasis on finding a curriculum reform specialist to work with the Puerto Rico Department of Education. Their job will be to select a provider for the curriculum and to identify key department of education stakeholders that will be involved in the process of curriculum reform.[130] Additionally, educators at the University of Puerto Rico are being called on to assist with professional development, teacher training, and opportunities to make up for lost instructional time due to COVID-19.[131]

Student Services Funding

Student services in Puerto Rico under the American Rescue Act are focused on opportunities for Social Emotional Learning in schools that identify as "high risk."

Schools exhibiting the largest percentage of risk factors will be provided with funding and support for student services. The qualification of high risk schools are (1) schools with students not achieving interim goals set forth by the Department of Education, (2) schools with students who have not presented a growth of 6% or more in the annual test, (3) schools with students who have not achieved proficiency in Spanish language in five years, (4) schools with more than five Spanish learners, and (5) schools with Spanish learners who belong to the Special Education Program (placed in a self-contained Special Education classroom).[132]

CAPITAL OUTLAY AND DEBT SERVICES

The entire Territory of Puerto Rico is facing a major debt crisis, more so than any other state or city in the United States. The Territory declared bankruptcy in 2017, facing $72 billion in debt. This exceeded the large bankruptcy declared in Detroit, Michigan in 2014 of $17 billion. Under the new debt restructuring, $33 billion will be cut from the $72 billion debt. Critics are worried that this will lead to major changes in Puerto Rico[133], noting specifically the 83 schools that will be closed by 2026 and the high percentages of families leaving Puerto Rico (estimated to be 15% of the current population by 2026) for better opportunities in the United States.[134]

TEACHER SALARIES

At the time of the writing of this chapter, Puerto Rico was experiencing a major teacher strike due to the low wages teachers receive in Puerto Rico. The current minimum salary for teachers is $1,750 per month, which had not been raised since 2014.[135] Under the new act, passed January 27th, 2022, minimum teacher salaries were to increase on average 27%[136], or roughly an additional $470 per month. This did not meet what the Puerto Rico Teachers' Association had asked for, which was an additional $950 per month. Puerto Rico faces an uphill battle in keeping teachers due to Puerto Rican teachers being in high demand and being actively recruited in both Florida and Texas.[137]

VIRTUAL EDUCATION

A percentage of the American Rescue Act funding was designated for virtual education in Puerto Rico. Specifically, funding is to be used to provide all public school students with laptops (currently 82% complete), to select an appropriate provider for online management learning systems, a voucher program to permit internet service in hard-to-reach areas of the Territory, and online social-emotional support to leverage school psychologists.[138] Additionally, the Puerto Rico Department of Education continues to support a 5-year initiative that was passed in 2015, which increases broadband speeds by 1000% from 2015 to 2019, laptops for all teachers, 100% support of Wi-Fi in all schools and classrooms by 2019, and 1:1 teacher and student educational devices while on a school campus.[139]

FEDERAL COVID-19 FUNDING

Out of all of the United States Territories, Puerto Rico received the largest amount of federal funding due to its size, with nearly $4 billion in education funding coming to Puerto Rico as direct aid as part of the American Rescue Plan Act. This money will be used to increase teacher salaries, provide support in hard-to-staff areas, and improve infrastructure throughout the island.[140]

ENDNOTES

1 Droessler, Holger. "Whose Pacific? US security interests in American Samoa from the Age of Empire to the Pacific Pivot." Pacific Asia Inquiry 4, no. 1 (2013): 58.

2 Ibid, 1.

3 Ibid, 1.

4 Dardani, Ross. "Citizenship in Empire: The Legal History of US Citizenship in American Samoa, 1899-1960." American Journal of Legal History 60, no. 3 (2020): 311-356.

5 Weaver, Michael W. "The territory federal jurisdiction forgot: the question of greater federal jurisdiction in American Samoa." Pac. Rim L. & Pol'y J. 17 (2008): 325.

6 Ballotpedia, "Article I, American Samoa Constitution." https://ballotpedia.org/Article_I,_American_Samoa_Constitution

7 Ibid, 6.

8 American Samoa Bar Association. "Division of Districts into Counties." https://new.asbar.org/code-annotated/5-0102-division-of-districts-into-counties/

9 Ropeti, Siamaua. "Student perspectives regarding school failure at the American Samoa community college." PhD diss., Walden University, 2015.

10 American Samoa Department of Education. "American Samoa Department of Education." https://www.doe.as/District/Schools

11 National Center for Education Statistics, "American Samoa Department of Education District Details." https://nces.ed.gov/ccd/districtsearch/district_detail.asp?Search=2&details=1&ID2=6000030&DistrictID=6000030

12 American Samoa 5 Year Plan. "American Samoa 5 Year Plan." https://www.imls.gov/sites/default/files/state-profiles/plans/americansamoa5yearplan.pdf

13 American Samoa Bar Association. "4.0105 Term of Office."

14 FIli Sagapolutele. "Unofficial results have Lemanu & Talauega winning 60+% of the vote." "Samoa News." https://www.samoanews.com/local-news/unofficial-results-have-lemanu-talauega-winning-60-vote.

15 Tapu, Ian Falefuafua. "Who Really Is a Noble?: The Constitutionality of American Samoa's Matai System." Asian Pac. Am. LJ 24 (2020): 61.

16 RNZ. "Teachers strike for the first time ever in American Samoa." https://www.rnz.co.nz/international/pacific-news/173182/teachers-strike-for-the-first-time-ever-in-american-samoa.

17 RNZ. "American Samoa teacher's strike said to have little impact." https://www.rnz.co.nz/international/pacific-news/173204/american-samoa-teacher's-strike-said-to-have-had-little-impact.

18 Ausage Fausia. "ECE strike over no pay for summer workshop is called off." https://www.samoanews.com/local-news/ece-strike-over-no-paychecks-summer-workshop-called.

19 Orphaned Starfish Association. "The OSF Story on CNN." https://www.osf.org/about-us#OurStory

20 Rural Health Information Hub. "American Samoa." https://www.ruralhealthinfo.org/states/american-samoa/organizations

21 H.R. 3729. "Northern Mariana Islands and American Samoa College Access Act." https://www.congress.gov/bill/117th-congress/house-bill/3729?r=3&s=1.

22 American Samoa Department of Commerce. "Educational Institutions and Enrollment." https://americansamoa.prism.spc.int/social/education/educational-institutions-and-enrollment.html

23 Ibid, 11.

24 Ibid, 22.

25 U.S. News and Report. "American Samoa Community College." https://www.usnews.com/best-colleges/american-samoa-community-college-667027.

26 IRS. "Bona Fide Residents of American Samoa—Tax Credits." https://www.irs.gov/individuals/bona-fide-residents-of-american-samoa-tax-credits.

27 Possession Exclusion. http://www.jdunman.com/ww/business/sbrg/publications/p57001.htm.

28 Ibid, 27.

29 Trading Economics. "Samoa Sales Tax Rate." https://tradingeconomics.com/samoa/sales-tax-rate.

30 Samoa News. "FY 2020 Ceiling is Same as Current Fiscal Year—$439.58 million." https://www.samoanews.com/local-news/fy-2020-ceiling-same-current-fiscal-year-43958-million.

31 Ibid, 31.

32 Fili Sagapolutele. "More than $140,000 included in the DOE budget to increase pay for senior personnel." https://www.samoanews.com/local-news/more-140k-included-doe-budget-increase-pay-senior-personnel

33 Afioga Mulipola Anarosa Ale Molio'o. "Budget Address 2021/2022." https://www.samoagovt.ws/wp-content/uploads/2021/09/ENG-Budget-Address-20212022-Final-for-Printing_14092021.pdf.

34 U.S. Department of the Interior. "Interior transmits $16,718,000 to American Samoa for Fiscal Year 21 Government Operations." https://www.doi.gov/oia/press/Interior-Transmits-%2416%2C718%2C000-to-American-Samoa-fo-Fiscal-Year-2021-Government-Operations

35 Fili Sagapolutele. "American Samoa Agrees to Improve Special Education Services." http://www.pireport.org/articles/2016/11/30/american-samoa-agrees-improve-special-education-services.

36 Ibid, 35.

37 Taleni. "Special Ed Awarded $6.9 million under IDEA." https://www.talanei.com/2017/06/26/special-ed-awarded-6-3-million-under-idea/.

38 Tanya Harris Joshua. "Interior Releases $9.5 million in FY16 Infrastructure for American Samoa." https://www.doi.gov/oia/interior-releases-95-million-fy16-infrastructure-funding-american-samoa.

39 Office of the Territorial Librarian. "The State Plan for the Library Services and Technology Act (LSTA) in American Samoa: FY 2018-2022." https://www.imls.gov/sites/default/files/state-profiles/plans/americansamoa5yearplan.pdf.

40 Bluesky Media Communications Release. "Blusky shares $20,000 among 7 high schools for tech-based initiatives." https://www.samoanews.com/bluesky-shares-20000-among-7-high-schools-technology-based-initiatives

41 Congresswoman Aumua Amata Coleman Radwagen. "House Passes Infrastructure Bill with Over 100 Million for American Samoa." https://radewagen.house.gov/media-center/press-releases/house-passes-infrastructure-bill-over-100-million-american-samoa.

42 School Buyers Online. "ASDOE Selects IXL to Support Math Instruction." https://www.schoolbuyersonline.com/doc/american-samoa-department-of-education-selects-ixl-to-support-math-instruction-0001

43 Fili Sagapolutele. "Special Programs Budget Earmarked for Football Development Doubles." https://www.samoanews.com/local-news/special-programs-budget-earmarked-football-development-doubles.

44 Ibid. 38.

45 Ausage Fausia. "House Endorses Teacher Salary Increase After Adding Amendments." https://www.samoanews.com/local-news/house-endorses-teacher-salary-increase-after-adding-amendments.

46 Fili Sagapolutele. "Laptops and iPads to Help Students With Virtual Learning Still Not Received." https://www.samoanews.com/local-news/laptops-and-ipads-help-students-virtual-learning-still-not-received.

47 Fili Sagapolutele. "ASCC Begins Fall Term with Enrollment Up—and Revenue as Well." https://www.samoanews.com/local-news/ascc-begins-fall-term-enrollment-and-revenue-well.

48 Fili Sagapolutele. "Education funding report shows lots of money allocated, little spent." https://www.samoanews.com/local-news/education-funding-report-shows-lots-money-allocated-little-spent.

49 Ibid, 26.

50 Doug Herman, "A Brief History of Guam." https://www.smithsonianmag.com/smithsonian-institution/brief-500-year-history-guam-180964508/

51 The Organic Act of Guam and Related Federal Laws Affecting the Governmental Structure of Guam. http://www.guamcourts.org/compileroflaws/GCA/OrganicAct/Organic%20Act.pdf

52 Guam Department of Education. "Guam School Directory." https://www.gdoe.net/District/Portal/gdoe-school-directory

53 Guam Department of Education. "Citizen Centric Fiscal Report 2020." https://www.gdoe.net/files/user/57/file/Guam%20Department%20of%20Education%20-%20FY2020%20Citizen%20Centric%20Report.pdf

54 Kim Fong Poon-McBrayer. "Contextualizing the Participation and Challenges in Education for All: The Case of Guam and Hong Kong." https://files.eric.ed.gov/fulltext/EJ1142324.pdf

55 Britannica. "Guam." https://www.britannica.com/place/Guam/Government-and-society

56 Guam Federation of Teachers. "Collective Bargaining Agreement." https://gftunion.com/wp-content/uploads/2020/04/GDOE-CBA.pdf

57 Guam Department of Education. "Curriculum and Instruction." https://www.gdoe.net/District/Department/5-Curriculum-Instruction/1434-Official-Student-Enrollment.html

58 Jolene Toves. "Report: GDOE Enrollment Down; Graduation Rate Up." https://www.postguam.com/news/local/report-gdoe-enrollment-down-graduation-rate-up/article_e33f3cca-5182-11ec-a314-131428700954.html

59 Manny Cruz. "Guam DOE: Enrollment Decline Linked to B.A.M. Scam, ; Charter Funding a Concern." https://www.guampdn.com/news/local/guam-doe-enrollment-decline-linked-to-b-a-m-scam-charter-funding-a-concern/article_c548f89c-dcf8-52be-b302-b36326ba60b3.html

60 Guam Department of Education. "Basic Financial Statements, Additional Information and Independent Auditor's Report: Year Ended September 30, 2020." https://opaguam.org/sites/default/files/2_-gdoe_fs20.pdf

61 John O' Conner. "Superintendent Looking at Funding Formula for Students." https://www.postguam.com/news/local/superintendent-looking-at-funding-formula-for-students/article_8946840a-9a1d-11e8-970c-230b4f4f5f8b.html

62 Richard Fee, Julie Fee, Peggy Snowden, Nicole Stuart, Dana Baumgartner. "The University of Guam Special Education Program: Preparing Special Education Teachers in a Very Diverse Culture." https://files.eric.ed.gov/fulltext/EJ1056451.pdf.

63 Congress. "All Information (Except Text) for H.R. 2437—IDEA Parity for Outlying Areas Act." https://www.congress.gov/bill/116th-congress/house-bill/2437/all-info.

64 The Guam Daily Post. "Let's Keep Special-Needs Students From Falling Through the Cracks." https://www.postguam.com/forum/editorial/lets-keep-special-needs-students-from-falling-through-the-cracks/article_bda1bd32-105d-11ec-9e9b-bbfbe8f46cd5.html

65 Jolene Toves. "27 Buses Added to DPW Fleet." https://www.postguam.com/news/local/27-buses-added-to-dpw-fleet/article_beda28ec-eaab-11eb-9a10-a7f98c270cb8.html

66 Jolene Toves. "Lack of Participation Leads to GDOE To Close Learning Centers." https://www.postguam.com/news/local/lack-of-participation-leads-gdoe-to-close-learning-centers/article_8d8939f6-62ea-11ec-910e-cfa5f50ae891.html.

67 Jolene Toves. "GDOE: Accelerated Learning not a "Hodgepodge" Approach." https://www.postguam.com/news/local/gdoe-accelerated-learning-not-a-hodgepodge-approach/article_c4b05cdc-5973-11ec-a5bc-73c31122abc0.html.

68 Carl Weinschenk. "Emergency Connectivity Fund Awards Pass Halfway Point with Latest Wave." https://www.telecompetitor.com/emergency-connectivity-fund-awards-pass-halfway-point-with-latest-wave/.

69 Isiah Aguon. "GCC Gains Certification for its Bachelor of Science in Career Technical Education Program." https://www.kuam.com/story/45501389/gcc-gains-certification-for-its-bachelor-of-science-in-career-technical-education-program

70 Phill Leon Guerrero. "$339K Awarded to Support Education, Health Care and Community Groups." https://www.postguam.com/news/local/339k-awarded-to-support-education-health-care-and-community-groups/article_0ad003e4-6887-11ec-9391-0f162eabb7c6.html.

71 Jolene Toves. "$2M in Federal Funds Set Aside To Help Sstudents Buy Uniforms." https://www.postguam.com/news/local/2m-in-federal-funds-set-aside-to-help-students-buy-uniforms/article_77bceb90-f4cc-11eb-9774-0b470c9e4f69.html.

72 U.S. Department of Education. "U.S. Department of Education Approves Guam's Implementation Plan for Use of American Rescue Plan Funds to Support K-12 Schools and Students." https://www.ed.gov/news/press-releases/us-department-education-approves-guams-implementation-plan-use-american-rescue-plan-funds-support-k-12-schools-and-students.

73 Jolene Toves. "Design for Sharks' New Home Wows Community; Construction Scheduled to Be Done By 2024." https://www.postguam.com/news/design-for-sharks-new-home-wows-community-construction-scheduled-to-be-done-by-2024/article_dc392dc8-1ac3-11ec-a9a4-e7b81975b776.html

74 Pacific News Center. "Groundbreaking Set for iLearn Academy Charter School Project." https://www.pncguam.com/groundbreaking-set-for-ilearn-academy-charter-school-project/.

75 Ibid, 56.

76 Ibid, 60.

77 Ibid, 60.

78 Ibid, 72.

79 Ibid, 72.

80 Commonwealth of the Northern Mariana Islands. "Public School System." https://www.cnmipss.org/.

81 New World Encyclopedia. "Northern Mariana Islands." https://www.newworldencyclopedia.org/entry/Northern_Mariana_Islands

82 Joel D. Pinaroc. "Lack of Experts on 'Special Education' Burdening School System—Attao." https://www.saipantribune.com/index.php/lack-of-experts-on-special-education-burdening-school-system-attao/.

83 Justine Nauta. "OVR Helps 175 Get Jobs or Pursue Higher Education." https://www.saipantribune.com/index.php/ovr-helps-175-get-jobs-or-pursue-higher-education/.

84 Press Release. "175 Headsets Given to PSS Special Education Services." https://www.saipantribune.com/index.php/175-headsets-given-to-pss-special-education-students/.

85 Moneth G. Deposa. "29 School Buses, 10 Vans Ready for Class Opening." https://www.saipantribune.com/index.php/29-school-buses-10-vans-ready-class-opening/.

86 Dennis b. Chan. "PSS Expects 2 New School Buses Next Year." https://www.saipantribune.com/index.php/pss-expects-2-new-school-buses-next-year/.

87 Press Release. "PSS Celebrates 9th Year of Educational Technology Program." https://www.saipantribune.com/index.php/pss-celebrates-9th-year-of-educational-technology-program/.

88 Saipan Tribune. "EDA Awards $6M for Vocational School at MHS." https://docs.google.com/document/d/1AyeGeollaGTrJO666bh6VR9fHsn52ascKZ-BogEiFVg/edit.

89 CNMI Scholarship Office. "Commonwealth of the Northern Mariana Islands: Vocational & Trade Aid." https://cnmischolarship.net/sec.asp?secID=14.

90 Kimberly B. Esmores. "PSS Allocates Funds to Hire Part-Time Nurses." https://www.saipantribune.com/index.php/pss-allocates-funds-to-hire-part-time-nurses/.

91 Kimberly B. Esmores. "PSS Working on Recruiting NMC Nursing Students Before the Start of the School Year." https://www.saipantribune.com/index.php/pss-working-on-recruiting-nmc-nursing-students-before-the-start-of-school-year/.

92 CNMI Public School System. "Office of Student and Support Services." https://cnmipss.org/office-student-and-support-services.

93 Justine Nauta. "BOE Approves Repairs for 3 Schools." https://www.saipantribune.com/index.php/boe-approves-repairs-for-3-schools/.

94 Ibid, 88.

95 Erwin Encinares. "NMI Schools Turns Focus on Digital Learning." https://www.saipantribune.com/index.php/nmi-schools-turns-focus-on-digital-learning/.

96 Kimberly B. Esmores. "PSS Shutters All Schools." https://www.saipantribune.com/index.php/pss-shutters-all-schools/.

97 U.S. Department of Education. "U.S. Department of Education Approves the Commonwealth of Northern Mariana Islands Public School System's Implementation Plan for Use of American Rescue Plan Funds to Support K-12 Schools and Students." https://www.ed.gov/news/press-releases/us-department-education-approves-commonwealth-northern-mariana-islands-public-school-systems-implementation-plan-use-american-rescue-plan-funds-support-k-12-schools-and-students.

98 Ibid, 97

99 Press Release. "Kilili: $74.4M for Marianas Education." https://www.saipantribune.com/index.php/kilili-74-4m-for-marianas-education/.

100 VINOW. "Virgin Islands History." https://www.vinow.com/general_usvi/history/.

101 The Virgin Islands Department of Education. "Vision—Mission—Goals." https://www.vide.vi/344-vision-mission-goals.html.

102 Government of the United States Virgin Islands. "Governor Bryan." https://www.vi.gov/governor-bryan/.

103 Community Foundation of the Virgin Islands. "Building Forward for Our Children Now!" https://cfvi.net/wp-content/uploads/2019/12/2019-KC-DB_Final-Version_11_6_2019_Additional-Reduced-Version.pdf.

104 Kyle Murphy. "With its Own Fleet Deteriorating, Abramson Enterprises Inc. will use Government Owned School Buses in Deal Still Being Negotiated." https://viconsortium.com/vi-education/virgin-islands-agreement-for-school-bus-service-in-st-croix-expected-to-be-reached-soon-abramson-enterprises-inc-to-use-government-owned-vehicles-.

105 United States Virgin of Islands Department of Health. "Infant and Toddler Program." https://doh.vi.gov/programs/infant-and-toddlers-program.

106 Staff Consortium. "St. Croix Students to Ride in New School Buses When School Resumes." https://viconsortium.com/vi-education/virgin-islands-st-croix-students-to-ride-in-new-school-buses-when-service-resumes-sept-29.

107 Ibid, 105.

108 Kelly Hill. "FCC Sends Out Another $603 Million in Emergency Connectivity Funds." https://www.rcrwireless.com/20211220/policy/fcc-sends-out-another-603-million-in-emergency-connectivity-funds.

109 United States Department of Agriculture. "USDA Invests $42 Million in Distance Learning and Telemedicine Infrastructure to Improve Education and Health Outcomes." https://www.usda.gov/media/press-releases/2021/02/25/usda-invests-42-million-distance-learning-and-telemedicine.

110 Staff Consortium. "My Brother's Workshop Announces Plan to Build St. Thomas Campus With Capacity of Over 1,000 Students; Project Kickstarted With $1 Million Match From Philanthropic Family." https://viconsortium.com/vi-education/virgin-islands-my-brothers-workshop-announces-plan-to-build-st-thomas-campus-with-capacity-of-over-1000-students-project-kickstarted-with-1-million-match-from-philanthropic-family-

111 Kyle Murphy. "My Brother's Workshop Breaks Ground on 1,000-Student Capacity Campus in St. Thomas." https://viconsortium.com/vi-education/virgin-islands-my-brothers-workshop-breaks-ground-on-1000-student-campus-in-st-thomas-.

[112] United States Department of Education. "Department of Elementary and Secondary Education—ARP-OA SEA Implementation Plans." https://oese.ed.gov/offices/education-stabilization-fund/outlying-areas/arp-oa-sea-implementation-plans/

[113] United States Department of Education. "Virgin Islands Department of Education State Educational Agency Plan for the American Rescue Plan Outlying Areas State Educational Agencies Fund." https://oese.ed.gov/files/2021/12/VIDE-ARPOASEA-Implementation-Plan.pdf.

[114] Co-authored with Devon Viola, BS; Graduate Student, Stetson University

[115] Library of Congress. "Puerto Rico." https://www.loc.gov/item/today-in-history/october-18/.

[116] United States Census. "Puerto Rico." https://www.census.gov/quickfacts/PR.

[117] Nicole Acevedo. "Puerto Rico's Progress Still Stalled Four Years After Maria." https://www.nbcnews.com/news/latino/puerto-rico-four-years-hurricane-maria-far-recovery-rcna2073.

[118] Nicole Johnson. "11 Largest School Districts in the Country and How they're Responding to COVID-19." https://www.indexjournal.com/news/national/11-largest-school-districts-in-the-country-and-how-theyre-responding-to-covid-19/collection_2ea5db44-a136-5600-8ad6-7d116561f7a6.html#7.

[119] Adrian Florido. "Puerto Rico Swears in a New Governor Who Inherits Multiple Crises." https://www.npr.org/2021/01/02/952862800/puerto-rico-swears-in-a-new-governor-who-faces-multiple-crises.

[120] Raquel Richard. "Why Isn't Puerto Rico a State?" https://www.history.com/news/puerto-rico-statehood.

[121] Jenniffer Gonzalez-Colon. "Statehood." https://gonzalez-colon.house.gov/statehood.

[122] Puerto Rico. "Administration, Finance, and Educational Research." https://education.stateuniversity.com/pages/1237/Puerto-Rico-ADMINISTRATION-FINANCE-EDUCATIONAL-RESEARCH.html.

[123] PR51ST. "Education in Puerto Rico." https://www.pr51st.com/education-in-puerto-rico/.

[124] National Center for Education Statistics. "Children and Youth with Disabilities." https://nces.ed.gov/programs/coe/indicator _cgg.asp.

[125] Rima Brusi and Isar Godreau. "Dismantling Public Education in Puerto Rico." https://d1wqtxts1xzle7.cloudfront.net/64981433/aftershocks_final_rima_isar_chapter-with-cover-page-v2.pdf?-Expires=1645388839&Signature=SZSe2yVDprdylFxdj4dmTAMeRgjOFTaRVpm4SudYlD-3VlBJ3-QEjBjmwfa2C0DTZr2qRWUEa73sU-iPVth1jQ91JZL4v4Yq722ekPTw71xYz99GG-cE-GQqfdm~PyLBD0ttEKCPbChNCVewc7MCRQ71Uj5caBSh6gSBPTvVtCe~bC7xFjC32R-0jVdFcAIffMCzDO3quLwLK2y-vgsn2DzmOmfGFRfvORo6REOSHnudyGGQW-VHx1Mfv-lzv7wdsURFpROCqQP~jQMygoW4CVHilS6~GJ0UHyxjYFTtIZm6BOngaQUeEUYnNttpkp-WujqsvAR4oPdqRFrlLumb4RGB6QQ__&Key-Pair-Id=APKAJLOHF5GGSLRBV4ZA

[126] U.S. Department of Education - Office of the Attorney General. "Final Audit Report: Puerto Rico Department of Education's (PRDE) Special Education Expenditures for the period, July 1, 2002, to December 2002." https://view.officeapps.live.com/op/view.aspx?src=https%3A%2F%2Fw-ww2.ed.gov%2Fabout%2Foffices%2Flist%2Foig%2Fauditreports%2Fa02d0020.doc&wdOrig-in=BROWSELINK.

[127] U.S. Department of Education. "Puerto Rico State Plan for the American Rescue Plan Elementary and Secondary School Emergency Relief Fund." https://oese.ed.gov/files/2021/11/PR-ARP-ESS-ER-State-Plan-Final.pdf.

[128] Financial Oversight & Management Board for Puerto Rico. "Federal COVID-19 Relief." https://www.puertoricoreport.com/wp-content/uploads/2021/04/FOMB-Presentation-26th-Public-Meeting-March-26-2021.pdf.

[129] U.S. Department of Education. "The Bipartisan Infrastructure Law will Deliver for Puerto Rico." https://www.transportation.gov/sites/dot.gov/files/2021-12/Puerto%20Rico.pdf.

[130] Ibid, 127.

[131] Andrew Ujifusa. "Top Federal Adviser on Puerto Rico's Schools Declares: 'We have to build trust.'" https://www.edweek.org/policy-politics/top-federal-adviser-on-puerto-ricos-schools-declares-we-have-to-build-trust/2021/11.

132 Puerto Rico Department of Education. "Consolidated State Plan." https://www2.ed.gov/admins/lead/account/stateplan17/prconsolidatedstateplanfinal.pdf.

133 Julio Ricardo Varela. "Puerto Rico's New Bankruptcy Plan Does Nothing for Most of the Island." https://www.msnbc.com/opinion/puerto-rico-s-new-bankruptcy-plan-does-nothing-most-island-n1287883.

134 Tatiana Diaz Ramos & Jose M. Encarnacion Martinez. "Department of Education is Planning a New Wave of School Closings." https://periodismoinvestigativo.com/2022/01/department-of-education-is-planning-a-new-wave-of-school-closings/.

135 Rafael Azul. "Puerto Rico: Teacher Strikes and Protests Continue Against Debt Payment Deal." https://www.wsws.org/en/articles/2022/02/14/puer-f14.html.

136 Associated Press. "Board Approves Fiscal Plan for Puerto Rico Amid Bankruptcy." https://www.cnbc.com/2022/01/27/board-approves-fiscal-plan-for-puerto-rico-amid-bankruptcy.html.

137 Ibid, 132

138 Ibid, 127.

139 Gigabit Island Plan. "Building Gigabit Capacity to Puerto Rico's Schools." https://www.connect-pr.org/sites/default/files/connected-nation/section5_buildinggigabitcapacitytopuertorico_schools.pdf.

140 Associated Press. "Puerto Rico to Receive $4 Billion in Federal Education Pandemic Relief Funds." https://www.cbsnews.com/news/puerto-rico-pandemic-relief-aid-4-billion/.

Printed in the USA
CPSIA information can be obtained
at www.ICGtesting.com
JSHW010711091123
51460JS00005B/19